2018

Radio Drama

Radio Drama

*A Comprehensive Chronicle of
American Network Programs,
1932–1962*

by MARTIN GRAMS, JR.

McFarland & Company, Inc., Publishers
Jefferson, North Carolina, and London

Library of Congress Cataloguing-in-Publication Data

Grams, Martin.
    Radio drama : a comprehensive chronicle of American network
programs, 1932–1962 / by Martin Grams, Jr.
       p.   cm.
    Includes index.
    ISBN 0-7864-0051-X (library binding : 50# alkaline paper)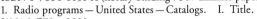
    1. Radio programs — United States — Catalogs.   I. Title.
PN1991.9.G73   2000
016.79144'75'0973 — dc21   99-29879

British Library Cataloguing-in-Publication data are available

Manufactured in the United States of America

*McFarland & Company, Inc., Publishers
   Box 611, Jefferson, North Carolina 28640
   www.mcfarlandpub.com*

To everyone who helped me with this book,
added small dates and title corrections, information,
and a gentle hand on a weary shoulder —
Greg Mank, Terry Salomonson, Jay Hickerson,
and of course, my loving family

TABLE OF CONTENTS

INTRODUCTION

Terry Salomonson once wrote, "If bad information is not stopped early enough, it becomes tomorrow's facts. There have been several new books published in recent years where you can see the same misleading and false information in one book after another. And this is when the misinformation starts and is very hard to stop." How right he is. A select handful of people have attempted to compile broadcast logs of various programs, in an attempt to preserve our broadcasting heritage and history. Still, much misinformation has been printed over the years.

With an eye to making reliable information available, I have compiled an alphabetical listing of over 300 broadcast logs, from the *Academy Award Theater* to *Your Story Parade*. All of the logs, to the best of my ability, are complete and accurate. In order to separate the true broadcasts from the misinformation, I have gone through scripts, newspaper listings and even existing recordings. The information for *The Cavalcade of America*, for example, came from archives at the DuPont Manufacturing Company. The *Suspense* log came directly from my previous publication, *Suspense: Twenty Years of Thrills and Chills*. Some broadcast listings such as *As Easy as A.B.C.* and *The Harold Lloyd Comedy Theater* came directly from the *New York Times*, while others such as *The Lives of Harry Lime* originated from a collector's catalog.

In an effort to compile the most comprehensive account of broadcast logs, I turned to other writers and log-compilers whose knowledge of particular programs was greater than my own. Fred Shay generously donated his work on *The Adventures of Superman*, and Chris Lembesis thoughtfully bestowed *The New Adventures of Philip Marlowe* and *This Is My Best*. Randy Eidemiller donated (a few with Lembesis) *Quiet Please* and *Dragnet*; Dan Haefele, *Crime Classics*; Will Murray, *Doc Savage*; and David L. Easter, *The Mystery Man*. Victor Girard provided information on *Great Plays* and supplied corrections and extra details for a few other logs.

A few collectors who have been gathering information over the years gave me the small leads and tid-bits needed to detail many of the logs: Steve Kelez, Gordon Payton, Dave Siegel, Ted Davenport, Bill Yunick, Judy Diamond, Mary Pat Grams, Harvey, and Stewart M. Wright of the Radio Historical Association of Colorado. I am also in debt to Jerry Haendiges and Jay Hickerson, who allowed me to reprint the many logs they had in their collection. All of these people I wish to thank from the bottom of my heart. They were very open in sharing their information, and they should be recognized appropriately.

Of those I need to thank, I cannot forget Terry Salomonson. He not only supplied numerous logs for the book, but he also proofread it, adding cast names, titles and dates I did not have. Without him, this book would not be as it is; all errors, of course, remain mine.

One last source of mention is the logs of the late Ray Stanich, the pioneer of radio documentation. He is not only credited for being the first man ever to sneak out of tour groups within the major broadcasting studios throughout New York City, but he also managed to sneak into the basements of NBC and CBS, spending many days and weeks going through script compilations of various radio programs, writing down hundreds of titles and dates and then typing them on his typewriter. Although I did not have the chance to meet him, I admire the man for his patience. Stanich's work circulated so much over the years that I found logs he compiled in the hands of more than a dozen collectors across the country — and they all had at least one log that the others didn't!

The broadcast logs themselves have been cross-referenced, a task that took numerous hours of proofing. Many programs such as *Stroke of Fate* and *CBS Is There* are listed with their exact script titles for the very first time. Each log includes the title of the program, a short broadcast history comprising the time of broadcast, directors, writers, and actors, a numbered episode list that provides the title, broadcast date, and whenever possible, the actual stars and performers.

Episodes for which the title is unknown are represented by either [No Title] or [-----]. I have seen numerous books with broadcast logs in which, instead of documenting the missing titles, the authors purposely skipped to the next broadcast and continued numbering. Readers were thus led to believe only twenty-four episodes were broadcast instead of twenty-six.

The cast lists inside are not always complete: many list only the guest performer, and others list no cast at all. Recordings for many of the programs listed inside do not exist, nor do scripts or other forms of documentation, so the inevitable blank spaces and unknown casts will remain, no matter how far one researches.

Many of these logs, such as *The Greatest Story Ever Told*, are appearing in print for the first time. Others, such as *The Electric Theater*, have been available from various collectors over the years. The only change I made to those previously available is updated information, corrected titles, corrected airdates, and so on.

Some programs listed inside were syndicated — that is, they were recorded and later broadcast across the country on numerous local radio stations on different days and at various times. Programs such as *Box 13*, then, were broadcast on different days across the country. Additionally, syndicated series were sometimes broadcast in an order different from the one listed. Unless otherwise noted, all broadcast times are East Coast.

THE PROGRAMS

Academy Award Theater

The Academy Awards ceremony has been a Hollywood tradition for more than 60 years. Nothing is more treasured than the coveted Oscar, and Hollywood stars have been known for taking drastic steps to acquire one of their own. In 1946, a half-hour anthology series premiered over the airwaves, using the Academy Award name. A drug manufacturing firm — the House of Squibb — was the sponsor of the program, paying $1,600 a week to use the name of the Academy of Motion Picture Arts and Sciences. The purpose? To present each week a different adaptation of a Hollywood film that either won or was nominated for an Academy Award in at least one category.

An Oscar-winning screenplay and an original story, "A Star Is Born" and "Arise, My Love," were two such presentations. The Oscar-winning music score for the 1939 film "Stagecoach" was a highlight in the sixth broadcast of the series. Ginger Rogers reprised her Oscar-winning film role of Christopher Morley in "Kitty Foyle." Bette Davis reprised her Oscar-winning performance in "Jezebel," as did Paul Muni in "Watch on the Rhine" and "The Story of Louis Pasteur."

Academy Award Theater started out as a Saturday-evening offering on CBS, from 7 to 7:30 pm, EST. On July 3, 1946, the series moved to Wednesday nights at 10 pm. It has been reported that the performers received $4,000 per appearance. For "The Maltese Falcon" broadcast, almost every major star from the film reprised his film role. Nigel Bruce was originally scheduled to star in "Suspicion," but because of illness, was unable to attend the production. Frank Wilson wrote the adaptations. Dee Engelbach was producer and director. Leith Stevens composed and conducted each musical score except for a handful of broadcasts that reprised the original film scores and songs. After nine months on the air, *Academy Award Theater* left the air, being replaced by *Hollywood Players*.

1. Jezebel (4/6/46; Bette Davis and Anne Revere)
2. Kitty Foyle (4/13/46; Ginger Rogers)
3. The Story of Louis Pasteur (4/20/46; Paul Muni)
4. The Great McGinty (4/20/46; Brian Donlevy and Gerald Mohr)
5. Snow White and the Seven Dwarfs (4/27/46; Walt Disney)
6. Stagecoach (5/4/46; Randolph Scott and Claire Trevor)
7. If I Were King (5/11/46; Ronald Colman)
8. My Sister Eileen (5/18/46; Janet Blair and Rosalind Russell)
9. The Informer (5/25/46; Wallace Ford and Victor McLaglen)

10. Arise My Love (6/1/46; Ray Milland)
11. The Ruggles of Red Gap (6/8/46; Charles Laughton)
12. Pride of the Marines (6/15/46; Rosemary DeCamp and John Garfield)
13. The Front Page (6/22/46; Adolphe Menjou and Pat O'Brien)
14. A Star Is Born (6/29/46; Janet Gaynor and Fredric March)
15. The Maltese Falcon (7/3/46; Mary Astor, Humphrey Bogart, Sydney Greenstreet, and Peter Lorre)
16. Young Mr. Lincoln (7/10/46; Henry Fonda)
17. The Prisoner of Zenda (7/17/46; Virginia Bruce and Douglas Fairbanks, Jr.)
18. Foreign Correspondent (7/24/46; Joseph Cotten)
19. Hold Back the Dawn (7/31/46; Olivia deHavilland and Jean Pierre Aumont)
20. Watch on the Rhine (8/7/46; Paul Lucas)
21. Vivacious Lady (8/14/46; Lana Turner)
22. Keys of the Kingdom (8/21/46; Gregory Peck)
23. One Sunday Afternoon (8/28/46; James Stewart)
24. Pinocchio (9/4/46)
25. Shadow of a Doubt (9/11/46; Joseph Cotten and June Vincent)
26. The White Cliffs of Dover (9/18/46; Irene Dunne)
27. Guest in the House (9/25/46; Kirk Douglas and Anita Louise)
28. My Man Godfrey (10/2/46; William Powell)
29. It Happened Tomorrow (10/9/46; Ann Blythe and Eddie Bracken)
30. Blood on the Sun (10/16/46; John Garfield)
31. The Devil and Miss Jones (10/23/46; Charles Coburn and Virginia Mayo)
32. Suspicion (10/30/46; Cary Grant and Ann Todd)
33. Cheers for Miss Bishop (11/6/46; Olivia deHavilland)
34. Night Train (11/13/46; Rex Harrison)
35. Brief Encounter (11/20/46; Greer Garson)
36. Lost Horizons (11/27/46; Ronald Colman)
37. Portrait of Jenny (12/4/46; Joan Fontaine and John Lund)
38. Enchanted Cottage (12/11/46; Peter Lawford and Joan Lorring)
39. Lost Angel (12/18/46; Margaret O'Brien)

The Adventurer's Club

Also known as *Strange Adventures* and *World's Adventurer's Club*, this 15-minute juvenile program ran a total of 32 broadcasts. Syndicated in 1932. Episode 23 featured no title. No relation to the 1947–48 series of almost the same name.

1. Papua Escape
2. Manchurian Limited
3. Pancho Villa's Treasure
4. The Borneo Diamond
5. The Frozen North
6. The Land of Doomed Souls
7. Land of Death
8. Land of Darkness
9. Land of the Black Hand
10. India — Land of Mystery
11. The Tattooed Rose
12. Norway's Luck
13. The Elephant's Graveyard
14. The Living Dead
15. The Treasure Hunt
16. Hidden Fangs
17. The Fire Dog
18. The Black White Man
19. Grains of Death
20. Hairy Wild Man
21. Malay Madness
22. The Pale Flame
23. [No Title]
24. The Fawn
25. Kaditcha
26. Mukin in the Kyber
27. The Madonna's Tear
28. Dead Men Walk
29. The Living Mummy
30. The Mad Monk of Angkor Wat
31. Vengeance
32. Continental Express

Adventurer's Club

Based on true stories, this Saturday morning program ran a full year, 52 episodes, originating from WBBM in Chicago. Broadcast over CBS from 11:30 to 12 pm. Sponsored by the W.A. Sheaffer Pen Company. Featured Ken Nordine.

1. The Dr. McGovern Story (1/11/47)
2. Major A.B. "Speed" Chandler Story (1/18/47)
3. The Lt. L. Keeler Story (1/25/47)
4. The S. Graham Story (2/1/47)
5. The Byron de Porok Story [part one] (2/8/47)
6. The Byron de Porok Story [part two] (2/15/47)
7. The Byron de Porok Story [part three] (2/22/47)
8. The Paul Cyr Story (3/1/47)
9. The Rhys Davies Story (3/8/47)
10. The John D. Craig Story (3/15/47)
11. The Fay–Cooper Cole Story (3/22/47)
12. The Don McGibeny Story (3/29/47)
13. The Chick Grimsley Story (4/5/47)
14. The Luther Gable Story (4/12/47)
15. The Nicol Smith Story (4/19/47)
16. The Ric Ricardo Story (4/26/47)
17. The Theren Wassen Story (5/3/47)
18. The Michael Fielding Story (5/10/47)
19. The E. Evers Story (5/17/47)
20. The C.J. Albrecht Story (5/24/47)
21. The "Speed" Chadler Story (5/31/47)
22. The Waldo Logan Story (6/7/47)
23. The Mike Fordney Story (6/14/47)
24. The Irving Johnson (6/21/47)
25. The Walter Buchen Story (6/28/47)
26. The Ralph Harris Story (7/5/47)
27. The Owen O'Neil Story (7/12/47)
28. The Hugh Darby Story (7/19/47)
29. The Bob Childs Story (7/26/47)
30. The Paul Havas Story (8/2/47)
31. The Charles Chapman Story (8/9/47)
32. The Jerry Jeswick Story (8/16/47)
33. The Norman Gerlach Story (8/23/47)
34. The Michael Field Story (8/30/47)
35. The Paul Cyr Story (9/6/47)
36. The William Thomas Story (9/13/47)
37. The Arthur Olsen Story (9/20/47)
38. The Dean Smith Story (9/27/47)
39. The Berry Brooks Story (10/4/47)
40. The Robert Foran Story (10/11/47)
41. The John Craig Story (10/18/47)
42. The Augustus Curtis Story (10/25/47)
43. The Frank Chesrow Story (11/1/47)
44. The George Voevodsky Story (11/8/47)
45. The Don McGibney Story (11/15/47)
46. The T.J. Callaghan Story (11/22/47)
47. The Bruce Thomas Story (11/29/47)
48. The Lewis Cotlow Story (12/6/47)
49. The Bob Becker Story (12/13/47)
50. The Bob Lorenz Story (12/20/47)
51. The Robert Foran Story (12/27/47)
52. The Junius Wood Story (1/3/48)

Adventures by Morse

This creepy mystery series was scripted by Carlton E. Morse, creator of *One Man's Family* and *I Love a Mystery*. Produced by Morse as a syndicated series, each episode ran 30 minutes and aired as a once-a-week program. Russell Thorson, David Ellis and Elliott Lewis all played the role of Captain Turner throughout the run. Jack Edwards played Skip Turner. Written in serial form, this series was divided into a ten-week story line followed by a three-week story line, followed by another ten-week story line, and so on. In fact, the first story of each adventure took off from the last story of the previous adventure. The official script titles are listed below, and it should be noted that Carlton E. Morse did not title all of his scripts. Broadcast on different days from coast to coast, the first date belongs to the West Coast run, the second date belongs to the East Coast run.

1. The City of the Dead (1/8/44; 10/26/44)
2. I've Dug Up Something Ghastly (1/15/44; 11/2/44)
3. The Body Walked In (1/22/44; 11/9/44)
4. Old Clawfoot Again (1/29/44; 11/16/44)
5. The Skeleton Walks In (2/5/44; 11/23/44)
6. The Ghoul in the Grave (2/12/44; 11/30/44)
7. Captain Friday Vanishes (2/19/44; 12/7/44)
8. The Kidnapping of Clawfoot (2/26/44; 12/14/44)
9. The Trail of the Phantom Church Bell (3/4/44; 12/21/44)
10. Where the Pearls Were Hidden (3/11/44; 12/28/44)
11. A Coffin for a Lady (3/18/44; 1/4/45)
12. Conversation in the Casket (3/25/44; 1/11/45)
13. The Deepest Grave in the World (4/1/44; 1/18/45)
14. The Cobra King Strikes Back (4/8/44; 1/25/45)
15. Something About Hooded Snakes (4/15/44; 2/1/45)
16. The Mad King Ankor (4/22/44; 2/8/45)
17. The Temple of the Gorillas (4/29/44; 2/15/45)
18. The Living Image of Cambodia (5/6/44; 2/22/45)
19. Terror of the Hollow Mountain (5/13/44; 3/1/45)
20. The Face of the Beast (5/20/44; 3/8/45)
21. It Was Not Cannibalism (5/27/44; 3/15/45)
22. The Fangs and Teeth of the Enemy (6/3/44; 3/22/45)
23. The Amazing end of the Expedition (6/10/44; 3/29/45)
24. The Girl on a Shipwrecked Island (6/17/44; 4/5/45)
25. The Pirate Is a Frightening Man (6/24/44; 4/12/45)
26. There Is More About Gracie Than Meets the Eye (7/1/44; 4/19/45)
27. Dead Men Prowl (7/8/44; 4/26/45)
28. The Prowler at Work (7/15/44; 5/3/45)
29. The Dead Do Walk at Night (7/22/44; 5/10/45)
30. Conversation with the Walking Dead (7/29/44; 5/17/45)
31. The Walking Dead Captured (8/5/44; 5/24/45)
32. Life History of Prowles (8/12/44; 5/31/45)
33. Four Go to Join the Prowling Dead (8/19/44; 6/7/45)
34. The Prowler With the Rope Around His Neck (8/26/44; 6/14/45)
35. The Prowler Dead Walks Again (9/2/44; 6/21/45)
36. The Prowling Dead Introduces Himself (9/9/44; 6/28/45)
37. You'll Be Dead in a Week (9/16/44; 7/5/46)
38. $200,000 to Lose (9/23/44; 7/12/45)
39. [No Title] (9/30/44; 7/19/45)
40. Land of the Living Dead (10/7/44; 7/26/45)
41. [No Title] (10/14/44; 8/2/45)
42. The Green Eyed Murderess Again (10/21/44; 8/9/45)
43. The Tree that Eats Flesh (10/28/44; 8/16/45)
44. [No Title] (11/4/44; 8/23/45)
45. [No Title] (11/11/44; 8/30/45)
46. The Terror of the Sacred City (11/18/44; 9/6/45)
47. [No Title] (11/25/44; 9/13/45)
48. [No Title] (12/2/44; 9/20/45)
49. [No Title] (12/9/44; 9/27/45)
50. It's Dismal to Die (12/16/44; 10/4/45)
51. [No Title] (12/23/44; 10/11/45)
52. Bad Medicine for the Doctor (12/30/44; 10/18/45)

Adventures in Industry

Syndicated documentary series dramatizing the origins of various industries in America, from Benjamin Franklin and his idea of fire insurance to the Iron Horse, also known as the locomotive. Broadcast Sunday evenings originating from WMCA in New York, from 7:30 to 8 pm, EST.

1. Electric Power (1/18/48)
2. Packaged Food Distribution (1/25/48)
3. Black Magic (2/1/48)
4. The Harbor (2/8/48)
5. The Stock Exchange (2/15/48)
6. Fire Insurance (2/22/48)
7. F.O.B. Calcutta (2/29/48)
8. Worth Street (3/7/48)
9. The Million Dollar Glass (3/14/48)
10. Under One Roof (3/21/48)
11. Behind Your Telephone (3/28/48)
12. The Iron Horse (4/4/48)
13. Hotels in New York City (4/11/48)
14. Life Begins at Fifty (4/18/48)

The Adventures of Ellery Queen

This radio series was a cross between *Information Please* and *Sherlock Holmes*. Each week the listeners would hear a short mystery drama involving a murder or theft, never giving away the ending. The guest panelists would then attempt to solve the mystery, each giving their own "possible" solution, and then hear the real solution to the crime. The radio audience loved this show because they too were allowed time to come up with their own possible solutions.

Broadcast over CBS, this series premiered on June 18, 1939, without a sponsor as a Sunday evening hour-long program, from 8 to 9 pm, EST. George Zachary produced and directed. Ken Roberts was the announcer. Frederic Dannay and Manfred B. Lee wrote the scripts. Bernard Herrmann, Leith Stevens and Lyn Murray composed and conducted the music. Beginning September 10, 1939, the series was broadcast from 10 to 11 pm, EST. Beginning February 25, 1940, the series went to a new half-hour format, broadcast from 8 to 8:30 pm. As of April 28, 1940, the program moved to 7:30 to 8 pm and gained a sponsor, Gulf Oil. Bert Parks became the announcer and the regular supporting cast was Hugh Marlowe, Santos Ortega, Ted de Corsia and Marian Shockley.

As of January 8, 1942, the program moved to Thursdays from 9:30 to 10 pm on the West Coast, and Saturday from 7:30 to 8 pm on the East Coast. Bromo Seltzer sponsored this run, and the program moved to NBC, where it aired on the West Coast on Thursday from 12:30 to 1 am and on the East Coast on Saturday 7:30 to 8 pm. (These shows list two dates, the first on the West Coast and the second on the East.) Charles Paul became the lead organist and Carlton Young replaced Hugh Marlowe. From July to September of 1943, Gulf Oil took over sponsorship again as a 13-week summer run consisting of repeat scripts. As of October 7, 1943, Ernest Chappell took over as the announcer, and Sydney

Smith took over Carlton Young's roles. Helen Lewis replaced Marian Shockley from October 7 to November 13, 1943.

As of January 24, 1945, the program moved back to CBS for Anacin, broadcast on Wednesday evenings from 7:30 to 8 pm. Don Hancock became the announcer. Sydney Smith, Santos Ortega, Ted de Corsia and Barbara Terrell were the supporting cast. Gertrude Warner joined the cast beginning June 13, 1945. As of October 9, 1946, Anthony Boucher replaced Frederic Dannay as the script writer, working with Manfred B. Lee. Charlotte Keane replaced Barbara Terrell.

As of June 1, 1947, the series moved to Sundays from 6:30 to 7 pm. Anacin was still sponsoring and Don Hancock was still announcer. Tom Victor took over as producer and director. Supporting performers now consisted of Larry Dobkin, Bill Smith, Charlotte Keane and Ed Latimer. Beginning this season, the program had moved to Hollywood instead of originating from New York. Chet Kingsbury became the organist.

As of November 27, 1947, the program moved to ABC on Thursday evenings from 7:30 to 8 pm, EST. There was no sponsor beginning with this episode, and the program would remain sustaining until the end of the run. Dick Woolen became the program's producer and director. Paul Masterson was the announcer. Rex Koury was the organist. The program would move ahead an hour, 8:30 to 9 pm, EST beginning January 29, 1948.

Episode 11 was later made into a nine-part adaptation distributed by Gulf Oil in May and June of 1940. The broadcasts of April 25, 1945, and October 16, 1946, were pre-empted by specials on the United Nations. Episode seven was the same script later performed on *The Ford Theatre* of January 4, 1948.

The guests listed below varied from East Coast to West Coast; the names listed below are those who appeared on that date, but not always on both coasts. The episodes listed below are from both broadcasts, the first on the West Coast and the second on the East Coast.

1. The Gum-Chewing Millionaire (6/18/39; Peter Arno, Ruth McKenney, and Colonel Stoopnagle)
2. The Last Man Club (6/25/39; Gelett Burgess, Ed Gardner, Princess A. Kropotkin, and Deems Taylor)
3. The Fallen Angel (7/2/39)
4. Napoleon's Razor (7/9/39; Lillian Hellman and Herman Shumlin)
5. The Impossible Crime (7/16/39)
6. George Spelvin, Murderer (7/23/39)
7. The Bad Boy (7/30/39)
8. The Flying Needle (8/6/39)
9. The Wandering Corpse (8/13/39)
10. The Thirteenth Clue (8/20/39; Margaret Bourke-Paige)
11. The Secret Partner (8/27/39)
12. The Million Dollar Finger (9/3/39)
13. The Three R's [broadcast only on West Coast] (9/10/39)
14. The Blue Curse [West Coast only] (9/17/39)
15. The Lost Treasure (9/24/39)
16. The Woman From Nowhere (10/1/39)
17. The Mother Goose Murders (10/8/39)
18. The March From Death (10/15/39; Harry Kurnitz)
19. The Haunted Cave (10/22/39)
20. The Dead Cat (10/29/39)
21. The Picture Puzzle (11/5/39)
22. The Cellini Cup (11/12/39)

100. The Bald-Headed Ghost (11/19/42; 11/21/42; Eva Gabor)
101. The Three Mothers (11/26/42; 11/28/42; Bernard Geis)
102. The Man in the Taxi (12/3/42; 12/5/42; Sally Rand)
103. The Gymnasium Murder (12/10/42; 12/12/42)
104. The Yellow Ledger (12/17/42; 12/19/42)
105. The Red and Green Boxes (12/24/42; 12/26/42)
106. The Man Who Was Murdered By Installments (12/31/42; 1/2/43; Peggy Wood)
107. The Singing Rat (1/7/43; 1/9/43; Ann Corio)
108. Mr. Short and Mr. Long (1/14/43; 1/16/43)
109. The Fairy Tale Murder (1/21/43; 1/23/43)
110. Tom, Dick and Harry (1/28/43; 1/30/43)
111. The Secret Enemy (2/4/43; 2/6/43)
112. The Broken Statues (2/11/43; 2/13/43)
113. The Two Swordsmen (2/18/43; 2/20/43; Herb Shriner)
114. The One-Legged Man (2/25/43; 2/27/43)
115. Number Thirteen Dream Street (3/4/43; 3/6/43; Nanette Fabray, Nancy Kelly, and Ed Sullivan)
116. The Incredible Murder (3/11/43; 3/13/43)
117. The Boy Detectives [aka The Great Nut Mystery] (3/18/43; 3/20/43; Jerry Lester)
118. The Circus Train (3/25/43; 3/27/43)
119. The Human Weapon (4/1/43; 4/3/43)
120. The Three Musketeers (4/8/43; 4/10/43)
121. Pharaoh Jones' Last Case (4/15/43; 4/17/43; Dorothy Arzner)
122. The Deadly Game (4/22/43; 4/24/43; John Nanavic)
123. The Three Gifts (4/29/43; 5/1/43)
124. The Eye Print (5/6/43; 5/8/43; Joan Caulfield, Celeste Holm, and Richard Widmark)
125. The Barbaric Murder (5/13/43; 5/15/43)
126. The Fortune Teller (5/20/43; 5/22/43)
127. The Death Traps (5/27/43; 5/29/43)
128. The Killer Who Was Going to Die (6/3/43; 6/5/43)
129. Crime, Inc. (6/10/43; 6/12/43; Guy Lombardo)
130. The Man With the Red Beard (6/17/43; 6/19/43; Joe Besser and Gypsy Rose Lee)
131. Sergeant Velie's Revenge (6/24/43; 6/26/43)
132. The Hidden Crime (7/1/43; 7/3/43)
133. The Double Triangle (7/8/43; Harry Von Zell)
134. The Man Who Could Double the Size of Diamonds (7/15/43)
135. The Fire Bug (7/22/43; Janet Blair and John Wayne)
136. The Honeymoon House (7/29/43)
137. The Mouse's Blood (8/5/43)
138. The Four Murderers (8/12/43)
139. The Good Samaritan (8/19/43; Ralph Edwards)
140. The Mysterious Traveler (8/26/43; Otto Preminger)
141. The Dark Cloud (9/2/43)
142. The Blind Bullet (9/9/43: Spike Jones)
143. The Fallen Gladiator (9/16/43; John Wayne)
144. The Treasure Hunt (9/23/43; Harry Hershfield)
145. The World Series Crime (9/30/43)
146. The Man With 10,000 Enemies (10/7/43)
147. The Hopeless Case (10/14/43)
148. The Frightened Star (10/21/43; Earl Carroll)
149. The Stolen Rembrandt (10/28/43)
150. The Vanishing Magician (11/4/43)
151. The Three Dollar Robbery (11/11/43)
152. The Bullet-Proof Man (11/18/43; Warren Hull, Paul Johnson, and Ed Sullivan)
153. The Train that Vanished (11/25/43; Jack Dempsey)
154. The Dying Message (12/2/43)
155. The Man Who Played Dead (12/9/43; Arthur Murray and Kathryn Murray)
156. The Unlucky Man (12/16/43)

228. The Runaway Husband (5/30/45)
229. The Iron Woman (6/6/45)
230. The Corpse of Mr. Entwhistle (6/13/45)
231. The Absent Automatic (6/20/45)
232. Mr. One and Mr. Two (6/27/45; Bennett Cerf)
233. Nikki's Rich Uncle (7/4/45)
234. The Shipyard Racket (7/11/45)
235. The Gentleman Burglar (7/18/45; Wendy Barrie)
236. The Torture Victim (7/25/45)
237. Nick the Knife (8/1/45)
238. The Clue in C Minor (8/8/45; Evelyn Keyes)
239. The Time of Death (8/15/45; Sally Eilers)
240. The Man Who Was Afraid (9/5/45)
241. The Blue Egg (9/12/45)
242. The Lost Soul (9/19/45)
243. The Green House (9/26/45)
244. Ellery Queen, Cupid (10/3/45)
245. The Kid Glove Killer (10/10/45)
246. The Other Man (10/17/45; Jan Clayton)
247. The Repentant Thief (10/24/45)
248. The Halloween Murder (10/31/45; Edward Everett Horton)
249. The Message in Red (11/7/45; Victory Jory)
250. The Happy Marriage (11/14/45)
251. The Ape's Boss (11/21/45)
252. The Doodle of Mr. O'Drew (11/28/45)
253. The Peddler of Death (12/5/45; Helen Hayes)
254. The Man With Two Faces (12/12/45)
255. The Curious Thefts (12/19/45)
256. The Man Who Loved Murders (12/26/45)
257. The Lost Hoard (1/2/46)
258. The Various Deaths of Mr. Frayne (1/9/46; Arthur Godfrey)
259. The Green Eye (1/16/46)
260. The Lovely Racketeer (1/23/46)
261. Ellery Queen's Tragedy (1/30/46)
262. The Fifteenth Floor (2/6/46; Marjorie Rambeau)
263. The Living Death (2/13/46)
264. The Three Fences (2/20/46; Willie Mosconi)
265. The Ninth Mrs. Pook (2/27/46; Craig Rice)
266. The Phantom Shadow (3/6/46)
267. The Clue of the Elephant (3/13/46)
268. The Man Who Waited (3/20/46; Orson Welles)
269. The Armchair Detective (3/27/46)
270. The Death Wish (4/3/46)
271. The Girl Who Couldn't Get Married (4/10/46)
272. Nikki Porter, Murder Victim (4/17/46)
273. The Man Who Bought One Grape (4/24/46)
274. The Rhubarb Solution (5/1/46)
275. The Nine Mile Clue (5/8/46; Red Barber)
276. The Crime in the Darkness (5/15/46)
277. The Hollywood Murder Case (5/22/46; Lucille Ball)
278. The Laughing Woman (5/29/46; Francis Lederer)
279. Mr. Warren's Profession (6/5/46)
280. The Great Spy Puzzle (6/12/46)
281. Cokey and the Pizza (6/19/46)
282. Double Die (6/26/46)
283. The War Bride (7/3/46)
284. The Confidential Butler (7/10/46)
285. The Ultra-Modern Murders (7/17/46)
286. The Golden Key (7/24/46; Ben Hecht)
287. The Man Who Got Away With Murder (7/31/46; Ray Bolger)
288. The First Night (8/7/46; Milton Berle)
289. The Bis to Cal (8/14/46)
290. The Gymnasium Murder (8/21/46)
291. The Doomed Man (8/28/46)
292. Ellery Queen, Criminal (10/9/46)
293. The Woman Who Died Several Times (10/23/46; John Carradine)
294. Ellery Queen's Rival (10/30/46)
295. The Crime of Inspector Queen (11/6/46; Paul Douglas)
296. The Uneasy Voyage (11/13/46)
297. The Prize Fighter's Birthday (11/20/46)
298. The Blackmail Victim (11/27/46)
299. The Ellery Queen, Gigolo (12/4/46)
300. The Old Man's Darling (12/11/46)
301. The Hurricane That Committed Murder (12/18/46)
302. Ellery Queen, Santa Claus (12/25/46)

303. The Unhappy New Year (1/1/47)
304. The Man Who Could Vanish
     (1/8/47)
305. The Lollipop Murders (1/15/47)
306. The Queen Solomon (1/22/47)
307. The Stone Age Detective (1/29/47)
308. The Haunted House (2/5/47; Victor Jory)
309. The Green Gorillas (2/12/47; Jose Ferrer)
310. The Big Brain (2/19/47)
311. The Strange Death of Mr. Entricson
     (2/26/47)
312. Nikki Porter, Killer (3/5/47; Alfred Drake)
313. The Crooked Man (3/12/47)
314. The Specialist in Cops (3/19/47; Bela Lugosi)
315. The Ten Thousand Dollar Bill
     (3/26/47)
316. The Man Who Murdered a City
     (4/2/47)
317. The Big Fix (4/9/47)
318. The Redheaded Blonde Brunette
     (4/16/47; Arthur Godfrey)
319. The Green Gorillas (6/1/47; Nina Foch)
320. The Sky Pirates (6/8/47)
321. The Atomic Murder (8/3/47)
322. The Foolish Girls (8/10/47)
323. Murder for Americans (8/17/47)
324. The Rats Who Walked Like Men
     (8/24/47)
325. The King's Horse (8/31/47)
326. Number Thirty-One (9/7/47)
327. Tragedy in Blue (9/14/47)
328. The Man Who Squared the Circle
     (9/21/47)
329. The Saga of Ruffy Rux (11/27/47)
330. -----(12/4/47)
331. Nikki Porter, Bride (12/11/47)
332. The Melancholy Dane (12/18/47)
333. -----(12/25/47)
334. -----(1/1/48)
335. The Head Hunter (1/8/48)
336. -----(1/15/48)
337. The Private Eye (1/22/48; Henry Morgan)
338. -----(1/29/48)
339. -----(2/5/48)
340. A Question of Color (2/12/48)
341. The Old Sinner (2/19/48)
342. -----(2/26/48)
343. The Human Weapon (3/4/48)
344. The Lynching of Mr. Q (3/11/48)
345. The Armchair Detective (3/18/48)
346. The Farmer's Daughter (3/25/48)
347. -----(4/01/48)
348. The K.I. Case (4/8/48)
349. -----(4/15/48)
350. Murder by Installments (4/22/48)
351. The Three Frogs (4/29/48)
352. One Diamond (5/6/48)
353. Nikki Porter, Starlet (5/13/48)
354. Misery Mike (5/20/48)
355. -----(5/27/48)

The Adventures of Frank Race

Syndicated adventure series with the lead character, Frank Race, as an attorney fighting for justice. This series was produced by Bruce Eells and syndicated at least twice, once on the East Coast, and a year later on the West Coast. Eells had a cute trick of acquiring a big-name star for a series, an audition pilot, and once the program was sold, dropped the star and subbed a smaller-name star for lower pay. Tom Collins from *Chandu the Magician* fame was the first Frank Race, later replaced by Paul DuBov beginning with episode 23. The music was written and performed by Ivan Ditmars. Scripts were written and directed by Joel Murcott and Buckley Angel. The following have two dates: the first date is the East Coast run, the second date, the West Coast. Mondays. Note: The audition for the West Coast was June 5, 1951, plus the first episode of the West Coast run was "T.A.O.T. Daring Debutante."

1. The Adventure of the Hackenshack Victory (5/1/49; 6/5/51)
2. The Adventure of the Darling Debutante (5/8/49; 6/11/51)
3. The Istanbul Adventure (5/15/49; 6/18/51)
4. The Adventure of the Seventeen Black (5/22/49; 6/25/51)
5. The Enoch Arden Adventure (5/29/49; 7/02/51)
6. The Adventure of the Vanishing President (6/5/49; 7/09/51)
7. The Adventure of the Baradian Letters (6/12/49; 7/16/51)
8. The Airborne Adventure (6/19/49; 7/23/51)
9. The Adventure of the Shanghai Incident (6/26/49; 7/30/51)
10. The Adventure of the Juvenile Passenger (7/3/49; 8/06/51)
11. The Adventure of the Reckless Daughter (7/10/49; 8/13/51)
12. The Adventure of the Silent Heart (7/17/49; 8/20/51)
13. The Adventure of the Garrulous Bartender (7/24/49; 8/27/51)
14. The Adventure of the Vanishing Favorite (7/31/49; 9/03/51)
15. The Adventure of the Embittered Secretary (8/7/49; 9/10/51)
16. The Adventure of the Talking Bullet (8/14/49; 9/17/51)
17. The Adventure of the Fat Man's Loot (8/21/49; 9/24/51)
18. The Adventure of the General's Lady (8/28/49; 10/01/51)
19. The Adventure of the Violent Virtuoso (9/4/49; 10/08/51)
20. The Adventure of the Fourth Round Knockout (9/11/49; 10/15/51)
21. The Adventure of Three on a Match (9/18/49; 10/22/51)
22. The Adventure of the Roughneck's Will (9/25/49; 10/29/51)
23. The Adventure of the Green Doubloon (10/2/49; 11/05/51)
24. The Adventure of the Sobbing Bodyguard (10/9/49; 11/12/51)
25. The Adventure of the Diver's Loot (10/16/49; 11/19/51)
26. The Adventure of the Mormon Country (10/23/49; 11/26/51)
27. The Adventure of the Brooklyn Accent (10/30/49; 12/03/51)
28. The Adventure of the Six Week Cure (11/6/49; 12/10/51)
29. The Adventure of the Fairway Beauties (11/13/49; 12/17/51)
30. The Adventure of the Runaway Queen (11/20/49; 12/24/51)
31. The Adventure of the Lady in the Dark (11/27/49; 12/31/51)
32. The Adventure of the Silent Tongue (12/4/49; 1/07/52)
33. The Adventure of the Candy Killing (12/11/49; 1/14/52)
34. The Adventure of the Undecided Bride (12/18/49; 1/21/52)
35. The Adventure of the Gold Worshipper (12/25/49; 1/28/52)
36. The Adventure of the House Divided (1/1/50; 2/04/52)
37. The Adventure of the Pharaoh's Staff (1/8/50; 2/11/52)
38. The Adventure of the Count Trefanno Crest (1/15/50; 2/18/52)
39. The Adventure of the Night Crawler (1/22/50; 2/25/52)
40. The Adventure of the Kettle Drum (1/29/50; 3/04/52)
41. The Adventure of the Loveable Character (2/5/50; 3/11/52)
42. The Adventure of the Black Friar's Bridge (2/12/50; 3/18/52)
43. The Adventure of the Big Top (2/19/50; 3/25/52)

The Adventures of Philip Marlowe

Broadcast over NBC and sponsored by Pepsodent. Van Heflin stars as Philip Marlowe. This short-run series was a summer replacement for *The Bob Hope Show*. Marlowe was already featured on the big screen in *Murder, My Sweet* (1944) and *The Lady in the Lake* (1946). Milton Geiger adapted the original Marlowe stories. The music was supplied by Lyn Murray. Wendell Niles announced. Marlowe returned in the fall of 1948, and the show was retitled *The New Adventures of Philip Marlowe*.

Audition: "Who Shot Waldo? (6/12/47)
1. The Red Wind (6/17/47)
2. Pit 13 (6/24/47)
3. A Daring Young Dame on the Flying Trapeze (7/1/47)
4. King in Yellow Case (7/8/47)
5. [title unknown; plot concerns Lucifer] (7/15/47)
6. Goldfish (7/22/47)
7. The Orange Dog (7/29/47)
8. Trouble Is My Business (8/5/47)

The Adventures of Sam Spade

On October 3, 1941, *The Maltese Falcon* premiered at the Strand. It was the first film directed by John Huston, the first time Bogart's name appeared over the title, and the film that established the character of Sam Spade in Hollywood limelight. Less than five years later, *The Adventures of Sam Spade* premiered over ABC radio, directed by "the Hitchock of the airwaves," William Spier.

Howard Duff was no Bogart, but his characterization of Sam Spade was nonetheless memorable. In the role of Suzy, Sam's secretary, was Lurene Tuttle. Jerry Hausner was Sam's lawyer, Sid Weiss. Lucien Morawek and Lud Gluskin composed and conducted the music. Dick Joy announced. Ann Lorraine and Bob Tallman were the first to write for the series, but Lorraine left shortly after the series premiered, being replaced by Gil Doud.

The program was first broadcast over ABC as a Friday night sustainer. Beginning September 29, 1946, the series was broadcast over CBS for Wildroot Cream Oil, Sunday evenings from 8 to 8:30 pm, EST. On September 25, 1949, *Sam Spade* moved to NBC but held on to the sponsor and time slot it had at CBS. Howard Duff left the role of Spade in September of 1950. In November of 1950, Steven Dunne took over the role, and the series concluded as a Friday night sustainer from 8:30 to 9 pm, EST.

Reportedly, CBS sold the show to NBC because of the fear that Dashiell Hammett was being investigated by the House Un–American Activities Committee. Episode six was based on a non–Sam Spade short story by Dashiel Hammett. Episodes 22 and 23 were later combined into an hour-long radio play presented on *Suspense* in January of 1948. Episode 105 featured Sandra Gould, filling in for a vacationing Lurene Tuttle, in the role of Sam's secretary,

The script titles are listed below, as well as the original broadcast date. For the episodes listing two dates, the first is the transcription date; the second is the actual broadcast date.

1. Sam and the Guiana Sovereign (7/12/46)
2. Sam and the Farewell Murders (7/19/46)
3. Sam and the Unhappy Poet (7/26/46)
4. Sam and Psyche (8/2/46)
5. Death and Company (8/9/46)
6. Two Sharp Knives (8/16/46)
7. Zig Zags of Treachery (8/23/46)
8. Sam and the Scythian Tiara (8/30/46)
9. The Corporation Murders (9/6/46)
10. The Dot Marlow Caper [part one] (9/13/46)
11. The Dot Marlow Caper [part two] (9/20/46)
12. The Count on Billy Burke (9/27/46)
13. The Blood Money Caper (9/29/46)
14. Gutting of Couffignal (10/4/46)
15. The Unwritten Law Caper (10/6/46)
16. The Ten Clues Caper (10/13/46)
17. The Fly Paper Caper (10/20/46)
18. The Midway Caper (10/27/46)
19. The Certified Czech Caper (11/3/46)
20. Sam and the Farewell Murders (11/10/46)
21. The Hot Ice Caper (11/17/46)
22. The Kandy Tooth Caper [part one] (11/24/46; Joseph Kearns)
23. The Kandy Tooth Caper [part two] (12/1/46; Joseph Kearns)
24. The Minks of Turk Caper (12/8/46)
25. The Picture Frame Caper (12/15/46)
26. Sam and the Three Wise Men (12/22/46)
27. The Golden Horseshoe (12/29/46)
28. The Llewelyn Caper (1/5/47)
29. The Cremona Clock Caper (1/12/47)
30. The False Face Caper (1/19/47)
31. The Agamemnon Caper (1/26/47)
32. The Dead Duck Caper (2/2/47)
33. The Girl With the Silver Eyes (2/9/47)
34. Inside Story on Kid Spade (2/16/47)
35. The Big Production Caper (2/23/47)
36. The Uncle Money Caper (3/2/47)
37. Orpheus and his Lute (3/9/47)
38. The Ignorance About Bliss (3/16/47)
39. Too Many Spades (3/23/47)
40. The Dancing Pearl Caper (3/30/47)
41. The Poisonville Caper (4/6/47)
42. The Double–Scar Caper (4/13/47)
43. The Scrooge of Portrero Caper (4/20/47)

44. The Debutante Caper (4/27/47)
45. Duet in Spades (5/4/47)
46. The Yule Log Caper (5/11/47)
47. The Assistant Murderer (5/18/47)
48. Jury Judy (5/25/47)
49. The Mishakoff Emeralds Caper (6/1/47)
50. The Calcutta Trunk Caper (6/8/47)
51. The Convertible Caper (6/15/47)
52. The Greek Letter Caper (6/22/47)
53. The Cosmic Harmony Caper (6/29/47)
54. The Simile Caper (7/6/47)
55. The Buff-Orpington Caper (7/13/47)
56. Sam and the Unhappy Poet (7/20/47)
57. The Gold Rush Caper (7/27/47)
58. The Crooked Neck Caper (8/3/47)
59. The Commonwealth Tankard Caper (8/10/47)
60. The Doctor's Dilemma Caper (8/17/47)
61. The Jade Dragon Caper (8/24/47)
62. The Corkscrew Caper (8/31/47)
63. The Forty-Nine Cent Caper (9/7/47)
64. The Cinderella Caper (9/14/47)
65. The April Caper (9/21/47)
66. The Madcap Caper (9/28/47)
67. The Adam Figg Caper (10/5/47)
68. The Tears of Buddha Caper (10/12/47)
69. The Untouchable Caper (10/19/47)
70. The Bonnie Fair Caper (10/26/47)
71. The Wrong Guy Caper (11/2/47)
72. The Bow Window Caper (11/9/47)
73. The Purple Poodle Caper (11/16/47)
74. The Caper With Eight Diamonds (11/23/47)
75. The Full House Caper (11/30/47)
76. The Palermo Vendetta Caper (12/7/47)
77. The Gumshoe Caper (12/14/47)
78. The Nick Saint Caper (12/21/47)
79. The Perfect Score Caper (12/28/47)
80. The One Hour Caper (1/4/48)
81. The Short Life Caper (1/11/48)
82. The Pike's Head Caper (1/18/48)
83. The Gold Key Caper (1/25/48)
84. The Nimrod Caper (2/1/48)
85. The Great Drought Caper (2/8/48)
86. The Goldie Gates Caper (2/15/48)
87. The Mason Crayson Caper (2/22/48)
88. The Grim Reaper Caper (2/29/48)
89. John's Other Wife's Other Husband (3/7/48)

238. The Spanish Prisoner Caper
     (3/9/51)
239. The Sinister Siren Caper (3/16/51)
240. The Kimberley Cross Caper
     (3/23/51)
241. The Vendetta Caper (3/11/51;
     3/30/51)

242. The Denny Shane Caper (4/6/51)
243. The Civic Pride Caper (4/13/51)
244. The Rowdy Dowser Caper
     (4/20/51)
245. The Hail and Farewell Caper
     (4/27/51)

The Adventures of Superman (1940–1949)*

First broadcast for a trial period in 1938 on some out-of-the-way radio stations, then brought back on February 12, 1940, as a thrice-a-week juvenile serial. Mutual never realized at the time how popular the show was and discontinued the program on March 9, 1942. The public, by submitting thousands of letters, convinced Mutual executives to continue the program. The series was revived on August 31, 1942, as a five-a-week, fifteen-minute series and continued till February 4, 1949. During the war years (1943–45), the menace went from comic book villains to Japanese and Germans. Bud Collyer was Superman throughout the entire run. *Superman* was broadcast on Mutual as a sustained serial until Kellogg's Pep began sponsoring the series on January 4, 1943. Pep continued until the end of 1946; the series returned sustaining. Batman and Robin first appeared on March 1, 1945, and were on the show many times until the end of the run. The titles listed below are actual script titles, as they appeared on the script covers.

1. The Baby from Krypton (2/12/40)
2. Clark Kent, Reporter (2/14/40)
3. Keno's Landslide (2/16/40)
4. Kent Captured by the Wolfe
   (2/19/40)
5. Locomotive Crew Freed (2/21/40)
6. The Silver Clipper (2/23/40)
7. The Atomic Beam Machine
   (2/26/40)
8. Fuel (2/28/40)
9. Threat to the Planet Building
   (3/1/40)
10. Fire in the Sterling Building (3/4/40)
11. Stabbing of June Anderson (3/6/40)
12. North Star Mining Company
    (3/8/40)
13. The Steamship Madison (3/11/40)
14. Plane to Canyon City (3/13/40)
15. Left to be Killed (3/15/40)
16. The Prison Riot (3/18/40)
17. The Steam Plant (3/20/40)
18. Wolfe vs. the Yellow Mask (3/22/40)

19. The Yellow Mask Escapes (3/25/40)
20–27. The Emerald of the Incas
    (3/27/40, 3/29, 4/1, 4/3, 4/5, 4/8,
    4/10, and 4/12/40)
28–33. Donnelli's Protection Racket
    (4/15/40, 4/17, 4/19, 4/22, 4/24, and
    4/26/40)
34–39. Airplane Disasters a Bridger Field
    (4/29/40, 5/1, 5/3, 5/6, 5/8, and
    5/10/40)
40–45. Buffalo Hills (5/13/40, 5/15, 5/17,
    5/20, 5/22, and 5/24/40)
46–51. Alonzo Craig: Arctic Explorer
    (5/27, 5/29, 5/31, 6/3, 6/5, and
    6/7/40)
52–57. H. Morton's Weather Predictions
    (6/10/40, 6/12, 6/14, 6/17, 6/19, and
    6/21/40)
58–63. Hans Hoebin's Doll Factory
    (6/24/40, 6/26, 6/28, 7/1, 7/3, and
    7/5/40)
64–69. Happyland Amusement Park

*Compiled by Fred Shay.

(7/8/40, 7/10, 7/12, 7/15, 7/17, and
7/19/40)

70–75. Lighthouse Point Smugglers
(7/22/40, 7/24, 7/26, 7/29, 7/31,
and 8/2/40)

76–78. Pillar of Fire at Graves End
(8/5/40, 8/7, and 8/9/40)

79–84. The Mayan Treasure (8/12/40,
8/14, 8/16, 8/19, 8/21, and
8/23/40)

85–96. Professor Thorpe's Bathesphere
(8/26/40, 8/28, 8/30, 9/2, 9/4,
9/6, 9/9, 9/11, 9/13, 9/16, 9/18, and
9/20/40)

97–102. The Curse of Dead Man's
Island (9/23/40, 9/25, 9/27, 9/30,
10/2, and 10/4/40)

103–117. The Yellow Mask and the Five
Million Dollar Jewel Robbery
(10/7/40, 10/9, 10/11, 10/14, 10/16,
10/18, 10/21, 10/23, 10/25, 10/28,
10/30, 11/1, 11/4, 11/6, and 11/8/40)

118–131. The Invisible Man (11/11/40,
11/13, 11/15, 11/18, 11/20, 11/22,
11/25, 11/27, 11/29, 12/2, 12/4, 12/6,
12/9, and 12/11/40)

132–145. The Howling Coyote
(12/13/40, 12/16, 12/18, 12/20,
12/23, 12/25, 12/27, 12/30/40,
1/1/41, 1/3, 1/6, 1/8, 1/10, and
1/13/41)

146–156. The Black Pearl of Osiris
(1/15/41, 1/17, 1/20, 1/22, 1/24,
1/27, 1/29, 1/31, 2/3, 2/5, and
2/7/41)

157–166. The Dragon's Teeth (2/10/41,
2/12, 2/14, 2/17, 2/19, 2/21, 2/24,
2/26, 2/28, and 3/3/41)

167–186. Last of the Clipper Ships
(3/5/41, 3/7, 3/10, 3/12, 3/14, 3/17,
3/19, 3/21, 3/24, 3/26, 3/28, 3/31,
4/2, 4/4, 4/7, 4/9, 4/11, 4/14, 4/16,
and 4/18/41)

187–195. The Nitrate Shipment
(4/21/41, 4/23, 4/25, 4/28, 4/30,
5/2, 5/5, 5/7, and 5/9/41)

196–201. The Grayson Submarine
(5/12/41, 5/14, 5/16, 5/19, 5/21, and
5/23/41)

202–213. Dr. Deutch and the Radium
Mine (5/26/41, 5/28, 5/30, 6/2, 6/4,
6/6, 6/9, 6/11, 6/13, 6/16, 6/18, and
6/21/41)

214–221. The White Plague (6/23/41,
6/25, 6/27, 6/30, 7/2, 7/4, 7/7,
and 7/9/41)

222–227. Fur Smuggling (7/12/41, 7/14,
7/16, 7/19, 7/21, and 7/23/41)

228–243. Dr. Roebling and the Voice
Machine (7/22/41, 7/28, 7/30, 8/1,
8/4, 8/6, 8/8, 8/11, 8/13, 8/15,
8/18, 8/20, 8/22, 8/25, 8/27, and
8/29/41; Frank Lovejoy)

244–258. Metropolis Football Team Poisoned (9/1/41, 9/3, 9/5, 9/8, 9/10,
9/12, 9/15, 9/17, 9/19, 9/22, 9/24,
9/26, 9/29, 10/1, and 10/3/41)

259–268. Crooked Oil Association
(10/6/41, 10/8, 10/10, 10/13, 10/15,
10/17, 10/20, 10/22, 10/24, and
10/27/41)

269–275. The Silver Arrow (10/29/41,
10/31, 11/3, 11/5, 11/7, 11/10, and
11/12/41)

276–290. The Pan-Am Highway
(11/14/41, 11/17, 11/19, 11/21, 11/24,
11/26, 11/28, 12/1, 12/3, 12/5, 12/8,
12/10, 12/12, 12/15, and 12/17/41)

291–300. The Mechanical Man
(12/19/41, 12/22, 12/24, 12/26,
12/29, 12/31, 1/2/42, 1/5, 1/7, and
1/9/42)

301–312. Lita, the Leopard Woman
(1/12/42, 1/14, 1/16, 1/19, 1/21, 1/23,
1/26, 1/28, 1/30, 2/2, 2/4, and
2/6/42)

313–320. The Ghost Car (2/9/42, 2/11,
2/13, 2/16, 2/18, 2/20, 2/23, and
2/25/42)

321–325. A Mystery for Superman
(2/27/42, 3/2, 3/4, 3/6, and
3/9/42)

326. Superman Comes to Earth
(8/31/42)

327. Eben Kent Dies in Fire, Clark Goes
to Metropolis (9/1/42)

328–338. The Wolfe (9/2/42, 9/3, 9/4,
9/7, 9/8, 9/9, 9/10, 9/11, 9/14,
9/15, and 9/16/42)

339–347. The Tiny Men (9/17/42, 9/18,
9/21, 9/22, 9/23, 9/24, 9/25, 9/28,
and 9/29/42)

348–357. Mystery in Arabia (9/30/42,
10/1, 10/2, 10/5, 10/6, 10/7, 10/8,
10/9, 10/12, and 10/13/42)

358–366. The Black Narcissus (10/14/42,
10/15, 10/16, 10/19, 10/20, 10/21,
10/22, 10/23, and 10/26/42)

367–385. The Headless Indian
(10/27/42, 10/28, 10/29, 10/30, 11/2,
11/3, 11/4, 11/5, 11/6, 11/9, 11/10, 11/11,
11/12, 11/13, 11/16, 11/17, 11/18, 11/19,
and 11/20/42)

386–398. The Midnight Intruder
(11/23/42, 11/24, 11/25, 11/26, 11/27,
11/30, 12/1, 12/2, 12/3, 12/4, 12/7,
12/8, and 12/9/42)

399–407. The Lost Continent of Atlantis
(12/10/42, 12/11, 12/14, 12/15, 12/16,
12/17, 12/18, 12/21, and 12/22/42)

408–414. The Mystery Ship (12/23/42,
12/24, 12/27, 12/28, 12/29, 12/30,
and 12/31/42)

415–429. The Tin Men (1/4/43, 1/5, 1/6,
1/7, 1/8, 1/11, 1/12, 1/13, 1/14, 1/15,
1/18, 1/19, 1/20, 1/21, and 1/22/43)

430–438. Trouble in Athabascus
(1/25/43, 1/26, 1/27, 1/28, 1/29, 2/1,
2/2, 2/3, and 2/4/43)

439–449. Island of Ghost Ships (2/5/53,
2/8, 2/9, 2/10, 2/11, 2/12, 2/15, 2/16,
2/17, 2/18, and 2/19/43)

450–465. The Model Plane Mystery
(2/22/43, 2/23, 2/24, 2/25, 2/26,
3/1, 3/2, 3/3, 3/4, 3/5, 3/8, 3/9,
3/10, 3/11, 3/12, and 3/15/43)

466–469. Dr. Cameron's Helicopter
(3/17/43, 3/18, 3/19, and 3/22/43)

470–485. The Vulture and The Thunderbolt Express (3/23/43, 3/24,
3/25, 3/26, 3/29, 3/30, 3/31, 4/1,
4/2, 4/5, 4/6, 4/7, 4/8, 4/9, 4/12,
and 4/13/43)

486–497. The Bainbridge Disaster
(4/14/43, 4/15, 4/16, 4/19, 4/20,
4/21, 4/22, 4/23, 4/26, 4/27, 4/28,
and 4/29/43)

498–511. Master of the Dream World
(4/30/43, 5/3, 5/4, 5/5, 5/6, 5/7,
5/10, 5/11, 5/12, 5/13, 5/14, 5/17,
5/18, and 5/19/43)

512–521. The Ghost Squadron
(5/20/43, 5/21, 5/24, 5/25, 5/26,
5/27, 5/28, 5/31, 6/1, and 6/2/43)

522–528. The Meteor From Krypton
(6/3/43, 6/4, 6/7, 6/8, 6/9, 6/10,
and 6/11/43)

529–543. Society of the Flamingo
(6/14/43, 6/15, 6/16, 6/17, 6/18, 6/21,
6/22, 6/23, 6/24, 6/25, 6/28, 6/29,
7/1, 7/2, and 7/5/43)

544–555. Mr. Prim and the Dragonfly

Adventure (7/6/43, 7/7, 7/8, 7/9,
7/12, 7/13, 7/14, 7/15, 7/16, 7/19,
7/20, and 7/21/43)

556–563. The Genie in the Bottle
(7/22/43, 7/23, 7/26, 7/27, 7/28,
7/29, 7/30, and 8/2/43)

564–574. The World of the Future
(8/3/43, 8/4, 8/5, 8/6, 8/9, 8/10,
8/11, 8/12, 8/13, 8/16, and 8/17/43)

575–588. The Civil Air Patrol (8/18/43,
8/19, 8/20, 8/23, 8/24, 8/25, 8/26,
8/27, 8/30, 8/31, 9/1, 9/2, 9/3, and
9/6/43)

589–596. Penrose Salvage Company
(9/7/43, 9/8, 9/9, 9/10, 9/13, 9/14,
9/15, and 9/16/43)

597–600. Mystery of the Death Plane
(9/17/43, 9/20, 9/21, and 9/22/43)

601–607. Adventures in the Capitol City
(9/23/43, 9/24, 9/27, 9/28, 9/29,
9/30, and 10/1/43)

608–615. German Submarine Menace
(10/4/43, 10/5, 10/6, 10/7, 10/8,
10/11, 10/12, and 10/13/43)

616–626. The New German Weapon
(10/14/43, 10/15, 10/18, 10/19, 10/20,
10/21, 10/22, 10/25, 10/26, 10/27,
and 10/28/43)

627–640. The Mystery of Prince Philip
(10/29/43, 11/1, 11/2, 11/3, 11/4, 11/5,
11/8, 11/9, 11/10, 11/11, 11/12, 11/15,
11/16, and 11/17/43)

641–656. Military Espionage (11/18/43,
11/19, 11/22, 11/23, 11/24, 11/25,
11/26, 11/29, 11/30, 12/1, 12/2, 12/3,
12/6, 12/7, 12/8, and 12/9/43)

657–672. Stolen War Information
(12/10/43, 12/13, 12/14, 12/15, 12/16,
12/17, 12/20, 12/21, 12/22, 12/23,
12/24, 12/27, 12/28, 12/29, 12/30/43,
and 1/3/44)

673–680. Lois and Jimmy Disappears
(1/4/44, 1/5, 1/6, 1/7, 1/10, 1/11, 1/12,
and 1/13/44)

681–689. The Green Death (1/14/44,
1/17, 1/18, 1/19, 1/20, 1/21, 1/22, 1/24,
1/25, and 1/26/44)

690–701. The Mystery of the $100,000
Stamp (1/27/44, 1/28, 1/31, 2/1, 2/2,
2/3, 2/4, 2/7, 2/8, 2/9, 2/10, and
2/11/44)

702–707. Mystery of the Transport Plane
Crashes (2/14/44, 2/15, 2/16, 2/17,
2/18, and 2/21/44)

708–714. Lighthouse Point (2/22/44, 2/23, 2/24, 2/25, 2/28, 2/29, and 3/1/44)

715–718. The Rocket Plane (3/2/44, 3/3, 3/6, and 3/7/44)

719–732. The Mystery of Clifftown (3/8/44, 3/9, 3/10, 3/13, 3/14, 3/15, 3/16, 3/17, 3/20, 3/21, 3/22, 3/23, 3/24, and 3/27/44)

733–753. The Mystery of the Golden Pigeon (3/28/44, 3/29, 3/30, 3/31, 4/3, 4/4, 4/5, 4/6, 4/7, 4/10, 4/11, 4/12, 4/13, 4/14, 4/17, 4/18, 4/19, 4/20, 4/21, 4/24, and 4/25/44)

754–774. Mystery of Desert Springs and The Birdmen (4/26/44, 4/27, 4/28, 5/1, 5/2, 5/3, 5/4, 5/5, 5/8, 5/9, 5/10, 5/11, 5/12, 5/15, 5/16, 5/17, 5/18, 5/19, 5/22, 5/23, and 5/24/44)

775–786. The Hurdy-Gurdy Man (5/25/44, 5/26, 5/29, 5/30, 5/31, 6/1, 6/2, 6/5, 6/6, 6/7, 6/8, and 6/9/44)

787–801. The North Woods Story (6/12/44, 6/13, 6/14, 6/15, 6/16, 6/19, 6/20, 6/21, 6/22, 6/22, 6/23, 6/26, 6/27, 6/28, 6/29, and 6/30/44)

802–810. The Seagull, North Pacific Adventure (7/3/44, 7/4, 7/5, 7/6, 7/7, 7/10, 7/11, 7/12, and 7/13/44)

811–821. The Mystery of the Aviation Freight Lines (7/14/44, 7/17, 7/18, 7/19, 7/20, 7/21, 7/24, 7/25, 7/26, 7/27, and 7/28/44)

822–832. The Society of the Crimson Robe (7/31/44, 8/1, 8/2, 8/3, 8/4, 8/7, 8/8, 8/9, 8/10, 8/11, and 8/14/44)

833–842. Ghosts of the Air (8/15/44, 8/16, 8/17, 8/18, 8/21, 8/22, 8/23, 8/24, 8/25, and 8/28/44)

843–851. The Scorpion (8/29/44, 8/30, 8/31, 9/1, 9/4, 9/5, 9/6, 9/7, and 9/8/44)

852–864. Der Teufel's Atomic Pistol (9/11/44, 9/12, 9/13, 9/14, 9/15, 9/18, 9/19, 9/20, 9/21, 9/22, 9/25, 9/26, and 9/27/44)

865–885. The Mystery of the Mummy Case (9/28/44, 9/29, 10/2, 10/3, 10/4, 10/5, 10/6, 10/9, 10/10, 10/11, 10/12, 10/13, 10/16, 10/17, 10/18, 10/19, 10/20, 10/23, 10/24, 10/25, and 10/26/44)

886–894. Dr. Roebling and the Voice Machine (10/27/44, 10/30, 10/31, 11/1, 11/2, 11/3, 11/6, 11/7, and 11/8/44)

895–906. Planet Utopia (11/16/44, 11/17, 11/20, 11/21, 11/22, 11/23, 11/24, 11/27, 11/28, 11/29, 12/1, and 12/4/44)

907–917. Lois's Uncle John and the Missing Plans (12/5/44, 12/6, 12/7, 12/8, 12/11, 12/12, 12/13, 12/14, 12/15, 12/18, and 12/19/44)

918–923. The Missing Santa Claus (12/20/44, 12/21, 12/22, 12/25, 12/26, and 12/27/44)

924–934. The Man in the Velvet Shoes (12/28/44, 12/29/44, 1/2/45, 1/3, 1/4, 1/5, 1/8, 1/9, 1/10, 1/11, and 1/12/45)

935–954. The Mystery of the Sleeping Beauty (1/15/45, 1/16, 1/17, 1/18, 1/19, 1/22, 1/23, 1/24, 1/25, 1/26, 1/29, 1/30, 1/31, 2/1, 2/2, 2/5, 2/6, 2/7, 2/8, and 2/9/45)

955–966. The Space Shell (2/12/45, 2/13, 2/14, 2/15, 2/16, 2/19, 2/20, 2/21, 2/22, 2/23, 2/26, and 2/27/45)

967–978. The Mystery of the Waxmen (2/28/45, 3/1, 3/2, 3/5, 3/6, 3/7, 3/8, 3/9, 3/12, 3/13, 3/14, and 3/15/45)

979–990. The Mystery of the Golden Nail (3/16/45, 3/19, 3/20, 3/21, 3/22, 3/23, 3/26, 3/27, 3/28, 3/29, 3/30, and 4/2/45)

991–999. The Ghost Car (4/3/45, 4/4, 4/5, 4/6, 4/9, 4/10, 4/11, 4/12, and 4/13/45)

1000–1008. The Boy King of Moravia (4/16/45, 4/17, 4/18, 4/19, 4/20, 4/23, 4/24, 4/25, and 4/26/45)

1009–1022. Lair of the Dragon (4/27/45, 4/30, 5/1, 5/2, 5/3, 5/4, 5/7, 5/8, 5/9, 5/10, 5/11, 5/14, 5/15, and 5/16/45)

1023–1032. The Mystery of the Counterfeit Money (5/17/45, 5/18, 5/21, 5/22, 5/23, 5/24, 5/25, 5/28, 5/29, and 5/30/45)

1033–1042. Valley of the Giants (5/31/45, 6/1, 6/4, 6/5, 6/6, 6/7, 6/8, 6/11, 6/12, and 6/13/45)

1043–1061. The Desert Adventure

(6/14/45, 6/15, 6/18, 6/19, 6/20, 6/21, 6/22, 6/25, 6/26, 6/27, 6/28, 6/29, 7/2, 7/3, 7/4, 7/5, 7/6, 7/9, and 7/10/45)

1062–1080. The Underseas Kingdom (7/11/45, 7/12, 7/13, 7/16, 7/17, 7/18, 7/19, 7/20, 7/23, 7/24, 7/25, 7/26, 7/27, 7/30, 7/31, 8/1, 8/2, 8/3, and 8/6/45)

1081–1087. The Flood (8/7/45, 8/8, 8/9, 8/10, 8/13, 8/14, and 8/15/45)

1088–1095. Black Market (8/24/45, 8/27, 8/28, 8/29, 8/30, 8/31, 9/3, and 9/4/45)

1096–1108. Dr. Blythe's Confidence Gang (9/5/45, 9/6, 9/7, 9/10, 9/11, 9/12, 9/13, 9/14, 9/17, 9/18, 9/19, 9/20, and 9/21/45)

1109–1110. The Meteor of Kryptonite (9/24/45 and 9/25/45)

1111–1120. The Scarlet Widow (9/26/45, 9/27, 9/28, 10/1, 10/2, 10/3, 10/4, 10/5, 10/8, and 10/9/45)

1121–1140. The Atom Man (10/10/45, 10/11, 10/12, 10/15, 10/16, 10/17, 10/18, 10/19, 10/22, 10/23, 10/24, 10/25, 10/26, 10/29, 10/30, 10/31, 11/1, 11/2, 11/5, and 11/6/45)

1141–1159. The Atom Man in Metropolis (11/7/45, 11/8, 11/9, 11/12, 11/13, 11/14, 11/15, 11/16, 11/19, 11/20, 11/21, 11/22, 11/23, 11/26, 11/27, 11/28, 11/29, 11/30, and 12/3/45)

1160–1185. Looking for Kryptonite (12/4/45, 12/5, 12/6, 12/7, 12/10, 12/11, 12/12, 12/13, 12/14, 12/17, 12/18, 12/19, 12/20, 12/21, 12/24, 12/25, 12/26, 12/27, 12/28, 12/31/45, 1/1/46, 1/2, 1/3, 1/4, 1/7, and 1/8/46)

1186–1199. The Talking Cat (1/9/46, 1/10, 1/11, 1/14, 1/15, 1/16, 1/17, 1/18, 1/21, 1/22, 1/23, 1/24, 1/25, and 1/28/46)

1200–1212. Is There Another Superman? (1/29/46, 1/30, 1/31, 2/1, 2/4, 2/5, 2/6, 2/7, 2/8, 2/11, 2/12, 2/13, and 2/14/46)

1213–1234. The Radar Rocket (2/15/46, 2/18, 2/19, 2/20, 2/21, 2/22, 2/25, 2/26, 2/27, 2/28, 3/1, 3/4, 3/5, 3/6, 3/7, 3/8, 3/11, 3/12, 3/13, and 3/14/46)

1235–1244. The Mystery of the Dragon's Teeth (3/15/46, 3/18, 3/19,

3/20, 3/21, 3/22, 3/25, 3/26, 3/27 and 3/28/46)

1245–1256. Story of the Century (3/29/46, 4/1, 4/2, 4/3, 4/4, 4/5, 4/8, 4/9, 4/10, 4/11, 4/12, and 4/15/46)

1257–1281. The Hate Mongers Organization (4/16/46, 4/17, 4/18, 4/19, 4/20, 4/23, 4/24, 4/25, 4/26, 4/29, 4/30, 5/1, 5/2, 5/3, 5/6, 5/7, 5/8, 5/9, 5/10, 5/13, 5/14, 5/15, 5/16, 5/17, and 5/20/46)

1282–1295. Al Vincent's Corrupt Political Machine (5/21/46, 5/22, 5/23, 5/24, 5/27, 5/28, 5/29, 5/30, 5/31, 6/3, 6/4, 6/5, 6/6, and 6/7/46)

1296–1311. Clan of the Fiery Cross (6/10/46, 6/11, 6/12, 6/13, 6/14, 6/17, 6/18, 6/19, 6/20, 6/21, 6/24, 6/25, 6/26, 6/27, 6/28, and 7/1/46)

1312–1333. Horatio F. Horn: Detective (7/2/46, 7/3, 7/4, 7/5, 7/8, 7/9, 7/10, 7/11, 7/12, 7/15, 7/16, 7/17, 7/18, 7/19, 7/22, 7/23, 7/24, 7/25, 7/26, 7/29, 7/30, and 7/31/46)

1334–1348. The Secret Menace Strikes (8/1/46, 8/2, 8/5, 8/6, 8/7, 8/8, 8/9, 8/12, 8/13, 8/14, 8/15, 8/16, 8/19, 8/20, and 8/21/46)

1349–1356. Candy Meyer's Big Story (8/22/46, 8/23, 8/26, 8/27, 8/28, 8/29, 8/30, and 9/2/46)

1357–1373. George Latimer, Crooked Political Boss (9/3/46, 9/4, 9/5, 9/6, 9/9, 9/10, 9/11, 9/12, 9/13, 9/16, 9/17, 9/18, 9/19, 9/20, 9/23, 9/24, and 9/25/46)

1374–1388. The Dead Voice (9/26/46, 9/27, 9/30, 10/1, 10/2, 10/3, 10/4, 10/7, 10/8, 10/9, 10/10, 10/11, 10/14, 10/15, and 10/16/46)

1389–1402. Counterfeit Money (10/17/46, 10/18, 10/21, 10/22, 10/23, 10/24, 10/25, 10/28, 10/29, 10/30, 10/31, 11/1, 11/4, and 11/5/46)

1403–1415. The Disappearance of Clark Kent (11/6/46, 11/7, 11/8, 11/11, 11/12, 11/13, 11/14, 11/15, 11/18, 11/19, 11/20, 11/21, and 11/22/46)

1416–1422. The Secret Letter (11/25/46, 11/26, 11/27, 11/28, 11/29, 12/2, and 12/3/46)

1423–1430. The Phony Song Publishing Company (12/4/46, 12/5, 12/6, 12/9, 12/10, 12/11, 12/12, and 12/13/46)

1431–1439. The Phony Housing Racket (12/16/46, 12/17, 12/18, 12/19, 12/20, 12/23, 12/24, 12/25, and 12/26/46)

1440–1448. The Phony Restaurant Racket (12/27/46, 12/30, 12/31/46, 1/1/47, 1/2, 1/3, 1/6, 1/7, and 1/8/47)

1449–1456. The Phony Inheritance Racket (1/9/47, 1/12, 1/13, 1/14, 1/15, 1/16, 1/17, and 1/20/47)

1457–1472. Drought in Freeville (1/21/47, 1/22, 1/23, 1/24, 1/27, 1/28, 1/29, 1/30, 1/31, 2/3, 2/4, 2/5, 2/6, 2/7, 2/10, and 2/11/47)

1473–1482. The Monkey Burglar (2/12/47, 2/13, 2/14, 2/17, 2/18, 2/19, 2/20, 2/21, 2/24, and 2/25/47)

1483–1496. Knights of the White Carnation (2/26/47, 2/27, 2/28, 3/3, 3/4, 3/5, 3/6, 3/7, 3/10, 3/11, 3/12, 3/13, 3/14, and 3/17/47)

1497–1512. The Man Without a Face (3/18/47, 3/19, 3/20, 3/21, 3/24, 3/25, 3/26, 3/27, 3/28, 3/31, 4/1, 4/2, 4/3, 4/4, 4/7, and 4/8/47)

1513–1525. The Mystery of the Lost Planet (4/9/47, 4/10, 4/11, 4/14, 4/15, 4/16, 4/17, 4/18, 4/21, 4/22, 4/23, 4/24/47, and 4/25/47)

1526–1537. The Phantom of the Sea (4/28/47, 4/29, 4/30, 5/1, 5/2, 5/5, 5/6, 5/7, 5/8, 5/9, 5/12, and 5/13/47)

1538–1570. Superman vs. Kryptonite (5/14/47, 5/15, 5/16, 5/19, 5/20, 5/21, 5/22, 5/23, 5/26, 5/27, 5/28, 5/29, 5/30, 6/2, 6/3, 6/4, 6/5, 6/6, 6/9, 6/10, 6/11, 6/12, 6/13, 6/16, 6/17, 6/18, 6/19, 6/20, 6/23, 6/24, 6/25, 6/26, and 6/27/47)

1571–1589. The Secret Rocket (9/29/47, 9/30, 10/1, 10/2, 10/3, 10/6, 10/7, 10/8, 10/9, 10/10, 10/13, 10/14, 10/15, 10/16, 10/17, 10/20, 10/21, 10/22, and 10/23/47)

1590–1613. The Ruler of Darkness (10/24/47, 10/27, 10/28, 10/29, 10/30, 10/31, 11/3, 11/4, 11/5, 11/6, 11/7, 11/10, 11/11, 11/12, 11/13, 11/14, 11/17, 11/18, 11/19, 11/20, 11/21, 11/24, 11/25, and 11/26/47)

1614–1631. Pennies for Plunder (11/27/47, 11/28, 12/1, 12/2, 12/3, 12/4, 12/5, 12/8, 12/9, 12/10, 12/11, 12/12, 12/15, 12/16, 12/17, 12/18, 12/19, and 12/22/47)

1632–1644. Hunger, Inc. (12/26/47, 12/29, 12/30, 12/31/47, 1/1/48, 1/2, 1/5, 1/6, 1/7, 1/8, 1/9, 1/12, and 1/13/48)

1645–1658. Dead Man's Secret (1/14/48, 1/15, 1/16, 1/19, 1/20, 1/21, 1/22, 1/23, 1/26, 1/27, 1/28, 1/29, 1/30, and 2/2/48)

1659–1669. Batman's Great Mystery (2/3/48, 2/4, 2/5, 2/6, 2/9, 2/10, 2/11, 2/12, 2/13, 2/16, and 2/17/48)

1670–1684. The Kingdom Under the Sea (2/18/48, 2/19, 2/20, 2/23, 2/24, 2/25, 2/26, 2/27, 3/1, 3/2, 3/3, 3/4, 3/5, 3/8, and 3/9/48)

1685–1701. The Mystery of the Stolen Costume (3/10/48, 3/11, 3/12, 3/15, 3/16, 3/17, 3/18, 3/19, 3/22, 3/23, 3/24, 3/25, 3/26, 3/29, 3/30, 3/31, and 4/1/48)

1702–1710. The Skin Game (4/2/48, 4/5, 4/6, 4/7, 4/8, 4/9, 4/12, 4/13, and 4/14/48)

1711–1723. The Crossword Puzzle Mystery (4/15/48, 4/16, 4/19, 4/20, 4/21, 4/22, 4/23, 4/26, 4/27, 4/28, 4/29, 4/30, and 5/3/48)

1724–1734. The Ghost Brigade (5/4/48, 5/5, 5/6, 5/7, 5/10, 5/11, 5/12, 5/13, 5/14, 5/17, and 5/18/48)

1735–1752. The Mystery of the Sleeping Beauty (5/19/48, 5/20, 5/21, 5/24, 5/25, 5/26, 5/27, 5/28, 5/31, 6/1, 6/2, 6/3, 6/4, 6/7, 6/8, 6/9, 6/10, and 6/11/48)

1753–1769. The Secret of Meteor Island (6/14/48, 6/15, 6/16, 6/17, 6/18, 6/21, 6/22, 6/23, 6/24, 6/25, 6/28, 6/29, 6/30, 7/1, 7/2, 7/5, and 7/6/48)

1770–1787. The Voice of Doom (7/7/48, 7/8, 7/9, 7/12, 7/13, 7/14, 7/15, 7/16, 7/19, 7/20, 7/21, 7/22, 7/23, 7/26, 7/27, 7/28, 7/29, and 7/30/48)

1788–1797. The Secret of the Genie (8/2/48, 8/3, 8/4, 8/5, 8/6, 8/9, 8/10, 8/11, 8/12, and 8/13/48)

1798–1808. The Mystery of the Letter (8/16/48, 8/17, 8/18, 8/19, 8/20, 8/23, 8/24, 8/25, 8/26, 8/27, and 8/30/48)

1809–1818. The Mystery of the Silver Buffalo (8/31/48, 9/1, 9/2, 9/3, 9/6, 9/7, 9/8, 9/9, 9/10, 9/13, and 9/14/48)

1819–1835. The Secret of Stone Ridge (9/15, 9/16, 9/17, 9/20, 9/21, 9/22, 9/23, 9/24, 9/27, 9/28, 9/29, 9/30, 10/1, 10/4, 10/5, 10/6, and 10/7/48)

1836–1852. The Mystery of the Unknown (10/8/48, 10/11, 10/12, 10/13, 10/14, 10/15, 10/18, 10/19, 10/20, 10/21, 10/22, 10/25, 10/26, 10/27, 10/28, 10/29, and 11/1/48)

1853–1862. Murder Scores a Touchdown (11/2/48, 11/3, 11/4, 11/5, 11/8, 11/9, 11/10, 11/11, 11/12, and 11/15/48)

1863–1875. The Riddle of the Mystery Message (11/16/48, 11/17, 11/18, 11/19, 11/22, 11/23, 11/24, 11/25, 11/26, 11/29, 11/30, 12/1, and 12/2/48)

1876–1886. The Vanishing Killers (12/3/48, 12/6, 12/7, 12/8, 12/9, 12/10, 12/13, 12/14, 12/15, 12/16, and 12/17/48)

1887–1894. Superman's Secret (12/20/48, 12/21, 12/22, 12/23, 12/24, 12/27, 12/28, and 12/29/48)

1895–1910. The Return of the Octopus (12/30/48, 12/31/48, 1/3/49, 1/4, 1/5, 1/6, 1/7, 1/8, 1/11, 1/12, 1/13, 1/14, 1/17, 1/18, 1/19, and 1/20/49)

1911–1921. The Mystery of the Spellbound Ships (1/21/49, 1/24, 1/25, 1/26, 1/27, 1/28, 1/31, 2/1, 2/2, 2/3, and 2/4/49)

The Adventures of Superman (1949–1951)*

Beginning February 7, 1949, *Superman* underwent a few noticeable changes. It was now broadcast on ABC as a thrice-a-week presentation — with the exception of late 1950, when the series broadcasted twice a week. The 15-minute program expanded to a full 30-minutes. Although many of the half-hour episodes were originals, about half of them were abridged adaptations of the serial adventures previously performed over the airwaves. Example: Episode six is actually an abridged adaptation of the July 22, 1941, to August 29, 1941, adventure. Bud Collyer was still playing the role of the alien superhero until June 6, 1950, when the role was handed over to Michael Fitzmaurice. An interesting tidbit: Superman was popular overseas, and during the 1950's *The Adventures of Superman* was broadcast from Australia with Leonard Teale in the title role.

1. The Frozen Death (2/7/49)
2. The Mystery of the Golden Eagle (2/9/49)
3. The Riddle of the Chinese Jade (2/11/49)
4. The Curse of the Devil's Creek (2/14/49)
5. The Lost Civilization (2/16/49)
6. The Mystery of the Voice Machine (2/18/49)
7. The Mystery of the Little Men (2/21/49)
8. The Story of Marina Baum (2/23/49)
9. Death Rides the Roller Coaster (2/25/49)
10. The Mystery of the Singing Wheels (2/28/45)
11. The Case of the Poisoned Town (3/2/49)
12. The Mystery of the Ten Thousand Dollar Ghost (3/4/49)
13. The Mystery of the Flying Monster (3/7/49)

Compiled by Fred Shay.

91. The Mystery of Butte Valley (8/2/50)
92. The Triangle of Crime (8/7/50)
93. The Portrait of Satan (8/9/50)
94. Eleven for Death (8/14/50)
95. The Mystery of the New Face (8/16/50)
96. The Eye of Balapur (8/21/50)
97. The Curse of the Devil's Creek (8/23/50)
98. Crime at a Bargain (8/28/50)
99. The Mystery of the Vibrating Death (8/30/50)
100. The Speedway of Terror (9/4/50)
101. The Case of the Double Double-Cross (9/7/50)
102. How Time Stood Still (9/12/50)
103. The Cat as Big as an Elephant (9/14/50)
104. The Lost King (9/19/50)
105. Crime by the Carload (9/21/50)
106. The Mystery of the Phantom Fleet (9/26/50)
107. Death on the Diamond (9/28/50)
108. The World's Greatest Secret (10/3/50)
109. The Ghost of Shipwreck Island (10/5/50)
110. The Riddle of the Mysterious Tapestry (10/10/50)
111. The Case of the Double Trouble (10/12/50)
112. Forecast for Crime (10/17/50)
113. The Horsemen of Doom (10/19/50)
114. The Vanishing Ships (10/24/50)
115. The Mystery of the Fortress of Fear (10/26/50)
116. Killer at Large (10/30/50)
117. Terror Under the Big Top (11/2/50)
118. The Mystery of Skull Cave (11/7/50)
119. The Return of Panic (11/9/50)
120. The Frozen Death (11/14/50)
121. The Mermaid's Ghost (11/16/50)
122. Murder on the Midway (11/21/50)
123. The Story of Marina Baum (11/23/50)
124. The Swiss Clock Killers (11/28/50)
125. The Secret of the Sahara (11/30/50)
126. The Achilles Heel (12/5/50)
127. Napoleon's Death Head (12/7/50)
128. The Mystery of the Voice Machine (12/12/50)
129. Glass Diamonds Spell Death (12/14/50)
130. The Case of the Precious Papers (12/19/50)
131. The Mystery of the Fabulous Fortune (12/21/50)
132. The Mystery of the Madcap Monkey (12/26/50)
133. Death in Disguise (12/28/50)
134. Fangs of Fury (1/2/51)
135. The Mystery of the Walking Doll (1/4/51)
136. Murder With Music (1/9/51)
137. The Case of the Mysterious Midgets (1/11/51)
138. The Mystery of the Stolen Costume (1/16/51)
139. Operation Danger (1/18/51)
140. The Mystery of the Reasoning Robot (1/23/51)
141. The Lizard Men (1/25/51)
142. The Ghost of Johnny Johnson (1/30/51)
143. The Counterfeit Murderers (2/1/51)
144. The Mystery of the Singing Wheels (2/6/51)
145. Death Sells A Picture (2/8/51)
146. The Diamond of Doom (2/13/51)
147. The Murder Trap (2/15/51)
148. Ride of Death (2/20/51)
149. The Diamond Pigeon (2/22/51)
150. The Marked Witness (2/27/51)
151. The Mystery of the Prehistoric Monster (3/1/51)

Africa Today

Produced in cooperation with the National Council of Churches, this seven-episode documentary series described the roles that religion and missionary work were playing in Africa. In the premiere broadcast, narrator Howard Price announced that this series was to be presented in six broadcasts, but seven episodes actually aired. Perhaps he mistook the two-part presentation as one broadcast. The premiere broadcast featured Ghana's Ambassador Daniel A. Chapman. Broadcast from 6 to 6:45 pm on Sunday evenings over station WLIB in New York.

1. The Role of Women (3/1/59)
2. The Hospital at Lambarene [part one] (3/8/59)
3. The Hospital at Lambarene [part two] (3/15/59)
4. The Music of Africa (3/22/59)
5. The Role of Missions (3/29/59)
6. Race Relations (4/5/59)
7. Emerging Africa (4/12/59)

An American Dialogue

Hosted by the Rev. Dr. Gustave Weiget, S.J., and Dr. Robert McAfee Brown, this late-night program presented short dramas followed by a lengthy panel discussion by the two hosts. The series dealt with discussions on Christianity. Broadcast on NBC from 11:30 to 12 pm, EST.

1. The Reformation (10/30/60)
2. The Sacral and the Secular [part one] (11/6/60)
3. The Sacral and the Secular [part two] (11/13/60)
4. Questions Protestants Ask Catholics [part one] (11/20/60)
5. Questions Protestants Ask Catholics [part two] (11/27/60)
6. The Ecumenical Issue (12/4/60)
7. Next Steps in the Dialogue (12/11/60)

An American in England

This special CBS series, in cooperation with the BBC, presented a look at England through the eyes and ears of Norman Corwin. In fact, all of the scripts were written by Norman Corwin. Edward R. Murrow produced and also appeared in a few broadcasts. Joseph Julian was the narrator. Benjamin Britten composed the music for the first six broadcasts, with Commander R. P. O'Donnell conducting. The last four episodes were composed and conducted by Lyn Murray.

The first six episodes of *An American in England* were broadcast on Monday from 10 to 10:30 pm, EST. The final four were broadcast Tuesday from 10 to 10:30 pm, EST. The September 7 broadcast was the only exception, aired from 9 to 9:30 because of Roosevelt's Fireside Chats.

The premiere broadcast, August 3, was actually a rebroadcast after short-wave interference interrupted transmission of the premiere performance on July

27. Shortwave interference made reception in the United States impossible for the sixth episode and prompted a network decision to complete the series in the Stateside studios of CBS rather than have them originate from England. Thus the reason for musicians and broadcast time changes. The sixth program was rebroadcast December 15, 1942.

1. London by Clipper (8/3/42; Angela Glynne, Betty Hardy, MacDonald Parke, John Snagge, Thorley Walters, and Arthur Young)
2. London to Dover (8/10/42; Leslie Bradley, Gerald Cooper, Terence de Marney, Dorothy Smith, John Snagge, Julian Somers, and Arthur Young)
3. Ration Island (8/17/42; Gwen Day Burrows, Terrence de Marney, Betty Hardy, Julian Somers, Arthur Young, and Gladys Young)
4. Women of Britain [aka Women at War] (8/24/42; Clifford Buckton, Olga Edwards, Dorothy Greene, Curigwen Lewis, Joan Miller, John Snagge, Julian Somers, and Arthur Young)
5. The Yanks Are Here (8/31/42; Lyn Evans, Richard George, Betty Hardy, Tommy Palmer, Harry Ross, and John Snagge)
6. An Anglo–American Angle (9/7/42; Laidman Browne, John Bryning, Clifford Buckton, Lyn Evans, Betty Hardy, MacDonald Parke, and Julian Somers)
7. Cromer (12/1/42; Frank Lovejoy)
8. Home is Where You Hang Your Helmet (12/8/42; Everett Sloane)
9. An Anglo–American Angle (12/15/42; Edna Best, Nicholas Joy, and Alfred Shirley)
10. Clipper Home (12/22/42; Joseph Julian)

American Portrait

Biographical dramas documenting the lives of famous (and some not-so-famous) Americans. Milton Bacon narrated the series, and various performers played the title roles. Broadcast over CBS from 6:15 to 6:45 pm, EST, originating from New York. The Kentucky Derby pre-empted the broadcast of May 4.

1. Alexander Hamilton (3/23/46; Dean Jagger)
2. Thomas Jefferson (3/30/46; Canada Lee and Arnold Moss)
3. Thomas Paine (4/6/46; Elspeth Eric and Alexander Scourby)
4. Roger Williams (4/13/46; Court Benson and Grace Matthews)
5. James J. Hill (4/20/46; House Jameson)
6. Henry Thoreau (4/27/46; Horace Braham, Jeanne Cagney, and Staats Cotsworth)
7. Benjamin Franklin (5/11/46; Eric Dressler)
8. Ralph Waldo Emerson (5/18/46; Horace Braham)
9. John Brown (5/25/46; Philip Bourneeuf)
10. John J. Audubon (6/1/46; Muriel Kirkland and Guy Sorel)
11. William Jennings Bryan (6/8/46; Helen Claire and Jay Jostyn)
12. Mark Hanna (6/15/46)
13. John and Washington Roebling (6/22/46)
14. Benjamin Rush, Physician and Patriot (6/29/46; Leon Janney)
15. Robert Owen (7/6/46)
16. Benjamin Rush, Physician and Patriot (7/13/46; Leon Janney)
17. Elizabeth Cady Stanton (7/20/46)
18. John Sutter (7/27/46)

19. Richard Henry Dana (8/3/46)
20. William James (8/10/46)
21. Cotton Mather (8/17/46)

22. Jane Adams (8/24/46)
23. Rutherford B. Hayes (8/31/46)
24. Samuel J. Tilden (9/7/46)

The American Story Teller

Mark Twain once wrote, "It was wonderful to find America, but it would have been more wonderful to miss it." The origin of America, from its discovery to the exploration of the West, is part of our historical integrity and ancestry. Archibald MacLeish wrote and narrated the entire series, described as "Literature of the New World." *The American Story Teller* was broadcast in 1944 over NBC on Friday evenings from 11:30 pm to 12 am, EST. In 1945, a second series using scripts from the previous run was presented over NBC, Saturday evenings from 7 to 7:30 pm. Arnold Moss was the narrator for the 1945 series.

1. The Discovery (2/5/44)
2. The Discoverers (2/12/44)
3. The Amerigo (2/19/44)
4. The Discovered (2/26/44)
5. The Indians View the Arrival (3/4/44)
6. The War on Indians (3/11/44)
7. The Accounts from the New-Found Land (3/18/44)
8. The Settlement (3/25/44)
9. The Colonial Experiance (4/1/44)
10. The Wars of Freedom (4/8/44)
11. The Westward Thrust (4/15/44)
12. The Moving Frontier (4/22/44)
13. The Bowed Shapes (4/29/44)
14. The Infection of Freedom (5/13/44)
15. The Loyalists (5/20/44)
16. Arms and the Man (5/27/44)
17. The Spiritual Tyranny (6/3/44)

18. The Industrial Revolution (6/10/44)
19. Doubling Our Heritage (6/17/44)
20. Western Waters and Westward Farers (7/1/44)
21. Oregon and China (7/8/44)
22. Bastile Day: The Franco-American Amity (7/15/44)
23. The Names for the Rivers (7/13/45)
24. The American Name (7/20/45)
25. The Discovered (7/27/45)
26. The American Gods (8/3/45)
27. The Many Dead (8/10/45)
28. Ripe Strawberries and Gooseberries and Sweet Single Roses (8/17/45)
29. Between Silence and the Surf (8/24/45)
30. Nat Bacon's Bones (8/31/45)
31. Socorro, When Your Sons Forget (9/7/45)

America's Lost Plays

Broadcast over NBC as a nine-week summer replacement for *Good News of 1939* and *Good News of 1940*. Sponsored by Maxwell House Coffee, the same sponsor of the *Good News* programs, this Thursday evening show was broadcast from 9 to 10 pm, EST.

1. The Minute Men of 1774 (7/6/39)
2. Flying Scud (7/13/39)
3. Eigermund (7/20/39)

4. A Trip to Chinatown (7/27/39)
5. The Two Orphans (8/3/39)
6. La Belle Russe (8/10/39)

7. The Count of Monte Cristo (8/17/39)
8. Mistress Nell [written by George C. Hazelton] (8/24/39)

9. Black Crook (8/31/39)

Arch Oboler's Plays

Arch Oboler wrote and directed each episode of this anthology series. Oboler was a popular figure over the radio, and shortly after his *Plays* program premiered, Hollywood stars began appearing in Oboler dramas for the meager pay of $21.00. Oboler became a widely known radio writer when his critically acclaimed "Alter Ego" won him a 1938 award as the best original drama of the year. James Cagney starred in "Johnny Got His Gun," a stomach-churning drama based on the Dalton Trumbo novel.

The series premiered over NBC, and was aired Saturday evenings from 10:00 to 10:30 pm, EST. Beginning with episode 28, *Plays* moved ahead a half-hour from 10:30 to 11 pm. Episodes 33 to 36 were broadcast from 9:00 to 9:30 pm. Beginning with episode thirty-seven, *Arch Oboler's Plays* began broadcast from 8:00 to 8:30 pm. In 1945, Oboler revised the series, this time over Mutual, with a summer run of 26 broadcasts, Thursday evenings from 10:00 to 10:30 pm, EST.

According to *Variety* magazine, Peter Lorre was originally scheduled to star in the drama "Nobody Died" on December 9, 1939. Lorre gave an advance notice that he was unable to attend, so the drama was pushed ahead one week. Lorre did not show up for the performance on December 16, and as a last-minute move, Jay Novello took Lorre's place. The broadcast of August 26, 1939, ran a full hour, instead of the usual 30 minutes. During the broadcast of episode 61, (aka "A Peculiar Comedy") the network lost the show temporarily and aired music for a time. "Lust for Life," broadcast on April 19, 1945, was originally scheduled for the broadcast of April 12, but was pre-empted the week after because of FDR's death. In the early sixties, Oboler revived his famed "Lights Out" radio series using some of the same plays he used on this program. The three short plays dramatized on episode #20 were previously written and dramatized on *The Fleischmann Hour* and *The Royal Gelatin Hour*.

1. The Ungliest Man in the World (3/25/39; Raymond Edward Johnson)
2. Mirage (4/1/39; Raymond Edward Johnson)
3. The Truth (4/8/39; Ray Collins)
4. The Ways of Men : Past, Present and Sum / Sole Survivors / The Laughing Man / Future (4/15/39; Raymond Edward Johnson)
5. Mr. Important (4/22/39; Martin Gabel)
6. The Cliff (4/29/39; Frank Lovejoy)
7. Engulfed Cathedral (5/6/39; Raymond Edward Johnson)
8. Baby (5/13/39; Ireene Wicker)
9. Crazy Town (5/20/39; Edmund O'Brien)
10. The Word (5/27/39)
11. Dark World / Steel / Humbug (6/3/39)
12. Nero's Wife (6/10/39)
13. Immortal Gentleman (6/17/39; Edmund O'Brien)

14. The Luck of Mark Street (6/24/39; Raymond Edward Johnson)
15. Visitor From Hades (7/1/39; Frank Lovejoy)
16. The Ivory Tower (7/8/39; Madame Nazimova)
17. The Shooting Star / Talisman / Eigerwund (7/15/39; Raymond Edward Johnson)
18. The Ugliest Man in the World (7/22/39; Raymond Edward Johnson)
19. Another World (7/29/39; Betty Garde)
20. The Brat/ Mr. Pip / Rich Kid (8/5/39)
21. History of a Mug (8/12/39)
22. Efficiency Island (8/19/39; Betty Caine)
23. This Lonely Heart (8/26/39; Madame Nazimova)
24. Love Story / The Valley / Mungahra (9/2/39; Santos Ortega)
25. And Adam Begot (9/9/39; Rosalinde Greene)
26. Suffer Little Children / Finale / I Do (9/16/39; Frank Lovejoy)
27. Mr. Whiskers (9/23/39; Morris Carnovsky)
28. Holiday 1939 (9/30/39; Raymond Edward Johnson)
29. The Machine / Happy Year / Autumn Flower (10/7/39)
30. The Word (10/14/39; Edmond O'Brien)
31. Perfect Party (10/21/39; Lurene Tuttle)
32. Profits Unlimited (10/28/39; Ray Collins and Paula Winslowe)
33. Young Mr. Trouble (11/4/39; Pamela Caveness and Billy Halop)
34. I'll Tell My Husband (11/11/39; Gale Sondergard)
35. Bathysphere (11/18/39; George Zucco)
36. Mirage (11/25/39; Nan Sutherland)
37. The Circle / Home Town / The Executioner (12/2/39)
38. Hometown / New World (12/9/39)
39. Nobody Died (12/16/39; Jay Novello)
40. These Are Your Brothers (12/23/39)
41. This Precious Freedom (12/30/39; Lou Merrill)
42. Money, Money, Money (1/6/40)
43. The Truth (1/13/40; Hans Conried, Lou Merrill, and Lurene Tuttle)
44. Sensitive Mr. Ginsberg (1/20/40)
45. Back to the Indians / The Day the Sun Exploded / Tongue-In-Cheek (1/27/40)
46. Hollywood Special (2/3/40; Gale Page)
47. Old Man Chump / Memoriam / Dark World (2/10/40)
48. Genghis Kahn (2/17/40)
49. The Women Stayed at Home (2/24/40; Elsa Lanchester)
50. Baby (3/2/40; Joan Crawford)
51. Johnny Got His Gun (3/9/40; James Cagney)
52. The Most Dangerous Game (3/16/40; Ronald Colman)
53. The Ivory Tower (3/23/40; Madame Nazimova)
54. Danger / Skyscraper (3/30/40)
55. Strange Morning (4/5/45)
56. Lust for Life (4/19/45; Martin Gabel and Raymond Edward Johnson)
57. The House I Live In (4/26/45; Raymond Massey, Mercedes McCambridge, Alfred Ryder, Ann Shephard, and Hester Sondegaard)
58. Love, Love, Love (5/3/45; Nanette Balbot, Bruce Elliot, Lisa Goan, Joseph Granby, Raymond Lawrence, Cathy Lewis, Truda Marsden, Frank Martin, Lou Merrill, Jane Morgan, Rose Ann Murray, Betty Reubin, Irene Tedrow, Lurene Tuttle, and Carlton Young)
59. Holiday 194X (5/10/45; Bea Benaderet, Bill Christy, Mary Jane Croft, Rhoda Elaine, Bruce Elliot, Norman Field, Joseph Granby, Lou Merrill, Raymond Severn, and Irene Tedrow)
60. Mr. Ten Percent (5/17/45; Everett Allen, Bob Bailey, Harold Cornsweet, Mary Jane Croft, Bruce Elliott, Harry Lang, Rose Ann Murray, Earle Ross, and Evelyn Scott)
61. Exercise in Horror (5/24/45; Bill Christy, Bruce Elliott, Lisa Goan, Harry Lang, Peter Lorre, Frank Martin, Jane Morgan, Frances Pasco, Victor Rodman, Bill Shaw, George Sorel, Theodore Von Eltz, Winifred Wolfe, and Will Wright)
62. Ostrich in My Bed / Report to My

Relatives (5/31/45; Mary Jane Croft, Bruce Elliott, Wally Maher)

63. Night (6/7/45; Everett Allen, Griff Barnett, Gloria Blondell, Bruce Elliott, Joseph Granby, Barney James, Elliott Lewis, Terese Lyon, Frank Martin, Edmund McDonald, Rose Ann Murray, Dorothy Scott, and Theodore Von Eltz)

64. Mr. Pyle (6/14/45; Burgess Meredith)

65. The Naked Mountain (6/21/45; Tommy Cook, Joel Davis, Franchot Tone, and Lurene Tuttle)

66. The Truth (6/28/45; Antony Ellis, Edmond Gwenn, and Rose Ann Murray)

67. Dr. Bluff (7/5/45; Morris Carnovsky, Mary Jane Croft, and Gloria Blondell)

68. A Gallery of Big Shots — Feminine (7/12/45; Mary Jane Croft, Barbara Eiler, Louise Erickson, Jane Morgan, Dorothy Scott, Lurene Tuttle, and Lynne Whitney)

69. Special to Hollywood (7/19/45; Bruce Elliott, Lou Merrill, and Gale Page)

70. My Chicago (7/26/45; Bea Benaderet, Tommy Cook, Joe Gilbert, Cathy Lewis, Truda Marson, Eddie McCambridge, and Evelyn Scott)

71. Parade (8/2/45; Dawn Bender, Olive Dearing, Van Heflin, Elliott Lewis, Frank Lovejoy, and Jane Morgan)

72. History of a Mug (8/9/45; John Alden, Bea Benaderet, Leo Cleary, Gerald Mohr, Jay Novello, Rose Ann Murray, Dorothy Scott, and Theodore Von Eltz)

73. Lust for Life (8/16/45; Helen Beverly, J. Edward Bomberg, Roman Bonan, Lloyd Bridges, Phil Brown, Morris Carnovsky, Hugo Hass, Ruth Nelson, and William Watts)

74. Facts of Men / I Do / Baby (8/23/45; Olive Deering, Mary Lansing, Frank Martin, Harry Standish, and Lurene Tuttle)

75. Mirage (9/6/45; Joan Blaine and Raymond Edward Johnson)

76. A Gallery of Big Shots — Masculine (9/13/45; Griff Barnett, Bill Johnstone, Cathy Lewis, Elliott Lewis, Lou Merrill, Sidney Miller, Elga Moret, Jane Morgan, and Theodore Von Eltz)

77. Rocket From Manhattan (9/20/45; Ervin Lee, Elliott Lewis, and Lou Merrill)

78. The Family Magashi (9/27/45; Elliott Lewis)

79. Mr. Miller (10/4/45; Eddie Cantor)

80. I Declare War (10/11/45; Paul Muni)

Arthur Hopkins Presents

Arthur Hopkins, one of Broadway's senior producers, decided to indulge in a bit of radio via NBC in 1944. Under the title *Arthur Hopkins Presents*, Hopkins hosted his own dramatic anthology series, featuring stage plays with stage actors. These one-hour dramatizations included some of his past hits, such as "Anna Christie," "Street Scene," "The Joyous Season," "A Successful Calamity," "Machinal," and "Holiday." Herbert Rice was the first director, Wynn Wright took to directing the series after the first few broadcasts. The entire program was heard on Wednesday evenings from 11:30 pm to 12:30 am, EST (with only one exception, the premiere broadcast, which was aired an hour earlier, from 10:30 to 11:30 pm, EST). Originally, the series was to premiere on the twelfth of April, but due to Hopkins' busy schedule the program premiered on the nineteenth. Sadly, two plays Hopkins originally intended to have dramatized, previous stage hits "Paris Bound" and "What Price Glory?" were never performed on this series before the program went off the air.

In episode two, Louis Calhern played Petra, a role created by John Barrymore on stage. Zasu Pitts was originally scheduled to star in episode 11, but asked for a postponement of her appearance. Edgar Stehli was originally scheduled to star in episode 18, but was not featured in the broadcast. Episode 29 featured a pre–*Mission: Impossible* Peter Graves in a small supporting role. Wyllis Cooper wrote the scripts for the first eight broadcasts; Gerald Holland, beginning with episode nine. Charles Newton, Frank Allen, and Ethel Ann Kreppel also wrote for the series. Morris Momorsky conducted the music for the series.

1. Our Town (4/19/44; Helen Carew, Phil Coolidge, Frank Craven, Mary Patton, Thomas Ross, Howard Smith, and Evelyn Varden)
2. Redemption (4/26/44; Louis Calhern and Dorothy Gish)
3. A Successful Calamity (5/3/44; Philip Merivale)
4. The Philadelphia Story (5/10/44; Vinton Hayworth and Katharine Hepburn)
5. Anna Christie (5/17/44; J. Edward Bromberg, Wendell Corey, and Pauline Lord)
6. Ah, Wilderness (5/24/44; Charita Bauer, Montgomery Clift, and Dudley Digges)
7. The Farmer Takes a Wife (5/31/44; Wendell Corey, Edgar Stehli, and June Walker)
8. Machinal (6/7/44; Sidney Blackmer, Zita Johann, and Harold Vermilyea)
9. The Circle (6/14/44; Horace Braham and Grace George)
10. The Late Christopher Bean (6/21/44; Charita Bauer, Sidney Blackmer, Helen Carew, Pauline Lord)
11. Mrs. Bumstead-Leigh (7/5/44; Sidney Blackmer, Josephine Hull, and Estelle Winwood)
12. The Last of Mrs. Cheyney (7/12/44; Nicholas Mary Phillips, and Roland Young)
13. The Lady with a Lamp (7/26/44; Helen Hayes, Nicholas Joy, and Edgar Stehli)
14. The Letter (8/2/44; Horace Braham and Geraldine Fitzgerald)
15. Yellow Jack (8/9/44; William Harrigan, Whitford Kane, Myron McCormack, and Edgar Stehli)
16. The Swan (8/16/44; Horace Braham, Staats Cotsworth, and Eva Le Gallienne)
17. The Deluge (8/23/44; Sidney Blackmer, Wendell Corey, Pauline Lord, and Edgar Stehli)
18. Justice (8/30/44; Bramwell Fletcher, Whitford Kane, and Estelle Winwood)
19. Excursion (9/6/44; Whitford Kane)
20. A Bill of Divorcement (9/13/44; Zita Johann and Edgar Stehli)
21. Buccaneer (9/20/44; Edgar Stehli and Estelle Winwood)
22. Her Master's Voice (9/27/44; Frances Fuller and Roland Young)
23. The Petrified Forest (10/4/44; Dorothy Knox and Bertram Tanswell)
24. Escape (10/11/44; Dennis King)
25. The Male Animal (10/18/44; Sidney Blackmer, Elliott Nugent, and Amanda Randolph)
26. Mr. Pimm Passes By (10/25/44; Violet Heming and Cecil Humphreys)
27. Beyond the Horizon (11/1/44; Jean Adair, Philip Huston, and Aline MacMahon)
28. Holiday (11/8/44; Tom Rutherford, Edgar Stehli, and Hope Williams)
29. Home Came the Steed (11/15/44; Sidney Blackmer, Frances Fuller, and Edgar Stehli)
30. Berkeley Square (11/22/44; Dennis King and Mary Patten)
31. Roadside (11/29/44; Ralph Bellamy and Ruth Elma Stevens)
32. Street Scene (12/13/44; Horace Braham and Erin O'Brien Moore)
33. Richard II [based off the play by William Shakespeare] (12/20/44; Dennis King)
34. The Bluebird (12/27/44; Alastair Kyle and Joyce Van Patten)
35. The Joyous Season (1/3/45; Lillian Gish)

As Easy as A.B.C.

This 13-week series on the work of the UNESCO (United Nations Educational, Scientific and Cultural Organization) was a presentation of United Nations Radio. The first episode presented highlights and clips of future programs. Broadcast nationally on CBS from 11:30 to 11:55 pm, EST. Some broadcasts presented two 15-minute dramas.

1. A Is for Alphabet (2/23/58; Jack Benny, Joe E. Brown, Eddie Cantor, Sir Cedric Hardwicke, Bob Hope, Danny Kaye, and Yehudi Menuhin)
2. B Is for Bargains (3/2/58; Myrna Loy, Edward G. Robinson, and Dinah Shore)
3. C Is for Charter / D Is for Dreams (3/9/58; Yul Brynner, Joseph Cotten, Frank Sinatra, Claude Dauphin, Walt Disney, and Ricardo Montalban)
4. E Is for Eve (3/16/58; Ingrid Bergman)
5. F Is for Firsts (3/23/58; Melvyn Douglas)
6. H Is for Humankind (3/30/58; Yul Brynner, Maurice Evans, H.V. Kaltenborn, and William Marshall)
7. I Is for Ideas / J Is for Julep (4/6/58; Yehudi Menuhn, Basil Rathbone, and Judy Holliday)
8. K Is for Knownothing / L Is for Library (4/13/58; Victor Borge, and Eva Marie Saint)
9. M Is for Membership / N Is for Name-Calling (4/20/58; Charlton Heston, Marlon Brando, and Sir Laurence Olivier)
10. O Is for Old Wives' Tales (4/27/58; Alfred Hitchcock, Boris Karloff, Peter Lorre, and Julienne Marie)
11. P Is for Project 32–33 / Q Is for Questions (5/4/58; Fred MacMurray, Danny Kaye, and Burt Lancaster)
12. V Is for Volumes (5/11/58; Rita Hayworth, Judy Holliday, Bob Hope, and Fred MacMurray)
13. Z Is for Zoo (5/18/58; Joe E. Brown, and Ginger McManus)

The Avenger

Similar to *The Shadow*, this program featured James Monks as Jim Brandon, famous biochemist. Brandon used numerous scientific devises to create a telepathic indicator and a diffusion capsule, the former enabling him to read the thoughts of anyone, the latter rendering him invisible. His assistant, beautiful Fern Collier, was the only person who knew the secret of the Avenger. Syndicated by Charles Michelson and penned by Walter Gibson, the creator of *The Shadow*, this series ran only half a year before going off the air. Dick Janiver later took over the lead role from Monks. James LaCurto also appeared in the supporting cast. The first date listed is for the West Coast, the second date for the East Coast.

1. The High Tide Murders (6/8/45; 10/25/45)
2. Mystery of the Giant Brain (6/15/45; 11/1/45)
3. Rendezvous With Murder (6/22/45; 11/8/45)
4. The Eyes of Shiva (6/29/45; 11/15/45)

5. The Coins of Death (7/6/45; 11/22/45)
6. Mystery of Dead Man's Rock (7/13/45; 11/29/45)
7. Tunnel of Disaster (7/20/45; 12/6/45)
8. The Crypt of Thoth (7/27/45; 12/13/45)
9. Melody of Murder (8/3/45; 12/20/45)
10. Fiery Death (8/10/45; 12/27/45)
11. Ghost Murder (8/17/45; 1/3/46)
12. The Blue Pearls (8/24/45; 1/10/46)
13. Wingate Heirs (8/31/45; 1/17/46)
14. Thoroughbred Murders (9/7/45; 1/24/46)
15. Department of Death (9/14/45; 1/31/46)
16. Keys of the City (9/21/45; 2/7/46)
17. Death in Mid-Air (9/28/45; 2/14/46)
18. The Hooded Circle (10/5/45; 2/21/46)
19. Death Rings the Bell (10/12/45; 2/28/46)
20. The Subway Ghost (10/19/45; 3/7/46)
21. The Cradle of Doom (10/16/45; 3/14/46)
22. Death Meets the Ghost (11/2/45; 3/21/46)
23. Murder Hits the Jackpot (11/9/45; 3/28/46)
24. Diploma of Death (11/16/45; 4/4/46)
25. Shot in the Dark (11/23/45; 4/11/46)
26. Death Counts to Ten (11/30/45; 4/18/46)

Battle Stations

The NBC Special Events Department, in cooperation with the Navy aired this dramatized report on the progress of the Navy in the war. Scripts written by Charles Gussman. Jack Cotello announcing. Music was composed by Leo Campeski, and the orchestra was conducted by Joseph Stopack. Joseph Mansfield directed. Broadcast by NBC as a partial summer replacement for *The Aldrich Family*, Thursday evenings from 8:30 to 9 pm, EST. Sponsored by Jell-O. Raymond Edward Johnson narrates.

1. The Battle of the Atlantic (8/5/43)
2. The Eastern Sea Frontier (8/12/43)
3. The Navy's Air Arm (8/19/43)
4. The Air Arm in WWI (8/25/43)

Best Plays

This series presented stage plays adapted for radio by Ernest Kinoy, Claris A. Ross and George Lefferts, and featured Hollywood and Broadway performers who had previously starred in the stage roles. Vincent Price reprised his stage role in Patrick Hamilton's "Angel Street"; Boris Karloff, his stage role of Jonathan Brewster in "Arsenic and Old Lace"; and Helen Hayes, her role in "Victoria Regina." Episode 14 presented two dramas.

Broadcast on NBC, the program never had a sponsor and began as a summer replacement for *Theater Guild on the Air*, broadcast 8:30 pm to 9:30 pm EST. Beginning with episode 15, the program moved to Friday at 9–10 pm and developed a new format. Beginning with episode 19, the series moved to Sundays and changed to a half-hour format, 8:30–9 pm.

John Chapman, drama critic of the New York *Daily News*, was the host; Fred Collins and Robert Denton shared announcing duties. William Welch supervised the entire program. Edward King directed for a time, and then Fred Weihe for the rest. Clarence Ross also adapted stage plays for the series.

1. Winterset (6/8/52; Burgess Meredith and Maureen Stapleton)
2. On Borrowed Time (6/15/52; David Anderson, Parker Fennelly, and Mildred Natwick)
3. Angel Street (6/22/52; Melville Cooper, Elizabeth Eustis, Judith Evelyn, and Vincent Price)
4. The Hasty Heart (6/29/52; Anne Burr and John Sylvester)
5. Arsenic and Old Lace (7/6/52; Jean Adair, Donald Cook, Boris Karloff, Edgar Stehli, and Evelyn Varden)
6. The Dark of the Moon (7/13/52; Alfred Drake)
7. The Voice of the Turtle (7/20/52; Audrey Christie, Elliott Nugent, and Martha Scott)
8. All My Sons (7/27/52; Ed Begley, John Larkin, and Alexander Scourby)
9. Outward Bound (8/3/52; Jean Adair, Alexander Scourby, and Chester Stratton)
10. Uncle Harry (8/10/52; Agnes Moorehead and Joseph Schildkraut)
11. The Philadelphia Story (8/17/52; Joan Alexander, Betty Furness, and Myron McCormick)
12. Home of the Brave (8/24/52; Donald Buka, Peter Capell, and Russell Hardie)
13. Blithe Spirit (8/31/52; John Loder, Mildred Natwick, and Haila Stoddard)
14. Bound East for Cardiff / The Long Voyage Home (9/7/52; Raymond Edward Johnson, Joan Lorring, and William Marshall) [Eugene O'Neill double feature]
15. Victoria Regina (10/3/52; Carl Esmond and Helen Hayes)
16. She Loves Me Not (10/10/52; Eddie Bracken and Ann Thomas)
17. High Tor (10/17/52; Burgess Meredith and Maureen Stapleton)
18. Biography (10/24/52; Faye Emerson)
19. Elizabeth the Queen (11/7/52; Eva Le Gallienne and Richard Waring)
20. The Mad Woman of the Chaillot (11/14/52; Aline MacMahon)
21. Missouri Legend (11/21/52; John Forsythe and Virginia Payne)
22. Rope (11/28/52; Hurd Hatfield and Victor Jory)
23. Skylark (12/5/52; Donald Cook and June Havoc)
24. Craig's Wife (12/12/52; John Beal, Judith Evelyn, Irene Hubbard, Ross Martin, William Redfield)
25. Night Must Fall (12/19/52; Mary Boland and Alfred Drake)
26. A Bell for Adano (12/26/52; Joe Di Santis, Arthur Kennedy, Gilbert Mack, Myron McCormick, Tony Randall, Louis Van Rooten, and Karl Weber)
27. Accent on Youth (1/2/53; Sally Forrest and Paul Lukas)
28. Men in White (1/9/53; Richard Basehart and Joan Lorring)
29. There Shall Be No Light (1/23/53; Florence Eldridge and Fredric March)
30. Camille (1/30/53; Eva Le Gallienne and Richard Waring)
31. John Loves Mary (2/6/53; Nina Foch and Van Johnson)
32. The Glass Menagerie (2/13/53; Geraldine Page)
33. Mr. Roberts (4/24/53; Wendell Holmes and Arthur Kennedy)
34. Susan and God (5/1/53; Judith Evelyn and Paul McGrath)
35. Of Mice and Men (5/8/53; Burgess Meredith and Anthony Quinn)
36. St. Helena (5/15/53; Dennis King)
37. Summer and Smoke (5/22/53; Geraldine Page)
38. The Amazing Dr. Clitterhouse (5/29/53; Sir Cedric Hardwicke)
39. Autumn Crocus (6/5/53; Carmen Mathews and Walter Slezak)

40. Another Language (6/21/53; Faye Emerson)
41. The Farmer Takes a Wife (6/28/53; John Forsythe and Joan Lorring)
42. Macbeth (7/12/53; Statts Cotsworth and Eva Le Gallienne)
43. The Rose Tattoo (7/19/53; Maureen Stapleton and Eli Wallach)
44. Kiss the Boys Goodbye (7/26/53; Helen Claire)
45. There's Always Juliet (8/2/53; Paul McGrath and Margaret Phillips)
46. The Male Animal (8/9/53; Elliot Nugent and Martha Scott)
47. Detective Story (8/16/53; Wendell Corey and Alexander Scourby)
48. Ladies in Retirement (8/23/53; Carmen Matthews, Mildred Natwick, and Evelyn Varden)
49. Tonight at 8:30 (8/30/53; Madeline Carroll and Jerome Cowan)
50. Kiss the Boys Goodbye (9/6/53; Helen Claire)
51. Ethan Frome (9/13/53; Geraldine Page)
52. The Petrified Forest (9/20/53; Cyril Ritchard)
53. The Mad Woman of Chaillot (9/27/53; Aline McMahon)

Best Seller

This anthology series featured adaptations of popular books and novels that were "best sellers" at the time. Authors and publishers had no problem with adaptations of their books being performed on this daily radio program, as it encouraged listeners to go out to their local book store and purchase a copy of their own. *Best Seller* originated from New York, but was broadcast nationally over the Blue Network, 3 to 3:30 pm, EST. Bret Morrison was the narrator for the series, broadcast five times a week.

1–5. The Ballad and the Source (6/4/45, 6/5, 6/6, 6/7, and 6/8/45)
6–10. The Upstart (6/11/45, 6/12, 6/13, 6/14, and 6/15/45)
11–15. Pride's Way (6/18/45, 6/19, 6/20, 6/21, and 6/22/45)
16–20. The Maiden with the Butterflies [based on the book by Tom Powers] (6/25/45, 6/26, 6/27, 6/28, and 6/29/45)
21–25. Ask No Quarter (7/2/45, 7/3, 7/4, 7/5, and 7/6/45)
26–30. The House on Clewe Street (7/9/45, 7/10, 7/11, 7/12, and 7/13/45)
31–35. The City of Trembling Leaves (7/16/45, 7/17, 7/18, 7/19, and 7/20/45)
36–40. The Wayfarers (7/23/45, 7/24, 7/25, 7/26, and 7/27/45)
41–45. Put Off Thy Shoes (7/30/45, 7/31, 8/1, 8/2, and 8/3/45)
46–50. Prekaska's Wife (8/6/45, 8/7, 8/8, 8/9, and 8/10/45)
51–55. Kitty (8/13/45, 8/14, 8/15, 8/16, and 8/17/45)
56–60. The Rickshaw Boy (8/20/45, 8/21, 8/22, 8/23, and 8/24/45)
61–65. Happy Time (8/27/45, 8/28, 8/29, 8/30, and 8/31/45)
66–70. Storm Tide (9/3/45, 9/4, 9/5, 9/6, and 9/7/45)
71–75. The Heritage of the River (9/10/45, 9/11, 9/12, 9/13, and 9/14/45)
76–80. A Lion Is in the Streets (9/17/45, 9/18, 9/19, 9/20, and 9/21/45)
81–85. I Married Them (9/24/45, 9/25, 9/26, 9/27, and 9/28/45)
86–90. The Peacock Sheds Its Tail (10/1/45, 10/2, 10/3, 10/4, and 10/5/45)
91–95. Burning Gold (10/8/45, 10/9, 10/10, 10/11, and 10/12/45)
96–100. Charity Strong (10/15/45, 10/16, 10/17, 10/18, and 10/19/45)
101–105. Rooster Crows (10/22/45, 10/23, 10/24, 10/25, and 10/26/45)
106–110. Ever After (10/29/45, 10/30, 10/31, 11/1, and 11/2/45)

111–115. The Perfect Round (11/5/45, 11/6, 11/7, 11/8, and 11/9/45)
116–120. The World, the Flesh and Father Smith (11/12/45, 11/13, 11/14, 11/15, and 11/16/45)

121–125. The Birth of Mischief (11/19/45, 11/20, 11/21, 11/22, and 11/23/45)
126–130. None So Blind (11/26/45, 11/27, 11/28, 11/29, and 11/30/45)

Beyond Tomorrow

Probably the first attempt at a pure science-fiction program for radio in the United States. The producer was William N. Robson and the series was directed by Mitchell Grayson. Henry Sylvern was responsible for the music and John Campbell, Jr., was host. In the cast were F. Lovejoy and Bret Morrison. Only three episodes are known to have been broadcast by CBS; possibly all of them were audition programs. Recorded in New York, conflicting information might date "The Outer Limit" February 23, 1950.

1. Requiem (4/5/50; Everett Sloane)
2. Incident at Switchpath (4/11/50)

3. The Outer Limit (4/13/50)

The Black Book

Mystery anthology series also known as *The Perfect Crime*, only three episodes broadcast. Sustaining on CBS, Sunday evenings from 4:15 to 4:30 pm, EST. Star Paul Frees played numerous roles.

Audition: Different Readings (11/2/51)
Audition: The Price of the Head (2/2/52; John Dehner)
1.On Schedule (2/17/52)

2. My Favorite Corpse (2/24/52)
3. Vagabond Murder (3/2/52; John Dehner)

The Black Chapel

This sustaining late-night mystery/horror program was broadcast over CBS, Thursday evenings from 11:45 pm to midnight, EST. *The Black Chapel* remained in this time slot when it moved to Fridays, beginning October 7, 1938. Ted Osborne starred.

1. The Mystery of the Penquin Palace (8/19/37)
2. The Franciscan Cross (8/26/37)
3. -----(9/2/37)

4. The Strange Case of Sister Filomena (9/9/37)
5. Dr. Roumanoff's Marvelous Microbe (9/16/37)

62. The Gruesome Case of the Halloween Joke (10/28/38)
63. The Weird Case of the Parisian Music Lover (11/4/38)
64. The Strange Case of Elias Wick (11/11/38)
65. The Mysterious Case of the Man in Gray (11/18/38)
66. The Ghastly Case of the Criminal in Command (11/25/38)
67. The Weird Case of the Maniacal Doctor Means (12/2/38)
68. The Weird Case of the Unexpected Guest (12/9/38)
69. The Hideous Tale of the Malevolent Butler (12/16/38)
70. The Tale of Four Dinner Guests and a Murderer (12/23/38)
71. Death Song Murder (12/30/38)
72. The Mahogany Coffin (1/6/39)
73. The Sinister Tale of the Strange Bequest (1/13/39)
74. The Direful Tale of the Midnight Listeners (1/20/39)
75. The Gruesome Tale of the Beautiful Witch (1/27/39)
76. The Horrible Tale of the Hounded Cripple (2/3/39)
77. The Rock-a-bye Baby Murder (2/10/39)
78. The Strange Case of Sylvester Black (2/17/39)
79. The Remarkable Case of the Surgeon's Hands (2/24/39)
80. The Strange Case of the Unknown Fingerprints (3/3/39)
81. The Horrible Case of Anthony Wolfe (3/10/39)
82. The Sinister Case of the Forest of Death (3/17/39)
83. The Eerie Case of the Midnight Seance (3/24/39)
84. The Macabre Case of the April Fool Joke (3/31/39)
85. The Tale the Dead Man Told (4/7/39)
86. The Fearful Case of the Black Point Spectre (4/14/39)
87. The Horrible Case of the Man Who Sold his Corpse (4/21/39)
88. The Uncanny Case of Jeremy James (4/28/39)
89. The Strange Hypnosis of Dr. Davidson (5/5/39)
90. The Uncanny Case of the Black Cat (5/12/39)
91. The Gruesome Case of the Sinking Death (5/19/39)
92. The Gruesome Case of the Mad Scientist (5/26/39)
93. The Uncanny Case of the Iron Maiden (6/2/39)
94. The Weird Case of the Catacombs (6/9/39)
95. The Gruesome Case of the Grinning Corpse (6/16/39)
96. The Sinister Case of Mr. Vorhees (6/23/39)
97. The Gruesome Mystery of the House on the Hill (6/30/39)
98. The Sinister Case of Leviticus Pettigrew (7/7/39)
99. The Uncanny Case of the Black Crow (7/14/39)
100. The Tale of the Monastery Crypt (7/21/39)

The Blue Beetle

This series started as a 30-minute detective program, broadcast twice a week for the first 12 programs, with Frank Lovejoy in the lead role as Patrolman Dan Garrett, the "Blue Beetle," for the first eight episodes. Frank Lovejoy was then replaced and, starting with the 13th broadcast, the series changed into a two-part, 15-minute series.

1. Smashing the Dope Ring (5/15/40)
2. Sabotage and Liquidation (5/17/40)
3. Murder For Profit (5/22/40)
4. Blasting the Dynamite Gang (5/24/40)

5. Invisible Ghost (5/29/40)
6. Death Rides on Horseback (5/31/40)
7. Death Strikes From the East (6/5/40)
8. Sea Serpent (6/7/40)
9. The Frame-Up (6/12/40)
10. Spirits Don't Talk (6/14/40)
11. Thoroughbreds Always Come Through (6/19/40)
12. Smashing the Arson Ring (6/21/40)
13. Rounding Up the Payroll Bandits [part one] (6/26/40)
14. Rounding Up the Payroll Bandits [part two] (6/28/40)
15. Crime, Inc. [part one] (7/3/40)
16. Crime, Inc. [part two] (7/5/40)
17. Saved by a Hair [part one] (7/10/40)
18. Saved by a Hair [part two] (7/12/40)
19. Finesse in Diamonds [part one] (7/17/40)
20. Finesse in Diamonds [part two] (7/19/40)
21. Sabotage, Inc. [part one] (7/24/40)
22. Sabotage, Inc. [part two] (7/26/40)
23. Smashing the Restaurant Racket [part one] (7/31/40)
24. Smashing the Restaurant Racket [part two] (8/2/40)
25. Two Rackets in One [part one] (8/7/40)
26. Two Rackets in One [part two] (8/9/40)
27. The Underground Goes Underground [part one] (8/14/40)
28. The Underground Goes Underground [part two] (8/16/40)
29. The Dancing Ghost of Rocking Hills [part one] (8/21/40)
30. The Dancing Ghost of Rocking Hills [part two] (8/23/40)
31. Whale of Pirates Folly [part one] (8/28/40)
32. Whale of Pirates Folly [part two] (8/30/40)
33. Asylum of Dr. Drear [part one] (9/4/40)
34. Asylum of Dr. Drear [part two] (9/6/40)
35. Jewell Mystery of Channel Island [part one] (9/11/40)
36. Jewell Mystery of Channel Island [part two] (9/13/40)

Blue Playhouse

In April of 1942, *Little Blue Playhouse* premiered, a Saturday morning children's program broadcast over ABC. Two months after *Little* went off the air, another version premiered, this time featuring adult dramas. *Blue Playhouse* premiered over the Blue Network, also on Saturday mornings, and was broadcast from 12 to 12:30 pm, EST.

1. The Awakening of Sleepy Sam (12/4/43)
2. Daughter of Vikings (12/11/43)
3. Scapegoat (12/18/43)
4. Footprints in the Snow (12/25/43)
5. C Four, H Six (1/1/44)
6. Trial Without Jury (1/8/44)
7. Buckeye on Bougainville (1/15/44)
8. The Rivers Run Red (1/22/44)
9. Trial to Light (1/29/44)
10. An Aggie Goes to War (2/5/44)
11. He Was a Working Man (2/12/44)
12. For His Brother (2/19/44)
13. World Horizon (2/26/44)
14. -----(3/4/44)
15. Shines Like Silver (3/11/44)
16. Skyhorse (3/18/44)
17. Write a Letter (3/25/44)
18. Black Magic (4/1/44)
19. Shoulder to Shoulder (4/8/44)
20. Homespun Philosopher (4/15/44)
21. Right Wax Street (4/22/44)
22. General Ike (4/29/44)
23. Lest We Forget (5/6/44)
24. Watch Tower (5/13/44)
25. What Hath God Wrought? (5/20/44)

Box 13   41

26. Blue and Gold (5/27/44)
27. Castle on the Hudson (6/3/44)
28. The Hundred Years (6/10/44)
29. Wonder Drug (6/17/44)
30. Aloysius Has a Son (6/24/44)
31. All Men are Equal (7/1/44)
32. Long Tom (7/8/44)
33. Liberty Cap (7/15/44)
34. The Least of These (7/22/44)

35. The Life of General C. Marshall (7/29/44)
36. They Shall Be Well Again (8/5/44)
37. Tennessee Diplomat (8/12/44)
38. The Daughters of Mercy (8/19/44)
39. Omm Jannie (8/25/44)
40. Daybreak for Our Carrier (9/2/44)
41. T.M.D. (9/9/44)

Box 13

The advertisement in the *Star-Times* read "Adventure Wanted. Will go anywhere, do anything. Box 13." Dan Holliday, newspaper reporter–turned–fiction writer, placed the ad. This was his way of gaining the next big story for the extra little cash to pay his rent. All sorts of people answered the ad — one week a psychopathic killer looking for fun, the next week a racketeer's victim. One week Holliday found himself trying to outsmart a blackmailing scheme, the next week he was in the South, battling a voodoo cult.

Box 13 was the brainstorm of Alan Ladd, the Hollywood actor who played the role of Dan Holliday. In the mid–1940s, Ladd and a couple of friends founded their own company, Mayfair Productions, to transcribe and syndicate their radio programs. Ladd was no fan of television, so he stayed on radio with his own mystery program. A total of 52 episodes were recorded and broadcast over Mutual. Sylvia Parker played the role of Suzy, Dan's secretary who scanned the mail every day. Betty Lou Gerson, Marsha Hunt, Alan Reed, Luis Van Rooten, John Beal, Frank Lovejoy, and Lurene Tuttle were but a few of the supporting cast. Verne Carstenson was the announcer, producer, and director. Russell Hughes wrote many of the scripts, as did Ladd. Rudy Schrager performed the music.

Box 13 was syndicated on many local radio stations. The dates below are from the national broadcast run over the Mutual network, first dates from the West Coast, and second dates belonging to the East Coast.

1. The First Letter (3/15/48, 8/22/48)
2. Insurance Fraud (3/22/48, 8/29/48)
3. Blackmail in Murder (3/29/48, 9/5/48)
4. Actor's Alibi (4/5/48, 9/12/48)
5. Extra Extra (4/12/48, 9/19/48)
6. Shanghied (4/19/48, 9/26/48)
7. Short Assignment (4/26/48, 10/3/48)
8. Double Mothers (5/3/48, 10/10/48)
9. A Book of Poems (5/10/48, 10/17/48)
10. The Great Torino (5/17/48, 10/24/48)
11. Suicide or Murder (5/24/48, 10/31/48)
12. Triple Cross (5/31/48, 11/7/48)
13. Damsel in Distress (6/7/48, 11/14/48)
14. Diamond in the Sky (6/14/48, 11/21/48)
15. Double Right Cross (6/21/48, 11/28/48)
16. Look Pleasant Please (6/28/48, 12/5/48)
17. The Haunted Artist (7/5/48, 12/12/48)

18. The Sad Night (7/12/48, 12/19/48)
19. Hot Box (7/19/48, 12/26/48)
20. The Better Man (7/26/48, 1/2/49)
21. The Professor and the Puzzle (8/2/48, 1/9/49)
22. The Dowager and Dan Holliday (8/9/48, 1/16/49)
23. Three to Die (8/16/48, 1/23/49)
24. The Philanthropist (8/23/48, 1/30/49)
25. Last Will and Nursery Rhyme (8/30/48, 2/6/49)
26. Delinquent's Dilemma (9/6/48, 2/13/49)
27. Flash of Light (9/13/48, 2/20/49)
28. Hare and Hound (9/20/48, 2/27/49)
29. Hunt and Peck (9/27/48, 3/6/49)
30. Death is a Doll (10/4/48, 3/13/49)
31. 113.5 (10/11/48, 3/20/49)
32. Dan and the Wonderful Lamp (10/18/48, 3/27/49)
33. Tempest in a Casserole (10/25/48, 4/3/49)
34. Mexican Maze (11/1/48, 4/10/49)

35. Sealed Instructions (11/8/48, 4/17/49)
36. Find Me, Find Death (11/15/48, 4/24/49)
37. Much Too Lucky (11/22/48, 5/1/49)
38. One of These Four (11/29/48, 5/8/49)
39. Daytime Nightmares (12/6/48, 5/15/49)
40. Death Is No Joke (12/13/48, 5/22/49)
41. Treasure of Hang Lee (12/20/48, 5/29/49)
42. Design for Danger (12/27/48, 6/5/49)
43. The Dead Man Walks (1/3/49, 6/12/49)
44. Killer at Large (1/10/49, 6/19/49)
45. Speed to Burn (1/17/49, 6/26/49)
46. House of Darkness (1/24/49, 7/3/49)
47. Double Trouble (1/31/49, 7/10/49)
48. The Bitter Bitten (2/7/49, 7/17/49)
49. The Perfect Crime (2/14/49, 7/24/49)
50. Archimedes and the Roman (2/21/49, 7/31/49)
51. The Clay Pigeon (2/28/49, 8/7/49)
52. Round Robin (3/7/49, 8/14/49)

*Broadway Is My Beat**

"Broadway is my beat. From Times Square to Columbus, the gaudiest, the most violent, the lonesomest mile in the world."

Starring Anthony Ross as Danny Clover, a detective of the New York Police Department. Larry Thor took over the role of Clover beginning with episode 17. The musical theme was "I'll Take Manhattan." Broadcast over CBS, Sunday from 5:30 to 6 pm. Robert Stringer supplied the music. The first 16 episodes were produced by Lester Gottlieb and directed by John Dietz. Episode 17 through the end of the series run were produced and directed by Elliott Lewis, written by Morton Fine and David Friedkin. The announcer was Bill Anders and music was by Wilbur Hatch and Alexander Courage.

Episode ninety featured an introduction by Bob Hope, talking about the overflowing river disaster at Topeka, Kansas, for two minutes of the program.

1. -----(2/27/49)
2. -----(3/6/49)
3. The Gordon Ellis Murder Case (3/13/49)
4. The Val Dane Murder Case (3/20/49)
5. The Eugene Bullock Murder Case (3/27/49)
6. The Jimmy Dorne Murder Case (4/3/49)

7. The Otto Procaush Murder Case (4/10/49)
8. -----(4/17/49)
9. The Henry Baker Murder Case (4/24/49)
10. The Mary Murdock Murder Case (5/1/49)
11. The Joan Gale Murder Case (5/8/49)
12. -----(5/15/49)

Compiled by Terry Salomonson. Copyright © 7/5/96 by Terry Salomonson.

13. The Julie Dixon Murder Case (5/22/49)
14. The Rhonda Lynn Murder Case (5/29/49)
15. The Joe Quento Murder Case (6/5/49)
16. The Eddie Amboy Murder Case (6/12/49)
17. The Jimmy Dean Murder Case (7/7/49)
18. The Otto Prokosh Murder Case (7/21/49)
19. The Paul Thomas Murder Case (7/28/49)
20. The Dr. Robbie McClure Murder Case (8/4/49)
21. The Jane Darwell Murder Case (8/11/49)
22. The Silks Bergen Murder Case (8/18/49)
23. The Val Dane Murder Case (8/25/49)
24. The Mei Ling Murder Case (11/5/49)
25. The Sgt. Gordon Ellis Murder Case (11/12/49)
26. The Eugene Bullock Murder Case (11/19/49)
27. The Mary Gilbert Murder Case (11/26/49)
28. The Sherman Gates Murder Case (12/3/49)
29. The Tori Jones Murder Case (12/10/49)
30. The Henry Baker Murder Case (12/17/49)
31. Nick Norman And Santa Claus (12/24/49)
32. The John Lomax Murder Case (12/31/49)
33. The Mary Murdock Murder Case (1/7/50)
34. The John Gale Murder Case (1/21/50)
35. The Roberto Segura Murder Case (1/31/50)
36. The Lt. Jimmy Hunt Murder Case (2/3/50)
37. The Julie Dixon Murder Case (2/10/50)
38. The Dion Hartley Murder Case (2/17/50)
39. The Ben Elliot Murder Case (2/24/50)
40. The Joe Quito Murder Case (3/3/50)
41. The Dr. Robert Stafford Murder Case (3/10/50)
42. The Charles And Jane Kimball Murder Case (3/17/50)
43. The Francie Greene Murder Case (3/24/50)
44. The Hope Anderson Murder Case (3/31/50)
45. The Earnie Cauldwell Murder Case (4/7/50)
46. The Tommy Stafford Murder Case (4/14/50)
47. The Elaine Hill Murder Case (4/21/50)
48. The Max Wendall Murder Case (4/28/50)
49. The Thelma Harper Murder Case (5/5/50)
50. The Marcia Dean Murder Case (5/12/50)
51. The Jane Arnold Murder Case (5/19/50)
52. The Ann Cornell Murder Case (5/26/50)
53. The Mario LaVecchia Murder Case (6/2/50)
54. The Ted Forestal & Ruth Ballard Murder Case (6/9/50)
55. The Morris Bernstein Murder Case (6/16/50)
56. The Steven Courtney Murder Case (6/23/50)
57. The Frank Conway Murder Case (6/30/50)
58. The Frank Briscoe Murder Case (7/3/50)
59. The Amelia Ramirez Murder Case (7/10/50)
60. The Celia Jordan Murder Case (7/24/50)
61. The Harry Brett Murder Case (7/31/50)
62. The Jack Jordon Murder Case (8/7/50)
63. The Mary Demming Murder Case (8/14/50)
64. Tom & Alice Corey And The Suicide Pact (8/21/50)
65. The Helen Carrol Murder Case (10/13/50)
66. The John Webster Murder Case (10/20/50)
67. The Harold Clark Murder Case (10/27/50)
68. The Laura Burton Murder Case (11/3/50)

69. The Johnny Hall Murder Case
    (11/10/50)
70. The Joan Fuller Murder Case
    (11/17/50)
71. The Shorty Dunne Murder Case
    (11/24/50)
72. The Kenneth Mitchell Murder Case
    (12/1/50)
73. The Mrs. Cotton Murder Case
    [might be The Ben Justin Murder
    Case] (12/8/50)
74. The Fred Bayer Murder Case (4/7/51)
75. The Thomas Hart Murder Case
    (4/14/51)
76. The Philip Hunt Murder Case
    (4/21/51)
77. The Georgia Gray Murder Case
    (4/28/51)
78. The Harry Foster Murder Case
    (5/5/51)
79. The Charles Crandell Murder Case
    (5/12/51)
80. The Eleanor Corbett Murder Case
    (5/26/51)
81. The Francesca Brown Murder Case
    (6/2/51)
82. The Earl Lawson Murder Case
    (6/9/51)
83. The Frank Dunn Murder Case
    (6/16/51)
84. The Ruth Larson Murder Case
    (6/23/51)
85. The Pablo Molari Murder Case
    (6/30/51)
86. The Joe Gruber Murder Case
    (7/8/51)
87. The Alice Gleason Murder Case
    (7/15/51)
88. The David Blaine Murder Case
    (7/22/51)
89. The Jimmy Sloan Murder Case
    (7/29/51)
90. The Howard Crawford Murder
    Case (8/5/51; Bob Hope)
91. The Richard Folger Murder Case
    (8/12/51)
92. The Roget, The Giant Murder Case
    (8/19/51)
93. The Elizabeth Price Murder Case
    (8/26/51)
94. The Anna Compton Murder Case
    (9/15/51)
95. The Tom Keeler Murder Case
    (9/22/51)
96. The Lars Nielson Murder Case
    (9/29/51)
97. The Lily Nelson Murder Case
    (10/6/51)
98. The Ed Koster Murder Case
    (10/13/51)
99. The Kurt Bower Murder Case
    (10/20/51)
100. The Ricardo Miguel Murder Case
    (10/27/51)
101. The Joe Blair Murder Case (11/3/51)
102. The Joey Macklin–John Howard
    Murder Case (11/10/51)
103. The Alex Raymond Murder Case
    (11/17/51)
104. The Paul Clark Murder Case
    (11/24/51)
105. The Clinton Pace Murder Case
    (12/1/51)
106. The Mary Smith Murder Case
    (12/8/51)
107. The Lucille Baker Murder Case
    (12/15/51)
108. The Buddy Malpaugh And The
    Jeweled Scimitar (12/22/51)
109. The Faye Welch Murder Case
    [might be The Ted Ebberly Mur-
    der Case] (12/29/51)
110. The John Dobson Murder Case
    (1/5/52)
111. The Larry Moore Murder Case
    (1/12/52)
112. The Lynn Halstead Murder Case
    (1/19/52)
113. The Russ Warner Murder Case
    (1/26/52)
114. The Herbie Jensen Murder Case
    (2/2/52)
115. The Carol Daly Murder Case
    [might be The Mary Stuart Mur-
    der Case] (2/9/52)
116. The Raymond Grant Murder Case
    (2/16/52)
117. The Jessica Howard Murder Case
    (2/23/52)
118. The Maria Osborne Murder Case
    (3/1/52)
119. The Eve Hunter Murder Case
    (3/8/52)
120. The Gordon Merrick Murder Case
    (3/15/52)
121. The John Mooney Murder Case
    (3/22/52)
122. The Joan Carson Murder Case

[might be The Celia Mason Murder Case] (3/29/52)
123. The John Elgin Murder Case (4/5/52)
124. The Lois Conrad Murder Case (4/12/52)
125. The Mark Allison Murder Case (4/19/52)
126. The Dave Selby Murder Case (4/26/52)
127. The Louis Webster Murder Case (5/3/52)
128. The Joe Quito Murder Case (5/10/52)
129. The Irene Hall Murder Case (5/17/52)
130. The Alice Mayo Murder Case (5/24/52)
131. The Harry Moore Murder Case (6/2/52)
132. The Wanda Korvat Murder Case (6/9/52)
133. The Lila Hunter Murder Case (6/16/52)
134. The Joey Croft Murder Case (6/23/52)
135. The Mason Victor Murder Case (6/30/52)
136. The Stacey Parker Murder Case (7/7/52)
137. The Joe Dane Murder Case (7/14/52)
138. The Leo Bruce Murder Case (7/21/52)
139. The Paul Tudor Murder Case (7/28/52)
140. The Georgie Beck Murder Case (8/2/52)
141. The Ralph Walker Murder Case (8/9/52)
142. The Joan Howard Murder Case (8/16/52)
143. The Dr. Lyle Murder Case (8/23/52)
144. The Althea Cornish Murder Case (8/30/52)
145. The Herbie Ford Murder Case (9/6/52)
146. The Joe Nelson Murder Case (9/13/52)
147. The Tony Blaire Murder Case (9/20/52)
148. The Paul Tracy Murder Case (9/27/52)
149. The Marty Connell Murder Case (10/4/52)
150. The Ruth Nelson Murder Case (10/11/52)
151. The Robert Turk Murder Case (10/18/52)
152. The Mary Trevor Murder Case (10/25/52)
153. The Amelia Lane Murder Case (11/1/52)
154. The Bob Foster Murder Case (11/8/52)
155. The Kenny Purdue Murder Case (11/15/52)
156. The Grace Cullen Murder Case (1/22/52)
157. The Johnny Clark Murder Case (11/29/52)
158. The Blanche Dermit Murder Case (12/6/52)
159. The Donald Wayne Murder Case (12/13/52)
160. The Charles Ralston Murder Case (12/20/52)
161. The Paul Clark Murder Case (12/27/52)
162. The Douglas Hayden Murder Case (1/3/53)
163. The Lona Hanson and the Fighter Murder Case (1/10/53)
164. The Joseph Brady Murder Case (1/17/53)
165. The Joey Condon Murder Case (1/24/53)
166. The Helen Selby Murder Case (1/31/53)
167. The Peggy Warner Murder Case (2/7/53)
168. The Artie Blanchard Murder Case (2/14/53)
169. The Joe Turner Murder Case (2/21/53)
170. The John Perry Murder Case (2/28/53)
171. The Rocking Man Murder Case (3/7/53)
172. The Mary Vardin Murder Case [might be The Tyler Gosden Murder Case] (3/14/53)
173. The George Haven Murder Case (3/21/53)
174. The John Stewart Murder Case (3/28/53)
175. The Barton Russell Murder Case (4/4/53)

176. The Frank Dayton Murder Case (4/11/53)
177. The Myra Fuller Murder Case (4/18/53)
178. The Harry Gray Murder Case (4/25/53)
179. The Margaret Royce Murder Case (5/2/53)
180. The Sybil Crane Murder Case (5/9/53)
181. The Barbara Hunt Murder Case (5/16/53)
182. The Joan Tracy Murder Case [might be The Robin Forrest Murder Case] (5/23/53)
183. The Ruth Shay Murder Case (5/30/53)
184. The John Nelson Murder Case (6/6/53)
185. The George Lane Murder Case (6/13/53)
186. The Joan Stanley Murder Case (6/20/53)
187. The Sophie Bretton Murder Case (6/27/53)
188. The John Rand Murder Case (7/4/53)
189. The Harry Brian Murder Case (7/11/53)
190. The Ted Lawrence Murder Case (7/18/53)
191. The Stacy Parker Murder Case (7/25/53)
192. The Joyce Tyler Murder Case (8/1/53)
193. The Jimmy Bruce Murder Case (8/8/53)
194. The Mrs. Webbs Murder Case (8/15/53)
195. The Joe, Herbie & Beebe Murder Case (8/22/53)
196. The Clair Scott Murder Case (8/29/53)
197. The Larry Burdette Murder Case (9/5/53)
198. The Michael Austin Murder Case (9/12/53)
199. The William Jackson Murder Case (9/19/53)
200. The Paul Tracey Murder Case (9/26/53)
201. The Frankie Spain Murder Case (10/3/53)
202. The Harriet Temple Murder Case (10/7/53)
203. The Cora Lee Murder Case (10/14/53)
204. The Lois Burton Murder Case (10/28/53)
205. The Paul Holland Murder Case (11/4/53)
206. The Donald Jordon Murder Case (11/13/53)
207. The Lou Martin Murder Case (11/20/53)
208. The Janice Bennett Murder Case (11/27/53)
209. The Peg Miller Murder Case (7/11/54)
210. The Julie Roland Murder Case (7/18/54)
211. The Katie Lane Murder Case (7/25/54)
212. The Floyd Decker Murder Case (8/1/54)

Cabin B-13

In 1943, *Suspense* presented a script entitled "Cabin B-13," penned by mystery writer John Dickson Carr, who was then a staff writer for the *CBS Mystery Program*. The radio play became an immediate hit after its initial broadcast, and has since (under different titles) been made into a movie, a novel, and in this case, a mystery series of its own.

Cabin B-13 was broadcast on CBS, with Arnold Moss as Dr. Fabian, the ship's doctor on a luxury liner. Moss was replaced by Alan Hewitt beginning with episode nine. Arnold Moss returned on episode 12. Carr was able to adapt many of his own short stories for the program. Episode five was adapted from Carr's story "House in Goblin Wood," episode nine from "Villa of the Damned," episode ten from "Clue in the Snow," and episode twelve from "The Silver Curtain." Later in the series, Carr began using scripts from other series he wrote for. Episodes 18 through 21 were originally written for the BBC radio series *Appointment with Fear* (1944–45), and episodes 22 to 24 were originally written for *Suspense* (1942–43).

The program had no sponsor. John Dietz directed. Alfredo Antoniti and Merle Kendrick supplied the music. The supporting cast was made up of many, including Cliff Carpenter, Janis Gilbert, Peter Capel, Mary Patton, Naomi Campbell, Joseph Curtin, Rod Hendrickson, and William Podmore. Broadcast over CBS, Monday evenings from 8:30 to 9 pm, EST, for the first eight broadcasts as a substitute for Arthur Godfrey's talent scouts. Episodes 9 to 11 were broadcast Tuesday from 10:30 to 11 pm, EST. Episodes 12 to 16 were broadcast on Sunday evenings from 8:30 to 9 pm, and from 10:30 to 11 pm beginning with the 17th episode.

1. A Razor in Fleet Street (7/5/48)
2. The Man Who Couldn't Be Photographed (7/12/48)
3. Death Has Four Faces (7/19/48)
4. The Blind-Folded Knife-Thrower (7/26/48)
5. No Useless Coffin (8/2/48)
6. The Nine Black Reasons (8/9/48)
7. The Count of Monte Carlo (8/16/48)
8. Below Suspicion (8/23/48)
9. The Power of Darkness (8/31/48)
10. The Footprint in the Sky (9/7/48)
11. The Man in the Iron Chest (9/14/48)
12. The Street of the Seven Daggers (10/3/48)
13. The Danger from Istanbul (10/10/48)
14. Death in the Desert (10/17/48)
15. The Island of Coffins (10/24/48)
16. The Man Who Couldn't be Photographed (10/31/48)
17. A Most Respectable Murder (11/7/48)
18. The Curse of the Bronze Lamp (11/14/48)
19. Lair of the Devil Fish (11/21/48)
20. The Dead Man's Knock (11/28/48)
21. The Man With Two Heads (12/5/48)
22. The Bride Vanishes (12/12/48)
23. Till Death Do Us Part (12/19/48)
24. The Sleep of Death (12/26/48)
25. The Dancer from Istanbul (1/2/49)

Calling All Cars

Broadcast over CBS on the West Coast only, this crime drama/police adventure was directed by William Robson and sponsored by Rio Grande Oil. The dramas were based on actual California police files. Episode 13 documented the actual facts involving the famed Mae West jewel robbery that hit the nation's headlines years before. Episode 35 documented the crimes and capture of John Dillinger. Dramatized true crime stories introduced by officers of the Los Angeles and other police departments. The show only ran in areas where Rio Grande gasoline was sold.

1. -----(11/29/33)
2. The Burma White Case (12/6/33)
3. The York Gang Holdup (12/13/33)
4. The Human Bomb (12/20/33)
5. The Cookie Vejar Killing (12/27/33)
6. The Missing Mexican Sheiks (1/3/34)
7. The Caliente Money Car Holdup (1/10/34)
8. The Skeele Kidnapping (1/17/34)
9. The Cure of the Grooved Bullets (1/24/34)
10. The Castor Oil Diamond Robbery (1/31/34)
11. The Smashed Windshield (2/7/34)
12. The Times Bombing Case (2/14/34)
13. The Mae West Jewel Robbery (2/21/34)

14. The Killer Hudson (2/28/34)
15. -----(3/7/34)
16. The Chloriform Murder (3/14/34)
17. The Dillinger Case (3/21/34)
18. The Spinoza Case (3/28/34)
19. The Red Rose Girl (4/4/34)
20. The Cut Rate Murder (4/11/34)
21. Hammers in Honduras (4/18/34)
22. Captain Courageous (4/25/34)
23. Murder at Southgate (5/2/34; Hanley Stafford)
24. The Little Phil Alquin (5/9/34)
25. The Gettle Kidnapping Case (5/16/34)
26. Seven Words and a Fingerprint (5/23/34)
27. The Dinner Party Bandits (5/30/34)
28. The Big Mail Robbery (6/6/34)
29. Murder of a Soul (6/13/34)
30. One of the Finest (6/20/34)
31. The Power and Light Holdup (6/27/34)
32. July Fourth Is a Radio Car (7/4/34)
33. Fingerprints Don't Lie (7/11/34)
34. The Manchuko Dope Ring (7/18/34)
35. The Execution of Dillinger (7/25/34)
36. Nightroglycerin Parson (8/1/34)
37. The Corpse in the Desert (8/8/34)
38. Crooks are Human Beings (8/15/34)
39. You Can't Kill a Cop (8/22/34)
40. Let the Sucker Pay (8/29/34)
41. Marks on the Bedroom Screen (9/5/34)
42. The Human Monkey (9/12/34)
43. The Ruth Judd Case (9/19/34)
44. Stop That Carl (9/26/34)
45. The Skid Row Dope Ring (10/2/34)
46. The Unwritten Law (10/9/34)
47. The One-Way Ride (10/16/34)
48. Trouser Cuff Clue (10/23/34)
49. The Perfect Crime (10/30/34)
50. Six Shots at Midnight (11/6/34)
51. A Thousand Pieces of Eight (11/13/34)
52. Death For a Diamond Ring (11/20/34)
53. Sometimes People Aren't Murdered (11/27/34)
54. Don't Get Chummy With a Watchman (12/4/34)
55. A Cup of Coffee, Some Strychnine Too (12/11/34)
56. The Moving Picture Murder (12/18/34)
57. The Human Side of a Cop (12/25/34)
58. Highlights of 1934 (1/1/35)
59. Crime Does Not Pay (1/8/35)
60. Two Against Six (1/15/35)
61. The San Quentin Prison Break (1/22/35)
62. The Necking Party Murder (1/29/35)
63. The Banker in the Well (2/5/35)
64. The Remote Control Sleuth (2/12/35)
65. Wreck of the Old Sixty-Nine (2/19/35)
66. The California Two-Man Crime Wave (2/26/35)
67. The Undercover Woman (3/5/35)
68. Thou Shalt Not Kill (3/12/35)
69. -----(3/19/35)
70. Rhythm of the Jute Mill (3/26/35)
71. The Aborted Revolution (4/2/35)
72. The Blonde Menace (4/9/35)
73. The Midnight Phantom (4/16/35)
74. The Wholesale Murder (4/23/35)
75. The Corpse in the Cellar (4/30/35)
76. The Wilting Chrysanthemum (5/7/35)
77. Murder in the Vineyard (5/14/35)
78. The Hightower Case (5/21/35)
79. Youth Rides Rough (5/28/35)
80. The Innocent Bride (6/4/35)
81. Hot Bonds (6/11/35)
82. The Chinese Puzzle (6/18/35)
83. Meet the Baron (6/25/35)
84. Oakland Payroll Robbery (7/2/35)
85. Murder by Blueprint (7/9/35)
86. The Human Claw (7/16/35)
87. The Opium Den (7/23/35)
88. Gun Drunk (7/30/35)
89. The Celestrial Journey (8/7/35)
90. The Vegetable Market Murder (8/14/35)
91. The Grinning Skull (8/21/35)
92. The Bad Dope (8/28/35)
93. Black Vengeance (9/4/35)
94. The Tunnel Bandits (9/11/35)
95. Eighteen Days of Freedom (9/18/35)
96. The Hollywood Kidnapping (9/25/35)
97. Escape (10/2/35)
98. Fire! Fire! Fire! (10/9/35)

99. Murder for Insurance (10/16/35)
100. The Lt. Crowley Murder (10/23/35)
101. The Murder Quartet (10/30/35)
102. Catching the Loose Kid (11/6/35)
103. Invitation to Murder (11/13/35)
104. Bank Bandits and Bullets (11/20/35)
105. -----(11/27/35)
106. Burglar Charges Collect (12/4/35)
107. Paroled (12/11/35)
108. A Corpse by the Road (12/18/35)
109. The Moran Jewelry Robbery (12/25/35)
110. The Ghost House (1/1/36)
111. Death Under the Sajuaro (1/8/36)
112. The Match Burglar (1/15/36)
113. The Corpse With a Face (1/22/36)
114. Bull in the China Shop (1/29/36)
115. Knives on the Barbary Coast (2/5/36)
116. Young Dillinger (2/12/36)
117. The Murder in the Back Room (2/19/36)
118. The Bloodstained Saw (2/26/36)
119. The Hundred Dollar Nightgown (3/4/36)
120. The Case of the June Bug (3/11/36)
121. The San Rafael Gang (3/18/36)
122. Think Before You Shoot (3/25/36)
123. Crime vs. Time (4/3/36)
124. One Good Turn Deserves Another (4/10/36)
125. Hang Me, Please (4/17/36)
126. The Beer Bottle Murder (4/24/36)
127. And A Little Child Shall Lead Them (5/1/36)
128. Weather Clear — Track Fast (5/8/36)
129. The Seventy-Four Day Stakeout (5/15/36)
130. Triple Cross (5/22/36)
131. The Throat That Didn't Bleed (5/29/36)
132. Drive 'Em Off the Dock (6/5/36)
133. Gold In Them Hills (6/11/36)
134. The Woman With The Stone Heart (6/18/36)
135. Reefers by the Acre (6/25/36)
136. Flaming Tick of Death (7/2/36)
137. The Crimson Riddle (7/9/36)
138. The Cockeyed Killer (7/16/36)
139. The Corpse in the Shack (7/23/36)
140. A Chance Meeting Murder (7/30/46)
141. Opium and Dough Don't Mix (8/6/36)

142. The Missing Messenger (8/13/36)
143. Body, Body, Whose Got the Body? (8/20/36)
144. All That Glitters (8/27/36)
145. The Body in the Mine (9/3/36)
146. Twenty Keys to Death (9/10/36)
147. The Verdugo Hills Murder (9/17/36)
148. The September Killer (9/24/36)
149. Hard to Kill (10/1/36)
150. The Holy Twenty-One (10/8/36)
151. Noblesse Obligue (10/15/36)
152. A Trap to Catch a Mailman (10/22/36)
153. The Army Game (10/29/36)
154. The Murder in Room Nine (11/5/36)
155. Nine Years a Safecracker (11/12/36)
156. The Corpse in the Red Necktie (11/19/36)
157. The Baby Dillinger Gang (11/26/36)
158. The Fire Detective (12/3/36)
159. The Criminal Policeman (12/10/36)
160. The Multiple Murders (12/17/36)
161. The Milkbottle Murder (12/21/36)
162. Fifty Cents For Life (12/28/36)
163. Banks and Bribes (1/4/37)
164. Curiosity Killed a Cat (1/11/37)
165. Death Is Box Office (1/18/37)
166. Dr. Nitro (1/25/37)
167. The Whistling Snowbirds (2/3/37)
168. The Laughing Killer (2/10/37)
169. Ten Tortured Extortionists (2/17/37)
170. The Banker Bandit (2/24/37)
171. The Honor Complex (3/3/37)
172. Desertion Leads to Murder (3/10/37)
173. Hit and Run Driver (3/17/37)
174. Trial by Talkie (3/24/37)
175. The Double Cross (3/31/37)
176. Death in the Morning (4/7/37)
177. Ransom Ring (4/14/37)
178. Pegleg Justice (4/21/37)
179. Murder Week (4/28/37)
180. The Ice House Murder (5/5/37)
181. John Doe Number 71 (5/12/37)
182. The Turk Burglars (5/19/37)
183. The Disappearing Scar (5/26/37)
184. The Cinder Dick (6/2/37)
185. The Man Who Lost His Face (6/9/37)
186. The Bamboo Snake (6/16/37)
187. The Desperate Choice (6/23/37)

188. The Case of the Performed Cigarette Lighter (6/30/37)
189. Kidnapped (7/7/37)
190. Man Overboard (7/14/37)
191. The Alibi (7/21/37)
192. The Bottle Trouble (7/28/37)
193. The Broken Xylophone (8/4/37)
194. The Manila Envelopes (8/11/37)
195. True Confession (8/18/37)
196. The Criminal Returns (8/26/37)
197. The Case of the One Pound Note (9/1/37)
198. Tobaccoville Road (9/7/37)
199. The Murder in Basin Street (9/14/37)
200. The Bone Button (9/21/37)
201. The Crimonson Crusader (9/28/37)
202. Sirens in the Night (10/5/37)
203. The Two-Edged Knife (10/12/37)
204. Death in the Forenoon (10/19/37)
205. The Bloodstained Coin (10/26/37)
206. The People vs. O'Brien (11/2/37)
207. The Phantom Radio (11/9/37)
208. Rhythm of the Wheels (11/16/37)
209. The Bad Man (11/23/37)
210. The Flat Nosed Pliers (11/30/37)
211. The Skeleton in the Desert (12/7/37)
212. The General Kills at Dawn (12/14/37)
213. The Shanghai Jester (12/21/37)
214. Sands of the Desert (12/28/37)
215. The Buccaneer (1/4/38)
216. Swing Low, Sweet Chariot (1/11/38)
217. The Tilted Pan (1/18/38)
218. Trail of the Numbered Bills (1/25/38)
219. The History of Dallas Eagan (2/1/38)
220. Flight from Freedom (2/8/38)
221. The Homicidal Hobo (2/15/38)
222. The Drunken Sailor (2/22/38)
223. The Broken Motel (3/1/38)
224. Death in the Moonlight (3/8/38)
225. The Peroxide Blond (3/15/38)
226. The Long Bladed Knife (3/22/38)
227. Murder with Mushrooms (3/29/38)
228. The Pink Nosed Pig (4/7/38)
229. The Roving Robbers (4/14/38)
230. Murder at Midnight (4/21/38)
231. The Pattering Parrot (4/28/38)
232. The Bloodstained Shoe (5/5/38)
233. The Ruined Suspenders (5/12/38)
234. The King's Ransom (5/19/38)
235. Muerte en Buenaventura (5/26/38)
236. The Greasy Trail (6/2/38)
237. The Turtle Necked Murderer (6/9/38)
238. The 25th Stamp (6/16/38)
239. The Incorrigible Youth (6/23/38)
240. The Big Shot (6/30/38)
241. The Kalsomined Kar (7/7/38)
242. The Man Who Talked (7/14/38)
243. A Murder Has Been Arranged (7/21/38)
244. Life, Liberty, and the Pursuit of Parker (7/28/38)
245. Murder on Eddy Street (8/4/38)
246. I Asked for It (8/11/38)
247. The Unbroken Spirit (8/18/38)
248. The Thirteenth Grave (8/25/38)
249. The Artful Dodger (9/1/38)
250. Murder on the Left (9/8/38)
251. The Embroidered Slip (9/15/38)
252. The Black Cat (9/22/38)
253. The Barking Dog (9/29/38)
254. The Tearless Magalane (10/6/38)
255. The Blond Paper Hanger (10/13/38)
256. The Abandoned Bricks (10/20/38)
257. The Swollen Face (10/27/38)
258. The Portuguese Crooner (11/3/38)
259. The Glass Gun (11/10/38)
260. The Four Lead Slugs (11/17/38)
261. The Rasping Voice (11/24/38)
262. Blind Man's Bluff (12/2/38)
263. The Poisoning Jezebel (12/9/38)
264. December Rhapsody (12/16/38)
265. Murder at Sundown (12/23/38)
266. Three Faces West (12/30/38)
267. The Grass Skirt (1/6/39)
268. The Silver Cord (1/13/39)
269. The Azure Ring (1/20/39)
270. The Baker's Bride (1/27/39)
271. The Careless Caretaker (2/3/39)
272. The Green Sedan (2/10/39)
273. The Bloodstained Wrench (2/17/39)
274. The Unconquerable Mrs. Shuttle (2/24/39)
275. The Lesson in Loot (3/3/39)
276. The Twenty Dollar Bill (3/10/39)
277. Flight in the Desert (3/17/39)
278. The Hunted Man (3/24/39)
279. The Rope Bound Truck (3/31/39)
280. The Man Who Walked Like an Ape (4/7/39)
281. Death in the Canyon (4/14/39)
282. The Bitter Wine (4/21/39)
283. The Man Who Ran Away (4/28/39)

284. The Gospel of Brother Ned (5/4/39)
285. You Can't Cheat an Honest Man (5/11/39)
286. Murder at Sunset (5/18/39)
287. The Bloodstained Car (5/25/39)
288. The Plague of the Black Locust (6/1/39)
289. The Old Grad Returns (6/8/39)
290. The Man With the Injured Knee (6/15/39)
291. In the Still of the Night (6/22/39)
292. The Wired Wrists (6/29/39)
293. The Wicked Flea (7/6/39)
294. The Squealing Rat (7/13/39)
295. The Twenty-Sixth Wife (7/20/39)
296. The Teardrop Charm (7/27/39)
297. The Body on the Promenade Deck (8/3/39)
298. The Missing Guns (8/10/39)
299. The Man with the Iron Pipes (8/17/39)
300. The Tenth Commandment (8/25/39)
301. Six of a Kind (9/1/39)
302. Murder in the Morning (9/8/39)

The Camel Screen Guild Players

Previously entitled *The Lady Esther Screen Guild Theater*, this series changed its title when it gained a new sponsor. Now under the sponsorship of Camel Cigarettes, this dramatic series continued featuring Hollywood stars in adaptations of movies. It was broadcast over CBS on Monday evenings. In less than a year after its premiere, Camel decided to change the title again, this time to *The Screen Guild Theater*, with Camel still sponsoring the series. Michael Roy was the announcer. William Lawrence was the director. Wilbur Hatch supplied the music. Harry Cronman adapted the movies into radio scripts. Bob Hope succeeded in breaking up the cast during the broadcast of October 13, 1947. Whenever possible, the original stars of the movies reprised their film roles.

1. The Bells of St. Mary's (10/6/47; Ingrid Bergman and Bing Crosby)
2. My Favorite Brunette (10/13/47; Bob Hope and Dorothy Lamour)
3. Elizabeth, the Queen (10/20/47; Brian Aherne and Bette Davis)
4. The Shocking Miss Pilgrim (10/27/47; Betty Grable and Tony Martin)
5. The Secret Life of Walter Mitty (11/3/47; Danny Kaye and Virginia Mayo)
6. Boomerang (11/10/47; Dana Andrews, Reed Hadley, Richard Widmark, and Jane Wyatt)
7. Secret Heart (11/17/47; David Bruce, Claudette Colbert, Walter Pidgeon, and Janet Waldo)
8. The Best Years of Our Lives (11/24/47; Myrna Loy, Fredric March, and Teresa Wright)
9. The Trouble with Women (12/1/47; Betty Hutton and Ray Milland)
10. Moss Rose (12/8/47; Ethel Barrymore, Ida Lupino, and Victor Mature)
11. Sweethearts (12/15/47; Nelson Eddy and Jeanette MacDonald)
12. Pinocchio (12/22/47; Fanny Brice and Hanley Stafford)
13. It's a Wonderful Life (12/29/47; Victor Moore, Donna Reed, and James Stewart)
14. The Fugitive (1/5/48; Ward Bond, Pedro de Cordoba, J. Carrol Naish, Gregory Peck, and Cesar Romero)
15. Desert Fury (1/12/48; Mary Astor, Wendell Corey, Burt Lancaster, and Elizabeth Scott)
16. Ivy (1/19/48; Joan Fontaine, Patrick Knowles, and John Sutton)
17. Brief Encounter (1/26/48; Tom

Conway, Irene Dunne, and Herbert Marshall)

18. The Dark Mirror (2/2/48; Lew Ayres and Loretta Young)
19. Johnny Come Lately (2/9/48; James Cagney and Agnes Moorehead)
20. Easy to Web (2/16/48; Van Johnson, Harry Von Zell, and Esther Williams)
21. The Foxes of Harrow (2/23/48; Rex Harrison, Gene Lockhart, and Maureen O'Hara)
22. The Bishop's Wife (3/1/48; Cary Grant, David Niven, and Loretta Young)
23. The Late George Apley (3/8/48; Edna Best, Ronald Colman, and Peggy Cummings)
24. Suddenly It's Spring (3/15/48; MacDonald Carey, Paulette Goddard, and Fred MacMurray)
25. Cheyenne (3/22/48; Dennis Morgan and Jane Wyman)
26. You Belong to Me (3/29/48; Linda Darnell and Robert Young)
27. One Way Passage (4/5/48; Ward Bond, Barbara Stanwyck, and Robert Taylor)
28. The Great Man Votes (4/12/48; Frank McHugh, George Murphy, Ronald Reagan, and Edward G. Robinson)
29. It Had to Be You (4/26/48; Lucille Ball and Cornell Wilde)
30. Next Time We Meet (5/3/48; Frank Albertson, Joseph Cotten, and Maureen O'Sullivan)
31. The Bachelor and the Bobbysoxer (5/10/48; Cary Grant, Myrna Loy, and Shirley Temple)
32. The Valiant (5/17/48; Edward Arnold, Jeanne Crain, and Gregory Peck)
33. The Casbah (5/24/48; Yvonne De Carlo, Peter Lorre, and Tony Martin)
34. Hold Back the Dawn (5/31/48; Charles Boyer and Ida Lupino)
35. Snow White (6/7/48; Jimmy Durante, Mary Jane Smith, and Margaret O'Brien)
36. Love Affair (6/14/48; Greer Garson and Walter Pidgeon)
37. Shadow of a Doubt (6/21/48; Vanessa Brown and Joseph Cotten)
38. Up in Central Park (6/28/48; Deanna Durbin, Dick Haymes, Charles Irwin, and Vincent Price)

The Campbell Playhouse

Literally overnight, Orson Welles became a legend and a star, duping America with his "War of the Worlds" broadcast on *The Mercury Theatre on the Air*. Campbell Soups decided to take a dare by sponsoring Welles' radio program and drop sponsorship of the famed *Hollywood Hotel*. Changing the *Mercury* name to *The Campbell Playhouse*, Campbell Soups gave Welles a bigger budget, allowing various stars of stage and screen to guest in the weekly dramas.

Edwin C. Hill introduced the premiere program of the series. Ernest Chappell was hired as announcer and pitchman. Dan Seymour of the earlier Mercury broadcasts subbed when Chappell could not attend. Bernard Herrmann composed and conducted for almost every episode, and Alexander Semmler subbed for Herrmann. As with *Mercury*, Orson Welles hosted each episode, acted, and added his usual touches to the final scripts.

Lionel Barrymore performed the villainous role of Ebenezer Scrooge in Charles Dickens' classic *A Christmas Carol* every year during the holiday season for almost twenty years, until his death in 1954. *The Campbell Playhouse* presented his annual Christmas special in 1939.

Helen Hayes appeared so frequently that many consider her a regular for the show. Author Daphne du Maurier spoke over the radio mike via telephone, direct from England, for the first broadcast of the series. George S. Kaufman not only wrote episode eight, but also performed in it as well. Pearl S. Buck appeared at the end of the nineteenth episode. Walter Huston's wife Nan Sutherland acted in a bit part in episodes 34 and 38. A real-life Foreign Legionnaire was made a guest speaker in the fifteenth episode. Warden Lewis of Sing-Sing prison is interviewed after the drama on the fourteenth episode. Richard Maney, a real-life press agent who was satirized in episode 16, also guested.

In episode 17, Helen Morgan reprised the role that made her famous in *Show Boat*, and the author of the musical made her acting debut as well. Episode 23 featured the first radio performance of Thornton Wilder's famous 1938 Pulitzer Prize–winning play, *Our Town*. In episode 37, Madeleine Carroll replaced Claudette Colbert, who was originally scheduled to star but was unable to attend the broadcast.

1. Rebecca (12/9/38; Margaret Sullavan, Ray Collins, Agnes Moorehead, and Mildred Natwick)
2. Call It a Day (12/16/38; Jeanne Dante, Beatrice Lillie, and Jane Wyatt)
3. A Christmas Carol (12/23/38; Joseph Cotten, Brenda Forbes, Alice Frost, Hiram Sherman, Arthur Anderson, Ray Collins, Anne Stafford, Kingsley Colton, and Alfred Shirley)
4. A Farewell to Arms (12/30/38; Katharine Hepburn)
5. Counselor at Law (1/6/39; Gertrude Berg, Arline MacMahon, Joseph Cotten, and Sam Liebowitz)
6. Mutiny on the Bounty (1/13/39; Dorothy Hall, Burgess Meredith, Carl Frank, Joseph Cotten, Frank Readick, Edgar Barrier, Memo Holt, Myron McCormick, Ray Collins, and Richard Wilson)
7. Chicken Wagon Family (1/20/39; Burgess Meredith)
8. I Lost My Girlish Laughter (1/27/39; Agnes Moorehead, Everett Sloane, and Joseph Cotten)
9. Arrowsmith (2/3/39; Helen Hayes, Ray Collins, Al Swenson, Karl Swenson, and Frank Readick)
10. The Green Goddess (2/10/39; Madelaine Carroll, Edgar Barrier, and Eustace Wyatt)
11. Burlesque (2/17/39; Sam Levene)
12. State Fair (2/24/39; Burgess Meredith and Phil Strong)
13. Royal Regiment (3/3/39; Mary Astor)
14. The Glass Key (3/10/39; Paul Stewart, Elspeth Eric, Everett Sloane, Myron McCormick, Laura Baxter, Howard Smith, Elizabeth Morgan, Ray Collins, and Edgar Barrier)
15. Beau Geste (3/17/39; Stefan Schnabel, Jackie Kelk, Laurence Olivier, and Edward Ryan)
16. Twentieth Century (3/24/39; Sam Levene, Elissa Landi, Teddy Bergman, and Edgar Kent)
17. Show Boat (3/31/39; Helen Morgan, Margaret Sullivan, William Johnstone, and Everett Sloane)
18. Les Miserables (4/7/39; Walter Huston)
19. The Patriot (4/14/39; Anna May Wong, Elliott Reid, Ray Collins, and Myron McCormick)
20. Private Lives (4/21/39; Getrude Lawrence, Naomi Campbell, and Edgar Barrier)
21. Black Daniel (4/28/39; Joan Bennett)
22. Wickford Point (5/5/39; John P. Marquand)
23. Our Town (5/12/39; Patricia Newton, John Craven, Parker Fennelly, and Agnes Moorehead)
24. The Bad Man (5/19/39; Ida Lupino,

William Allen, Diana Stevens, and Edwin Jerome)

25. American Cavalcade (5/26/39; Cornelia Otis Skinner, Frank Readick, Kenny Delmar, Bill Harrigan, Kingsley Colton, Howard Smith, Everett Sloane, Agnes Moorehead, Ray Collins)

26. Victoria Regina (6/2/39; Helen Hayes)

27. Peter Ibbetson (9/10/39; Helen Hayes, Everett Sloane, George Coulouris, Agnes Moorehead, Eustace Wyatt, Vera Allen, John Emery, and Richard Wilson)

28. Ah, Wilderness (9/17/39; Joan Tetzel, Paul Stewart, Joseph Cotten, and Arlene Francis)

29. What Every Woman Knows (9/24/39; Alfred Shirley, Naomi Campbell, and Helen Hayes)

30. The Count of Monte Cristo (10/1/39; George Coulouris, Agnes Moorehead, and Edgar Barrier)

31. Algiers (10/8/39; Paulette Goddard)

32. Escape (10/15/39; Wendy Barrie, Jack Smart, Bea Benaderet, Harriet Kaye, and Ray Collins)

33. Liliom (10/22/39; Helen Hayes, Bill Adams, Agnes Moorehead, Joan Tetzel, and Joseph Cotten)

34. The Magnificent Ambersons (10/29/39; Walter Huston, Ray Collins, and Bea Benaderet)

35. The Hurricane (11/5/39; Mary Astor, Bea Benaderet, and Edgar Barrier)

36. The Murder of Roger Ackroyd (11/12/39; Edna May Oliver, Alan Napier, Mary Taylor, Brenda Forbes, Ray Collins, George Coulouris, and Everett Sloane)

37. The Garden of Allah (11/19/39; Madeleine Carroll, Everett Sloane, and George Coulouris)

38. Doddsworth (11/26/39; Fay Bainter, Dennis Green, and Brenda Forbes)

39. Lost Horizon (12/3/39; Sigrid Gurie)

40. Vanessa (12/10/39; Helen Hayes and Alfred Shirley)

41. There's Always a Woman (12/17/39; Marie Wilson, Mary Taylor, and Georgia Backus)

42. A Christmas Carol (12/24/39; Lionel Barrymore, George Coulouris, and Bea Benaderet)

43. Vanity Fair (1/7/40; Helen Hayes, Betty Garde, and Joseph Holland)

44. Theodora Goes Wild (1/14/40; Ray Collins, Mary Taylor, and Loretta Young)

45. The Citadel (1/21/40; Geraldine Fitzgerald, Everett Sloane, and George Coulouris)

46. It Happened One Night (1/28/40; William Powell, Miriam Hopkins, and John Houseman)

47. Broome Stages (2/4/40; Helen Hayes)

48. Mr. Deeds Goes to Town (2/11/40; Gertrude Lawrence, Agnes Moorehead, and Joseph Cotten)

49. Dinner at Eight (2/18/40; Lucille Ball, Hedda Hopper, and Charles Trowbridge)

50. Only Angels Have Wings (2/25/40; Joan Blondell, George Coulouris, and Regis Toomey)

51. A Rabble in Arms (3/3/40; William Allen, Georgia Backus, Guy Repp, and Richard Wilson)

52. Craig's Wife (3/10/40; Richard Bear, Janet Beecher, Bea Benaderet, and Regis Toomey)

53. Huckleberry Finn (3/17/40; William Allen, Walter Catlett, Jackie Cooper, and Robert Warwick)

54. June Moon (3/24/40; Bea Benaderet, Jack Benny, Virginia Gordon, and Benny Rubin)

55. Jane Eyre (3/31/40; Madeleine Carroll, Cecilia Loftus, Edgar Barrier, Robert Coot, George Coulouris, and Serita Wooten)

Canterbury Tales

Based on the stories of Geoffrey Chaucer, this syndicated anthology series ran a total of seven episodes. It was broadcast over WNYC in New York, 2 to 3 pm, EST.

1. The Shipman's Tale / The Prioress' Tale (7/20/50)
2. The Monk's Tale / The Nun's Priest's Tale (7/27/50)
3. The Pardoner's Preamble and Tale (8/3/50)
4. The Merchant's Preamble and Tale (8/10/50)
5. The Squire's Tale (8/17/50)
6. The Franklin's Tale (8/24/50)
7. The Canon Yeoman's Preamble and Tale (8/31/50)

The Carrington Playhouse

Anthology series, broadcast on Mutual from 8 to 8:30 pm, EST.

1. The Balzac Murder (2/21/46; Frank Lovejoy and Michael Fitzmaurice)
2. Wait for Me (2/28/46)
3. At Midnight on the Thirty-First of March (3/7/46)
4. -----(3/14/46)
5. The Sparrow (3/21/46)
6. Up in the Clouds (3/28/46)
7. Letters to Irene (4/4/46)
8. Design for Murder (4/11/46)
9. Ride a Cock Horse (4/18/46)
10. Eternity Express (4/25/46)
11. Elmer and the Wise Guys (5/2/46)
12. Victoria (5/9/46; Martha Scott)
13. -----(5/16/46)
14. The Portrait of a Girl (5/23/46)
15. The Jumping Sailor (5/30/46)
16. My Dear Aunt Caroline (6/6/46)
17. The Sitter (6/13/46)
18. Country Squire (6/20/46)
19. Not a Match in the House (6/27/46)
20. The Simple Songs (7/4/46)
21. Mind Over Matter (7/11/46)
22. Me, I'm Sentimental (7/18/46)
23. Love Is a Funny Thing (7/25/46)
24. The Show Must Go On (8/1/46)
25. Your Time Is Up (8/8/46)
26. The Portrait of a Girl (8/15/46)
27. Enter Youth (8/22/46)
28. Love Me, Love My Ghost (8/29/46)
29. Make Mine Murder (9/5/46)
30. Here's Dust in Your Eye (9/12/46)
31. Johnny Lately (9/19/46)
32. Satire on Radio (9/26/46)

Case Dismissed

This program was broadcast over WMAQ and NBC as a Saturday night sustained offering.

1. Criminal Liability (1/30/54)
2. Pitfalls of Buying a House (2/6/54)
3. Necessity of a Legal Will (2/13/54)
4. Child Support (2/20/54)
5. Installment Buying (2/27/54)
6. Adoption (3/6/54)
7. Landlord and Tenant (3/13/54)
8. Rights When Arrested (3/20/54)
9. Liability for Minors (3/27/54)
10. Eye Witness (4/3/54)
11. Libel and Slander (4/17/54)
12. Juvenile Delinquency (4/24/54)

Casey, Crime Photographer

Continuation of the *Casey* series, previously titled *Casey, Press Photographer*. Sponsored initially by Anchor-Hocking Glass, the Toni Company took over sponsorship on April 1, 1948. Philip Morris then took over sponsorship August 4, 1949, and on October 26, 1950 the series went sustaining. Broadcast over CBS, Thursday evenings from 9:30 to 10 pm, EST. John Dietz produced and directed. Music was supplied by the Al Bleyer Orchestra. Lew White was the organist. Staats Cotsworth starred in the lead role of Casey. Interesting trivia: For the broadcast of August 21, 1947, the lead character Casey did not appear in the program! In January of 1954, the series changed titles for one last time to *Crime Photographer*. Writers included Alonzo Dean Cole, Milton J. Kramer and Harry Ingram. Tony Marvin was announcer until episode 233.

179. The Demon Miner (3/20/47)
180. Blood Pact (3/27/47)
181. The Girl on the Dock (4/3/47)
182. The Ugly Duckling (4/10/47)
183. The Box of Death (4/17/47)
184. The Gentle Stranger (4/24/47)
185. King of the Apes (5/1/47)
186. The Laughing Killer (5/8/47)
187. Mad Dog (5/15/47)
188. Pickup (5/22/47)
189. Out of the Past (5/29/47)
190. The Haunted House (6/5/47)
191. In the Sweet Name of Charity (6/12/47)
192. Find the Papers (6/19/47)
193. A Package for Annie (6/26/47)
194. Acquitted (7/3/47)
195. The Lady Killer (7/10/47)
196. Casey and the Self-Made Hero (7/17/47)
197. Photo of the Dead (7/24/47; Arnold Moss)
198. Bright New Star (7/31/47)
199. Death in Lover's Lane (8/7/47; Ed Begley, Roger De Koven, and Peter Capell)
200. The Chivalrous Gunman (8/14/47)
201. The Busman's Holiday (8/21/47; Ralph Bell)
202. Hide-Out (8/28/47; Joseph Julian)
203. The Loaded Dice (9/4/47)
204. Graveyard Gertie (9/11/47; Abby Lewis)
205. The Tobacco Pouch (9/18/47; Mandel Kramer)
206. The Treasure Cave (9/25/47)
207. The Miscarriage of Justice (10/2/47; Joe di Santis and Santos Ortega)
208. The Wedding Breakfast (10/9/47)
209. The Camera Bug (10/16/47)
210. The Lady in Distress (10/23/47)
211. Great Grandfather's Rent Receipt (10/30/47; Karl Swenson)
212. The Case of the Blonde Lipstick (11/6/47)
213. Too Many Angels (11/13/47; Peter Capell)
214. Earned Reward (11/20/47; Joseph Julian)
215. After Turkey Comes The Bill (11/27/47)
216. The Serpent Goddess (12/4/47; Ted de Corsia and Raymond Edward Johnson)
217. The New Will (12/11/47)
218. The Life of the Party (12/18/47)
219. The Santa Claus of Bums' Blvd. (12/25/47; Bob Dryden)
220. Hot New Year's Party (1/1/48; Joseph Julian)
221. Queen of the Amazons (1/8/48; Hope Emerson)
222. The Miracle (1/15/48)
223. Ex-Convict (1/22/48)
224. The Piggy Bank Robbery (1/29/48; Bill Adams)
225. Music to Die By (2/5/48; Raymond Edward Johnson)
226. Key Witness (2/12/48)
227. Witchcraft (2/19/48)
228. The Fix (2/26/48)
229. Tough Guy (3/4/48; Joseph Julian)
230. Fog (3/11/48; Peter Capell)

231. Murder in Black and White (3/18/48)
232. Blind Justice (3/25/48)
233. Sleeping Dogs Awake (4/1/48)
234. A Present for Percy (4/8/48)
235. The Considerate Burglar (4/15/48)
236. You Die Today (4/22/48)
237. Half Guilty (4/29/48)
238. X marks the Spot (5/6/48)
239. Dead Man's Fortune (5/13/48)
240. My Brother's Keeper (5/20/48)
241. Gun Wanted (5/27/48)
242. Murderers, Ltd. (6/3/48)
243. Letters from Mexico (6/10/48)
244. Wife Number Eight (6/17/48)
245. No Tears for Terry (6/24/48)
246. Missing Heiress (7/1/48)
247. Old Joe (7/8/48)
248. Farewell Performance (7/15/48)
249. In For Trouble (7/22/48)
250. Man Hater (7/29/48)
251. The Pirates (8/12/48)
252. On the Record (8/19/48)
253. Kangaroo Court (8/26/48)
254. My Little Feathered Friends (9/2/48)
255. Winning Streak (9/9/48)
256. Two Thousand Suspects (9/16/48)
257. Finger Man (9/23/48)
258. A Poison Pen (9/30/48)
259. Old Blankety Blank (10/7/48)
260. Only Saps Work for Wages (10/21/48)
261. Election Bet (10/28/48)
262. The Ghost See-ers (11/4/48)
263. The Mystery Man (11/11/48)
264. String of Beads (11/18/48)
265. Holiday (11/25/48)
266. The Wild Man (12/2/48)
267. The Genius (12/9/48)
268. Blackout (12/16/48)
269. Two Days Before Christmas (12/23/48)
270. Meet the Wife (12/30/48)
271. The Box of Ashes (1/6/49)
272. Tiger on the Loose (1/13/49)
273. Action Photograph (1/20/49)
274. Pick up your Marbles (1/27/49)
275. Unwelcome Party (2/3/49)
276. The Grandson of Mr. Smith (2/10/49)
277. The Chinese Room (2/17/49)
278. Blood Money (2/24/49)
279. You Are the Killer (3/3/49)
280. The Scene of the Crime (3/10/49)
281. An Attempt to Murder (3/17/49)
282. Terror (3/24/49)
283. I'll See You Hanged (3/31/49)
284. Murder in the Air (4/7/49)
285. Too Many Knives (4/14/49)
286. Rest Cure (4/21/49)
287. Death from the Dead (4/28/49)
288. The Wolverine (5/5/49)
289. The Booby Trap (5/12/49)
290. Cupid Is a Killer (5/19/49)
291. The Return from the Grave (5/26/49)
292. Brotherly Hate (6/2/49)
293. Deadline — Midnight (6/9/49)
294. Notice — to the Public (6/16/49)
295. The Dragon Head (6/23/49)
296. The Lily (6/30/49)
297. Murder Farm (7/7/49)
298. Crazy Like a Fox (7/14/49)
299. Durable Dennis (7/21/49)
300. Murder-Go-Round (7/28/49)
301. Sell-Out (8/4/49)
302. The Death of a Stranger (8/11/49)
303. Big Danger (8/18/49)
304. The Snow Ball (8/25/49)
305. Scrub Woman (9/1/49)
306. Peace Mission (9/8/49)
307. The Maniac (9/15/49)
308. The Blackmailer (9/22/49)
309. Unstandard Model (9/29/49)
310. The Weasel (10/6/49)
311. Museum of Murder (10/13/49)
312. -----(10/20/49)
313. The Vampire (10/27/49)
314. Fall of the Cards (11/3/49)
315. Thunderbolt (11/10/49)
316. The Upholsterer (11/17/49)
317. A Gift for Thanksgiving (11/24/49)
318. Murder at Auction (12/1/49)
319. Witness for the Prosecution (12/8/49)
320. Appointment for Murder (12/15/49)
321. A Picture (12/22/49)
322. The Chisler (12/29/49)
323. Justice (1/5/50)
324. The Love Story (1/12/50)
325. Wanted — A Gun (1/19/50)
326. Unsolved Murder (1/26/50)
327. Four Forefingers (2/2/50)
328. The Bad Hunch (2/9/50)
329. The Girl Hitch-Hiker (2/16/50)
330. The Jinx (2/23/50)
331. The Bad Little Babe (3/2/50)

Casey, Press Photographer

Continuation of the *Casey* series, previously entitled *Flashgun Casey*. Still sustaining with no sponsor, this series was heard over CBS, Saturday from 11:30 pm to 12 am, EST. On July 15, 1944, the series moved to an earlier time slot, 5 to 5:30 pm. On September 12, 1944, the series moved to Tuesdays, heard from 11:30 pm to 12 am, EST. John Dietz produced and directed. In July of 1945, the program changed its name again, this time to *Casey, Crime Photographer*.

71. The Substitutes (11/28/44)
72. Trial Balloon (12/5/44)
73. A Girl Named Kate (12/12/44)
74. Group Photograph (12/19/44)
75. The Unknown Caller (12/26/44)
76. Engagement Ring (1/2/45)
77. Key to Room 424 (1/9/45)
78. The Professional Widow (1/16/45)
79. Beware of the Dog (1/23/45)
80. Don't Call the Cops (2/6/45)
81. Suicide Note (2/13/45)
82. Diamonds and Tombstones (2/20/45)
83. Complete Acquittal (3/6/45)
84. The Picture in the Park (3/13/45)
85. Incredible Evidence (3/20/45)
86. The White Monster (3/27/45)
87. The Impossible Crime (4/3/45)
88. Account Settled (4/10/45)
89. Outline in Clay (4/17/45)
90. Gambler's Luck (4/24/45)
91. The Killer's Kid (5/1/45)
92. Free Confession (5/15/45)
93. The Unexpected Guest (5/22/45)
94. A Degree of Arson (5/29/45)
95. The Invisible Man (6/5/45)
96. The Strange Case of Mr. Strange (6/12/45)
97. Vacation in Maine (6/19/45)
98. Man Overboard (6/26/45)
99. The Cat's Paw (7/4/45)

The Cavalcade of America

In 1935, the Dupont Manufacturing Company began sponsoring a radio program as a means of enhancing the company's image and bringing great events in American history to an audience of millions. From biographies of famous American inventors and little known war heroes, this program employed the best talent of Hollywood and Broadway for the leads. A board of "historical advisers" was established to choose material and to authenticate each facet of the broadcast. Headed by Dr. Frank Monaghan of Yale University, the series also included Carl Carmer and Marquis James.

Roger Pryor, Paul Stewart, Homer Fickett and Jack Zoller were the producers and directors over the years. Donald Voohees was the musical director for the East Coast performances, and Robert Armbruster for the West Coast performances. Bud Collyer, Bill Hamilton and Cy Harrice were the announcers.

Episodes 40 to 50 was a special summer series entitled "Cavalcade of America in Music." Episodes 90 to 101 constituted another special summer series of musical presentations. The broadcast of September 14, 1942, featured a speech by the former Ambassador to Japan, Joseph C. Grew, on the occasion of awarding the Army-Navy E Award at the Remington Arms Plant in Bridgeport, Connecticut. Episode 408 was not really broadcast, pre-empted due to election specials. Episode 407 was Clark Gable's first appearance on radio since he returned from service. Walter Huston was the host for a few months beginning September 18, 1944. When DuPont tried an experimental short-run television version in 1952, it proved a success and within a few months, the radio series was dropped for a more permanent schedule on television.

1. No Turning Back (10/9/35; Walter Hampden)
2. The Will to Conquest Distance (10/16/35)
3. The Spirit of Competition (10/23/35; Franchot Tone)
4. The Will to Rebuild (10/30/35; Frank Craven)
5. Faith in Education (11/6/35)
6. Woman's Emancipation (11/13/35; Fay Bainter)
7. Willingness to Share (11/20/35)
8. Community Self Reliance (11/27/35)
9. Heroism in Medical Science (12/4/35)
10. The Will to Explore (12/11/35)
11. Defiance of Nature (12/18/35)
12. The Humanitarian Urge (12/25/35)
13. The Declaration of Independence (1/1/36)
14. Women in Public Service (1/8/36)
15. Building and Architecture (1/15/36)
16. Speed of Words (1/22/36)
17. Enterprise (1/29/36)
18. Loyalty to Family (2/5/36)
19. Abraham Lincoln: A True American (2/12/36)
20. The Bridge Builders (2/19/36)
21. Heroes of the Sea (2/26/36)
22. Songs that Inspired the Nation (3/4/36)
23. Perseverance (3/11/36)
24. They Also Serve (3/18/36)
25. Conservation (3/25/36)
26. Winning Fame for American Literature (4/1/36)
27. Opportunity (4/8/36)
28. Railroad Builders (4/15/36)
29. Safety First (4/22/36)
30. Self Reliance (4/29/36)
31. The Artistic Impulse (5/6/36)
32. Tillers of the Soil (5/13/36)
33. Hardiness (5/20/36)
34. Resourcefulness (5/27/36)
35. Songs of Home (6/3/36)
36. Heroes of Texas (6/17/36)
37. Steamboat Builders (6/24/36)
38. American Journalism (7/1/36)
39. Victor Herbert, Master of Melody (7/8/36)
40. The Development of Band Music in America [part one] (7/15/36)
41. The Development of Band Music in America [part two] (7/22/36)
42. The Development of Band Music in America [part three] (7/29/36)
43. The Development of Band Music in America [part four] (8/5/36)
44. The Development of Band Music in America [part five] (8/12/36)
45. The Development of Band Music in America [part six] (8/19/36)
46. The Evolution of Dance Music in America (8/26/36)
47. American Musical Comedy and Operetta (9/2/36)
48. Modern American Orchestral Music (9/9/36)
49. The Orchestra of Today and How it Grew (9/16/36)
50. Music of the Movies (9/23/36)
51. Showmanship (9/30/36)
52. A Helping Hand (10/7/36)
53. Sentinels of the Deep (10/14/36)
54. John Winthrop, Pioneer of Chemical Science (10/21/36)
55. Edward MacDowell, Pioneer in American Music (11/4/36)
56. Transcontinental Journeys (11/11/36)
57. The Story of Rubber (11/18/36)
58. Songs of Sentiment (11/25/36)
59. The Seeing Eye (12/2/36)
60. The Story of Christmas Seals (12/9/36)
61. The Man Who Had Two Careers (12/16/36)
62. A Tribute to Ernestine Schumann-Heink (12/23/36)
63. Yankee Independence (12/30/36)
64. Winning Prestige for the American Stage (1/6/37)
65. John Hyatt, Father of Plastics (1/13/37)
66. Songs of the Sea (1/20/37)
67. Pioneer Woman Physician (1/27/37)
68. Minute Men of the Air (2/3/37)
69. The Man Who Couldn't Grow Old (2/10/37)
70. The Ounce of Prevention (2/17/37)
71. Winning Recognition for American Singers (2/24/37)
72. National Parks Pioneers (3/3/37)
73. Stephen Girard (3/10/37)
74. James Fenimore Cooper, First American Novelist (3/17/37)
75. The House of Glass (3/24/37)
76. The McGuffy Readers (3/31/37)

77. Admiral Peary Discovers the Pole (4/7/37)
78. Songs of the Gay Nineties (4/14/37)
79. The Golden Touch (4/21/37)
80. George Washington, Scientific Farmer (4/28/37)
81. Songs of the South (5/5/37)
82. The Story of Dynamite (5/12/37)
83. Thomas A. Edison, the Man (5/19/37)
84. Songs of the American Indian (5/26/37)
85. The Story of American Dyes (6/2/37)
86. The Eighth Wonder of the World [drama about the Grand Coulee Dam] (6/9/37)
87. Stars of Destiny (6/16/37)
88. The Pine Tree Shilling (6/23/37)
89. Luther Burbank, the Plant Wizard (6/30/37)
90. The Cavalcade of Music: Irving Berlin [part one] (7/7/37; Conrad Thibault)
91. The Cavalcade of Music: George Gershwin [part two] (7/14/37)
92. The Cavalcade of Music: Richard Rogers [part three] (7/21/37)
93. The Cavalcade of Music: Vincent Youmons [part four] (7/28/37)
94. The Cavalcade of Music: Rudolph Friml [part five] (8/4/37)
95. The Cavalcade of Music: Jerome Kern [part six] (8/11/37)
96. The Cavalcade of Music: Sigmund Romberg [part seven] (8/18/37)
97. The Cavalcade of Music: Arthur Schwartz [part eight] (8/25/37)
98. The Cavalcade of Music: Victor Herbert [part nine] (9/1/37)
99. The Cavalcade of Music: Nacio Herb Brown [part ten] (9/8/37)
100. The Cavalcade of Music: Cole Porter [part eleven] (9/15/37)
101. The Cavalcade of Music: Donald Voorhees [part twelve] (9/22/37)
102. Edwin Booth, Pioneer American Actor (9/29/37)
103. Mary Lyon, Pioneer Woman Educator (10/6/37)
104. William Penn and the Holy Experiment (10/13/37)
105. John Jacob Astor (10/20/37)
106. Clara Louise Kellogg (10/27/37)
107. Elmer Ambrose Sperry (11/3/37)
108. John Bartram's Garden (11/10/37)
109. The Seeing Eye (11/17/37)
110. Sara Josepha Hale (11/24/37)
111. Ottmar Mergenthaler (12/1/37)
112. The Constitution of the United States (12/8/37)
113. The Glory of the Vanquished (12/15/37)
114. The Master Navigator (12/22/37)
115. Ernestine Schumann-Heink (12/29/37; Jeanette Nolan)
116. James Buchanan Eads, Pioneer American Engineer (1/5/38)
117. Blazing Trails for Science (1/12/38)
118. The Big Brothers (1/19/38)
119. The Pathfinder (1/26/38)
120. Francis Scott Key (2/2/38; Bill Adams and House Jameson)
121. Oliver Wendell Holmes (2/9/38)
122. The Louisiana Purchase (2/16/38)
123. Noah Webster, the Nation's School Master (2/23/38)
124. Anne Sullivan Macy (3/2/38)
125. The Last of the Scouts (3/9/38)
126. Captain Robert Gray and the Columbia River (3/16/38)
127. John James Audubon (3/23/38)
128. Charlotte Cushman (3/30/38)
129. The Search for Iron (4/6/38)
130. Thomas Jefferson and American Education (4/13/38)
131. The 4-H Club Movement (4/20/38)
132. Maria Mitchell: First American Woman Scientist (4/27/38)
133. Songs of the Mississippi (5/4/38; Everett Clarke, Charles Harrison and Phil Dewey)
134. The Colonization of California (5/11/38)
135. Benjamin Franklin (5/18/38)
136. Child Welfare in the U.S. (5/25/38)
137. Samuel Slater (6/1/38)
138. King Coal: The Story of Anthracite (6/8/38)
139. Doctor John Gorrie (6/15/38)
140. The Swedes Land in Delaware (6/22/38)
141. Eluthere Irenee Du Pont (6/29/38)
142. Knute Rockne (12/5/38; Kenny Delmar, Frank Readick, and Ted Reid)
143. Peter Stuyvesant (12/12/38)

144. Will Rogers [written and narrated by Cal Tinney] (12/19/38)
145. Paul Bunyon (12/26/38; Bill Pringle)
146. John Honeyman (1/2/39; Frank Readick)
147. Edward Bok (1/9/39)
148. Stephen Foster (1/16/39; Ted Jewett)
149. Alexander Graham Bell (1/23/39)
150. Mark Twain (1/30/39)
151. Nathan Hale (2/6/39; Ted Reid)
152. Allan Pinkerton (2/13/39)
153. Kit Carson (2/20/39; Bill Adams)
154. George Gershwin (2/27/39)
155. The Texas Rangers (3/6/39)
156. Marie Dressler (3/13/39; Agnes Moorehead)
157. The American Clipper (3/20/39)
158. The League of the Long House (3/27/39)
159. The Pioneer Mother: Eliza Ann Brooks (4/3/39; Agnes Moorehead)
160. John Howard Payne (4/10/39; Ted Reid)
161. Patrick Henry (4/17/39)
162. Baseball (4/24/39)
163. Washington and the Crown (5/1/39; Bill Adams)
164. Juliette Low (5/8/39)
165. Mr. Justice Holmes (5/15/39; Bill Adams)
166. Dolly Madison (5/22/39; Agnes Moorehead)
167. Elothere Irenee Du Pont (5/29/39; Ed Jerome)
168. Amerigo Vespucci (1/2/40; Burgess Meredith)
169. Sam Houston, the Raven [part one of two] (1/9/40; Walter Huston)
170. Mehitabel Wing (1/16/40; Jeanette Nolan)
171. Tisquantum, Strange Friend of the Pilgrims (1/23/40; Sam Jaffe)
172. Thomas Jefferson (1/30/40; John Beal)
173. Jean Laffite (2/6/40; William Johnstone)
174. Abraham Lincoln: The War Years [based on Carl Sandburg's novel] (2/13/40; Raymond Massey)
175. Anne Royall (2/20/40; Ethel Barrymore)
176. Enoch Crosby, The Spy (2/27/40; Henry Hull)
177. The Stolen General (3/5/40; John Garfield)
178. The Raven Wins Texas [part two] (3/12/40; Walter Huston)
179. Jordan's Banks (3/19/40; Elliott Reid)
180. The Story of John Fitch (3/26/40; Thomas Mitchell)
181. Benedict Arnold (4/2/40; Claude Rains)
182. America Sings: The Songs of Stephen Foster [narrated by Channing Pollack] (4/9/40)
183. Daniel Boone (4/16/40; John McIntire)
184. Robert E. Lee (4/23/40; Philip Merivale)
185. Thomas Paine (4/30/40; Frank Readick)
186. Nancy Hanks (5/7/40; Agnes Moorehead)
187. Roger Williams (5/14/40; Ray Collins)
188. Jane Addams of Hull House (5/21/40; Helen Hayes)
189. Show Boat [based on the novel by Edna Ferber, with Rogers and Hammerstein music] (5/28/40)
190. John Sutter (6/4/40; Edwin Jerome)
191. Victor Herbert (6/11/40; John McIntire)
192. Susan B. Anthony (6/18/40; Cornelia Otis Skinner)
193. Walter Reed (6/25/40; John McIntire)
194. The Lost Colony (10/2/40; Ray Collins and Loretta Young)
195. Valley Forge (10/9/40; Ray Collins, Kenny Delmar, Edwin Jerome, William Johnstone, John McIntire, Jeanette Nolan, and Karl Swenson)
196. The Pathfinder of the Seas (10/16/40; Ray Collins, Kenny Delmar, Edwin Jerome, John McIntire, Jeanette Nolan, and Karl Swenson)
197. Ann Rutledge and Lincoln [written by Norman Corwin] (10/23/40; Ray Collins, Edwin Jerome, John McIntire, Agnes Moorehead, Jeanette Nolan, Karl Swenson)
198. The Red Death (10/30/40; Ray

Collins, George Coulouris, John
McIntire, Agnes Moorehead,
Jeanette Nolan, and Elliott Reid)
199. Wild Bill Hickcock: The Last of
Two Gun Justice [includes original
ballads sung by Woody Gutherie]
(11/6/40; Kenny Delmar)
200. Doctor Franklin Goes to Court
(11/13/40; Ray Collins, George
Coulouris, Kenny Delmar, Sarah
Fussell, John McIntire, Elliott
Reid, and Karl Swenson)
201. The Farmer Takes a Wife (11/20/40;
William Johnstone, Nancy Kelly,
John McIntire, Agnes Moorehead,
Jeanette Nolan, and Howard
Smith)
202. Light in the Hills (11/27/40; Ray
Collins, John McIntire, Agnes
Moorehead, Jeanette Nolan, and
Karl Swenson)
203. The Battle Hymn of the Republic
(12/4/40; Alexander Woolcott)
204. John Brown (12/11/40; John McIn-
tire)
205. The Undefended Border [written by
Stephen Vincent Benet] (12/18/40;
Raymond Massey)
206. The Green Pastures (12/25/40;
Juano Hernandez and the Hall
Johnson Choir)
207. Will Rogers [written and narrated
by Cal Tinney] (1/1/41)
208. Mightier Than the Sword (1/8/41;
William Johnstone)
209. As a Man Thinketh (1/15/41; John
McIntire, Agnes Moorehead,
Jeanette Nolan, and Claude Rains)
210. Wait for the Morning (1/22/41;
Anne Sterrett)
211. Dr. Franklin Takes It Easy (1/29/41;
Sarah Fussell and John McIntire)
212. Henry Clay of Kentucky (2/5/41;
Ray Collins)
213. Abraham Lincoln: The War Years
(2/12/41; Raymond Massey)
214. Plain Mr. President (2/19/41;
George Coulouris, John McIntire,
Jeanette Nolan and Karl Swenson)
215. Edgar Allan Poe (2/26/41; Charita
Bauer, Edwin Jerome, William
Johnstone, John McIntire, Agnes
Moorehead, Jeanette Nolan, and
Karl Swenson)

216. Voice in the Wilderness (3/5/41;
George Coulouris, Henry Hull,
Agnes Moorehead, and Karl Swenson)
217. Black Rust (3/12/41; William Johnstone)
218. I Sing a New World (3/19/41; John
McIntire)
219. Down to the Sea (3/26/41; William
Johnstone)
220. Edwin Booth (3/31/41; Paul Muni)
221. Ode to a Nightingale (4/7/41; Karl
Swenson)
222. A Passage to Georgia (4/14/41;
Alfred Shirley)
223. Henry Bergh, Founder of the
A.S.P.C.A. [written and narrated
by Albert Payson Terhune]
(4/21/41; Karl Swenson)
224. The Heart and the Fountain
(4/28/41; Madeleine Carroll)
225. The Trials and Triumphs of Horatio
Alger (5/5/41; Kenny Delmar)
226. Theodosia Burr (5/12/41; Anne Sterrett)
227. David Crockett (5/19/41; John
McIntire)
228. Johns Hopkins (5/26/41; John
McIntire and Karl Swenson)
229. Anna Ella Carroll: The Woman in
Lincoln's Cabinet (6/2/41; Agnes
Moorehead)
230. Young Andrew Jackson (6/9/41; Ray
Collins, John McIntire, Agnes
Moorehead, and Karl Swenson)
231. Annie Oakley (6/16/41; Ray Collins,
Agnes Moorehead, and Karl Swenson)
232. Joel Chandler Harris [written by
Arthur Miller] (6/23/41; Karl
Swenson)
233. Jean Pierre Blanchard (6/30/41;
Edwin Jerome)
234. The Mystery of the Spotted Death
(7/7/41; John McIntire)
235. Anne Hutchinson (7/14/41; Agnes
Moorehead)
236. O. Henry (7/21/41; Karl Swenson)
237. Clifford Holland (7/28/41; William
Johnstone)
238. Josephine Baker (8/4/41; Agnes
Moorehead)
239. Red Lanterns on St. Michaels
[based on the story by Thornwall

Jacobs] (8/11/41; William Johnstone, John McIntire, Agnes Moorehead, and Frank Readick)

240. Stephen Arnold Douglas (8/18/41; Kenny Delmar)

241. Sacajawea (8/25/41; Edwin Jerome, Ted Jewitt, John McIntire, and Jeanette Nolan)

242. Leif Ericsson (9/1/41; John McIntire, Jeanette Nolan, Everett Sloane, and Karl Swenson)

243. Geronimo (9/8/41; Kenny Delmar, Edwin Jerome, John McIntire, Jeanette Nolan, and Everette Sloane)

244. City of Illusion (9/15/41; Kenny Delmar, Agnes Moorehead, Frank Readick, and Karl Swenson)

245. Native Land [part one] (9/22/41; Burgess Meredith and Carl Sandburg)

246. Native Land [part two] (9/29/41; Judith Anderson and Burgess Meredith)

247. Bolivar, the Liberator (10/6/41; Paul Muni)

248. Waters of the Wilderness (10/13/41; Bea Benaderet, Kay Francis, Gale Gordon, Jack Mathers, Lou Merrill, Gerald Mohr, and Agnes Moorehead)

249. All That Money Can Buy [based on the Stephen Vincent Benet story "The Devil and Daniel Webster"] (10/20/41; Edward Arnold, James Craig, Jane Darwell, Walter Huston, Anne Shirley)

250. Captain Paul [adapted by John Driscoll and Arthur Miller] (10/27/41; Claude Rains)

251. One Foot in Heaven (11/3/41; Florence Eldridge, Fredric March, and Norman Vincent Peale)

252. Drums Along the Mohawk (11/10/41; Henry Fonda and Jeanette Nolan)

253. They Died with Their Boots On (11/17/41; Errol Flynn)

254. So Red the Rose (11/24/41; Joan Bennett, Jeanette Nolan, and Karl Swenson)

255. Cimarron (12/1/41; Irene Dunne and Gale Gordon)

256. Men in White (12/8/41; Franchot Tone and Betty Garde)

257. The Great Man Votes (12/15/41; Ray Collins and Orson Welles)

258. The Green Pastures (12/22/41; Juano Hernandez and the Hall Johnson Choir)

259. The Gorgeous Hussey (12/29/41; Paulette Goddard)

260. Valley Forge (1/5/42; Lionel Barrymore)

261. The Gentleman from Paris (1/12/42; Charles Boyer and Gayne Whitman)

262. An American Is Born [written and directed by Arch Oboler] (1/19/42; Bette Davis)

263. Tomorrow and Tomorrow (1/26/42; Madeleine Carroll)

264. Captains of the Clouds (2/2/42; Reginald Denny, Alan Hale, James Cagney, and Dennis Morgan)

265. Abraham Lincoln: The War Years (2/9/42; Raymond Massey)

266. The Dark Angel (2/16/42; William Johnstone, Merle Oberon, and Karl Swenson)

267. Arrowsmith (2/23/42; Lou Merrill, Tyrone Power, and Lurene Tuttle)

268. Accent on Youth (3/2/42; Ellen Drew, Arlene Francis and Walter Pidgeon)

269. Wait for the Morning (3/9/42; Madeline Carroll)

270. Dear Brutus (3/16/42; Charita Bauer and Fredric March)

271. Angels on Horseback (3/23/42; Kenny Delmar and Myrna Loy)

272. The Silent Heart (3/30/42; Ingrid Bergman)

273. Yellow Jack (4/6/42; Tyrone Power)

274. A Continental Uniform (4/13/42; Gale Gordon and Basil Rathbone)

275. In This Crisis (4/20/42; Ray Collins, Gale Gordon, and Claude Rains)

276. This Side of Hades (4/27/42; Loretta Young)

277. The Printer was a Lady (5/4/42; Lynn Fontaine and John McIntire)

278. A Tooth for Paul Revere [written by Stephen Vincent Benet] (5/11/42; Raymond Massey)

279. Remember the Day (5/18/42; Claudette Colbert, Tommy Cook, and Elliott Lewis)

280. Young Tom Jefferson (5/25/42; Ray Collins and Tyrone Power)
281. Clara Barton (6/1/42; Madeleine Carroll)
282. The Colossus of Panama (6/8/42; Walter Huston)
283. The Lady and the Flag (6/15/42; Paulette Goddard)
284. The Battle of the Ovens [written by Arthur Miller] (6/22/42; Jean Hersholt)
285. Hymn From the Night (6/29/42; Helen Hayes)
286. The Gentleman from the Islands (7/6/42; Alfred Lunt)
287. Man of Iron (7/13/42; Dean Jagger)
288. The Wild Young Man (7/20/42; Dean Jagger)
289. Man of Design (7/27/42; Karl Swenson)
290. This Our Exile [written by Henry Wadsworth Longfellow] (8/3/42; Madeleine Carroll)
291. I, Mary Washington (8/10/42; Madeleine Carroll)
292. Theodore Roosevelt, Man of Action (8/17/42; Edward Arnold)
293. The Giant of the Meadow (8/24/42; Ralph Bellamy)
294. Prophet Without Honor (8/31/42; Charles Laughton)
295. Soldier of a Free Press (9/7/42; Claude Rains)
296. Untitled [Joseph C. Crew Speech on A-Navy E Award] (9/14/42)
297. Eagle to Britain (9/21/42; Kenny Delmar)
298. Juarez [aka Thunder from the Mountains] [written by Arthur Miller] (9/28/42; Orson Welles)
299. I Was Married on Bataan [written by Arthur Miller] (10/5/42; Madeleine Carroll)
300. Admiral of the Ocean Sea (10/12/42; Karl Swenson and Orson Welles)
301. That They Might Live (10/19/42; Madeleine Carroll)
302. In the Best Tradition (10/26/42; Orson Welles)
303. Toward a Farther Star (11/2/42; Madeleine Carroll and Frank Readick)
304. Torpedo Lane (11/9/42; Dean Jagger, Edwin Jerome, and Ann Thomas)
305. Alaska Under Arms (11/16/42; Arlene Francis)
306. Feast from the Harvest [narrated by Louis Bromfield] (11/23/42)
307. Sister Kenny (11/30/42; Madeleine Carroll)
308. The Road to Victory (12/7/42; Carl Sandburg and the Delta Rhythm Boys)
309. The Man Who Wouldn't Be President (12/14/42; Edward Arnold, William Farnum, Joseph Kearns, and Agnes Moorehead)
310. A Child Is Born [written by Stephen Vincent Benet] (12/21/42; Lynn Fontaine and Alfred Lunt)
311. The Eagle's Nest [adapted by Arthur Miller] (12/28/42; Paul Muni)
312. Between them Both (1/4/43; Nancy Kelly)
313. Diary on a Pig Boat (1/11/43; Edwin Jerome)
314. Soldiers of the Tide (1/18/43; Dennis Morgan)
315. The Flying Tigers (1/25/43; Ralph Bellamy)
316. To the Shores of Tripoli (2/1/43; Joseph Cotten)
317. The Perfect Tribute (2/8/43; Edwin Jerome)
318. War Comes to Dr. Morgan (2/15/43; Arlene Francis and Elliott Nugent)
319. The Plot to Kidnap Washington (2/22/43; Edmund Gwenn and Adelaide Klein)
320. Diary of a Saboteur (3/1/43; Mildred Natwick and Joseph Schildkraut)
321. The Eighteenth Captain (3/8/43; Ralph Bellamy)
322. A Case for the F.B.I. (3/15/43; Edward G. Robinson)
323. Lifetide (3/22/43; Alfred Lunt)
324. The Cook on the P-T Boat Writes Home (3/29/43; William Bendix)
325. Submarine Astern (4/5/43; Ray Milland)
326. The Lengthening Shadow (4/12/43; Fredric March)
327. Listen for the Sound of Wings [written by Arthur Miller] (4/19/43; Paul Lukas)

328. Soldiers in High Boots (4/26/43; Jon Hall and Reed Hadley)
329. Soldiers in Greasepoint (5/3/43; Kay Francis, Mitzi Mayfair, and Martha Raye)
330. Fat Girl (5/10/43; Edward Arnold and Hans Conried)
331. Nurses Under Sealed Orders (5/17/43; Geraldine Fitzgerald)
332. Pharmacist's Mate, First Class (5/24/43; Alfred Drake and Michael O'Shea)
333. Mr. Lincoln's Wife (5/31/43; Helen Hayes)
334. The Enemy Is Listening (6/7/43; Everett Sloane)
335. Make Way for the Lady (6/14/43; Madeleine Carroll)
336. The Unsinkable Marblehead (6/21/43; Dean Jagger)
337. Sky Nursemaid (6/28/43; Maureen O'Sullivan and Frank Readick)
338. Listen to the People [written by Stephen Vincent Benet] (7/5/43; Ethel Barrymore)
339. Soldier of the Cloth (7/12/43; Ralph Bellamy)
340. The Schoolhouse at the Front (7/19/43; George Tobias)
341. Diamonds at War (7/26/43; Charles Coburn)
342. Nine Men Against the Arctic (8/2/43; Dean Jagger)
343. Short Cut to Tokyo (8/9/43; Ralph Bellamy)
344. The Major and the Mules (8/16/43; Warren William)
345. The Weapon that Saves Lives (8/23/43; Edmund Lowe)
346. Dear Funny Face (8/30/43; Wendy Barrie and Alfred Drake)
347. Double Play (9/6/43; Brian Donlevy and Kent Smith)
348. Iron Camels (9/13/43; Pat O'Brien and Wally Maher)
349. The Vengeance of Torpedo Eight (9/20/43; Randolph Scott)
350. The Hatred Hero of 1776 (9/27/43; Basil Rathbone and Ruth Warrick)
351. Continue Unloading (10/4/43; John Garfield and Wally Maher)
352. Bob Hope Reports (10/11/43; Bob Hope stars is a recreation of his first tour of the front in June, 1943.)

353. The General Wore Calico (10/18/43; Jane Darwell and Wally Maher)
354. Take Her Down! (10/25/43; Robert Young)
355. Burma Surgeon (11/1/43; George Brent)
356. Joe Dyer Ends a War (11/8/43; Beulah Bondi and James Craig)
357. Twelve Desperate Miles (11/15/43; Edward Arnold)
358. Soldiers of the Soil [based on the film by the same name] (11/22/43; Russell Hayden and Carroll Nye)
359. The Wise Mad General (11/29/43; Warner Baxter and Lloyd Nolan)
360. Navy Doctor (12/6/43; Brian Donlevy and Will Geer)
361. Check Your Heart at Home [based on a novel by Jane Goodell] (12/13/43; Shirley Booth and Burl Ives)
362. A Child Is Born [previously performed on 12/21/42] (12/20/43; Helen Hayes and Philip Merivale)
363. U-Boat Prisoner (12/27/43; Richard Arlen)
364. Bullseye for Sammy (1/3/44; Alfred Drake and Jackie Kelk)
365. Here Is Your War [true story of Ernie Pyle, based on his book] (1/10/44; James Gleason)
366. Terence O'Toole, M.P. (1/17/44; George Murphy)
367. The Doctor Shoots a Cannon (1/24/44; Preston Foster, Otto Kruger, and Gene Lockhart)
368. The Sailor Takes a Wife (1/31/44; Dick Powell and Ona Munson)
369. Prologue to Glory (2/7/44; Raymond Massey)
370. G.I. Valentine (2/14/44; Frances Langford, June Lockhart, and Tony Romano)
371. The Purple Heart Comes to Free Meadows (2/21/44; Wendy Barrie, Parker Fennelly, Dick Foran, and Guy Kibbee)
372. Junior Angel (2/28/44; Jane Darwell and Virginia Weidler)
373. Odyssey to Freedom (3/6/44; Brian Donlevy)
374. Song From Spokane [life story of opera star Patrice Munsel]

(3/13/44; Edwin Jerome, Jessie Royce Landis, and Patrice Munsel)
375. G.I. Circuit (3/20/44; Joe E. Brown and Ann Sothern)
376. So Sorry–No Mercy (3/27/44; Pat O'Brien)
377. Ambulance Driver, Middle East (4/3/44; Alan Ladd)
378. The First Commando (4/10/44; Alfred Drake and Everett Sloane)
379. A Mask for Jefferson (4/17/44; Walter Huston)
380. The Story of Penicillin (4/24/44; George Coulouris)
381. The Adventures of Mark Twain (5/1/44; Fredric March)
382. Autobiography of an Angel (5/8/44; Helen Hayes)
383. The Blessings of Liberty (5/15/44; John Garfield)
384. A Ship to Remember (5/22/44; Preston Foster, John Hodiak, and Edward Marr)
385. Sing a War Song (5/29/44; Kay Armen and Deems Taylor)
386. Treason (6/5/44; Joseph Cotten and Richard Whorf)
387. My Fighting Congregation (6/12/44;) Brian Donlevy and Wally Maher)
388. Tokyo Spearhead (6/19/44; Richard Conte and Stuart Erwin)
389. What Price Freedom? (6/26/44; Herbert Marshall)
390. My Friend McNair (7/3/44; Jose Ferrer, Everett Sloane, and Barbara Weeks)
391. From Emporia, Kansas (7/10/44; Parker Fennelly and Frank Readick)
392. Boomerang (7/17/44; Frank Lovejoy and Everett Sloane)
393. Lovely Lady (7/24/44; Ted de Corsia and Edwin Jerome)
394. The Conquest of Quinine (7/31/44; House Jameson)
395. A Walk in the Sun (8/7/44; Larry Haines, Frank Lovejoy, and Everett Sloane)
396. The Gals They Left Behind (8/14/44; Shirley Booth, Helen Claire, Parker Fennelly, and Patsy O'Shea)
397. The Story of Canine Joe [written by Arthur Miller] (8/21/44; Everett Sloane)
398. Yankee from Olympus (8/28/44; Karl Swenson)
399. What Makes a Hero? (9/4/44; Staats Cotsworth and Richard Widmark)
400. The Doctor Gets the Answer (9/11/44; Donald Buka and Edwin Jerome)
401. Hymn from the Night (9/18/44; Rosalind Russell)
402. Lifetide (9/25/44; Walter Pidgeon)
403. Voice on the Stairs (10/2/44; Edward G. Robinson)
404. Valley Forge (10/9/44; Walter Huston)
405. Report From the Pacific (10/16/44; Jerry Colonna, Bob Hope, and Frances Langford)
406. The Girl Lincoln Loved [written by Norman Corwin] (10/23/44; Joan Fontaine and John McIntire)
407. Take Her Down (10/30/44; Clark Gable)
408. Jane Adams of Hull House (11/6/44; Loretta Young)
409. The Laziest Man in the World (11/13/44; Charles Laughton)
410. The Admiral (11/20/44; Robert Montgomery)
411. Witness for the People (11/27/44; Fay Bainter and Ray Collins)
412. Doughnut Girl (12/4/44; Lana Turner)
413. Conquest of Pain (12/11/44; Brian Donlevy)
414. Doctor in Crinoline (12/18/44; Loretta Young)
415. America for Christmas (12/25/44; Walter Huston)
416. Westward the Women (1/1/45; Ann Harding)
417. Name, Rank, Serial Number (1/8/45; John Beal, William Holden, and Kent Smith)
418. Immortal Wife (1/15/45; Ida Lupino and Frank Graham)
419. Penny Fancy (1/22/45; Claire Trevor)
420. A Race for Lennie (1/29/45; Vincent Price and Richard Whorf)
421. The Road to Berlin (2/5/45; Bing Crosby and Jeannie Darrell)

422. The Man Who Taught Lincoln
(2/12/45; Walter Huston and John
McIntire)
423. Washington and the Traitor
(2/19/45; Herbert Marshall)
424. Flight Nurse (2/26/45; Marsha
Hunt and Marjorie Reynolds)
425. Bernadine, I Love You [written by
Arthur Miller] (3/5/45; William
Bendix)
426. Seven Iron Men (3/12/45; Walter
Brennan and Richard Whorf)
427. Sign Here, Please (3/19/45; Bob
Bailey and Burgess Meredith)
428. Grandpa and the Statue (3/26/45;
Charles Laughton and Arthur
Shields)
429. My Wayward Parents (4/2/45; Anne
Baxter and Brian Donlevy)
430. Robinson Crusoe, USN (4/9/45;
Chester Morris)
431. Doctora in Mexico (4/16/45;
Frances X. Bushman and Irene
Dunne)
432. Weapon 4-H (4/23/45; Skip
Homeier and Virginia Weidler)
433. The Philippines Never Surrendered
[written by Arthur Miller]
(4/30/45; Edward G. Robinson)
434. Artist to the Wounded (5/7/45;
Geraldine Fitzgerald)
435. Weather Is a Weapon (5/14/45;
Dana Andrews)
436. How to Build Paradise (5/21/45;
Robert Young)
437. Recon Pilot [based on an army
training film of the same name]
(5/28/45; William Holden)
438. The Lieutenants Come Home
(6/4/45; Bob Bailey and Marjorie
Reynolds)
439. The Law West of the Pecos
(6/11/45; Walter Brennan and Barton Yarborough)
440. Party Line (6/18/45; Verna Felton,
Agnes Moorehead, and Jane Morgan)
441. DDT (6/25/45; Richard Whorf)
442. Assignment For the Prof. (8/27/45;
Burgess Meredith)
443. Cargo Over Burma (9/3/45; Richard
Conte and Michael O'Shea)
444. Sawdust Underground (9/10/45;
Bob Bailey and John Hodiak)

445. Nellie Was a Lady (9/17/45; Agnes
Moorehead)
446. The Battle to Stay Alive (9/24/45;
Robert Young)
447. 200,000 Fliers (10/1/45; Pat O'Brien)
448. The Spy on the Kilocycles (10/8/45;
Henry Fonda)
449. Children, This Is Your Father
(10/15/45; Tommy Bernard, Gale
Gordon, and Loretta Young)
450. Johnny Comes Home (10/22/45;
Marsha Hunt, Howard McNear,
and Robert Walker)
451. My Son John (10/29/45; Humphrey
Bogart, Jerry Hausner, and Alan
Reed)
452. The Builders of the Bridge (11/5/45;
Claire Trevor)
453. A Sailor Who Had to Have a Horse
(11/12/45; Mary Jane Croft and
Jimmy Stewart)
454. I Count the Days (11/19/45; Signe
Hasso)
455. Traveler to Arkansas (11/26/45;
Lloyd Nolan)
456. Direction Home (12/3/45; Mary
Jane Croft, Howard Duff, and
Thomas Mitchell)
457. Big Boy Blue (12/10/45; Henry
Fonda)
458. The Magnificent Meddler (12/17/45;
George Sanders)
459. Names on the Land (12/24/45;
Frank Morgan)
460. Ten in Texas (12/31/45; Walter
Brennan)
461. Build Me Straight (1/7/46; Joseph
Cotten and Claire Trevor)
462. Venture in Silk Hat (1/14/46;
Howard Duff and Franchot Tone)
463. The Camels Are Coming (1/21/46;
Francis X. Bushman, Laraine Day,
and Joel McCrea)
464. Commencement in Khaki (1/28/46;
Dana Andrews, Nancy Kelly, and
Eddie Marr)
465. Children of Ol' Man River (2/4/46;
Janet Blair, Francis X. Bushman,
and John Hodiak)
466. Remembered Day (2/11/46; Georgia
Backus and Walter Pidgeon)
467. Young Major Washington (2/18/46;
Gregory Peck, George Sorel, and
Stan Waxman)

468. Star in the West (2/25/46; William Johnstone and Ida Lupino)
469. The Case of the Tremendous Trifle (3/4/46; Betty Arnold, Brian Donlevy, and Horace Murphy)
470. The Doctor With Hope in his Hands (3/11/46; Edward G. Robinson and Ian Wolfe)
471. Alaskan Bush Pilot (3/18/46; Frances X. Bushman, Dick Foran, and Gale Page)
472. The General's Wife (3/25/46; William Johnstone and Agnes Moorehead)
473. When Cupid Was a Pup (4/1/46; Jerry Hausner, Sammie Hill, Elliott Lewis, and Cornel Wilde)
474. Circus Day (4/8/46; Ted Donaldson, Anne Revere, and Dick Ryan)
475. The Great McGraw (4/15/46; William Johnstone and Pat O'Brien)
476. Meet Artie Greengroin (4/22/46; William Bendix, Francis X. Bushman, and Paula Winslowe)
477. Thirst Without End (4/29/46; James Cagney)
478. The Unsinkable Mrs. Brown (5/6/46; Helen Hayes and Cameron Prud'Homme)
479. Storm (5/13/46; John Beal and Dane Clark)
480. The Petticoat Jury (5/20/46; Jean Arthur, Ted Osborne, and Cameron Prud'Homme)
481. Spin a Silver Dollar (5/27/46; Helen Hayes)
482. I Guess It's Here to Stay (6/3/46; Everett Sloane and Gladys Thornton)
483. My Freshman Husband (6/10/46; Geraldine Fitzgerald)
484. Algerian Adventure (6/17/46; George Murphy)
485. Cruise of the Cashalot (6/24/46; Cameron Andrews, Aldelaide Klein, and Everett Sloane)
486. Passport to Freedom (8/26/46; Paul Lukas)
487. With Cradle and Clock (9/2/46; Francis X. Bushman, Jeff Chandler, and Herbert Marshall)
488. Danger : Women at Work (9/9/46; Fay Bainter, Howard Duff, and June Foray)

489. General Benjamin Franklin (9/16/46; Charles Laughton, Kathleen Lockhart, and George Zucco)
490. The Old Fall River Line (9/23/46; Brian Donlevy and Theodore Von Eltz)
491. One Wagon Westward (9/30/46; Skip Homeier)
492. That They May Live (10/7/46; Robert Young)
493. The Hickory Tree (10/14/46; Hans Conried, Agnes Moorehead, and Walter Tetley)
494. Mr. Conyngham Sweeps the Seas (10/21/46; Douglas Fairbanks, Jr. and George Zucco)
495. Flying Tigers Fly Again (10/28/46; George Murphy)
496. An Honorable Titan (11/4/46; Frances Chaney and Robert Young)
497. Country Lawyer (11/11/46; Edward Arnold and Eddie Firestone, Jr.)
498. The Pinkerton Man (11/18/46; Lee Bowman, William Johnstone, and Wally Maher)
499. Parade (11/25/46; Jean Hersholt)
500. Mother of Freedom (12/2/46; Francis X. Bushman, William Conrad, and Ann Harding)
501. Wings to Glory (12/9/46; John Hodiak)
502. That Powell Girl (12/16/46; Peggy Ann Garner)
503. The DuPont Chorus [Christmas music, no drama] (12/23/46)
504. The Rain Fakers (12/30/46; Burgess Meredith)
505. The Woman on Lime Rock (1/6/47; Shirley Booth)
506. The Prairie Burner (1/13/47; Louise Allbritton and Ralph Bellamy)
507. Builder of the Soo (1/20/47; William Holden and Marsha Hunt)
508. A Chance for Jimmy (1/27/47; Basil Rathbone)
509. The Magnificent Failure (2/3/47; Burgess Meredith)
510. The Voice of the Wizard (2/10/47; Dane Clark, Donna Reed, and Chester Stratton)
511. Man Against the Mountain (2/17/47; Chester Morris)

512. Abigail Opens the White House (2/24/47; Ida Lupino and John McIntire)
513. Mr. Pullman's Palace Car (3/3/47; Robert Young)
514. The Stirring Blood (3/10/47; Bob Bailey, Lee Bowman, and Una Merkel)
515. The Man With Green Fingers (3/17/47; Lionel Barrymore)
516. The Man Who Stepped Aside (3/24/47; John McIntire and Thomas Mitchell)
517. Kansas Marshall (3/31/47; Henry Fonda)
518. That Skipper From Stonington (4/7/47; Dana Andrews and Anita Louise)
519. The Peanut Vendor (4/14/47; Don Ameche)
520. The Doctor and the President (4/21/47; Douglas Fairbanks, Jr., Maureen O'Sullivan, and George Zucco)
521. Frontier Widow (4/28/47; Anne Baxter)
522. The School for Men (5/5/47; Bob Bailey and Gregory Peck)
523. Page One (5/12/47; John Hodiak and Jack Kruschen)
524. Witness by Moonlight (5/19/47; Joseph Cotten)
525. Under the Big Top (5/26/47; Robert Young)
526. The Stirring Blood (6/2/47; Lee Bowman and Una Merkel)
527. Lady of Distinction (6/9/47; Ida Lupino and Jeanette Nolan)
528. Woman Alone (6/16/47; Virginia Bruce)
529. The Iron Horse (8/18/47; Walter Brennan and Robert Young)
530. The Red Stockings (8/25/47; John Hodiak, Gerald Mohr, and Jane Morgan)
531. Mission to Cuba (9/1/47; Lee Bowman, Herb Butterfield, and Nestor Paiva)
532. Kitchen Scientist (9/8/47; Bob Bailey, Ida Lupino, Alan Reed, and Dorothy Scott)
533. Return to Glory (9/15/47; Lionel Barrymore and Jane Morgan)
534. The Girl Who Ran for President (9/22/47; Virginia Bruce and Alan Reed)
535. Big Boy (9/29/47; Brian Donlevy, Howard McNear, and Alan Reed)
536. Of Such Is the Kingdom (10/6/47; Henry Fonda)
537. The Forge (10/13/47; Howard McNear, Ronald Reagan, and Alan Reed)
538. The Oath (10/20/47; June Duprez and William Powell)
539. The Admiral Who Had No Name (10/27/47; House Jameson and Robert Montgomery)
540. The Flame (11/3/47; Helen Hayes)
541. The Unnatural Death (11/10/47; Lee Bowman)
542. Hurry Up 'Yost (11/17/47; Thomas Mitchell and Bill Stern)
543. Us Pilgrims (11/24/47; Mercedes McCambridge and George Tobias)
544. Towards the Horizon (12/1/47; Van Heflin)
545. Diamond In the Sky (12/8/47; Gene Lockhart, June Lockhart, and Kathleen Lockhart)
546. The Day they Gave Babies Away (12/15/47; Claude Jarman, Jr.)
547. The DuPont Chorus [Christmas music, no drama] (12/22/47)
548. Powhatan's Daughter (12/29/47; Joan Caulfield, Lamont Johnson, and Ian Martin)
549. The Justice and the Lady (1/5/48; Dorothy Gish and Basil Rathbone)
550. The Conscience of Black Dan'l (1/12/48; Thomas Mitchell)
551. Sheriff Teddy (1/19/48; Joel McCrea)
552. The Perfect Union (1/26/48; Robert Taylor)
553. Good Morning, Miss Tyckman (2/2/48; Helen Hayes and House Jameson)
554. Mr. Lincoln Goes to the Play (2/9/48; Joe di Santis, Alice Reinheart, and Robert Young)
555. The Alerting of Mr. Pomerantz (2/16/48; Bob Dryden and Paul Muni)
556. This Way to Tomorrow (2/23/48; Paul Lukas and William Redfield)
557. The Black Duster (3/1/48; Cameron Prud'Homme, Rosemary Rice, and Cornel Wilde)

558. No Greater Love (3/8/48; Joseph Bell, Edwin Jerome, Dorothy McGuire, and Lyle Sudrow)

559. Paging Miss Ellen (3/15/48; Geraldine Fitzgerald)

560. The President and the Doctor (3/22/48; Thomas Mitchell and Basil Rathbone)

561. Roses in the Rain (3/29/48; Ralph Bellamy and Joan Caulfield)

562. Woman of Steel (4/5/48; Helen Hayes, Cameron Prud'Homme, and Everett Sloane)

563. The Man Who Took the Freedom Train (4/12/48; Eddie Albert and Shirley Booth)

564. Winner Takes Life (4/19/48; Jackie Cooper, Paul Lukas, and Ann Rutherford)

565. Lee of Virginia (4/26/48)

566. Thunder on the Hudson (5/3/48; Julie Hayden and Robert Mitchum)

567. Village Doctor (5/10/48; Melvyn Douglas)

568. Queen of Heartbreak Trail (5/17/48; Irene Dunne)

569. The Enlightened Professor (5/24/48; Gale Gordon and Franchot Tone)

570. Who Walk Alone (5/31/48; Louis Calhern and MacDonald Carey)

571. The Last Frontier (6/7/48; Bob Dryden, Ray Milland, and Cameron Prud'Homme)

572. Chautauqua Fable (6/14/48; William Powell, Rosemary Rice, and Agnes Young)

573. Skylark Song (6/21/48; Lucille Ball)

574. The Common Glory (6/28/48; Basil Rathbone)

575. The Exiled Heart (7/5/48; Rosemary De Camp, Elliott Reid, and Alice Reinheart)

576. Break the News (7/12/48; Parker Fennelly and John Lund)

577. Gettysburg (9/13/48; Joan Lorring and Dick Powell)

578. The Proud Way (9/20/48; Laraine Day and House Jameson)

579. Incident at Niagra (9/27/48; Anita Louise and Robert Montgomery)

580. Action at Santiago (10/4/48; John Dall and Robert Trout)

581. Home to the Heritage (10/11/48; Fay Bainter and Walter Pidgeon)

582. The Darkest Hour (10/18/48; Burt Lancaster)

583. Bryant's Station (10/25/48; Irene Dunne and Chuck Webster)

584. The Blue Cockade (11/1/48; Linda Darnell and John Hodiak)

585. Garden Key (11/8/48; Paul Muni)

586. The Burning Bush (11/15/48; Juano Hernandez)

587. U.S. Pilgrims (11/22/48; George Tobias)

588. The Betrayal (11/29/48; Alan Hewitt and Dorothy McGuire)

589. Oliver Wendell Holmes MacLanahan (12/6/48; Pat O'Brien)

590. Family Circle [Cornelia Otis Skinner is author and performer] (12/13/48; Douglas Fairbanks, Jr. and Patricia Ryan)

591. The DuPont Chorus [Christmas songs, no drama] (12/20/48)

592. The Indigo Girl (12/27/48; Staats Cotsworth and Gene Tierney)

593. The Gift of Johnny Appleseed (1/3/49; John Lund)

594. Experiment at Monticello (1/10/49; Rex Harrison)

595. Secret Operation (1/17/49; Les Damon and John Payne)

596. The Queen's Handmaid (1/24/49; Madeleine Carroll)

597. One Last Romance (1/31/49; Walter Hampden and Una O'Connor)

598. The Store That Winked Out (2/7/49; Zachary Scott and Lyle Sudrow)

599. A Valentine for Sophia (2/14/49; Glenn Ford and Patricia Ryan)

600. The Unheroic Hero (2/21/49; Douglas Fairbanks, Jr. and Lamont Johnson)

601. Pink Lace (2/28/49; Janet Blair)

602. Journey Among the Lost (3/7/49; Jean Arthur)

603. My Hunt After the Captain (3/14/49; Conrad Nagel)

604. Letter From Europe (3/21/49; Charles Boyer and House Jameson)

605. Boy Wanted (3/28/49; Virginia Bruce)

606. Citizen Mama (4/4/49; Irene Dunne)

607. Dinner at Belmont (4/11/49; Janet Blair, Les Damon, and Marjorie Maude)

608. Honest John Gaminski and the Thirteen Uncle Sams (4/18/49; Oscar Homolka)

609. Lady on a Mission (4/25/49; Dorothy McGuire)

610. When We're Green We Grow (5/2/49; Helen Claire and Jane Darwell)

611. Heard 'Round the World (5/9/49; Donald Crisp and Elliott Reid)

612. The House Near Little Dock Street (5/16/49; Ginger Rogers)

613. Woman With A Sword (5/23/49; Madeleine Carroll, Ed Jerome, and Charles Webster)

614. Reluctant Rebel (5/30/49; Robert Cummings and Agnes Young)

615. The Return of the Lodger (6/6/49; Ian Martin, Edgar Stehli, and Richard Widmark)

616. Footlights on the Frontier (6/13/49; Ivan Cury and Walter Hampden)

617. Ridin' Shotgun (6/20/49; Ralph Bellamy and Jeanette Nolan)

618. The Homecoming of Sou Chan (6/27/49; Kenny Delmar)

619. Wire to the West (8/30/49; Parker Fennelly, Raymond Massey, and Cameron Prud'Homme)

620. Lay that Musket Down (9/6/49; Bob Dryden and Paul Henried)

621. Joe Palmer's Beard (9/13/49; Brian Donlevy, Donald Rose, and Agnes Young)

622. Troublesome Jane (9/20/49; Kenny Delmar, Ruth Hussey, John Nesbitt)

623. The Immortal Blacksmith [John Nesbitt is the writer and host] (9/27/49; Parker Fennelly, Jean Gillespie, and John Griggs)

624. The Lady Becomes a Governor (10/4/49; Staats Cotsworth and Dorothy McGuire)

625. This Little Plot of Ground (10/11/49; Cornel Wilde)

626. Remember Anna Zenger (10/18/49; Rosalind Russell)

627. Life Line (10/25/49; Dane Clark and Les Damon)

628. Strike a Blow for Liberty (11/1/49; Tyrone Power)

629. Signal to the World (11/8/49; Cary Grant)

630. The Greatest Risk (11/15/49; Charlotte Manson and Ray Milland)

631. Us Pilgrims (11/22/49; Peter Donald, Mercedes McCambridge, Dan Ocko, and George Tobias)

632. Spindletop (11/29/49; Henry Fonda, Larry Haines, Malcolm Keen, and Gertrude Warner)

633. The Wall of Silence (12/6/49; Gene Tierney)

634. South of Cape Horn (12/13/49; Parker Fennelly, Ian Martin, and Mickey Rooney)

635. The DuPont Chorus [Christmas music, no drama] (12/20/49)

636. A Cup of Coffee with Lew (12/27/49; Gene Lockhart and Lowell Thomas)

637. The Incomparable Doctor (1/3/50; Ivan Cury, Charles Laughton, Elliott Reid, and Melville Ruick)

638. Honor Bound (1/10/50; Joan Caulfield and John Lund)

639. The Golden Needle (1/17/50; Dorothy McGuire)

640. The Interchangeable Mr. Whitney (1/24/50; Robert Taylor)

641. Ordeal by Fire (1/31/50; Edward Arnold)

642. The Thinking Heart [prose by Carl Sandburg and Walt Whitman] (2/7/50; Raymond Massey and Beatrice Pearson)

643. Enterprise U.S.A. (2/14/50; Lee Bowman and James Monks)

644. Reveille (2/21/50; Walter Hampden and Arnold Moss)

645. Young Man in a Hurry (2/28/50; Virginia Payne and Cornel Wilde)

646. Mr. Peale and the Dinosaur (3/7/50; Parker Fennelly, Agnes Moorehead, and Claude Rains)

647. Crazy Judah (3/14/50; Douglas Fairbanks, Jr.)

648. I, Mary Peabody (3/21/50; Susan Douglas, Anne Seymour, Elizabeth Taylor, Richard Waring)

649. General Forrest Rides Again (3/28/50; John Gibson and Richard Widmark)

650. Decision in the Valley (4/4/50; Robert Cummings)

651. Citizen Straus (4/11/50; Parker Fennelly and Melvyn Douglas)
652. Lady of Johnstown (4/18/50; Virginia Bruce and John Larkin)
653. The Firefly Lamp (4/25/50; William Holden and Brenda Marshall)
654. I Can and I Will (5/2/50; Lee Bowman)
655. Never Marry a Stranger (5/9/50; Nelson Case and Martha Scott)
656. The Sword of Kentucky (5/16/50; Wanda Hendrix, Lon McAllister, and Robert Young)
657. A Portrait of the Author (5/23/50; Basil Rathbone)
658. Miss Vinnie and Mr. Lincoln (5/30/50; Bill Adams, Barbara Bel Geddes, and Berry Kroeger)
659. The Conqueror (6/6/50; Denise Alexander, Carl Eastman, William Eythe, Parker Fennelly and Dan Ocko)
660. The Redemption of Lottie Moon (6/13/50; Lucille Ball)
661. Experiment in Humanity (6/20/50; Edward Arnold)
662. I Speak for Democracy (6/27/50; Susan Douglas)
663. John Yankee (8/29/50; Kathleen Cordell and Basil Rathbone)
664. The Iron Mountain (9/5/50; Dane Clark and Staats Cotsworth)
665. The Man With the Cargo of Water (9/12/50; Richard Widmark)
666. Golden Harvest (9/19/50; Ed Begley and Lon McAllister)
667. Yankee Doodle Debby (9/26/50; Joan Caulfield
668. Six Men of Wood (10/3/50; Bob Hastings, Robin Morgan, Gertrude Warner, and Robert Young)
669. Emma (10/10/50; Ozzie Davis and Ginger Rogers)
670. Wizards of Whiting (10/17/50; Ralph Bellamy and Lee Bowman)
671. Juliet in Pigtails (10/24/50; Margaret O'Brien)
672. Whither Thou Goest (10/31/50; Wesley Addy and Loretta Young)
673. Improvement Noted (11/7/50; Cornel Wilde)
674. Sir Galahad in Manhattan (11/14/50; Ray Milland)
675. The Stepping Stones (11/21/50; Susan Douglas, Douglas Fairbanks, Jr., and Walter Hampden)
676. The Rose and the Thorns (11/28/50; Dorothy McGuire)
677. The Grand Design (12/5/50; Charles Boyer and Staats Cotsworth)
678. Ulysses in Love (12/12/50; Denise Alexander, Patsy Campbell, and Ronald Reagan)
679. The DuPont Chorus [Christmas music, no drama] (12/19/50)
680. A Mockingbird Sang at Chickamauga (12/26/50; Lee Bowman)
681. An American from France [later staged on 5/6/52] (1/2/51; Joseph Cotten and Walter Hampden)
682. Spindletop (1/9/51; Robert Cummings, Dan Ocko, Chester Stratton, and Teresa Wright)
683. There Stands Jackson (1/16/51; Charles Dingle and John Hodiak)
684. The Metal of the Moon (1/23/51; Bill Adams, Montgomery Clift, and Dan Ocko)
685. Keepsakes [narrated by Wesley Addy] (1/30/51; Margaret Draper, and Raymond Massey)
686. Greeley of the Tribune (2/6/51; Brian Donlevy)
687. Fibre 66 (2/13/51; Wesley Addy, Lee Bowman, and Judy Parrish)
688. Mary of Murray Hill (2/20/51; Joan Fontaine)
689. The Case of Harold Thomas (2/27/51; Dane Clark and George Petrie)
690. Whale Off (3/6/51; Louis Calhern)
691. Uncle Eury's Dollar (3/13/51; Robert Cummings and Juano Hernandez)
692. Mr. Statler's Story (3/20/51; Charles Dingle and John Lund)
693. The King of Nantucket (3/27/51; Donald Crisp and Robert Preston)
694. The Reluctant Pioneer (4/3/51; Bill Adams, June Havoc, Jeffrey Lynn, and Roland Winters)
695. Once More the Thunderer (4/10/51; Laraine Day and Franchot Tone)
696. Man of Action (4/17/51; Dane Clark)
697. No Doll for Abigail (4/24/51; Joan Bennett)

698. The Raft (5/1/51; Hazel Logan and Robert Montgomery)
699. The Duel with Aunt Rebecca (5/8/51; Richard Carlson, Charles Dingle, and Raymond Massey)
700. Militant Angel (5/15/51; Margaret Sullavan and Barbara Weeks)
701. Top Secret (5/22/51; Robert Young)
702. The Torchbearer (5/29/51; Richard Greene and Basil Rathbone)
703. Path to the Stars (6/5/51; Claire Niesen and Barry Sullivan)
704. The Silent Service (6/12/51; Jack Grimes and Dick Powell)
705. Chinese Daughter (6/19/51; Diana Lynn and Anne Seymour)
706. They Shall Have Music (6/26/51; Paul Lukas and Jan Miner)
707. Sound the Great Bell (7/3/51; Lee Bowman and Susan Douglas)
708. Towards a New World (9/4/51; Alice Frost, Mercer McLeod, and Basil Rathbone)
709. No One Is Alone (9/11/51; Laraine Day, Les Damon, Thomas Mitchell, and Dan Ocko)
710. Girl on a Mission (9/18/51; Joan Caulfield)
711. Listen My Children (9/25/51; Kenny Delmar and Robert Ryan)
712. Sequel at Seventy (10/2/51; Parker Fennelly, Walter Hampden, George Petrie, and Guy Repp)
713. The Fields Are Green (10/9/51; Bob Hastings, Audie Murphy, and Rosemary Rice)
714. The Ship the Nazis Had to Get (10/16/51; Ray Milland)
715. Loyal Lady (10/23/51; Diana Lynn)
716. Navy Blue (10/30/51; Robert Cummings, Kenny Delmar, Santos Ortega, and George Petrie)
717. Seven Hundred Boiled Shirts (11/6/51; Ginger Rogers)
718. A New Commandment (11/13/51; Douglas Fairbanks, Jr.)
719. The Path of Praise (11/20/51; Walter Hampden)
720. Incident at Lancaster (11/27/51; MacDonald Carey, Robert Dryden, and Frank Readick)
721. The Sitting Duck (12/4/51; William Holden)
722. The Giant Who Stepped Over the Mountain (12/11/51; Tyrone Power)
723. The DuPont Chorus [Christmas music, no drama] (12/18/51)
724. The Day they Gave Babies Away (12/25/51; Bobby Driscoll)
725. Sixteen Sticks in a Bundle (1/1/52; Ethel Waters)
726. A Prisoner Named Brown (1/8/52; Gregory Peck)
727. A Port of Missing Men (1/15/52; Harold Huber, Dan Ocko, Ruth Yorke, and Loretta Young)
728. As If a Door Were Opening (1/22/52; Robert Dryden, John Hodiak, Arnold Moss, Kermit Murdock, and Ross Martin)
729. The Night There Was No President (1/29/52; Robert Dryden, Parker Fennelly, Sarah Fussell, Ed Jerome, Ian Martin, Guy Repp, Dean Stockwell, and Gertrude Warner)
730. Thunder of Justice (2/5/52; Parker Fennelly, Ian Martin, Dorothy McGuire, and Cameron Prud'Homme)
731. With Malice Toward None (2/12/52; John Griggs, Raymond Massey, and Scott Tennyson)
732. Three Words (2/19/52; Bill Lipton, Kermit Murdock, Richard Purdy, and Claude Rains)
733. Doctor Commando (2/26/52; Wendell Corey and Les Damon)
734. Romance at Fort Crawford (3/4/52; Vera Allen, Bill Adams, Les Barker, and Arlene Dahl)
735. Adventure on the Kentucky (3/11/52; Don Briggs, Les Barker, Richard Widmark, and Dick York)
736. The Marine Who Was 200 Years Old (3/18/52; William Bendix)
737. Breakfast at Nancy's (3/25/52; Susan Hayward)
738. The Devil's Staircase (4/1/52; Joseph Bell, Grace Matthews, Ray Milland, and Dan Ocko)
739. The Nurse who Forgot Fear (4/8/52; Nina Foch, John Newland, and Judith Parish)
740. Fly High, Fly Low (4/15/52; Bill Adams, Lee Bowman, Parker Fennelly, and Melville Ruick)
741. Yankee and the Scales (4/22/52;

Robert Dryden, Cameron Prud'Homme, and Mark Stevens)

742. Going Up (4/29/52; Robert Cummings)

743. An American From France (5/6/52; Walter Hampden and John Lund)

744. The Prisoner of Castle Thunder (5/13/52; Robert Taylor)

745. The Green Wall (5/20/52; Les Damon and John Hodiak)

746. The Valley of the Swans (5/27/52; Louise Allbritton, Dana Andrews, Dan Ocko, and Luis Van Rooten)

747. The Long Gray Line (6/3/52; Staats Cotsworth and Cornel Wilde)

748. Daughter with Wings (6/10/52; Joan Caulfield, Arnold Moss, Dan Ocko, and Chester Stratton)

749. The Quality of Courage (6/17/52; MacDonald Carey, Bernard Lenrow, and Dick York)

750. The Dark Heart (6/24/52; Joseph Bell, Vinnie Burrows, Dan Ocko, George Petrie, Karl Weber, and Jane Wyman)

751. Patriot with the Chestnut Curls (8/26/52; Vera Allen, Joan Caulfield, and Neva Patterson)

752. The Melody Man (9/2/52; Ed Begley, Robert Cummings, Dan Ocko, and Judith Parish)

753. How High the Flame (9/9/52; Court Benson, MacDonald Carey, Charles Dingle, Ginger Jones)

754. Man of Great Importance (9/16/52; Lee Bowman)

755. A Woman's Way (9/23/52; Patricia Neal)

756. The Gig of the Saginaw (9/30/52; Ed Begley, Gary Merrill, and Pat O'Malley)

757. One Way Out (10/7/52; Staats Cotsworth and John Lund)

758. The Saga of Jerry O'Brien (10/14/52; Dennis O'Keefe)

759. Ready on the Right (10/21/52; Jackie Cooper, Edwin Jerome, Arnold Moss, and Rosemary Rice)

760. That Moore Girl (10/28/52; Ann Blyth)

761. One Nation Indivisible (11/11/52; Thomas Mitchell)

762. Away All Boarding Parties (11/18/52; Wendell Corey)

763. The Path of Praise (11/25/52; Walter Hampden)

764. A Thousand to One (12/2/52; Joseph Bell, Lee Bowman, and Les Damon)

765. Listen My Children (12/9/52; Mandel Kramer, Dan Ocko, George Petrie, Rosemary Rice, and Richard Widmark)

766. Barbed-Wire Christmas (12/16/52; Kermit Murdock, Edmund O'Brien, and Dan Ocko)

767. Christmas in America (12/23/52; Walter Hampden, and DuPont Employee Choir)

768. Billy the Kid (12/30/52; Staats Cotsworth and Van Johnson)

769. A Medal for Miss Walker (1/6/53; Dorothy McGuire)

770. Down Brake (1/13/53; Ed Begley, Charles Dingle, Parker Fennelly, Ted Osborne, Cornel Wilde)

771. Bless This House (1/20/53; MacDonald Carey)

772. The Nugget and the Law (1/27/53; Ed Begley, Glenn Ford, and Arthur Maitland)

773. The Short Straw (2/3/53; Les Damon and Irene Dunne)

774. Operation Miracle (2/10/53; Robert Preston)

775. Dangerous Mission (2/17/53; MacDonald Carey and Berry Kroeger)

776. Life on the Mississippi (2/24/53; Raymond Massey)

777. Star and the Shield (3/3/53; Broderick Crawford)

778. The Secret Road (3/10/53; Lee Bowman, Tom Collins, Robert Dryden, John Griggs, Arnold Moss, and Karl Weber)

779. The River Finds a Master (3/17/53; Robert Young)

780. One Came Through (3/24/53; Wendell Corey)

781. A Time to Grow (3/31/53; Joseph Bell, Ian Martin, Thomas Mitchell, Dan Ocko, George Petrie, Guy Sorel, Chester Stratton, Scott Tennyson, and Luis Van Rooten)

The Cavalcade of Literature

The Cavalcade of Literature was another program directed by and starring Orson Welles. Originating from New York City as a short-run summer series, it presented adaptations of Shakespeare plays in consecutive segments. After the tenth broadcast, Welles left the series to star in another, entitled *Lady Esther Presents Orson Welles*, which premiered on September 15th. When Welles dropped out of the series, so did the Shakespeare plays, leaving room for patriotic type dramas. Broadcast 8 to 8:30 pm, EST.

1. Julius Caesar [part one] (7/12/41)
2. Julius Caesar [part two] (7/19/41)
3. Julius Caesar [part three] (7/26/41)
4. Twelfth Night [part one] (8/2/41)
5. Twelfth Night [part two] (8/9/41)
6. The Merchant of Venice [part one] (8/16/41)
7. The Merchant of Venice [part two] (8/23/41)
8. The Merchant of Venice [part three] (8/30/41)
9. The Merchant of Venice [part four] (9/6/41)
10. The Merchant of Venice [part five] (9/13/41)
11. The White Cliffs of Dover (9/20/41; Lynn Fontaine)
12. Air-Raid (9/27/41)

CBS Is There

"CBS asks you to imagine that our microphone is present at this unforgettable moment … all things are as they were then, except, when CBS is there, *you* are there!" Without the use of a physical time machine, CBS presented cleverly written scripts involving fictional on-the-spot interviews during historical moments in world history, as they happened. Listeners were invited to tune in to reporter John Daly as he interviewed troops beginning an advance attack at the Battle of Gettysburg. The week after, listeners heard people speaking into the radio microphone, describing the commotion of a gunshot that was fired and the news of Abraham Lincoln's assassination.

Produced and directed by Robert Lewis Shayon, this series quickly became a popular radio program not just for history professors, but for those who wanted to hear what the excitement could have been like when the Alamo was attacked, when Julius Caesar was stabbed, and Justice Samuel Chase became impeached. Irve Tunick wrote the scripts (he also wrote for *Radio's Cavalcade of America*, another history program), having to read and study numerous history books to gather facts surrounding famous world events. Other writers included Michael Sklar and Joseph Liss. John Daly was not the only newsman heard interviewing famous and not-so-famous people. Others included Don Hollenbeck and Richard C. Hottelet. Announcers included: Ken Roberts, Jackson Beck, Harry Marble, and Guy Sorel. It was created by Goodman Ace.

Episode five was not broadcast on certain stations on the East Coast. Walter Hampden guest starred in episode twenty-two. The first seven episodes were broadcast on Monday evenings at 9–9:30 pm EST. Episodes eight through twenty-three were broadcast on Sunday afternoon from 2 to 2:30. After 23 broadcasts, the series under went a title change, in an attempt to gather a larger listening audience. For the continuation of this series, see *You Are There*. The titles listed below are official script titles.

1. The Assassination of Abraham Lincoln (7/7/47)
2. The Storming of the Bastille (7/14/47)
3. Columbus Discovers America (7/21/47)
4. Witchcraft Trials At Salem (7/28/47)
5. How Sir Alfred Drake Defeats the Spanish Armada (8/4/47)
6. The Defense of the Alamo (8/11/47)
7. The Last Days of Pompeii (8/18/47)
8. The Exile of Napoleon (12/7/47)
9. The Assassination of Abraham Lincoln (12/14/47)
10. The Sailing of the Pilgrims (12/21/47)
11. The Storming of the Bastille (12/28/47)
12. The Salem Witchcraft Trials (1/4/48)
13. The Burr-Hamilton Duel (1/11/48)
14. The Signing of the Magna Carta (1/18/48)
15. The Defense of the Alamo (1/25/48)
16. How Sir Alfred Drake Defeats the Spanish Armada (2/1/48)
17. The Dreyfus Case (2/8/48)
18. The Assassination of Julius Caesar (2/15/48)
19. The Battle of Gettysburg (2/22/48)
20. The Execution of Joan of Arc (2/29/48)
21. The Oklahoma Land Run (3/7/48)
22. The Death of Socrates (3/14/48; Walter Hampden)
23. Philadelphia, July 4, 1776 (3/21/48)

CBS Radio Workshop

Similar to its predecessor, *The Columbia Workshop*, this anthology series presented experimental dramas using the latest techniques of sound innovation. Take "King of the Cats," a fantasy about an orchestra leader who conducted with his tail. "The Legend of Jimmy Blue Eyes" featured William Conrad narrating the poetry and prose against a backdrop of 1920s New Orleans blues. Various producer, directors and writers were involved in this project. Jack Johnstone, Dee Englebach, William N. Robson, Elliott Lewis, Tony Schwartz, William Froug, and others. Ray Noble, Amerigo Moreno and Leith Stevens supplied the music. Without a sponsor, this experimental series lasted a little more than a year. Broadcasts originated from both New York and California, allowing talent from the East Coast, as well as the West Coast, to emerge. Broadcast Friday evenings from 8:30 to 9 pm, EST. Beginning November 4, 1956, the series moved to Sundays from 4 to 4:30 pm, EST.

1. Brave New World [part one, Aldous Huxley narrates] (1/27/56; William Conrad, Joseph Kearns, and Lurene Tuttle)
2. Brave New World [part two, Aldous Huxley narrates] (2/3/56; William Conrad, Joseph Kearns, and Lurene Tuttle)
3. Storm (2/10/56)
4. Seasons of Disbelief / Hail and Farewell [Ray Bradbury narrates] (2/17/56; John Dehner and Virginia Gregg)
5. Colloquy #1: An Interview with William Shakespeare (2/24/56; Frank Baxter, Hans Conried, Raymond Hill, and Ben Wright)
6. The Voice of New York [Clifton Fadiman narrates] (3/2/56)

7. Report on E.S.P. (3/9/56; Raymond Burr, Lillian Buyeff, Sam Edwards, Stacy Harris, Bert Holland, John McIntire, and Russell Thorson)

8. Cops and Robbers (3/16/56; Elspeth Eric, Larry Haines, Ken Lynch, and John Sylvester)

9. The Legend of Jimmy Blue Eyes [William Conrad narrates] (3/23/56; Sam Edwards and Georgia Ellis)

10. The Ex-Urbanites [Eric Sevareid narrates] (3/30/56)

11. Speaking of Cinderella –If the Show Fits (4/6/46; Harry Bartell, Jeanne Bates, Virginia Gregg, Jack Kruschen, Peter Leeds, Jeanette Nolan, Vic Perrin, Vincent Price, and Lurene Tuttle)

12. Jacob's Hands [written by Aldous Huxley] (4/13/56; Herb Butterfield, Lawrence Dobkin, Christopher Isherwood, Helen Kleeb, Vic Perrin, and Janet Stewart)

13. Living Portrait –William Zeckendorf, Tycoon (4/20/56; Bob Hite and Martin Weldon)

14. The Record Collectors (4/27/56; John Dancer, Lyn Murray, Margaret Whiting, Margaret Young)

15. The Toldeo War (5/4/56)

16. The Enormous Radio [William Conrad narrates] (5/11/56; Hans Conried, Virginia Gregg, Helen Kleeb, Charlotte Lawrence, Eve McVey, Irene Tedrow, and George Walsh)

17. Lovers, Villains and Fools (5/18/56; Helen Hayes)

18. The Little Prince (5/25/56; Dick Beals, Raymond Burr, Joseph Kearns, and Ben Wright)

19. A Matter of Logic (6/1/56; Parley Baer, William Conrad, and Mary Jane Croft)

20. Bring on the Angels [from the notes of H.L. Mencken] (6/8/56; Mason Adams, Jackson Beck, Walter Kinsella, Ian Martin, and Luis Van Rooten)

21. The Stronger (6/15/56; Adelaide Bishop)

22. Another Point of View : Hamlet Revisited (6/22/56; William Conrad, John McIntire, Ben Wright)

23. The Eternal Joan (6/29/56; Roger De Koven, Robert Dryden, John Gibson, Lewis Kronenberger, Jack Manning, Ed Prentiss, Guy Repp, and Luis Van Rooten)

24. Portrait of Paris [by David Shornburn] (7/6/56)

25. The Case of the White Kitten (7/13/56; Mason Adams, Audrey Christie, Kenny Delmar, Ed Latimer, and Berry Kroeger)

26. Portrait of London (7/20/56; Sarah Churchill)

27. Star Boy (7/27/56)

28. Subways Are for Sleeping (8/3/56)

29. Only Johnny Knows (8/10/56; Catherine Anderson, Jackson Beck, Sarah Fussell, Joseph Julian, Ian Martin, Ed Prentiss, and Lawson Zerbe)

30. Colloquy # 2: Dissertation on Love [narrated by Frank Baxter] (8/17/56; Sam Hill, Peter Leeds, Shephard Menken, and Ben Wright)

31. Figger Fallup's Billion Dollar Failure [aka The Billion Dollar Failure of Figure Fallop] (8/24/56; Robert Dryden, Joseph Julian, and Elaine Rost)

32. Colloquy # 3: A Study of Satire (8/31/56; Stan Freeberg)

33. The Hither and Thither of Danny Dither (9/7/56)

34. A Pride of Carrots [aka Venus Well Served] [narrated by Robert Nathan, the author] (9/14/56; Ted Bliss, Daws Butler, June Foray, Robert Nathan, Alan Reed, and Bill Thompson)

35. Oedipus Complex (9/21/56; Roger De Koven, Robert Dryden, Elspeth Eric, Joseph Julian, Jack Manning, and Guy Repp)

36. Roughing It [written by Mark Twain] (10/5/56; Daws Butler, Eddie Marr, and Howard McNear)

37. A Writer at Work [written by Hector Chevigny] (10/12/56; Jan Miner)

38. Legend of Annie Christmas [narrated by William Conrad] (10/19/56)

39. When the Mountain Fell (10/26/56)

40. Biography of the White House [aka 1600 Pennsylvania Avenue] (11/2/56)

41. Colloquy # 4: Joe Miller's Joke Book (11/4/56; Frank Baxter, Virginia

Gregg, Joseph Kearns, Peter Leeds, Howard McNear, Jay Novello, and Ben Wright)

42. Report on the We'uns (11/11/56; Edgar Barrier, June Foray, Byron Kane, and Jay Novello)

43. Sounds of the Nation (11/18/56; Leon Janney, Dick Noel, and Luis Van Rooten)

44. The King of the Cats [written by Stephen Vincent Benet] (11/25/56; Byron Kane, Joseph Kearns, Jeanette Nolan, and Jay Novello)

45. The Day the Roof Fell In (12/2/56; Jackson Beck, Leon Janney, Joseph Julian, and Berry Kroeger)

46. I Was the Duke [aka A Portrait of a Juvenile Delinquent] (12/9/56)

47. The Big Event [aka The Law of Averages] (12/16/56; Ralph Bell, Roger De Koven, and William Redfield)

48. All Is Bright (12/23/56)

49. No Time for Heartaches (1/13/57; Daws Butler, Hans Conried, June Foray, Byron Kane, Jay Novello, Amanda Randolf, Sophie Tucker, and Maragret Whiting)

50. Disaster! Fire at Malibu (1/20/57; William Conrad, Joe di Santis, Lou Krugman, James Nusser, Barney Phillips, Sam Pierce, and Larry Thor)

51. The Crazy Life (1/27/57; Elspeth Eric, Henry Morgan, Bryna Raeburn, and Luis Van Rooten)

52. La Grane Greteche [aka The Opera] (2/3/57; Avery Klaffland and George R. Mills)

53. 1489 Words (2/10/57; William Conrad)

54. The Space Merchants [part one] (2/17/57; Ralph Bell, Ralph Camargo, Robert Dryden, Virginia Kaye, Ian Martin, Ed Prentiss, and Robert Readick)

55. The Space Merchants [part two] (2/24/57; Ralph Bell, Ralph Camargo, Robert Dryden, Virginia Kaye, Ian Martin, Ed Prentiss, and Robert Readick)

56. Ballad of the Iron Horse (3/3/57; Daws Butler, William Conrad, Dick Crenna, Joe di Santis, Jack Kruschen, and Jack Moyles)

57. Air Raid [aka Prevarications of Mr. Peeps] [restaged from *The Columbia Workshop* of 10/27/38] (3/10/57; John Dehner, Frank Goss, Betty Noyes, Anne Whitfield, and Ben Wright)

58. The Endless Road (3/17/57; Dick Beals, Ralph Bell, Robert Dryden, Dan Ocko, and Guy Repp)

59. Harmonica Solo (3/24/57; Joe di Santis, Lou Krugman, Jack Kruschen, and Shepard Menken)

60. A Dog's Life [aka Adopting a Dog] (3/31/57; Ralph Bell and Tony Schwartz)

61. Japanese Drama [aka Japanese Theater / No Plays of Japan] (4/7/57; William Conrad, John Dehner, Virginia Gregg, and Ben Wright)

62. Carlotta's Serape (4/14/57; Brooks Atkinson, Staats Cotsworth, and Luis Van Rooten)

63. The Son of Man (4/21/57; Raymond Burr, Victor Jory, Herbert Marshall, Vincent Price, and Robert Young)

64. Light Ship (4/28/57; Ralph Bell, Dan Ocko, Santos Ortega, and Luis Van Rooten)

65. Nightmare (5/5/57; Edgar Barrier, Mary Jane Croft, Elliott Lewis, Barney Phillips, Paula Winslowe)

66. The Long Way Home (5/12/57; Roger De Koven, Wendell Holmes, William Redfield, Guy Repp)

67. Heaven Is in the Sky (5/19/57; Frank Goss)

68. I Have Three Heads (5/26/57; Jackson Beck, Ralph Bell, Ian Martin, and Bill Quinn)

69. Epitaphs [aka Spoon River Anthology] (6/2/57; Parley Baer, Virginia Christine, Richard Crenna, John Dehner, John McIntire, Howard McNear, Jeanette Nolan, and Lurene Tuttle)

70. The Seven Hills of Rome (6/9/57)

71. Housing Problem (6/16/57; Daws Butler, Shepard Menken, and Shirley Mitchell)

72. Meditations of Ecclesiastas (6/23/57; Senator John F. Kennedy and Edward R. Murrow)

73. The Battle of Gettysburg (6/30/57; Raymond Burr, Daws Butler, and John Dehner)

74. You Could Look It Up [by James

Thurber] (7/7/57; Ralph Bell, Sarah Fussell, Larry Haines, Harold Huber, Joseph Julian, and Del Sharbutt)

75. The Silent Witness (7/14/57; Raymond Burr)

76. The Green Hills of Earth [based on the story by Robert Heinlein] (7/21/57; Jackson Beck, Berry Kroeger, Ian Martin, Dan Ocko, and Everett Sloane)

77. Never Bet the Devil Your Head [written by Edgar Allan Poe] (7/28/57; Eleanor Audley, Dick Beals, Alan Botzer, Daws Butler, John Dehner, Hugh Douglas, and Howard McNear)

78. The Heart of Man (8/4/57; Ralph Camargo, Berry Kroeger, Bill Mason, Guy Repp, and Luis Van Rooten)

79. Malihina Magic [aka Vacations] (8/11/57; Lillian Buyeff, Virginia Gregg, Jack Kruschen, Sam Pierce, Joe di Santis, Lurene Tuttle, and Ben Wright)

80. The Celestrial Omnibus (8/18/57; Peter Lazer, Luis Van Rooten, and Lee Vines)

81. Sweet Cherries of Charleston (8/25/57; Parley Baer, Harry Bartell, Paul Frees, Roy Glenn, Ed Marr)

82. Grief Drives a Black Sedan (9/1/57; Ralph Bell, Alice Frost, Larry Haines, Jay Johnson, Bill Mason, and Lee Vines)

83. People Are No Good (9/8/57)

84. Time Found Again (9/15/57; Jan Miner, Ted Osborne, and Dwight Weist)

85. Young Man Axlebrod (9/22/57)

Challenge of the Yukon

Created by Thomas Dougall, this juvenile program lay in the same tradition as *The Lone Ranger*, substituting the Northwest, aka the Yukon, for the Wild West. With his trusty wonder dog Yukon King, Sergeant Preston fought evil and always captured the ruthless for a fair trial. Writers included Fran Striker, Betty Joyce, Bob Green, Mildred Merrill, Dan Beattie, Felix Holt, Tom Dougall, Jim Lawrence, and Steve McCarthy.

Challenge of the Yukon started out in fifteen-minute broadcasts on Thursdays from WXYZ, Detroit, went to Tuesdays on February 4, 1947, and back to Thursdays beginning February 20, 1947. On March 12, 1947, the series was heard on Wednesdays. A new thirty-minute format began a Tuesday run on ABC, sponsored by Quaker Oats on June 12, 1947, moved to Saturdays beginning July 12, 1947, Thursdays on September 11, 1947, Saturdays on November 1, 1947, Wednesdays on July 28, 1948. The program moved into a three-day-a-week format, Monday, Wednesday, and Friday beginning September 6, 1948, moved to once-a-week on Wednesdays beginning June 15, 1949, and returned to three-a-week format on September 12, 1949.

The series took a move from ABC to Mutual beginning January 2, 1950, still three-a-week format; on January 1 and 8 of 1951, it was Monday from 5:30 to 6 pm, EST, and on January 20, 1951, the series moved to Saturdays. Beginning January 27, 1951, the program was heard Saturday and Sunday. On July 10, 1951, the

Compiled by Terry Salomonson. Copyright © 10/17/88 by Terry Salomonson.

series moved to a three-a-week format, Sundays, Tuesdays and Thursdays. On November 13, 1951, the program changed its name to *Sergeant Preston of the Yukon*.

1. -----(2/3/38)	51. -----(1/19/39)	101. -----(1/4/40)
2. -----(2/10/38)	52. -----(1/26/39)	102. -----(1/11/40)
3. -----(2/17/38)	53. -----(2/2/39)	103. -----(1/18/40)
4. -----(2/24/38)	54. -----(2/9/39)	104. -----(1/25/40)
5. -----(3/3/38)	55. -----(2/16/39)	105. -----(2/1/40)
6. -----(3/10/38)	56. -----(2/23/39)	106. -----(2/8/40)
7. -----(3/17/38)	57. -----(3/2/39)	107. -----(2/15/40)
8. -----(3/24/38)	58. -----(3/9/39)	108. -----(2/22/40)
9. -----(3/31/38)	59. -----(3/16/39)	109. -----(2/29/40)
10. -----(4/7/38)	60. -----(3/23/39)	110. -----(3/7/40)
11. -----(4/14/38)	61. -----(3/30/39)	111. -----(3/14/40)
12. -----(4/21/38)	62. -----(4/6/39)	112. -----(3/21/40)
13. -----(4/28/38)	63. -----(4/13/39)	113. -----(3/28/40)
14. -----(5/5/38)	64. -----(4/20/39)	114. -----(4/4/40)
15. -----(5/12/38)	65. -----(4/27/39)	115. -----(4/11/40)
16. -----(5/19/38)	66. -----(5/4/39)	116. -----(4/18/40)
17. -----(5/26/38)	67. -----(5/11/39)	117. -----(4/25/40)
18. -----(6/2/38)	68. -----(5/18/39)	118. -----(5/2/40)
19. -----(6/9/38)	69. -----(5/25/39)	119. -----(5/9/40)
20. -----(6/16/38)	70. -----(6/1/39)	120. -----(5/16/40)
21. -----(6/23/38)	71. -----(6/8/39)	121. -----(5/23/40)
22. -----(6/30/38)	72. -----(6/15/39)	122. -----(5/30/40)
23. -----(7/7/38)	73. -----(6/22/39)	123. -----(6/6/40)
24. -----(7/14/38)	74. -----(6/29/39)	124. -----(6/13/40)
25. -----(7/21/38)	75. -----(7/6/39)	125. -----(6/20/40)
26. -----(7/28/38)	76. -----(7/13/39)	126. -----(6/27/40)
27. -----(8/4/38)	77. -----(7/20/39)	127. -----(7/4/40)
28. -----(8/11/38)	78. -----(7/27/39)	128. -----(7/11/40)
29. -----(8/18/38)	79. -----(8/3/39)	129. -----(7/18/40)
30. -----(8/25/38)	80. -----(8/10/39)	130. -----(7/25/40)
31. -----(9/1/38)	81. -----(8/17/39)	131. -----(8/1/40)
32. -----(9/8/38)	82. -----(8/24/39)	132. -----(8/8/40)
33. -----(9/15/38)	83. -----(8/31/39)	133. -----(8/15/40)
34. -----(9/22/38)	84. -----(9/7/39)	134. -----(8/22/40)
35. -----(9/29/38)	85. -----(9/14/39)	135. -----(8/29/40)
36. -----(10/6/38)	86. -----(9/21/39)	136. -----(9/5/40)
37. -----(10/13/38)	87. -----(9/28/39)	137. -----(9/12/40)
38. -----(10/20/38)	88. -----(10/5/39)	138. -----(9/19/40)
39. -----(10/27/38)	89. -----(10/12/39)	139. -----(9/26/40)
40. -----(11/3/38)	90. -----(10/19/39)	140. -----(10/3/40)
41. -----(11/10/38)	91. -----(10/26/39)	141. -----(10/10/40)
42. -----(11/17/38)	92. -----(11/2/39)	142. -----(10/17/40)
43. -----(11/24/38)	93. -----(11/9/39)	143. -----(10/24/40)
44. -----(12/1/38)	94. -----(11/16/39)	144. -----(10/31/40)
45. -----(12/8/38)	95. -----(11/23/39)	145. -----(11/7/40)
46. -----(12/15/38)	96. -----(11/30/39)	146. -----(11/14/40)
47. -----(12/22/38)	97. -----(12/7/39)	147. -----(11/21/40)
48. -----(12/29/38)	98. -----(12/14/39)	148. -----(11/28/40)
49. -----(1/5/39)	99. -----(12/21/39)	149. -----(12/5/40)
50. -----(1/12/39)	100. -----(12/28/39)	

150. The Shadow of the Gallows (12/12/40)
151. The Gold of Burning River (12/19/40)
152. The Wedding at Taranga (12/26/40)
153. Mantrap (1/2/41)
154. Murder in the Black Forest (1/9/41)
155. Beyond the Rainbow (1/16/41)
156. The Case of the Frightened Lady (11/23/41)
157. Partners Wanted (1/30/41)
158. The Spotted Parka (2/6/41)
159. The Man in the Red Coat (2/13/41)
160. A Case of Identity (2/20/41)
161. The Dark Trail (2/27/41)
162. South Wind Over White Horse (3/6/41)
163. To Have and To Hold (3/13/41)
164. The Case of the Insurance Blanks (3/20/41)
165. The Case of the Torn Fur (3/27/41)
166. Deadfall (4/3/41)
167. The Law of Frozen Flats (4/10/41)
168. The Trail of Rose Tremaine (4/17/41)
169. El Dorado Thirty Three (4/24/41)
170. Dead Man's Hand (5/1/41)
171. Second Homecoming (5/8/41)
172. The Doctor Takes a Case (5/15/41)
173. The Hand of the Storm King (5/22/41)
174. North of the Circle (5/29/41)
175. The Locked Door (6/5/41)
176. Blind Man's Bluff (6/12/41)
177. A Scrap of Deerskin (6/19/41)
178. -----(6/26/41)
179. -----(7/3/41)
180. -----(7/10/41)
181. -----(7/17/41)
182. A Corner in Dogs (7/24/41)
183. The Long Trail Home (7/31/41)
184. The Pay Off (8/7/41)
185. Eight Hours to Dawson (8/14/41)
186. A Message to Pierre (8/21/41)
187. Find the Woman (8/28/41)
188. The Hundred Mile Test (9/4/41)
189. Buried Treasure (9/11/41)
190. The Shadow of the Past (9/18/41)
191. White Wolf (9/25/41)
192. Quarantine (10/2/41)
193. Payment on Demand (10/9/41)
194. The Big Story (10/16/41)
195. Non Stop to Skagway (10/23/41)
196. Seal Hunt (10/30/41)

197. Seven Day Option (11/6/41)
198. The Wolf Pack (11/13/41)
199. The Trap at Big Pine Creek (11/20/41)
200. Trail Robbery (11/27/41)
201. Ghost Town (12/4/41)
202. Wanted (12/11/41)
203. King of the Rescue (12/18/41)
204. The Cache at Bitter Creek (12/25/41)
205. The Raid at Christmas Cove (1/1/42)
206. One Night in Dawson (1/8/42)
207. Prisoner's Base (1/15/42)
208. Materia Medica (1/22/42)
209. Reunion (1/29/42)
210. Diamonds (2/5/42)
211. Christmas Eve (2/12/42)
212. Turnabout (2/19/42)
213. A Deathbed Promise (2/26/42)
214. Gratitude (3/5/42)
215. Turn to the Right (3/12/42)
216. Murder by Law (3/19/42)
217. Two Sisters (3/26/42)
218. Reprieve for a Night (4/2/42)
219. Delayed Conviction (4/9/42)
220. Double Deal (4/16/42)
221. The Will (4/23/42)
222. Return to Skagway (4/30/42)
223. The Dawson Fire (5/7/42)
224. Blue River (5/14/42)
225. Lucky Streak (5/21/42)
226. Test for Traitors (5/28/42)
227. Land Office Business (6/4/42)
228. The Trail of Twenty Years (6/11/42)
229. The King of Rapids City (6/18/42)
230. The Lynch Mob (6/25/42)
231. Diphtheria (7/2/42)
232. Dead Dog (7/9/42)
233. Rock Slide (7/16/42)
234. Soapy Jones (7/23/42)
235. The Cheechako (7/30/42)
236. The Eagle Mine (8/6/42)
237. Peril at Peace River (8/13/42)
238. Malachuck Pass (8/20/42)
239. Birthday Party (8/27/42)
240. Smallpox (9/3/42)
241. King Remembers (9/10/52)
242. Construction Gang (9/17/42)
243. Loon Lake (9/24/42)
244. The Melvin Brothers (10/1/42)
245. Gold at Lame Dog Creek (10/8/42)
246. Carson's Express (10/15/42)
247. Double Alibi (10/22/42)

248. Alibi (10/29/42)
249. Stolen Nuggets (11/5/42)
250. Promice to Avenge (11/12/42)
251. Alibi (11/19/42)
252. The Brass Button (11/26/42)
253. Sight Unseen (12/3/42)
254. Pretense to Homicide (12/10/42)
255. Chinook Gold (12/17/42)
256. Rat Poison (12/24/42)
257. Corporal Standish (12/31/42)
258. Wolf Call (1/7/43)
259. Wind River Trail (1/14/43)
260. Partners at Haunted Lake (1/21/43)
261. Carlin Creek (1/28/43)
262. Sealskin Evidence (2/4/43)
263. To the Highest Bidder (2/11/43)
264. Mounties Ain't Much (2/18/43)
265. Circumstantial Evidence (2/25/43)
266. The Tenderfoot (3/4/43)
267. Extortion (3/11/43)
268. The Eyes of Talooga (3/18/43)
269. The Double-Cross (3/25/43)
270. Yukon Story (4/1/43)
271. Renegade at Silver Ridge (4/8/43)
272. King's Sixth Sense (4/15/43)
273. Fur Base (4/22/43)
274. Gambler's Pay-Off (4/29/43)
275. All that Glitters (5/6/43)
276. Wolf Trap (5/13/43)
277. What's In a Name (5/20/43)
278. Ace of Spades (5/27/43)
279. Golden Journey (6/3/43)
280. Reunion (6/10/43)
281. Cue for Murder (6/17/43)
282. The Price of a Getaway (6/24/43)
283. A Brother's Treachery (7/1/43)
284. Assayed for Death (7/8/43)
285. Meeting the Terms of a Contract (7/15/43)
286. Till a Man's Proven Dead (7/22/43)
287. A Swindler Swindled (7/29/43)
288. Dealing in Death (8/5/43)
289. A Footprint in Leather (8/12/43)
290. Caught By a Button (8/19/43)
291. The Last Days of a Freight Line (8/26/43)
292. When the Law Helps an Orphan (9/2/43)
293. A Swill o' Gunpowder (9/9/43)
294. King's Ransom (9/16/43)
295. Murder on Train Time (9/23/43)
296. A Previewed Confession (9/30/43)
297. Attempted Manslaughter (10/7/43)
298. Lantern Rock (10/14/43)

299. The Ring on His Finger (10/21/43)
300. The Tell-Tale Bullet (10/28/43)
301. A Date to Remember (11/4/43)
302. Belated Revenge (11/11/43)
303. Return to the Crime (11/18/43)
304. King Spots Murder (11/25/43)
305. Self Defense or Murder (12/2/43)
306. By Hook or by Crook (12/9/43)
307. The Eleventh Hour (12/16/43)
308. Murder in ABC's (12/23/43)
309. No Escape for a Murderer (12/30/43)
310. Revenge in the Yukon (1/6/44)
311. Forgery and Murder (1/13/44)
312. Macbeth's Bloody Knife (1/20/44)
313. Wolf Pack (1/27/44)
314. Cabin on the Trail (2/3/44)
315. Lady Luck Claim (2/10/44)
316. As A Man Thinketh (2/17/44)
317. The Hannagan Brothers (2/24/44)
318. The Great Dog King (3/2/44)
319. The Vallera Diamond (3/9/44)
320. Paul Matthews (3/16/44)
321. King Meets Soapy Smith (3/23/44)
322. A Pack of Bacon (3/30/44)
323. Edward Carson (4/6/44)
324. The Plaid Coat (4/13/44)
325. Belle Brady's Gesture (4/20/44)
326. Preston's Right Hand Man (4/27/44)
327. A Woman Scorned (5/4/44)
328. Outlaw Dog (5/11/44)
329. The Outlaw's Nemesis (5/18/44)
330. The Idol (5/25/44)
331. A Joke Led to the gallows (6/1/44)
332. Reverend Jim (6/8/44)
333. The Man From Missouri (6/15/44)
334. Design for Murder (6/22/44)
335. The Duke Bows To A King (6/29/44)
336. Unscheduled Escape (7/6/44)
337. The Lady's Locket (7/13/44)
338. Lucky Walters (7/20/44)
339. Of Dogs and Horses (7/27/44)
340. Maintiens Le Droit (8/3/44)
341. The Plan that Failed (8/10/44)
342. King Breaks the Wheel of Fortune (8/17/44)
343. A Rendezvous (8/24/44)
344. Smokey (8/31/44)
345. A Frame-Up That Failed (9/7/44)
346. Death and the Flickering Eye (9/14/44)
347. A Masquerade (9/21/44)

348. Eyes for the Blind (9/28/44)
349. A Wrong Righted (10/5/44)
350. King Saves the Day (10/12/44)
351. Suzanne Verrill (10/19/44)
352. The Case History of a Mountie (10/26/44)
353. Seahorse City's Editor (11/2/44)
354. King Found the Clue (11/9/44)
355. Florabelle's Adventure (11/16/44)
356. Paula Buchanan (11/23/44)
357. King Meets a Grizzley (11/30/44)
358. Trial by Fire (12/7/44)
359. One Went to the Gallows (12/14/44)
360. How Connelly Paid the Law (12/21/44)
361. Preston's Dilemma (12/28/44)
362. Trap for a Mountie (1/4/45)
363. Man-Hunt (1/11/45)
364. Murder on the Trail (1/18/45)
365. The Fugitives (1/25/45)
366. King Led the Way (1/30/45)
367. An Unlucky Gambler (2/6/45)
368. Guilty by Proxy (2/13/45)
369. Wilderness Girl (2/20/45)
370. Glynns Canyon (2/27/45)
371. Trail Scent (3/6/45)
372. The Dog-Head Nugget (3/13/45)
373. Silver Point Renegades (3/20/45)
374. Landslide (3/27/45)
375. Blizzard in the Yukon (4/3/45)
376. Back Door of the Mountain (4/10/45)
377. Her Weight in Gold (4/24/45)
378. Spawn of the North (5/1/45)
379. The Dog Team Race (5/8/45)
380. God of the Mountain (5/15/45)
381. A Boy and a Dog (5/22/45)
382. Ambush (5/29/45)
383. Trap Robber (6/5/45)
384. Medicine Man (6/12/45)
385. Thunder (6/19/45)
386. Recovered Claim (6/26/45)
387. Old Tom (7/3/45)
388. The Brass Button (7/10/45)
389. Escape (7/17/45)
390. Skipper (7/24/45)
391. The Chase (7/31/45)
392. The Map (8/7/45)
393. Arctic Chase (8/14/45)
394. Maw Baker's Pies (8/21/45)
395. Magnanimous Ghost (8/28/45)
396. Bear Trap (9/4/45)
397. Alibi (9/11/45)

398. Big Bill (9/18/45)
399. The Red Mitten (9/25/45)
400. Chechako (10/2/45)
401. The Black Bear (10/9/45)
402. Scorpion Sam's Gold (10/16/45)
403. Dynamite Provides (10/23/45)
404. The Trail (10/30/45)
405. The Last Laugh (11/6/45)
406. The Irish Wolf Hound (11/13/45)
407. Father Donovan (11/20/45)
408. Long Fall Canyon (11/27/45)
409. The Bonanza Belle (12/4/45)
410. The Dachshund (12/11/45)
411. Christmas Present (12/18/45)
412. New Year's Eve (12/29/45)
413. The Grave Robbers (1/5/46)
414. The Mail Team (1/10/46)
415. Preston Takes Over (1/17/46)
416. Jane Gets Her Man (1/24/46)
417. The Blind Man (1/31/46)
418. The Cure (2/14/46)
419. Mabel (2/21/46)
420. The Shamaness (2/28/46)
421. Mad Wolf (3/7/46)
422. The Bully (3/14/46)
423. Hold Up (3/21/46)
424. The Rivals (3/28/46)
425. The Return of Pete Hunt (4/4/46)
426. Ned's Wife (4/11/46)
427. Rex (4/18/46)
428. Torn Parka (4/25/46)
429. Balmy Bill (5/2/46)
430. Eskimo Justice (5/9/46)
431. Shrimp Togan (5/16/46)
432. Chap (5/23/46)
433. The Mitten (5/30/46)
434. Annie Jones (6/6/46)
435. The Great Dane (6/13/46)
436. How Preston Got King (6/20/46)
437. The Sharp Shooter (6/27/46)
438. The Pup That Ate Too Much (7/4/46)
439. Flash (7/11/46)
440. Preston Breaks A Rule (7/18/46)
441. Beaver Dam (7/25/46)
442. The Silver Fox (8/1/46)
443. Blind Wolf (8/8/46)
444. The Mute Speaks (8/15/46)
445. Grizzly Martin (8/22/46)
446. Preston Goes to Jail (8/29/46)
447. The Man Who Couldn't Remember (9/5/46)
448. The Epidemic (9/12/46)
449. Preston Sells King (9/19/46)

450. Blind Man's Claim (9/26/46)
451. The Wooden Case (10/3/46)
452. One-Man Cat (10/10/46)
453. False Alarm (10/17/46)
454. The Deer Head (10/24/46)
455. Timber Wolf (10/31/46)
456. Trap in the Mountains (11/7/46)
457. The Choice (11/14/56)
458. The Cat Collar (11/21/46)
459. Thanksgiving in the Wilderness (11/28/46)
460. The Watch Dog (12/5/46)
461. The Dog Fight (12/12/46)
462. Christmas Present (12/19/46)
463. The Man Who Limped (12/26/46)
464. The False Beard (1/2/47)
465. Zeb (1/9/47)
466. The Black Dog (1/16/47)
467. A Question of Ethics (1/23/47)
468. The Gold Fang (1/30/47)
469. Pet Bear (2/4/47)
470. The Substitution (2/11/47)
471. The Red Parka (2/20/47)
472. The Hermit of Nugget Hill (2/27/47)
473. The Coffin (3/6/47)
474. Sunshine Stones (3/12/47)
475. The Birthday Present (3/19/47)
476. The Big Stone House (3/26/47)
477. The Dancing Bear (4/2/47)
478. The Story of Big John (4/9/47)
479. The Torn Sleeve (4/16/47)
480. The Mad Trapper (4/23/47)
481. The Red Setter (4/30/47)
482. The Usurpers (5/14/47)
483. The Maniac (5/21/47)
484. Lost Mitten (5/28/47)
485. The Wolf Cub (6/12/47)
486. Grizzley (6/19/47)
487. Pet Bear (6/26/47)
488. The Puppy (7/3/47)
489. Sam's Gold (7/12/47)
490. The Man in the Fur Cap (7/19/47)
491. A Dog named Mabel (7/26/47)
492. Messenger of Mercy (8/2/47)
493. Derelict Dog (8/9/47)
494. The Revenge of Steve Carlton (8/23/47)
495. Clue to a Killer (8/30/47)
496. The Stolen Pups (9/6/47)
497. The Northern Pursuit (9/11/47)
498. The Fraud (9/18/47)
499. Reprisal (9/25/47)
500. The Proof (10/2/47)
501. The Malamute Pup (10/9/47)
502. The Last Cabin (10/16/47)
503. Rex (10/23/47)
504. Sam's Wife (11/1/47)
505. King's Escape (11/8/47)
506. The Limping Dog (11/15/47)
507. King Gets His Man (11/22/47)
508. Tara (11/29/47)
509. The Marked Cards (12/6/47)
510. White Man's Law (12/13/47)
511. The Shepherd Dog (12/27/47)
512. The Silent One (1/3/48)
513. Tago, the Half Breed (1/10/48)
514. The Bridge (1/17/48)
515. The Loyalty of Chief (1/24/48)
516. The Pamphlet (1/31/48)
517. The Red Herring (2/7/48)
518. The Klondike Palace (2/14/48)
519. Aunt Em (2/21/48)
520. Silvertip (2/28/48)
521. The Debt (3/6/48)
522. Witness for the Crown (3/13/48)
523. King Comes Home (3/20/48)
524. The Wire Haired Terrier (3/27/48)
525. The Scent of Murder (4/3/48)
526. The Lesson (4/10/48)
527. Rusty (4/24/48)
528. False Alibi (5/1/48)
529. The Mail Robbery (5/8/48)
530. The Million Dollar Case (5/15/48)
531. Murder at the El Dorado (5/22/48)
532. The Rainbow Claims (5/29/48)
533. Starvation Camp (6/5/48)
534. The Sweetwater Fire (6/19/48)
535. Breakup (6/26/48)
536. King of the Castle (7/3/48)
537. The Wolf Dog (7/10/48)
538. Pit of Disaster (7/24/48)
539. Canyon Trap (7/28/48)
540. The Tattooed Star (8/4/48)
541. King's Revenge (8/11/48)
542. Vindication (8/18/48)
543. Rusky (8/25/48)
544. The Champion (9/1/48)
545. Shots in the Dark (9/6/48)
546. Winner by Proxy (9/8/48)
547. King's Feud (9/10/48)
548. The Fraud (9/13/48)
549. Trader Muldoon (9/15/48)
550. The Showdown (9/17/48)
551. Lost Indian Mine (9/20/48)
552. Icebound (9/22/48)
553. Old Ben's Gold (9/24/48)
554. Pot Luck Killers (9/27/48)

555. Ghost Town (9/29/48)
556. Find the Body (10/1/48)
557. The Extra Uniform (10/4/48)
558. Record Run (10/6/48)
559. Parson Shorty Meadows (10/8/48)
560. The Red Ace (10/11/48)
561. Mine of Good Hope (10/13/48)
562. White Hawk (10/15/48)
563. Underground Ambush (10/18/48)
564. The False Trail (10/20/48)
565. The Poisoner of Chiliwaw (10/22/48)
566. Samaritan of the Trail (10/25/48)
567. Preston Turns the Tables (10/27/48)
568. The Phantom Gang (10/29/48)
569. The Call of Duty (11/1/48)
570. The Man with the Red Hair (11/3/48)
571. Death on the Trail (11/5/48)
572. The Wilderness Uprising (11/8/48)
573. Ben Yancy's Legacy (11/10/48)
574. Shadow (11/12/48)
575. The Second Chance (11/15/48)
576. Manhunt (11/17/48)
577. The St. Bernard Dog (11/19/48)
578. Mutiny on the Penguin (11/22/48)
579. Old Moby's Cabin (11/24/48)
580. Lost River Roundup (11/26/48)
581. Strike at Pelican Creek (11/29/48)
582. The Black Husky (12/1/48)
583. The Sergeant's Right (12/3/48)
584. Timber (12/6/48)
585. The Dawson Fire (12/8/48)
586. The Trap in Cabin Four (12/10/48)
587. Escape to the North (12/13/48)
588. Marlow's Gang (12/15/48)
589. Faith in a Mountie (12/17/48)
590. The Emerald in the Nugget (12/20/48)
591. The Man in the Red Coat (12/22/48)
592. Injun Devil (12/27/48)
593. Arrowhead Frame-Up (12/29/48)
594. Case of Frank Weaver (12/31/48)
595. King Takes Over (1/3/49)
596. Bonanza 47 (1/5/49)
597. Jim Beldens' Secret (1/7/49)
598. King Proves His Worth (1/10/49)
599. Peril for Preston (1/12/49)
600. Lem Baileys Pet Bear (1/14/49)
601. White Water (1/17/49)
602. Jimmy's Birthday Cake (1/19/49)
603. Skagway Patrol (1/21/49)
604. Mystery in the Cave (1/24/49)

605. The Moose River Murder (1/26/49)
606. Lost River Ambush (1/28/49)
607. The Mongrel (1/31/49)
608. On One Condition (2/2/49)
609. The Trail of Grizzley Grayson (2/4/49)
610. Rogue's Progress (2/7/49)
611. Sergeant Preston Faces Death (2/9/49)
612. Ambush (2/11/49)
613. The Coward (2/14/49)
614. Double Cross Creek (2/16/49)
615. The Dog With the Gold Tooth (2/18/49)
616. The Magic Light (2/21/49)
617. Signal in Green (2/23/49)
618. Danger Signal (2/25/49)
619. River Pirates (2/28/49)
620. Ambush at Forty-Mile (3/2/49)
621. The Music Hall Murder (3/4/49)
622. Trail Mates (3/7/49)
623. Bulldog Charm (3/9/49)
624. The Meal the Convicted (3/1/49)
625. The White Huskie (3/14/49)
626. The Klondike Queen (3/16/49)
627. The Caribou Case (3/18/49)
628. The Black and White Pup (3/21/49)
629. The Devil Dog (3/23/49)
630. Letters to a Killer (3/25/49)
631. Conover's Crime (3/28/49)
632. Crumpled Handbill (3/30/49)
633. The Killer (4/1/49)
634. The Remittance Man (4/4/49)
635. Dead Man's Man (4/6/49)
636. The Knife Throwers (4/8/49)
637. The Lucky Shirt (4/11/49)
638. The Trail of the Werewolf (4/13/49)
639. Trouble at Forty-Mile (4/15/49)
640. The Luck of the Newtons (4/18/49)
641. The Empty Coffin (4/20/49)
642. The Doomed Witness (4/22/49)
643. The Bear Trap (4/25/49)
644. The Perfect Crime (4/27/49)
645. Fire in the Sky (4/29/49)
646. Escape to the North (5/2/49)
647. The Sparrow (5/4/49)
648. The Case of the Hard-Hearted Hermit (5/6/49)
649. Race to Twenty-Mile (5/9/49)
650. The Million Dollar Deadline (5/11/49)
651. The Skagway-Mail (5/13/49)
652. The Counter Plan (5/16/49)
653. The Bad Penny (5/18/49)

654. Adventure in Selkirk (5/20/49)
655. The Duel (5/23/49)
656. Death and the Lucky Seven (5/25/49)
657. The Skull in the Stone (5/27/49)
658. The Case of the Turncoat Mountie (5/30/49)
659. The Case of the Frightened Child (6/1/49)
660. The Case of the Canyon Hold-Up (6/3/49)
661. The Missing Code (6/6/49)
662. The Case of the Yellow Ribbon (6/8/49)
663. A Boy and His Dog (6/10/49)
664. The Uphill Sled (6/15/49)
665. King Takes Over (6/22/49)
666. The Case of the Beautiful Swindler (6/29/49)
667. The Case of the Crown Fire (7/6/49)
668. Trickery in the River (7/13/49)
669. The Case of the Kind Hearted Killer (7/20/49)
670. The Case of the Unwilling Guardian (7/27/49)
671. The Renegade Huskie (8/3/49)
672. What Price King (8/10/49)
673. The Case of the Friendly Enemies (8/17/49)
674. The Yellow Kitten (8/24/49)
675. The Minster's Missing Money (8/31/49)
676. The Case of the Detective Who Liked Excitement (9/7/49)
677. The Fab-Tan Gold Robbery (9/12/49)
678. The Boy Who Feared Dogs (9/14/49)
679. The Case of the Wishbone (9/16/49)
680. Fire on the Trail (9/19/49)
681. King and the Baxter Gang (9/21/49)
682. The Case of the River Pirates (9/23/49)
683. Ambush Near Selkirk (9/26/49)
684. The Case of the Sourdough's Dog (9/28/49)
685. The Phantom Witness (9/30/49)
686. The Scent of Blood (10/3/49)
687. Murder on the Mountain (10/5/49)
688. The Generous Hobo (10/7/49)
689. Allen McRea's Birthday Present (10/10/49)

690. The Burning Cabin (10/12/49)
691. The Great Charlotta (10/14/49)
692. The Doctor Disappears (10/17/49)
693. Hazel Crest Decision (10/19/49)
694. Rescue in the Forest (10/21/49)
695. The Missing Money (10/24/49)
696. Bad Boy (10/26/49)
697. The Last Will (10/28/49)
698. Nipper Moves Himself (10/31/49)
699. Bear Trap (11/2/49)
700. Dr. Blake's Surrender (11/4/49)
701. Trapped (11/7/49)
702. The Miser and the Mob (11/9/49)
703. The Old Timer (11/11/49)
704. The Senator Finds a Treasure (11/14/49)
705. Note of Evidence (11/16/49)
706. The Brother's Promise (11/18/49)
707. The King Emperor (11/21/49)
708. The Stolen Box (11/23/49)
709. The Barbary Gang (11/25/49)
710. Grubstake for Vickers (11/28/49)
711. Forty-Eight Hours to Pay (11/30/49)
712. Outlaws Twin (12/2/49)
713. Dance at Caribou Creek (12/5/49)
714. The Return of Tom Becket (12/7/49)
715. Swindlers Luck (12/9/49)
716. Copper Gulch Patrol (12/12/49)
717. The Wainwright Cache (12/14/49)
718. The Black Bag (12/16/49)
719. Missing Gold (12/19/49)
720. The Shanghaied Sergeant (12/21/49)
721. The Sergeant's Present (12/23/49)
722. Journey For Revenge (12/26/49)
723. Swindler's Luck (12/28/49)
724. The Prodigal Father (12/30/49)
725. Rainbow's End (1/2/50)
726. Jeff Marco's Gang (1/4/50)
727. The Battle at Bradley's (1/6/50)
728. Barry Jeffer's Trust (1/9/50)
729. Red Devil (1/11/50)
730. The Miner's Meeting (1/13/50)
731. The Diamond Collar (1/16/50)
732. The Long Trail (1/18/50)
733. No Epitaph for Tombstone (1/20/50)
734. The Ten Thousand Dollar Rewards (1/23/50)
735. The Trap that Failed (1/25/50)
736. The Ghost Raider (1/27/50)
737. Casper Mott's Adventure (1/30/50)
738. Circumstantial Evidence (2/1/50)

739. Blind Man's Bluff (2/3/50)
740. Jailbreak (2/6/50)
741. The Runaway Heir (2/8/50)
742. Flaming Valley (2/10/50)
743. The Haunted Mine (2/13/50)
744. The Black Cat (2/15/50)
745. Alias Al Gibson (2/17/50)
746. The Murdered Witness (2/20/50)
747. Trails End (2/22/50)
748. Uncle Joe's Luck (2/24/50)
749. Guardian for Jimmy (2/27/50)
750. When Thief Catches Thief (3/1/50)
751. The Innocent Criminal (3/3/50)
752. Wolf Creek (3/6/50)
753. Restitution (3/8/50)
754. The Lost Lady (3/10/50)
755. Hidden Evidence (3/13/50)
756. Secret Orders (3/15/50)
757. The Man Who Fled (3/17/50)
758. The Cascade Case (3/20/50)
759. The Fugitive Bride (3/22/50)
760. The Wolf Cub (3/24/50)
761. Canyon Cache (3/27/50)
762. Mystery of the Ridge (3/29/50)
763. Twenty Little Indians (3/31/50)
764. Unfinished Note (4/3/50)
765. The Two Bullets (4/5/50)
766. Showdown on Shotgun Creek (4/7/50)
767. Rusty Wins a Home (4/10/50)
768. Den of Thieves (4/12/50)
769. The Yukon Pirates (4/14/50)
770. A Slight Case of Poison (4/17/50)
771. The Gullible Grubstaker (4/19/50)
772. A Job for Jim (4/21/50)
773. The Three Black Dots (4/24/50)
774. The Blackwood Treasure (4/26/50)
775. Blacky Does His Bit (4/28/50)
776. The Runaway Princess (5/1/50)
777. The Young One (5/3/50)
778. The Servants of the Queen (5/5/50)
779. The Sleeping Man (5/8/50)
780. Convict's Son (5/10/50)
781. Madge and the Mounties (5/12/50)
782. The Gold Convoy (5/15/50)
783. The Hangman's Noose (5/17/50)
784. Miaku's Vow (5/19/50)
785. Pursuit by Night (5/22/50)
786. Trouble with Running Dog (5/24/50)
787. Wand?? Diamond (5/26/50)
788. Notorious Chet Craig (5/29/50)
789. The Dead Man's Trail (5/31/50)
790. The Angel of Death (6/2/50)

791. Six Gun Clue (6/5/50)
792. Jose's Return (6/7/50)
793. Revenge From Beyond (6/9/50)
794. The Bag of Gold (6/28/50)
795. Race of the River Boats (7/7/50)
796. The Diamond Solitaire (7/10/56)
797. Stolen Gold (7/19/50)
798. The Spread Eagle Raid (7/26/50)
799. The Beaverton Legacy (8/2/50)
800. A Change of Mind (8/9/50)
801. Ten Thousand Counterfeit (8/16/50)
802. The Branded Pelts (8/23/50)
803. Logan's Luck (8/30/50)
804. Cal Dorset's Hair (9/6/50)
805. The Gold Behind the Waterfall (9/11/50)
806. The Polar Quest (9/13/50)
807. Left to Die (9/15/50)
808. The Sack of Sand (9/18/50)
809. The Malamute Express (9/20/50)
810. The Torn Map (9/22/50)
811. Diagram of Danger (9/25/50)
812. The Red Raiders (9/27/50)
813. Dog Crazy (9/29/50)
814. The Malacca Cane (10/2/50)
815. The Vagabond (10/4/50)
816. The Criminal Collie (10/6/50)
817. The Blue Paper (10/9/50)
818. Harper's Castle (10/11/50)
819. A Dog Named Sparky (10/13/50)
820. Fugitive From Bald Rock (10/16/50)
821. The Masked Gunman (10/18/50)
822. Out of the Night (10/20/50)
823. Heart of a Killer (10/23/50)
824. Dead Man's Whistle (10/25/50)
825. A Call to Action (10/27/50)
826. Undercover (10/30/50)
827. Contention (11/1/50)
828. Whistling in the Dark (11/3/50)
829. A Friend in Need (11/6/50)
830. The Ghost Riders (11/8/50)
831. White Flash (11/10/50)
832. The Clue of the Silver Pup (11/13/50)
833. Passport to Death (11/15/50)
834. The Telltale Knife (11/17/50)
835. The Wrong Map (11/20/50)
836. The Rebel Yell (11/22/50)
837. Death Waits on the River (11/24/50)
838. The Man in the Canyon (11/27/50)
839. Gold Fever (11/29/50)
840. Spider Burke's Daughter (12/1/50)
841. Wild Dog (12/4/50)

842. The Indian Sign (12/6/50)
843. The Notorious Hawk Cooper (12/8/50)
844. Danger at Devil's Gorge (1/20/51)
845. Murder on Fox Run (1/27/51)
846. Escape by Night (1/28/51)
847. White Fox For Marie (2/3/51)
848. Storm the Pass (2/4/51)
849. The King of Keena Creek (2/10/51)
850. The Trail Robbers (2/11/51)
851. Wrong Trail (2/17/51)
852. Honest Young Man (2/18/51)
853. Blackmailer's Payoff (2/24/51)
854. Vanished Loot (2/25/51)
855. Job for Jim Lackey (3/3/51)
856. The Russian Rubies (3/4/51)
857. Secret of the Closed Room (3/10/51)
858. Doctor Redcoat (3/11/51)
859. The Third Strike (3/17/51)
860. Never Be Missed (3/18/51)
861. The Counterfeit Heiress (3/24/51)
862. Old Faithful (3/25/51)
863. Cabin 102 (3/31/51)
864. The Blue Scarf (4/1/51)
865. Trappers Trail (4/7/51)
866. Take It Easy (4/8/51)
867. The Blind Husky (4/14/51)
868. Team-Mates (4/15/51)
869. Rowdy's Choice (4/21/51)
870. Indian Dream (4/22/51)
871. Assist Axpress Agent (4/28/51)
872. Rookie's First Case (4/29/51)
873. Sentinel On the Ridge (5/5/51)
874. Fur Thieves (5/6/51)
875. Cabin Code (5/12/51)
876. The Sleeping Sentry (5/13/51)
877. Toy Pick and Shovel (5/19/51)
878. The Green Bottle (5/20/51)
879. On the Dalton Trail (5/26/51)
880. A Dog for Bobby (5/27/51)
881. Wilderness Post (6/2/51)
882. The Black Onyx (6/3/51)
883. Black and White Checked (6/9/51)
884. Number One Challenger (6/10/51)
885. Ghost of Louie Lachine (6/16/51)
886. Broken Promise (6/17/51)
887. Picture for Mickey (6/23/51)
888. Fiery Night (6/24/51)
889. The Curse of Moluk (6/30/51)
890. The Stuffed Shirt (7/1/51)
891. Stranded in Skagway (7/7/51)
892. Murder at the Flood (7/8/51)
893. Gold Rush Patrol (7/10/51)
894. A Boy Called Jack (7/12/51)
895. Thieves Progress (7/19/51)
896. Elephants and King (7/17/51)
897. Tom Barry's Return (7/19/51)
898. The Trail's End (7/22/51)
899. Landslide (7/24/51)
900. The Innocent Fugitives (7/26/51)
901. The Sunset Bell (7/29/51)
902. Chinese Box (7/31/51)
903. And Far Away (8/2/51)
904. The Widow's Son (8/5/51)
905. When Traveler's Meet (8/7/51)
906. The Man Who Feared Dogs (8/9/51)
907. Ambush in Bellary Flats (8/12/51)
908. Trail Sailor Joe (8/14/51)
909. Against Time (8/16/51)
910. The Red Parka (8/19/51)
911. The Champion (8/21/51)
912. The Scent of Death (8/23/51)
913. Bullets for Preston (8/26/51)
914. The Collies Return (8/28/51)
915. Red Coated Crook (8/30/51)
916. Boy Alone (9/2/51)
917. The Grudge (9/4/51)
918. Junior Partner (9/6/51)
919. Divided on Murder (9/9/51)
920. Gold Catch (9/11/51)
921. The Landlady (9/13/51)
922. The Killer Cree (9/16/51)
923. Three Men in Black (9/18/51)
924. Chance Meeting (9/20/51)
925. Trapper's Gold (9/23/51)
926. Shadow of a Doubt (9/25/51)
927. Uncle Ben (9/27/51)
928. Arctic Patrol (9/30/51)
929. King's Pal Streak (10/2/51)
930. Open and Shut (10/4/51)
931. Fire in the Forest (10/7/51)
932. Man in Hiding (10/9/51)
933. Double Indemnity (10/11/51)
934. Forgotten Grubstake (10/14/51)
935. The Caribou Stampede (10/16/51)
936. Golconda Claim (10/18/51)
937. The Mutiny's Survivor (10/21/51)
938. Snowslide (10/23/51)
939. Claim 22 (10/25/51)
940. Father of the Heir (10/28/51)
941. Reward for Shiloh (10/30/51)
942. Trail to Trouble (11/1/51)
943. The Diamond Solitaire (11/4/51)
944. Forbidden Ground (11/6/51)
945. Si Atkin's Gold (11/8/51)
946. The Forgetful Killer (11/11/51)

Charlie Wild, Private Detective

Charlie Wild was a tough New York private eye who got into at least one fight per episode. Although this show originated from New York, it worked simultaneously with television. Technically, this series was broadcast over radio in two series. The first was over NBC for the Wildroot Company, Inc., Sunday evenings from 6:30 to 7 pm, EST. On November 12, the series moved back an hour, broadcast from 5:30 to 6 pm, EST. George Petrie played the role of Charlie. William Rogers was the announcer. Peter Barry wrote the scripts. Lawrence White and Edwin Marshall produced and Carlo De Angelo directed, Stanley Niss took over directing on May 13. Music was supplied by C. Sherrill.

The second series began on January 7, 1951, broadcast over CBS, Sunday evenings from 6 to 6:30 pm, EST. Kevin O'Morrison took over as Charlie. On television, it was almost the same. Beginning a couple of weeks before the second season, on December 22, 1950, *Charlie Wild, Private Detective* premiered over television with O'Morrison in the lead. Reportedly, O'Morrison tired of doing the same role twice in one week (once on radio and once on television), so on March 18, John McQuade took over the role. Weeks later, in May, McQuade assumed the role on television. In July of 1951, the radio show was dropped, leaving the television series to continue for another year.

1. The Case of the Gunning for Joey (9/24/50)
2. The Case of the Custom-Built Triangle (10/1/50)
3. The Case of the Hungry O'Gar (10/8/50)
4. The Case of the Cautious Klopstock (10/15/50)
5. The Case of the Barleymore Massacre (10/22/50)
6. The Case of the Murderous Urge (10/29/50)
7. -----(11/5/50)
8. The Case of the Jump to Ralston (11/12/50)
9. The Case of the Loveless Chick (11/19/50)
10. The Case of the Abandoned Lulu (11/26/50)
11. The Case of the News from Jaspar (12/3/50)
12. The Case of the Killer Who Didn't (12/10/50)
13. The Case of the Doom at Retail (12/17/50)
14. The Case of the Very Mean Lisa (1/7/51)
15. The Case of the Bloody Rampage (1/14/51)
16. The Case of the Costly Info (1/21/51)
17. The Case of the Boomerang Guilt (1/28/51)
18. The Case of the Three Cornered Frame (2/4/51)
19. The Case of the Exclusive Gardenia (2/11/51)
20. -----(2/18/51)
21. The Case of the Sad-Eyed Clam (2/25/51)
22. -----(3/4/51)
23. The Case of the Long Count to Ten (3/11/51)
24. -----(3/18/51)
25. The Case of the Dear Departed Wife (3/25/51)
26. The Case of the Triple Cross (4/1/51)
27. The Case of the Counterfeit Corpse (4/8/51)
28. The Case of the Family Affair (4/15/51)
29. The Case of the Old Acquaintance (4/22/51)
30. The Case of the Redheaded Angel (4/29/51)

31. The Case of the Sour Sugar (5/6/51)
32. The Case of the Nappatuck Niche
    (5/13/51)
33. The Case of the House Guest
    (5/20/51)
34. The Case of the Half-Steps to Taps
    (5/27/51)
35. The Case of the Blues in the Morning
    (6/3/51)

36. The Case of the Galloping Mink
    (6/10/51)
37. The Case of the Clouded Title
    (6/17/51)
38. The Case of the Ten Gallon Hat
    (6/24/51)
39. The Case of the Tarnished Angel
    (7/1/51)

The Chase

It was once said that the best way to thrill an audience is by adding a chase scene. And that was the topic of this suspense series. Whether it was adventure, comedy, horror, mystery, crime or science-fiction, this program made good on its promise of drawing the protagonist into a web of lies and situations too complicated for him to understand. A chase followed. Created by Lawrence Klee of *Mr. Keen* fame. Fred Collins announced. Fred Weihe, Walter McGraw, Edward King, and Daniel Sutter were the directors. Broadcast over NBC, Sunday evenings from 6:30 to 7 pm, EST. Beginning July 3, 1952, this Thursday evening series was heard 8:30 to 9 pm, EST. On September 21, 1952, *The Chase* moved back to Sundays, 4 to 4:30 pm, EST. A few of the scripts used were previously performed on *The Clock* and *Inner Sanctum Mysteries*.

1. The Big Cat (4/27/52)
2. Harry Troll's Diamond (5/4/52)
3. Countess Treanna (5/11/52)
4. Elliott Preston Is Framed for Murder
   (5/18/52)
5. They Thought He Was Dead
   (5/25/52)
6. Sunken Gold (6/1/52)
7. Strictly for the Horses (6/8/52)
8. Spy (6/15/52)
9. Bald Artie Bender (6/22/52)
10. Stephan, Monica, and $1,000,000
    (6/29/52)
11. Doug Burton and a Mysterious Trav-
    eler (7/10/52)
12. Joey (7/17/52)
13. The Apprentice (7/24/52)
14. The Painting (8/7/52)
15. The Amusement Park (8/14/52)
16. The Promotion (8/21/52)
17. The Chinese Buddha (9/21/52)
18. Twenty Million Bum (9/28/52)
19. Flight From Istanbul (10/5/52)
20. The Cat's Meow (10/12/52)

21. Man Hunt (10/19/52)
22. Iron Curtain Express (10/26/52)
23. Long Distance (11/2/52)
24. Career Girl (11/9/52)
25. My Love Is a Ghost (11/16/52)
26. Blackout (11/23/52)
27. The Most Dangerous Game [based
    on the story by Richard Connell]
    (11/30/52)
28. Dangerous Journey (12/7/52)
29. The Murder (12/14/52)
30. The Sound of Murder (12/21/52)
31. No Contact (12/28/52)
32. The Fortune Hunter (1/4/53)
33. Professor Calvin and the Voice
    (1/11/53)
34. Killer at Large (1/18/53)
35. The Creeper [based on Joseph Rus-
    coll's story] (1/25/53)
36. The Little Man Who Wasn't There
    (2/1/53)
37. Worth More than Life Itself (2/8/53)
38. The Million Dollar Chase (2/15/53)
39. Jailbreak (2/22/53)

40. A Frame for Murder (3/1/53)
41. Special Delivery (3/8/53)
42. The Lady Is a Corpse (3/15/53)
43. Woman for Man (3/22/53)
44. Murderer's Row (3/29/53)
45. Bank Robbery, Kidnapping (4/5/53)
46. Kingdom Lost (4/19/53)
47. Leading Man Talent Search (4/26/53)

48. Circumstantial Evidence (5/3/53)
49. The Hold-Up (5/17/53)
50. Tiger Lily (5/24/53)
51. The Evil Puppet (5/31/53)
52. Million Dollar Hunt (6/7/53)
53. The Playboy (6/14/53)
54. The Monster (6/21/53)
55. Harry, the Talking Horse (6/28/53)

The Chicago Theater of the Air

The Chicago Theater grew out of a listener survey conducted by Chicago station WGN in 1940. What eventually resulted was probably one of the most popular radio programs offering condensed grand opera and dramatic operettas. On May 9, 1940, this series premiered over WGN, and by October, *The Chicago Theater of the Air* went national over the Don Lee Mutual network as a sustained Saturday offering.

Marion Claire starred in each broadcast for the first seven years. Claire left the program in 1947, reportedly because she wanted to retire from singing. Instead, Claire became the show's production supervisor. History lectures discussing the evening's performance were supplied by Col. Robert R. McCormick.

For the casts, Jack LaFrandre, the program director, chose the best dramatic radio talent available. Marvin Miller, Barbara Luddy, Betty Lou Gerson, Bret Morrison, Willard Waterman, Betty Winkler, Rita Ascot, and Les Tremayne were a few. Leading musical roles were performed by Thomas L. Thomas, Ruth Slater, Selma Kaye, George Tozzi, Graciela Rivera, Jane Lawrence, Ann Ayars, Dorothy Staiger, Thomas Hayward, Bruce Foote, Attilio Baggiore, Earl Willkie, Winifred Heidt, Morton Bowe, Andzia Kuzak and others. Singer Allan Jones guested on a few episodes. (Jones appeared with the Marx Brothers' "A Night at the Opera.")

The first twenty episodes were broadcast 10:05 to 11 pm, CST. Episodes 21 through 25 were broadcast 9:45 pm, CST. Episodes 26 through 28 were 9 to 10 pm, CST. Episodes 39 through 43 were 8:30 to 9:30 pm, CST. Episodes 44 through 130 were 9 to 10 pm, CST. From episode 141 to the end of the series, 10 to 11 pm, CST. The final two broadcasts, July 3 and September 11 of 1954, were special presentations aired, in an unsuccessful attempt to revive the series.

1. The Vagabond King (10/5/40; Conrad Thibault)
2. The Chocolate Soldier (10/12/40; James Melton)
3. Madame Butterfly (10/19/40; C. Kellerman)
4. Robin Hood (11/9/40; J. Carter)
5. The Desert Song (11/16/40; Richard Bonelli)

6. Eileen (11/23/40; James Melton)
7. Countess Maritza (11/30/40; Igor Gorin)
8. Sweethearts (12/7/40)
9. Rio Rita (12/14/40; Conrad Thibault)
10. Rose Marie (12/21/40; Robert Weede)
11. The New Moon (12/28/40; Conrad Thibault)

12. The Chocolate Soldier (1/4/41)
13. Sari (1/11/41; Igor Gorin)
14. Cyrano de Bergerac (1/18/41; Richard Bonelli and Conrad Thibault)
15. Blossom Time (1/25/41; Igor Gorin)
16. Naughty Marietta (2/1/41; Jan Pearce)
17. Carmen (2/8/41)
18. Countess Maritza (2/15/41; Igor Gorin)
19. My Maryland (2/22/41; James Melton)
20. I, Pagliacci (3/1/41; Igor Gorin and F. Jagel)
21. The Merry Widow (10/4/41; Allan Jones)
22. The New Moon (10/11/41; Thomas L. Thomas)
23. Sari (10/18/41; Igor Gorin)
24. Sweethearts (10/25/41; J. Carter)
25. Naughty Marietta (11/1/41; J. Carter)
26. The Fortune Teller (11/8/41; Igor Gorin)
27. The Desert Song (11/15/41; J. Brownlee)
28. Carmen (11/22/41; Jan Pearce)
29. The Mikado (11/29/41; Attilio Baggiore)
30. Rio Rita (12/6/41; Thomas L. Thomas)
31. I, Pagliacci (12/13/41; Igor Gorin)
32. Babes in Toyland (12/20/41; Attilio Baggiore)
33. Orchestral show (12/27/41)
34. Eileen (1/3/42; Jan Pearce)
35. H.M.S. Pinafore (1/10/42; Attilio Baggiore)
36. Faust (1/17/42; J. Brownlee and F. Jagel)
37. The New Moon (1/24/42; Thomas L. Thomas)
38. Countess Maritza (1/31/42; Thomas L. Thomas)
39. Blossom Time (2/7/42; Robert Weede)
40. Rose of Algiers (2/14/42; Jan Pearce)
41. America Marches On — A Salute to R.O.T.C. (2/21/42; Charles Kullman)
42. My Maryland (2/28/42; J. Brownlee and Walter Cassel)
43. America Loves a Melody (4/12/42)
44. The New Moon (10/3/42; Thomas L. Thomas)
45. The Chocolate Soldier (10/10/42)
46. Rio Rita (10/17/42; Thomas L. Thomas)
47. H.M.S. Pinafore (10/24/42; Attilio Baggiore)
48. Robin Hood (10/31/42; Felix Knight)
49. La Boheme (11/7/42; Charles Kullman)
50. The Fortune Teller (11/14/42; Thomas L. Thomas)
51. Mademoiselle Modiste (11/21/42; M. Berini and Jeanette MacDonald)
52. Bohemian Girl (11/28/42; Attilio Baggiore)
53. Naughty Marietta (12/5/42; M. Berini)
54. Carmen (12/12/42; M. Berini, Bruce Foote, and Virginia Haskins)
55. Babes in Toyland (12/19/42; Attilio Baggiore)
56. America Loves a Melody (12/26/42; Thomas L. Thomas)
57. The Merry Widow (1/2/43)
58. Yeoman of the Guard (1/9/43; M. Berini)
59. The Desert Song (1/16/43; Thomas L. Thomas)
60. Martha (1/23/43; E. Conley)
61. Sweethearts (1/30/43; Felix Knight)
62. The Vagabond King (2/6/43; Ruth Slater and Thomas L. Thomas)
63. Faust (2/13/43)
64. The Red Mill (2/20/43; Thomas L. Thomas)
65. Music in the Air (2/27/43; Thomas L. Thomas)
66. Madame Pompadour (3/6/43; M. Berini)
67. Eileen (3/13/43; M. Berini)
68. Cavalleria Rusticana (3/20/43; E. Conley)
69. Bittersweet (3/27/43)
70. Heritage of Hereafter (6/5/43; A. Raffaelli)
71. Paper Hearts (6/12/43; Nancy Carr and Thomas L. Thomas)
72. Beyond the Beyond (6/26/43)
73. A Century and 67 (7/3/43; Thomas L. Thomas)
74. Scheherazade (7/10/43)
75. Peter Gynt [aka The Great Pretender] (7/17/43)
76. A Midsummer Night's Dream (7/24/43)

77. New World [aka The Life of A. Dvorak] (7/31/43)
78. Prologue to Destiny (8/7/43; Attilio Baggiore)
79. About the Girl (9/11/43; Atillio Baggiore, Marion Claire, and Thomas L. Thomas)
80. Painted Memories (9/18/43; Attilio Baggiore and Marion Claire)
81. Optical Enchantment (9/25/43)
82. H.M.S. Pinafore (10/2/43; Marion Claire and John Dudley)
83. Roberta (10/9/43; Thomas L. Thomas)
84. Bittersweet (10/16/43; Donald Dame)
85. Mignon (10/23/43; J. Gerard and E. Leuning)
86. The Chocolate Soldier (10/30/43; Morton Bowe)
87. The Desert Song (11/6/43; Thomas L. Thomas)
88. Carmen (11/13/43; Attilio Baggiore)
89. Rose Marie (11/20/43; Attilio Baggiore)
90. Music in the Air (11/27/43; Thomas L. Thomas)
91. Special Christmas Seal Program (12/4/43)
92. The Student Prince (12/11/43; Bruce Foote and John B. McCormack)
93. Hansel and Gretel (12/18/43; Bruce Foote and Ruth Slater)
94. Christmas Music (12/25/43; Thomas L. Thomas)
95. Madame Pompadour (1/1/44; Grace Russell)
96. Puccini (1/8/44)
97. The Vagabond King (1/15/44; Robert Weede)
98. The Belle of New York (1/22/44)
99. Naughty Marietta (1/29/44; Morton Bowe and Ruth Slater)
100. The Firefly (2/5/44; Attilio Baggiore and Ruth Slater)
101. My Maryland (2/12/44; Bruce Foote and A. Raffaelli)
102. La Boheme (2/19/44; Richard Tucker)
103. Blossom Time (2/26/44; Igor Gorin)
104. Countess Maritza (3/4/44; Igor Gorin)
105. The Count of Luxemburg (3/11/44; Grace Russell)
106. Sweethearts (3/18/44; Grace Russell)
107. Faust (3/25/44; Bruce Foote and J. Laderonte)
108. The New Moon (4/1/44; Bruce Foote)
109. H.M.S. Pinafore (4/8/44; Attilio Baggiore)
110. The Merry Widow (4/15/44; Grace Russell)
111. The Tales of Hoffmann (4/22/44; Grace Russell)
112. Sari (4/29/44; S. Dickenson and A. Raffaelli)
113. Minstrel of the Masses (7/1/44; Attilio Baggiore and Ruth Slater)
114. A Midsummer Night's Dream (7/8/44; Attilio Baggiore and Virginia Haskins)
115. Peer Gynt (7/15/44; Bruce Foote, Virginia Haskins and Ruth Slater)
116. A Woman of Arles [aka L'Arlesienne] (7/22/44; Bruce Foote and Ruth Slater)
117. Prince of Pathos (7/29/44; Bruce Foote, Virginia Haskins, and Ruth Slater)
118. Court of the Moon (8/5/44; Bruce Foote, Virginia Haskins, and A. Raffaelli)
119. Hertertiana Festival (8/12/44; Attilio Baggiore, Bruce Foote, and Virginia Haskins)
120. Chicagoland Music Festival (8/19/44)
121. A Life in Operatasia (8/26/44; Bruce Foote and Virginia Haskins)
122. Rebel of Salzburg [aka The Life of Mozart] (9/2/44; Bruce Foote and Virginia Haskins)
123. Pioneer from Brooklyn [aka The Life of George Gershwin] (9/9/44; Reinhold Schmidt)
124. D-Day 1787 (9/16/44)
125. White Shadows (9/23/44; Bruce Foote and Virginia Haskins)
126. Chimes of San Sebastian (9/30/44; Bruce Foote and Virginia Haskins)
127. A Student at Oak Manor (10/7/44; Bruce Foote and Virginia Haskins)
128. Vanished Voices (10/14/44; Bruce Foote, Virginia Haskins, and Ruth Slater)
129. Legend of Deepwell Crossing (10/21/44; Bruce Foote, Virginia Haskins, and Ruth Slater)

130. Peter and the Pumpkin (10/28/44; Bruce Foote and Virginia Haskins)
131. The Sacred Trust of John Q. Public (11/4/44; Bruce Foote and Ruth Slater)
132. The Great Waltz (11/11/44; Morton Bowe)
133. The New Moon (11/18/44; Bruce Foote and Earl Willkie)
134. The Chocolate Soldier (11/25/44; Earl Wilkie)
135. Carmen (12/2/44; Bruce Foote and Richard Tucker)
136. A Waltz Dream (12/9/44; Grace Russell, Ruth Slater, and Earl Wilkie)
137. Sari (12/16/44; Igor Gorin, A. Raffaelli, and Earl Wilkie)
138. Hansel and Gretel (12/23/44; Bruce Foote and Ruth Slater)
139. The Belle of New York (12/30/44; Earl Wilkie)
140. Naughty Marietta (1/13/45; A. Raffaelli)
141. The Queen of Spades (1/20/45; M. Berini)
142. Rio Rita (1/27/45; Bruce Foote)
143. La Tosca (2/3/45; Bruce Foote and Richard Tucker)
144. Good News (2/10/45; Bruce Foote and B. Milliner)
145. The Desert Song (2/17/45; Bruce Foote, A. Raffaelli, and Earl Wilkie)
146. Gypsy Love (2/24/45; Bruce Foote and Grace Russell)
147. Mignon (3/3/45; Richard Tucker)
148. The Merry Widow (3/10/45; Grace Russell)
149. Eileen (3/17/45; Morton Bowe)
150. Faust (3/24/45; J. Laderonte)
151. Girl Crazy (3/31/45; Morton Bowe and B. Milliner)
152. Hit the Deck (4/7/45; Penny Perry and A. Raffaelli)
153. The Three Musketeers (4/21/45; Igor Gorin)
154. Mademoiselle Modiste (4/28/45; Bruce Foote and A. Raffaelli)
155. Maytime (5/5/45; Richard Tucker and Earl Wilkie)
156. Sweethearts (5/12/45)
157. The Vagabond King (5/19/45; Bruce Foote)
158. Bittersweet (5/26/45; A. Raffalelli)

159. Gershwin Music (6/16/45; Bruce Foote and Penny Perry)
160. Valley of the Shadow (7/28/45; Ruth Slater and Earl Wilkie)
161. Starlight Interlude (8/11/45; Bruce Foote and Penny Perry)
162. Chicagoland Music Festival (8/18/45; Gladys Swarthout and Lawrence Tibbet)
163. Prince of Pathos (9/1/45; Marion Claire, Bruce Foote, and Ruth Slater)
164. Debussy Fantasy (9/15/45; A. Raffaelli)
165. The Song of Norway (9/22/45; Bruce Foote)
166. Naughty Marietta (9/29/45; Morton Bowe)
167. Carmen (10/6/45; Richard Tucker)
168. La Boheme (10/13/45; Richard Tucker)
169. Music in the Air (10/20/45; Bruce Foote)
170. The Gypsy Princess (10/27/45; Richard Tucker and Earl Wilkie)
171. Bittersweet (11/3/45; Allan Jones)
172. La Tosca (11/10/45; Richard Tucker)
173. The Vagabond King (11/17/45; Bruce Foote)
174. Gypsy Love (11/24/45; Bruce Foote)
175. The Prince of Pilsen (12/1/45; A. Raffaelli)
176. The Three Musketeers (12/8/45; Bruce Foote)
177. Hansel and Gretel (12/15/45)
178. Babes in Toyland (12/22/45; A. Raffaelli and Penny Perry)
179. Girl Crazy (12/29/45; Skip Farrell and B. Milliner)
180. Sweethearts (1/5/46; Bruce Foote)
181. Lohengrin (1/12/46; Morton Bowe)
182. The Merry Widow (1/19/46; Thomas Hayward)
183. The Bartered Bride (1/26/46; Morton Bowe)
184. Rio Rita (2/2/46; Bruce Foote and Penny Perry)
185. Madame Butterfly (2/9/46; Richard Tucker)
186. -----(2/16/46; J. Herrick)
187. Othello (2/23/46; Bruce Foote and Richard Tucker)
188. The Mikado (3/2/46; A. Raffaelli)
189. Secret of Suzanne (3/9/46; J. Huehn)

190. Eileen (3/16/46; Morton Bowe)
191. Sari (3/30/46; Morton Bowe and J. Novotna)
192. The New Moon (4/6/46; Walter Cassel)
193. Cavalleria Rusticana (4/13/46; Richard Tucker)
194. H.M.S. Pinafore (4/20/46; Thomas Hayward)
195. Faust (4/27/46; Thomas Hayward)
196. The Fortune Teller (5/4/46; Thomas Hayward)
197. The Gondoliers (5/11/46; J. Tome and George Tozzi)
198. Mignon (5/18/46; Richard Tucker)
199. Mademoiselle Modiste (5/25/46; A. Raffaelli)
200. Hansel and Gretel (12/14/46; Ruth Slater)
201. Babes in Toyland (12/21/46; Andzia Kuzak and A. Raffaelli)
202. The Prince of Pilsen (12/28/46; J. Browne, L. Fehr, and A. Raffaelli)
203. The Merry Widow (1/4/47; Thomas Hayward)
204. Rigoletto (1/11/47)
205. Madame Pompadour (1/18/47; Morton Bowe)
206. Sweethearts (1/25/47; Morton Bowe and V. Parker)
207. Carmen (2/1/47; D. Beattle and Ruth Slater)
208. -----(2/8/47; D. Beattle and Earl Wilkie)
209. The Marriage of Figaro (2/15/47; D. Beattle, W. Kerner, and Andzia Kuzak)
210. The Gondoliers (3/1/47; J. Carter and S. Dickensen)
211. Naughty Marietta (3/8/47; Bruce Foote, Ruth Slater, and Richard Tucker)
212. Eileen (3/15/47; Richard Tucker)
213. Music in the Air (3/22/47; Bruce Foote, V. Parker, and Ruth Slater)
214. Iolanthe (3/29/47; John Barclay and Ruth Slater)
215. The Red Mill (4/5/47; Andzia Kuzak, Ruth Slater, and Earl Wilkie)
216. Sari (4/12/47; Bruce Foote and Raymond Paige)
217. The Mikado (4/19/47; J. Carter and Bruce Foote)

218. Cavalleria Rusticana (4/26/47; George Tozzi and Richard Tucker)
219. I, Pagliacci (5/3/47; Morton Bowe, Dorothy Staiger, and George Tozzi)
220. The Three Musketeers (5/10/47; Bruce Foote, V. Parker, and Earl Wilkie)
221. Faust (5/17/47; Bruce Foote)
222. Mademoiselle Modiste (5/24/47; J. Carter)
223. The Great Waltz (5/31/47; Morton Bowe)
224. Roberta (11/1/47; Bruce Foote and Jane Lawrence)
225. -----(11/8/47; Morton Bowe and Andzia Kuzak)
226. Rigoletto (11/15/47; E. Conley and Virginia Haskins)
227. The Merry Widow (11/22/47; Morton Bowe and Ruby Mercer)
228. The Firefly (11/29/47; J. Browne and R. Nielson)
229. Madame Butterfly (12/6/47; E. Conley, B. Lewis, and Ruth Slater)
230. Hansel and Gretel (12/13/47; Virginia Haskins and Ruth Slater)
231. Babes in Toyland (12/20/47; Andzia Kuzak and R. Neilson)
232. Martha (12/27/47; Virginia Haskins and N. Ventura)
233. The Student Prince (1/3/48; Glenn Burris and E. Clementi)
234. I, Pagliacci (1/10/48; V. Parker and Richard Tucker)
235. Countess Maritza (1/17/48; D. Bolger and Ruth Slater)
236. Naughty Marietta (1/24/48; Thomas Hayward and Andzia Kuzak)
237. The Marriage of Figaro (1/31/48; D. Beattle and Virginia Haskins)
238. Faust (2/7/48; R. Marshall and F. Yeand)
239. Sweethearts (2/14/48; Morton Bowe and B. Taylor)
240. La Traviata (2/21/48; Virginia Haskins and Richard Tucker)
241. Katinka (2/28/48; Bruce Foote and Andzia Kuzak)
242. Eileen (3/6/48; E. Conley and V. Parker)
243. The Red Mill (3/13/48; Bruce Foote and Virginia Haskins)
244. Sunny (3/20/48; Bruce Foote and Andzia Kuzak)

245. H.M.S. Pinafore (3/27/48; E. Clementi and Ricky Nelson)
246. Apple Blossoms (4/3/48; M. Stewart and Richard Tucker)
247. The Desert Song (4/10/48; Bruce Foote and Michael Stewart)
248. The Chimes of Normandy (4/17/48; Glenn Burris and Virginia Haskins)
249. Blossom Time (4/24/48; M. Delany and R. Marshall)
250. Cavalleria Rusticana (5/1/48; John Barclay, E. Clementi, and E. Reichart)
251. The Chocolate Soldier (5/15/48; Morton Bowe and Virginia Haskins)
252. The New Moon (5/22/48; Bruce Foote and Dorothy Sarnoff)
253. The Girl With the Yale Eyes (6/20/48)
254. The Vagabond King (10/9/48; Nancy Carr, Bruce Foote, Ruth Slater)
255. Il Trovatore (10/16/48; Selma Kaye, Bruce Foote, and Richard Tucker)
256. The Merry Widow (10/23/48; V. Gard and Richard Tucker)
257. Martha (10/30/48; E. Conley, D. Gramm, Virginia Haskins, and Ruth Slater)
258. The Magic Flute (11/6/48; Bruce Foote, D. Gramm, Doris Lloyd, and F. Yeand)
259. Naughty Marietta (11/13/48; Nancy Carr and Richard Tucker)
260. Manon (11/20/48; E. Conley, Virginia Haskins, and Ruth Slater)
261. The Pink Lady (11/27/48; Morton Bowe, Virginia Haskins, and Earl Wilkie)
262. Good News (12/4/48; Bruce Foote and N. King)
263. Hansel and Gretel (12/11/48; Bruce Foote, Virginia Haskins, and Ruth Slater)
264. La Boheme (12/18/48; Nancy Carr and Richard Tucker)
265. Lohengrin (12/25/48; R. Marshall and F. Yeand)
266. Die Fledermaus (1/1/49; Morton Bowe and Michael Stewart)
267. Faust (1/8/49; Nancy Carr and E. Conley)
268. H.M.S. Pinafore (1/15/49; Bruce Foote, A. Norman, and Ruth Slater)
269. Aida (1/22/49; Bruce Foote, R. Marshall, and Ruth Slater)
270. Sweethearts (1/29/49; Morton Bowe and Nancy Carr)
271. The Chocolate Soldier (2/5/49; Morton Bowe and Virginia Haskins)
272. When Johnny Comes Marching Home (2/12/49; Nancy Carr, Bruce Foote, and Earl Wilkie)
273. Sunny (2/19/49; Nancy Carr, Bruce Foote, and Earl Wilkie)
274. The Prince of Pilsen (2/26/49; J. Browne, Everett Clarke, and T. Mills)
275. Rigoletto (3/5/49; Virginia Haskins, Raymond Scott, and Richard Tucker)
276. Eileen (3/12/49; Nancy Carr, Bruce Foote, Virginia Haskins, Richard Tucker)
277. No, No Nanette (3/19/49; Bruce Foote and Virginia Haskins)
278. Rio Rita (4/2/49; Nancy Carr and Bruce Foote)
279. The Mikado (4/9/49; Bruce Foote, Virginia Haskins, and T. Mills)
280. Cavalleria Rusticana (4/16/49; Reinhold Schmidt, Michael Stewart, Richard Tucker)
281. The New Moon (4/23/49; Nancy Carr and Bruce Foote)
282. Madame Pompadour (4/30/49; Morton Bowe and Nancy Carr)
283. The White Eagle (5/7/49; Morton Bowe, Andzia Kuzak, and Earl Wilkie)
284. The Desert Song (5/14/49; S. Russell and Thomas L. Thomas)
285. The Gondoliers (5/21/49; J. Carter, Bruce Foote, and V. Parker)
286. I, Pagliacci (5/28/49; Nancy Carr and Richard Tucker)
287. Chicagoland Music Festival (8/20/49; Nancy Carr and Lauritz Melchior)
288. The Student Prince (10/1/49; Nancy Carr, Bruce Foote, and D. Poleri)
289. My Romance (10/8/49; Nancy Carr and Richard Tucker)
290. La Boheme (10/15/49; Nancy Carr and Richard Tucker)
291. The Mikado (10/22/49; John Barclay, N. Lozzi, and D. Poleri)

292. The Pink Lady (10/29/49; Virginia Haskins and D. Poleri)
293. The Chocolate Soldier (11/5/49; Virginia Haskins and D. Poleri)
294. Madame Butterfly (11/12/49; Nancy Carr and D. Poleri)
295. The Gondoliers (11/19/49; J. Carter, Bruce Foote, and Andzia Kuzak)
296. The Vagabond King (11/26/49; Nancy Carr, G. Lane, and Thomas L. Thomas)
297. Countess Maritza (12/3/49; Nancy Carr and Thomas L. Thomas)
298. Manon (12/10/49; Virginia Haskins and D. Poleri)
299. Hansel and Gretel (12/17/49; Bruce Foote, Virginia Haskins, and Ruth Slater)
300. Babes in Toyland (12/24/49; M. Hadden and D. Poleri)
301. The Merry Widow (12/31/49; Nancy Carr, D. Poleri, and Earl Wilkie)
302. Frederica (1/7/50; Nancy Carr and D. Poleri)
303. The Desert Song (1/14/50; Nancy Carr and Thomas L. Thomas)
304. Iolanthe (1/21/50; John Barclay and Ruth Slater)
305. Robin Hood (1/28/50; Virginia Haskins and D. Poleri)
306. The Pirates of Penzance (2/4/50; John Barclay and Virginia Haskins)
307. Music in the Air (2/11/50; Nancy Carr and Thomas L. Thomas)
308. The Fortune Teller (2/18/50; D. Gramm and Virginia Haskins)
309. The Cat and the Fiddle (2/25/50; Nancy Carr and Bruce Foote)
310. No, No Nannette (3/4/50; Virginia Haskins and Richard Tucker)
311. I, Pagliacci (3/11/50; Nancy Carr and Richard Tucker)
312. Naughty Marietta (3/18/50; Nancy Carr and Richard Tucker)
313. Yeoman of the Guard (3/25/50; John Barclay and Nancy Carr)
314. Rose Marie (4/1/50; Nancy Carr, Bruce Foote, and D. Poleri)
315. Blossom Time (4/8/50; Nancy Carr, D. Poleri, and Thomas L. Thomas)
316. The Bartered Bride (4/15/50; J. Carter, E.M. Holm, and Earl Wilkie)
317. Mademoiselle Modiste (4/22/50; Nancy Carr and J. Carter)
318. Bittersweet (4/29/50; Nancy Carr, Bruce Foote, and D. Poleri)
319. The Gypsy Princess (5/6/50; Nancy Carr and Richard Tucker)
320. La Traviata (5/13/50; Nancy Carr, Bruce Foote, and Richard Tucker)
321. Katinka (5/20/50; Nancy Carr and Bruce Foote)
322. Faust (5/27/50; Nancy Carr and D. Poleri)
323. The Life of Robert Burns (6/16/50; D. Gramm and Ruth Slater)
324. Thais (6/24/50; Nancy Carr and Bruce Foote)
325. Minstrel of the Masses (7/1/50)
326. Swan of Tuonela (7/15/50; D. Poleri)
327. Neapolitan Nights (7/22/50; D. Poleri)
328. Rebel of Salzburg (7/29/50; Nancy Carr and Bruce Foote)
329. In the Shadow of the Foote (8/5/50; Elaine Malbin)
330. A Midsummer Night's Dream (8/12/50; Ruth Slater and Rowene [Jane] Williams)
331. Chicagoland Music Festival (8/19/50; Alec Templeton)
332. The Saga of Casey Jones (9/1/50; Bruce Foote)
333. Peter Gynt [aka The Great Pretender] (10/7/50; D. Gramm and Carl Smith)
334. The Vagabond King (10/21/50; Nancy Carr and Thomas L. Thomas)
335. Madame Butterfly (10/28/50; Nancy Carr and D. Poleri)
336. The Only Girl (11/4/50; with L. Murphy and D. Poleri)
337. La Boheme (11/11/50; Nancy Carr, Bruce Foote, and D. Poleri)
338. The New Moon (11/18/50; Nancy Carr and Bruce Foote)
339. One Touch of Venus (11/25/50; Nancy Carr and Bruce Foote)
340. My Romance (12/2/50; Nancy Carr, Thomas L. Thomas, and Earl Wilkie)
341. Hit the Deck (12/9/50; L. Murphy and R. Nielson)
342. Hansel and Gretel (12/16/50; Bruce Foote, Virginia Haskins, and Raymond Scott)

343. Damascus Diary (12/23/50; Nancy Carr and Bruce Foote)
344. Carmen (12/30/50; Bruce Foote, L. Murphy, and Carl Smith)
345. Aida (1/6/51; Bruce Foote, Ruth Slater, and Richard Tucker)
346. The Mikado (1/13/51; L. Murphy, D. Poleri, and Ruth Slater)
347. The Desert Song (1/20/51; Nancy Carr and Thomas L. Thomas)
348. The Blue Paradise (1/27/51; Bruce Foote and Elaine Malbin)
349. Bittersweet (2/3/51; Nancy Carr, J. Carter, and Bruce Foote)
350. Faust (2/10/51; Nancy Carr, Bruce Foote, and D. Poleri)
351. Sweethearts (2/17/51; Nancy Carr, L. Kaller, and D. Poleri)
352. Paganini (2/24/51; Nancy Carr and D. Poleri)
353. The Red Mill (3/3/51; John Barclay, Bruce Foote, and Elaine Malbin)
354. The Student Prince (3/10/51; Bruce Foote, L. Murphy, and D. Poleri)
355. The Cat and the Fiddle (3/17/51; Nancy Carr and Bruce Foote)
356. Cavalleria Rusticana (3/24/51; Bruce Foote, M. Roberts, and Richard Tucker)
357. Frederica (3/31/51; Nancy Carr and D. Poleri)
358. I, Pagliacci (4/7/51; Nancy Carr and Richard Tucker)
359. Apple Blossoms (4/14/51; Nancy Carr and Thomas L. Thomas)
360. Rigoletto (4/21/51; Elaine Malbin and D. Poleri)
361. Aida (10/6/51; Nancy Carr and Richard Tucker)
362. The Desert Song (10/13/51; M. Roberts and Thomas L. Thomas)
363. Countess Maritza (10/20/51; Nancy Carr and Igor Gorin)
364. Anything Goes (10/27/51; Bruce Foote and L. Read)
365. The Merry Widow (11/3/51; M. Roberts and Earl Wilkie)
366. Die Fledermaus (11/10/51; M. Roberts and Earl Wilkie)
367. The Chocolate Soldier (11/17/51; Nancy Carr and Earl Wilkie)
368. Brigadoon (11/24/51; Nancy Carr and Bruce Foote)
369. No, No, Nanette (12/1/51; Nancy Carr and Bruce Foote)
370. A Connecticut Yankee (12/8/51; Bruce Foote and P. Mullens)
371. Sunny (12/15/51; John Browne and Bruce Foote)
372. Where the Saints Have Trod (12/22/51; A. Addison and Bruce Foote)
373. The Count of Luxemburg (12/29/51; Nancy Carr, D. Poleri, and Earl Wilkie)
374. My Romance (1/5/52; Nancy Carr and Thomas L. Thomas)
375. Paganini (1/12/52; Nancy Carr and D. Poleri)
376. Naughty Marietta (1/19/52; A. Bertocci and P. Clabassi)
377. Bittersweet (1/26/52; Nancy Carr, Patrick Knowles, and R. Morton)
378. Madame Pompadour (2/2/52; J. Carter and Virginia Haskins)
379. H.M.S. Pinafore (2/9/52; John Brown and Bruce Foote)
380. Rose Marie (2/16/52; Nancy Carr and Bruce Foote)
381. The Mikado (2/23/52; C. Nelson and E. Warner)
382. One Touch of Venus (3/1/52; Nancy Carr and Bruce Foote)
383. Roberta (3/8/52; Nancy Carr and Bruce Foote)
384. Eileen (3/15/52; W. Fredericks and C. Vannes)
385. The Pink Lady (3/22/52; J. Carter and H. George)
386. The New Moon (3/29/52; Nancy Carr and Bruce Foote)
387. Blossom Time (4/5/52; D. Aiken, N. Murphy, and J. Scott)
388. The Only Girl (4/12/52; D. Aiken, N. Murphy, and J. Scott)
389. Rigoletto (4/19/52; Adelaide Bishop and Richard Tucker)
390. The Student Prince (4/26/52; Bruce Foote and D. Poleri)
391. I, Pagliacci (5/3/52; Nancy Carr and Richard Tucker)
392. The Bartered Bride (5/10/52; A. Garrels and R. Herbert)
393. The Vagabond King (5/17/52; Nancy Carr and Thomas L. Thomas)
394. Tosca (10/4/52; Nancy Carr and D. Poleri)

395. The Song of Norway (10/11/52; Nancy Carr and Thomas L. Thomas)
396. The Merry Widow (10/18/52; Nancy Carr, Thomas Hayward, and Earl Wilkie)
397. Robin Hood (10/25/52; John Browne and C. Nelson)
398. The Cat and the Fiddle (11/1/52; Nancy Carr and Bruce Foote)
399. Countess Maritza (11/8/52; Nancy Carr and Igor Gorin)
400. The Vagabond King (11/15/52; Nancy Carr and Thomas L. Thomas)
401. Lakme (11/22/52; J. Carter, Bruce Foote, and M. Hill)
402. Carmen (11/29/52; J. Druary, G. Lane, and M. Powell)
403. The Desert Song (12/6/52; H. George and Thomas L. Thomas)
404. The Wizard of Oz (12/13/52; V. Stevens and Earl Wilkie)
405. Damascus Diary (12/20/52; Nancy Carr and Bruce Foote)
406. A Connecticut Yankee (12/27/52; John Browne and Bruce Foote)
407. Floradora (1/3/53; Bruce Foote and A. Jordan)
408. Faust (1/10/53; Nancy Carr and J. Crain)
409. Samson and Delilah (1/17/53; G. Lane and R. Marshall)
410. Eva (1/24/53; Nancy Carr and C. Curtis)
411. The Student Prince (1/31/53; Bruce Foote and L. Murphy)
412. My Maryland (2/7/53; Nancy Carr and Thomas L. Thomas)
413. Sweethearts (2/14/53; Ann Ayars and C. Curtis)
414. Rio Rita (2/21/53; Bruce Foote and V. Stevens)
415. Naughty Marietta (2/28/53; D. Cunningham, H. George, and T. McDuffy)
416. My Romance (3/7/53; Nancy Carr and Thomas L. Thomas)
417. One Touch of Venus (3/14/53; Nancy Carr and Bruce Foote)
418. Bittersweet (3/21/53; Nancy Carr and Bruce Foote)
419. Martha (3/28/53; Nancy Carr and D. Poleri)
420. Ghosts of Gethiemane (4/4/53; R. Marshall and M. Roberts)

421. Katinka (4/11/53; Nancy Carr and Bruce Foote)
422. H.M.S. Pinafore (4/18/53; John Browne, Bruce Foote, and Ruth Slater)
423. Eileen (4/25/53; S. Hamilton and D. Poleri)
424. Paganini (5/2/53; Nancy Carr and D. Poleri)
425. Gypsy Baron (10/10/53; M. Roberts, Ruth Slater, and Earl Wilkie)
426. Music in the Air (10/17/53; Nancy Carr and Thomas L. Thomas)
427. La Boheme (10/24/53; Nancy Carr, H. George, and D. Poleri)
428. Lakme (10/31/53; D. Cunningham, Bruce Foote, and M. Hill)
429. The Merry Widow (11/7/53; W. Boehme and Nancy Carr)
430. My Romance (11/14/53; Nancy Carr and Thomas L. Thomas)
431. Tosca (11/21/53; Nancy Carr and Bruce Foote)
432. Bloomer Girl (11/28/53; Bruce Foote and M. Powell)
433. Samson and Delilah (12/5/53; G. Lane and R. Marshall)
434. The Vagabond King (12/12/53; Nancy Carr, G. Lane, and Thomas L. Thomas)
435. Gems of Literature and Song (12/19/53; G. Kriese and Thomas L. Thomas)
436. The Wizard of Oz (12/26/53; V. Stevens)
437. The Pink Lady (1/2/54; W. Boehme and H. George)
438. Eva (1/9/54; W. Boehme and Nancy Carr)
439. The Desert Song (1/16/54; M. Roberts and Thomas L. Thomas)
440. Faust (1/23/54; Nancy Carr, D. Cunningham, and Bruce Foote)
441. Madame Butterfly (1/30/54; Nancy Carr and D. Cunningham)
442. The Circus Princess (2/6/54; M. Roberts and Earl Wilkie)
443. My Maryland (2/13/54; Nancy Carr and Bruce Foote)
444. H.M.S. Pinafore (2/20/54; John Browne and R. Nielsen)
445. Paganini (2/27/54; J. Crain and M. Roberts)

446. Rose Marie (3/6/54; Nancy Carr and H. Noel)
447. Finian's Rainbow (3/13/54; Nancy Carr and Bruce Foote)
448. Final Chapter in the Life of Benedict Arnold (7/3/54; Maurice Copeland)
449. None But the Lonely Heart (9/11/54)

Citizens of the World

Originally, this series was intended to have a lengthened broadcast run, but was cut short after two broadcasts. Documentary biographies on various figures of present-day events. Broadcast over NBC from 2:30 to 3 pm, EST.

1. The Story of Ralph Bunche (2/24/51)
2. Major General William Dean (3/3/51)

Cloak and Dagger

This NBC anthology series was based on the files of the O.S.S. Agents during WWII, who took dangerous missions behind enemy lines, knowing they may never return alive. Raymond Edward Johnson starred as the Hungarian Giant and Gilbert Mack was Impy the Midget. Sherman Marks directed. Broadcast on Sunday evenings, the program moved to Fridays from 8 to 8:30 pm, EST, beginning with episode fifteen, and the final two broadcasts were back to Sundays. Originated from New York. Broadcast Sunday afternoon from 4 to 4:30 pm, EST, announcers were Karl Weber and Robert Warren. John Gart supplied the music. Winifred Wolfe and Jack Gordon wrote the scripts. The cast included: Ross Martin, Bill Zuckert, Berry Kroeger, Larry Haines, Everett Slone, Leon Janney, Jan Miner, Karl Weber, Ralph Bell, Guy Repp, Martin Balsam, Lili Darvass, and Francis Robinson. Mel Ferrer guested on episode 21.

1. File 2218 (5/7/50; Joseph Julian)
2. The Trojan Horse (5/14/50)
3. The Brenner Pass Story (6/4/50)
4. The People in the Pass Story (6/11/50)
5. The Kachlin Story (6/18/50)
6. Direct Line to Bombers (6/25/50)
7. The Eyes of Buddha (7/2/50)
8. The Trap (7/9/50)
9. The Secret Box (7/23/50)
10. Swastika on the Windmill (7/30/50)
11. Recommendation From Rommell (8/6/50)
12. The Roof of the World (8/13/50)
13. Norwegian Incident (8/20/50)
14. The Black Radio (8/27/50)
15. War of Words (9/1/50)
16. Over Ground Railroad (9/8/50)
17. Seeds of Doubt (9/15/50)
18. Operation Sellout (9/22/50)
19. The Last Mission (9/29/50)
20. Delay on Route (10/6/50)
21. Wine of Freedom (10/15/50)
22. Windfall (10/22/50)

The Clock

This mystery/suspense series was broadcast over ABC as a sustaining program. *The Clock* was originally produced in England, and after it picked up the interest of ABC officials, they decided to move the program to New York. Beginning with episode seventy, the productions orginated from Hollywood, where Cathy and Elliott Lewis were able to provide more suspenseful tales of mystery, using scripts previously performed on *Suspense* and *The Whistler*. Gene Kirby was the announcer. Lawrence Klee wrote the scripts early in the run. Clark Andrews and William Spier beginning with episode #72 directed. Bernard Green supplied the music. The narrator was described as "Father Time." Ed Rosenberg and Larry White produced.

Episodes one through nine were broadcast Sunday evenings from 8:30 to 9 pm, EST; episodes ten through thirty-five, Sundays from 7:30 to 8 pm; episodes thirty-six through forty-three, Monday evenings from 9 to 9:30 pm; episodes forty-four through sixty-five, Thursdays from 8:30 to 9 pm; episodes sixty-six through seventy-seven, Thursday evenings from 9:30 to 10 pm; and episode seventy-eight to the end of the series, Sunday from 7:30 to 8 pm.

1. Wilbur (11/3/46)
2. The Actor (11/10/46; Wendy Clayfair and John Mellion)
3. All the Money in the World (11/17/46)
4. The Story of Mr. Littlefield (11/24/46)
5. One-Eyed Cat (12/1/46)
6. Jungle Dreams (12/8/46)
7. Aunt Emmy (12/15/46)
8. The Hunter and the Hunted (12/22/46)
9. A Helping Hand [aka Chance and Coincidence] (12/29/46)
10. Reference Please (1/5/47)
11. Lively Ghost (1/12/47)
12. The Vanished Wife [aka The Other Woman] (1/19/47)
13. Spangler's Attic (1/26/47)
14. The Bank Vault (2/2/47)
15. The Hitch-hiker (2/9/47)
16. Dr. Carter's Experiment (2/23/47)
17. The Man Who Lived Once Before (3/2/47; James Muntz and Alice Rhinehart)
18. The Good Valet (3/9/47)
19. Island of Women (3/16/47)
20. Petty Cousin Amy (3/23/47)
21. The Past or the Present (3/30/47)
22. The Man With the Strange Trunk (4/6/47)
23. Star-Crossed Lovers (4/13/47)
24. Hollywood Heartache (4/20/47)
25. The Criminal Mind [aka The Perfect Crime] (4/27/47)
26. Guilty as Always (5/4/47)
27. Only Death Is Timeless (5/11/47)
28. Uncle Amos (5/18/47)
29. Angel with Two Faces (5/25/47; Wendy Clayfair, Guy Dallman, Joselene Huntfield, John Mellion, and Al Thomas)
30. -----(6/1/47)
31. Coming Events (6/8/47)
32. Island Paradise (6/15/47)
33. The Man Who Couldn't Lose (6/22/47)
34. Behind the Mask (6/29/47)
35. The Hypnotist (7/6/47)
36. The Manicurist (7/14/47; Fran Lafferty and Charles Webster)
37. Rendezvous With Death (7/21/47; Gus Fowler)
38. Flaming Frances (7/28/47; John Busell, Margaret Christianson, and Margo Lee)
39. The Criminal Mind (8/4/47)
40. The Dream House (8/11/47)
41. Mental Telepathy (8/18/47)
42. Professor Leonard Higgens (8/25/47)
43. Retribution in the Bull Ring (9/1/47)
44. The Sentimental Cop (9/4/47; Tom

Hughes, Brian James, Leon Peters,
and Jody Sterling)
45. Trouble at Key West (9/11/47)
46. Strike Back From the Grave, Ophelia
(9/18/47)
47. Retribution (9/25/47; Joe Di Santis
and Jean Ellen)
48. Jekyll and Hyde Gangster (10/2/47)
49. Lefty and Delilah (10/9/47)
50. The Mystery of Loring Square
(10/16/47)
51. The Leach (10/23/47)
52. Leon (10/30/47)
53. Consuelo (11/6/47)
54. Exclusive Story (11/13/47)
55. Lover Boy (11/20/47)
56. Aunt Emmy (11/27/47)
57. Daisy (12/4/47)
58. The Companion (12/11/47)
59. The Cruncher (12/18/47)
60. Past or Present (12/25/47)
61. The Girl With the Animal Charm
(1/1/48)
62. Roberta (1/8/48)

63. Monks (1/15/48)
64. Brenda (1/22/48)
65. Lemuel Springer (1/29/48)
66. Valerie Lathrop (2/5/48)
67. Electro (2/12/48)
68. Martha (2/19/48)
69. Vivian Ellis (2/26/48)
70. Nicky (3/4/48)
71. Jonathan Wales (3/11/48)
72. The House in Cypress Canyon
(3/18/48)
73. Hazel and Charlie (3/25/48)
74. House of Beauty (4/1/48)
75. John Barbie and Son (4/8/48)
76. Can't We Be Friends? (4/15/48)
77. The Search for Isabel (4/22/48)
78. Bad Dreams (4/25/48; Elliott Lewis
and Jeanette Nolan)
79. Bank Holiday (5/2/48; Cathy Lewis
and Elliott Lewis)
80. Liz (5/9/48; Joseph Kearns and
Lurene Tuttle)
81. While Best Remembered (5/16/48)
82. My Wife Geraldine (5/23/48)

Columbia Presents Corwin

Norman Corwin established himself as a CBS staff writer by writing numerous radio plays of charm and wit for previous shows such as *The Columbia Workshop* and *Americans at Work*. This series featured productions written and directed by Corwin, ranging from humor to war propaganda. Premiering in 1944, *Columbia Presents Corwin* ran a total of twenty-two broadcasts. As a summer replacement for *Inner Sanctum Mysteries*, the Corwin program returned for an eight-week presentation in 1945. The entire 1944 series originated from New York except for episodes fourteen through eighteen, which originated from Hollywood. The entire 1945 series originated from Hollywood.

"The Lonesome Train" described the long, dark journey of the great Iron Horse that carried the body of the late Abraham Lincoln. "Movie Primer," told in music and verse, made fun of the film industry. The life of Carl Sandburg was dramatized in one broadcast, as was Walt Whitman's. "The Moat Farm Murder" presented a one man tour de force performance with Charles Laughton in the lead.

Musicians for the program varied from episode to episode and included Bernard Herrmann, Lud Gluskin, Lyn Murray, Jeff Alexander, Josh White, Carmen Dragon, Langston Hughes, Mary Lou Williams, Fred Steiner, Betty Comden and Adolph Green. Episode three was not scripted by Corwin, but by Millard

Lampell and Earl Robinson. Corwin himself played a small role in episode four. Episodes ten through twelve constituted a three-part dramatic presentation of "Unusual Cities." Episode seven was entitled "Untitled," which received so many queries from listeners that the drama was repeated a few weeks later. After the closing credits of the July 17, 1945, broadcast, Groucho Marx ad-libbed a line, causing Keenan Wynn to start laughing so hard over the mike that he couldn't continue. For the final broadcast of the series, violinist David Frisina helped out with the music with Dragon and Gluskin.

The broadcast "Fourteen August" featured a moving and dramatic antiwar reading by Orson Welles. Five days later, on August 19, an expanded broadcast of this beautiful hymn of praise and victory was broadcast, featuring Orson Welles and Olivia de Havilland.

1. Movie Primer (3/7/44; Ralph Bell, Ted de Corsia, Peter Donald, Alex Englander, Frank Gallop, Yung Ying Hsu, Donna Keath, Tony Marvin, Minerva Pious, Everett Sloane, and Hester Sondergaard)

2. The Long Name None Could Spell (3/14/44; Carl Frank, Martin Gabel, Michael Ingram, Joseph Julian, Kermit Murdock, William L. Shirer, and Giuliana Taberna)

3. The Lonesome Train (3/21/44; Burl Ives, Raymond Massey, and Earl Wrightson)

4. Savage Encounter (3/28/44; Joan Alexander, Carl Frank, and Arnold Moss)

5. The Odyssey of Runyon Jones (4/4/44; Michael Artist, Roy Fant, Hester Sondergaard, Arthur Vinton)

6. You Can Dream, Inc. (4/11/44; Ralph Bell, Lon Clark, Ruth Gilbert, John Griggs, Joseph Julian, Harry Marble, Kermit Murdock, Minerva Pious, Samuel Raskyn, Eleanor Sherman, Robert Trout)

7. Untitled (4/18/44; Charme Allen, Allen Drake, Michael Ingram, Joseph Julian, Donna Keith, Paul Mann, Fredric March, Hester Sondergaard)

8. Dorie Got a Medal (4/25/44; Jim Bacus, Laura Duncan, the Golden Gate Quartet, Earl Hyman, Canada Lee, Rosetta Lenoir, Ken Renard, Josh White, and Mary Lou Williams)

9. The Cliché Expert (5/2/44; Jackson Beck, Ralph Bell, Allen Drake, Robert Dryden, Adolph Green, John McGovern, Kermit Murdock, Robert Trout, and Roland Young)

10. Cromer (5/9/44; Roland Bottomley, Jay Malcolm Dunn, Burford Hampden, Nora Howard, Nicholas Joy, Joseph Julian, Frank Lovejoy, John Moore, Kermit Murdock, Minerva Pious, and Bertram Tanswell)

11. New York: A Tapestry for Radio (5/16/44; Walter Burke, Ed Cullen, Tana de Gamez, Martin Gable, Richard Huey, Sid Kassell, Donna Keith, Paul Mann, Minerva Pious, Sam Raskyn, and Hester Sondergaard)

12. Tel Aviv (5/23/44; Joan Alexander, Olive Deering, Margaret Foster, Maurice Franklin, Robert Harris, Mordecai Kossover, Paul Mann, Myron McCormick, and Martin Wolfson)

13. Untitled (5/30/44; Charme Allen, Allen Drake, Michael Ingram, Joseph Julian, Donna Keith, Paul Mann, Fredric March, Hester Sondergaard)

14. Carl Sandburg (6/6/44; Harry Bartel, Bob Bruce, Hans Conried, Charles Laughton, Joan Lorring, Mercedes McCambridge, Franklin Parker, Dick Ryan, Lurene Tuttle, and Will Wright)

15. Wolfiana (6/13/44; Hans Conried, Joseph Forte, Charles Laughton,

Peter Leeds, Elliott Lewis, Franklin Parker, Alfred Ryder, and Janet Scott)

16. Walt Whitman (6/20/44; John Dehner, Charles Laughton, Wally Maher, and Peggy Miller)

17. Home for the Forth (7/4/44; Dane Clark, Byron Kane, Betsy Kelly, Joan Lorring, Wally Maher, Paul McVey, and Regina Wallace)

18. The Moat Farm Murder (7/18/44; Elsa Lanchester, Charles Laughton, and Raymond Lawrence)

19. El Capitan and the Corporal (7/25/44; Bob Dryden, Burl Ives, Joseph Julian, Katherine Locke, Paul Mann, Kermit Murdock, Minerva Pious, Sam Raskyn, and Cecil Roy)

20. A Pitch to Reluctant Buyers (8/1/44; Martin Gabel)

21. A Very Fine Type Girl (8/8/44; Kathleen Carnes, Robert Dryden, Larry Haines, Joseph Julian, Paul Mann, Kermit Murdock, Minerva Pious, Eleanor Sherman, and Hester Sondergaard)

22. There Will Be Time Later (8/15/44; Shannon Day, Robert Dryden, House Jameson, and Paul Mann)

23. Unity Fair (7/3/45; Alfred Drake, Harry Lang, Groucho Marx, June Richmond, Bill Shaw, William Spier, Elmore Vincent, Joe Worthy, and Keenan Wynn)

24. Daybreak (7/10/45; Ronald Colman and Corrinha Murra)

25. The Undecided Molecule (7/17/45; Robert Benchley, Elliott Lewis, Norman Lloyd, Groucho Marx, Vincent Price, Sylvia Sidney, and Keenan Wynn)

26. New York: A Tapestry for Radio (7/24/45; Oliver Deering, Eddie Harburg, Gerald Keane, Merton Koplin, Eddie Marr, Maxine Marx, Paul McVey, Orson Welles, and Joe Worthy)

27. A Walk with Nick (7/31/45; John Hodiak, Elliott Lewis, and Joan Lorring)

28. Savage Encounter (8/7/45; Glenn Ford)

29. Fourteen August (8/14/45; Orson Welles)

30. L'Affaire Gumpert (8/21/45; Emil Corwin, Elsa Lanchester, Charles Laughton, and David Persina)

The Columbia Workshop

The Columbia Workshop was an experimental series devoted to the development of new techniques and personalities in radio presentations, with the premise that the idea — not the story — came first. Some episodes were awful, while others received critical acclaim. Under the direction of numerous CBS staff writers and actors, including Norman Corwin, Bernard Herrmann, Irving Reis, Orson Welles, William N. Robson, and Maw Wylie. *The Columbia Workshop* premiered as a low-budget radio series was granted a bigger budget and gained fame shortly after the broadcast of April 11, 1937. Afterwards, top writers, from Dorothy Parker to Lord Dunsany, began contributing to the series.

The broadcasts of "Alice in Wonderland" and "Alice Through the Looking Glass" were performed with music instead of sound effects. "The Constitution of the United States" featured a strict reading, to music, of the Constitution, with no frills added. The broadcast of November 24, 1938, was a musical presentation of "Beauty and the Beast," in opera form, written by Vittorio Giannini's Radio Opera. The September 1939 presentation of "The Fall of the City" featured five-hundred UCLA students at the L.A. Colosseum. The April 4, 1937, broadcast was scripted by students of radio writing at New York University. The studio orchestra used bells instead of conventional instruments for the broadcast of April 9, 1938. "Ecce Homo," broadcast on May 21, 1938, was the first — possibly the only — radio documentary by Pare Lorentz, the famous documentary filmmaker. Edwin Granberry's controversial "A Trip to Czardis" was broadcast on July 27, 1939.

Episode nineteen honored the 100th anniversary of the patent office. Episode twenty-four, based loosely on *Gulliver's Travels,* starred Eustace Wyatt, who also wrote the script. Episode eighty-nine was produced by the head of the BBC's drama department. Episode 158 was based on the Ellery Queen mystery "The Case of the Mysterious Leap Year." Vittorio Giannini's Radio Opera performed "Blennerhassett" in October of 1939. "My Heart Is in the Highlands" was broadcast on January 11, 1940. It was originally scheduled for the week before, but at the last minute was pushed ahead a week. "Gator Boy," broadcast in November of 1941, was an observance of Freedom Day. A few weeks later, "Citizen for Tomorrow" was dramatized in celebration of the 150th anniversary of the Bill of Rights.

Premiered on Saturday evenings from 8 to 8:30 pm, EST, until February 28, 1937, when the series moved ahead to Sundays from 7 to 8 pm. All of the broadcasts of December 1937 were broadcast on Thursday at 10:30 pm. On January 8, 1938, the series moved back to Saturdays, beginning at 7 pm and occasionally 7:30 pm. On September 15, 1938, the program moved back to Thursday evenings at 10 to 10:30 pm. On January 9, 1939, the series broadcasted on Mondays at 10:30 pm. July 6, 1939, moved to Thursdays, and May 5, 1940, to Sundays at 10:30 pm. Beginning in May of 1941, Norman Corwin took over the writing assignments, and the program went under a new title, *Twenty-Six by Corwin.* On November 16, 1941, the program changed back to its original title of *The Columbia Workshop,* broadcast on Sunday evenings again. On June 12, 1942, *Columbia* was broadcast on Friday at 10:30 pm, and beginning July 13, 1942, Monday at the same time. The broadcast of November 8, 1942, was on Sunday, after which *Columbia* underwent another title change to *Columbia Presents Corwin.* Months later CBS went back once again to *The Columbia Workshop,* beginning February of 1946 at Saturday afternoons at 2:30 pm; Corwin directed, but did not write. On April 21, 1946, the program went back to Sunday at 4 pm. The final run began September 21, 1946, on Saturday evenings beginning at 6:15 pm; the series had another title change, *Once Upon a Tune,* which ended the series.

The broadcast of May 23, 1937, featured a news bulletin of the death of John D. Rockefeller. The broadcast of September 12, 1937, was actually a short-wave broadcast from the BBC. The broadcast of November 30, 1939, featured a promo for *The Pursuit of Happiness.* Two special ninety-minute broadcasts were presented by "The Old Vic Theater Company of London, England" on June 2 and 9 of 1946, broadcast at a special time, 3–4:30 pm. At the beginning of the June 30, 1946, broadcast, an atom bomb program advisory was posted. A documentary on the life of Marconi was presented on December 9, 1937, the 36th anniversary of the first transatlantic radio message. The broadcast of March 7, 1940, was brought to the big screen under a different title during the mid–1940's. In 1956, CBS revived the series for one last time, under the title *The CBS Radio Workshop*.

1. Comedy of Danger / Finger of God (7/18/36; Arnold Moss, Orson Welles, and Eustace Wyatt)
2. Broadway Evening (7/25/36)
3. Cartwheel / Technical Radio Demonstration (8/1/36; Arlene Francis)
4. Experiment / Roadside Incident (8/8/36)
5. Case History [written by Milton Geiger] (8/15/36)
6. There Must Be Something Else / The March of the Molecules (8/22/36; Dr. Cauldwell of the old Federal Communications Commission)
7. 1986 A.D. (8/29/36)
8. San Quentin Prison Break [written and narrated by William N. Robson] (9/5/36)
9. A Voyage to Brobdingnag (9/12/36; Ray Collins)
10. Hamlet: Acts I and II (9/19/36; George Gaul, Edgerton Paul, Rosamon Pinchot, Alexander Scourby, Hiram Sherman, Sidney Smith, and Orson Welles)
11. The Dream Makers / Shadows that Walk in Night (9/26/36)
12. St. Louis Blues (10/3/36)
13. Sound Demonstration (10/10/36)
14. Dauber (10/17/36; David Ross)
15. Letting the Cat Out of the Bag (10/24/36)
16. Music for Radio : Vocabulary of Music (11/7/36; Deems Taylor)
17. Hamlet: Act III (11/14/36; Joseph Cotten, Laura Hale, Miss Frank Hall, Whitford Kane, Shirley Oliver, Santos Ortega, Edgerton Paul, Hiram Sherman, Sidney Smith, and Orson Welles)
18. Electrical Demonstration / Two Hundred Were Chosen (11/21/36)
19. Patent System (11/28/36; Richard Collins)
20. Rhythm of the Jute Hill [written by William N. Robson] (12/12/36)
21. The Gods of the Mountain [based on the story by Lord Dunsany] (12/19/36)
22. The Happy Prince [based on the story by Oscar Wilde] (12/26/36)
23. Public Domain: Characters of Fiction Freed From the Copyright Lane (1/2/37)
24. The Control Engineer / A Voyage to Lilliput (1/9/37; Clyde Barrie and Eustace Wyatt)
25. An Incident of the Cosmos / Control Engineering [written by Paul X. Anderson] (1/16/37)
26. The Signalman [based on the story by Charles Dickens] (1/23/37)
27. The Evolution of the Negro Spiritual [written by Leopold Proser] (1/30/37)
28. The Rime of the Ancient Mariner [based on the poem by Samuel T. Coleridge] (2/6/37)
29. The Human Ear [aka Pitch Perception] [Conducted by Dr. John Steinberg] (2/13/37; Mark Warnow and Dr. Steinberg of the Bell Telephone Labs)
30. Macbeth (2/28/37; Orson Welles)
31. Split Seconds [written by Irving Reis] (3/14/37; Carlton Young)
32. Danse Macabre [written by Helen Bergway and George Zachary] (3/21/37)
33. The Eve of St. Agnes (3/28/37; Arlene Francis and David Ross)
34. Big Ben / The Crisis (4/4/37)
35. The Fall of the City [written by Archibald MacLeish] (4/11/37; Burgess Meredith and Orson Welles)
36. R. U. R. (4/18/37)

37. St. Louis Blues (4/25/37; Kenny Delmar)
38. Drums of Conscience (5/2/37)
39. Supply and Demand [written by Irving Reis] (5/9/37)
40. Paul Revere [written by Steven Vincent Benet] (5/16/37; Parker Fennelly)
41. Night at the Inn [based on the stage play by Lord Dunsany] (5/23/37)
42. Discovery (5/30/37)
43. Downbeat of Murder (6/6/37)
44. The Young King [based on the story by Oscar Wilde] (6/13/37)
45. Red Head Baker (6/20/37)
46. The Babouk (6/27/37; Ken Roberts)
47. Mr. Sycamore (7/4/37)
48. The Tell-Tale Heart [based on the short story by Edgar Allan Poe] (7/11/37)
49. Fifty Grand [based on the story by Ernest Hemingway] (7/18/37; Edmund MacDonald)
50. A Matter of Life and Death [based on the story by Leopold Atlas] (7/25/37)
51. Daniel Webster and the Sea Serpent [written by Steven Vincent Benet] (8/1/37; Gene Morgan)
52. An Incident of the Cosmos / The Last Citation (8/8/37)
53. Escape [part one] (8/15/37; Orson Welles)
54. Escape [part two] (8/22/37; Orson Welles)
55. The Half-Pint Flask (8/29/37)
56. S.S. San Pedro (9/5/37)
57. Death of a Queen (9/12/37; Edward R. Murrow and Leanne Quartermane)
58. Riders to the Sea (9/19/37)
59. Alice in Wonderland [part one] (9/26/37; Helen Claire and Ken Roberts)
60. Alice in Wonderland [part two] (10/3/37; Helen Claire and Ken Roberts)
61. Meridian 7-1212 (10/10/37)
62. The Killers / Illusion [based on the stories by Ernest Hemingway] (10/17/37)
63. I've Got the Tune [Composed by Marc Blitztein] (10/24/37; Norman Lloyd)
64. Sweeps (10/31/37; George Coulouris, Kenny Delmar, House Jameson, and Santos Ortega)
65. The Horla [based on the short story by Guy De Maupassaunt] (11/7/37; Santos Ortega)
66. Supply and Demand / Dead End (11/14/37)
67. Georgia Transport (11/21/37)
68. The First Violin (11/28/37)
69. Marconi (12/9/37)
70. Metzengerstein [based on the story by Edgar Allan Poe] (12/16/37)
71. Alice's Adventures Through the Looking Glass [part one] (12/23/37; Helen Claire, House Jameson, Agnes Moorehead, and Lurene Tuttle)
72. Alice's Adventures Through the Looking Glass [part two] (12/30/37; Helen Claire, House Jameson, Agnes Moorehead, and Lurene Tuttle)
73. The Ghost of Benjamin Sweet [part one of a two-part broadcast: see 3/5/38] (1/8/38; Karl Swenson)
74. The House That Jack Didn't Build (1/15/38; David Ross)
75. Robert Owens (1/22/38; Bert Parks)
76. Madame Curie [written by Eve Curie] (1/29/38; House Jameson)
77. Andrea del Sarto (2/5/38)
78. Be Prepared [written by Richard Linkroum and Guy Della-Cioppa] (2/12/38)
79. The Well of Saints (2/19/38)
80. Night Patrol (2/26/38)
81. The Ghost of Benjamin Sweet [part two from 1/8/38] (3/5/38; Karl Swenson)
82. H'assan (3/12/38)
83. Wedding of the Meteors / An Industrial Fantasy (3/19/38)
84. J. Smith and Wife (3/26/48)
85. Seven Waves Away (4/2/38; Van Helfin)
86. The Broken Feather (4/9/38)
87. The Terrible Meek (4/16/38)
88. Never Come Monday (4/23/38; Sir Cedric Hardwicke)
89. Four Into Seven Won't Go (4/30/38)
90. The Fisherman and His Soul [based on the story by Oscar Wilde] (5/7/38)

91. Melodramas [music by Bernard Herrmann and David Ross, poet] (5/14/38; David Ross)
92. Ecce Homo [aka Behold, the Man, A Symphony of Reality and An Industrial Symphony] (5/21/38)
93. Bury the Dead (5/28/38; Frank Lovejoy)
94. Tranga Man, Fine Gah [aka Strong Man, Fine Girl] (6/4/38)
95. Surrealism in Sound and From Ohh to Aah [music by Satie and Hindemith] (6/11/38)
96. Reunion (6/18/38)
97. Never Come Monday (6/25/38)
98. The Constitution of the United States (7/2/38)
99. The Red Badge of Courage [based on the novel by Stephen Crane] (7/9/38; Chester Stratton)
100. National Headliners (7/16/38)
101. Murder in the Cathedral (7/23/38)
102. Tristram [based on a story by E.A. Robinson] (7/30/38; Richard Kollmar)
103. The Devil and Daniel Webster [based on the story by Stephen Vincent Benet] (8/6/38)
104. The Brushwood Boy (8/13/38)
105. Pelleas et Melisande (8/27/38)
106. Outward Bound [based on the stage play by Sutton Vane] (9/15/38)
107. He Doubles in Pipes [aka Joe Swing Returns] (9/22/38; Pee Wee Erwin and Van Heflin)
108. The Lighthouse Keeper (9/29/38; Ray Collins and Luis Van Rooten)
109. The Brushwood Boy [based on the story by Rudyard Kipling] (10/13/38)
110. The Happy Journey to Trenton and Camden [based on the story by Thorton Wilder] (10/20/38)
111. Air Raid [based on a story by Archibald MacLeish] (10/27/38; Aline McMahon and Orson Welles)
112. Poetic License [written by Norman Corwin] (11/3/38)
113. A Drink of Water [story by Wilbur D. Steele] (11/10/38)
114. Luck [story by Wilbur D. Steele] (11/17/38; Walter Greaza, Frank Readick, and Luis Van Rooten)
115. Beauty and the Beast (11/24/38; Agnes Moorehead and Robert Simon)
116. The Giant's Stair [story by Wilbur D. Steele] (12/1/38)
117. Man With a Gun / Fall of Jericho [aka Man With a Gun / Simeon] (12/8/38)
118. A Trip to Czardis (12/15/38; Ray Collins, Elsie Mae Gordon, Jack Grimes, and Ed Latimer)
119. Bread on the Waters [written by Arch Oboler] (12/22/38; Frank Lovejoy and Santos Ortega)
120. Crosstown Manhattan (12/29/38)
121. Orphan Ego (1/5/39)
122. Forgot in the Rains (1/9/39; Ronald Liss, Santos Ortega, Stefan Schnabel, and Ruth Yorke)
123. Mr. Whipple Is Worried (1/16/39)
124. Sooth [aka Prophesy] [story by Wilbur Daniel Steele] (1/23/39)
125. Now Playing: Tomorrow [written by Arthur Laurents] (1/30/39; Arlene Francis and Karl Swenson)
126. Do Not Open for 5,000 Years [written by William N. Robson] (2/6/39)
127. Nine Prisoners (2/20/39)
128. Jury Trial (2/27/39)
129. The Winged Victory (3/6/39; Zita Johann and Frank Lovejoy)
130. In the Train (3/13/39)
131. A Letter From Home [directed by Nila Mack] (3/20/39; Karl Swenson)
132. Pepito Inherits the Earth (3/27/39)
133. A Rendezvous with Kit Carson (4/3/39; Ray Collins and Dean Jagger)
134. They Fly Through the Air with the Greatest of Ease [written by Norman Corwin] (4/10/39; House Jameson)
135. This Is Radio: An Ear Essay on Broadcasting (4/17/39; Davidson Taylor)
136. Seems Radio Is Here to Stay [written by Norman Corwin] (4/24/39; House Jameson)
137. Wet Saturday [based on the short story by John Collier] (5/1/39; Agnes Moorehead)

138. Wild Man (5/8/39; Walter Bruce, Mitzi Gould, and Frank Readick)
139. The Law Beaters [based on a story by Richard Connell] (5/15/39; John Griggs and James van Dyke)
140. Private Throgg (5/29/39; Parker Fennelly)
141. Highboy (6/5/39)
142. A Handful of Dust [based on a story by Evelyn Waugh] (6/12/39; Lowell Gilmore and Alfred Shirley)
143. Journalism in Tennessee / Salesmanship [based on a story by Mark Twain] (6/19/39; Arnold Moss, Luis Van Rooten, Everett Sloane, and Karl Swenson)
144. The Half-Pint Flask [based on the story by DuBose Heyward] (7/6/39)
145. Never Come Monday (7/13/39)
146. John Brown's Body [based on the story by Stephen Vincent Benet] (7/20/39; Ray Collins and Luis Van Rooten)
147. A Trip to Czardis (7/27/39)
148. The Ghost of Benjamin Sweet (8/3/39)
149. Radio Play (8/10/39; Orth Bell, John Gibson, Mitzi Gould, Beatrice Kay, Hank Ladd, Joe Latham, William Morgan, and Everett Sloane)
150. A Drink of Water (8/17/39; Alice Frost and Adelaide Klein)
151. Meridian 7-1212 (8/24/39)
152. Apartment to Let [based on the story by Dorothy Parker] (8/31/39; Allen Campbell, Ed Gardner, and Marie Wilson)
153. So This Is Radio [written by Norman Corwin] (9/7/39)
154. The Use of Man [based on the story by Lord Dunsany] (9/14/39; Horace Braham, George Coulouris, and Ian Martin)
155. Now It's Summer (9/21/39; Karl Swenson)
156. The Fall of the City (9/28/39; Myron McCormick, Burgess Meredith, Dorothy Meredith, Ted Osborne, and Earle Ross)
157. The Great Microphone Mystery (10/5/39)
158. Wake Up and Die (10/12/39; Elsie Mae Gordon and Frank Lovejoy)

159. William Ireland's Confession [written by Arthur Miller] (10/19/39; Ian Martin)
160. Blennerhassett (10/26/39)
161. A Letter From Above (11/16/39)
162. A Circular Tour [based on the story by W.W. Jacobs] (11/23/39)
163. The Wonderful Day (11/30/39)
164. As You Like It [based on the play by William Shakespeare] (12/7/39; Margaret Webster)
165. The Story of Dogtown Common (12/14/39)
166. Mr. Cohen Takes a Walk (12/21/39; Frank Lovejoy)
167. Higher Than A Kite (12/28/39; Rosemary De Camp, Anne Elstner, Frank Lovejoy, Santos Ortega)
168. My Heart Is in the Highlands (1/11/40; Santos Ortega)
169. An Event From the Life of Fanny Kimball (1/18/40; Elsa Lanchester)
170. Heavenly Rest: A Hymn for Lost Americans (1/25/40; Dean Carlton and John Griggs)
171. Coals to Newcastle (2/1/40; Orth Bell, Peter Donald, Parker Fennelly, and Hester Sondergaard)
172. Double Exposure (2/15/40; Carlton Young)
173. An Autobiography of an Egotist (2/22/40; House Jameson)
174. The Great Microphone Mystery (2/29/40; Mel Allen, Howard Barlow, Ted Husing, Beatrice Kay, John Reed King, Nila Mack, Burgess Meredith, and Robert Trout)
175. My Client, Curly [adapted by Norman Corwin from a story by Lucille Fletcher] (3/7/40)
176. Outside This World / Dialogue With Music / Fraternity Meeting (3/14/40)
177. The Taming of the Shrew [based on the play by William Shakespeare] (3/21/40)
178. My Client, Curley (4/4/40)
179. Three Strikes, You're Out [aka Three Strokes You're Out ... The Romance for a Piano Tuner] (4/18/40; Ray Collins, Jack Grimes, Frank Lovejoy, Adrian Martin)

180. America was Promises (4/25/40; Archibald MacLeish)
181. The Honest Captain (5/5/40; Arthur Anderson, Cameron Andrews, Orth Bell, Vincent Donohue, Parker Fennelly, Gene Leonard, and Agnes Moorehead)
182. A Day in Manhattan (5/12/40; Arnold Moss, Santos Ortega, and Carlton Young)
183. Mexican Concert (5/19/40)
184. The Dark Valley (6/2/40; Dame May Whitty)
185. No Complications (6/9/40; Frances Chaney and Phillip Trent)
186. In April Once (6/23/40; Roger DeKoven, Maurice Tarplin, and Wallace Warner)
187. The Man With the One Track Mind [written by Lucille Fletcher] (6/30/40; Beatrice Kay and Mandel Kramer)
188. The Cock-eyed Wonder (7/7/40; William Bendix, Ed Gardner, Walter Kinsella and Richard Widmark)
189. Fish Story (7/14/40; Teddy Hart and Mark Smith)
190. The Canvas Kisser (7/21/40; Peter Donald, Ed Gardner, and Walter Kinsella)
191. Carmilla (7/28/40; Bill Johnstone and Jeanette Nolan)
192. Nightmare at Noon / Radio in the Rain (8/11/40; Martin Gabel and Dwight Weist)
193. The 500 Hats of Bartholomew Cubbins [based on the Dr. Seuss story, directed by Nila Mack] (8/18/40; Jack Grimes, Parker Fennelly, and Howard Lindsay)
194. I Followed the Seals (8/25/40; Ed Gardner, Beatrice Kay, and Frank Lovejoy)
195. Alf, the All-American Fly (9/1/40; Arthur Elmer, Mandel Kramer, Dan Seymour, and Dwight Weist)
196. The Major Goes Over the Hill [aka Big Boy Blue] (9/8/40; Helen Dumont, Ed Gardner, and Vicki Vola)
197. Mr. Charles (9/15/40; Anne Elstner, Roger DeKoven, and Luis Van Rooten)
198. Elsie Dinsmore's Childhood [aka Well Look Who's Here] (9/22/40)
199. The Pussy Cat and the Expert Plumber Who Was a Man [written by Arthur Miller] (9/29/40)
200. The Age of the Fish / They Also Serve (10/6/40; Martin Gabel, Walter Kinsella, Eddie Ryan, Jr.)
201. A Man's House (10/20/40)
202. Fulton Fish Market (10/27/40; Bob Edge)
203. The Constitution of the United States (11/3/40)
204. Bartok: Sonata for Two Pianos [aka Piano Recital] (11/10/40; Mr. and Mrs. Bela Bartok, and Harry Clark)
205. I Get the Blues From Revues (11/17/40; Joan Banks, Peter Donald, Len Doyle, Frank Lovejoy, and Al Rinker)
206. The Dynasts (11/24/40; Martin Gabel, House Jameson, and Alexander Kirkland)
207. And To Think That I Saw It on Mulberry Street [based on the story by Dr. Seuss; directed by Nila Mack] (12/1/40; Ted de Corsia, Jack Grimes, House Jameson, and Sybil Trent)
208. The Trojan Women (12/8/40; George Coulouris and Jessica Tandy)
209. Symptoms of Being 35 / In the Fog (12/15/40; George Coulouris, Ed Latimer, Everett Sloane, and Richard Widmark)
210. The Plot to Overthrow Christmas [written by Norman Corwin] (12/22/40; Ray Collins, Martin Gabel, Luis Van Rooten, Everett Sloane, and Karl Swenson)
211. Dr. Johnson in Scotland (12/29/40; Peter Donald, Ian Martin, Warren Sweeney, Eustace Wyatt)
212. Love in Thirty-Two Bars (1/5/41; Freda Gibson, John Griggs, Frank Lovejoy, Ted Osborne, and Charles Webster)
213. Cassidy and the Devil (1/12/41; Kenny Delmar, Ted de Corsia, Walter Kinsella, Arthur Vinton)
214. This Is From David (1/26/41; Agnes Moorehead and Larry Robinson)

215. Help Me Hannah (2/2/41; Helen Chase, Betty Garde, Ed Latimer, and Eustace Wyatt)
216. Dress Rehearsal [scripted by Charles Jackson and J. Mosman] (2/9/41)
217. A Crop of Beans (2/16/41; Ted de Corsia, Agnes Moorehead, and Linda Watkins)
218. Wings for an Eagle (2/23/41; Donald Cook)
219. Roadside (3/2/41; Wesley Addy, Burl Ives, and Joe Latham)
220. The Still Small Voice (3/9/41; Craig McDonnell and Arthur Vinton)
221. Cassidy and the Devil (3/16/41; Ted de Corsia, Kenny Delmar, Walter Kinsella, Arthur Vinton)
222. Out of the Air (3/23/41; Hiram Sherman)
223. The Creation / The Congo (3/30/41)
224. The Rocking Horse Winner [musical version of the D. H. Lawrence short story] (4/6/41)
225. The Glory Machine / The House / The Brooklyn Cantata (4/13/41; Frank Lovejoy and Tony Marvin)
226. The Reluctant Dragon [adapted and directed by Nila Mack] (4/20/41)
227. Jason Was a Man (4/27/41; Eddie Green)
228. Gator Boy (11/16/41; Ed Latimer, James McCallion, Larry Robinson, and Tom Tully)
229. Soundtrack of the Life of a Careful Man (11/23/41; Arnold Moss)
230. Double Ugly (11/30/41; Jim Backus, Jackson Beck, Isabel Jewell, and Eddie Mayeoff)
231. Citizen for Tomorrow (12/14/41)
232. Miracle in Manhattan (12/21/41; Ed Gardner)
233. Who Wants to Be Born These Days? (12/28/41; Dolores Gillen)
234. Fish on the Bathroom Floor (1/4/42; Carl Eastman)
235. Freedom of Speech (1/11/42; John Daly)
236. At the Sign of the Lark (1/18/42; Peg Allenby, John McGovern, and Walter Slezak)
237. The Man Without a Shadow (1/25/42; Ted Osborne, Walter Slezak, Maurice Tarplin, and

Lurene Tuttle (Tuttle plays all seven female parts)
238. Jenny, the Bus That Nobody Loved (2/1/42; Jim Backus, the Cab Calloway Orchestra, and Tom Tully)
239. Portrait of Jenny [based on the novel by Robert Nathan] (2/8/42; Santos Ortega and Betty Philson)
240. Opus for Lute and Lyre [directed by Nila Mack] (2/15/42; Arthur Allen, Orth Bell, Kingsley Cotton, and Parker Fennelly)
241. The Plot of Mr. Greenberg (2/22/42; Jim Backus, Ed Latimer, Eddie Mayeoff, Guy Repp, and Tom Tully)
242. When the Bough Breaks (3/1/42; Richard Widmark)
243. The Test (3/8/42)
244. A Child's History of Hot Music [story and script by Joseph Ruscoll] (3/15/42)
245. The Green Receipt (3/22/42; Jack Grimes and Craig McDonnell)
246. Solomon and Balkis (3/29/42; Eileen Farrell)
247. The Miracle of the Danube (4/5/42; Maxwell Anderson, Berry Kroeger, Ted Osborne, and Joseph Schildkraut)
248. He Should Have Stood in Elba (4/12/42; Jackson Beck, Joseph Julian, and Ed Latimer)
249. Play Ball (4/19/42; Eddie Mayehoff, Robert Readick, and Gertrude Warner)
250. Looking for Susie (5/3/42; Jim Backus, Eddie Mayehoff, and Joe Di Santis)
251. Flight to Arras (5/10/42; Vincent Price)
252. Good Morning Mr. Crumb [directed by Nila Mack] (5/17/42)
253. Midnight Blue (5/24/42; Jim Backus, Jackson Beck, and Myron McCormick)
254. The City That Wears a Slouch Hat [music by John Cage] (5/31/42; Les Tremayne)
255. The Little One (6/7/42; Chester Stratton)
256. Inside a Kid's Head [aka Richie, the Great and A Tour Through

the Brain of Richie Price] (6/12/42;
Skip Homeier)

257. It Couldn't Happen to a Nicer Kid
[written by Henry Denker]
(6/19/42; Arnold Moss and Ted
Osborne)

258. History Is on the March: Broadcast
from the Year, 1812 (6/26/42)

259. Tag #1-184-463 (7/3/42; June
Allyson and James Monks)

260. Let Me Tell You About My Operation (7/13/42)

261. Someone Else [written by Lucille
Fletcher] (7/20/42; Martin Gabel)

262. Reveille Pass (7/27/42; Anne
Sedgewick and Chester Stratton)

263. Laughter for the Leader (8/3/42;
Eric Dressler, Robert Dryden,
Craig McDonnell, and Ted
Osborne)

264. The Music of Mountains (8/10/42;
House Jameson)

265. All Out for Comedy (8/17/42; Eddie
Green, Pinky Lee, and the Delta
Rhythm Boys)

266. Hold 'Em Yale (8/24/42)

267. All Out for Comedy / The Columbia Sketchbook (8/31/42; Jim
Backus, Art Carney, Minerva Pious,
and Alan Reed)

268. Cafe Society Stars (9/7/42)

269. Portrait of Jenny (9/14/42; Ted de
Corsia and Santos Ortega)

270. My Kid Brother (9/21/42)

271. Florrie and the Country Green
(9/28/42; Parker Fennelly)

272. Rebirth of Barrow's Inlet / The Story
of an American Town (10/12/42;
Frank Gallop and the Delta
Rhythm Boys)

273. Remodeled Brownstone [written by
Lucille Fletcher] (10/19/42; Martin
Gabel)

274. Proclaim the Morning (11/8/42;
David Ross)

275. Homecoming (2/2/46; Bob Dryden
and Will Geer)

276. Anniversary (2/9/46; Art Carney and
Ted Osborne)

277. Just a Plain Blue Suit (2/16/46; Larry
Haines and Charlotte Holland)

278. Hard Luck Story (2/23/46; Ralph
Bell, Robert Dryden, John Gibson,
and Ted Osborne)

279. Slim (3/2/46; Bob Dryden and
Elliott Reid)

280. Thanks for the Memories (3/9/46;
Warren Bryant)

281. Four Quartetes [based on the story
by T.S. Eliot] (3/16/46)

282. Act of Faith [aka Last Delegate]
(3/23/46; Bob Dryden and Ruth
Nelson)

283. A Very Honorable Guy [based on
the story by Damon Runyon]
(3/30/46; Sandy Becker, Ed Begley, Joe Di Santis, Elspeth Eric,
and John Gibson)

284. The Last Speech (4/6/46; Eric
Dressler and Eileen Farrell)

285. Joe Peabody's Dream (4/13/46; Kermit Murdock and Minerva Pious)

286. The Play Room (4/21/46)

287. A Study in Bells / The House
(4/28/46; Eric Dressler and Bob
Dryden)

288. The Remarkable Gentleman from
Yorkshire [aka Sam Small's Better
Half] (5/5/46; Hal Young)

289. No Children at Play (5/12/46;
George Coulouris, Paul Henreid,
Alan Hubbard, Lee Price, and
Lurene Tuttle)

290. The Trial [based on the Franz Kafka
novel] (5/19/46; Karl Swenson and
Lurene Tuttle)

291. The Fisherman and the Jinni
(5/26/46; Joan Alexander)

292. Richard III (6/2/46; Laurence
Olivier and Ralph Richardson)

293. Peer Gynt (6/9/46; Laurence Olivier
and Ralph Richardson)

294. Sometime Every Summertime [writ-
ten and directed by Fletcher
Markle] (6/16/46; Bob Dryden,
Alan Hewitt, Patricia Jowdry, Paul
Mann, Marceila Markham, Larry
Robinson, Martin Wolfson)

295. How Radar Saved Democracy
(6/23/46; Berry Kroeger and Martin Wolfson)

296. This Is the Singing Country (1776-
1864) (6/30/46; Berry Kroeger and
Pete Seeger)

297. The Day That Baseball Died
[arranged by Stan Lomax] (7/7/46)

298. Three's Company [written by
Fletcher Markle] (7/14/46)

299. Pied Piper of Hamelin (7/21/46; Frank Lovejoy, Donald Ogden, and Artie Shaw)
300. Legend in Brocade (7/28/46; Sara Burton, Berry Kroeger, and Harold Young)
301. Happy Thoughts for a Hot Afternoon (8/4/46; Byron McGrath, Greg Morton, Kermit Murdock)
302. Wilbur, the Psycho-Neurotic Auto (8/11/46; Art Carney, Ethel Everett, Earl Hammond, Arnold Stang, and Sam Wanamaker)
303. Modern Exhibit [music by Woody Herman and Igor Stravinsky] (8/18/46; Woody Herman and Chet Huntley)
304. Path in the Door (8/25/46; Jay Novello and Elliott Reid)
305. The Last Delegate (9/15/46; Don Appell, Horace Braham, Alfred Shirley, Everett Sloane, and Carl Weber)
306. The Midnight Town Is Full of Boys [directed by Fletcher Markle] (9/21/46)
307. The Day that Baseball Died (9/28/46; Art Carney, Santos Ortega, and Bill Slater)
308. Studies in Jealousy (10/5/46)
309. Bruisy and Willy (10/12/46)
310. Moby Dick [part one of two] (10/19/46; Charles Irving, Neil O'Malley, and Sidney Smith)
311. Moby Dick [part two] (10/26/46; Charles Irving, Neil O'Malley, and Sidney Smith)
312. Lee Fountain Comes of Age (11/2/46; Kenny Delmar, Bob Dryden, Julian Liss, Ted Osborne, and Lawson Zerbe)
313. Farewell to Altamont [based on the story *Look Homeward Angel* by Thomas Wolfe] (11/9/46; Art Carney)
314. The Man Who Could Bring Pictures to Life (11/16/46)
315. The Tin Whistle (11/23/46; John Beals and Al Hodge)
316. It Shouldn't Happen to a Man (11/30/46; Cathy Lewis, Elliott Lewis, and Jay Novello)
317. The Parade (12/7/46; Kermit Murdock and Betty Philson)
318. Alice and the Echo (12/14/46; Joe Di Santis, Kermit Murdock, and Martin Wolfson)
319. The Day They Gave Babies Away (12/21/46)
320. Rain, Rain, Go Away (12/28/46; Arthur Q. Bryan, Jerry Hausner, Jack Kruschen, Elliott Lewis, Ed Max, Norma Jean Nilsson, and Sarah Selby)
321. Tongues of Fire (1/4/47)
322. The Surreal Marriage (1/11/47; Irene Hubbard, Ronald Liss, and Ted Osborne)
323. My Life with Ernest Rule (1/18/47; Charlotte Holland)
324. Natural History of Nonsense (1/25/47; Jack Grimes and William Keane)

Crime Classics *

Broadcast over CBS, dramatizing true-life crimes from Lizzie Borden, suspected ax murderer, to body snatchers Burke and Hare. Lou Merril was host "Thomas Hyland." Bernard Herrmann supplied the music. Elliott Lewis and Ken McMannus were the directors. Morton Fine and David Friedkin were the script writers. Elliott Lewis also produced. Bob Lemond, Roy Rowan and Larry Thor shared announcing duties. Broadcast on Mondays from 8 to 8:30 pm, EST, as a

*Compiled by Dan Haefele.

summer replacement for *Suspense*, and then a prime-time run on Wednesdays from 9:30 to 10 pm, beginning September 30, 1953.

Audition Show: The Crime of Bathsheba Spooner (12/3/52; Herb Butterfield, Mary Jane Croft, Sam Edwards, Georgia Ellis, William Johnstone, Tudor Owen, and Ben Wright)

1. The Crime of Bathsheba Spooner (6/15/53; Herb Butterfield, Mary Jane Croft, Sam Edwards, Georgia Ellis, William Johnstone, Tudor Owen, and Ben Wright)
2. The Shockingly Peaceful Passing of Thomas Edwin Bartlett, Greengrocer (6/22/53; Herb Butterfield, Betty Harford, and Terry Kilburn)
3. The Checkered Life and Sudden Death of Colonel James Fisk, Junior (6/29/53; Mary Jane Croft, Tony Ellis, Betty Harford, William Johnstone, Irene Tedrow, and Martha Wentworth)
4. The Shrapnelled Body of Charles Drew, Senior (7/6/53; Tony Ellis, Paul Frees, Betty Harford, William Johnstone, Terry Kilburn, Irene Tedrow, and Ben Wright)
5. The Terrible Deed of John White Webster and his Crime that Shocked the Nation (7/13/53; Herb Butterfield, Jean Howell, Junius Matthews, Jay Novello, Larry Thor, Martha Wentworth, and Paula Winslowe)
6. The Death of a Picture Hanger (7/20/53; Sam Edwards, Paul Frees, Joe Granby, Joseph Kearns, Charlotte Lawrence, Clayton Post, and Paula Winslowe)
7. The Final Day of General Ketchum and How He Died (7/27/53; Hy Averback, Bill Bissell, Herb Butterfield, Sarah Selby, Russell Simpson, Paula Winslowe, and Dave Young)
8. Mr. Thrower's Hammer (8/3/53; Alistair Duncan, William Johnstone, Joseph Kearns, Jay Novello, Tudor Owen, Eric Snowden, and Paula Winslowe)
9. The Ax and the Droot Family: How They Fared (8/10/53; Herb

Butterfield, Mary Jane Croft, Charles Davids, Sam Edwards, Paul Frees, and Clayton Post)
10. The Incredible Trial of Laura D. Fair (8/17/53; Herb Butterfield, Mary Jane Croft, Joe Granby, William Johnstone, Florence Walcott, Paula Winslowe, and Jean Wood)
11. The Alsop Family: How It Diminished and Grew Again (8/24/53; Herb Butterfield, Betty Harford, Terry Kilburn, Raymond Lawrence, Ellen Morgan, Richard Peel, and Ben Wright)
12. Your Loving Son, Nero (8/31/53; Hy Averback, Edgar Barrier, William Conrad, Betty Lou Gerson, Sam Hill, and Martha Wentworth)
13. The Torment of Henrietta Robinson (9/7/53; Sam Edwards, Betty Harford, Sam Hill, Lamont Johnson, Joseph Kearns, Paula Winslowe, and Ben Wright)
14. The Bloody, Bloody Banks of Fall River (9/30/53; Herb Butterfield, Paul Frees, Betty Harford, William Johnstone, Jeanette Nolan, Sarah Selby, and Irene Tedrow)
15. The Hangman and William Palmer Who Won (10/7/53; Alastair Duncan, Betty Harford, Joseph Kearns, Ellen Morgan, Jay Novello, and Ben Wright)
16. The Seven Layered Arsenic Cake of Madame Lafarge (10/14/53; Edgar Barrier, William Conrad, Joseph Kearns, Eve McVey, Irene Tedrow)
17. Billy Bonny Bloodletter: Also Known as 'The Kid' (10/21/53; Tony Barrett, Harry Bartell, Dick Beals, Lillian Buyeff, William Conrad, Sam Edwards, Barney Phillips, Clayton Post, and Fred Shields)
18. John Hayes, His Head, and How They Were Parted (10/28/53; Charles Davis, Alastair Duncan, Betty Harford, William Johnstone, Jeanette Nolan, Richard Peel, and Ben Wright)
19. Raschi Among the Crocodiles and the

Prank He Played (11/4/53; Edgar Barrier, William Conrad, Jack Edwards, Jack Kruschen, Eric Snowden, Jane Webb, and Ben Wright)

20. Blackbeard's Fourteenth Wife: Why She Was No Good For Him (11/11/53; William Conrad, Alastair Duncan, Betty Harford, Joseph Kearns, Jack Kruschen, Richard Peel, and Ben Wright)

21. The Triangle on the Round Table (11/18/53; Edgar Barrier, Bob Cole, William Conrad, Lamont Johnson, William Johnstone, Ellen Morgan, and Ben Wright)

22. The Killing Story of William Corder and the Farmer's Daughter (11/25/53; Betty Harford, Joseph Kearns, Alma Lawton, Donald Lawton, Jeanette Nolan, and Richard Peel)

23. If a Body Need a Body, Just Call Burke and Hare (12/2/53; Charles Davis, Betty Harford, William Johnstone, Jack Kruschen, Jeanette Nolan, Jay Novello, and Richard Peel)

24. The Assassination of Abraham Lincoln (12/9/53; Herb Butterfield, William Conrad, Mary Jane Croft, Jack Edwards, Betty Lou Gerson, Roy Glenn, Sam Hill, Junius Matthews, Barney Phillips, Clayton Post, and Irene Tedrow)

25. John and Judith, Their Crime, and Why They Didn't Get to Enjoy It (12/16/53; Alec Harford, Betty Harford, Jeanette Nolan, Irene Tedrow, Norma Varden, and Ben Wright)

26. Coyle and Richardson: Why They Hung in a Swinging Breeze (12/30/53; Herb Butterfield, Charles Calvert, Georgia Ellis, Gladys Holland, Clayton Post, and Walter Tetley)

27. The Younger Brothers : Why Some of Them Grew No Older (1/6/54; Bill Bissell, Jimmy Eagles, Sam Edwards, Barney Phillips, Clayton Post, and Walter Tetley)

28. How Supan Got the Hook Outside Bombay (1/13/54; Julie Bennett, Lillian Buyeff, William Conrad, Alastair Duncan, Byron Kane, and Jack Kruschen)

29. Madeline Smith, Maid or Murderess: Which? (1/20/54; John Dehner, Betty Harford, William Johnstone, and Florence Walcott)

30. The Boorn Brothers and the Hangman: A Study In Nip and Tuck (1/27/54; Herb Butterfield, William Conrad, Virginia Gregg, Lamont Johnson, Joseph Kearns, Jack Kruschen, Irene Tedrow)

31. The Incredible History of John Shepard (2/3/54; Alistair Duncan, Jerry Deamond, Betty Harford, Ellen Morgan, Richard Peel, Dee J. Thompson, and Ben Wright)

32. Twenty-Three Knives Against Caesar (2/10/54; Hy Averback, Edgar Barrier, Harry Bartell, Betty Harford, Lou Krugman, Marvin Miller, and Irene Tedrow)

33. Jean Baptiste Troppmann: Killer of Many (2/17/54; Dix Davis, Larry Dobkin, Jack Edwards, Joseph Kearns, Kurt Martell, Junius Matthews, and Irene Tedrow)

34. The Good Ship Jane: Why She Became Floatsam (2/24/54; Herb Butterfield, Paul Frees, William Johnstone, Gary Montgomery, Steve Roberts, and Ben Wright)

35. Roger Nems: How He, Though Dead, Won the Game (3/3/54; Alistair Duncan, Betty Harford, Gary Montgomery, Ellen Morgan, Richard Peel, and Ben Wright)

36. New Hampshire, the Tiger and Brad Ferguson: What Happened Then (3/10/54; Parley Baer, Jeanne Bates, Mary Jane Croft, John Dehner, Lamont Johnson, Jack Kruschen, Jane Webb, and Paula Winslowe)

37. Old Sixtoes: How He Stopped Construction on the B.B.C. and I (3/17/54; Herb Butterfield, Jack Edwards, Jack Kruschen, Jane Webb, and Ben Wright)

38. Francisco Pizarro: His Heart on a Golden Knife (3/24/54; Hy Averback, Edgar Barrier, Harry Bartell, William Conrad, John Dehner, and Jack Kruschen)

39. Robby-Boy Balfour: How He Wrecked a Big Prison's Reputation (3/31/54; Norman Field, Virginia

Gregg, Betty Harford, William Johnstone, Steve Roberts, and Ben Wright)

40. A General's Daughter, Czar's Lieutenant and the Linen Closet: A Russian Tragedy (4/7/54; Hy Averback, Lillian Buyeff, John Dehner, Vic Perrin, Barney Phillips, and Irene Tedrow)
41. James Evans, Fireman: How He Extinguished a Human Torch (4/14/54; Alistair Duncan, Betty Harford, Richard Peel, Florence Walcott, Paula Winslowe, and Ben Wright)
42. Caesar Borgia: His Most Difficult Murder (4/21/54; Hy Averback, Edgar Barrier, Whitfield Connor, William Conrad, Betty Lou Gerson, Lamont Johnson, and Larry Thor)
43. Widow Magee and the Three Gypsies — A Vermont Fandango (4/28/54; Hy Averback, William Conrad, Sam Hill, and Shepard Menken)
44. Bunny Baumler: His Close Brush With Fame (5/5/54; Edgar Barrier, Howard McNear, Jack Kruschen, Benny Rubin, Irene Tedrow, Martha Wentworth, and Paula Winslowe)
45. Mr. Clarke's Skeleton in Mr. Aram's Closet: The Noise it Made (5/12/54;

Herb Butterfield, Mary Jane Croft, Charles Davis, Betty Harford, William Johnstone, Ellen Morgan, Richard Peel, and Ben Wright)

46. The Lethal Habit of Marquise De Brinvilliers (5/26/54; Herb Butterfield, Mary Jane Croft, Joseph Kearns, Lamont Johnson, Shepard Menken, Truda Marsden, Barney Phillips, and Irene Tedrow)
47. Mr. Jonathon Jewett: How, Most Peculiarly, He Cheated the Hangman (6/2/54; John Dehner, Byron Kane, Elliott Lewis, Junius Matthews, Lee Miller, and Vic Perrin)
48. The Assassination of Leon Trotsky (6/9/54; Edgar Barrier, Herb Butterfield, Charles Calvert, Miliza Kahlke, Barney Phillips, and Irene Tedrow)
49. The Death of a Baltimore Birdie and Friend (6/16/54; Charles Calvert, Mary Jane Croft, Ted de Corsia, Jerry Hausner, and Paula Winslowe)
50. Ali Pasha; A Turkish Delight (6/23/54; Edgar Barrier, Lillian Buyeff, Hans Conried, Jack Kruschen, Kurt Martell, Vic Perrin, and Paula Winslowe)
51. Good Evening. My Name Is Jack the Ripper (6/30/54)

Crime Does Not Pay

From 1935 to 1947, MGM studios released a short-subject series of two-reelers entitled *Crime Does Not Pay*. The plots, similar to *Gangbusters*, dealt with racketeering, espionage, thefts, and murder — and portraying the detective force in high pursuit. It was no surprise that two years after the final reel of the series was completed, MGM syndicated a radio series using the same title and format. First broadcast over WMGM in New York City, Monday evenings at 7:30 pm, EST. Hosted by Donald Buka. Beginning with episode fifty-six, the series was broadcast on Wednesday evenings, at the same time slot. Only seventy-eight episodes were recorded. Episodes one and fifty-two featured a starring performance of host Donald Buka. Episode nine featured Cameron Mitchell, who had appeared in one of the earlier filmed two-reeled subjects and who was at that time an up-and-coming talent. Episode fifty-one was originally scheduled for broadcast on September 25, 1950, but was pre-empted and pushed ahead a week.

When the last of the seventy-eight episodes was broadcast on April 11, 1951, WMGM began rebroadcasting the episodes again, in order, starting with "Kid with a Gun" on April 18, 1951. The rebroadcasts lasted only until the repeat of episode twenty-six, "Ingenious Woman," on October 10, 1951.

A final broadcast run of these crime dramas was made available on the Mutual network, Monday evenings at 8:30 pm, running from January 7, 1952, to December 22, 1952. Not all of the episodes were featured in this Mutual run, and they were not broadcast in the same order as its predecessor. The entire series remained sustaining.

1. Kid With a Gun (10/10/49; Donald Buka)
2. All-American Fake (10/17/49; Sidney Blackmer)
3. Death Is a Song (10/24/49; Margo)
4. Kid Twist (10/31/49; William Prince)
5. Trigger Man's Moll (11/7/49; Nancy Kelly)
6. The Body of the Crime (11/14/49; Parker Fennelly)
7. Summertime Take (11/21/49; Charles Karvin)
8. A Female of the Species (11/28/49; Ken Lynch)
9. A Piece of Rope (12/5/49; Cameron Mitchell)
10. Gasoline Cocktail (12/12/49; Bela Lugosi)
11. Dead Pigeon (12/19/49; Myron McCormick)
12. Glossy Finish (12/26/49; Martin Gabel)
13. Clothes Make the Woman (1/2/50; Jean Muir)
14. The Law of the Jungle (1/9/50; Anne Baxter)
15. Speech Is Silver (1/16/50; Richard Hart)
16. Devil in the Dark (1/23/50; Helmut Dantine)
17. The Snatcher (1/30/50; Ralph Forbes)
18. Kid Sister (2/6/50; Marsha Hunt)
19. For He's A Jolly Good Fellow (2/13/50; John Beal)
20. Death on the Doorstep (2/20/50; Donald Curtis)
21. Kangaroo Court (2/27/50; Richard Derr)
22. What's in a Name? (3/6/50; Helen Craig)
23. Death on Blake Street (3/13/50; Russell Hardie)
24. The Man Who Never Was Caught (3/20/50; Alan Baxter)
25. Thick as Thieves (3/27/50; Everett Sloane)
26. Ingenious Woman (4/3/50; Barbara O'Niel)
27. The Bagman (4/10/50; Ian Keith)
28. The Rum Runner (4/17/50; J. Edward Bromberg)
29. Visiting Fireman (4/24/50; Arleen Whelan)
30. Six, Two and Seven (5/1/50; Alfred Ryder)
31. Don't Write, Telephone (5/8/50; Jack LaRue)
32. Between Dark and the Daylight (5/15/50; Lionel Stander)
33. Second Hand Pistols (5/22/50; Ronald Colman)
34. Imported Headache (5/29/50; Joseph Buloff)
35. Fishmonger's Fortune (6/5/50; George Reeves)
36. Short Circuit (6/12/50; Hurd Hatfield)
37. Clip Joint (6/19/50; Alexander Kirkland)
38. The Professor Pulls the Switch (6/26/50; John Loder)
39. The Lady Loves Kittens (7/3/50; Anna Lee)
40. Once Too Often (7/10/50; Herbert Rudley)
41. Burglar Alarm (7/17/50; Betty Furness)
42. Horseshoes Are For Luck (7/24/50; Neil Hamilton)
43. Beauty and the Beast (7/31/50; Everett Sloane)
44. Giddyap Horsie (8/7/50; Richard Webb)

45. The Gangster Was a Lady (8/14/50; Blanche Yurka)
46. Murder Makes Book (8/21/50; Joseph Wiseman)
47. Father's Day (8/28/50; Richard Hart)
48. The Weak Spot (9/4/50; Margo)
49. Horse Face (9/11/50; Frank Albertson)
50. You Gotta Have What to Eat? (9/18/50; Horace MacMahon)
51. Sucker's Bait (10/2/50; Ed Begley)
52. Rigger's Racket (10/9/50; Donald Buka)
53. Voice of Death (10/16/50; John Loder)
54. The Recruit (10/23/50; Charles Karvin)
55. Escort for Hire (10/30/50; Mary Wickes)
56. The Big Book (11/8/50; Donald Curtis)
57. Mow the Man (11/15/50; Ward Wilson)
58. The Celluloid Candle (11/22/50; Ralph Forbes)
59. The Doll (11/29/50; Sara Haden)
60. Kid Shive (12/6/50; Dickie Moore)
61. Two Gun Annie (12/13/50; Joan Lorring)
62. Strange Town (12/20/50; Morris Carnovsky)
63. Building Blocks (12/27/50; Richard Dere)
64. Death on the Upgrade (1/3/51; Donald Woods)
65. Edge of the Desert (1/10/51; Harvey Stephens)
66. Cards and Spades (1/17/51; Susan Douglas)
67. The Old Mob Goes (1/24/51; Ian Keith)
68. Love Is Not All (1/31/51; Ralph Forbes)
69. Heir Apparent (2/7/51; Pamela Reed)
70. Carnival Frail (2/14/51; Diana Barrymore)
71. Tough Customer (2/21/51; John Shelton)
72. For Sweet Charity (2/28/51; Romney Brent)
73. Operation Payroll (3/7/51; Harold Vermelyea)
74. Diamond Trumped (3/14/51; Ralph Meeker)
75. Through the Hoop (3/21/51; Una O'Connor)
76. Plug-Ugly (3/28/51; Edmond Ryan)
77. Front Boy (4/4/51; Bramwell Fletcher)
78. Violets, Sweet Violets (4/11/51; Robert Lowery)

Crime Photographer

Previously entitled *Casey, Press Photographer*. Broadcast sustaining over CBS, Wednesday evenings from 9 to 9:30 pm, EST. Beginning September 12, 1945, the series was heard 10:30 to 11 pm, EST. On October 20, 1945, CBS moved the program to Saturday afternoons from 1:30 to 2 pm. On December 3, 1945, the program moved to Monday from 10:30 to 11 pm. On March 12, 1946, the series was heard on Tuesday from 10 to 10:30 pm. Beginning June 3, 1946, *Crime Photographer* was heard on Monday evenings from 8:30 to 9 pm as a partial summer replacement for *The Joan Davis Show*.

Staats Cotsworth was Casey. Al Bleyer and his orchestra supplied the music. Lew White was the organist. John Dietz directed. The American Hocking Glass company took over sponsorship beginning August 8, 1946. In March of 1947, the series changed its title again, this time to *Casey, Crime Photographer*. After *Casey, Crime Photographer*, the series went back to this title on January 13, 1954, as a Wednesday-night sustainer from 9 to 9:30 pm, EST. On October 8, 1954, the series moved to a new time slot, Fridays from 8 to 8:30 pm, EST.

100. The Double Cross (7/11/45)
101. Uncle John (7/18/45)
102. The Retired Camera (7/25/45)
103. Danger for Blondes (8/1/45)
104. The Bird Expert (8/8/45)
105. Hot Ice (8/15/45)
106. A Tiger on the Loose (8/22/45)
107. The Chamber of Horrors (8/29/45)
108. Gun Boy (9/5/45)
109. A Walk in the Rain (9/12/45)
110. Death Insurance (9/19/45)
111. One of the Family (9/26/45)
112. Cupid Is a Killer (10/20/45)
113. -----(10/27/45)
114. The Case of the Battered Playboy (11/3/45)
115. The Last of the Faradays (11/10/45)
116. The Little Man Who Wasn't There (11/17/45)
117. Strictly Confidential (11/24/45)
118. No Evidence (12/3/45)
119. The Considerate Burglar (12/10/45)
120. Death of a Rattlesnake (12/17/45)
121. Two New $100 Bills (12/24/45)
122. A Date with Hester (12/31/45)
123. Earned Reward (1/7/46)
124. The Finger of Death (1/14/46)
125. The Fighting Fool (1/21/46)
126. Iron Mike (1/28/46)
127. The Prince of Darkness (2/4/46)
128. Killers Can Be Beautiful (2/11/46)
129. -----(2/18/46)
130. Graveyard Gertie (2/25/46)
131. Motive for Murder (3/4/46)
132. Beaten by a Nose (3/12/46)
133. Family Argument (3/19/46)
134. Buccaneer's Cove (3/26/46)
135. The Body was Buried Deep (4/2/46)
136. The Joker (4/23/46)
137. The Butterfly (4/30/46)
138. The Man That Nobody Liked (5/7/46)
139. The Reunion (6/3/46)
140. Mr. Big (6/10/46)
141. Social Afternoon (6/17/46)
142. The Poker Game (6/24/46)
143. Bloodless Murder (7/1/46)
144. The Man Called John Doe (7/8/46)
145. A Tooth for a Tooth (7/15/46)
146. A Girl Named Kate (7/22/46)
147. Three Sapphires (8/8/46)
148. Unlucky Day (8/15/46)
149. The Fat Lady Dies (8/22/46)

150. The Red Raincoat (8/29/46)
151. The Handkerchief (9/5/46)
152. Johnnie's Got a Gun (9/12/46)
153. The Duke of Skid Row (9/19/46)
154. The Bronze Peacock (9/26/46)
155. -----(10/3/46)
156. The Carved Bed (10/10/46)
157. The Tip Off (10/17/46)
158. The Prison Break (10/24/46)
159. The Halloween Story (10/31/46)
160. Missing Persons (11/7/46)
161. The Cuckoo (11/14/46)
162. The Searchlight and the Tomb (11/21/46)
163. The Thanksgiving Dinner (11/28/46)
164. Room 1110 (12/5/46)
165. Dangerous Characters (12/12/46)
166. Christmas Shopping (12/19/46)
167. The Buried Evidence (12/26/46)
168. The Last of the Faradays (1/2/47)
169. Dead Pigeon (1/9/47)
170. The Surprising Corpse (1/16/47)
171. The Purloined Payroll (1/23/47)
172. Held for Ransom (1/30/47)
173. The Gray Kitten (2/6/47)
174. Please Be My Valentine (2/13/47)
175. The Twenty Minute Alibi (2/20/47)
176. The Red Headed Kid (2/27/47)
177. The Mysterious Lodger (3/6/47)
178. The Undercover Man (3/13/47)
Continuation from title change.
369. The Road Angel (1/13/54)
370. Source of Information (1/20/54)
371. -----(1/27/54)
372. -----(2/3/54)
373. -----(2/10/54)
374. -----(2/17/54)
375. Portrait of the Artist (2/24/54)
376. -----(3/3/54)
377. -----(3/10/54)
378. -----(3/17/54)
379. -----(3/24/54)
380. Dateline (3/31/54)
381. -----(4/7/54)
382. Full Circle (4/14/54)
383. Casey Visits A Circus (4/21/54)
384. Yellow Streak (5/12/54)
385. -----(5/19/54)
386. The Legacy (5/26/54)
387. -----(6/2/54)
388. -----(6/9/54)
389. -----(6/16/54)
390. -----(6/23/54)

391. -----(6/30/54)
392. -----(7/7/54)
393. -----(7/14/54)
394. -----(7/21/54)
395. Target Unknown (7/28/54)
396. -----(8/4/54)
397. -----(8/11/54)
398. -----(8/18/54)
399. The Moth (8/25/54)
400. The Man in Brown (9/1/54)
401. For the Family Honor (9/8/54)
402. Death in the Rain (9/15/54)
403. Street Carnival (9/22/54)
404. The Strangling Ghost (9/29/54)
405. The Protection Racket (10/8/54)
406. Life for Sale (10/15/54)
407. The Football (10/22/54)
408. Black Magic (10/29/54)
409. Showdown (11/5/54)
410. Widgeon Is a Ducky Word! (11/12/54)
411. Poor Little Rich Kid (11/19/54)
412. No Publicity (11/26/54)
413. Juanita (12/3/54)
414. What's in a Name? (12/10/54)
415. Ex-Cop (12/17/54)
416. A Red Wagon for Junior (12/24/54)
417. A Dead Man's Message (12/31/54)
418. Unbury the Dead (1/7/55)
419. Peaches (1/14/55)
420. Criminal for a Day (1/21/55)
421. The Watchdog (1/28/55)
422. The Late Unlamented (2/4/55)
423. Valentine (2/11/55)
424. One Grave for Three (2/18/55)
425. Panic (2/25/55)
426. The Bogey-Man Story (3/4/55)
427. The Homicide Ring (3/11/55)
428. Check and Double Check (3/18/55)
429. The Death Watch (3/25/55)
430. Death Visits Five (4/1/55)
431. Top Secret (4/8/55)
432. Battleground (4/15/55)
433. Casey Visits a Circus (4/22/55)

Crisis in War Town

Recorded in New York and syndicated across the United States in 1949, this series was a successor to *War Town*. Victor Jory was narrator for the entire series, except for "Paper Doll" with Dean Jagger and "Soldiers in Grease Paint" with Ralph Bellamy. Jon Gart supplied the music. Robert Lewis Shayon produced and directed, and Earle McGill occasionally subbed. Eloise Walton wrote the majority of the scripts; Max Ehrlich, Irve Tunick and Phyllis Parker also scripted.

1. Johnny Jerry (Wendy Barrie, Ben Cooper, Rod Hendrickson, and Irene Hubbard)
2. White Elephant Sale (Betty Caulfield, Rosemary Rice, and Susan Thorne)
3. The Hungry Heart (Arlene Francis, Patsy O'Shea, Dorothy Sands, and Gladys Thornton)
4. Sitting Duck (Richard Basehart, Joseph Boland, Robert Readick, and Charles Webster)
5. Hero Stuff (Michael Artist, Helen Claire, Ben Cooper, Alistair Kyle, and Jack Taylor)
6. The Square Peg (Barry Hopkins, Walter Kinsella, Nora Marlowe, and Robert Readick)
7. The Man Who Came Back (Madeleine Pierce, Joan Tetzel, and Richard Widmark)
8. The Little Green Horse (Owen Alden, Jeanne Cagney, Ben Cooper, Maxine Flood, Lorna Lynn, and Gladys Thornton)
9. The Way Back (Francis De Sales, John Lund, Guy Repp, and Allen Wood)
10. Heartbreak Island (Lon Clark, Berry Kroeger, Alistair Kyle, Guy Repp, and Al Ward)

11. The Marvelous Unknown (Elspeth Eric, Don MacLaughlin, Gladys Thornton, and Vicki Vola)
12. Paper Doll (Helen Claire, Peggy Conklin, Woody Parker, Al Ward, and Richard Widmark)
13. Soldiers in Greasepaint (Jim Backus, Leon Janney, Ted Jewett, and Jack Tyler)

The Cruise of the Poll Parrot

Syndicated by Poll Parrot Shoes (International Shoe Company). An enjoyable children's adventure serial about a whaling trip in 1858. Dave Ward announced.

1– 26. The Treasure Hunt [26 parts] (9/25/37, 10/2, 10/9, 10/16, 10/23, 10/30, 11/6, 11/13, 11/20, 11/27, 12/4, 12/11, 12/18, 12/25/37, 1/1/38, 1/8, 1/15, 1/22, 1/29, 2/5, 2/12, 2/19, 2/26, 3/5, 3/12, and 3/19/38)

27 – 39. The Mysterious Island [13 parts] (3/26/38, 4/2, 4/9, 4/16, 4/23, 4/30, 5/7, 5/14, 5/21, 5/28, 6/4, 6/11, and 6/18/38)

The Damon Runyon Theater

Damon Runyon was a master story teller whose New York City characters during the twenties and thirties were unforgettable. Prohibition was in kick, and gambling was illegal. But that didn't mean there were no gambling houses hidden throughout the city. The main character was a con named Broadway (played to perfection by John Brown), who had a weakness for stories. One week Broadway found himself in the midst of the largest pie eating contest on the East Coast, and the week after, Broadway met a practical joker whose jokes went a bit too far.

All of the scripts were written by Russell Hughes and Alan Ladd, and all of the episodes were adaptations of Damon Runyon's original short stories. Richard Sanville directed the broadcasts. A production of Alan Ladd's syndicated Mayfair production company. The supporting cast included; Joe Du Val, Eddie Marr, Gerald Mohr, Frank Lovejoy, Alan Reed, Luis Van Rooten, Jack Webb, and William Conrad.

Because this program was syndicated, there are no official broadcast dates. Some newspaper listings indicate the series premier was on January 2, 1949, while others, such as WOR (Mutual) in New York, suggest June 22, 1950. Some stations even repeated episodes after they had finished broadcasting the entire series. Others only presented a handful to fill in time slots for short-run summer replacements. The dates below belong to just one of the many stations across the country that presented the series. When stations did air all fifty-two episodes, they were broadcast in the order listed below.

1. Little Miss Marker (8/8/50)
2. Tobias the Terrible (8/15/50)
3. Butch Minds the Baby (8/22/50)
4. Breach of Promise (8/29/50)
5. A Nice Price (9/5/50)
6. The Idyll of Miss Sarah Brown (9/12/50)
7. Romance in the Roaring Forties (9/19/50; William Conrad)
8. The Lemon Drop Kid (9/26/50)
9. The Hottest Guy in the World (10/3/50)
10. All Horse Players Die Broke (10/10/50)
11. Princess O'Hara (10/17/50)
12. For A Pal (10/24/50)
13. A Piece of Pie (10/31/50)
14. Barbecue (11/7/50)
15. Blonde Mink (11/14/50)
16. Leopard's Spots (11/21/50)
17. Dancing Dan's Christmas (11/28/50)
18. Pick the Winner (12/5/50)
19. The Brain Goes Home (12/12/50)
20. Hold 'em Yale! (12/19/50)
21. Old Em's Kentucky Home (12/26/50)
22. Blood Pressure (1/2/51)
23. Lonely Heart (1/9/51)
24. Broadway Complex (1/16/51)
25. Madame La Gimp (1/23/51; Frank Lovejoy)
26. Baseball Hattie (1/30/51)
27. The Big Umbrella (2/6/51)
28. Earthquake (2/13/51)
29. The Bloodhounds of Broadway (2/20/51)
30. The Lily of St. Pierre (2/27/51)
31. It Comes Up Mud (3/6/51)
32. Broadway Financier (3/13/51)
33. Bred for Battle (3/20/51)
34. So You Won't Talk! (3/27/51)
35. Social Error (4/3/51)
36. Cemetery Bait (4/10/51)
37. The Melancholy Dane (4/17/51)
38. The Brakeman's Daughter (4/24/51)
39. The Lacework Kid (5/1/51)
40. Maybe a Queen (5/8/51)
41. Joe Terrace (5/15/51)
42. Lillian (5/22/51)
43. Palm Beach Santa Claus (5/29/51)
44. Tight Shoes (6/5/51)
45. That Ever-Loving Wife of Hymie's (6/12/51)
46. A Light In France (6/19/51)
47. A Story Goes with It (6/26/51)
48. Dark Dolores (7/3/51; Jack Webb)
49. What, No Butler? (7/10/51)
50. Neat Strip (7/17/51)
51. Sense of Humor (7/24/51)
52. Dream Street Rose (7/31/51)

Dangerously Yours

It is probably safe to say that almost all major Hollywood stars had their own radio program, Victor Jory being no exception. *Dangerously Yours* was an anthology vehicle starring Jory. Jean Holloway wrote most of the scripts for this series, a few of which were adaptations of popular stage plays and movies; others were originals. Mark Warnow supplied the music. Richard Sanville directed, Nick Dawson produced. Sponsored by Vicks Vapo Rub and broadcast Sunday at 2 to 2:30 pm, EST. Two audition recordings were made, but only one of them was rebroadcast over the air as a regular episode. On October 22, 1944, the series, remaining in the same time slot, underwent a title change, becoming *The Matinee Theater.*

Audition: Masquerade (6/20/44)
Audition: The Highwayman (6/21/44)
1. The Highwayman (7/2/44; Gertrude Warner)
2. The Pirate of Orleans (7/9/44; Gertrude Warner)
3. The Man from the South (7/16/44; Gertrude Warner)
4. Knight of the Seas [aka A Man Named Jones] (7/23/44)
5. Rogue of Paris (7/30/44)
6. Cortez the Conquistador (8/6/44;

Inge Adams, Ralph Bell, and Juano Hernandez)
7. God's Country and the Woman (8/13/44; Claire Neisen)
8. Monsieur Beaucaire (8/20/44; Jackson Beck, Gertrude Warner, and Joan Westmore)
9. Bothwell of Scotland Yard (8/27/44; Alfred Shirley and Gertrude Warner)
10. The Sheik (9/3/44; Jackson Beck and Gertrude Warner)

11. The Firebrand (9/10/44; Kermit Murdock, Joan Tetzel, and Gertrude Warner)
12. The Shadow of the Raven (9/17/44; Janice Gilbert and Gertrude Warner)
13. Berkeley Square (9/24/44; Gertrude Warner)
14. Windward Passage (10/1/44; Gertrude Warner)
15. Assignment in Brittany (10/8/44)
16. Front Page (10/15/44)

Dark Fantasy

Anthology series dramatizing horror, science-fiction and murder tales, broadcast locally over WKY in Oklahoma City until January 2, 1942, when the series went national over NBC as a Friday-night sustainer. Scott Bishop, who wrote a few scripts for *The Sealed Book* and *The Mysterious Traveler*, wrote the scripts for this series. Keith Painton acted out many characterizations in the broadcasts. "Seance" was the same script as "A Delicate Case for Murder."

1. The Man Who Came Back (11/14/41)
2. The Soul of Shan Hai Huan (11/21/41)
3. The Thing from the Sea (11/28/41)
4. The Demon Tree (12/5/41)
5. Men Call Me Mad (12/19/42)
6. The House of Bread (12/26/41)
7. Resolution, 1841 (1/2/42)
8. The Curse of the Neanderthal (1/9/42)
9. Debt from the Past (1/16/42)
10. Headless Death (1/23/42)
11. Death Is a Savage Deity (1/30/42)
12. The Sea Phantom (2/6/42)
13. W Is for Werewolf (2/13/42)
14. A Delicate Case of Murder (2/20/42)
15. Spawn of the Subhuman (2/27/42)
16. The Man with the Scarlet Satchel (3/6/42)

17. Superstition Be Hanged (3/13/42)
18. Pennsylvania Turnpike (3/20/42)
19. Convoy for Atlantis (3/27/42)
20. The Thing from the Darkness (4/3/42)
21. Edge of the Shadow (4/10/42)
22. Curare (4/17/42)
23. The Screaming Skulls (4/24/42)
24. The Letter From Yesterday (5/1/42)
25. A Cup of Gold (5/8/42)
26. Funeral Arrangements Completed [aka Coffin for Two] (5/15/42)
27. Dead Hands Reaching (5/22/42)
28. Rendezvous with Satan (5/29/42)
29. I Am Your Brother (6/5/42)
30. The Sleeping Death (6/12/42)
31. Seance (6/19/42)

Death Valley Days

This series began in 1930 as a means of promoting the products of the Pacific Borax Company (20 Mule Team Borax / Boraxo). The stories were all based on fact and revolved around the legends and lore of Death Valley, California, where Borax was mined. This western anthology was created by Ruth Woodman, a New York advertising-agency scriptwriter who had never seen the place. And ironically, the program originated from Hollywood, California!

After the series went on the air, Woodman made frequent trips to the area recording tales and stories of the land, to be later used as plot material for the series. Woodman wrote scripts for the entire series, along with Ruth Adams Knight. The only recurring character for the series was the "Old Ranger," played throughout the years by Jack MacBryde, Tim Daniel Frawley, Harry Humphrey, and George Rand. John White was the balladeer ("The Lonesome Cowboy"). Harry Glantz was the trumpeter, and Joseph Bonime directed the orchestra. George Hicks was the announcer. Dresser Dahlstead was the narrator. In 1944, the series changed its title to *Death Valley Sheriff*, and in 1945, to *The Sheriff*. In 1952, the series left radio for television, under its original title of *Death Valley Days*, and enjoyed another long and successful run.

First broadcast over NBC Tuesday evenings from 9 to 9:30, EST. On August 17, 1931, the series moved to the Blue Network, Monday evenings from 8 to 8:30 pm, later 8:30 to 9 from 8/17/31 and 10/6/32. On October 6, 1932, the series moved to Thursdays from 9 to 9:30 pm. On September 4, 1936, Fridays from 8:30 to 9 pm. Beginning June 10, 1938, *Death Valley Days* moved back to NBC, Friday evenings from 9:30 to 10 pm. Beginning October 7, 1939, Saturdays from 9:30 to 10 pm. Beginning May 3, 1940, Fridays from 8:30 to 9 pm. Beginning July 3, 1941, CBS began broadcasting the series, Thursdays from 8 to 8:30 pm. On July 2, 1942, the series moved to Thursdays from 8:30 to 9 pm.

1. Death Valley Days (9/30/30)
2. Panamint, the Town of Sudden Death (10/7/30)
3. She Burns Green (10/14/30)
4. The Hold Up of Aaron Winters (10/21/30)
5. The Story of Bellerin' Teck (10/28/30)
6. -----(11/4/30)
7. Twenty Mule Teams Makes Its First Trip (11/11/30)
8. Little Bullfrog Nugget (11/18/30)
9. Lost Breyfogle Mine (11/25/30)
10. Philander Lee, the Squaw Man (12/2/30)
11. The Story of Swamper Ike (12/9/30)
12. Death Valley Sandstorm (12/16/30)
13. Christmas at Furnace Creek Inn (12/23/30)
14. The Tiger Lil of Rhyolite (12/30/30)
15. Sky Pilot (1/6/31)
16. -----(1/13/31)
17. Jimmy Dayton's Courtship (1/20/31)
18. Jimmy Dayton's Last Adventure (1/27/31)
19. Jayhawker's Reunion (2/3/31)
20. The Chivaree (2/10/31)
21. Jim and Me Found Tonopah (2/17/31)
22. Twenty Mule Team's First Trip (2/24/31)
23. Runout of Rhyolite (3/3/31)
24. The Discovery of Panamint (3/10/31)
25. The Bandits of Panamint (3/17/31)
26. The Story of Death Valley Scotty (3/24/31)
27. Easter Sunrise Service (3/31/31)
28. Twenty Mule Teamsters Songfest (4/7/31)
29. Claim-Jumpin' Jennie of Rhyolite (4/14/31)
30. Iron Horse Reaches Rhyolite (4/21/31)

466. The Yankee Pirate (10/21/39)
467. Sing for Your Supper (10/28/39)
468. Norin' On the Desert (11/4/39)
469. To Big Charlie from Little Charlie (11/11/39)
470. The Joshua Tree (11/18/39)
471. Reno (11/25/39)
472. King of California (12/2/39)
473. Stormy and Sandy (12/9/39)
474. Peter Lassen (12/16/39)
475. Christmas, 1849 (12/23/39)
476. Mrs. Smith Recieves (12/30/39)
477. Soapy Smith (1/6/40)
478. For Molly-With Love (1/13/40)
479. Mother-In-Law McGimsey (1/20/40)
480. The Owens Valley Earthquake (1/27/40)
481. -----(2/3/40)
482. Nevada, the Battle Born (2/10/40)
483. -----(2/17/40)
484. A Highway Turns Aside (2/24/40)
485. Duff, or the French Cook (3/2/40)
486. The Green Hand (3/9/40)
487. Abe Curry, The Father of Carson (3/16/40)
488. Sermons in Stones (3/23/40)
489. Milton Sharpe, Highwayman (3/30/40)
490. Master and Man (4/6/40)
491. Billie Derick (4/13/40)
492. Biggest Wagons in the World (4/20/40)
493. School for Brides (4/27/40)
494. The Story of Borax Bill (5/3/40)
495. Mammy Pleasant (5/10/40)
496. The Twelve Pound Nugget (5/17/40)
497. Lottie (5/24/40)
498. The Great Unknown (5/31/40)
499. The Curry Engine Company (6/7/40)
500. Reform of the Bindle Stiff (6/14/40)
501. Crazy Quilt (6/21/40)
502. California's First Fourth of July Celebration (6/28/40)
503. The Fire Queen (7/5/40)
504. Crazy With the Heat (7/12/40)
505. The Grape Vine Root (7/19/40)
506. Treasure of Jean Lafitte (7/26/40)
507. Moonstruck (8/2/40)
508. The Donkey Serenade (8/9/40)
509. Buffalo Bill in London (8/16/40)
510. Oofty Goofty (8/23/40)

511. Bill Stewart's Courtship (8/30/40)
512. Kit Carson, Story Book Hero (9/6/40)
513. Woman Who Lied About Her Age (9/13/40)
514. The Black Pearl (9/20/40)
515. Death Valley Fiesta (9/27/40)
516. Dogs of the Mist (10/4/40)
517. Hannah Clapp, Schoolmarm (10/11/40)
518. The Blue Silk Umbrella (10/18/40)
519. Justin Gates (10/25/40)
520. The Old Ames Press (11/1/40)
521. The Missouri Reds (11/8/40)
522. The Ride on the Flume (11/15/40)
523. Double Damask (11/22/40)
524. The Widow's Bible (11/29/40)
525. Bringing Home the Bacon (12/6/40)
526. Samaritans at Stone Cabin (12/13/40)
527. A Tale of the Christ (12/20/40)
528. Captain Sutter's Christmas Dinner (12/27/40)
529. The Squaw Who Walked Alone (1/3/41)
530. The Holy Terror (1/10/41)
531. The Desert Beauty Shop (1/17/41)
532. The Lost Pearl Shop (1/24/41)
533. Lone Operator (1/31/41)
534. Helen Holmes (2/7/41)
535. Ships of the Desert (2/14/41)
536. The Dream that Came True (2/21/41)
537. God's in His Heaven (2/28/41)
538. Field of Honor (3/7/41)
539. The Whisker Derby (3/14/41)
540. Mazeppa (3/21/41)
541. Words and Music (3/28/41)
542. Sweet Shasta Town (4/4/41)
543. Parson of Gold Hill (4/11/41)
544. Playing With Fire (4/18/41)
545. Cherokee's Courtship (4/25/41)
546. Old Stephan (5/2/41)
547. The Pleasure Wagon (5/9/41)
548. Age Before Beauty (5/16/41)
549. In Memoriam (5/30/41)
550. Root Hog (6/6/41)
551. Friday the Thirteenth (6/13/41)
552. Mr. Pelton Helps a Widow (6/20/41)
553. Sam Kee and Uncle Sam (6/27/41)
554. Ishi, the Last of the Yahis (7/3/41)
555. Henry Cronkhite's Suspenders (7/10/41)

556. The Miracle of the Sea Gulls
     (7/17/41)
557. Running Water (7/24/41)
558. Covered Wagon Baby (7/31/41)
559. Rose Bush of Tombstone (8/7/41)
560. Corpse in the Express Car (8/14/41)
561. Ghost of the Great White Sands
     (8/21/41)
562. Homeliest Man in Nevada (8/28/41)
563. Australia Next (9/4/41)
564. Bill Stewart Acquires a Toga
     (9/11/41)
565. Prelude to a Party (9/18/41)
566. Shot-With-Luck Rollins (9/25/41)
567. 3,000 Miles to Fame (10/2/41)
568. Bandit Who Kissed and Ran
     (10/9/41)
569. The Governor's Lady (10/16/41)
570. Rockin' Chair Charlie (10/23/41)
571. El Gran Hombre (10/30/41)
572. Angel's Serenade (11/6/41)
573. How the Old Chief Said Thank You
     (11/13/41)
574. St. Louis Sam (11/20/41)
575. White Medicine Man (11/27/41)
576. The Desert Lighthouse (12/4/41)
577. God and the Klickitats (12/11/41)
578. The Great Diamond Hoax
     (12/18/41)
579. Cornish Miners' Christmas Carols
     (12/25/41)
580. Moving Out of Minnie (1/1/42)
581. Anna Mouron (1/15/42)
582. Two-Bits (1/22/42)
583. Quejo, the Bandit (1/29/42)
584. Mr. Godiva (2/5/42)
585. What Manner of Man (2/12/42)
586. Ten in Texas (2/19/42)
587. Flight in the Dark (2/26/42)
588. The Seventh Day (3/5/42)
589. School Keeps (3/12/42)
590. California's Paul Revere (3/19/42)
591. Sego Lilies (3/26/42)
592. Diamond Bill (4/2/42)
593. Two Gun Man (4/9/42)
594. Mr. Pinkerton of Placerville
     (4/16/42)
595. Dr. Montezuma (4/23/42)
596. Bigfoot (4/30/42)
597. Staheli's Brass Band (5/7/42)
598. The Three Telegraphers (5/14/42)
599. Silverheels (5/21/42)
600. Thirty Cents a Mile (5/28/42)
601. The Chinese Never Forget (6/4/42)

602. Dr. Thorne's Lost Mine (6/11/42)
603. All God's Chillun' Got Shoes
     (6/18/42)
604. Basket Meeting (6/25/42)
605. The Gold That Grows on Trees
     (7/2/42)
606. Bullet that Left no Mark (7/9/42)
607. The Rescue of Ted (7/16/42)
608. On the Arizona Strip (7/23/42)
609. Mr. Kettle's Political Career
     (7/30/42)
610. The Murder Brand (8/6/42)
611. Captain Jeffords and Chief Cochise
     (8/13/42)
612. Uncle Billy Cools His Heels
     (8/20/42)
613. Buck and Jess (8/27/42)
614. Putting Teeth in the Law (9/3/42)
615. Perennial Beau (9/10/42)
616. A Hunting We Will Go (9/17/42)
617. Rocky (9/24/42)
618. The Man Who Walked to His
     Death (10/1/42)
619. By the Skin of his Teeth (10/8/42)
620. That Thing Called Savvy (10/15/42)
621. To Hank Foster (10/22/42)
622. Courtship on the Roof (10/29/42)
623. Little Men of the Valley (11/5/42)
624. Two Hearts They Couldn't Change
     (11/12/42)
625. California's First Ice Man (11/19/42)
626. Harvest at Fort Rock (11/26/42)
627. The Lady Says No (12/3/42)
628. Round Trip to Michigan (12/10/42)
629. Cranky Charlie (12/17/42)
630. Cornish Miners' Christmas Carols
     (12/24/42)
631. Red Eye Joe Signs the Pledge
     (12/31/42)
632. The Lost Cement Mine (1/7/43)
633. Faith of Our Fathers (1/14/43)
634. The Ghost of White Cap (1/21/43)
635. Contrary Minded (1/28/43)
636. Felix's Last Fight (2/4/43)
637. Americans All (2/11/43)
638. Including the Scandinavian
     (2/18/43)
639. Pat and the Payroll (2/25/43)
640. Here Lies a Vermonter (3/4/43)
641. Hi Jolly (3/11/43)
642. Yes, Jenny (3/18/43)
643. George I of the Mojave (3/25/43)
644. Discover's Fate (4/1/43)
645. Old Zack (4/8/43)

646. Prunes (4/15/43)
647. Mrs. Isabel Tries Her Hand at Teaching (4/22/43)
648. The Rose of Monterey (4/29/43)
649. Flight to Glory (5/6/43)
650. More Buckshot (5/13/43)
651. Mine With the Iron Door (5/20/43)
652. California's First Postman (5/27/43)
653. Lucky Baldwin (6/3/43)
654. Brass Band of Quong Kee (6/10/43)
655. The Alcan Highway Builder (6/17/43)
656. An Indian Never Forgets (6/24/43)
657. Hidden Treasure of Cucamonga (7/1/43)
658. Methodist Mining Company (7/8/43)
659. The Devil's Dream (7/15/43)
660. Gold and Ice (7/22/43)
661. The Run of the Western Four (7/29/43)
662. Man Tracker (8/5/43)
663. The Mother of Texas (8/12/43)
664. The Schoolhouse Ghost (8/19/43)
665. Comanche Captive (8/26/43)
666. Tribute to a Long Line Skinner (9/2/43)
667. Ham n' Eggs álà Farallones (9/9/43)
668. Mystery of Suicide Gulch (9/16/43)
669. The Well of Sacrifice (9/23/43)
670. Surgeon and the Sutler (9/30/43)
671. Descent into Darkness (10/7/43)
672. Wheelbarrow John (10/14/43)
673. Silas Haight's Bear Fight (10/21/43)
674. Wild Bill and the Sky Pilot (10/28/43)
675. Diary of a Pioneer (11/4/43)
676. Lord of the Chipmunk (11/11/43)
677. -----(11/18/43)
678. There Were Once Two Traveling Salesmen (11/25/43)
679. The Crutch Brand (12/2/43)
680. The Cow that Starts A War (12/9/43)
681. Underground Escape (12/16/43)
682. Blizzard Baby (12/23/43)
683. Lend-Lease 1849 (12/30/43)
684. Dad Fairbanks (1/6/44)
685. Walt's White Thing (1/13/44)
686. The Pied Piper of Leola (1/20/44)
687. Father and Son (1/27/44)
688. When Kit Carson Fought a Duel (2/3/44)
689. The Ghost of Sam Howard (2/10/44)
690. The Washington Elm (2/17/44)
691. Hellfire of the Gospel (2/24/44)
692. The Doughnut Bride (3/2/44)
693. The Strange Case of Josiah Wilbarger (3/9/44)
694. The Luck of the Irish (3/16/44)
695. Just Like a Man (3/23/44)
696. Waters of the Hassayampa (3/30/44)
697. The Story of Scott's Bluff (4/6/44)
698. Road Across the Mountains (4/13/44)
699. Wild Man of the West (4/20/44)
700. Woman's Place (4/27/44)
701. Longest Beard in the World (5/4/44)
702. Aleutian-Bound (5/11/44)
703. Lost Butcher Knife Mine (5/18/44)
704. Bread Upon the Waters (5/25/44)
705. Brownie and Rosie (6/1/44)
706. Man Who Trailed Himself (6/8/44)
707. House that Zach Built (6/15/44)
708. Chips for Mother, Too (6/22/44)
709. The Jingo and Johnny Mine (6/29/44)
710. Lost Woman of San Nicolas (7/6/44)
711. Buried Alive (7/13/44)
712. Good Samaritan of Death Valley (7/20/44)
713. The World's a Stage (7/27/44)
714. Well Done, Thou Good and Faithful Servant (8/3/44)

Detour

This psychological drama series presented stories dealing with life-or-death situations. The first thirteen episodes were written by Laurence Klee, previously dramatized from *The Clock*, but retitled. After episode thirteen, all new stories were presented, written by Don Witty, Bernard Dougall, Ira Marion, Michael Sklar and Melina Parlmer. Broadcast over ABC, Wednesday evenings from 9 to 9:30 pm, sustaining.

1. The Artificial Tree (6/21/50)
2. The Story of Adam Stewart (6/28/50)
3. The Story of Red Fulton (7/5/50)
4. The Story of Nora Spencer (7/12/50)
5. The Story of Mark Waynard (7/19/50)
6. The Story of Wilbur Cooke (7/26/50)
7. The Story of Eve Clifford (8/2/50)
8. The Story of Frederic Spangler (8/9/50)
9. The Story of Vera Bascomb (8/16/50)
10. The Story of Leonard Keeler (8/23/50)
11. The Story of Fletcher (8/30/50)
12. The Story of Arlene (9/6/50)
13. The Story of Rex Pound (9/13/50)
14. The Story of David Vaughn (9/20/50)
15. The Story of Eddie Sayers (9/27/50)
16. The Story of Steve Rednik (10/4/50)
17. Strange Lady (10/11/50)
18. The Story of Leta Parano (10/18/50)
19. The Hitch-hiker (10/25/50)
20. A Lad Named David (11/1/50)
21. The Story of Agatha Reed (11/8/50)

Dimension X

Dimension X was ahead of its time. The science-fiction boom did not pick up for another couple of years, and serious science fiction was not yet on radio until *Dimension X* premiered. Originating from New York, this NBC series presented adaptations of various novels and short stories from Ray Bradbury's "The Martian Chronicles" and "Marionettes, Inc." to Robert Bloch's "Almost Human." Kurt Vonnegut, Robert Heinlein, and Isaac Asimov's stories were featured as well.

Van Woodward was the first to produce the series, and William Welch later took over. Edward King was the first director, later replaced by Fred Weihe. Norman Rose was the narrator. Albert Berman supplied the music. Bill Chambers was the engineer and Robert Warren was the announcer. Ernest Kinoy adapted many of the scripts. The episode "Destination: Moon" was based on the George Pal film that was in the theaters at the time, which helped to promote the movie. Episode forty-five was not an untitled story; rather the title itself was "Untitled Story." Episode eleven featured two fifteen-minute stories, both written by Ray Bradbury.

1. The Outer Limit (4/8/50; Joseph di Santis, Wendell Holmes, and Joseph Julian)
2. With Folded Hands (4/15/50; Alexander Scourby)
3. Report on the Barnhouse Effect (4/22/50; Ed Jerome, Bill Quinn, and Karl Weber)
4. No Contact (4/29/50; Donald Buka, Cameron Prud'Homme, and Luis Van Rooten)
5. Knock (5/6/50; Joan Alexander, Arnold Moss, and Luis Van Rooten)
6. Almost Human (5/13/50; Jack Grimes and Santos Ortega)

7. The Lost Race (5/20/50; Matt Crowley, Roger De Koven, and Joseph Julian)
8. To the Future (5/27/50; John Larkin and Jan Miner)
9. The Embassy (6/3/50; Joseph Julian and Berry Kroeger)
10. The Green Hills of Earth (6/10/50)
11. There Will Come Soft Rains / Zero Hour (6/17/50; Denise Alexander, Roger De Koven, Rita Lynn)
12. Destination: Moon (6/24/50; Joe di Santis and Wendell Holmes)
13. A Logic Named Joe (7/1/50; Roger De Koven and Joseph Julian)
14. Mars Is Heaven (7/7/50; Peter Capel and Wendell Holmes)
15. The Man in the Moon (7/14/50; Santos Ortega and Luis Van Rooten)
16. Beyond Infinity (7/21/50; Les Damon, Joe di Santis, E. A. Krumschmidt, and Lada Staviski)
17. The Potters of Firsk (7/28/50; Wendell Holmes, Raymond Edward Johnson, and Karl Weber)
18. Perigi's Wonderful Dolls (8/4/50; Joan Alexander, Joe di Santis, and Les Tremayne)
19. The Castaways (8/11/50; Greg Morton and Santos Ortega)
20. The Martian Chronicles (8/18/50; Inga Adams, Donald Buka, and Roger De Koven)
21. The Parade (8/25/50; Joe Curten, Berry Kroeger, and Alexander Scourby)
22. The Roads Must Roll (9/1/50; Ralph Bell and Wendell Holmes)
23. The Outer Limit (9/8/50; Joseph di Santis, Wendell Holmes, and Joseph Julian)
24. Hello, Tomorrow (9/15/50; Nancy Olsen)
25. Dr. Grimshaw's Sanitarium (9/22/50; Roger De Koven and Karl Weber)
26. And the Moon Be Still and Bright (9/29/50; Wendell Holmes and Alexander Scourby)
27. No Contact (10/28/50; Donald Buka, Cameron Prud'Homme, and Luis Van Rooten)
28. The Professor Was a Thief (11/5/50; John Gibson, John Larkin, and Arthur Maitland)
29. Shanghaied (11/12/50; Bill Griffis and John Sylvester)
30. Competition (11/19/50; Elaine Ross and Les Tremayne)
31. Universe (11/26/50; Mason Adams and Peter Capel)
32. The Green Hills of Earth (12/24/50)
33. Mars Is Heaven (1/7/51; Peter Capel and Wendell Holmes)
34. The Martian Death March (1/14/51)
35. The Last Objective (6/3/51; Ralph Bell, Jack Grimes, Wendell Holmes, and Lawson Zerbe)
36. Nightmare (6/10/51; John Gibson and Rita Lynn)
37. Pebble in the Sky (6/17/51; Susan Douglas and Santos Ortega)
38. Child's Play (6/24/51; Patsy Campbell, Leon Janney, and Karl Weber)
39. Time and Time Again (7/12/51; David Anderson)
40. Dwellers in Silence (7/19/51; Bill Griffis, Peter Capel, and Gertrude Warner)
41. Courtesy (7/26/51)
42. Universe (8/2/51; Mason Adams and Peter Capel)
43. The Veldt (8/9/51; Joan Alexander, Bill Quinn, and Leslie Woods)
44. The Vital Factor (8/16/51; Raymond Edward Johnson, John McGovern, and Luis Van Rooten)
45. Untitled Story (8/23/51; Bernard Lenrow, George Petrie, and Ann Sargeant)
46. Marionettes, Inc. (8/30/51; Ross Martin, Kermit Murdock, and Martin Rudy)
47. First Contact (9/8/51)
48. Kaleidoscope (9/15/51; Joan Alexander, Joseph di Santis, and Leon Janney)
49. Requiem (9/22/51; Rod Hendrickson, Owen Jordan, and Bill Quinn)
50. Nightfall (9/29/51; John McGovern, Cameron Prud'Homme, and Lyle Sudrow)

Disaster!

Documentary on the Red Cross Disaster Service. Sponsored by the Red Cross. Broadcast over ABC at different times and on different days. The first seventeen episodes were broadcast 5:05 to 5:30 pm, EST. Episode eighteen was a special broadcast from 6:35 to 7 pm, EST. Episodes nineteen through thirty-one were broadcast from 5:05 to 5:30 pm, EST. Episodes thirty-two through forty-five were broadcast Sunday afternoon from 12:30 to 1 pm, EST. The broadcasts were first transcribed in New York and later broadcast nationally. Recorded interviews with victims and disaster workers were featured after the dramas.

The dramas reenacted disaster scenes that featured the Red Cross providing relief and service to those in need. The broadcast of June 10, 1956, for example, concerned itself with the western floods that inundated northern California and parts of Oregon and Nevada. The broadcast of July 29, 1956, compared rescue operations during the earthquakes in San Francisco in 1906 to the earthquake in Colombia in 1955.

1. The Texas City Explosion of April 16, 1947 (5/22/55; Jackson Beck)
2. The Current Southwest Tornadoes (5/29/55)
3. The Vanport Story (6/5/55; Norman Rose)
4. The Story of the Tornado that Struck Flint, Michigan, in June 1953 (6/12/55)
5. The Story of the Floods of 1951 (6/19/55; Norman Rose)
6. The Story of the Youngstown, Ohio, Tornado of March 1955 (6/26/55)
7. The New England Forest Fires of 1946 (7/3/55; Norman Rose)
8. The Missouri Valley Floods of 1952 (7/10/55; Raymond Edward Johnson)
9. -----(7/17/55)
10. The Panhandle Tornadoes of 1947 (7/24/55)
11. Operation Snowbound [documentary on the 1949 blizzard] (7/31/55; Raymond Edward Johnson)
12. -----(8/7/55)
13. -----(8/14/55)
14. The Vicksburg, Missouri Tornado of 1953 (8/21/55; Norman Rose)
15. How the Northeastern States are Rebuilding After Recent Floods (8/28/55)
16. The Southern Tornadoes of 1952

(9/4/55; Norman Rose)
17. The Pennsylvania and Connecticut Reports on Rehabilitation Work with Victims of Recent Eastern States Floods (9/11/55)
18. The First Disaster (5/20/56; E. Roland Harriman)
19. The Western Floods of 1955-56 (6/10/56)
20. The Hawaiian Tidal Wave of April, 1946 (6/17/56)
21. Boston's Coconut Grove Fire in November, 1942 (6/24/56)
22. Southwest Texas Flood of 1954 (7/1/56)
23. The Navaho Indian Operation (7/8/56)
24. The Story of the Black Friday Tornadoes of June, 1952 (7/15/56)
25. Operation Brotherhood (7/22/56)
26. Comparison of Rescue Operation of Earthquake Disasters (7/29/56)
27. The Flash Floods of 1954 in Pennsylvania, West Virginia and Ohio (8/5/56)
28. The Woman Without a Face (8/12/56)
29. Ships in the Night (8/19/56)
30. The Story of the Rebuilding of Damaged or Destroyed Homes (8/26/56)
31. How Labor and the Red Cross Work Together (9/2/56)

32. The Story of Hurricane Audrey (7/7/57)
33. The January 1957 Floods in Eastern Kentucky, Virginia, and West Virginia (7/14/57)
34. The 1951 Mine Explosion in West Krankfort, Illinois (7/21/57)
35. The Texas/Oklahoma/Arkansas Tornadoes of April, 1957 (7/28/57)
36. The Hawaiian Tidal Wave of March, 1957 (8/4/57)
37. Galveston Hurricane and Flood of September, 1900 (8/11/57)
38. The Southern Tornadoes of 1957 (8/18/57)
39. Labor and the Red Cross (9/1/57)
40. The Ohio/Mississippi Valley Flood of 1937 (9/8/57)
41. The Missouri/Kansas Tornadoes of May, 1957 (9/15/57)
42. The Oklahoma Floods and Storms of May, 1957 [part one] (9/22/57)
43. The Oklahoma Floods and Storms of May, 1957 [part two] (9/29/57)
44. The Fargo, North Dakota Tornado of 1957 (10/6/57)
45. The East Texas Floods of April, 1957 (10/13/57)

Doc Savage*

The *Doc Savage Magazine* was only a year old in 1934 when a radio adaptation of the preserver of law and order premiered over the Don-Lee Network. All of the scripts were written by Lester Dent, the creator of *Doc Savage*. The twenty-six episodes, broadcast in syndication, were heard only on the West Coast (KHJ, Los Angeles) and then rebroadcast when the series went national in October. The cast for this series is unknown, and never announced when the program was on the air. Sponsored by Cystex. Broadcast Sunday evenings, 9 to 9:15 pm, PST, during the West Coast run.

1. The Red Death (2/10/34)
2. The Golden Legacy (2/17/34)
3. The Red-Laced Quest (2/24/34)
4. The Sniper in the Sky (3/3/34)
5. The Evil Extortionists (3/10/34)
6. Black Light Magic (3/17/34)
7. Radium Scramble (3/24/34)
8. Death Had Blue Hands (3/31/34)
9. The Sinister Sleep (4/7/34)
10. The Southern Star Mystery (4/14/34)
11. The Impossible Sleep (4/21/34)
12. The Too-Talkative Parrot (4/28/34)
13. The Blue Angel (5/5/34)
14. The Green Ghost (5/12/34)
15. Blocks of Fear (5/19/34)
16. The Phantom Terror (5/26/34)
17. Mantrap Mesa (6/2/34)
18. Fast Workers (6/9/34)
19. The Needle in a Chinese Haystack (6/16/34)
20. The Monk Called it Justice (6/23/34)
21. The White-Haired Devil (6/30/34)
22. The Oilfield Ogres (7/7/34)
23. The Fainting Lady (7/14/34)
24. Poisoned Cargo (7/21/34)
25. Find Curly Morgan (7/28/34)
26. The Growing Wizard (8/4/34)
27. The Red Death (10/6/34)
28. The Golden Legacy (10/13/34)
29. The Red-Laced Quest (10/20/34)
30. The Sniper in the Sky (10/27/34)
31. The Evil Extortionists (11/3/34)
32. Black Light Magic (11/10/34)
33. Radium Scramble (11/17/34)
34. Death Had Blue Hands (11/24/34)
35. The Sinister Sleep (12/1/34)
36. The Southern Star Mystery (12/8/34)
37. The Impossible Sleep (12/15/34)

*Compiled by Will Murray.

38. The Too-Talkative Parrot (12/22/34)
39. The Blue Angel (12/29/34)
40. The Green Ghost (1/5/35)
41. Blocks of Fear (1/12/35)
42. The Phantom Terror (1/19/35)
43. Mantrap Mesa (1/26/35)
44. Fast Workers (2/2/35)
45. The Needle in a Chinese Haystack
    (2/9/35)

46. The Monk Called It Justice (2/16/35)
47. The White-Haired Devil (2/23/35)
48. The Oilfield Ogres (3/2/35)
49. The Fainting Lady (3/9/35)
50. Poisoned Cargo (3/16/35)
51. Find Curly Morgan (3/23/35)
52. The Growing Wizard (3/30/35)

Doc Savage, Man of Bronze

This program, a revival of the original 1934–35 series, originated from WMCA in New York, and was broadcast only as a local radio station program. Sustained, this program was broadcast on Wednesday afternoon, 5 to 5:30 pm, EST. The scripts were written by Edwards Gruskin, and starred Bernard Lenrow and Earl George. Only twenty-six episodes were broadcast; the last three were repeats of earlier scripts. In 1985, *Doc Savage* was revised over network radio again, this time on National Public Radio for two serial adventures.

1. Doc Savage (1/6/43)
2. The Return from Death (1/13/43)
3. A Note of Death (1/20/43)
4. Murder Charm (1/27/43)
5. Death Stalks the Morgue (2/3/43)
6. I'll Dance on Your Grave (2/10/43)
7. Murder Is a Business (2/17/43)
8. The Living Evil (2/24/43)
9. Journey into Oblivion (3/3/43)
10. The Hour of Murder (3/10/43)
11. The Pharaoh's Wisdom (3/17/43)
12. Society Amazonia (3/24/43)
13. Insect Menace (3/31/43)
14. Subway to Hell (4/7/43)

15. The Monster of the Sea (4/14/43)
16. The Voice That Cried "Kill"
    (4/21/43)
17. The Cult of Satan (4/28/43)
18. When Dead Men Walk (5/5/43)
19. The Screeching Ghost (5/12/43)
20. Ransom or Death (5/19/43)
21. Murder Man (5/26/43)
22. The Miracle Maniac (6/2/43)
23. The Skull Man (6/9/43)
24. The Voice That Cried "Kill"
    (6/16/43)
25. The Living Evil (6/23/43)
26. Murder Is a Business (6/30/43)

Doctors Then and Now

Presented on NBC in cooperation with the American Medical Association, *Doctors Then and Now* was a series of dramatizations dealing with a century of American Medical History. The program presented stories from the lives of men who had contributed to Medical progress. The initial broadcast told of Dr. James Marion Sims, who won international fame for his work in gynecology. Scripts were written by William Murphy. Norman Felton directed. Broadcast on Saturday afternoons from 4 to 4:30 pm, EST, the final two broadcasts were 4:30–5 pm. After each drama, a guest speaker, always a doctor, gave a short speech about the advances of the medical field.

1. The Story of Dr. James Sims (12/7/46)
2. The Story of Dr. Samuel J. Crumbine (12/14/46)
3. -----(12/28/46)
4. The Story of Dr. Crawford W. Long (1/4/47)
5. The Story of Dr. Stephen Smith (1/11/47)
6. The Story of Francois Marie Prevost (1/18/47)
7. The Story of Dr. John S. Bobbs (1/25/47)
8. The Medicine in Chicago and Dr. John Evans (2/1/47)
9. The Life of Dr. Nathan Smith, Founder of Dartmouth Medical College (2/8/47)
10. The Career of Dr. Marcus Whitman, First American Doctor to Cross the Continental Divide (2/15/47)
11. The Story of Dr. John A Waggoner (2/22/47)
12. The Story of Dr. Ephraim McDowell (3/1/47)
13. The Story of Dr. Daniel Drake (3/8/47)
14. The Story of Dr. Howard Kelly (3/15/47)
15. The Life of Father Anthony Ravalli (3/22/47)
16. The Life of Dr. Victor H. Stickney (3/29/47)
17. The Life of Dr. Douglas Houghton (4/5/47)
18. The Life of Joseph P. Widney (4/12/47)
19. The Life of John T. Huff (4/19/47)
20. The Story of Dr. Anson Jones (4/26/47)
21. The Story of Dr. John (5/3/47)
22. The Life of John Peter Mettauer (5/10/47)
23. The Story of Hot Springs Arkansas, and Dr. George Lawrence (5/17/47)
24. -----(5/24/47)
25. The Life of Dr. John Frederick May (5/31/47)
26. The Life of Dr. Beatty Marchmont (6/7/47)
27. -----(6/14/47)

Dr. Christian

This dramatic series dealt with the life of a fictional Dr. Christian (named after Hans Christian Andersen) who lived his life helping others in need — much like Mayberry with a doctor instead of a sheriff. One week he was a kindly town philosopher, and the week after he played cupid. One week he may be saving an old woman from a burning house, and the week after he was involved in a murder case. Jean Hersholt played the role of Dr. Christian for the entire run, a role that made him famous almost overnight. The only other recurring character was Dr. Christian's secretary, Judy Price, a role first played by Helen Claire. Lurene Tuttle took over the role by the early forties, replaced afterwards by Claire again in the mid-forties. By 1947, Rosemary de Camp was Judy, bowing out in the early fifties for Kathleen Fitz.

When the program premiered, it was initially called *Dr. Christian of River's End* and, for a time, *The Vaseline Program*, because it was sponsored by Vaseline. Broadcast over CBS, first on Sunday afternoons from 2:30 to 3 pm, EST. Beginning October 18, 1938, the program featured new music and was heard on

Tuesday evenings from 10 to 10:30 pm, EST. Beginning November 1, 1939, *Dr. Christian* was heard on Wednesday evenings from 10 to 10:30 pm, EST. Finally, the program settled on Wednesday evenings from 8:30 to 9 pm, beginning January 3, 1940, remaining in this time slot for the remainder of the run.

In 1941, the producers came up with a great idea to encourage listeners of the program to participate in the productions. A contest was held in which the listeners were allowed to submit their own stories and scripts for the series. Writers of those that would be used were paid an average $500. Each season, the best script would be awarded $2,000, with the first award given in June of 1942. This annual contest brought in more than 10,000 manuscripts a year.

The first ten broadcasts originated from New York, as did episodes 36 through 41, 58 through 62, 82 through 84, 11, 207, 319, 338, and 341 through 343. All of the other broadcasts originated from Hollywood. Episodes 341, 342 and 343 featured Claude Rains as Dr. Alexander Webb while Jean Hersholt returned home to Copenhagen, Denmark, to survey needs for the National War Fund. (Hersholt was heard at the end of episode 343 via shortwave.) Episode 201 featured an all Negro cast except for Hersholt and Tuttle. Episode 24 featured Robert Mitchell and the St. Branden's Boys Choir. Note: The first 25 episodes may not be the exact script titles, as titles were not announced on the program until episode twenty-six.

1. Operation in a Shack (11/7/37)
2. The Steve and Charlotte Story (11/14/37)
3. The Tanzy Story (11/21/37)
4. Susan and the Opera Singer (11/28/37)
5. The Blind Boy Story (12/5/37)
6. The Mother-In-Law Story (12/12/37)
7. The Young Fellow Who Stole an Auto (12/19/37)
8. The Woman Who Runs Dress Store (12/26/37)
9. Kidnapped Husband (1/2/38)
10. Auto Accident (1/9/38)
11. The Flood Story (1/16/38)
12. Dog Story (1/23/38)
13. The New Stove (1/30/38)
14. The Man with the Paralyzed Arm (2/6/38)
15. Widow Wants to Mary Doctor (2/13/38)
16. War Story (2/20/38)
17. Milk Racket [part one] (2/27/38)
18. Milk Racket [part two] (3/6/38)
19. Milk Racket [part three] (3/13/38)
20. The Story of Prisoner's Child (3/20/38)
21. The Story of Windy and the Truth Pills (3/27/38)
22. The Story of Harry Monroe and a Scarf (4/3/38)
23. Landslide (4/10/38)
24. The Dishonest Boy (4/17/38)
25. Joe Perino (4/24/38)
26. Baby on the Doorstep (10/18/38)
27. Boy Loves Girl (10/25/38)
28. Dr. Christian for Mayor (11/1/38)
29. Tony Donella (11/8/38)
30. The Accident (11/15/38)
31. Corner Stone (11/22/38)
32. The Seeing Eye [part one] (11/29/38)
33. The Seeing Eye [part two] (12/6/38)
34. The Pirate of Rivers End (12/13/38)
35. Danny Gets Married (12/20/38)
36. The Glamour Girl (12/27/38)
37. The Neediest Case (1/3/39)
38. Guest of Honor (1/10/39)
39. Back to Youth (1/17/39)
40. Chains (1/24/39)
41. The Music Box (1/31/39)
42. Have a Heart (2/7/39)
43. Angel Beware (2/14/39)
44. Washington Had His Delaware (2/21/39)
45. Puppy Love (2/28/39)

344. Dr. Christian Award Winners — # 4 (6/27/45)
345. Dave's in Love (7/4/45)
346. Always A Woman (7/11/45)
347. Joyous Heart (7/18/45)
348. The Liar (7/25/45)
349. The Legend of Khorassam (8/1/45)
350. Christmas Deferred (8/8/45)
351. Canine Justice (8/15/45)
352. Leave It to Love (8/22/45)
353. Puff (8/29/45)
354. Much to Do About Marty (9/5/45)
355. Room Clerk (9/12/45)
356. Our Daughter Barbara (9/19/45)
357. The Wolf Named Navy Blue (9/26/45)
358. Love to Mama (10/3/45)
359. Chain Letter (10/10/45)
360. The Attic Stairway Murder Mystery (10/17/45)
361. Playboy (10/24/45)
362. Sterling Silver (10/31/45)
363. The Last Awakening (11/7/45)
364. The Long Lane (11/14/45)
365. The Philandering Ghost (11/21/45)
366. Retreat to Kindness (11/28/45)
367. Girl Trouble (12/5/45)
368. Susan Comes Marching Home (12/12/45)
369. The Little Carpenter (12/19/45)
370. Mission Accomplished (12/26/45)
371. What It Takes (1/2/46)
372. Curare (1/9/46)
373. Scandal in the Fourth Dimension (1/16/46)
374. Mr. Sourpuss (1/23/46)
375. Miss Minnie (1/30/46)
376. Requiem for a Hero (2/6/46)
377. The Hoofer (2/13/46)
378. The Girl with the Golden Gauntlets (2/20/46)
379. Forbidden Hill (2/27/46)
380. One for the Money (3/6/46)
381. Two Notes (3/13/46)
382. Man to Man (3/20/46)
383. The Vagabond Veteran (3/27/46)
384. Big and Little Johnny (4/3/46)
385. Boost for Heaven (4/10/46)
386. Live Wire (4/17/46)
387. The Junction (4/24/46)
388. Clue of the Left-Handed Matches (5/1/46)
389. Mother Trouble (5/8/46)
390. The Devil That Calls in the Night (5/15/46)
391. Hero in the Doghouse (5/22/46)
392. Pattern Completed (5/29/46)
393. The Love Bug (6/5/46)
394. The Other Side of the Page (6/12/46)
395. Dr. Christian Award Winners —#5 (6/19/46)
396. The Ghost-Ridden Doctor (6/26/46)
397. Two Loves Had Marian (7/3/46)
398. Spotlight on Grandma (7/10/46)
399. The Silver Cup (7/17/46)
400. Squeegee (7/24/46)
401. World Champion (7/31/46)
402. Marriage Masquerade (8/7/46)
403. Angel's flight (8/14/46)
404. Wedding Bells (8/21/46)
405. Adventure in Tutoring (8/28/46)
406. By Death Deferred (9/4/46)
407. Annabella and I (9/11/46)
408. The Atomic Vitamin (9/18/46)
409. Lorelei (9/25/46)
410. The Brought-On Saint (10/2/46)
411. A Loose Nut in the Living Machine (10/9/46)
412. Out of the Bog (10/16/46)
413. None But the Beautiful (10/23/46)
414. A Man of his Stamp (10/30/46)
415. To All Men (11/6/46)
416. As Old as He Feels (11/13/46)
417. Sergeant Snafu (11/20/46)
418. No Heart So Lonely (11/27/46)
419. Without Appointment (12/4/46)
420. Cupid in Bobby-Sox (12/11/46)
421. Two Too Many (12/18/46)
422. So You Don't Believe in Christmas (12/25/46)
423. Diagnosis (1/1/47)
424. Cross-Country Wedding (1/8/47)
425. Bewitched (1/15/47)
426. Manuel (1/22/47)
427. Dr. Christian Tells a Lie (1/29/47)
428. Guest From India (2/5/47)
429. Aftermath (2/12/47)
430. Home Is the Son (2/19/47)
431. The Ring (2/26/47)
432. The Mark of Buddha (3/5/47)
433. Davey's in Love (3/12/47)
434. The Ghost-Ridden Doctor (3/19/47)
435. The Stone Lions (3/26/47)
436. Party Line (4/2/47)

437. The Case of the Twin Keys (4/9/47)
438. Doctor's Orders (4/16/47)
439. The Silent Seymours (4/23/47)
440. Tombstone Tommie (4/30/47)
441. The Silver Lining (5/7/47)
442. Where There's Smoke (5/14/47)
443. The Bright Shield (5/21/47)
444. Show Me First Your Penny (5/28/47)
445. Strange Caller (6/4/47)
446. Wife of a Hero (6/11/47)
447. Dr. Christian Award Winners —#6 (6/18/47)
448. Coming in on a Cloud (6/25/47)
449. For Better or For Worse (7/2/47)
450. The Century Plant (7/9/47)
451. Death and Life of Jonathan Lord (7/16/47)
452. A Pearl Gray Fedora (7/23/47)
453. The Street Called 'Now' (7/30/47)
454. Paid in Full (8/6/47)
455. Heritage (8/13/47)
456. Princess (8/20/47)
457. And the Sun Stood Still (8/27/47)
458. The Oath (9/3/47)
459. The Lovin' Hearted (9/10/47)
460. The Norton Nose (9/17/47)
461. Twenty Year Promise (9/24/47)
462. The Boy From Texas (10/1/47)
463. His Father's Son (10/8/47)
464. Dr. Christian's Cinderella (10/15/47)
465. Bible in the Window (10/22/47)
466. The Crystal Bowl (10/29/47)
467. Anniversary Party (11/5/47)
468. The Doctor Takes a Son (11/12/47)
469. -----(11/19/47)
470. Cupid's Boomerang (11/26/47)
471. Gold Girl (12/3/47)
472. Love's Old Sweet Dream (12/10/47)
473. There's No Accounting for Tastes (12/17/47)
474. Dr. Christian Pulls Some Strings (12/24/47)
475. Genius Hits a Snag (12/31/47)
476. Eyes to See With (1/7/48)
477. Strange Gesture (1/14/48)
478. Little White Lie (1/21/48)
479. Commander Halliday Returns (1/28/48)
480. A Wish for Elizabeth (2/4/48)
481. The Legacy (2/11/48)
482. Candid Shot (2/18/48)
483. Next Car Going Up (2/25/48)

484. Fool's Gold (3/3/48)
485. Born to Dance (3/10/48)
486. The Decision (3/17/48)
487. The Black Patch (3/24/48)
488. Lucky Accident (3/31/48)
489. The Climax Comes Up Bobby-Sox (4/7/48)
490. The Trap (4/14/48)
491. The Broken Taboo (4/21/48)
492. Little Boy Marine (4/28/48)
493. Now That Spring Is Here (5/5/48)
494. Winner's Circle (5/12/48)
495. Dr. Christian Award Winners —#7 (5/19/48)
496. The Little Boy Laughed (5/26/48)
497. S & H, Inc. (6/2/48)
498. Call in the Night (6/9/48)
499. Love's Young Dream (6/16/48)
500. Compensation (6/23/48)
501. My Decision (6/30/48)
502. Often a Bridesmaid (7/7/48)
503. Double Double-Cross (7/21/48)
504. Big Brother (7/28/48)
505. Fresh as a Daisy (8/4/48)
506. Taylor-Made Dreams (8/11/48)
507. The Other Mother (8/18/48)
508. Night Time (8/25/48)
509. Long Years of Remembering (9/1/48)
510. Where Angels Fear to Tread (9/8/48)
511. Like Father, Like Son (9/15/48)
512. The Lost Vision (9/22/48)
513. Stranger in Our House (9/29/48)
514. Father by Proxy (10/6/48)
515. Moon Madness (10/13/48)
516. The Lord's Prayer (10/20/48)
517. Confidence Regained (10/27/48)
518. Home Town (11/3/48)
519. Two Is a Crowd (11/10/48)
520. Cactus Joe (11/17/48)
521. The Re-Education of Bill Benton (11/24/48)
522. The Man Who Talked (12/1/48)
523. He That Is Great (12/8/48)
524. A Child Is Born (12/15/48)
525. Listen, The Bells Are Ringing (12/22/48)
526. Shirt Baby (12/29/48)
527. Obsession (1/5/49)
528. The Big One That Got Away (1/12/49)
529. Doctor of Law (1/19/49)
530. Bring Home the Bacon (1/26/49)

531. Her Husband's Ghost (2/2/49)
532. Time and Love (2/9/49)
533. Phantom in the Studio (2/16/49)
534. Career Woman (2/23/49)
535. I Choose Daddy (3/2/49)
536. Sense of Humor (3/9/49)
537. Who Would Not Sing for David? (3/16/49)
538. Mademoiselle from River's End (3/23/49)
539. Optical Illusion (3/30/49)
540. The Full Treatment (4/6/49)
541. The Toy Pistol (4/13/49)
542. The Lie (4/20/49)
543. Poor Henry (4/27/49)
544. One-Dog Ambulance (5/4/49)
545. The River Rats (5/11/49)
546. Dr. Christian Award Winners —#8 (5/18/49)
547. Stolen Glory (5/25/49)
548. Dr. Christian's Magic (6/1/49)
549. The Perfectionist (6/8/49)
550. Is Good — Eggs (6/15/49)
551. Three Springs of Bittersweet (6/22/49)
552. Wanted: A Wife (6/29/49)
553. The Wedding Present (7/6/49)
554. Sammy Hits the Jackpot (7/13/49)
555. Two-Way Promise (7/20/49)
556. Fate Breaks an Arm (7/27/49)
557. The Immigrant (8/3/49)
558. Operation Angela (8/10/49)
559. White Magic (8/17/49)
560. The Oxygen Tent (8/24/49)
561. Tradition of the Towel (8/31/49)
562. The Magic Cell (9/7/49)
563. Cloudburst (9/14/49)
564. Miss Tittleworth's Will (9/21/49)
565. Rendezvous in Paris (9/28/49)
566. Dangerous Age for Ellen (10/5/49)
567. Angel With a Black Eye (10/12/49)
568. Say it With Music (10/19/49)
569. Squish-Face (10/26/49)
570. Old Battle-Ax (11/2/49)
571. Who Would Not Sing for David? (11/9/49)
572. Girl in the Mist (11/16/49)
573. The Teakettle: She Sing (11/23/49)
574. To Live a Dream (11/30/49)
575. Lucky Thirteen (12/7/49)
576. Miss Baltimore (12/14/49)
577. Santa's Sunday Punch (12/21/49)
578. Bon Voyage, Miss Tweedie (12/28/49)

579. Clear Conscience (1/4/50)
580. The Other Road (1/11/50)
581. Peel Rubber (1/18/50)
582. Ghost in the House (1/25/50)
583. Winner Takes Corrigan (2/1/50)
584. The Redheads (2/8/50)
585. Whirlpool's Rim (2/15/50)
586. The Generals Ride the Night (2/22/50)
587. Granny Hears the Truth (3/1/50)
588. Heaven's with Mom and Dad (3/8/50)
589. Remarkable Fortune of Joe Baker (3/15/50)
590. The Rainbow Trail (3/22/50)
591. The Sawdust Transfusion (3/29/50)
592. Complications of the Heart (4/5/50)
593. The Journey (4/12/50)
594. Show in the Street (4/19/50)
595. The Babysitter (4/26/50)
596. All Things Come Home (5/3/50)
597. The Giggler (5/10/50)
598. Dr. Christian Award Winners —#9 (5/17/50)
599. The Language for Pamela (5/24/50)
600. Prescription for Pamela (5/31/50)
601. The Noblest Motive (6/7/50)
602. The Green Cat (6/14/50)
603. Cupid Walks a Picket Line (6/21/50)
604. The General's Sword (6/28/50)
605. A Flower for Mom (7/5/50)
606. Tell Her So (7/12/50)
607. Ghost Story (7/19/50)
608. A Little Bit of Glory (7/26/50)
609. Just Call Me Aunt Letty (8/2/50)
610. The Brother Act (8/9/50)
611. Will O' the Wisp (8/16/50)
612. Top Dog (8/23/50)
613. One Touch of Genius (8/30/50)
614. The Return of Johnny Sinclair (9/6/50)
615. Housing for Two (9/13/50)
616. A Million for Your Thoughts (9/20/50)
617. Old Sarge (9/27/50)
618. Love Is a Two-Sided Thing (10/4/50)
619. A Time to Remember (10/11/50)
620. The Eldest (10/18/50)
621. Don't Look Down (10/25/50)
622. The Class of 1908 Elects (11/1/50)
623. The Lopsided Halo (11/8/50)

715. -----(8/13/52)
716. Dear Elizabeth (8/20/52)
717. A Rugged Individualist (8/27/52)
718. The Will of Caleb Johnson (9/3/52)
719. The Better Part (9/10/52)
720. Little Black Part (9/17/52)
721. For the Sake of Honor (9/24/52)
722. Courage Is Contagious (10/1/52)
723. Second Chance (10/8/52)
724. The Common Denominator (10/15/52)
725. Fear Not (10/22/52)
726. A Slight Case of Politics (10/29/52)
727. The Lady From South Creek (11/5/52)
728. A Woman's Place (11/12/52)
729. Take Me Home, Perry (11/19/52)
730. The Ghost on Crutches (11/26/52)
731. Doc, You Made a Miracle (12/3/52)
732. Double Trouble (12/10/52)
733. Boy Doll (12/17/52)
734. Substitute for Santa (12/24/52)
735. Old Man Marsh (12/31/52)
736. For Everything You Gain (1/7/53)
737. Firm Is the Rock (1/14/53)
738. Ballad of the Married Bachelor (1/21/53)
739. A Monument for My Father (1/28/53)
740. The Pinafore Sash (2/4/53)
741. Maid of Honor (2/11/53)
742. Pitcher's Battle (2/18/53)
743. The Perils of Parenthood (2/25/53)
744. The Fork of the Road (3/4/53)
745. The Return of Helen Haines (3/11/53)
746. The Sound of the Bells (3/18/53)
747. Triplets Are Not Uncommon (3/25/53)
748. Aunt Belle (4/1/53)
749. Mother's Day (4/8/53)
750. The Stubborn One (4/15/53)
751. A Case of Conscience (4/22/53)
752. The Head That Swells (4/29/53)
753. Fingerprints (5/6/53)
754. Leave It to Lucy (5/13/53)
755. Dr. Christian Award Winners —#12 (5/20/53)
756. The Boy Who Saw Good (5/27/53)
757. Mind Over Menu (6/3/53)
758. The Gordon Nose (6/10/53)
759. Pony Ride (6/17/53)
760. Hubby's Hobby (6/24/53)
761. The Mighty Mite (7/1/53)
762. Postman Who Wanted To Sit (7/8/53)
763. The Amazing Hour (7/15/53)
764. Cry to the World (7/22/53)
765. Heroes (7/29/53)
766. Mr. Thraser's Preview (8/5/53)
767. Romano and Son (8/12/53)
768. The Man Was Independent (8/19/53)
769. Baby's Choice (8/26/53)
770. Inheritance (9/2/53)
771. Reluctant Grandma (9/9/53)
772. Mr. Fulton's Fancy (9/16/53)
773. Bread for Marty (9/23/53)
774. Like Mother Used to Make (9/30/53)
775. Room 316 (10/7/53)
776. Girl Like Mom (10/14/53)
777. The Piano (10/21/53)
778. Second Son (10/28/53)
779. Grandpa Ferguson (11/4/53)
780. Cigars for Two (11/11/53)
781. Loveletter Killer (11/18/53)
782. Puppets on a String (11/25/53)
783. Silver Spoon (12/2/53)
784. Package From Paris (12/9/53)
785. Man Size (12/16/53)
786. Tony's Parcel (12/23/53)
787. Butch (12/30/53)
788. Evenhanded Justice (1/6/54)

Dragnet *

"Ladies and Gentlemen ... the story you are about to hear is true. Only the names have been changed to protect the innocent." Based on actual L.A.P.D. police files, *Dragnet* presented the day-to-day drudgery of police work. Broadcast over

*Compiled by Chris Lembesis and Randy Eidemiller.

NBC, this long-running detective/crime series ran on television and radio for more than a decade. In 1954, Warner Brothers released a big-screen version of the popular radio/television series, with Jack Webb still in the role of Sergeant Joe Friday.

The series was sustaining until October 6, 1949, when Fatima Cigarettes took over as sponsor. Chesterfield began sponsoring on September 14, 1952. *Dragnet* featured multiple sponsors beginning September 27, 1955. The first four broadcasts were heard on Friday evenings, episodes five through thirteen on Thursdays, episodes fourteen through eighteen on Saturdays, and from October 6, 1949, to September 11, 1952, Thursdays. Beginning September 14, 1951, the program was broadcast Sundays from 9:30 to 10 pm, and beginning September 1, 1953, on Tuesdays.

Barton Yarborough was Friday's partner until December 20, 1951. Barney Phillips took over beginning December 27, 1951; Martin Milner, beginning April 17, 1952; Harry Bartell, May 1, 1952; Martin Milner, again on May 8; Herb Ellis, beginning May 15; Ken Peters, on June 12, 1952; Victor Perrin, beginning June 19; Ken Patterson, on August 14, 1952; and Herb Ellis, beginning August 21, 1952. Charles McGraw played the role of Ed Backstrand for the first three broadcasts, before being replaced by Raymond Burr. Peggy Webber played the part of Sgt. Joe Friday's mother.

Scripts were written by James Moser, John Robinson, Paul Coates, Richard Breen, Earl Schley, Robert Ryf, Frank Burt, Ben Alexander and Jack Webb. Webb was so associated with police work that when he died on December 23, 1982, flags were flown at half staff at Police Headquarters in Parker Center and at substations throughout Los Angeles.

1. Nickel Plate Gun (6/3/49)
2. Fast Trigger Gun (6/2/49; Frank Lovejoy)
3. The Werewolf (6/17/49)
4. Shotgun Cop Kill (6/24/49)
5. The Big Pipe (7/7/49)
6. Red Light Bandit (7/14/49)
7. The Big Bomb (7/21/49)
8. The Big Missing (7/28/49)
9. Benny Trounsel (8/4/49)
10. Maniac Murderer (8/11/49; Raymond Burr)
11. The Big Affair (8/18/49)
12. Police Academy — Mario Koski (8/25/49)
13. Myra, The Redhead (9/1/49)
14. Eric Kelby (9/3/49)
15. Sullivan Kidnap (9/10/49)
16. James Vickers (9/17/49)
17. Brick-Bat Slayer (9/24/49)
18. Tom Laval (10/1/49)
19. Second Hand Killer (10/6/49)
20. The Big Buy (10/13/49)
21. The Big Lamp (10/20/49)
22. The Big Drink (10/27/49)
23. The Big Help (11/3/49)
24. The Big Bar (11/10/49)
25. Harry Girard (11/17/49)
26. Mother-In-Law Murder (11/24/49)
27. Spring St. Gang (12/1/49)
28. Jade Thumb Rings (12/8/49)
29. Garbage Chute Murder (12/15/49)
30. .22 Rifle for Christmas (12/22/49)
31. Flowerland Roof Murder (12/29/49)
32. The Big Escape (1/5/50)
33. The Big Man (Part One) (1/12/50)
34. The Big Man (Part Two) (1/19/50)
35. Child Killer (2/2/50)
36. The Big Girl (2/9/50)
37. The Big Gifter (2/23/50)

38. The Big Kill (3/2/50)
39. The Big Thank You (3/9/50)
40. The Big Boys (3/16/50)
41. The Big Gangster (Part One) (3/23/50)
42. The Big Gangster (Part Two) (3/30/50)
43. The Big Book (4/6/50)
44. The Big Watch (4/13/50)
45. The Big Trial (4/20/50)
46. The Big Job (4/27/50)
47. The Big Badge (5/4/50)
48. The Big Knife (5/11/50)
49. The Big Pug (5/18/50)
50. The Big Key (5/25/50)
51. The Big Fake (6/1/50)
52. The Big Smart Guy (6/8/50)
53. The Big Press (6/15/50)
54. The Big Mink (6/22/50)
55. The Big Grab (6/29/50)
56. The Big Frame (7/6/50)
57. The Big Bomb (7/13/50)
58. The Big Gent (Part One) (7/20/50)
59. The Big Gent (Part Two) (7/27/50)
60. The Big Dare (8/3/50)
61. The Big Actor (8/10/50)
62. The Big Youngster (8/17/50)
63. The Big Chance (8/24/50)
64. The Big Check (8/31/50)
65. The Big Poison (9/7/50)
66. The Big Make (9/14/50)
67. The Big Pair (9/21/50)
68. The Big Death (9/28/50)
69. The Big .38 (10/5/50)
70. The Big Quack (10/12/50)
71. The Big Grandma (10/19/50)
72. The Big Meet (10/26/50)
73. The Big Church (11/2/50)
74. The Big Mother (11/9/50)
75. The Big Parrot (11/16/50)
76. The Big Betty (11/23/50)
77. The Big Car (11/30/50)
78. The Big Picture (12/7/50)
79. The Big Break (12/14/50)
80. .22 Rifle for Christmas (12/21/50)
81. The Big Family (12/28/50)
82. The Big Holdup (1/4/51)
83. The Big Jump (1/11/51)
84. The Big Dance (1/18/51)
85. The Big Tomato (1/25/51)
86. The Big Children (2/1/51)
87. The Big Cast (2/8/51)
88. The Big Crime (2/15/51)
89. The Big Couple (2/22/51)
90. The Big Partner (3/1/51)
91. The Big New Years (3/8/51)
92. The Big Ben (3/15/51)
93. The Big Trunk (3/22/51)
94. The Big Lover (3/29/51)
95. The Big Friend (4/5/51)
96. The Big Threat (4/12/51)
97. The Big Speech (4/19/51)
98. The Big Saint (4/26/51)
99. The Big Casing (5/3/51)
100. The Big Drills (5/10/51)
101. The Big Blast (5/17/51)
102. The Big Mailman (5/24/51)
103. The Big Bindle (5/31/51)
104. The Big Impostor (6/7/51)
105. The Big Building (6/14/51)
106. The Big Run (6/21/51)
107. The Big Cliff (6/28/51)
108. The Big Love (7/5/51)
109. The Big Set-Up (7/12/51)
110. The Big Sophomore (7/19/51)
111. The Big Late Script (7/26/51)
112. The Big Cop (8/2/51)
113. The Big Screen (8/9/51)
114. The Big Winchester (8/16/51)
115. The Big In-Laws (8/23/51)
116. The Big Crazy (8/30/51)
117. The Big Seventeen (9/6/51)
118. The Big Waiter (9/13/51)
119. The Big Sour (9/20/51)
120. The Big September Man (9/27/51)
121. The Big Want Ad (10/4/51)
122. The Big Shoplift (10/11/51)
123. The Big Story Man (10/18/51)
124. The Big Market (10/25/51)
125. The Big Lease (11/1/51)
126. The Big Hit and Run Killer (11/8/51)
127. The Big Bungalow (11/15/51)
128. The Big Hands (11/22/51)
129. The Big Affair (11/29/51)
130. The Big Canaries (12/6/51)
131. The Big Overtime (12/13/51)
132. .22 Rifle for Christmas (12/20/51)
133. The Big Sorrow (12/27/51)*
134. The Big Red (Part One) (1/3/52)
135. The Big Red (Part Two) (1/10/52)
136. The Big Juvenile Division (1/17/52)
137. The Big Court (1/24/52)
138. The Big Almost No-Show (1/31/52)

Show is dedicated to Barton Yarborough who had died unexpectedly.

139. The Big Honeymoon (2/7/52)
140. The Big Phonecall (2/14/52)
141. The Big Producer (2/21/52)
142. The Big Plant (2/28/52)
143. The Big Evans (3/6/52)
144. The Big Fire (3/13/52)
145. The Big Border (3/20/52)
146. The Big Rose (3/27/52)
147. The Big Streetcar (4/3/52)
148. The Big Show (4/10/52)
149. The Big Bunco (4/17/52)
150. The Big Elevator (4/24/52)
151. The Big Safe (5/1/52)
152. The Big Gamble (5/8/52)
153. The Big Mail (5/15/52)
154. The Big Shakedown (5/22/52)
155. The Big Fourth (5/29/52)
156. The Big Whiff (6/5/52)
157. The Big Donation (6/12/52)
158. The Big Jules (6/19/52)
159. The Big Roll (6/26/52)
160. The Big Trio (7/3/52)
161. The Big Hate (7/10/52)
162. The Big Signet (7/31/52)
163. The Big Impression (8/7/52)
164. The Big Drive (8/14/52)
165. The Big Paper (8/21/52)
166. The Big Test (8/28/52)
167. The Big Ray (9/4/52)
168. The Big Tear (9/11/52)
169. The Big Bull (9/14/52)
170. The Big Shot (9/21/52)
171. The Big Brain (9/28/52)
172. The Big Jolt (10/5/52)
173. The Big Lie (10/12/52)
174. The Big Pill (10/19/52)
175. The Big Number (10/26/52)
176. The Big Light (11/2/52)
177. The Big Dive (11/9/52)
178. The Big Walk (11/16/52)
179. The Big Guilt (11/23/52)
180. The Big Shirt (11/30/52)
181. The Big Mole (12/7/52)
182. The Big Eavesdrop (12/14/52)
183. .22 Rifle for Christmas (12/21/52)
184. The Big Mask (Part One)
      (12/28/52)
185. The Big Mask (Part Two) (1/4/53)
186. The Big Small (1/11/53)
187. The Big String (1/18/53)
188. The Big Lay-Out (1/25/53)

189. The Big Strip (2/1/53)
190. The Big Press (2/8/53)
191. The Big Tooth (2/15/53)
192. The Big Smoke (2/22/53)
193. The Big Want (3/1/53)
194. The Big Laugh (3/8/53)
195. The Big Impossible (3/15/53)
196. The Big Informant (3/22/53)
197. The Big Dream (3/29/53)
198. The Big Chet (4/5/53)
199. The Big Compulsion (4/12/53)
200. The Big Rip (4/19/53)*
201. The Big Scrapbook (4/26/53)
202. The Big Carney (5/3/53)
203. The Big Joke (5/10/53)
204. The Big False Move (5/17/53)
205. The Big Gun (Part One) (5/24/53)
206. The Big Gun (Part Two) (5/31/53)
207. The Big Will (6/7/53)
208. The Big Lilly (6/14/53)
209. The Big Revolt (6/21/53)
210. The Big Ham (6/28/53)
211. The Big Bop (9/1/53)
212. The Big Lift (9/8/53)
213. The Big Cab (9/15/53)
214. The Big Slip (9/22/53)
215. The Big Try (9/29/53)
216. The Big Little Mother (10/6/53)
217. The Big Plea (10/13/53)
218. The Big Paint (10/20/53)
219. The Big Fraud (10/27/53)
220. The Big Rain (11/3/53)
221. The Big Kid (11/10/53)
222. The Big Flight (11/17/53)
223. The Big Present (11/24/53)
224. The Big Odd (12/1/53)
225. The Big Pick (12/8/53)
226. The Big Brink (12/15/53)
227. The Big Little Jesus (12/22/53)
228. The Big Steal (12/29/53)
229. The Big Listen (1/5/54)
230. The Big Switch (1/12/54)
231. The Big Bill (1/19/54)
232. The Big Bid (1/26/54)
233. The Big Filth (2/2/54)
234. The Big Broad (2/9/54)
235. The Big Sucker (2/16/54)
236. The Big Pipe (2/23/54)
237. The Big TV (3/2/54)
238. The Big Cup (3/9/54)
239. The Big Rod (3/16/54)

* *Interuption for a special news bulletin giving names of wounded POWs returned from Freedom village.*

240. The Big Mustache (3/23/54)
241. The Big Confession (3/30/54)
242. The Big Saw (4/6/54)
243. The Big Note (4/13/54)
244. The Big Net (4/20/54)
245. The Big Lift (4/27/54)
246. The Big Stop (5/4/54)
247. The Big Look (5/11/54)
248. The Big Help (5/18/54)
249. The Big Watch (5/25/54)
250. The Big Cowboy (6/1/54)
251. The Big Student (6/8/54)
252. The Big Cat (6/15/54)
253. The Big Customer (6/22/54)
254. The Big Chick (6/29/54)
255. The Big Search (7/6/54)
256. The Big Rescue (7/13/54)
257. The Big Heel (7/20/54)
258. The Big Match (7/27/54)
259. The Big Stand (8/3/54)
260. The Big Wish (8/10/54)
261. The Big Cad (8/17/54)
262. The Big Shock (8/24/54)
263. The Big Office (8/31/54)
264. The Big Trunk (9/7/54)
265. The Big Cut (9/14/54)
266. The Big Try (9/21/54)
267. The Big Bible (9/28/54)
268. The Big Handsome Bandit (10/5/54)
269. The Bar Tar Baby (10/12/54)
270. The Big Manakin (10/19/54)
271. The Big Key (10/26/54)
272. The Big Locker (11/2/54)
273. The Big Coins (11/9/54)
274. The Big Dog (11/16/54)
275. The Big Switch (11/23/54)
276. The Big Gone (11/30/54)
277. The Big Dig (12/7/54)
278. The Big Lens (12/14/54)
279. The Big Little Jesus (12/21/54)
280. The Big Underground (12/28/54)
281. The Big Mug (1/4/55)
282. The Big Complex (1/11/55)
283. The Big Token (1/18/55)
284. The Big Bounce (1/25/55)
285. The Big Bird (2/1/55)
286. The Big Gap (2/8/55)
287. The Big Hat (2/15/55)
288. The Big Slug (2/22/55)
289. The Big Set-Up (3/1/55)
290. The Big Father (3/8/55)
291. The Big Set (3/15/55)
292. The Big Talk (3/22/55)

293. The Big Death (3/29/55)
294. The Big No-Tooth (4/5/55)
295. The Big Tie (4/12/55)
296. The Big Deal (4/19/55)
297. The Big Child (4/26/55)
298. The Big Momma (5/3/55)
299. The Big Revision (5/10/55)
300. The Big Squealer (5/17/55)
301. The Big Siege (5/24/55)
302. The Big Sisters (5/31/55)
303. The Big Limp (6/7/55)
304. The Big Fall Guy (6/14/55)
305. The Big Grab (6/21/55)
306. The Big Convertible (6/28/55)
307. The Big Rush (7/5/55)
308. The Big Genius (7/12/55)
309. The Big Bobo (7/19/55)
310. The Big Housemaid (7/26/55)
311. The Big Sheet (8/2/55)
312. The Big Missus (8/9/55)
313. The Big Beer (8/16/55)
314. The Big Blonde (8/23/55)
315. The Big Fellow (8/30/55)
316. The Big Ruling (9/6/55)
317. The Big Daughter (9/13/55)
318. The Big Close (9/20/55)
319. The Big Shot (9/27/55)
320. The Big Brain (10/4/55)
321. The Big Jolt (10/11/55)
322. The Big Lie (10/18/55)
323. The Big Pill (10/25/55)
324. The Big Number (11/1/55)
325. The Big Light (11/8/55)
326. The Big Dive (11/15/55)
327. The Big Walk (11/22/55)
328. The Big Guilt (11/29/55)
329. The Big Shirt (12/6/55)
330. The Big Mole (12/13/55)
331. .22 Rifle for Christmas (12/20/55)
332. The Big Mask (Part One) (12/27/55)
333. The Big Mask (Part Two) (1/3/56)
334. The Big Small (1/10/56)
335. The Big String (1/17/56)
336. The Big Lay-Out (1/24/56)
337. The Big Strip (1/31/56)
338. The Big Press (2/7/56)
339. The Big Tooth (2/14/56)
340. The Big Smoke (2/21/56)
341. The Big Want (2/28/56)
342. The Big Laugh (3/6/56)
343. The Big Impossible (3/13/56)
344. .22 Rifle for Christmas (3/20/56)
345. The Big Informant (3/27/56)

346. The Big Dream (4/3/56)
347. The Big Chet (4/10/56)
348. The Big Compulsion (4/17/56)
349. The Big Rip (4/24/56)
350. The Big Scrapbook (5/1/56)
351. The Big Carney (5/8/56)
352. The Big Joke (5/15/56)
353. The Big False Move (5/22/56)
354. The Big Gun (Part One) (5/29/56)
355. The Big Gun (Part Two) (6/5/56)
356. The Big Will (6/12/56)
357. The Big Lilly (6/19/56)
358. The Big Revolt (6/26/56)
359. The Big Ham (9/18/56)
360. The Big Bop (9/25/56)
361. The Big Lift (10/2/56)
362. The Big Cab (10/9/56)
363. The Big Slip (10/16/56)
364. The Big Flight (10/23/56)

365. The Big Present (10/30/56)
366. The Big Odd (11/6/56)
367. The Big Pick (11/13/56)
368. The Big Brink (11/20/56)
369. The Big Steal (11/27/56)
370. The Big Listen (12/4/56)
371. The Big Switch (12/11/56)
372. The Big Bill (12/18/56)
373. The Big Little Jesus (12/25/56)
374. The Big Bid (1/1/57)
375. The Big Filth (1/8/57)
376. The Big Broad (1/15/57)
377. The Big Sucker (1/22/57)
378. The Big Pipe (1/29/57)
379. The Big TV (2/5/57)
380. The Big Cup (2/12/57)
381. The Big Rod (2/19/57)
382. The Big Mustache (2/26/57)

Dramatic Workshop

A generic title to a generic program. This series of one-act plays — some of which were originally two or three acts edited down to one act — was broadcast on Tuesday evenings from 9 to 9:30 pm, EST. A few were originals, but others were adaptations of works such as Franz Kafka's "The Warden of the Tomb," Shakespeare's "As You Like It," M. David Samples' "Out of Order" and Stephen Vincent Benet's "The Devil and Daniel Webster." Arch Oboler's classic drama "The Mother-In-Law" from the 1943 season of *Lights Out!* was dramatized. Episode seven was presented by the Theater Studio of New York, where the series originated (from station WEVD-FM). Episode eight featured the original Off Broadway cast of "The Buffalo Skinner." The highlight of the series was an exclusive interview with playwright Arthur Miller, which was later repeated for the final broadcast.

1. Charlie, Esquire (6/16/59)
2. The Tortoise and the Hare (6/23/59)
3. The Theater of the Soul (6/30/59)
4. The Twenty-Five Cent White Cap (7/7/59)
5. The Warden of the Tomb (7/14/59)
6. The Mother-In-Law (7/21/59)
7. The Devil and Daniel Webster (7/28/59)

8. The Buffalo Skinner (8/4/59)
9. [Interview with Arthur Miller] (8/11/59)
10. The Death of Odysseus (8/18/59)
11. As You Like It (8/25/59)
12. Out of Order (9/1/59)
13. [Interview with Arthur Miller] (9/8/59)

The Easy Aces

The Easy Aces was created around 1930 on station KMBC in Kansas City. Goodman Ace was a movie and drama critic for the old *Kansas City Journal-Post* in 1928. After reading comics over the radio on Sundays, he began doing *The Movie Man*, based on his newspaper reviews, and eventually, by accident, *The Easy Aces* came to be. On March 1, 1932, *The Easy Aces* went national over CBS, staying on the air for more than a decade.

Anacin dropped sponsorship on January 17, 1945, leaving Goodman Ace to find work in other series such as *The Danny Kaye Show*. Out of work, he and Jane dusted off some old transcriptions of the originals from 1937 to 1938 and let ZIV Productions syndicate them from 1945 to 1946. Broadcast five times a week, for fifteen minutes. In February of 1948, the show was revived in a half-hour format under a new title, *Mr. Ace and Jane*. Note: This is the 1945–46 syndication, only descriptive titles are given.

1. Jane Talks About a Book She Doesn't Like
2. Jane Buys Two Suits for Her Brother
3. Johnny Argues with Ace
4. Johnny Will Work in Everett's Store
5. Johnny Works in the Warehouse
6. What Is Johnny Doing at Night?
7. Plans to Catch a Gang of Fur Thieves
8. Jane and Alice Tip Off the Thieves
9. Mr. Neff Talks Jane Into Selling Everett Some Land
10. Neff Tries to Tell Jane About the Land
11. Ace and Jane Argue About Answering the Phone
12. Jane Talks to Everett About the Land
13. Talking About the Price of the Land
14. Talking About the Land with Jane
15. Ace Is Surprised About Jane and Neff
16. Everett Buys the Land from Jane
17. Ace Can't Get his Regular Lawyer
18. The New Lawyer Needs a New Suit
19. Ace and Jane Get Ready for the Trial
20. Neff's Lawyer Gets Ace's Suit of Clothes
21. Neff's Lawyer Comes Back Over for a Vest
22. Jane Studies the Questions of the Trial
23. Jane Gets a Little Mixed Up in Court
24. Jane Gets Fined for Contempt-of-Court
25. Neff Agrees to a $5,000 Settlement
26. Jane Tries to Explain About Money to Ace
27. Ace Finds Out About His Suit of Clothes
28. Jane Learns to Play Bridge
29. Jane's Game-Winning Plan for Bridge
30. Bridge Game Starts with Phone Calls
31. Daniel Boone Hides at the Aces
32. Ace Finds Out About the Boy in His Basement
33. Jane Wants to Adopt the Little Boy
34. Ace and Jane Talk About Children
35. Daniel Boone Must Go
36. Ace and Jane Decide Not to Adopt
37. Daniel Boone Leaves
38. A Prize Fighter Is Discovered
39. Kookie Might Be a Good Prizefighter
40. A Newspaper Friend Gets a Fight for Kookie
41. Jane Helps with Kookie's First Fight
42. Could the Fight Be Rigged?
43. Kookie Is Set Up for a Knock Out
44. Jane Takes $1,000 for Kookie to Throw the Fight
45. Kookie Wins and Ace Finds Out About the Bribe
46. Ace Works Late, Mrs. Benton Thinks Otherwise
47. Jane Tries to Find Out what Ace Is Doing
48. Ace Agrees to Help Out His Artist Sister
49. Ace Tells Marge About Her Portrait
50. Jane Tries to Make Ace Jealous with Phone Calls
51. Jane Has an Old Boyfriend Show Up
52. Ace Gets His Portrait Completed
53. Jane Meets "The Other Woman"

The Electric Theater

On April 12, 1902, Thomas L. Talley's Electric Theater opened its doors, located at 262 South Main Street in Los Angeles. It became the first theater to show exclusively movies. So it was no surprise when electric companies agreed to sponsor an anthology series based on stage plays and film adaptations, and to hire Helen Hayes, "The First Lady of the Theater," as host and star. It was broadcast Sunday evenings on CBS, at 9–9:30 pm. Hayes hosted each episode and played the female lead for each drama, except for a few episodes during the beginning of the series.

1. One Sunday Afternoon (10/3/48; Francesca Bruning and Henry Fonda)
2. The Amazing Dr. Clitterhouse (10/10/48; Basil Rathbone)
3. Rebound (10/17/48; Margaret Sullavan)

4. The Admirable Crichton (10/24/48; Anne Burr and Herbert Marshall)
5. The Lady Is Willing (10/31/48; Marlene Dietrich)
6. Accent on Youth (11/7/48; Louis Calhern and Jessica Tandy)
7. Victoria Regina (11/14/48)
8. The Sobbin' Women [written by Stephen Vincent Benet] (11/21/48; John Morley)
9. Angel Street (11/28/48; Martin Gabel)
10. Dark Victory (12/5/48; Don Briggs)
11. What Every Woman Knows (12/12/48; Barry Doig)
12. The Littlest Angel [written by Charles Tassewell] (12/19/48)
13. Arrowsmith (1/2/49; Jeff Morrow)
14. Being Nice to Emily (1/9/49)
15. Young Woodley (1/16/49; James Lipton)
16. Skylark (1/23/49; Dick Kollmar)
17. The Enemy (1/30/49)
18. The Ghost and Mrs. Muir (2/6/49)
19. The Wren [written by Booth Tarkington] (2/13/49; Donald Murphy)
20. The Recluse (2/20/49; Sydney Smith)
21. The Farmer Takes a Wife (2/27/49; John Morley)
22. A Study in Charcoal (3/6/49; Karl Malden)
23. Autumn Crocus (3/13/49; Tonio Selwart)
24. Saturday's Children (3/20/49; Cliff Carpenter)
25. The Farmer Takes A Wife (3/27/49; John Morley)
26. Shadow of the Heart (4/3/49; Jack Manning)
27. My Little Boy (4/10/49; Arthur Cassell)
28. The Seven Miracles of Gubbio (4/17/49)
29. Manhattan Pastorale (4/24/49; Tonio Selwart)
30. Brief Encounter [written by Noel Coward] (5/1/49)
31. No Room for Peter Pan (5/8/49; Ivan Cury)
32. Love From a Stranger (5/15/49; Dan O'Herlihy)
33. My Favorite Wife (5/22/49; Myron McCormick)
34. His Name Is Jason (5/29/49; Alexander Scourby)

Encore Theater

This thirteen-episode summer series featured movie adaptations of stories involving characters connected with the medical profession. Sponsored by Schenley Laboratories, Inc. Broadcast from Hollywood over CBS, Tuesday evening from 9:30 to 10 pm, EST. Leith Stevens composed and conducted the music. Frank Graham was the announcer. Bill Lawrence produced and directed. Jean Holloway wrote all but one of the scripts; Milton Geiger wrote the script for "The Prisoner of Shark Island." Loretta Young was originally scheduled to star in "Now, Voyager," but Young was unable to attend, and was replaced by Maureen O'Sullivan.

1. The Magnificent Obsession (6/4/46; Griff Barnett, Victor Rodman, Earle Ross, Eric Snowden, Lurene Tuttle, and Cornell Wilde)
2. The Life of Louis Pasteur (6/11/46; Griff Barnett, Paul Lukas, Lou Merrill, Gerald Mohr, Terry O'Sullivan, GeGe Pearson, Lurene Tuttle, and George Zucco)
3. Yellow Jack (6/18/46; Ken Christy, Ronald Colman, Norman Field, Jerry Hausner, and Ed Max)
4. Green Light (6/25/46; Jim Backus, Pedro de Cordoba, Cathy Lewis, Jane Morgan, Lurene Tuttle, and Robert Young)

5. Men in White (7/2/46; Griff Barnett, Elliott Lewis, GeGe Pearson, Lurene Tuttle, and Robert Taylor)
6. The White Angel (7/9/46; Eleanor Audley, Virginia Bruce, Norman Field, Earle Ross, Eric Snowden, and Ben Wright)
7. Now, Voyager (7/16/46; Cathy Lewis, Elliott Lewis, Jane Morgan, Maureen O'Sullivan, Jeanine Roose, and George Zucco)
8. Dr. Ehrlich's Magic Bullet (7/23/46; Charles Bickford, Norman Field, Frank Nelson, Barney Phillips, and Paula Winslowe)
9. Dark Victory (7/30/46; Gerald Mohr, Frank Nelson, Susan Peters, and Franchot Tone)
10. A Man to Remember (8/6/46) Griff Barnett, Lionel Barrymore, Ken Christy, Howard Duff, Jack Edwards, Jr., Jerry Hausner, and Earle Ross)
11. The Prisoner of Shark Island (8/13/46; Joe Du Val, Jack Edwards, Jr., Norman Field, Jerry Hausner, Barney Phillips, Earle Ross, Zachary Scott, and Paula Winslowe)
12. Nurse Edith Cavell (8/20/46; Ken Christy, Jack Edwards, Jr., Verna Felton, Norman Field, Jerry Hausner, Ida Lupino, Jane Morgan, and Barney Phillips)
13. Disputed Passage (8/27/46; Hume Cronyn, Dennis O'Keefe, and Lurene Tuttle)

The Endless Frontier

This short-run series starred Raymond Massey in a variety of Western and war dramas. Broadcast over NBC Sunday afternoons from 1:30 to 2 pm, EST.

1. Our Daily Bread (1/27/52)
2. The Search (2/3/52)
3. The Trouble Shooter (2/10/52)
4. Only One to a Customer (2/17/52)
5. Private First Class Bill Smith, Man Alive (2/24/52)

*Escape**

Escape was another CBS production that presented dramas of high adventure and intrigue. Designed to free the listeners from the four walls of their homes to high adventure. *Escape* was a collaboration of numerous writers, actors, sound effects men, producers and directors. With the opening theme of "Night on Bald Mountain," *Escape* premiered in July of 1947, originally as a short-run summer series, and staying on radio until September of 1954.

Originals scripts, adaptations of short stories, and novels were presented. Works by Robert Louis Stevenson, Sir Arthur Conan Doyle, H. G. Wells, Joseph Conrad, Rudyard Kipling, Edgar Allan Poe, Algernon Blackwood, Ambrose Bierce, M. R. James, John Collier, and F. Scott Fitzgerald were a few of the stories presented. George Stewart's novel "The Earth Abides" was performed in two parts in November of 1950, presenting a realistic drama of what the end of

Compiled by Terry Salomonson. Copyright © 1992 by Terry Salomonson.

the world would be like. Writers for the series included Kathleen Hite, John and Gwen Bagni, Antony Ellis, Joel Murcott, Morton Fine and David Friedkin.

Organ music was played by Ivan Ditmars. Musical scores were conceived by Cy Feuer, Leith Stevens, Wilbur Hatch, and Dee Castillo. Bill Gould and Cliff Thorsness, two sound effects men, claimed that their most difficult challenge was reproducing the sound of thousands of rats in "Three Skeleton Key." Other sound effects men involved were Bill James, Tom Hanley, David Light and Ray Kemper. Directors included Antony Ellis, William N. Robson, and Norman McDonnell. Announcers were Roy Rowan and Paul Frees.

Escape had two different sponsors during its run. From January 17, 1950, to February 14, 1950, the broadcasts were sponsored by the Ford Motor Company. The second sponsorship was by the Richfield Oil Company from April 21, 1950, through August 4, 1950, and again on August 18, for a total of fifteen programs. For the broadcast of November 29, 1949, Gracie Allen made a cameo after the drama to pitch *The Burns and Allen Program*, as she did on numerous radio programs over CBS that particular week.

Escape was broadcast on the East and West coasts, airing different episodes in different cycles. Episodes marked ECB were East Coast broadcasts. Episodes marked WCB were West Coast broadcasts. Episodes without ECB or WCB were broadcast nationally. To fill in a time-slot on one occasion, the show was broadcast twice a week, on a Saturday and Sunday. To prevent confusion, all broadcasts are listed in their consecutive air-date order. Episodes seventy-two, seventy-four, and seventy-six were three Sunday *Escape* special broadcasts. In episode eighty-seven, Jeff Chandler guested under the pseudonym of Ira Grosell.

A pilot program, *Out of This World*, similar to another CBS program called *Forecast*, presented an experimental script entitled "Dead of Night," broadcast on February 28, 1947. The same recording was also used on March 21, 1947, as the audition of *Escape*. So there are two audition programs for *Escape*.

Audition: *Out of This World* Dead of Night (2/28/47)

Audition: Dead of Night (3/21/47)

1. The Man Who Would Be King (7/7/47; John Dehner, Jack Kruschen, and Ben Wright)
2. Operation: Fleur de Lis (7/14/47; Elliott Lewis, Jack Webb, and Peggy Webber)
3. Diamond as Big as the Ritz (7/21/47; Jack Edwards, Jr., Linda Mason, and Danny Merrill)
4. Typhoon (7/28/47; Cy Kendall, Frank Lovejoy, and Raymond Lawrence)
5. Sire de Maletroit's Door (8/4/47; Ramsey Hill, Elliott Lewis, and Peggy Webber)
6. The Ring of Thoth (8/11/47; Joan Banks and Jack Webb)
7. The Fourth Man (8/18/47; William Johnstone and Joseph Kearns)
8. The Most Dangerous Game (10/1/47; Hans Conried and Paul Frees)
9. Run of the Yellow Mail (10/8/47)
10. A Shipment of Mute Fate (10/15/47; Raymond Lawrence and Jack Webb)
11. The Fall of the House of Usher (10/22/47; Paul Frees, Sheraton Hall, and Ramsey Hill)
12. Pollack and the Porrah Man (10/29/47; Luis Van Rooten and Barton Yarborough)
13. Evening Primrose (11/5/47; Eleanor Audley, Paul Frees, Elliott Lewis, and Pat Lowry)

14. The Young Man with the Cream of Tarts (11/12/47; William Johnstone and Barton Yarborough)
15. Casting the Runes (11/19/47; William Conrad, John McIntire, and Ian Wolfe)
16. The Country of the Blind (11/26/47; William Conrad, Paul Frees, and Peggy Webber)
17. Taboo (12/3/47; William Conrad, Morgan Farley, Paul Frees, and Marta Metrovich)
18. An Occurrence at Owl Creek Bridge (12/10/47; Harry Bartell and Luis Van Rooten)
19. Wild Oranges (12/17/47; William Conrad, Paul Frees, Jack Kruschen, and Jeanette Nolan)
20. Back for Christmas (12/24/47; Eleanor Audley, Paul Frees, and Marta Metrovich)
21. Confession (12/31/47; William Conrad, Ramsay Hill, Raymond Lawrence, and Peggy Webber)
22. Second Class Passenger (1/7/48, East Coast Production; Harry Bartell, Cathy Lewis, and Jeanette Nolan)
23. Second Class Passenger (1/10/48, West Coast Production; Harry Bartell and Jeanette Nolan)
24. Leiningen vs. the Ants (1/14/48, ECB; William Conrad, Don Diamond, and Lou Merrill)
25. Leiningen vs. the Ants (1/17/48, WCB; William Conrad, Don Diamond, and Lou Merrill)
26. Papa Benjamin (1/21/48, ECB; Joan Banks, Harry Bartell, Frank Lovejoy, and Luis Van Rooten)
27. Papa Benjamin (1/24/48, WCB; Joan Banks, Harry Bartell, Frank Lovejoy, and Luis Van Rooten)
28. Three Good Witnesses (1/28/48, ECB; Harry Bartell, Morgan Farley, Jeanette Nolan, Jack Webb, and Barton Yarborough)
29. Three Good Witnesses (1/31/48, WCB; Harry Bartell, Morgan Farley, Jeanette Nolan, Jack Webb, and Barton Tarborough)
30. The Vanishing Lady (2/1/48, ECB; Hy Averback, Joan Banks, and Ramsay Hill)
31. The Vanishing Lady (2/7/48, WCB; Hy Averback, Joan Banks, and Ramsay Hill)
32. Snake Doctor (2/8/48, ECB; William Conrad, Paul Frees, Fred Howard, and Ruth Perrott)
33. Snake Doctor (2/14/48, WCB; William Conrad, Paul Frees, Fred Howard, and Ruth Perrott)
34. Ancient Sorceries (2/15/48, ECB; Kay Brinker, Jeff Corey, Paul Frees, and Ann Morrison)
35. Ancient Sorceries (2/21/48, WCB; Kay Brinker, Jeff Corey, Paul Frees, and Ann Morrison)
36. How Love Came to Professor Guildea (2/22/48, ECB; Parley Baer, Harry Bartell, and Luis Van Rooten)
37. How Love Came to Professor Guildea (2/28/48, WCB; Parley Baer, Harry Bartell, and Luis Van Rooten)
38. The Grove of Ashtaroff (2/29/48, ECB; Kay Brinker, William Conrad, and Paul Frees)
39. The Grove of Ashtaroff (3/6/48, WCB; Kay Brinker, William Conrad, and Paul Frees)
40. Jimmy Goggles — the God (3/7/48, ECB; Paul Frees, Luis Van Rooten, and Jack Webb)
41. Jimmy Goggles — the God (3/13/48, WCB; Paul Frees, Luis Van Rooten, and Jack Webb)
42. The Log of the Evening Star (3/14/48, ECB; Gale Page, Alan Reed, and Jack Webb)
43. The Log of the Evening Star (3/20/48, WCB; Gale Page, Alan Reed, and Jack Webb)
44. Misfortune's Isle (3/21/48, ECB; William Conrad, Paul Frees, and Virginia Gregg)
45. Misfortune's Isle (3/27/48, WCB; William Conrad, Paul Frees, and Virginia Gregg)
46. A Shipment of Mute Fate (3/28/48, ECB; Harry Bartell, Berry Kroeger, and Peggy Webber)
47. Action (4/4/48; Joseph Kearns, Berry Kroeger, and Luis Van Rooten)
48. The Brute (4/11/48; Parley Baer, Wilms Herbert, and Dan O'Herlihy)
49. The Drums of Fore and Aft (4/18/48; Jimmy Ogg, Eric Rolfe, Gil Stratton, Jr., and Peggy Webber)

50. The Forth Man (4/25/48; Joseph Kearns, Berry Kroeger, Lou Merrill, and Jay Novello)
51. John Jock Todd (5/2/48; Tony Barrett, Don Diamond, Wilms Herbert, and Jack Kruschen)
52. The Time Machine (5/9/48; Kay Brinker, Jeff Corey, and Eric Rolfe)
53. The Match (5/16/48; Clark Cunny, Wilms Herbert, Frank Lovejoy, and Nestor Paiva)
54. Leiningen vs. the Ants (5/23/48; William Conrad, Don Diamond, Lou Krugman, and Jay Novello)
55. Beau Geste (6/6/48; Wilms Herbert, Berry Kroeger, Jay Novello, Peggy Webber, and Ben Wright)
56. The Country of the Blind (6/27/48; Paul Frees, Wilms Herbert, Berry Kroeger, and Peggy Webber)
57. A Tooth for Paul Revere (7/4/48; Parley Baer, Harry Bartell, William Conrad, and Berry Kroeger)
58. She (7/11/48; Kay Brinker, Lawrence Dobkin, Wilms Herbert, Berry Kroeger, and Ben Wright)
59. Habit (7/18/48; John Denher, Wilms Herbert, Berry Kroeger, and Luis Van Rooten)
60. The Man Who Would Be King (8/1/48; John Dehner, Wilms Herbert, and Ben Wright)
61. The Fugitive (8/15/48; Gloria Blondell, John Dehner, Wilms Herbert, Luis Van Rooten, and Ben Wright)
62. S. S. San Pedro (8/22/48; Harry Bartell, Jeff Corey, John Dehner, Don Diamond, and Jay Novello)
63. Diamond as Big as the Ritz (8/29/48; Sam Edwards, Danny Merrill, and Peggy Webber)
64. Dream of Armageddon (9/5/48; John Dehner, Betty Lou Gerson, Stacy Harris, Jack Kruschen, Charlotte Lawrence, and Eric Rolfe)
65. Evening Primrose (9/12/48; Harry Bartell, William Conrad, and Constance Cavandish)
66. The Man Who Could Work Miracles (9/19/48; John Dehner, Wilms Herbert, Ben Wright)
67. The Lost Special (2/12/49; Parley Baer, Edgar Barrier, John Dehner,

Lawrence Dobkin, Paul Frees, and Ben Wright)
68. Orient Express (2/19/49; Edgar Barrier, Harry Bartell, Hans Conried, and Gloria Grant)
69. Red Wine (2/26/49; Edgar Barrier, William Conrad, Hans Conried, and Gloria Grant)
70. Conqueror's Isle (3/5/49; Jeff Chandler, David Ellis, Berry Kroeger, and Lou Krugman)
71. He Who Rides the Tiger (3/12/49; Edgar Barrier, Jack Kruschen, Maria Palmer, and Ben Wright)
72. A Shipment of Mute Fate (3/13/49; Lois Corbett, David Ellis, John Lund, and Vivi Janiss)
73. Finger of Doom (3/19/49; Louise Arthur, Edgar Barrier, Harry Bartell, Ed Begley, Kay Miller, Peter Proust, and Joy Terry)
74. The Country of the Blind (3/20/49; Harry Bartell, Edgar Barrier, William Conrad, Byron Kane, Edmund O'Brien, and Peggy Webber)
75. Adaptive Ultimate (3/26/49; Edgar Barrier, Lawrence Dobkin, Frank Gerstle, and Stacy Harris)
76. Diamond as Big as the Ritz (3/27/49; Sam Edwards, Nina Klowden, and Hugh Thomas)
77. Confidential Agent (4/2/49; Parley Baer, Herb Butterfield, Berry Kroeger, and Ben Wright)
78. When the Man Comes, Follow Him (4/9/49; Paul Dubov, Junius Matthews, and Barney Phillips)
79. The General Died at Dawn (4/16/49; Lawrence Dobkin, Jack Kruschen, and Ben Wright)
80. The Great Impression (4/23/49; Jeanne Bates, John Dehner, and Ben Wright)
81. The Fourth Man (7/7/49; Lawrence Dobkin, Joseph Kearns, Barney Phillips, and Ben Wright)
82. The Drums of the Fore and Aft (7/14/49; Wilms Herbert, Tudor Owen, and Ben Wright)
83. Action (7/21/49; Joseph Kearns, Bill Johnstone, Ben Wright, Maria Palmer, and Jeff Corey)
84. Second Class Passenger (7/28/49;

Parley Baer, Paul Dubov, Georgia Ellis, and Ben Wright)

85. Leiningen vs. the Ants (8/4/49; Gerald Mohr and Tudor Owen)
86. Red Wine (8/11/49; Robert Boone, Lawrence Dobkin, and Victor Perrin)
87. Snake Doctor (8/18/49; William Conrad, Paul Frees, Ira Grosell, and Bill Lally)
88. Evening Primrose (8/25/49; Harry Bartell, Lois Corbett, Georgia Ellis, Wilms Herbert, Vivi Janiss, Ruth Perrott, and Ben Wright)
89. The Fortune of Vargas (9/21/49; Hans Conried and Victor Mature)
90. Wild Oranges (9/28/49; William Conrad, Van Heflin, Betty Lou Gerson, and Edmund MacDonald)
91. The Primitive (10/8/49; Ted de Corsia, Paul Frees, Lucille Meredith, and Ian Wolfe)
92. The Sure Thing (10/15/49; Fay Baker, William Conrad, John Hoyt, and Ian Wolfe)
93. Night in Havana (10/22/49; Tony Barrett, William Conrad, Jeff Corey, Alan Reed, and Jack Webb)
94. The Blue Wall (10/29/49; William Conrad, Ted de Corsia, Peter Leeds, and Benny Rubin)
95. Flood on the Goodwins (11/1/49; Jack Edwards, Will Geer, and Barton Yarborough)
96. Plunder of the Sun (11/8/49; Tony Barrett, Charlie Lung, Lucille Meredith, and Gerald Mohr)
97. Three Skeleton Key (11/15/49; Harry Bartell, William Conrad, and Elliott Reid)
98. Maracas (11/22/49; Joan Banks, William Conrad, Ted de Corsia, and Paul Frees)
99. Letter from Jason (11/29/49; Kay Brinker, William Conrad, Will Geer, and Frank Lovejoy)
100. Command (12/6/49; Ted de Corsia, Sam Edwards, William Johnstone, and Elliott Reid)
101. Bordertown (12/13/49; Bea Benaderet, William Conrad, Ted de Corsia, and Jack Webb)
102. Figure a Dame (12/20/49; Paul Frees and Frank Lovejoy)

103. Seeds of Greed (12/27/49; Tony Barrett, Gary Merrill, and Ben Wright)
104. The Pistol (1/3/50; Betty Lou Gearson, Eddie Mahr, Charles McGraw, and Gerald Mohr)
105. The Vanishing Lady (1/10/50; Joan Brooks, John Hoyt, Anthony Ross, and Ben Wright)
106. The Sure Thing (1/17/50; Fay Baker, Harry Bartell, Jeff Corey, Paul Frees, Ramsey Hill, Ruth Perrott, Anthony Ross, and Ian Wolfe)
107. Treasure, Inc. (1/24/50; Harry Baretell, John Hoyt, Mary Lansing, and Frank Lovejoy)
108. Present Tense (1/31/50; Joan Banks, Harry Bartell, Jeff Corey, Paul Frees, William Lally, Charles McGraw, Tom Tully, and Vincent Price)
109. The Outer Limit (2/7/50; Jeff Corey, Frank Lovejoy, Charles McGraw, and Stan Waxman)
110. Two If By Sea (2/14/50; John Dehner, Paul Frees, Marta Metrovich, and Barton Yarborough)
111. The Red Mark (2/21/50; William Conrad, Will Geer, Junius Matthews, and Barbara Whiting)
112. The Man Who Won the War (2/28/50; Jeff Corey, John Dehner, Paul Frees, Joseph Kearns, Charlie Lung, Ian Wolfe, and Barton Yarborough)
113. Port Royal (3/10/50; William Conrad, John Dehner, Charles McGraw, and Dee Tatum)
114. Three Skeleton Key (3/17/50; Harry Bartell, Jeff Corey, and Vincent Price)
115. Danger at Matecumbe (3/24/50; Harry Bartell, Robert Clark, Ted de Corsia, Lawrence Dobkin, Jerry Hausner, Frank Lovejoy, Dee Tatum, Rick Vallin, and Marie Windsor)
116. Green Splotches (3/31/50; Ted de Corsia, Jay Novello, and Barton Yarborough)
117. The Ambassador of Poker (4/7/50; William Conrad, John Dehner, Benson Fong, Ramsey Hill,

Richard Loo, Lucille Meredith, Elliott Reid, Rick Vallin, and Ben Wright)

118. The Golden Snake (4/14/50; Tony Barrett, John Hoyt, Jeanette Nolan, and Rick Vallin)

119. The Shanghai Document (4/21/50; Joan Banks, Charlie Lung, and Ben Wright)

120. Something for Nothing (4/28/50; Frances Chaney, William Conrad, and Ann Morrison)

121. The Man Who Stole the Bible (5/5/50; Harry Bartell, Nanette Boardman, Paul Frees, Will Geer, Peter Leeds, Lou Merrill, Mary Shipp, Rick Vallin, and Ben Wright)

122. The Rim of Terror (5/12/50; Hans Conried, Nancy Kelly, and Barton Yarborough)

123. Pass to Berlin (5/19/50; Stacy Harris, Peggy Webber, and Ben Wright)

124. Command (5/26/50; Harry Bartell, David Ellis, John Hoyt, Wally Maher)

125. Mars Is Heaven (6/2/50; Florence Bates, Jeff Corey, William Johnstone, and Ian Wolfe)

126. The Big Sponge (6/9/50)

127. Serenade for a Cobra (6/16/50; Joseph Kearns, Charles McGraw, and Jay Novello)

128. Sundown (6/23/50; John Dehner, Ted Osborne, and Barton Yarborough)

129. Bloodbath (6/30/50; Ted de Corsia, Wally Maher, and Vincent Price)

130. A Shipment of Mute Fate (7/7/50; William Conrad, David Ellis, David Light, and Sarah Selby)

131. Shark Bait (7/14/50; John Dehner, Paul Frees, Will Geer, Steve Roberts, and Mary Shipp)

132. Yellow Wake (7/21/50; William Conrad, John Hoyt, and George Opperman, Jr.)

133. Poison (7/28/50; William Conrad and Jack Webb)

134. Two Came Back (8/4/50; Joan Banks, Paul Frees, Stacy Harris, and Ben Wright)

135. The Red Forest (8/11/50; William

Conrad, Georgia Ellis, Paul Frees, and Ben Wright)

136. The Footprint (8/18/50; Charles Davis, Ramsey Hill, Tom Holland, and Lou Krugman)

137. Crossing Paris (8/25/50; Howard McNear, Jay Novello, and Barney Phillips)

138. Your Grandfather's Necktie (8/26/50)

139. A Sleeping Draught (10/1/50; John Dodsworth, Bruce Payne, and Ben Wright)

140. Roulette (10/8/50; Edgar Barrier, John Dehner, and Georgia Ellis)

141. The Power of Hammer (10/15/50; Edgar Barrier, Don Diamond, and Ann Morrison)

142. The Time Machine (10/22/50; John Dehner, Lawrence Dobkin, and Georgia Ellis)

143. Seven Hours to Freedom (10/29/50; Lou Krugman, Jack Moyles, and Stan Waxman)

144. The Earth Abides [Part One] (11/5/50; Michael Ann Barrett, John Dehner, and Lawrence Dobkin)

145. The Earth Abides [Part Two] (11/12/50; John Dehner, Jeffrey Silver, and Peggy Webber)

146. Journey Into Fear (11/19/50; Edgar Barrier, Shimon Ruskin, and Rolfe Sedan)

147. Funeral Fires (11/26/50; Don Diamond, Georgia Ellis, Lamont Johnson, and Ben Wright)

148. This Side of Nowhere (12/3/50; Virginia Gregg, Lou Krugman, and Ralph Moody)

149. A Passenger to Bali (12/10/51; Michael Ann Barrett, Lou Merrill, and Bruce Payne)

150. Wild Jack Rhett (12/17/50; Parley Baer, Jeanne Bates, John Dehner, Lawrence Dobkin, Paul Dubov, Sam Edwards, Lou Krugman, Junius Matthews, and Russell Simpson)

151. The Cave (12/24/50; John Dehner, Georgia Ellis, Ileene Erskin, Wilms Herbert, Lou Krugman, Charlie Lung, Jay Novello, and Peggy Webber)

152. The Man Who Could Work

Miracles (12/31/50; John Dehner
and Ben Wright)

153. Conquest (1/7/51; William Conrad,
Lawrence Dobkin, Ramsey Hill,
and Lou Krugman)

154. A Bullet for Mr. Smith (1/14/51;
Jeanne Bates, Lawrence Dobkin,
and Jack Kruschen)

155. The Killer Mine (2/11/51; Tony Barrett, John Dehner, Eileen Erskine,
and Raymond Lawrence)

156. The Follower (2/18/51; William
Conrad, Georgia Ellis, Virginia
Gregg, and Lou Krugman)

157. The Island (7/11/51; Michael Ann
Barrett, Harry Bartell, and
William Conrad)

158. Macao (7/18/51; Michael Ann Barrett, Raymond Burr, Stacy Harris,
and Lou Krugman)

159. The Earth Men (7/25/51; Parley
Baer, Harry Bartell, Hans Con-
ried, John Dehner, Lawrence
Dobkin, Georgia Ellis, Byron
Kane, Lou Krugman, Jack
Kruschen, and Sindey Miller)

160. The Gladiator (8/1/51; Lillian
Buyeff, William Conrad, Byron
Kane, and Ted Osborne)

161. Up Periscope (8/8/51; Hy Averback,
Edgar Barrier, Harry Bartell,
Byron Kane, Lou Krugman,
Charles Lung, and Ben Wright)

162. A Rough Shoot (8/15/51; John
Dehner, Lawrence Dobkin, Lou
Krugman, and Stan Waxman)

163. Silent Horror (8/22/51; Harry
Bartell, Georgia Ellis, Jack
Kruschen, and Stan Waxman)

164. The Man Who Stole the Bible
(8/29/51; Nan Boardman, Sam
Pierce, and Ben Wright)

165. Gringo (10/12/52; Parley Baer,
Edgar Barrier, Lillian Buyeff, and
William Conrad)

166. The Price of the Head (10/19/52;
Parley Baer, William Conrad, and
Lawrence Dobkin)

167. Robert of Huntington (10/26/52;
Edgar Barrier, William Conrad,
and Lawrence Dobkin)

168. The Running Man (11/2/52;
Michael Ann Barrett, Jeanne Bates,
Don Diamond, Byron Kane,

Ralph Moody, Victor Perrin, and
Barney Phillips)

169. The Return (11/9/52; Edgar Barrier,
Jeanne Bates, Lawrence Dobkin,
and Paul Dubov)

170. The Loup-Garou (11/16/52; John
Dehner, Georgia Ellis, Forrest
Lewis, and Tom Tully)

171. Transport to Terror (11/23/52;
Edgar Barrier, William Conrad,
and Georgia Ellis)

172. Pagosa (11/30/52; Parley Baer,
William Conrad, John Dehner,
and Georgia Ellis)

173. Incident at Quito (12/7/52; Tony Barrett, Jack Kruschen, and Larry Thor)

174. Four Went Home (12/14/52; John
Dehner, Jack Kruschen, Peter
Leeds, and Bob Sweeny)

175. The Man Who Liked Dickens
(12/21/52; Ramsey Hill, Joseph
Kearns, and Terry Kilburn)

176. Nightmare in the Sun (12/28/52;
Tony Barrett, Lillian Buyeff, Don
Diamond, and Jack Kruschen)

177. A Dangerous Man (1/4/53; John
Dehner, Tom Holland, Ralph
Moody, and Chief Thundercloud)

178. Conqueror's Isle (1/11/53; Harry
Bartell, Eddie Firestone, Ramsey
Hill, and John Stevenson)

179. A Matter of Conscience (1/18/53;
Parley Baer, Harry Bartell, Jack
Kruschen, and Ben Wright)

180. Diary of Madman (1/25/53; Edgar
Barrier, Barney Phillips, Paul
Richards, and Ben Wright)

181. A Study in Wax (2/1/53; William
Conrad and Stacy Harris)

182. Jetsam (2/8/53; John Dehner,
Lawrence Dobkin, Charlie Lung,
and Ben Wright)

183. Wild Jack Rhett (2/15/53; Parley
Baer, Harry Bartell, John Dehner,
and Lawrence Dobkin)

184. I Saw Myself Running (2/22/53;
Georgia Ellis, Sammie Hill, and
John Stevenson)

185. The Tramp (3/1/53; Alec Harford,
Charlie Lung, Jay Novello, Tudor
Owen, and Ben Wright)

186. The Island (3/8/53; Michael Ann
Barrett, William Conrad, Stacy
Harris, and Jack Kruschen)

187. The Man With the Steel Teeth (3/15/53; Harry Bartell, Jack Kruschen, and Charlotte Lawrence)

188. Pressure (3/22/53; William Conrad and Bob Sweeny)

189. The Invader (3/29/53; Fay Baker, Edgar Barrier, Bill Bissel, Paul Frees, Peter Leeds, Leroy Leonard, and Howard McNear)

190. A Sleeping Draught (4/5/53; John Doddsworth, Charlie Lung, and Richard Peel)

191. Classified Secret (4/12/53; Parley Baer, Charlotte Lawrence, Peter Leeds, and Leroy Leonard)

192. El Guitarrero (4/19/53; Lillian Buyeff, Eddie Firestone, and Jack Kruschen)

193. The Derelict (4/26/53; Charlotte Lawrence, Charlie Lung, and Ben Wright)

194. Lili and the Colonel (5/3/53; Lou Krugman, Paula Winslowe, and Ben Wright)

195. The Vessel of Wrath (5/10/53; Parley Baer, Alan Reed, Eric Snowden, and Dave Young)

196. North of Polaris (5/17/53; Hy Averback, William Conrad, Eddie Firestone, and Vivi Janiss)

197. The Blue Hotel (5/24/53)

198. A Good Thing (5/31/53; Anthony Barrett, Herb Butterfield, John Dehner, and Jack Kruschen)

199. The Voyages of Sinbad (6/7/53; Amanda Blake, Herb Butterfield, Whitfield Connor, Ted de Corsia, Georgia Ellis, Larry Thor, and Ben Wright)

200. Clear for Action (6/14/53; William Conrad, John Dehner, John Stevenson, and Ben Wright)

201. The Faraway Island (6/21/53; Anthony Barrett, Edgar Barrier, and Ted de Corsia)

202. The One-Eighth Apache (6/28/53; Parley Baer, Harry Bartell, and Lawrence Dobkin)

203. A Source of Irritation (7/5/53; Hy Averback, Paul Frees, Jack Kruschen, and Ben Wright)

204. The Out Station (7/12/53; Dick Beals, Alistaire Duncan, Terry Kilburn, and Dave Young)

205. The Open Boat (7/19/53; Edgar Barrier, William Conrad, Bob Sweeney, and Tom Tully)

206. The Notebook (7/26/53; William Conrad, John Dehner, and Joseph Kearns)

207. The Red Forrest (8/2/53; Parley Baer, John Dehner, Georgia Ellis, Jay Novello, and Tom Tully)

208. Three Skeleton Key (8/9/53; Paul Frees, Jay Novello, and Ben Wright)

209. The Thirteenth Truck (8/16/53; Hy Averback, Dick Beals, Alistaire Duncan, Alec Harford, Jack Kruschen, and Charlie Lung)

210. The Man From Tomorrow (8/23/53; Lawrence Dobkin, Vivi Janniss, and Barney Phillips)

211. The Game (8/30/53; John Dehner, Sam Edwards, and Eddie Firestone)

212. The Train from Olbefelde (9/6/53; William Conrad, Lawrence Dobkins, and Fritz Feld)

213. The Abominable Snowman (9/13/53; Hy Averback, Tony Barrett, Edgar Barrier, William Conrad, and Jack Kruschen)

214. The Log (9/20/53; Dick Beals, Lawrence Dobkin, Frank Gerstle, Byron Kane, Curt Martell, James Nusser, Alan Reed, and Eric Snowden)

215. The Untouchable (9/27/53; Parley Baer, Charles Davis, and Jack Kruschen)

216. Zero Hour (10/4/53; William Johnstone, Mary McGovern, Eve McVey, and Paula Winslowe)

217. Elementals (10/11/53; Tony Barrett, Georgia Ellis, Byron Kane, and Ben Wright)

218. The Bird of Paradise (3/11/54; Jeanne Bates, John Dehner, and Lawrence Dobkin)

219. Violent Night (3/18/54; William Conrad, Don Diamond, and Joyce McCluskey)

220. The Second Shot (3/25/54; John Dehner, Ellen Morgan, Victor Perrin, and Ben Wright)

221. The Return (4/1/54; Edgar Barrier, Jeanne Bates, Lawrence Dobkin, and Paul Dubov)

222. The Scarlet Plague (4/8/54; John Dehner, Sam Edwards, Virginia Gregg, and Victor Perrin)
223. Affair at Mandrake (4/15/54; Dick Beals, Joseph Kearns, and Jerry Montgomery)
224. The Adversary (5/20/54; Alec Harford, Charlie Lung, and Barney Phillips)
225. An Ordinary Man (6/3/54; Tony Barrett, Edgar Barrier, Harry Bartell, and Virginia Gregg)
226. Benchillina and the Fisherman (6/10/54; Lawrence Dobkin, Vic Perrin, and Paula Winslowe)
227. Bloodwaters (6/17/54; Lillian Buyeff, Jack Kruschen, Victor Perrin, and Barney Phillips)
228. Judgement Day at Crippled Deer (6/24/54; Lou Krugman, James Nusser, and Clayton Post)
229. The Dark Wall (7/1/54; John Dehner, Fritz Feld, Joyce McClusky, Nester Paiva, and Ben Wright)
230. The Birds (7/10/54; John Dehner, John Dodsworth, Virginia Gregg, Ann Morrison, Anne Whitfield, and Ben Wright)
231. Eye of Evil (7/17/54; Lynn Allen, Parley Baer, John Dehner, Jack Kruschen, and Ben Wright)
232. Flood on the Goodwins (7/24/54; Betty Lou Gearson, Will Geer, and Barton Yarborough)
233. Night of the Guns (7/31/54; Lillian Buyeff, Herb Ellis, Byron Kane, and Jay Novello)
234. The Price of the Head (8/7/54; Hans Conried, Mary Jane Croft, and Ben Wright)
235. The Coward (8/14/54; Herb Butterfield, Virginia Gregg, Lou Merrill, and Barney Phillips)
236. Two and Two Make Four (8/21/54; Joyce McCluskey, Shep Menken, and Tudor Owen)
237. The King of Owanatu (8/28/54; Anthony Barrett, Joseph Kearns, and Clayton Post)
238. The Boiling Sea (9/4/54; Ted de Corsia, Jim Hayward, Jack Moyles, and Clayton Post)
239. Carnival in Vienna (9/11/54; Robert Boone, Lillian Buyeff, Jack Kruschen, and Barney Phillips)
240. The Target (9/18/54; Whitfield Conner, Hans Conried, Mary Jane Croft, and Melisa Milo)
241. The Heart of Kali (9/25/54; Paul Frees, Lou Merrill, Clayton Post, and Paul Richards)

The Eternal Light

Dramas based on Jewish literature, history and music. Sponsored by the Jewish Theological Seminary and broadcast Sunday mornings/afternoons on NBC. Premiered on October 8, 1944, as of 1992, the series was still being broadcast over the radio! During the summer, for many years, the program presented a series of dramas entitled "The Words We Live By." From April 20, 1958, to May 11, 1958, *The Eternal Light* broadcast four special presentations celebrating Israel's tenth anniversary. The broadcasts of 1959 were rebroadcasts of previous scripts, the most popular plays previously presented, in honor of the fifteenth anniversary of the series. *The Eternal Light* was first heard from 12 to 12:30 pm, and later moved to 12:30 pm in the late forties, remaining in that time slot for many years.

Some scripts such as "Watchman, What of the Night?" described the last days of Isaac Rosenberg, the poet, who was killed in WWI. "An American Ballad" presented the story of Rabbi Henry Cohen. "Not Even Ten" featured a dramatization of Sodom and Gomorra. "A Song for Queen Esther" was Morton Wishengrad's musical rendition of the biblical story. "The Return of Danny Miller" was a Veterans drama, repeated many times over the years.

1. R. I. Refugee (10/8/44)
2. Emanuel (10/15/44)
3. Jacob and the Indians (10/22/44)
4. Tabernacle in Duke's Place (10/29/44)
5. Black Death (11/5/44)
6. -----(11/12/44)
7. Candelabra of the Steppes (11/19/44)
8. Temple of K' Ai Feng' Fu (11/26/44)
9. Maimonides (12/3/44)
10. Maccabees (12/10/44)
11. The Founding of the Synagogue (12/17/44)
12. The Vineyard of Yahneh (12/24/44)
13. Esther the Queen (12/31/44)
14. -----(1/7/45)
15. Solomon Schecter (1/14/45)
16. Rabbi Israel Salater (1/21/45)
17. The Battle of the Warsaw Ghetto (1/28/45; Raymond Massey)
18. Waldemar Mordicai Haffkins (2/4/45)
19. Mr. Lincoln and the Rabbi (2/11/45)
20. Rebecca Grate (2/18/45)
21. Emma Lazarus (2/25/45)
22. The Life of Sholom Aleichem (3/4/45)
23. Cyrus Adler (3/11/45)
24. Rabbi Isaac M. Wise (3/18/45)
25. Second Exodus (3/25/45)
26. Passover (4/1/45)
27. Seed and Dream (4/8/45)
28. Henrietta Szold [part one] (4/15/45)
29. Henrietta Szold [part two] (4/22/45)
30. The Death of Akiba (4/29/45)
31. The Life of Rabbi Meir (5/6/45)
32. The Book of Ruth (5/13/45)
33. As a Driven Leaf (5/20/45)
34. The Story of an American (5/27/45)
35. The Lie (6/3/45)
36. Jacob and the Indians (6/10/45)
37. The Tabernacle in Duke's Place (6/17/45)
38. The Bar Mitzvah of Private Cohen (6/24/45)
39 -----(7/1/45)
40. Juke Box Boys and the Synagogue (7/8/45)
41. Hear Ye Sons [part one] (7/15/45)
42. Hear Ye Sons [part two] (7/22/45)

43. The Man Who Flew to Heaven (7/29/45)
44. Jeremiah (8/5/45)
45. Young Joseph [part one, based on the novel by Thomas Mann] (8/12/45; Ludwig Lewisohn)
46. The Day of Prayer [part two] (8/19/45)
47. Joseph in Egypt [aka Joseph and His Brothers] [part three] (8/26/45)
48. Joseph the Provider (9/2/45)
49. If Not Higher (9/16/45)
50. Solomon Schelter (10/7/45)
51. -----(10/14/45)
52. Talmud (10/21/45)
53. The Unbroken Circle (10/28/45)
54. Lillian Wald (11/4/45)
55. R. I. Refugee (11/11/45)
56. The Day of the Shadow (11/18/45)
57. Thomas Kennedy (11/25/45)
58. Maccabees (12/2/45)
59. Lantern in the Inferno (12/9/45)
60. A Chassidic Tale (12/16/45)
61. Sound of Music (12/23/45)
62. The Voice of Rachel (12/30/45)
63. Jonah (1/6/46)
64. Parable of Reb Yisroel (1/13/46)
65. My Cousin Avigdor (1/20/46)
66. Isaac M. Wise (1/27/46)
67. The Sabbath of Chayyim, the Porter (2/3/46)
68. Postmaster of Quincy (2/10/46)
69. The Pastor of Eindhoven (2/17/46)
70. Moses Mendelssohn (2/24/46)
71. Ransom of Rabbi Meir (3/3/46)
72. My Favorite Assassin (3/10/46)
73. Great Purim Scandal (3/17/46)
74. Rahel (3/24/46)
75. The Cow That Coughed (3/31/46)
76. Hand of the Hunter (4/7/46)
77. Tender Grass (4/14/46)
78. When I Think of Seraye (4/21/46)
79. Waldemar M. W. Haffkine (4/28/46)
80. Quiet Life in Hampshire (5/5/46)
81. To Conquer the Sea (5/12/46)
82. A Pity for the Living (5/19/46)
83. Savior to Barnow (5/26/46)
84. Hunger (6/2/46; F. H. Laguardia)
85. The Remarkable Adventures of Deuteronomy Katz (6/9/46)

174. The Trees of Galilee (3/7/48; Melvyn Douglas)
175. The Island in the Wilderness (3/14/48; Edward G. Robinson)
176. Esther (3/21/48; Benjamin H. Swig)
177. Hoe Uriel Got Into Heaven (3/28/48)
178. The Physician of Birkenau (4/4/48)
179. The Man Who Remembered Lincoln (4/11/48)
180. The Passover of Rembrandt Van Rijn (4/18/48)
181. The Man from Omaha (5/2/48)
182. The Things I Saw (5/9/48)
183. The River Jordan (5/16/48)
184. How They Knocked the Devil Out of Uncle Ezra (5/23/48)
185. The Return of Danny Miller (5/30/48)
186. Boaz Makes Up His Mind (6/6/48)
187. The Dream of Jacob Meyer (6/20/48)
188. -----(6/27/48)
189. An American Ballad (7/4/48; Tom Glazer)
190. Cain and Abel (7/11/48)
191. Jacob and Esau (7/18/48)
192. Joseph and Benjamin [aka Joseph and His Brothers] (7/25/48)
193. Special Performance (8/1/48)
194. The Wise Men of Chelm (8/8/48)
195. The Head of the Table (8/15/48)
196. Portland, U.S.A. (8/22/48)
197. The Woman Rich in Time (8/29/48)
198. Messenger of Prayer (9/5/48)
199. The Book of Books (9/12/48)
200. Tzipporah (9/19/48)
201. The Man Who Hated God (9/26/48)
202. All These Barren Hills (10/3/48)
203. The Congregation of the Dead (10/10/48)
204. The Creation (10/17/48)
205. Josiah (10/24/48)
206. The Man With the Kiss of God (10/31/48)
207. The Light from the Darkness (11/7/48)
208. The Sentence of Life (11/14/48)
209. The Man Who Touched the Stars (11/21/48)
210. In Henry's Back Yard (11/28/48)
211. The Sneeze of Schomele (12/5/48)

212. The Trolley Bible of the Broadway Line (12/12/48)
213. His Excellency of Vilna (12/19/48)
214. The Great Outcry (12/26/48)
215. The Seven Who Came Home (1/2/49)
216. The Merry Jests of Hershel Ostropolier (1/9/49)
217. Trial and Error (1/16/49)
218. The Four Spinsters of Gimel (1/23/49)
219. Who Can Build a House? (1/30/49)
220. The Man Who Knew Carver (2/6/49)
221. The Physician and the Sorcerer (2/13/49)
222. Gandhi (2/20/49)
223. Lizzie and the Whiskers (2/27/49)
224. The Case of Ivor Haug (3/6/49)
225. The Lot of Esther (3/13/49)
226. A Magic Power (3/20/49)
227. A Green Thumb in the City (3/27/49)
228. An Adventure in Time (4/3/49)
229. The Slave (4/10/49)
230. One Little Nanny-Goat (4/17/49)
231. Out of Darkness (4/24/49)
232. The Portrait of Dedication (5/1/49)
233. The Second Sun (5/8/49)
234. Welcome Home (5/15/49)
235. The Trial of Jonathan Green (5/22/49)
236. Solomon: Man of Peace (5/29/49)
237. The Way of My Uncle Gedalia (6/5/49)
238. A Dreamer's Journey (6/12/49)
239. Aarn the Cobbler and the Western Wall (6/19/49)
240. An Incident at Sea (6/26/49)
241. The Sealed Tunnel (7/3/49)
242. The Words We Live By [part one] (7/10/49)
243. The Words We Live By [part two] (7/17/49)
243. The Words We Live By [part three] (7/24/49)
244. The Words We Live By [part four] (7/31/49)
245. The Words We Live By [part five] (8/7/49)
246. The Words We Live By [part six] (8/14/49)
247. The Words We Live By [part seven] (8/21/49)

248. The Words We Live By [part eight] (8/28/49; Dr. Juduh I. Goldin)
249. The Words We Live By [part nine] (9/4/49; Dr. Ludwig Lewisohn)
250. The Words We Live By [part ten] (9/11/49; Benjamin A. Cohen)
251. A New Amen (9/18/49)
252. The Fourth Confession (10/2/49)
253. Moses Mendessohn (10/23/49)
254. How They Knocked the Devil Out of Uncle Ezra (10/30/49)
255. The Return of Danny Miller (11/6/49)
256. Emma Lazarus (11/13/49; Margaret Webster)
257. In Henry's Backyard (11/20/49)
258. The Light From the Darkness (11/27/49; Eva Le Gallienne)
259. Joseph and Benjamin (12/4/49)
260. An American Ballad (12/11/49; Tom Glazer)
261. The River Jordan (12/18/49)
262. How Uriel Got to Heaven (12/25/49)
263. Gandhi (1/1/50)
264. The Thief and the Hangman (1/8/49; Mel Ferrer)
265. Brandeis (1/15/49; Sam Jaffe)
266. The Education of a Labor Leader (1/22/50; Ezra Stone)
267. The Embers Still Burn (1/29/50)
268. Dream No More (2/5/50)
269. Passport to the World (2/12/50)
270. The White Circus Horse (2/19/50)
271. A Song for Queen Esther (2/26/50; Tom Glazer)
272. The Promising Young Man (3/5/50)
273. Mrs. Steinberg's Partner in Heaven (3/12/50)
274. The Tender Grass (3/26/50)
275. Miracle in the Making (4/16/50)
276. The Death of Akiba (4/23/50)
277. On Wings of Eagles (4/30/50)
278. Milton Steinberg: A Memorial (5/7/50)
279. Operation Baby Sitters (5/14/50)
280. The Glowing Coals of Wisdom (5/21/50)
281. The Man Who Changed his Mind (5/28/50)
282. The Lance of Justice (6/4/50)
283. Investment in People (6/11/50)
284. Cardoza (6/18/50)
285. Prophet, What Do You See? (7/30/50; Cord Meyer, Jr.)

286. The Words We Live By [part one] (8/6/50; Norman Cousins)
287. The Words We Live By [part two] (8/13/50; Dr. Alice V. Keleher)
288. The Words We Live By [part three] (8/20/50; Dr. Channing Tobias)
289. The Words We Live By [part four] (8/27/50; Dr. Ruth Gruber)
290. The Words We Live By [part five] (9/3/50; Dr. Ordway Tead)
291. Rosh Hashonah Program (9/10/50)
292. The Song of Berditchev (9/17/50)
293. Ecclesiastes (9/24/50)
294. This Side of the Jordan (10/1/50)
295. A Duty of Conscience (10/8/50; John Garfield)
296. Young Man in a Hurry (10/15/50; Lilli Darvas and Leon Janney)
297. A Segment of My Times (10/22/50; Roger DeKoven and Ross Martin)
298. The Builders (10/29/50; Peter Cappell and Charlotte Holland)
299. The Wall (11/5/50)
300. The Way to Willingness (11/12/50)
301. The Preacher of Salem (11/19/50)
302. The Faithful City (11/26/50)
303. Thou Shalt Teach Them Diligently (12/3/50; Julia Richman)
304. The Top that Ran Away (12/10/50)
305. Preacher of Providence (12/17/50)
306. David and Jonathan (12/24/50; Donald Buka)
307. Watchman, What of the Night? (12/31/50)
308. The Rabbi-Hillel (1/7/51)
309. Judith (1/14/51)
310. The Camel and I (1/21/51)
311. The Yeleds of Yeled (1/28/51)
312. Charity Box (2/4/51)
313. The Lincoln Highway (2/11/51; Tom Glazer)
314. The Prince and the Prophet (2/18/51)
315. David and Absalom (2/25/51)
316. How the World Came to Yanovke (3/4/51)
317. Transmigration of a Melody (3/11/51)
318. Little Purim (3/18/51)
319. The Alphabet of Life (3/25/51)
320. Call of the Torah (4/1/51)
321. Rise Up and Walk (4/8/51)
322. These Rocks Are Mine (4/15/51)
323. Man Is Not Alone (4/29/51)

468. The Days of My Life (3/14/54)
469. The Purim Play (3/21/54)
470. Hosea (3/28/54)
471. The Children of Liberty (4/4/54)
472. City of the Dream (4/11/54)
473. Once Upon a Sunday (4/18/54; David Wayne and Martha Scott)
474. The Gift (5/2/54)
475. The Smallest Ship (5/9/54)
476. One Tree in the Desert [story of Abraham and the burning bush] (5/16/54)
477. The Dragon's Tail (5/23/54)
478. The Last Penny (5/30/54)
479. Ruth Comes Home (6/6/54)
480. A Bridge for Sarah (6/13/54)
481. The Court Without a Gavel (6/20/54; Supreme Court Justice William O. Douglas)
482. For Those Who Dream (6/27/54)
483. The Words We Live By: Supporting Cast of the Bible [part one] (7/4/54; Marc Van Doren and Maurice Samuel)
484. The Words We Live By: Supporting Cast of the Bible [part two] (7/11/54; Marc Van Doren and Maurice Samuel)
485. The Words We Live By: Supporting Cast of the Bible [part three] (7/18/54; Marc Van Doren and Maurice Samuel)
486. The Words We Live By: Supporting Cast of the Bible [part four] (7/25/54; Marc Van Doren and Maurice Samuel)
487. The Words We Live By: Supporting Cast of the Bible [part five] (8/1/54; Marc Van Doren and Maurice Samuel)
488. The Words We Live By: Supporting Cast of the Bible [part six] (8/8/54; Marc Van Doren and Maurice Samuel)
489. The Words We Live By: Supporting Cast of the Bible [part seven] (8/15/54; Marc Van Doren and Maurice Samuel)
490. The Words We Live By: Supporting Cast of the Bible [part eight] (8/22/54; Marc Van Doren and Maurice Samuel)
491. The Words We Live By: Supporting Cast of the Bible [part nine] (8/29/54; Marc Van Doren and Maurice Samuel)
492. The Words We Live By: Supporting Cast of the Bible [part ten] (9/5/54; Marc Van Doren and Maurice Samuel)
493. Rendezvous with Liberty (9/12/54)
494. Valley Forge (9/19/54)
495. As a Wind that Blows (9/26/54)
496. The Sealed Tunnel (10/3/54)
497. Jacob and the Indians (10/10/54)
498. Pugnacious Commodore (10/17/54)
499. Emma Lazarus (10/24/54)
500. The Mark of Cain (10/31/54)
501. The Cow That Coughed (11/7/54)
502. Education of a Labor Leader (11/14/54)
503. An American Sampler (11/21/54)
504. The Lie (11/28/54)
505. An American Ballad (12/5/54)
506. Easy to be an Angel (12/12/54)
507. A Light in the Darkness (12/19/54)
508. The Voice (12/26/54)
509. The Solid Oak Floor (1/2/55)
510. The Bible Blueprint (1/9/55)
511. The Sum of Man (1/16/55)
512. The Kidduan Cup (1/23/55)
513. Once Upon a Time (1/30/55)
514. The Transgression of Judel Kinderschein (2/6/55; Joseph Schildkraut)
515. David and Solomon (2/13/55; Walter Brennan)
516. How Rabbi Kalman Disappeared (2/20/55)
517. Different Drums (2/27/55)
518. There Is Always Purim (3/6/55)
519. The Root and the Flower (3/13/55)
520. The Upwards Road (3/20/55)
521. And Two Walked Backwards (3/27/55)
522. Departure into Freedom (4/3/55)
523. The Well of Dothan (4/10/55)
524. The Story of a Rich Man (4/17/55)
525. Four Hours To Midnight (4/24/55)
526. The Little Shoemaker (5/1/55)
527. A Meal for the Poor (5/8/55)
528. Northeast of Gaza (5/15/55)
529. All the Room in the World (5/22/55)
530. The Pious Ox (5/29/55)
531. Walt Whitman and I (6/5/55)
532. Light Against the Dark (6/12/55)
533. Einstein (6/19/55)

534. Operation Hebrew (6/26/55)
535. The Words We Live By: Stories of the Hebrew Prophets [part one] (7/3/55; Mark Van Doren and Maurice Samuel)
536. The Words We Live By: Stories of the Hebrew Prophets [part two] (7/10/55; Mark Van Doren and Maurice Samuel)
537. The Words We Live By: Stories of the Hebrew Prophets [part three] (7/17/55; Mark Van Doren and Maurice Samuel)
538. The Words We Live By: Stories of the Hebrew Prophets [part four] (7/24/55; Mark Van Doren and Maurice Samuel)
539. The Words We Live By: Stories of the Hebrew Prophets [part five] (7/31/55; Mark Van Doren and Maurice Samuel)
540. The Words We Live By: Stories of the Hebrew Prophets [part six] (8/7/55; Mark Van Doren and Maurice Samuel)
541. The Words We Live By: Stories of the Hebrew Prophets [part seven] (8/14/55; Mark Van Doren and Maurice Samuel)
542. The Words We Live By: Stories of the Hebrew Prophets [part eight] (8/21/55; Mark Van Doren and Maurice Samuel)
543. The Words We Live By: Stories of the Hebrew Prophets [part nine] (8/28/55; Mark Van Doren and Maurice Samuel)
544. The Words We Live By: Stories of the Hebrew Prophets [part ten] (9/4/55; Mark Van Doren and Maurice Samuel)
545. The Words We Live By: Stories of the Hebrew Prophets [part eleven] (9/11/55; Mark Van Doren and Maurice Samuel)
546. The Words We Live By: Stories of the Hebrew Prophets [part twelve] (9/25/55; Mark Van Doren and Maurice Samuel)
547. The Season of Gladness (10/16/55)
548. A Visit from Lord Baltimore (10/23/55)
549. Judgment for Idolatry (10/30/55)
550. Treasure of the Dead Sea Caves (11/6/55)
551. -----(11/13/55)
552. A Wrestling with an Angel (11/20/55)
553. Not Without Tears (11/27/55)
554. The Top That Ran Away (12/4/55)
555. Triumph in Samaria (12/11/55)
556. A Formal Accusation (12/18/55)
557. A Song for the Conqueror (12/25/55)
558. The Man Who Knew Lincoln (1/1/56; Raymond Massey)
559. The Human Element (1/8/56)
560. The Harp of King David (1/15/56; Richard Todd)
561. The Day (1/22/56)
562. Ben Franklin and the Liberty Bell (1/29/56; Louis Calhern)
563. A Very Special Village (2/5/56)
564. Mr. Flanagan, the Chaplain and Mr. Lincoln (2/12/56; Maurice Copeland)
565. A Song for Queen Esther (2/19/56)
566. The First Ingredient (2/26/56)
567. The Most Precious Gift (3/4/56)
568. Journey to Canaan (3/11/56)
569. Instant of Creation (3/18/56)
570. The Passover of Rembrandt Van Rijn (3/25/56)
571. Nor Reach the Uplands (4/1/56)
572. My Unpredictable Story-Telling Father (4/8/56)
573. It's a Long Walk to Jerusalem (4/15/56)
574. A Man Is Not a Thing (4/22/56)
575. The Cedar and the Reed (4/29/56)
576. The House with Blue Curtains (5/6/56)
577. The Ordination (5/13/56)
578. Ben Franklin, American (5/20/56; Ralph Bellamy)
579. The Guardian Angel of Genesee County (5/27/56)
580. Another June Third (6/3/56)
581. A Garden East-ward (6/10/56)
582. The Man Who Rode Like Revere (6/17/56)
583. The Rabbi With the Ink-Stained Hands (6/24/56)
584. Highlights About the First Five Books of the Bible [part one] (7/1/56; Mark Van Doren and Maurice Samuel)
585. Highlights About the First Five Books of the Bible [part two]

(8/4/57; Marc Van Doren and Maurice Samuel)

642. The Words We Live By: The Wisdom Books of the Bible [part six] (8/11/57; Marc Van Doren and Maurice Samuel)

643. The Words We Live By: The Wisdom Books of the Bible [part seven] (8/18/57; Marc Van Doren and Maurice Samuel)

644. The Words We Live By: The Wisdom Books of the Bible [part eight] (8/25/57; Marc Van Doren and Maurice Samuel)

645. The Words We Live By: The Book of Job [part nine] (9/1/57; Marc Van Doren and Maurice Samuel)

646. The Words We Live By: The Endings of the Wisdom Books of the Bible [part ten] (9/8/57; Marc Van Doren and Maurice Samuel)

647. My Friend, the Conductor (9/15/57)

648. Take With You Words (9/22/57)

649. Wash the Stain Away (9/29/57)

650. Callused Hands (10/6/57)

651. The Case of the Glastonbury Cows (10/13/57)

652. Only the Heart (10/20/57)

653. The Great Discovery (10/27/57)

654. The Song of Deborah (11/3/57)

655. The Return of Danny Miller (11/10/57)

656. Elijah the Tishbite (11/17/57)

657. Photographer in Buckskin (11/24/57)

658. David and Johnathan (12/1/57)

659. A Lifetime Is Just Long Enough (12/8/57)

660. A Simple Matter (12/15/57)

661. The Key to David's Suitcase (12/22/57)

662. The Friend and Peter Stuyvesant (12/29/57)

663. The Parable of Reb Yisroel (1/5/58)

664. My Father's Talis (1/12/58)

665. A Heart of Wisdom (1/19/58)

666. Honey on the Book: The Life of Louis M. Rabinowitz (1/26/58; Theodore Bikel and Eli Wallach)

667. Wisdom of the Fathers (2/2/58)

668. Sam's Farm (2/9/58)

669. Abbie Could See (2/16/58; Alexander Scourby)

670. The Big Road (2/23/58; Bob Ross and Bill Williams)

671. The Golden Egg (3/2/58)

672. Tree at My Window (3/9/58)

673. The Uses of Adversity (3/16/58)

674. Journey to the Promised Land (3/23/58)

675. My Son, the Convict (3/30/58)

676. Icarua in a Wheelchair (4/13/58)

677. The River Jordan (4/20/58)

678. The Camel and I (4/27/58)

679. Quiet Street (5/4/58)

680. These Rocks Are Mine (5/11/58)

681. A Boy's Quiet Voice (5/18/58)

682. The Hour Is Now (6/1/58)

683. In His Father's House (6/8/58)

684. Summer of Decision (6/15/58)

685. Cantillation — Interpreter of the Bible (6/22/58)

686. David Dubinsky, Man of Labor (6/29/58)

687. The Words We Live By: Great Words in Literature of the Bible [part one] (7/6/58; Marc Van Doren and Maurice Samuel)

688. The Words We Live By: Great Words in Literature of the Bible [part two] (7/13/58; Marc Van Doren and Maurice Samuel)

689. The Words We Live By: Great Words in Literature of the Bible [part three] (7/20/58; Marc Van Doren and Maurice Samuel)

690. The Words We Live By: Great Words in Literature of the Bible [part four] (7/27/58; Marc Van Doren and Maurice Samuel)

691. The Words We Live By: Great Words in Literature of the Bible [part five] (8/3/58; Marc Van Doren and Maurice Samuel)

692. The Words We Live By: Great Words in Literature of the Bible [part six] (8/10/58; Marc Van Doren and Maurice Samuel)

693. The Words We Live By: Great Words in Literature of the Bible [part seven] (8/17/58; Marc Van Doren and Maurice Samuel)

694. The Words We Live By: Great Words in Literature of the Bible [part eight] (8/24/58; Marc Van Doren and Maurice Samuel)

695. The Words We Live By: Great

Words in Literature of the Bible [part nine] (8/31/58; Marc Van Doren and Maurice Samuel)

696. The Words We Live By: Great Words in Literature of the Bible [part ten] (9/7/58) Marc Van Doren and Maurice Samuel
697. The High Places (9/14/58)
698. To Begin Again (9/21/58)
699. An Orange from Sharon (9/28/58)
700. As Deep Waters (10/5/58)
701. Four-and-a-Half Feet of Faith (10/12/58)
702. Two Ounces of Lead (10/19/58)
703. Moses Levy in the Wilderness (10/26/58)
704. The Horse and his Rider (11/2/58)
705. The Return of Danny Miller (11/9/58)
706. The Garments of Truth (11/16/58)
707. This Precious Ground (11/23/58)
708. One Man's Faith (11/30/58)
709. The Maccabees (12/7/58)
710. -----(12/14/58)
711. -----(12/21/58)
712. -----(12/28/58)
713. Jeremiah (1/4/59)
714. Lullaby for Ruth (1/11/59)
715. Enter to Learn, Depart to Serve (1/18/59)
716. Sweet Hemlock (1/25/59)
717. Is All Vanity? (2/1/59)
718. We're All Human (2/8/59)
719. As a Wind That Blows (2/15/59)
720. Not Even Ten (2/22/59)
721. Ben Franklin and the Liberty Bell (3/1/59)
722. An American Ballad (3/8/59)
723. The Bible Blueprint of the Holy Land (3/15/59)
724. The Root and the Flower (3/22/59)
725. The Song of Berditschev (3/29/59)
726. Mrs. Steinberg's Partner in Heaven (4/5/59)
727. Children of Liberty (4/12/59)
728. The Battle of the Warsaw Getto (4/19/59)
729. Light from the Darkness [written by Sylvia Berger] (4/26/59)
730. Walt Whitman and I (5/3/59; Dore Schary)
731. My Unpredictable Story-Telling Father (5/10/59)
732. Little Sakiki (5/17/59)

733. Watchman, What of the Night? (5/24/59)
734. The Words We Live By: The Legends of the Bible (5/30/59; Mark Van Doren and Maurice Samuel)
735. The Legends of the Bible: The Creation [part one] (6/7/59; Mark Van Doren and Maurice Samuel)
736. The Legends of the Bible: The Creation [part two] (6/14/59; Mark Van Doren and Maurice Samuel)
737. The Legends of the Bible: The Creation [part three] (6/21/59; Mark Van Doren and Maurice Samuel)
738. The Legends of the Bible: Adam and Eve and the Fall (6/28/59; Mark Van Doren and Maurice Samuel)
739. The Legends of the Bible: Ten Generations (7/5/59; Mark Van Doren and Maurice Samuel)
740. The Legends of the Bible: Noah and the Flood (7/12/59; Mark Van Doren and Maurice Samuel)
741. The Legends of the Bible: The Patriarchs [part one] (7/19/59; Mark Van Doren and Maurice Samuel)
742. The Legends of the Bible: The Patriarchs [part two] (7/26/59; Mark Van Doren and Maurice Samuel)
743. The Legends of the Bible: The Patriarchs [part three] (8/2/59; Mark Van Doren and Maurice Samuel)
744. The Legends of the Bible: Moses in the Wilderness [part one] (8/9/59; Mark Van Doren and Maurice Samuel)
745. The Legends of the Bible: Moses in the Wilderness [part two] (8/16/59; Mark Van Doren and Maurice Samuel)
746. The Legends of the Bible: The Judges (8/23/59; Mark Van Doren and Maurice Samuel)
747. The Legends of the Bible: The Kings (8/30/59; Mark Van Doren and Maurice Samuel)
748. The Legends of the Bible: The Prophets (9/6/59; Mark Van Doren and Maurice Samuel)
749. Goldstone's Folly (9/13/59)

750. A Skillful Song (9/20/59)
751. Each New Day (9/27/59)
752. The World Will Know (10/11/59)
753. Thou Wast a Slave in Egypt [part one] (11/1/59)
754. Thou Wast a Slave in Egypt [part two] (11/8/59)
755. Rachel (11/15/59)
756. An Unlikely Story (11/22/59)
757. Advocate of the People (11/29/59)
758. The Sign of the Seal (12/6/59)
759. The Protector (12/13/59)
760. Treaty for the People (12/20/59)
761. From Bergen-Belsen to Wuppertal (12/27/59)
762. A Voyage to Inner Space (1/3/60)
763. How Manny Got Into the Seventh Grade (1/10/60)
764. The Survivors (1/17/60)
765. A Pattern for Peace (1/24/60)
766. A Fruitful Hill (1/31/60)
767. The Language of Hope (2/7/60)
768. The Song of My People (2/14/60)
769. The Blessing (2/21/60)
770. Chaim, the Shoe-maker (2/28/60)
771. A Summer's Reading (3/6/60)
772. The Seed and the Dream (3/13/60)
773. As a Driven Leaf (3/20/60)
774. The Blessed Tailor (3/27/60)
775. Are You Listening, King Solomon? (4/3/60)
776. A Still Small Voice (4/10/60)
777. Monument to Remembrance (4/17/60)
778. The Golden Chain (4/24/60)
779. The Raven and the Dove (5/1/60)
780. These Children (5/8/60)
781. The Circus Clown (5/15/60)
782. Andrea's Room (5/22/60)
783. Come Under the Wings (5/29/60)
784. Message to the World [story about the late Nate B. Spingold, motion-picture executive] (6/5/60; Joan Crawford and Franchot Tone)
785. The Psalms as Great Human Documents [part one] (6/12/60; Marc Van Doren and Maurice Samuel)
786. The Psalms as Great Human Documents [part two] (6/19/60; Marc Van Doren and Maurice Samuel)
787. The Psalms as Great Human Documents [part three] (6/26/60; Marc Van Doren and Maurice Samuel)
788. The Psalms as Great Human Documents [part four] (7/3/60; Marc Van Doren and Maurice Samuel)
789. The Psalms as Great Human Documents [part five] (7/10/60; Marc Van Doren and Maurice Samuel)
790. The Psalms as Great Human Documents [part six] (7/17/60; Marc Van Doren and Maurice Samuel)
791. The Psalms as Great Human Documents [part seven] (7/24/60; Marc Van Doren and Maurice Samuel)
792. The Psalms as Great Human Documents [part eight] (7/31/60; Marc Van Doren and Maurice Samuel)
793. The Psalms as Great Human Documents [part nine] (8/7/60; Marc Van Doren and Maurice Samuel)
794. The Psalms as Great Human Documents [part ten] (8/14/60; Marc Van Doren and Maurice Samuel)
795. The Psalms as Great Human Documents [part eleven] (8/21/60; Marc Van Doren and Maurice Samuel)
796. The Psalms as Great Human Documents [part twelve] (8/28/60; Marc Van Doren and Maurice Samuel)
797. The Psalms as Great Human Documents [part thirteen] (9/4/60; Marc Van Doren and Maurice Samuel)
798. The Psalms as Great Human Documents [part fourteen] (9/11/60; Marc Van Doren and Maurice Samuel)
799. Let There Be Light (9/18/60)
800. The Third Confession [script by Yom Kippur] (9/25/60)
801. The Season of Hope (10/2/60)
802. Land of Deliverance (10/9/60)
803. The World Turned Right Side Up (10/16/60)
804. Jacob and the Indians [based on the Stephen Vincent Benet story] (10/23/60)
805. Portrait of a Man (11/6/60)
806. Pugnacious Commodore (11/13/60)
807. Reminder of the Covenant (11/20/60)
808. Pioneer of the Panhandle (11/27/60)
809. The Rabbi with the Ink-Stained Hands (12/4/60)
810. A Deal with the Devil (12/11/60)

811. A Special Kind of Hero (12/18/60)
812. The Search (12/25/60)
813. The Leaf Shall be Green (1/1/61)
814. The Hidden Cord (1/8/61)
815. These Are My Brothers (1/15/61)
816. From All My Teachers (1/22/61)
817. The Talmudic Stove (1/29/61)
818. Leave a Little for God (2/5/61)
819. The Days of a Poet (2/12/61)
820. Primer for the Sighted (2/19/61)
821. A Song for Queen Esther (2/26/61)
822. To Plow the Sea (3/5/61)
823. Who Stands on Trial? (3/12/61)
824. The Trial of the Two Mothers (3/19/61)
825. Bitter Herb (3/26/61)
826. The Battle of the Warsaw Getto [written by Morton Wishengrad] (4/9/61)
827. The Roots of Independence (4/16/61)
828. Investigation at Medziboz (4/23/61)
829. The World and I (4/30/61)
830. A Memorial to Rabbi Abraham Isaac Kook (5/7/61)
831. The Prayer Shaws (5/14/61)
832. Love and Human Devine [part one] (5/28/61; Marc Van Doren and Maurice Samuel)
833. Love and Human Devine [part two] (6/4/61; Marc Van Doren and Maurice Samuel)
834. Love and Human Devine [part three] (6/11/61; Marc Van Doren and Maurice Samuel)
835. Love and Human Devine [part four] (6/18/61; Marc Van Doren and Maurice Samuel)
836. Love and Human Devine [part five] (6/25/61; Marc Van Doren and Maurice Samuel)
837. Love and Human Devine [part six] (7/2/61; Marc Van Doren and Maurice Samuel)
838. Love and Human Devine [part seven] (7/9/61; Marc Van Doren and Maurice Samuel)
839. Love and Human Devine: The Tragedy of Dinah [part eight] (7/16/61; Marc Van Doren and Maurice Samuel)
840. Love and Human Devine: Saul, David and Jonathan [part nine] (7/23/61; Marc Van Doren and Maurice Samuel)
841. Love and Human Devine: David [part ten] (7/30/61; Marc Van Doren and Maurice Samuel)
842. Love and Human Devine: Love That Failed [part eleven] (8/6/61; Marc Van Doren and Maurice Samuel)
843. Love and Human Devine: Ruth [part twelve] (8/13/61; Marc Van Doren and Maurice Samuel)
844. Love and Human Devine: Tobit [part thirteen] (8/20/61; Marc Van Doren and Maurice Samuel)
845. Love and Human Devine: The Song of Songs [part fourteen] (8/27/61; Marc Van Doren and Maurice Samuel)
846. Love and Human Devine: Bible Translation [part fifteen] (9/3/61; Marc Van Doren and Maurice Samuel)
847. Tears of Paradise (9/10/61)
848. Called to Nineveh (9/17/61)
849. A Song of Ascent (9/24/61)
850. A Lifetime Is Just Long Enough (10/1/61)
851. Lighthouse to the Past (10/8/61)
852. The Mark of a Free Man (10/15/61)
853. The Walls (10/22/61)
854. The Odyssey to Amsterdam (10/29/61)
855. The Years in the Wilderness (11/5/61)
856. Newsprint for a Dream [written by Johanna Johnston] (11/12/61)
857. Our Uncle Arthur (11/19/61)
858. A Cigar Box and a Promise (11/26/61)
859. The Caves of Bar Kochba (12/3/61)
860. The Genie in the Lamp (12/10/61)
861. The Mounds of Assyria (12/17/61)
862. The Tablet of Siloam (12/24/61)
863. The Secret of the Lachish Letters (12/31/61)
864. The Rabbi with the Ink-Stained Hands (1/7/62)
865. Mr. Flanagan, the Chaplain and Mr. Lincoln (1/14/62)
866. The Man Who Knew Lincoln (1/21/62)
867. The Postmaster of Quincey (1/28/62)
868. The Big Road (2/4/62)
869. Mr. Lincoln and the Rabbi (2/11/62)

870. The Hand of Essu (2/18/62)
871. The Miracle-Maker (2/25/62)
872. The Inheritance (3/4/62)
873. A World Dialogue (3/11/62)
874. A Song for Queen Esther (3/18/62)
875. One Hundred Children (3/25/62)
876. The Hill of Hope (4/1/62)
877. The Faces of Man (4/8/62)
878. Little Sakiki (4/15/62)
879. The Yellow Star (4/22/62)
880. In the House of Pilgrimage (4/29/62)
881. One Hundred Hours (5/6/62)
882. The 6,000 Year-Old Man (5/13/62)
883. The Masoretic Crown (5/20/62)
884. The Words We Live By: Democracy and the Bible [part one] (5/27/62; Mark Van Doren and Maurice Samuel)
885. The Words We Live By: The Bible as the Wellspring of Democracy [part two] (6/3/62; Mark Van Doren and Maurice Samuel)
886. The Words We Live By: The Sanctity of the Individual [part three] (6/10/62)
887. The Words We Live By: The Sabbath as a Democratic Institution [part four] (6/17/62; Mark Van Doren and Maurice Samuel)
888. The Words We Live By: The Sabbath as a Democratic Institution [part five] (6/24/62; Mark Van Doren and Maurice Samuel)
889. The Words We Live By: The Giving of the Law as a Democratic Act [part six] (7/1/62; Mark Van Doren and Maurice Samuel)
890. The Words We Live By: Human Relations in Democracy and the Bible [part seven] (7/8/62; Mark Van Doren and Maurice Samuel)

891. The Words We Live By: Human Relations in Democracy and the Bible [part eight] (7/15/62; Mark Van Doren and Maurice Samuel)
892. The Words We Live By: Education, Democracy and the Bible [part nine] (7/22/62; Mark Van Doren and Maurice Samuel)
893. The Words We Live By: Education, Democracy and the Bible [part ten] (7/29/62; Mark Van Doren and Maurice Samuel)
894. The Words We Live By: A Democratic and Biblical Point of View [part eleven] (8/5/62; Mark Van Doren and Maurice Samuel)
895. The Words We Live By: A Democratic and Biblical Point of View [part twelve] (8/12/62; Mark Van Doren and Maurice Samuel)
896. The Words We Live By: Problems of War and Democracy [part thirteen] (8/19/62; Mark Van Doren and Maurice Samuel)
897. The Words We Live By: Problems of War and Democracy [part fourteen] (8/26/62; Mark Van Doren and Maurice Samuel)
898. The Words We Live By: The Vision of a Perfect World [part fifteen] (9/2/62; Mark Van Doren and Maurice Samuel)
899. Some Fascinating Minor Figures of the Bible (9/9/62; Mark Van Doren and Maurice Samuel)
900. The Story of Ruth, the Moabitess (9/16/62; Mark Van Doren and Maurice Samuel)
901. The Story of Rebekeh (9/23/62; Mark Van Doren and Maurice Samuel)
902. The Reluctant Deliverer (10/7/62)

Everyman's Theater

Produced, directed and written by Arch Oboler, this NBC anthology series was heard on Friday evenings from 9:30 to 10 pm, EST, sponsored by Oxydol. Richard Strauss' "Death and Transfiguration" was used as the opening and closing theme. The premiere broadcast was a miniature version of a 1939 *Arch Oboler's Plays* drama. The program was preempted on November 1 by a presidential speech. For the broadcast of November 22, 1940, Joan Crawford starred in three short dramas. Boris Karloff reprised his *Lights Out!* role in "Cat Wife." Episode eight was later redramatized on the *Cavalcade of America*.

1. This Lonely Heart (10/4/40; Alla Nazimova)
2. This Precious Freedom (10/11/40; Raymond Massey)
3. Cat Wife (10/18/40; Raymond Edward Johnson and Boris Karloff)
4. Mr. and Mrs. Chump (10/25/40; Walter Huston)
5. I'll Tell My Husband (11/8/40; Mary Astor and Edmund MacDonald)
6. Flying Yorkshireman (11/15/40; Elsa Lanchester and Charles Laughton)
7. The Word / Two / Eve (11/22/40; Joan Crawford)
8. An American Is Born (11/29/40; Elisabeth Bergner)
9. Visitor From Hades (12/6/40; Helen Mack)
10. Mr. Whiskers (12/13/40; Lee J. Cobb)
11. The Woman Stayed at Home (12/20/40; Norma Shearer)
12. These Are Your Brothers (12/27/40; Brian Donlevy)
13. Suffer the Little Children (1/3/41; Martha Scott)
14. Flight From Destiny (1/10/41; Thomas Mitchell)
15. Papa Jonathan (1/17/41; Howard Duff)
16. Of Human Bondage (1/24/41; Bette Davis)
17. Madame Affamee (1/31/41; Marlene Dietrich)
18. Special to Hollywood (2/7/41; Gale Page)
19. Immortal Gentleman (2/14/41; Franchot Tone)
20. Mr. Ginsburg (2/21/41; Benny Rubin)
21. The Family (2/28/41; Alla Nazimova)
22. You and I (3/7/41; Walter Huston)
23. The Ugliest Man in the World (3/14/41; Raymond E. Johnson)
24. The Listener [by Louis Bromfield] (3/21/41; Mona Hungerford)
25. Baby (3/28/41; Martha Scott)

Everything for the Boys

This series, although successful, did not surface on radio as it was originally intended. Originally, the series was to be a collaboration of Arch Oboler's writing and directing skills, along with Ronald Colman as host. A twenty-minute drama was to be acted out by a new guest each week, followed by a two-way shortwave conversation between the guests and service men stationed in foreign places. A selection of popular stage plays and novels was made on the basis of a careful survey of service men's preferences. Oboler's task was to then adapt the novels and stage plays for radio, being allowed to submit one Oboler original of his own. Oboler had no budget restrictions to worry about in casting for the novels and plays he adapted for this series, but he was somewhat concerned about talent before the program premiered, for a monetary reason. "The motion picture studios," he said, "are behind twelve and forty-five days in their shooting schedules due to the flu epidemic and are inclined to think radio can take care of itself."

On NBC, Tuesday evening at 7:30 pm, EST, *Everything for the Boys* premiered, with an adaptation of Robert E. Sherwood's stage hit, "The Petrified

Forest." Frank Martin was the announcer, Gordon Jenkins supplied the music, and the Electric Auto-Lite Company was the sponsor. What happened afterwards was disastrous. The subsequent offerings of "A Connecticut Yankee," "Rebecca," "Three Men on a Horse" and "Cyrano de Bergerac" were supposed to be next, but copyright conflicts halted production. As a last minute solution to the lack of scripts, Oboler turned to Robert E. Sherwood and paid for the rights to other Sherwood stories such as "Lost Horizon" and "Berkeley Square." Oboler began pulling scripts from previous radio programs that he wrote for and the script solution came to be.

Eventually Ronald Colman and Arch Oboler left for other radio productions, and the program was revamped by Dick Haymes as star. For the new version, the dramas were dropped. Instead, poems were read and songs were sung. This was done in order to provide servicemen on Allied fighting fronts whatever they wanted in the way of dramatic entertainment. Dick Haymes starred in the broadcast of June 13, 1944, and he remained as a regular until June 25, 1945. After the drama "Death Takes a Holiday," Ingrid Bergman sang "As Time Goes By" to servicemen. Ella Mae Morse sang "Milkman, Keep Those Bottles Quiet" after "Holy Matrimony," which was an adaptation of A. Bennett's "Buried Alive." After the drama of 2/15/44, Ronald Colman read "High Flight" by John G. McGee. After the drama of 3/21/44, Colman read a "Letter to General Montgomery from General Nye." After the drama of 3/28/44, Colman read "Letter to a Soldier's Wife from India." The broadcast of 1/25/44 was originally titled "Knuckles," but was changed shortly before broadcast.

1. The Petrified Forest (1/18/44; Ginger Rogers)
2. Lady of the House (1/25/44; Irene Dunne)
3. Lost Horizon (2/1/44; Janet Blair, Norman Field, and Mercedes McCambridge)
4. Berkeley Square (2/8/44; Greer Garson)
5. A Man to Remember (2/15/44; Bob Burns)
6. The Woman Stayed at Home (2/22/44; Mercedes McCambridge)
7. Rogue Male (2/29/44; Merle Oberon)
8. Of Human Bondage (3/7/44; Hans Conried and Bette Davis)
9. The Ghost Goes West (3/14/44; Anne Baxter)
10. A Girl of the Road (3/21/44; Martha Scott)
11. An Ostrich in Bed (3/28/44; Joan Bennett)
12. This Living Book (4/4/44; Bob Bailey, Dennis Day, Lou Merrill, and Mercedes McCambridge)
13. The Citadel (4/11/44; Ida Lupino)
14. The Jervis Bay Goes Down (4/18/44; Ella Logan)
15. Death Takes a Holiday (4/25/44; Ingrid Bergman, Hans Conried, and Luis Van Rooten)
16. Holy Matrimony (5/2/44; Ruth Chatterton and Ella Mae Morse)
17. This Above All (5/9/44; Olivia de Havilland)
18. Blithe Spirit (5/16/44; Edna Best, Mercedes McCambridge, and Loretta Young)
19. Quality Street (5/23/44; Agnes Moorehead and Maureen O'Sullivan)
20. The House I Live In (5/30/44; Dinah Shore)
21. Durante Takes Over (6/6/44; Jimmy Durante and Jose Iturbi)
22. Reunion in Vienna (6/13/44; Claudette Colbert and Dick Haymes)

Famous Trials

Series on outstanding trials in American History, discussed by Professor William M. Kunstler of New York University. Each episode featured a prominent professor or doctor who was expert on the subject of the week, to give their view points after each drama.

1. The United States vs. Hiss (5/22/59)
2. The Commonwealth vs. Sacco and Vanzetti (5/29/59)
3. The Commonwealth vs. Lizzie Borden (6/5/59)
4. The State of Illinois vs. Leopold and Loeb (6/12/59)
5. The United States vs. Julius and Ethel Rosenberg (6/19/59)
6. The Mass. Bay Colony vs. Anne Hutchinson (6/26/59)
7. The State of New York vs. Nan Patterson (7/3/59)
8. The State of Tennessee vs. John Thomas Scopes (7/10/59)
9. The Greer Case (7/24/59)
10. The Crown vs. Dr. Crippen (7/31/59)
11. The Crows vs. William Joyce (8/7/59)

Fannie Hurst Presents

Anthology series, hosted by Fannie Hurst. Broadcast Saturday mornings over ABC, 10 to 10:30 am, EST.

1. -----(7/8/44)
2. Carousel (7/15/44; Sam Jaffee)
3. God Made Little Apples (7/22/44)
4. The Golden Fish (7/29/44)
5. Nightshade (8/5/44)
6. The Vertical City (8/12/44)
7. Hattie Turner vs. Hattie Turner (8/19/44)
8. Home James (8/26/44)
9. A Petal on the Current (9/2/44)
10. The Wrath (9/9/44)
11. The Candy Butcher (9/16/44)
12. He Shall Not Pass (9/23/44)
13. The Good Provider (9/30/44; Sam Jaffee)
14. Give This Little Girl a Hand (10/7/44; Betty Garde)
15. Ice Water, Please (10/14/44)
16. Do-Re-Me-Fah (10/21/44)
17. The Golden Fleece (10/28/44)
18. The Laugh Was on Harry (11/4/44)
19. The Sieve of Fulfillment (11/11/44)
20. Higginbottom of Cincinnati (11/18/44)
21. An American Scene (11/25/44)
22. The Squirrel Cage (12/2/44)
23. Rosemary for Remembrance (12/9/44)
24. Elaine, Daughter of Elaine (12/16/44)
25. Who Are You? (12/23/44)
26. Madagascar Ho! (12/30/44)

Fantasies from Lights Out!

Lights Out! was so popular that even when it went off the air, it couldn't be helped that a short-run revival of the series would return for a summer series.

This revival went under a title other than *Lights Out!* and only seven episodes were broadcast; it was preempted on August 18. All of the scripts were written by Wyllis Cooper, ranging from science-fiction to down-to-earth murder. The final broadcast was entitled "Lights Out," the same name as the program, but was more on the patriotic side, concerning a veteran on Decoration day.

1. The Safe Crackers (7/14/45; Will Geer and William Griffis)
2. Reunion After Death (7/21/45; Sarah Burton and Alexander Scourby)
3. The Rocket Ship (7/28/45; Lon Clark and Edgar Stehli)
4. Lady from the Lake (8/4/45; June Allyson, William Griffis, and A. Kohl)
5. Did the Murder Happen? (8/11/45; Vinton Hayworth and Betty Winkler)
6. Man in the Middle (8/25/45; S. Leigh)
7. Lights Out (9/1/45; J. Floyd)

Favorite Story

Syndicated series released by Ziv. Hollywood stars were asked what their favorite novel or short story was, and an adaptation was performed using various radio performers such as Howard Duff, Frank Lovejoy, Jack Webb, and Janet Waldo. Examples: George Burns and Gracie both agreed that their favorite story was "The Mystery of Room 323." Helen Trauble said her favorite story was "The Man Who Married a Dumb Wife," Ruth Gordon loved "Tom Sawyer," Barry Fitzgerald's favorite story was "Jamie Freel," and Henry Fonda's favorite story was "Cashel Byron's Profession." Lauritz Melchoir's favorite was "The Man Who Made Gold." Eva Le Gallienne's was "Marco Polo," Walter Wagner's was "Mutiny on the Bounty," and Garson Cainon's was "The Brownings." Ethel Barrymore chose "The Young Years." Ironically, Ed Wynn claimed that "The Bottle Imp" was his favorite, and Fred Allen's favorite was "Frankenstein." Not too surprising, Clyde Beatty said that "Ben Hur" was his favorite story. Others who chose their favorite stories were Eleanor Roosevelt, Irving Berlin, Sinclair Lewis, Ozzie and Harriet, and Alfred Hitchcock.

The first date below is from the East Coast. The second date is the broadcast date from the West Coast, Tuesday evenings. Others stations across the country broadcast different days. Over Mutual, for one example, episode twenty, "Alice in Wonderland" was broadcast on December 28, 1948.

Jack Hayes supplied the sound effects. There were various sponsors due to syndication, Bullocks for instance over Mutual. Claude Sweeten supplied the music. Jerome Lawrence and Robert Lee (both of whom would later be involved with *The Railroad Hour*) wrote, produced, and directed the series. True Boardman was the narrator for many broadcasts. Ronald Colman, who starred in the lead on occasion, was the host. Lyle Bond was the announcer.

1. Les Miserables (9/13/47; 6/25/46)
2. The Diamond Lens (9/20/47; 7/2/46; William Conrad)
3. Little Women (9/27/47; 7/9/46)
4. Wuthering Heights (10/4/47; 7/16/46; William Conrad and Janet Waldo)
5. A Connecticut Yankee in King Arthur's Court (10/11/47; 7/23/46)
6. Cyrano de Bergerac (10/18/47; 7/30/46)
7. David Copperfield (10/25/47; 8/6/46)
8. The Queen of Spades (11/1/47; 8/13/46)
9. The Adventures of Huckleberry Finn (11/8/47; 8/20/46; Jimmy Lydon and Ed MacDonald)
10. The Arabian Nights (11/15/47; 8/27/46)
11. Jane Eyre (11/22/47; 9/3/46)
12. Vanity Fair (11/29/47; 9/10/46)
13. Joan of Arc (12/6/47; 9/17/46)
14. Frankenstein (12/13/47; 9/24/46)
15. 20,000 Leagues Under the Sea (12/20/47; 10/1/46)
16. The Importance of Being Ernest (12/27/47; 10/8/46)
17. Dr. Jekyll and Mr. Hyde (1/10/48; 10/15/46)
18. The Man Who Sold His Shadow to the Devil (1/17/48; 10/22/46)
19. Lodging for the Night (1/24/48; 10/29/46; William Conrad and Janet Waldo)
20. Alice in Wonderland (1/31/48; 11/5/46; Arthur Q. Bryan, June Foray, Lurene Tuttle, Herb Vigran)
21. Rapaccini's Daughter (2/7/48; 11/12/46)
22. Moby Dick (2/14/48; 11/19/46; William Conrad, Howard Duff, and Frank Lovejoy)
23. Great Expectations (2/21/48; 11/26/46)
24. The Phantom Rickshaw (2/28/48; 12/3/46)
25. The Sire De Maletroit's Door (3/6/48; 12/10/46)
26. God Sees the Truth but Waits (3/13/48; 12/17/46)
27. Debt Collector (3/20/48; 12/24/46)
28. Gulliver's Travels (3/27/48; 12/31/46)
29. Mayerling (4/3/48; 1/7/47)
30. Mister Shakespeare (4/10/48; 1/14/47)
31. Casey at the Bat (4/17/48; 1/21/47)
32. The Light That Failed (4/24/48; 1/28/47)
33. The Man Without a Country (5/1/48; 2/4/47)
34. Mary, Queen of Scotts (5/8/48; 2/11/47)
35. Dr. Heidegger's Experiment (5/15/48; 2/18/47)
36. Oliver Twist (5/22/48; 2/25/47)
37. The Legend of Sleepy Hollow (5/29/48; 3/4/47)
38. The Three Musketeers (6/5/48; 3/11/47)
39. The Mystery of Room 323 (6/12/48; 3/18/47; Janet Waldo)
40. Tom Sawyer (6/19/48; 3/25/47; Skip Homeier and Jimmy Lydon)
41. Peter Ibbetson (6/26/48; 4/1/47)
42. The Necklace (7/3/48; 4/8/47)
43. Jamie Freel (7/10/48; 4/15/47)
44. The Strange Mr. Bartlesby (7/17/48; 4/22/47)
45. Lost Horizon (7/24/48; 4/29/47)
46. Lady of the Lamp (7/31/48; 5/6/47)
47. The Moonstone (8/7/48; 5/13/47)
48. Pride and the Prejudice (8/14/48; 5/20/47)
49. The Bottle Imp (8/21/48; 5/27/47; Jeff Corey and Mary Jane Croft)
50. Cashel Byron's Profession (8/28/48; 9/23/47; Dan O'Herlihy)
51. Ben Hur (9/4/48; 9/30/47; John Beal and Marvin Miller)
52. Mutiny on the Bounty (9/11/48; 10/7/47)
53. The Man Who Made Gold (9/18/48; 10/14/47)
54. Washington Square (9/25/48; 10/21/47)
55. Mrs. Lecks and Mrs. Aleshine (10/2/48; 10/28/47)
56. Marco Polo (10/9/48; 11/4/47; Norman Field and Roland Morris)
57. The Man From Yesterday (10/16/48; 11/11/47)
58. A Tale of Two Cities (10/23/48; 11/18/47)
59. Aladdin's Lamp (10/30/48; 11/25/47)
60. The Suicide Club (11/6/48; 12/2/47)
61. Inside a Kid's Head (11/13/48; 12/9/47)
62. A Doll's House (11/20/48; 12/16/47)
63. Crime Silvestre Bonnard (11/27/48; 12/23/47)

64. Looking Backward (12/4/48; 12/30/47)
65. The Tell-Tale Heart (12/11/48; 1/6/48)
66. The Brownings (12/18/48; 1/13/48; William Conrad, Betty Lou Gerson, and Berry Kroeger)
67. The Window (12/25/48; 1/20/48)
68. The Glass Eye (1/1/49; 1/27/48; Byron Kane and Lurene Tuttle)
69. The Sunken City (1/8/49; 2/3/48)
70. The Aspern Papers (1/15/49; 2/10/48)
71. The Man Who Married a Dumb Wife (1/22/49; 2/17/48; Bea Benaderet and Peter Rankin)
72. The Young Years (1/29/49; 2/24/48; William Conrad and William Johnstone)
73. Green Mansions (2/5/49; 3/2/48)
74. The Vendetta (2/12/49; 3/9/48)
75. Son's Veto (2/19/49; 3/16/48)
76. Rhythm (2/26/49; 3/23/48)
77. The Bet (3/5/49; 3/30/48)
78. The Valiant (3/12/49; 4/6/48)
79. The Maniac (3/19/48; 4/13/48)
80. Youth (3/26/48; 4/20/48)
81. The Blue Danube (4/2/48; 4/27/48)
82. Jest of Hahalaba (4/9/48; 5/4/48)
83. A Piece of String (4/16/49; 5/11/48)
84. The Strange Valley [adaptation of H. G. Wells' "The Country of the Blind"] (4/23/49; 5/18/48)
85. A Work of Art (4/30/49; 5/25/48)
86. All My Children (5/7/49; 6/1/48)
87. The Assignation (5/14/49; 6/8/48)
88. Long Ago (5/21/49; 9/14/48)
89. The Time Machine (5/28/49; 9/21/48)
90. The Monkey's Paw (6/4/49; 9/28/48)
91. Copper Penny (6/11/49; 10/5/48)
92. Roll Call of the Reef (6/18/49; 10/12/48)
93. The Gambler (6/25/49; 10/19/48)
94. Francesca Da Rimini (7/2/49; 10/26/48)
95. Judgement of Paris (7/9/49; 11/2/48)
96. The Flying Dutchman (7/16/49; 11/9/48)
97. Around the World in Eighty Days (7/23/49; 11/16/48)
98. The Dynamiter (7/30/49; 11/23/48; Jeff Chandler, William Conrad, and Janet Waldo)
99. The Magic Shop (8/6/49; 11/30/48)
100. Enoch Soames (8/13/49; 12/7/48)
101. How Much Land Does a Man Need? (8/20/49; 12/14/48)
102. When the Door Opened (8/27/49; 12/21/48)
103. Change of Face (9/3/49; 12/28/48)
104. The Young Man That Stroked Cats (9/10/49; 1/4/49)
105. Turn of the Screw (9/17/49; 1/11/49)
106. The Man Who Corrupted Hadleyburg (9/24/49; 1/18/49)
107. Pacific Crossing (10/1/49; 1/25/49)
108. The Substitute (10/8/49; 2/1/49)
109. Billy the Kid (10/15/49; 2/8/49)
110. The Gift of Laughter (10/22/49; 2/15/49; Hans Conried)
111. The Passing of the Third Floor Back (10/29/49; 2/22/49)
112. Lifeline (11/5/49; 3/1/49)
113. The Magnificent Lie (11/12/49; 3/8/49; William Conrad)
114. Brushwood Bay (11/19/49; 3/15/49)
115. In the Time of the Terror (11/26/49; 3/22/49)
116. Doll in the Pink Silk Dress (12/3/49; 3/29/49)
117. Little Minister (12/10/49; 4/5/49)
118. Journey to Bethlehem (12/17/49; 4/12/49)
119. A Christmas Carol (12/24/49; 4/19/49)

The Fifth Horseman

Short-run series produced to convince the American public to accept a plan to put all nuclear weapons under U.N. control. Produced by the Public Service, this piece of early Cold War propaganda dramatized the argument that no one could win a nuclear conflict, portraying the horrors of life after a nuclear holocaust. The program was broadcast over NBC as a summer series, Thursday evenings from 10:30 to 11 pm, EST. Pat O'Brien was originally scheduled to star in episode four, but was replaced by Robert Young.

1. Rehearsal (7/4/46; Henry Fonda)
2. Dawn (7/11/46; William Bendix)
3. Promise (7/18/46; Glenn Ford)
4. Crisis (7/25/46; Howard McNear and Robert Young)
5. Zero Minus One (8/1/46; George Coulouris and William Johnstone)
6. Doomsday ("The Day of Doom" NY Times; [8/8/46] Dane Clark)
7. Aftermath (8/15/46; J. Carrol Naish)
8. Memo to Mankind (8/22/46; Charles Bickford)

Flashgun Casey

More popularly known as *Casey, Crime Photographer*, this series was based on the character created by George Harmon Coxe. Casey was a detective reporter who did his reporting with a camera. One week he caught a murderer in the making and found himself on the run. The week after Casey noticed something wrong in one of his pictures, and solved the crime of the week. Jackson Beck and Bernard Lenrow played the role of Police Inspector Logan. John Gibson was the bartender at the Blue Note. Leslie Woods, June Allyson, Alice Reinhart, Betty Furness and Jan Miner played Casey's girlfriend Annie Williams, who often got herself caught up in trouble. Albert Ward was the director. A. Renier and R. L. Landy were the producers. Alonzo Deen Cole wrote most of the scripts. Tony Marvin, Bob Hite and Bill Cullen were announcers. Matt Crowley, later replaced by Staats Cotsworth, was Casey.

First broadcast on Wednesday evenings from 11:30 pm to 12 am, EST. Beginning August 12, 1943, the series was heard on Thursdays from 11:30 pm to 12 am, EST. Beginning October 30, 1943, the series moved to Saturdays, same time slot.

The program started out as *Flashgun Casey* on 7/7/43 to 4/1/44. The title changed to *Casey, Press Photographer* from 4/8/44 to 6/26/45, *Crime Photographer* from 7/4/45 to 3/13/47, *Casey, Crime Photographer* from 3/20/47 to 11/16/50, and back to *Crime Photographer* from 1/13/54 to the end of the run. Premiered sustaining until American Hocking Glass took up sponsorship from 8/8/46 to 3/25/48. Originated from New York, CBS. The role of Casey was originally played by Matt Crowley and later, Staats Cotsworth.

Started out Wed 11:30–12 mid. 8/12/43–10/21/43 Thursdays 11:30–12 mid., 10/30/43–end of run on Sat 11:30–12 mid. John Dietz produced and directed. The music was supplied by Al Bleyer and his orchestra. The organ music was supplied by Lew White.

1. The Case of the Switched Plates (7/7/43)
2. Murder Off the Record (7/14/43)
3. The Lost Melody (7/21/43)
4. Love Is a Whisper (7/28/43)
5. The Case of the Painted Walls (8/4/43)
6. Murder Comes in Threes (8/12/43)
7. No Answer (8/19/43)
8. Hoodoo for Hire (8/26/43)
9. The Case of the Whispering Gun (9/2/43)
10. -----(9/9/43)
11. -----(9/16/43)
12. The Kidnapping of the Rare Book Dealer (9/23/43)
13. Murder For Breakfast (9/30/43)
14. The Case of the Indignant Lady (10/7/43)
15. Picture in the Park (10/14/43)
16. Five Thousand Dollar Reward (10/21/43)
17. A Butterfly Dies (10/30/43)
18. Death in the Dentist's Chair (11/6/43)
19. Ghosts Work for Money (11/13/43)
20. The Killer's Kid (11/20/43)
21. Man With the Crippled Arm (11/27/43)
22. The Last Will and Testament (12/4/43)
23. Mystery Girl (12/11/43)
24. Set to Kill (12/18/43)
25. Christmas Is a Family Day (12/25/43)
26. Casey Begins a New Year (1/1/44)
27. Casey Goes Into Society (1/8/44)
28. Casey Compounds a Felony (1/15/44)
29. Casey Remains to Dance (1/22/44)
30. Casey and the House with the Hedge (2/5/44)
31. Casey and the Man Called John Doe (2/12/44)
32. The Mystery of the Ten Dollar Bills (2/19/44)
33. The Clue in the Clouds (2/26/44)
34. Casey and the Strong Woman (3/4/44)
35. Man Overboard (3/11/44)
36. Casey and the Self-Made Hero (3/18/44)
37. Star Witness (3/25/44)
38. The Case of the Glowing Ghost (4/1/44)

For This We Fight

Panel discussions with small dramas, featuring senators and representatives as panel members. Senator Joseph H. Ball of Minnesota was on one broadcast, Senator Claude D. Pepper of Florida was on another. About three guests were featured in each broadcast, with an occasional guest of popular recognition. Broadcast over NBC Saturday evening from 7 to 7:30 pm, EST.

1. Underwriting Victory (6/5/43)
2. Science and the Future (6/12/43; David Sarnoff)
3. The United Nations (6/19/43)
4. Peace Through World Trade (6/26/43)
5. Making the World Secure (7/3/43)
6. Alternatives for War (7/10/43)
7. Marvin Jones, Food Administrator (7/17/43)
8. World Problems of Labor (7/24/43)
9. The World of Sight and Sound (7/31/43; Walt Disney)
10. Education for Freedom (8/7/43)
11. Justice and Human Rights (8/14/43)
12. The Role of the Americans (8/21/43; Archibald MacLeish)
13. The Role of the United States in the Post-War World (8/28/43)
14. The America We're Fighting For (9/4/43)
15. Post-War Jobs: Responsibility of Business (9/11/43)
16. Post-War Jobs: Responsibility of Labor (9/18/43)
17. What Future for Farmers? (9/25/43)
18. Tomorrow's Transportation (10/2/43)
19. New Plans for Education? (10/9/43)

20. Financing Post-War Prosperity
(10/16/43)
21. Better Houses and Cheaper
(10/23/43)
22. Public Works in Post-War America
(10/30/43)
23. Getting Goods to Consumers
(11/6/43)
24. Better Health Care (11/13/43)

25. Security for Everyone (11/20/43)
26. Congress Faces Post-War America
(11/27/43)
27. Bases of Permanent Peace (12/4/43)
28. The U. N.'s Plan for Tomorrow
(12/11/43)
29. Community Post-War Planning
(12/18/43)
30. Spiritual Issues of Peace (12/25/43)

The Ford Theater

This hour-long anthology series was sponsored by Ford Motors. Howard Lindsay was the host. Lyn Murray composed and conducted the music. George Zachary directed the first season, replaced by Fletcher Markle for the second season. Broadcast Friday evenings over NBC from 5 to 6 pm, EST. Beginning with episode forty, the series was heard from 9 to 10 pm, over CBS.

1. A Connecticut in King Arthur's Court [based on the story by Mark Twain] (10/5/47; Maude Adams) and Karl Swenson
2. The Great McGinty (10/12/47)
3. On Borrowed Time (10/19/47)
4. A Coffin for Dimitrious (10/26/47; Wendell Holmes)
5. Ah, Wilderness (11/2/47; Eric Dressler and Anne Seymour)
6. The Power and the Glory (11/9/47; Les Damon, Mitzi Gould, and Vicki Vola)
7. Carmen Jones (11/16/47; Irving Barnes, Valerie Black, Maurice Ellis, Juano Hernandez, Luther Saxon, Murial Smith, Earle Sitnore, and Alton Warren)
8. George Washington Slept Here (11/23/47; Claudia Morgan and Karl Swenson)
9. Dangerous Crossing (11/30/47; Staats Cotsworth, Anne Seymour, and Vicki Vola)
10. We Hold These Truths (12/7/47; Mason Adams, Wendell Holmes, and Linda Reid)
11. Cimarron (12/14/47; Gary Merrill and Barbara Weeks)
12. The Man Who Played God (12/21/47; Santos Ortega and Anne Seymour)
13. Father, Dear Father (12/28/47; Fran Carden, Elsie Hitz, Ed Jerome, and Bert Parks)
14. The Adventure of the Bad Boy (1/4/48; Ted de Corsia, Hugh Marlowe, and Santos Ortega)
15. Storm in a Teacup (1/11/48; Wendell Holmes, Amzie Strickland, and Les Tremayne)
16. Girl Crazy (1/18/48; Ted de Corsia, Larry Douglas, and Monica Lewis)
17. Arsenic and Old Lace (1/25/48; Jean Adair, John Alexander, Josephine Hull, and Edgar Stehli)
18. The Green Pastures (2/1/48; Maurice Evans, Juano Hernandez, Avon Long, and Earl Sydnor)
19. Abe Lincoln in Illinois (2/8/48; Muriel Kirkland and Karl Swenson)
20. Abe Lincoln in Washington (2/15/48; Muriel Kirkland and Karl Swenson)
21. The Bishop Misbehaves (2/22/48)
22. The Count of Monte Cristo (2/29/48; Lauren Gilbert)
23. Twentieth Century (3/7/48; Arnold Moss and Barbara Weeks)
24. Autumn Crocus (3/14/48)
25. It's a Gift (3/21/48)
26. The Informer (3/28/48; Paul Douglas, Bryan Herbert, and Una O'Connor)

27. The Goose Hangs High (4/4/48; Anne Seymour and Gladys Thornton)
28. The Murder of Roger Ackroyd [based on the novel by Agatha Christie] (4/11/48; Harold Huber)
29. The Silver Cord (4/18/48; John Sylvester, Les Tremayne, Evelyn Varden, and Barbara Weeks)
30. Personal Appearance (4/25/48; Arlene Francis, Gary Merrill, Virginia Payne, and Joan Tighe)
31. Alice Adams (5/2/48)
32. Front Page [based on the play by Ben Hecht and Charles McArthur] (5/9/48; Ed Begley and Everett Sloane)
33. Counselor at Law (5/16/48; Lauren Gilbert and Les Tremayne)
34. A Star Is Born (5/23/48)
35. Laura (5/30/48; Virginia Gilmore and John Larkin)
36. Michael and Mary (6/6/48; Luther Adler, Florida Friebus, and Alexander Kirkland)
37. My Sister Eileen (6/13/48; Shirley Booth and Virginia Gilmore)
38. The Late Christopher Bean (6/20/48)
39. Arrowsmith (6/27/48; Lauren Gilbert)
40. Madame Bovary (10/8/48; Marlene Dietrich, Van Heflin, and Claude Rains)
41. Double Indemnity (10/15/48; Joan Bennett and Burt Lancaster)
42. Tom, Dick, and Harry (10/22/48; Eddie Albert and Lucille Ball)
43. Of Human Bondage (10/29/48; Joan Lorring and Ray Milland)
44. The Damask Cheek (11/5/48; Dorothy McGuire)
45. Camille (11/12/48; Ingrid Bergman)
46. The Male Animal (11/19/48; Eddie Albert and Barbara Bel Geddes)
47. Secret Agent (11/26/48; Douglas Fairbanks, Jr.)
48. The Big Street (12/3/48; Lucille Ball and John Garfield)
49. Page Miss Glory (12/10/48; Joan Blondell and MacDonald Carey)
50. The Gentle People (12/17/48; Gene Kelly)
51. Pilgrim's Inn (12/24/48; Geraldine Fitzgerald)
52. Becky Sharp (12/31/48; Miriam Hopkins)
53. Talk of the Town (1/7/49; Jean Arthur and Ronald Colman)
54. Boomerang (1/14/49; Dana Andrews)
55. Anna Christie (1/21/49; Joan Lorring and Ray Milland)
56. The Woman in the Window (1/28/49; Linda Darnell, Stephen McNally, and E.G. Robinson)
57. No Time for Love (2/4/49; Claudette Colbert, Glenn Ford, and Vincent Price)
58. The Awful Truth (2/11/49; Bob Hope)
59. Shadow of a Doubt (2/18/49; Ann Blyth and Ray Milland)
60. The Palm Beach Story (2/25/49; Anne Baxter and MacDonald Carey)
61. The Horn Blows at Midnight (3/4/49; Jack Benny, Hans Conried, Joseph Kearns, Shirley Mitchell, Jane Morgan, Jeanette Nolan, Claude Rains, and Miriam Wolfe)
62. Welcome, Stranger (3/11/49; Ann Blyth, Bing Crosby, and Barry Fitzgerald)
63. Holy Matrimony (3/18/49; Charles Laughton)
64. The Show-Off (3/25/49; Dan Dailey)
65. Wuthering Heights (4/1/49; Montgomery Clift)
66. Lightnin' (4/8/49; Walter Huston)
67. Elmer, the Great (4/15/49; Paul Douglas)
68. Skylark (4/22/49; Bette Davis)
69. Intermezzo (4/29/49; Fredric March)
70. Ladies in Retirement (5/6/49; Ida Lupino)
71. Alice Adams (5/13/49; Dorothy McGuire)
72. Crime Without Passion (5/20/49; Margo and Claude Rains)
73. To Mary, with Love (5/27/49; Burgess Meredith)
74. Haunted Honeymoon (6/3/49; Douglas Fairbanks, Jr.)
75. Craig's Wife (6/10/49; Ruth Hussey)
76. Peg o' My Heart (6/17/49; Ann Blyth)
77. A Farewell to Arms (6/24/49; Helen Hayes)
78. Cluny Brown (7/1/49; Leveen MacGrath and Walter Pidgeon)

Forecast

In order for the Columbia Broadcasting System to know what radio listeners had an interest in, a pilot program entitled *Forecast* premiered in the summer of 1940. This series presented two half-hour presentations — occasionally an hour-long presentation — which were broadcast over the airwaves, with the announcer making mention that if anyone who tuned in to the program liked what they heard, write to CBS. This way, CBS would know exactly what programs the listening audience wanted to hear. And the result was illuminating. The "Suspense" drama of July 22, 1940, later became a prime-time anthology series that would broadcast over twenty years! "Duffy's Tavern" of the week after, returned in the fall as a prime-time comedy that became a milestone in radio comedy. "Hopalong Cassidy" was presented on August 11, 1941, but it was not until nine years later that it became a regular series.

As a summer replacement for the *Lux Radio Theater*, *Forecast* returned the summer after for a second series. Both series were heard over CBS on Monday evenings at 9 p.m. The listings below are the presentations of the dates supplied, the top drama listed being the first of the two. If only one drama is listed, then the program was presented for a full hour. Trivia and tidbits: Booth Tarkington was the author of "The American Theater." Film director Alfred Hitchcock directed the "Suspense" broadcast. Raymond Massey narrated the drama of August 18, 1941. "Bethel Merriday" was an adaptation of Sinclair Lewis' story. Dickie Jones, the star of Walt Disney's animated film *Pinocchio*, which was released in the theaters in February, guested in "Of Stars and States." Paramount Studios had just released a Hopalong Cassidy picture in the theaters and as a publicity stunt, and an attempt to create a regular series on the radio, the August 11, 1941, broadcast featured a very corny and juvenile Hopalong, with music and songs!

1. Battle of Music (7/15/40; Arlene Francis, Freda Gibson, Frankie Hyers, and Raymond Paige) "The American Theater: The Gentleman from Indiana" Fredric March
2. When You Were Twenty-One (7/22/40; Joan Edwards, Rush Hughes, and Danny Kaye) "Suspense: The Lodger" Noreen Gammill, Edmund Gwenn, Herbert Marshall, and Lurene Tuttle
3. Angel (7/29/40; Elliott Lewis and Loretta Young) "Duffy's Tavern" Larry Adler, Mel Allen, Ed Gardner, Gertrude Niesen, and F. Chase Taylor
4. Of Stars and States (8/5/40; Nan Grey, Hedda Hopper, Mary Martin, Ann Miller, and Red Ryder)
5. The Life of the Party (8/12/40; Fred Hall, Hildegarde, Cortez Peters, David Ross, and Shirley Wayne) "Leave It to Jeeves" Edward Everett Horton, Donald Morrison, Alan Mowbray, and Helen Wood
6. Back Where I Came From (8/19/40; Len Doyle, Clifton Fadiman, Burl Ives, and Alan Lomax) "Ever After / To Tim, at Twenty [the latter is written by Norman Corwin] Roy Atwell, Edna Best, Elsa Lanchester, Charles Laughton, Mark Smith, and Richard Whorf
7. Jubilee (8/26/40; Duke Ellington,

Wonderful Smith, and Ethel Waters) "Bethel Merriday" Norman Corwin, Howard Da Silva, Byron Kane, Lurene Tuttle, and Paula Winslowe
8. One Thousand and One Nights (7/14/41; Marlene Dietrich)
9. Memories of Mischa, the Magnificent (7/21/41; Mischa Auer and Arthur Q. Bryan) "51 East 51" Erik Rhodes, Lionel Stander, and Kay Thompson
10. Pibby and the Houlihans (7/28/41; Dudley Digges) "Deductions Deluxe: The Mystery of the Painted Poodle" Verna Felton, Adolphe Menjou, Vera Teasdale, and Arthur Q. Bryan
11. Song Without End (8/4/41; Burgess Meredith and Margo)

12. Class of '41 (8/11/41; Jim Backus, Abe Burrows, Gwen Davies, and Arnold Stang) "Hopalong Cassidy [William Boyd did not star in this broadcast.] Lou Merrill and Gerald Mohr
13. The Country Lawyer (8/18/41; Edgar Barrier, Bea Benaderet, Arthur Q. Bryan, Berry Kroeger, Grace Leonard, Knox Manning, and Ed Max)
14. Three Wishes (8/25/41; Lynn Fontaine, Alfred Lunt, and Paul Robeson) "Search for a Sponsor: A Tour of Hollywood" Bert Lahr, Tony Martin, and Linda Ware
15. Jubilee (9/1/41; Duke Ellington and Ethel Waters)

Fort Laramie

About a hundred miles from the city of Laramie on the Wyoming prairie stands the historical Fort Laramie, a United States Army military post. The fort, once a supply depot for lengthy military campaigns against the Sioux and the Cheyenne, remains a tourist site. In 1956, Norman MacDonnell (of *Gunsmoke* fame), brought to CBS radio a series of dramas based on the fort. Its stories were hard and cruel. Men on the program died by freezing, drowning, typhoid and smallpox, but only four died of gunshot wounds. Captain Lee Quince (played by Raymond Burr) was in charge of the fort, with such personnel as Sergeant Goerss (Vic Perrin, later the control voice of *The Outer Limits*), Lt. Seiberts (Harry Bartell, Doc on radio's *Gunsmoke*), and Major Daggett (played by Jack Moyles). Amerigo Moreno performed the music. The sound effects men were Bill James, Ray Kemper, and Tom Hanley.

Dan Cubberly was the announcer. Writers included John Meston, John Dunkel, Gil Doud, Les Crutchfield, E. Jack Neuman, William N. Robson, and Kathleen Hite.

Audition: For Creed (7/25/55; with John Dehner)
1. Playing Indian (1/22/56; Lawrence Dobkin, Paul DuBov, Joyce McCluskey, James Nusser, Clayton Post, and Dan Riss)
2. The Boatwright's Story (1/29/56; Jan Arvan, Joseph Cranston, Sam Edwards, Lou Krugman, and Bob Sweeney)
3. Squaw Man (2/5/56; Edgar Barrier,

Frank Moody, and Eleanor Tanin)
4. The Woman at Horse Creek (2/12/56; Virginia Christine, John Dehner, and Barney Phillips)
5. Boredom (2/19/56; Howard Culver, Sam Edwards, Jack Kruschen, and Vivi Janniss)
6. Captain's Widow (2/26/56; Joe Cranston, Virginia Gregg, Helen Kleeb, Jack Kruschen, Jim Nusser)

7. Shavetail (3/4/56; Joseph Cranston and John Dehner)
8. Hattie Pelfrey (3/11/56; Sam Edwards and Virginia Gregg)
9. The Beasley Girls (3/18/56)
10. The Coward (3/25/56; Lynn Allen, John Dehner, Paul DuBov, and Clayton Post)
11. Lost Child (4/1/56; Dick Beals, Lawrence Dobkin, Ralph Moody, and Clayton Post)
12. Stagecoach Stop (4/15/56; Frank Cady, Sam Edwards, Jack Kruschen, Howard McNear, Shirley Mitchell, Jeanette Nolan, and Eleanore Tanin)
13. The New Recruit (4/22/56; John Dehner, Lawrence Dobkin, Paul DuBov, Sam Edwards, Lou Krugman, and James Nusser)
14. Capture (4/29/56; Frank Cady, Lou Krugman, Lee Millar, Ralph Moody, Jack Moyles, and Jeff Silver)
15. Never the Twain (5/6/56; Lillian Buyeff, John Dehner, Don Diamond, Ralph Moody, and John Stephenson)
16. War Correspondents (5/13/56; Parley Baer, Lawrence Dobkin, Sam Edwards, and Lou Krugman)
17. Gold (5/20/56; Frank Gerstle, Virginia Gregg, Howard McNear, Ralph Moody, and Clayton Post)
18. Sergeant's Baby (5/27/56; Dick Crenna, Virginia Gregg, Howard McNear, and Ralph Moody)
19. Don't Kick My Horse (6/3/56; Lawrence Dobkin, Tim Graham, Jack Kruschen, and James Nusser)
20. Young Trooper (6/10/56; Frank Cady, Eve McVey, and Jeff Silver)
21. Winter Soldier (6/17/56; Joseph Cranston, Howard Culver, Paul DuBov, and James Nusser)
22. The Loving Cup (6/24/56; Helen Kleeb)
23. Trooper's Widow (7/1/56; Lynn Allen, Jeanne Bates, Lawrence Dobkin, and Jack Moyles)
24. Talented Recruits (7/8/56; Parley

Baer and John Dehner)
25. Old Enemy (7/15/56; Paul DuBov, Sam Edwards, James Nusser, and Herb Vigran)
26. Spotted Tail's Return (7/22/56; John Dehner, Tim Graham, Lou Krugman, and Ralph Moody)
27. Nature Boy (7/29/56; Parley Baer, John Dehner, Virginia Gregg, Howard McNear, and Shirley Mitchell)
28. The Massacre (8/5/56; John Dehner, Lawrence Dobkin, Sam Edwards, Tim Graham, and Lou Krugman)
29. The Assembly Line (8/12/56; John Dehner, Vivi Janiss, and Joseph Kearns)
30. Goodbye Willa (8/19/56; Parley Baer, John Dehner, Paul DuBov, and Virginia Gregg)
31. The Chaplain (8/26/56; Dolores Brown, John Dehner, and Virginia Gregg)
32. The Return of Hattie Pelfrey (9/2/56; Paul DuBov, Sam Edwards, and Virginia Gregg)
33. The Buffalo Hunters (9/9/56; James Nusser and Barney Phillips)
34. The Payroll (9/16/56; Sam Edwards, Howard McNear, Jack Moyles, and Clayton Post)
35. The Woman at Horse Creek (9/23/56; Virginia Christine, John Dehner, and Barney Phillips)
36. A Small Beginning (9/30/56; Howard Culver, Jess Curt Patrick, John Dehner, Sam Edwards, Lawrence Dobkin, and Lou Kruschen)
37. Galvanized Yankee (10/7/56; Parley Baer, Frank Cady, Paul DuBov, and Sam Edwards)
38. Still Waters (10/14/56; Sam Edwards, Howard McNear, and Jeanette Nolan)
39. Indian Scout (10/21/56; Lawrence Dobkin)
40. Army Wife (10/28/56; Parley Baer, Sam Hill, and Helen Kleeb)

The Forty Million

A syndicated series of six broadcasts, intended for child health awareness. First broadcast over NBC beginning November 8, 1952, from 7:30 to 8 pm, EST. The series was first heard over NBC. WNYC in New York had also broadcast the syndicated series, 8:30 to 9 pm, EST. First date is the NBC run, the second, the WNYC run.

1. Death Was Catching (11/8/53; 7/18/53; Josephine Hull)
2. Friend of the Bride (11/15/53; 7/25/53; Gene, Kathleen, and June Lockhart)
3. Villain in Hiding: Malnutrition (11/22/53; 8/1/53; Ben Grauer)
4. Accidentally Speaking (11/29/53; 8/8/53; Gene Lockhart)
5. Davey Kills a Giant (12/6/53; 8/15/53; June Lockhart)
6. Sound Bodies for Sound Minds (12/13/53; 8/22/53; Peter Roberts)

Four Great Makers

This series, more documentation than drama, dealing with contemporary architecture, was broadcast over station WNYC in New York Sunday afternoons from 3:00 to 4 pm, EST, except for episode five, which was broadcast from 3 to 4:30 pm.

1. The Four Great Makers of Contemporary Architecture (5/21/61)
2. Dr. Ludwig Mies Van Der Rohe (5/28/61)
3. The Future of the Skyscraper (6/4/61)
4. The City: Doomed or Dominant Factor in Our Future? (6/11/61)
5. The House for the Modern Family: Urban Towers or Suburban Idyllis? (6/18/61)
6. A House for the Modern Family (6/25/61)

The Frances Langford Show

As a summer replacement for the Burns and Allen show, Frances Langford starred in her own musical/dramatic series, which ran for thirteen broadcasts. Each program featured songs by Langford, aided by "Eloise and the Maxwell House Coffee Chorus"—which was really the Dick Davis Chorus. A skit representing a glimpse of "the American scene," was featured as well. The music was supplied by Carmen Dragon. Toby Reed, the announcer, appeared in the skits, and Carmen Dragon also had a speaking part on several shows. Under the sponsorship of Maxwell House Coffee, the same sponsor of Burns and Allen, the program was broadcast Thursday evenings at 8:30–9 pm on NBC. Langford sang songs of George

Gershwin in the second broadcast, and a melody of songs by George M. Cohen for episode five. Songs written especially for Hollywood pictures were featured in episode ten. Supporting cast included Barbara Fuller, Earle Ross, and Sam Edwards.

1. Going to a Baseball Game (6/5/47)
2. Holly's Graduation (6/12/47)
3. Family Picnic (6/19/47)
4. Father Gives Away the Bride (6/26/47)
5. Taking Holly to her First Country Club Dance (7/3/47)
6. Summer Barbecue (7/10/47)
7. Sunday Evening Concert in the Park (7/17/47)
8. Performing Macbeth for the Women's Club (7/24/47)
9. The Founder's Day Parade (7/31/47)
10. The Surprise Birthday Party for Frances (8/7/47)
11. Church Social (8/14/47)
12. Cleaning the House and Going on a Hayride (8/21/47)
13. College Days (8/28/47)

The Free Company

This series, featuring stories of the Bill of Rights, enjoyed a variety of talented writers, directors, and actors. Broadcast on CBS, sustaining, on Sunday afternoons from 2–2:30 pm. Burgess Meredith was the host. Writers varied from episode to episode and included Maxwell Anderson, Stephen Vincent Benét, Robert Sherwood, Marc Connelly, William Saroyan, Walter Van Tilburg Clark, and Archibald MacLeish. Orson Welles supposedly wrote the April 6 broadcast. Norman Corwin directed "A Start in Life." James Boyd, chairman of the Free Company, made an appearance in episode five.

1. The People with Light Coming Out of Them (2/23/41; Henry Fonda, John Garfield, Edmund Gwenn, and Nancy Kelly)
2. The Mole on Lincoln's Cheek (3/2/41; Charles Bickford and Robert Young)
3. An American Crusader (3/9/41; Gail Patrick and Franchot Tone)
4. One More Free Man (3/16/41; Betty Field, Elia Kazan, Margo, Myron McCormick, and Dorothy McGuire)
5. Freedom's a Hard Bought Thing (3/23/41; Eric Burroughs, Georgette Harvey, The Juanita Hall Singers, and Harrington Lewis)
6. The Ox-Bow Incident (3/30/41)
7. His Honor, the Mayor (4/6/41; Ray Collins, Agnes Moorehead, Erskine Sanford, Everett Sloane, Paul Stewart, and Orson Welles)
8. A Start in Life (4/13/41; Canada Lee and Luis Van Rooten)
9. The States Talking (4/20/41)
10. The Miracle of the Danube (4/27/41; Paul Muni)
11. Above Suspicion (5/4/41; Paul Lukas)
12. American Pilgrimage: Benjamin Franklin, Philadelphia, PA (5/11/41)

The Free World Theater

NBC Blue, sustaining, Sundays 6:05 pm–6:30 pm. From April 18 to the end of the run the show began at 6:30–7 p.m. Produced, directed, and written by Arch Oboler. Episode two was based on the statement by Thomas Mann. Musical variety; dramatic portion regarding The World of Tomorrow.

1. The People March (2/21/43; Alla Nazimova and Conrad Veidt)
2. Tomorrow (2/28/43; Mona Freeman, Marshall Thompson, and Orson Welles)
3. Your Day Is Coming (3/7/43; Dinah Shore)
4. Rip Van Dinkle of Nuremberg (3/14/43)
5. White House Kitchen (3/21/43; Harry Carey and Jane Darwell)
6. Music for Freedom (3/28/43)
7. The Siege of Stalingrad (4/4/43; Claudette Colbert)
8. Night Flight (4/11/43; Paul Henried)
9. Fiesta (4/18/43; Paul Henried)
10. S.S. Middleton (4/25/43)
11. China to America (5/2/43; Lee J. Cobb, Joseph Cotten, and Chester Morris)
12. The Last Will and Testament of John Smith (5/9/43; James Cagney)
13. Mother's Day in Modern Berlin (5/16/43)
14. Something About Joe (5/23/43; Lena Horne, Rex Ingram, and Hazel Scott)
15. The Man with a Beard (5/30/43; Jackie Cooper)
16. General Armchair (6/6/43; Edward Arnold)
17. The Second Battle of Warsaw (6/13/43)
18. In Memory of a Hero (6/20/43; Charles Colburn)
19. V-Day (6/27/43)

Frontier Fighters

Broadcast during the 1930s, this syndicated series ran for a total of thirty-nine broadcasts, each fifteen minutes long. Dramatizing historical events from American history, it told of explorers and settlers who risked their lives for the land we carelessly disregard as "dirt" and "soil." One episode chronicled the life of John A. Sutter, the man who dreamed of "Sutterville," and whose dreams were smashed by the start of what became known as "The Gold Rush." Wild Bill Hickcock, General Custer and his losing battle against what he thought was a small group of Indians, and Black Bart, the Wells Fargo stagecoach robber, were documented.

1. Robert LaSalle
2. The Lewis and Clark Expedition
3. Zebulon Mt. Pike
4. John C. Freemont
5. Kit Carson
6. Jebediah S. Smith
7. Marcus Whitman
8. John McLaughlin
9. The Donner Party
10. The Fall of the Alamo
11. Stephen W. Kearney
12. Brigham Young
13. Joseph L. Meek
14. Lyman A. Cutler and George C. Pickett

Frontier Gentleman

Produced and directed by Antony Ellis, this western was one of many broadcast over CBS following the success of *Gunsmoke*. John Dehner starred as Jeremy Bryant Kendall, reporter for *The London Times*, who wrote colorful accounts of his travels throughout the Western United States. As entertaining as it was, this series only lasted forty-one broadcasts (one was a repeat) sustaining, Sunday evenings, before leaving the air. The supporting cast included Harry Bartell, Lawrence Dobkin, Stacy Harris, Joseph Kearns, Jack Kruschen, Jack Moyles, and husband and wife team John McIntire and Jeanette Nolan.

Frontier Town

Western with Jeff Chandler as lawyer Chad Remington. Syndicated from 1952 to 1953 for a total of forty-seven broadcasts. Beginning with episode twenty-four, Reed Hadley played the role of Chad until the end of the series.

1. The Return to Dos Rios
2. His Name Is John Smith
3. Tod Ford
4. Marie
5. The Poisoned Waterhole
6. Emily Bracket
7. The Seminole Strip
8. The Chavez Family
9. The Opening of Tioga Reserve
10. Death and Texas
11. Six-Gun Justice
12. The Return of the Badmen
13. The Valley of Lawless Men
14. The Guns of Wrath
15. Her Name Is Bourbon Kate
16. The Railroad, Dam, and the Water Works
17. Land Grab
18. The Jailbird Rangers
19. Five Gun Final
20. Valley of the Varmints
21. All Trails Lead to Trouble
22. Forest Fire
23. Thunder Over Texas
24. Gun Trouble Valley
25. Branding the Badlands
26. South of Santa Fe
27. Maverick Town
28. The Coach Arrived Missing
29. Western Empire
30. The Six-Gun Lawyer
31. Sundown Valley
32. The Glory Trail
33. Trouble Rides the Rails
34. Open Range
35. The Chase
36. Bullets for Boothill
37. On the Prod
38. The Trail Drive
39. Fort Disaster
40. End of the Trail
41. Canyon of Wanted Men
42. Days of the Road Agent
43. Stampede
44. The Badlands
45. Boom Town
46. Where Men Are Men
47. Lady Luck

French Twentieth Century Writers

Six talks, the first dealing with Romain's "Men of Good Will." Dr. Francis Carmody of the University of California leads the discussions. Broadcast from 1 to 2 pm, EST. Syndicated.

1. Men of Good Will (7/17/60)
2. A Discussion on André Gide (7/24/60)
3. The Stories of Marcel Proust (7/31/60)
4. A Study of Paul Valery (8/7/60)
5. A Discussion on André Malraux (8/14/60)
6. Revisiting Jean Giradoux (8/21/60)

General Electric Theater

Sponsored by the General Electric Company and originating from Hollywood, this drama series presented guest stars in various dramas. Produced and directed by Jaime del Valle. Ken Carpenter was host. Music by Wilbur Hatch. Broadcast over CBS, Thursday evenings, 8:30 to 9 pm, EST.

1. Random Harvest (7/9/53; Ronald Colman and Benita Hume)
2. Bachelor (7/16/53; Cary Grant)
3. Penny Serenade (7/23/53; Irene Dunne)
4. The Old Man's Bride (7/30/53; Van Johnson)
5. Bachelor Girl (8/6/53; Jane Wyman)
6. The Virginian (8/13/53; William Holden)
7. Spring Over Brooklyn (8/20/53; Alan Young)
8. Sometime Every Summertime (8/27/53; Dorothy McGuire)
9. A Bell for Adano (9/3/53; John Hodiak)
10. State Fair (9/10/53; Ann Blyth)
11. Cyrano de Bergerac (9/17/53; James and Pamela Mason)
12. The Enchanted Cottage (9/24/53; Joan Fontaine)
13. The Old Man's Bride (10/1/53; Van Johnson)

Great Moments from Great Plays

Sponsored by Philip Morris, this anthology series presented adaptations of popular stage plays. Elmer Rice's "Street Scene" featured Edmund O'Brien in the lead role, while John Steinbeck's "Of Mice and Men" featured Frank Readick and Alan Reed. Broadcast over CBS, Friday evenings beginning at 9:00 pm, EST. Ray Bloch supplied the music. Carroll O'Connor was the announcer except for the final two broadcasts, which featured Nelson Case as the announcer.

1. Outward Bound (3/21/41)
2. You Can't Take It With You (3/28/41)
3. Street Scene (4/4/41; Edmund O'Brien)
4. Three Men on a Horse (4/11/41; Sam Levene)
5. On Borrowed Time (4/18/41; Henry Hull)
6. Dead End (4/25/41; Elia Kazan, Arnold Stang, and Arthur Vinton)
7. Burlesque (5/2/41)
8. Ceiling Zero (5/9/41; Ray Collins, William Johnstone, and Agnes Moorehead)
9. Of Mice and Men (5/16/41; Frank Readick and Alan Reed)
10. Accent on Youth (5/23/41; Alice Frost, William Johnstone, and Alan Reed)
11. Butter and Egg Man (5/30/41; Alan Reed, Paul Stewart, and Kennan Wynn)
12. Whistling in the Dark (6/6/41; Milton Berle)
13. Private Lives (6/13/41; Alan Reed)
14. The Milky Way (6/20/41)
15. Counselor at Law (6/27/41)
16. One Sunday Afternoon (7/4/41)
17. Room Service (7/11/41)
18. The Amazing Dr. Clitterhouse (7/18/41)
19. Death Takes a Holiday (7/25/41)

20. Blind Alley (8/1/41; Claude Rains and
    Everett Sloane)

21. Ladies of the Jury (8/8/41; Alice Frost,
    Alan Reed, and Everett Sloane)

Great Plays

Originally broadcast from New York on Sunday afternoons, *Great Plays* was an attempt to capture the *Radio Guild* listening audience. *Radio Guild* was known for its Monday afternoon time-slot and presented adaptations of famous novels and stage plays from the literary works of William Shakespeare, Leo Tolstoy, J. M. Barrie, and Lennox Robinson. This program had numerous directors who took turns producing and directing the broadcasts on what seemed to be an almost-regular rotation: Harry MacFayden, James Church, Albert N. Williams, Edmund Wolf, and Charles Warburton who not only directed, but also wrote many of the scripts. Other script writers were George Maynard, Lester O'Keefe, Joseph Bell, Charles Newton, Welborn Kelly, Helen Jerome, Ernest Boyd, Arthur Goodrich, and Edith Hamilton. The first eleven broadcasts were produced by Blevins Davis.

The music was first performed by Joseph Honty, and by October of 1939, Allan Sly and Frank Black started working beside Honty in the musical department. Later, Tom Bennett, Harold Sanford, Gayle Kubik, and Ernie Watson invaded the musical performances. Burns Mantle was drama commentator from October of 1938 to May of 1939, except for episodes 32 and 33, in which Brooks Atkinson subbed. Barrett H. Clark was commentator by November of 1941.

The performances originated from New York. The first eleven episodes were broadcast over NBC Blue 5–6 pm, EST, except for episode ten from 5:15 to 6 pm due to racing. Episodes 12–40, Sunday 1–2 pm. Episodes 41–69, Sunday 2–3 pm. Episodes 70–99, Sunday 3–4 pm (this run might have gone under the title of *Great Plays Cavalcade*). Episodes 100 and 101, Sunday 3–4 pm. Episode 102, Sunday 3–4 pm (two thirty-minute dramas, *second drama may not be a broadcast of Great Plays, in which case the show was broadcast 3–3:30 pm*). Episodes 103–119, Sunday 2–3 pm. Episode 120–end of series, Sunday 2–2:30 pm. The entire series was broadcast over the Blue Network.

Episode thirty-two was originally titled "Camille," but the title was changed in full during the actual broadcast. Episode thirty-seven, written by George Bernard Shaw, was broadcast at a special time, 12:45 to 2 pm. Pert Kelton, comedian, starred in episode seventy-one. Episode seventy-seven featured excerpts from "The Spanish Tragedy," "Antonio's Revenge," "The Revenger's Tragedy," "The White Devil" and "The Duchess of Malfi." Episode eighty featured two Nativity plays. Episode eighty-two featured excerpts from "The Country Wife,"

"The Conquest of Grenada," "Oranxib," "The Man of Mode," "The Way of the World" and "Venice Preserved."

1. The Birds [based on the play by Aristophanes] (2/26/38)
2. Everyman (3/5/38; Boys Choir from the Cathedral of St. John the Divine)
3. The Great Magician (3/12/38)
4. Tamburlaine (3/19/38)
5. A Midsummer Night's Dream (3/26/38)
6. The School for Husbands (4/2/38)
7. Love for Love (4/9/38)
8. The School for Scandal (4/16/38)
9. The Silver King (4/23/38)
10. The Playboy of the Western World (4/30/38)
11. Valley Forge [based on Maxwell Anderson's play] (5/7/38)
12. The Trojan Woman (10/16/38; Jerome Lester, Harry Mostair, and Blanche Yurka)
13. Everyman (10/23/38; Ian MacAllaster and Alfred Shirley)
14. The Great Magician (10/30/38)
15. The Tragical History of Dr. Faustus (11/6/38; Carl Benton Reid and Charles Webster)
16. A Midsummer Night's Dream (11/13/38)
17. Julius Caesar (11/20/38; John Anthony, Floyd Buckley, and Ken Daniel)
18. Othello (11/27/38; Walter Hampden and Selena Royle)
19. Le Cid [based on the Pierre Corneille play] (12/4/38; Richard Kollmar)
20. Life Is a Dream (12/11/38; Winifred Holm and Carl Benton Reid)
21. Le Bourgeois Gentilhomme (12/18/38; Richard Gordon and Junius Matthews)
22. The Nervous Wreck [comedy] (1/1/39)
23. She Stoops to Conquer (1/8/39; [based on the play by Goldsmith] Margalo Gilmore)
24. The School for Scandal (1/15/39)
25. Mary Stuart (1/22/39; Jane Cowl and Dennis Hoey)
26. Hernani [based on the Victor Hugo play] (1/19/39; Neil O'Malley and

Luis Van Rooten)
27. Richelieu (2/5/39; Phillip Clark, Walter Hampden, Dennis Hoey, and Carlton Young)
28. The Octaroon (2/12/39; Roger De Koven, Parker Fennelly, and Jane Wyatt)
29. Redemption [based on the Leo Tolstoy play] (2/19/39)
30. The Doll House [based on the play by Henrik Ibsen] (2/26/39; Ruth Gordon)
31. Patience [an adaptation of the Gilbert and Sullivan Operetta] (3/5/39)
32. The Lady of Camelias (3/12/39; Staats Cotsworth, Jane Cowl, Dennis Hoey, and Edmund O'Brien)
33. Cyrano de Bergerac (3/19/39; Wesley Addy, Staats Cotsworth, and Martha Scott)
34. Peter Pan (3/26/39; Eva Le Gallienne)
35. The Blue Bird [based on the Maurice Maeterlinck play] (4/2/39)
36. Justice [based on the Galsworthy play] (4/9/39)
37. Back to Methuselah (4/16/39)
38. Oliver Cromwell (4/23/39; William Podmore and Alfred Shirley)
39. The White-Headed Boy (4/30/39; Liam Redmond)
40. Elizabeth the Queen [based on Maxwell Anderson's play] (5/7/39; Wesley Addy and Mady Christians)
41. Antigone [based on the play by Sophocles] (10/15/39)
42. Alcestis (10/22/39; Helen Claire)
43. Everyman (10/29/39; Alexander Kirkland)
44. Edward II (11/5/39; Raymond Edward Johnson, Edmund O'Brien, and Alfred Shirley)
45. Romeo and Juliet (11/12/39; Wesley Addy, Horace Braham, and John McGovern)
46. Much Ado About Nothing (11/19/39; Raymond Edward Johnson and Ireene Wicker)
47. Macbeth (11/26/39; Florence Malone and Alfred Shirley)
48. Volpone [based on the Ben Johnson

play] (12/3/39; Ralph Locke and Selena Royle)
49. Tartuffe (12/10/39; Chester Stratton)
50. The Beggar's Opera (12/17/39; Eric Dressler, Betty Garde, Karl Swenson, and Ireene Wicker)
51. The Man Named Christmas (12/24/39)
52. The Rivals (1/7/40; Eric Dressler, Ian Martin, Alfred Shirley, and Charles Webster)
53. William Tell (1/14/40; Wesley Addy, Richard Gordon, and William Redfield)
54. Ruy Blas [based on the Victor Hugo play] (1/21/40; Arnold Moss and Edmund O'Brien)
55. Rip Van Winkle (1/28/40)
56. Arrah-na-Pogue (2/4/40; Richard Gordon, Thelma Ritter, Ireene Wicker, and Eustace Wyatt)
57. Peer Gynt (2/11/40; Richard Gordon, Junius Matthews, and Ireene Wicker)
58. The Playboy of the Western World (2/18/40; Walter Kinsella)
59. The Pirates of Penzance [based on the Gilbert and Sullivan Operetta] (2/25/40; Walter Preston)
60. The Second Mrs. Tanqueray (3/3/40; Florence Malone)
61. Secret Service (3/10/40; Helen Claire, Bob Dryden, Alice Frost, Ruth Gilbert, Onslow Stevens, Harold Vermilyea, and Robert Walker)
62. L'Aiglon (3/17/40; Thomas Gomez, Ian Martin, and Harold Vermilyea)
63. Captain Jinks of the Horse Marines (3/24/40)
64. The Three Sisters [based on the Chekov play] (3/31/40; Morris Carnovsky, Olive Dearing, and Walter Slezak)
65. Pelleas and Melisande (4/7/40; Harold Vermilyea)
66. Strife (4/14/40; Dennis Hoey, Ireene Wicker, and Eustace Wyatt)
67. Liliom (4/21/40)
68. The Return of Peter Grimm (4/28/40; Richard Gordon)
69. Winterset [based on the play by Maxwell Anderson] (5/5/40;

Myron McCormick)
70. From Greece to Broadway (10/13/40)
71. The Birds [based on the play by Aristophanes] (10/20/40; Pert Kelton)
72. Everyman (10/27/40; Alexander Kirkland)
73. The Tragedy of Dr. Faustus (11/3/40)
74. Love's Labor Lost (11/10/40; Richard Gordon and Carlton Young)
75. The Merry Wives of Windsor (11/17/40; Ian Martin and Agnes Moorehead)
76. The Tempest (11/24/40; John Abbott, Sir Cedric Hardwicke, Jessica Tandy, and Ireene Wicker)
77. The Revenge Tragedies (12/1/40; Peter Capell, Olive Dearing, Ian Martin, and Stefan Schnable)
78. Le Cid (12/8/40; Richard Kollmar)
79. Imaginary Invalid [based on the play by Moliere] (12/15/40)
80. The Second Shepherd's Play (12/22/40)
81. The Pigeon (12/29/40; Eustace Wyatt)
82. The English Restoration Drama (1/5/41)
83. The Barber of Seville (1/12/41; George Coulouris, Sylvia Field, Jay Jostyn, and Santos Ortega)
84. The Rivals (1/19/41; Eric Dressler, Ralph Forbes, and Florence Reed)
85. A Summary of Early American Drama (1/26/41)
86. The Thunderbolt (2/2/41; Alfred Shirley and Eustace Wyatt)
87. Rosmersholm [based on the Henrik Ibsen play] (2/9/41)
88. Cyrano de Bergerac (2/16/41; Florence Eldridge and Fredric March)
89. A Summary of the Victorian Age (2/23/41)
90. The Climbers (3/2/41)
91. The Well of the Saints (3/9/41)
92. The Swan (3/16/41)
93. The American Theater, 1920-1940 (3/23/41)
94. Robert E. Lee (3/30/41)
95. The Beggar on Horseback (4/6/41)
96. The Servant in the House (4/13/41)
97. Trelawny of the Wells (4/20/41)

Great Scenes from Great Plays

Broadcast on Mutual, Friday evenings beginning 8:00 pm, EST. Walter Hampden was master of ceremonies and also the star of the first broadcast. Highlights of the series include Raymond Massey performing Stephen Vincent Benét's "The Devil and Daniel Webster"— the role Edward Arnold was originally scheduled to play. Henry Fonda reprised his film role of Abraham Lincoln in "Young Mr. Lincoln." A musical drama was presented on Christmas Eve, with Gladys Swarthout and Lawrence Tibbett in the lead. Eddie Albert and his real-life wife Margo starred in the classic, "The Farmer Takes a Wife." After twenty-two broadcasts without a sponsor, Mutual dropped the series.

1. Cyrano de Bergerac (10/1/48; Walter Hampden)
2. The Corn Is Green (10/8/48; Jane Cowl)
3. The Barretts of Wimpole Street (10/15/48; Basil Rathbone and Beatrice Straight)
4. Dark Victory (10/22/48; Walter Abel and Celeste Holm)
5. On Borrowed Time (10/29/48; Parker Fennelly and Boris Karloff)

6. Little Women (11/5/48; Betty Caulfield, Joan Caulfield, and Susan Douglas)
7. A Tale of Two Cities (11/12/48; Brian Aherne)
8. Enchanted Cottage (11/19/48; Gene Tierney)
9. What Every Woman Knows (11/26/48; Gertrude Lawrence)
10. The Devil and Daniel Webster (12/3/48; Raymond Massey)
11. The Old Lady Shows Her Medals (12/10/48; Fay Bainter)
12. Young Mr. Lincoln (12/17/48; Henry Fonda)
13. The Silent Stars (12/24/48; Gladys Swarthout and Lawrence Tibbett)
14. You and I (12/31/48; Otto Kruger and Peggy Wood)
15. The Citadel (1/7/49; Walter Pidgeon)
16. The Farmer Takes a Wife (1/14/49; Eddie Albert and Margo)
17. Icebound (1/21/49; Cornel Wilde)
18. The Goose Hangs High (1/28/49; Walter Abel)
19. The World We Made (2/4/49; Jessica Tandy)
20. Dead End (2/11/49; John Payne)
21. A Doll's House (2/18/49; Brian Aherne and Ingrid Bergman)
22. The Lady with a Lamp (2/25/49; Madeline Carroll)

The Greatest Story Ever Told (1938–39 Series)

Sponsored by Philip Morris, this series featured adaptations of short stories and novels. Also billed under the title *Johnny Presents*, "*Johnny*" presented musicals and drama, often in increments of a few months, and then changing to another format. From August to September of 1938, "*Johnny*" presented "Psychic Detective." From October to December of 1938, "*Johnny*" presented "Canadian Mounted Police Stories." From December of 1938 to June of 1939, "The Greatest Story Ever Told." In June of 1939, "The Perfect Crime." Below is a complete broadcast log of *The Greatest Story Ever Told*. Broadcast over CBS, Saturday evenings from 8 to 8:30 pm, EST. Max Marcin wrote the scripts.

1. Back Pay [based on the story by Hillary Blake] (12/10/38)
2. Markheim [based on the story by Robert Louis Stevenson] (12/17/38)
3. The Gift of the Magi [based on the short story by O. Henry] (12/24/38)
4. The Signal Tower [based on the story by W. Camp] (12/31/38)
5. The Monkey's Paw [based on the short story by W. W. Jacobs] (1/7/39)
6. The Valiant (1/14/39)
7. A Lick Penny Lover [based on the story by O. Henry] (1/21/39)
8. The Tell-Tale Heart [based on the short story by Edgar Allan Poe] (1/28/39; Luther Adler)
9. The Last of the Troubadours [based on the story by O. Henry] (2/4/39)
10. The Bishop's Candlesticks [from "Les Miserables"] (2/11/39)
11. The Hiding of Black Bill [based on the story by O. Henry] (2/18/39)
12. Cyrano de Bergerac (2/25/39; Donald Montgomery)
13. The Cop and the Anthem [based on the story by O. Henry] (3/4/39)
14. William Wilson [based on the short story by Edgar Allan Poe] (3/11/39)
15. Peer Gynt (3/18/39; D. Montgomery)
16. Vanity and Some Sables [based on the story by O. Henry] (3/25/39)
17. A Harlem Tragedy [based on the story by O. Henry] (4/1/39)

The Greatest Story Ever Told (1947–56 series)

Originally based on the book of the same name by Fulton Oursler — who was then the religious editor of *Reader's Digest* — this series dramatized events and stories told of and from Jesus Christ, "the greatest story ever lived." Goodyear Tires was the sponsor, and in an attempt to put quality productions ahead of their product, used no commercial advertisements, just a simple tagline reminding listeners of its sponsorship. Each Sunday afternoon, listeners tuned in to hear another dramatization of the life of Christ, or a tale told by Christ. This made the program the first radio series to simulate the voice of Christ as a continuous character, played by Warren Parker. Marx Loeb was the director, Leonard Blair was the assistant director. Wadill Catchings was producer. William Stoess composed the music, led by a full orchestra and a sixteen-voice chorus.

The series was broadcast on Sunday evenings on ABC, 6:30–7:00 pm, EST, and beginning 5:30 pm as of episode 116. Sponsored by Goodyear Tire and Rubber Company, the same company that invented an effective "static eliminator" for radios back in 1943.

The various scripts, written by Henry Denker, usually left the audience with a moral to live by for the rest of the week. "The Golden Rule" was one of the more popular laws revisited, while "The Prodigal Son" returned at least once every season. "Where Are the Nine?" concerned the story of the lepers and "John the Baptist" invited us along for his famed meeting with Jesus. Human interest morals were even integrated into the scripts. "He That Is Faithful" concerned man's integrity during tribulation. "The Second Mile" featured a youth's conquest of hatred. "If the House Be Worthy" expressed the conflict of love and power. "Blessed Are the Meek" allotted victory over despair, "The Widow's Mite" taught us a lesson in humility, and "The Fruitless Fig Tree" taught a lesson in forgiveness.

1. The Good Samaritan (1/26/47)
2. The Unmerciful Steward (2/2/47)
3. The Prodigal Son (2/9/47)
4. Turn the Other Cheek (2/16/47)
5. Ten Talents (2/23/47)
6. Faith Is as a Mustard Seed (3/2/47)
7. The Second Mile (3/9/47)
8. The Story of Lazarus (3/16/47)
9. The Betrayal (3/23/47)
10. The Crucifixion (3/30/47)
11. The Resurrection (4/6/47)
12. Nicodemus, The Man Who Came by Night (4/13/47)
13. John the Baptist (4/20/47)
14. The Golden Rule (4/27/47)
15. Cast the First Stone (5/4/47)
16. They Which See Not Shall See (5/11/47)
17. The Soldier's Servant (5/18/47)
18. Unto the Least of These (5/25/47)
19. The Fruitless Fig Tree (6/1/47)
20. The Chief Seat at the Wedding (6/8/47)
21. The Mote in Thy Brother's Eye (6/15/47)
22. Ask and Ye Shall Receive (6/22/47)
23. The Lost Sheep (6/29/47)
24. As Ye Would That Men Should Do To You (7/6/47)
25. The Loaves and the Fishes (7/13/47)
26. Be Not Afraid (7/20/47)
27. The Pearl of Great Price (7/27/47)
28. A House Built on Rock (8/3/47)
29. Lord, Make Me Clean (8/10/47)
30. The Parable of the Lost Coin (8/17/47)
31. Call Not Any Man a Fool (8/24/47)
32. The Calling of Matthew (8/31/47)
33. If Thine Eye Offend Thee (9/7/47)
34. Who Shall Desire to be First? (9/14/47)
35. Where Are the Nine? (9/21/47)
36. The Kingdom of God Is Within You (9/28/47)
37. The Troubled Waters (10/5/47)
38. The Wind and the Sea Obeyed Him (10/12/47)
39. Let Us Grow Together (10/19/47)
40. Who Is Most Forgiven? (10/26/47)
41. The Greater Shield (11/2/47)
42. And It Shall Be Given to You (11/9/47)
43. All Ye Are Brethren (11/16/47)
44. Thy Soul Shall Be Required (11/23/47)
45. And Her Name Was Mary (11/30/47)
46. Blessed Among Women (12/7/47)
47. Go and Be Counted (12/14/47)
48. No Room at the Inn (12/21/47)
49. Flight Into Egypt (12/28/47)
50. Our Father Which Art in Heaven (1/4/48)
51. A Little Leaven (1/11/48)
52. The Strength Within (1/18/48)
53. The Good Samaritan (1/25/48)
54. Seventy Times Seven (2/1/48)
55. In the Place of Others (2/8/48)
56. The Courage to Try Again (2/15/48)
57. Blessed are the Meek (2/22/48)
58. They Did Not Receive Him (2/29/48)
59. Blessed Are They That Mourn (3/7/48)
60. Blessed Are the Peacemakers (3/14/48)
61. The Betrayal and the Crucifixion (3/21/48)
62. The Resurrection (3/28/48)
63. The Hand to the Plow (4/4/48)
64. The Hunger Within (4/11/48)
65. That Ye Be Not Judged (4/18/48)
66. Unto These, My Brethren (4/25/48)
67. First, Be Reconciled (5/2/48)
68. Sufficient Unto the Day (5/9/48)
69. Thou Shalt Be Recompensed (5/16/48)
70. If You Have Faith (5/23/48)
71. Whosoever Is Angry (5/30/48)
72. Disputed Boundary (6/6/48)
73. The Challenge (6/13/48)
74. The Greater Miracle (6/20/48)
75. -----(6/27/48)
76. Of Such Is the Kingdom (9/12/48)
77. Men With the Mark (9/19/48)
78. The Idle Word (9/26/48)
79. By Their Fruits (10/3/48)
80. Greater Love Hath No Man (10/10/48)
81. Flight of the Children (10/17/48)
82. The Unbelieving (10/24/48)
83. Ye Who Are Heavy Laden (10/31/48)
84. The Pursued (11/7/48)
85. The Reward Is Great (11/14/48)
86. A Blade from Damascus (11/21/48)
87. A Child in the House (11/28/48)
88. Where Thieves Break Through (12/5/48)
89. Let Your Light Shine (12/12/48)
90. Unto You This Day (12/19/48)
91. The Star of Peace (12/26/48)

The Green Lama

"Om mani padme hum!" The chant of justice. *The Green Lama* was actually Jethro Dumont, a wealthy New York adventurer who spent ten years in a monastery of lamas in Tibet, where he was granted special crime fighting powers. Paul Frees played the role of Jethro Dumont and Ben Wright was Tulku, your everyday faithful Tibetan servant.

Larry Thor was the announcer. Richard Aurandt supplied the music. Norman MacDonnell, later James Burton, produced and directed. Richard Foster and William Froug wrote the scripts and also produced some of the episodes. *The Green Lama* was created by Foster, a pulp magazine writer. Broadcast from Hollywood as a short-run summer series, over CBS, Sunday evenings from 5:30 to 6 pm, EST. Broadcast on Saturday evenings from 7 to 7:30 pm, EST, beginning with episode six.

Audition: The Man Who Never Existed (5/17/49)
1. The Man Who Never Existed (6/5/49)
2. The Man Who Stole a Pyramid (6/12/49)
3. The Girl With No Name (6/19/49)
4. The Million Dollar Chopsticks (6/26/49)
5. The Last Dinosaur (7/3/49)
6. The Return of Madame Pompadour (7/16/49)
7. Tapestry in Purple (7/23/49)
8. The African Diamond Affair (7/30/49)
9. The Gumbo Man (8/6/49)
10. The Case of the Dangerous Dog (8/13/49)
11. The Case of the Patient Prisoner (8/20/49)

The Gulf Screen Guild Show/Theater

The Gulf Screen Guild Show was a charity show, donating all of the stars' fees to the Motion Picture Relief Fund. Sponsored by Gulf Gasoline, this series premiered in 1939 and featured numerous guest stars every week. Original dramas, comedy skits and music were presented. The program was broadcast on Sunday evenings over CBS, 7:30 to 8:30 pm, EST.

On November 26, 1939, the series changed its name to *The Gulf Screen Guild Theater*, and began presenting adaptations of movies instead of the varieties originally presented. Now at thirty minutes and with fewer guests, *Gulf* gained such prestige that when one Hollywood star called in sick, producers were swamped with offers from others to take his place. In April of 1942, the series went off the air for the summer and returned in the fall under a new name, *The Lady Esther Screen Guild Theater.*

For *The Gulf Screen Guild Show,* George Murphy was master of ceremonies for the first twenty-two broadcasts; Roger Pryor took over the job as host until April of 1942 (with the exception of Roland Young on episode twenty-one and Reginald Gardiner on episode twenty-two). Episodes marked "Variety" indicate that no specific drama was presented, just various comedic shorts, dramas and songs. Announcements claimed that film directors such as Frank Capra, Leo McCarey, Busby Berkeley and others directed broadcasts: Not true. The announcement was made each week only to gain audience attention and Hollywood appeal.

Writers for the *Gulf Show* were Earl Brecher, Sam Perrin, Frank Butler, Everett Freeman, Eddie Morgan, and Leonard Spigelgass. Writers (and adapters) for the *Gulf Theater* were Bill Morrow, Ed Beloin, Charles Tazewell, Keith Fowler, Frank Galen, Sam Perrin, and Bill Hampton. Oscar Bradley composed the music for *Gulf Theater,* Frank Tours conducted. Harry Von Zell was the first announcer for *Gulf Theater,* Bud Hiestand later took over the announcing job.

In episode five, Jane Withers successfully performed an entire *Gulf Screen Guild* show in one minute. Rufe Davis sang his memorable rendition of "Mama Don't Allow" in episode eight. Patsy Kelly attempted to sing like Deanna Durbin in episode sixteen and her voice cracked! Episode eighteen starred Claudette Colbert as herself in a biography about how she broke into the movies. In episode twenty-eight, bloopers struck the stage as Gary Cooper forgot his lines and the sound effects didn't work! Fred Allen interviewed Robert Benchley in episode thirty-one. Noel Coward's comedy of romance and divorce was presented on October 13, 1940. Episodes fifty-four and ninety-four were scripted by Norman Corwin. Episode 112 was based on a short story by Damon Runyon.

Bette Davis received the first Redbook Award in episode thirty-nine, after starring in a script written by Arch Oboler. Reportedly, Bette Davis made her first radio appearance in a comedy, featured in episode forty-seven (and she also sang!). After "Ninotchka," a preview of *The Adventures of Ellery Queen* was heard since Gulf Gasoline sponsored the *Ellery Queen* series when the *Gulf Theater* went off the air for the summer. The broadcast of October 20, 1940, was actually untitled, but the script concerned Jack Benny and his attempts to hire Claudette Colbert for the *Gulf Screen Guild Theater*. Mary Pickford presented an award to *The Gulf Screen Guild Theater* after the drama of April 20, 1941. "Alice Adams" was announced as the first all-dramatic role for Deanna Durbin.

1. Variety (1/8/39; Jack Benny, Joan Crawford, Reginald Gardiner, Judy Garland, and Ralph Morgan)
2. Miss Brown of Worcester (1/15/39; Fred Astaire, Herbert Marshall, Franklin Pagnborne, and Loretta Young)
3. Can We Forget? (1/22/39; Louise Beavers, Bette Davis, Robert Montgomery, and Basil Rathbone)
4. Variety (1/29/39; Mary Boland, Marlene Dietrich, Frank Morgan, and Cliff Nazarro)
5. The Junior Screen Guild Show (2/5/39; Bing Crosby, Hugh Herbert, Little Jane Wither, and the Yacht Club Boys)
6. Three Days in March (2/12/39; Olivia de Havilland, Billy Gilbert, Akim Tamiroff, and Spencer Tracy)
7. A Song for Clotilde (2/19/39; Jeanette MacDonald, Robert Taylor, and Charles Winninger)
8. A Review (2/26/39; Gracie Allen, George Burns, Rufe Davis, Melvyn Douglas, and Shirley Ross)
9. Bridge of Mercy (3/5/39; Lionel Atwill, Josephine Hutchinson, George Irving, and Paul Muni)
10. Tailored by Toni (3/12/39; Spring Byington, Edward Everett Horton, Carole Lombard, and James Stewart)
11. Zazazu (3/19/39; Fanny Brice, Bob Hope, Martha Raye, and Hanley Stafford)
12. Never of This World (3/26/39; Kay Francis, Leslie Howard, Mary Nash, Irving Pichel, and Virginia Weidler)
13. A Mug, A Moll, and A Mountaineer (4/2/39; Bob Burns, Warren Hymer, Edna May Oliver, George Raft, the Bryan Sisters, and Virginia Verrill)
14. Variety (4/9/39; Joan Bennett, Rosemary Lane, The King's Men, Mickey Rooney, and Rudy Vallee)
15. The Fingers of Providence (4/16/39; James Cagney, Andy Devine, Priscilla Lane, and Donald Meek)
16. A Review (4/23/39; Gary Cooper, Deanna Durbin, Patsy Kelly, and Parkyakarkus)
17. Alone in Paris (4/30/39; Herman Bing, Walter Connelly, Irene Dunne, and Cary Grant)
18. Thwarted Ambitions (5/7/39; Joe E. Brown, Claudette Colbert, Melvyn Douglas, The King's Men, and Phil Regan)
19. Variety (5/14/39; Mischa Auer, Billie Burke, Jerry Colonna, Jackie Oakie, Roger Pryor, and Betty Jane Rhodes)
20. A Review (5/21/39; Robert Benchley, Constance Bennett, Errol Flynn, Reginald Gardiner, Gertrude Niesen, and Maxie Rosenbloom)
21. A Review (5/28/39; Nelson Eddy, Douglas Fairbanks, Jr., Jim and Marian Jordan, Ann Sheridan, and Roland Young)
22. Variety (6/4/39; Reginald Gardiner, Jean Hersholt, Dick Powell, Tyrone Power, Rosalind Russell, Lionel Stander, and Marie Wilson)
23. Variety (9/24/39; Judy Garland, Cary Grant, Mickey Rooney, and Ann Sothern)
24. Imperfect Lady (10/1/39; Clark Gable, Harriet Lindsey, and Ginger Rogers)
25. Variety (10/8/39; Connie Boswell, Gary Cooper, Marlene Dietrich, and Bob Hope)
26. None Shall Part Us (10/15/39; Lew Ayers, Ronald Colman, Joan Crawford, and Montegue Love)

27. Variety (10/22/39; Gracie Allen, George Burns, James Cagney, and Gloria Jean)
28. We Were Dancing (10/29/39; Binnie Barnes, Hedda Hopper, Adolphe Menjou, and Robert Montgomery)
29. Going My Way (11/5/39; Edward Arnold, James Stewart, and Loretta Young)
30. The Beachcomber (11/12/39; Jean Hersholt, Elsa Lanchester, and Charles Laughton)
31. Variety (11/19/39; Fred Allen, Robert Benchley, and John Charles Thomas)
32. Enchanted Cottage (11/26/39; Helen Hayes and Fredric March)
33. Accent on Youth (12/3/39; Johnny Mac Brown, Gertrude Lawrence, and Herbert Marshall)
34. Mr. Jinks Goes to Sea (12/10/39; Bing Crosby, Andy Devine, and Jean Parker)
35. Smilin' Through (12/17/39; Louis Hayward, Basil Rathbone, and Norma Shearer)
36. Blue Bird (12/24/39; Nelson Eddy and Shirley Temple)
37. Variety (12/31/39; Gene Autry, Eddie Cantor, and Little Josephine)
38. The Petrified Forest (1/7/40; Joan Bennett, Humphrey Bogart, and Tyrone Power)
39. This Lonely Heart [script by Arch Oboler] (1/14/40; Bette Davis)
40. Firebrand (1/21/40; Douglas Fairbanks, Jr., Paulette Goddard, and Frank Morgan)
41. Private Worlds (1/28/40; Charles Boyer, Claudette Colbert, and Isabel Jewell)
42. I Met Him in Paris (2/4/40; Melvyn Douglas, Ann Sothern, and Robert Young)
43. Single Crossing (2/11/40; Myrna Loy and James Stewart)
44. Next Time We Live (2/18/40; James Cagney, Olivia de Havilland, and Jeffrey Lynn)
45. Blind Alley (2/25/40; Joseph Calliela, Isabel Jewell, and Edward G. Robinson)
46. Winter in Paris (3/3/40; Don Ameche, Maureen O'Sullivan, and Warren William)

47. Ballerina, Slightly with Accent (3/10/40; Bette Davis and William Powell)
48. The Awful Truth (3/17/40; Ralph Bellamy, Carole Lombard, and Robert Young)
49. Morning Glory (3/24/40; Miriam Hopkins and Adolphe Menjou)
50. Allergic to Love (3/31/40; Fred Mac-Murray and Barbara Stanwyck)
51. Vivacious Lady (4/7/40; Charles Colburn, Fred MacMurray, and Ginger Rogers)
52. Elmer the Great (4/14/40; Elvia Allman, Bob Hope, and Ann Sheridan)
53. Ninotchka (4/21/40; Rosalind Russell and Spencer Tracy)
54. The Shop Around the Corner (9/29/40; Frank Morgan, James Stewart, and Margaret Sullavan)
55. Red Dust (10/6/40; Clark Gable, Rita Johnson, Jeffrey Lynn, and Ann Sothern)
56. Private Lives (10/13/40; Vivien Leigh and Laurence Olivier)
57. [Untitled] (10/20/40; Edward Arnold, Jack Benny, Claudette Colbert, Ernst Lubitsch, and Basil Rathbone)
58. Jezebel (10/27/40; Jean Arthur, Jeffrey Lynn, Mary Nash, and Walter Pidgeon)
59. The Great Man Votes (11/3/40; John Barrymore, Thomas Mitchell, and Virginia Weidler)
60. History Is Made at Night (11/10/40; Lionel Atwill, Charles Boyer, and Greer Garson)
61. A Star Is Born (11/17/40; Adolphe Menjou, Burgess Meredith, and Loretta Young)
62. Allergic to Ladies (11/24/40; Errol Flynn, Nan Grey, Alan Hale, and Jane Wyman)
63. Desire (12/1/40; Marlene Dietrich and Fred MacMurray)
64. Torrid Zone (12/8/40; Joan Bennett, James Cagney, Brian Donlevy, and George Tobias)
65. Seventh Heaven (12/15/40; Annabella and Tyrone Power)
66. Juggler of Notre Dame (12/22/40; Ronald Colman and Nelson Eddy)
67. Drink a Glass of Sassafras (12/29/40;

Fay Bainter, William Holden, and Martha Scott)

68. Love Affair (1/5/41; Madeleine Carroll and Melvyn Douglas)
69. Waterloo Bridge (1/12/41; Brian Aherne and Joan Fontaine)
70. Magnificent Obsession (1/19/41; Don Ameche and Myrna Loy)
71. If She Could Only Cook (1/26/41; Humphrey Bogart, Alice Faye, and Herbert Marshall)
72. Destry Rides Again (2/2/41; Walter Brennan, Henry Fonda, Paulette Goddard, and Lloyd Nolan)
73. No Time for Comedy (2/9/41; Walter Abel, Mary Astor, Hattie McDaniel, Norma Shearer, and Franchot Tone)
74. Brother Orchid (2/16/41; Donald Crisp, Carole Landis, and Pat O'Brien)
75. Alter Bound (2/23/41; Bing Crosby, Betty Grable, and Bob Hope)
76. Jane Eyre (3/2/41; Brian Aherne and Bette Davis)
77. [Untitled] (3/9/41; Edward Arnold, Joan Bennett, Gary Cooper, Francis Langford, and Jim and Marian Jordan)
78. My Love Came Back (3/16/41; Olivia de Havilland, Charles Winninger, and Robert Young)
79. My Favorite Wife (3/23/41; Irene Dunne, Franklin Pangborne, and Robert Montgomery)
80. His Girl Friday (3/30/41; Cary Grant and Rosalind Russell)
81. Lucky Partners (4/6/41; William Powell and Ginger Rogers)
82. True Confessions (4/13/41; Carole Lombard and Fred MacMurray)
83. Hired Wife (4/20/41; Joan Blondell, Melvyn Douglas, and Mary Pickford)
84. Meet John Doe (9/28/41; Edward Arnold, Gary Cooper, and Barbara Stanwyck)
85. Strawberry Blonde (10/5/41; James Cagney, Jack Carson, and Olivia de Havilland)
86. Alice Adams (10/12/41; Deanna Durbin and Alan Marshall)
87. Nothing Sacred (10/19/41; James Gleason, Barbara Stanwyck, and Robert Taylor)

88. Good-Bye Mr. Chips (10/26/41; Greer Garson and Basil Rathbone)
89. The Amazing Doctor Clitterhouse (11/2/41; Humphrey Bogart, Marsha Hunt, and E.G. Robinson)
90. Babes in Arms (11/9/41; Judy Garland and Mickey Rooney)
91. Penny Serenade (11/16/41; Irene Dunne and Cary Grant)
92. If You Could Only Cook (11/23/41; Humphrey Bogart, Priscilla Lane, and Adolphe Menjou)
93. The Perfect Specimen (11/30/41; Melvyn Douglas, Betty Grable, and Dame May Whitty)
94. Between Americans (12/7/41; Orson Welles)
95. My Life with Caroline (12/14/41; George Barbie, William Powell, and Ann Sothern)
96. The Juggler of Our Lady (12/21/41; Ronald Colman and Nelson Eddy)
97. Long Engagement (12/28/41; Madeline Carroll, George Murphy, and Gene Raymond)
98. High Sierra (1/4/42; Humphrey Bogart and Claire Trevor)
99. Love Affair (1/11/42; Myrna Loy and Herbert Marshall)
100. Sergeant York (1/18/42; Walter Brennen, Gary Cooper, and Joan Leslie)
101. Torrid Zone (1/25/42; Jack Carson, Paulette Goddard, Betty Grable, and George Raft)
102. Bachelor Mother (2/1/42; Charles Colburn, Laraine Day, and Henry Fonda)
103. Mr. and Mrs. Smith (2/8/42; Errol Flynn and Lana Turner)
104. Liberty's a Lady (2/15/42; Loretta Young)
105. Love Is News (2/22/42; James Gleason, Betty Grable, and Kay Kyser)
106. Midnight (3/1/42; Joan Bennett and Robert Young)
107. Too Many Husbands (3/8/42; Bing Crosby, Bob Hope, and Hedy Lamarr)
108. Come and Get It (3/15/42; Edward Arnold, Walter Brennen, and Laraine Day)
109. How Green Was My Valley (3/22/42; Sara Allgood, Donald

Crisp, Roddy McDowall, Maureen O'Hara, Walter Pidgeon, and Rhys Williams)
110. Parent by Proxy (3/29/42; Jack Benny, Paulette Goddard, and Frank Nelson)
111. Philadelphia Story (4/5/42; Henry Fonda, Greer Garson, and Fred MacMurray)
112. Tight Shoes (4/12/42; Lucille Ball, Red Skelton, and George Tobias)
113. A Woman's Face (4/19/42; Bette Davis, Conrad Veidt, and Warren William)

Gunsmoke

This popular western starred William Conrad as Marshall Matt Dillon, Georgia Ellis as Kitty, Howard McNear as Doc Adams, and Parley Baer as Chester. Dodge City was violent — from scalped victims of Indians to innocent bystanders being shot in the street. Three audition programs were recorded, Rye Billsbury was in the lead role for the June 11, 1949 recording. On July 13, 1949, a second pilot was recorded with Howard Culver as Matt Dillon. On March 9, 1951, John Dehner starred in the third pilot. Trivia: for the broadcast entitled "The Cast" (December 12, 1953), Howard McNear could not play Doc, so Paul Frees stood in. Episode eighty-eight featured special guitar music performed by Al Hendrickson. The title to episode 127 stands for exactly what you think it stands for.

Audition : Mark Dillon Goes to Gouge an Eye (Recorded 7/13/49; Howard Culver, June Foray, and Victor Perrin)
1. Billy the Kid (4/26/52; Harry Bartell, Dick Beals, Don Diamond, Paul DuBov, and Mary Lansing)
2. Ben Thompson (5/3/52; Michael Ann Barrett, Harry Bartell, Don Diamond, Lawrence Dobkin, Sam Edwards, and Bob Griffin)
3. Jaliscoe (5/10/52; Harry Bartell, Vivi Janniss, Lou Krugman, Jack Kruschen, Johnny McGovern, and Barney Phillips)
4. Dodge City Killer (5/17/52; Lillian Buyeff, Lawrence Dobkin, Paul DuBov, Lou Krugman, Ralph Moody and Ben Wright)
5. Ben Slade's Saloon (5/24/52; Hy Averback, Dick Beals, Herb Ellis, Jack Kruschen, and Ann Morrison)
6. Carmen (5/31/52; Michael Ann Barrett, Harry Bartell, Don Diamond, and Jeanette Nolan)
7. Buffalo Killers (6/7/52; Lillian Buyeff, John Dehner, Lawrence Dobkin, Sam Edwards, Tom Holland, Mary Lansing, and Stan Waxman)
8. Jailbait Janet (6/14/52; Harry Bartell, John Dehner, Paul DuBov, and Sam Hill)
9. Heat Spell (6/21/52; John Dehner, Paul Frees, Jack Kruschen, Nestor Paiva, and John Stephenson)
10. The Ride Back (6/28/52; Larry Dobkin)
11. Never Pester Chester (7/5/52; Don Diamond, Paul DuBov, Lou Krugman, Jack Kruschen, and Gil Stratton, Jr.)
12. The Boughten Bride (7/12/52; Lawrence Dobkin, Herb Ellis, Frank Gerstle, Jonathan Hole, Mary Lansing, Jim Nusser, John Stephenson, and Patricia Walter)
13. Doc Holiday (7/19/52; Harry Bartell, Lee Millar, Ralph Moody, Nestor Paiva, and Tom Tully)

14. Gentleman's Disagreement (7/26/52; Lynn Allen, Larry Dobkin, Barney Phillips, and Tom Tully)
15. Renegade White (8/2/52; Harry Bartell, Lawrence Dobkin, Jack Kruschen, and Herb Vigran)
16. The Kentucky Tolmans (8/9/52; Harry Bartell, Virginia Gregg, Joseph Kearns, Lou Krugman, Peter Leeds, and Junius Matthews)
17. The Lynching (8/16/52; Joan Danton, John Dehner, Paul DuBov, Lee Millar, Ralph Moody, and Tom Tully)
18. Shakespeare (8/23/52; Hans Conried and Mary Lansing)
19. The Juniper Tree (8/30/52; Michael Ann Barrett, John Dehner, Paul DuBov, Vivi Janniss, and Bill Lally)
20. The Brothers (9/6/52; Harry Bartell, Paul DuBov, Joe DuVal, Lou Krugman, and Victor Perrin)
21. Home Surgery (9/13/52; John Dehner, Lawrence Dobkin, and Sam Hill)
22. Drop Dead (9/20/52; Harry Bartell, Joe DuVal, Lou Krugman, and Barney Phillips)
23. The Railroad (9/27/52; John Dehner, Jeanette Nolan, and Tom Tully)
24. Cain (10/3/52; Harry Bartell and Lawrence Dobkin)
25. Hinka-Do (10/10/52; John Dehner, Byron Kane, Ralph Moody, and Jeanette Nolan)
26. Lochinvar (10/17/52; Herb Ellis, Vivi Janniss, Barney Phillips, and Tom Tully)
27. The Mortgage (10/24/52; Harry Bartell, Dick Beals, Lawrence Dobkin, Joe DuVal, Jim Nusser, and Paula Winslowe)
28. Overland Express (10/31/52; Lawrence Dobkin, Lou Krugman, Junius Mathews, Ralph Moody, Jim Nusser, and Victor Perrin)
29. Tara (11/7/52; John Dehner, Joe DuVal, Sam Hill, Vivi Janniss, and Ralph Moody)
30. The Square Triangle (11/14/52; Harry Bartell, Lillian Buyeff, Lawrence Dobkin, and Jack) Kruschen
31. Fingered (11/21/52; Harry Bartell, Paul DuBov, Jack Kruschen, Jeanette Nolan, and John McIntire)
32. Kitty (11/29/52; John Dehner, Lawrence Dobkin, Mary Lansing, and Bob Sweeny)
33. I Don't Know (12/6/52; Michael Ann Barrett, Dick Beals, John Dehner, Lawrence Dobkin, and Lee Millar)
34. Post Martin (12/13/52; Jeanne Bates, Sam Edwards, and Ralph Moody)
35. Christmas Story (12/20/52; Harry Bartell, John Dehner, and Lawrence Dobkin)
36. The Cabin (12/27/52; Harry Bartell, John Dehner, and Vivi Janniss)
37. Westbound (1/3/53; John Dehner, Lawrence Dobkin, Sam Edwards, Jim Nusser, Barney Phillips and Tom Tully)
38. Word of Honor (1/10/53; Harry Bartell, John Dehner, and Larry Dobkin)
39. Paid Killer (1/17/53; Harry Bartell, Lawrence Dobkin, Jack Kruschen, and Ralph Moody)
40. The Old Lady (1/24/53; Parley Baer, Harry Bartell, Sam Edwards, Jeanette Nolan, and Herb Vigran)
41. Cavalcade (1/31/53; Larry Dobkin, Paul DuBov, Jack Kruschen, and Vivi Janniss)
42. Cain (2/7/53; Harry Bartell and Lawrence Dobkin)
43. The Round-Up (2/14/53; Harry Bartell, John Dehner, Lawrence Dobkin, Lou Krugman, and James Nusser)
44. Meshougah"* (2/21/53; Michael Ann Barrett, Ted Bliss, John Dehner, Lawrence Dobkin, Lou Krugman, Victor Perrin, and Bob Sweeny)
45. Trojan War (2/28/53; Harry Bartell, John Dehner, Lawrence Dobkin, Paul DuBov, Louise Fitch, and Tom Tully)
46. Absalom (3/7/53; Harry Bartell, John Dehner, Sam Edwards, Charlotte Lawrence, and Barney Phillips)
47. Cyclone (3/14/53; Harry Bartell, Joseph Cranston, Lawrence Dobkin, Jerry Hausner, and Vivi Janniss)
48. Pussy Cats (3/21/53; Michael Ann

*Meshougah is a Yiddish word that means "crazy."

Barrett, John Dehner, Lawrence Dobkin, Jack Kruschen, and Tom Tully)

49. Quarter Horse (3/28/53; Harry Bartell, Lawrence Dobkin, Joseph Kearns, Lou Krugman, and Johnny McGovern)

50. Jayhawkers (4/4/53; Harry Bartell, Lawrence Dobkin, Sam Edwards, Jack Kruschen, and Jim Nusser)

51. Gonif (4/11/53; John Dehner, Lawrence Dobkin, Jack Kruschen, and Barney Phillips)

52. Bum's Rush (4/18/53; Harry Bartell, John Dehner, Lawrence Dobkin, Lou Krugman)

53. The Soldier (4/25/53; Harry Bartell, Lawrence Dobkin, Paul Frees, and Victor Perrin)

54. Tacetta (5/2/53; Lillian Buyeff, Lawrence Dobkin, Paul DuBov, and Tom Tully)

55. The Buffalo Hunter (5/9/53; Harry Bartell, Dick Beals, John Dehner, Lawrence Dobkin, and William Oiler)

56. The Big Con (5/16/53; Harry Bartell, Joseph Cranston, Lawrence Dobkin, Paul DuBov, Peter Leeds, Ralph Moody, and James Nusser)

57. Print Asper (5/23/53; John Dehner, Sam Edwards, and Joseph Kearns)

58. Fall Semester (5/30/53; Harry Bartell, John Dehner, and John McIntire)

59. Sundown (6/6/53; Michael Ann Barrett, John Dehner, Lawrence Dobkin, and John McIntire)

60. Spring Term (6/13/53; Harry Bartell, John Dehner, Lou Krugman, and Victor Perrin)

61. Wind (6/20/53; John Dehner, Virginia Gregg, and James Griffith)

62. Flashback (6/27/53; Lawrence Dobkin, Joe DuVal, Sam Edwards, and Lou Krugman)

63. Dirt (7/4/53; Joseph Cranston, Lawrence Dobkin, Sam Edwards, Joyce McCluskey, Pat McGeehan, and Elaine Williams)

64. Grass (7/11/53; Harry Bartell, Lawrence Dobkin, and Ralph Moody)

65. Wild West (7/18/53; Michael Ann Barrett, John Dehner, Joseph

Kearns, John McGovern, and Nestor Paiva)

66. Hickcock (7/25/53; Harry Bartell, John Dehner, Lawrence Dobkin, Joe DuVal, and John McIntire)

67. Boy (8/1/53; John Dehner, Lawrence Dobkin, and Charlotte Lawrence)

68. Sky (8/8/53; Sam Edwards, Vivi Janiss, Helen Kleeb, Lou Krugman, Mary Lansing, Ralph Moody, and Jim Nusser)

69. Moon (8/15/53; Harry Bartell, John Dehner, Vivi Janiss, and Victor Perrin)

70. Gone Straight (8/22/53; Harry Bartell, John Dehner, Paul DuBov, Helen Kleeb, James Nusser, and Tom Tully)

71. Jesse (8/29/53; Harry Bartell, John Dehner, Larry Dobkin, and Sam Edwards)

72. The Sutler (9/5/53; Harry Bartell, Juli Conger, John Dehner, Joseph Kearns, and James Nusser)

73. Prairie Happy (9/12/53; Lillian Buyeff, John Dehner, Lawrence Dobkin, James Nusser, Victor Perrin)

74. There Was Never a Horse (9/19/53; John Dehner, Lawrence Dobkin, and Ralph Moody)

75. Fawn (9/26/53; Edgar Barrier, Leo Curley, John Dehner, Lawrence Dobkin and Helen Kleeb)

76. How to Kill a Friend (10/3/53; Harry Bartell, John Dehner, and Lawrence Dobkin)

77. How to Die for Nothing (10/10/53; Harry Bartell, John Dehner, Lawrence Dobkin, and Victor Perrin)

78. Yorky (10/17/53; Dick Beals, John Dehner, and Lawrence Dobkin)

79. The Buffalo Hunter (10/24/53; Dick Beals, Jack Edwards, Louis Jean Heydt, and Tom Tully)

80. How to Kill a Woman [aka How to Kill a Road Ranch] (10/31/53; John Dehner, Lawrence Dobkin, and Jack Edwards)

81. Stolen Horses (11/7/53; Paul Frees, Helen Kleeb, Ralph Moody, and James Nusser)

82. Professor Lute Bone (11/14/53; John Dehner, Lawrence Dobkin, Paul DuBov and Barney Phillips)

83. Custer (11/21/53; John Dehner and

Sam Edwards)
84. Kick Me (11/28/53; Harry Bartell, Lawrence Dobkin, Frank Gerstle, Byron Kane and Ralph Moody)
85. The Lamb (12/5/53; Harry Bartell, Lawrence Dobkin, Herb Ellis, and Victor Perrin)
86. The Cast (12/12/53; Sam Edwards, Paul Frees, and Tom Tully)
87. Big Girl Lost (12/19/53; Harry Bartell, Lawrence Dobkin, Joyce McCluskey, and Victor Perrin)
88. The Guitar (12/26/53; Harry Bartell, John Dehner, Lawrence Dobkin, and Victor Perrin)
89. Stage Holdup (1/2/54; John Dehner, Lawrence Dobkin, and Victor Perrin)
90. Joke's on Us (1/9/54; Ted Bliss, John Dehner, Sam Edwards, Herb Ellis, and Helen Kleeb)
91. The Bear (1/16/54; John Dehner, Lawrence Dobkin, Lou Krugman, and Jim Nusser)
92. Nina (1/23/54; Lillian Buyeff, Lawrence Dobkin, James Eagle, and Victor Perrin)
93. Gunsmuggler (1/30/54; Harry Bartell, John Dehner, Lawrence Dobkin, Jack Edwards, and Barney Phillips)
94. Big Broad (2/6/54; John Dehner, Virginia Gregg, and Victor Perrin)
95. The Killer (2/13/54; Howard Culver, Lawrence Dobkin, Richard Deacon, and Victor Perrin)
96. Last Fling (2/20/54; John Dehner, Helen Kleeb, and Ralph Moody)
97. Bad Boy (2/27/54; Charles Bastin, John Dehner, Paul DuBov, and Sam Edwards)
98. The Gentleman (3/6/54; Harry Bartell, John Dehner, and Eleanore Tanin)
99. Confederate Money (3/13/54; Harry Bartell, James Ogg, Victor Perrin, and Barney Phillips)
100. Old Friend (3/20/54; John Dehner, Lawrence Dobkin, and Victor Perrin)
101. Blood Money (3/27/54; Harry Bartell, John Dehner, and Jim Nusser)
102. Mr. and Mrs. Amber (4/3/54; Harry Bartell, John Dehner, Lawrence Dobkin, Frances Drew, Helen Kleeb, Ralph Moody, and Jim Nusser)
103. Greater Love (4/10/54; John Dehner, Frank Gerstle, Joyce McClusky, and Ralph Moody)
104. What the Whiskey Drummer Heard (4/17/54; Edgar Barrier, John Dehner, and Victor Perrin)
105. Murder Warrant (4/24/54; John Dehner, Lawrence Dobkin, Joe DuVal, Sam Edwards, and Jim Nusser)
106. Cara (5/1/54; Harry Bartell, John Dehner, Jill Jarmyn, and Victor Perrin)
107. The Constable (5/8/54; John Dehner Joseph Kearns, Jack Kruschen, Fred MacKaye and Victor Perrin)
108. The Indian Horse (5/15/54; Harry Bartell, John Dehner, Ralph Moody, and Paul Savage)
109. Monopoly (5/22/54; Herb Ellis, Joseph Kearns, Jack Kruschen, and Victor Perrin)
110. Feud (5/29/54; John Dehner, Lawrence Dobkin, and Virginia Gregg)
111. The Blacksmith (6/5/54; Jeanne Bates, John Dehner, Jack Kruschen, and Victor Perrin)
112. The Cover Up (6/12/54; Joseph Kearns, Helen Kleeb, Clayton Post, and Paul Savage)
113. Going Bad (6/19/54; Harry Bartell, Sam Edwards, Vivi Janiss, and Edward Penney)
114. Claustrophobia (6/26/54; John Dehner, Lawrence Dobkin, Jack Kruschen, and Victor Perrin)
115. Word of Honor (7/3/54; Harry Bartell, John Dehner, and Larry Dobkin)
116. Hack Prine (7/5/54; Harry Bartell, John Dehner, Lawrence Dobkin, and Victor Perrin)
117. Texas Cowboys (7/12/54; Harry Bartell, John Dehner, Lawrence Dobkin, and Victor Perrin)
118. The Queue (7/19/54; Edgar Barrier, John Dehner, Lawrence Dobkin, and Paul DuBov)
119. Matt for Murder [aka How to

Catch a Marshall] (7/26/54; John Dehner, James Nusser, and Victor Perrin)

120. No Indians (8/2/54; Harry Bartell, John Dehner, Lawrence Dobkin, Joseph Kearns and Victor Perrin)

121. Joe Phy (8/9/54; John Dehner, Ralph Moody, and Victor Perrin)

122. Mavis McCloud (8/16/54; Harry Bartell, John Dehner, Sam Edwards, and Eleanore Tanin)

123. Young Man with a Gun (8/23/54; John Dehner, Lawrence Dobkin, Sam Edwards, and Vivi Janiss)

124. Obie Tater (8/30/54; Virginia Gregg, Joseph Kearns, Victor Perrin, and Barney Phillips)

125. The Handcuffs [aka The Promise] (9/6/54; John Dehner, Lawrence Dobkin, Joe Forte, Jack Kruschen, and Irene Tedrow)

126. Dooley Surrenders (9/13/54; Harry Bartell, James Nusser, and Victor Perrin)

127. The F.U. (9/20/54; John Dehner and Lawrence Dobkin)

128. Helping Hand (9/27/54; Joseph Cranston, John Dehner, Lawrence Dobkin, and Sam Edwards)

129. Matt Gets It (10/2/54; Harry Bartell, John Dehner, Paul DuBov, and Victor Perrin)

130. Love of a Good Woman (10/9/54; John Dehner, Vivi Janiss, and James Nusser)

131. Kitty Caught (10/16/54; John Dehner, Lawrence Dobkin, and Joe DuVal)

132. Ma Tennis (10/23/54; Harry Bartell, Sam Edwards, Virginia Gregg, and Lee Millar)

133. The Patsy (10/30/54; Lawrence Dobkin, Jill Jarmyn, Jack Kruschen, Jim Nusser, and Victor Perrin)

134. Smoking Out the Beedles (11/6/54; Harry Bartell, Joseph Cranston, Lawrence Dobkin, and Jeanette Nolan)

135. Wrong Man (11/13/54; John Dehner, Lawrence Dobkin, Vivi Janiss, and Victor Perrin)

136. How to Kill a Woman (11/20/54; Lawrence Dobkin, Victor Perrin, and Clayton Post)

137. Cooter (11/27/54; Harry Bartell, John Dehner, and Victor Perrin)

138. Cholera (12/4/54; Virginia Christine, Sam Edwards, Ralph Moody, Clayton Post and Victor Perrin)

139. Bone Hunters (12/11/54; Frank Cady, John Dehner, and Herb Ellis)

140. Magnus (12/18/54; Robert Easton)

141. Kitty Lost (12/25/54; John Dehner, James Nusser, Victor Perrin, and Barney Phillips)

142. The Bottle Man (1/1/55; Lawrence Dobkin, Ralph Moody, and Eleanore Tanin)

143. Robin Hood (1/8/55; Harry Bartell, Frank Cady, Joe Cranston, Lawrence Dobkin, Helen Kleeb)

144. Chester's Murder (1/15/55; Lawrence Dobkin, Joyce McClusky, James Nusser, and Victor Perrin)

145. Sins of the Father (1/22/55; Harry Bartell, Lillian Buyeff, Lawrence Dobkin, Joe DuVal, and Clayton Post)

146. Young Love (1/29/55; Frank Cady, Don Diamond, Sam Edwards, Victor Perrin and Eleanore Tanin)

147. Cheyennes (2/5/55; Harry Bartell, Larry Dobkin, Ralph Moody, Victor Perrin, Barney Phillips)

148. Chester's Hanging (2/12/55; Joseph Cranston, Paul DuBov, James Nusser, and Clayton Post)

149. Poor Pearl (2/19/55; Harry Bartell, Virginia Christine, and Victor Perrin)

150. Crack-Up (2/26/55; Harry Bartell and John Dehner)

151. Kite's Reward (3/5/55; John Dehner, Joe DuVal, Sam Edwards, and Victor Perrin)

152. The Trial (3/12/55; Harry Bartell, John Dehner, Lawrence Dobkin, and Victor Perrin)

153. The Mistake (3/19/55; John Dehner, Lou Krugman, and James Nusser)

154. Horse Deal (3/26/55; Harry Bartell, Joe Cranston, Sam Edwards, James Nusser, and Victor Perrin)

155. Bloody Hands (4/2/55; John

Dehner and Lawrence Dobkin)

156. Skid Row (4/9/55; Harry Bartell, Barney Phillips, and Eleanore Tanin)

157. The Gypsum Hill Feud (4/16/55; John Dehner, Vivi Janiss, and Victor Perrin)

158. Born to Hang (4/23/55; John Dehner, Lawrence Dobkin, Joseph Kearns, and James Nusser)

159. Reward for Matt (4/30/55; Sam Edwards, Helen Kleeb, and Jeanette Nolan)

160. Potato Road (5/7/55; Virginia Gregg, John McIntire, and Victor Perrin)

161. Robber Bridegroom (5/14/55; Harry Bartell, Jeanne Bates, Clayton Post, Lawrence Dobkin, and Frank Gerstle)

162. The Liar from Blackhawk (5/21/55; John Dehner, Paul DuBov, Victor Perrin, and Barney Phillips)

163. Cow Doctor (5/28/55; John Dehner, Sam Edwards, and Vivi Janiss)

164. Jealousy (6/4/55; Harry Bartell, Don Diamond, Virginia Gregg, and Victor Perrin)

165. Trust (6/11/55; John Dehner, Joseph Kearns, James Nusser, Victor Perrin, and Clayton Post)

166. The Reed Survives (6/18/55; Michael Ann Barrett, Edgar Barrier, Sam Edwards, Ralph Moody)

167. The Army Trial (6/25/55; Harry Bartell, Lawrence Dobkin, Vivi Janiss, and James Nusser)

168. General Parcley Smith (7/2/55; John Dehner, Joe DuVal, and Victor Perrin)

169. Uncle Oliver (7/9/55; Harry Bartell and Victor Perrin)

170. Twenty-Twenty (7/16/55; Joseph Cranston, James Nusser, and Victor Perrin)

171. Ben Tolliver's Stud (7/23/55; Sam Edwards, James Nusser, and Eleanore Tanin)

172. Tap Day for Kitty (7/30/55; Michael Ann Barrett, John Dehner, and Virginia Gregg)

173. Innocent Broad (8/6/55; Paul DuBov, Lawrence Dobkin, Victor Perrin, and Eleanore Tanin)

174. Johnny Red (8/13/55; Larry Dobkin, Paul DuBov, Sam Edwards, Virginia Gregg, and Victor Perrin)

175. Indian Scout (8/20/55; Harry Bartell, Lawrence Dobkin, Joseph Kearns, and Barney Phillips)

176. Doc Quits (8/27/55; Frank Cady, Lawrence Dobkin, Ann Morrison, and James Nusser)

177. Change of Heart (9/3/55; Virginia Christine, Joe DuVal, Sam Edwards, and Victor Perrin)

178. Alarm at Pleasant Valley (9/10/55; John Dehner, Sam Edwards, John James, Helen Kleeb, Victor Perrin, and Eleanore Tanin)

179. Thoroughbreds (9/17/55; Harry Bartell, John Dehner, and Lawrence Dobkin)

180. Indian White (9/24/55; Harry Bartell, John Dehner, Virginia Gregg, Joseph Kearns, Ralph Moody, and Sammy Ogg)

181. The Barton Boy (10/1/55; Dick Beals, Virginia Christine, and Lawrence Dobkin)

182. Good Girl-Bad Company (10/8/55; Virginia Christine and John Dehner)

183. The Coward (10/9/55; John Dehner, Sam Edwards, and Victor Perrin)

184. Trouble in Kansas (10/16/55; Harry Bartell, Lawrence Dobkin, and Barney Phillips)

185. Brush at Elkader (10/23/55; Harry Bartell, Lawrence Dobkin, Paul DuBov, James Nusser, and Victor Perrin)

186. The Choice (10/30/55; Harry Bartell, Lawrence Dobkin, Sam Edwards, and Barney Phillips)

187. Second Choice (11/6/55; Sam Edwards, Joseph Kearns, and Victor Perrin)

188. The Preacher (11/13/55; Joseph Cranston, John Dehner, and Lawrence Dobkin)

189. Dutch George (11/20/55; John Dehner, James Nusser, and Victor Perrin)

190. Amy's Good Deed (11/27/55; Harry

Bartell and Virginia Gregg)

191. Sunny Afternoon (12/4/55; Virginia Christine, John Dehner, and Ralph Moody)

192. Land Deal (12/11/55; John Dehner, Lawrence Dobkin, Vivi Janiss, and Victor Perrin)

193. Scared Kid (12/18/55; John Dehner, Sam Edwards, Ann Morrison, and Eleanore Tanin)

194. Twelfth Night (12/25/55; John Dehner, Helen Kleeb, and Victor Perrin)

195. Pucket's New Year (1/1/56; Ralph Moody and James Nusser)

196. Doc's Revenge (1/8/56; John Dehner and Victor Perrin)

197. How to Cure a Friend (1/15/56; Harry Bartell, John Dehner, Larry Dobkin, and Ralph Moody)

198. Romeo (1/22/56; John Dehner, Sam Edwards, Joyce McClusky, and James Nusser)

199. Bureaucrat (1/29/56; Harry Bartell, John Dehner, and Victor Perrin)

200. Legal Revenge (2/5/56; Lawrence Dobkin, Stacy Harris, and Helen Kleeb)

201. Kitty's Outlaw (2/12/56; Victor Perrin and Barney Phillips)

202. New Hotel (2/19/56; Harry Bartell, John Dehner, Larry Dobkin, Joe DuVal, and Victor Perrin)

203. Who Lives by the Sword (2/26/56; John Dehner, Sam Edwards, and Clayton Post)

204. The Hunter (3/4/56; Harry Bartell, Sam Edwards, and Nestor Paiva)

205. Bringing Down Father (3/11/56; Lawrence Dobkin, William Idelson, and Victor Perrin)

206. The Man who Would be Marshal (3/18/56; Harry Bartell, John Dehner, and James Nusser)

207. Hanging Man (3/25/56; John Dehner, Lawrence Dobkin, and Virginia Gregg)

208. How to Sell a Ranch (4/1/56; Harry Bartell, Joe DuVal, Kathy Marlowe, and Ralph Moody)

209. Widow's Mite (4/8/56; Virginia Christine and John Dehner)

210. The Executioner (4/15/56; John Dehner, Sam Edwards, and Victor Perrin)

211. Indian Crazy (4/22/56; Lawrence Dobkin and Helen Kleeb)

212. Doc's Reward (4/29/56; John Dehner and Victor Perrin)

213. The Photographer (5/6/56; Harry Bartell, Lawrence Dobkin, and James Nusser)

214. Cows and Cribs (5/13/56; Frank Cady, Virginia Christine, John Dehner, Jeanette Nolan, and Victor Perrin)

215. Buffalo Man (5/20/56; John Dehner, Lawrence Dobkin, Helen Kleeb, and Victor Perrin)

216. Man Hunter (5/27/56; John Dehner, Lawrence Dobkin, and Ken Lynch)

217. The Pacifist (6/3/56; Harry Bartell, Paul DuBov, James Nusser, and Victor Perrin)

218. Daddy-O (6/10/56; Lawrence Dobkin and John McIntire)

219. Cheap Labor (6/17/56; Harry Bartell, Jeanne Bates, Larry Dobkin, Victor Perrin, Barney Phillips)

220. Sunday Supplement (6/24/56; Harry Bartell, John Dehner, Joseph Kearns, Lou Krugman, and Ralph Moody)

221. Gun for Chester (7/1/56; Lawrence Dobkin)

222. Passive Resistance (7/8/56; Harry Bartell, John Dehner, Jack Moyles, and Ralph Moody)

223. Letter of the Law (7/15/56; Paul DuBov, Joseph Kearns, Helen Kleeb, Victor Perrin, and Will Wright)

224. Lynching Man (7/22/56; Harry Bartell, John Dehner, Lawrence Dobkin, Jack Moyles, James Nusser, and Victor Perrin)

225. Lost Rifle (7/29/56; Dick Beals, John Dehner, Jack Kruschen, and Victor Perrin)

226. Sweet and Sour (8/5/56; Lynn Allen, Harry Bartell, and Lawrence Dobkin)

227. Snakebite (8/12/56; Lawrence Dobkin, Joseph Kearns, and Victor Perrin)

228. Annie Oakley (8/19/56; Harry Bartell, Paul DuBov, and Jeanette

Dehner, Lawrence Dobkin, and
Joseph DuVal)

277. Cow Doctor (7/28/57; John Dehner,
Sam Edwards, and Vivi Janiss)

278. Big Hands (8/4/57; Victor Perrin)

279. Jayhawkers (8/11/57)

280. The Peace Officer (8/18/57)

281. Grass (8/25/57; John Dehner)

282. Jobe's Son (9/1/57; John Dehner
and Victor Perrin)

283. Loony McCluny (9/8/57; Lawrence
Dobkin, Virginia Gregg, and Jess
Kirkpatrick)

284. Child Labor (9/15/57)

285. Custer (9/22/57)

286. Another Man's Poison (9/29/57;
Victor Perrin)

287. The Rooks (10/6/57; Harry Bartell,
John Dehner, Don Diamond,
Lawrence Dobkin, James Nusser,
Victor Perrin, and Barney Phillips)

288. The Margin (10/13/57; John Dehner
and Victor Perrin)

289. Professor Lute Bone (10/20/57)

290. Man and Boy (10/27/57; Victor
Perrin)

291. Bull (11/3/57; John Dehner and
Sam Edwards)

292. Gunshy (11/10/57; Victor Perrin)

293. The Queue (11/17/57)

294. Odd Man Out (11/24/57; Harry
Bartell, John Dehner, and
Lawrence Dobkin)

295. Jud's Woman (12/1/57; Victor Perrin)

296. Long As I Live (12/8/57; John
Dehner)

297. Ugly (12/15/57; John Dehner and
Victor Perrin)

298. Twelfth Night (12/22/57)

299. Where'd They Go? (12/29/57; Virginia Gregg, Joseph Kearns, and
Ralph Moody)

300. Pucket's New Year (1/5/58; Ralph
Moody and James Nusser)

301. Second Son (1/12/58; John Dehner,
Victor Perrin, and Ben Wright)

302. Moo Moo Raid (1/19/58; John
Dehner and Victor Perrin)

303. One for Lee (1/26/58; John Dehner
and Ralph Moody)

304. Kitty's Killing (2/2/58; John
Dehner)

305. Joke's On Us (2/9/58)

306. Bruger's Folly (2/16/58)

307. The Surgery (2/23/58; John
Dehner)

308. The Guitar (3/2/58; Harry Bartell,
John Dehner, Lawrence Dobkin,
and Victor Perrin)

309. Laughing Gas (3/9/58; John
Dehner, Ralph Moody, and Victor
Perrin)

310. Real Sent Sonny (3/16/58)

311. Indian (3/23/58)

312. Why Not (3/30/58; John Dehner)

313. Yorky (4/6/58)

314. Livvie's Loss (4/13/58; John
Dehner, Jeanette Nolan, and Victor Perrin)

315. The Partners (4/20/58; Virginia
Christine, John Dehner, Sam
Edwards, James Nusser, and Bar-
ney Phillips)

316. The Squaw (4/27/58; Lillian Buyeff,
Frank Cady, Dick Crenna, Ralph
Moody, and Victor Perrin)

317. How to Die for Nothing (5/10/58;
Harry Bartell, Lawrence Dobkin,
Jack Moyles, Victor Perrin)

318. Little Bird (5/11/58; Harry Bartell,
Lillian Buyeff, and John McIntire)

319. The Stallion (5/18/58; Lawrence
Dobkin, Ralph Moody, and James
Nusser)

320. Blue Horse (5/25/58; Harry Bartell,
Dick Crenna, and Victor Perrin)

321. Quarter-Horse (6/1/58)

322. Hot Horse Hyatt (6/8/58; Dick
Beals, John Dehner, and Jack
Moyles)

323. Old Flame (6/15/58; Jeanne Bates,
John Dehner, and Joseph Kearns)

324. Target (6/22/58; Tommy Cook,
John Dehner, and Ralph Moody)

325. What the Whiskey Drummer Heard
(6/29/58; John Dehner)

326. Chester's Choice (7/6/58; Harry
Bartell, Lawrence Dobkin, and Jess
Kirkpatrick)

327. The Proving Kid (7/13/58; Virginia
Christine, John Dehner, and Victor Perrin)

328. Marshal Proudfoot (7/20/58; John
Dehner)

329. The Cast (7/27/58)

330. Miguel's Daughter (8/3/58; Lynn
Allen, Dick Crenna, Lawrence

Dobkin, and Victor Perrin)

331. A House Ain't a Home (8/10/58; John Dehner, Sam Hill, Ralph Moody, and Victor Perrin)

332. The Piano (8/17/58; Virginia Gregg and Victor Perrin)

333. The Blacksmith (8/24/58; John Dehner)

334. I Thee Wed (8/31/58; Harry Bartell, Virginia Christine, and John Dehner)

335. Tried It-Didn't Like It (9/7/58; Jeanne Bates, Dick Beals, and Victor Perrin)

336. False Witness (9/14/58; Harry Bartell, Sam Edwards, and James Nusser)

337. Big Girl Lost (9/21/58)

338. Kitty's Rebellion (9/28/58; John Dehner, Sam Edwards, and Victor Perrin)

339. Tag, You're It (10/5/58; Dick Crenna, Virginia Christine, and Victor Perrin)

340. Doc's Showdown (10/12/58; Irene Andres, John Dehner, Lawrence Dobkin, Sam Edwards, and Helen Kleeb)

341. Kick Me (10/19/58)

342. The Tragedian (10/26/58; John Dehner, James Nusser, Victor Perrin, and James Westerfield)

343. Old Man's Gold (11/2/58; Harry Bartell, John Dehner, and Ralph Moody)

344. Target : Chester (11/9/58; John Dehner, Lawrence Dobkin, Sam Edwards, and Victor Perrin)

345. Brush at Elkader (11/16/58; Harry Bartell, Lawrence Dobkin, Victor Perrin, James Westerfield, and Ben Wright)

346. The Correspondent (11/23/58; Harry Bartell, Lawrence Dobkin, and Sam Edwards)

347. Burning Wagon (11/30/58; Lawrence Dobkin, Virginia Gregg, and Tom Hanley)

348. The Grass Asp (12/7/58; Harry Bartell, James Nusser, and Victor Perrin)

349. Kitty's Injury (12/14/58; Jeanne Bates, John Dehner, and Victor Perrin)

350. Where'd They Go? (12/21/58; Vir-

ginia Gregg, Joseph Kearns, and Ralph Moody)

351. The Choice (12/28/58; Harry Bartell, Sam Edwards, and Barney Phillips)

352. The Coward (1/4/59; Lawrence Dobkin, Joseph Kearns, and Jack Moyles)

353. The Wolfer (1/11/59; Lawrence Dobkin, Tom Hanley, and Victor Perrin)

354. Kangaroo (1/18/59; Harry Bartell, Jack Edwards, Sam Edwards, and Joseph Kearns)

355. The Boots (1/25/59; Dick Beals, Lawrence Dobkin, and Victor Perrin)

356. The Bobsy Twins (2/1/59; Jeanne Bates, Sam Edwards, Joseph Kearns, Ralph Moody, Jack Moyles, and James Nusser)

357. Groat's Grudge (2/8/59; Harry Bartell, Frank Cady, Lawrence Dobkin, and Jess Kirkpatrick)

358. Body Snatch (2/15/59; Howard Culver, Ralph Moody, Jack Moyles, James Nusser and Victor Perrin)

359. Sarah's Search (2/22/59; Clark Gordon, Ann Morrison, and Victor Perrin)

360. Big Tom (3/1/59)

361. Maw Hawkins (3/8/59; Sam Edwards, Jeanette Nolan, and Victor Perrin)

362. Incident at Indian Ford (3/15/59; Jeanne Bates, Jack Moyles, and Victor Perrin)

363. The Trial (3/22/59; Harry Bartell, Lawrence Dobkin, Joseph Kearns, and Victor Perrin)

364. Laurie's Suitor (3/29/59; Eleanore Berry, Lawrence Dobkin, Sam Edwards, and Victor Perrin)

365. Trapper's Revenge (4/5/59; Lawrence Dobkin, Ralph Moody, and Victor Perrin)

366. Chester's Mistake (4/12/59; James Nusser)

367. Third Son (4/19/59; Sam Edwards, Ken Lynch, Ralph Moody, and Barney Phillips)

368. The Badge (4/26/59; Harry Bartell and Victor Perrin)

369. Unwanted Deputy (5/3/59; Jeanne

Lawrence Dobkin, Ralph Moody)

406. Fiery Arrest (1/17/60; Harry Bartell, Jeanne Bates, Sam Edwards, Victor Perrin and Barney Phillips)

407. Bless Me Till I Die (1/24/60; Harry Bartell, Virginia Christine, Lawrence Dobkin, Ralph Moody)

408. Chester's Dilemma (1/31/60; John Dehner, Barbara Eiler, Joseph Kearns, and Victor Perrin)

409. Delia's Father (2/7/60; Virginia Christine, Lawrence Dobkin, and Bartlett Robinson)

410. Distant Drummer (2/14/60; Harry Bartell, Joseph Kearns, Ralph Moody, James Nusser, Victor Perrin, and Barney Phillips)

411. Mr. and Mrs. Amber (2/21/60; Jeanne Bates, Harry Bartell, Virginia Gregg, Ralph Moody, James Nusser, Victor Perrin and Barney Phillips)

412. Prescribed Killing (2/28/60; Jeanne Bates, Virginia Christine, and Lawrence Dobkin)

413. Blood Money (3/6/60)

414. Unloaded Gun (3/13/60; Harry Bartell, Dick Beals, Sam Edwards, Victor Perrin and Barney Phillips)

415. The Constable (3/20/60)

416. Indian Baby (3/27/60; Jeanne Bates, Ralph Moody, and Victor Perrin)

417. Greater Love (4/3/60)

418. Dave's Lesson (4/10/60; Harry Bartell, Sam Edwards, Joseph Kearns, and Ralph Moody)

419. Solomon River (4/17/60; Virginia Perrin)

420. Stage Snatch (4/24/60; Lawrence Dobkin, Ralph Moody, and Victor Perrin)

421. Nettie Sitton (5/1/60; Virginia Gregg)

422. Wrong Man (5/8/60; Harry Bartell, Lawrence Dobkin, Sam Edwards, Jack Moyles and Victor Perrin)

423. Tall Trapper (5/15/60; Victor Perrin and Barney Phillips)

424. Marryin' Bertha (5/22/60; Virginia Gregg, Joseph Kearns, Victor Perrin, and Ben Wright)

425. Bad Seed (5/29/60; John Dehner, Sam Edwards, and Eve McVey)

426. Fabulous Silver Extender (6/5/60; Harry Bartell, Joseph Kearns, Jack Moyles, and Victor Perrin)

427. Kitty Accused (6/12/60; Dick Beals, Virginia Christine, Victor Perrin, and Barney Phillips)

428. Homely Girl (6/19/60; John Dehner, Virginia Gregg, and Victor Perrin)

429. Line Trouble (6/26/60; Harry Bartell, Lawrence Dobkin, Joe Kearns, Ralph Moody and Jack Moyles)

430. Little Girl (7/3/60; Lawrence Dobkin, Joseph Kearns, and Ann Morrison)

431. Reluctant Violence (7/10/60; John Dehner, Lawrence Dobkin, Sam Edwards, Joseph Kearns, and Barney Phillips)

432. Busted-Up Guns (7/17/60; Virginia Gregg, Ralph Moody, and Victor Perrin)

433. The Impostor (7/24/60; Jeanne Bates, Lawrence Dobkin, and Victor Perrin)

434. Stage Smash (7/31/60; Dick Beals, John Dehner, James Nusser, Victor Perrin and Barney Phillips)

435. Old Fool (8/7/60; Sam Edwards, Virginia Gregg, Joseph Kearns, and Peggy Webber)

436. The Noose (8/14/60; Harry Bartell, John Dehner, Lawrence Dobkin, Victor Perrin, Barney Phillips, Bartlett Robinson, and Ben Wright)

437. Dangerous Bath (8/21/60; Jeanne Bates, Lawrence Dobkin, and Sam Edwards)

438. The Tumbleweed (8/28/60; Virginia Christine, Joseph Kearns, Victor Perrin, Barney Phillips)

439. Peace Officer (9/4/60; Virginia Christine and Barney Phillips)

440. About Chester (9/11/60; Lynn Allen Harry Bartell, John Dehner, Victor Perrin and Bartlett Robinson)

441. Two Mothers (9/18/60; Jeanne Bates Virginia Christine, and John Dehner)

442. Doc Judge (9/25/60; Harry Bartell, John Dehner, and James Nusser)

443. The Big Itch (10/2/60; Lynn Allen and Sam Edwards)

444. Born to Hang (10/9/60)

445. Crack-Up (10/16/60)
446. Newsma'am (10/23/60; Harry Bartell, Jeanne Bates, Victor Perrin, and Barney Phillips)
447. Never Pester Chester (10/30/60)
448. Jedro's Woman (11/6/60; Virginia Christine, Lawrence Dobkin, and James Nusser)
449. The Big Con (11/13/60)
450. The Professor (11/20/60; Lawrence Dobkin, Ralph Moody, Victor Perrin, and Barney Phillips)
451. Dirt (11/27/60)
452. Kitty's Good Neighboring (12/4/60; Virginia Christine, John Dehner, Victor Perrin, and Barney Phillips)
453. The Cook (12/11/60; Harry Bartell, Jeanne Bates, John Dehner, Lawrence Dobkin, Sam Edwards, Victor Perrin, Bartlett Robinson, and Ben Wright)
454. Hero's Departure (12/18/60; John Dehner, Sam Edwards, Jack Moyles, and Victor Perrin)
455. Minnie (12/25/60; John Dehner, Virginia Gregg, and Victor Perrin)
456. Spring Term (1/1/61)
457. Old Faces (1/8/61; Harry Bartell, Jeanne Bates, John Dehner, and Lawrence Dobkin)
458. The Wake (1/15/61; John Dehner and Virginia Gregg)
459. Hard Virtue (1/22/61; Harry Bartell, Jeanne Bates, John Dehner, and Victor Perrin)
460. Harriet (1/29/61; John Dehner, Eve McVey, Barney Phillips, and Ben Wright)
461. Love of Money (2/5/61; Virginia Christine, John Dehner, and Lawrence Dobkin)
462. Daddy-O (2/12/61)
463. Kitty Love (2/19/61; John Dehner)
464. Joe Sleet (2/26/61; Harry Bartell and Victor Perrin)
465. Melinda Miles (3/5/61; John Dehner, Sam Edwards, Victor Perrin, and Anne Whitfield)
466. Sweet and Sour (3/12/61; Lynn Allen and Lawrence Dobkin)
467. Joe Phy (3/19/61; John Dehner, Ralph Moody, and Victor Perrin)
468. No Indians (3/26/61)
469. Chester's Inheritance (4/2/61; Harry Bartell, Ralph Moody, Jack Moyles, and Victor Perrin)
470. Hangman's Mistake (4/9/61; Lawrence Dobkin, Ken Lynch, and Victor Perrin)
471. Cooter (4/16/61)
472. Father and Son (4/23/61; Harry Bartell, Lillian Buyeff, Ralph Moody, and Victor Perrin)
473. Ex-Urbanites (4/30/61; Harry Bartell, John Dehner, and Victor Perrin)
474. Ma's Justice (5/7/61; Virginia Christine, Dick Crenna, John Dehner, Sam Edwards, Victor Perrin)
475. The Lady Killer (5/14/61; Lynn Allen, Harry Bartell, John Dehner, and Lawrence Dobkin)
476. Chester's Rendezvous (5/21/61; Jeanne Bates, John Dehner, and James Nusser)
477. The Sod-Buster (5/28/61; Jeanne Bates, John Dehner, Ralph Moody, and Barney Phillips)
478. Cows and Cribs (6/4/61)
479. Doc's Visitor (6/11/61; John Dehner, Sam Edwards, Virginia Gregg, Ralph Moody, James Nusser, and Victor Perrin)
480. Letter of the Law (6/18/61; Paul DuBov, Joseph Kearns, Helen Kleeb, Victor Perrin, and Will Wright)

Hallmark Playhouse

With the opening theme of Charles Williams' "Dream of Olwne," *Hallmark Playhouse* opened each week with a drama of top quality and a Hollywood actor in the starring role. James Hilton, author of *Goodbye, Mr. Chips, Lost Horizon,* and *Random Harvest*, was the host of this series, bowing out near the end of the series. Lionel Barrymore took over afterwards. Scripts for the series were previously performed on such programs as *Suspense*, *Academy Award Theatre*, and *The Cavalcade of America*. Jean Holloway, Ring Lardner, Louis Bromfield, Jack Rubin, and Joel Murcott were just a few of the script writers.

The program was sponsored by Hallmark Cards. Frank Goss was the announcer. Produced and directed by Dee Engelbach. William Gaye later took over as producer. Lyn Murray composed and conducted the music, as did David Rose. Broadcast over CBS Thursday evenings from 10 to 10:30 pm, EST, until episode ninety-nine, when the show moved back to 9:30 to 10 pm. Beginning with episode one-hundred and forty-one, the series was broadcast from 8:30 to 9 pm. Beginning September 7, 1952, the series moved to Sunday evenings from 9 to 9:30 pm, EST.

In December of 1952, Lionel Barrymore starred in his annual "Christmas Carol" presentation. Episode thirty-eight featured Meredith Wilson in a biography of early life. For the broadcast of June 1, 1950, a special hour-long episode was broadcast from Kansas City and designed to commemorate its Centennial. Episode fifty-three was the same script performed on *Suspense* in 1945. Episode one-hundred and eighty was previously performed on *The Cavalcade of America*.

1. The Devil and Daniel Webster [written by Stephen Vincent Benet] (6/10/48; John McIntire and Alan Reed)
2. Mrs. Union Station (6/17/48; Mary Jane Croft, David Ellis, Joseph Kearns, Mary Lansing, Elliott Lewis, and Frank Nelson)
3. Unless Love Is Music (6/24/48; Joan Banks, Bea Benaderet, William Johnstone, and Alan Ordley)
4. Penny Serenade (7/1/48; Ed Begley, Frank Lovejoy, Gerald Mohr, Margaret MacDonald, Frances Robinson, and Anne Whitfield)
5. Pride and Prejudice [based on the novel by Jane Austen] (7/8/48)
6. Girls Are Like Boats (7/22/48; Ann Blythe)
7. Phantom Philly (7/29/48)
8. Afterward (8/5/48; Lurene Tuttle)
9. The Old Nest (8/12/48)
10. Drums Along the Mohawk (8/19/48)
11. State Fair (8/26/48; Ann Blythe)
12. To Mary, with Love (9/2/48)
13. Cimarron [based on the story by Edna Ferber] (9/9/48; Irene Dunne and Gerald Mohr)
14. Goodbye, Mr. Chips (9/16/48; Ronald Colman)
15. Captain January (9/23/48; Lionel Barrymore and Luana Patton)
16. Elmer, the Great (10/7/48; Jeff Chandler, Bob Hope, and Gerald Mohr)
17. Arrowsmith [based on the story by Sinclair Lewis] (10/14/48; John Lund)
18. Mrs. Parkington (10/21/48; Rosalind Russell)
19. O'Halloran's Luck [written by Stephen Vincent Benet] (10/28/48; Edmund O'Brien and Dan O'Herlihy)
20. My Friend Flicka (11/4/48; Jeff Chandler and Claude Jarmon, Jr.)
21. The Wild Swans [based on a story by Hans Christian Andersen] (11/11/48; Jean Hersholt)
22. My Financial Career (11/18/48; Jack Benny, Stephen Leacock, and Jack Kirkwood)
23. Free Land (11/25/48; Jack Kirkwood and Martha Scott)

24. Old Man Minnick [written by Edna Ferber] (12/2/48; Victor Moore)
25. Woman with a Sword (12/9/48; Ida Lupino)
26. The Desert Shall Rejoice (12/16/48; John Hodiak)
27. The Story of Silent Night (12/23/48; Gerald Mohr)
28. Lost Horizon (12/30/48; Herbert Marshall)
29. MacCleod's Folly (1/6/49; Robert Young)
30. Clay Shuttered Door [based on the story by Helen Rose Hull] (1/13/49; Jane Wyman)
31. Parnassus on Wheels [based on the novel by Christopher Morey] (1/20/49; Ruth Hussey)
32. The Failure (1/27/49; Ward Bond and Jeff Chandler)
33. Abe Lincoln : The Prairie Years [based on the book by Carl Sandburg] (2/3/49; Gregory Peck)
34. Smilin' Through (2/10/49; Lew Ayres)
35. Random Harvest (2/17/49; Joan Fontaine)
36. So Big [based on the story by Edna Ferber] (2/24/49; Virginia Bruce, Jeff Chandler, and Howard McNear)
37. Berkeley Square (3/3/49; David Niven, Frances Robinson, and Lurene Tuttle)
38. And There I Stood with My Piccolo (3/10/49; Jeff Chandler and Meredith Wilson)
39. Our Own Kind (3/17/49; Barry Fitzgerald)
40. Wyatt Earp, Frontier Marshall (3/24/49; Richard Conte and Gerald Mohr)
41. Immortal Wife (3/31/49; Paul McVey and Lorreta Young)
42. Morning Glory (4/7/49; Elizabeth Taylor)
43. One Foot in Heaven (4/14/49; George Brent)
44. Kitty Foyle (4/21/49; June Allyson, Tim Peters, and Whitfield Connor)
45. A Tree Grows in Brooklyn (4/28/49; James Dunn and Claudia Marshall)
46. Mother (5/5/49; Linda Darnell and Verna Felton)
47. You Could Look It Up [based on the James Thurber story] (5/12/49; Jerry Austin, William Frawley, and Gerald Mohr)
48. The Enchanted Cottage (5/19/49; Lurene Tuttle and Richard Widmark)
49. The Barker (5/26/49; Charles Bickford, Gloria Blondell, and Lurene Tuttle)
50. I Like It Here (6/2/49; Paul Lukas and Howard McNear)
51. Yankee from Olympus (9/8/49; Robert Young)
52. Anna and the King of Siam (9/15/49; Deborah Kerr)
53. So Well Remembered (9/22/49)
54. August Heat (9/29/49; Ed Begley and Fred MacMurray)
55. National Velvet (10/6/49; Roddy McDowell and Anne Whitfield)
56. The Virginian (10/13/49; MacDonald Carey)
57. Let the Hurricane Roar (10/20/49; Ann Blythe and Sam Edwards)
58. The Story of Dr. Sericold (10/27/49; Verna Felton and Edmund Gwenn)
59. Colonel Effingham's Raid (11/3/49; Charles Colburn and Gerald Mohr)
60. Bride of Fortune (11/10/49; Irene Dunn and John McIntire)
61. A Letter to Mr. Priest (11/17/49; Lew Ayres)
62. The Courtship of Miles Standish [based on the story by Henry Wadsworth Longfellow] (11/24/49; William Conrad, David Niven)
63. Cheers for Miss Bishop (12/1/49; Martha Scott)
64. Christopher and Columbus (12/8/49; Frank Lovejoy and Dorothy McGuire)
65. Wedding Morning (12/15/49; Robert Walker)
66. The Story of Silent Night (12/22/49)
67. Father Flannagan of Boy's Town (12/29/49; Dana Andrews)
68. The Egg and I (1/5/50; Claudette Colbert and Frank Nelson)
69. The Way West (1/12/50; Joel McCrea)
70. Around the World in Eighty Days (1/19/50; Ronald Colman and Hans Conried)
71. Green Grass of Wyoming (1/26/50; Fanny Hill and Lon McAllister)

72. Wine of Youth (2/2/50; Hans Conried, Ida Lupino, and Ben Wright)
73. Lincoln and the Baltimore Plot (2/9/50; Victor Jory)
74. April 25th, as Usual [based on the story by Edna Ferber] (2/16/50; Ethel Barrymore and Tom Tully)
75. The Autobiography of Will Rogers (2/23/50; Edward Arnold, Ted deCorsia, and Will Rogers, Jr.)
76. The Indestructible Julia (3/2/50; Katina Paxinou and Tom Tully)
77. Home to the Hermitage (3/9/50; Burgess Meredith and Jeanette Nolan)
78. Three Wishes of Jamie McRuin (3/16/50; Richard Todd)
79. Richard Carvel (3/23/50; Douglas Fairbanks, Jr.)
80. Pioneer Preacher (3/30/50; Charles Bickford)
81. The Arbutus of Bonnet (4/6/50; Ann Blythe)
82. Appassionata (4/13/50; Charles Boyer)
83. My Sister Eileen (4/20/50; Rosalind Russell)
84. They Came to a River (4/27/50; Jeanne Crain)
85. Victoria Regina (5/4/50; Joan Fontaine)
86. Marmee (5/11/50; Teresa Wright)
87. The Wayfarers (5/18/50; Lloyd Nolan)
88. Knee Pants (5/25/50; Bobby Driscoll)
89. The Story of Kansas City (6/1/50; Jane Wyman and Robert Young)
90. The Story of Tom Edison (9/7/50; Van Heflin)
91. The Big Build-Up (9/14/50; Dana Andrews)
92. West of the Hill (9/21/50; Elizabeth Taylor)
93. The Barefoot Mailman (9/28/50; John Hodiak)
94. The Story of Florence Nightingale (10/5/50; Irene Dunne)
95. Final Tribute (10/12/50; Edmund Gwenn)
96. Not Wanted (10/19/50; D. Blackwell)
97. The Legend of Sleepy Hollow (10/26/50; Lionel Barrymore)
98. Mistress of the White House (11/2/50; Teresa Wright)
99. Great Expectations (11/9/50; Richard Todd)
100. Enchanted April (11/16/50; Joan Fontaine)
101. Home to Thanksgiving (11/23/50; Jane Wyman)
102. Decatur (11/30/50; Richard Widmark)
103. The Third Ingredient (12/7/50; Ann Blythe)
104. The Promise (12/14/50; Robert Young)
105. The Story of Silent Night (12/21/50; The Lyn Murray Chorus)
106. Patrick Calls Me Mother (12/28/50; Martha Scott)
107. The Life of Theodore Roosevelt (1/4/51; Broderick Crawford)
108. Farmer in the Dell (1/11/51; Charles Bickford)
109. Old Soldiers Never Die (1/18/51; Raymond Massey)
110. The Golden Horde (1/25/51; Bruce Cabot)
111. Goodbye, Mr. Chips (2/1/51; Deborah Kerr)
112. Abraham Lincoln : A Man for the Ages (2/8/51; Joseph Cotten)
113. Cinderella (2/15/51; Judy Garland)
114. Valley Forge (2/22/51; Van Heflin)
115. Monsieur Beaucaire (3/1/51; Douglas Fairbanks, Jr.)
116. Deepwood (3/8/51; Rosalind Russell)
117. The Long Winter (3/15/51; Edward Arnold)
118. The Long Love (3/22/51; Van Johnson and Lurene Tuttle)
119. Waterloo Bridge (3/29/51; Douglas Fairbanks, Jr. and Veronica Lake)
120. Rest and be Thankful (4/5/51; Dorothy McGuire)
121. Joy Street (4/12/51; Irene Dunne)
122. F.O.B. America (4/19/51; Robert Cummings)
123. Two Years Before the Mast (4/26/51; Edmund O'Brien)
124. A Breath of Air (5/3/51; Sarah Churchill)
125. A Man's Mother (5/10/51; Ethel Barrymore)
126. Benjamin Franklin (5/17/51; Lionel Barrymore)

127. Scudda Ho, Scudda Hay (5/24/51; Lon McAllister)
128. The Quest of John Chapman (5/31/51; Lew Ayres)
129. Whistling in the Dark (6/7/51; Edward Everett Horton)
130. True Confessions (6/14/51; Rosalind Russell)
131. Payment Deferred (6/21/51; Hume Cronyn and Jessica Tandy)
132. Double Identity (6/28/51; Gloria Swanson)
133. Bachelor Mother (7/5/51; Paulette Goddard)
134. Front Page (7/12/51; Lee Tracy)
135. Night Must Fall (7/19/51; Dan Duryea)
136. No Time for Comedy (7/26/51; Rosalind Russell)
137. A Double Life (8/2/51; Douglas Fairbanks, Jr.)
138. Petrified Forest (8/9/51; Wendell Corey)
139. Ball of Fire (8/16/51; Wendy Barrie and Franchot Tone)
140. An Inspector Calls (8/23/51; Vanessa Brown)
141. Accent on Youth (8/30/51; Joan Caulfield and Jeffrey Lynn)
142. Ladies of the Jury (9/6/51; Lucille Watson)
143. Francis Scott Key (9/13/51; Robert Young)
144. The Prisoner of Zenda (9/20/51; Douglas Fairbanks, Jr.)
145. The Web of Destiny (9/27/51; Jane Wyman)
146. Country Lawyer (10/4/51; Fred MacMurray)
147. Wild Orchard (10/11/51; Ann Blythe)
148. Cashel Byron's Profession (10/18/51; Joseph Cotten)
149. John Adams and the American Revolution (10/25/51; Van Heflin)
150. Evangeline (11/1/51; Joan Fontaine)
151. 20,000 Leagues Under the Sea (11/8/51; Louis Jordan)
152. Mississippi Bubble (11/15/51; Ray Milland)
153. The Widened Heart (11/22/51; Ann Harding)
154. Salad Days (11/29/51; Ronald Reagan)
155. The Night of the Hayride (12/6/51; Loretta Young)
156. Story of John Hancock (12/13/51; Dana Andrews, Herb Butterfield, Ted deCorsia, Virginia Gregg, William Johnstone, Ted Osborne, and Norma Varden)
157. The Story of Silent Night (12/20/51)
158. Stephen Foster (12/27/51; MacDonald Carey)
159. The Camerak (or Tamerak; Tree (1/3/52) Lon McAllister)
160. Horse and Buggy Doctor (1/10/52; Lionel Barrymore)
161. Madam Clair (1/17/52; Agnes Moorehead)
162. Singing in the Wilderness (1/24/52; Jean Pierre Aumont)
163. Westward Ho! (1/31/52; Joseph Cotten)
164. Percussion (2/7/52; Deborah Kerr)
165. Robert Schumann (2/14/52; Joan Fontaine)
166. Powder Mission (2/21/52; Barry Sullivan)
167. The Mother of the Groom (2/28/52; Ruth Hussey)
168. Man Without a Home (3/6/52; Joseph Cotten)
169. This Pleasant Leave (3/13/52; Deborah Kerr)
170. Time Remembered (3/20/52; Jane Wyman)
171. Yankee's Doorkeeper (3/27/52; Lionel Barrymore)
172. Lisa Lilywhite (4/3/52; Angela Lansbury)
173. Ben Hur (4/10/52; Jeff Chandler)
174. Doubtful Valley (4/17/52; Richard Widmark)
175. Professor (4/24/52; Joan Fontaine)
176. Lorna Doone (5/1/52; David Niven)
177. Whistler's Mother (5/8/52; Jane Wyman)
178. Marquis de Lafayette (5/15/52; Jean Pierre Aumont)
179. Marsha Byrnes (5/22/52; Barbara Stanwyck)
180. Lewis and Clark (5/29/52; Van Heflin 9/7/52)
181. The Pathfinder (9/14/52; Van Heflin) Powder Mission (9/21/52)
182. Nebraska Coast (9/28/52; Fred MacMurray)

183. Mansfield Park (10/5/52; Angela Lansbury)
184. Young Mr. Disraeli (10/12/52; Joseph Cotten)
185. Lady of the Lake (10/19/52; Joan Fontaine)
186. Preble's Boy (10/26/52; MacDonald Carey)
187. Daniel Webster (11/2/52; Lionel Barrymore)
188. Covered Bridge (11/9/52; Anne Baxter)
189. Thunder Shower (11/16/52; Edward Arnold)
190. Standish Outstandish (11/23/52; John Hodiak (11/30/52?)
191. Miracle on Blotter (12/7/52; Joan Fontaine)
192. Home for Christmas (12/14/52; Ann Blythe)
193. A Christmas Carol (12/21/52; Parley Baer, Lionel Barrymore, Hans Conried, Ted de Corsia, Virginia Gregg, and Ben Wright)
194. A Man Named Peter (12/28/52; Joseph Cotten and Lurene Tuttle)
195. Wave High the Banner (1/4/53; MacDonald Carey)
196. January Thaw (1/11/53; Irene Dunne)
197. Forty Odd (1/18/53; Ruth Hussey)
198. Big Family (1/25/53; Fred MacMurray)
199. Trenton '76 (2/1/53; Jane Wyman)

The Harold Lloyd Comedy Theater

Sponsored by Old Gold, this program is also known as *The Old Gold Comedy Theater*, *The Comedy Theater of the Air* and *The Harold Lloyd Theater*. Harold Lloyd, whose adventures on building ledges and swinging clock hands were a highlight of his silent film days, emerged from retirement to be master of ceremonies for this radio anthology/comedy series. Direct from Hollywood, broadcast over NBC on Sunday evenings from 10:30–11 pm, EST. The first three broadcasts originated from New York, after which the series was broadcast from Hollywood, California. The program of April 15, 1945, was pre-empted due to FDR's death. Carl Hoff was the musical director and conductor. Jimmy Wallington was the announcer.

1. The Palm Beach Story (10/29/44; Claudette Colbert and Robert Young)
2. Ball of Fire (11/5/44; Lucille Ball and Walter Pidgeon)
3. True to Life (11/12/44; Rosemary DeCamp, Victor Moore, and Dick Powell)
4. Vivacious Lady (11/19/44; Lee Bowman and Linda Darnell)
5. Clarence [story by Booth Tarkington] (11/26/44; Joseph Cotten)
6. Take a Letter, Darling (12/3/44; Susan Hayward and John Hodiak)
7. Louder Please [story by Norman Krasna] (12/10/44; Julie Bishop and Adolphe Menjou)
8. Lucky Partners (12/17/44; Sheldon Leonard, Herbert Marshall, and Jane Wyman)
9. Bachelor Mother (12/24/44; Brenda Marshall and Louis Hayward)
10. Room Service (12/31/44; Stu Erwin, Donald McBride, Jackie Oakie, and Cara Williams)
11. The Lady Eve (1/7/45; Ralph Bellamy, Betty Field, and Guy Kibbee)
12. Nothing but the Truth (1/14/45; Anne Baxter and Alan Young)
13. The Show-Off (1/21/45; Fred Allen, Joseph Curtin, Alice Frost, and Claudia Morgan)
14. Appointment for Love (1/28/45; Virginia Bruce and Paul Henreid)

15. My Favorite Wife (2/4/45; Joel McCrea, Constance Moore, and Gail Patrick)
16. A Girl, a Guy and a Gob (2/11/45; Lucille Ball and George Murphy)
17. The Milky Way (2/18/45; Eve Arden, Jimmy Gleason, and Robert Walker)
18. You Can't Ration Love (2/25/45; Dick Haymes and Betty Rhodes)
19. Standing Room Only (3/4/45; Paulette Goddard and Burgess Meredith)
20. The Magnificent Dope (3/11/45; Janet Blair, Tom Drake, and William Gargan)
21. A Lady Takes a Chance [adapted by Louis Vittes] (3/18/45; Randolph Scott and Gene Tierney)
22. Brewster's Millions (3/25/45; Mischa Auer, Dennis O'Keefe, and Helen Walker)
23. The Major and the Minor (4/1/45; Joan Fontaine and Sonny Tufts)
24. A Slight Case of Murder (4/8/45; Allen Jenkins and Edward G. Robinson)
25. The Nervous Wreck (4/22/45; Jack Haley and Martha O'Driscoll)
26. Scatterbrain (4/29/45; Judy Canova)
27. Hired Wife (5/6/45; Joan Bennett and Robert Paige)
28. She Loves Me Not (5/13/45; Freddie Bartholomew, Tom Drake, and Maria Montez)
29. Boy Meets Girl (5/20/45; Chester Morris, Ann Sothern, and Lee Tracy)
30. June Moon (5/27/45; Jack Carson and Frank McHugh)
31. Having Wonderful Time (6/3/45; Tom Conway, June Duprez, and Pat O'Brien)
32. Tom, Dick and Harry (6/10/45; June Allyson)

Have Gun, Will Travel

Have Gun, Will Travel, unlike many programs during the fifties, originated on television first, then made a transition to radio. This popular western premiered on CBS television in September of 1957, and was last telecast in September of 1963. From November of 1958 to November of 1960, *Have Gun, Will Travel* was heard on CBS radio, Sunday evenings from 6:05 to 6:30 pm, EST. This meant that for two years, *Have Gun* could be heard or seen twice in one week.

On radio, John Dehner played Paladin, a college-educated man who attended West Point to start a military career. Instead, he served in the Civil War and as a result of a mistake he had made in the past, he chose to lead a different sort of life, one in which his skills could help others. Paladin became a "hired gun," described by many of his clients as a "paid bounty hunter." One week Paladin was hired to bring back a daughter who ran off with the lover her father did not approve of. The week after, an old man would offer to pay Paladin to kill the men who stole his land and gold mine. By the end of the episode Paladin's conscience had guided him through the rights and wrongs, as he had made decisions that occasionally went against the men (or women) who hired him.

Paladin never had a sidekick or deputy beside him. Hey Boy was the comic relief of the series, a bellhop working where Paladin resided, the Carlton Hotel, in San Francisco, California. Hey Boy would open almost every broadcast with a telegram or introduction from a client requesting Paladin's services. Hey Boy's girlfriend, Miss Wong, also worked at the hotel, but was featured only on occasion.

Most of the early episodes of the radio series were adaptations of the television dramas (a couple were written by *Star Trek* creator Gene Roddenbury). Ann Doud, Albert Aley, John Dawson, Les Crutchfield, Frank Michael and William N. Robson were a few who wrote for the series. Hugh Douglas was the announcer. Norman MacDonnell was the first producer/director of the series, replaced by Frank Paris beginning in mid–1959. Ben Wright played the role of Hey Boy; Virginia Gregg was Miss Wong. The series was created by Herb Meadow and Sam Rolfe; the latter would go on to create the famed television show *The Man from U.N.C.L.E.*

There were numerous sponsors for this series; Pepsi-Cola, Winston Cigarettes, Columbia Phonographs, Ex-Lax, Dristan, Fitch Shampoo, Camel Cigarettes, Yardley, Fritos, Kellogg's Cereals, A.T.&T., and Sylvania Flash Bulbs. Episode forty-four featured Debbie Reynolds in a *Look* magazine commercial. Don Ameche and Frances Langford were featured in a "Bickersons" commercial in episode thirty-six. Episode sixty-nine featured Burgess Meredith in a Super Sixty Hearing Glasses commercial. From mid to late 1960, Edgar Bergen and Charlie McCarthy were heard on Guardian Maintenance commercials.

1. Strange Vendetta (11/23/58; Harry Bartell, Lillian Buyeff, Howard Culver, Joseph Kearns, Ralph Moody, and Victor Perrin)
2. Food to Wickenberg (11/30/58; Lynn Allen, Harry Bartell, Jack Edwards, Frank Gerstle, Eve McVey, and Victor Perrin)
3. Ella West (12/7/58; Lynn Allen, Harry Bartell, Sam Edwards, Lawrence Dobkin, and Barney Phillips)
4. The Outlaw (12/14/58; Frank Cady, Lawrence Dobkin, Sam Edwards, Joseph Kearns, Jean Landsworth, and Ralph Moody)
5. The Hanging Cross (12/21/58; Dick Beals, Virginia Christine, Jess Curt Patrick, Ann Morrison, Victor Perrin, and Roy Woods)
6. No Visitors (12/28/58; Jean Bates, Lou Krugman, and Victor Perrin)
7. Helen of Abejinian (1/4/59; Lynn Allen, Lillian Buyeff, Virginia Christine, Richard Crenna, and Lawrence Dobkin)
8. The Englishman (1/11/59; Harry Bartell, Jean Bates, Virginia Christine, Ralph Moody, James Nusser, and Barney Phillips)
9. Three Bells to Perdido (1/18/59; William Alice, Jean Bates, Lillian Buyeff, Howard Culver, Don Diamond, Paul DuBov, and Joseph Kearns)
10. The Teacher (1/25/59; Harry Bartell, Joel Davis, Helen Kleeb, and Richard Perkins)
11. Matter of Ethics (2/1/59; Virginia Christine, Jack Edwards, Jack Kruschen, Olan Soule, Victor Perrin, and Roy Woods)
12. Killer's Widow (2/8/59; Joseph Kearns, Victor Perrin, and Eleanor Tanin)
13. Return of Doctor Thackeray (2/15/59; Jean Bates, Harry Bartell, Lawrence Dobkin, Sam Edwards, and Lou Krugman)
14. Winchester Quarantine (2/22/59; Edgar Barrier, Harry Bartell, Lillian Buyeff, Lawrence Dobkin, Joseph Kearns, and Barney Phillips)

15. Hey Boy's Revenge (3/1/59; Edgar Barrier, Paul DuBov, Joseph Kearns, and Lou Krugman)
16. Monster of Moonridge (3/8/59; Jean Bates, Larry Dobkin, Virginia Christine, Jess Curt Patrick)
17. Death of a Young Gunfighter (3/15/59; Harry Bartell, Lillian Buyeff, Lawrence Dobkin, Clark Gordon, and Barney Phillips)
18. The Five Books of Owen Deaver (3/22/59; Jess Curt Patrick, Paul DuBov, Sam Edwards, Helen Kleeb, and Ken Lynch)
19. Sense of Justice (3/29/59; Lynn Allen, Harry Bartell, Richard Perkins, and Barney Phillips)
20. Maggie Banion (4/5/59; Lynn Allen, Harry Bartell, and Barney Phillips)
21. The Colonel and the Lady (4/12/59; Lillian Buyeff, Lawrence Dobkin, Frank Gerstle, Eve McVey, and Jack Moyles)
22. Birds of a Feather (4/19/59; Joseph Kearns and James Nusser)
23. The Gunsmith (4/26/59; Lawrence Dobkin and Ralph Moody)
24. Gun Shy (5/3/59; Richard Crenna, Barbara Eiler, Jeanette Nolan, Vic Perrin, and Barney Phillips)
25. The Statue of San Sebastian (5/10/59; Dick Beals, Perry Cook, Lawrence Dobkin, and James Nusser)
26. Silver Queen (5/17/59; Lynn Allen, Harry Bartell, Joseph Kearns, and James Nusser)
27. In an Evil Time (5/24/59; Harry Bartell and Joseph Kearns)
28. Blind Courage (5/31/59; Sam Edwards, Barbara Eiler, Jack Moyles, and Tracy Roberts)
29. Roped (6/7/59; Jeanne Bates, Joseph Kearns, and Victor Perrin)
30. Bitter Wine (6/14/59; Lawrence Dobkin, Waldo Emerson, and Blanche Hawkins)
31. North Fork (6/21/59; Harry Bartell, Joseph Kearns, Jess Kirkpatrick, Lou Krugman, Victor Perrin)
32. Homecoming (6/28/59; Harry Bartell, Lou Krugman, Ken Lynch, Jack Moyles, and Barney Phillips)
33. Comanche (7/5/59; Sam Edwards, Barbara Eiler, Jack Moyles, and Victor Perrin)
34. Young Gun (7/12/59; Harry Bartell, Virginia Christine, Harry Cook, Sam Edwards, and Vic Perrin)
35. Deliver the Body (7/19/59; Harry Bartell, Richard Crenna, Bartlett Robinson, and James Westerfield)
36. The Wager (7/26/59; Lynn Allen, Lawrence Dobkin, Victor Perrin, and Barney Phillips)
37. High Wire (8/2/59)
38. Finn Alley (8/9/59; Waldo Emerson, Patty Gallagher, and Joseph Kearns)
39. The Lady (8/16/59; Virginia Christine)
40. Bonanza (8/23/59; Harry Batrell, Helen Kleeb, James Nusser, and Bartlett Robinson)
41. Love Birds (8/30/59; Jack Moyles and Richard Perkins)
42. All That Glitters (9/6/59; Eleanor Barry, Don Diamond, Jack Edwards, and Victor Perrin)
43. Treasure Hunt (9/13/59; Virginia Christine, Joseph Cranston, Joel Davis, and Barney Phillips)
44. Stardust (9/20/59; Jeanne Bates, Tim Graham, and Norma Jean Nilsson)
45. Like Father (9/27/59; Paul Dubov, Sam Edwards, Shirley Mitchell, Ralph Moody, Ann Morrison, and Jack Moyles)
46. Contessa Marie Desmoulins (10/4/59)
47. Stopover in Tombstone (10/11/59; Lawrence Dobkin, James Nusser, Bartlett Robinson, and Peggy Webber)
48. Brothers Lost (10/18/59; Lawrence Dobkin, Tim Graham, and Ann Morrison)
49. When in Rome (10/25/59; Ralph Moody, Jack Moyles, Victor Perrin, and Barney Phillips)
50. Wedding Day (11/1/59; Parley Baer, Eleanor Berry, Sam Edwards, Robert Robertson, and Bartlett Robinson)
51. Assignment in Stone's Crossing (11/8/59; Harry Bartell, Joseph Cranston, Victor Perrin, and Bartlett Robinson)
52. Landfall (11/15/59; Virginia Christine, Virginia Gregg, Lou Krugman, Ralph Moody, and Barney Phillips)
53. Fair Fugitive (11/22/59; Harry Bartell, Lillian Buyeff, and Don Diamond)

54. Bitter Vengeance (11/29/59; Jeanne Bates and Barney Phillips)
55. Anything I Want (12/6/59; Victor Perrin and Walter Stocker)
56. Out of Evil (12/13/59; Lynn Allen, Virginia Christine, Joseph Kearns, and Walter Stocker)
57. Range Carnival (12/20/59; Dick Beals, Lillian Buyeff, Ralph Moody, Jack Moyles, and Vic Perrin)
58. About Face (12/27/59; Lynn Allen, Harry Bartell, Lawrence Dobkin, and Sam Edwards)
59. Return Engagement (1/3/60)
60. The Lonely One (1/10/60; Jeanne Bates, Paul Dubov, and Jack Moyles)
61. French Leave (1/17/60; Harry Bartell, Marvin Miller, Shirley Mitchell, and Barney Phillips)
62. Nataemhon (1/24/60; Lilian Buyeff and Joseph Kearns)
63. Bad Bert (1/31/60; Larry Dobkin, James Nusser, Bartlett Robinson and Peggy Webber)
64. The Boss (2/7/60; Larry Dobkin, Tim Graham, Ann Morrison, Vic Perrin and Herb Vigron)
65. Bring Him Back Alive (2/14/60)
66. That Was No Lady (2/21/60; Harry Bartell, Howard McNear, Jeanette Nolan, and Victor Perrin)
67. Dollhouse in Diamond Springs (2/28/60; Harry Bartell, Betty Harper, and Clayton Post)
68. Somebody Out There Hates Me (3/6/60; Harry Bartell, Don Diamond, and Tim Graham)
69. Montana Vendetta (3/13/60; Paul Dubov, Ralph Moody, and Barney Phillips)
70. Caesar's Wife (3/20/60; Lynn Allen, Larry Dobkin, Bill Idelson and Jack Moyles)
71. They Told Me You Were Dead (3/27/60; Lillian Buyeff, Lou Krugman, Ralph Moody, James Nusser and Bartlett Robinson)
72. Shanghai Is a Verb (4/3/60; Edgar Barrier, Harry Bartell, Virginia Christine, Tim Graham, Charles Lung, and Barney Phillips)
73. So True, Mr. Barnum (4/10/60; Lawrence Dobkin, Sam Edwards, and Barney Phillips)
74. Prunella's Fella (4/17/60; Larry Dobkin, Bill Idelson, Vic Perrin and Peggy Webber)
75. Irish Luck (4/24/60; Harry Bartell, Jeanne Bates and Jack Moyles)
76. Dressed to Kill (5/1/60; Parley Baer, Eleanor Barry, Jack Edwards, Jack Moyles and Jim Nusser)
77. Pat Murphy (5/8/60; Lawrence Dobkin, Virginia Gregg, Frank Katy, and Victor Perrin)
78. Lina Countryman (5/15/50; Russell Arms, Harry Bartell, Jeanne Bates, and Charles Lung)
79. Lucky Penny (5/22/60; Joseph Kearns and Ralph Moody)
80. Dusty (5/29/60; Dick Beals, Sam Edwards, Shirley Mitchell, and Bartlett Robinson)
81. Apache Concerto (6/5/60; Eleanor Barry, Larry Dubov, Joseph Kearns and Barney Phillips)
82. The Search for Wyllie Dawson (6/12/50; Harry Bartell, Don Diamond, Jack Edwards, Bartlett Robinson, and Peggy Webber)
83. Too, Too Solid Town (6/19/50; Joseph Kearns, Vic Perrin, and Barney Phillips)
84. Doctor From Vienna (6/26/50; Harry Bartell, Shirley Mitchell, and Peggy Webber)
85. Dad-Blamed Luck (7/3/60; Virginia Christine, Virginia Gregg, Forrest Lewis, Jack Moyles, and Barney Phillips)
86. Five Days to Yuma (7/10/60; Parley Baer, Tim Graham, Joseph Kearns, Jack Moyles, William Redfield, and Peggy Webber)
87. Little Guns (7/17/60; Lawrence Dobkin, Virginia Gregg, Joseph Kearns, and William Redfield)
88. Delta Queen (7/24/60; Harry Bartell)
89. My Son Must Die (7/31/60; Lillian Buyeff, Virginia Gregg, Vic Perrin, and Anne Whitfield)
90. Visa [Part One] (8/7/60; Harry Bartell, Don Diamond, Jack Edwards, and Billy Idelson)
91. Extended Visa [Part Two] (8/14/60; Russell Arms, Harry Bartell, Don Diamond, and Billy Idelson)
92. The Warrant (8/21/60; Harry Bartell,

Lawrence Dobkin, and Victor Perrin)

93. For the Birds (8/28/60; Virginia Gregg, Hugh Katy, Joseph Kearns, and Bartlett Robinson)
94. Eat Crow (9/4/60; Virginia Gregg, Ralph Moody, Vic Perrin, and Barney Phillips)
95. Deadline (9/11/60; Jeanne Bates, Lawrence Dobkin, Tim Graham, and Charlie Lung)
96. Nellie Watson's Boy (9/18/60; Sam Edwards and Ken Lynch)
97. Bringing Up Ollie (9/25/60; Russell Arms, Ralph Moody, and Anne Whitfield)
98. Talika (10/2/60; Lillian Buyeff, Don Diamond, Ken Lynch, and Victor Perrin)
99. Sam Crow (10/9/60; Forrest Lewis, Shirley Mitchell, and Jack Moyles)
100. Stardust (10/16/60; Jeanne Bates, Lawrence Dobkin, Tim Graham, and Anne Whitfield)
101. Hell Knows No Fury (10/23/60; Lynn Allen, Russell Arms, Jack Moyles, and Olan Soule)
102. Oil (10/30/60; Billy Idelson, Frank Katy, Marvin Miller, Ralph Moody, and Jack Moyles)
103. The Odds (11/6/60; Harry Bartell, Dick Beals, and Barney Phillips)
104. The Map (11/13/60; Virginia Christine, Tim Graham, Ken Lynch, and Victor Perrin)
105. Martha Nell (11/20/60; Sam Edwards, Charles Lung, Jack Moyles, Bartlett Robinson, and Anne Whitfield)
106. From Here to Boston (11/27/60; Lynn Allen, John James, Vic Perrin and Bartlett Robinson)

Hello, Americans

Under the auspices of the CIA, Orson Welles produced and directed this series of dramas and documentaries concerning Latin America. Carmen Miranda was guest on the first broadcast, musician Tito Guizar was featured in the eighth. Orson Welles was, of course, narrator and performer. Lud Gluskin supplied the music. Broadcast over CBS, Sunday evenings from 8 to 8:30 pm, EST. Orson Welles was unable to attend the eighth broadcast because of illness. Due to the lack of a sponsor, the series bowed out after twelve broadcasts.

1. The Life of Carmen Miranda (11/15/42; Carmen Miranda)
2. The Christ of the Andes (11/22/42; Ray Collins, Hans Conried, Pedro de Cordova, Gerald Mohr, Agnes Moorehead, and Edmund O'Brien)
3. Santa Domingo — Haiti (11/29/42; Ray Collins and Hans Conried)
4. The Alphabet of the Islands [part one] (12/6/42; Ray Collins, Hans Conried, Agnes Moorehead, Ted Reid, and Miguelito Valdez)
5. The Alphabet of the Islands [part two] (12/13/42; Lou Merrill and Gerald Mohr)
6. The Story of Abendigo, the Slave (12/20/42; Norman Field, Gerald Mohr, and Ted Reid)
7. The Bad Will Ambassador (12/27/42; John Tucker Battle, Hans Conried, Pedro de Cordova, Norman Field, and Ted Reid)
8. Rhythms of the Americas (1/3/43; Tito Guizar, Dick Joy, Sir Lancelot, and Miguelito Valdez)
9. Mexico (1/10/43; Ray Collins, Hans Conried, Laird Cregar, Lou Merrill, and Agnes Moorehead)
10. Deed to the Town (1/17/43; Joseph Cheshire, Ed Jerome, Jack Mass, Frank Readick, Louise Solomon, and Karl Swenson)

11. Romantic Rhythms of the Americas (1/24/43; Migualito Lopez and Carlos Romariz)

12. Pan-Americanism (1/31/43; Ray Collins)

Here's to Youth

Taking over the time slot of *That They Might Live*, this NBC series was broadcast Saturday afternoons from 1 to 1:30 pm, EST. A few Hollywood stars guested on these broadcasts, dramas dealing with moral and social issues and directed towards the young. *Here's to Youth* originated from New York, but the final episodes originated from London, England.

1. Young Americans in Crisis (1/15/44; Helen Hayes)
2. Trailer Town's Children (1/22/44)
3. Dad's in the Army (1/29/44)
4. Till the Boy Comes Home (2/5/44)
5. Latchkey Children (2/12/44)
6. Our Nomad Families (2/19/44)
7. Danger — Mother Working (2/26/44)
8. The Melting Pot Boils (3/4/44)
9. Help Wanted (3/11/44)
10. Johnny Comes Marching Home (3/18/44)
11. Castle Orchestra (3/25/44)
12. Johnny Comes Marching Home (4/1/44)
13. Strength for America (4/8/44)
14. -----(4/15/44)
15. -----(4/22/44)
16. -----(4/29/44)
17. -----(5/6/44; Governor Earl Warren of California)
18. -----(5/13/44)
19. Freedom's Children (5/20/44)
20. School's Out (5/27/44)
21. Talent in the Balance (6/3/44)
22. Life Begins at Seventeen (6/10/44)
23. Play it Safe (6/17/44)
24. A Lost Parent (6/24/44)
25. Life Without Father (7/1/44)
26. Good Old Summertime (7/8/44; Eddie Cantor)
27. What Price Violence? (7/15/44)
28. World Without End (7/22/44)
29. Autumn Leaves (7/29/44; Alan Hale)
30. School, A War Time Job (8/5/44)
31. Faith of Our Fathers (8/12/44)
32. Service of Youth [part one] (8/19/44)
33. Service of Youth [part two] (8/26/44)

Heritage

Sponsored by *Life* magazine, this series presented historical dramas involving world history. It was broadcast on ABC Thursday evenings 8:30–9 pm, EST. This documentary drama series presented different ways of life and history ranging from Benjamin Franklin's innovative ideas, Napoleon's conquest of the Western World from witchcraft, the Salem Trials, and the tradition of Knighthood. Geoffrey Chaucer's "The Wife of Bath" was dramatized in episode five. The influence of the little red schoolhouse on American education was presented in episode sixteen. Joe College, a Medieval student of Life, for whom higher-education institutions are now named, was dramatized by Eddie Albert. Half way through the series, various Hollywood stars began appearing on the program in an attempt to raise the ratings. For the New Year, a documentary on how time has been kept track of throughout the ages was presented. Tales of Boccaccio's *The Decameron* were presented in episode fifteen.

1. The Theories of Leonardo da Vinci (12/11/52)
2. Bill Shakespeare in America (12/18/52)
3. Christmas Traditions (12/25/52)
4. Time (1/1/53)
5. The Wife of Bath (1/8/53)
6. The Cultural Influence of Benjamin Franklin (1/15/53)
7. Freedom of Curiosity (1/22/53)
8. Languages (1/29/53)
9. Marco Polo (2/5/53)
10. Joseph Lister (2/12/53)
11. Knighthood (2/19/53)
12. The Lewis and Clark Expedition (2/26/53)
13. Blood [part one] (3/5/53)
14. Blood [part two] (3/12/53)
15. The Decameron (3/19/53)
16. School Days (3/26/53)
17. The English Bible (4/2/53)
18. The Extraordinary Doctor (4/9/53)
19. The Man of Liberty (4/16/53; Raymond Massey)
20. Plague (4/23/53; Boris Karloff)
21. The Crusades (4/30/53; Sir Cedric Hardwicke)
22. Napoleon (5/7/53; Conrad Nagel)
23. Joe College, 1273 A.D. (5/14/53; Eddie Albert)
24. Samuel Johnson (5/21/53; Brian Aherne)
25. The History of the Coronation (5/28/53; Basil Rathbone)
26. Semmelweis, His Medical Contributions (6/4/53)
27. Commodore Perry's Historic Visit to Japan (6/11/53)
28. The Louisiana Purchase (6/18/53)
29. The Conquest of Mt. Everest (6/25/53)
30. The Jews in America (7/2/53)
31. The Magna Carta (7/9/53)
32. The Story of the Mails (7/16/53)
33. Women (7/23/53)
34. The Civil War (7/30/53)
35. The Story of Simon Bolivar (8/6/53)
36. The Puritans (8/13/53)
37. Lafayette in America (8/20/53)
38. Witchcraft (8/27/53)
39. How Old Is Mother Earth? (9/3/53)
40. The Farmer and Politics (9/10/53)
41. The Canterbury Tales (9/17/53)
42. Ballads of Our Contemporary Ancestors (9/24/53)

A History of Western Music

This musical anthology lasted only three episodes before being pulled from the air. Many others were originally scheduled. It was broadcast over NBC, Sunday afternoons from 4 to 4:30 pm, EST.

1. Gregorian Chant to the Twentieth Century (9/5/54)
2. The Thirteenth and Fourteenth Century [part one] (9/12/54)
3. The Thirteenth and Fourteenth Century [part two] (9/19/54)

Hollywood Hotel

Known as the first "blackmailing" radio program aimed towards Holly-wood stars, this series featured various twenty-minute adaptations of movies, current and past, chosen by Louella Parsons. Parsons was the host of the series, and as powerful as she was — writing the largest-circulated Hollywood gossip columns in the country — Hollywood stars had no other choice but to appear on her program. Parsons had so much influence in Hollywood that a bad review from her mouth meant no returns at the box office. A good review from Parsons made many a movie soar to the top of the weekly charts. The fact that a movie from almost every major Hollywood studio was featured on this program proved just how much power Louella Parsons had. Films from Twentieth-Century Fox, MGM, RKO, United Artists, Republic, Columbia, Paramount, Goldwyn, and others can be found in the log below.

The Campbell Soups Company was the sponsor for the entire run. The series went off the air in December of 1938 when Campbell decided to drop sponsorship for a more favorable series, *The Campbell Playhouse.* The "War of the Worlds" panic broadcast in October attracted their attention, and the company left *Hollywood Hotel* for a promising up-and-comer named Orson Welles. Dick Powell was the master of ceremonies from episode 1 to 118 (except 102 and 103), Fred MacMurray from 119 to 133, Jerry Cooper from 134 to 153 and 167 to 172, Ken Murray from 154 to 166 and 173 to 179, Frank Parker from 180 to 192, Herbert Marshall from 193 to 198, and William Powell from 199 to 205.

Raymond Paige was the orchestra leader and led the music for each drama, being replaced by Victor Young beginning September 9, 1938. Frances Langford was a featured singer throughout the entire series when she was subbed by Lois Ravel from 10/23/36 to 11/6/36, Shirley Ross from 4/16/37 to 5/7/37, and Loretta Lee from 11/19/37 to 12/3/37. George MacGarret was the first director, later being replaced by Bill Backer, who stepped down on December 18, 1937. Fred Ibbet began on December 25, 1937, finishing off on April 8, 1938. Brewster Morgan began April 15, 1938, and directed till the end of the series.

Wyllis Cooper wrote all of the scripts for the first 192 episodes; John McClain took over afterwards. Duane Thompson played "Sally," the telephone girl. Comedian El Brendel appeared on the first nine episodes.

Louella Parsons interviewed the Hollywood guests each week, about their film roles and their personal lives. After *Hollywood Hotel* went off for the summer of 1938, it returned sans Parsons, who needed time to work on her column writing. William Powell took over as host and emcee for this last run.

From October 5, 1934, to April 26, 1935, *Hollywood Hotel* was broadcast on CBS, Friday evenings from 9:30 to 10:30 pm, EST. From May 3, 1935, to December 2, 1938, the program moved back a half-hour from 9 to 10 pm, EST. Episode 167 presented two dramas, broadcast at a special time. "Tom Sawyer" was broadcast from 4 to 5 pm, and Lionel Barrymore's annual presentation, "A Christmas Carol," was broadcast from 5 to 5:45 pm.

1. Imitation of Life (10/5/34; Claudette Colbert and Warren William)
2. Clive of India (10/12/34; Ronald Colman and Loretta Young)
3. China Seas (10/19/34; Jean Harlow)
4. Du Barry (10/25/34; Dolores Del Rio, Victor Jory, and Reginald Owen)
5. Music in the Air (11/2/34; John Boles and Gloria Swanson)
6. Within the Law (11/9/34; Myrna Loy and William Powell)
7. Outcast Lady (11/16/34; Constance Bennett and Herbert Marshall)
8. Flirtation Walk (11/23/34; Al Jolson and Ruby Keeler)
9. Lives of a Bangal Lancer (11/30/34; Gary Cooper and Sir Guy Standing)
10. Rhumba (12/7/34; Carole Lombard, Lynne Overman, and George Raft)
11. Carnival (12/14/34; Sally Eilers and Lee Tracy)
12. After Office Hours (12/21/34; Stuart Erwin and Clark Gable)
13. Romance in Manhattan (12/28/34; Francis Lederer)
14. Living on Velvet (1/4/35; George Brent and Kay Francis)
15. Under Pressure (1/11/35; Edmund Lowe and Victor McLaglen)
16. Rejuvenation of Aunt Mary (1/18/35; James Busch, L. Harmer, and May Robson)
17. Roberta (1/25/35; Fred Astaire and Irene Dunne)
18. The Whole Town's Talking (2/1/35; Jean Arthur and Edward G. Robinson)
19. The Wedding Night (2/8/35; Ralph Bellamy and Anna Sten)
20. Follies Bergere (2/15/35; Maurice Chevalier)
21. Les Miserables (2/22/35; Frederic March)
22. Paris in the Spring (3/1/35; Mary Ellis and Tullio Carminatti)
23. Vanesa (3/8/35; Ruth Gordon, Robert Montgomery, and May Robson)
24. Becky Sharp (3/15/35; Frances Dee, Miriam Hopkins, and Alan Mowbray)
25. Sarah and Son (3/22/35; Ruth Chatterton and Louis Hayward)
26. The Traveling Saleslady (3/29/35; Joan Blondell, Glenda Farrell, and William Gargan)
27. Alibi Ike (4/5/35; Joe E. Brown, Roscoe Karns, and William Frawley)
28. Let 'Em Have It (4/12/35; Richard Arlen, Virginia Bruce, and Bruce Cabot)
29. The Flame Within (4/19/35; Edmund Goulding, Ann Harding, and Herbert Marshall)
30. Goin' to Town (4/26/35; Paul Cavanaugh and Mae West)
31. Love Me Forever (5/3/35; Michael Bartlett and Grace Moore)
32. [No Drama] (5/10/35; Bert Wheeler and Bob Woolsey)
33. The Girl from Tenth Avenue (5/17/35; Bette Davis and Ian Hunter)
34. Under the Pampas Moon (5/24/35; Warner Baxter, Ketti Gallien, and J. Caroll Naish)
35. [No Drama] (5/31/35; Maria Jeritza)
36. In Caliente (6/7/35; Leo Carillo, Dolores Del Rio, and Pat O'Brien)
37. So Red the Rose (6/14/35; Randolph Scott and Margaret Sullavan)
38. Return of Peter Grimm (6/21/35; Lionel Barrymore and Georgie Breakstone)
39. Thunder in the Night (6/28/35; Una O'Connor, Edmund Lowe, and Karen Morley)
40. The Last Outpost (7/5/35; Cary Grant, Gertrude Michael, and Claude Rains)
41. She Married Her Boss (7/12/35; Claudette Colbert, Jean Dixon, and Melvyn Douglas)
42. Dark Angel (7/19/35; Fredric March, Herbert Marshall, and Merle Oberon)
43. The Valiant (7/26/35; Paul Muni and Jean Muir)
44. The Gay Deception (8/2/35; Frances Dee and Frances Lederer)

45. China Seas (8/9/35; Clark Gable and Jean Harlow)
46. Virginia House (8/16/35; D. Dickerson, Stepin Fetchit, and Walter C. Kelly)
47. Rich Man's Daughter (8/23/35; Joan Bennett, Billie Burke, and George Raft)
48. Page Miss Glory (8/30/35; Marian Davies, Frank McHugh, and Pat O'Brien)
49. A Tale of Two Cities (9/6/35; Elizabeth Allen and Ronald Colman)
50. Peter Ibbetson (9/13/35; Gary Cooper and Ann Harding)
51. Hands Across the Table (9/20/35; Carole Lombard and Marie Prevost)
52. Barbary Coast (9/27/35; Miriam Hopkins and Joel McCrea)
53. Rose of the Rancho (10/4/35; John Boles and Gladys Swarthout)
54. The Magnificent Obsession (10/11/35; Irene Dunne, Sarah Haden, and Robert Taylor)
55. Shipmates Forever (10/18/35; Ruby Keeler, Joe King, and Dick Powell)
56. A Night at the Opera (10/25/35; Chico Marx, Groucho Marx, Harpo Marx, and Mary Pickford)
57. I Found Stella Parish (11/1/35; Kay Francis, Ian Hunter, and Baby Sybil Jason)
58. Annie Oakley (11/8/35; Preston Foster and Barbara Stanwyck)
59. Her Master's Voice (11/15/35; Laura H. Crewes, Edward Everett Horton, and Ian Hunter)
60. Captain Blood (11/22/35; Olivia de Havilland, Errol Flynn, and Basil Rathbone)
61. Riff Raff (11/29/35; Joseph Calleia, Jean Harlow, and Spencer Tracy)
62. Ah, Wilderness (12/6/35; Lionel Barrymore, Eric Linden, and Cecelia Parker)
63. Professional Soldier (12/13/35; Constance Collier, Freddie Bartholomew, and Victor McLaglen)
64. Desire (12/20/35; Gary Cooper and Marlene Dietrich)
65. Show Boat (12/27/35; Dick Powell, Helen Westley, and Charles Winninger)
66. The Lady Consents (1/10/36; Ann Harding and Herbert Marshall)
67. Next Time We Love (1/17/36; James Stewart and Margaret Sullavan)
68. Don't Get Personal (1/24/36; James Dunn and Sally Eilers)
69. Sutter's Gold (1/31/36; Edward Arnold and Binnie Barnes)
70. These Three (2/7/36; Marian Hopkins, Otto Kruger, Joel McCrea, and Merle Oberon)
71. Small Town Girl (2/14/36; Janet Gaynor, Lewis Stone, and Robert Taylor)
72. Love Before Breakfast (2/21/36; Preston Foster and Carole Lombard)
73. Country Doctor (2/28/36; Jean Hersholt and Dorothy Peterson)
74. Everybody's Old Man (3/6/36; Irwin Cobb, N. Foster, and Rochelle Hudson)
75. Thirteen Hours By Air (3/13/36; Joan Bennett, Fred MacMurray, and Zasu Pitts)
76. Little Lord Fauntleroy (3/20/36; Freddie Bartholomew, Dolores Costello, and C. Aubrey Smith)
77. The Informer (3/27/36; Heather Angel, Margot Grahame, and Victor McLaglen)
78. I Married a Doctor (4/3/36; Gracie Allen, George Burns, Josephine Hutchinson, Guy Kibbee, and Pat O'Brien)
79. The Moon's Our Home (4/10/36; Henry Fonda and Margaret Sullavan)
80. And So They Were Married (4/17/36; Mary Astor, Edith Fellows, and Bert Lytell)
81. Big Brown Eyes (4/24/36; Joan Bennett and Cary Grant)
82. Dangerous (5/1/36; Bette Davis and Allan Jones)
83. Bullets or Ballots (5/8/36; Joan Blondell, Kay Kenny, James Melton, and Edward G. Robinson)
84. The Case Against Mrs. Ames (5/15/36; George Brent and Madeleine Carroll)
85. To Mary, With Love (5/22/36; Warner Baxter, Ian Hunter, Myrna Loy, and Claire Trevor)
86. The White Angel (5/29/36; Kay Francis, Ian Hunter, and Donald Woods)

87. The Bride Walks Out (6/5/36; Helen Broderick, Gene Raymond, and Barbara Stanwyck)
88. The Devil-Doll (6/19/36; Lionel Barrymore and Maureen O'Sullivan)
89. My American Wife (6/26/36; Francis Lederer and Ann Sothern)
90. Ramona (7/3/36; Don Ameche, Katherine DeMille, Kent Taylor, and Loretta Young)
91. Sing, Baby Sing (7/10/36; Alice Faye, Ted Healy, Patsy Kelly, Adolph Menjou)
92. Anthony Adverse [part one] (7/17/36; Olivia de Havilland, Claude Rains, Gale Sondergaard, and Donald Woods)
93. Anthony Adverse [part two] (7/24/36; Olivia de Havilland, Claude Rains, Gale Sondergaard, and Donald Woods)
94. Adventure in Manhattan (7/31/36; Jean Arthur and Joel McCrea)
95. His Brother's Wife (8/7/36; Barbara Stanwyck and Robert Taylor)
96. Walking on Air (8/14/36; Gene Raymond and Ann Southern)
97. Dodsworth (8/21/36; Ruth Chatterton and Walter Huston)
98. China Clipper (8/28/36; Ross Alexander, Pat O'Brien, and Beverly Roberts)
99. Romeo and Juliet (9/4/36; Edna May Oliver and Norma Shearer)
100. Winterset (9/11/36; Eduardo Cianelli, Margo, and Burgess Meredith)
101. Valiant Is the Word for Carrie (9/18/36; Gladys George, Isabel Jewel, and Arline Judge)
102. Give Me Your Heart (9/25/36; Gracie Allen, George Brent, George Burns, and Kay Francis)
103. Can This Be Dixie? (10/2/36; Slim Summerville, Ruth Warwick, and Jane Withers)
104. Charge of the Light Brigade (10/9/36; Olivia de Havilland and Errol Flynn)
105. The Devil Is a Sissy (10/16/36; Freddie Bartholomew, Jackie Cooper, and Mickey Rooney)
106. The Plough and the Stars (10/23/36; Preston Foster and Barbara Stanwyck)
107. Come and Get It (10/30/36; Edward Arnold and Frances Farmer)
108. Three Men On A Horse (11/6/36; Joan Blondell, Guy Kibbee, and Frank McHugh)
109. Born to Dance (11/13/36; Buddy Ebsen, Clark Gable, Jean Harlow, Allan Jones, Myrna Loy, Una Merkel, Eleanor Powell, James Stewart, and Robert Taylor)
110. Theodora Goes Wild (11/20/36; Melvyn Douglas and Irene Dunne)
111. Garden of Allah (11/27/36; Mary Astor and Charles Boyer)
112. Maid of Salem (12/4/36; Claudette Colbert and Fred MacMurray)
113. Lloyds of London (12/11/36; Madeline Carroll, Tyrone Power, and Douglas Scott)
114. One in a Million (12/18/36; The Ritz Bros., Alice Faye, Sonja Henie, and Adolph Menjou)
115. A Christmas Carol (12/25/36; John Barrymore)
116. Career Woman (1/1/37; Isabel Jewell, Claire Trevor, and Michael Whalen)
117. Three Smart Girls (1/8/37; Alice Brady, Deanna Durbin, and Charles Winninger)
118. Swing High, Swing Low (1/15/37; Carol Lombard, Fred MacMurray, and Tony Martin)
119. God's Country and the Woman (1/22/37; George Brent and Beverly Roberts)
120. Green Light (1/29/37; Errol Flynn and Anita Louise)
121. On the Avenue (2/5/37; Irving Berlin, Eddie Cantor, Madeline Carroll, and Alice Faye)
122. Sea Devils (2/12/37; Preston Foster, Ida Lupino, and Victor MacLaglen)
123. Black Legion (2/19/37; Humphrey Bogart and Gloria Dickson)
124. Interns Can't Take Money (2/26/37; Gracie Allen, George Burns, Joel McCrea, Hal Roach, and Barbara Stanwyck)
125. Nancy Steele Is Missing (3/5/37;

June Lang, Warden Lawes, Peter Lorre, Victor MacLaglen, and Paul Muni)

126. Love Is News (3/12/37; Gracie Allen, George Burns, Tyrone Power, Oscar Straus and Loretta Young)
127. Top of the Town (3/19/37; Mischa Auer, Hugh Herbert, George Murphy, and G. Niesen)
128. Call It a Day (3/26/37; Olivia de Havilland, Ian Hunter, Anita Louise, and Roland Young)
129. Maytime (4/2/37; Jeanette MacDonald)
130. The Woman I Love (4/9/37; Colin Clive, Louis Hayward, and Miriam Hopkins)
131. Marked Woman (4/16/37; Humphrey Bogart, Eduardo Ciannelli, and Bette Davis)
132. Wake Up and Live (4/23/37; Ben Bernie, Alice Faye, Jack Haley, and Walter Winchell)
133. A Star Is Born (4/30/37; Andy Devine, Gracie Fields, Janet Gaynor, Fredric March, and Adolph Menjou)
134. The Prince and the Pauper (5/7/37; Errol Flynn, and Bill and Bobby Mauch)
135. The Go-Getter (5/14/37; George Brent, C. Wakefield Cadman, Anita Louise, Charles Winninger)
136. I Met Him in Paris (5/21/37; Claudette Colbert, Melvyn Douglas, and Robert Young)
137. Cafe Metropole (5/28/37; Tyrone Power, Jack Smart, and Loretta Young)
138. Kid Galahad (6/4/37; Bette Davis and Edward G. Robinson)
139. A Day at the Races (6/11/37; Gus Edwards, George Jessel, Al Jolson, Chico Marx, Groucho Marx, and Harpo Marx)
140. Last Train from Madrid (6/18/37; Gail Patrick, Anthony Quinn, and Gilbert Roland)
141. Singing Marine (6/25/37; Hugh Herbert, Allan Jenkins, and Dick Powell)
142. Between Two Women (7/2/37; Virginia Bruce, Maureen O'Sullivan,

and Franchot Tone)
143. It's All Yours (7/9/37; Madeleine Gray, Frances Lederer, and J.P. Nugent)
144. Broadway Melody of 1938 (7/16/37; Judy Garland, Eleanor Powell, Robert Taylor, and Sophie Tucker)
145. Exclusive (7/23/37; Ida Lupino, Fred MacMurray, and Charlie Ruggles)
146. Make a Wish (7/30/37; Bobby Breen, Marion Claire, and Basil Rathbone)
147. High, Wide and Handsome (8/6/37; Irene Dunne and Randolph Scott)
148. One Mile From Heaven (8/13/37; Douglas Fowley, Judge B. Lindsay, and Claire Trevor)
149. Dead End (8/20/37; Humphrey Bogart, Andrea Leeds, and Joel McCrea)
150. One Hundred Men and a Girl (8/27/37; Deanna Durbin, Andrea Leeds, and Joel McCrea)
151. Mr. Dodd Takes the Air (9/3/37; Kenny Baker, George Jessel, Frank McHugh, and Gertrude Michael)
152. Wife, Doctor and Nurse (9/10/37; Warner Baxter and Loretta Young)
153. That Certain Woman (9/17/37; Donald Crisp, Bette Davis, Ian Hunter, Anita Louise)
154. Life Begins in College (9/24/37; The Ritz Bros., Joan Davis, and Gloria Stewart)
155. [No drama] (10/1/37; John Beal, Gladys George, and Warren William)
156. Lancer Spy (10/8/37; Dolores Del Rio, Peter Lorre, and George Sanders)
157. The Awful Truth (10/15/37; Ralph Bellamy, Irene Dunne, and Cary Grant)
158. The Barrier (10/22/37; Leo Carrillo, J. Ellison, and Jean Parker)
159. Hurricane (10/29/37; Mary Astor, Jon Hall, Andrea Leeds, and C. Aubrey Smith)
160. Damsel in Distress (11/5/37; Gracie Allen, Fred Astaire, George Burns, and Joan Fontaine)
161. The Great Garrick (11/12/37; Brian Aherne and Olivia de Havilland)

162. Second Honeymoon (11/19/37; Sally Blaine, Stuart Erwin, Tyrone Power, and M. Weaver)
163. First Lady (11/26/37; Kay Francis, Preston Foster, and Vera Teasdale)
164. True Confession (12/3/37; Carole Lombard and Fred MacMurray)
165. The Lady Misbehaves (12/10/37; Sally Eilers, Neil Hamilton, and Joseph Schildkraut)
166. Bulldog Drummond's Revenge (12/17/37; Elaine Barrie, John Barrymore, and John Howard)
167. Tom Sawyer (12/25/37; Victor Jory, Tommy Kelly, Jackie Moran, and May Robson) "A Christmas Carol (12/25/37; Lionel Barrymore)
168. She's Got Everything (12/31/37; Victor Moore, Gene Raymond, and Ann Sothern)
169. Tovarich (1/7/38; Amos 'n' Andy, Charles Boyer, Claudette Colbert, Melville Cooper, and Basil Rathbone)
170. Hollywood Hotel (1/14/38; Hugh Herbert, Lola Lane, and Dick Powell)
171. In Old Chicago (1/21/38; Don Ameche, John Barrymore, Alice Faye, Brian Donlevy, and Tyrone Power)
172. Radio City Revels (1/28/38; Kenny Baker, Bob Burns, Ann Miller, and Jackie Oakie)
173. Little Miss Roughneck (2/4/38; Leo Carillo and Edith Fellows)
174. Dangerous to Know (2/11/38; Lloyd Nolan, Gail Patrick, Akim Tamiroff, and Anna May Wong)
175. Swing Your Lady (2/18/38; Humphrey Bogart, Louise Fazenda, Frank McHugh, and Nat Pendleton)
176. Romance in the Dark (2/25/38; John Barrymore, John Boles, and Gladys Swarthout)
177. I Met My Love Again (3/11/38; Joan Bennett, Henry Fonda, and Tim Hope)
178. A Slight Case of Murder (3/18/38; Amos 'n' Andy, R. Donnelly, Allen Jenkins, and E.G. Robinson)
179. Jezebel (3/25/38; George Brent, Bette Davis, Henry Fonda, and Helen Gahagan)

180. Good-bye Broadway (4/1/38; Alice Brady, Frank Parker, and Charles Winninger)
181. Battle of Broadway (4/8/38; Brian Donlevy, Louise Hovick, and Victor McLaglen)
182. The Adventures of Marco Polo (4/15/38; Gary Cooper, Sigrid Gurie, Alan Hale, and Basil Rathbone)
183. Fools for Scandal (4/22/38; Fernand Gravet and Carole Lombard)
184. Four Men and A Prayer (4/29/38; Richard Greene, David Niven, George Sanders, Loretta Young)
185. Coconut Grove (5/6/38; Ben Blue, Harriet Hilliard, and Fred MacMurray)
186. My Bill (5/13/38; Kay Francis, Bonita Granville, and J. Lytell)
187. Gold Diggers in Paris (5/20/38; Allen Jenkins, H. Herbert, and Rosemary Lane)
188. Under Western Stars (5/27/38; Smiley Burnett, Carol Hughes, and Roy Rogers)
189. Blockade (6/3/38; Joan Bennett, Leo Carillo, Henry Fonda, and Walter Wagner)
190. White Banners (6/10/38; Fay Bainter, Jackie Cooper, Bonita Granville, and Claude Rains)
191. Mother Carey's Chickens (6/17/38; Fay Bainter, J. Ellison, Ruby Keeler, and Anne Shirley)
192. Always Goodbye (6/24/38; Herbert Marshall, Cesar Romero, and Barbara Stanwyck)
193. The Dark Angel (9/9/38; Claudette Colbert)
194. Bulldog Drummond (9/16/38; Charles Butterworth, Hanley Stafford, and H.B. Warner)
195. The Big Softie (9/23/38; Vince Barnett and Josephine Hutchinson)
196. History Is Made at Night (9/30/38; Joan Bennett and Thomas Mitchell)
197. I Met Him in Paris (10/7/38; John McLean, David Niven, and Ginger Rogers)
198. Berkeley Square (10/14/38; Heather Angel and Charles Butterworth)
199. Of Human Bondage (10/21/38; Margaret Sullavan)

200. By Candlelight (10/28/38; Melville Cooper and Ida Lupino)
201. Trouble in Paradise (11/4/38; Miriam Hopkins)
202. Journey's End (11/11/38; Melville Cooper, Burgess Meredith, and H.B. Warner)
203. Tovarich (11/18/38; Charles Butter-worth, J. Calleia, and Louise Rainer)
204. Death Takes a Holiday (11/23/38; Amos 'n' Andy, Gail Paige, and C. Aubrey Smith)
205. The Canary Murder Case (12/2/38; Humphrey Bogart, Glenda Farrell, and Thomas Mitchell)

Hollywood Players

Sponsored by Cresta Blanca Wines, this series was placed in the time slot previously held by *Academy Award Theater*. Adaptations of various movies were presented, with "a company of Hollywood's greatest stars" such as John Garfield, Gregory Peck, Bette Davis, Paulette Goddard, Claudette Colbert, and Joseph Cotten appearing in a semi-rotating basis. The series was broadcast over CBS, Tuesday evenings from 9:30 to 10 pm, EST. Beginning January first, *Hollywood Players* was heard on Wednesday from 10 to 10:30 pm, EST. B. Katz was the orchestra leader. Frank Singham was the announcer. Janet Leigh made her radio debut on the seventeenth broadcast, a special Christmas presentation.

1. The Small Servant (9/3/46; Bette Davis and Rex Harrison)
2. Fallen Sparrow (9/10/46; John Garfield)
3. Skylark (9/17/46; Claudette Colbert)
4. Pride of the Yankees (9/24/46; Joseph Cotten)
5. Rebecca (10/1/46; Joseph Cotten and Joan Fontaine)
6. Golden Boy (10/8/46; John Garfield)
7. Elizabeth the Queen (10/15/46; Bette Davis)
8. Sullivan's Travels (10/22/46; Gregory Peck)
9. Nothing Sacred (10/29/46; Joseph Cotten)
10. Kitty (11/5/46; Paulette Goddard)
11. Heaven Can Wait (11/12/46; Gregory Peck)
12. Affairs of Susan (11/19/46; Joan Fontaine)
13. The Glass Key (11/26/46; Gene Kelly)
14. Standing Room Only (12/3/46; Paulette Goddard)
15. No Time for Comedy (12/10/46; Gregory Peck)
16. Constant Nymph (12/17/46; Joan Fontaine)
17. All Through the House (12/24/46; Joseph Cotten, John Garfield, Gene Kelly, Janet Leigh, and Gregory Peck)
18. Fifth Avenue Girl (1/1/47; Paulette Goddard)
19. Woman in the Window (1/15/47; John Garfield)
20. Random Harvest (1/22/47; Joseph Cotten)
21. Dark Victory (1/29/47; Hume Cronyn and Maureen O'Hara)
22. And Now Tomorrow (2/5/47; Gene Kelly)
23. Diary of a Chambermaid (2/12/47; Paulette Goddard)
24. The Major and the Minor (2/19/47; Joan Fontaine)
25. Vivacious Lady (2/26/47; Paulette Goddard)

Hollywood Sound Stage

Previously titled *The Screen Guild Theater*, this series presented thirteen broadcasts before changing back to its original name. Sustaining, broadcast over CBS, Thursday evenings from 10 to 10:30 pm, EST.

1. The Dark Mirror (12/13/51; Bette Davis and Gary Merrill)
2. Brief Encounter (12/20/51; Joan Fontaine and Herbert Marshall)
3. Call Northside 777 (12/27/51; Dana Andrews and Thomas Gomez)
4. The Secret Heart (1/3/52; Claudette Colbert)
5. Shadow of a Doubt (1/10/52; Ann Blyth and Jeff Chandler)
6. The Ox-Bow Incident (1/17/52; Edward Arnold and Charlie Ruggles)
7. The Postman Always Rings Twice (1/24/52; Eleanor Parker and Richard Widmark)
8. Thirteen Rue Madeleine (1/31/52; Douglas Fairbanks, Jr.)
9. The Informer (2/7/52; Paul Douglas, Isabel Jewell, and Tom Peters)
10. One Way Passage (2/14/52; Frank Lovejoy and Ruth Roman)
11. The Champion (2/21/52; Kirk Douglas and Marilyn Maxwell)
12. Boomerang (2/28/52; Tyrone Power and Jane Wyatt)
13. Dark Victory (3/6/52; Barbara Stanwyck and Carlton Young)

Hollywood Star Playhouse

With original dramas and big name stars in the lead roles, this anthology series brought mystery, comedy, and even serious dramas of life to radio listeners for almost three years. It was broadcast over CBS, Monday evenings from 8 to 8:30 pm, EST, for the first season. The sponsor was Emerson Drug (Bromo Seltzer). There were no sponsors for the second season, broadcast over ABC, Thursday evenings from 8 to 8:30 pm, EST. American Baker sponsored the third season, and the title of the program changed to *Baker's Theater of Stars*. This third run was broadcast over NBC, Sunday afternoons from 5 to 5:30 pm, EST.

For the CBS run, Jeff Alexander supplied the music, and Herb Rawlinson was host. Basil Adlam supplied the music for the ABC run, and Orval Anderson and Irving Howard were hosts. Wendell Holmes was the announcer for the third season. Jack Johnstone produced and directed each broadcast for all three seasons, and Norman Brokenshire was also announcer.

Scripts were originals and adaptations, penned by various writers, including Harold Swanton and Milton Geiger. Episodes 39, 103, 119, 122, and 134 were previously performed on *Suspense*. Episode seven was later dramatized for an episode of television's *Alfred Hitchcock Presents*. Episode forty-two was scripted by Maurice Zimm. Episode one hundred and thirty-two was written by Arch Oboler. Episode eighty-six was based on a short story by Guy de Maupassant. Episode one hundred and four was actually a pilot for a new radio series entitled

"Safari," which was to star Ray Milland. The response from listeners was not too enthusiastic, and nothing became of it. Episode ninety-nine, however, received critical acclaim, and less than a year later, James Stewart starred in his own radio program entitled *The Six Shooter*.

1. Nor Gloom of Night (4/24/50; James Stewart)
2. Hospital Zone — Quiet (5/1/50; Broderic Crawford)
3. Confession (5/8/50; Ray Milland)
4. The Pattern in the Rug (5/15/50; Claire Trevor)
5. Clash by Moonlight (5/22/50; John Lund)
6. Real as Death (5/29/50; Evelyn Keyes)
7. Bang! Bang! You're Dead (6/5/50; David Brian)
8. Sacrifice (6/12/50; Edward Arnold)
9. Venom (6/19/50; Lurene Tuttle and Cornel Wilde)
10. Sound Off, My Love (6/26/50; Dorothy McGuire)
11. A Deep Red Mist (7/3/50; John Hodiak)
12. The Archer (7/10/50; Wendell Corey)
13. Jill Came Tumbling After (7/17/50; Audrey Totter)
14. Honeymoon into Terror (7/24/50; Lee Bowman)
15. The Cave (7/31/50; Van Heflin)
16. Filler for Adventure (8/7/50; Ronald Reagan)
17. Street of Jewels (8/14/50; Dick Powell)
18. Final Entry (8/21/50; Victor Mature)
19. Flute in the Night (8/28/50; Herbert Marshall)
20. Outpost (9/4/50; Richard Widmark)
21. Death Takes a Honeymoon (9/11/50; Mercedes McCambridge)
22. A Question of Time (9/18/50; Anne Baxter)
23. The Man Who Knew Tomorrow (9/25/50; William Powell)
24. Dead or Alive (10/2/50; Ida Lupino)
25. Of Night and the River (10/9/50; Joseph Cotten)
26. Reluctant Witness (10/16/50; Robert Ryan)
27. Death in the Desert (10/23/50; Edmund O'Brien)
28. Black Death (10/30/50; Robert Cummings)
29. Not the Nervous Type (11/6/50; Barbara Stanwyck)
30. Exhibit A (11/13/50; Mel Ferrer)
31. Drums of Yesterday (11/20/50; Rosalind Russell)
32. Strange Vengeance (11/27/50; Barry Sullivan)
33. Revolution (12/4/50; John Payne)
34. Never Count on Murder (12/11/50; Patricia Neal)
35. The Tangled Web (12/18/50; William Holden)
36. Lefty Gallagher's Christmas Carol (12/25/50; Dane Clark)
37. What It's Really Like (1/1/51; Alan Ladd)
38. Dream Job (1/8/51; Joan Bennett)
39. Statement in Full (1/15/51; Joan Crawford)
40. Rabbit Foot (1/22/51; Dick Haymes)
41. Later Than You Think (1/29/51; Victor Mature)
42. Calculated Risk (2/5/51; Vincent Price)
43. Never Count on Murder (2/12/51; Patricia Neal)
44. Death Is a White Swan (2/19/51; Edmund Gwenn)
45. The Face (2/26/51; David Niven)
46. The Unknown (3/5/51; Howard Duff)
47. The Secret Room (3/12/51; MacDonald Carey)
48. The Redheaded Man (3/19/51; Richard Widmark)
49. You'll Never Know When (3/26/51; Anne Baxter)
50. The Perfect Mrs. Chesney (4/2/51; Angela Lansbury)
51. Ledge of Death (4/9/51; Barry Sullivan)
52. The God they Call Gold (4/16/51; Jeff Chandler)
53. Father's Day (4/23/51; Barbara Stanwyck)

54. The Long Way Back (4/30/51; David Brian)
55. Death Is a Right Hook (5/7/51; Dan Dailey)
56. A Ride With a Stranger (5/14/51; William Holden)
57. Specter of the Red Balloon (5/21/51; Mel Ferrer)
58. They Call Me Lucky (5/28/51; John Lund)
59. The Trap (6/4/51; Dean Stockwell)
60. On a Windy Night (6/11/51; Dana Andrews)
61. Blackout (6/18/51; Robert Young)
62. Wanted: Beneficiary [broadcast on a Tuesday] (6/26/51; Dane Clark)
63. The Envelope (7/2/51; Richard Basehart)
64. Knee High to a Corpse (7/9/51; Mickey Rooney)
65. Mindin' My Business (7/16/51; Frank Lovejoy)
66. I Am a Coward (7/26/51; Barbara Stanwyck)
67. Until Death Do Us Part (8/2/51; MacDonald Carey)
68. A Wonderful Disposition (8/9/51)
69. An Obit for Joe (8/16/51; Barry Sullivan)
70. Big Wave (8/23/51; Claire Trevor)
71. Until Midnight (8/30/51; Lee Bowman)
72. Cathedral in the Fens (9/6/51; Douglas Fairbanks, Jr.)
73. Dust of Doomsday (9/13/51; William Bendix)
74. Hour of Truth (9/20/51; Joan Banks, Gerald Mohr, Alan Reed, and Vincent Price)
75. The Professor Stays at Home (9/27/51)
76. The Gun and Miss Greenfield (10/4/51; Anne Baxter)
77. Postage Due (10/11/51; Cornel Wilde)
78. Killer's Moon (10/18/51; Eve Arden)
79. Wedding Present (10/25/51; George Murphy)
80. It Always Comes Up Tails (11/1/51; M. Mitchell)
81. Jack of Diamonds (11/8/51; John Payne)
82. The Night the Moon Went Out (11/15/51; Cesar Romero)
83. No One Will Ever Know (11/22/51; Ray Milland)
84. The Brother of the Ox (11/29/51; Richard Widmark)
85. Solo for the Bowstring (12/6/51; Tyrone Power)
86. The Diary of a Madman (12/13/51; John Lund)
87. The Night Before Dawn (12/20/51; Herbert Marshall)
88. Year of the Devil (12/27/51; Robert Cummings)
89. You're Driving Me Crazy (1/3/52; Dennis O'Keefe)
90. The Frontier (1/10/52; William Conrad, Paul Frees, Virginia Gregg, and Claire Trevor)
91. The Deep Grave (1/17/52; MacDonald Carey)
92. A Letter from Laura (2/24/52; Jane Wyman)
93. Father's Day (3/2/52; Claire Trevor)
94. Hospital Zone — Quiet (3/9/52; Paul Douglas)
95. Companion Wanted (3/16/52; Deborah Kerr)
96. Death Is a Right Hook (3/23/52; Barry Sullivan)
97. Blind Flight (3/30/52; Audrey Totter)
98. The Patient Stranger (4/6/52; Gary Merrill)
99. The Six Shooter (4/13/52; James Stewart)
100. Dream Job (4/20/52; Diana Lynn)
101. Nor Gloom of Night (4/27/52; Alan Young)
102. The Wrong Pair of Shoes (5/4/52; Lee Bowman)
103. Drury's Bones (5/11/52; Herbert Marshall)
104. Safari (5/18/52; Joan Banks, William Conrad, Paul Frees, and Ray Milland)
105. Mrs. Teckey (5/25/52; Barbara Stanwyck)
106. The Man on the Road (6/1/52; Cesar Romero)
107. The Long Shot (6/8/52; David Niven)
108. The Nemesis (6/15/52; Cornel Wilde)
109. Final Entry (6/22/52; Van Heflin)
110. Real as Death (6/29/52; Gloria Grahame)

111. Blonde Puzzle (7/6/52; MacDonald Carey)
112. Not the Nervous Type (7/13/52; Mercedes McCambridge)
113. Step Right Up and Die (7/20/52; John Lund)
114. Tampico Incident (7/27/52; Tony Curtis)
115. The Third Fate (8/3/52; Barbara Stanwyck)
116. Avalanche (8/10/52; Edmund O'Brien)
117. Haunt Me Not (8/17/52; Deborah Kerr)
118. One Minute to Twelve (8/24/52; Richard Basehart)
119. Statement in Full (8/31/52; Marilyn Monroe)
120. The Tenth Planet (9/7/52; Joseph Cotten)
121. The Reluctant Witness (9/14/52; Dennis O'Keefe)
122. The Last Chance (9/21/52; Charlton Heston)
123. Ambush for Two (9/28/52; Barry Sullivan)
124. -----(10/5/52)
125. Sitting Duck (10/12/52; Dane Clark)
126. Nothing to Lose (10/19/52; Ray Milland and Claire Trevor)
127. Quicksand (10/26/52; Dana Andrews)
128. The Big One (11/2/52; M. Mitchell)
129. Double Disaster (11/9/52; Lynn Bari)
130. Diamonds of Gulaga (11/16/52; Cesar Romero)
131. The Joyful Beggar (11/23/52; William Holden)
132. The Word (11/30/52; John Lund)
133. Memory of the Future (12/7/52; Ronald Reagan)
134. End of Aunt Delia (12/14/52; Cornel Wilde)
135. Santa Is No Saint (12/21/52; Broderic Crawford)
136. All Brides Are Beautiful (12/28/52; Ruth Hussey)
137. Match Point (1/4/53; Joanne Dru)
138. The Soil (1/11/53; Barry Sullivan)
139. Blackout (1/18/53; Richard Conte)
140. Encore (1/25/53; Janet Leigh)
141. -----(2/1/53)
142. -----(2/8/53)
143. -----(2/15/53)

Hollywood Stars on Stage

Another anthology series featuring big-name stars from Hollywood. Broadcast over ABC, Sunday evenings from 9:30 to 10 pm, EST. The scripts were originals. The final broadcast of the series was scripted by Arch Oboler.

1. The Joyful Beggar (10/7/51; Jean Wallace and Cornel Wilde)
2. Girl or Ghost? (10/14/51; Arlene Dahl)
3. Operation Manhunt (10/21/51; Bruce Cabot)
4. Come Spring Again (10/28/51; David Brian)
5. The Perfect Gentleman (11/4/51; MacDonald Carey)
6. Daybreak for Two (11/11/51; Anita Louise)
7. The Trouble with Luke Casper (11/18/51; Cesar Romero)
8. Miss Burdie's Public Affair (11/25/51; Ann Rutherford)
9. Some Small Nobility (12/2/51; Joan Bennett)
10. I Thee Kill (12/9/51; John Payne)
11. Beloved Rogue (12/16/51; Vincent Price)
12. The Double Double-Cross (12/23/51; Dan Duryea)
13. Big Ben (12/30/51; Lynn Bari)

Hollywood Star Time

Hollywood Star Time premiered on May 29, 1944, as a fifteen minute, five-a-week afternoon series of interviews with various Hollywood actors. This format soon died off, leaving the Blue Network on November 24, 1944. A little more than a year later, in January of 1946, CBS revived the program, this time as an anthology series of adaptations of movies with Hollywood stars. General Motors and Frigidaire were the sponsors. (General Motors had also sponsored the previous 1944 series as well.)

Robert L. Redd was the director for the entire series. Tom McAvity was the first producer, bowing out on December 21, 1946. Jack Johnstone began producing the series beginning December 28, 1946. Alfred Newman supplied the music; Johnny Green took over the musical chore beginning December 28, 1946. Wendell Niles was the announcer.

The program was broadcast over CBS, Sunday afternoons from 2:30 to 3 pm, EST. Beginning with episode twenty-three, *Hollywood Star Time* was broadcast Saturday evenings from 8 to 8:30 pm, EST. The final episode of the series was broadcast on Thursday evening, 10:30 to 11 pm, EST.

1. Seventh Heaven (1/6/46; Jeanne Crain and Tyrone Power)
2. Laura (1/13/46; Gene Tierney and Clifton Webb)
3. Daytime Wife (1/20/46; Linda Darnell and John Payne)
4. A Tree Grows in Brooklyn (1/27/46; James Dunn, Peggy Ann Garner, Joseph Kearns and Lurene Tuttle)
5. Shock (2/3/46; Lynn Bari, Michael Dunn, and Vincent Price)
6. My Gal Sal (2/10/46; June Havoc and Victor Mature)
7. Mark of Zorro (2/17/46; Cornel Wilde)
8. Home in Indiana (2/24/46; Jeanne Crain and Lon McCallister)
9. Swamp Water (3/3/46; Dana Andrews and Anne Baxter)
10. The Return of Frank James (3/10/46; Henry Fonda and Burl Ives)
11. Cafe Metropole (3/17/46; Nancy Guild and Cesar Romero)
12. Junior Miss (3/24/46; Peggy Ann Garner and Alan Joslyn)
13. Strange Triangle (3/31/46; Signe Hasso, Lloyd Nolan, and John Shepperd)
14. Hangover Square (4/7/46; Linda Darnell, Fay Marlow, and Vincent Price)
15. Diamond Horseshoe (4/14/46; Betty Grable and Frank Latimer)
16. Song of Bernadette (4/21/46; Charles Bickford, Vanessa Brown, Lee J. Cobb, and Vincent Price)
17. Kidnapped (4/28/46; Douglas Fairbanks, Jr., Roddy MacDowall, and Lurene Tuttle)
18. House on 92nd Street (5/5/46; William Eythe, Signe Hasso, and Lloyd Nolan)
19. Riders of the Purple Sage (5/12/46; Lynn Bari and George Montgomery)
20. The Lodger (5/19/46; Cathy Lewis and Vincent Price)
21. The Man Who Broke the Bank at Monte Carlo (5/26/46; Rex Harrison)
22. Second Honeymoon (6/2/46; Lynn Bari and George Brent)
23. Murder, My Sweet (6/8/46; Joan Bennett and Dick Powell)
24. Morning Glory (6/15/46; Olivia de Havilland and Reed Hadley)
25. Double Indemnity (6/22/46; Alan Ladd)
26. It Happened Tomorrow (6/29/46; Robert Young)
27. The Suspect (7/6/46; Charles Laughton)
28. Christmas in July (7/13/46; Eddie Bracken and Diana Lynn)

29. Mr. and Mrs. Smith (7/20/46; Robert Montgomery)
30. Hot Spot (7/27/46; Brian Donlevy, Vincent Price, and Lurene Tuttle)
31. The Major and the Minor (8/3/46; Joan Caulfield and Robert Young)
32. O.S.S. (8/10/46; Robert Cummings)
33. Conflict (8/17/46; George Brent and Sydney Greenstreet)
34. O.S.S. (8/24/46; Brian Donlevy)
35. Lost Horizon (8/31/46; Herbert Marshall)
36. Mission Perilous (9/7/46; Dane Clark and Sylvia Sydney)
37. Holiday (9/14/46; Judy Garland)
38. The Lady Eve (9/21/46; Joan Blondell and John Lund)
39. The Most Dangerous Game (9/28/46; Robert Cummings)
40. Intermezzo (10/5/46; Herbert Marshall)
41. Death Takes a Holiday (10/12/46; Walter Pidgeon)
42. Welcome Home (10/19/46; John Lund)
43. Bedulia (10/26/46; Gene Tierney)
44. Holy Matrimony (11/2/46; Frank Morgan)
45. One Way Passage (11/9/46; Herbert Marshall and Theresa Wright)
46. Three Men on a Horse (11/16/46; Dennis Day)
47. Scandal in Paris (11/23/46; David Niven and Akim Tamiroff)
48. Stagecoach (11/30/46; Virginia Bruce and John Hodiak)
49. Dulcy (12/7/46; George Burns and Gracie Allen)
50. Mad About Music (12/14/46; Ann Blyth and Herbert Marshall)
51. Three Wise Guys (12/21/46; James Dunn and Herbert Marshall)
52. A Star Is Born (12/28/46; Diana Lynn and Herbert Marshall)
53. Captain January (1/4/47; Charles Dingle and Margaret O'Brien)
54. It's A Date (1/11/47; Mary Astor and Vanessa Brown)
55. June Moon (1/18/47; Mickey Rooney)
56. Elmer the Great (1/25/47; Harold Peary)
57. Hired Wife (2/1/47; Jane Wyman)
58. The Letter (2/8/47; Herbert Marshall, Vincent Price, and Ann Todd)
59. Talk of the Town (2/15/47; Marguerite Chapman and Cary Grant)
60. Journey Into Fear (2/22/47; Herbert Marshall)
61. It Started With Eve (3/1/47; Van Heflin and Audrey Totter)
62. My Name Is Julia Ross (3/8/47; Herbert Marshall, Ann Todd, and Dame May Whitty)
63. Petrified Forest (3/15/47; Ann Baxter and Herbert Marshall)
64. Blind Spot (3/22/47; Chester Morris)
65. Love Is News (3/27/47; Bob Hope)

Hopalong Cassidy

The name Hopalong Cassidy was familiar in every American home during the forties and fifties. The hero in black rode across the plains — with his horse Topper and his sidekick California Carlson — in a fight for law and order. Syndicated by Commodore Productions and Artists, Inc., this program was broadcast for a total of one-hundred and four episodes. Hopalong Cassidy made his first radio appearance on the *Forecast* series (see log) in 1941, in an attempt to adapt the popular movie western to radio. The audition show never made it to a regular prime-time run, and the idea was scrapped. Later, in 1948, Commodore began transcribing radio dramas using William Boyd in the lead role of Hopalong.

The role of California Carlson was played by Andy Clyde for the first twelve pisodes, as well as episodes 14–20, 22, 23, 25, 26, and 53–104. Joe DuVal acted out the role of California for episodes 28–35 and 37–52. Hopalong Cassidy did not have a sidekick for episodes 13, 21, 24, 27 and 36.

Scripts were written by Buckley Angel, Dean Owen, Robert T. Smith, Howard Swart, Wayne Yarnell, Harold Swanton, John Barkley, and numerous others. Episode twenty-five was based on the Hopalong Cassidy motion picture *Silent Conflict* (1948). Episode three was based on *The Marauders* (1947), episode twenty-nine came from *Borrowed Trouble* (1948), and episode thirty-nine from *Sinister Journey* (1948). Albert Glasser supplied the music.

The list of broadcasts below includes two sets of dates. The first date is the date of transcription (the recording date) and the second date is the actual broadcast date over Mutual. They were not broadcast in the same order as they were recorded. Because the series was syndicated, the dates may have varied across the country, and some stations may have even added sponsor breaks, such as General Foods for the first nine months of 1950, and Cella Vineyards in a short run of repeats over CBS' Mountain States network. First broadcast over Mutual as a Sunday afternoon feature at 4 pm, EST, the program went to CBS 8:30 pm as of September 30, 1950.

Audition on *Forecast:* Hopalong Cassidy (8/11/41)

1. Dead Man's Hand (5/11/48; 1/1/50)
2. The Rainmaker of Eagle Nest Mountain (1/1/48; 1/8/50)
3. The Coltsville Territory (2/4/48; 1/15/50)
4. Mystery of Skull Valley (8/4/48; 1/22/50)
5. The Renegades of the San Rafael (8/9/48; 1/29/50)
6. The Phantom Bandido (8/10/48; 2/5/50)
7. Murder on the Trial (8/16/48; 2/12/50)
8. Hoppy Takes a Chance (8/17/48; 2/19/50)
9. Voice of the Dead (8/24/48; 2/26/50)
10. Ten Strike Gold (8/27/48; 3/5/50)
11. Red Cloud Mesa (8/31/48; 3/12/50; Frank Lovejoy)
12. The Empty Saddle (9/7/48; 3/19/50)
13. The Failure (9/10/48; 3/26/50)
14. The Bandits of Ridge Creek (9/28/48; 4/2/50)
15. Killers of Sandy Gulch (10/4/48; 4/9/50)
16. Red Death (10/5/48; 4/16/50)
17. Coyote's Creed (10/11/48; 4/23/50)
18. Bullets for Ballots (10/11/48; 4/30/50)
19. The Green Valley Payoff (10/18/48; 5/7/50)
20. The Man Who Made Willy Whirl (10/26/48; 5/14/50)
21. Range War (11/1/48; 5/21/50)
22. Letter from the Grave (11/15/48; 5/28/60)
23. Death Paints a Picture (11/16/48; 6/4/50)
24. Border to Nowhere (11/22/48; 6/11/50)
25. The Medicine Man (11/30/48; 6/18/50; Frank Lovejoy)
26. The Flying Outlaw (12/10/48; 6/25/50)
27. The Sundown Kid (1/25/49; 7/2/50)
28. Hoppy Sees Red (1/31/49; 7/9/50)
29. Hoppy and the Schoolmarm (2/1/49; 7/16/50)
30. The King of Cinnabar (2/3/49; 7/23/50; Howard McNear)
31. The Shell Game (2/7/49; 7/30/50; Joseph Kearns)
32. Blood Money (2/8/49; 8/6/50)
33. The Disappearing Deputy (2/14/49; 8/13/50)
34. The Whistling Ghosts (2/15/49; 8/20/50)
35. An Old Spanish Custom (3/21/49; 8/27/50; Joseph Kearns)

97. California or Bust (3/23/51; 1/26/52)
98. Death Comes Invited (3/26/51; 2/2/52)
99. Bullfight (3/28/51; 2/9/52; Barton Yarborough)
00. Women of Windy Ridge (3/20/51; 2/16/52)
101. Right Rope, Wrong Neck (4/2/51; 3/1/52)
102. Stampede at Semple Crossing (4/4/51; 3/1/52)
103. Cowtown Troubleshooters (8/10/51; 3/8/52)
104. The Santa Claus Rustlers (12/7/50; 3/15/52)

Horizons West

This thirteen-part serial was told in thirty-minute chapters, syndicated in the fifties, documenting the lives and exploration of Lewis and Clark to the West. Stars Harry Bartell as Lewis and John Anderson as Clark. The announcer was Michael Rye.

1. Mr. Jefferson's Dream
2. The Confrontation
3. Dakota Winter
4. Into the Unknown
5. The Great Falls
6. Shoshone Country
7. To the Pacific
8. Fort on the Columbia
9. Homeward Bound
10. Decision at Travelers' Rest
11. Clark and the Horse Thieves
12. Lewis and the Black Feet
13. Down the Missouri to St. Louis

The Hour of Mystery

Sponsored by United States Steel, this short-run series was a summer replacement for *The Theater Guild on the Air* and was broadcast over ABC, Sunday evenings from 10 to 11 pm, EST. Adaptations of popular mystery novels were presented each week with a Hollywood star as guest. Eric Ambler's "Journey Into Fear" was presented in the premiere broadcast. Cornell Woolrich's "The Black Angel" was presented for the second episode. Craig Rice's "The Lucky Stiff," Earle Stanley Gardner's "The Case of the Lame Canary" and F. Van Wyck Mason's "The Singapore Exile Murder" were a few of the highlights of the series.

1. Journey Into Fear (6/9/46; Laurence Olivier)
2. The Black Angel (6/16/46; Geraldine Fitzgerald)
3. Turn on the Heat (6/23/46; Frank Sinatra)
4. Above Suspicion (6/30/46; Brian Aherne and Wendy Barrie)
5. The Glass Key (7/7/46; Ralph Bellamy)
6. The Burning Court (7/14/46; John Beal)
7. The Singapore Exile Murder (7/21/46; Roger Pryor)
8. Murder, My Sweet (7/28/46; William Holden)
9. The Lucky Stiff (8/4/46; William Bendix)

10. Death in the Mind (8/11/46; John Loder)
11. The Phantom Lady (8/18/46; Franchot Tone)
12. The Case of the Lame Canary (8/25/46; Victor Jory)
13. The Thirty-Nine Steps (9/1/46; David Niven)

I Love Adventure

This short-run summer series was broadcast in 1948, written and directe by Carlton E. Morse. Morse was also the creator of *I Love a Mystery*, a popula radio program running more than twelve years. *I Love Adventure* followed th continuing adventures of the main characters from *Mystery*, Doc, Jack and Reg gie. Rex Koury supplied the organ music. Dresser Dahlstead was the announcer Broadcast over ABC on Sunday evenings. Michael Raffetto played the role c Jack Packard, and Tom Collins was Reggie Yorke for the first eight episodes Then, without any explanation, Reggie was not heard on the program; he wa replaced by Doc Long, played by Barton Yarborough. There was no sponsor.

Audition: Grandma, What Big Teeth You Have (5/21/45)
1. The China Coast Incident (4/25/48)
2. The Great Airmail Robbery (5/2/48)
3. The Devil's Sanctuary (5/9/48)
4. The Pearl of Great Price (5/16/48)
5. The $100,000,000 Manhunt (5/23/48)
6. The Finishing School Kidnapping (5/30/48)
7. But Grandma, What Big Teeth You Have (6/7/48)
8. The Man With the Third Green Eye (6/13/48)
9. The Girl in the Street (6/20/48)
10. The Kwan Moon Dagger (6/28/48)
11. Assignment With a Displaced Person (7/4/48)
12. The Hearse on the Highway (7/11/48)
13. The Ambassador Richardo Santos Affair (07/18/48)

I Love a Mystery

Carlton E. Morse, famed radio writer for numerous radio programs sucl as *One Man's Family* and *I Love Adventure*, made his mark in radio with the ever popular *I Love a Mystery*. *Mystery* told the story of three men, Doc Long, Jacl Packard, and Reggie Yorke, who wandered the world in search of adventure. An what adventure they went through! From werewolves to vampires, to psycho pathic women and killer zombies.

I Love a Mystery premiered on the West Coast over NBC as a five-a-weel daytime serial from 3:15 to 3:30 pm, PST. Beginning October 2, 1939, Fleis chmann took up sponsorship and the popular mystery program went national 7:15 to 7:30 pm, EST. Beginning April 4, 1940, Fleischmann no longer spon sored the series, and the program went to a once-a-week format, Thursda evenings from 8:30 to 9 pm, EST. On September 30, 1940, Fleischmann took up sponsorship again, and the series moved to the Blue Network, Monday evenings from 8 to 8:30 pm, EST. Beginning March 22, 1943, the series moved to CBS, now sponsored by Proctor and Gamble (Ivory Soap), back to its original five-a-week format from 7 to 7:15 pm, EST. On October 3, 1949, the series moved to Mutual, without a sponsor, staying in this five-a-week time slot until the program left the air in 1952.

During the West Coast run, Michael Raffetto, Barton Yarborough, Walter Paterson and Gloria Blondell were the lead performers. Paterson left the series after episode 333. The entire series was broadcast from California until October 3, 1949, when the series moved to New York over Mutual. Jim Boles, Russell Thorson, Tony Randall and Mercedes McCambridge were the lead performers, performing reruns of previous scripts. In 1945, *I Love a Mystery* was released in theaters as a big-screen adventure with Nina Foch and Barton Yarborough in the leads, and led to two sequels.

1.–14. The Case of the Roxy Mob (1/16/39, 1/17, 1/18, 1/19, 1/20, 1/23, 1/24, 1/25, 1/26, 1/27, 1/30, 1/31, 2/1 and 2/2/39)

15.–26. Trouble at Sea (2/3/39, 2/6, 2/7, 2/8, 2/9, 2/10, 2/13, 2/14, 2/15, 2/16, 2/17 and 2/20/39)

27.–51. The Case of the Nevada Man Killer (2/21/39, 2/22, 2/23, 2/24, 2/27, 2/28, 3/1, 3/2, 3/3, 3/6, 3/7, 3/8, 3/9, 3/10, 3/13, 3/14, 3/15, 3/16, 3/17, 3/20, 3/21, 3/22, 3/23, 3/24 and 3/27/39)

52.–70. Turn of the Wheel (3/29/39, 3/30, 3/31, 4/3, 4/4, 4/5, 4/6, 4/7, 4/10, 4/11, 4/12, 4/13, 4/14, 4/17, 4/18, 4/19, 4/20, 4/21, 4/24 and 4/25/39)

71.–85. Whose Body Got Buried? (4/26/39, 4/27, 4/28, 5/1, 5/2, 5/3, 5/4, 5/5, 5/8, 5/9, 5/10, 5/11, 5/12, 5/15 and 5/16/39)

86.–100. Escapade of the Desert Hog (5/17/39, 5/18, 5/19, 5/22, 5/23, 5/24, 5/25, 5/26, 5/29, 5/30, 5/31, 6/1, 6/2, 6/5 and 6/6/39)

101.–115. Blood on the Boarder (6/7/39, 6/8, 6/9, 6/12, 6/13, 6/14, 6/15, 6/16, 6/19, 6/20, 6/21, 6/22, 6/23, 6/26 and 6/27/39)

116.–130. Flight to Death (6/28/39, 6/29, 6/30, 7/3, 7/4, 7/5, 7/6, 7/7, 7/10, 7/11, 7/12, 7/13, 7/14, 7/17 and 7/18/39)

131.–145. Murder: Hollywood Style (7/19/39, 7/20, 7/21, 7/24, 7/25, 7/26, 7/27, 7/28, 7/31, 8/1, 8/2, 8/3, 8/4, 8/7 and 8/8/39)

146.–160. Incident Concerning Death (8/9/39, 8/10, 8/11, 8/14, 8/15, 8/16, 8/17, 8/18, 8/21, 8/22, 8/23, 8/24, 8/25, 8/28 and 8/29/39)

161.–178. The Battle of the Century (8/30/39, 8/31, 9/1, 9/4, 9/5, 9/6, 9/7, 9/8, 9/11, 9/12, 9/13, 9/14, 9/15, 9/18, 9/19, 9/20, 9/21 and 9/22/39)

179.–193. Blue Phantom (10/2/39, 10/3, 10/4, 10/5, 10/6, 10/9, 10/10, 10/11, 10/12, 10/13, 10/16, 10/17, 10/18, 10/19 and 10/20/39)

194.–213. The Fear That Creeps Like a Cat (10/23, 10/24, 10/25, 10/26, 10/27, 10/30, 10/31, 11/1, 11/2, 11/3, 11/6, 11/7, 11/8, 11/9, 11/10, 11/13, 11/14, 11/15, 11/16 and 11/17/39)

214.–228. The Thing That Cried in the Night (11/20/39, 11/21, 11/22, 11/23, 11/24, 11/27, 11/28, 11/29, 11/30, 12/1, 12/4, 12/5, 12/6, 12/7 and 12/8/39)

229.–243. Bury Your Dead, Arizona (12/11/39, 12/12, 12/13, 12/14, 12/15, 12/18, 12/19, 12/20, 12/21, 12/22, 12/25, 12/26, 12/27, 12/28 and 12/29/39)

244.–258. San Diego Murders (1/1/40, 1/2, 1/3, 1/4, 1/5, 1/8, 1/9, 1/10, 1/11, 1/12, 1/15, 1/16, 1/17, 1/18 and 1/19/40)

259.–278. Temple of the Vampires
(1/22/40, 1/23, 1/24, 1/25, 1/26,
1/29, 1/30, 1/31, 2/1, 2/2, 2/5, 2/6,
2/7, 2/8, 2/9, 2/12, 2/13, 2/14, 2/15
and 2/16/40)

279.–293. Brooks Kidnapping (2/19/40,
2/20, 2/21, 2/22, 2/23, 2/26, 2/27,
2/28, 2/29, 3/1, 3/4, 3/5, 3/6, 3/7
and 3/8/40)

294.–308. Murder in Turquoise Pass
(3/11/40, 3/12, 3/13, 3/14, 3/15, 3/18,
3/19, 3/20, 3/21, 3/22, 3/25, 3/26,
3/27, 3/28 and 3/29/40)

309.–333. The Snake with the Diamond
Eyes (4/1/40, 4/2, 4/3, 4/4, 4/5, 4/8,
4/9, 4/10, 4/11, 4/12, 4/16, 4/17, 4/18,
4/19, 4/22, 4/23, 4/24, 4/25, 4/26,
4/29, 4/30, 5/2, 5/3 and 5/6/40)

334.–359. The Tropics Don't Call It
Murder (9/30/40, 10/3, 10/7, 10/10,
10/14, 10/17, 10/21, 10/24, 10/28,
10/31, 11/4, 11/7, 11/11, 11/14, 11/18,
11/21, 11/25, 11/28, 12/2, 12/5, 12/9,
12/12, 12/16, 12/19, 12/23 and
12/26/40)

360.–377. The Case of the Transplanted
Castle (1/6/41, 1/9, 1/13, 1/16, 1/20,
1/23, 1/27, 1/30, 2/3, 2/6, 2/10, 2/13,
2/17, 2/20, 2/24, 2/27, 3/3 and
3/6/41)

378.–395. Murder on February Island
(3/10/41, 3/13, 3/17, 3/20, 3/24,
3/27, 3/31, 4/3, 4/7, 4/10, 4/14, 4/17,
4/21, 4/24, 4/28, 5/1, 5/5 and
5/8/41)

396.–411. Eight Kinds of Murder
(5/12/41, 5/15, 5/19, 5/22, 5/26,
5/29, 6/2, 6/5, 6/9, 6/12, 6/16, 6/19,
6/23, 6/26, 6/30, and 7/3/41)

412.–427. The Monster in the Mansion
(10/6/41, 10/9, 10/13, 10/16, 10/20,
10/23, 10/27, 10/30, 11/3, 11/6, 11/10,
11/13, 11/17, 11/20, 11/24 and
11/27/41)

428.–447. Secret Passage to Death (12/1,
12/4, 12/8, 12/11, 12/15, 12/18, 12/22,
12/25, 12/29/41, 1/1/42, 1/5, 1/8,
1/12, 1/15, 1/19, 1/22, 1/26, 1/29, 2/2
and 2/5/42)

448.–465. Terror of Frozen Corpse Lodge
(2/9/42, 2/12, 2/16, 2/19, 2/23,
2/26, 3/2, 3/5, 3/9, 3/12, 3/16, 3/19,
3/23, 3/26, 3/30, 4/2, 4/6 and
4/9/42)

466.–491. Pirate Loot of the Island of
Skulls (4/13/42, 4/16, 4/20, 4/23,
4/27, 4/30, 5/4, 5/7, 5/11, 5/14, 5/18,
5/21, 5/25, 5/28, 6/1, 6/4, 6/8, 6/11,
6/15, 6/18, 6/22, 6/25, 6/29, 7/2,
7/3 and 7/6/42)

492.–506. The Girl in the Gilded Cage
(3/22/43, 3/23, 3/24, 3/25, 3/26,
3/29, 3/30, 3/31, 4/1, 4/2, 4/5, 4/6,
4/7, 4/8 and 4/9/43)

507.–526. Blood of the Cat (4/12/43,
4/13, 4/14, 4/15, 4/16, 4/19, 4/20,
4/21, 4/22, 4/23, 4/26, 4/27, 4/28,
4/29, 4/30, 5/3, 5/4, 5/5, 5/6 and
5/7/43)

527.–545. The Killer of Circle M
(5/10/43, 5/11, 5/12, 5/13, 5/14, 5/17,
5/18, 5/19, 5/20, 5/21, 5/24, 5/25,
5/26, 5/27, 5/28, 6/1, 6/2, 6/3 and
6/4/43)

546.–575. Stairway to the Sun (6/7/43,
6/8, 6/9, 6/10, 6/11, 6/14, 6/15, 6/16,
6/17, 6/18, 6/21, 6/22, 6/23, 6/24,
6/25, 6/28, 6/29, 6/30, 7/1, 7/2,
7/5, 7/6, 7/7, 7/8, 7/9, 7/12, 7/13,
7/14, 7/15 and 7/16/43)

576.–590. The Graves of Whamperjaw,
Texas (7/19/43, 7/20, 7/21, 7/22,
7/23, 7/26, 7/27, 7/28, 7/29, 7/30,
8/2, 8/3, 8/4, 8/5 and 8/6/43)

591.–605. Murder Is the Word for It
(8/9/43, 8/10, 8/11, 8/12, 8/13, 8/16,
8/17, 8/18, 8/19, 8/20, 8/23, 8/24,
8/25, 8/26 and 8/27/43)

606.–630. Decapitation of Jefferson
Monk (8/30/43, 8/31, 9/1, 9/2, 9/3,
9/6, 9/7, 9/8, 9/9, 9/10, 9/13, 9/14,
9/15, 9/16, 9/17, 9/20, 9/21, 9/22,
9/23, 9/24, 9/27, 9/28, 9/29, 9/30,
and 10/1/43)

631.–656. My Beloved Is a Vampire
(10/4/43, 10/5, 10/6, 10/7, 10/8,
10/11, 10/12, 10/13, 10/14, 10/15,
10/18, 10/19, 10/20, 10/21, 10/22,
10/25, 10/26, 10/27, 10/28, 10/29,
11/1, 11/2, 11/3, 11/4 and 11/5/43)

657.–676. The Hermit of San Felipe
Atabapo (11/8/43, 11/9, 11/10, 11/11,
11/12, 11/15, 11/16, 11/17, 11/18, 11/19,
11/22, 11/23, 11/24, 11/25, 11/26, 11/29,
11/30, 12/1, 12/2 and 12/3/43)

677.–691. The Deadly Sin of Richard
Coyle (12/6/43, 12/7, 12/8, 12/9,
12/10, 12/13, 12/14, 12/15, 12/16,

12/17, 12/20, 12/21, 12/22, 12/23 and 12/24/43)

692.–735. The Twenty Traders of Timbuktu (12/27/43, 12/28, 12/29, 12/30 and 12/31/43, 1/3/44, 1/4, 1/5, 1/6, 1/7, 1/10, 1/11, 1/12, 1/13, 1/14, 1/17, 1/18, 1/19, 1/20, 1/21, 1/24, 1/25, 1/26, 1/27, 1/28, 1/31, 2/1, 2/2, 2/3, 2/4, 2/7, 2/8, 2/9, 2/10, 2/11, 2/14, 2/15, 2/16, 2/17, 2/18, 2/21, 2/22, 2/23 and 2/24/44)

736.–755. The African Jungle Mystery (2/28/44, 2/29, 3/1, 3/2, 3/3, 3/6, 3/7, 3/8, 3/9, 3/10, 3/13, 3/14, 3/15, 3/16, 3/17, 3/20, 3/21, 3/22, 3/23 and 3/24/44)

756.–775. The Widow with the Amputation (3/27/44, 3/28, 3/29, 3/30, 3/31, 4/3, 4/4, 4/5, 4/6, 4/7, 4/10, 4/11, 4/12, 4/13, 4/14, 4/17, 4/18, 4/19, 4/20 and 4/21/44)

776.–790. I Am the Destroyer of Women (4/24/44, 4/25, 4/26, 4/27, 4/28, 5/1, 5/2, 5/3, 5/4, 5/5, 5/8, 5/9, 5/10, 5/11 and 5/12/44)

791.–805. You Can't Pin A Murder on Nevada (5/15/44, 5/16, 5/17, 5/18, 5/19, 5/22, 5/23, 5/24, 5/25, 5/26, 5/29, 5/30, 5/31, 6/1 and 6/2/44)

806.–810. The Corpse in Compartment C, Car 75 (6/5/44, 6/6, 6/7, 6/8 and 6/9/44)

811.–830. The Thing That Wouldn't Die (6/12/44, 6/13, 6/14, 6/15, 6/16, 6/19, 6/20, 6/21, 6/22, 6/23, 6/26, 6/27, 6/28, 6/29, 6/30, 7/4, 7/5, 7/6 and 7/7/44)

831.–851. The Case of the Terrified Comedian (7/10/44, 7/11, 7/12, 7/13, 7/14, 7/17, 7/18, 7/19, 7/20, 7/21, 7/24, 7/25, 7/26, 7/27, 7/28, 7/31, 8/1, 8/2, 8/3, 8/4 and 8/7/44)

852.–861. The Man Who Hated to Shave (8/8/44, 8/9, 8/10, 8/11, 8/14, 8/15, 8/16, 8/17, 8/18 and 8/21/44)

862.–882. Temple of Vampires (8/22/44, 8/23, 8/24, 8/25, 8/28, 8/29, 8/30, 8/31, 9/1, 9/4, 9/5, 9/6, 9/7, 9/8, 9/11, 9/12, 9/13, 9/14, 9/15 and 9/18/44)

883.–897. The Bride of the Werewolf (9/19/44, 9/20, 9/21, 9/22, 9/25, 9/26, 9/27, 9/28, 9/29, 10/2, 10/3, 10/4, 10/5, 10/6 and 10/9/44)

898.–920. The Monster in the Mansion (10/10/44, 10/11, 10/12, 10/13, 10/16, 10/17, 10/18, 10/19, 10/20, 10/23, 10/24, 10/25, 10/26, 10/27, 10/30, 10/31, 11/1, 11/2, 11/3, 11/6, 11/7, 11/8 and 11/9/44)

921.–940. Portrait of a Murderess (11/16/44, 11/17, 11/20, 11/21, 11/22, 11/23, 11/24, 11/27, 11/28, 11/29, 11/30, 12/1, 12/4, 12/5, 12/6, 12/7, 12/8, 12/11, 12/12 and 12/13/44)

941.–952. Find Elsa Holberg, Dead or Alive (12/14/44, 12/15, 12/18, 12/19, 12/20, 12/21, 12/22, 12/25, 12/26, 12/27, 12/28 and 12/29/44)

953.–972. The Fear That Creeps Like a Cat (10/3/49, 10/4, 10/5, 10/6, 10/7, 10/10, 10/11, 10/12, 10/13, 10/14, 10/17, 10/18, 10/19, 10/20, 10/21, 10/24, 10/25, 10/26, 10/27 and 10/28/49)

973.–987. The Thing That Cries in the Night (10/31/49, 11/1, 11/2, 11/3, 11/4, 11/7, 11/8, 11/9, 11/10, 11/11, 11/14, 11/15, 11/16, 11/17 and 11/18/49)

988.–1002. Bury Your Dead, Arizona (11/21/49, 11/22, 11/23, 11/24, 11/25, 11/28, 11/29, 11/30, 12/1, 12/2, 12/5, 12/6, 12/7, 12/8 and 12/9/49)

1003.–1017. The Million Dollar Curse (12/12/49, 12/13, 12/14, 12/15, 12/16, 12/19, 12/20, 12/21, 12/22, 12/23, 12/26, 12/27, 12/28, 12/29 and 12/30/49)

1018.–1037. Temple of Vampires (1/2/50, 1/3, 1/4, 1/5, 1/6, 1/9, 1/10, 1/11, 1/12, 1/13, 1/16, 1/17, 1/18, 1/19, 1/20, 1/23, 1/24, 1/25, 1/26 and 1/27/50)

1038.–1055. Battle of the Century (1/30/50, 1/31, 2/1, 2/2, 2/3, 2/6, 2/7, 2/8, 2/9, 2/10, 2/13, 2/14, 2/15, 2/16, 2/17, 2/20, 2/21 and 2/22/50)

1056.–1081. The Tropics Don't Call It Murder (2/23/50, 2/24, 2/27, 2/28, 3/1, 3/2, 3/3, 3/6, 3/7, 3/8, 3/9, 3/10, 3/13, 3/14, 3/15, 3/16, 3/17, 3/20, 3/21, 3/22, 3/23, 3/24, 3/27, 3/28, 3/29 and 3/30/50)

1082.–1106. The Case of the Nevada Man Killer (3/31/50, 4/3, 4/4, 4/5, 4/6, 4/7, 4/10, 4/11, 4/12, 4/13, 4/14, 4/17, 4/18, 4/19, 4/20, 4/21, 4/24, 4/25, 4/26, 4/27, 4/28, 5/1, 5/2, 5/3 and 5/4/50)

1107.–1126. The Turn of the Wheel (5/5/50, 5/8, 5/9, 5/10, 5/11, 5/12, 5/15, 5/16, 5/17, 5/18, 5/19, 5/22, 5/23, 5/24, 5/25, 5/26, 5/29, 5/30, 5/31, and 6/1/50)

1127.–1141. The Blue Phantom Murders (6/2/50, 6/5, 6/6, 6/7, 6/8, 6/9, 6/12, 6/13, 6/14, 6/15, 6/16, 6/19, 6/20, 6/21 and 6/22/50)

1142.–1167. The Snake With the Diamond Eyes (6/23/50, 6/26, 6/27, 6/28, 6/29, 6/30, 7/3, 7/4, 7/5, 7/6, 7/7, 7/10, 7/11, 7/12, 7/13, 7/14, 7/17, 7/18, 7/19, 7/20, 7/21, 7/24, 7/25, 7/26, 7/27 and 7/28/50)

1168.–1182. Flight to Death (7/31/50, 8/1, 8/2, 8/3, 8/4, 8/7, 8/8, 8/9, 8/10, 8/11, 8/14, 8/15, 8/16, 8/17 and 8/18/50)

1183.–1197. Murder in Turquoise Pass (8/21/50, 8/22, 8/23, 8/24, 8/25, 8/28, 8/29, 8/30, 8/31, 9/1, 9/4, 9/5, 9/6, 9/7 and 9/8/50)

1198.–1212. Whose Body Got Buried? (9/11, 9/12, 9/13, 9/14, 9/15, 9/18, 9/19, 9/20, 9/21, 9/22, 9/25, 9/26, 9/27, 9/28 and 9/29/50)

1213.–1227. Escape of the Desert Hog (10/2, 10/3, 10/4, 10/5, 10/6, 10/9, 10/10, 10/11, 10/12, 10/13, 10/16, 10/17, 10/18, 10/19 and 10/20/50)

1228.–1242. Blood on the Boarder (10/23/50, 10/24, 10/25, 10/26, 10/27, 10/30, 10/31, 11/1, 11/2, 11/3, 11/6, 11/7, 11/8, 11/9 and 11/10/50)

1243.–1254. Trouble at Sea (11/13/50, 11/14, 11/15, 11/16, 11/17, 11/20, 11/21, 11/22, 11/23, 11/24, 11/27 and 11/28/50)

1255.–1269. Incident Concerning Death (11/29/50, 11/30, 12/1, 12/4, 12/5, 12/6, 12/7, 12/8, 12/11, 12/12, 12/13, 12/14, 12/15, 12/18 and 12/19/50)

1270.–1283. The Case of the Roxy Mob (12/20/50, 12/21, 12/22, 12/25, 12/26, 12/27, 12/28 and 12/29/50, 1/1/51, 1/2, 1/3, 1/4, 1/5 and 1/8/51)

1284.–1301. The Case of the Transplanted Castle (1/9/51, 1/10, 1/11, 1/12, 1/15, 1/16, 1/17, 1/18, 1/19, 1/22, 1/23, 1/24, 1/25, 1/26, 1/29, 1/30, 1/31, and 2/1/51)

1302.–1319. Murder on February Island (2/2/51, 2/5, 2/6, 2/7, 2/8, 2/9, 2/12, 2/13, 2/14, 2/15, 2/16, 2/19, 2/20, 2/21, 2/22, 2/23, 2/26 and 2/27/51)

1320.–1342. The Monster in the Mansion (2/28/51, 3/1, 3/2, 3/5, 3/6, 3/7, 3/8, 3/9, 3/12, 3/13, 3/14, 3/15, 3/16, 3/19, 3/20, 3/21, 3/22, 3/23, 3/26, 3/27, 3/28, 3/29 and 3/30/51)

1343.–1358. Eight Kinds of Murder (4/2/51, 4/3, 4/4, 4/5, 4/6, 4/9, 4/10, 4/11, 4/12, 4/13, 4/16, 4/17, 4/18, 4/19, 4/20 and 4/23/51)

1359.–1378. Secret Passage to Death (4/24/51, 4/25, 4/26, 4/27, 4/30, 5/1, 5/2, 5/3, 5/4, 5/7, 5/8, 5/9, 5/10, 5/11, 5/14, 5/15, 5/16, 5/17, 5/18 and 5/21/51)

1379.–1396. Terror of Frozen Corpse Lodge (5/22/51, 5/23, 5/24, 5/25, 5/28, 5/29, 5/30, 5/31, 6/1, 6/4, 6/5, 6/6, 6/7, 6/8, 6/11, 6/12, 6/13 and 6/14/51)

1397.–1422. The Pirate Loot of the Island of Skulls (6/15/51, 6/18, 6/19, 6/20, 6/21, 6/22, 6/25, 6/26, 6/27, 6/28, 6/29, 7/2, 7/3, 7/4, 7/5, 7/6, 7/9, 7/10, 7/11, 7/12, 7/13, 7/16, 7/17, 7/18, 7/19 and 7/20/51)

1423.–1437. Brooks Kidnapping (7/23/51, 7/24, 7/25, 7/26, 7/27, 7/30, 7/31, 8/1, 8/2, 8/3, 8/6, 8/7, 8/8, 8/9 and 8/10/51)

1438.–1452. Murder: Hollywood Style (8/13/51, 8/14, 8/15, 8/16, 8/17, 8/20, 8/21, 8/22, 8/23, 8/24, 8/27, 8/28, 8/29, 8/30 and 8/31/51)

1453.–1467. The Girl in the Gilded Cage (9/3/51, 9/4, 9/5, 9/6, 9/7, 9/10, 9/11, 9/12, 9/13, 9/14, 9/17, 9/18, 9/19, 9/20 and 9/21/51)

1468.–1487. Blood on the Cat (9/24/51, 9/25, 9/26, 9/27, 9/28, 10/1, 10/2, 10/3, 10/4, 10/5, 10/8, 10/9, 10/10, 10/11, 10/12, 10/15, 10/16, 10/17, 10/18 and 10/19/51)

1488.–1507. The Case of the Terrified Comedian (10/22/51, 10/23, 10/24, 10/25, 10/26, 10/29, 10/30, 10/31, 11/1, 11/2, 11/5, 11/6, 11/7, 11/8, 11/9, 11/12, 11/13, 11/14, 11/15 and 11/16/51)

1508.–1527. The Killer of the Circle M (11/19/51, 11/20, 11/21, 11/22, 11/23, 11/26, 11/27, 11/28, 11/29, 11/30, 12/3, 12/4, 12/5, 12/6, 12/7, 12/10, 12/11, 12/12, 12/13 and 12/14/51)

1528.–1542. Murder Is the Word For It (12/17/51, 12/18, 12/19, 12/20, 12/21, 12/24, 12/25, 12/26, 12/27, 12/28, 12/31/51, 1/1/52, 1/2, 1/3 and 1/4/52)

1543.–1572. Stairway to the Sun (1/7/52, 1/8, 1/9, 1/10, 1/11, 1/14, 1/15, 1/16, 1/17, 1/18, 1/21, 1/22, 1/23, 1/24, 1/25, 1/28, 1/29, 1/30, 1/31, 2/1, 2/4, 2/5, 2/6, 2/7, 2/8, 2/11, 2/12, 2/13, 2/14 and 2/15/52)

1573.–1587. The Graves of Whamper-jaw, Texas (2/18/52, 2/19, 2/20, 2/21, 2/22, 2/25, 2/26, 2/27, 2/28, 2/29, 3/3, 3/4, 3/5, 3/6 and 3/7/52)

1588.–1612. The Decapitation of Jefferson Monk (3/10/52, 3/11, 3/12, 3/13, 3/14, 3/17, 3/18, 3/19, 3/20, 3/21, 3/24, 3/25, 3/26, 3/27, 3/28, 3/31, 4/1, 4/2, 4/3, 4/4, 4/7, 4/8, 4/9, 4/10 and 4/11/52)

1613.–1637. My Beloved Is a Vampire (4/14/52, 4/15, 4/16, 4/17, 4/18, 4/21, 4/22, 4/23, 4/24, 4/25, 4/28, 4/29, 4/30, 5/1, 5/2, 5/5, 5/6, 5/7, 5/8, 5/9, 5/12, 5/13, 5/14, 5/15 and 5/16/52)

1638.–1657. The Hermit of San Felipe Atabapo (5/19/52, 5/20, 5/21, 5/22, 5/23, 5/26, 5/27, 5/28, 5/29, 5/30, 6/2, 6/3, 6/4, 6/5, 6/6, 6/9, 6/10, 6/11, 6/12 and 6/13/52)

1658.–1672. The Deadly Sin of Sir Richard Doyle (6/16/52, 6/17, 6/18, 6/19, 6/20, 6/23, 6/24, 6/25, 6/26, 6/27, 6/30, 7/1, 7/2, 7/3 and 7/4/52)

1673.–1682. The Man Who Hated to Shave (7/7/52, 7/8, 7/9, 7/10, 7/11, 7/14, 7/15, 7/16, 7/17 and 7/18/52)

1683.–1702. The African Jungle Mystery (7/21/52, 7/22, 7/23, 7/24, 7/25, 7/28, 7/29, 7/30, 7/31, 8/1, 8/4, 8/5, 8/6, 8/7, 8/8, 8/11, 8/12, 8/13, 8/14 and 8/15/52)

1703.–1722. The Cobra King Strikes Back (9/1/52, 9/2, 9/3, 9/4, 9/5, 9/8, 9/9, 9/10, 9/11, 9/12, 9/15, 9/16, 9/17, 9/18, 9/19, 9/22, 9/23, 9/24, 9/25 and 9/26/52)

1723.–1742. The Widow with the Amputation (9/30/52, 10/1, 10/2, 10/3, 10/6, 10/7, 10/8, 10/9, 10/10, 10/13, 10/14, 10/15, 10/16, 10/17, 10/20, 10/21, 10/22, 10/23, 10/24 and 10/27/52)

1743.–1757. I Am the Destroyer of Women (10/28/52, 10/29, 10/30, 10/31, 11/3, 11/4, 11/5, 11/6, 11/7, 11/10, 11/11, 11/12, 11/13, 11/18 and 11/19/52)

1758.–1772. The Bride of the Werewolf (11/20/52, 11/21, 11/24, 11/25, 11/26, 11/27, 11/28, 12/1, 12/2, 12/3, 12/4, 12/5, 12/8, 12/9 and 12/10/52)

1773.–1784. Find Elsa Holberg, Dead or Alive (12/11/52, 12/12, 12/15, 12/16, 12/17, 12/18, 12/19, 12/22, 12/23, 12/24, 12/25 and 12/26/52)

Image Minorities

This series documented the immigration history, cultural traits, assimilation patterns and contemporary status of various racial and religious groups in the United States. Originally meant to be a four-week series, *Image Minorities* ran for fifteen weeks before going off the air. Bob Considine narrated each broadcast. The first episode featured then–Vice President Richard Nixon and former Immigration Commissioner Edward Corsi. Various guests gave support in various broadcasts, such as James Cagney and Pat O'Brien in episode five, concerning the

Irish in America. Anne Bancroft and Jimmy Durante, both Italian, were featured in episode seven. Episode one concerned sources of prejudice and discrimination against minority groups. The program was broadcast in syndication on various stations across the country. The dates below are from WRCA in New York. Broadcast Monday through Thursday from 8:40 to 10 pm, EST, with the exception of episode two, 8:45 to 10 pm, EST.

1. Historical Background of Immigration (6/2/59; Edward Corsi and Richard Nixon)
2. The American Indian (6/3/59; Allie Reynolds and Maria Tallchief)
3. Negroes in America (6/4/59; Harry Belafonte, Thurgood Marshall, and Jackie Robinson)
4. Minority Influences in American Music (6/8/59)
5. The Irish in America (6/9/59; James Cagney, Peggy Cass, James A. Farley, James T. Farrell, and Pat O'Brien)
6. Germans and Scandinavians in America (6/10/59; Edgar Bergen, Conrad Hilton, Celeste Holm, and Lotte Lenya)
7. The Italians in America (6/11/59; Anne Bancroft, Jimmy Durante, and Phil Rizzuto)
8. Minority Influences in American Music (6/15/59; Morton Gould)
9. The Orientals in America (6/16/59; Keye Luke and Pat Suzuki)
10. The Jews in America (6/17/59; Abe Burrows, Fannie Hurst, and Shelley Winters)
11. East Europeans in America (6/18/59; Stan Musial and Akim Tamiroff)
12. Minority Influences in American Music (6/22/59)
13. Puerto Ricans and Mexicanism in the U.S. (6/23/59; Mel Ferrer)
14. Small Groups in America (6/24/59)
15. The Outlook for Minorities (6/25/59; Mel Allen and Abe Burrows)

In the Name of the Law

Syndicated crime series broadcast in 1936.

1. The Robbery (5/31/36)
2. Who Framed Francis? (6/7/36)
3. I Dreamed Mother was Poisoned (6/14/36)
4. Red Ryan's Prison Break (6/21/36)
5. The July Fourth Picnic (6/28/36)
6. The Phantom Gang (7/5/36)
7. I Bumped Off Hubby (7/12/36)
8. Narcotics in the Trunk (7/19/36)
9. Nothing Ever Happens in Chinatown (7/26/36)
10. I Didn't Do Nothing (8/2/36)
11. She Was Murdered (8/8/36)
12. He Did It. Or Did He? (8/16/36)

Inheritance

Dramatic presentations of American historic figures and history. "But for the Courage of a Woman" presented the story of Jane Sullivan in the American Revolution. "The Nutmegger and the Turtle" featured the story of the development of America's first secret weapon. "The Story of Elizabeth Blackwell" dramatized the life of the first woman physician. Many of the scripts were previously written for and dramatized on *The Cavalcade of America*. Replacing *Last Man Out* in April of 1954, this series became popular, running for two seasons over NBC, 10 to 10:30 pm, EST. When *Fibber McGee and Molly* moved into the same time slot as *Inheritance*, the series moved to a Sunday afternoon 4:30 to 5 pm time slot. Beginning November 21, the series was heard from 5 to 5:30 pm, EST.

1. When Washington Refused a Crown (4/4/54)
2. The Story of Oliver Pollack (4/11/54)
3. The Mountain Men [story of Hugh Glass, hunter/trapper] (4/18/54)
4. Lincoln's Reconstruction Policy (4/25/54; Milo J. Warner)
5. The Story of Elizabeth Blackwell (5/2/54)
6. The Story of the San Francisco Earthquake and Fire (5/9/54; Les Tremayne)
7. -----(5/16/54)
8. The Lewis and Clark Expedition (5/23/54)
9. The Nutmegger and the Turtle (5/30/54; Truman Wold)
10. But for the Courage of a Woman (6/6/54)
11. The Story of the Texas Rangers (6/13/54; Milo J. Warner, past Commander, American Legion)
12. Whipple's War [story of 1775] (6/20/54)
13. The Story of a Soldier (6/27/54)
14. The Story of the Liberty Bell (7/4/54; Arthur J. Connell)
15. America's Greatest Bargain (7/11/54)
16. Victory on Lake Erie (7/18/54; Paul V. McNutt)
17. -----(7/25/54)
18. -----(8/1/54)
19. The Gingerbread Man (8/8/54)
20. The Flag That Talks (8/15/54)
21. The Mail Had Wings (8/22/54)
22. Gibraltar on the Hudson (9/19/54; Paul Cavanaugh)
23. The Young Davy Crockett (9/26/54)
24. The Sequoia (10/3/54)
25. The Hand That Rocked the Cradle (10/10/54)
26. Mother Bickerdyke [story of the Civil War Nurse] (10/17/54; Mrs. William H. Corwith)
27. Gorgas and the Panama Canal (10/24/54)
28. The Whale Hunters (10/31/54)
29. Horatio Alger (11/7/54)
30. Nancy Hanks (11/14/54)
31. What Is America? (11/21/54)
32. Harvest of the Stony Fields (11/28/54)
33. Paul Revere (12/5/54)
34. The Man Without a Country [story of Edward Everett Hale] (12/12/54)
35. The Cordwainers (12/19/54)
36. The Vanguard (12/26/54)
37. Log of the Louisiana (1/2/55; Seaborn P. Collins)
38. The Life of George Washington Carver (1/9/55)
39. Bradford [foundation of Plymouth Colony] (1/16/55)
40. Johnny Appleseed (1/23/55)
41. The Peacemaker (1/30/55)
42. My Friend David (2/6/55)
43. The Lincoln Portrait (2/13/55)
44. -----(2/20/55)
45. Cheese on a Raft (2/27/55)
46. Adventurer's Laughter (3/6/55)
47. He Died Free (3/13/55)
48. -----(3/20/55)
49. Their Rights and Nothing Less (3/27/55)
50. The Story of Benjamin Rush (4/3/55)
51. Thanks for America (4/17/55)
52. -----(4/24/55)
53. Proclaim Liberty (5/1/55)

Inner Sanctum Mysteries

Famed for the creaking door that opened and closed each episode, this mystery/horror series presented tales of murder and madness. During the first couple of years, adaptations of tales written by Poe and de Maupassant were featured, but original scripts were eventually used. The series was broadcast from New York; Himan Brown produced and directed. Ed Herlihy, Dwight Weist, and A.C. Anthony (during Mars' sponsorship) were the announcers throughout the years. *Inner Sanctum Mysteries* was so popular that it later spawned a series of movies from Universal Studios with Lon Chaney, Jr., in the leads, and even a short-run television series. Lew White supplied the organ music. Raymond Edward Johnson played the host "Raymond," who opened and closed each episode with awful ... and morbid ... jokes and puns. Paul McGrath took over the role of Raymond beginning with the broadcast of May 29, 1945, and later it was House Jameson.

The series was first broadcast over the Blue Network and sponsored by Carter Liver Pills, Tuesday evenings from 9:35 to 10 pm, EST. Beginning March 16, 1941, Carter moved the series to ABC, Sunday evenings from 8:30 to 9 pm, EST.

Beginning September 4, 1943, Colgate Palmolive began sponsoring the series over CBS, Saturday evenings from 8:30 to 9 pm, EST. On November 22, 1944, the series moved to Wednesdays from 9 to 9:30 pm. Lever Brothers (Lipton Tea) took up sponsorship on January 2, 1945, and *Inner Sanctum* was heard on Tuesdays from 9 to 9:30 pm. On July 29, 1946, Bromo Seltzer took over as sponsor, and the program moved to Mondays from 8 to 8:30 pm, EST. Finally, Mars Candy took over sponsorship beginning September 4, 1950, and the program moved to ABC, Monday evenings from 8 to 8:30 pm. In the summer of 1952, the Pearson Pharmaceutical Company, Inc., decided to sponsor a short-run revival of the program, using scripts previously written and performed on the program. This last run was heard on Sunday evenings from CBS.

1. Death For Sale (1/7/41)
2. Nursery Rhyme Murders (1/14/41)
3. The Magic Curse (1/21/41)
4. The Vampire Strikes (1/28/41)
5. Murder in the Air (2/4/41)
6. Mystery of the Howling Dog (2/11/41)
7. The Strangled Snake (2/18/41)
8. The Case of the Blood Type (2/25/41)
9. -----(3/4/41)
10. -----(3/11/41)
11. The Man of Steel (3/16/41; Boris Karloff)
12. The Man Who Hated Death (3/23/41; Boris Karloff)
13. The Mad Doctor (3/30/41; George Coulouris)
14. Death in the Zoo (4/6/41; Boris Karloff)
15. The Bells of Death (4/13/41)
16. Fog (4/20/41; Boris Karloff)
17. Death in a Dream (4/27/41)
18. The Horla [based on the Guy de Maupassaunt story] (5/4/41; Paul Lukas)
19. Imperfect Crime (5/11/41; Boris Karloff)
20. Dead Freight (5/18/41; Peggy Conklin and Myron McCormick)

21. Death Is a Joker (5/25/41; Paul Lukas)
22. Fall of the House of Usher [based on the Edgar Allan Poe story] (6/1/41; Boris Karloff)
23. The Cabala (6/8/41; Donald Cook and Claudia Morgan)
24. Murder in the Mind (6/15/41; Paul Lukas)
25. Green-Eyed Bat (6/22/41; Boris Karloff)
26. The Man Who Painted Death (6/29/41; Boris Karloff or Paul Lukas)
27. Doom of Damballa (7/6/41)
28. Death Is a Murderer (7/13/41; Boris Karloff)
29. The Eye of Shiva (7/20/41; Paul Lukas)
30. The Button (7/27/41)
31. The Tell-Tale Heart [based on the short story by Edgar Allan Poe] (8/3/41; Boris Karloff)
32. The Death Ship (8/10/41)
33. The Dark Squadron (8/17/41; Paul Lukas)
34. The Wail of Death (8/24/41)
35. The Hands of Death (8/31/41; George Coulouris)
36. Hunter From Beyond (9/7/41)
37. The Stallion of Death (9/14/41)
38. Death Goes to a Party (9/21/41; Ralph Forbes)
39. The Haunting Face (9/28/41; Claude Rains)
40. Dead Man's Rock (10/5/41; Everett Sloane)
41. Horror Hotel (10/12/41)
42. Hell Is Where You Find It (10/19/41; Burgess Meredith)
43. Terror on Bailey Street (10/26/41; Boris Karloff)
44. Nocturne of Death (11/2/41; Everett Sloane)
45. The Living Dead (11/9/41)
46. The Corpse Who Came to Dinner (11/16/41; Arnold Moss)
47. The Man From Outside (11/23/41)
48. The Accusing Corpse (11/30/41)
49. The Island of Death (12/7/41)
50. The Song of Doom (12/14/41)
51. The Man From Yesterday (12/21/41; Myron McCormick and Anne Seymour)

52. Death Has Claws (12/28/41; Santos Ortega)
53. Appointment for Murder (1/4/42)
54. Scarlet Widow (1/11/42)
55. Dead Reckoning (1/18/42; Arthur Vinton)
56. Death Has a Sculptor (1/25/42)
57. Death Has Wings (2/1/42)
58. The Phantom Express (2/8/42)
59. Death Strikes Twice (2/15/42)
60. Pact of Death (2/22/42)
61. Ghost Town (3/1/42)
62. The Black Swamp (3/8/42)
63. The Mask of Death (3/15/42)
64. Death Strikes Back (3/22/42)
65. Death, the Huntsman (3/29/42)
66. Fall of the House of Usher (4/5/42; Boris Karloff)
67. The Haunted Mine (4/12/42)
68. Blackstone (4/19/42; Boris Karloff)
69. The Man Who Died Again (4/26/42)
70. Study for Murder (5/3/42; Boris Karloff)
71. Death Calls at 12:00 (5/10/42)
72. The Last Performance (5/17/42)
73. The Cone (5/24/42; Boris Karloff)
74. Death Wears My Face (5/31/42; Boris Karloff)
75. Strange Request (6/7/42; Boris Karloff)
76. Terrible Vengeance (6/14/42)
77. The Grey Wolf (6/21/42; Boris Karloff)
78. Meeting in the Madhouse (6/28/42)
79. Terror Is a Double-Edged Sword (7/5/42)
80. Road to Death (7/12/42)
81. The Garden of Death (7/19/42)
82. Strange Cat (7/26/42)
83. Death Keeps a Date (8/2/42)
84. Death Has Four Faces (8/9/42)
85. Moon Murders (8/16/42)
86. Dead Man's Magic (8/23/42)
87. Visitor at Midnight (8/30/42)
88. Design for Dying (9/6/42)
89. Death Four Faces (9/13/42)
90. The Dead Walk at Night (9/20/42)
91. The Man Who Played With Death (9/27/42; Claude Rains)
92. Death's Revenge (10/4/42)
93. The King of Darkness (10/11/42; Claude Rains)
94. The Killer and the Moth (10/18/42)
95. The Deadly Parrot (10/25/42)

96. The Gunman and the Ghost (11/1/42; Arnold Moss)
97. The Laughing Murderer (11/8/42; Claude Rains)
98. Return from the Unknown (11/15/42)
99. The Cat and the Killer (11/22/42)
100. The Murders in the Morgue (11/29/42; Peter Lorre)
101. The Mummy's Curse (12/6/42)
102. The Man Who Returned from the Dead (12/13/42)
103. The Doomed Ship (12/20/42)
104. Dig My Grave (12/27/42; Peter Lorre)
105. Mystery of the Great Forest (1/3/43)
106. The Killer Pleads Guilty (1/10/43)
107. The Ring of Death (1/17/43; Chester Morris)
108. The Hound of Death (1/24/43)
109. Death at Moordan Castle (1/31/43)
110. The Black Seagull (2/7/43; Peter Lorre)
111. River of Blood (2/14/43)
112. Screams in the Night (2/21/43; Martha Scott)
113. The Button (2/28/43)
114. The Black Seagull (3/7/43; Peter Lorre)
115. Woman of Death (3/14/43)
116. Death on Merle Street (3/21/43)
117. Double Death (3/28/43)
118. The Ring of Doom (4/4/43)
119. The Dead Want Company (4/11/43)
120. The Unforgettable Face (4/18/43)
121. The Voice in the Night (4/25/43)
122. Death Builds A House (5/2/43)
123. One Must Die (5/9/43)
124. Death From A Stranger (5/16/43)
125. Death Comes Calling (5/23/43; Arnold Moss)
126. Fog (5/30/43)
127. The House Where Death Lived (6/6/43)
128. Murder by Mistake (6/13/43)
129. The Smiling Killer (6/20/43)
130. The House by the Sea (6/27/43)
131. Cups of Death (7/4/43)
132. Mr. De Capello (7/11/43)
133. The Temple of Isis (7/18/43)
134. -----(7/25/43)
135. The Horla [based on the story by Guy de Maupassant] (8/1/43; Arnold Moss)
136. The House of Death (8/8/43)
137. Death and the Lady Diana (8/15/43)
138. The Bog-Oak Necklace (8/22/43)
139. The Thirteenth Chime (8/29/43; Arnold Moss)
140. Death and the Detective (9/4/43; Everett Sloane)
141. Mr. Zenith (9/11/43)
142. Return to Death (9/18/43)
143. The Smiling Skull (9/25/43; Miriam Hopkins)
144. The Man Who Died Twice (10/2/43; Arnold Moss)
145. Death Walks on Padded Feet (10/9/43)
146. Accusing Corpse (10/16/43; Martin Gabel and Marian Hopkins)
147. Death's Candle Stick (10/23/43)
148. The Man Who Had No Heart (10/30/43)
149. Death Shines a Light (11/6/43)
150. Death Is a Blind Man (11/13/43; Joseph Cotten)
151. Vision of Death (11/20/43)
152. Death Strikes the Keys (11/27/43; Orson Welles)
153. Death has a Vacancy (12/4/43)
154. Speak of the Dead (12/11/43)
155. Dreadful Tapestry (12/18/43; Judith Evelyn)
156. Death Is a Madman (12/25/43; Leslie Woods)
157. The Train to Glory (1/1/44; Joseph Julian)
158. The Death Laugh (1/8/44; Laird Cregar)
159. The Huntress (1/15/44; Martin Gabel)
160. The Song of Doom (1/22/44; Laird Cregar)
161. The Dead Walk Tonight (1/29/44; Martin Gabel)
162. Dealer in Death (2/5/44; Laird Cregar)
163. Death Dream (2/12/44; Martin Gabel)
164. Death Steals the Scene (2/19/44)
165. Mysterious Stranger (2/26/44; Ann Sheperd)
166. The Wolf Woman (3/4/44; Akim Tamiroff)
167. Valse Triste [written by Arch Oboler] (3/11/44)

168. The Wings of Death (3/18/44; Akim Tamiroff)
169. The Room for the Standing Dead (3/25/44; Leslie Woods)
170. The Shriveled Head (4/1/44; Lionel Barrymore)
171. Death Tonight Can Wait (4/8/44; Leslie Woods)
172. The Walking Skull (4/15/44)
173. Screams in the Night (4/22/44; Mary Astor)
174. The Laughing Murderer (4/29/44; Adolph Menjou)
175. Death in the Bolero (5/6/44; Margo)
176. The Silent Hands (5/13/44; Mary Astor)
177. The Dead Refuse to Die (5/20/44; Berry Kroeger)
178. The Haunted Guitar (5/27/44; Margo)
179. Black Angel (6/3/44)
180. Death Is a Joker (6/10/44; Boris Karloff)
181. The Mind Reader (6/17/44; Peter Lorre)
182. Cypress Island (6/24/44; Leslie Woods)
183. Death Is a Delusion (7/1/44)
184. The Hanging Puppet (7/8/44)
185. The Spider and the Lady (7/15/44)
186. The Blue Tie (7/22/44)
187. The Mad House [part one] (7/29/44; Margo)
188. The Mad House [part two] (8/5/44; Margo)
189. Toccato Murder (8/19/44)
190. Tomb of Ramhotys (8/26/44)
191. Murder in the Museum (9/2/44)
192. Boy Butcher (9/9/44)
193. One Foot in the Grave (9/16/44; Peter Lorre)
194. The Dream (9/23/44; Orson Welles)
195. Premonition (9/30/44; Anne Seymour)
196. Dead Man's Vengeance (10/7/44)
197. The Deadly Ring (10/14/44)
198. The Grave of Maria Chandell (10/21/44)
199. A Dead Woman's Tale (10/28/44; Louise Rainer)
200. Blind Man's Bluff (11/4/44)
201. The House of Death (11/11/44)

202. The Cursed Twins (11/18/44; Berry Kroeger)
203. The Living Dead (11/22/44; Judith Evelyn)
204. The Voice on the Wire (11/29/44; Mary Astor)
205. The Color Blind Formula (12/6/44; Richard Widmark)
206. The Man Who Died Smiling (12/13/44; Joseph Julian)
207. The Frightened Lady (12/20/44; Leslie Woods)
208. Death Dream (12/27/44; Santos Ortega)
209. The Murdered Do Not Die (1/2/45; Clifton Webb)
210. Desert Death (1/9/45)
211. Death and the Dolls (1/16/45; Leslie Woods)
212. Death Is an Artist (1/23/45; Lee Bowman)
213. The Hand (1/30/45; Judith Evelyn)
214. Death in the Depths (2/6/45; Santos Ortega)
215. Ends of the Earth (2/13/45; Richard Arlen)
216. No Coffin for the Dead (2/20/45; Les Tremayne)
217. The Phantom Bell (2/27/45; Santos Ortega)
218. The Last Refrain (3/6/45; Wendy Barrie)
219. Island of the Dead (3/13/45; Karl Swenson)
220. Train to Glory (3/20/45; Jerry Wayne)
221. Mrs. Bluebird (3/27/45; Claudia Morgan)
222. The Meek Die Slowly (4/3/45; Victor Moore)
223. The Bog Oak Necklace (4/10/45; Miriam Hopkins)
224. The Judas Clock (4/17/45; Jackson Beck, Berry Kroeger, and Santos Ortega)
225. Song of the Slasher (4/24/45; Arnold Moss)
226. The Girl and the Gallows (5/1/45; Wendy Barrie)
227. The Black Art (5/15/45; Simone Simon)
228. Dead to Rights (5/22/45; Elspeth Eric and Santos Ortega)
229. Musical Score (5/29/45; Berry Kroeger)

230. Death Across the Board (6/5/45; Jackson Beck and Raymond Massey)
231. Portrait of Death (6/12/45; Leslie Woods)
232. Dead Man's Holiday (6/19/45; Myron McCormick)
233. Dead Man's Debt (6/26/45; Joseph Julian)
234. Dead Man's Deal (8/28/45; Larry Haines)
235. The Murder Prophet (9/4/45; Wendy Barrie)
236. The Last Story (9/11/45; Richard Widmark)
237. Terror By Night (9/18/45; Ann Shepherd)
238. The Lonely Sleep (9/25/45; Karl Swenson)
239. The Shadow of Death (10/2/45; Richard Widmark)
240. Death By Scripture (10/9/45; Stefan Schnabel)
241. Till Death Do Us Part (10/16/45; Larry Haines)
242. The Corridor of Doom (10/23/45; Boris Karloff)
243. Elixir Number Four [aka The Man Who Couldn't Die] (10/30/45; Boris Karloff)
244. The Wailing Wall (11/6/45; Jackson Beck and Boris Karloff)
245. The Dreadful Hunch (11/13/45; Richard Widmark)
246. Boomerang (11/20/45; Martin Gabel)
247. Death Can Be Beautiful (11/27/45; Karl Swenson)
248. A Puppet for Murder (12/4/45; Larry Haines)
249. The Dark Chamber (12/11/45; Kenneth Lynch)
250. The Undead (12/18/45; Anne Seymour)
251. The Littlest Angel (12/25/45; Helen Hayes)
252. Phantom Music Box (1/1/46; Santos Ortega)
253. The Creeping Wall (1/8/46; Irene Wicker)
254. The Edge of Death (1/15/46; Larry Haines)
255. The Confession (1/22/46; Santos Ortega)
256. The Blood of Cain (1/29/46; Mercedes McCambridge)
257. Skeleton Bay (2/5/46; Betty Lou Gerson)
258. The Man Who Couldn't Die (2/12/46; Richard Widmark)
259. You'll Never Escape (2/19/46; Kenny Lynch)
260. I Walk in the Night (2/26/46; Larry Haines)
261. Accident (3/5/46; Charlotte Holland)
262. The Strands of Death (3/12/46; Santos Ortega)
263. Murders in the Morgue (3/19/46; Victor Moore)
264. Death Is a Double Crosser (3/26/46; Lawson Zerbe)
265. The Night Is My Shroud (4/2/46; Ann Shepherd)
266. Lady with a Plan (4/9/46; Elspeth Eric)
267. The Lonely Hearts Killer (4/16/46; Orson Welles)
268. Make Ready My Grave (4/23/46; Joan Banks and Richard Widmark)
269. Dead Man's Turn (4/30/46; Larry Haines)
270. You Can Die Laughing (5/7/46; Santos Ortega)
271. Screams in the Night (5/14/46; Anne Shepherd)
272. Detour to Terror (5/21/46; Mason Adams)
273. Murder in the Night (5/28/46; Santos Ortega)
274. Eight Steps to Murder (6/4/46; Berry Kroeger)
275. Bury Me Not (6/11/46; Mercedes McCambridge)
276. I Want to Report a Murder (6/18/46; Santos Ortega)
277. One More Murder (7/29/46; Larry Haines)
278. Asleep in the Deep (8/5/46; Mercedes McCambridge)
279. Preview for Murder (8/12/46; Lawson Zerbe)
280. Specter of the Rose [based on a story by Ben Hecht] (8/19/46)
281. The Long Wait is Over (8/26/46; Joseph Julian)
282. The Missing Claw (9/2/46; Leslie Woods)

283. Murder Comes at Midnight (9/9/46; Mercedes McCambridge)
284. Murder to a Metronome (9/16/46; Anne Shepherd)
285. The Dead Laugh (9/23/46; Mercedes McCambridge and Santos Ortega)
286. Death Rides a Dollar Bill (9/30/46; Larry Haines)
287. The Listener (10/7/46; Freddie Bartholomew)
288. Strange Passenger (10/14/46; Mason Adams)
289. The Black Dog (10/21/46; Leslie Woods)
290. The Sister (10/28/46; Anne Shepherd)
291. Death's Old Sweet Song (11/4/46; Mercedes McCambridge)
292. Nightmare (11/11/46; Les Tremayne)
293. Highway to Death (11/18/46; Larry Haines)
294. No Rest for the Dead (11/25/46; Anne Shepherd)
295. But the Dead Walk Alone (12/2/46; Mercedes McCambridge)
296. Invisible Demon (12/9/46; Joseph Julian)
297. Whistle While I Die (12/16/46; Les Tremayne)
298. The Lonely Room (12/23/46; Mason Adams)
299. The Open Grave (12/30/46; Leslie Woods)
300. Death Pays the Freight (1/6/47; Larry Haines)
301. Payable at Death (1/13/47; Lawson Zerbe)
302. Witch Man (1/20/47; Berry Kroeger)
303. The Silent Hand (1/27/47; Stefan Schnabel)
304. Death Bound (2/3/47; Richard Widmark)
305. The Ghost in the Garden (2/10/47; Leslie Woods)
306. Moonlight Is for Murder (2/17/47; Larry Haines)
307. Journey Into Death (2/24/47; Karl Swenson)
308. The Corpse That Nobody Loved (3/3/47; Wendy Barrie)
309. The Deadly Kiss (3/10/47; Richard Widmark)
310. Bury Me Deep (3/17/47; Charlotte Holland)
311. Black Is for Death (3/24/47; Everett Sloane)
312. The Ghost of Jeremiah (3/31/47; Berry Kroeger)
313. The Girl Who Wouldn't Die (4/7/47; Mason Adams)
314. Death Is My Brother (4/14/47; Larry Haines)
315. Hour of Darkness (4/21/47; Karl Swenson)
316. The Case of the Living Corpse (4/28/47; Anne Shepherd)
317. Don't Dance on My Grave (5/5/47; Charlotte Holland and Arnold Moss)
318. The Dead Man Tells a Tale (5/12/47; Arlene Blackburn)
319. Terror By Night (5/19/47; Anne Shepherd)
320. Never to Die Again (5/26/47; Everett Sloane)
321. The Fear of Death (6/2/47; Richard Widmark)
322. The Rest of My Natural Life (6/9/47; Charlotte Holland)
323. The Man on the Slab (6/16/47; Arnold Moss)
324. Over My Dead Body (6/23/47; Larry Haines)
325. The Man and the Knife (6/30/47; Les Tremayne)
326. Nightmare (7/7/47; Elspeth Eric)
327. I Must Not Die Alone (7/14/47; Everett Sloane)
328. Death Accentuates the Negative (7/21/47; Anne Shepherd)
329. Murderer at Large (7/28/47; Joseph Julian)
330. The White Witch (8/4/47; Elspeth Eric)
331. Night of Death (8/11/47; Richard Widmark)
332. Adventure in the Macabre (8/18/47; Larry Haines)
333. The Body in the Closet (8/25/47; Karl Swenson)
334. Last Time I Killed Her (9/1/47; Arnold Moss)
335. The Deadly Ring (9/8/47; Richard Widmark)
336. Till the Day I Kill You (9/15/47)
337. As Long As I Live (9/22/47; Santos Ortega)

338. The Hands of Death (9/29/47; Myron McCormick)
339. A Time to Die (10/6/47; Mercedes McCambridge)
340. The Last Tour (10/13/47; Charles Irving)
341. The Mind Reader (10/20/47; Charlotte Holland)
342. Till Death Do Us Part (10/27/47; Mercedes McCambridge and Everett Sloane)
343. The Carnival of Death (11/3/47; Santos Ortega)
344. The Murderer Would Not Die (11/10/47; Karl Swenson)
345. The Conquest of Death (11/17/47; Larry Haines)
346. Tell it to the Dead (11/24/47; Everett Sloane)
347. Bernice (12/1/47; Karl Swenson)
348. Blood on the Roses (12/8/47; Mason Adams)
349. Death Pays the Black Keys (12/15/47; Everett Sloane)
350. Madame Midnight (12/22/47; Joseph Julian)
351. Death Out of Mind (12/29/47; Larry Haines and Ann Shephard)
352. The Flaming Corpse (1/5/48; Everett Sloane)
353. Tempo in Blood (1/12/48; Mason Adams and Everett Sloane)
354. Murder Counts to Four (1/19/48; Ted Osborne)
355. The Doomed (1/26/48; Mercedes McCambridge and Karl Swenson)
356. Death Trap (2/2/48; Evelyn Varden)
357. The Mislaid Corpse (2/9/48; Everett Sloane)
358. The Black Art (2/16/48; Ted Osborne)
359. Death Takes a Lonely Road (2/23/48; Mason Adams)
360. Dream Another Grave (3/1/48; Ted Osborne)
361. The Magic Tile (3/8/48; Mercedes McCambridge and Everett Sloane)
362. Ring Around the Morgue (3/15/48; Larry Haines)
363. Kill Me Tonight (3/22/48; Anne Shepherd)
364. Lady Killer (3/29/48; Everett Sloane)
365. Murder Is My Destiny (4/5/48; Karl Swenson)
366. Vampire (4/12/48; Arnold Moss)
367. Death Paints Its Face (4/19/48; Arnold Moss)
368. Doorway to Death (4/26/48; Joseph Julian)
369. Murder On My Mind (5/3/48; Larry Haines)
370. The Murder Mirror (5/10/48; Karl Swenson)
371. A Touch of Death (5/17/48; Anne Shepherd)
372. Murder Wears Polka Dots (5/24/48; Everett Sloane)
373. The Murdered Never Die (5/31/48; Joseph Julian)
374. The Kane Curse (6/7/48; Mason Adams)
375. The Mark of Murder (6/14/48; Karl Swenson)
376. The Death Trap (6/21/48; Evelyn Varden)
377. The Corpse Laughs Last (6/28/48; Mason Adams)
378. Death Demon (7/5/48; Anne Seymour and Everett Sloane)
379. Death Is a Magician (7/12/48; Larry Haines)
380. The Eyes of My Murderer (7/19/48; Donald Buka)
381. Murder Takes a Honeymoon (7/26/48; Ann Shepherd and Everett Sloane)
382. The Murder Ship (8/2/48; Mason Adams)
383. House of Doom (8/9/48; Charlotte Holland, Myron McCormick, Santos Ortega, Anne Seymour)
384. Paint My Coffin Black (8/16/48; Lawson Zerbe)
385. Only the Dead Will Know (8/23/48; Charlotte Holland and Sam Wanamaker)
386. Next Time I Live (8/30/48; Mason Adams and Anne Shepherd)
387. Death Rides a Riptide (9/6/48; Arlene Blackburn and Lawson Zerbe)
388. The Murder Carousel (9/13/48; Larry Haines)
389. Hangman's Island (9/20/48; Mason Adams and Elspeth Eric)
390. Murder by Prophesy (9/27/48; Joseph Julian, Santos Ortega, and Lawson Zerbe)

391. Death in the Universe (10/11/48; Lawson Zerbe)
392. Death of a Doll (10/18/48; Mason Adams and Ted Osborne)
393. The Phantom Dancer (10/25/48; Mercedes McCambridge)
394. Flight from Fear (11/1/48; Elspeth Eric)
395. The Front Page Murder (11/8/48; Myron McCormick)
396. Death Watch in Boston (11/15/48; Mason Adams and Ted Osborne)
397. The Monkey Called Death (11/22/48; Larry Haines)
398. Murder For Keeps (11/29/48; Arnold Moss)
399. The Cause of Death (12/6/48; Berry Kroeger and Santos Ortega)
400. Murder Faces East (12/13/48; Charlotte Holland and Karl Swenson)
401. Between Two Worlds (12/20/48; Mason Adams and Ann Shephard)
402. The Painted Corpse (12/27/48; Larry Haines)
403. Fearful Voyage (1/3/49; Elspeth Eric and Arnold Moss)
404. Murder Comes to Life (1/10/49; Charles Irving and Santos Ortega)
405. Mark My Grave (1/17/49; Santos Ortega and Lawson Zerbe)
406. The Deadly Dummy (1/24/49; Mason Adams and Elspeth Eric)
407. The Devil's Fortune (1/31/49; Jackson Beck, Charles Irving, and Karl Swenson)
408. Death Demon (2/7/49; Everett Sloane and Leslie Woods)
409. Birdsong for a Murderer (2/14/49; Arline Blackburn and Ted Osborne)
410. The Flame of Death (2/21/49; Charlotte Holland and Les Treymane)
411. The Roses Are Red (2/28/49; Larry Haines)
412. Murder by Coincidence (3/7/49; Everett Sloane)
413. Death and the Detective (3/14/49; Charles Irving)
414. Only the Dead Die Twice (3/21/49; Larry Haines and Alice Reinhart)
415. Appointment with Death (3/28/49; Charlotte Holland and Karl Swenson)
416. Death Wears a Lonely Smile (4/4/49; Mercedes McCambridge and Everett Sloane)
417. Murder Off the Record (4/11/49; Mason Adams and Elspeth Eric)
418. The Death Deal (4/18/49; Mercedes McCambridge, Arnold Moss, and Everett Sloane)
419. Death Is the Winner (4/25/49; Larry Haines)
420. The Deadly Double (5/2/49; Karl Swenson)
421. The Corpse on the Town (5/9/49; Charles Irving)
422. The Unburied Dead (5/16/49; Everett Sloane and Leslie Woods)
423. Strange Passenger (5/23/49; Mason Adams)
424. The Corpse Is Lonely (5/30/49; Larry Haines)
425. Death on the Highway (6/6/49; Ted Osborne and Alice Reinhart)
426. The Curious Corpse (6/13/49; Mercedes McCambridge)
427. The Corpse Without a Conscience (6/20/49; Everett Sloane and Karl Swenson)
428. Model for a Murder (6/27/49; Arnold Moss)
429. Pattern for Fear (7/4/49; Cameron Prud'Homme and Everett Sloane)
430. Death Song (7/11/49; Mason Adams)
431. Deadly Fare (7/18/49; Larry Haines and Everett Sloane)
432. Murder Wears a Straw Hat (7/25/49; Mason Adams)
433. Dead Level (8/1/49; Berry Kroeger)
434. Death Takes First Prize (8/8/49; Joseph Julian)
435. Dead Heat (8/15/49; Mercedes McCambridge and Karl Swenson)
436. Mind Over Murder (8/22/49; Elspeth Eric and Everett Sloane)
437. Death's Little Brother (8/29/49; Larry Haines)
438. Murder Rides the Carousel (9/5/49; Leslie Woods and Lawson Zerbe)
439. The Vengeful Corpse (9/12/49; Karl Swenson and Barbara Weeks)
440. Honeymoon with Death (9/19/49; Mason Adams, Arlene Blackburn, and Mercedes McCambridge)
441. Strike Me Dead (9/26/49; Berry Kroeger)

442. Catch a Killer (10/3/49; Larry Haines and Barbara Weeks)
443. The Devil's Workshop (10/10/49; Mason Adams and Joan Banks)
444. Image of Death (10/17/49; Jean Ellen and Berry Kroeger)
445. Night Is my Shroud (10/24/49; Kenneth Lynch and Ann Shepard)
446. A Corpse for Halloween (10/31/49; Larry Haines, Berry Kroeger, and Mercedes McCambridge)
447. Make Deep My Grave (11/7/49; Martin Gabel)
448. The Wish to Kill (11/14/49; Karl Swenson and Leslie Woods)
449. Time to Die (11/21/49; Lawson Zerbe)
450. The Illusion of Murder (11/28/49; Mason Adams)
451. Wake Up and Die (12/5/49; Larry Haines)
452. The Touch of Death (12/12/49; Charlotte Holland)
453. Beyond the Grave (12/19/49; Martin Gabel)
454. The Enchanted Ghost (12/26/49; Frank Sinatra)
455. Blood Relative (1/2/50; Charlotte Holland)
456. Killer at Large (1/9/50; Larry Haines)
457. The Scream (1/16/50; Barbara Weeks)
458. The Hitch-hiking Corpse (1/23/50; Kenneth Lynch)
459. Skeleton Bay [originally scheduled for 1/16/50, but was postponed] (1/30/50; Charlotte Holland)
460. The Deadly Face (2/6/50; Arnold Moss)
461. Not Quite Dead (2/13/50; Everett Sloane)
462. The Obituary (2/20/50; Mason Adams)
463. The Death Grip (2/27/50; Martin Gabel)
464. The Haunted (3/6/50; Arnold Moss)
465. Diamonds for a Corpse (3/13/50; Larry Haines)
466. A Corpse in the Parlor (3/20/50; Kenneth Lynch)
467. Murder Mansion (3/27/50; Arnold Moss and Everett Sloane)
468. The Touch of Terror (4/3/50; Charlotte Holland)
469. The Cry of Death (4/10/50; Berry Kroeger)
470. Beneficiary: Death (4/17/50; Everett Sloane and Barbara Weeks)
471. The Corpse Said No (9/4/50; Larry Haines)
472. Death Watch (9/11/50; Robert Sloane)
473. Dead Man's Holiday (9/18/50; Peter Cappel)
474. The Dead Are Never Lonely (9/25/50; Mason Adams)
475. Cry Ghosts (10/2/50; Ken Lynch)
476. Death Wish (10/9/50; Peter Cappel)
477. The Hangman (10/16/50; Santos Ortega)
478. The Empty Grave (10/23/50; Ralph Bell)
479. Twice Dead (11/6/50; Larry Haines)
480. Skeleton in the Sun (11/13/50; Ken Lynch)
481. No Escape (11/20/50; Charlotte Holland)
482. One Coffin Too Many (11/27/50; Ralph Bell)
483. Beyond the Grave (12/4/50; Mason Adams, Lester Coppel, and Mercedes McCambridge)
484. Two in a Grave (12/11/50; Karl Swenson)
485. Murder by Consent (12/18/50; Ken Lynch)
486. The Enchanted Ghost (12/25/50; Larry Haines)
487. The Phantom Music Box (1/1/51)
488. Terror in the Night (1/8/51; Ralph Bell)
489. The Sound of Death (1/15/51; Peter Cappel)
490. The Lonesome Corpse (1/22/51; Ken Lynch)
491. The Finger of Death (1/29/51; Larry Haines)
492. The Snow-White Scarf (2/5/51; Mason Adams)
493. Fear of Night (2/12/51; Everett Sloane)
494. The Smile of the Dead (2/19/51; Larry Haines)
495. The Man From the Grave (2/26/51; Ralph Bell and Peter Cappel)
496. Death Proposal (3/5/51; Charlotte Holland)

497. Live a Little, Die a Little (3/12/51; Everett Sloane)
498. The Skeleton in a Trunk (3/19/51; Lawson Zerbe)
499. The Unseen (3/26/51; Mandel Kramer)
500. The Deadly Purse (4/2/51; Arnold Moss)
501. Time to Kill (4/9/51; Ralph Bell)
502. -----(4/16/51; Larry Haines)
503. -----(4/23/51; Ken Lynch)
504. -----(4/30/51)
505. Death Is a Right Hook (5/7/51; Larry Haines)
506. -----(5/14/51; Mason Adams)
507. -----(5/21/51; Arnold Moss)
508. The Unforgiving Corpse (5/28/51; Luis Van Rooten and Lawson Zerbe)
509. A Corpse There Was (6/4/51)
510. The Death Watch (6/11/51; Barbara Weeks)
511. The Ghost in the Garden (6/18/51; Lesley Woods)
512. Birdsong for a Murderer (6/22/52; Boris Karloff)
513. Terror By Night (6/29/52; Agnes Moorehead)
514. Death Pays the Freight (7/6/52; Everett Sloane)
515. Death for Sale (7/13/52; Boris Karloff)
516. The Listener (7/20/52; Paul McGrath and Agnes Moorehead)
517. The Murder Prophet (7/27/52; Agnes Moorehead)
518. Murder Off the Record (8/3/52; Kenneth Lynch)
519. The Magic Tile (8/10/52; Anne Seymour)
520. The Corpse Laughs Last (8/17/52; Wendell Corey)
521. No Rest for the Dead (8/24/52; Barbara Weeks)
522. Strange Passenger (8/31/52; Wendell Corey)
523. The Meek Die Slowly (9/7/52; Arnold Moss)
524. Till Death Do Us Part (9/14/52; Mason Adams)
525. The Corpse Nobody Loved (9/21/52; Joan Lorring)
526. The Dead Walk at Night (9/28/52; Donald Buka)
527. Death Pays the Freight (10/5/52; Everett Sloane)

Inspector Thorne

Sustaining detective series starring Karl Weber in the lead role of Inspector Thorne. This short summer series was broadcast over NBC from 9 to 9:30 pm, EST, Friday evenings. The final four episodes were broadcast on Thursday evenings at the same time-slot. Staats Cotsworth starred as Inspector Thorne in the final broadcast.

1. The Fabulous Divorce Pay-Off Murder Case (7/20/51)
2. The Vacant Lot Murder Case (7/27/51)
3. The Golden Girl Murder Case (8/3/51)
4. The Defrosted Refrigerator Murder Case (8/10/51)
5. The High Style Murder Case (8/17/51)
6. The Master Mind Murder Case (8/24/51)
7. The Dark Cigarette Murder Case (8/31/51)
8. The Nickels and Dimes Murder Case (9/6/51)
9. The Two Finances Murder Case (9/13/51)
10. The Empty Ash Tray Murder Case (9/20/51)
11. The Society Writer Murder Case (9/27/51)

Intrigue

Dramatic anthology series using stories of distrust. Joseph Schildkraut was the narrator and actor of each episode. Directed by Charles Vanda. Sustaining. Broadcast on Wednesday evenings over CBS from 9:30 to 10 pm, EST.

1. Rogue Male (7/24/46)
2. Dawn Over the Amazon (7/31/46)
3. Sinister Errand (8/7/46)
4. The Great Impersonator (8/21/46; P. Oppenheimer)
5. Smiler with the Knife (8/28/46; Virginia Bruce)
6. The Dreyfus Case (9/4/46; Joseph Schildkraut)
7. Basil Zaboroff (9/11/46)

Jerry at Fair Oaks

This syndicated juvenile serial was a continuation of *Jerry of the Circus*. Our hero of that series now goes to Fair Oaks, a military school. Each episode ran fifteen minutes, broadcast from 1937 to 1938.

1. Roommate Assigned
2. Meeting Red, Tubby and Harold
3. Learning about Demerits
4. Meeting Ted and William
5. Red Gets 13 Demerits
6. Ready for the Polo Team Tryouts
7. Tryout Against Two Others
8. Three-way Tie, Cards Drawn
9. Financing an Invention
10. Harold Almost Drowns
11. Runaway Horse Stopped
12. $250.00 Turned Down
13. Invention was Too Late
14. Jerry Paints the Smoke Stack
15. Jerry Gets Caught
16. Cleaning the Paint
17. Top of the List
18. Splendor
19. Paul Rides Splendor
20. Saddle Loosened
21. The Court Martial
22. The Hopeless Case
23. Jerry Found Innocent
24. Bomber Crash
25. Harold Leaves
26. Treasure Hunt Planned
27. Treasure Hunt Begins
28. Someone Falls in Hole
29. Getting Help
30. Red Is Rescued
31. Red Is Recovering
32. The Boat to the Island
33. Seeing Smoke
34. Plot for Safety
35. Guy Linwell Arrives
36. Suspicious of Man
37. Yorga Wants Secrets
38. Letter Taken
39. Harold Disappears
40. Yorga Spotted
41. Traced to Farm House
42. All are Arrested
43. Guy Will Teach
44. Bruce Campbell Arrives
45. Pony and Polo Interest
46. Red Talks with Sgt. Alden
47. Mr. X Arrives at Fair Oaks
48. Jerry and Lee Meet Mr. X
49. Splendor Is Sick
50. Bumps Comes to See the Meet
51. Lee and Tubby Fight with Red
52. The Meet
53. Celebrating Victory
54. Punishment for Fighting with Red
55. Bruce and Jerry Argue
56. Mrs. Gardner Takes a Hand
57. Disagreement With Bruce Is Settled
58. Practice Basketball Game

Jerry of the Circus

This juvenile series was syndicated in 1937. Each episode ran for fifteen minutes. Followed by a second serial, *Jerry at Fair Oaks.*

80. Race About to Start
81. Blaze Wins the Race
82. Spike Rejoins the Circus
83. An Abandoned Kitten
84. Counterfeit Money Passed
85. Forty Ten-Dollar Bills Passed
86. Joe Hadley Hired
87. Spike Is Suspected
88. Patsy Accepts a Date
89. Belco Suspected
90. Spike Suspected More
91. Hadley Arrests Spike
92. Tony Tonetti Spotted
93. Hadley Arrests Belco
94. Circus Lot Floods
95. Fake Invitation Sent to Boris
96. Boris Gets the Invitation
97. -----
98. -----
99. Fast Landing
100. A Bet for Dan
101. Too Many Monkeys
102. $117.00 Receipt Increase
103. Restless Animals
104. Storm Warnings
105. Circus Hit by Cyclone

106. Borrowing $25,000
107. Patsy Leaves Early
108. Jerry Inherits Forty Acres
109. Boris and Jason Fight
110. Patsy Wins $25,000
111. Boris Eyes the Money
112. Jason Is Clawed by the Cat
113. Jason Quickly Recovers
114. Boris Starts Dissension
115. A Strike Is Possible
116. The Strike Begins
117. Strikers Are Worried
118. The Strike Ends
119. A New Scheme by Boris
120. Rex Runs Away
121. Speed Demonstrates
122. Advice for Patsy
123. Boris Has a New Plot
124. Spud's Tricks Fool Jerry
125. Spud's Bad Trick
126. Financial Troubles for Mr. Randall
127. Patsy Loans the Circus Money
128. Jerry Sells His Land
129. Jerry Chooses Fair Oaks
130. Jerry Leaves the Circus

John Barrymore and Shakespeare
see *Streamlined Shakespeare*

Jurgen's Hollywood Playhouse

Sponsored by Jurgen's Lotion, this series was part of the *Romance* series, retitled because of a new sponsor. Also billed as *The Playhouse of Romance*, adaptations of popular stories and original dramas were presented. Lyn Murray supplied the music. Broadcast over CBS, Thursday evenings from 9 to 9:30 pm, EST.

1. Stone Walls (9/4/52)
2. Motive for Murder (9/11/52)
3. Mayerling (9/18/52)
4. Bayou Song (9/25/52)
5. Glass Hero (10/2/52)
6. Valley of the Shadow (10/9/52)
7. Long Arm (10/16/52)

8. San Francisco Incident (10/23/52)
9. The Bribe (10/30/52)
10. Two Languages (11/6/52)
11. One — oh — One (11/13/52)
12. The Fine Line (11/20/52)
13. September Times Two (11/27/52)
14. Red (12/4/52)

15. Heiress from Red Horse (12/11/52)   17. Wild Oranges (1/1/53)
16. The Bachelor (12/18/52)   18. False Holiday (1/8/53)

Kaleidoscope

This variety series was a three-hour-long, Saturday afternoon feature, broadcast over NBC from 2–5 pm, EST. Bob Hope was the host for the first two broadcasts, being replaced by Charlton Heston in episode three. It is not known who was host from episode four to the end of the series, because none of the broadcasts exist. Each week brought three hours of musical presentations, dramas, readings, and speeches with various guests from Britain and America. The presentations are listed in the order they were presented on the programs. "Mr. President" from episode seven was a documentary on the American tradition of White House delegations. The popular "The Quick and the Dead," the H-Bomb documentary presented over numerous radio stations across the country every year, was restaged for episode eight. Carl Sandburg was interviewed in episode eight. Many of the presentations were recordings of various shows broadcast in the past. Eventually, the Shakespearean dramas and plays were abandoned, leaving the series with more musical presentations. Episode thirty-two featured a recording of Groucho Marx's "Hooray for Captain Spalding."

1. The Lady's Not for Burning (1/17/53; Pamela Brown Don Giovanni) [Mozart's musical]
2. Twelfth Night (1/24/53; The Beggar's Opera Alec Guinness)
3. An Inspector Calls [based on the story by J.B. Priestley] (1/31/53; Sir Ralph Richardson The Marriage of Figaro [Mozart's musical] Bertrand Russell)
4. Fighter Pilot (2/7/53; Marius Goring The Door in the Wall [based on the story by H.G. Welles] Clifford Curzon)
5. The Father (2/14/53; Robert Harris Il Re Pastore [Mozart's musical])
6. The Importance of Being Ernest (2/21/53; Edith Evans and Sir John Gielgud The Fairy Queen [Purcell's Opera] Bertrand Russell)
7. Richard II, Part I (2/28/53; Michael Redgrave Mr. President [Henry Purcell's Opera])
8. Richard II, Part II (3/7/53; Michael Redgrave Carl Sandburg Exclusive

The Quick and the Dead Down in the Valley [Kurt Weill's Opera])
9. Uncle Vanya (3/14/53; La Traviata [Verdi Opera] Licia Albanese The International Situation with Anthony Eden, British Foreign Secretary)
10. Measure for Measure (3/21/53; Claire Bloom La Traviata [part two] Poems Written and Read by Archibald MacLeish Carnival of the Animals [based on Saint-Saens])
11. La Boheme (3/28/53; Licia Albanese and Jan Peerce Measure for Measure [based on Shakespeare's play, part two] Claire Bloom Tennessee Williams Reads his Works)
12. Strife (4/4/53; Ernest Jay Die Fledermaus [Strauss] Patrice Munsel, Jan Peerce, and Rise Stevens)
13. Bible Readings (4/11/53; Charles Laughton The Voice of FDR [documentary] Sing Out Sweet Land Alfred Drake and Burl Ives)
14. Othello [Verdi Opera] (4/18/53; On

Acting Shakespeare discussed by Alec Guinness Hamlet [excerpts] Laurence Olivier Romeo and Juliet Pamela Brown and Sir John Gielgud)

15. The Man Who Could Work Miracles (4/25/53; Poetry of Our Times [part one] Katherine Anne Porter H.M.S. Pinafore More Bible Readings Charles Laughton)

16. Mikado (5/2/53; Queen Elizabeth Edith Evans) Music from the film Ivanhoe Poetry of Our Times [part two] Katherine Anne Porter

17. Call Me Madam (5/9/53; Ethel Merman Songs of the Auvergne Madeline Grey Woodland Suite [MacDowell composition] Poetry of Our Times [part three] Katherine Anne Porter Plymouth Adventure [film music])

18. The Pirates of Penzance (5/16/53; Poetry of Our Times [part four] Katherine Anne Porter Symphony No. 5 1/2 [based on the Don Gillis composition])

19. Poetry of Our Times [part five] (5/23/53; Katherine Anne Porter)

20. The Treatment of Freedom Choral (5/30/53; Boston Symphony and the Harvard Glee Club The Mississippi Suite [based on the Grofe composition] Susan Reed Sings Folk Songs Folk Songs of the Civil War)

21. Excerpts from the Works of Herbert, Romberg, Friml, Rogers and Hart (6/6/53)

22. Yeomen of the Guard (6/13/53; Folk Songs Burl Ives Poetry of Our Times [part six] Katherine Anne Porter)

23. Iolanthe (6/20/53)

24. Gondoliers [based on Gilbert and Sullivan] (6/27/53; Show Business Memories John Barrymore and Maurice Chevalier)

25. The Living Declaration (7/4/53; Claude Rains Songs of America Fred Waring Early American Songs Margaret Truman, and the Robert Shaw Chorale Stephen Foster Melodies Nelson Eddy)

26. Ruddigore [based on Gilbert and Sullivan] (7/11/53)

27. The Shrine Chanter Concert (7/18/53)

28. -----(7/25/53)

29. The Discovery of Boswell's Journals [documentary] (8/1/53; Portrait of a Prairie Town Don Gillis)

30. -----(8/8/53)

31. The Summer Opera Festival [music by Verdi, Wagner, and Puccini] (8/15/53)

32. Humor to Music (8/22/53; Spike Jones, Beatrice Lillie, Groucho Marx, and Ogden Nash)

33. Boston Pops Concert (8/29/53; Jan Peerce, Ezio Pinza, and Eleanor Steber)

34. -----(9/5/53)

The Lady Esther Screen Guild Theater

Previously titled *The Gulf Screen Theater*, Lady Esther took over the sponsorship (as a last minute decision) from Gulf Oil. Broadcast Monday evenings from Hollywood, over CBS from 10:00 to 10:30 pm, EST, the series comprised adaptations of movies with Hollywood stars in the lead roles. Episode fifty-seven was based on the play "A Design for Scandal." Basil Rathbone substituted for Brian Aherne at the last moment for episode twelve. Episode seventy, entitled "Thank Your Lucky Stars," was a revue featuring music from the war-time film. During the performance of episode ninety-five, "The Ghost Goes West," someone belched over the air, causing a moment of silence during the broadcast. In January of 1945, Bing Crosby performed selected scenes from "Going My Way." Norman Corwin's "My Client Curley," originally performed over *The Columbia*

Workshop, was performed again on *Lady Esther*, February of 1946. In 1947, Lady Esther dropped sponsorship, and Camel Cigarettes took over, causing the title to change to *The Camel Screen Guild Theater*.

1. Yankee Doodle Dandy (10/19/42; James Cagney, Betty Grable, Rita Hayworth, and Walter Huston)
2. A Yank in the RAF (10/26/42; Betty Grable, Tyrone Power, and John Sutton)
3. My Favorite Wife (11/2/42; Barbara Stanwyck and Robert Taylor)
4. Take a Letter, Darling (11/9/42; Cary Grant and Rosalind Russell)
5. Good-Bye, Mr. Chips (11/16/42; Merle Oberon and Basil Rathbone)
6. Bachelor Mother (11/23/42; Fred MacMurray and Ann Sothern)
7. Ball of Fire (11/30/42; Paulette Goddard, Richard Hayden, and Kay Kyser)
8. Mrs. Miniver (12/7/42; Greer Garson and Walter Pidgeon)
9. Mr. and Mrs. Smith (12/14/42; Ralph Bellamy, Joan Bennett, and Robert Young)
10. The Juggler of Our Lady (12/21/42; Ronald Colman and Nelson Eddy)
11. The Male Animal (12/28/42; Jack Carson, Olivia de Havilland, and Joel McCrea)
12. Suspicion (1/4/43; Nigel Bruce, Joan Fontaine, and Basil Rathbone)
13. Holiday Inn (1/11/43; Fred Astaire, Bing Crosby, and Dinah Shore)
14. To Be or Not to Be (1/18/43; Jon Hall, Dianna Lewis, and William Powell)
15. Across the Pacific (1/25/43; Mary Astor, Humphrey Bogart, and Sydney Greenstreet)
16. Dodsworth (2/1/43; Bette Davis, Walter Huston, and Nan Sutherland)
17. Hold Back the Dawn (2/8/43; Charles Boyer, Susan Hayward, and Margaret Lindsay)
18. They Got Me Covered (2/15/43; Bob Hope, Dorothy Lamour, and Philis Ruth)
19. Louisiana Purchase (2/22/43; Annabella, William Gaxton, and Victor Moore)
20. This Above All (3/1/43; Virginia Bruce, Herbert Marshall, and Alan Mowbray)
21. Stand by for Action (3/8/43; Brian Donlevy, Charles Laughton, and Chester Morris)
22. Palm Beach Story (3/15/43; Claudette Colbert, Randolph Scott, and Rudy Vallee)
23. For Me and My Gal (3/22/43; Judy Garland, Gene Kelly, George Murphy, and Dick Powell)
24. This Thing Called Love (3/29/43; George Brent, Alice Faye, Allyn Joslyn, and Robert Young)
25. Journey for Margaret (4/5/43; Anita Louise, Margaret O'Brien, Billy Severn, and Robert Young)
26. Pittsburgh (4/12/43; Marlene Dietrich, Randolph Scott, and John Wayne)
27. Woman of the Year (4/19/43; Katharine Hepburn and Spencer Tracy)
28. Casablanca (4/26/43; Ingrid Bergman, Humphrey Bogart, and Paul Henried)
29. Nothing But the Truth (5/3/43; Lucille Ball, Humphrey Bogart, and Frank Morgan)
30. Johnny Eager (5/10/43; John Garfield, Carole Landis, and Robert Paige)
31. Whistling in Dixie (5/17/43; Virginia Grey, Red Skelton, and Claire Trevor)
32. Shadow of a Doubt (5/24/43; Joseph Cotten and Deanna Durbin)
33. Rebecca (5/31/43; Brian Aherne, Joan Fontaine, and Agnes Moorehead)
34. The Devil and Miss Jones (6/7/43; Charles Coburn, Laraine Day, Joseph Kearns, and George Murphy)
35. Love Is News (6/14/43; Jack Benny, James Gleason, and Ann Sheridan)
36. Back Street (6/21/43; Charles Boyer and Martha Scott)
37. Remember the Day (6/28/43; Franchot Tone and Loretta Young)
38. Tennessee Johnson (7/5/43; Lionel

Barrymore, Gary Cooper, and Ruth Hussey)

39. Human Comedy (7/12/43; Frank Morgan and Mickey Rooney)
40. Men in White (7/19/43; Louise Allbritton, James Craig, and Jean Hersholt)
41. Once Upon a Honeymoon (7/26/43; Linda Darnell and Ray Milland)
42. Come Live with Me (8/2/43; Hedy Lamarr, John Loder, and Vincent Price)
43. Spitfire (8/9/43; Heather Angel, Reginald Gardner, and Basil Rathbone)
44. The Pied Piper (8/16/43; Roddy McDowall and Monty Wooley)
45. Skylark (8/23/43; Preston Foster, Allyn Joslyn, and Ginger Rogers)
46. The Moon Is Down (8/30/43; Sir Cedric Hardwicke and Lewis Stone)
47. The Major and the Minor (9/6/43; Warner Baxter, Diana Lynn, and Ruth Warrick)
48. Birth of the Blues (9/13/43; Bing Crosby, Johnny Mercer, and Ginny Simms)
49. The Maltese Falcon (9/20/43; Mary Astor, Humphrey Bogart, Sydney Greenstreet, and Peter Lorre)
50. Thank Your Lucky Stars (9/27/43; Eddie Cantor, Dennis Morgan, and Dinah Shore)
51. Hi Diddle Diddle (10/4/43; Mary Boland, Dennis O'Keefe, and Martha Scott)
52. Love Affair (10/11/43; Luis Alberni, Virginia Bruce, and Herbert Marshall)
53. My Sister Eileen (10/18/43; Brian Aherne, Louis Alberni, Rosalind Russell, and George Tobias)
54. Edge of Darkness (10/25/43; John Garfield, Ralph Morgan, and Maureen O'Hara)
55. You Belong to Me (11/1/43; Don Ameche and Mary Astor)
56. George Washington Slept Here (11/8/43; Jack Carson and Carole Landis)
57. Remember the Day (11/15/43; Olivia de Havilland and Walter Pidgeon)
58. Immortal Sergeant (11/22/43; Charles Irwin, Alan Mobray, Maureen O'Sullivan and Franchot Tone)

59. Theodora Goes Wild (11/29/43; Irene Dunne, Cary Grant, and Hanley Stafford)
60. Only Yesterday (12/6/43; Joseph Cotten and Loretta Young)
61. Holy Matrimony (12/13/43; Fay Bainter and Frank Morgan)
62. The Youngest Profession (12/20/43; Edward Arnold, Jean Porter, and Virginia Weidler)
63. Let's Face It (12/27/43; Bill Goodwin, Bob Hope, and Jane Wyman)
64. The North Star (1/3/44; Anne Baxter, Farley Granger, Walter Huston, and Jane Withers)
65. Watch on the Rhine (1/10/44; Bette Davis and Paul Lukas)
66. I Love You Again (1/17/44; Paulette Goddard, William Powell, and Charles Winninger)
67. Iron Major (1/24/44; Pat O'Brien and Ruth Warrick)
68. Lucky Jordan (1/31/44; Barbara Britton, Alan Ladd, Marjorie Main, and Harry Von Zell)
69. True to Life (2/7/44; Joan Leslie and Dick Powell)
70. Gentleman Jim (2/14/44; Ward Bond, Errol Flynn, Alexis Smith, and Grant Withers)
71. A Design for Scandal (2/21/44; Carole Landis and Robert Young)
72. Three Men on a Horse (2/28/44; Isabel Jewell, Charles Laughton, and Ann Sothern)
73. The Gay Divorcee (3/6/44; Spring Byington, Gloria DeHaven, Edward Everett Horton, and Frank Sinatra)
74. Tuttles of Tahiti (3/13/44; Florence Bates, Charles Bickford, Elsa Lanchester and Charles Laughton)
75. Constant Nymph (3/20/44; Charles Boyer, Geraldine Fitzgerald, Maureen O'Hara and Alexis Smith)
76. Why Jack Is Not Going to Appear on the Show (3/27/44; Jack Benny, Michael Curtiz, Jean Hersholt, Basil Rathbone, and Barbara Stanwyck)
77. Hello Frisco, Hello (4/3/44; Jackie Oakie, Dick Powell, and Ginny Simms)
78. A Farewell to Arms (4/10/44; Gary Cooper, Pedro de Cordova, and Joan Fontaine)

79. High Sierra (4/17/44; Humphrey Bogart and Ida Lupino)
80. Snow White (4/24/44; Edgar Bergen, Charlie McCarthy, Billy Gilbert, and Jane Powell)
81. A Night to Remember (5/1/44; Lucille Ball and Brian Donlevy)
82. Dark Angel (5/8/44; Ronald Colman, Donald Crisp, and Merle Oberon)
83. Priorities on Parade (5/15/44; Jerry Colonna, Bing Crosby, Betty Rhodes, and Vera Vague)
84. Up in Mabel's Room (5/22/44; Mischa Auer, Jinx Falkenburg, Dennis O'Keefe and Marjorie Reynolds)
85. Congo Maisie (5/29/44; John Hodiak and Ann Sothern)
86. The Amazing Dr. Clitterhouse (6/5/44; Lloyd Nolan, Edward G. Robinson, and Claire Trevor)
87. No Time for Love (6/12/44; Claudette Colbert, Hedda Hopper, and Fred MacMurray)
88. My Son, My Son (7/3/44; Heather Angel, Freddie Bartholomew, and Herbert Marshall)
89. The Informer (7/10/44; Charles Bickford, Reginald Denny, Wallace Ford, and Isabel Jewell)
90. Make Your Own Bed (7/17/44; Jack Carson, Alan Hale, and Jane Wyman)
91. Night Must Fall (7/24/44; James Cagney, Rosemary DeCamp, and Dame May Whitty)
92. The Good Fairy (7/31/44; Deanna Durbin, June Lockhart, and Fredric March)
93. Alias the Deacon (8/7/44; Noah Beery, Jr., Martha O'Driscoll, and Charles Winninger)
94. Nervous Wreck (8/14/44; Mary Astor, Edward Everett Horton, and Edgar Kennedy)
95. The Ghost Goes West (8/21/44; Marsha Hunt, Charles Irving, Herbert Marshall, Eugene Pallatte, and Basil Rathbone)
96. The Uninvited (8/28/44; Betty Field, Ruth Hussey, and Ray Milland)
97. Too Many Husbands (9/4/44; Bill Goodwin, Donna Reed, and Frank Sinatra)
98. Phantom Lady (9/11/44; Walter Abel, Louise Allbritton, Ralph Bellamy, and David Bruce)
99. The Ox-Bow Incident (9/18/44; Edward Arnold, Harry Davenport, and William Eythe)
100. It Happened Tomorrow (9/25/44; Frank Craven, Linda Darnell, and Dick Powell)
101. Shopworn Angel (10/2/44; Laraine Day, Adolphe Menjou, and Robert Walker)
102. A Girl, a Guy, and a Gob (10/9/44; Lucille Ball, William Gargan, and George Murphy)
103. Mad About Music (10/16/44; Eric Blore, Gloria Jean, and Herbert Marshall)
104. Ninotchka (10/23/44; Signe Hasso and Robert Young)
105. Anna Karenina (10/30/44; Ingrid Bergman and Gregory Peck)
106. Holiday (11/13/44; Joseph Cotten and Loretta Young)
107. Once Upon a Holiday (11/20/44; John Hodiak and Lana Turner)
108. You Belong to Me (11/27/44; Lee Bowman and Paulette Goddard)
109. China Seas (12/4/44; Lucille Ball, Douglas Dumbrill, Clark Gable, Anna Lee, and Herbert Rawlinson)
110. San Diego, I Love You (12/11/44; Louise Allbritton, Jon Hall, and Edward Everett Horton)
111. The Age of Innocence (12/18/44; Jane Morgan, Merle Oberon, and John Payne)
112. Pinocchio (12/25/44; Fanny Brice and Hanley Stafford)
113. Mr. and Mrs. Smith (1/1/45; Louise Allbritton, Joan Blondell, Stuart Erwin, and Preston Foster)
114. Going My Way (1/8/45; Bing Crosby, Barry Fitzgerald, Paul Lukas, and George Murphy)
115. Three Is a Family (1/15/45; Fay Bainter, Helen Broderick, Hattie McDaniel, and Charles Ruggles)
116. Love Before Breakfast (1/22/45; David Bruce, Virginia Bruce, and Brian Donlevy)
117. No Time for Comedy (1/29/45; Jack Carson and Alexis Smith)

118. Joan of the Ozarks (2/5/45; Joe E. Brown, Judy Canova, and Frank Nelson)
119. Belle of the Yukon (2/12/45; Bob Burns, Gail Patrick, Randolph Scott, and Dinah Shore)
120. Take a Letter, Darling (2/19/45; Don Ameche, Linda Darnell, and Franklyn Pangborn)
121. Shop Around the Corner (2/26/45; Felix Bressart, Van Johnson, and Phyllis Thaxter)
122. Double Indemnity (3/5/45; Fred MacMurray and Barbara Stanwyck)
123. So This Is Washington (3/12/45; Edward Arnold, Jimmy Gleason, and Lum and Abner)
124. Next Time We Love (3/19/45; Robert Cummings and Joan Fontaine)
125. The Princess and the Pirate (3/26/45; Virginia Bruce, Bob Hope, and Virginia Mayo)
126. This Gun for Hire (4/2/45; Alan Ladd and Veronica Lake)
127. Abroad with Two Yanks (4/9/45; William Bendix, Dennis O'Keefe, and Marjorie Reynolds)
128. The Mask of Dimitrios (4/16/45; Sydney Greenstreet, Peter Lorre, and Zachary Scott)
129. Flesh and Fantasy (4/23/45; Charles Boyer and Ella Raines)
130. Ramona (4/30/45; Anne Baxter, Joseph Cotten, Reed Hadley, and Loretta Young)
131. Heaven Can Wait (5/7/45; John Carradine, Susan Hayward, and Walter Pidgeon)
132. First Love (5/14/45; Peter Lawford, Shirley Temple, and Arthur Treacher)
133. The Desert Song (5/21/45; Bruce Cabot, Hans Conried, Dennis Morgan, and Francia White)
134. Joy of Living (5/28/45; Louise Allbritton and Robert Young)
135. The Heavenly Body (6/4/45; Reed Hadley, William Powell, and Ann Sothern)
136. Parson from Panamint (6/11/45; Don DeFore, Ellen Drew, and Charles Ruggles)

137. Alibi Ike (6/18/45; Jack Carson, Alan Hale, and Joan Lorring)
138. New Wine (6/25/45; Robert Benchley, Marguerite Chapman, Paul Henried, and Ilona Massey)
139. Standing Room Only (7/2/45; Robert Benchley, Marguerite Chapman, and Ray Milland)
140. Romance (7/9/45; Signe Hasso and Gregory Peck)
141. Flesh and Fantasy (7/16/45; Vincent Price, Edward G. Robinson, and Dame May Whitty)
142. Smilin' Through (7/23/45; Larraine Day, Van Heflin, and C. Aubrey Smith)
143. Voice of Bugle Anne (7/30/45; Lionel Barrymore, Noah Beery, Jr., and Martha O'Driscoll)
144. The Little Foxes (8/6/45; Bette Davis, Charles Dingle, Otto Kruger, and Teresa Wright)
145. Gildersleeve's Bad Day (8/13/45; Harold Peary)
146. Laura (8/20/45; Dana Andrews, David Bruce, Herbert Marshall, Gene Tierney, and Clifton Webb)
147. The Great McGinty (8/27/45; Brian Donlevy, Ruth Hussey, and Akim Tamiroff)
148. Flesh and Fantasy (9/3/45; John Hodiak and Claire Trevor)
149. Private Worlds (9/10/45; Frank Albertson, Claudette Colbert, Isabell Jewell, and Herbert Marshall)
150. The Valiant (9/17/45; Humphrey Bogart, Pedro deCordoba, Dorothy McGuire and Robert Middlemas)
151. Kiss the Boys Good-Bye (9/24/45; Johnny Mercer, Dinah Shore, and Sonny Tufts)
152. Those Endearing Young Charms (10/1/45; Virginia Bruce, Bill Williams, and Robert Young)
153. My Life with Caroline (10/8/45; Brian Aherne, Mary Astor, and Allyn Joslyn)
154. Model Wife (10/15/45; Rod Cameron, Martha O'Driscoll, and Robert Paige)
155. If You Could Only Cook (10/22/45; Linda Darnell, Dennis O'Keefe, and Lionel Stander)

156. You Only Live Once (10/29/45; Henry Fonda and Sylvia Sidney)
157. Hail, the Conquering Hero (11/5/45; Eddie Bracken and Donna Reed)
158. My Favorite Wife (11/12/45; Greer Garson and Richard Ney)
159. Paris Underground (11/19/45; Constance Bennett and Gary Cooper)
160. Biography of a Bachelor Girl (11/26/45; Louise Allbritton, Joseph Cotten, and Harry Von Zell)
161. Vivacious Lady (12/3/45; Janet Blair and Jimmy Stewart)
162. Along Came Jones (12/10/45; Gary Cooper, William Demarest, and Ona Munson)
163. Ruggles of Red Gap (12/17/45; Charles Laughton and Charlie Ruggles)
164. Pinocchio (12/24/45; Fannie Brice and Hanley Stafford)
165. Pillow to Post (12/31/45; Ida Lupino and John Payne)
166. The Lost Weekend (1/7/46; Frank Faylen, Barry Fitzgerald, Ray Milland, Billy Wilder, and Jane Wyman)
167. History Is Made at Night (1/14/46; Virginia Bruce and Paul Lukas)
168. Suspicion (1/21/46; Nigel Bruce and Loretta Young)
169. Brother Rat (1/28/46; Ronald Reagan and Wayne Morris)
170. My Client Curley (2/4/46; John Brown and Ted Donaldson)
171. Don Juan Quilligan (2/11/46; William Bendix and Phil Silver)
172. Over Twenty-One (2/18/46; Irene Dunne, Alexander Knox, and Raymond Walburn)
173. Wuthering Heights (2/25/46; Reed Hadley, Merle Oberon, and Cornel Wilde)
174. Getting Gertie's Garter (3/4/46; Lucille Ball, Dennis O'Keefe, and Barry Sullivan)
175. When Irish Eyes Are Smiling (3/11/46; June Haver and Dick Haymes)
176. Love Is News (3/18/46; Linda Darnell, James Gleason, and Bob Hope)
177. On Borrowed Time (4/1/46; Lionel Barrymore, Agnes Moorehead, and Vincent Price)
178. A Night to Remember [aka The Barbary Coast] (4/8/46; Brian Donlevy and Claire Trevor)
179. Her First Beau (4/15/46; Walter Brennen, Lon McAllister, and Elizabeth Taylor)
180. The Perfect Specimen (4/22/46; Jack Carson, Betty Grable, and Dame May Whitty)
181. The Cowboy and the Lady (4/29/46; Olivia de Havilland, Patsy Moran, and Gregory Peck)
182. Bachelor Mother (5/6/46; Francis X. Bushman, David Niven, and Ginger Rogers)
183. Talk of the Town (5/13/46; Virginia Bruce, Ronald Colman, and Allyn Joslyn)
184. Guest Wife (5/20/46; Claudette Colbert, Dick Foran, and Fred MacMurray)
185. The Firebrand (5/27/46; Douglas Fairbanks, Jr., Virginia Field, and Frank Morgan)
186. Lightnin' (6/3/46; Florence Bates, Barbara Britton, Harry Davenport, and George Murphy)
187. The House on 92nd Street (6/10/46; Signe Hasso, William Lundigan, Lloyd Nolan, and Lucille Meredith)
188. Marriage Is a Private Affair (6/17/46; John Hodiak and Lana Turner)
189. The Barbaray Coast (6/24/46; Mary Astor and Charles Bickford)
190. Come Live With Me (7/1/46; Leon Ames, Henry Fonda, and Ilona Massey)
191. The Great O'Malley (7/8/46; William Bendix, Howard Duff, Charles Irving, and Anita Louise)
192. Naughty Marietta (7/15/46; Allan Jones and Irene Manning)
193. The Glass Key (7/22/46; Ward Bond, Alan Ladd, and Marjorie Reynolds)
194. Naughty Marietta (7/29/46; Allan Jones and Irene Manning)
195. Christmas in Connecticut (8/5/46; Leon Belasco, Ronald Reagan, and Jane Wyman)

196. The Devil and Miss Jones (8/12/46; Van Johnson, Guy Kibbee, and Donna Reed)
197. Hired Wife (8/19/46; Brian Aherne, Lucille Ball, and Porter Hall)
198. The Bells of St. Mary's (8/26/46; Ingrid Bergman, Joan Carroll, and Bing Crosby)
199. Weekend for Three (9/2/46; Lynn Bari, Dennis O'Keefe, and Harry Von Zell)
200. Waterloo Bridge (9/9/46; Isabel Jewell, Barbara Stanwyck, and Robert Taylor)
201. Arrowsmith (9/16/46; Anne Baxter, Barbara Britton, Jean Hersholt, and Gregory Peck)
202. Susan and God (9/23/46; Bette Davis, Walter Pidgeon, and Paula Winslowe)
203. Junior Miss (9/30/46; Peggy Ann Garner, Allyn Joslyn, and Barbara Whitting)
204. The Old Lady Shows her Medals (10/7/46; Ethel Barrymore, Lionel Barrymore, and Douglas Fairbanks, Jr.)
205. Michael and Mary (10/21/46; Herbert Marshall and Ann Todd)
206. Adorable (10/28/46; Arthur Q. Bryan, Charles Coburn, Peter Lawford, and Shirley Temple)
207. Experiment Perilous (11/4/46; George Brent, Ruth Hussey, and Adolph Menjou)
208. The First Year (11/11/46; Harriet Hilliard and Ozzie Nelson)
209. Blind Alley (11/18/46; Broderick Crawford, Isabel Jewell, and Edward G. Robinson)
210. Arsenic and Old Lace (11/25/46; Eddie Albert, Verna Felton, Boris Karloff, and Jane Morgan)
211. Love Letters (12/2/46; Rex Harrison and Loretta Young)
212. The Last of Mrs. Cheyney (12/9/46; Nigel Bruce, Joan Fontaine, and Alan Marshal)
213. This Love of Ours (12/16/46; Joseph Cotten, Sue England, and Merle Oberon)
214. Snow White (12/23/46; Edgar Bergen, Charlie McCarthy, Charles Kemper, and Mary Jane Smith)
215. Pinocchio (12/30/46; Fanny Brice and Hanley Stafford)
216. The Yearling (1/6/47; Claude Jarmon, Jr., Gregory Peck, and Jane Wyman)
217. Parent by Proxy (1/13/47; Jack Benny and Paulette Goddard)
218. Dragonwyck (1/20/47; Glenn Langan, Vincent Price, and Teresa Wright)
219. Swell Guy (1/27/47; Ann Blyth and Joseph Cotten)
220. Gaslight (2/3/47; Charles Boyer and Susan Hayward)
221. Heavenly Days (2/10/47; Jim and Marian Jordan)
222. You Belong to Me (2/17/47; Don Ameche and Carole Landis)
223. Stork Club (2/24/47; Betty Hutton and Charlie Ruggles)
224. Kitty Foyle (3/3/47; Olivia de Havilland, Henry Fonda, and William Lundigan)
225. A Tree Grows in Brooklyn (3/10/47; Anne Baxter and Peggy Ann Garner)
226. Philadelphia Story (3/17/47; Cary Grant, Katharine Hepburn, and James Stewart)
227. The Moon Is Our Home (3/24/47; Virginia Bruce, Fred MacMurray, and Robert Young)
228. Brewster's Millions (3/31/47; Dennis O'Keefe)
229. Christmas in July (4/7/47; Eddie Bracken and Virginia Welles)
230. Bluebeard's Eighth Wife (4/14/47; Claudette Colbert and Fred MacMurray)
231. Too Many Husbands (4/21/47; Lucille Ball, Bob Hope, and Frank Sinatra)
232. Stork Bites Man (4/28/47; Jackie Cooper, Anita Louise, Emory Parnell, and Gus Schilling)
233. Pardon My Past (5/5/47; Marguerite Chapman, William Demarest, and John Hodiak)
234. Brief Encounter (5/12/47; Herbert Marshall, Lilli Palmer, and Eric Snowden)
235. The Best Years of Our Lives (5/19/47; Dana Andrews, Virginia Mayo, and Donna Reed)

36. Johnny Apollo (5/26/47; Dorothy Lamour, Lloyd Nolan, and Tyrone Power)
37. Saturday's Children (6/2/47; Jim Backus, John Garfield, Michael Raffetto, and Jane Wyman)
38. Outward Bound (6/9/47; Sara Allgood, David Niven, Henry Wilcox, and Dame May Whitty)

239. The Postman Always Rings Twice (6/16/47; John Garfield and Lana Turner)
240. Rose Marie (6/23/47; Leon Belasco, Nelson Eddy, Verna Felton, and Jeanette MacDonald)
241. The Strange Love of Martha Ivers (6/30/47; Kirk Douglas, Ida Lupino, and Dick Powell)
242. My Reputation (7/7/47)

Landmarks of Radio

Broadcast over NBC as a short-run spring/early summer series, from 8:00 o 8:30 pm, EST, this anthology series presented dramas that the producers and directors felt would be "landmarks of radio." Broadcasts originated from New York with Arnold Moss as host, occasionally narrating. Episode five presented two short dramas. William Faulkner's "Smoke" was presented in June.

1. Brigade Exchange (4/6/40)
2. Every Mother's Son (4/13/40; James Bell and Richard Gordon)
3. The Flowers Are Not for You to Pick (4/20/40)
4. The Day Before the Monsoon Came (4/27/40)
5. Danger / The Death-House Bottle (5/4/40)

6. Benjamin Franklin (5/11/40; Dudley Digges)
7. Council for Defense (5/18/40)
8. The First Born (5/25/40)
9. The Good Provider (6/1/40)
10. Prepare to Die (6/8/40; Colleen Ward)
11. Smoke (6/15/40)
12. The Life of Dr. Andrew Taylor Still (6/22/40)

Les Miserables

Seven-part miniseries based on the Victor Hugo Novel. Orson Welles produced, directed and starred. The supporting cast consisted of Martin Gabel, Agnes Moorehead, Alice Frost, Ray Collins, Adelaide Klein, Estelle Levy, Frank Readick, Virginia Welles, Everett Sloane, William Johnstone, and Hiram Sherman — most of whom would later be known as "The Mercury Theater Players." The broadcasts originated from New York, and were heard over the Don-Lee Mutual Network.

1. The Bishop (7/23/37)
2. Jabar (7/30/37)
3. The Trial (8/6/37)
4. Cosette (8/13/37)

5. The Grave (8/20/37)
6. The Barricade (8/27/37)
7. The Final Episode (9/3/37)

Lights Out! (1942–43 series)

Lights Out! was one of the most popular late-night horror programs ever to be broadcast over the radio. The series premiered over WENR in Chicago on January 1, 1934, and by April of 1935, the series had gone national. Wyllis Cooper was one of the earliest writers of the series, followed by Arch Oboler in June of 1936. NBC dropped the program in August of 1939, and *Lights Out!* remained off the air until Ironized Yeast sponsored a one-year revival. Broadcast over CBS on Tuesday evenings from 8 to 8:30 pm, EST. Frank Martin was the announcer for Ironized Yeast. Some of the scripts were written for earlier broadcast runs of *Lights Out!* while others were new scripts written by Oboler.

The classic "Chicken Heart" episode was immortalized when comedian Bill Cosby reminisced about the effect that the particular episode had on him when he was a child. Actors who played supporting roles for the 1942-43 series were Theodore Von Eltz, Templeton Fox, Irene Tedrow, Ted Maxwell, Tom Lewis and Earle Ross. These broadcasts originated from New York and Hollywood.

1. What the Devil (10/6/42; Gloria Blondell and Wally Maher)
2. Revolt of the Worms (10/13/42)
3. Poltergeist (10/20/42)
4. Mungahra (10/27/42)
5. Across the Gap (11/3/42)
6. Bon Voyage (11/10/42)
7. Come to the Bank (11/17/42)
8. Chicken Heart (11/24/42)
9. Mr. Maggs (12/1/42)
10. Scoop (12/8/42)
11. Knock at the Door (12/15/42)
12. Meteor Man (12/22/42)
13. Valse Triste (12/29/42; Gloria Blondell, Joseph Kearns, Wally Maher, Lou Merrill, Dinah Shore)
14. The Fast One (1/5/43)
15. The Mirror (1/12/43)
16. Cat Wife (1/19/43)
17. Projective Mr. Dorgan (1/26/43)
18. Until Dead (2/2/43)
19. He Dug it Up (2/9/43)
20. Oxycloride X (2/16/43)
21. They Met at Dorset (2/23/43)
22. The Sea (3/2/43)
23. The Ball (3/9/43)
24. The Dream (3/16/43)
25. The Flame (3/23/43)
26. Money, Money, Money (3/30/43)
27. Superfeature (4/6/43)
28. Archer (4/13/43)
29. Kill (4/20/43)
30. Execution (4/27/43)
31. Heavenly Jeep (5/4/43)
32. Murder in the Script Department (5/11/43)
33. Spider (5/18/43; Lou Merrill)
34. The Little Old Lady (5/25/43; Noreen Gammill, Cathy Lewis, Lou Merrill, Shirley Mitchell, and Jay Novello)
35. The Ugliest Man in the World (6/1/43; Raymond Edward Johnson and Ann Shepherd)
36. Organ (6/8/43)
37. Prelude to Murder (6/15/43)
38. Nature Study (6/22/43)
39. Bathysphere (6/29/43)
40. The Cliff (7/6/43)
41. Visitor From Hades (7/13/43)
42. Profits Unlimited (7/20/43)
43. The Little People (7/27/43)
44. Murder Castle (8/3/43)
45. Sakhalin (8/10/43)
46. State Executioner (8/17/43)
47. Sub Basement (8/24/43)
48. Immortal Gentleman (8/31/43)
49. Lord Marley's Guest (9/7/43; Mary Jane Croft and June Duprez)
50. The Word (9/14/43)
51. Mirage (9/21/43)
52. The Author and the Thing (9/28/43; Mercedes MacCambridge and Arch Oboler)

Little Blue Playhouse

This juvenile Saturday morning series, presenting patriotic dramas aimed toward the younger audience, was broadcast over ABC from 11:30 am to 12 pm, EST. Many of the broadcasts were biographies of young people who were (and still are) an influence to other young children. The program ended in October of 1943, being replaced by *Land of the Lost*, but returned a year later under a new title, *Blue Playhouse*, an adult version of the same series.

1. -----(4/4/42)
2. The Boy With the Powder Horn (4/11/42)
3. The Girl Behind the Gun (4/18/42)
4. Boyscout on the Burma Road (4/25/42)
5. The Story of Nathan Hale (5/2/42)
6. Indian Princess Goes to Court (5/9/42)
7. Captain Jones of the U.S. Navy (5/16/42)
8. World War Ace (5/23/42)
9. Little Spartan (5/30/42)
10. Around the World to the Land Down Under (6/6/42)
11. The Story of a Flag (6/13/42)
12. Big Six (6/20/42)
13. Florence Nightingale (6/27/42)
14. The Life of Admiral Robert Peary (7/4/42)
15. General George A. Custer (7/11/42)
16. The Man Who Beat the Sun (7/18/42)
17. Davy Crockett Plows a Furrow Straight (7/25/42)
18. The Girl Who Won the Heart of the Nation (8/1/42)
19. The Greatest Show on Earth (8/8/42)
20. The Story of John Cullen, Coast Guard Hero (8/15/42)
21. The World at My Fingertips (8/22/42)
22. The Schoolroom for Democracy (8/29/42)
23. The Story of Jacob Riis (9/5/42)
24. Forward the Nation (9/12/42)
25. First Woman in White (9/19/42)
26. -----(9/26/42)
27. The Story of Charles Goodyear (10/3/42)
28. Hero of San Pasqual (10/10/42)
29. The Minstrel Man (10/17/42)
30. -----(10/24/42)
31. The Raven's Destiny (10/31/42)
32. The Life of Francis Scott Key (11/7/42)
33. Invincible Louisa (11/14/42)
34. The Life of George Washington Carver (11/21/42)
35. The Life of Sara Josepha Hale (11/28/42)
36. The Life of Father Flanagan (12/5/42)
37. The Life of Dr. William P.G. Morton (12/12/42)
38. -----(12/19/42)
39. The Story of Helen Keller (12/26/42)
40. The Life of Eddie Rickenbaker (1/2/43)
41. The Life of George Washington Carver (1/9/43)
42. -----(1/16/43)
43. A President Walks with Courage [part one] (1/23/43)
44. A President Walks with Courage [part two] (1/30/43)
45. Steamboat Down the River (2/6/43)
46. Young Tom Edison (2/13/43)
47. The Life of David Carter Beard (2/20/43)
48. The Fighting Billy Mitchell (2/27/43)
49. The Life of Jane Adams (3/6/43)
50. The Life of Mme. Chiang Kai-Shek (3/13/43)
51. The Life of J. Edgar Hoover (3/20/43)
52. The Life of Andrew Jackson (3/27/43)
53. The Life of Barney Ross (4/3/43)
54. The Pride of the Yankees (4/10/43)
55. Thomas Jefferson, the Farmer (4/17/43; Jackie Kelk)
56. Mr. England [part one] (4/24/43)
57. Mr. England [part two] (5/1/43)
58. Flying Bantam (5/8/43)

The Lives of Harry Lime

For anyone who has not seen Carol Reed's masterpiece *The Third Man*, heartily recommend it. Orson Welles gives one of his best performances as Harr Lime, war-profiteer, double-crosser, thief, wanted by every policeman in ever country of the world. Only months after the movie premiered in the theater Lang/Worth syndications began planning a series, based on the Lime characte And Orson Welles was the lead choice. After negotiations, Lang acquired Welle for two series, *The Black Museum* and *The Lives of Harry Lime*. Both series wou star Welles. There were a total of fifty-two episodes for each program, and wit a large budget, others stars such as Sebastian Cabot and Dana Wynter would pla small roles in various episodes.

In the end of *The Third Man*, Harry Lime was shot by an old friend, so a introduction was added to the beginning of each episode, explaining that thes adventures took place before Lime died in the feature film. The series wa recorded in IBC Studios, in Portland Place, London, England. Others in the ca on occasion were Agnes Bernelle and Robert Arden.

Anton Karas's zither music, which was featured in the film, was used fc the opening and closing theme for the series. Tig Roe directed all of the episode and they were produced by Harry Alan Towers. Ernest Borneman wrote man of the episodes, probably about half of them. Sigmund Miller, Irvan Ashkinaz Bud Lesser, Robert Cenedella, and Peter Lyon wrote an occasional episode a well. Orson Welles wrote a handful as well, such as episodes "Too Many Crooks, "Operation Music Box," "Dead Candidate," "Two Is Company," and others. Th episode "Greek Meets Greek" was adapted by Welles a few years later as a scree play and became known as *Mr. Arkadin*. The episode "Buzzo Gospel" was late published as a novel by Gallimard under the title *Une Grosse Legume*.

In 1952, while *The Lives of Harry Lime* aired over the American airwave News of the World published, in a Pocket Book edition, stories adapted fror the actual radio scripts, three of which were from Orson Welles' radio plays "It in the Bag," "The Golden Fleece," and "A Ticket to Tangier." Mutual brough the series to America and broadcast it in 1951–1952, along with *The Black Museum,* which was narrated by Welles, and had the same production company, producer, and director. Kriswick Jenkinson wrote all of the *Black Museum* scripts, and was presented by arrangement with MGM Radio Attractions.

1. Too Many Crooks (8/3/51)
2. See Naples and Live (8/10/51)
3. Clay Pigeon (8/17/51)
4. A Ticket to Tangier (8/24/51)
5. Voodoo (8/31/51)
6. The Bohemian Star (9/7/51)
7. Love Affair (9/14/51)
8. Rogue's Holiday (9/21/51)
9. Work of Art (9/28/51)
10. Operation Music Box (10/5/51)
11. Golden Fleece (10/12/51)
12. Blue Bride (10/19/51)
13. Every Frame Has a Silver Lining (10/26/51)
14. Mexican Hat Trick (11/2/51)
15. Art Is Long and Lime Is Fleeting (11/9/51)
16. In Pursuit of a Ghost (11/16/51)
17. Horse Play (11/23/51)
18. Three Farthings for Your Thought (11/30/51)
19. The Third Woman (12/7/51)
20. An Old Moorish Custom (12/14/51)
21. It's a Knockout (12/21/51)
22. Two Is Company (12/28/51)
23. Cher Chez le Gem (1/4/52)
24. The Hands of Glory (1/11/52)
25. The Double Double Cross (1/18/52)
26. 5,000 Pengoes and a Kiss (1/25/52)
27. The Dark Enchantress (2/1/52)
28. The Earl on Troubled Waters (2/8/52)
29. The Dead Candidate (2/15/52)
30. It's in the Bag (2/22/52)
31. Hyacinth Patrol (2/29/52)
32. Turnabout Is Foul Play (3/7/52)
33. Violets, Sweet Violets (3/14/52)
34. Faith, Hope, and Lime (3/21/52)
35. Pleasure Before Business (3/28/52)
36. Fools Gold (4/4/52)
37. Man of Mystery (4/11/52)
38. The Painted Smile (4/18/52)
39. Harry Lime Joins the Circus (4/25/52)
40. Susie's Cue (5/2/52)
41. Viva la Chance (5/9/52)
42. The Elusive Vermeer (5/16/52)
43. Murder on the Riviera (5/23/52)
44. Pearls of Bohemia (5/30/52)
45. A Night in the Harem (6/6/52)
46. Blackmail Is a Nasty Word (6/13/52)
47. The Professor Regrets (6/20/52)
48. The Hard Way (6/27/52)
49. Paris Is Not the Same (7/4/52)
50. Honeymoon (7/11/52)
51. The Blue Caribou (7/18/52)
52. Greek Meets Greek (7/25/52)

Lives of the Great

Syndicated in 1934, this short-run series dramatized the lives of famous people who have been considered a "great" in American history (plus one Englishman). No one knows what census or poll was taken to determine who in America's history is considered a "great," but the twelve fifteen-minute broadcasts were the only episodes recorded. They were broadcast in the order listed below.

1. Thomas Edison
2. Benjamin Franklin
3. Ulysses S. Grant
4. Benjamin Disraeli
5. Mark Twain
6. Henry Clay
7. Robert E. Peary
8. Andrew Jackson
9. Robert E. Lee
10. P.T. Barnum
11. Abraham Lincoln
12. Buffalo Bill Cody

The Lonesome Road

This documentary series on alcoholism was broadcast over the American Broadcasting Company, Monday evenings from 8:45 to 9 pm, EST.

1. The Way Problem Drinkers Can Get Help (9/10/51)
2. To Help Him If He Wishes (9/17/51)
3. For the Non-Alcoholic [part one] (9/24/51)
4. For the Non-Alcoholic [part two] (10/1/51)
5. New Drugs: An Interim Report (10/8/51)
6. Alcoholism and Youth (10/15/51)

Luke Slaughter of Tombstone

Another CBS western series broadcast during the late fifties, this one lasting only sixteen episodes. Sam Buffington starred as Luke Slaughter, Civil War cavalryman–turned–Arizona cattleman. The series was directed by William N. Robson. Fred Van Hartesveldt wrote the scripts. The music was composed by Wilbur Hatch. It was broadcast over CBS, as a sustaining Sunday evening feature.

1. Duel on the Trail (2/23/58)
2. Tracks Out of Tombstone (3/2/58)
3. Yancey's Pride (3/9/58)
4. Page's Progress (3/16/58)
5. The Homesteaders (3/23/58)
6. The Aaron Holcomb Story (3/30/58)
7. Wagon Train (4/13/58)
8. The Henry Fell Story (4/20/58)
9. Death Watch (4/27/58)
10. Worth Its Salt (5/4/58)
11. Heritage (5/11/58)
12. Drive to Fort Huachuca (5/18/58)
13. Outlaw Kid (5/25/58)
14. Cattle Drive (6/1/58)
15. Big Business (6/8/58)
16. June Bride (6/15/58)

The Lux Radio Theatre

This anthology series ran for more than twenty years and presented the best of Broadway and Hollywood. The program was first broadcast from New York with Antony Stanford directing, and dramas of both stage and screen were presented. Lux Soap was the sponsor, and the budget was high enough to pay for top talent, even if it meant paying for the plane flights of West Coast stars to the East. On June 1, 1936, *The Lux Radio Theatre* began broadcasting from Hollywood, with Cecil B. DeMille as the host and director. The program picked up popularity, and every Hollywood star flocked to the microphone.

On January 22, 1945, DeMille hosted his final *Lux* broadcast, standing up for what he felt was morally right in relation to a tax being collected throughout the movie industry. Various Hollywood stars became host beginning January

29; William Keighley was hired as permanent host beginning November 5, 1945. Irving Cumming began hosting September 8, 1952. *Lux* was entitled the *Summer Theatre* during the summer of 1953, and guest hosts included Ken Carpenter and Don Wilson.

The New York broadcasts were heard over NBC, Sunday evenings from 2:30 to 3:30 pm, EST. Beginning July 29, 1935, *Lux* became a Monday night feature over CBS from 9 to 10 pm, EST. On September 14, 1954, the series moved back to NBC, Tuesdays from 9 to 10 pm, EST.

Episode 112 featured the first radio appearance of newlyweds Dick Powell and Joan Blondell. Episode 136 featured a memorial at the end of the program for Jean Harlow, who had recently died. Cecil B. DeMille announced at the beginning of episode 140 that Amelia Earhart was originally scheduled to appear at the end of the program, but could not because she was reported to have been lost at sea. Episode 227 was billed as "Charles Laughton's first dramatic radio appearance in America."

1. Seventh Heaven (10/14/34; Miriam Hopkins)
2. What Every Woman Knows (10/21/34; Helen Hayes)
3. The Barker (10/28/34; Walter Huston)
4. Sailin' Through (11/4/34; Jane Cowl)
5. The Nervous Wreck (11/11/34; June Walker)
6. Rebound (11/18/34; Ruth Chatterton)
7. Mrs. Dane's Defense (11/25/34; Ethel Barrymore)
8. Let Us Be Gay (12/2/34; Tallulah Bankhead)
9. Berkley Square (12/9/34; Leslie Howard)
10. Turn to the Right (12/16/34; James Cagney)
11. The Goose Hangs High (12/23/34; Walter Connolly)
12. Daddy Long Legs (12/30/34; John Boles)
13. The Green Goddess (1/6/35; Claude Rains)
14. Counselor at Law (1/13/35; Paul Muni)
15. The Late Christopher Bean (1/20/35; Walter Connolly)
16. The Bad Man (1/27/35; Walter Huston)
17. Peg O' My Heart (2/3/35; Margaret Sullavan)
18. The First Year (2/10/35; Lila Lee)
19. The Old Soak (2/17/35; Wallace Beery)
20. Nothing But the Truth (2/24/35; Frank Morgan)
21. Lilac Time (3/3/35; Jane Cowl)
22. Holiday (3/10/35; Claudette Colbert)
23. Her Master's Voice (3/17/35; Roland Young)
24. Secrets (3/24/35; Irene Dunne)
25. The Romantic Age (3/31/35; Leslie Howard)
26. The Prince Chap (4/7/35; Gary Cooper)
27. The Broken Wing (4/14/35; Lupe Velez)
28. Little Women (4/21/35; Dorothy Gish and Lillian Gish)
29. Ada Beats the Drum (4/28/35; Mary Boland)
30. Adam and Eva (5/5/35; Cary Grant)
31. The Bishop Misbehaves (5/12/35; Walter Connolly and Jane Wyatt)
32. The Lion and the Mouse (5/19/35; Ruth Chatterton)
33. Michael and Mary (5/26/35; Elissa Landi)
34. The Vinegar Tree (6/2/35; Billie Burke)
35. Candlelight (6/9/35; Robert Montgomery)
36. The Patsy (6/16/35; Loretta Young)
37. Polly with a Past (6/23/35; Ina Claire)
38. Elmer the Great (6/30/35; Joe E. Brown)

39. Bunty Pulls the Strings (7/29/35; Helen Hayes)
40. Lightnin' (8/5/35; Wallace Beery)
41. Man in Possession (8/12/35; Robert Montgomery)
42. Ladies of the Jury (8/19/35; Mary Boland)
43. The Church Mouse (8/26/35; Ruth Gordon and Otto Kruger)
44. Whistling in the Dark (9/2/35; Charles Ruggles)
45. Petticoat Influence (9/9/35; Ruth Chatterton)
46. Leah Kleschna (9/16/35; Judith Anderson and Conrad Nagel)
47. Mary, Mary Quite Contrary (9/23/35; Ethel Barrymore)
48. Alias Jimmy Valentine (9/30/35; Richard Barthelmess)
49. The Wren (10/7/35; Helen Chandler)
50. Within the Law (10/14/35; Joan Crawford)
51. Merely Mary Ann (10/21/35; Joan Bennett)
52. Dulcy [written by George S. Kaufman and Marc Connelly] (10/28/35; Leslie Adams, Donald Foster, Stuart Fox, Gene Lockhart, Zasu Pitts, Harold Vermilyea, and Cliff Walker)
53. The Milky Way (11/4/35; Charles Butterworth)
54. His Misleading Lady (11/11/35; Clark Gable)
55. Sherlock Holmes (11/18/35; William Gillette)
56. Way Down East (11/25/35; Dorothy Gish and Lillian Gish)
57. The Swan (12/2/35; Elissa Landi)
58. The Showoff (12/9/35; Joe E. Brown)
59. The Truth (12/16/35; Grace George)
60. Applesauce (12/23/35; Jack Oakie)
61. The Queen's Husband (12/30/35; Frank Morgan)
62. The Third Degree (1/6/36; Sylvia Sidney)
63. The Boss (1/13/36; Edward G. Robinson)
64. A Prince There Was (1/20/36; Ricardo Cortez)
65. Grumpy (1/27/36; John Barrymore)
66. Green Grow the Lilacs (2/3/36; John Boles)
67. The Bride the Sun Shines On (2/10/36; Douglas Fairbanks, Jr.)
68. The Old Soak (2/17/36; Wallace Beery)
69. Peter Pan (2/24/36; Freddie Bartholomew)
70. Alias the Deacon (3/2/36; Victor Moore)
71. Girl of the Golden West (3/9/36; Eva Le Gallienne)
72. The Last of Mrs. Chayney (3/16/36; Miriam Hopkins)
73. The Song and Dance Man (3/23/36; George M. Cohen)
74. Bought and Paid For (3/30/36; Bette Davis)
75. Kick-In (4/6/36; Ann Sothern)
76. Shore Leave (4/13/36; Lee Tracy)
77. Harmony Lane (4/20/36; Lawrence Tibbett)
78. Undercover (4/27/36; Richard Barthelmess)
79. The Music Master (5/4/36; Jean Hersholt)
80. Bittersweet (5/11/36; Irene Dunne)
81. Get-Rich-Quick Wallingford (5/18/36; George M. Cohen)
82. East Is West (5/25/36; Fay Bainter)
83. The Legionnaire and the Lady (6/1/36; Marlene Dietrich, Clark Gable, Jesse Lasky, Wally Maher)
84. The Thin Man (6/8/36; Theda Bara, W.S. Van Dyke, Myrna Loy, Barbara Luddy, Wally Maher, Bret Morrison, and William Powell)
85. Burlesque (6/15/36; Daniel Frohman, Al Jolson, Ruby Keeler, Lou Merrill, and Frank Nelson)
86. The Dark Angel (6/22/36; James Montgomery Flagg, Herbert Marshall, and Merle Oberon)
87. Irene (6/29/36; D.W. Griffith, Jeanette MacDonald, and Regis Toomey)
88. The Voice of Bugle Ann (7/6/36; Lionel Barrymore, Porter Hall, Hal Roach, and Anne Shirley)
89. The Brat (7/13/36; Marion Davies and Joel McCrea)
90. The Barker (7/20/36; Claudette Colbert and Walter Huston)
91. Chained (7/27/36; Joan Crawford and Franchot Tone)
92. Main Street (8/3/36; Fred MacMurray and Barbara Stanwyck)
93. The Jazz Singer (8/10/36; Al Jolson)

94. The Vagabond King (8/17/36; John Boles and Evelyn Venable)
95. One Sunday Afternoon (8/24/36; Agnes Ayres, Alan Hale, Jack Oakie, and Helen Twelvetrees)
96. Cheating Cheaters (8/31/36; June Lang and George Raft)
97. Is Zat So? (9/7/36; Robert Armstrong, James Cagney, A.H. Gianini, Sheila Graham, Boots Mallory, Lou Merrill, and Frank Nelson)
98. Quality Street (9/14/36; Brian Aherne and Ruth Chatterton)
99. Trilby (9/21/36; Peter Lorre and Grace Moore)
100. The Plutocrat (9/28/36; Wallace Beery, Walt Disney, Eric Linden, Cecelia Parker, Marjorie Rambeau, Clara Kimball Young, and Victor Young)
101. Elmer the Great (10/5/36; Lou Gerhig and Joe E. Brown)
102. The Curtain Rises (10/12/36; Ginger Rogers and Warren William)
103. Captain Applejack (10/19/36; Frank Morgan and Maureen O'Sullivan)
104. Saturday's Children (10/26/36; Mona Barry, Olivia de Havilland, Fred Perry, and Robert Taylor)
105. The Virginian (11/2/36; Gary Cooper, Helen Mack, and Sidney Skolsky)
106. Alias Jimmy Valentine (11/9/36; Maude Evans, Allen Jenkins, Pat O'Brien, and Melvyn Purvis)
107. Conversation Piece [written by Noel Coward] (11/16/36; Marjorie Gateson, Adolphe Menjou, Lily Pons, and George Sanders)
108. The Story of Louis Pasteur (11/23/36; Adrian, William K. Howard, Crawford Kent, Fritz Lieber, Barbara Luddy, and Paul Muni)
109. Polly of the Circus (11/30/36; Lionel Barrymore, James Gleason, Gavin Gordon, Robert L. Ripley, and Loretta Young)
110. The Grand Duchess and the Waiter (12/7/36; Vince Barnett, Elissa Landi, Gene Lockhart, Alma Krueger, Lou Merrill, Robert Montgomery, and Frank Nelson)
111. Madame Sans-Gene (12/14/36; C.

Henry Gordon, Jean Harlow, Claude Rains, and Robert Taylor)
112. The Golddiggers (12/21/36; Joan Blondell and Dick Powell)
113. Cavalcade (12/28/36; Elsa Buchanan, Madeleine Carroll, Noel Coward, Herbert Marshall, David Niven, Una O'Connor, and Douglas Scott)
114. Men in White (1/4/37; Virginia Bruce, Frances Farmer, Edith Head, and Spencer Tracy)
115. The Gilded Lily (1/11/37; Claudette Colbert and Fred MacMurray)
116. The Criminal Code (1/18/37; Paul Guilfoyle, Noah Madison, Lou Merrill, Frank Nelson, Beverly Roberts, Edward G. Robinson, and Lou Ross)
117. Tonight or Never (1/25/37; Luis Alberni, Melvyn Douglas, and Jeanette MacDonald)
118. Mr. Deeds Goes to Town (2/1/37; Jean Arthur, Gary Cooper, Fay Gillis, Sidney Skolsky, and Barbara Stanwyck)
119. Graustark (2/8/37; Gene Raymond and Anna Sten)
120. Brewster's Millions (2/15/37; Lionel Bellmore, Jack Benny, Mary Livingstone, and Lou Merrill)
121. Captain Blood (2/22/37; Charles Courtney, Donald Crisp, Olivia de Havilland, Errol Flynn, Herbert Marshall, Basil Rathbone, and Henry Stephenson)
122. Cappy Ricks (3/1/37; Richard Arlen, Byron K. Folger, Peter B. Kine, and Charles Winninger)
123. Madame Butterfly (3/8/37; Pedro De Cordova, Cary Grant, Crawford Kent, and Grace Moore)
124. Desire (3/15/37; Marlene Dietrich, Ernst Lubitsch, Otto Kruger, and Herbert Marshall)
125. Death Takes a Holiday (3/22/37; Arthur Byron, Florence Eldridge, Kay Johnson, Gene Lockhart, and Fredric March)
126. Dulcy (3/29/37; Gracie Allen, George Burns, Hedda Hopper, Elliott Nugent, and Victor Rodman)
127. A Farewell to Arms (4/5/37; Clark

166. Poppy (3/7/38; W.C. Fields, Helen Grant, John Payne, Anne Shirley)
167. The Boss (3/14/38; Edward Arnold and Fay Wray)
168. The Man Who Played God (3/21/38; George Arliss)
169. Naughty Marietta (3/28/38; Lawrence Tibbett)
170. Dark Victory (4/4/38; Melvyn Douglas and Barbara Stanwyck)
171. Mary Burns, Fugitive (4/11/38; Henry Fonda and Miriam Hopkins)
172. Mad About Music (4/18/38; Deanna Durbin, Herbert Marshall, and Gail Patrick)
173. Dangerous (4/25/38; Don Ameche and Madeleine Carroll)
174. The Prisoner of Shark Island (5/2/38; John Carradine, Gary Cooper, and Fay Wray)
175. My Man Godfrey (5/9/38; Carole Lombard, David Niven, Gail Patrick, and William Powell)
176. The Girl from 10th Avenue (5/16/38; George Brent and Loretta Young)
177. The Letter (5/23/38; Walter Huston and Merle Oberon)
178. I Met My Love Again (5/30/38; Joan Bennett and Henry Fonda)
179. A Doll's House (6/6/38; Joan Crawford and Basil Rathbone)
180. Theodora Goes Wild (6/13/38; Irene Dunne and Cary Grant)
181. Manslaughter (6/20/38; Florence Eldridge and Fredric March)
182. Jane Eyre (6/27/38; Helen Hayes and Robert Montgomery)
183. I Found Stella Parish (7/4/38; George Brent and Herbert Marshall)
184. Spawn of the North (9/12/38; Dorothy Lamour, Fred MacMurray, and George Raft)
185. Morning Glory (9/19/38; Ralph Bellamy and Barbara Stanwyck)
186. Seven Keys to Baldpate (9/26/38; Jack Benny, Mary Livingstone, and Efrem Zimbalist)
187. Another Dawn (10/3/38; Madeleine Carroll and Franchot Tone)
188. Viva Villa (10/10/38; Wallace Beery)
189. Seventh Heaven (10/17/38; Don Ameche and Jean Arthur)
190. Babbitt (10/24/38; Edward Arnold and Fay Bainter)
191. That Certain Woman (10/31/38; Carole Lombard and Basil Rathbone)
192. Next Time We Love (11/7/38; Joel McCrea and Margaret Sullavan)
193. The Buccaneer (11/14/38; Clark Gable, Gertrude Miche, and Akim Tamiroff)
194. Confession (11/21/38; Richard Greene and Miriam Hopkins)
195. Interference (11/28/38; Leslie Howard and Herbert Marshall)
196. The Princess Comes Across (12/5/38; Madeleine Carroll and Fred MacMurray)
197. The Scarlet Pimpernel (12/12/38; Olivia De Havilland, Dennis Green, and Leslie Howard)
198. Kid Galahad (12/19/38; Joan Bennett, Alice Frost, Wayne Morris, and Edward G. Robinson)
199. Snow White and the Seven Dwarfs (12/26/38; Walt Disney)
200. The Perfect Specimen (1/2/39; Joan Blondell and Errol Flynn)
201. Mayerling (1/9/39; Robert Barrett, Janet Gaynor, Alma Kruger, and William Powell)
202. Front Page Woman (1/16/39; Paulette Goddard and Fred MacMurray)
203. Cardinal Richelieu (1/23/39; Florence Arliss, George Arliss, Edward Lambert, and Cesar Romero)
204. The Arkansas Traveler (1/30/39; Bob Burns)
205. The Count of Monte Cristo (2/6/39; Sidney Blackmer, Alton Cook, Josephine Hutchinson, Paul Lukas, Robert Montgomery, Lloyd Nolan, and Victor Rodman)
206. The Return of Peter Grimm (2/13/39; Edward Arnold, Lionel Barrymore, Alan Ladd, and Maureen O'Sullivan)
207. Stage Door (2/20/39; Eve Arden, Adolph Menjou, Ginger Rogers, and Rosalind Russell)
208. Ceiling Zero (2/27/39; Ralph Bellamy, James Cagney, Jeanne Cagney, and Stuart Erwin)

246. Sing You Sinners (1/15/40; Ralph Bellamy, Bing Crosby, Elizabeth Patterson, and Charles Peck)
247. Bachelor Mother (1/22/40; Frank Albertson, Fredric March, Eddie Marr, and Ginger Rogers)
248. Intermezzo (1/29/40; Ingrid Bergman and Herbert Marshall)
249. The Young At Heart (2/5/40; Don Ameche and Ida Lupino)
250. The Sidewalks of London (1/12/40; Claude Allister, Elsa Lanchester, and Charles Laughton)
251. Made For Each Other (2/19/40; Verna Felton, Carole Lombard, Fred MacMurray, and Eddie Marr)
252. Swing High, Swing Low (2/26/40; Virginia Bruce, Una Merkel, and Rudy Vallee)
253. Trade Winds (3/4/40; Mary Astor, Joan Bennett, and Errol Flynn)
254. My Son, My Son (3/11/40; Brian Aherne, Madeleine Carroll, and Josephine Hutchinson)
255. The Rains Came (3/18/40; Jim Ameche, George Brent, Kay Francis, and Jean Parker)
256. Remember the Night (3/25/40; Beulah Bondi, Arthur Q. Bryan, Jack Carr, Sterling Holloway, Fred MacMurray, and Barbara Stanwyck)
257. Love Affair (4/1/40; Irene Dunne, Gale Gordon, Lou Merrill, and William Powell)
258. Mama Loves Papa (4/8/40; Arthur Q. Bryon, Jim and Marion Jordan, and Victor Rodman)
259. The Underpup (4/15/40; Robert Cummings, Nan Grey, and Gloria Jean)
260. Abe Lincoln in Illinois (4/22/40; Fay Bainter and Raymond Massey)
261. Smilin' Through (4/29/40; Barbara Stanwyck, Robert Taylor, and H.B. Warner)
262. Our Town (5/6/40; Fay Bainter, Beulah Bondi, Frank Craven, William Holden, Thomas Mitchell, and Martha Scott)
263. True Confession (5/13/40; Ruth Donnelly, Fred MacMurray, and Loretta Young)
264. Midnight (5/20/40; Don Ameche,

Claudette Colbert, Gale Gordon, Victor Rodman, Rolfe Sedan)
265. Vigil in the Night (5/27/40; Olivia de Havilland)
266. Alexander's Ragtime Band (6/3/40; Alice Faye, Ray Milland, and Robert Preston)
267. Till We Meet Again (6/10/40; George Brent, Merle Oberon, and Pat O'Brien)
268. After the Thin Man (6/17/40; Arthur Q. Bryan, Myrna Loy, Eddie Marr, and William Powell)
269. Show Boat (6/24/40; Irene Dunne, Verna Felton, Allan Jones, and Charles Winninger)
270. Alias the Deacon (7/1/40; Bob Burns, Wally Maher, Rolfe Sedan, and Helen Wood)
271. To the Ladies [written by George S. Kaufman] (7/8/40; Helen Hayes and Otto Kruger)
272. Manhattan Melodrama (9/9/40; Don Ameche, Myrna Loy, and William Powell)
273. Love Is News (9/16/40; Madeleine Carroll and Bob Hope)
274. The Westerner (9/23/40; Walter Brennan, Gary Cooper, Doris Davenport, and Lou Merrill)
275. His Girl Friday (9/30/40; Jack Carson, Claudette Colbert, Fred MacMurray, and Edwin Max)
276. Wings of the Navy (10/7/40; George Brent, Olivia de Havilland, and John Payne)
277. The Littlest Rebel (10/14/40; Preston Foster, Claude Rains, and Shirley Temple)
278. Lillian Russell (10/21/40; Edward Arnold, Alice Faye, Verna Felton, and Victor Mature)
279. Strike Up the Band (10/28/40; Judy Garland, Mickey Rooney, and John Scott Trotter)
280. Wuthering Heights (11/4/40; Ida Lupino, Basil Rathbone, and Martha Wentworth)
281. Nothing Sacred (11/11/40; Joan Bennett, Douglas Fairbanks, Jr., and Eddie Waller)
282. The Rage of Manhattan (11/18/40; Annabella and Tyrone Power)
283. Jezebel (11/25/40; Brian Donlevy,

Verna Felton, Jeffrey Lynn, and Loretta Young)

284. Knute Rockne, All-American (12/2/40; Donald Crisp, Pat O'Brien, Ronald Reagan, and Fay Wray)

285. My Favorite Wife (12/9/40; Laurence Olivier, Gail Patrick, and Rosalind Russell)

286. Fifth Avenue Girl (12/16/40; Edward Arnold, John Howard, Joan Perry, and Ginger Rogers)

287. Young Tom Edison (12/23/40; Beulah Bondi, Mickey Rooney, and Virginia Weidler)

288. A Little Bit of Heaven (12/30/40; Gloria Jean)

289. Vivacious Lady (1/6/41; Don Ameche, Alice Faye, Fred MacKaye, and Rolfe Sedan)

290. Libel (1/13/41; Ronald Colman, Otto Kruger, and Frances Robinson)

291. The Cowboy and the Lady (1/20/41; Gene Autry)

292. Captain January (1/27/41; Gene Lockhart, Shirley Temple, and Charles Winninger)

293. Rebecca (2/3/41; Ronald Colman and Ida Lupino)

294. The Moon's Our Home (2/10/41; Clara Blandick, Carole Lombard, and James Stewart)

295. Johnny Apollo (2/17/41; Dorothy Lamour and Burgess Meredith)

296. The Whole Town's Talking (2/24/41; Jim and Marion Jordan)

297. My Bill (3/3/41; Dix Davis, Kay Francis, and Warren William)

298. The Awful Truth (3/10/41; Constance Bennett, Gloria Gordon, and Bob Hope)

299. Cheers for Miss Bishop (3/17/41; Hans Conried, William Gargan, and Martha Scott)

300. Flight Command (3/24/41; Ted Bliss, Ruth Hussey, Walter Pidgeon, and Robert Taylor)

301. Stablemates (3/31/41; Wallace Beery, Sidney Miller, Mickey Rooney, and Fay Wray)

302. The Stand-In (4/7/41; Warner Baxter, Joan Bennett, Hans Conried, Stanley Ferrar, Earl Keane)

303. Dust Be My Destiny (4/14/41; Arthur Q. Bryan, John Garfield, and Claire Trevor)

304. The Letter (4/21/41; Bette Davis, Herbert Marshall, James Stephenson)

305. Wife, Husband, and Friend (4/28/41; George Brent, Hans Conried, and Priscilla Lane)

306. Kitty Foyle (5/5/41; James Craig, Verna Felton, Dennis Morgan, and Ginger Rogers)

307. Craig's Wife (5/12/41; Beulah Bondi, Herbert Marshall, Jane Morgan, and Rosalind Russell)

308. Model Wife (5/19/41; Joan Blondell, Verna Felton, Fred MacKaye, and Dick Powell)

309. Virginia City (5/26/41; Hans Conried, Errol Flynn, Gale Gordon, and Martha Scott)

310. They Drive by Night (6/2/41; Lucille Ball, George Raft, and Lana Turner)

311. Mr. and Mrs. Smith (6/9/41; Jack Arnold, Bill Goodwin, Bob Hope, and Carole Lombard)

312. The Lady from Cheyenne (6/16/41; Edward Arnold, Forrest Taylor, Robert Preston, and Loretta Young)

313. The Shop Around the Corner (6/23/41; Don Ameche, Leo Cleary, and Claudette Colbert)

314. I Love You Again (6/30/41; Jack Arnold, Cary Grant, Myrna Loy, and Frank McHugh)

315. Algiers (7/7/41; Charles Boyer, Jeff Corey, and Hedy Lamarr)

316. Tom, Dick, and Harry (9/8/41; Alan Marshall, Burgess Meredith, George Murphy, Ginger Rogers)

317. Lost Horizon (9/15/41; Lynn Carver, Ronald Colman, and Donald Crisp)

318. Lydia (9/22/41; Joseph Cotten, Dix Davis, Merle Oberon, and Edna May Oliver)

319. Third Finger, Left Hand (9/29/41; Douglas Fairbanks, Jr., Howard McNear, and Martha Scott)

320. Unfinished Business (10/6/41; Don Ameche, Arthur Q. Bryan, and Irene Dunne)

359. Love Affair (7/6/42; Bea Benaderet, Charles Boyer, Tristram Coffin, and Irene Dunne)
360. H.M. Pulham, Esquire (7/13/42; Josephine Hutchinson, Hedy Lamarr, and Robert Young)
361. The Philadelphia Story (7/20/42; Cary Grant, Ruth Hussey, Katharine Hepburn, Jimmy Stewart)
362. This Above All (9/14/42; James Kirkwood, Tyrone Power, and Barbara Stanwyck)
363. How Green Was My Valley (9/21/42; Donald Crisp, Roddy MacDowall, Maureen O'Hara, and Walter Pidgeon)
364. The Magnificent Dope (9/28/42; Don Ameche, Lynn Bari, Arthur Q. Bryan, and Henry Fonda)
365. Love Crazy (10/5/42; Gale Gordon, Joseph Kearns, Hedy Lamarr, and William Powell)
366. Morning Glory (10/12/42; Bea Benaderet, Judy Garland, Adolph Menjou, and John Payne)
367. My Favorite Blonde (10/19/42; Virginia Bruce, Bob Hope, Charles Seel, and Horace Willard)
368. Wake Island (10/26/42; Broderick Crawford, Brian Donlevy, and Robert Preston)
369. A Woman's Face (11/2/42; Brian Aherne, Lillian Bond, Ida Lupino, and Conrad Veidt)
370. Sullivan's Travels (11/9/42; Veronica Lake)
371. To Mary, with Love (11/16/42; Bea Benaderet, Irene Dunne, Otto Kruger, and Ray Milland)
372. The Gay Sisters (11/23/42; Barbara Stanwyck and Robert Young)
373. Broadway (11/30/42; Janet Blair and George Raft)
374. The War Against Mrs. Hadley (12/7/42; Edward Arnold, Fay Bainter, and Van Johnson)
375. Algiers (12/14/42; Charles Boyer, Gene Lockhart, J. Carrol Naish, and Loretta Young)
376. The Pied Piper (12/21/42; Anne Baxter, Roddy MacDowall, Frank Morgan, and Ralph Morgan)
377. A Star Is Born (12/28/42; Arthur Q. Bryan, Judy Garland, Jane Morgan, and Walter Pidgeon)
378. The Bugle Sounds (1/4/43; Wallace Beery, Leo Cleary, Marjorie Rambeau, and Horace Willard)
379. She Knew the Answers (1/11/43; Eve Arden, Joan Bennett, and Preston Foster)
380. My Gal Sal [written by Theodore Dreiser] (1/18/43; Norman Field, Mary Martin, Dick Powell)
381. This Gun for Hire (1/25/43; Joan Blondell, Arthur Q. Bryan, Laird Cregar, and Alan Ladd)
382. The Show-Off (2/1/43; Beulah Bondi, Una Merkel, Harold Peary, and Paula Winslowe)
383. The Maltese Falcon (2/8/43; Laird Cregar, Gail Patrick, and Edward G. Robinson)
384. Are Husbands Necessary? (2/15/43; Gracie Allen, Arthur Q. Bryan, George Burns, Norman Field)
385. This Is the Army [featured an all Army cast] (2/22/43)
386. The Lady Is Waiting (3/1/43; George Brent, Ann Doran, Kay Francis, and Lillian Randolph)
387. Reap the Wild Wind (3/8/43; Paulette Goddard and Ray Milland)
388. Libel (3/15/43; Edna Best, Ronald Colman, Otto Kruger, and Fredrick Worlock)
389. Each Dawn I Die (3/22/43; Lynn Bari, Norman Field, Franchot Tone, and George Raft)
390. Crossroads (3/29/43; Lana Turner)
391. The Road to Morocco (4/5/43; Bing Crosby, Bob Hope, and Ginny Simms)
392. Once Upon a Honeymoon (4/12/43; Brian Aherne, Claudette Colbert, Laird Cregar, Albert Dekker)
393. A Night to Remember (4/19/43; Wally Maher, Bradley Page, Ann Sothern, and Robert Young)
394. The Lady Has Plans (4/26/43; Cary Grant, Rita Hayworth, and William Powell)
395. The Navy Comes Through (5/3/43; Ruth Hussey, George Murphy, and Pat O'Brien)
396. Now Voyager (5/10/43; Albert Dekker, Paul Henreid, Ida Lupino, Dame May Whitty)

397. The Talk of the Town (5/17/43; Jean Arthur, Ronald Colman, Cary Grant, and Lynn Whitney)

398. Hitler's Children (5/24/43; Bonita Granville, Otto Kruger, Walter Reed, and Kent Smith)

399. The Major and the Minor (5/31/43; Joan Lorring, Ray Milland, and Ginger Rogers)

400. My Friend Flicka (6/7/43; George Brent, Rita Johnson, and Roddy MacDowall)

401. The Philadelphia Story (6/14/43; Roland Drew, Robert Taylor, Loretta Young, and Robert Young)

402. In Which We Serve (6/21/43; Edna Best, Ronald Colman, Pat O'Malley, and Vernon Steele)

403. The Great Man's Lady (6/28/43; Joseph Cotten, Faye MacKenzie, Chester Morris, and Barbara Stanwyck)

404. My Sister Eileen (7/5/43; Brian Aherne, Janet Blair, Rosalind Russell, and Akim Tamiroff)

405. Air Force (7/12/43; Harry Carey, Art Gilmore, Fred MacKaye, Eddie Marr, and George Raft)

406. The Phantom of the Opera (9/13/43; Nelson Eddy, Susanna Foster, and Basil Rathbone)

407. Flight for Freedom (9/20/43; George Brent, Chester Morris, and Rosalind Russell)

408. Ladies in Retirement (9/27/43; Brian Aherne, Edith Barrett, Ida Lupino, and Dame May Whitty)

409. The Pride of the Yankees (10/4/43; Virginia Bruce, Edgar Buchanan, Gary Cooper, Verna Felton)

410. Heaven Can Wait (10/11/43; Don Ameche, Cliff Clark, Verna Felton, and Maureen O'Hara)

411. Mr. Lucky (10/18/43; Laraine Day, Cary Grant, Arthur Hohl, and Eddie Marr)

412. Slightly Dangerous (10/25/43; Gene Lockhart, Victor Mature, and Lana Turner)

413. So Proudly We Hail (11/1/43; Claudette Colbert, Paulette Goddard, Veronica Lake, Sonny Tufts)

414. Salute to the Marines (11/8/43; Louise Arthur, Fay Bainter, Noah Beery, and Wallace Beery)

415. Hello, Frisco, Hello (11/15/43; Alice Faye, Eddie Marr, Truda Marsden, and Robert Young)

416. China (11/22/43; William Bendix, Robert Harris, Alan Ladd, and Loretta Young)

417. The Navy Comes Through (11/29/43; Pat O'Brien, Chester Morris, and Ruth Warrick)

418. Mrs. Miniver (12/6/43; Greer Garson, Raymond Lawrence, Susan Peters, and Walter Pidgeon)

419. Five Graves to Cairo (12/13/43; Anne Baxter, J. Carrol Naish, Walter Pidgeon, Otto Preminger, and Franchot Tone)

420. Dixie (12/20/43; Cliff Clark, Bing Crosby, Dorothy Lamour, and Barry Sullivan)

421. Kathleen (12/27/43; Bea Benaderet, Frances Gifford, Herbert Marshall, Shirley Temple)

422. Shadow of a Doubt (1/3/44; Verna Felton, William Powell, and Teresa Wright)

423. The Constant Nymph (1/10/44; Charles Boyer, Maureen O'Sullivan, and Alexis Smith)

424. War Loan Drive (1/17/44)

425. Casablanca (1/24/44; Edgar Barrier, Alan Ladd, Hedy Lamarr, John Loder)

426. Random Harvest (1/31/44; Ronald Colman, Greer Garson, and Raymond Lawrence)

427. His Butler's Sister (2/7/44; Deanna Durbin, Jay Novello, Pat O'Brien, and Robert Paige)

428. The Fallen Sparrow (2/14/44; Maureen O'Hara, Walter Slezak, and Robert Young)

429. Wake Up and Live (2/21/44; Bob Crosby, James Gleason, Marilyn Maxwell, and Frank Sinatra)

430. Guadalcanal Diary (2/28/44; William Bendix, Preston Foster, John McIntire, and Lloyd Nolan)

431. The Letter (3/6/44; Bette Davis, Charles Lung, Herbert Marshall, and Vincent Price)

432. In Old Oklahoma (3/13/44; Albert Dekker, Roy Rogers, Martha Scott, and Martha Wentworth)

433. The Hard Way (3/20/44; Anne Baxter, Miriam Hopkins, Charles Seel, and Franchot Tone)
434. The Phantom Lady (3/27/44; Brian Aherne, Alan Curtis, Chester Morris, and Ella Raines)
435. Destroyer (4/3/44; Marguerite Chapman, Dennis O'Keefe, and Edward G. Robinson)
436. The Happy Land (4/10/44; Don Ameche, Walter Brennan, Frances Dee, Bob Haines, Joan Lorring)
437. Coney Island (4/17/44; Alan Ladd, Dorothy Lamour, and Chester Morris)
438. This Land Is Mine (4/24/44; Edgar Barrier, Cliff Clark, Charles Laughton, and Maureen O'Sullivan)
439. Appointment for Love (5/1/44; Olivia De Havilland, Dennis Greene, and Paul Lukas)
440. Penny Serenade (5/8/44; Edgar Buchanan, Joseph Cotten, Irene Dunne, and John McIntire)
441. Action in the North Atlantic (5/15/44; Julie Bishop, Raymond Massey, and George Raft)
442. Springtime in the Rockies (5/22/44; Edgar Barrier, Betty Grable, Carmen Miranda, Dick Powell)
443. Old Acquaintance (5/29/44; Bob Bailey, Miriam Hopkins, Otto Kruger, and Alexis Smith)
444. Jane Eyre (6/5/44; Orson Welles and Loretta Young)
445. Naughty Marietta (6/12/44; Nelson Eddy, Verna Felton, Jeanette MacDonald, and Jay Novello)
446. Lost Angel (6/19/44; James Craig, Marsha Hunt, Margaret O'Brien, and Keenan Wynn)
447. Christmas in July (6/26/44; Lionel Barrymore, Linda Darnell, Howard McNear, and Dick Powell)
448. It Happened Tomorrow (7/3/44; Don Ameche and Anne Baxter)
449. Maytime (9/4/44; Nelson Eddy and Jeanette MacDonald)
450. Break of Hearts (9/11/44; Rita Hayworth and Orson Welles)
451. Suspicion (9/18/44; Olivia De Havilland, Gloria Gordon, Charles

Irwin, and William Powell)
452. Lucky Partners (9/25/44; Don Ameche and Lucille Ball)
453. Home in Indiana (10/2/44; Walter Brennan, Charlotte Greenwood, and Charles Seel)
454. In Old Chicago (10/9/44; John Hodiak, Cy Kendall, Dorothy Lamour, and Robert Young)
455. Seventh Heaven (10/16/44; Billy Gilbert, Jean Hersholt, Jennifer Jones, and Van Johnson)
456. The Story of Dr. Wassel (10/23/44; Gary Cooper)
457. Standing Room Only (10/30/44; Arthur Q. Bryan, Verna Felton, Paulette Goddard, and Fred MacMurray)
458. The Pied Piper (11/6/44; Signe Hasso, Frank Morgan, and Margaret O'Brien)
459. Magnificent Obsession (11/13/44; Don Ameche, Claudette Colbert, and Frank Sinatra)
460. It Started With Eve (11/20/44; Susanna Foster, Charles Laughton, and Dick Powell)
461. Dark Waters (11/27/44; Preston Foster, Thomas Mitchell, and Merle Oberon)
462. The Unguarded Hour (12/4/44; Laraine Day, Gloria Gordon, Robert Montgomery, Roland Young)
463. Casanova Brown (12/11/44; Joan Bennett, Gary Cooper, and Thomas Mitchell)
464. Berkley Square (12/18/44; Ronald Colman and Maureen O'Sullivan)
465. The Vagabond King (12/25/44; Katherine Grayson, Dennis Morgan, and J. Carroll Naish)
466. Bride by Mistake (1/1/45; Laraine Day, John Hodiak, Marsha Hunt)
467. I Never Left Home (1/8/45; Jerry Colonna, Bob Hope, Frances Langford, and Tony Romano)
468. The Master Race (1/15/45; George Coulouris, Nancy Gates, Stanley Ridges, and Charles Seel)
469. Tender Comrades [based on a story by Dalton Trumbo] (1/22/45; Olivia De Havilland, June Duprez, and Dennis O'Keefe)

549. Mrs. Parkington (11/25/46; Greer Garson and Walter Pidgeon)
550. Meet Me in St. Louis (12/2/46; Tom Drake, Judy Garland, Gale Gordon, and Margaret O'Brien)
551. Together Again (12/9/46; Jeff Donnell, Irene Dunne, Walter Pidgeon, and Alan Reed)
552. Killer Kates (12/16/46; Jack Benny, James Gleason, Gail Patrick, Alan Reed, and Eric Snowden)
553. Do You Love Me? (12/23/46; Dick Haymes, John McIntire, Maureen O'Hara, and Barry Sullivan)
554. Crack-up (12/30/46; Lynn Bari, Lester Matthews, and Pat O'Brien)
555. Till the End of Time (1/6/47; Tony Barrett, Laraine Day, Robert Mitchum, and Bill Williams)
556. The Green Years (1/13/47; Charles Coburn, Hume Cronyn, Tom Drake, and Gale Gordon)
557. Anna and the King of Siam (1/20/47; Irene Dunne and Rex Harrison)
558. Cluny Brown (1/27/47; Charles Boyer and Olivia de Havilland)
559. National Velvet (2/3/47; Donald Crisp, Mickey Rooney, and Elizabeth Taylor)
560. Frenchman's Creek (2/10/47; Joan Fontaine, Gerald Mohr, David Niven, and Alan Reed)
561. Devotion (2/17/47; Virginia Bruce, Vincent Price, and Jane Wyman)
562. Kitty (2/24/47; Paulette Goddard)
563. Somewhere in the Night (3/3/47; Lynn Bari, William Johnstone, John Hodiak, and Carol Smith)
564. It's Wonderful Life (3/10/47; Victor Moore, Donna Reed, and James Stewart)
565. Leave Her to Heaven (3/17/47; Kay Christopher, Tommy Cook, Gene Tierney, and Cornel Wilde)
566. Smokey (3/24/47; Joel McCrea and Constance Moore)
567. How Green Was My Valley (3/31/47; Donald Crisp, David Niven, and Maureen O'Sullivan)
568. Alexander's Ragtime Band (4/7/47; Dick Haymes, Al Jolson, Dinah Shore, Tyrone Power, and Margaret Whiting)

569. Monsieur Beaucaire (4/14/47; Joan Caulfield and Bob Hope)
570. My Reputation (4/21/47; George Brent and Barbara Stanwyck)
571. My Darling Clementine (4/28/47; Richard Conte, Cathy Downs, Henry Fonda, Paula Winslowe)
572. The Egg and I (5/5/47; Claudette Colbert, William Johnstone, and Fred MacMurray)
573. Johnny O'Clock (5/12/47; Janice Carter, Marguerite Chapman, Lee J. Cobb, and Dick Powell)
574. It Happened on Fifth Avenue (5/19/47; Don DeFore, Victor Moore, Charles Ruggles, Gale Storm)
575. Vacation from Marriage (5/26/47; Van Heflin and Deborah Kerr)
576. The Jazz Singer (6/2/47; William Johnstone, Al Jolson, and Gail Patrick)
577. The Animal Kingdom (6/9/47; Dennis Morgan and Jane Wyman)
578. The Other Love (6/16/47; George Brent and Barbara Stanwyck)
579. Cynthia (6/23/47; Mary Astor and Elizabeth Taylor)
580. A Stolen Life (8/23/47; Bette Davis and Glenn Ford)
581. Three Wise Fools (9/1/47; Lionel Barrymore and Margaret O'Brien)
582. Margie (9/8/47; Jeanne Crain and Glenn Langan)
583. The Seventh Veil (9/15/47; Joseph Cotten, Gale Gordon, Joseph Kearns, and Ida Lupino)
584. Two Years Before the Mast (9/22/47; MacDonald Carey, Jeff Chandler, Howard da Silva, Wanda Hendrix, Alan Ladd, and Luis Van Rooten)
585. The Web (9/29/47; Edmund O'Brien, Maria Palmer, and Vincent Price)
586. Undercurrent (10/6/47; Jeff Chandler, Katharine Hepburn, William Johnstone, and Robert Taylor)
587. Great Expectations (10/13/47; Ann Blyth, Lee J. Cobb, Robert Cummings, Howard da Silva)
588. 13 Rue Madeleine (10/20/47; Vanessa Brown, Richard Conte, Robert Montgomery, Lloyd Nolan)

589. Stairway to Heaven (10/27/47; Ray Milland and Lloyd Nolan)
590. Singapore (11/3/47; Ava Gardner and Fred MacMurray)
591. Dark Corner (11/10/47; Lucille Ball, Joseph Kearns, Wally Maher, and Mark Stevens)
592. Nobody Lives Forever (11/17/47; William Conrad, Ronald Reagan, and Jane Wyman)
593. Saratoga Trunk (11/24/47; Ida Lupino, Jay Novello, Zachary Scott, and Ben Wright)
594. The Ghost and Mrs. Muir (12/1/47; Charles Boyer and Madaleine Carroll)
595. Ride the Pink Horse (12/8/47; Thomas Gomez, Wanda Hendrix, and Robert Montgomery)
596. Magic Town (12/15/47; James Stewart and Jane Wyman)
597. Miracle on 34th Street (12/22/47; Edmund Gwenn, Maureen O'Hara, John Payne, Natalie Wood)
598. Anchors Aweigh (12/29/47; Katherine Grayson, Gene Kelly, and Frank Sinatra)
599. The Farmer's Daughter (1/5/48; Joseph Cotten and Loretta Young)
600. The Kiss of Death (1/12/48; Jeff Chandler, Coleen Gray, Victor Mature, and Richard Widmark)
601. The Yearling (1/19/48; Claude Jarman, Jr., Gregory Peck, and Jane Wyman)
602. Notorious (1/26/48; Ingrid Bergman, Joseph Cotten, Joseph Kearns, and Gerald Mohr)
603. Mother Wore Tights (2/2/48; Dan Dailey and Betty Grable)
604. Lady in the Lake (2/9/48; Gerald Mohr, Robert Montgomery, and Audrey Totter)
605. The Jolson Story (2/16/48; Ludwig Dunath, Al Jolson, and Evelyn Keyes)
606. T-Men (2/23/48; Dennis O'Keefe and Gail Patrick)
607. Bad Bascomb (3/1/48; Wallace Beery and Margaret O'Brien)
608. Spellbound (3/8/48; Herb Butterfield, Joseph Cotten, William Johnstone, Gerald Mohr, and Valli)
609. Irish Eyes are Smiling (3/15/48; Dick Haymes)
610. A Woman's Vengeance (3/22/48; Ann Blyth and Charles Boyer)
611. I Love You Again (3/29/48; William Powell and Ann Sothern)
612. Daisy Kenyon (4/5/48; Dana Andrews, Jeff Chandler, Ida Lupino, Eddie Marr, and Gerald Mohr)
613. Perfect Marriage (4/12/48; Ray Milland and Lizabeth Scott)
614. Random Harvest (4/19/48; Ronald Colman, Greer Garson, and Lurene Tuttle)
615. Dear Ruth (4/26/48; Joan Caulfield, Billy de Wolfe, and William Holden)
616. Cloak and Dagger (5/3/48; Herb Butterfield, Jeff Chandler, Lilli Palmer, and Ronald Reagan)
617. Intrigue (5/10/48; Jeff Chandler, June Havoc, and George Raft)
618. Homestretch (5/17/48; Maureen O'Hara and Cornel Wilde)
619. I Walk Alone (5/24/48; Burt Lancaster and Lizabeth Scott)
620. Miracle of the Bells (5/31/48; Jeff Chandler, Fred MacMurray, Frank Sinatra, and Valli)
621. Relentless (6/7/48; Claire Trevor and Robert Young)
622. Jane Eyre (6/14/48; Ingrid Bergman, Robert Montgomery, Janet Scott, and Stan Waxman)
623. You Were Meant for Me (6/28/48; Dan Dailey and Donna Reed)
624. I Remember Mama (8/30/48; Barbara Bel Geddes, Irene Dunne, and Oscar Homolka)
625. Mr. Peabody and the Mermaid (9/6/48; William Powell)
626. Another Part of the Forest (9/13/48; Tony Barrett, Ann Blyth, Walter Huston, and Vincent Price)
627. Gentleman's Agreement (9/20/48; Anne Baxter, Jeff Chandler, and Gregory Peck)
628. Tap Roots (9/27/48; Susan Hayward and Van Heflin)
629. Stallion Road (10/4/48; Ronald Reagan, Zachary Scott, and Alexis Smith)

630. Larceny (10/11/48; Joan Caulfield and John Payne)
631. Razor's Edge (10/18/48; Ida Lupino and Mark Stevens)
632. Secret Heart (10/25/48; Deborah Kerr and Walter Pidgeon)
633. Pitfall (11/8/48; Dick Powell, Lizabeth Scott, and Jane Wyatt)
634. Body and Soul (11/15/48; William Conrad, John Garfield, Marie Windsor, and Jane Wyman)
635. The Big Clock (11/22/48; Ray Milland and Maureen O'Sullivan)
636. Brief Encounter (11/19/48; Greer Garson and Van Heflin)
637. The Foxes of Harrow (12/6/48; John Hodiak and Maureen O'Hara)
638. The Seventh Veil (12/13/48; Ingrid Bergman and Robert Montgomery)
639. Miracle on 34th Street (12/20/48; Edmund Gwenn, Maureen O'Hara, and John Payne)
640. Luck of the Irish (12/27/48; Dana Andrews, Anne Baxter, Jack Benny, and Cecil Kellaway)
641. The Mating of Millie (1/3/49; Glenn Ford)
642. The Velvet Touch (1/10/49; Sydney Greenstreet and Rosalind Russell)
643. You Gotta Stay Happy (1/17/49; Joan Fontaine and James Stewart)
644. High Barbaree (1/24/49; Van Johnson)
645. Street with No Name (1/31/49; Ed Begley, John McIntire, Lloyd Nolan, Mark Stevens, and Richard Widmark)
646. Captain from Castile (2/7/49; Jean Peters and Cornel Wilde)
647. Sitting Pretty (2/14/49; Ed Begley, Gale Gordon, Maureen O'Hara, Clifton Webb, Robert Young)
648. The Unafraid (2/21/49; Joan Fontaine and Burt Lancaster)
649. Apartment for Peggy (2/28/49; Jeanne Crain, Edmund Gwenn, William Holden, Howard McNear)
650. Red River (3/7/49; Walter Brennan, Jeff Chandler, Joanne Dru, and John Wayne)
651. What a Woman (3/14/49; Robert Cummings and Rosalind Russell)
652. That Wonderful Urge (3/21/49; Don Ameche and Gene Tierney)
653. The Accused (3/28/49; Robert Cummings and Loretta Young)
654. Family Honeymoon (4/4/49; Claudette Colbert and Fred MacMurray)
655. The Song of Bernadette (4/11/49; Anne Baxter and Charles Bickford)
656. The Treasure of Sierra Madre (4/18/49; Humphrey Bogart, Walter Huston, and Frank Lovejoy)
657. When My Baby Smiles At Me (4/25/49; William Conrad, Dan Dailey, and Betty Grable)
658. Miss Tatlock's Millions (5/2/49; Wanda Hendrix and John Lund)
659. The Paradine Case (5/9/49; Joseph Cotten and Valli)
660. April Showers (5/16/49; Jack Carson and Dorothy Lamour)
661. To the Ends of the Earth (5/23/49; Signe Hasso and Dick Powell)
662. Anna and the King of Siam (5/30/49; Irene Dunne and James Mason)
663. Mildred Pierce (6/6/49; Rosalind Russell and Zachary Scott)
664. The Bachelor and the Bobby Soxer (6/13/49; Cary Grant, Shirley Temple, and Esther Williams)
665. Merton of the Movies (6/20/49; Arlene Dahl and Mickey Rooney)
666. Every Girl Should Be Married (6/27/49; Betsy Drake and Cary Grant)
667. June Bride (8/29/49; Bette Davis and James Stewart)
668. Saigon (9/5/49; John Lund and Lizabeth Scott)
669. Deep Waters (9/12/49; Dana Andrews, Shepard Menken, Donna Reed, Anne Revere, Jeffrey Silver)
670. Green Dolphin Street (9/19/49; Joan Banks, Van Heflin, Peter Lawford, and Lana Turner)
671. Emperor Waltz (9/26/49; Ann Blyth and Bing Crosby)
672. It Happens to Be Spring (10/3/49; Ray Milland)
673. Mr. Blandings Builds His Dream House (10/10/49; Irene Dunne and Cary Grant)

674. Mother Was a Freshman (10/17/49; Van Johnson, Rhoda Williams, and Loretta Young)
675. Scudda Hoo, Scudda Hay (10/24/49; June Haver and Lon McAllister)
676. A Portrait of Jenny (10/31/49; Anne Baxter, Herb Butterfield, and Joseph Cotten)
677. High Wall (11/7/49; Van Heflin and Janet Leigh)
678. Mother Wore Tights (11/14/49; Joan Banks, Dan Dailey, Betty Grable, and William Johnstone)
679. Sorrowful Jones (11/21/49; Lucille Ball and Bob Hope)
680. Key Largo (11/28/49; Edmund O'Brien, Debbie Reynolds, Claire Trevor, Edward G. Robinson)
681. Dear Ruth (12/5/49; Joan Caulfield and William Holden)
682. Street With No Name (12/12/49; Stephen McNally and Mark Stevens)
683. The Bishop's Wife (12/19/49; David Niven and Tyrone Power)
684. My Dream Is Yours (12/26/49; Jack Carson)
685. To Each His Own (1/2/50; Olivia de Havilland and John Lund)
686. Sorry, Wrong Number (1/9/50; Burt Lancaster and Barbara Stanwyck)
687. Mr. Belvedere Goes to College (1/16/50; Colleen Gray, Robert Stack, and Clifton Webb)
688. I'll Be Yours (1/23/50; William Bendix, Ann Blyth, Robert Cummings, and Willard Waterman)
689. California (1/30/50; Ray Milland and Lizabeth Scott)
690. Red, Hot, and Blue (2/6/50; Betty Hutton and John Lund)
691. The Stratton Story (2/13/50; June Allyson and James Stewart)
692. A Letter to Three Wives (2/20/50; Linda Darnell and Paul Douglas)
693. Easy to Wed (2/27/50; Van Johnson and Esther Williams)
694. Slattery's Hurricane (3/6/50; William Conrad, Richard Conte, Veronica Lake, Maureen O'Hara)
695. Little Women (3/13/50; June Allyson, Peter Lawford, Janet Leigh, and Margaret O'Brien)

696. Father Was a Fullback (3/20/50; Paul Douglas and Maureen O'Hara)
697. The Man Who Came to Dinner (3/27/50; Lucille Ball and Clifton Webb)
698. Come to the Stable (4/3/50; Hugh Marlowe and Loretta Young)
699. The Snake Pit (4/10/50; Leo Genn and Olivia de Havilland)
700. Every Girl Should Be Married (4/17/50; Cary Grant and Betsy Drake)
701. Mrs. Mike (4/24/50; Dick Powell and Gene Tierney)
702. All My Sons (5/1/50; Edward Arnold, Scott Brady, and Burt Lancaster)
703. The Life of Riley (5/8/50; William Bendix, John Brown, Rosemary DeCamp, and Meg Randall)
704. The Lady Takes a Sailor (5/15/50; Dennis Morgan and Jane Wyman)
705. Jolson Sings Again (5/22/50; Barbara Hale and Al Jolson)
706. Night Song (5/29/50; Dana Andrews and Joan Fontaine)
707. Bride For Sale (6/5/50; Claudette Colbert and Robert Young)
708. The Corn Is Green (6/12/50; Richard Basehart, Herb Butterfield, and Olivia De Havilland)
709. John Loves Mary (6/19/50; Patricia Neal, Ronald Reagan, and Alan Reed)
710. The Bride Goes Wild (6/26/50; June Allyson and Van Johnson)
711. My Foolish Heart (8/28/50; Dana Andrews and Susan Hayward)
712. One Sunday Afternoon (9/4/50; Dennis Morgan, Patricia Neal, and Ruth Roman)
713. The Heiress (9/11/50; Louis Calhern, Olivia de Havilland, and Van Heflin)
714. Pinky (9/18/50; Ethel Barrymore and Jeanne Crain)
715. Good Sam (9/25/50; Joel McCrea and Ann Sheridan)
716. Flamingo Road (10/2/50; Jane Wyman)
717. Love That Brute (10/9/50; Paul Douglas and Jean Peters)

718. House of Strangers (10/16/50; Anne Baxter and Richard Conte)
719. A Woman of Distinction (10/23/50; Cary Grant and Rosalind Russell)
720. Double Indemnity (10/30/50; Fred MacMurray and Barbara Stanwyck)
721. Rebecca (11/6/50; Eleanor Audley, Vivien Leigh, and Lawrence Olivier)
722. Wabash Avenue (11/13/50; Betty Grable and Victor Mature)
723. Pretty Baby (11/20/50; Betsy Drake and Dennis Morgan)
724. You're My Everything (11/27/50; Anne Baxter and Phil Harris)
725. Apartment for Peggy (12/4/50; Jeanne Crain)
726. BF's Daughter (12/11/50; Stewart Granger and Barbara Stanwyck)
727. Holiday Affair (12/18/50; Laraine Day and Robert Mitchum)
728. The Wizard of Oz (12/25/50; Judy Garland)
729. The Barkleys of Broadway (1/1/51; George Murphy and Ginger Rogers)
730. Once More My Darling (1/8/51; Ann Blyth and Van Heflin)
731. The Farmer's Daughter (1/15/51; Joseph Cotten and Loretta Young)
732. Broken Arrow (1/22/51; Jeff Chandler, William Conrad, Burt Lancaster, and Debra Paget)
733. Treasure Island (1/29/51; Bobby Driscoll and James Mason)
734. Louisa (2/5/51; Ruth Hussey and Ronald Reagan)
735. Battleground (2/12/51; John Hodiak, Van Johnson, Ricardo Montalban, George Murphy, Marshall Thompson, and James Whitmore)
736. Dear Wife (2/19/51; Joan Caulfield and William Holden)
737. When Johnny Comes Marching Home (2/26/51; Joanne Dru and James Stewart)
738. Panic in the Streets (3/5/51; Paul Douglas and Richard Widmark)
739. She Wore a Yellow Ribbon (3/12/51; Mel Ferrer and John Wayne)
740. The Red Danube (3/19/51; Peter Lawford, Janet Leigh, and Walter Pidgeon)

741. Seventh Heaven (3/26/51; Charles Farrell, Janet Gaynor, Jean Moorehead, and Alan Reed)
742. Where the Sidewalk Ends (4/2/51; Dana Andrews and Anne Baxter)
743. The Third Man (4/9/51; Joseph Cotten and Evelyn Keyes)
744. Oh, You Beautiful Doll (4/16/51; Joan Caulfield, Bob Crosby, and George Jessel)
745. Family Honeymoon (4/23/51; Claudette Colbert and Fred MacMurray)
746. Down to the Sea in Ships (4/30/51; Lionel Barrymore and Richard Widmark)
747. Cheaper by the Dozen (5/7/51; Betty Lou Gerson, Clifton Webb, and Rhonda Williams)
748. Brief Encounter (5/14/51; Richard Basehart and Olivia de Havilland)
749. Love Letters (5/21/51; William Holden and Loretta Young)
750. Bright Leaf (5/28/51; Virginia Mayo and Gregory Peck)
751. A Ticket to Tomahawk (6/4/51; Anne Baxter and Dan Dailey)
752. Our Very Own (6/11/51; Farley Granger and Diana Lynn)
753. Edward, My Son (6/18/51; Deborah Kerr and Walter Pidgeon)
754. The Reformer and the Redhead (6/25/51; June Allyson and Dick Powell)
755. The Mudlark (8/27/51; Irene Dunne and Sir Cedric Hardwicke)
756. Payment on Demand (9/3/51; Bette Davis and Barry Sullivan)
757. Fancy Pants (9/10/51; Lucille Ball, Verna Felton, and Bob Hope)
758. Sunset Boulevard (9/17/51; William Conrad, Nancy Gates, William Holden, and Gloria Swanson)
759. Movietime — USA [50th Anniversary of Movies with an All-star cast] (9/24/51; Mary Alden, Ann Blyth, Claudette Colbert, Gary Cooper, Bing Crosby, Dan Dailey, Joann Drew, Gene Kelly, Robert Ryan, Forrest Tucker, John Wayne, Jane Wyman)
760. All About Eve (10/1/51; Anne Baxter, Bette Davis, Reginald Gardner, and Gary Merrill)

761. Borderline (10/8/51; Fred MacMurray and Claire Trevor)
762. Mister 880 (10/15/51; Dana Andrews and Edmund Gwenn)
763. Margie (10/22/51; Jeanne Crain and Hugh Marlowe)
764. I'd Climb the Highest Mountain (10/29/51; Susan Hayward and William Lundigan)
765. That Forsythe Woman (11/5/51; Greer Garson and Walter Pidgeon)
766. Winchester '73 (11/12/51; James Stewart)
767. Samson and Delilah (11/19/51; Hedy Lamarr and Victor Mature)
768. To Please a Lady (11/26/51; John Hodiak, Adolphe Menjou, and Donna Reed)
769. Strangers on a Train (12/3/51; Frank Lovejoy, Ray Milland, and Ruth Roman)
770. The Lemon Drop Kid (12/10/51; Bob Hope and Marilyn Maxwell)
771. The Men (12/17/51; William Holden and Teresa Wright)
772. Alice in Wonderland (12/24/51; Kathryn Beaumont, Jerry Colonna, Verna Felton, Gale Gordon, Sterling Holloway, and Ed Wynn)
773. Bird of Paradise (12/31/51; Jeff Chandler, Louis Jourdan, and Debra Paget)
774. Duchess of Idaho (1/7/52; Van Johnson and Esther Williams)
775. Goodbye My Fancy (1/14/52; Barbara Stanwyck and Robert Young)
776. Captain Horatio Hornblower (1/21/52; Virginia Mayo and Gregory Peck)
777. Branded (1/28/52; Mona Freeman and Burt Lancaster)
778. Showboat (2/4/52; Ava Gardner, Kathryn Grayson, and Howard Keel)
779. Kim (2/18/52; Errol Flynn and Dean Stockwell)
780. My Blue Heaven (2/25/52; Dan Dailey and Betty Grable)
781. Young Man with a Horn (3/3/52; Kirk Douglas and Jo Stafford)
782. Follow the Sun (3/10/52; Anne Baxter, Burgess Meredith, and Gary Merrill)
783. Top O' the Mountain (3/17/52; Ann Blyth and Barry Fitzgerald)
784. Come to the Stable (3/24/52; Loretta Young)
785. I Can Get It for You Wholesale (3/31/52; Dan Dailey and Susan Hayward)
786. Union Station (4/7/52; William Holden and Nancy Olsen)
787. Royal Wedding (4/14/52; George Murphy and Jane Powell)
788. Crisis (4/21/52; Robert Taylor)
789. No Highway in the Sky (4/28/52; Marlene Dietrich, Evelyn Eaton, and James Stewart)
790. On Moonlight Bay (5/5/52; Gordon MacRae and Jane Wyman)
791. Riding High (5/12/52; Rhonda Fleming and Fred MacMurray)
792. The Magnificent Yankee (5/19/52; Louis Calhern and Ann Harding)
793. Room for One More (5/26/52; Cary Grant and Phyllis Thaxter)
794. Two Weeks with Love (9/8/52; Ricardo Montalban, Jane Powell, and Debbie Reynolds)
795. Here Comes the Groom (9/15/52; Fred MacMurray and Jane Wyman)
796. I'll Never Forget You (9/22/52; Debra Paget and Tyrone Power)
797. Adam and Evelyn (9/29/52; Stewart Granger, Jean Simmons, and Chester Stratton)
798. The Model and the Marriage Broker (10/6/52; Hans Conried, Jeanne Crain, Verna Felton, Jack Kruschen, and Thelma Ritter)
799. Five Fingers (10/13/52; James Mason)
800. My Six Convicts (10/20/52; Dana Andrews, Sheldon Leonard, and Millard Mitchell)
801. My Son John (10/27/52; Fay Bainter, Dean Jagger, and John Lund)
802. Viva Zapata (11/3/52; William Conrad, Paul Frees, Charlton Heston, and Jean Peters)
803. Grounds for Marriage (11/10/52; Herb Butterfield, Kathryn Grayson, and Van Johnson)
804. Submarine Command (11/17/52; William Holden, Sheldon Leonard, and Alexis Smith)
805. The Blue Veil (11/24/52; Herb Butterfield, Gloria Blondell, William Conrad, and Jane Wyman)

806. King Solomon's Mines (12/1/52; Stewart Granger and Deborah Kerr)
807. Strictly Dishonorable (12/8/52; Ted de Corsia, Fernando Lamas, and Janet Leigh)
808. The African Queen (12/15/52; Humphrey Bogart, Hans Conried, and Greer Garson)
809. Les Miserables (12/22/52; Ronald Colman, Robert Newton, and Debra Paget)
810. Westward the Women (12/29/52; Denise Darcel and Robert Taylor)
811. Phone Call from a Stranger (1/5/53; Verna Felton, Gary Merrill, and Shelley Winters)
812. The Will Rogers Story" or "The Story of Will Rogers (1/12/53; Will Rogers, Jr. and Jane Wyman)
813. Appointment with Danger (1/19/53; William Conrad, Colleen Gray, and William Holden)
814. September Affair (1/26/53; Joseph Cotten and Joan Fontaine)
815. Captain Carey, USA (2/2/53; Wanda Hendrix, Charlton Heston, and Jeanette Nolan)
816. With a Song in My Heart (2/9/53; Susan Hayward, Thelma Ritter, Robert Wagner, David Wayne)
817. Lady in the Dark (2/16/53; Judy Garland and John Lund)
818. You're My Everything (2/23/53; Jeanne Crain and Dan Dailey)
819. Close to My Heart (3/2/53; Ray Milland and Phyllis Thaxter)
820. The People Against O'Hara (3/9/53; Janet Leigh and Walter Pidgeon)
821. This Woman Is Dangerous (3/16/53; Leif Erickson, Virginia Mayo, and Dennis Morgan)
822. Fourteen Hours (3/23/53; Paul Douglas and Terry Moore)
823. Miracle of Our Lady of Fatima (3/30/53; J. Carroll Naish and Carroll Whitney)
824. Angels in the Outfield (4/6/53; Donna Cochran, Janet Leigh, and George Murphy)
825. Just For You (4/13/53; Dick Haymes and Jane Wyman)
826. Deadline, USA (4/20/53; Dan Dailey, Dick Haymes, Debra Paget)
827. Somebody Loves Me (4/27/53; Gene Barry, Betty Hutton, and David Wayne)
828. Wait Till the Sun Shines Nellie (5/4/53; Jean Peters, Phyllis Thaxter, and Les Tremayne)
829. The Bishop's Wife (5/11/53; Cary Grant, Olan Soule, and Phyllis Thaxter)
830. The Girl in White (5/18/53; June Allyson and Steve Forrest)
831. Lure of the Wilderness (5/25/53; Jeffery Hunter and Jean Peters)
832. High Tor (6/1/53; William Holden)
833. China Run (6/8/53; Virginia Mayo)
834. The Lady and the Tumbler (6/15/53; Fred MacMurray)
835. The Fall of Maggie Phillips (6/22/53; William Conrad, Verna Felton, and Dorothy McGuire)
836. One More Spring (6/29/53; Jeanne Crain)
837. Cynara (7/6/53; Joseph Cotten)
838. The Physician in Spite of Himself (7/13/53; Robert Young)
839. The Birds [based on the novel by Daphne Du Maurier] (7/20/53; Herbert Marshall)
840. One Foot in Heaven (7/27/53; Dana Andrews and Steve Forrest)
841. Romance to a Degree (8/3/53; Parley Baer, Joseph Cotten, John Dehner, and Verna Felton)
842. Leave Her to Heaven (8/10/53; Joan Fontaine)
843. Edward, My Son (8/17/53; Walter Pidgeon)
844. The Affairs of Susan (8/24/53; Anne Baxter)
845. Our Last September (8/31/53; Claire Trevor)
846. My Cousin Rachel (9/7/53; Olivia De Havilland and Ron Randell)
847. The Steel Trap (9/14/53; Joseph Cotten and Theresa Wright)
848. I Confess (9/21/53; Cary Grant and Phyllis Thaxter)
849. The President's Lady (9/28/53; Joan Fontaine and Charlton Heston)
850. Our Very Own (10/5/53; Joan Evans, Terry Moore, and Robert Wagner)
851. Breaking the Sound Barrier (10/12/53; Lamont Johnson,

Dorothy McGuire, and Robert Newton)

852. Taxi (10/19/53; Dan Dailey, Colleen Gray, Jack Kruschen, and Eddie Marr)

853. Skirts Ahoy (10/26/53; Virginia Gregg, Barry Sullivan, and Esther Williams)

854. Because of You (11/2/53; June Allyson, Jeff Chandler, and Jeanette Nolan)

855. Thunder on the Hill (11/9/53; Claudette Colbert and Barbara Rush)

856. It Grows on Trees (11/16/53; Ginger Rogers)

857. The Browning Version (11/23/53; Ronald Colman, Robert Douglas, and Benita Hume)

858. Undercurrent (11/30/53; Joan Fontaine and Mel Ferrer)

859. Man on a Tightrope (12/7/53; Terry Moore and Edward G. Robinson)

860. Million Dollar Mermaid (12/14/53; Steve Dunn, Walter Pidgeon, and Esther Williams)

861. Peter Pan (12/21/53; Kathryn Beaumont, John Carradine, Bobby Driscoll, and Bill Thompson)

862. June Bride (12/28/53; Irene Dunne and Fred MacMurray)

863. The Day the Earth Stood Still (1/4/54; Michael Rennie and Jean Peters)

864. Has Anybody Seen My Gal? (1/11/54; Rock Hudson, Piper Laurie, and Gene Lockhart)

865. The Winslow Boy (1/18/54; Brian Aherne, Ray Milland, and Dorothy McGuire)

866. People Will Talk (1/25/54; Jeanne Crain and Cary Grant)

867. Laura (2/1/54; Gene Tierney)

868. The Third Man (2/8/54; Ray Milland and Ruth Roman)

869. Trouble Along the Way (2/15/54; Jack Carson and June Haver)

870. September Affair (2/22/54; Dana Andrews and Eleanor Parker)

871. Mississippi Gambler (3/1/54; Linda Christian and Tyrone Power)

872. The Glass Menagerie (3/8/54; Fay Bainter, Tom Brown, Frank Lovejoy, and Jane Wyman)

873. Jeopardy (3/15/54; Tony Barrett, Barbara Stanwyck, and Barry Sullivan)

874. Carbine Williams (3/22/54; Wendell Corey, Jean Hagen, and Ronald Reagan)

875. A Blueprint for Murder (3/29/54; Dan Dailey and Dorothy McGuire)

876. Welcome Stranger (4/5/54; Pat Crowley, Barry Fitzgerald, and Cary Grant)

877. Strangers on a Train (4/12/54; Dana Andrews, Robert Cummings, and Virginia Mayo)

878. The Star (4/19/54; Ida Lupino and Edmund O'Brien)

879. Detective Story (4/26/54; Kirk Douglas and Eleanor Parker)

880. Going My Way (5/3/54; Stanley Clements, Barry Fitzgerald, and William Lundigan)

881. Holy Matrimony (5/10/54; Fay Bainter and Charles Laughton)

882. The Corn Is Green (5/17/54; Claudette Colbert and Cameron Mitchell)

883. The Model and the Marriage Broker (5/24/54; Jeanne Crain and Thelma Ritter)

884. What a Woman (5/31/54; Robert Cummings and Rosalind Russell)

885. The Naked Jungle (6/7/54; Charlton Heston and Donna Reed)

886. Mildred Pierce (6/14/54; Hal March, Zachary Scott, and Claire Trevor)

887. Pickup on South Street (6/21/54; Stephen McNally, Terry Moore, and Thelma Ritter)

888. Goodbye My Fancy (6/28/54; Rosalind Russell and Robert Young)

889. Wuthering Heights (9/14/54; Samuel Goldwyn, Cameron Mitchell, and Merle Oberon)

890. So Big (9/21/54; Ida Lupino and Robert Stack)

891. How Green Was My Valley (9/28/54; Donald Crisp, Donna Reed, Michael Rennie, Alexis Smith)

892. The Turning Point (10/5/54; Joanne Dru and Fred MacMurray)

893. Great Expectations (10/12/54; Rock Hudson and Barbara Rush)

94. David and Bathsheba (10/19/54; William Conrad, Hans Conried, Arlene Dahl, Michael Rennie)

95. The Song of Bernadette (10/26/54; Charles Bickford and Ann Blyth)

96. The Big Trees (11/2/54; Nancy Gates and Van Heflin)

97. My Man Godfrey (11/9/54; Julia Adams, Jeff Chandler, and Alan Reed)

98. Mother Didn't Tell Me (11/16/54; Frank Lovejoy and Dorothy McGuire)

99. All About Eve (11/23/54; Ann Blyth, William Conrad, and Claire Trevor)

00. The Blue Gardenia (11/30/54; Dana Andrews, William Conrad, and Ruth Roman)

01. Battleground (12/7/54; William Conrad, Van Johnson, and George Murphy)

02. Secret of the Incas (12/14/54; Charlton Heston and Nicole Maurey)

03. Miracle on 34th Street (12/21/54; Edmund Gwenn)

04. The Iron Mistress (12/28/54; John Lund and Virginia Mayo)

05. Mother Wore Tights (1/4/54; Dan Dailey and Mitzi Gaynor)

06. Island in the Sky (1/11/54; William Conrad and Dick Powell)

07. The Awful Truth (1/18/54; William Conrad, Irene Dunne, and Cary Grant)

08. Sangaree (1/25/54; William Conrad, Arlene Dahl, and Cesar Romero)

09. Five Fingers (2/1/54; Hans Conried, and James and Pamela Mason)

10. War of the Worlds (2/8/54; Dana Andrews and Pat Crowley)

911. Treasure of the Sierra Madre (2/15/54; Walter Brennan and Edmund O'Brien)

912. Shane (2/22/54; Alan Ladd and Ruth Hussey)

913. The Bishop's Wife (3/1/54; Herb Butterfield, Cary Grant, and Phyllis Thaxter)

914. The Walls of Jericho (3/8/54; Terry Moore and Cornel Wilde)

915. Gentleman's Agreement (3/15/54; Ray Milland)

916. Rawhide (3/22/54; Parley Baer, William Conrad, Jeffrey Hunter, and Donna Reed)

917. Trouble Along the Way (3/29/54; Joanne Dru, Sherry Jackson, Van Johnson, and Howard McNear)

918. Come Fill the Cup (4/5/54; Mona Freeman and Van Heflin)

919. Stairway to Heaven (4/12/54; Dick Beals, William Conrad, David Niven, and Barbara Rush)

920. Forever Female (4/19/54; Ginger Rogers)

921. The Story of Alexander Graham Bell (4/26/54; Robert Cummings)

922. Elephant Walk (5/3/54; Joan Fontaine)

923. Together Again (5/10/54; Maureen O'Hara)

924. Little Boy Lost (5/17/54; Dick Powell)

925. Now Voyager (5/24/54; Dorothy McGuire)

926. Rope of Sand (5/31/54; Barry Sullivan)

927. Edward My Son (6/7/54; Walter Pidgeon)

Macabre

This was an original Armed Forces Radio Service production, using enlisted men as actors. Although the series originated in the South Pacific, this program was broadcast in America from late 1961 to early 1962 in a short run of eight broadcasts.

1. The Final Resting Place (11/13/61)
2. The Weekend (11/20/61)
3. The Man in the Mirror (11/27/61)
4. The House in the Garden (12/4/61)
5. The Midnight Horseman (12/11/61)
6. The Avenger (12/18/61)
7. The Chrystalline Man (1/1/62)
8. The Edge of Evil (1/8/62)

Magic Island

This juvenile adventure serial deals with the search for a long-lost girl on mysterious magic island somewhere in the South Seas. Catch phrases throughout the story are "golly whiskers," "ice water freckles," and "two fried holes in blanket." Broadcasts originated from either Chicago or New York, syndicated throughout the country in 1936, leaving no opening and closing, which was don by local announcers. Each episode ran twelve minutes. Stars William Johnstone

1. Jerry Hall's Proposal
2. Leaving for the Magic Island
3. The Strange Windstorm
4. The Strange Bank of Fog
5. Tex Bradford Prepares His Straightascope
6. Island in the Viewer
7. Pulled In by a Magnetic Force
8. Joan Is Found on Euclidia
9. G-47 Uses His Ray Gun
10. False Radio Message
11. Island Secrets
12. The Last Radio Message
13. Joan Stays on the Yacht
14. The Cloth Factory on the Island
15. Staged Escape Attempt
16. Soundproof Seaweed Cloth
17. The Homing Pigeon
18. The Pigeons are Released
19. The Secret Formula
20. G-47 Has the Pigeon and the Formula
21. A Different Formula
22. Trapped in an Elevator
23. The Elevator Escape
24. Stolen Oxygen Tank
25. Battleships Approach
26. Magic Island Prepares to Submerge
27. Radio Signals Within the Island
28. Joan and Jerry Board the Submarine
29. A Woman Commander
30. A Message to Johnson
31. Joan and Jerry Ray Gunned
32. Submarine Heads for Johnson's Ship
33. The Submarine Surfaces
34. Johnson Speeds Away
35. Tex Contacts Johnson
36. Johnson's Ship Runs Out of Fuel
37. Gregory's Yacht is Pulled Out into the Light
38. Commander Talks to Johnson
39. Everyone Arrives
40. McLeod Poses as Johnson
41. Help From the Sub Commander
42. The Gas is Released
43. Jerry and Joan Escape
44. Transferring Oil
45. Escape Attempt Tonight
46. Power Shutdown Plan
47. Joan Fires at Jerry
48. Escape From Guard
49. Ready to Throw Switches
50. The Alarm Sound
51. Swim for the Boat
52. Island Sinks and a Successful Escape
53. Lighted Buoys Mark the Route
54. Out of Fuel
55. Magic Island Sub Catches Up
56. Sub Tows the Yacht Back to Magic Island
57. Two Guards Knocked Out
58. In a Chamber Ninety Feet Underground
59. Island Gets Ready to Move
60. Chamber Filling with Water
61. Tex Is Ray Gunned
62. Safe for Three Days
63. Keystone Notes
64. Locked in Rooms
65. Reunited
66. Stealing a Sub

Making Democracy Work for You and Me

This program was made up of open-ended forums led by Senator Estes Kefauver and was broadcast over WMCA in New York, Friday evenings from 9:30 to 9:45 pm, EST.

Mama Bloom's Brood

Syndicated in 1934, each episode ran fifteen minutes. These are probably descriptive titles.

1. New Dresses
2. Abe Morganstein
3. Girls are Late
4. Sidney Comes to Dinner
5. A Picnic Proposed
6. A Picnic Planned
7. Finding a Place
8. Jake's Lawsuit
9. Gold Mine Investment
10. Thetta's Lesson
11. Jake Buys a New Car
12. Planning an Afternoon Party
13. Engagement Announced
14. Sidney Goes to Work for Jake
15. Red Uniform Profit
16. Where's Sidney?
17. $175 Dress Bargain
18. Making the Wedding List
19. Sidney's Visit at Night
20. Sara Is Jealous
21. Honeymoon in Europe Rumor
22. Mrs. Fink Told Off
23. Blank Checks
24. The Day Before the Wedding
25. The Wedding Day Arrives
26. Another Engagement
27. New Furniture
28. Yhetta and Herold Elope
29. Out of Honeymoon Money
30. Harold Becomes a VIP
31. Should Papa Retire?
32. Papa Wants a Vacation
33. Travel Plans Changed
34. Should Sam Retire?
35. First to Hollywood
36. Grandparents Soon
37. Mr. Greenville's Offer
38. $800 Price
39. The Hollywood Trip Begins
40. The Bridge Game
41. Indian Trouble
42. In the Pictures
43. Papa Buys In
44. Sidney and Harold Are Also In
45. A Controlling Interest
46. Getting Used To It
47. Learning the Ropes
48. Things Run Smoothly
49. Marsha Vallee's Temper Tantrum
50. Back to Norman
51. One Hundred Suits of Armor
52. One Hundred More Arrive
53. A Super Picture
54. Movie Premiere
55. Mama Is Homesick
56. Yascha Bloom Akoff
57. New Name Accepted
58. Shooting Gallery
59. Papa's Dancing Partner
60. Sara Is Jealous
61. New Neighbors
62. Movie Plot Problem
63. Sara has Twins
64. Going to the Hospital
65. Getting to Sleep
66. Shopping for a New Suit
67. The Book for Babies
68. Nathan and Rachel
69. The Fortune Teller
70. Arthur S. Mollington
71. Almost Caught at Pinochle
72. To the Restaurant'
73. The Magician's Show
74. $250 Super Picture
75. Sneak Preview
76. Retirement
77. [Title Unknown]
78. The Final Episode

Man with a Question

Syndicated series about blindness. Broadcast over ABC, Sunday afternoons from 12 to 12:30 pm, EST.

1. Children and Blindness (1/9/55; Eva Le Gallienne)
2. Blindness in the Orient (1/16/55; Lowell Thomas)
3. The U.N.'s Concern with Blindness (1/23/55; Dr. Ralph Bunche)
4. Aids and Devices for the Blind (1/30/55; John Gunther)

Man's Right to Knowledge

Now here's a series of intellectual dinner conversations. "Pardon me, could you please pass the salt shaker. And while you are reaching across the table, what are your views on authority and freedom in the Ancient Mediterranean World?" Various guests from all walks of religion and ethics were featured, in what was more of a panel discussion than dramatic presentation. Episode ten was written by Swami Nikhilananda, Hindu Master, and read by Joseph Campbell of Sarah Lawrence College. Dr. Grayson Kirk was the host. The first thirteen episodes were broadcast over CBS, Sunday afternoons from 1 to 1:30 pm, EST.

1. Ancient Mediterranean View of Man (1/3/54)
2. An Asian View of Man (1/10/54; Sir Sarvepalli Radhakrishnan)
3. Judaeo, Christian View of Man (1/17/54; Dr. William F. Albright)
4. -----(1/24/54; Joseph Wood Krutch)
5. Authority and Freedom in the Ancient Mediterranean World (1/31/54; Dr. William Linn Westermann)
6. Authority and Freedom in the Ancient Asian World (2/7/54; Dr. Hu Shih)
7. Freedom and Authority in the Middle Ages (2/14/54; Rev. Martin Cyril D'Arcy)
8. Freedom and Authority in the Modern World (2/21/54; Professor Robert M. McIver)
9. The Old World and the New Humanism (2/28/54; Dr. George Sarton)
10. The Universe as Pure Being (3/7/54)
11. Knowledge and Faith in Medieval Europe (3/14/54; Professor Francois L. Ganshof of Belgium)
12. Inquiry and Reason Today (3/21/54; Dr. H.J. Bhabha of Bombay)
13. The Idea of a University as an Aspect of Tradition and Change (3/28/54)
14. The Nature of Things: Matter [part one] (10/3/54; Professor Howard P. Robertson)
15. The Nature of Things: Matter [part two] (10/10/54; Dr. Wolfgang Pauli of Switzerland)
16. The Nature of Things: Life (10/17/54; Dr. Herman J. Muller)
17. Versions of Man (10/24/54; Professor Henry A. Murray)
18. Human Organization: Law and Freedom (10/31/54; John Lord O'Brian)
19. Human Organization: Use of Resources (11/7/54; Prof. Eli Ginzberg and Jean Monnet)
20. Human Organization: Physical Well-Being (11/14/54; Dr. Brock Chisholm)
21. Human Relations: War and Peace (11/21/54; Dr. Hans Speier)
22. Religion as an Aspect of the Human Spirit (11/28/54; Dr. Paul J. Tillich)
23. Visual Arts and the Human Spirit (12/5/54; Dr. William G. Constable)
24. Literature and the Human Spirit (12/12/54; Sir Herbert Read)
25. Music and the Human Spirit (12/19/54; Aaron Copland)
26. Prospects in the Arts and Sciences (12/26/54; Dr. J. Robert Oppenheimer)

Matinee Theater

Previously titled *Dangerously Yours*, this anthology series starred Victor Jory in dramas based on stage plays, movies, and even a few originals. Jean Holloway wrote most of the scripts. David Victor and Herbert Little, Jr., also wrote. Music was composed and conducted by Mark Warnow. Nick Dawson produced, and Richard Sanville directed. Gertrude Warner costarred with Victor Jory in all but the final broadcast. Sponsored by Vicks VapoRub, broadcast over CBS, Sunday afternoons from 2 to 2:30 pm, EST. Martin Gabel was narrator of most of the dramas. Harry Marble was the announcer. Jory himself starred in all but the broadcast of January 21, 1945. Near the end of the series, scripts from *Dangerously Yours* were performed.

1. Wuthering Heights (10/22/44)
2. Beloved Enemy (10/29/44)
3. My Beloved Wife (11/5/44; Martha Sleeper and Betty Winkler)
4. Penny Serenade (11/12/44; Betty Winkler)
5. The Scarlet Pimpernel (11/19/44; Jackson Beck)
6. Mr. and Mrs. Smith (11/26/44; Betty Winkler)
7. Jane Eyre (12/3/44)
8. Hold Back the Dawn (12/10/44; Jackson Beck and Betty Winkler)
9. Elizabeth the Queen (12/17/44; Judith Evelyn)
10. A Stable in Bethlehem, USA [based on a story by Charles Tazewell] (12/24/44; Jackson Beck)
11. No Time For Love (12/31/44)
12. Random Harvest (1/7/45)
13. Smilin' Through (1/14/45; Janice Gilbert, Claire Niesen, and Karl Swenson)
14. Rebecca (1/21/45; Blanche Yurka)
15. Beautiful Dreamer (1/28/45; Betty Winkler)
16. Dark Victory (2/4/45)
17. Reap the Wild Wind (2/11/45; Helen Claire)
18. Intermezzo (2/18/45)
19. The Highwayman (2/25/45; Phil Clark, Burford Hampden, Alfred Shirley, and Guy Sprawl)
20. Night Bus (3/4/45)
21. Rendezvous at Mayerling (3/11/45; Claire Niesen)
22. The Pirate of Orleans (3/18/45; Jackson Beck and Janice Gilbert)
23. 'Till We Meet Again (3/25/45; Kermit Murdock)
24. The Love Story of Elizabeth Barrett and Robert Browning (4/1/45)
25. A Man Named Jones (4/8/45; Inge Adams and Arnold Moss)

Medicine USA

Sponsored by the American Medical Association, this production starred Charles Laughton narrating various techniques and advances in the medical field. Originally broadcast as a six-episode syndicated series. Laughton narrated each episode, broadcast on Sunday afternoons over NBC from 1:30 to 2 pm, EST.

The A.M.A. decided that the series was so successful that they produced a second series under the same name. The second series consisted of seven broadcasts, and featured various Hollywood stars instead of one. The second run was broadcast over NBC from 8:30 to 9 pm, EST.

1. Alcoholism (3/30/52)
2. Psychiatry (4/6/52)
3. The Span of Life (4/13/52)
4. New Ideas in Communicable Diseases (4/20/52)
5. New Perspective in the Role of Exercises and Athletics in Health (4/27/52)
6. The Impact of Medicine on the Life Pattern of Americans (5/4/52)
7. Grow Old Along with Me (3/21/53; Pat O'Brien)
8. Our Hidden Wealth (3/28/53; Claude Rains)
9. Rural Health (4/4/53; H.V. Kaltenborn, commentator)
10. The Closing World (4/11/53; Kim Hunter)
11. Arthritis (4/18/53; Robert Preston)
12. Man's Fight Against Pain (4/25/53; Helen Hayes)
13. The Long Journey Home (5/2/53; Vanessa Brown)

The Mercury Summer Theater on the Air

This short-run summer series was a revival of the predecessor, *The Mercury Theater on the Air*, first broadcast in 1938. Sponsored by Pabst Beer, this thirty-minute anthology/drama series presented dramas previously performed on other Orson Welles programs. Bernard Herrmann composed and conducted the music, replaced near the end of the series by Lucien Morawek and Lud Gluskin. Ken Roberts was the announcer for the first four broadcasts, Jim Ameche for episodes five through eight, and Jimmy Wallington beginning with episode nine. The series was broadcast over CBS on Friday evenings, from 10 to 10:30 pm, EST. Welles starred in and directed each episode, with one exception. Episode seven was performed, produced, and directed by Fletcher Markle, leaving Orson Welles with the job of host. Episode three was previously performed on *Suspense* with Welles in the lead role. Episode six was also previously performed on *Suspense*, but Welles was not in the original *Suspense* production. Norman Corwin adapted the Emily Brontë novel for episode four. Corwin also scripted episode eight.

1. Around the World in Eighty Days (6/7/46)
2. The Count of Monte Cristo (6/14/46)
3. The Hitch-hiker (6/21/46; Alice Frost)
4. Jane Eyre (6/28/46; Alice Frost)
5. A Passenger to Bali (7/5/46; Stefan Schnable, Alfred Shirley, Everett Sloane, and Guy Sprawl)
6. The Search for Henri Leferre (7/12/46)
7. Life with Adam (7/19/46; Betty Garde, Grace Matthews, and Hedley Rennie)
8. The Moat Farm Murder (7/26/46; Mercedes McCambridge)
9. Golden Honeymoon / Romeo and Juliet (8/2/46; Mercedes McCambridge)
10. Hell On Ice (8/9/46; John Brown, Elliott Reid, and Lurene Tuttle)
11. Abednego, the Slave (8/16/46; John Brown, Carl Frank, Agnes Moorehead, and Elliott Reid)
12. I'm a Fool / The Tell-Tale Heart (8/23/46)
13. Moby Dick (8/30/46)
14. The Apple Tree / Cynnara (9/6/46)
15. King Lear (9/13/46; Edgar Barrier, Norman Field, Agnes Moorehead, Elliott Reid, and Lurene Tuttle)

The Mercury Theater on the Air

Broadcast over CBS, this hour-long anthology series featured adaptation of popular novels and stories. Orson Welles directed and starred in each episode Radio performers such as Joseph Cotten and Agnes Moorehead were hear numerous times throughout the series in supporting roles, and Welles himsel often played more than one role. This series was originally titled *First Person Sin gular* and broadcast on Monday evenings from 9 to 10 pm, EST. Beginning wit episode ten, the series under went a title change, becoming *The Mercury The ater on the Air*, and was broadcast on Sunday evening from 8 to 9 pm, EST, com peting with what was then the highest rated radio program, *The Chase an Sanborn Hour,* with Edgar Bergen and Charlie McCarthy.

On October 30, 1938, Welles and his staff presented an adaptation of H G. Wells' science-fiction novel *War of the Worlds,* and unlike the other drama Welles performed previously, this one was modernized for the 1930s. The resul was pockets of widespread panic across the nation, especially on the East Coast sending hundreds into the streets and churches. Orson Welles became a house-hold name overnight, signing up with RKO studios to produce and direct hi own films, making Welles one of the youngest Hollywood stars of his time to do so. After twenty-two broadcasts, the Campbell Soup Company decided to begin sponsoring *Mercury,* retitling the program *The Campbell Playhouse.* Later in 1941, Lady Esther took up sponsorship, and the title changed again to *Lad Esther Presents Orson Welles.* In 1946, Pabst Blue Ribbon signed as sponsor, an the title changed to *The Mercury Summer Theater on the Air.*

Bernard Herrmann, who was then a staff musician at CBS, composed an conducted the music for this series. Davidson Taylor was Production Supervi-sor. Dan Seymour was the announcer. Welles wrote the script for episode nin supposedly hours before the actual broadcast, and came up short before the hou was up. As an inspiration, Welles began reading passages and quotes from vari-ous books as "previews of things to come." Episode nineteen was originall planned to be a dramatization of Van Dine's "The Bishop Murder Case," but "A Passenger to Bali" was presented instead. Arthur Anderson of *Let's Pretend* fame starred in the lead role of Robert Louis Stevenson's "Treasure Island."

1. Dracula (7/11/38; Ray Collins, George Coulouris, Elizabeth Farah, Martin Gabel, Agnes Moorehead, and Karl Swenson)
2. Treasure Island (7/18/38; Arthur Anderson, Ray Collins, George Coulouris, and Agnes Moorehead)
3. A Tale of Two Cities (7/25/38; Edgar Barrier, Ray Collins, Kenny Delmar, Frank Readick, and Eustace Wyatt)
4. The Thirty-Nine Steps (8/1/38)
5. I'm A Fool / My Little Boy / The Open Window (8/8/38; Edgar Bar-rier and Ray Collins)
6. Abraham Lincoln (8/15/38; Ray Collins, George Coulouris, Agnes Moorehead, and Karl Swenson)
7. The Affairs of Anatole (8/22/38; Ray

Collins, Arlene Francis, Alice Frost, and Helen Lewis)

8. The Count of Monte Cristo (8/29/38; Edgar Barrier, Ray Collins, George Coulouris, and Eustace Wyatt)
9. The Man Who Was Thursday (9/5/38; Edgar Barrier, Ray Collins, Joseph Cotten, and George Coulouris)
10. Julius Caesar (9/11/38; George Coulouris and Martin Gable)
11. Jane Eyre (9/18/38)
12. The Immortal Sherlock Holmes (9/25/38; Edgar Barrier, Ray Collins, and Eustace Wyatt)
13. Oliver Twist (10/2/38)
14. Hell On Ice (10/9/38; William Allen, Ray Collins, Bud Collyer, Joseph Cotten, Frank Readick, Thelma Schnay, Howard Smith, and Karl Swenson)
15. Seventeen (10/16/38; Patty Chapman, Ray Collins, Joseph Cotten, Marilyn Erskine, Morgan Farley, Ruth Ford, Betty Garde, Elliott Reid, and Mary Wickes)

16. Around the World in Eighty Days (10/23/38; William Allen, Edgar Barrier, Ray Collins, Arlene Francis, Frank Readick, Stefan Schnabel, Karl Swenson, and Eustace Wyatt)
17. War of the Worlds (10/30/38; Ray Collins, Kenny Delmar, and Joseph Cotten)
18. The Heart of Darkness / Life With Father (11/6/38; William Allen, Arthur Anderson, Edgar Barrer, Ray Collins, George Coulouris, Alice Frost, Frank Readick, Alfred Shirley, Anne Stafford, and Mary Wickes)
19. A Passenger to Bali (11/13/38; Ray Collins, George Coulouris, Frank Readick, Alfred Shirley, and Eustace Wyatt)
20. Pickwick Papers (11/20/38; Edgar Barrier, Ray Collins, Brenda Forbes, William Pringle, Frank Readick, Elliott Reid, Alfred Shirley, William Todmore, Mary Wickes, and Eustace Wyatt)
21. Clarence (11/27/38)
22. The Bridge of San Luis Rey (12/4/38)

MGM Musical Comedy Theater

MGM has been recognized for the musicals they produced during the forties and fifties. *Singing in the Rain, Babes on Broadway, Meet Me in Saint Louis,* and *An American in Paris* need no introduction. Here, under the supervision of MGM officials, musical adaptations of MGM films were transcribed, featuring stars under contract to the studio. The series was recorded on the MGM lot, so actors such as Walter Pidgeon and Mickey Rooney were available twenty-four hours a day.

After a summer hiatus, the show resumed with one new program and a rebroadcast of the first twelve programs of the series. A total of twenty-seven episodes were recorded and broadcast not just for entertainment value but also to promote the upcoming releases MGM had to offer. Broadcast over Mutual, Wednesday evenings from 8 to 9 pm, EST.

The first twenty-six episodes were sponsored by C. Antel Company. After a short summer hiatus, the series returned to Mutual for a second broadcast run, same day and time, but with two differences: R.J. Reynolds was now sponsoring, and all but the first were rebroadcasts.

1. Holiday in Mexico (1/2/52; Walter Pidgeon and Jane Powell)
2. No Leave, No Love (1/9/52; Monica Lewis, Barry Sullivan, and Keenan Wynn)
3. It Happened in Brooklyn (1/16/52; Mimi Benzell and Russel Nype)
4. Cuban Love Song (1/23/52; Alfred Drake and Olga San Juan)
5. Born to Dance (1/30/52; Vera-Ellen, Georgia Ellis, and Johnny Johnston)
6. Going Hollywood (2/6/52; Denise Darcel, Mary McCarty, and Andy Russell)
7. Honolulu (2/13/52; Robert Alda and Carole Bruce)
8. Yolanda and the Thief (2/20/52; Boris Karloff and Lisa Kirk)
9. Ship Ahoy (2/27/52; Jackie Cooper, Bert Lahr, and Martha Wright)
10. Lady Be Good (3/5/52; Lex Barker, Arlene Dahl, and Phyllis Kirk)
11. Babes on Broadway (3/12/52; Kitty Kallen and Mickey Rooney)
12. On an Island with You (3/19/52; Polly Bergen, Edward E. Horton, and Earl Wrightson)
13. Two Sisters from Boston (3/26/52; Lauritz Melchoir and Jules Munshin)
14. The Kissing Bandit (4/2/52; John Conte and Olga San Juan)
15. Two Girls on Broadway (4/9/52; Joan Blondell, Rosemary Clooney, and Dick Foran)
16. Born to Sing (4/16/52; Connie Haines and Russell Nype)
17. Three Darling Sisters (4/25/52; Edith Fellows, Basil Rathbone, and Gladys Swarthout)
18. The Barkleys of Broadway (4/30/52; Yvonne deCarlo and Alfred Drake)
19. Luxury Liner (5/7/52; Igor Gorin, Patrice Munsel, and Audrey Totter)
20. For Me and My Gal (5/14/52; Johnnie Desmond and Peggy Lee)
21. Neptune's Daughter (5/21/52; Jules Munshin, Carl Revazza, and Fran Warren)
22. Fiesta (5/28/52; Nannette Fabray and Aldo Ray)
23. Two Girls and a Sailor (6/4/52; Howard Keel, Patsy Kelly, and Monica Lewis)
24. Summer Holiday (6/11/52; Carlton Carpenter, Kitty Kallen, and Annette Warren)
25. Everybody Sing (6/18/52; Eileen Barton and John Raitt)
26. Hullabaloo (6/25/52; Arlene Dahl, Ray Middleton, and Arnold Stang)
27. Dancing Co-Ed (10/1/52; Gloria deHaven, Johnny Johnston, and Patsy Kelly)
28. Holiday in Mexico (10/8/52; Walter Pidgeon and Jane Powell)
29. No Leave, No Love (10/15/52; Monica Lewis, Barry Sullivan, and Keenan Wynn)
30. It Happened in Brooklyn (10/22/52; Mimi Benzell and Russel Nype)
31. Babes on Broadway (11/5/52; Kitty Kallen and Mickey Rooney)
32. Born to Dance (11/12/52; Vera-Ellen, Georgia Ellis, and Johnny Johnston)
33. On an Island with You (11/19/52; Polly Bergen, Edward E. Horton, and Earl Wrightson)
34. Yolanda and the Thief (11/26/52; Boris Karloff and Lisa Kirk)
35. Ship Ahoy (12/3/52; Jackie Cooper, Bert Lahr, and Martha Wright)
36. Going Hollywood (12/10/52; Denise Darcel, Mary McCarty, and Andy Russell)
37. Lady Be Good (12/17/52; Lex Barker, Arlene Dahl, and Phyllis Kirk)
38. Honolulu (12/24/52; Robert Alda and Carole Bruce)

MGM Theater of the Air

Throughout the early fifties, the movie studios were in a gradual financial decline. Attendance was falling. Television kept people glued to their living rooms instead of the movie theaters. In one of many attempts to multiply theater attendance, MGM introduced a transcribed series entitled the *MGM Theater of he Air.* It was supervised by MGM vice president Howard Dietz, who also hosted the program.

Sustaining with no sponsor, this series was broadcast over WMGM in New York from 7:30 to 8:30 pm, EST. From May 4, 1951, to December 20, 1952, recorded broadcasts were repeated in the exact order in which they were originally heard from October of 1949 to April 20, 1951. The second rebroadcast run went out national over Mutual, Saturday evenings from 8:30 to 9:30 pm, EST.

Audition: Anna Karenina (c.1949; Marlene Dietrich and Arnold Moss.)

1. Vacation From Marriage (10/14/49; Deborah Kerr)
2. Johnny Eager (10/21/49; Van Heflin)
3. The Canterville Ghost (10/28/49; Charles Laughton)
4. The Shopworn Angel (11/4/49; Margaret Sullavan)
5. Married Bachelor (11/11/49; Burgess Meredith)
6. Citadel (11/18/49; Florence Eldridge and Fredric March)
7. A Stranger in Town (11/25/49; Edward Arnold)
8. The Prize Fighter and the Lady (12/1/49; John Garfield)
9. Anna Karenina (12/9/49; Marlene Dietrich and Arnold Moss)
10. The Youngest Profession (12/16/49; Margaret O'Brien)
11. H.M. Pulham, Esq. (12/23/49; Brian Aherne)
12. Hideout (12/30/49; Cornel Wilde)
13. Three Loves Has Nancy (1/6/50; Ann Sothern)
14. Crossroads (1/13/50; Rex Harrison)
15. Slightly Dangerous (1/20/50; Celeste Holm)
16. Riptide (1/27/50; Madeleine Carroll)
17. Stablemates (2/3/50; Mickey Rooney)
18. Third Finger, Left Hand (2/10/50; Melvyn Douglas and Arlene Francis)
19. Queen Christina (2/17/50; Lilli Palmer and Basil Rathbone)
20. Come Live With Me (2/24/50; Peter Lawford)
21. Undercurrent (3/3/50; Robert Taylor)
22. Dramatic School (3/10/50; Martin Gabel and Luise Rainer)
23. Fast Company (3/24/50; Nina Foch and George Murphy)
24. Reckless (3/31/50; June Havoc)
25. Three Hearts for Julia (4/7/50; Jane Wyatt)
26. The Big House (4/14/50; Pat O'Brien)
27. Feminine Tough (4/21/50; Louise Allbritton and Marsha Hunt)
28. Unholy Partners (4/28/50; George Raft)
29. They Met in Bombay (5/5/50; Herbert Marshall)
30. Chained (5/12/50; Ava Gardner)
31. A Tale of Two Cities (5/19/50; Maurice Evans)
32. His Brother's Wife (5/26/50; Franchot Tone)
33. Joe Smith, American (6/2/50; Ronald Reagan)
34. Young Ideas (6/9/50; Peggy Ann Gardner and Miriam Hopkins)
35. Camille (6/16/50; Marlene Dietrich)
36. Escape (6/23/50; William Holden and Brenda Marshall)
37. The Duke Steps Out (7/7/50; Jack Carson)
38. Stepping Out (7/14/50; Lee Bowman)
39. My Dear Miss Aldrich (7/21/50; Donna Reed)
40. Public Hero Number One (7/28/50; William Eythe and Nina Foch)
41. A Letter to Evie (8/4/50; Hume Cronyn and Marsha Hunt)
42. Stamboul Quest (8/11/50; Angela Lansbury)
43. Vanishing Virginian (8/18/50; Edward Arnold)
44. See Here, Private Hargrove (8/25/50; Eddie Albert)
45. William Tell (9/1/50; Raymond Massey)
46. Guilty Hands (9/15/50; Gene Lockhart and June Lockhart)
47. Billy the Kid (9/22/50; Zachary Scott)
48. Vanity Fair (9/29/50; Jessica Tandy)
49. I Take This Woman (10/6/50; Ralph Bellamy)

50. Love Crazy (10/13/50; Arlene Francis)
51. Thunder Afoot (10/27/50; Brian Donlevy)
52. Hold That Kiss (11/3/50; Ruth Hussey)
53. A Yank at Oxford (11/10/50; Dane Clark)
54. The Count of Monte Cristo (11/17/50; Jose Ferrer)
55. Our Blushing Brides (11/24/50; Jane Wyatt)
56. Kid Gloves Killer (12/1/50; William Holden)
57. Dance, Fool, Dance (12/8/50; Barbara Stanwyck)
58. The Man in the Iron Mask (12/15/50; Brian Aherne)
59. The Sailor Takes a Wife (12/22/50; Tom Drake and Bonita Granville)
60. Woman of the Year (12/29/50; Madeleine Carroll)
61. Red Dust (1/5/51; Veronica Lake)
62. Faithful to My Fashion (1/12/51; Ann Rutherford)
63. Apache Trail (1/19/51; William Lundigan)
64. Mill on the Floss (1/26/51; Sarah Churchill)
65. High Wall (2/2/51; John Payne)
66. Too Hot to Handle (2/9/51; Mel Ferrer and Anita Louise)
67. Easy to Wed (2/16/51; Van Johnson)
68. The Spy (2/23/51; Cornel Wilde)
69. A Stranger's Return (3/2/51; Charles Colburn)
70. I Love You Again (3/9/51; Lee Bowman and Coleen Gray)
71. Hold Your Man (3/16/51; Jeffrey Lynn and Patricia Neal)
72. Lady of the Tropics (3/23/51; Signe Hasso and John Ireland)
73. Manhattan Melodrama (3/30/51; John Hodiak and Janis Paige)
74. Life Is a Headache (4/6/51; Joan Bennett)
75. Wife Versus Secretary (4/13/51; Laraine Day)
76. We Who Are Young (4/20/51; Richard Conte)

Molle Mystery Theater

This mystery series ran for more than a decade under different titles, the first being *The Molle Mystery Theater*. Featured the best in mystery and detective fiction, selected and introduced by Geoffrey Barnes, the on-the-air pseudonym of Bernard Lenrow. Stories by Edgar Allan Poe, Raymond Chandler, Dashiell Hammett, and numerous others were adapted. By episode 229, most of the scripts were originals.

Molle premiered over NBC, Tuesday evenings from 9 to 9:30 pm, EST. Beginning October 5, 1945, *Molle* began broadcasting Friday evenings from 10 to 10:30 pm, EST. Beginning June 29, 1948, *Molle* moved to CBS, Tuesday evening, from 8 to 8:30 pm, EST. Roc Rogers narrated the first ninety-one broadcasts. Bernard Lenrow took over the narration after Rogers, till June 25, 1948. Dan Seymour was the announcer early in the series' run; George Putnam during the later years. Molle Shaving Cream was the first sponsor, later joined by Ironized Yeast and Double Dandereen by late 1945 to early 1946.

Script writers for the series who adapted the novels and short stories were Eric Arthur, Walter Brown Newman, and numerous others. Jack Miller supplied the music, later Alexander Semmler. Episode 170 was based on a story by radio actor Arnold Moss, who also starred in the production. The broadcasts originated from New York.

1. The Tell-Tale Heart [based on the short story by Edgar Allan Poe] (9/7/43)
2. The Flying Death Squad [based on the story by Edgar Wallace] (9/14/43)
3. The Leavenworth Case (9/21/43)
4. Death Lights a Candle (9/28/43)
5. Dark Eyes of London [based on the story by Edgar Wallace] (10/5/43)
6. The Sunday Pigeon Murders [based on the story by Craig Rice] (10/12/43)
7. The Murders in the Rue Morgue [based on the story by Edgar Allan Poe] (10/19/43)
8. Death in the Doll's House (10/26/43)
9. The Big Sleep [based on the story by Raymond Chandler] (11/2/43)
10. Crime of Violence [based on the story by Rufus King] (11/9/43)
11. Mourned on Sunday (11/16/43)
12. File for Record (11/23/43)
13. A Dreadful Memory [based on the story by Cornell Woolrich] (11/30/43)
14. Murder in the Madhouse (12/7/43)
15. Lady in the Lake [based on the story by Raymond Chandler] (12/14/43)
16. Stalk the Hunter (12/21/43)
17. Homicide for Hannah (12/28/43)
18. The Mystery of the Seven Keys (1/4/44)
19. The Most Dangerous Game [based on the short story by Richard Connell] (1/18/44)
20. Thursday Turkey Murders [based on the story by Craig Rice] (1/25/44)
21. Talent for Murder (2/1/44)
22. The Crimson Circle [based on the story by Edgar Wallace] (2/8/44)
23. You Only Hang Once (2/15/44)
24. The Gorgeous Ghoul Murder Case (2/22/44)
25. Farewell, My Lovely [based on the story by Raymond Chandler] (2/29/44)
26. The Cat and the Canary (3/7/44)
27. The Monkey's Paw [based on the short story by W.W. Jacobs] (3/14/44)
28. Going, Going, Gone (3/21/44)
29. The Dead Don't Care (3/28/44)
30. Affair of the Splintered Heart (4/4/44)
31. Criminal at Large [based on the story by Edgar Wallace] (4/11/44)
32. If I Die Before I Wake (4/18/44)
33. Love From a Stranger [based on the story by Agatha Christie] (4/25/44)
34. Murder Masks Miami (5/2/44)
35. Sister of Cain [based on the story by Mary Collins] (5/9/44)
36. The Dain Curse [based on the story by Dashiell Hammett] (5/16/44)
37. Home Sweet Homicide [based on the story by Craig Rice] (5/23/44)
38. Great Impersonation (5/30/44)
39. Agony Column (6/13/44)
40. Death Talks Out of Turn (6/20/44)
41. The Cat Saw Murder (6/27/44)
42. Bunches of Knuckles [based on the story by Jack London] (7/4/44)
43. Murder Ad Lib (7/11/44)
44. Goldfish [based on the story by Raymond Chandler] (7/18/44)
45. The Fifty Candles (7/25/44)
46. Death in the Doghouse (8/1/44)
47. The Mark of Gregory (8/8/44)
48. Murder in Havana (8/15/44)
49. The Case of the Talking Pillow (8/22/44)
50. Crime Without Passion [based on the story by Ben Hecht] (8/29/44)
51. Murder Through the Looking Glass [based on the story by Michael Venning] (9/5/44)
52. Give the Guy Rope (9/12/44)
53. Murder in the City Hall [based on the story by Raymond Chandler] (9/19/44)
54. The Death Rose [based on the story by Cornell Woolrich] (9/26/44)
55. Insidious Dr. Fu Manchu (10/3/44)
56. The Wheel Spins [aka The Lady Vanishes] [based on the story by Ethel Lina White] (10/10/44)
57. Murder Without Crime (10/17/44)
58. The Comic Strip Killer (10/24/44)
59. The Interruption [based on the story by W.W. Jacobs] (11/14/44)
60. The Dilemma (11/21/44)
61. Nightmare [based on the story by Cornell Woolrich] (11/28/44)
62. A Crime to Fit the Punishment (12/5/44)
63. The Bottle Imp [based on the story by Robert Louis Stevenson] (12/12/44)

64. The Man in the Velvet Hat (12/19/44)
65. The Letter [based on the story by Sommerset Maugham] (12/26/44)
66. Witness for the Prosecution [based on the story by Agatha Christie] (1/2/45)
67. Too Busy to Die (1/9/45)
68. Rumor, Inc. [based on the story by Anthony Boucher] (1/16/45)
69. Red Wine [based on the story by Lawrence G. Blockman] (1/23/45)
70. Deadline at Dawn [based on the story by Cornell Woolrich] (1/30/45)
71. The Hands of Mr. Ottermole [based on the short story by Thomas Burke] (2/6/45)
72. Two Sharp Knives [based on the story by Dashiell Hammett] (2/13/45)
73. The Mystery of the Blue Jar [based on the story by Agatha Christie] (2/20/45)
74. Yours Truly, Jack the Ripper [based on the story by Robert Bloch] (2/27/45)
75. The Man Who Murdered in Public [based on the story by Roy Vickers] (3/6/45)
76. His Heart Could Break [based on the story by Craig Rice] (3/13/45)
77. After Dinner Story [based on the story by Cornell Woolrich] (3/20/45)
78. The Gay Falcon (3/27/45)
79. The Eleventh Juror (4/3/45)
80. Journey Into Fear (4/10/45)
81. The Perfect Crime (4/17/45)
82. The Cask of Amontillado [based on the short story by Edgar Allan Poe] (4/24/45)
83. The Clock (5/1/45)
84. The Lady in the Morgue (5/15/45)
85. The Level Crossing (5/22/45)
86. The Adaptive Ultimate (5/29/45)
87. The Beckoning Fair One [based on the story by Oliver Onions] (6/5/45)
88. Breakdown (6/12/45)
89. The Gioconda Smile [based on the story by Aldous Huxley] (6/19/45)
90. Marijuana [based on the story by

Cornell Woolrich] (6/26/45)
91. Rex Sackler (7/3/45)
92. Angel Face (10/5/45)
93. A Death Is Caused [based on the story by Cornell Woolrich] (10/12/45)
94. Leg Man [based on the story by Cornell Woolrich] (10/19/45)
95. Ghost With a Gun [based on the story by Anthony Boucher] (10/26/45)
96. Who Took the Corpse? (11/2/45)
97. Not Quite Perfect (11/9/45)
98. The Rat Is a Mouse [based on the story by Hal Ellison] (11/16/45)
99. Post Mortem [based on the story by Cornell Woolrich] (11/23/45)
100. The Men From Yesterday (12/7/45)
101. I Wouldn't Be in Your Shoes [based on the story by Cornell Wollrich] (12/14/45)
102. The Doctor, his Wife, and the Clock (12/21/45)
103. Blind Man's Bluff (12/28/45)
104. The Blind Spot (1/4/46)
105. Dime a Dance [based on the story by Cornell Woolrich] (1/11/46)
106. Ladies in Retirement (1/18/46)
107. Burn, Witch, Burn [based on the novel by A. Merritt] (1/25/46)
108. Mathematics for Murder [based on the story by Cornell Woolrich] (2/1/46)
109. The Comic Strip Murder (2/8/46)
110. Beautiful Silence (2/15/46)
111. Late Night [based on the story by Cornell Woolrich] (2/22/46)
112. Code Number Two [based on the story by Edgar Wallace] (3/1/46)
113. Red Wine (3/8/46)
114. The Case of the Missing Mind [based on the story by James Ruscoll] (3/15/46)
115. Alibi for Murder (3/22/46)
116. The Creeper [based on a story by James Ruscoll] (3/29/46)
117. Murder in the City Hall (4/5/46)
118. Night Must Fall [based on the play by Emlyn Williams] (4/12/46)
119. Follow that Cab (4/19/46)
120. The Doctor and the Lunatic [based on the story by Richard Connell] (4/26/46)
121. Murder Without Crime (5/3/46)

story by Cornell Woolrich]
(8/29/47)
188. Death Wears a Mask (9/5/47)
189. Death Goes Shopping (9/12/47)
190. Zelma's Boy (9/19/47)
191. Kiss Me Good-Bye [based on the
story by Billy Rose] (9/26/47)
192. Night Must Fall (10/3/47)
193. Lucky Guy (10/10/47)
194. Rx For Death (10/17/47)
195. Now You See Her (10/31/47)
196. Primer for Murder [based on the
story by James Ruscoll] (11/7/47)
197. The Four Fatal Jugglers (11/14/47)
198. Check Number B-131 (11/21/47)
199. Two Men in a Furnished Room
(11/28/47)
200. The World of S. Craig (12/5/47)
201. Four-Time Loser (12/12/47)
202. I Wouldn't Be in Your Shoes
(12/26/47; Martin Gabel)
203. Yours Truly, Jack the Ripper
(1/2/48)
204. Dig Your Own Grave [based on the
story by James Ruscoll] (1/9/48)
205. The Last Laugh (1/16/48)
206. Nemesis (1/23/48)
207. Long Distance (1/30/48)
208. Triangle of Death [based on the
story by James Ruscoll] (2/6/48)
209. The Long Count (2/13/48)
210. Murder Is a Matter of Opinion
[based on the story by Jules
Archer] (2/20/48)
211. Double Disaster Clause (2/27/48)
212. The Ear Ring [based on the story by
Cornell Woolrich] (3/5/48)
213. The Pick-Up Killer [based on the
story by James Ruscoll] (3/12/48)
214. The Great Mellagio (3/19/48)
215. A Question of Survival (3/26/48)
216. The Betrayer (4/2/48)
217. House of A Thousand Doors
(4/9/48)
218. Five Bullets for Baldwin [based on
the story by James Ruscoll]
(4/16/48)
219. Killer at Large (4/23/48)
220. Make No Mistake (4/30/48; Alan
Baxter)
221. Inescapable Corpse (5/7/48)
222. Close Shave (5/14/48; Kay Stevens)
223. Solo Performance (5/21/48; Elizabeth Morgan and Everett Sloane)

224. Deadly Nuisance (5/28/48)
225. The Champ (6/4/48)
226. On Stage Murder (6/11/48)
227. Farewell Performance (6/18/48)
228. Doctor Discord (6/25/48; Martin
Gabel and Everett Sloane)
229. Deed for the Day (6/29/48)
230. The Elephant's Tail (7/6/48)
231. Silent as the Grave (7/13/48)
232. The Reading of the Will (7/20/48)
233. The Honest Cop (7/27/48)
234. The Woman I Married (8/3/48)
235. The Squealer (8/10/48)
236. Newsstand Maggie (8/17/48)
237. Death and the Weeping Bride
(8/24/48)
238. The Murder in the Family (8/31/48)
239. The Garden of Death (9/7/48)
240. The Case of the Clock Strike Murder (9/14/48)
241. The Case of Death and the Fourth
Man (9/21/48)
242. The Case of Death and the Helping
Hand (9/28/48)
243. Murder in High Places (10/5/48)
244. Murder and the Housing Shortage
(10/12/48)
245. The Case of the Dead Man's Gun
(10/19/48)
246. The Alimony Murder Case
(10/26/48)
247. The Step-Mother Murder Case
(11/9/48)
248. The Tip-Off Murder Case
(11/23/48)
249. The Case of Death's End Honeymoon (11/30/48)
250. The Marriage of Convenience Murder Case (12/7/48)
251. The Windfall Murder Case (12/14/48)
252. The Wedding Anniversary Murder
Case (12/21/48)
253. The Case of Murder and the
Banker's Wife (12/28/48)
254. The Fabulous Garage Murder Case
(1/4/49)
255. The Double Motive Murder Case
(1/11/49)
256. The Fifty Dollar Murder Case
(1/18/49)
257. The Meat Market Murder Case
(1/25/49)
258. The Musical Clue Murder Case
(2/1/49)

259. The Case of the $100,000 Reward for One Man's Murder (2/8/49)
260. The Case of the Mother Who Said No (2/15/49)
261. The Big Fence Murder Case (2/22/49)
262. The Career Woman Murder Case (3/1/49)
263. The Case of the Murder and the Lonely Man (3/8/49)
264. The Trained Nurse Murder Case (3/15/49)
265. The Genial Host Murder Case (3/22/49)
266. The Scrap of Paper Murder Case (3/29/49)
267. The Secret Marriage Murder Case (4/5/49)
268. The Case of the Murder and the Milk and the Water Clerk (4/12/49)
269. The Twin Bed Murder Case (4/19/49)
270. The Book of Death Murder Case (4/26/49)
271. The Masked Men Murder Case (5/3/49)
272. The Gas Oven Murder Case (5/10/49)
273. The Message of Death Murder Case (5/17/49)
274. The Rich Widow Murder Case (5/24/49)
275. The Clue from the Past Murder Case (5/31/49)
276. The Murder Clue of the Overflowing Mailbox (6/7/49)
277. The Mysterious Murder at the Clefton Hotel (6/14/49)
278. The Murder at High Noon (6/21/49)
279. The Dead Cat Murder Case (6/28/49)
280. The Case of the Man Who Was Killed Twice (7/5/49)
281. The Stick-up Murder Case (7/12/49)
282. The Wheel of Death Murder Case (7/19/49)
283. The Murder Clue of the New Shoes (7/26/49)
284. The Sleeping Watch Dog Murder Case (8/2/49)
285. The Case of the Murder and the Man Who Looked Like an Ape (8/9/49)
286. The Case of the Old Woman's False Teeth (8/16/49)
287. The Dream Girl Murder Case (8/23/49)
288. The Hunted (8/30/49)
289. The Second Wife Murder Case (9/6/49)
290. The Case of the Girls Who Were Slaves (9/13/49)
291. The Case of the Blackmailing Jam Murder Case (9/20/49)
292. The Case of the Girl Who Laughed at Murder (9/27/49)
293. The Stamp of the Scarlet Heart (10/4/49)
294. The Girl Meets Boy Murder Case (10/11/49)
295. The Rented Bungalow Murder Case (10/18/49)
296. The Crystal Gazer Murder Case (10/25/49)
297. The Case of the Man Who Came Home Murdered (11/1/49)
298. The Broken Date Murder Case (11/8/49)
299. Murder in High Society (11/15/49)
300. The Funeral Wreath Murder Case (11/22/49)
301. The Missing Heiress (11/29/49)
302. The Adopted Daughter Murder Case (12/6/49)
303. The Glamorous Pickpocket Murder Case (12/20/49)
304. The Wedding Eve Murder Case (12/27/49)
305. The Brass Bed Murder Case (1/3/50)
306. The Instant Poison Murder Case (1/10/50)
307. The Birthday Gift Murder Case (1/17/50)
308. The Other Woman Murder Case (1/24/50)
309. The Four of Diamonds Murder Case (1/31/50)
310. The Beautiful Nurse Murder Case (2/7/50)
311. The Forbidden Romance Murder Case (2/14/50)
312. The Friend in Need Murder Case (2/21/50)
313. The Homely Bride Murder Case (2/28/50)

314. The New Step-Mother Murder Case (3/7/50)
315. The Mysterious Stranger Murder Case (3/14/50)
316. The Beautiful Doll Murder Case (3/21/50)
317. The Jealous Husband Murder Case (3/28/50)
318. The Mother-In-Law Murder Case (4/4/50)
319. The Wedding Picture Murder Case (4/11/50)
320. The Best Dressed Woman Murder Case (4/18/50)
321. The Nice Young Man Murder Case (4/25/50)
322. The Shanghai Dance Murder Case (5/2/50)
323. The Forbidden Garden Murder Case (5/9/50)
324. The Jilted Bride Murder Case (5/16/50)
325. The Devoted Husband Murder Case (5/23/50)
326. The Lonely Widow Murder Case (5/30/50)
327. The Separate Bedroom Murder Case (6/6/50)
328. The Out-of-Town Murder Case (6/13/50)
329. The Rich Dowager Murder Case (6/20/50)
330. The Handsome Millionaire Murder Case (6/27/50)
331. The Blue Thread Murder Case (7/4/50)
332. The Screaming Parrot Murder Case (7/11/50)
333. The Mallory Mansion Murder Case (7/18/50)
334. The Divorce Agreement Murder Case (7/25/50)
335. The Missing Women Murder Case (8/1/50)
336. The House They Rented Murder Case (8/8/50)
337. The Glamour Girl Murder Case (8/15/50)
338. The Pointing Finger Murder Case (8/22/50)
339. The Dream-Come-True Murder Case (8/29/50)
340. The Evil Man Murder Case (9/5/50)
341. The Boss Comes to Dinner Murder Case (9/12/50)
342. The Vanishing Necklace Murder Case (9/19/50)
343. The Poisoned Pigeon Murder Case (9/26/50)
344. The Divorce Mill Murder Case (10/3/50)
345. The Poisoned Room Murder Case (10/10/50)
346. The Woman Who Told Murder (10/17/50)
347. The High Voltage Murder Case (10/24/50)
348. The Snapshot Clue Murder Case (10/31/50)
349. The Alienation of Affection Murder Case (11/7/50)
350. The Terrified Witness Murder Case (11/14/50)
351. The Marry Me Or Else Murder Case (11/21/50)
352. The Poison Pen Letter Murder Case (11/28/50)
353. The Child for Sale Murder Case (12/5/50)
354. The Orphaned Sisters Murder Case (12/12/50)
355. The Glamorous Model Murder Case (12/19/50)
356. The Rich Heiress Murder Case (12/26/50)
357. The Horrible Daughter-in-Law Murder Case (1/2/51)
358. The Famous Movie Star Murder Case (1/9/51)
359. The Beautiful Gold-Digger Murder Case (1/16/51)
360. The Thirty Days to Live Murder Case (1/23/51)
361. The Last Meeting Murder Case (1/30/51)
362. The Wife Swapping Murder Case (2/6/51)
363. The Stingy Aunt Murder Case (2/13/51)
364. The Prince Charming Scandal (2/20/51)
365. The Chorus Girl's Dream (2/27/51)
366. The Mother Against Daughter Murder Case (3/6/51)
367. The Cinderella Murder Case (3/13/51)
368. The Invisible Hand Clue (3/20/51)

Moon Over Africa

Broadcast from 1937 to 1938, this syndicated serial consisted of twenty-six chapters. It might have originated from South Africa, but it was broadcast in America. This great adventure serial follows Professor Anton Edwards, his daughter and fiancé, and a preserved human head carried around in a basket that babbles in a foreign tongue that only their African guide can decipher, as they search for Atlantis — in the depths of the African jungle!

1. The Talking Head
2. The Atlantis Quest
3. Jungle Trance
4. The Sacred Python
5. The Rhinoceros Hill
6. Captured by Cannibals
7. Escape
8. A New Land
9. Inside the Volcano
10. Prisoners in the Palace
11. Sacrificed
12. Revolution
13. The Secret of the Talking Head
14. Passage of the Rock
15. Witch Woman of the Rock
16. Back to the Jungle
17. The Eyes of the Moon
18. The Leopard Cult
19. Leopard Woman
20. The Devil Doll
21. White Magic
22. Native Revenge
23. The Whispering Forest of Death
24. Treachery
25. The Orchids of Death
26. The Treasure of the Ancients

Murder at Midnight

Anthology series devoted to tales of terror and horror, eventually taking place near or at midnight, when our fears are the weakest. Raymond Morgan, a former Long Island minister who had given up his cloth for a career in radio, was the host. The stories themselves were creepy. One involved a severed hand with a mind of its own and another featured the body of a scientist, possessed by alien beings from another world. James Ruscoll, Max Ehrlich, William Norwood, and Robert Newman were just some of the script writers. Charles Paul supplied the organ music. Anton M. Leader, who would later direct a year of *Suspense,* was the director. The program was a syndicated, transcribed series that was recorded in New York and later broadcast as far west as Los Angeles. Because the program was syndicated, there are numerous dates to various broadcasts. The very first time the series was broadcast over radio was over Mutual in New York — these dates are listed below. In the summer of 1950 (May–July), a small handful of broadcasts were repeated as a short summer series.

"The Ace of Death" was actually an adaptation of Robert Louis Stevenson's "The Suicide Club." "A Week Ago Wednesday" was originally a script written for *Suspense.* "Death Tolls a Requiem" was originally scheduled to be broadcast on January 20, 1947, but was pre-empted and aired at a later date.

1. The Dead Hand (9/16/46; Betty Caine, Barry Hopkins, Berry Kroeger, and Lawson Zerbe)
2. The Man Who Was Death (9/23/46; Frank Barrens)
3. The Secret of XR-3 (9/30/46; Karl Swenson)
4. Wherever I Go (10/7/46)
5. The Trigger Man (10/14/46; Berry Kroeger)
6. The Death Goblet (10/21/46)
7. The Heavy Death (11/4/46)
8. Nightmare (11/11/46; Elspeth Eric)
9. The Dead Come Back (11/18/46)
10. The Creeper (11/25/46; Betty Caine, Carl Frank, Barry Hopkins, Berry Kroeger, and Lawson Zerbe)
11. The Man Who Died Yesterday (12/2/46)
12. Till Death Do Us Part (12/9/46; Eric Dressler)
13. Murder's a Lonely Business (12/16/46; Wendell Holmes and Helen Shields)
14. The House Where Death Lived (12/23/46)
15. The Kabbala (12/30/46; James Van Dyke)
16. The Ace of Death (1/6/47; John Briggs and Karl Swenson)
17. The House That Time Forgot (1/13/47)
18. A Week Ago Wednesday (1/20/47)
19. The Thirteenth Floor (1/27/47)
20. The Man With the Black Beard (2/3/47; Mercedes McCambridge)
21. The Black Curtain (2/10/47; Eric Dressler, Winston O'Keefe, and Santos Ortega)
22. The Outcast (2/17/47; Abby Lewis, James Monks, and Martin Wilson)
23. Terror Out of Space (2/24/47; Stephen Chase, Elspeth Eric, John Harvey, Grace Keddy, and George Topaldi)
24. Death's Worshipper (3/10/47; Charles Emery and Beth Johnson)
25. Death Tolls a Requiem (3/17/47; Ed Begley, Michael Fitzmaurice, and Arthur Maitland)
26. Red Wheels (3/24/47; Frank Behrens, Craig McDonnell, and John Sylvester)
27. The Ape Song (3/31/47; Brad Barker, Raymond Edward Johnson, Alfred Shirley, and Ruth Yorke)
28. The Line Is Dead (4/7/47)
29. Death Ship (4/14/47)
30. We Who Are About to Die (4/21/47)
31. The Living Dead (4/28/47)
32. Island of the Dead (5/5/47)
33. Corridor of Doom (5/12/47; Santos Ortega)
34. City Morgue (5/19/47; Santos Ortega)
35. The Dark Chamber (5/26/47)
36. Death Is No End (6/2/47)
37. The Dark Cellar (6/9/47)
38. Murder Is Not Enough (6/16/47)
39. The Man Who Died Yesterday (6/30/47)
40. The Face of the Dragon (7/7/47)
41. Fatal Interruption (7/14/47)

42. The Dispossessed (7/21/47)
43. The Appointment (7/28/47)
44. Glory Train (8/4/47)
45. The Face (8/11/47)
46. The Black Swan (8/18/47; Carl Frank and Betty Caine)

47. Dead Man's Turn (8/25/47)
48. The Mark of Cain (9/1/47)
49. Death Across the Board (9/8/47)
50. Murder Out of Mind (9/15/47; Charlotte Holland)

Music Depreciation

Patterned after NBC's *Chamber Music Society of Lower Basin Street*, this program presented swinging tunes and arrangements of songs originally written in other styles. Comedy commentary by Rubin Gained was offered during each broadcast. Tony La Frano was the announcer. Featured the music of the Les Paul Trio and the Frank DeVol Orchestra. Broadcast only on the West Coast, this series never had a sponsor.

Broadcast over Mutual, the series was replaced by *California Melodies* in April of 1945. The broadcast of December 24, 1944, was preempted by a special broadcast of *California Melodies*. During the broadcast of March 25, 1945, the sound man accidentally set off a cap gun during one of the songs.

1. The Minute Waltz (10/29/44; Herb Jeffries and Illinois Jaquet)
2. Black and Blue Danube (11/5/44; Dale Jones and Eddie Smith)
3. Night Ride (11/12/44; Pat Kay and Rafael Mendez)
4. Syncopation / Minuet in G (11/19/44; Joe Green and Marjorie Himes)
5. Little Boy Blue / Schubert's Serenade (11/26/44; Peggy Lee and Murray McEhern)
6. Strike Up the Band (12/3/44; Dan Grissom and Milton Rascin)
7. The Continental (12/10/44; Debbie Clair and Billy May)
8. Song of India (12/17/44; Skeets Herfurt and Martha Tilton)
9. Bori Bori / Pavan (12/31/44; Andre Previn and Margaret Whiting)
10. La Cucaracha (1/7/45; Shorty Sherock and Helen Ward)
11. Volga Boatman (1/14/45; Matty Malneck, and The Four Notes)
12. Deep Night (1/21/45; Pat Kay and Michael Riley)
13. Mexican Hat Dance (2/4/45; Jack Jenney, and The Thrusher Sisters)
14. Caravan (2/11/45; Dave Mathews and Dave Street)
15. Lullaby of Broadway (2/18/45; Nora Martin and Andre Previn)
16. Tico Tico (2/25/45; The Meltones, Willie Smith, and Mel Tormé)
17. La Cucaracha (3/4/45; Anita Boyer and Al Burton)
18. Great Day (3/11/45; Dave Matthews and Mary Ann Mercer)
19. The Donkey Serenade (3/18/45; Neil Hefty, and the Barry Sisters)
20. Bim, Bam, Boom (3/25/45; Milton Delugg and Buddy DeVito)
21. Parisian Market (4/1/45; Corkey Corcoran and Kay Starr)
22. There's a Small Hotel (4/8/45; Paul Carley and Julie Kinsler)
23. The National Emblem March (4/22/45; Robert Armstrong, and the Smart Set)

The Mysterious Traveler

Broadcast on Mutual as a Sunday-night sustained show, this series never had a sponsor. It spawned comic books and later a television show. The sound of a train was heard, followed by the host, a mysterious man who, each week, told a different tale that brought chills, most of which were in the tradition of the soon-to-be E.C. Comics. Not gory but horrifying.

In one episode, a man married a beautiful woman who turns out to be the queen of all the cats in the world. In another, two soldiers find themselves on an island, battling giant crabs. Murderers try to hide out for a time before the police eventually catch up with them, a man sees a mysterious woman dressed in black at every location of someone's death, and a submarine stuck on the bottom of the ocean floor hears banging from the outside — the dead of other wrecks trying to come in.

Maurice Tarplin played the host, known as the Mysterious Traveler, in each and every episode. Robert A. Arthur and David Kogan wrote the scripts, as well as producing and directing the entire series.

1. The Hands that Killed (12/5/43)
2. Death at Storm house (12/12/43)
3. King of the World (12/19/43)
4. Devil Island (12/26/43)
5. The Clock Struck Midnight (1/2/44)
6. The Visiting Corpse (1/9/44)
7. The Strange Journal of Professor Drake (1/16/44)
8. Murderer Unknown (1/23/44)
9. House of Death (1/30/44)
10. The Man Who Knew Too Much (2/6/44)
11. To Have and to Hold (2/13/44)
12. Ugliest Woman Alive (2/20/44)
13. The Good Die Young (2/27/44)
14. Design for Death (3/5/44)
15. Statement by the Accused (3/12/44)
16. Welcome Aboard (3/19/44)
17. Stranger in the House (3/26/44)
18. Out of the Past (4/2/44)
19. Beware of Tomorrow (4/9/44)
20. The Accusing Corpse (4/16/44)
21. Escape by Death (4/23/44)
22. Murder Spins the Plot (4/30/44)
23. I'll Die Laughing (5/7/44)
24. Ghost Makers (5/14/44)
25. The Man Who Could Vanish (5/21/44)
26. In Loving Memory (5/28/44)
27. Murder Must Be Paid For (6/4/44)
28. Death Spins a Web (6/11/44)
29. The Man With the Stolen Face (6/18/44)
30. Blood on the Moon (6/25/44)
31. Queen of the Cats (7/2/44)
32. Broadway Here I Come (7/9/44)
33. Death Rings Down the Curtain (7/16/44)
34. The Man Who Couldn't Die (7/23/44)
35. Till Death Do Us Part (7/30/44)
36. My Beloved Must Die (8/6/44)
37. Flight From Fear (8/13/44)
38. Time On My Hands (8/20/44)
39. The Unknown Enemy (8/27/44)
40. The Bell of Life (9/10/44)
41. A Dream of Death (9/17/44)
42. Death Laughs Last (9/24/44)
43. The Man the Insects Hated (10/7/44)
44. Mind Over Murder (10/14/44)
45. Voice of the Dead (10/21/44)
46. Invitation to Death (10/28/44)
47. She Shall Have Music (11/11/44)
48. Journey With Death (11/18/44)
49. Footsteps of Fate (11/25/44)
50. The Cat and the Mouse (12/2/44)
51. Murder Without Crime (12/9/44)
52. You Only Die Twice (12/16/44)
53. Christmas Present (12/23/44)
54. Embarrassing Corpse (12/30/44)
55. They Who Sleep (1/6/45)
56. Escape through Time (1/13/45)

57. Letter from the Dead (1/20/45)
58. Death Needs a Witness (1/27/45)
59. Farewell Appearance (2/3/45)
60. Murder Is So Fatal (2/10/45)
61. Wanted for Murder (2/17/45)
62. Concerto for Death (2/24/45)
63. Murder Is No Accident (3/3/45)
64. Case of Charles Foster (3/10/45)
65. Blood Money (3/17/45)
66. Death Comes to Adolph Hitler (3/24/45)
67. Murder Goes Free (3/31/45)
68. Seven Years to Wait (7/14/45)
69. It Might Be You (7/21/45)
70. Summer Heat (7/28/45)
71. Death Is My Companion (8/4/45)
72. Mortal Clay (8/11/45)
73. Dynasty of Death (8/18/45)
74. Death Is the Visitor (8/25/45)
75. No One on the Line (9/1/45)
76. Symphony of Death (9/8/45)
77. As I Lie Dying (9/15/45)
78. The Strange Death of Charles DuVal (9/22/45)
79. Death Plays the Tune (9/29/45)
80. Friend of the Dead (12/1/46)
81. Death Is in the Wind (12/8/46)
82. Death Is a Dream (12/15/46)
83. Between Two Worlds (12/22/46)
84. If You Believe (12/29/46)
85. New Year's Nightmare (1/5/47)
86. No Grave Can Hold Me (1/12/47; Richard Coogan and Santos Ortega)
87. Death Is the Dealer (1/19/47)
88. You Won't Escape Me (1/26/47)
89. Voice from Tomorrow (2/2/47)
90. Five Miles Down (2/9/47)
91. Murder in Masquerade (2/16/47)
92. The Cat Died Twice (2/23/47)
93. Dig My Grave Deep (3/2/47)
94. Woman in Black (3/9/47)
95. Death Wears my Face (3/16/47)
96. Voice of Murder (3/23/47)
97. Death Is My Prisoner (3/30/47)
98. You Only Hang Once (4/6/47)
99. Dark Destiny [aka Death Laughs Last] (4/13/47)
100. Flight from Fear (4/20/47)
101. House of Silence (4/27/47)
102. Destination Death (5/4/47)
103. Design for Death (5/11/47)
104. Die She Must (5/18/47)
105. Mind Over Murder (5/25/47;

Ralph Bell and Chuck Webster)
106. She Walks with Death (6/1/47)
107. I Died Last Night (6/8/47)
108. Death Is the Judge (6/15/47)
109. Meet Me at the Morgue (6/22/47)
110. Murder Without Crime (6/29/47)
111. The Locomotive Ghost (7/6/47)
112. Dark Is the Night (7/13/47)
113. Their Cold Companion (7/20/47)
114. The Man the Insects Hated (7/27/47)
115. I Dreamed of Dying (8/3/47)
116. Nightmare (8/10/47)
117. Murder Goes Free (8/24/47)
118. Murder at Their Heels (8/31/47)
119. Vacation From Life (9/7/47)
120. The Big Payoff (9/14/47)
121. Island of Fear (9/21/47)
122. Deep Is My Grave (9/28/47)
123. Death Rides the Storm (10/7/47)
124. Death Is My Host (10/14/47)
125. Death Is My Caller (10/21/47)
126. Invitation to Death (10/28/47)
127. Murder at the Dawn of Time (11/4/47)
128. My Date Is with Death (11/11/47)
129. Death Guides My Hand (11/25/47)
130. Death Cancels All Debts (12/2/47)
131. Death Must Have Revenge (12/9/47)
132. Christmas Present (12/16/47)
133. Mr. Trimble's Christmas (12/23/47)
134. Escape to 2480 (12/30/47)
135. Death Is at the Throttle (1/6/48)
136. Death Must Wait (1/13/48)
137. The Man in the Black Derby (1/20/48)
138. Death Has a Vacancy (1/27/48)
139. Life Is But a Dream (2/3/48)
140. I'll Dance on Your Coffin (2/10/48)
141. Chance of a Lifetime (2/17/48)
142. The Man Who Died Twice (2/24/48)
143. The Ivory Elephant (3/2/48)
144. Alibi for Murder (3/9/48)
145. They Struck It Rich (3/16/48)
146. Seven Years to Wait (3/23/48)
147. Death Is a Dream (3/30/48)
148. When Killers Meet (4/6/48)
149. They'll Never Believe Me (4/13/48)
150. Murder in Jazz Time (4/20/48)
151. The Little Man Who Wasn't There (4/27/48)
152. They Who Sleep (5/4/48)

247. The Dark Underworld (3/21/50)
248. No Grave So Deep (3/28/50)
249. The Man from Singapore (4/4/50)
250. Operation Tomorrow (4/11/50)
251. Death at Fifty Fathoms [aka Death Comes to Adolph Hitler] (4/18/50)
252. I Died Last Night (4/25/50; Eric Dressler and Bret Morrison)
253. S.O.S. (5/2/50)
254. The Big Dive (5/9/50)
255. Voices at Midnight (5/16/50)
256. The Lady in Red (5/23/50)
257. Beyond the Law (5/30/50)
258. Killer at Large (6/6/50)
259. Death Has Two Faces (6/13/50)
260. Die She Must (6/20/50)
261. Journey Through Time (6/27/50)
262. Five Miles Down (7/4/50)
263. Ring Twice for Death (7/11/50)
264. Killer Comes Home (7/18/50)
265. Gun for Hire (7/25/50)
266. Footsteps Behind You (8/1/50)
267. Blood Money (8/8/50)
268. Vacation from Life (8/15/50)
269. Nightmare (8/22/50)
270. Murder Has a Price (8/29/50)
271. Mind Over Matter (9/5/50)
272. Tomorrow Is Forever (9/12/50)
273. Design for Death (9/19/50)
274. Into the Unknown (9/26/50)
275. What's in It for Me? (10/3/50)
276. The Final Hour (10/10/50)
277. The Cat's Paw (10/17/50)
278. House of Silence (10/14/50)
279. Their Cold Companion (10/31/50)
280. The Big Money (11/14/50)
281. Escape to 2480 (11/21/50)
282. Thirteen Steps to Death (11/28/50)
283. Two Lethal Ladies (12/5/50)
284. A Present for Santa (12/12/50)
285. The Survivors (12/19/50)
286. Between Two Worlds (12/26/50)
287. Never Say Die (1/2/51)
288. Death Cancels All Debts (1/9/51)
289. Diamond Fever (1/16/51)
290. Easy, Easy Money (1/23/51)
291. I'll Dance on Your Grave (1/30/51)
292. Death Is But a Dream (2/6/51)
293. Money in the bank (2/13/51)
294. When Killers Meet (2/20/51)
295. The Ivory Elephant (2/27/51)
296. World of Tomorrow (3/6/51)
297. Knives of Death (3/13/51)
298. A Coffin for Charley (3/20/51)
299. The Man Who Died Twice (3/27/51)
300. X Marks the Spot (4/3/51)
301. Fifty Thousand, B.C. (4/10/51)
302. The Little Man Who Wasn't There (4/17/51)
303. Chance of a Lifetime (4/24/51)
304. The Planet Zevius (5/1/51)
305. Death in the Swamps (5/15/51)
306. Judgment Day (5/22/51)
307. Fatal Mistake (5/29/51)
308. The Unexpected (6/5/51)
309. Big Jackpot (6/12/51)
310. Another Man's Murder (6/19/51)
311. I Won't Walk Alone (6/26/51)
312. Restless Skeleton (7/3/51)
313. Death Writes a Letter (7/10/51)
314. They'll Never Believe Me (7/17/51)
315. Visitors from Infinity (7/24/51)
316. Terror by Night (8/7/51)
317. The Chase (8/14/51)
318. When the Dead Return (8/21/51)
319. Fire in the Sky (8/28/51)
320. Death Has a Thousand Faces (9/4/51)
321. Strange Destiny (9/11/51)
322. Some Only Sleep (9/18/51)
323. Four Fatal Callers (9/25/51)
324. What Happened Last Night (10/2/51)
325. The Man Who Knew Everything (10/9/51)
326. Death Needs a Substitute (10/16/51)
327. This Is Murder Calling (10/23/51)
328. Miracle on 10th Avenue (10/30/51)
329. Behind the Locked Door (11/6/51)
330. Speak of the Devil (11/13/51)
331. The Most Famous Man in the World (11/20/51)
332. Murder Has a Price (11/27/51)
333. Token of Friendship (12/4/51)
334. Hide Out (12/11/51)
335. Make Mine Murder (12/18/51)
336. Christmas Story (12/25/51)
337. Stamps from Eldorado (1/1/52)
338. It's Only Money (1/8/52)
339. Key Witness (1/15/52; Ralph Bell and Karl Webber)
340. Change of Address (1/22/52)
341. Stranger in the House (1/29/52)
342. The Man Who Frightened Himself (2/5/52)
343. Death Plays the Tune (2/12/52)
344. Strange New World (2/19/52)

Mystery in the Air

When *The Bud Abbott and Lou Costello Show* took a short summer hiatus, as did most radio comedies, Camel Cigarettes, the sponsor of the comedy series, decided to continue sponsoring the same time slot, but with a series of the opposite nature. Peter Lorre, one of the more popular of the horror stars during the forties, was the star of this thirteen-week horror series, which presented a different tale of terror each week. Ben Hecht's "The Marvelous Barastro" was performed one week, while "Nobody Loves Me," a script previously performed by Lorre on *Suspense*, was another. The most notable episode was Nelson Bond's "The Mask of Medusa," which sparked the best of Lorre, from a calm to maniacal madman before the drama ended. The program was broadcast over NBC, Thursday evenings from 10 to 10:30 pm, EST.

Henry Morgan was the "Voice of Mystery," the host of each episode. Michael Roy read the closing credits. The entire series was broadcast from Hollywood. Cal Coon was the director. Paul Baron composed the musical scores.

1. The Tell-Tale Heart (7/3/47)
2. Leinengen vs. the Ants (7/10/47)
3. Touch of Your Hand (7/17/47)
4. The Interruption (7/24/47)
5. Nobody Loves Me (7/31/47)
6. The Marvelous Barastro (8/7/47; John Brown, Howard Culver, Barbara Eiler, Jane Morgan, and Russell Thorson)
7. The Lodger (8/14/47; Conrad Binyon, Barbara Eiler, Raymond Lawrence, Agnes Moorehead, Rolfe Sedan, and Eric Snowden)
8. The Horla (8/21/47; Ken Christy, Howard Culver, Jack Edwards, Jr., Lurene Tuttle, Peggy Webber, and Ben Wright)
9. Beyond Good and Evil (8/28/47; John Brown, Howard Culver, Jack Edwards, Jr., Russell Thorson, and Peggy Webber)
10. The Mask of Medusa (9/4/47; Phyllis Christie Morris, Lucille Meredith, Russell Thorson, Stanley Waxman, Peggy Webber, and Ben Wright)
11. The Queen of Spades (9/11/47; Jack Edwards, Jr., Luis Van Rooten, Rolfe Sedan, Lurene Tuttle, Stanley

Waxman, Peggy Webber, and Ben
Wright)
12. The Black Cat (9/18/47)
13. Crime and Punishment (9/25/47;

Herb Butterfield, Joseph Kearns,
Luis Van Rooten, Gloria Ann Simp-
son, Peggy Webber, and Ben
Wright)

The Mystery Man*

This five-a-week daytime mystery series featured adaptations of various novels from the top mystery writers of the time. Sponsored by General Mills, Inc. (Gold Medal Flour and Wheaties), this program was broadcast over NBC from 2:15 to 2:30 pm, EST. The host of the program, The Mystery Man, was played by Jay Jostyn throughout the entire series, except for the fourth adventure, in which Joe Latham played the lead role *and* the Mystery Man. Film fans take note: MacDonald Carey was a supporting performer for the first adventure.

1.–40. The Window at the White Cat (3/24/41 to 5/16/41; [by Mary Roberts Rinehart] Ray Bramley, MacDonald Carey, Claire Granville, Mona Hungerford, Vicki Vola, and Lawson Zerbe.)

41.–80. The Bannister Case (5/19/41 to 7/11/41; [by Jonathan Stagg] Vera Allen, Charita Bauer, Neil Fitzgerald, Joe Helgeson, Don McLaughlin, Marilyn Miller, and Kay Strozzi.)

81.–100. The Circular Staircase (7/14/41— 8/8/41; [by Mary Roberts Rinehart] Brad Barker, Winfield Hooey, Edward Jepson, Frances Oliver, Florence Pendleton, Sid Smith, Ethel Wilson.)

101.–125. The Mystery of the Priceless Ambergris (8/11/41 to 9/12/41; [by Phoebe Atwood Taylor] Sarah Burton, Morgan Farley, Eunice Howard, Bartlett Robinson, and Margaret Wycherly.)

126.–155. The Black Curtain (9/15/41 to 10/24/41; [based on the novel by Cornell Woolrich] Ray Bramley, Templeton Fox, Bernard Lenrow, Beatrice Miller, Gladys Thorton, Lawson Zerbe.)

156.–180. The Glass Slipper (10/27/41 to 11/28/41; [by Mignon Eberhart] George Baxter, Malcolm Dunn, Bernard Lenrow, Donald MacDonald, Charita Mauer, Hester Sondergaard, and Gertrude Warner.)

181.–210. Red Roses and White Roses (12/1/41 to 1/9/42; [by Q. Patrick] Delma Byron, Stanley Harrison, and Chester Stratton.)

211.–130.A Woman Named Smith (1/12/42 to 2/6/42; [by Marie Conway Demler] Joseph Branby, Doris Dalton, Margaret Douglas, Mercedes Gilbert, Alexander Kirkland, and Adrienne Marden.)

131.–156. The Dark Garden (2/9/42 to 3/16/42; [by Mignon Eberhart] Teresa Dale, H. Davis, Dick Janaver, Basil Longhrane, Jerry Macy, Gladys Thornton, and Elizabeth Sutherland.)

Compiled by David L. Easter.

NBC Presents Eugene O'Neill

This was a special four-part NBC series showcasing never-before-broadcast plays penned by Eugene O'Neill. Broadcast on Monday evenings from 9:30 to 10 pm, EST. Sustaining. Hollywood stars were paid by NBC to star in the presentations; Helen Hayes, Richard Kollmar, and Henry Hull were a few.

1. Beyond the Horizon (8/2/37; Helen Hayes, James Meighan, and Neil O'Malley)
2. The Fountain (8/9/37; John Anthony, Ray Bromley, Francesca Bruning, Joseph Curtain, Joseph Julian, Ian Keith, Richard Kollmer, Arthur Mateland, William Shelley, Irene Tedrow, Stan Waxman, and Charles Webster)
3. Where the Cross Is Made (8/16/37; Helen Choat, Parker Fennelly, Henry Hull, and Robert Strauss)
4. The Straw (8/23/37; Allan McAteer, James Meighan, Mary Michael, Neil O'Malley, Irene Tedrow, and Peggy Wood)

NBC Radio Theater

This anthology was a series of plays based on original stories submitted to a national contest. Some creative ideas surfaced. The winners received a small check, as well as their sixty minutes of fame. Pat O'Brien hosted this sustaining program, broadcast over NBC, Sunday evenings from 5:05 to 6 pm, EST. In "The Disappearing Santa Claus," Charles Colburn guested as an old man who finds himself kidnapped when the newspapers mistakenly print he owns millions. Dane Clark portrayed a scientist on a trip to Mars in "Destination Mars," and Spring Byington portrayed an elderly grandmother with a system for beating the horses in "Ladies' Day at the Track."

1. Berlin Interlude (9/18/55; Joan Banks and Frank Lovejoy)
2. Maybe Tomorrow (9/25/55; Adolph Menjou)
3. The Girl Who Came Back (10/2/55; Joan Bennett)
4. About Face (10/9/55; Barry Sullivan)
5. Quality of Mercy (10/16/55; Mona Freeman)
6. Cellar Attraction (10/23/55; Zasu Pitts)
7. Secret of the Sea (10/30/55; Pat O'Brien)
8. Destination Mars (11/6/55; Dane Clark)
9. The Dream Department (11/13/55; Dennis Day)
10. Soft Hand and a Six Gun (11/20/55; Maureen O'Hara)
11. Clown (11/27/55; Kennan Wynn)
12. Runaway Flight (12/4/55; Claire Trevor)
13. The Glass Idol (12/11/55; Joseph Cotten)
14. The Disappearing Santa Claus (12/18/55; Charles Coburn)
15. Second Christmas (12/25/55; Otto Kruger)
16. Twelve Strong Men (1/1/56; Pat O'Brien)
17. Dedication (1/8/56; Teresa Wright)
18. By Hook or Crook (1/15/56; Joan Banks)

19. Tim Hogan's Millions (1/22/56; James Dunn)
20. The Fall of a Tyrant (1/29/56; Cesar Romero)
21. Miss Adventure (2/5/56; Diana Lynn)
22. Old Bristol Head (2/12/56; Piper Laurie and Les Tremayne)
23. Ladies' Day at the Track (2/19/56; Spring Byington)
24. Ring Round Rosey (2/26/56; Dan Duryea)
25. The Lost Age (3/4/56; Paul Douglas)
26. The K Street Legacy (3/11/56; Mary Astor)

NBC Star Playhouse

Another anthology series featuring top Hollywood stars in adaptations of stage plays. A select handful of the broadcasts were actually repeat recordings of another show, *Best Plays*, with a new opening theme added. With John Chapman as host, the series was broadcast over NBC, Sunday evenings from 6:30 to 7:30 pm, EST. Beginning with episode six, the series was heard from 8:30 to 9:30 pm, EST. There was no sponsor for this series.

1. What Every Woman Knows (10/4/53; Helen Hayes)
2. A Bell for Adano (10/11/53; Florence Eldridge, Fredric March, and Myron McCormick)
3. No Time for Comedy (10/18/53; Rex Harrison and Lilli Palmer)
4. Grand Hotel (10/25/53; Marlene Dietrich)
5. Victoria Regina (11/1/53; Helen Hayes)
6. Moby Dick (11/8/53; Fredric March)
7. Cluny Brown (11/15/53; Celeste Holm)
8. Twentieth Century (11/22/53; Rex Harrison and Lilli Palmer)
9. There Shall Be No Night (11/29/53; Fredric March)
10. Cashel Byron's Profession (12/6/53; Angela Lansbury)
11. Farewell to Arms (12/13/53; Florence Eldridge and Fredric March)
12. Second Man (12/20/53; Rex Harrison and Anna Lee)
13. Alice in Wonderland (12/27/53; Margaret O'Brien)
14. The Champion (1/3/54; James Cagney)
15. For Whom the Bell Tolls (1/10/54; John Forsythe and Margo)
16. John Loves Mary (1/17/54; Nina Foch and Van Johnson)
17. A Slight Case of Murder (1/24/54; Edward G. Robinson)
18. Sunset Blvd. (1/31/54; Jeffrey Lynn)
19. Biography (2/7/54; Joan Fontaine)
20. Lost Weekend (2/14/54; Glenn Ford)
21. Major and the Minor (2/21/54; June Allyson)
22. The Lady Eve (2/28/54; Barbara Stanwyck)
23. Dream Girl (3/7/54; Judy Holliday)
24. Julius Caesar (3/14/54; Alfred Drake)
25. Great Expectations (3/21/54; Cyril Ritchard)
26. Madame Bovary (3/28/54; Joan Fontaine)
27. Angel Street (4/4/54; Melville Cooper, Judith Evelyn, and Vincent Price)
28. Death of a Salesman (4/11/54; Fredric March)

NBC University Theater of the Air

Originally entitled *The World's Great Novels*, this anthology series presented hour-long adaptations of popular novels, tied to college-supervised home-study courses. From Herman Melville to Sinclair Lewis, novels of adventure, comedy and horror were featured. Broadcast over NBC without a sponsor for its entire run, the program originated from Hollywood and was produced and directed by Andrew C. Love.

The first five episodes were broadcast on Friday evenings from 9 to 10 pm, EST. Episodes 6, 7 and 8 were 30 minutes, from 9 to 9:30 pm, EST. Episodes 9 through 45 were broadcast Sunday afternoons from 2:30 to 3:30 pm, EST. Episodes 46 through 57 were broadcast Saturday evenings from 6:30 to 7:30 pm, EST. Episodes 58 through 108 were broadcast Sunday afternoons from 2 to 3 pm, EST. Episodes 109 through 112 were broadcast Sunday afternoons from 3 to 3:30 pm, EST. Episodes 113 and 114 were broadcast Thursday evenings from 10 to 11 pm, EST. Episodes 115 and 116 were broadcast Sunday evenings from 10:30 to 11 pm, EST. Episodes 117 to 118 were broadcast Saturday evenings from 6:30 to 7 pm, EST. Episodes 119 to the end of the series were broadcast Wednesday from 10:30 to 11 pm, EST.

The series was entitled *The NBC Theater of the Air*, sans "University," for a brief period of time from October 2, 1949, to April 16, 1950.

Numerous script writers were involved with the project, among them, George Lefferts, Earl Hammer, Ernest Kinoy, Alan Circle, Frank Welles, Milton Wayne, John C. Wilson, James Speed, and Vincent McConner. Music was supplied by Albert Harris and Henry Russell. Don Rickles was the announcer for the series from May 7 to 21, 1950. James Hilton was the host for the May 28, 1950, broadcast, as well as commentator for numerous broadcasts. From June 11, 1950, to October 22, 1950, Wade Arnold produced the series. Harrison Smith, president of the *Saturday Review of Literature* was guest speaker in episode thirteen. Episode 45 featured the widow of E. M. Forster. Edward Weeks of the *Atlantic Monthly* is the commentator on the July 16, 1949, broadcast.

1. Main Street [based on the story by Sinclair Lewis] (7/30/48; Leon Ames, Vanessa Brown, Charles Seel, and Lyn Whitney)
2. A Farewell to Arms (8/6/48; John Beal, John Lund, Byron Kane, and Lurene Tuttle)
3. Number One (8/13/48; Frank Gerstle, Wally Maher, Marvin Miller, and Barry Sullivan)
4. Noon Wine (8/20/48; John Beal, Beulah Bondi, Lou Merrill, and Russell Thorson)
5. Romantic Comedians (8/27/48; Georgia Backus, Albert Dekker, and Noreen Gammill)
6. Candide (9/3/48; Eddie Bracken, Hans Conried, June Foray, Rolfe Sedan, and Richard Warren)
7. The Story of Peter Ibbertson (9/10/48; Charles Lung, Joseph Schieldkraut, and Anne Whitfield)
8. The Purloined Letter (9/17/48; Theodore Von Eltz, Adolph Menjou, John Newland and David Wolfe)
9. Gulliver's Travels (9/26/48; Ken

Christy, Gale Gordon, Henry Hull,
and Jack Kruschen)

10. Lord Jim [based on the story by
Joseph Conrad] (10/3/48; Brian
Aherne, Norman Field, Jack
Kruschen, Donald Morrison, and
Vic Perrin)

11. An American Tragedy (10/10/48;
Lynn Allen, John Dehner, Clifton
Fadiman, Noreen Gammill, George
Montgomery, Ralph Montgomery,
and Theodore Von Eltz)

12. The History of Mr. Polly [based on
the H.G. Welles story] (10/17/48;
Arthur Q. Bryan, Ramsey Hill,
Boris Karloff, and Ben Wright)

13. They Stopped to Folly (10/24/48;
Jack Edwards, Paul Frees, and Jane
Webb)

14. Justice [based on the story by John
Gallsworth] (10/31/48; Nigel Bruce
and Dan O'Herlihy)

15. Arrowsmith (11/7/48; Steven Chase,
John Dehner, Joe Forte, Van Heflin,
and Jane Wells)

16. Of Human Bandage (11/14/48; Brian
Aherne, Clifton Fadiman, and
Angela Lansbury)

17. The Short, Happy Life of Francis
Macomber (11/21/48; Preston Foster
and Ramsey Hill)

18. A Passage to India (11/28/48; Parley
Baer, Alma Laughton, and Joseph
Schildkraut)

19. Three Soldiers [based on the story by
John Dos Passos] (12/5/48; Georgia
Backus, Dane Clark, Larry Dobkin,
Scott Elliott, and Inga Yolas)

20. After Many A Summer Dies the Swan
[based on the story by Aldus Hux-
ley] (12/12/48; Tony Barrett, Alan
Hale, Paul Henried, and Earl
Keene)

21. Alice in Wonderland (12/26/48;
Arthur Q. Bryan, Dick Ryan, and
Dinah Shore)

22. Main Street (1/2/49; Leon Ames,
Vanessa Brown, John Dehner, and
Gayne Whitman)

23. The Grapes of Wrath (1/9/49; Jane
Darwell, John Dehner, Gwen
Delano, and Wally Maher)

24. All the King's Men [based on the
story by Robert P. Warren] (1/16/49;

Paul Frees, Wayne Morris, and Luis
Van Rooten)

25. Ministry of Fear (1/23/49; Alan
Mowbray)

26. Noon Wine (1/30/49; Beulah Bondi)

27. Guilliver's Travels (2/6/49; Parley
Baer, Barry Drew, Henry Hull, and
Hugh Thomas)

28. Tom Jones (2/13/49; Tom Conway)

29. Pride and Prejudice (2/20/49; Angela
Lansbury, George Pembroke, and
Ben Wright)

30. The Heart of Midlothian (2/27/49;
Whitfield Connor, Maureen O'Sullivan, and Ben Wright)

31. Tales of Edgar Allan Poe (3/6/49;
Joseph Schildkraut)

32. The Pickwick Papers (3/13/49;
Charles Coburn, Norma Vardon,
and Ben Wright)

33. The Marble Fawn (3/20/49; Hy
Averback, Lynn Bari, John Dehner,
Berry Kroeger, and Jane Webb)

34. The History of Henry Esmond, Esq.
(3/27/49; Crawford Kent, Donald
Morrison, Edmund O'Brien)

35. Jane Eyre (4/3/49; Deborah Kerr,
Doris Lloyd, Harry Martin, and
Eric Snowden)

36. Moby Dick (4/10/49; Hy Averback,
John Beal, John Dehner, Henry
Hull, and Ralph Moody)

37. The Adventures of Huckleberry Finn
(4/17/49; Hal Gibney, Charles Seel,
and Dean Stockwell)

38. The Way of All Flesh (4/24/49; Tom
Conway, Ramsey Hill, Alma
Laughton, and Phyllis Morris)

39. The Mayor of Casterbridge (5/1/49;
Reginald Gardiner, Ramsey Hill,
and Tudor Owen)

40. The Red Badge of Courage (5/8/49;
John Agar, John Dehner, and Mark
Van Doren)

41. Heart of Darkness (5/15/49; Brian
Aherne, Whitfield Connor, Doris
Lloyd, and Ben Wright)

42. The Age of Innocence (5/22/49; Bennett Cerf, Steven Chase, and John
Sutton)

43. The Ambassadors (5/29/49; Henry
Daniell, Alma Laughton, and Lynn
Whitney)

44. The Short, Happy Life of Francis

McComber (6/5/49; Ralph Bates, Preston Foster and Ramsey Hill)
45. A Passage to India [based on the E.M. Forster story] (6/12/49; Alma Laughton and Joseph Schildkraut)
46. What Makes Sammy Run (6/18/49; Paul Stewart)
47. Brighton Rock (6/25/49; Paul Stewart)
48. The Ides of March [based on the Thornton Wilder story] (7/2/49; Georgia Backus, Henry Hull, Reese Marin, and Doris Singleton)
49. Good-Bye, Mr. Chips (7/9/49; Herbert Marshall, Johnny McGovern, and Dan O'Herlihy)
50. Point of No Return (7/16/49; Steven Chase, John Dehner, Kent Smith, and Lynne Whitney)
51. How Green Was My Valley (7/23/49; Donald Crisp)
52. This Side of Paradise (7/30/49; Lynn Allen, John Dehner, Gloria Grant, Tom Holland, Guy Madison, and Gayne Whitman)
53. The Death of a Heart [based on a story by Elizabeth Brown] (8/6/49; Dennis Hoey, Donald Morrison, and Maureen O'Sullivan)
54. The Big Sky (8/13/49; R. Hutton)
55. The Crusaders (8/20/49; Ken Christy, Jeff Corey, Cesar Romero, and Stan Waxman)
56. 1984 (8/27/49; David Niven)
57. Precious Bane (9/3/49; Eleanor Audley, Alec Harford, Dan O'Herlihy, and Maureen O'Sullivan)
58. Penrod [based on the Booth Tarkington story] (9/25/49; Byron Kane, John McGovern, Florence Ravenau, and Theodore Von Eltz)
59. Portrait of a Lady [based on the Henry James story] (10/2/49; Larry Dobkin and Gayne Whitman)
60. The House of Mirth [based on the short story by Edith Wharton] (10/9/49; Virginia Gregg)
61. Sister Carrie (10/16/49; Marvin Miller, Kay Stewart, and Lynne Whitney)
62. The Romantic Comedian (10/23/49)
63. Dark Laughter [based on a story by Sherwood Anderson] (10/30/49; Parley Baer, Gloria Hunter, and Vivi Janniss)
64. Dodsworth (11/6/49; Paul Frees, Ramsey Hill, Monty Margetts, and Dan O'Herlihy)
65. Babylon Revisited [based on the book by F. Scott Fitzgerald] (11/13/49; John Crosby, John Dehner, Jerry Hausner, Doris Singleton, and Anne Whitfield)
66. For Whom the Bell Tolls (11/20/49; Georgia Backus, Nestor Paiva, and Lester Sharp)
67. Point of No Return (11/27/49; Steven Chase, John Dehner, Frank Gerstle, and Lynne Whitney)
68. The Wild Palms [based on the William Faulkner story] (12/4/49; Helen Andrews, Clark Gordon, Shepard Menken, Nestor Paiva, and Gloria Ann Simpson)
69. You Can't Go Home Again (12/18/49; Norman Cousins, Marvin Miller, and Nestor Paiva)
70. Great Expectations (1/1/50; Terry Kilburn, Donald Morrison, and Norma Varden)
71. Manhattan Transfer (1/8/50; Paul Frees, Lena Larr, Don Randolph, and Gayne Whitman)
72. The Ides of March (1/15/50; Whitfield Connor, Jim Nusser, and Edward Weeks)
73. At Heaven's Gate (1/22/50; Paul Frees, Glen Denning, Felix Nelson, and Betty Nigelous)
74. Flowering Judas / Pale Horse, Pale Rider [both stories by Katherine Anne Porter] (1/29/50; Marlene Ames, Alma Laughton, and Jack Kruschen)
75. The Track of the Cat (2/5/50; Steven Chase, John Dehner, Ralph Moody, and Lynne Whitney)
76. The Light That Failed (2/12/50; Henry Autland, Crawford Kent, Dan O'Herlihy, and Tudor Owen)
77. Victory [based on the Joseph Conrad story] (2/16/50; Whitfield Connor, Don Diamond, Ramsey Hill, and Herbert Rawlinson)
78. The Patrician (2/24/50; Ramsey Hill, Robin Hughes, and Margaret Webster)
79. Tono Bungay [based on the H.G.

Wells story] (3/5/50; Tom Dylan, Alma Laughton, Tom McKee)

80. There Is No Convention (3/12/50; Nan Boardman, William Lally, and Norma Vardon)
81. Angel Pavement (3/19/50; Constance Cavandish, Naomi Stevens, Hugh Thomas, and Ben Wright)
82. Howard's End [based on the E.M. Forster story] (3/26/50; Terry Kilburn and Alma Laughton)
83. Mrs. Dalloway (4/2/50; Robin Hughes and Doris Lloyd)
84. The Nazarene (4/9/50; Steven Chase, Jim Nusser, Nestor Paiva, and Herbert Rawlinson)
85. After Many a Summer Dies the Swan (4/16/50)
86. Portrait of the Artist as a Young Man (4/23/50; Jerry Farber and Dan O'Herlihy)
87. Sons and Lovers [based on the D.H. Lawrence story] (4/30/50; Alma Laughton, Virginia McDowell, and Tudor Owen)
88. England Made Me (5/7/50; Constance Cavendish, Marvin Miller, Naomi Stevens, and Ben Wright)
89. Prater Violet (5/14/50; Whitfield Connor, John Dosworth, Fritz Feld, Alec Harford, Harry Martin)
90. The House in Paris [based on the story by Elizabeth Bowen] (5/21/50; Charles Davis, Alma Laughton, and Anne Whitfield)
91. Imperial Palace (5/28/50; Fritz Feld, Donald Morrison, and Marion Richman)
92. Gallion's Reach (6/4/50; Don Diamond, Danny Ocko, Herbert Rawlinson, and Ben Wright)
93. Monsieur Vincent (6/11/50; Pedro de Cordoba, Eddie Firestone, Eve McVey, and Nestor Paiva)
94. The Wild Palms [based on the William Faulkner story] (6/18/50; Helen Andrews, Clark Gordon, Wally Maher, Shepard Menken, and Nestor Paiva)
95. The Doctor in Spite of Himself (6/25/50; Tony Barrett, Jack Kruschen, Naomi Stevens, and Stan Waxman)
96. The Chips Are Down (7/2/50;

Steven Chase, Charles Davis, Noreen Gammill, and Lee Millar)

97. The Time of Man (7/9/50; Jeff Corey, John Dehner, Paul McVey, John Stevenson, and Kay Stewart)
98. The Treasure of Franchard [based on the Robert Lewis Stevenson story] (7/16/50; Parley Baer, Paul Frees, Charles Seel, and Lynne Whitney)
99. The Adventures of Huckleberry Finn (7/23/50; Georgia Backus, Larry Dobkin, and Jack Kruschen)
100. Trent's Last Case (7/29/50; Raymond Lawrence, Dan O'Herlihy, and Ben Wright)
101. A Connecticut Yankee in King Arthur's Court (8/6/50; Alec Harford, Ramsey Hill, Wally Maher, Herbert Rawlinson, and Hugh Thomas)
102. The Track of the Cat (8/13/50)
103. High Winds in Jamaica (8/20/50; John Dosworth, Felix Nelson, Jeanine Roose and Norma Varden)
104. Hedda Gabler (8/27/50; Virginia Christine, Paul Frees, Vivi Janniss, and John Stevenson)
105. The Crime of Sylvester Bonnard (9/3/50; Gail Bonnie, Eddie Firestone, and Rolfe Sedan)
106. Lost Horizon (9/10/50; John Dodsworth, Robin Hughes, Doris Lloyd, and Nestor Paiva)
107. Portrait in the Mirror [based on the Charles Morgan story] (9/17/50; Constance Cavendish, Terry Kilborn, Dan O'Herlihy, and Tudor Owen)
108. Don Quixote [based on the Cervantes story] (9/24/50; Hans Conried, Lou Merrill, Jay Novello)
109. Jonathan Wilde (10/1/50; Joan Banks, Eileen Erskine, Alec Harford, and Tudor Owen)
110. Candide (10/8/50; Sam Edwards, Alma Laughton, Shepard Menken, and Jay Novello)
111. Northanger Abby [based on the Jane Austen story] (10/15/50; Gilbert Fry, Crawford Kent, Virginia McDowell, Norma Vardon, and Nelson Welch)
112. Pere Goriot [based on the de Balzac

story] (10/22/50; Michael Ann Barrett, Steven Chase, Vivi Janniss, Dan O'Herlihy, and Stanley Waxman)

113. The Red and the Black (11/2/50; Lucille Alex, Earl Lee, Donald Morrison, and Gayne Whitman)
114. Great Expectations (11/9/50)
115. Les Miserables (11/12/50)
116. Baron of Grogswig (11/19/50)
117. Bartley, the Scrivener (12/2/50)
118. Madame Bovary (12/9/50)
119. The Gambler (12/27/50; Georgia Ellis, Scott Forbes, Dan O'Herlihy, and Nestor Paiva)
120. The Kreutzer Sonata [based on the Leo Tolstoy story] (1/3/51; Paul DuBov, Stanley Ferrar, Vivi Janniss, and Whitfield Connor)
121. Daisy Miller (1/17/51; Georgia Backus, Don Randolph, and Kay Stewart)
122. The Man that Corrupted Hadleyburg (1/24/51; Gail Bonney, Ted Von Eltz, Earl Lee, and Gayne Whitman)
123. The Withered Arm (2/14/51; Betty Harford, Virginia McDowell, Donald Morrison, George Pembroke, and Naomi Stevens)

The New Adventures of Nero Wolfe

One of my personal favorites in American cinema is the 1944 film *Between Two Worlds*. Based on the 1923 stage play *Outward Bound*, written by Sutton Vane, the plot concerned a group of people in war-torn London who find themselves on a boat, its destination unknown. Before the end of the film, they all realize they are dead and will walk down the gang plank towards Heaven or Hell. Sydney Greenstreet was the St. Peter figure, hosting Judgment Day during the last third of the picture, giving a tour de force performance.

For *The New Adventures of Nero Wolfe*, Greenstreet played Nero Wolfe, a fat man whose eye for detail and deductive reasoning solved numerous cases without his leaving the office. One week a Broadway singer received life-threatening notes and was afraid to leave her hotel room. During the Christmas season, Wolfe put a stop to a psychotic who was killing everyone dressed like Santa Claus. The role of Nero Wolfe was played by J.B. Williams, Santos Ortega, Luis Van Rooten and even Francis X. Bushman in previous broadcast runs, but none so fittingly as Greenstreet. A role similar to his *Between Two Worlds*.

Archie Goodwin was Wolfe's secretary, played by numerous radio actors throughout the entire series. Wally Maher was Archie in the first episode. Lamont Johnson was Archie in the second episode, followed by Herb Ellis, Larry Dobkin, Gerald Mohr and Harry Bartell.

J. Donald Wilson was the producer and director of the series. Wilson was previously a script writer for CBS, having written some of the earliest scripts for *The Whistler* series. Don Stanley was the announcer. *The New Adventures of Nero Wolfe* was an Edwin Fadiman program. The supporting cast consisted of many, including Howard McNear, Grace Leonard, Victor Rodman, Jeanne Bates, Betty Lou Gerson, Victor Perrin, William Johnstone and Peter Leeds.

1. The Case Stamped For Murder (10/20/50)
2. The Case of the Careworn Cuff (10/27/50)
3. The Case of the Dear, Dead Lady (11/3/50)
4. The Case of the Headless Hunter (11/10/50)
5. The Case of the Careless Cleaner (11/17/50)
6. The Case of the Beautiful Archer (11/24/50)
7. The Case of the Brave Rabbit (12/1/50)
8. The Case of the Impolite Corpse (12/8/50)
9. The Case of the Girl Who Cried Wolfe (12/15/50)
10. The Case of the Slaughtered Santas (12/22/50)
11. The Case of the Bashful Body (12/29/50)
12. The Case of the Deadly Sell-Out (1/5/51)
13. The Case of the Killer Cards (1/12/51)
14. The Case of the Calculated Risk (1/19/51)
15. The Case of the Phantom Fingers (1/26/51)
16. The Case of the Vanishing Shells (2/2/51)
17. The Case of the Party For Death (2/9/51)
18. The Case of the Malevolent Medic (2/23/51)
19. The Case of the Hasty Will (3/2/51)
20. The Case of the Disappearing Diamonds (3/9/51)
21. The Case of the Midnight Ride (3/16/51)
22. The Case of the Final Page (3/23/51)
23. The Case of the Tell-Tale Ribbon (3/30/51)
24. A Slight Case of Perjury (4/6/51)
25. The Case of the Lost Heir (4/20/51)
26. The Case of Room 304 (4/27/51)

The New Adventures of Philip Marlowe*

This program was based on the fictional detective created by Raymond Chandler. Gerald Mohr starred as Marlowe. With the exception of a brief sponsorship in 1950 by Ford, the entire series was sustained. It was broadcast over CBS, Sunday evening, Saturday as of January 8, 1949, Tuesday evenings as of February 7, 1950, Wednesday as of June 14, 1950, and Friday as of July 28, 1950. In the summer of 1951, *The New Adventures of Philip Marlowe* was broadcast over CBS, Sunday evenings from 8:30 to 9 pm, EST, as a summer replacement for *Hopalong Cassidy*.

Scripts were written by Mel Dinelli, Robert Mitchell, and Gene Leavett. Music was composed and conducted by Richard Aurandt and Wilbur Hatch. Roy Rowan and Paul Masterson were announcers. Norman MacDonnell and Richard Howell produced and directed. Gracie Allen made a quick cameo after the drama of episode sixty.

1. The Red Wind (9/26/48; Joan Banks, Jeff Corey, Wilms Herbert, and Berry Kroeger)
2. The Persian Slippers (10/3/48; Jeff Corey, Virginia Gregg, Frank Richards, and Gil Stratton, Jr.)
3. The Panama Hat (10/10/48; Jeff Corey, Wilms Herbert, Lou Krugman, and Shep Menkin)
4. Where There's A Will (10/17/48; Parley Baer, Don Diamond, Wilms Herbert, and Ted Von Eltz)

*Compiled by Chris Lembesis.

5. The Heart of Gold (10/24/48; Gloria Blondell, John Dehner, Jack Moyles, and Ben Wright)
6. The Blue Burgonet (10/31/48; Hans Conried, Howard McNear, and Alan Reed)
7. The Flaming Angel (11/7/48; Joan Banks, David Ellis, Jack Kruschen, and Kay Miller)
8. The Silent Partner (11/14/48; Edgar Barrier, Grace Lenard, and Ben Wright)
9. The Perfect Secretary (11/21/48; Parley Baer, Harry Bartell, Lillian Buyeff, and Sydney Miller)
10. The Hard Way Out (11/28/48; Jeff Corey, Barbara Fuller, and Luis Van Rooten)
11. The Unhappy Medium (12/5/48; Earl Keen, Junius Matthews, and Jay Novello)
12. The Jade Tear Drop (12/12/48; Jeff Corey, Lou Krugman, and Peter Leeds)
13. The Three Wiseguys (12/19/48; Hans Conried, Lois Corbett, Paul Dubov, and Wilms Herbert)
14. The Old Acquaintance (12/26/48; Edgar Barrier, Gloria Blondell, Jeff Corey, and Stan Waxman)
15. The Restless Day (1/8/49; Edgar Barrier, John Dehner, Virginia Gregg, and Jack Moyles)
16. The Black Halo (1/15/49; Joan Banks, Paul Frees, and Jack Kruschen)
17. The Orange Dog (1/22/49; Edgar Barrier, Ed Begley, Jeff Corey, and Jack Kruschen)
18. The Easy Mark (1/29/49; Paul Dubov, Laurette Filbrandt, Ken Harvey, and Sylvia Simms)
19. The Long Rope (2/5/49; Fay Baker, Lillian Buyeff, Jeff Corey, and Junius Matthews)
20. The Lonesome Reunion (2/12/49; Edgar Barrier, Jeff Chandler, Virginia Gregg, and Jack Kruschen)
21. The Flying Trapeze (2/19/49; Parley Baer, Wilms Herbert, and Jay Novello)
22. The Big Mistake (2/26/49; Edgar Barrier, Jeff Chandler, Virginia Gregg, and Jack Kruschen)
23. The Friend From Detroit (3/5/49; Ed Begley, Jeff Corey, Virginia Gregg, and Peter Leeds)
24. The Grim Hunters (3/12/49; Dick Benedict, Laurette Filbrandt, Alan Reed, and Mary Shipp)
25. The Dancing Hands (3/19/49; Ed Begley, Paul Frees, Bert Holland, and Lou Krugman)
26. The Green Flame (3/26/49; Parley Baer, Fay Baker, Larry Dobkin, and Howard McNear)
27. The Last Laugh (4/2/49; John Dehner, Paul Dubov, and Doris Singleton)
28. The Name to Remember (4/9/49; Jeanne Bates, Jerry Hausner, and Yvonne Peattie)
29. The Heat Wave (4/16/49; Ed Begley, Vivi Janiss, and Barney Phillips)
30. The Cloak of Kamehameha (4/23/49; John Dehner, Paul Frees, Clarke Gordon, and Berry Kroeger)
31. The Lady in Mink (4/30/49; Lynn Allen, Whitfield Conner, Jim Eagles, and Ann Morrison)
32. The Feminine Touch (5/7/49; Barbara Eiler, Virginia Gregg, Wilms Herbert, and Peter Prouse)
33. The Promise to Pay (5/14/49; John Dehner, William Johnstone, and Jack Kruschen)
34. The Night Tide (5/21/49; Michael Ann Barrett, Howard Culver, and Lou Krugman)
35. The Ebony Link (5/28/49; Edgar Barrier, Jeanne Bates, and Larry Dobkin)
36. The Unfair Lady (6/4/49; Parley Baer, Hans Conried, Paul Dubov, and Nestor Paiva)
37. The Pigeon's Blood (6/11/49; Gloria Blondell, Herb Butterfield, and Barney Phillips)
38. The Busy Body (6/18/49; Lynn Allen, Lois Corbett, Peter Leeds, and John Stevenson)
39. The Key Man (6/25/49; Parley Baer, Larry Dobkin, Howard McNear, and Shep Menkin)
40. The Dude From Manhattan (7/2/49; Herb Butterfield, Charlotte Lawrence, and D.J. Thompson)
41. The Quiet Number (7/9/49; Frances Chaney, Georgia Ellis, Barney Phillips, and Jack Webb)

2. The Headless Peacock (7/16/49; Joan Banks, Howard McNear, Jack Moyles, and Cliff Thorsness)
3. The Mexican Boat Race (7/30/49; Harry Bartell, Ralph Moody, and Nestor Paiva)
4. The August Lion (8/6/49; Jeanne Bates, Larry Dobkin, Barney Phillips, and D. J. Thompson)
5. The Indian Giver (8/13/49; Hans Conried, Howard Culver, Betty Lou Gerson, and Jay Novello)
6. The Lady Killer (8/20/49; Jeanne Bates, Paul Dubov, Ann Morrison, and Don Randolph)
7. The Eager Witness (8/27/49; John Dehner, Larry Dobkin, Junius Matthews, and Ben Wright)
8. The Bum's Rush (9/3/49; Herb Butterfield, Hans Conried, and Ann Morrison)
9. The Rust in Hickory (9/10/49; Edgar Barrier, John Dehner, Mary Lansing, and Charles McGraw)
0. The Baton Sinister (9/17/49; Georgia Ellis, Hugh Thomas, Theodore Von Eltz, and Ben Wright)
1. The Fatted Calf (9/24/49; Parley Baer, David Ellis, Vivi Jannis, and Howard McNear)
2. The Tail of the Mermaid (10/1/49; Michael Ann Barrett, John Dehner, and Wilms Herbert)
3. The Open Window (10/8/49; Ed Begley, Paul Dubov, Betty Lou Gerson, and Jay Novello)
4. The Strange Hold (10/15/49; Vivi Janiss, Charlotte Lawrence, and Theodore Von Eltz)
5. The Smokeout (10/22/49; Parley Baer, John Dehner, Barney Phillips, and Hugh Thomas)
6. The Green Witch (10/29/49; Edgar Barrier, Lois Corbett, Paul Frees, and Eve McVey)
57. The Fine Italian Hand (11/5/49; Georgia Ellis, Vivi Janiss, and Barney Phillips)
58. The Gorgeous Lyre (11/12/49; Edgar Barrier, Peter Leeds, and Tudor Owen)
59. The Sweet Thing (11/19/49; Jack Edwards, Verna Felton, Mary Lansing, and Stan Waxman)
60. The Birds on the Wing (11/26/49; Lois Corbett, Jim Eagles, and Jack Moyles)
61. The Kid on the Corner (12/3/49; Harry Bartell, Virginia Gregg, Wilms Herbert, and Gil Stratton, Jr.)
62. The Little Wishbone (12/10/49; Jeanne Bates, Larry Dobkin, William Johnstone, and Ann Morrison)
63. The Lowest Bid (12/17/49; Parley Baer, Jeff Corey, Paul Dobov, Tudor Owen, and Vic Perrin)
64. Carol's Christmas (12/24/49; Edgar Barrier, Mary Landing, Ann Morrison, and Anne Whitfield)
65. The House that Jacqueline Built (12/31/49; Lois Corbett and Howard McNear)
66. The Torch Carriers (1/7/50; Harry Bartell, Sam Hill, and Vivi Janiss)
67. The Covered Bridge (1/14/50; Wilms Herbert, Jack Kruschen, Barney Phillips, and Ben Wright)
68. The Bid for Freedom (1/21/50; Jeanne Bates, Jack Edwards, Jr., and Yvonne Peattie)
69. The Hairpin Turn (1/28/50; Tony Barrett, Olive Deering, Ralph Moody, and Jay Novello)
70. The Long Arm (2/7/50; Georgia Ellis, Bert Holland, Sidney Miller, Ted Osborne, and Tom Tully)
71. The Grim Echo (2/14/50; Verna Felton, Frank Gerstle, Sam Hill, and Junius Matthews)
72. The Ladies Night (2/21/50; Lillian Buyeff and Jeanette Nolan)
73. The Big Step (2/28/50; Jeanne Bates, Paul Dubov, Vivi Janiss, and Peter Leeds)
74. The Monkey's Uncle (3/7/50; Ed Begley, Ann Morrison, Bob Sweeney, and Stan Waxman)
75. The Vital Statistic (3/14/50; Larry Dobkin, Charlotte Lawrence, Elliott Reid, and Doris Singleton)
76. The Deep Shadow (3/21/50; Jeff Corey, Larry Dobkin, Verna Felton, and Jack Kruschen)
77. The Sword of Cebu (3/28/50; Jeanne Bates, Paul Frees, Byron Kane, and Barney Phillips)

The New Adventures of Sherlock Holmes

On March 24, 1939, *The Hound of the Baskervilles* premiered in the theaters, introducing Basil Rathbone and Nigel Bruce as Holmes and Watson. The film was such a huge success that thirteen other Sherlock Holmes films were released within the next seven years. Seven months after the success of *Baskervilles*, Basil Rathbone and Nigel Bruce reprised their film roles for a prime-time broadcast run over the Blue Network.

Bromo Quinine sponsored the series since the first broadcast, replaced by Petri Wines beginning May 7, 1943. The Semler Company began sponsoring *Holmes* on October 12, 1946. It was first broadcast over the Blue Network Monday evening from 8:30 to 9 pm, EST. Beginning September 29, 1940, the series moved to Sunday from 8:30 to 9 pm, EST. Beginning October 5, 1941, the series moved to NBC, Sunday evenings from 10:30 pm, EST. On May 7, 1943, the series premiered over Mutual on Friday evenings from 8:30 to 9 pm, EST. Mutual moved the series to Monday from 8:30 to 9 pm, EST, beginning October 4, 1943. ABC began broadcasting the series on October 12, 1946, Saturday evenings from 9:30 to 10 pm, EST. It moved to Mondays at 8:30 to 9 pm, EST, beginning January 13, 1947.

After the broadcast of May 27, 1946, Basil Rathbone dropped from the series to star in his own mystery program, *Tales of Fatima*. Tom Conway replaced Rathbone till the end of the run. Nigel Bruce remained faithful to the Watson character throughout the entire run, to the announcer (the sponsor's pitchman) as the opener. Knox Manning was the announcer for the first year or two, with Owen Babbe taking over in 1943. Bill Forman, who previously played the role of *The Whistler* for a while, took over the announcing job by 1945. Jack Slattery and Bob Campbell began announcing after Forman during the same year. Harry Bartell became the announcer, interviewing Watson by September of 1945.

Scripts (previously written and performed for other *Holmes* series), were written by Edith Meiser, who later assisted Leslie Charteris, creator and author of *The Saint*, who wrote under the pen name of Bruce Taylor. Dennis Green, Anthony Boucher (and occasionally Charteris) were writing the bulk of the scripts by 1945, dropping from the later shows in favor of Max Ehrlich, Howard Merrill and Leonard Lee. Adaptations of Conan Doyle stories were used at first, with original scripts being added to the series by 1943. Luis Hector, who played the role of Holmes for a brief run in 1935, played the villainous Moriarty throughout most of this series.

Lou Coslowe supplied the music beginning with the premiere broadcast in 1939, replaced by Dean Fosler by 1945. Harold Kemp was the first producer, replaced by Tom McKnight in early 1940, and Russell Seeds by late 1941. Glenhall Taylor produced the program shortly after Russel Seeds took over, staying with the program until the end.

1. The Sussex Vampire (10/2/39)
2. The Silver Blaze (10/9/39)
3. The Speckled Band (10/16/39)
4. The Twisted Lip (10/23/49)
5. The Devil's Foot (10/30/39)
6. The Bruce-Partington Plans (11/6/39)
7. The Lion's Mane (11/13/39)
8. The Adventure of the Dying Detective (11/20/39)
9. The Creeping Man (11/27/39)
10. The Adventure of Charles Augustus Milverton (12/4/39)
11. The Musgrave Ritual (12/11/39)
12. Wisteria Lodge (12/18/39)
13. The Adventure of the Three Garridebs (12/25/39)
14. The Blue Carbuncle (1/1/40)
15. The Adventure of the Priority School (1/8/40)
16. The Greek Interpreter (1/15/40)
17. The Cardboard Box (1/22/40)
18. The Second Stain (1/29/40)
19. The Adventure of the Abbey Grange (2/5/40)
20. The Golden Prince Nez (2/12/40)
21. The Blanched Soldier (2/19/40)
22. The Reigate Puzzle (2/26/40)
23. The Twisted Lip (3/4/40)
24. The Empty House (9/29/40)
25. The Copper Beeches (10/6/40)
26. The Noble Bachelor (10/13/40)
27. The Engineer's thumb (10/20/40)
28. The Red Headed League (10/27/40)
29. The Problem of Thor Bridge (11/3/40)
30. The Crooked Man (11/10/40)
31. The Norwood Builder (11/17/40)
32. The Three Students (11/24/40)
33. The Dancing Men (12/1/40)
34. Black Peter (12/8/40)
35. The Naval Treaty (12/15/40)
36. The Boscombe Valley Mystery (12/22/40)
37. The Missing Three Quarter (12/29/40)
38. The Adventure of the Mazarin Stone (1/5/41)
39. The Hound of the Baskervilles [part one] (1/12/41)
40. The Hound of the Baskervilles [part two] (1/19/41)
41. The Hound of the Baskervilles [part three] (1/26/41)
42. The Hound of the Baskervilles [part four] (2/2/41)
43. The Hound of the Baskervilles [part five] (2/9/41)
44. The Hound of the Baskervilles [part six] (2/16/41)
45. The Resident Patient (2/23/41)
46. The Speckled Band (3/2/41)
47. The Adventure of Shocombe Old Place (3/9/41)
48. The Illustrious Client (10/5/41)
49. The Six Napoleans (10/12/41)
50. The Case with the Two Solutions (10/19/41)
51. The Solitary Cyclist (10/26/41)
52. The Case of the Walking Corpse (11/2/41)
53. The Stockbroker's Clerk (11/9/41)
54. The Adventure of the Missing Papers (11/16/41)
55. The Hindu in the Wicker Basket (11/23/41)
56. A Case of Identity (11/30/41)
57. The Mystery of Mrs. Warren's Key (12/7/41)
58. The Mystery of the Dark Gentleman (12/14/41)
59. The Mystery of Donald's Death (12/21/41)
60. The Gloria Scott Case (12/28/41)
61. The Adventure of the Second Stain (1/4/42)
62. The Haunted Bagpipe (1/11/42)
63. The Three Garridebs (1/18/42)
64. The Lion's Mane (1/25/42)
65. The Five Orange Pips (2/1/42)
66. The Adventure of the Voodoo Curse (2/8/42)
67. The Dark Tragedy of the Circus (2/15/42)
68. The Sussex Vampire (2/22/42)
69. The Giant Rat of Sumatra (3/1/42)
70. -----(3/8/42)
71. The Copper Beeches (5/7/43)
72. The Man with the Twisted Lip (5/14/43)
73. The Devil's Foot (5/21/43)
74. The Red Headed League (5/28/43)
75. The Engineer's Thumb (6/4/43)
76. The Case of Silver Blaze (6/11/43)
77. The Adventure of the Dying Detective (6/18/43)
78. Wisteria Lodge (6/25/43)
79. The Adventure of the Priority School (7/2/43)

80. The Creeping Man (7/9/43)
81. The Musgrave Ritual (7/16/43)
82. The Greek Interpreter (7/23/43)
83. Murder in the Waxworks (7/30/43)
84. The Missing Leonardo Da Vinci (8/6/43)
85. The Syrian Mummy (8/13/43)
86. The Missing Dancer (8/20/43)
87. The Adventure of the Cardboard Box (8/27/43)
88. The Adventure of the Retired Colorman (9/3/43)
89. The Bruce-Partington Plans (9/10/43)
90. The Case of the Dying Rose Bush (9/17/43)
91. The Missing Black Bag (9/24/43)
92. The Speckled Band (10/1/43)
93. The Dundas Separation Case (10/8/43)
94. The Old Russian Woman (10/15/43)
95. -----(10/22/43)
96. Ricoletti of the Club Foot (10/25/43)
97. The Brother's Footsteps (11/1/43)
98. The Shocking Affair of the S.S. Friesland (11/8/43)
99. The Apparition at Sadler's Wells (11/15/43)
100. Murder at the Park (11/22/43)
101. The Case of the Mrs. Farintosh's Opal Tiara (11/29/43)
102. The Camberwell Poisoning Case (12/6/43)
103. The Adventure of the Jumping Jack (12/13/43)
104. The Adventure of the Missing Black Dog (12/20/43)
105. The Adventure of the Tired Captain (12/27/43)
106. The Incredible Mystery of Mr. James Philmore (1/3/44)
107. The Unlucky White Horse (1/10/44)
108. The Case of the Departed Banker (1/17/44)
109. The Amateur Mendicant Society (1/24/44)
110. The Dog that Howled at the Night (1/31/44)
111. Death at Cornwall (2/7/44)
112. The Case of the Red Leeches (2/14/44)
113. The Adventure of Doctor Moore Agar (2/21/44)
114. The Case of the Missing Bullion (2/28/44)
115. Death on the Scottish Express (3/6/44)
116. The Peculiar Persecution of John Vincent Harding (3/13/44)
117. The Man Who Drowned in Paddington Station (3/20/44)
118. The Haunted Bag Pipes (3/27/44)
119. The Fingerprints that Couldn't Lie (4/3/44)
120. The Man Who Was Hanged (4/10/44)
121. The Singular Contents of the Ancient British Barrow (4/17/44)
122. The Dentist Who Used Wolfsbane (4/24/44)
123. Holmes and the Half Man (5/1/44)
124. The Adventure of the Phantom Iceberg (5/8/44)
125. The Adventure of the Missing Bloodstains (5/15/44)
126. The Adventure of the Superfluous Pearl (5/22/44)
127. The Adventure of Skull and Bones (6/5/44)
128. The Monster of Gyre (6/12/44)
129. The Man with the Twisted Lip (6/19/44)
130. The Adventure of the Dissimilar Body (6/26/44)
131. The Adventure of the Amateur Mendicant Society (7/3/44)
132. The Adventure of the Devil's Foot (7/10/44)
133. The Sinister Wind Bells (7/17/44)
134. The Strange Case of the Aluminum Crutch (7/24/44)
135. The Case of the Giant Rat of Sumatra (7/31/44)
136. The Case of the Lighthouse, Frightened Politician, and Trained Cormorant (8/7/44)
137. Murder by Remote Control (8/14/44)
138. The Case of the Missing Corpse (8/21/44)
139. The Adventure of the African Leopard Men (8/28/44)
140. Dimitrious the Divine (9/4/44)
141. Guardian of the Dead (9/11/44)
142. The Invisible Necklace (9/18/44)
143. The Vampire of Cadiz (9/25/44)
144. The Two Hundred Year Old Murderer (10/2/44)

145. The Third Hunchback (10/9/44)
146. The Missing Treaty (10/16/44)
147. The League of Unhappy Orphans (10/23/44)
148. The Haunted Chateau (10/30/44)
149. Murder Under the Big Top (11/6/44)
150. The Strange Case of the Veiled Horseman (11/13/44)
151. The Secret of Glaive (11/20/44)
152. The Case of the Tell-Tale Bruises (12/4/44)
153. The Island of the Uffa (12/11/44)
154. The Wandering Miser (12/18/44)
155. The Blue Carbuncle (12/25/44)
156. Should an Old Acquaintance be Forgotten? (1/1/45)
157. The Play's the Thing (1/8/45)
158. Dr. Anselmo (1/15/45)
159. The Elusive Umbrella (1/22/45)
160. The Werewolf of Vair (1/29/45)
161. The Dead Adventures (2/5/45)
162. The Newmarket Killers (2/12/45)
163. The Mystery of the Surrey Inn (2/19/45)
164. The Disappearance of Lady Frances Carfax (2/26/45)
165. The Doomed Sextet (3/5/45)
166. The Erratic Windmill (3/12/45)
167. The Secret of Stonehinge (3/19/45)
168. The Book of Tobit (3/26/45)
169. The Amateur Mendicant Society (4/2/45)
170. The Viennese Strangler (4/9/45)
171. The Remarkable Worm (4/16/45)
172. The Notorious Canary Trainer (4/23/45)
173. The Unfortunate Tobacconist (4/30/45)
174. The Purloined Ruby (5/7/45)
175. On the Flanders [aka In Flanders Fields] (5/14/45)
176. The Paradol Chamber (5/21/45)
177. Dance of Death (5/28/45)
178. The Limping Ghost (9/3/45)
179. Colonel Warburton's Madness (9/10/45)
180. Out of Date Murder (9/17/45)
181. The Eyes of Mr. Leyton (9/24/45)
182. The Problem of Thor Bridge (10/1/45)
183. The Vanishing Elephant (10/8/45)
184. The Manor House Case (10/15/45)
185. The Great Gandolfo (10/22/45)

186. Murder in the Moonlight (10/29/45)
187. The Fifth of November [aka The Gunpowder Plot] (11/5/45)
188. The Speckled Band (11/12/45)
189. The Case of the Double Zero (11/19/45)
190. The Case of the Accidental Murderess (11/26/45)
191. Murder in the Casbah (12/3/45)
192. A Scandal in Bohemia (12/10/45)
193. The Second Generation (12/17/45)
194. The Night Before Christmas (12/24/45)
195. The Strange Case of the Iron Box (12/31/45)
196. The Hampton Heath Killer [aka Murderer in Wax] (1/7/46)
197. Murder Beyond the Mountains [aka Murder in the Himalayas] (1/14/46)
198. The Tell-Tale Pigeon Fathers (1/21/46)
199. Sweeny Todd, The Demon Barber (1/28/46)
200. The Cross of Damascus [aka The Indiscretion of Mr. Edwards] (2/4/46)
201. The Guileless Gyspy (2/11/46)
202. The Camberwell Poisoning Case (2/18/46)
203. Murder at the Opera [aka The Terrifying Cats] (2/25/46)
204. The Submarine Caves (3/4/46)
205. The Adventure of the Living Doll (3/11/46)
206. The Adventure of the Blarney Stone (3/18/46)
207. The Girl with the Gazelle (3/25/46)
208. The April Fool's Adventure (4/1/46)
209. The Disappearing Scientists (4/8/46)
210. Mystery of the Headless Monk (4/15/46)
211. The Tankerville Club Scandal (4/22/46)
212. The Waltz of Death (4/29/46)
213. The Man with the Twisted Lip (5/6/46)
214. The Strange Adventure of the Uneasy Chair (5/13/46)
215. The Haunting of Sherlock Holmes (5/20/46)
216. The Singular Affair of the Baconian Cipher (5/27/46)

217. The Stuttering Ghost (10/12/46)
218. The Case of the Black Angus (10/19/46)
219. The Clue of the Hungry Cat (10/26/46)
220. The Adventure of the Original Hamlet (11/2/46)
221. -----(11/9/46)
222. The Mystery of the Murdered Violinist (11/16/46)
223. The Adventure of Sally Martin (11/23/46)
224. The Strange Death of Mrs. Abernetty (11/30/46)
225. The Case of the Coptic Compass (12/7/46)
226. The Vanishing Emerald (12/14/46)
227. The Grand Old Man (12/21/46)
228. The White Cockerel (12/28/46)
229. The Darlington Substitution Case (1/4/47)
230. The Devil's Foot (1/11/47)
231. The Babbling Butler (1/20/47)
232. The Unfortunate Brides (1/27/47)
233. The Adventure of the Dying Detective (2/3/47)
234. The Persecuted Millionaire (2/10/47)
235. The Haunted Bagpipes (2/17/47)
236. The Horseless Carriage (2/24/47)
237. Queue for Murder (3/3/47)
238. The Egyptian Curse (3/10/47)
239. The Creeping Man (3/17/47)
240. The Scarlet Worm (3/24/47)
241. The Maltree Abbey (3/31/47)
242. The Tolling Bell (4/7/47)
243. The Carpathian Horror (4/14/47)
244. The Lion's Mane (4/21/47)
245. The Island of Death (4/28/47)
246. The Pointless Robbery (5/5/47)
247. The Voodoo Curse (5/12/47)
248. The Harley Street Murders (5/19/47)
249. The Adventure of a Submerged Baronet (5/26/47)
250. The Red Headed League (6/2/47)
251. Murder in the Locked Room (6/9/47)
252. Death in the North Sea (6/16/47)
253. The Adventure of the Speckled Band (6/23/47)
254. The Adventure of the Innocent Murderess (6/30/47)
255. The Iron Maiden (7/7/47)

New World A-Coming

Originating from New York, this series dramatized stories concerning minority groups. Canada Lee starred in the first twenty-three broadcasts. *New World* premiered as a Sunday afternoon feature over WMCA from 3:00 to 3:30 pm, EST. Beginning with episode forty-nine, the series moved to another day and time, 9:30–10 pm, EST. The broadcast of November 5, 1946, was preempted due to election returns. The broadcast of October 8, 1946, was a documentary of the life and time of Senator Theodore G. Bilbo.

1. [This episode was untitled] (3/5/44; Roi Ottley and Muriel Smith)
2. The Negro: Fascism and Democracy (3/12/44; Muriel Smith and Leigh Whipper)
3. The Negro in Early America (3/19/44; Muriel Smith and Leigh Whipper)
4. The Story of the Negro in Entertainment (3/26/44; Hazel Scott)
5. Ghettoes: The Black Belt, Their History (4/2/44; Muriel Smith and Leigh Whipper)
6. The Negro and Health (4/9/44; Maurice Ellis)
7. The Story of Negro Humor (4/16/44; Josh White)
8. The Story Behind the Headlines in the Negro Press (4/23/44; Maxine Sullivan)
9. The Story of the Negro Church in New York City (4/30/44; Josh

White, and the Young People's
Choir)

10. Arrangement in Black and White
(5/7/44; Roi Ottley and Hester Sondergaard)

11. The Colored Orphan Asylum [aka
Riverdale Children's Association]
(5/14/44)

12. The Story of James Pearson (5/21/44)

13. The Story of Ted Morgan, a Negro
Reporter (5/28/44; Maurice Ellis)

14. Life in the Ghetto (6/4/44; Dr.
Algernon Black)

15. A Statement by the Negro Commu-
nity on D-Day (6/11/44; Marian
Anderson, Roi Ottley, and Dr.
Channing Tobias)

16. The Mammy Legend (6/18/44; Georgette Harvey and Erik Roberts)

17. The Story of Negro Music (6/25/44;
Billie Holliday, Benny Morton, Slam
Stewart, and Art Tatum)

18. The Vermont Experiment: Harlem
Youth on Vermont Farms (10/22/44)

19. Music at War (10/29/44; David
Brooks, Josh White, and Dooley
Wilson)

20. Executive Order #8802: Presidential
Committee on Fair Employment
Practices (11/5/44; Muriel Smith and
Frank Wilson)

21. The Barbara Latham Story: The Story
of Harlem Hospitals (11/12/44;
Celeste Holm, Hilda Simms, and
Murial Smith)

22. A Tribute to W.C. Handy (11/19/44;
Josh White and Leigh Whipper)

23. Parachutes for Democracy: The Story
of the First Negro-Owned and
Operated War Factory (11/26/44)

24. Heroes of the Sky: The Story of the
All-Negro 99th Fighter Squadron of
the U.S. Army (12/3/44)

25. The American Negro Theater
(12/10/44; Alvin Childress, Ruby
Dee, Frederick O'Neal, and Hilda
Simms)

26. We Deliver the Goods (12/17/44;
Charles Perry)

27. Christmas Program (12/24/44; Lester
Grainger, Roi Ottley, and Dr.
Channing Tobias)

28. I Teach Negro Girls (12/31/44; Paula
Bauersmith)

29. Host Spots USA: The Story of Labor
Tensions in the Face of Negro
Migrations to the West (1/7/45;
Frank Wilson)

30. Freedom Road [part one] (1/14/45;
Will Geer, Frederick O'Neal,
Alexander Scourby, Hilda Simms)

31. Freedom Road [part two] (1/21/45;
Will Geer, Frederick O'Neal,
Alexander Scourby, Hilda Simms)

32. Roll Call (1/28/45; Canada Lee and
Myron McCormick)

33. There Are Things to Do (2/4/45;
Miriam Hopkins and Canada Lee)

34. They Knew Later (2/11/45; Georgia
Burke and Canada Lee)

35. The Story of Blood Plasma (2/18/45;
Dr. Everett R. Clinchy and Canada
Lee)

36. Furlough Home (2/25/45; David
Brooks, William Franklin, Muriel
Smith, and Dooley Wilson)

37. Negroes in Housing (3/4/45; Frederick O'Neal, Alexander Scourby and
Muriel Smith)

38. The Story of Negroes and Health
(3/11/45; Georgia Burke and Canada
Lee)

39. Negroes in Labor (3/18/45; Ruby
Dee, Joseph Julian, and Canada Lee)

40. The Story of Ted Morgan, a Negro
Reporter (3/25/45; Maurice Ellis)

41. The Negro in Early American History
(4/1/45; Muriel Smith and Leigh
Whipper)

42. White Folks Do Some Funny Things
(4/8/45; Canada Lee)

43. Special Memorial to Franklin D.
Roosevelt (4/15/45; William
Franklin, Canada Lee, Muriel
Smith, and Dr. Channing Tobias)

44. The Story of Negro Nurses (4/22/45;
Georgia Burke, Canada Lee, and
Hilda Simms)

45. Report from the Western Front
(4/29/45; Frederick O'Neal and
Canada Lee)

46. Blood Flows Red (5/6/45; Georgia
Burke, Charles Perry, and Norman
Rose)

47. The Meaning of V-E Day to Negroes
(5/20/45)

48. The Wind at my Back: The Story of
Sergeant William Makepeace

Nick Carter, Master Detective

This is a continuation of the detective series originally entitled *The Return of Nick Carter*, with the same cast and time slot. Beginning June 12, 1949, the program was broadcast on Sunday evenings from 6:30 to 7 pm, EST. The cast included Lon Clark as Nick Carter, Charlotte Manson, Ed Latimer, and John Kane. Beginning September 28, 1952, Libby began sponsoring the series, 6 to 6:30 pm, EST. The series was sustaining beginning July 19, 1953. Harrison Products sponsored the remaining broadcast run beginning June 12, 1955.

336. The Case of the Black-Magic Murder (4/18/48)
337. The Case of the Fatal Redhead (4/25/48)
338. The Case of the Super-Charged Corpse (5/2/48)
339. The Case of the Nameless Blonde (5/9/48)
340. The Case of the Salesman of Death (5/16/48)
341. The Case of the Tattooed Cobra (5/23/48)
342. The Case of the Littlest Gangster (5/30/48)
343. The Case of the Saltwater Fence (6/6/48)
344. The Case of the Unexpected Corpse (6/13/48)
345. The Case of the Flowery Farewell (6/20/48)
346. The Case of the King's Apology (6/27/48)
347. The Case of the Frightened Fingers (7/4/48)
348. The Case of the Doctor's Last Call (7/11/48)
349. The Case of Blackbeard's Map (7/18/48)
350. The Case of the Deadly Passer (7/25/48)
351. The Case of the Midway Murders (8/1/48)
352. The Case of the Curtained Corpse (8/8/48)
353. The Case of the Professional Beggar (8/15/48)
354. The Case of the Red Arrow (8/22/48)
355. The Case of the Failing Eyes (8/29/48)
356. The Case of the Quiet Room-mate (9/5/48)
357. The Case of the Great Impersonation (9/12/48)
358. The Case of the Homely Bride (9/19/48)
359. The Case of the Candidate's Corpse (9/26/48)
360. The Case of the Substitute Slayer (10/3/48)
361. The Case of the Unwanted Wife (10/10/48)
362. The Case of the Walt-Water Fence (10/17/48)

363. The Case of the Bull and the Bear (10/24/48)
364. The Case of the Wrong Mr. Wright (10/31/48)
365. The Case of the Forgetful Killer (11/7/48)
366. The Case of the Clue Called X (11/14/48)
367. The Case of the Red Thumb (11/21/48)
368. The Case of the Frightened Grandfather (11/28/48)
369. The Case of the Bloodstained Alibi (12/5/48)
370. The Case of the Counterfeit Corpse (12/12/48)
371. The Case of the Five-Hundred Witnesses (12/19/48)
372. The Case of the Disappearing Bandit (12/26/48)
373. The Case of the Dying Stamps (1/2/49)
374. The Case of the Disappearing Doctor (1/9/49)
375. The Case of the Corpse Named Smith (1/16/49)
376. The Case of the Bad Samaritan (1/23/49)
377. The Case of the Blind Witness (1/30/49)
378. The Case of the Man Who Married Murder (2/6/49)
379. The Case of the Perfect Crime (2/13/49)
380. The Case of the Killer in the Dark (2/20/49)
381. The Case of the Deadly Torch Bearer (2/27/49)
382. The Case of the Would-Be Crook (3/6/49)
383. The Case of the Living Corpse (3/13/49)
384. The Case of the Bronze Dragon (3/20/49)
385. The Case of the Genial Gambler (3/27/49)
386. The Case of the Lady Arsenal (4/3/49)
387. The Case of Death in the Dark (4/10/49)
388. The Case of the Cupid Killer (4/17/49)
389. The Case of the Marvelous Mabel (4/24/49)

390. The Case of the Seven Sinister Steps (5/1/49)
391. The Case of the Troubled Bridegroom (5/8/49)
392. The Case of the Unlucky Corpses (5/15/49)
393. The Case of the Green Flame (5/22/49)
394. The Case of the Kidnapped Corpse (5/29/49)
395. The Case of the Coffee Killers (6/5/49)
396. The Case of the Guilty Bystanders (6/12/49)
397. The Case of the Perfect Alibi (6/19/49)
398. The Case of the Custom-Made Corpse (6/26/49)
399. The Case of the Brick Oven Corpse (7/3/49)
400. The Case of the Dead Survivors (7/10/49)
401. The Case of the Poisonous Grape Wine (7/17/49)
402. The Case of the Laughing Skull (7/24/49)
403. The Case of the Green Diamond Murders (7/31/49)
404. The Case of the Phantom Policeman (8/7/49)
405. The Case of the Vital Three Hours (8/14/49)
406. The Case of the Unlucky Seven (8/21/49)
407. The Case of the Screaming Corpse (8/28/49)
408. The Case of the Rainbow Dream (9/4/49)
409. The Case of the Man Who Died Later (9/11/49)
410. The Case of the Vanishing Weapon (9/18/49)
411. The Case of the Purloined Penicillin (9/25/49)
412. The Case of the Obsolete Broker (10/2/49)
413. The Case of the Orange Lady (10/9/49)
414. The Case of the Columbus Log (10/16/49)
415. The Case of the Deadly Carnation (10/23/49)
416. The Case of the Careful Killer (10/30/49)
417. The Case of the Deadly Toy Soldier (11/6/49)
418. The Case of the Man Who Died Laughing (11/13/49)
419. The Case of the Killers on Parade (11/20/49)
420. The Case of the Mistaken Murder (11/27/49)
421. The Case of the Music Box Murder (12/4/49)
422. The Case of the Festival of Death (12/11/49)
423. The Case of the Sighing House (12/18/49)
424. The Case of the Phantom Shoplifter (12/25/49)
425. The Case of the Perfect Penman (1/1/50)
426. The Case of the Flaming Crime (1/8/50)
427. The Case of the Forgotten Murder (1/15/50)
428. The Case of the Murder Without a Corpse (1/22/50)
429. The Case of the Chinese Motto Murder (1/29/50)
430. The Case of the Corpse Who Came Back (2/5/50)
431. The Case of the Son's Confession (2/12/50)
432. The Case of the Unimportant Murder (2/19/50)
433. The Case of the Painted Heel (2/26/50)
434. The Case of the Thirteenth Clue (3/5/50)
435. The Case of the Short Blonde Hair (3/12/50)
436. The Case of the Hot Rod Murder (3/19/50)
437. The Case of the Beggar's League (3/26/50)
438. The Case of the Reluctant Witness (4/2/50)
439. The Case of the Big Key (4/9/50)
440. The Case of the Guilty Corpse (4/16/50)
441. The Case of the Murderer's Haven (4/23/50)
442. The Case of the Purple Tiger (4/30/50)
443. The Case of the Murder for Charity (5/7/50)
444. The Case of the Greedy Ghost (5/14/50)

445. The Case of the Hypnotic Hostess (5/21/50)
446. The Case of the Hole in the Wall (5/28/50)
447. The Case of the Purloined Arrow (6/4/50)
448. The Case of the Dead Client (6/11/50)
449. The Case of the Kindergarten Murders (6/18/50)
450. The Case of the Purple Clue (6/25/50)
451. The Case of the Penny Arcade Murder (7/2/50)
452. The Case of the Corpse Who Changed His Mind (7/9/50)
453. The Case of the Murder Dreamer (7/16/50)
454. The Case of the Sleeper Murders (7/23/50)
455. The Case of the Restless Corpse (7/30/50)
456. The Case of the Twice-Murdered Man (8/6/50)
457. The Case of the Jealous Pitcher (8/13/50)
458. The Case of the Greedy Thieves (8/20/50)
459. The Case of the Murder Frame (8/27/50)
460. The Case of the Misled Skeletons (9/3/50)
461. The Case of the Broken Glasses (9/10/50)
462. The Case of the Little Gray Man (9/17/50)
463. The Case of the High Note Murder (9/24/50)
464. The Case of the Waiting Murder (10/1/50)
465. The Case of the Olgari Curse (10/8/50)
466. The Case of the Deadly Diamonds (10/15/50)
467. The Case of the Phantom Fortune (10/22/50)
468. The Case of the Careful Killer (10/29/50)
469. The Case of the Foolproof Murder (11/5/50)
470. The Case of the Murder Marathon (11/12/50)
471. The Case of the Peculiar Penthouse (11/19/50)
472. The Case of the Baffling Bullets (11/26/50)
473. The Case of the Dead Dummy (12/3/50)
474. The Case of the Lovelorn Letter (12/10/50)
475. The Case of the Last Survivor (12/17/50)
476. The Case of the Sinister Santa Claus (12/24/50)
477. The Case of the Wrong Number (12/31/50)
478. The Case of the Vanished Loot (1/7/51)
479. The Case of the Million Dollar Motive (1/14/51)
480. The Case of the Necessary Corpse (1/21/51)
481. The Case of the Pock-Marked Thumbnail (1/28/51)
482. The Case of the Bewildered Beauty (2/4/51)
483. The Case of the Hitch-hike Killer (2/11/51)
484. The Case of the Old Man's Darling (2/18/51)
485. The Case of the Vanished Villain (2/25/51)
486. The Case of the Horror Hotel (3/4/51)
487. The Case of the Innocent Killer (3/11/51)
488. The Case of the Confused Bystander (3/18/51)
489. The Case of the Gangster's Bride (3/25/51)
490. The Case of the Misunderstood Merchant (4/1/51)
491. The Case of the Golden Hand (4/8/51)
492. The Case of the Wealthy Widow (4/15/51)
493. The Case of the Triple Identity (4/22/51)
494. The Case of the Fabulous Fraud (4/29/51)
495. The Case of the Terrified Swami (5/6/51)
496. The Case of the Murder Mansion (5/13/51)
497. The Case of the Punch-Board Murder (5/20/51)
498. The Case of the Gentle Killers (5/27/51)

499. The Case of the Innocent Lifer
(6/3/51)

500. The Case of the Peculiar Puzzle
(6/10/51)

501. The Case of the Unmarked Snow
(6/17/51)

502. The Case of the Fraudulent Fires
(6/24/51)

503. The Case of the Frightened Ghost
(7/1/51)

504. The Case of the Generous Crook
(7/8/51)

505. The Case of the Portrait of Death
(7/15/51)

506. The Case of the Hot Briefcase
(7/22/51)

507. The Case of the Baffled Bride
(7/29/51)

508. The Case of the Mother Goose
Murders (8/5/51)

509. The Case of the Hot Ice (8/12/51)

510. The Case of the Desperate Driver
(8/19/51)

511. The Case of the Murder Memory
(8/26/51)

512. The Case of the Merry-Go-Round
Murder (9/2/51)

513. The Case of the Warehouse Murder
(9/9/51)

514. The Case of the Impossible Crime
(9/16/51)

515. The Case of the Browbeaten Brain
(9/23/51)

516. The Case of Murder on the Mound
(9/30/51)

517. The Case of the Vengeful Gangster
(10/7/51)

518. The Case of the Blindman's Bluff
(10/14/51)

519. The Case of the Five-Hundred Suspects (10/21/51)

520. The Case of the Kidnapped Train
(10/28/51)

521. The Case of the Baffling Bell
(11/4/51)

522. The Case of the Skid Row Murders
(11/11/51)

523. The Case of the Kidnapped Bus
(11/18/51)

524. The Case of the Wounded Clock
(11/25/51)

525. The Case of the Vanishing Roadhouse (12/2/51)

526. The Case of the Murdering Caper
(12/9/51)

527. The Case of the Borrowed Timers
(12/16/51)

528. The Case of the Invisible Star
(12/23/51)

529. The Case of the Twin Murders
(12/30/51)

530. The Case of the Bootleg Dog
(1/6/52)

531. The Case of the Red Moon
(1/13/52)

532. The Case of the Suspicious Silver-
smith (1/20/52)

533. The Case of the Folsom Point
(1/27/52)

534. The Case of the Mathematical
Clock (2/3/52)

535. The Case of the Three Times Murder (2/10/52)

536. The Case of the Murder by the
Dozen (2/17/52)

537. The Case of the Champlain-Twelve
(2/24/52)

538. The Case of the Fifteen-Story Murder (3/2/52)

539. The Case of the Bloodstained Alibi
(3/9/52)

540. The Case of the Cautious Colonel
(3/16/52)

541. The Case of the Frosted Window
(3/23/52)

542. The Case of the Malacca Cane
(3/30/52)

543. The Case of the Mysterious Mr. X
(4/6/52)

544. The Case of the Impulsive Killer
(4/13/52)

545. The Case of the Lost Star (4/20/52)

546. The Case of the Freeze-Out
(4/27/52)

547. The Case of the Deadly Diamonds
(5/4/52)

548. The Case of the Blue Madonna
(5/11/52)

549. The Case of Mana Joe, Junk Dealer
(5/18/52)

550. The Case of the Red Dragon (5/25/52)

551. The Case of Mr. Bluebeard (6/1/52)

552. The Case of the Beautiful Corpse
(6/8/52)

553. The Case of the Oxford Needles
(6/15/52)

554. The Case of the Forty Fishermen
(6/22/52)

555. The Case of the Phantom Fortune (6/29/52)
556. The Case of the Recipe for Murder (7/6/52)
557. The Case of the Curious Cat (7/13/52)
558. The Case of the Lying Corpse (7/20/52)
559. The Case of the Lying Widow (7/27/52)
560. The Case of the Ironclad Alibi (8/3/52)
561. The Case of the Death Assignment (8/10/52)
562. The Case of the Vanishing Gun (8/17/52)
563. The Case of the Tired Bullet (8/24/52)
564. The Case of the Caribbean Cruise (8/31/52)
565. The Case of the Man Who Paid Twice (9/7/52)
566. The Case of the Devil's Dish-Pan (9/14/52)
567. The Case of the Mailbox Murder (9/21/52)
568. The Case of the Murder Museum (9/28/52)
569. The Case of the Rehearsal for Death (10/5/52)
570. The Case of the Unwelcome Guest (10/12/52)
571. The Case of the Reformed Delinquent (10/26/52)
572. The Case of the Decoy Story (10/26/52)
573. The Case of the Merry Little Men (11/2/52)
574. The Case of the Box of Rogue (11/9/52)
575. The Case of the Counterfeit Face (11/16/52)
576. The Case of the King-Sized Frame (11/23/52)
577. The Case of the Little Black Book (11/30/52)
578. The Case of the Murder Memoirs (12/7/52)
579. The Case of the Whistling Ghost (12/14/52)
580. The Case of the Blazing Diamonds (12/21/52)
581. The Case of the Wrong Spot (12/28/52)
582. The Case of the Prescription for Death (1/4/53)
583. The Case of the Invisible Man (1/11/53)
584. The Case of the Nightmare That Came True (1/18/53)
585. The Case of the Anonymous Corpse (1/25/53)
586. The Case of the Green Corduroy Bandit (2/1/53)
587. The Case of the Firebug Murder (2/8/53)
588. The Case of the Golden Gods (2/15/53)
589. The Case of the Style-Show Sapphires (2/22/53)
590. The Case of the Purloined Pussycat (3/1/53)
591. The Case of the Jalopy Jinx (3/8/53)
592. The Case of the Echoing Clue (3/15/53)
593. The Case of the Golden Cow (3/22/53)
594. The Case of the Unlikely Grave (3/29/53)
595. The Case of the Impossible Murder (4/5/53)
596. The Case of the Body in the Well (4/12/53)
597. The Case of the Useless Engagement Ring (4/19/53)
598. The Case of the Dangerous Alibi (4/26/53)
599. The Case of the Red-Headed Herring (5/3/53)
600. The Case of the Fly-Leaf Murder (5/10/53)
601. The Case of the Visiting Vampire (5/17/53)
602. The Case of the Murderous Booby-Traps (5/24/53)
603. The Case of the Short Snorter (5/31/53)
604. The Case of the Unlikely Horseshoe (6/7/53)
605. The Case of the Desert Drowning (6/14/53)
606. The Case of the Man Who Got Away with Murder (6/21/53)
607. The Case of the Diamond Trail (6/28/53)
608. The Case of the Phantom Accident (7/5/53)

663. The Case of the Bad-Tempered Twin (8/1/54)
664. The Case of Death in a Straw Hat (8/8/54)
665. The Case of the Murder Diary (8/15/54)
666. The Case of the Lovelorn Corpse (8/22/54)
667. The Case of the Crimson Clue (8/29/54)
668. The Case of the Crossword Puzzle Clue (9/5/54)
669. The Case of the Stray Bullet Murder (9/12/54)
670. The Case of the Forgotten Murder (9/19/54)
671. The Case of the Preview for Murder (9/26/54)
672. The Case of the Panama Lady (10/3/54)
673. The Case of the Freight Train (10/10/54)
674. The Case of the Murder in a Convertible (10/17/54)
675. The Case of the Girl on the Loose (10/31/54)
676. The Case of the Murder on Reflection (11/7/54)
677. The Case of the Ghost Train (11/14/54)
678. The Case of Charlie Mahoney (11/21/54)
679. The Case of the Man Who Wasn't There (11/28/54)
680. The Case of the Framing of Dixie Schultz (12/5/54)
681. The Case of the Frustrated Ego (12/12/54)
682. The Case of the Man from Suez (12/19/54)
683. The Case of the Little Man Who Cried (12/26/54)
684. The Case of the Perilous Switch (1/2/55)
685. The Case of the Hijackers (1/9/55)
686. The Case of the Pact with the Devil (1/16/55)
687. The Case of the Girl on the Run (1/23/55)
688. The Case of the Man with the Dark Eyes (1/30/55)
689. The Case of the Option on a Wife (2/6/55)
690. The Case of the Righteous Hoodlum (2/13/55)
691. The Case of the Constant Telephone (2/20/55)
692. The Case of the Corpse That Moved (2/27/55)
693. The Case of the Man Without a Face (3/6/55)
694. The Case of the Mountain Secret (3/13/55)
695. The Case of the Bootleg Ivory Hunter (3/20/55)
696. The Case of the Three-Headed Lama (3/27/55)
697. The Case of Marty Jones (4/3/55)
698. The Case of Lupo Moreno (4/10/55)
699. The Case of Baron Leopold (4/17/55)
700. The Case of the Circus Fire (4/24/55)
701. The Case of the Missing Code Book (5/1/55)
702. The Case of the Three-Sided Knife (5/8/55)
703. The Case of the Roads That Crossed (5/15/55)
704. The Case of the John Ignatius Pilgrim (5/22/55)
705. The Case of the Voodoo Drums (5/29/55)
706. The Case of the Framing of Nick Carter (6/5/55)
707. The Case of the Missing Bride (6/12/55)
708. The Case of the Jungle Doctor (6/19/55)
709. The Case of the Diamond Smugglers (6/26/55)
710. The Case of the Ruby Thompson (7/3/55)
711. The Case of the Trial by Tempest (7/10/55)
712. The Case of the Would-Be Citizen (7/17/55)
713. The Case of the Madame Yaznik (7/24/55)
714. The Case of the Specter of Brunheim Castle (7/31/55)
715. The Case of the Moonlight Swim (8/7/55)
716. The Case of the Sarasan's Return (8/14/55)
717. The Case of the Man Who Was There Too Late (8/21/55)

718. The Case of the Dragon Society
     (8/28/55)
719. The Case of the Guilty Victim
     (9/4/55)
720. The Case of the Slave Runners

(9/11/55)
721. The Case of the Pagan Gods
     (9/18/55)
722. The Case of the Counterfeit Pass-
     ports (9/25/55)

Once Upon a Tune

This series presented original musical dramas, the majority as a radio car-
toon (comical). "Special Delivery" concerned a mailman's last day at his job; "The
Sentimental Locomotive" was a cleverly written musical about a locomotive very
much in love with a French girl locomotive; Adam and the animals on the very
first day was presented in "When the World Was New"; and the final broadcast
presented an interesting look at the things that can happen when Father Time
takes a vacation. Heralded as an original music/comedy series which defied pre-
cise definition, these half-hour shows were the combined handiwork of writer
Ray Darby and composer Morris Surdin, citizen of Canada, whose novel presentations had been one of the Canadian Broadcasting Corporation's most popular programs.

The series was broadcast sustaining over CBS, Sunday afternoons from 2:30
to 3 pm, EST. After its first three broadcasts, *Once Upon a Tune* took over the
time slot of *The Columbia Workshop*, Saturday from 6:15 to 6:45 pm, EST. The
final four episodes were broadcast on Saturday evenings from 8 to 8:30 pm,
EST. The broadcasts originated from New York, with a supporting cast of Joe
di Santis, Jack Grimes, Sandy Becker, Parker Fennelly, Arnold Stang and Minerva Pious. Mae Questel, the voice of Betty Boop, guested in episode fourteen.

1. Tugboat Danny (1/5/47)
2. Special Delivery (1/12/47)
3. Tortilla Jones (1/19/47)
4. The Natural History of Nonsense
   [written by Bergen Evans] (1/25/47)
5. The Sentimental Locomotive (2/1/47)
6. On of Our Bongs Is Missing (2/8/47)
7. Henry, the Spook (2/15/47)
8. Two Bits (2/22/47)
9. Atom From the Apple (3/1/47)
10. Ferdinand the Bullfrog (3/8/47)
11. Tortilla Jones (3/15/47)
12. No More Rainy Saturdays (3/22/47)
13. The Sentimental Locomotive
    (3/29/47)
14. The Wabbits of Warren (4/5/47)
15. Head in the Clouds (4/12/47)
16. When the World Was New (4/19/47)
17. Time Unlimited (4/26/47)

One World Flight

Norman Corwin, CBS staff writer, was the first recipient of the "One World
Flight" award, and in homage to the award, Corwin wrote a thirteen-episode

series using the award as the title of the program. All of the scripts were written, hosted and narrated by Corwin, commenting about his trip around the world, the places he saw and the people he met. Lyn Murray composed and conducted the music, with Guy Della Cioppa assisting the productions. The series was broadcast sustaining over CBS, Tuesday evenings from 10 to 10:30 pm, EST.

Nobel Prize winner Frederick Joliot-Curie made an appearance in the third broadcast. United States Commissioner Walter Robertson was featured in episode nine. United States Ambassador Paul V. McNutt was featured in the tenth broadcast.

1. Introduction (1/14/47)
2. England (1/21/47; Prime Minister Clement Attlee)
3. France, Denmark, Norway, and Sweden (1/28/47; Louis Aragon, Kersten Hesselgren, Frederick Joliot-Curie, Baroness Eren Krona, Paul Nelson, and Maurice Schumann)
4. Poland (2/4/47; Madame Rabecwisz)
5. Soviet Union (2/11/47; Michael Borodin, Sergei Eisenstein, Aram Katchaturian, David Zaslavsky)
6. Czechoslovakia (2/18/47)
7. Italy (2/25/47; Sergio Amidei, Roberto Rossellini, and Palmiro Togliatti)
8. Egypt and India (3/4/47; Jawaharlal Nehru and Viceroy Lord Wavell)
9. China (3/11/47; Chou En-lai, Pung She Pay, and Walter Robertson)
10. Philippines (3/18/47; Paul V. McNutt and Manuel Roxas)
11. Australia (3/25/47; J.B. McKell)
12. New Zealand (4/1/47; Peter Fraser)
13. A Final Summary (4/8/47)

On Stage

This dramatic series featured adaptations of popular novels, stories and poems, as well as many originals. From sentimental tales to horror, this program represented the best radio actors could put together with a little persistence and a love of their job. Cathy and Elliott Lewis were the stars of the program, which, behind the microphone was referred to as "The Cathy and Elliott Lewis Show." Elliott Lewis was producing and directing the popular *Suspense* program at the same time he produced and directed this series, keeping him very busy indeed. Famed musician and conductor Ray Noble composed the theme song, "The Cathy and Elliott Theme." If a radio actor wrote his own radio script, he knew he could turn to Cathy or Elliott to have it dramatized over the air. George Walsh was the announcer. Fred Steiner, Lucien Morawek and Lud Gluskin supplied the music.

At first broadcast over CBS, sustaining, Thursday evening from 9 to 9:30 pm, EST, beginning September 9, 1953, the series moved to Wednesday from 9 to 9:30 pm, EST. On February 3, 1954, *On Stage* moved ahead an hour, airing from 10 to 10:30 pm, EST. Finally, the program went back to its original time slot on Thursday evenings from 9 to 9:30 pm, EST, beginning June 17, 1954, remaining there until the end of the series.

The scripts were sometimes experimental, but always dealt with relationships. Episode seventeen, "Happy Anniversary Album," was actually Cathy and Elliott Lewis' tenth wedding anniversary; this broadcast was written as a celebration. Radio actor Bob Sweeney wrote and narrated "A Fifth of Tears." Episode fifteen was a dramatized adaptation of the popular poem by Ernest Lawrence Thayer.

1. The String Bow Tie (1/1/53)
2. Beirut by Sunrise (1/8/53; Edgar Barrier, Byron Kane, and Ben Wright)
3. A Poetic Tragedy (1/15/53)
4. Cargo (1/22/53)
5. Public Furlough (1/29/53)
6. A Corner of Autumn (2/5/53)
7. The Party (2/12/53)
8. Four Meetings (2/19/53; Jeanette Nolan and Ben Wright)
9. A Fifth of Tears (2/26/53)
10. Call Me A Cab (3/12/53; Mary Jane Croft, Shirley Gordon, Howard McNear, and Peggy Webber)
11. Eddie (3/19/53; Jerry Hausner, Clayton Post, and Peggy Webber)
12. Dig, the Thief (3/26/53; Ken Christy, Hal Gerard, Byron Kane, John McIntire, Lee Millard, GeGe Pearson, and Bob Sweeney)
13. The Lady or the Tiger (4/2/53; Sammy Hill, Junius Matthews, and Alan Reed)
14. The Bunch of Violets (4/9/53; Dick Beals, Byron Kane, Charlotte Lawrence, Lou Merrill, and Peggy Webber)
15. Casey at the Bat (4/16/53; Hy Averback, Herb Butterfield, Byron Kane, Peter Leeds, Hal March, Howard McNear, and Sidney Miller)
16. Skin Deep (4/23/53)
17. Happy Anniversary Album (4/30/53; Ray Noble)
18. The Bear (5/7/53; Byron Kane and Horace Murphy)
19. Statement of Fact (5/14/53; Joan Danton, Byron Kane, Joseph Kearns, Jack Kruschen, Truda Marsden, and Tyler McVey)
20. Conrad in Quest of his Youth (5/21/53)
21. The Hanging at Four Oaks (5/28/53; Edgar Barrier, Harry Bartell, Byron Kane, Johnny McGovern, and Barney Phillips)
22. And a Fond Farewell (6/4/53; Byron Kane)
23. East Lynn (6/11/53)
24. An Ideal Couple (6/18/53; Tom Dixon and Paul Frees)
25. A Day to Remember (6/25/53)
26. The Midnight Ride of Paul Revere (7/2/53; Richard Shandly)
27. Man of Independent Mind (7/9/53)
28. Miracle for Julie (7/16/53)
29. The Fling (7/23/53; Herb Butterfield and Sam Hill)
30. The Girl I Tried to Love (7/30/53)
31. A Month of Sundays (8/13/53)
32. Canary Yellow (8/20/53; Lou Merrill and GeGe Pearson)
33. Child in the Room (8/27/53)
34. I Love You, I Love You, Gezundheit! (9/9/53)
35. The Crustacean (9/16/53; Parley Baer and Larry Thor)
36. Penny Ante (9/23/53)
37. Loving [three short plays] (9/30/53; William Conrad, Byron Kane, Barney Phillips and Clayton Post)
38. Great Dane (10/7/53)
39. Ditty and Mr. Jasper (10/14/53)
40. Take My Hand, My Love (10/21/53)
41. Cellar Door (10/28/53)
42. Vickie (11/4/53)
43. The Marathon (11/11/53)
44. A Circle of Wheels (11/18/53; Whitfield Connor)
45. New York Is a Nice Place to Visit, But I Wouldn't Want to Live There (11/25/53)
46. Our American Cousin (12/2/53)
47. Passing Strange (12/9/53)
48. Candide (12/16/53; Edgar Barrier, Byron Kane, Jack Kruschen, Howard McNear, Larry Thor, Martha Wentworth, and Ben Wright)
49. Happy Holidays (12/30/53)

50. Gopher Man (1/6/54)
51. Camille (2/3/54)
52. Tragedy Off Hollywood Boulevard (2/10/54)
53. Heartbreak (2/17/54)
54. The Dreamer (3/3/54)
55. Crusade of Stanley Finston (3/10/54)
56. Occurrence Up A Side Street (3/17/54)
57. Heaven's to Betsy (3/24/54)
58. Three Anniversaries (3/31/54)
59. Hidden Heart (4/7/54)
60. The Referee (4/14/54)
61. A Man and his Mountain (4/21/54)
62. Giant's Fireplace (4/28/54)
63. Fork in the Road (6/17/54)
64. Younger Sister (6/24/54)
65. Some Days it Just Doesn't Pay (7/1/54)
66. Welcome Home Dan (7/8/54)
67. The Book of Next Month (7/15/54)
68. Interlude (7/22/54)
69. The Telegram (7/29/54)
70. Diversion (8/5/54)
71. Driftwood (8/12/54)
72. Stanley Finston, Stockbroker (8/19/54)
73. The Prize Fighter (8/26/54)
74. Lovely Dead Letter (9/2/54)
75. Saralee, You Are Lovely As the Summer Night (9/9/54)
76. Sleepytime Gal (9/16/54)
77. Fascination (9/23/54)
78. Circle of Wheels (9/30/54)

Palmolive Beauty Box Theater

A series of light operettas. John Barclay starred in the early shows, with support from Jane Froman, Rose Kirkman, and others. The ratings, however, sagged the longer the program remained on the air, so in order to keep the program from dropping off the air, Gladys Swarthout was added. This didn't seem to help much, and after three-and-a-half years, the *Palmolive Beauty Box Theater* went off the air for good.

Nat Shilkret's Orchestra supplied the music until August 9, 1935, when Al Goodman took over the remainder of the series. Jessica Dragonette was added to the cast on January 13, 1937, remaining on the program until the end. First broadcast over NBC, Tuesday evenings from 10 to 11 pm, EST, beginning August 9, 1935, *Palmolive* moved to the Blue Network, Fridays from 9 to 10 pm, EST. On January 11, 1936, *Palmolive* moved again, this time to CBS, Saturday evenings from 8 to 9 pm, EST. A year later on January 13, 1937, the program moved one last time, remaining on Wednesday evenings from 9:30 to 10 pm, EST. Otto Harbach was commentator during the 1935-36 Blue season. The final season consisted mostly of repeats, with the final broadcast consisting of request performances from faithful listeners. The entire series was sponsored by Palmolive Soap.

1. The Vagabond King (4/3/34; Theodore Webb)
2. Student Prince (4/10/34; Paul Oliver)
3. Rogue Song [part one] (4/17/34; John Barclay)
4. Rogue Song [part two] (4/24/34; John Barclay)
5. Blossom Time (5/1/34; James Melton)
6. Eileen (5/8/34; James Melton)
7. My Maryland (5/15/34; John Barclay)
8. The Chocolate Soldier (5/22/34; John Barclay)
9. Carmen (5/29/34; James Melton)
10. Sweethearts (6/5/34; James Melton)

11. Rio Rita (6/12/34)
12. Bittersweet (6/19/34)
13. Countess Maritza (6/24/34)
14. Robin Hood (7/3/34; Marie Wilson)
15. M'lle Modiste (7/10/34; John Barclay)
16. Blue Paradise (7/17/34; Rose Kirkman)
17. Floradora (7/24/34)
18. Madame Butterfly (7/31/34; Mario Chamlee)
19. The Red Mill (8/7/34)
20. Prince of Pilsen (8/14/34)
21. H.M.S. Pinafore (8/21/34; Gloria La Voy)
22. The White Eagle (8/28/34; John Barclay)
23. Count of Luxembourg (9/4/34)
24. The Vagabond King (9/11/34)
25. Fortune Teller (9/18/34)
26. Girl of the Golden West (9/25/34)
27. Miss Springtime (10/2/34)
28. Student Prince (10/9/34)
29. Dearest Enemy (10/16/34)
30. Sari (10/23/34)
31. Bohemian Girl (10/30/34; Annie Jameson)
32. Cyrono De Bergerac (11/6/34)
33. Hit the Deck (11/13/34)
34. Naughty Marietta (11/20/34; Annie Jameson)
35. Pink Lady (11/27/34; John Barclay)
36. Connecticut Yankee (12/4/34; Jane Froman)
37. Princess Flavia (12/11/34)
38. The Mikado (12/18/34)
39. Babes in Toyland (12/23/34; John Barclay)
40. Lady Be Good (1/1/35; Jane Froman)
41. New Moon (1/8/35)
42. Girl Crazy (1/15/35; Jane Froman)
43. Paganini (1/22/35)
44. Desert Song (1/29/35)
45. The Only Girl (2/5/35; John Barclay)
46. Lady in Ermine (2/12/35; Peggy Allenby)
47. The Great Waltz (2/19/35; Francia White)
48. Good News (2/25/35)
49. Rogue Song [part one] (3/5/35; John Barclay)
50. Rogue Song [part two] (3/12/35; John Barclay)
51. One Night of Love (3/19/35; Francia White)
52. The Merry Widow (3/26/35; John Barclay)
53. The Pirates of Penzance (4/2/35)
54. Apple Blossoms (4/9/35)
55. Naughty Marietta (4/16/35; Francia White)
56. I Pagliacci (4/23/35; Jan Pearce)
57. Princess Pat (4/30/35)
58. Blossom Time (5/7/35)
59. Circle Princess (5/14/35; Francia White)
60. The Chocolate Soldier (5/21/35)
61. Jenny Lind (5/28/35; Sylvia Brema)
62. Prince of Pilsen (6/4/35)
63. Madame Pompadour (6/11/35)
64. Eileen (6/18/35; Francia White)
65. Chimes of Normandy (6/25/35; Francia White)
66. My Maryland (7/2/35)
67. Mississippi (7/9/35)
68. Die Fledermaus (7/16/35)
69. Bittersweet (7/23/35)
70. Iolanthe (7/30/35)
71. Desert Song (8/9/35; Rose Bampton)
72. Love Me Forever (8/16/35; Jan Pearce and Francia White)
73. Countess Maritza (8/23/35; Frank Parker)
74. Natoma (8/30/35)
75. Rio Rita (9/6/35)
76. The Love Song (9/13/35; John Barclay and Frank Parker)
77. Carmen (9/20/35; Rose Bampton)
78. Dream Girl (9/27/35)
79. Student Prince (10/4/35; Francia White)
80. La Boheme (10/11/35)
81. Maytime (10/18/35)
82. Here's to Romance (10/25/35)
83. Sari (11/1/35)
84. Land of Smiles (11/8/35; Rose Bampton)
85. The Three Musketeers (11/15/35)
86. Stars Over Broadway (11/22/35; Jane Froman)
87. The Gondoliers (12/6/35)
88. The Merry Widow (12/13/35)
89. I Dream Too Much (12/20/35; Helen Jepson)
90. Manon (12/27/35)
91. Rose of the Rancho (1/11/36)
92. Irene (1/18/36)
93. Waltz Dream (1/25/36; Jessica Dragonette)
94. Rose of Algeria (2/1/36)

95. The Vagabond King (2/8/36)
96. The Great Waltz (2/15/36)
97. New Moon (1/13/37)
98. Desert Song (1/20/37)
99. Student Prince (1/27/37)
100. Rio Rita (2/3/37)
101. Countess Maritza (2/10/37)
102. My Maryland (2/17/37)
103. Blossom Time (2/24/37)
104. Street Song (3/3/37)
105. Land of Smiles (3/10/37)
106. Two Tickets to Romance (3/17/37)
107. Hits from the Classics (3/24/37)
108. Naughty Marietta (3/31/37)
109. M'lle Modiste (4/7/37)
110. The Chocolate Soldier (4/14/37)
111. The Vagabond King (4/21/37)
112. Lady in Ermine (4/28/37)
113. The Merry Widow (5/5/37)
114. Eileen (5/12/37)
115. Rogue Song [part one] (5/19/37)
116. Rogue Song [part two] (5/26/37)

117. The Only Girl (6/2/37)
118. Irene (6/9/37)
119. Maytime (6/16/37)
120. Sari (6/23/37)
121. Pink Lady (6/30/37)
122. Sweethearts (7/7/37)
123. Bittersweet (7/14/37)
124. Princess Pat (7/21/37)
125. Madame Pompadour (7/28/37)
126. The Dream Girl (8/4/37)
127. Prince of Pilsen (8/11/37)
128. The Three Musketeers [part one] (8/18/37)
129. The Three Musketeers [part two] (8/25/37)
130. Robin Hood (9/1/37)
131. Blue Paradise (9/8/37)
132. A Waltz Dream (9/15/37)
133. Dearest Enemy (9/22/37)
134. Count of Luxembourg (9/29/37)
135. [Request numbers] (10/6/37)

Parade of Progress

Sponsored by International Foods, this documentary series dramatized the manufacturing and processing of food items and their distribution across the country — from the origin of glass bottles and their uses in preserving food products to the countries that grow and import spices used on modern-day food. Hosted by Charlotte Manson, the series was broadcast over the Blue Network on Thursday evenings from 8 to 8:30 pm, EST.

1. The Story of Wheat (1/26/39)
2. The Story of Canning (2/2/39)
3. The Story of Glass Bottles (2/9/39)
4. The Story of Packaging (2/16/39)
5. The Story of Oats and Corn (2/23/39)
6. The Story of Tea (3/2/39)
7. The Story of Frosted Foods (3/9/39)

8. The Story of Spices (3/16/39)
9. The Story of Cracker Barrel (3/23/39)
10. The Story of Desserts (3/30/39)
11. The Story of Beverages (4/6/39)
12. The Story of Meat (4/13/39)
13. The Story of Cheese (4/20/39)
14. The Story of Soap (4/27/39)
15. The Story of Coffee (5/4/39)

Parade of the States

Sponsored by General Motors, this nationwide series, presenting a roadside advantage to in-home tourism, was broadcast over NBC Red, Monday evenings from 9:30 to 10 pm, EST. Each broadcast featured a different state of the Union, offering trivia, facts, short skits, state songs and famous tourist sites. The program originated from NBC studios in New York City. Under the direction of Erno Rapee and his orchestra, all forty-eight states (not including Alaska and Hawaii) were featured on this series. Charles Webster was the announcer. David Bain was the imitator, performing the voices of many famous people from across the nation. John Anthony was narrator. Episodes ten and thirty-three featured Alfred P. Sloan, Jr., then the president of General Motors Corporation.

1. Virginia (10/19/31; John Powell)
2. Arizona (10/26/31)
3. Connecticut (11/2/51)
4. Alabama (11/9/31)
5. Oklahoma (11/16/31)
6. Massachusetts (11/23/31)
7. Idaho (11/30/31)
8. Ohio (12/7/31)
9. Georgia (12/14/31)
10. Michigan (12/21/31; Alfred P. Sloan, Jr.)
11. California (12/28/31)
12. Delaware (1/4/32)
13. New York (1/11/32)
14. Florida (1/18/32)
15. Nevada (1/25/32)
16. Illinois (2/1/32; Attilo Baggiore)
17. Louisiana (2/8/32; Viola Philo and Theodore Webb)
18. New Mexico (2/15/32; Gladys Rice)
19. The District of Columbia (2/22/32)
20. Mississippi (2/29/32; Rollin Smith, and the Rosamond Johnson Choir)
21. Utah (3/7/32)
22. Tennessee (3/14/32)
23. New Jersey (3/21/32; Phil Dewey)
24. Missouri (3/28/32; Yvonne D'Arle)
25. South Carolina (4/11/32; Phil Dewey and Elizabeth Lennox)
26. Texas (4/18/32; Phil Dewey)
27. Nebraska (4/25/32; Jay Alden Edkins and Elizabeth Lennox)
28. Kentucky (5/2/32; Fred Hufsmith)
29. Maryland (5/9/32)
30. Arkansas (5/16/32)
31. Colorado (5/23/32; Fred Hufsmith)
32. Indiana (5/30/32; Veronica Wiggins)
33. Oregon (6/6/32; Alfred P. Sloan, Jr.)
34. Vermont (6/13/32; Thedore Webb)
35. Washington (6/20/32)
36. Minnesota (6/27/32; Fred Hufsmith)
37. Pennsylvania (7/4/32)
38. North Dakota (7/11/32; Theodore Webb)
39. Maine (7/18/32; Carol Edwards)
40. Wyoming (7/25/32; Phil Dewey)
41. Wisconsin (8/1/32; Elizabeth Lennox and Theodore Webb)
42. Rhode Island (8/8/32; Theodore Webb)
43. South Dakota (8/15/32; Phil Dewey)
44. New Hampshire (8/29/32; Martha Attwood)
45. Iowa (9/5/32; Viola Philo and Clarence Whitehall)
46. West Virginia (9/12/32)
47. Kansas (9/19/32; Frank Luther)
48. North Carolina (9/26/32)
49. Montana (10/3/32; John Fogarty)
50. Territorial Possessions (10/10/32; Fred Hufsmith, and The Hernandez Brothers)
51. The United States: All America Night (10/17/32; Phil Dewey, Lottice Howell, Angelita Loya, and Aileen Stanley)

The People Act

Not much is known about this show, except that *The People Act* was a syndicated series of twenty-six episodes, featuring real-life dramas. The purpose of the dramas was to instruct the public in problem solving, with recorded interviews from eyewitnesses and those who actually participated in the events. Originally broadcast over CBS in January of 1952, from 10:05–10:30 pm, EST, the series, being syndicated, was rebroadcast on numerous local radio stations after the CBS run. The first date is the initial CBS broadcast.

1. A Story of Gary, Indiana (1/6/52; 11/1/52)
2. The Arlington Story (1/13/52; 11/8/52)
3. The Blairsville Story (1/20/52; 11/15/52)
4. The Kansas City Story (1/27/52; 11/22/52)
5. The Vermont Story (2/3/52; 11/29/52)
6. The Chicago Story (2/10/52; 12/6/52)
7. The Tupelo, Missouri Story (2/17/52; 12/13/52)
8. The New Sharon, Maine Story (2/24/52; 12/20/52)
9. The Tin Top, Kansas Story (3/2/52; 12/27/52)
10. The Mt. Adams Area, Washington Story (3/9/52; 1/3/53)
11. The Syracuse Story (3/16/52; 1/10/53)
12. The Story of Bellville, Illinois (3/23/52; 1/17/53)
13. The Story of Kings County, Washington (3/30/52; 1/24/53)
14. The People in Binghamton, New York (4/6/52 ; 1/31/53)
15. The People in Scranton, Pennsylvania (4/13/52; 2/7/53)
16. The People on Jackson Street, Seattle (4/20/52; 2/14/53)
17. The People in Newark, New Jersey (4/27/52; 2/21/53)
18. The People in San Joaquin, California (5/4/52; 2/28/53)
19. The People in Georgia and Etawah, Indiana (5/11/52; 3/7/53)
20. The People in Owatonna, Minnesota (5/18/52; 3/14/53)
21. The People in New York (5/25/52; 3/21/53)
22. The People in Santa Barbara, California (6/1/52; 3/28/53)
23. The People in Alexandria, Minnesota (6/8/52; 4/4/53)
24. The People in Jerome County, Idaho (6/15/52; 4/11/53)
25. The People in Delaware, Ohio (6/22/52; 4/18/53)
26. The People in the U.S.A. (6/29/52; 4/25/53)

People Under Communism

During the fifties and sixties, radio programs began turning their attention towards anticommunism dramas. *I Was a Communist for the F.B.I.* was just one of many. *People Under Communism*, an adult education series, was another. Originating from WNYC in New York on Sunday afternoons from 5–5:30 pm, EST, Arnold Moss was narrator. The series was then syndicated, and aired across the nation after the initial broadcasts. The first date is the original broadcast run, the second belongs to a rebroadcast run, in New York again, but over another station, from 12 noon to 12:30 pm.

1. Terror as a Symbol of Power (12/7/52; 5/4/58)
2. Music to Order (12/14/52; 5/11/58)
3. The Men Who Make the MIGS (12/21/52; 5/18/58)
4. Drama to Order (12/28/52; 5/25/58)
5. Literature to Order (1/4/53; 6/1/58)
6. Pattern of World Conflict (1/11/53; 6/8/58)
7. The Music and the Dream (1/18/53; 6/15/58)

Philco Radio Playhouse

Sponsored by Philco, this anthology series featured original radio dramas and top Hollywood stars in the leads and was broadcast over the ABC Network, Thursday evening from 9 to 9:30 pm, EST. Beginning September of 1953, the program moved to Wednesday, 8 to 8:30 pm, EST. Highlights included Michael Redgrave as Horatio Hornblower and Hedda Hopper actually acting out a performance in the broadcast of September 30, 1953. This program originated from Hollywood and New York, which allowed a wide variety of actors to play the roles. Joseph Cotten guested on the program so many times during the second season that he could have been mistaken for a regular!

1. The Hunted (4/16/53; Robert Cummings)
2. My Husband, Mr. Forsythe (4/23/53; Cesar Romero)
3. Checkmate (4/30/53; Gary Merrill and Cesar Romero)
4. Country Lawyer (5/7/53; Bert Lytell and Cesar Romero)
5. Justice (5/14/53; Henry Barnard)
6. The Pen Is Mightier Than People (5/21/53; Arthur Treacher)
7. Horatio Hornblower (5/28/53; Michael Redgrave)
8. The Guardsman (6/4/53; Rex Harrison and Lilli Palmer)
9. Colonel Flack (6/11/53; Frank McHugh and Alan Mowbray)
10. The Chain (6/18/53; Everett Sloane)
11. Who's the Boss? (6/25/53; Betty Furness)
12. Point to View (7/2/53; Burgess Meredith)
13. Jet Fighter (7/9/53; Leon Janney and George Peatrie)
14. Fade Out (9/30/53; Sidney Blackmer and Hedda Hopper)
15. Dr. Hudson's Secret Journal (10/7/53; Joseph Cotten)
16. Routine Assignment (10/14/53; Kevin McCarthy)
17. A Cowboy for Chris (10/21/53; Billy de Wilde and Fredric March)
18. Dusty Drawer (10/28/53; Joseph Cotten)
19. Double Jeopardy (11/4/53; Kevin McCarthy)
20. Marcia Akers (11/11/53; Olive Dearing)
21. Bulletin 20 (11/18/53; Bert Lytell)
22. Thin Air (11/25/53; John Beal)
23. Second Oldest Profession (12/2/53; William Prince)
24. The End Is Known (12/9/53; Joseph Cotten and Kim Hunter)
25. Wacky, the Small Boy (12/16/53; Joseph Cotten and House Jameson)
26. In Beauty like the Night (12/23/53; Eileen Burns and Joseph Wiseman)
27. Decoy (12/30/53; Ralph Bellamy and Joseph Cotten)
28. The Room (1/6/54; Joseph Cotten and Arlene Francis)
29. Hear My Heart Speak (1/13/54; Joseph Cotten and Kim Stanley)
30. Brat Farrar (1/20/54; Joseph Cotten and Cathleen Nesbitt)
31. A Member of the Family (1/27/54; Luis Van Rooten)

Philip Morris Playhouse

Sponsored by Philip Morris Cigarettes, this anthology program took the time slot of *Great Moments from Great Plays*, another program Philip Morris sponsored. *Playhouse* featured original dramas as well as movie adaptations with various Hollywood stars as the leads. *Playhouse* originated from New York until January of 1942, when the program migrated to Hollywood. Stars such as Madeline Carroll and John Garfield were appearing almost monthly. Nelson Case was the announcer, replaced by Carl Frank beginning December 26, 1941. Ray Bloch supplied the music. The series was broadcast over CBS, Friday evenings from 9 to 9:30 pm, EST.

Episode fifty-five featured a documentary drama of the life of Eddie Cantor, with Cantor in the lead. Orson Welles reprised his role of Ronald Adams in Lucille Fletcher's "The Hitch-Hiker," from a performance he gave on *Suspense* only a month before!

This format remained on the air until February 22, 1944, diverting from radio until 1948. Philip Morris decided to sponsor other programs, as it had with *Great Moments from Great Plays*. In late 1948, the cigarette giant decided to revive the program, under its original title, but with a few changes. Still broadcast from Hollywood, William Spier, previous director of *Suspense*, took charge, bringing suspenseful tales of mystery and murder to the program. Hollywood stars still appeared on the program, but no dramas based on film adaptations were used (a big handful of *Suspense* scripts were featured). Art Ballingen was the announcer. Lucien Morawek and Lud Gluskin, both of whom worked closely with Spier on *Suspense*, supplied the music. The broadcast came over CBS, Friday from 10 to 10:30 pm, EST.

The program went off the air for a year, and when it returned in 1951, Spier was no longer director. Charles Martin was now director, and Lehman Engel was in charge of the music duties. The show once again featured adaptations of movies such as "Double Indemnity," "The Front Page" and "Night Must Fall." Alexander Semmler supplied the music. At first broadcast over CBS, Thursday from 10 to 10:30 pm, EST, *Playhouse* moved back a half-hour, to 9:30 to 10 pm, EST. In September of 1951, the title of the program was changed to the *Philip Morris Playhouse on Broadway*.

1. Dark Victory (8/15/41; Agnes Moorehead and Sylvia Sidney)
2. Front Page (8/22/41; Everett Sloane)
3. Five Came Back (8/29/41; Elia Kazan and Everett Sloane)
4. Yellow Jack (9/5/41; House Jameson and Everett Sloane)
5. One Way Passage (9/12/41; Alice Frost and Everett Sloane)
6. Angels with Dirty Faces (9/19/41; Frank Lovejoy and Everett Sloane)
7. A Man to Remember (9/26/41; Claude Rains)
8. June Moon (10/3/41; Eddie Cantor)
9. The Little Foxes (10/10/41; Tallulah Bankhead and Everett Sloane)
10. Wuthering Heights (10/17/41; Raymond Massey, Flora Robson, and Sylvia Sidney)
11. Night Must Fall (10/24/41; Burgess Meredith, Maureen O'Sullivan, and Flora Robson)
12. My Favorite Wife (10/31/41; Madeline Carroll and Burgess Meredith)
13. Made for Each Other (11/7/41; Burgess Meredith and Martha Scott)
14. The Devil and Miss Jones (11/14/41; Everett Sloane and Lana Turner)

15. Girl in the News (11/21/41; Joan Bennett)
16. You Only Live Once (11/28/41; Burgess Meredith)
17. Stage Door (12/5/41; Geraldine Fitzgerald and Robert Young)
18. The Petrified Forest (12/12/41; Rita Johnson and Franchot Tone)
19. The Lady Vanishes (12/19/41; Errol Flynn and Flora Robson)
20. Four Daughters (12/26/41; Jeffrey Lynn and Burgess Meredith)
21. Each Dawn I Die (1/2/42)
22. We Are Not Alone (1/9/42; Raymond Massey)
23. Angels Over Broadway (1/16/42; Pat O'Brien)
24. The Great McGinty (1/23/42; Brian Donlevy)
25. Brother Orchid (1/30/42; George Raft)
26. Vivacious Lady (2/6/42; Madeline Carroll)
27. Story of Louis Pasteur (2/13/42; Walter Huston)
28. Kid Galahad (2/20/42; Edward Arnold)
29. True Confession (2/27/42; Rita Johnson)
30. The Letter (3/6/42; Betty Field)
31. Golden Boy (3/13/42; John Garfield)
32. The Criminal Code (3/20/42; John Garfield and Claude Rains)
33. Goodbye, Mr. Chips (3/27/42; Florence Eldridge and Fredric March)
34. Mister V (4/3/42; Sir Cedric Harwicke)
35. I Wake Up Screaming (4/10/42; Carole Landis)
36. The Man Who Played God (4/17/42; Raymond Massey)
37. Sullivan's Travels (4/24/42; Melvyn Douglas)
38. Arise My Love (5/1/42; Madeline Carroll)
39. That Uncertain Feeling (5/8/42; Roland Young)
40. Personal Appearance (5/15/42; Dorothy Lamour)
41. The Lady Has Plans (5/22/42; Madeline Carroll)
42. Bachelor Mother (5/29/42; Martha Scott)
43. Broadway (6/5/42; George Raft)
44. No Time for Comedy (6/12/42; Madeline Carroll)
45. Take a Letter Darling (6/19/42; Melvyn Douglas)
46. Friendly Enemies (6/26/42; Charlie Ruggles and Charles Winninger)
47. This Gun for Hire (7/3/42; Marlene Dietrich and William Holden)
48. The Man Who Came to Dinner (7/10/42; Monty Woolley)
49. My Favorite Blonde (7/17/42; Milton Berle)
50. The Male Animal (7/24/42; William Holden)
51. Man Hunt (7/31/42; Robert Montgomery)
52. A Gentleman at Heart (8/7/42; Milton Berle)
53. The Maltese Falcon (8/14/42; Edward Arnold)
54. Remember the Day (8/21/42; Madeline Carroll)
55. The Life of Eddie Cantor (8/28/42; Eddie Cantor)
56. High Sierra (9/4/42; Bruce Cabot)
57. A Star Is Born (9/11/42; Ralph Bellamy)
58. Underground (9/18/42; Claude Rains)
59. Crime Without Passion [based on the story by Ben Hecht] (9/25/42; Orson Welles)
60. Ball of Fire (10/2/42; Dorothy Lamour)
61. They All Kissed the Bride (10/9/42; Paulette Goddard)
62. The Hitch-Hiker (10/15/42; Orson Welles)
63. His Girl Friday (10/23/42; Paulette Goddard)
64. Meet John Doe (10/30/42; Melvyn Douglas)
65. Rebecca (11/6/42; Herbert Marshall)
66. The Pied Piper (11/13/42; Monty Woolley)
67. Nothing Sacred (11/20/42; Melvyn Douglas)
68. To Be or Not to Be (11/27/42; Milton Berle and Ann Rutherford)
69. This Above All (12/4/42; Joan Fontaine)
70. Crime and Punishment (12/11/42; Peter Lorre)
71. Intermezzo (12/18/42; E. Bergner)

72. Love Affair (12/25/42; Diana Barrymore)
73. Penny Serenade (1/1/43; Madeline Carroll)
74. Fifth Avenue Girl (1/8/43; Virginia Bruce)
75. Private Worlds (1/15/43; Anita Louise)
76. Mr. and Mrs. Smith (1/22/43; Virginia Buce)
77. The Glass Key (1/29/43; George Raft)
78. The Immortal Sergeant (2/5/43; Henry Fonda)
79. Bedtime Story (2/12/43; Madeline Carroll)
80. George Washington Slept Here (2/19/43; Phil Baker)
81. Life Begins at 8:30 (2/26/43; Monty Woolley)
82. Proof Through the Night (3/5/43; Jane Cowl)
83. All This and Heaven Too (3/12/43; Madeline Carroll)
84. The Crystal Ball (3/19/43; Susan Hayward)
85. In Which We Serve (4/2/43; Sir Cedric Hardwicke)
86. I Married a Witch (4/9/43; Ray Milland)
87. Shop Around the Corner (4/16/43; Madeline Carroll)
88. Tin Pan Alley (4/23/43; Dick Powell)
89. The Rage of Paris (4/30/43; Annabella)
90. I Married an Angel (5/7/43; Zorina)
91. Roberta (5/14/43; Mary Martin)
92. The Thirty-Nine Steps (5/21/43; Madeline Carroll)
93. Tom, Dick, and Harry (5/28/43; Paulette Goddard)
94. The Gay Divorce (6/4/43; Mary Martin)
95. You Belong to Me (6/11/43; Paulette Goddard)
96. Kiss the Boys Good-Bye (6/18/43; Mary Martin)
97. This Thing Called Love (6/25/43; Elisa Landi and Ray Milland)
98. The Meanest Man in the World (7/2/43; Maureen O'Sullivan and Roland Young)
99. The Fleet's In (7/9/43; Betty Hutton and Jerome Lester)
100. Hello Frisco, Hello (7/16/43; Dorothy Lamour)
101. Too Many Husbands (7/23/43; Carole Landis)
102. Now Voyager (7/30/43; Madeline Carroll)
103. Anything Goes (8/6/43; Betty Hutton)
104. The Palm Beach Story [based on the Damon Runyon short story] (8/13/43; Joan Blondell)
105. Love Crazy (8/20/43; Carole Landis)
106. The Hard Way (8/27/43; Gene Tierney)
107. Casablanca (9/3/43; Raymond Massey)
108. Make Way for Tomorrow (9/10/43; Jean Hersholt)
109. The Philadelphia Story (9/17/43; Miriam Hopkins)
110. The Fallen Sparrow (9/24/43; John Garfield)
111. Talk of the Town (10/1/43; Lana Turner)
112. The Lady Is Waiting (10/8/43; Ann Sothern)
113. Suspicion (10/15/43; Madeline Carroll)
114. Hold Back the Dawn (10/22/43; Jean Pierre Aumont and Wendy Barrie)
115. Alibi Ike (10/29/43; Bert Lahr)
116. First Comes Courage (11/5/43; Madeline Carroll)
117. Shadow of a Doubt (11/12/43; Orson Welles)
118. The More the Merrier (11/19/43; Rita Hayworth)
119. There's Always a Woman (11/26/43; Joan Blondell)
120. Journey Into Fear (12/3/43; Brian Aherne)
121. In Old Chicago (12/10/43; Ginny Simms)
122. Wake Island (12/17/43; Brian Donlevy)
123. Joan of Paris (12/24/43; Michele Morgan)
124. Remember the Night (12/31/43; Richard Arlen and Wendy Barrie)
125. Christmas in July (1/7/44; Dick Powell)

126. Light That Failed (1/14/44; Brian Aherne)
127. Manpower (1/21/44; Marlene Dietrich)
128. Magnificent Obsession (1/28/44; Joan Fontaine)
129. My Sister Eileen (2/4/44; Lucille Ball)
130. Here Comes Mr. Jordan (2/11/44; Franchot Tone)
131. The Lodger (2/18/44; Wendy Barrie and Laird Cregar)
132. The Silver Frame (11/5/48; Burt Lancaster)
133. Angel Face (11/12/48; Lucille Ball)
134. Postage Due (11/19/48; Rosalind Russell)
135. Murder Plot (11/26/48; Jeanette Nolan)
136. Harry King's Ransom (12/3/48; Robert Young)
137. Deadly Is the Diamond (12/10/48; June Havoc)
138. Cat and Mouse (12/17/48; Dennis O'Keefe)
139. The One Millionth Joe (12/24/48; Michael O'Shea)
140. Widow in Name Only (12/31/48; Herbert Marshall)
141. First Act of Murder (1/7/49; John Lund)
142. The Man Who Dreamed of Murder (1/14/49; Paul Henried)
143. The Search for Isabel (1/21/49; Eddie Bracken)
144. Going Down, Please (1/28/49; Donald O'Connor)
145. The Dead Never Cry (2/4/49; Claire Trevor)
146. Time Table (2/11/49; Gene Kelly)
147. The Painted Limerick (2/18/49; Celeste Holm)
148. Leona's Room (2/25/49; Vincent Price)
149. The Well (3/4/49; Dan Dailey)
150. Lady from the Sea (3/11/49; Marlene Dietrich)
151. Letter of Condolence (3/18/49; Harold Peary)
152. Banquo's Chair (3/25/49; Claude Rains)
153. Apology (4/1/49; Elliott Lewis)
154. Run Away from Murder (4/8/49; Donald O'Connor)
155. Night Man (4/15/49; Ida Lupino)
156. August Heat (4/22/49; Ronald Colman)
157. The Diary of Saphronia Winters (4/29/49; Agnes Moorehead)
158. Murder Needs an Artist (5/6/49; Vincent Price)
159. Four Hours to Kill (5/13/49; Howard Duff)
160. Copper Turns Green (5/20/49; Chester Morris)
161. Spoils for Victor (5/27/49)
162. Lady Killer (6/3/49; Cathy Lewis)
163. Drop Dead (6/10/49)
164. The Expert (6/17/49)
165. Into the Mist (6/24/49)
166. Texas Killing (7/1/49; Elliott Lewis)
167. Babe Lincoln (7/8/49; June Havoc)
168. Open the Door for Murder (7/15/49)
169. The Third Grace (7/22/49)
170. The Iron Man (7/29/49)
171. The Heiress (3/15/51; Richard Carlson)
172. Long Love (3/22/51; Van Johnson)
173. Waterloo Bridge (3/29/51; Douglas Fairbanks, Jr.)
174. Blind Alley (4/5/51; Edmund O'Brien)
175. The Governor (4/12/51; Walter Abel and Martha Scott)
176. Homecoming (4/19/51; Chester Morris)
177. No Sad Songs for Me (4/26/51; Maureen Sullivan)
178. Uncle Harry (5/3/51; Lucille Watson)
179. Accused (5/10/51; Joan Bennett)
180. Take a Letter Darling (5/17/51; Rosaling Russell)
181. Crime Without Passion (5/24/51; Joseph Schildkraut)
182. Black Chiffon (5/31/51; Lillian Gish)
183. Springtime for Henry (6/7/51; Edward Everett Horton)
184. True Confession (6/14/51; Rosalind Russell)
185. Payment Deferred (6/21/51; Hume Cronyn and Jessica Tandy)
186. Double Indemnity (6/28/51; Gloria Swanson)
187. Bachelor Mother (7/5/51; Paulette Goddard)
188. Front Page (7/12/51; Lee Tracy)

189. Night Must Fall (7/19/51; Dan Duryea)
190. No Time for Comedy (7/26/51; Rosalind Russell)
191. A Double Life (8/2/51; Douglas Fairbanks, Jr.)
192. The Petrified Forest (8/9/51; Wendell Corey)

193. Ball of Fire (8/16/51; Franchot Tone)
194. An Inspector Calls (8/23/51; Vanessa Brown)
195. Accent on Youth (8/30/51; Joan Caulfield)
196. Ladies of the Jury (9/6/51; Lucille Watson)

Philip Morris Playhouse on Broadway

Previously entitled *Philip Morris Playhouse*, this Hollywood-based program continued presenting dramas, of both stage and screen, with top stars in the lead roles. Alexander Semmler and Ray Bloch were now supplying the music for the series. Elizabeth Lawrence was announcer. At first broadcast over NBC, Tuesday evenings from 10:30 to 11 pm, EST, beginning January 13, 1952, it was heard over CBS, Sunday evening 10–10:30 pm, EST. Beginning December 3, 1951, CBS moved the program to Wednesdays from 8:30 to 9 pm, EST.

1. The Great McGinty (9/11/51; Paul Douglas)
2. The Amazing Dr. Clitterhouse (9/18/51; Lew Ayres)
3. Brief Encounter (9/25/51; David Niven)
4. Angel Street (10/2/51; Joseph Cotten)
5. September Affair (10/9/51; Joan Fontaine)
6. Champion (10/16/51; Dennis O'Keefe)
7. This Thing Called Love (10/23/51; Rosalind Russell)
8. A Star Is Born (10/30/51; Douglas Fairbanks, Jr.)
9. Shop Around the Corner (11/6/51; Richard Greene)
10. I'll Be Seeing You (11/13/51; Nina Foch)
11. We Are Not Alone (11/20/51; Rex Harrison)
12. Remember the Day (11/27/51; Rosalind Russell)
13. The Killers (12/4/51; Chester Morris)
14. Philomel Cottage (12/11/51; Madeline Carroll)
15. Little Foxes (12/18/51; Noel Mast)
16. David's Star of Bethlehem (12/25/51; Loretta Young)
17. Stage Door (1/1/52; Adolph Menjou)
18. Talk of the Town (1/13/52; Ronald Colman)
19. 711 Ocean Drive (1/20/52; Edmund O'Brien)
20. Princess O'Rourke (1/27/52; June Allyson)
21. Seventh Veil (2/3/52; David Niven)
22. Journey Into Nowhere (2/10/52; Boris Karloff)
23. [Contest Winners — No Drama] (2/17/52)
24. One Saturday Afternoon (2/24/52; Hume Cronyn)
25. Criminal Code (3/2/52; Dane Clark)
26. Vivacious Lady (3/9/52; Barbara Stanwyck)
27. In a Lonely Place (3/16/52; Joseph Cotten)
28. Sullivan's Travels (3/23/52; Ray Milland)
29. Take One False Step (3/30/52)
30. Room Beyond (4/6/52; Nina Foch)
31. Giaconda Smile (4/13/52; Rex Harrison)
32. Each Dawn I Die (4/20/52; Chester Morris)

33. Romantic Years (4/27/52; Paulette Goddard)
34. Dark Victory (5/4/52; Lew Ayres)
35. Nightmare (5/11/52; Dane Clark)
36. I Married an Angel (5/18/52; Patricia Morrison)
37. Rebecca (5/25/52; Melvyn Douglas)
38. Outward Bound (6/1/52; Boris Karloff)
39. Murder Without Crime (6/8/52; Vincent Price)
40. The Will (6/15/52; R. Comstock and Joyce Rogers)
41. The Professor Gambles (6/22/52; Arlene Dahl)
42. Kitty Doone (6/29/52; Miriam Hopkins)
43. Killer at Large (7/6/52; Dane Clark)
44. We Strangers (7/13/52; Peter Lorre)
45. Holiday (7/20/52; Jeffrey Lynn)
46. The Whole Town's Talking (7/27/52; Janet Garner and Janet Paige)
47. My Dear Relatives (8/3/52; Jack Carter)
48. Temptation (8/10/52; Wanda Hendrix)
49. Petticoat Fever (8/17/52; Melvyn Douglas)
50. Crime and Punishment (8/24/52; Charlton Heston)
51. Professor Gambles (8/31/52; Arlene Dahl)
52. Too Many Husbands (9/7/52; Eve Arden)
53. The Silver Cord (9/14/52; Lucille Watson)
54. The Jewelry Robbery (9/21/52; Constance Bennett)
55. Lady and the Murderer (9/28/52; Jerome Cowan and Rosaland Russell)
56. The Letter (10/5/52; Marlene Dietrich)
57. Broken Dishes (10/12/52; Veronica Lake)
58. Guest in the House (10/19/52; Nina Foch)
59. My Man Godfrey (10/26/52; Arthur Treacher)
60. Sunset Boulevard (11/2/52; Miriam Hopkins)
61. Butter and Egg Man (11/9/52; Eddie Bracken)
62. The Big Clock (11/16/52; Wendell Corey)
63. Standing Room Only (11/23/52; Paulette Goddard)
64. Practically Yours (11/30/52; Gloria De Haven)
65. Suddenly It's Spring (12/3/52; Sally Forrest and Jeffrey Lynn)
66. Man Against Town (12/10/52; Boris Karloff)
67. Manhattan Serenade (12/17/52; Joan Fontaine)
68. David's Star of Bethlehem (12/24/52; Nina Foch)
69. Palm Beach Story (12/31/52; Paulette Goddard)
70. Detective Story (1/7/53; Van Johnson)
71. Hold Back the Dawn (1/14/53; Joseph Cotten)
72. Candle Light (1/21/53; Charles Calvet)
73. Big Ride (1/28/53; Glenn Ford)
74. The Two Mrs. Carrolls (2/4/53; James Mason)
75. Man's Weakness (2/11/53; MacDonald Carey)
76. Wednesday's Child (2/18/53; Madeline Carroll)
77. His Brother's Keeper (2/25/53; Franchot Tone)
78. Plan for Escape (3/4/53; Nina Foch)
79. Thelma Jordan (3/11/53; Marlene Dietrich)
80. Appointment with Danger (3/18/53; Zachary Scott)
81. Mr. Barry's Etchings (3/25/53; Charles Colburn)
82. Miss Tatlock's Millions (4/1/53; Eddie Bracken)
83. Thelma Jordon (4/8/53; Arlene Dahl)
84. Dead Past (4/15/53; Boris Karloff)
85. Make Me Happy, Make Me Sad (4/22/53; Richard Widmark)
86. Life Begins at 9:30 (4/29/53; Roland Young)
87. Her Cardboard Lover (5/6/53; Madeline Carroll)
88. The Turning Point (5/13/53; Dane Clark)
89. Miracle of Morgan's Creek (5/20/53; Janet Leigh)
90. Salty O'Rourke (5/27/53; John Lund)
91. No Man of Her Own (6/3/53; Arlene Dahl)

92. Hired Wife (6/10/53; Paulette Goddard)
93. Shop at Sly Corner (6/17/53; Boris Karloff)
94. Hail the Conquering Hero (6/24/53; Eddie Bracken)
95. The Web (7/1/53; Jeff Chandler)
96. The Sacrifice (7/8/53; Franchot Tone)
97. Lost Weekend (7/15/53; Melvyn Douglas)
98. The Eleventh Juror (7/22/53; Ronald Reagan)
99. My Favorite Wife (7/29/53; Madeline Carroll)
100. Three Men on a Horse (8/5/53; Eddie Bracken)
101. The Lady Eve (8/12/53; Deborah Kerr)
102. The Night Has a Thousand Eyes (8/19/53; Peter Lorre)
103. Love Letters (8/26/53; Joseph Cotten)
104. Blind Alley (9/2/53; Van Heflin)

Phyl Coe *Radio Mysteries*

Syndicated mystery series, broadcast in 1932. Each episode ran fifteen minutes.

1. The Case of the Dead Musician
2. The Case of the Missing Masterpiece
3. The Mystery of the Death Ray Tube
4. The Murder in the Sky
5. Death Boards the Sea Serpent
6. The Double X Mystery
7. The Mystery of the Last Will and Testament
8. The Case of the Stolen Sables
9. Who Murdered Senator Floyd?
10. The Case of the Laughing Ghost
11. The Case of the Fallen Star
12. The Jagged Rock Mystery

Plays by Ear

This series, written by and occasionally starring Hector Chevigny, was a short-run summer replacement for *The Cavalcade of America*, broadcast over NBC, Monday evenings from 8 to 8:30 pm, EST.

1. Shower Thy Blessings (6/23/47)
2. Complex for Millions (6/30/47; Joseph Curtin)
3. Uncommon Stock (7/7/47)
3. Freedom and Weep (7/14/47)
4. Winter of Discontent (7/21/47)
5. Golden Wedding (7/28/47)
6. The Life and Works of President Pewter (8/4/47)
7. The Short Career of Dictator Jones (8/11/47)

Plays for Americans

One of many dramatic series written, produced and directed by Arch Oboler. Most of the dramas consisted of World War II propaganda, supporting troops overseas and filling the loved ones back home with hope. Various stars c Hollywood guested in the broadcasts, from Bette Davis to James Stewart "Chicago, Germany" presented a very scary view of what America would be lik if the Germans were to win the war.

Broadcast over NBC, Sunday afternoons from 4:30 to 5 pm, EST, the pro gram was eventually moved to 5:30.

1. Johnny Quinn, U.S.N. (2/1/42; Olivia deHavilland and Alfred Rider)
2. Paul Reverski (2/8/42; Tommy Cook)
3. Memo to Berchtesgaden (2/15/42; Raymond Massey)
4. Ghost Story (2/22/42; Elliott Lewis)
5. The Chinese Way (3/1/42; Alla Nazimova)
6. The Way to Go Home (3/8/42; Thomas Mitchell)
7. A Letter at Midnight (3/15/42; James Stewart)
8. Have You Seen Him? (3/22/42; Edna Best)
9. Hate (3/29/42; Conrad Veidt)
10. Miracle in 3-B (4/5/42; Rosemary de Camp)
11. Soliloquy with Death (4/12/42; Bette Davis)
12. Blood Story (4/19/42; Jean Hersholt and Dick Powell)
13. The Welburns — A Confidential Report (4/26/42; Elliott Lewis and Mercedes McCambridge)
14. The Last in the World (5/3/42; Burgess Meredith)
15. Execution (5/10/42; Elisabeth Bergner
16. Bomber to Tokyo (5/17/42; Ralph Bellamy and Robert Taylor)
17. Chicago, Germany (5/24/42; Joan Blondell)
18. Gangster in the House (5/31/42; Mercedes McCambridge)
19. Back Where You Came From (6/7/42; Claude Rains)
20. Adolf and Mrs. Runyon (6/21/42; Bette Davis)
21. Johnny Quinn, U.S.N. (7/5/42; Martha Scott)

Police Headquarters

Syndicated police dramas broadcast in 1932. Each episode ran fifteen min-utes over NBC; only thirty-nine were made.

1. The Rod Dugan Murder
2. The Laundry Truck Kidnapping
3. The Warehouse Job
4. The James Davis Murder
5. Antonio Moretti
6. Jake Miller Knifed
7. The $40,000 Payroll Shipment
8. The Helen Marsh Murder
9. The Tommy Wood Murder
10. The Life Insurance Scheme
11. The Wagner Hotel Murder
12. The Phony Payroll Check
13. The Silver Collection
14. The McKenzie Death
15. A Man Stealing Food
16. The Tommygun Murders
17. The Telephone Suicide
18. Boxing Match Death
19. The $80,000 Robbery
20. Infiltrating the Mob
21. The Andy Green Murder
22. Two Officers Disappear
23. The Mrs. North Robbery
24. The Mrs. Smallwood Murder
25. Dr. Thornton's Wife Disappears
26. A Small Girl Found Chained
27. The Williams Brothers
28. Jim Bradley, Jewel Thief
29. Dad Higgins Dies
30. John Fleming Confesses

1. The Bank Swindle
2. The Deadly Poker Game
3. Judge Carleton Missing
4. The William Spencer Murder
5. The High Flights Race

36. The $190,000 Money Transfer
37. A Body Stolen
38. Tommy Evans Is Run Down
39. A Mystery Writer Dies

The Private Files of Rex Saunders

A short-run summer detective series, this one starring Rex Harrison in the lead role. Supporting cast consisted of Alice Frost, Everett Sloane, Leon Janney, and Anne Seymour. The broadcasts originated from New York, NBC, Wednesday evenings from 8:30 to 9 pm. Directed by Himan Brown.

Audition: Game With Death (4/13/51)
1. The Lady with Hate in Her Heart (5/2/51)
2. A Shocking Still Life (5/9/51)
3. Done to Death (5/16/51)
4. The Game with Death (5/23/51)
5. Shallow Graves (5/30/51)
6. The Plan in the Killer's Mind (6/6/51)
7. A Trip to the Death House (6/13/51)
8. Murder Deep in a Killer's Mind

(6/20/51)
9. To Murder or Not to Murder (6/27/51)
10. A Masquerade (7/4/51)
11. Murder Is a Silent Companion (7/11/51)
12. Until Death Do Us Part (7/18/51)
13. Worth More Than Its Weight in Murder (7/25/51)
14. The Human Game (8/1/51)
15. Shakespeare (8/8/51)

Profiles in Crime

Much like *Gangbusters*, this documentary series presented dramas regarding organized racketeering. "The Garbage Man" presented the life and crime of Vincent Jimmy Squillante, while "The Man Who Ran New Jersey" documented in two broadcasts the life of Longie Zwillman. A three-part documentary on Lucky Luciano began on March 16, and a special three-part presentation on the Appalachian Underworld Gathering began at the end of April. Broadcast over WMCA in New York on Monday evenings at 10:35–11 pm, EST.

1. The Hood Who Runs Boxing (2/23/59)
2. The Garbage Man (3/2/59)
3. Gangland's Prime Minister: Frank Costello (3/9/59)
4. Lucky Luciano: What Makes Him Lucky? [part one of three] (3/16/59)
5. How Lucky Can You Get? [part two] (3/23/59)

6. The Man Hitler Got Out of Jail [part three] (3/30/59)
7. The Man Who Ran New Jersey [part one of two] (4/6/59)
8. The Death of an Invisible Man [part two] (4/13/59)
9. Vito Genovese: Gangland's Mr. Big (4/20/59)

10. Joseph Barbara, the Host at Appalachian (4/27/59)
11. Joe Barbara's Appalachian Barbecue (5/4/59)
12. Gangland's Summit Conference (5/11/59)
13. Meyer Lansky: International Gambling Prince (5/18/59)
14. Big John Ormento: Harlem's Narcotics King (5/25/59)
15. Joe Profaci: Big Man in Brooklyn (6/1/59)
16. Albert Ackalitis: Muscle on the Docks (6/8/59)
17. Gerry Catena: Jersey's Juke Box Prince [part one] (6/15/59)
18. Gerry Catena: Jersey's Juke Box Prince [part two] (6/22/59)
19. Mr. X: The Mysterious Millionaire (6/29/59)
20. Russell Bufalino: Gangland's Garment Industry Boss (7/6/59)
21. Mike Miranda: Tomorrow's Underworld Emperor (7/13/59)

The Prudential Family Hour of Stars

This series was originally *The Prudential Family Hour*, which was broadcast from 1941 to September 26, 1948, as a Sunday evening feature. The week after on October 3, the series underwent a title change, and offered dramas instead of music. Sponsored by the Prudential Insurance Company, *The Family Hour of Stars*, also known as *The Prudential Family Hour of Stars*, was broadcast on CBS every Sunday evening at 6 pm, EST. Because the series originated from Hollywood, a different movie star appeared on the program each week. The dramas were produced by Ken Burton and directed by Jack Johnstone, with the music supplied by Carmen Dragon. Truman Bradley was the first announcer, later replaced by Frank Goss. Supporting cast varied each week, and a few were Lurene Tuttle, Parley Baer, Herb Vigran, Joseph Kearns, Alan Reed, Jerry Hausner, Paul Frees, and Isabel Jewell.

The first half of the series presented original dramas or adaptations of short stories and novels, with almost the same handful of guests each week — Gregory Peck, Barbara Stanwyck, Humphrey Bogart, Ginger Rogers, Jane Wyman, and Ray Milland. In the summer of 1949, two slight changes occurred. Adaptations of previously released films were dramatized instead of original dramas or short stories, and the guest cast started growing, allowing a wider variety of Hollywood actors other than Stanwyck, Milland and Rogers to appear.

The episodes entitled "The Word" and "Big Ben" were written by Arch Oboler. Others who scripted were Walter Brown Newman, Douglas Heyes, Don Quinn, and Jean Holloway. Edward Arnold reprised his film role in an adaptation of Stephen Vincent Benét's "The Devil and Daniel Webster," as Arnold had done on many radio programs before. Episodes fifty-one and sixty-two were previously performed on *The Cavalcade of America*. Joseph Cotten starred in "Easter Bonnet," a special Easter episode broadcast on Easter Sunday.

1. John James, Vice President (10/3/48; Gregory Peck)
2. The Long Way Home (10/10/48; Robert Taylor)
3. Destination (10/17/48; Humphrey Bogart)
4. The Flowering Thorn (10/24/48; Barbara Stanwyck)
5. By-Line, Nellie Bly (10/31/48; Ginger Rogers)
6. The Deeper Shadow (11/7/48; Frank Lovejoy and Ray Milland)
7. Moonlight Sonata [based on the story by Alexander Woollcott] (11/14/48; Barbara Stanwyck)
8. The Secret Diary and Mistress Croft (11/21/48; Ginger Rogers)
9. Driven Snow (11/28/48; Gregory Peck)
10. The Mink Gloves (12/5/48; Humphrey Bogart)
11. Lady Alice and Dog Biscuit (12/12/48; Jane Wyman)
12. The Lullaby of Christmas (12/19/48; Gregory Peck)
13. Unfinished Business (12/26/48; Ray Milland)
14. Yesterday's Town (1/2/49; Jane Wyman)
15. Some Small Nobility (1/9/49; Barbara Stanwyck)
16. Joyful Bum (1/16/49; Ray Milland)
17. Post Mortem [based on the short story by Cornell Woolrich] (1/23/49; Burt Lancaster)
18. The Man on the Third Floor (1/30/49; Gregory Peck)
19. The Trouble with Luke Casper (2/6/49; Van Johnson)
20. Appointment in Springfield (2/13/49; Ginger Rogers)
21. Three Hours (2/20/49; Bette Davis and Ray Milland)
22. The Asking Price (2/27/49; Robert Taylor)
23. Impact (3/6/49; Gregory Peck)
24. Pink Peril (3/13/49; Victor Jory)
25. Fun with Dynamite (3/20/49; Ray Milland)
26. The Capture of Kitty Stone (3/27/49; Ginger Rogers)
27. Angel (4/3/49; Jane Wyman)
28. The Word (4/10/49; Bette Davis)
29. Easter Bonnet (4/17/49; Joseph Cotten)
30. The Love Tree (4/24/49; Victor Jory)
31. Storm and the Cypress (5/1/49; Barbara Stanwyck)
32. Big Ben (5/8/49; Bette Davis)
33. Break-down (5/15/49; James Cagney)
34. Ho, Ho, Ho for Emily (5/22/49; Ginger Rogers)
35. Luck Is a Lady (5/29/49; Ray Milland)
36. My Man Godfrey (6/5/49; John Lund)
37. Exit Linda (6/12/49; Ava Gardner)
38. Petticoat Fever (6/19/49; Richard Widmark)
39. Encore (6/26/49; Diana Lynn)
40. One Life to Lose (7/3/49; Kirk Douglas)
41. Dulcy (7/10/49; Celeste Holm)
42. I Give You Maggie (7/17/49; John Payne)
43. Rebecca [based on the novel by Daphne Du Maurier] (7/24/49; Audrey Totter)
44. To Mary, with Love (7/31/49; Herbert Marshall)
45. Hold Back the Dawn (8/7/49; Wanda Hendrix)
46. The Wookey (8/14/49; Heather Angel and Edmund Gwenn)
47. Penny Serenade (8/21/49; Joan Bennett)
48. The Firebrand (8/28/49; Victor Jory)
49. The Big Job (9/4/49; John Hodiak)
50. The Uninvited Guest (9/11/49; Wendell Corey)
51. The Devil and Daniel Webster [based on the story by Stephen Vincent Benét] (9/18/49; Edward Arnold)
52. Seventh Heaven (9/25/49; Jane Powell)
53. Love Affair (10/2/49; Irene Dunne)
54. Berkeley Square (10/9/49; Ronald Colman)
55. One Sunday Afternoon (10/16/49; Dana Andrews)
56. Mary of Scotland (10/23/49; Loretta Young)
57. Winterset (10/30/49; Kirk Douglas)
58. Quality Street (11/6/49; Ronald Colman and Maureen O'Sullivan)
59. My Favorite Wife (11/13/49; William Powell)
60. A Farewell to Arms (11/20/49; Jane Wyman)

61. The Barretts of Whimpole Street (11/27/49; Irene Dunne)
62. Yellow Jack (12/4/49; Dana Andrews)
63. Mrs. Moonlight (12/11/49; Loretta Young)
64. The Promise (12/18/49; Jane Wyman)
65. The Small One (12/25/49; Ronald Colman)
66. The Great Gatsby (1/1/50; Kirk Douglas)
67. Eliza (1/8/50; Irene Dunne)
68. George Washington Slept Here (1/15/50; Dana Andrews)
69. Ballerina (1/22/50; Diana Lynn)
70. The Short, Happy Life of Francis Macomber (1/29/50; James Stewart)
71. Night Must Fall (2/5/50; Kirk Douglas)
72. Skylark (2/12/50; Jane Wyman)
73. Mrs. Parkington (2/19/50; Irene Dunne)
74. Philadelphia Story (2/26/50; Gene Kelly)

Pulitzer Prize Plays

This summer series featured dramas that had won the Pulitzer Prize, from Jessie Lynch Williams' *Why Marry?* to Eugene O'Neill's *Anna Christie*. For episode three, Owen Davis, Jr., performed his father's great play *Icebound*. Broadcast on the Blue Network, Thursday evenings beginning at 10 pm, EST, and running for a full hour, the series moved to 9 pm beginning with episode six. The show was preempted on August 4, 1938, for a concert special. Chrystal Herne created *Craig's Wife* in 1925. In episode four, the play became such a success that it was later taken to a Broadway theater, where Frank Wilson played the role of Abraham on stage.

1. Craig's Wife (6/2/38; Chrystal Herne and Florence Malone)
2. Anna Christie [based on the play by Eugene O'Neill] (6/9/38; William Shelley and Barbara Weeks)
3. Icebound (6/16/38; Owen Davis, Jr.)
4. In Abraham's Bosom [based on the Paul Green play] (6/23/38; Juano Hernandez and Frank Wilson)
5. Why Marry? (6/30/38; Vivian Martin)
6. Both Your Houses [based on Maxwell Anderson's play] (7/7/38)
7. Men in White (7/14/38)
8. Alison House (7/21/38)
9. Beyond the Horizon [based on the play by Eugene O'Neil] (7/28/38; Margalo Gilmore, Earle Larimore, and James Meighan)
10. They Knew What They Wanted (8/11/38; Pauline Lord)
11. Strange Interlude [part one] [based on the play by Eugene O'Neill] (8/18/38)
12. Strange Interlude [part two] (8/25/38)

Quiet Please*

Wyllis Cooper, creator of the famed late-night horror program *Lights Out!* created this fantasy program filled with more imagination than most children

*Compiled by Chris Lembesis and Randy Eidemiller.

dream of. Ernest Chappell was the announcer and main protagonist who each week would converse with the audience and then relate his present-day circumstances. One week we found ourselves beside two human-looking aliens on an alien planet, looking up at the stars and wondering whether there was life — and love — on other planets. The week after, we found ourselves in an Egyptian tomb with two archeologists who find a miniature model of earth, learning what it really meant to have the whole earth in their hands.

Robin Hood and his Merry Men battled Hitler and his troops, a jealous wife fought a battle against a bed of killer lilies (her husband being the object of possession) and a time traveler found love not in the future, but in the past. The annual Christmas broadcast, "Berlin, 1945," dramatized a group of Army buddies who, eating a Christmas dinner amongst the rubble of war-torn Europe, received a visit from the Son of Man. Other episodes presented singing caterpillars from outer space, the ghost of a twelve-year old girl who sang and played the piano in the attic, and a giant invisible spider surfaced from a recently drilled oil well.

Cooper wrote all of the scripts, and the entire series originated from New York. The episodes were transcribed, however, since numerous episodes were broadcast in different parts of the country, on different days and times. The following is the broadcast log for the New York run.

The first four episodes were test run on Mutual, Sunday afternoons from 3:30 to 4 pm. Responses were good, so the program returned on July 20, 1947, for a prime-time run. The series alternated from Sunday, Wednesday, and, finally, Monday in February of 1948 from 9:30 to 10 pm. On September 19, 1948, *Quiet Please* moved to ABC, 5:30 to 6 pm. On May 21, 1949, ABC moved the program to Saturdays 9 to 9:30 pm. Shortly after *Quiet Please* left radio, Cooper arranged with ABC to broadcast the fantasy series on television, but it lasted only six broadcasts before going off the air permanently.

Audition: How Are You Pal? (5/22/47; Charme Allen and Vicki Vola)
1. Nothing Behind the Door (6/8/47; Martin Lawrence, Pat O'Malley, and James Van Dyke)
2. I've Been Looking for You (6/15/47; Claudia Morgan, Peggy Stanley, and Martin Wolfson)
3. We Were Here First (6/22/47; Walter Black, Nancy Douglas, and Kermit Murdock)
4. The Ticket Taker (6/29/47; Floyd Buckley, Lon Clark, Pat O'Malley, and Rock Rogers)
5. Cornelia (7/20/47; Walter Black, Anne Seymour, and Peggy Stanley)
6. I Remember Tomorrow (7/27/47; Frederick Bell, Frank Dane, and Kermit Murdock)
7. Inquest (8/3/47; Sylvia Cole, John Morley, Pat O'Malley, and James Van Dyke)
8. Bring Me to Life (8/10/47; Walter Black, Walter Bryan, and Helen Marcy)
9. A Mile High and a Mile Deep (8/17/47)
10. Mirror, Mirror on the Wall (8/24/47)
11. A Ribbon of Lincoln Green (8/31/47)
12. Retreat at Dunkerque (9/3/47)
13. Three Sides to a Story (9/8/47)
14. The Big Box (9/15/47)
15. Be a Good Dog, Darling (9/22/47)

16. The Low Road (9/29/47)
17. Not Enough Time (10/6/47; Donald Briggs, Catherine Meschel, and Nancy Sheridan)
18. Camera Obscura (10/13/47; Charita Bauer)
19. The Girl with the Flaxen Hair (10/20/47)
20. Don't Tell Me About Halloween (10/27/47; Charita Bauer, Jim Boles, and Peggy Stanley)
21. Take Me Out to the Graveyard (11/3/47; Donald Briggs, Evelyn Juster, and Edward Latimer)
22. Three (11/10/47; Vinton Hayworth, Kermit Murdock, Cameron Prud'homme, and Les Tremayne)
23. Kill Me Again (11/17/47; James Monks, Pat O'Malley, and Peggy Stanley)
24. In Memory of Bernadine (11/24/47; Melville Ruick and Nancy Sheridan)
25. Come In, Eddie (12/1/47; Arthur Cole and Les Tremayne)
26. Some People Don't Die (12/8/47; William Adams, Sid Cassell, Ted Osborne, and Anne Seymour)
27. Little Fellow (12/15/47; Lon Clark, Betty Garde, and Pat O'Malley)
28. Berlin, 1945 (12/22/47)
29. Rain on New Year's Eve (12/29/47; Muriel Kirkland and Pat O'Malley)
30. Little Visitor (1/5/48; Charme Allen, Audrey Christie, and Michael Odist)
31. The Room Where the Ghosts Lived (1/12/48; Claudia Morgan and James Van Dyke)
32. Baker's Dozen (1/19/48; Murray Forbes, Ed Latimer, Lotte Stavisky, and Harry Worth)
33. Green Light (1/26/48; Gus Gordon, William Huggins, and Anne Seymour)
34. The Pathetic Fallacy (2/2/48; Charita Bauer, Michael Fitzmaurice, and Vicki Vola)
35. A Red and White Guidon (2/9/48; Floyd Buckley, Arthur Cole, and Pat O'Malley)
36. Whence Came You (2/16/48; Don Briggs and Murray Forbes)
37. Wear the Dead Man's Coat (2/23/48; Edward Latimer, Martin Lawrence, and Leora Thatcher)

38. Sketch for a Screenplay (3/1/48; James Monks, Lotte Stavisky, and Frank Thomas, Jr.)
39. Never Send to Know (3/8/48; Nancy Sheridan and Edgar Stehli)
40. The Meeting at Ticonderoga (3/15/48)
41. A Night to Forget (3/22/48; Lon Clark, Polly Cole, Murray Forbes, James Monks, Kermit Murdock, and Jack Tyler)
42. Quiet Please (3/29/48)
43. I Always Marry Juliet (4/5/48; Margaret Draper, Abby Lewis, James Monks, and Anne Seymour)
44. Twelve to Five (4/12/48; Connie Duffin, Edward Latimer, Marry Lee Joel, Connie Lempke, and Jack Lescoulie)
45. Clarissa (4/19/48; Peggy Stanley and Bruno Wick)
46. Thirteen and Eight (4/26/48; Murray Forbes, Pat O'Malley, and Edward Ragge)
47. How Beautiful Upon the Mountain (5/3/48; Roy Irving)
48. There Are Shadows Here (5/10/48; Sidney Cassell, Edward Latimer, Alan Sparrow, and Frank Thomas, Jr.)
49. Gem of the Purest Ray (5/17/48; Charita Bauer, Martin Lawrence, and Edgar Stehli)
50. In the House Where I Was Born (5/24/48; Pat O'Malley, Betty Ragge, Cecil Roy, Lotte Stavisky)
51. Below Fifth Avenue (5/31/48)
52. One Hundred Thousand Diameters (6/7/48)
53. Not Responsible After Thirty Years (6/14/48; Court Benson, Pat O'Malley, and Nancy Sheridan)
54. Let the Lilies Consider (6/28/48; James Boles, Kathleen Cordell, and Peggy Stanley)
55. Vahine Tahiti (7/5/48; Charita Bauer, Roy Irving, Pat O'Malley, Charles Penman and Harriet Priestly)
56. As Long As I Live (7/19/48; Alice Reinhart, Lotte Stavisky, and Bruno Wick)
57. The Man Who Stole a Planet (7/26/48; Hilda Palmer and Phil Tonkin)

58. It Is Later Than You Think (8/2/48; Donald Briggs, Edward Latimer, and Abby Lewis)
59. The Thing on the Fourable Board (8/9/48; Pat O'Malley, Cecil Roy, and Daniel Sutter)
60. Presto Change-O, I'm Sure (8/16/48; Brad Barker, Edward Latimer, Peggy Stanley and Edgar Stehli)
61. Three Thousand Words (8/23/48; Donald Briggs, Lon Clark, Kathleen Naday, and Anne Seymour)
62. Motive (8/30/48)
63. The Third Man's Story (9/6/48; Lon Clark, Arthur Cole, and Alice Reinhart)
64. Symphony in D Minor (9/13/48; Charita Bauer, Pat O'Malley, and James Van Dyke)
65. Anonymous (9/19/48; Athena Lord, Peggy Stanley, and Daniel Sutter)
66. Light the Lamp for Me (9/26/48; Floyd Buckley, Kathleen Naday, and Pat O'Malley)
67. Meet John Smith, John (10/3/48; G. Swain Gordon and Nancy Sheridan)
68. Beezer's Cellar (10/10/48; Charles Eggleston, Lotte Stavisky, and Warren Stevens)
69. And Jeannie Dreams of Me (10/17/48; Sarah Fussell, Anna Morath, and Claudia Morgan)
70. Good Ghost (10/24/48; Arthur Cole, Murray Forbes, and Ruth Last)
71. Calling All Souls (10/31/48; Kermit Murdock, Mary Patton, and Ralph Scuman)
72. Adam and the Darkest Ray (11/7/48; William Adams and Kathleen Cordell)
73. The Evening and the Morning (11/14/48; Bess Johnson and Martin Lawrence)
74. One for the Book (11/21/48; Charles Eggleston, Melville Ruick, and Daniel Sutter)
75. My Son John (11/28/48; Kathleen Cordell and Warren Stevens)
76. Very Unimportant Person (12/5/48; James Monks, Nancy Sheridan, and Frank Thomas, Jr.)
77. Read Me This Riddle (12/12/48)
78. The Gothic Tale (12/19/48)
79. Berlin, 1945 (12/26/48; James Goss, Frank Latimer, James Monks, Melville Ruick, Warren Stevens, and Frank Thomas, Jr.)
80. The Time of the Big Snow (1/2/49; Sarah Fussell, Abby Lewis, Cecil Roy, and Vicki Vola)
81. Portrait of a Character (1/9/49; Charles Eggleston and Athena Lord)
82. Is This Murder? (1/16/49; Joyce Gordon and Dan O'Herlihy)
83. Summer Good-Bye (1/23/49; Kathleen Cordell)
84. Northern Lights (1/30/49; Cecil Roy and Daniel Sutter)
85. Tap the Heat, Bogdan (2/6/49; Carl Emory, Pat O'Malley, and Lotte Stavisky)
86. Valentine (2/13/49; Jack Arthur, Anne Seymour, and Leona Thatcher)
87. Where Do You Get Your Ideas? (2/20/49)
88. If I Should Wake Before I Die (2/27/49; Donald Briggs)
89. The Man Who Knew Everything (3/6/49; Arthur Cole, James Goss, and Jean McBride)
90. Dark Rosaleen (3/13/49; Charita Bauer, Mark Forbes, Edward Latimer, and Leora Thatcher)
91. The Smell of High Wines (3/20/49; Walter Black, Murray Forbes, and Frank Thomas, Jr.)
92. A Time to Be Born and a Time to Die (3/27/49; Helen Choate, Joyce Gordon, Athena Lord, and Edgar Stehli)
93. The Venetian Blind Man (4/3/49)
94. Dialogue for a Tragedy (4/10/49; Kathleen Cordell, John Seymour, and Ellen Sparrow)
95. Shadow of the Wings (4/17/49; Cecil Roy)
96. The Vale of Glencoe (4/24/49; Helen Choate and Pat O'Malley)
97. Dark Gray Magic (5/1/49; Polly Cole and James Monks)
98. The Other Side of the Stars (5/8/49; Mark Forbes and Jane White)

99. The Little Morning (5/15/49; Merrill Joles and Betty Ragge)
100. The Oldest Man in the World (5/21/49; Donald Briggs and Nancy Sheridan)
101. In the House Where I Was Born (5/28/49; Pat O'Malley, Betty Ragge, Cecil Roy, Lotte Stavisky)
102. Tanglefoot (6/4/49; Jack Lescoulie)
103. The Hat, the Bed, and John J. Catherine (6/11/49; Nancy Sheridan)
104. Pavane (6/18/49; Donald Briggs, Joan Laser, and Anne Seymour)
105. Quiet Please (6/25/49; Vinton Hayworth, Claudia Morgan, and Lotte Stavisky)

Radio City Playhouse

Directed and narrated by Harry W. Junkin, this anthology series featured originals tales as well as adaptations from America's top writers such as Ray Bradbury, John Galsworthy, Cornell Woolrich, and Stephen Vincent Benét. Broadcast on NBC, the stories — most of them at least — dealt with life or death situations. Some of the scripts originated from *The Whistler*, *Suspense*, and *Author's Playhouse*. Richard P. McDonough was the production supervisor. Fred Collins and Bob Warren shared announcing duties. The first three episodes were broadcast on Saturday evening at 10 pm EST, and was broadcast at 10:30 pm beginning with episode four. Episodes eight, nine and ten were broadcast on Monday evenings at 10:30 pm. Episodes eleven, twelve, and thirteen were broadcast on Saturday evening at 8 pm. Episodes fourteen through fifty-four were broadcast on Monday at 10:30 pm. The series finally settled on Sunday at 5 pm beginning with episode fifty-five, and staying at this time slot until the final broadcast.

The premiere broadcast, "Long Distance," concerned a woman attempting to contact authorities by phone regarding new evidence that would save her husband from death row. "Portrait of Lenore" was inspired by the movie *Laura*.

1. Long Distance (7/3/48; Jan Miner)
2. Ground Floor Window (7/10/48)
3. Of Unsound Mind (7/17/48; Casey Allen, Phil Sterling, and Jean Tatum)
4. Whistle, Daughter, Whistle (7/31/48)
5. Special Delivery (8/7/48)
6. Hit and Run (8/14/48; Casey Allen, Fran Carlon, Lon Clark, and Donald Hastings)
7. Fanny (8/21/48)
8. Long Distance (8/23/48)
9. Betrayal (8/30/48)
10. King of the Moon (9/6/48)
11. Mother (9/11/48)
12. Soundless (9/18/48)
13. Dark Hour (9/25/48)
14. The Promise (11/8/48)
15. The First and the Last (11/15/48)
16. The Door (11/22/48)
17. Temporarily Purple (11/29/48)
18. Five Extra Nooses (12/6/48)
19. Heritage of Wimpole Street (12/13/48)
20. The Three Men (12/20/48)
21. Strange Identity (12/27/48)
22. A Matter of Life and Death (1/3/49)
23. Correction [based on the story by C.L. Hutching] (1/10/49)
24. Portrait of Lenore (1/17/49; Bernard Grant and Jan Miner)

Radio Guild

This is probably one of the earliest known radio programs to present quality dramas stage plays and originals to the radio audience. Radio was still in its infancy during the early thirties, but the Blue Network decided to give it the go-ahead, resulting in a highly successful dramatic series that remained on the air for nine years. The program remained sustaining through the entire run.

Dramas of every kind were presented, from adaptations of Shakespeare plays to Rudyard Kipling stories. John Galsworthy's "Justice" and Maeterlinck's "The Bluebird" were performed more than once. From June 4, 1937, to July of

1937, *Radio Guild* presented a string of comedies. In November of 1935, a string of royal tragedies were presented, lasting three months. The broadcast of June 3, 1938, featured Shakespeare's *Cymbeline*, with the fifth act rewritten by George Bernard Shaw. No drama was presented for the broadcast of December 24, 1938. Instead, Maude Adams guested in what was nine numbers of carols and verses. By 1939, original dramas were being written for the series, along with adaptations of popular dramas and stories.

The series premiered Wednesday afternoons 4–5 pm, EST. Episode 47 was 4–4:55 pm. Beginning with episode 48, the series was broadcast Fridays, 4–5 pm. Episodes 71 and 72 were 4:15 to 5:15 on Fridays. Episode 73 was 4:30 to 5:15 pm. Beginning with episode 74, the airtime was 4:15 to 5:15 pm, still on Friday; beginning with 87, 4:30 to 5:15 pm; beginning with episode 93, 4:15 to 5:15 pm. Beginning with episode 45, the show was broadcast 4 to 5 pm, Mondays; episodes 194 and 195 were 4:15 to 5:15 pm; beginning with episode 196, 3–4 pm, Mondays, EST. Beginning April 29, 1935, *Radio Guild* was heard 4:30–5:30 pm; beginning October 9, 1936, 3:30–4:30 pm. On November 6, 1936, the show moved to Friday 4–5 pm, and Thursday as of 9/26/35. Beginning April 23, 1937, *Radio Guild* went back to its old time-slot, 3–4 pm. On July 9, 1938, *Radio Guild* went to a new thirty-minute format, beginning 8:30 pm. Beginning September 1, 1938, it was broadcast 8–9 pm. The broadcast of October 6, 1938, was 8:30–9 pm. Beginning October 13, 1938, *Radio Guild* was broadcast 8–8:30 pm; beginning November 5, 1938, 8:30–9 pm. On March 26, 1939, the program moved to Sunday evenings at 7:30–8 pm; beginning September 17, 1939, 7–8 pm. On November 1, 1939, *Radio Guild* moved to Wednesday, 9 pm. On January 27, 1940, the program moved to Saturday, 8:30–9 pm; beginning June 29, 1940, 8–8:30 pm. And beginning August 24, 1940, *Radio Guild* was broadcast 9:30–10 pm, and there it remained until the end of the run. [Exceptions to the above broadcast schedules can be found throughout the log.]

1. Romeo and Juliet (11/6/29)
2. The Tragedy of Love (11/13/29)
3. Milestones (11/20/29)
4. The Doll's House (11/27/29)
5. An Ideal Husband (12/4/29)
6. Easter (12/11/29)
7. The Ship (12/18/29)
8. Prunella (12/25/29)
9. Captain Applejack (1/1/30)
10. The Lady from the Sea (1/8/30)
11. As You Like It (1/15/30)
12. Lucky Sam McCarver (1/22/30)
13. The Love Match (1/29/30)
14. The Climbers (2/5/30)
15. Rollo's Wild Oats (2/12/30)
16. The Ship (2/19/30)
17. The Romantic Age (2/26/30)
18. -----(3/5/30)
19. The Sunken Bell (3/12/30)
20. King Argimenes and the Unknown Warrior (3/26/30)
21. The Melting Pot (4/2/30)
22. Monna Vanna (4/9/30)
23. My Lady's Dress (4/16/30)
24. Mrs. Dane's Defense (4/23/30)
25. Dulcy (4/30/30)
26. The Dover Road (5/7/30)
27. The Girl with the Green Eyes (5/14/30)
28. The Mollusk (5/21/30)
29. The Vicar of Wakefeld (5/28/30)
30. The Romantic Young Lady (6/11/30)
31. A Successful Calamity (7/2/30)
32. Tartuffe (7/9/30)

33. Mr. Pim Passes By (7/23/30)
34. The Sea Woman's Cloak (7/30/30)
35. She Stoops to Conquer (8/6/30)
36. Michael and His Lost Angel (8/13/30)
37. Beau Brummel (8/27/30)
38. The Witching Hour (9/3/30)
39. Captain Applejack (9/10/30)
40. The Magical City [broadcast from 3:40 to 4:30 pm] (9/17/30)
41. The Romantic Age (9/24/30)
42. King Argimenes and the Unknown Warrior / Le Tartuffe [broadcast 4:15–5 pm] (10/1/30)
43. Redemption (10/8/30)
44. Magic (10/15/30)
45. The Truth [part one] (10/29/30)
46. The Truth [part two] (11/5/30)
47. Iphigenia in Aulis (11/14/30)
48. Julius Caesar (11/21/30)
49. Peer Gynt (11/28/30)
50. The Green Goddess (12/5/30)
51. The Doll's House (12/12/30; Dudley Digges and Eva Le Gallienne)
52. Milestones (12/19/30)
53. Servant in the House (12/26/30; Charles Rann Kennedy)
54. The Melting Pot (1/2/31)
55. The Second Mrs. Tanqueray (1/9/31)
56. Romeo and Juliet (1/16/31; Eva Le Gallienne and Rollo Peters)
57. Beau Brummel (1/23/31)
58. The Merchant of Venice (1/30/31)
59. Redemption (2/6/31; Florence Malone)
60. Jane Clegg (2/13/31; Ernest Cossort and Margaret Wycherley)
61. The Importance of Being Ernest (2/20/31)
62. The Romantic Age (2/27/31)
63. Paola and Francesca (3/6/31)
64. Lady Windermere's Fan (3/13/31; Margaret Anglin)
65. Hamlet [part one] (3/20/31; Florence Malone and William S. Rainey)
66. Hamlet [part two] (3/27/31; Florence Malone and William S. Rainey)
67. The Terrible Meek (4/3/31)
68. Mrs. Pim Passes By (4/10/31)
69. Macbeth (4/17/31; Florence Malone and Charles Webster)

70. Will Shakespeare (4/24/31; Florence Malone and William S. Rainey)
71. The School for Scandal (5/1/31)
72. Peter Ibbetson (5/8/31)
73. The Girl with the Green Eyes (5/15/31; Blythe Daly)
74. Mary, Mary, Quite Contrary (5/22/31)
75. The Ship (5/29/31)
76. A Successful Calamity (6/5/31)
77. The Lady from the Sea (6/12/31)
78. Captain Applejack (6/19/31)
79. The Swan (6/26/31)
80. Dulcy (7/3/31)
81. The Queen's Husband (7/10/31)
82. The Famous Mrs. Fair (7/17/31)
83. Mrs. Dane's Defense (7/24/31)
84. The Dover Road (7/31/31)
85. Beverly's Balance (8/7/31)
86. The Great Adventure (8/14/31)
87. The Magical City (9/4/31)
88. Rollo's Wild Oats (9/11/31)
89. The Show-Off (9/18/31)
90. Beau Brummel (9/25/31)
91. Craig's Wife (10/2/31)
92. Agamemnon (10/9/31)
93. Faustus (10/16/31)
94. A Midsummer Night's Dream (10/23/31)
95. Julius Caesar (10/30/31)
96. Hamlet [part one] (11/6/31)
97. Hamlet [part two] (11/13/31)
98. The Merchant of Venice (11/20/31)
99. Le Bourgeois Gentilhomme (11/27/31)
100. She Stoops to Conquer (12/4/31)
101. A School for Scandal (12/11/31)
102. The Rivals (12/18/31)
103. The Servant of the House (12/25/31)
104. The Importance of Being Ernest (1/1/32)
105. Peer Gynt (1/8/32)
106. Redemption (1/15/32)
107. Dear Brutus (1/22/32)
108. Prunella (1/29/32)
109. Milestones (2/5/32)
110. Paolo and Francesca (2/12/32)
111. The Second Mrs. Tanqueray (2/19/32)
112. King Argimenes and the Unknown Warrior / The Queen's Enemies / The Lost Silk Hat [three short dramas] (2/26/32)

113. Cyrano de Bergerac (3/4/32)
114. The Dover Road (3/11/32)
115. The Great Divide (3/18/32)
116. The Terrible Meek [broadcast 3–4 pm] (3/25/32; C.R. Kennedy and Edith Wynne Matthison)
117. The Truth (4/1/32)
118. The Doll's House (4/8/32)
119. The Melting Pot (4/15/32)
120. The Jest (4/22/32)
121. Beggar on Horseback (4/29/32)
122. Camille (5/6/32)
123. Richelieu (5/13/32)
124. Arrah-Na-Pogue (5/20/32)
125. David Garrick (5/27/32)
126. Rip Van Winkle (6/3/32)
127. London Assurance (6/10/32)
128. Uncle Tom's Cabin (6/17/32)
129. Don Caesar de Bazan (6/24/32)
130. Caste (7/1/32)
131. The Corsican Brothers (7/8/32)
132. Lady of Lyons (7/15/32)
133. The Colleen Bawn (7/22/32)
134. The Bells (7/29/32)
135. A Scrap of Paper (8/5/32)
136. The Hunchback of Notre Dame (8/12/32)
137. Cricket of the Hearth (8/19/32)
138. Kathleen Mavourneen (8/26/32)
139. Frou Frou (9/2/32)
140. Dr. Jekyll and Mr. Hyde (9/9/32)
141. The Count of Monte Cristo (9/16/32)
142. The Inspector General (9/23/32)
143. A Doctor in Spite of Himself (9/30/32)
144. Redemption (10/7/32)
145. Antigone (10/10/32)
146. Faustus (10/17/32)
147. Coriolanus (10/24/32)
148. Romeo and Juliet (10/31/32)
149. Henry V (11/7/32)
150. As You Like It (11/14/32)
151. Richard III (11/21/32)
152. Le Tartuffe [based on the play by Moliere] (11/28/32)
153. The School for Scandal (12/5/32)
154. Lady Windermere's Fan (12/12/32)
155. L'Arlesienne (12/19/32)
156. The Passing of the Third Floor Back (12/26/32)
157. The Doll's House (1/2/33)
158. Trelawny of the Wells (1/9/33)
159. Michael and His Lost Angel (1/16/33)
160. L'Aigion (1/23/33)
161. Peter Ibbetson (1/16/33)
162. Sherwood (2/6/33)
163. The Climbers (2/13/33)
164. The Romantic Age (2/20/33)
165. John Ferguson (2/27/33)
166. The Great Divide (3/6/33)
167. The Melting Pot (3/13/33)
168. The Admirable Crichton (3/20/33)
169. The Blue Bird (3/27/33)
170. The Witching Hour (4/3/33)
171. Clarence (4/10/33)
172. Prunella (4/17/33)
173. Will Shakespeare (4/24/33)
174. Engaged (5/1/33)
175. The Bells (5/8/33)
176. Ignomar (5/15/33)
177. Rich Elieu (5/22/33)
178. Tragedy of Love (5/29/33)
179. Ruy Blas (6/5/33)
180. Camille (6/12/33)
181. Rip Van Winkle (6/19/33)
182. Fachon the Cricket (6/26/33)
183. David Garrick (7/3/33)
184. Kathleen Mavourneen (7/10/33)
185. A Scrap of Paper (7/17/33)
186. Cyrano de Bergerac (7/24/33)
187. Silas Marner (7/31/33)
188. Cricket of the Hearth (8/7/33)
189. Lady from the Sea (8/14/33)
190. The Importance of Being Ernest (8/21/33)
191. The Iron Master (9/11/33)
192. Dr. Jekyll and Mr. Hyde (9/18/33)
193. Hedda Gabler [based on the play by Ibsen] (9/25/33)
194. She Stoops to Conquer (10/9/33)
195. Julius Caesar (10/16/33)
196. The Wild Duck (10/23/33)
197. The Scarecrow (10/30/33)
198. The Sunken Bell (11/6/33)
199. Mrs. Moonlight (11/13/33)
200. The White-Headed Boy (11/20/33)
201. R.U.R. [based on the Capek story] (11/27/33)
202. The Passing of the Third Floor Back (12/4/33)
203. The Whole Town's Talking (12/11/33)
204. Once in a Lifetime (12/18/33)
205. A Kiss for Cinderella (1/1/34)
206. Saturday's Children (1/8/34)
207. The Creaking Chair (1/15/34)

208. Justice (1/22/34)
209. John Ferguson (1/29/34)
210. A Bill of Divorcement (2/5/34)
211. If Booth Had Missed (2/12/34)
212. Loyalties (2/19/34)
213. The Romantic Young (2/26/34)
214. The Swan (3/5/34)
215. The Blue Bird (3/12/34)
216. The Mollusk (3/19/34)
217. Old Man Minick (3/26/34)
218. Captain Applejack (4/2/34)
219. Dear Brutus (4/9/34)
220. Enter Madame (4/16/34)
221. The Tempest [based on the play by William Shakespeare] (4/23/34)
222. Rose of the Ranches (4/30/34)
223. The Romantic Age (5/7/34)
224. L'Arlesienne (5/14/34)
225. Rip Van Winkle (5/21/34)
226. The Count of Monte Cristo [based on the novel by Alexander Dumas] (5/28/34)
227. The Fortune Hunter (6/4/34)
228. Frou Frou (6/11/34)
229. Camille (6/18/34)
230. The Shopkeeper Turns Gentleman (6/25/34)
231. Ruy Blas (7/2/34)
232. An Ideal Husband (7/9/34)
233. The Man in the Iron Mask [based on the novel by Alexander Dumas] (7/16/34)
234. The Octoroon (7/23/34)
235. The Corsican Brothers (7/30/34)
236. The Rivals (8/6/34)
237. A Midsummer Night's Dream (8/13/34)
238. Ingomar (8/20/34)
239. Arrah-Na-Pogue [based on the Boucicault play] (8/27/34)
240. Thomas A. Beckett (9/10/34)
241. Othello (9/17/34)
242. David Garrick (9/24/34)
243. Our Boys (10/1/34)
244. Virginius (10/8/34)
245. Death Takes a Holiday (10/15/34)
246. The Young Mrs. Winthrop (10/22/34)
247. The Vinegar Tree (10/29/34)
248. The Young Mrs. Winthrop (11/5/34)
249. The Fantastic Battle (11/12/34)
250. Macbeth (11/19/34; Dame Sybil Thorndike and Charles Warburton)
251. Justice (11/26/34)
252. Virginius (12/3/34)
253. The Bells (12/10/34)
254. A Scrap of Paper (12/17/34)
255. The Passing of the Third Floor Back (12/24/34)
256. Twelfth Night [based on the Shakespeare play] (12/31/34)
257. Engaged (1/7/35)
258. The Corsican Brothers (1/14/35)
259. A Tale of Two Cities (1/21/35)
260. Dr. Faustus [based on the Marlowe play] (1/28/35)
261. Old Words to New Music [broadcast began 2:45 pm] (2/4/35)
262. When We Were Twenty-One (2/11/35)
263. A Celebrated Case (2/18/35)
264. Quarrel Island (2/25/35)
265. Henry IV (3/4/35)
266. Black Peril (3/11/35)
267. The Man with a Load of Mischief (3/18/35)
268. The Silver Box (3/25/35)
269. The Feast of the Jest (4/1/35)
270. The Wild Duck (4/8/35)
271. The World and His Wife (4/15/35)
272. Good-Bye, Mr. Chips (4/22/35)
273. Pas Seul (4/29/35)
274. Cyrano de Bergerac [part one] (5/6/35)
275. Cyrano de Bergerac [part two] (5/13/35)
276. Old Bannerman (5/20/35)
277. Dolly Madison (5/27/35)
278. The Three Musketeers [part one] (6/3/35)
279. The Three Musketeers [part two] (6/10/35)
280. Our American Cousin (6/17/35)
281. Raleigh (6/24/35)
282. Uncle Tom's Cabin (7/1/35)
283. Clear All Wires (7/15/35)
284. Chopin (7/22/35)
285. A Midsummer Night's Dream (7/29/35)
286. She [based on the H. Rider Haggard novel] (8/5/35)
287. Justice (8/12/35)
288. John Ferguson (8/19/35)
289. The Solitaire Man (8/26/35)
290. The Great Adventure (9/26/35)
291. The Sunken Bell (10/3/35)

292. The School for Scandal (10/10/35)
293. Much Ado About Nothing (10/17/35)
294. Lady Windermere's Fan (10/24/35)
295. Treasure Island (10/31/35)
296. King John (11/7/35)
297. Richard II (11/14/35)
298. Henry IV (11/21/35)
299. King Henry IV, Part I (12/5/35)
300. King Henry IV, Part II [part one] (12/12/35)
301. King Henry IV, Part II [part two] (12/19/35)
302. King Henry V, Part I (12/26/35)
303. King Henry V, Part II (1/2/36)
304. King Henry VI, Part I (1/9/36)
305. King Henry VI, Part II (1/16/36)
306. King Henry VI, Part III (1/23/36)
307. King Richard II (1/30/36)
308. King Richard III (2/6/36)
309. King Henry VIII (2/13/36)
310. Diamond Studs (2/20/36)
311. Milady (2/27/36)
312. Twenty Years After (3/5/36)
313. The Man in the Iron Mask (3/12/36)
314. Lost Horizon [based on the James Hilton novel] (3/19/36)
315. John Gabriel Bjorkman (3/26/36)
316. The Pillars of Society (10/9/36)
317. Wings Over Westralia (10/16/36)
318. Richelieu (10/23/36)
319. Tartuffe (10/30/36)
320. Ruy Blas (11/6/36)
321. The Rivals (11/13/36)
322. The Doctor in Spite of Himself (11/20/36)
323. Twelfth Night [based on the play by Shakespeare] (11/27/36)
324. The Inspector General (12/4/36)
325. The Bluebird (12/11/36)
326. Boar's Head and Yule Log (12/18/36; [performed from the Hoosac School in Hoosick, NY])
327. Three Pills in a Bottle / A Game of Chess (1/8/37)
328. Dr. Faustus (1/15/37)
329. When We Were Twenty-One (1/22/37)
330. She Stoops to Conquer (1/29/37)
331. Enemy of Society [based on the play by Ibsen] (2/5/37)
332. This Was a Man (2/12/37)
333. Queen's Enemy / Lend Me Five Shillings (2/19/37)
334. Old Man Minick (2/26/37)
335. The Merry Wives of Windsor (3/5/37)
336. Nero (3/12/37)
337. -----(3/19/37)
338. The Terrible Meek [broadcast from 4–4:30 pm] (3/26/37)
339. His Majesty, Bunker Bean (4/2/37)
340. Leah Kleschna (4/9/37)
341. A Florentine Tragedy (4/16/37)
342. Shakespeareana [dramas of selections from some of his best known plays] (4/23/37)
343. The Goose Hangs High (4/30/37)
344. Shavings (5/7/37)
345. Makropoulos Secret (5/21/37)
346. Evangeline (5/28/37)
347. Her Husband's Wife [comedy] (6/4/37)
348. Apron Strings [comedy] (6/11/37)
349. Mama's Affair [comedy] (6/18/37)
350. Clear All Wires (6/25/37)
351. The Marriage of Kitty [comedy by Cosmo Gordon-Lennox] (7/2/37)
352. Adam and Eva (7/9/37)
353. Quarrel Island (7/16/37)
354. What Happened to Jones [written by George Broadhurst] (7/23/37)
355. Young Woodley (8/6/37)
356. -----(8/13/37)
357. Witness for the Defense (8/27/37)
358. So Wing the Wind [broadcast 3–3:45 pm] (9/3/37)
359. Mirandolinne [comedy] (9/10/37)
360. Mirandolinne [part two] (9/17/37)
361. -----(9/24/37)
362. Road to Yesterday (10/1/37)
363. Paolo and Francesa (10/15/37)
364. Like Falling Leaves (10/22/37; Lisa Sergio)
365. -----(10/29/37)
366. Salome (11/5/37)
367. Anthony and Cleopatra [based on the play by William Shakespeare] (11/12/37)
368. Lend Me Five Shillings and the Black Silk Hat (11/19/37)
369. Magda (11/26/37)
370. Cricket of the Hearth (12/3/37)
371. -----(12/10/37)
372. Tidings Brought to Mary (12/17/37)
373. Dust of the Road [broadcast 2–2:25 pm] (12/24/37)

374. Miss Lulu Betts (12/31/37)
375. Rosmersholm [based on the play by Ibsen] (1/7/38; Mariana Flory)
376. Makropoulos Secret (1/14/38)
377. Within the Law (1/21/38; Sheila Barrett)
378. First Lady of the Land (1/28/38)
379. The Romancers (2/4/38)
380. This Was a Man (2/11/38)
381. There's Always Juliet [based on the play by John Van Druten] (2/18/38)
382. The Critic (3/4/38)
383. The Far Off Hills (3/11/38)
384. Thomas A. Becket [based on Tennyson's play] (3/18/38)
385. Magda (3/25/38)
386. -----(4/1/38)
387. Sherwood [written by Alfred Noyes] (4/8/38)
388. Julius Caesar (4/22/38)
389. Madame Sans Gens (4/29/38)
390. The Communters (5/6/38; Taylor Holmes)
391. The Bells (5/13/38)
392. The Inspector General (5/20/38)
393. -----(5/27/38)
394. Cymbeline [broadcast 3:15 to 4 pm] (6/3/38)
395. Episode in Red (7/9/38)
396. On Naseby Hill (7/16/38)
397. The Pie Cure [written by Merritt P. Allen] (7/23/38)
398. The Ineffable Essence of Nothing (7/30/38)
399. The Death of a King (8/6/38)
400. Festival (8/13/38)
401. By the Grace of Dishwater (8/20/38)
402. Humbug Weed (8/27/38)
403. The Nine Day's Queen (9/1/38)
404. Men, Women and Goats [written by Charles O'Brien Kennedy] (9/8/38)
405. The Valiant (9/15/38)
406. Edna's Fruit Hat (9/22/38)
407. Ballad of Youth [based on a story by Alfred Kreymborg] (9/29/38)
408. The Gold Bug [based on the story by Edgar Allan Poe] (10/6/38)
409. The Phantom Rickshaw [based on the Rudyard Kipling story] (10/13/38; Burford Hampden, Eunice Howard, Florence Malone, and Eustace Wyatt)
410. Old Gray Mare (10/20/38)
411. Uncle Eban (10/27/38)
412. Samson Agonistes (11/5/38)
413. A Saint in the Making: The Life of Mother Cabrini (11/12/38)
414. Thanks to Thanksgiving (11/19/38)
415. Protection (11/26/38)
416. The Ineffable Essence of Nothing [written by Reginald MacDougall] (12/3/38)
417. The Dark Voice (12/10/38)
418. Of Good Family (12/17/38)
419. Christmas Eve Special (12/24/38; Maude Adams)
420. The Green Angel (12/31/38)
421. Safe Deposit (1/7/39)
422. Celestial Influence (1/14/39)
423. American Song (3/26/39; Jay Jostyn)
424. Dr. Abernathy (4/9/39)
425. Best Two Out of Three (4/16/39)
426. Haunted House (4/25/39)
427. Paris Evening (4/30/39)
428. Back Number Up (5/7/39; Arthur Allen and Parker Fennelly)
429. The Man Who Was Tomorrow (5/14/39; Peter Donald and Eric Dressler)
430. The Fish Widowers (5/21/39)
431. Silver Candlestick (5/28/39)
432. The Towers of Hatred (6/4/39; Arnold Moss)
433. The Piper (6/11/39)
434. The Bagman's Uncle [based on Charles Dickens short story] (6/18/39)
435. Robert Herrick (6/25/39)
435. Ghostly Business (7/2/39)
436. Two Drones (7/9/39)
437. Kid Star (7/16/39; Phyllis Creore)
438. Tie 'Em Up Perkins (7/23/39)
439. Dust in Their Eyes (7/30/39)
440. First Selectman, in Person (8/6/39)
441. The Cottingham's Last Banshee (8/13/39)
442. Sob Stuff (8/20/39)
443. The Man with the Lantern (9/3/39)
444. Words Set to Music (9/10/39)
445. Health and Beauty, Inc. (9/17/39)
446. This Honorable Court (9/24/39)
447. Moonlight Sonata [based on the short story by Alexander Woollcott] (11/1/39)

448. Speed (11/8/39)
449. All American (11/15/39)
450. Turkey Soup (11/22/39)
451. The Shrinking Mr. Pertwie (11/29/39; Peggy Allen and Robert Strauss)
452. The Four-Sided Triangle (12/6/39)
453. Mr. Throgg's Trial Balance (12/20/39)
454. Aunt Phillis Coffee (1/3/40)
455. His Brother's Keeper (1/10/40)
456. Peter Lovely's Pigeons (1/17/40)
457. Marry the Girl (1/27/40)
458. Going Home / Moon Road (2/3/40)
459. A Most Tragic Brutus (2/10/40; Henry Hull, Jr. and Edmund O'Brien)
460. All Quiet at Silver Valley (2/17/40)
461. My Godfather (2/24/40)
462. Laughing Duck (3/2/40)
463. Johnny Pye and the Fool Killer (3/9/40)
464. Drink Deep (3/16/40)
465. The Fish Widowers (3/23/40)
466. Now Playing Heaven (3/30/40)
467. The Withering Glare of Amelia Peck [aka The Flood Is Rising] (4/6/40; Peter Donald and Agnes Moorehead)
468. The Ineffable Essence of Nothing

(4/13/40; Ian MacAllaster and Ian Martin)
469. The Comeback (4/20/40)
470. Incredible Clanahan (4/27/40)
471. Paris Evening (5/4/40)
472. The Four-Sided Triangle (5/11/40)
473. Me and Eddie [comedy] (5/18/40)
474. Beat Out the Count (5/25/40)
475. The Girl Who Knows What You're Thinking (6/1/40)
476. The Clinic (6/8/40)
477. The Brother of Pinky Chance (6/15/40)
478. The Crazy Heart Blues (6/22/40)
479. Elise (6/29/40)
480. -----(7/6/40)
481. Escape (7/13/40)
482. By the Grace of Dishwater (7/20/40)
483. Ripe for the Picking (7/27/40)
484. And Six Came Back (8/10/40)
485. The Traitor (8/17/40)
486. Adam and Eve on a Raft / When Your Time Comes / A Piece of Ice (8/24/40)
487. -----(8/31/40)
488. The Perfect Marriage (9/7/40)
489. Life's Hungry Man (9/14/40)
490. Things in Common (9/21/40)
491. Height of Fashion (9/28/40)
492. -----(10/5/40)

Radio Reader's Digest

As the title implies, this was a radio version of the popular digest, featuring adaptations of short stories, essays, and other enjoyable pleasures. Many of the programs had more than one skit performed. Directed by Robert Nolan, the program had Ernest Chappell as announcer. Lyn Murray supplied the music, replaced by N. Van Cleef beginning December 10, 1944. Conrad Nagel was master of ceremonies, replaced by Bob Trout on December 17, 1944. Deems Taylor was emcee on December 24, 1944. Quentin Reynolds took over as emcee on December 31, 1944. Edwin C. Hill filled in on August 6, 1944, Lowell Thomas on July 30, 1944. The broadcasts originated from New York over CBS for Campbell Soups, Sunday evenings from 9 to 9:30 pm, EST.

1. War Gyps / Picturesque Speech / Casey Jones (9/13/42)
2. Back for Christmas [based on the

John Collier story] (9/20/42; Charles Laughton and Roland Young)

3. Flight of the Chetniks / The Lost Gold Piece (9/27/42; Henry Hull, Vincent Price, Joseph Schildkraut)
4. Most Unforgettable Character I Have Ever Met (10/4/42; Madelline Carroll and Edgar Kennedy)
5. I Was a German Hostage / Woman with the Green Eyes (10/11/42; Wendy Barrie, Orson Welles, and Monty Woolley)
6. Miss Victoria (10/18/42; Joan Fontaine)
7. Missionary and the Gangster (10/25/42; Claude Rains)
8. Mama Mosquito / Reward of Mercy (11/1/42; Eva Le Gallienne and Sir Cedric Hardwicke)
9. What of It? / A Visit to Berchesgarden (11/8/42; Paul Muni and Alexander Woollcott)
10. They Called Her Mouse / The Clock Strikes (11/15/42; Shirley Booth and Stanley Ridges)
11. Unscheduled Operation / The Tooth, The Whole Tooth, and Nothing But the Tooth (11/22/42; Brian Aherne and Robert Benchley)
12. From Pillar to Post / Love Story of Mark Twain (11/29/42; Charles Butterworth and Vincent Price)
13. So Long Son / Sabotage–Secret War Against America (12/6/42; Joseph Calliela and Raymond Massey)
14. The Man Who Won the War (12/13/42; Ronald Colman)
15. The Only Wise Man / The Fred Harvey Girls (12/20/42; Helen Hayes and Conrad Nagel)
16. Miss Vilda's Dream (12/27/42; Abbey Players of Dublin and Alexander Woollcott)
17. Mrs. Corey, Unforgettable / Dwellers in the Shadow (1/3/43; Frazier Hunt and Martha Scott)
18. Thousand Dollar Bill / Stuka Horror Over Greece (1/10/43; Ralph Bellamy and Robert St. John)
19. Greatest Hoax in History (1/17/43; Joan Anderson and George Coulouris)
20. French Underground (1/24/43; Claude Rains)
21. Education for Death (1/31/43; Peter Lorre)
22. The Knife (2/7/43; George Raft)
23. Wartime America at Night (2/14/43; Tom Collins and Kate Smith)
24. No African Campaign (2/21/43; Lowell Thomas)
25. Rhoda Monroe (2/28/43; Ethel Waters)
26. The Necklace / War Manpower Chief (3/7/43; Miriam Hopkins and Paul V. McNutt)
27. A Doctor in Lennox (3/14/43; Sidney Smith)
28. To My Lost Husband (3/21/43; Madeline Carroll)
29. Hostages (3/28/43; Paul Lukas)
30. The Last Days of St. Pierre (4/4/43; James Monks and Kent Smith)
31. Life of Nobel (4/11/43; Janet Blair and Charles Boyer)
32. Blacksmith of Brandon (4/18/43; Edward G. Robinson)
33. Two for a Penny (4/25/43; Claudia and Ralph Morgan)
34. The Unsinkable Mrs. Brown (5/2/43; Tallulah Bankhead)
35. Bill's Little Girl (5/9/43; Michael O'Shea)
36. Judge's Last Opinion (5/16/43; Herbert Marshall)
37. Forgotten Inventor (5/23/43; Jean Hersholt)
38. Polish Corridor (5/30/43; Leslie Woods)
39. Tom's Last Forage (6/6/43; Juano Hernandez)
40. The Story of Ann Sullivan (6/13/43)
41. One Alaska Night (6/20/43; Claire Niesen)
42. Illustrative Anecdote (6/27/43; Don Chisholm)
43. Fletch and Brother Joseph (7/4/43)
44. Sutter's Gold (7/11/43)
45. Face of Judas Iscariot (7/18/43)
46. R. Wagner–Music Monster / The Great Invention (7/25/43)
47. Archer–Shee Case (8/1/43)
48. Dinner in the Evening / The Juggler (8/8/43)
49. The Portrait of Extravagance (8/15/43)
50. The Corpse at the Table / Submarine Genius (8/22/43)
51. Man-God of Japan (8/29/43)
52. The Trapper and His Dog (9/5/43)

53. So It Happened to Me Too (9/12/43; James Cagney)
54. Open Door in Marriage (9/19/43; Carole Landis)
55. Is There a Scarcity of Husbands? (9/26/43; Walter Pidgeon)
56. Whirligig of Life (10/3/43; Ann Sothern)
57. Warning to Office Wives (10/10/43; Lana Turner)
58. Giraud's Brilliant Escape (10/17/43; Raymond Massey)
59. He Adopted Us (10/24/43; Greer Garson)
60. What They Call Bravery (10/31/43; Orson Welles)
61. Nurses on Horseback (11/7/43; Joan Blondell)
62. The High Cost of Dying (11/14/43)
63. Getting Along with Women (11/21/43)
64. Braves on the Warpath (11/28/43; Ralph Bellamy)
65. Lifeline (12/5/43)
66. Thank You Hitler / A Piece of String (12/12/43)
67. Dead Reckoning (12/19/43)
68. Murder Is My Business / Afterthought (12/26/43)
69. An Eye for an Eye (1/2/44; Joan Fontaine)
70. Not Too Close (1/9/44)
71. The Runt of a Horse / Story of a Scoop (1/16/44)
72. Flight Surgeon / The Gusher (1/23/44)
73. Hobo in Japan (1/30/44)
74. And So They Married (2/6/44)
75. Hate (2/13/44; Peter Capell)
76. The Rock / But Your Honor (2/20/44)
77. Dead Men on Leave / Progress Under Protest (2/27/44)
78. Dig in / Gung Ho! (3/5/44)
79. Rumanian Boomerang / Operation as Arranged (3/12/44)
80. Auction Sale / Tall Tale / Tough Guy (3/19/44)
81. Two Men and a Jeep / Hi, Toots / Hot Shorts (3/26/44)
82. Fair and Square (4/2/44)
83. The Inside Story of Hess Flight (4/9/44)
84. Going Home / Talent Scout (4/16/44)
85. Boomerang / That's the Spirit (4/23/44)
86. A Bug for Detail / Remember (4/30/44)
87. Our Good Friends, the Head Hunters (5/7/44)
88. Check Your Hat / Every Child (5/14/44)
89. Accidental Immortals / Pearl Harbor (5/21/44)
90. Imagination / Mary White (5/28/44)
91. Fraudulent Ant / D.D.T. (6/4/44)
92. To Love and Cherish / Right Time of Home (6/11/44)
93. Big, Bad Buccaneer / Happy Landing (6/18/44)
94. Five Short Clocks (6/25/44; F. Chaliapin)
95. Summers Are Not Fish (7/2/44)
96. Who Invented It? / It Takes All Kinds (7/9/44)
97. Drama in Everyday Life (7/16/44)
98. Correction Please / Real 1-A (7/23/44)
99. -----(7/30/44; Lowell Thomas)
100. Pathway in the Night (8/6/44)
101. Light of the World (8/13/44)
102. Red Badge of Courage (8/20/44)
103. France Without Law (8/27/44)
104. When a Man Leaves Prison / Hot Magic (9/3/44)
105. Outshining Mata Hari / True Greatness (9/10/44)
106. Death in the Alps / Larceny on a Lark (9/17/44)
107. Murder in the Big Bow / And So They Married (9/24/44)
108. Genius in Exile / Who Is That Man? (10/1/44; J. Whistler)
109. Fannie Farmer (10/8/44; Major A. de Seversky)
110. Woodland Tragedy / Gentle Amazon (10/15/44)
111. Tone Up Your Voice (10/22/44)
112. Power of Suggestion / Bed Quilt (10/29/44)
113. Woman Who Died Twice / Magic Words (11/5/44)
114. Tongue Twisters (11/12/44; Ted Husing)
115. Gettysburg Address / Gingereich Spot (11/19/44)

116. Alcoholism / Child Psychology (11/26/44)
117. Standing Room Only / Portrait of a Giant (12/3/44)
118. Oliver W. Holmes / Sing: Or Is it? (12/10/44)
119. My Talk with Joseph Stalin (12/17/44)
120. A Miserable Merry Christmas (12/24/44)
121. A Guy Called Ike (12/31/44)
122. G-Men of the Airwaves (1/7/45; G. Sterling of FCC)
123. American Rangers / A Warm Welcome (1/14/45)
124. Quicken the Spirit (1/21/45; Bob Hope and the U.S.O. Entertainers)
125. Prophet With Honor / Miracles at Milton (1/28/45; General De Gaulle)
126. Return of the Troubadours / He Knows How to Interest People (2/4/45; Burl Ives)
127. So That's How It Started / He Loved Me Truly (2/11/45)
128. Lowest Form of Humor (2/18/45; Tom Howard and G. Shelton)
129. Wings Over Jordan (2/25/45)
130. Life in These United States [part one] / Ripleyana (3/4/45; Burl Ives and Robert Ripley)
131. Life in These United States [part two] (3/11/45; Dunninger and Burl Ives)
132. St. Patrick's Day / Signs of Spring (3/18/45)
133. Signs of the Times / Nylons (3/25/45)
134. George S. Patton (4/1/45; Burl Ives)
135. Your Witness / A Song for Today (4/8/45)
136. Ernie Makes Thirty (4/22/45; Burl Ives)
137. Reverend John Elingsberg (4/29/45; Reverend John Elingsberg)
138. National Council of Domestic Employment (5/6/45; Shirley Davis)
139. [special appearance by Claire Phillips, widow of a Bataan soldier] (5/13/45)
140. Not Charity, but a Chance (5/20/45; Burl Ives)
141. Case Dismissed (5/27/45; Burl Ives)
142. Lillian / Nine Million New Cars (6/3/45)
143. Nothing Rotten in Denmark (6/10/45; Burl Ives)
144. Home from America (6/17/45; Burl Ives)
145. Soldier, Sailor, Beware (6/24/45)
146. Information Please, Dogs of War (7/1/45)
147. Burr's Acres (7/8/45; Alfred Lunt)
148. Cadet Nurse Corps / Police Files (7/15/45)
149. -----(7/22/45)
150. Behind the Lines / Surprise Ending (7/29/45)
151. Shangri-La / A Hero Comes Home (8/5/45)
152. -----(8/12/45)
153. Family Sessions, Inc. (9/9/45; Johnny Desmond)
154. Emergencies / Britain's Pet Spy (9/16/45)
155. Command Performance (9/23/45; Irving Berlin)
156. Good Morning Teacher / The Gusher / Canceled Resurrection (9/30/45)

The Railroad Hour

   The Railroad Hour was a series of musical dramas, abridged operettas featuring stars of stage and screen. Gordon MacRae was the host, and by January of 1949, MacRae was the male lead, and female guests were featured. Sponsored by the Association of American Railroads, this series featured a full orchestra conducted by Carmen Dragon. Top name screen stars were dropped by January of

1949 to allow a lower but still ample budget, using musical stars of opera (and the fact that this program was competing against *Suspense* might also may have been another reason for dropping Hollywood talent).

At first broadcast over ABC, Monday evenings from 8 to 8:45 pm, EST, on October 2, 1949, the series shrank in length, broadcast from 8 to 8:30 pm. On October 3, 1949, the series moved to NBC. The opening and closing theme was (not too surprisingly) "I've Been Working on the Railroad."

1. Good News (10/4/48; Jane Powell and Dinah Shore)
2. Anything Goes (10/11/48; Victor Moore and Margaret Whiting)
3. The Cat and the Fiddle (10/18/48; Adolphe Menjou and Rise Stevens)
4. The Student Prince (10/26/48; Ken Baker and Dorothy Kirsten)
5. Roberta (11/1/48; Eddie Bracken and Jan Clayton)
6. Rio Rita (11/8/48; Leo Carillo, Marian Hutton, Margo, and Sweeny and Marx)
7. Vagabond King (11/15/48; Francis X. Bushman, Lucille Norman, and Dorothy Kirsten)
8. Hit the Deck (11/22/48; Frances Langford)
9. New Moon (11/29/48; Nadine Conner and Rudy Vallee)
10. Girl Crazy (12/6/48; William Bendix, Doris Day, and Joan Edwards)
11. Sally (12/13/48; Leon Errol and Dinah Shore)
12. Holiday Inn (12/20/48; George Murphy and Martha Tilton)
13. Desert Song (12/27/48; Francis X. Bushman, Nadine Conner, and Sterling Holloway)
14. Whoopee (1/3/49; Eddie Cantor, Jeff Chandler, and Irene Wilson)
15. The Red Mill (1/10/49; Gene Kelly and Lucille Norman)
16. Naughty Marietta (1/17/49; Jeanette MacDonald)
17. Blossom Time (1/24/49; Patrice Munsel)
18. Bitter Sweet (1/31/49; Jeanette MacDonald)
19. Rose Marie (2/7/49; Patrice Munsel)
20. Sweethearts (2/14/49; Jane Powell)
21. Lady Be Good (2/21/49; Groucho Marx)
22. Song of Norway (2/28/49; M. Kosetz)
23. The Merry Widow (3/7/49; Jeanette MacDonald)
24. Eileen (3/14/49; Irene Manning)
25. State Fair (3/21/49; Jo Stafford and Eileen Wilson)
26. Best Foot Forward (3/28/49)
27. Mademoiselle Modiste (4/4/49; Dorothy Kirsten)
28. The Firefly (4/11/49; Nadine Connor)
29. Apple Blossoms (4/18/49; Jeanette MacDonald)
30. Fortune Teller (4/25/49; Patricia Munsel)
31. Showboat (5/2/49; Lucille Norman)
32. Kiss Me Kate (5/9/49; Lucille Norman)
33. Robin Hood (5/16/49; Lucille Norman)
34. Porgy and Bess (5/23/49; Lucille Norman)
35. The Life of C.J. Bonds (5/30/49; Lucille Norman)
36. Oklahoma (6/6/49; Lucille Norman)
37. The Stephen Foster Story (6/13/49; Lucille Norman)
38. Brooks/Van Heusen Salute (6/20/49; Lucille Norman)
39. Chicago Fair Salute (6/27/49; Lucille Norman)
40. Miss Liberty (7/4/49; Lucille Norman)
41. The John McHugh Story (7/11/49; Lucille Norman)
42. Bandwagon (7/18/49; Lucille Norman)
43. Tin Pan Alley Salute (7/25/49; Lucille Norman)
44. E. Nevin Salute (8/1/49; Lucille Norman)
45. Brigadoon (8/8/49; Lucille Norman)
46. Gordon / Warren Salute (8/15/49; Lucille Norman)

47. Call Me Mister (8/22/49; Lucille Norman)
48. I. Green Salute (8/29/49; Lucille Norman)
49. Wizard of Oz (9/5/49; Lucille Norman)
50. Hogey Carmichael Salute (9/12/49; Lucille Norman)
51. N. H. Brown Salute (9/19/49; Lucille Norman)
52. Rogers and Hammerstein Salute (9/26/49; Lucille Norman)
53. Showboat (10/3/49; Dorothy Kirsten and Lucille Norman)
54. New Moon (10/10/49; Ilona Massey)
55. The Chocolate Soldier (10/17/49; Nadine Conner)
56. Music in the Air (10/24/49; Jane Powell)
57. Blossom Time (10/31/49; Lucille Norman)
58. The Great Waltz (11/7/49; J. Novotna)
59. Vagabond King (11/14/49; Lucille Norman)
60. No, No Nanette (11/21/49; Doris Day)
61. Student Prince (11/28/49; Jane Powell)
62. The Mikado (12/5/49; Kenny Baker and E. Case)
63. Desert Song (12/12/49; Patricia Munsel)
64. Rose Marie (12/19/49; Patricia Munsel)
65. Snow White (12/26/49; Jane Powell)
66. The Red Mill (1/2/50; Lucille Norman)
67. Bittersweet (1/9/50; Dorothy Kirsten)
68. Louisiana Purchase (1/16/50; Lloyd Norman)
69. The Merry Widow (1/23/50; Dorothy Kirsten)
70. Brigadoon (1/30/50; Jane Powell)
71. Apple Blossoms (2/6/50; Dorothy Kirsten)
72. Sweet Hearts (2/13/50; Jane Powell)
73. The Count of Luxembourg (2/20/50; Nadine Conner)
74. Mademoiselle Modiste (2/27/50; Jane Powell)
75. H.M.S. Pinafore (3/6/50; Lloyd Norman)
76. Little Nellie Kellie (3/13/50; Jane Powell)
77. The Only Girl (3/20/50; Dorothy Warenskjold)
78. Sunny (3/27/50; Jo Stafford)
79. Song of Norway (4/3/50; D. Coulter and Ileen Petina)
80. Naughty Marietta (4/10/50; Nadine Conner)
81. Madame Sherry (4/17/50; Marion Bell)
82. The Prince of Pilsen (4/24/50; Nadine Conner)
83. Sally (5/1/50; Marion Bell)
84. The Pink Lady (5/8/50; Michael Checkov and Lucille Norman)
85. Robin Hood (5/15/50; Dorothy Kirsten)
86. Princess Pat (5/22/50; Dorothy Kirsten and Lucille Norman)
87. Review of 1927 (5/29/50; Lucille Norman)
88. Review of 1937 (6/5/50; Lucille Norman)
89. Review of 1931 (6/12/50; Lucille Norman)
90. Review of the Gay Nineties (6/19/50; Lucille Norman)
91. Review of 1925 (6/26/50; Lucille Norman)
92. Review of 1900–1905 (7/3/50; Lucille Norman)
93. Review of 1934 (7/10/50; Lucille Norman)
94. Review of 1905–1910 (7/17/50; Lucille Norman)
95. Review of 1938 (7/24/50; Lucille Norman)
96. Review of 1915–1920 (7/31/50; Lucille Norman)
97. Review of 1932 (8/7/50; Lucille Norman)
98. Review of 1926 (8/14/50; Lucille Norman)
99. Review of 1935 (8/21/50; Lucille Norman)
100. Review of 1929 (8/28/50; Lucille Norman)
101. Review of 1922 (9/4/50; Lucille Norman)
102. Review of 1933 (9/11/50; Lucille Norman)

103. Review of 1910–1915 (9/18/50; Lucille Norman)
104. Review of 1924 (9/25/50; Lucille Norman)
105. Allergo (10/2/50; Nadine Conner)
106. Roberta (10/9/50; Ginny Simms)
107. Countess Maritza (10/16/50; Dorothy Warenskjold)
108. Revenge with Music (10/23/50; Nadine Conner)
109. Showboat (10/30/50; Dorothy Kirsten)
110. Irene (11/6/50; Eileen Wilson)
111. Orange Blossoms (11/13/50; Dorothy Warenskjold)
112. Snow White (11/20/50; Ileen Woods)
113. A Connecticut Yankee (11/27/50; Ginny Simms)
114. The Firefly (12/4/50; Dorothy Sarnoff)
115. The Pirates of Penzance (12/11/50; Lucille Norman)
116. Brigadoon (12/18/50; Marion Bell)
117. Christmas Songs (12/25/50; Lucille Norman)
118. Review of 1950 (1/1/51; Lucille Norman)
119. Carousel (1/8/51; Patricia Morrison)
120. The Student Prince (1/15/51; E. Case)
121. Dearest Enemy (1/22/51; Nadine Conner)
122. New Moon (1/29/51; Dorothy Kirsten)
123. The Cat and the Fiddle (2/5/51; F. Yeand)
124. Sari (2/12/51; V. Della Chiesa)
125. Song of Norway (2/19/51; Ileen Petina)
126. Two Hearts in Three Quarter Time (2/26/51; Marion Bell)
127. Vagabond King (3/5/51; Ileen Petina)
128. Rosalinda (3/12/51; A. Dickey)
129. Apple Blossoms (3/19/51; Dorothy Kirsten)
130. Fortune Teller (3/26/51; Nadine Conner)
131. Annie Laurie (4/2/51; Dorothy Warenskjold)
132. The Great Waltz (4/9/51; Dorothy Kirsten)
133. One Touch of Venus [part one] (4/16/51; Ginny Simms)

134. One Touch of Venus [part two] (4/23/51; Nadine Conner)
135. Music in the Air (4/30/51; Jo Stafford)
136. High Button Shoes (5/7/51; Margaret Whiting)
137. Nina Rosa (5/14/51; Mimi Benzell)
138. The Chocolate Soldier (5/21/51; Marion Bell)
139. Katinka (5/28/51; A. Dickey)
140. Very Warm for May (6/4/51; A. Dickey)
141. Gypsy Princess (6/11/51; J. Novotna)
142. The Boys from Syracuse (6/18/51; E. Case)
143. The Merry Widow (6/25/51; Nadine Conner)
144. Beautiful Dreamer (7/2/51; Dorothy Warenskjold)
145. Casey at the Bat (7/9/51; Dorothy Warenskjold)
146. Springtime in Paris (7/16/51; Dorothy Warenskjold)
147. The Luck of Roaring Camp (7/23/51; Dorothy Warenskjold)
148. The Pirates of Picadilly (7/30/51; Dorothy Warenskjold)
149. The Big Top (8/6/51; Dorothy Warenskjold)
150. A Thousand and One Nights (8/13/51; Dorothy Warenskjold)
151. Long Ago (8/20/51; Dorothy Warenskjold)
152. Danny Freel (8/27/51; Dorothy Warenskjold)
153. Innocents Abroad (9/3/51; Dorothy Warenskjold)
154. Journey Into the Sun (9/10/51; Dorothy Warenskjold)
155. Rip Van Winkle (9/17/51; Dorothy Warenskjold)
156. The Emperor of San Francisco (9/24/51; Dorothy Warenskjold)
157. State Fair (10/1/51; Dorothy Kirsten)
158. Madame Sherry (10/8/51; Nadine Conner)
159. Martha (10/15/51; Dorothy Kirsten)
160. Sweethearts (10/22/51; Mimi Benzell)
161. Holiday Inn (10/29/51; Dorothy Kirsten)
162. Rose Marie (11/5/51; Dorothy Kirsten)
163. Bohemian Girl (11/12/51; Dorothy Kirsten)

164. Jubilee (11/19/51; Dorothy Kirsten)
165. Mademoiselle Modiste (11/26/51; Dorothy Kirsten)
166. Marinka (12/3/51; Gladys Swarthout)
167. The Red Mill (12/10/51; Rise Stevens)
168. Rosalie (12/17/51; Nadine Conner)
169. The Happy Prince (12/24/51; Lucille Norman)
170. Review of 1951 (12/31/51; Lucille Norman)
171. Blossom Time (1/7/52; Nadine Conner)
172. I Married an Angel (1/14/52; Nadine Conner)
173. Desert Song (1/21/52; Mimi Benzell)
174. The Three Musketeers (1/28/52; Dorothy Warenskjold)
175. East Wind (2/4/52; Mimi Benzell)
176. Orange Blossoms (2/11/52; Patricia Morrison)
177. Frederika (2/18/52; Dorothy Kirsten)
178. The Firefly (2/25/52; Dorothy Kirsten)
179. The White Eagle (3/3/53; Lucille Norman)
180. The Cat and the Fiddle (3/10/53; Dorothy Kirsten)
181. Sari (3/17/53; Margaret Truman)
182. Kiss Me Kate (3/24/53; Partice Munsel)
183. Countess Maritza (3/31/53; B. Thebom)
184. Roberta (4/7/53; Nadine Conner)
185. Rosalinda (4/14/53; Dorothy Warenskjold)
186. Erminie (4/21/53; N. Tageman)
187. The Pink Lady (4/28/53; Nadine Conner)
188. Sunny (5/5/53; Virginia Haskins)
189. Spring Is Here (5/12/53; A. Dickey)
190. The Great Waltz (5/19/53; Lucille Norman)
191. My Maryland (5/26/53; Dorothy Kirsten)
192. Minstrel Boy (6/2/53; Dorothy Warenskjold)
193. Swedish Nightingale (6/9/53; Dorothy Warenskjold)
194. The Right Dress (6/16/53; Dorothy Warenskjold)

195. The Little Minister (6/23/53; Dorothy Warenskjold)
196. Springtime in Paris (6/30/53; Dorothy Warenskjold)
197. Scheherazade (7/7/53; Lucille Norman)
198. The Necklace (7/14/53; Dorothy Warenskjold)
199. Love Song (7/21/53; Dorothy Warenskjold)
200. The Pirate of New Orleans (7/28/53; Dorothy Warenskjold)
201. Starlight (8/4/53; Lucille Norman)
202. The Brownings (8/11/53; Dorothy Warenskjold)
203. Miss Cinderella (8/18/53; Dorothy Warenskjold)
204. Fantasy Impromptu (8/25/53; Dorothy Warenskjold)
205. The Pirates of Picadilly (9/1/53; Dorothy Warenskjold)
206. Swan Lake (9/8/53; Dorothy Warenskjold)
207. Maestro (9/15/53; Dorothy Warenskjold)
208. Golden Curtain (9/22/53; Lucille Norman)
209. Annie Laurie (9/29/53; Lucille Norman)
210. Maytime (10/6/53; Dorothy Kirsten)
211. A Waltz Dream (10/13/53; Dorothy Kirsten)
212. Naughty Maurietta (10/20/53; Dorothy Kirsten)
213. Gypsy Princess (10/27/53; B. Thebom)
214. Seventh Heaven (11/3/53; Ann Ayars)
215. Dearest Enemy (11/10/53; Eileen Farrell)
216. On Your Toes (11/17/53; Marion Bell)
217. Vagabond King (11/24/53; Mimi Benzell)
218. Babes in Toyland (12/1/53; Lucille Norman)
219. Gypsy Baron (12/8/53; Mimi Benzell)
220. Holiday Inn (12/15/53; Dorothy Kirsten)
221. Christmas Party (12/22/53; Dorothy Kirsten)
222. Review of 1952 (12/29/53; Dorothy Warenskjold)

223. My Romance (1/5/53; Nadine Conner)
224. Two Hearts in Three Quarter Time (1/12/53; Marion Bell)
225. Showboat (1/19/53; Dorothy Kirsten)
226. The Merry Widow (1/26/53; Dorothy Kirsten)
227. Carousel (2/2/53; Nadine Conner)
228. Miss Liberty (2/9/53; Nadine Conner)
229. Blue Paradise (2/16/53; Nadine Conner)
230. Bittersweet (2/23/53; Dorothy Warenskjold)
231. Rose of Algeria (3/2/53; Lucille Norman)
232. Up in Central Park (3/9/53; Mimi Benzell)
233. Eileen (3/16/53; Lucille Norman)
234. Lute Song (3/23/53; Mimi Benzell)
235. Princess Pat (3/30/53; Elaine Malbin)
236. Sally (4/6/53; Lucille Norman)
237. Fortune Teller (4/13/53; Dorothy Warenskjold)
238. El Capitan (4/20/53; Ann Ayars)
239. The Pink Lady (4/27/53; Nadine Conner)
240. Mary (5/4/53; Dorothy Kirsten)
241. Rosalind (5/11/53; Dorothy Kirsten)
242. Circus Princess (5/18/53; Dorothy Kirsten)
243. Irene (5/25/53; Dorothy Warenskjold)
244. Quality Street (6/1/53; Dorothy Warenskjold)
245. Dear Yesterday (6/8/53; Dorothy Warenskjold)
246. Love Story (6/15/53; Dorothy Warenskjold)
247. New Wine (6/22/53; Dorothy Warenskjold)
248. The Man Without a Country (6/29/53; Dorothy Warenskjold)
249. Penny Whistle (7/6/53; Dorothy Warenskjold)
250. Friml Story (7/13/53; Dorothy Warenskjold)
251. Starlight (7/20/53; Dorothy Warenskjold)
252. Golden Express (7/27/53; Dorothy Warenskjold)
253. On Wings of Song (8/3/53; Dorothy Warenskjold)
254. Trilby (8/10/53; Dorothy Warenskjold)
255. Luck of Roaring Camp (8/17/53; Dorothy Warenskjold)
256. Hope Is a Woman (8/24/53; Dorothy Warenskjold)
257. Lorna Doone (8/31/53; Dorothy Warenskjold)
258. Night Music (9/7/53; Dorothy Warenskjold)
259. The Million Dollar Bank Note (9/14/53; Dorothy Warenskjold)
260. Minstrel Boy (9/21/53; Dorothy Warenskjold)
261. Familiar Stranger (9/28/53; Dorothy Warenskjold)
262. The Student Prince (10/5/53; Dorothy Warenskjold)
263. Showboat (10/12/53; Dorothy Warenskjold)
264. Sunny (10/19/53; Lucille Norman)
265. The Firefly (10/26/53; Dorothy Warenskjold)
266. Rosalinda (11/2/53; Elaine Malbin)
267. Roberta (11/9/53; Dorothy Kirsten)
268. The Merry Widow (11/16/53; Dorothy Kirsten)
269. The Chocolate Soldier (11/23/53; V. Haskins)
270. State Fair (11/30/53; Lucille Norman)
271. Sweethearts (12/7/53; Elaine Malbin)
272. The Cat and the Fiddle (12/14/53; Dorothy Kirsten)
273. Snow White (12/21/53; Dorothy Warenskjold)
274. Review of 1953 (12/28/53; Dorothy Kirsten)
275. Vagabond King (1/4/54; J.S. Smith)
276. Gypsy Baron (1/11/54; Mimi Benzell)
277. The Girl from Utah (1/18/54; Ann Ayars)
278. Music in the Air (1/25/54; Mimi Benzell)
279. Maytime (2/1/54; Nadine Conner)
280. The Schumann Story (2/8/54; Dorothy Warenskjold)
281. Through the Years (2/15/54; Dorothy Kirsten)
282. Martha (2/22/54; Gladys Swarthout)

283. The Great Waltz (3/1/54; Elaine Malbin)
284. The Red Mill (3/8/54; Eileen Farrell)
285. Minstrel Boy (3/15/54; Lucille Norman)
286. Irene (3/22/54; Elaine Malbin)
287. The Three Musketeers (3/29/54; Dorothy Warenskjold)
288. Great Day (4/5/54; Mimi Benzell)
289. Babes in Toyland (4/12/54; Lucille Norman)
290. Smiles (4/19/54; Elaine Malbin)
291. Rose Marie (4/26/54; V. Haskins)
292. Birthday (5/3/54; Lucille Norman)
293. Wonderful One-Horse Shay (5/10/54; Lucille Norman)
294. Around the World in Eighty Days (5/17/54; Lucille Norman)
295. Penny Whistle (5/24/54; Lucille Norman)
296. Homecoming (5/31/54; Nadine Conner)
297. Rosalie (6/7/54; Nadine Conner)
298. The Pink Lady (6/14/54; Lucille Norman)
299. New Moon (6/21/54; Lucille Norman)

Religion — Defied and Defended

This program had sermons, dialogues and dramas presenting religion from both sides of the pulpit, from the believers and the deceivers. Half of each episode defends religion, while the other half defies, leaving the audience to choose between common good and common bad. The Rev. James A. Pike and the Rev. Dr. John M. Krumm were the two who debated on each episode, broadcast over ABC Sunday evenings from 9:35 to 10 pm, EST. This series lasted a mere five broadcasts.

1. Isn't Religion Unscientific? (7/11/53)
2. How Can We Know Which Is the True Religion? (7/18/53)
3. Aren't Moral and Spiritual Values Enough? (7/25/53)
4. I Have My Own Religion (8/1/53)
5. Doesn't Evil Disprove God? (8/8/53)

Report on Africa

This series presented a look at social distinction in Africa, and how it affects the African-American community. Diverse opinions and a contributing investigation of the problems of Africa were the main offering of the program, which was broadcast locally from New York City over WNYC, from 3 to 4 pm.

1. South Africa: The Land and the People (9/2/56)
2. South Africa: The Problem of Apartheid (9/9/56; Sir Ernest Oppenheimer)
3. Lake Victoria (9/16/56)
4. Journey by the Niger (9/30/56)
5. The Fullness of the Nile (10/7/56)
6. Experiment in Partnership (10/14/56)
7. The Gold Coast Experiment (10/21/56)
8. Kenya (10/28/56)

The Return of Nick Carter

Of the detective series originating from the old pulp magazines, this was one of the most successful. In the classic tradition of detective fiction, Nick Carter would gather tons of clues, piece them together, and reveal the guilty party at the end. Afterwards, Carter would explain each clue to his friends Patsy Bowen and Scubby Wilson. The murderer or thief would then be arrested.

Lon Clark was Nick Carter, with Helen Chaote as Patsy. Ed Latimer was Sergeant Matty and John Kane was Scubby. The entire production was written, produced and directed at WOR in New York by Jock MacGregor. Music was by Lew White, later George Wright. The series was broadcast over Mutual, Sunday evenings from 5:30 to 6 pm, EST; beginning with episode three, Tuesday 9:30–10 pm and starting with episode fourteen, Monday from 9:30 to 10 pm. *Nick Carter* moved to Wednesday from 7 to 7:30 pm for episodes thirty through thirty-three and beginning with episode thirty-four, 8:30 to 9 pm.

Starting with episode fifty-four, the program went to a four or five-a-week format, alternating from 9:15 to 9:30 pm to 9:30 to 9:45 pm. On October 8, 1944, Lin-X Home Brighteners became the first sponsor of *Nick Carter*, and the program went back to its original once-a-week, thirty-minute format, now Sundays 3:30–4 pm.

On April 22, 1945, Lin-X dropped sponsorship, but the show remained in the same day and time slot. Beginning March 5, 1946, *Nick Carter* moved to Tuesdays, 3:30 to 4 pm, EST. On August 18, 1946, Old Dutch Cleanser began sponsorship, pushing the program to Sundays from 6:30 to 7 pm, EST. Charlotte Manson took over the role of Patsy at this point; the rest of the cast remained the same.

On December 8, 1946, the series changed its title to *Nick Carter, Master Detective*. The first two broadcasts were technically audition programs, allowing Mutual a couple of weeks for the listeners to respond. These two episodes were titled *Nick Carter, Master Detective*. By episode three, the program fastened itself to *The Return of Nick Carter* and a prime-time run.

1. The Strange Dr. Devolo (4/11/43)
2. The Voice of Crime (4/18/43)
3. The Mystery of the Indian Idols (4/27/43)
4. The Mystery of the Old Red Mill (5/4/43)
5. Seven Drops of Blood (5/11/43)
6. Three Blind Mice (5/18/43)
7. The Skeleton in the Closet (5/25/43)
8. The Purloined Portraits (6/1/43)
9. Murder in Bronze (6/8/43)
10. Insured for Death (6/15/43)
11. The Forgotten Alibi (6/22/43)
12. Endowment for Murder (6/29/43)
13. The Echo of Death (7/6/43)
14. Death Across the Tracks (7/12/43)
15. Death's Double Deal (7/19/43)
16. The Mystery of the Devil's Treasure (7/26/43)
17. Murder in the Crypt (8/2/43)
18. Murder on Skull Island (8/9/43)
19. Carnival of Death (8/16/43)
20. Dead Man's Reef (8/23/43)
21. Ragoff Broach (8/30/43)
22. The Tattooed Twin (9/6/43)
23. Igloo of Burning Death (9/13/43)

Rocky Fortune

Starring Frank Sinatra as Rocky Fortune, private detective (Rocky took various jobs and also took a variety of trouble), this series was broadcast over NBC, Tuesday evenings from 9:30 to 10 pm, EST. Fred Weihe and Andrew Love directed. The scripts were written by George Lefferts and Ernest Kinoy. Even with Sinatra's name associated with the series, there remained no sponsor! As soon as the movie *From Here to Eternity* took hold at the box office, reviving Sinatra's film career, Sinatra stopped doing any further radio programming of this type.

1. Oyster Shucker (10/6/53)
2. Insurance Fraud [aka Steven in a Rest Home] (10/13/53)
3. Shipboard Jewel Robbery (10/20/53)
4. Pint-Sized Payroll Bandit (10/27/53)
5. Messenger for Murder (11/10/53)
6. A Hepcat Kills the Canary (11/17/53)
7. Murder on the Isle (11/24/53)
8. Murder Among the Statues (12/1/53)
9. Carnival One Way (12/8/53)
10. Companion to a Chimp (12/15/53)
11. The Plot to Murder Santa Claus (12/22/53)
12. Prize Fight Setup (12/29/53)
13. On the Trail of a Killer (1/5/54)
14. Rodeo Murder (1/12/54)
15. The Museum Murder (1/19/54)
16. Hauling Nitro (1/26/54)
17. Football Fix (2/2/54)
18. Catskills Cover-up (2/9/54)
19. The Too Much Married Blond (2/16/54)
20. Decoy for Death (2/23/54)
21. The Doctor's Dilemma (3/2/54)
22. Incident in a Bar (3/9/54)
23. Psychological Murder (3/16/54)
24. Rocket Racket (3/23/54)
25. Boarding House Double-Cross (3/30/54)

Romance

Anthology series featuring different dramas, originals and adaptations having some sort of romance brewing between the central characters, this series also featured various guests of stage and screen.

First broadcast over CBS first as a sustainer, Mondays from 11:30 pm to 12 am, EST, beginning July 19, the series was heard from 9 to 9:30 pm, and beginning September 6, 1943, 11:30 pm to 12 am. On November 30, 1943, *Romance* moved to Tuesdays at 10 pm; on February 29, 1944, it began at 11:30 pm. Colgate began sponsoring the program in July of 1944, and the series changed its title to *Theater of Romance.*

In April of 1947, the series went back to its original title and was heard on Wednesday from 7:30 to 8 pm, EST. Beginning June 30, 1947, *Romance* moved to Monday evenings from 10 to 10:30 pm. A number of changes followed: beginning October 18, 1947, Saturday from 7:30 to 8 pm; beginning February 4, 1948, Wednesday from 9:30 to 10 pm; beginning July 5, 1948, Monday from 10:30 to 11 pm; beginning August 6, 1948, Fridays from 8:30 to 9 pm; and beginning October 23, 1948, Saturdays from 10:30 to 11 pm.

From June 20, 1950, to August 8, 1950, *Romance* was heard on Tuesdays from 9 to 9:30 pm, sponsored by Wrigley, as a summer replacement for *Life with Luigi.* Broadcasts on January 6 and 13 of 1951 were heard on Saturday evening from 11:30 to 12 pm. From July 2, 1951, to August 20, 1951, it was on Mondays from 9 to 9:30 pm. The September 8, 1951, broadcast was heard on Saturday from 12:30 to 1 am; from September 15 to 29, 1951, it was Saturday from 11:30 pm to 12 am, and from December 23, 1951, to January 6, 1952, Sunday from 8:30 to 9 pm. From June to September of 1952, Lux sponsored, Monday from 9 to 9:30 pm. Afterwards, the title changed again, this time to *Jurgen's Hollywood Playhouse* and *The Playhouse of Romance.*

It returned to its original *Romance* title on June 4, 1953, Thursday evenings from 9 to 9:30 pm. On September 12, 1953, the series moved to Saturday mornings, its final resting place, at first 11 to 11:30 pm, and finally 12:05 to 12:30 pm beginning May 22, 1954.

The program was broadcast from Hollywood. Orchestra conductors included Ben Ludlow, Alexander Courage and Lyn Murray. Scripts were written by numerous people, including Lucille Fletcher, Ross Murray, Jean Holloway, C.S. Monroe, Charles Jackson, Antony Ellis, and Kathleen Hite.

The narrator was Frank Gallop beginning January 25, 1944. The "Voice of Romance" in 1943 was Kay Brinker, later to be replaced by Doris Dalton. Earl McGill produced and Marx Loeb directed in 1943. Charles Vanda directed in 1944, Norman McDonell from 1950 to 1954, Fred MacKaye from 1953 to 1955, William Froug from 1955 to 1956, and Antony Ellis from 1956 to 1957.

1. Smilin' Through (4/19/43)
2. Berkeley Square (4/26/43)
3. There's Always Juliet (5/3/43)
4. Wuthering Heights (5/10/43)
5. Firebrand (5/17/43)
6. Accent on Youth (5/24/43)
7. Seventh Heaven (5/31/43)
8. Bride the Sun Shines On (6/7/43)
9. If I Were King (6/14/43)
10. One Sunday Afternoon (6/21/43)
11. Camille [written by Lucille Fletcher] (6/28/43)

2. Someone Else [written by Lucille Fletcher] (7/5/43)
3. The Three Musketeers (7/12/43)
4. Sun Field (7/19/43)
5. The Apple Tree (7/26/43)
6. Michael and Mary (8/2/43)
7. The Portrait of Jenny (8/9/43)
8. The Scarlet Pimpernel (8/16/43)
9. Lady Hamilton [written by Jean Holloway] (8/23/43; Sarah Burton, Madeleine Carroll, and Alfred Shirley)
20. Mrs. Moonlight (8/30/43; Julie Hayden and Ted Osborne)
21. Wild Oranges (9/6/43)
22. Immortal Bachelor (9/13/43)
23. Dark Victory (9/20/43; Carl Frank and Barbara Weeks)
24. The Barker (9/27/43; Heime K. Bacus, Eric Dressler, Jackie Kelk, and Peg Zinke)
25. The Prisoner of Zenda (10/4/43)
26. Don't Ever Love Me (10/11/43)
27. Shining Hour (10/18/43)
28. Elizabeth of Austria (10/25/43; Alice Frost, Ed Jerome, and Myron McCormick)
29. Daddy Long Legs (11/1/43; Myron McCormick, Gladys Thornton, and Florence Williams)
30. Rupert of Henzau (11/15/43)
31. Squaring the Circle (11/22/43)
32. Accent on Youth (11/30/43; Gloria Blondell)
33. Berkeley Square (12/7/43; Brian Aherne)
34. Dark Victory (12/14/43)
35. -----(12/28/43)
36. Goodbye, Mr. Chips (1/4/44)
37. Peg O' My Heart (1/11/44)
38. Squaring the Circle (1/18/44)
39. Elizabeth of Austria (1/25/44; Peter Capell, Alice Frost, and John Moore)
40. A Quiet Wedding (2/1/44; Frank Lovejoy and Betty Winkler)
41. Manslaughter (2/8/44)
42. Seventh Heaven (2/22/44; Ralph Bell, Lamont Johnson, and Joey Giffen)
43. A Lady in Love (2/29/44)
44. My Man Godfrey (3/7/44)
45. Enchanted Hearth (3/14/44)
46. Farmer Takes a Wife (3/21/44)

47. -----(3/28/44)
48. Trelawney of the Wells (4/4/44)
49. Death Takes a Holiday (4/11/44)
50. Jane Eyre (4/18/44)
51. Petticoat Fever (4/25/44)
52. Romantic Young Lady (5/2/44)
53. One Sunday Afternoon (5/9/44)
54. Excess Baggage (5/16/44)
55. Love Song (5/23/44)
56. Holiday (5/30/44)
57. Pride and Prejudice (6/6/44)
58. -----(6/13/44)
59. The Boomerang (6/20/44)
60. There's Always Juliet (4/23/47)
61. Isles of Spices and Lilies (4/30/47)
62. Petticoat Fever (5/7/47)
63. Kitty Foyle (5/14/47)
64. One Sunday Afternoon (5/21/47)
65. Pride and Prejudice (5/28/47)
66. Seventeen (6/4/47)
67. The Apple Tree (6/11/47)
68. June Moon (6/18/47)
69. Peg O' My Heart (6/25/47)
70. The Dark Angel (6/30/47)
71. Great Expectations (7/14/47)
72. My Man Godfrey (7/21/47)
73. Rich Boy (10/18/47)
74. Outward Room (11/1/47)
75. The Light That Failed (11/8/47)
76. The Camel's Back (11/15/47)
77. She Loves Me Not (11/22/47)
78. Jamaica Inn (11/29/47)
79. Personal Appearance (12/6/47)
80. Lorna Doone (12/13/47)
81. A Stand-In for Santa Claus (12/20/47)
82. The Cocktail Reporter (12/27/47)
83. Outward Room (2/4/47)
84. Pearls Are a Nuisance (2/11/47)
85. The Citadel (2/18/47)
86. The Light That Failed (2/25/47)
87. In the Hands of the Senecas (3/3/47)
88. Little Minister (3/10/47)
89. The Apple Tree (3/17/47)
90. Cluny Brown (7/5/47)
91. -----(7/12/47)
92. The Dark Angel (7/19/47)
93. Cocktail Reporter (7/26/47)
94. Portrait of a Man with Red Hair (8/6/47)
95. Mason Shows (8/13/47)
96. June Moon (8/20/47)
97. Kitty Foyle (10/23/47)
98. Windward Passage (10/30/47)

99. Disputed Passage (11/6/47)
100. Long Engagement (11/13/47)
101. The Highwayman (11/20/47)
102. Quiet Wedding (11/27/47)
103. Wuthering Heights (12/4/47)
104. Daddy Long Legs (12/11/47)
105. Somebody Loves Me (12/18/47)
106. The Messiah (12/25/47)
107. For Business Reasons (1/1/49)
108. The Pirate of Orleans (1/8/49)
109. The Doll in the Pink Silk Dress (1/15/49)
110. Vigil for Chris (1/22/49)
111. Young Woman's Darling (1/29/49)
112. The Man from the North (2/5/49)
113. The Apple Tree (6/20/50)
114. Quiet Wedding (6/27/50)
115. Germelshausen (7/4/50)
116. Let There Be Honor (7/11/50)
117. Carmen (7/18/50)
118. Wild Oranges (7/25/50)
119. Mayerling (8/1/50)
120. Off-Shore Pirate (8/8/50)
121. For Business Reasons (1/6/51)
122. Vigil for Chris (1/13/51)
123. Two Live Again (7/2/51)
124. Sword and the Knitting Needle (7/9/51)
125. China Run (7/16/51)
126. Columbia (7/23/51)
127. The Token (7/30/51)
128. Pagosa (8/6/51)
129. Den of Thieves (8/13/51)
130. Marriage of Lit Lit (8/20/51)
131. Purple and Fine Linen (9/8/51)
132. Damascus Steel (9/15/51)
133. The Woman Who Wouldn't Run (9/22/51)
134. Germelshausen (9/29/51)
135. Home on Fasseri (12/23/51)
136. Mail-Order Bride (12/30/51)
137. Impressario (1/6/52)
138. Monte Carlo (6/2/52)
139. Mad 44 (6/9/52)
140. Murder Island (6/16/52)
141. Glass Wall (6/23/52)
142. I Am Not a Stranger (6/30/52)
143. Red Angel (7/7/52)
144. This Above All (7/14/52)
145. Paradise Package (7/28/52)
146. Return to Tomorrow (8/4/52)
147. Den of Thieves (8/11/52)
148. Old Man's Bride (8/18/52)
149. Barrier Reef (8/25/52)
150. Hour of Truth (9/1/52)
151. Latin Affair (6/4/53)
152. Home on Fasseri (6/11/53)
153. Palermo and Return (6/18/53)
154. September Times Two (6/25/53)
155. The Pool (7/2/53)
156. Development in Portugal (7/9/53)
157. The Big Hello (7/16/53)
158. Flight 71 (7/23/53)
159. Very Considerate Burglar (7/30/53)
160. I Am Not a Stranger (8/6/53)
161. Martinique (8/13/53)
162. Hour of Truth (8/20/53)
163. Captain Huckabee's Beard (8/27/53)
164. A Simple Affair (9/3/53)
165. Bachelor's Quarters (9/10/53)
166. Portrait of Stephanie (9/12/53)
167. Miggles (9/19/53)
168. Treadmill (9/26/53)
169. Autumn Heroes (10/3/53)
170. Intermezzo (10/10/53)
171. Goodbye, Mr. Chips (10/17/53)
172. Rapaccini's Daughter (10/24/53)
173. Portrait of Jenny (10/31/53)
174. Point of View (11/7/53)
175. Egg Farm (11/14/53)
176. Pagosa (12/12/53)
177. A Warm Coat for Mommy (12/19/53)
178. The Citadel (12/26/53)
179. Frenchman's Creek (5/22/54)
180. Affair at Aden (5/29/54)
181. Lost Horizon (6/5/54)
182. Amalfi Summer (6/12/54)
183. Lord Sweeney (6/19/54)
184. The Kreutzen List (6/26/54)
185. Sometime Every Summertime (7/3/54)
186. Cordoba (7/10/54)
187. Valiant Lady (7/17/54)
188. Long Way Home (7/24/54)
189. The Fling (7/31/54)
190. Flight to Athens (8/7/54)
191. Isle of the Windward (8/14/54)
192. Paris Encounter (8/21/54)
193. Silhouette (8/28/54)
194. The Postmistress of Laurel Run (9/4/54)
195. The Return of Maria Sanchez (9/11/54)
196. Heiress from Red Horse (9/18/54)
197. The Way to the Castle (9/25/54)
198. Down East (10/1/54)

293. Face of Love (7/28/56)
294. Gentle Torment (8/4/56)
295. The Gypsy (8/11/56)
296. Fielder's Choice (8/18/56)
297. The Cadiz Fly (8/25/56)
298. The Vortegs (9/1/56)
299. Bill Gunn's Mermaid (9/8/56)
300. The Man from Venus (9/15/56)
301. The Law and Miss Deborah (9/22/56)
302. Captain Willis' Wonderful Paddle Wheel (9/29/56)
303. Earthquake (10/6/56)
304. The Bell That Couldn't Ring (10/13/56)
305. Theatricals at Medicine Hat (10/20/56)
306. Lovely Dead Letter (10/27/56)
307. Egg Farm (11/3/56)
308. Log of the Black Parrot (11/10/56)
309. Long Way Home (11/17/56)
310. Women of the Seventh (12/1/56)
311. The Guitar (12/8/56)
312. The Indian Sign (12/15/56)
313. The Cave (12/22/56)
314. A Quiet Little Party (12/29/56)
315. Uncle Fats and the Goose Step (1/5/57)

The Romance of Famous Jewels

This syndicated series, consisting of fifteen-minute broadcasts about various diamonds and jewels, their history and value, was broadcast during the 1930s.

1. The Sancey Diamond
2. The Mysterious Opal
3. The Pigott Diamond
4. The Great Mogul Diamond
5. The Orloff Diamond
6. Treasure of Caballo Cunco
7. The Alfred Jewel
8. Queen Elizabeth's Ring
9. Mssr. Silhouette
10. The Jonker's Diamond
11. Anne Boleyn's Diamond
12. The Matan Diamond

Romance of the Ranchos

Dramatizing southern California history, this CBS series originated from station KNX in California. Howard McNear and Pat McGeehan starred. Fran Graham was the "Wandering Vacaro." Sponsored by the Title Insurance and Trust Company, the series was initially broadcast on Sundays, then Wednesday as of episode four.

1. San Rafael (9/7/41)
2. Santa Gertrudes (9/14/41)
3. San Jose (9/21/41)
4. Aguaje De La Centinela (10/1/41)
5. Rodeo De Las Aguas (10/8/41)
6. San Pedro and Palos Verdes (10/15/41)
7. Paso De Martolo Viejo (10/22/41)
8. Ex Mission De San Fernando (10/29/41)
9. Los Cerritos and Los Alamitos (11/5/41)
10. Tiburcio Vasquez (11/12/41)
11. San Vincente Y Santa Monica (11/9/41)
12. San Francisco (11/26/41)
13. San Antonio (12/3/41)
14. Benjamin D. Wilson [part one] (12/10/41)
15. Benjamin D. Wilson [part two] (12/17/41)
16. Christmas at San Gabriel (12/24/41)
17. San Jose de Buenos Ayres (12/31/41)

18. Joseph Chapman (1/7/42)
19. Azusa Dalton (1/14/42)
20. Jedediah Smith (1/21/42)
21. Rancho La Puente (1/28/42)
22. Santa Catalina Island (2/4/42)
23. Hugo Reid (2/11/42)
24. La Ballona (2/18/42)
25. Juan Flaco (2/25/42)
26. Phineas Banning (3/8/42)

27. Rancho San Francisquito (3/15/42)
28. Water Development (3/22/42)
29. Joaquin Murietta (3/29/42)
30. Rancho San Pasqual (4/5/42)
31. Don Juan Temple (4/12/42)
32. Rancho La Brea (4/19/42)
33. Pueblo of Los Angeles (4/26/42)
34. Transportation (5/3/42)
35. Carrillo Family (5/10/42)

Satellite Seven

Broadcast over the BBC, various East Coast radio stations presented this thrilling series simultaneously in 1958. The announcer referred to *Satellite Seven* as part science-fiction, part mystery, part spy tale, and part adventure. *Satellite Seven* revolved around a British space mission to be the first to photograph the far side of the moon and a spy's mission to sabotage the project. Aimed at a juvenile audience, reality came close to home when a little more than a year after, in October of 1959, the Soviet Union sent a satellite into orbit around the moon, photographing for the first time the far side of the moon, changing science-fiction to science-fact.

1. The Mysterious Island (4/30/58)
2. The Whispering Voices (4/30/58)
3. Counter Spy (5/7/58)
4. The Launching Day (5/7/58)

5. The Late Night Rendezvous (5/14/58)
6. Zero Hour (5/14/58)
7. The Spy (5/21/58)
8. The Moon Messenger (5/21/58)

Screen Director's Playhouse

This radio program, unlike the majority of the Hollywood drama programs, was devoted to the director, not the actor. For thirty minutes, a dramatization of a specific film was performed, using the original cast whenever possible, and then the director was given a few minutes at the end of the program to talk about his film and recollect various scenes and moments with the cast members. Adaptors for the series were Milton Geiger, Richard Allen Simmons, Jack Rubin and Nat Wolf. Music was composed and conducted by Henry Russell, later to be replaced by William Lava, followed by Robert Armbruster by April of 1950. Bill Cairn started out as an associate producer for the show, later becoming the director of the program. Warren Lewis began directing on April 19, 1951. Howard Wiley was the producer.

Screen Director's Playhouse premiered sustaining over NBC, Sunday evenings from 8:30 to 9 pm, EST. Beginning July 1, 1949, the show was sponsored by Pabst

Blue Ribbon Beer and broadcast on Friday evenings from 9 to 9:30 pm, EST. On October 3, 1949, Pabst dropped sponsorship, *Playhouse* went sustaining again, and broadcast on Monday evenings from 10 to 10:30 pm, EST. On November 11, 1949, the series moved to Friday from 10 to 10:30 pm, EST. Beginning January 6, 1950, RCA began sponsoring the series, broadcast on Friday from 9 to 9:30 pm, EST. On November 9, 1950, *Playhouse* moved to Thursday evenings, sponsored by Anacin and Chesterfield. On November 16, 1950, *Playhouse* went to a new sixty-minute format. On September 7, 1951, the series moved to Fridays from 8 to 9 pm. When the program premiered, the series aired under the title *Screen Director's Guild* and *Screen Director's Assignment*, until July of 1949, when the title became *Screen Director's Playhouse*.

Frank Barton was the first announcer for the series; Jimmy Wallington took over the announcing duties when Pabst Blue Ribbon sponsored. The President of the Screen Director's Guild made an appearance on the February 13, 1949, broadcast. Violinist Isaac Stern supplied the music for the broadcast of April 19, 1951, although the music was previously transcribed. For the broadcast of January 25, 1951, the music bridges, played by Dr. Samuel Hoffman, are played on a "theramin," as in the original film. Bob Hope and Bing Crosby were featured in the Chesterfield commercials. Although there was an attempt to get the original director of each film on each episode, sometimes a substitute was placed. Leo McCarey, the producer of *My Favorite Wife*, took the place of director Garson Kanin on December 7, 1950. The real Mrs. Mike, on whose life the book and film were based, was interviewed after the drama of November 30, 1950.

1. Stagecoach (1/9/49; Ward Bord, Claire Trevor, and John Wayne)
2. Let's Live a Little (1/16/49; Robert Cummings, Betty Lou Gerson, and Richard Wallace)
3. The Exile (1/23/49; Raymond Burr, Douglas Fairbanks, Jr., Carl Harbor, Lou Krugman, Paul McVey, Max Ophuls, and Janet Waldo)
4. Mr. and Mrs. Smith (1/30/49; Mary Jane Croft, Verna Felton, Alfred Hitchcock, Patrick McGeehan, Robert Montgomery, and Carlton Young)
5. Hired Wife (2/6/49; Ed Begley, Joan Banks, Herb Litton, Betty Moran, Dan Riss, Rosalind Russell, William Seiter, and Carlton Young)
6. Magnificent Obsession (2/13/49; Irene Dunne, Barbara Eiler, John Lund, Ralph Moody, Dan Riss, Willard Waterman, and Anne Whitfield)
7. The Prisoner of Zenda (2/20/49; Ronald Colman and Benita Hume)
8. Night Has a Thousand Eyes (2/27/49; William Demerest, Paul Frees, and Edward G. Robinson)
9. A Foreign Affair [hour-long special] (3/6/49; Marlene Dietrich, John Lund, Rosalind Russell, Herb Vigran, and Billy Wilder)
10. You Were Meant For Me (3/13/49; Jim Backus, Lloyd Bacon, Dan Dailey, Norman Field, Betty Lynn, Dan Riss, Irene Tedrow, William Tracy)
11. The Perfect Marriage (3/20/49; Lewis Allen, Bob Bailey, Gayle Bonney, Leif Erickson, Ruth Perrott, Dan Riss, Dorothy Thompson, Barton Yarborough, and Loretta Young)
12. Suddenly, It's Spring (3/27/49; Margaret Brayton, Hal Gerard, Virginia Gregg, Mitchell Leisen, Frank Lovejoy, Fred MacMurray, and Dan Riss)
13. The Ghost Breakers (4/3/49; Ken

Christy, Jack Edwards, June Foray, Bob Hope, Sheldon Leonard, George Marshall, Shirley Mitchell, Betty Moran, Donald Morrison, and Dan Riss)

14. Music for Millions (4/10/49; June Allyson, Henry Coster, Joseph Kearns, Betty Moran, GeGe Pearson, Herbert Rawlinson, Dan Riss, Wilms Herbert, and Anne Whitfield)

15. The Best Years of Our Lives (4/17/49; Dana Andrews, Ken Christy, David Ellis, Virginia Gregg, Howard McNear, Gerald Mohr, Earle Ross, Theodore Von Eltz, Janet Waldo, and William Wyler)

16. The Sky's the Limit (4/24/49; Fred Astaire, Harry Bartell, Sharon Douglas, Edward H. Griffith, Edwin Max, Jay Novello, Dan Riss and Barton Yarborough)

17. The Trouble with Women (5/1/49; Grif Barnett, Bob Bruce, Mary Jane Croft, Florence Halop, Sidney Lanfield, Frank Lovejoy, Ray Milland, Ralph Moody, Dan Riss, Herb Vigran, and Sarajane Wells)

18. It's a Wonderful Life (5/8/49; Georgia Backus, Arthur Q. Bryan, Herb Butterfield, Frank Capra, Hans Conried, Barbara Eiler, Joseph Granby, Jimmy Stewart, and Irene Tedrow)

19. Hold Back the Dawn (5/15/49; Jeanne Bates, Charles Boyer, Vanessa Brown, Raymond Burr, John Dehner, and Mitchel Leisen)

20. Her Husband's Affairs (5/22/49; Lucille Ball, Ken Christy, Hans Conried, Wilms Herbert, Elliott Lewis, Herbert Litton, Jay Novello, Dan Riss, and S. Sylvan Simon)

21. Trade Winds (5/29/49; Tay Garnett, Wally Maher, Fredric March, Betty Moran, James Nusser, GeGe Pearson, Dan Riss and Lurene Tuttle)

22. The Killers (6/5/49; Tony Barrett, William Conrad, Gwen Deleno, Sam Edwards, Frank Gerstle, Burt Lancaster, Dan Riss, Robert Siodmak, and Shelley Winters)

23. Mr. Blandings Builds His Dream House (7/1/49; Herb Butterfield,

Ruby Dandridge, Frank Gerstle, Cary Grant, Wilms Herbert, Betty Moran, Frances Robinson, Willard Waterman and Anne Whitfield)

24. The Big Clock (7/8/49; Tony Barrett, William Conrad, Larry Dobkin, John Farlow, Ray Milland, and Maureen O'Sullivan)

25. Yellow Sky (7/15/49; Gloria Blondell, Sam Edwards, Paul Frees, Wally Maher, Gregory Peck, and William Wellman)

26. Casbah (7/22/49; John Berry, Herb Butterfield, Tony Martin, Marta Toren, and Lurene Tuttle)

27. Saigon (7/29/49; Leslie Fenton and Alan Ladd)

28. Fort Apache (8/5/49; Tony Barrett, Ward Bond, John Ford, Paul McVey, Lou Merrill and John Wayne)

29. Jezebel (8/12/49; Bette Davis, Paul Frees, Gerald Mohr, Ralph Moody, and William Tyler)

30. Love Crazy (8/19/49; Gloria Blondell, Hans Conried, William Johnstone, William Powell, Dan Riss, Mary Shipp, Malcolm St. Clair, and Gil Stratton)

31. Appointment for Love (8/26/49; Charles Boyer, Virginia Gregg, Jerry Hausner, Howard McNear, William Seiter, and Gale Storm)

32. Apartment for Peggy (9/2/49)

33. The Human Comedy (9/9/49; Clarence Brown, Francis X. Bushman, Mickey Rooney, and Barton Yarborough)

34. Whispering Smith (9/16/49; Alan Ladd)

35. Don't Trust Your Husband (9/23/49; Fred MacMurray)

36. Pride of the Yankees (9/30/49; Gary Cooper)

37. The Senator Was Indiscreet (10/3/49; Jeanne Bates, William Conrad, Peggy Dow, Paul Frees, Jack Kruschen, Jay Novello, and William Powell)

38. Criss Cross (10/10/49; Jeff Corey, Betty Lou Gerson, Burt Lancaster, Betty Morgan, Stan Waxman)

39. Pitfall (10/17/49; Raymond Burr, Andre de Toth, Sam Edwards, Virginia Gregg, Ralph Moody, Dick Powell, and Jane Wyatt)

40. Love Letters (10/24/49; Joseph Cotten, William Dieterle, Barbara Eiler, Alma Laughton, Dan O'Herlihy, and Ben Wright)
41. Remember the Night (10/31/49; Gerald Mohr and Barbara Stanwyck)
42. Body and Soul (11/11/49; William Conrad, Hans Conried, Steve Dunne, Barbara Eiler, John Garfield, Jerry Hausner, Wally Maher, Ralph Moody, and Robert Rossen)
43. The Uninvited (11/18/49; Lewis Allen, John Dehner, June Foray, Alma Laughton, Ray Milland, and Mary Shipp)
44. The Spiral Staircase (11/25/49; John Dehner, Steve Dunne, Dorothy McGuire, Jane Morgan, Dan Riss, and Robert Siodmak)
45. All My Sons (12/2/49; Helen Andrews, Jeff Chandler, Jack Edwards, Irving Reis, Edward G. Robinson, and Irene Tedrow)
46. Call Northside 777 (12/9/49; Bill Conrad, Paul Frees, Stacy Harris, Henry Hathaway, and James Stewart)
47. The Affairs of Susan (12/16/49; Steve Dunne, Joan Fontaine, Wilms Herbert, William Seiter, Willard Waterman, and Barton Yarborough)
48. Miracle on 34th Street (12/23/49; Paul Frees, Edmund Gwenn, George Seaton, Willard Waterman, and Natalie Wood)
49. One Way Passage (12/30/49; John Dehner, Don Diamond, Peggy Dow, Steve Dunne, Tay Garnett, and William Powell)
50. Magic Town (1/6/50; Hans Conried, Virginia Gregg, Jerry Hausner, Sam Hayes, Eddie Marr, George Marshall, and Jimmy Stewart)
51. Tomorrow Is Forever (1/13/50; Jeff Chandler, Claudette Colbert, Sam Edwards, John McIntire, and Irving Pichel)
52. Mr. Lucky (1/20/50; Ken Christy, Cary Grant, Hank Potter, and Francis Robinson)
53. It Had to Be You (1/27/50; Joan Fontaine, Wilms Herbert, Gerald Mohr, Frank Nelson, Jay Novello, and Alfred Werker)
54. The Sea Wolf (2/3/50; Herb Butterfield, Michael Curtiz, Paul Frees, Wilms Herbert, Lou Merrill, Edward G. Robinson, and Lurene Tuttle)
55. This Thing Called Love (2/10/50; Joan Banks, Paul DuBov, Steve Dunne, Alexander Hall, Harry Lang, and Rosalind Russell)
56. It's In the Bag (2/17/50; Fred Allen, John Brown, Hans Conried, Sheldon Leonard, Frank Nelson, Alan Reed, Lurene Tuttle, and Richard Wallace)
57. Incendiary Blonde (2/24/50; Betty Hutton)
58. The Paleface (3/3/50; Bob Hope, Norman McLeod, and Jane Russell)
59. Portrait of Jenny (3/10/50; Eleanor Audley, Frank Barton, Joseph Cotten, Barbara Eiler, Wilms Herbert, Ramsey Hill, Norma Jean Nilsson, Victor Perrin, and Lurene Tuttle)
60. Champion (3/17/50; Frank Barton, Kirk Douglas, Jack Edwards, Frank Lovejoy, Rita Lynn, Dan Riss, and Mark Robson)
61. Chicago Deadline (3/24/50; Lewis Allen, Jim Backus, Raymond Burr, and Alan Ladd)
62. The Dark Mirror (3/31/50; Francis X. Bushman, John Dehner, David Ellis, and Olivia De Havilland)
63. The Fighting O'Flynn (4/7/50; Frank Barton, Raymond Burr, Douglas Fairbanks, Jr., Paul Frees, Frank Gerstle, Ramsey Hill, Dan O'Herlihy, and Arthur Pierson)
64. It Happens Every Spring (4/14/50; Parley Baer, Lloyd Bacon, Frank Barton, Ted de Corsia, Ann Diamond, Eddie Fields, Ray Milland, Frank Nelson, and Dan Riss)
65. A Kiss in the Dark (4/21/50; Hans Conried, Delmar Daves, Olan Soule, and Jane Wyman)
66. Rope of Sand (4/28/50; Frank Barton, Corinne Calvert, William Dieterle, Norman Field, William Johnstone, Burt Lancaster, Donald Morrison, and Stan Waxman)
67. When My Baby Smiles at Me (5/5/50; Hy Averback, Frank Barton, Betty

Grable, Walter Lang, Paul McVey, Herb Vigran, and Barton Yarborough)

68. Butch Minds the Baby (5/12/50; Frank Barton, Gail Bonney, Broderick Crawford, Steve Dunne, Wilms Herbert, Jerry Hausner, Edwin Max, Frances Robinson, Albert S. Rogel, and Herb Vigran)

69. Miss Grant Takes Richmond (5/19/50; Lloyd Bacon, Lucille Ball, Frank Barton, Jeanne Bates, Arthur Q. Bryan, Steve Dunne, Norman Field, Frank Nelson, and Herb Vigran)

70. Flamingo Road (5/26/50; David Brian, Joan Crawford, and Michael Curtiz)

71. She Wouldn't Say Yes (6/2/50; Hy Averback, Alexander Hall, Frank Nelson, and Rosalind Russell)

72. Mr. Blandings Builds his Dream House (6/9/50; Betsy Drake, Cary Grant, and Hank Potter)

73. A Star Is Born (6/16/50; Fredric March)

74. The Strange Love of Martha Ivers (6/23/50; Eleanor Audley, Ken Christy, Jack Edwards, Wilms Herbert, Lou Merrill, Gerald Mohr, Joel Nessler, Norma Jean Nilsson, Jeffrey Silvers, Barbara Stanwyck, and Gayne Whitman)

75. Cinderella (6/30/50; Verna Felton)

76. Shadow of a Doubt (11/9/50; Hy Averback, Gail Bonney, Lois Corbett, Betsy Drake, Cary Grant, Earle Ross, and Anne Whitfield)

77. Lifeboat (11/16/50; Tallulah Bankhead, Jeff Chandler, Ann Diamond, Barbara Eiler, Roy Glenn, Wilms Herbert, Alfred Hitchcock, Sheldon Leonard, and Henry Rowland)

78. Cluncy Brown (11/23/50; Charles Boyer, Joseph Mankiewicz, Dorothy McGuire, and Billy Wilder)

79. Mrs. Mike (11/30/50; Michael Ann Barrett, Joseph Cotten, Hal Gerard, Joe Granby, Byron Kane, Evelyn Keyes, Louis King, Leone Ledoux, Ralph Moody, Frank Nelson, Janet Scott, and Martha Wentworth)

80. My Favorite Wife (12/7/50; Irene Dunne, Cary Grant, Leo McCarey, and Frank Nelson)

81. Lady Gambles (12/14/50; Paul Avery, Georgia Bacus, Tony Barrett, William Conrad, John Dehner, Michael Gordon, Byron Kane, Stephen McNally, Ruth Perrott, and Barbara Stanwyck)

82. Miracle on 34th Street (12/21/50; Gail Bonney, William Conrad, David Ellis, Edmund Gwenn, Ralph Moody, Jack Moyles, Frank Nelson, Joel Nessler, Herbert Rawlinson, Joan Ray, and Lurene Tuttle)

83. Alias Nick Beal (12/28/50; Tony Barrett, Raymond Burr, Herb Butterfield, Lois Corbett, Frank Gerstle, Jack Kruschen, Ray Milland, Jan Sterling, and Theodore Von Eltz)

84. Prince of Foxes (1/4/51; Lynn Allen, Raymond Burr, Herb Butterfield, William Conrad, Douglas Fairbanks, Jr., Henry King, Joyce McKenzie, Lou Merrill, and Ben Wright)

85. Ivy (1/11/51; Eleanor Audley, Ken Christy, Charles Drake, Joan Fontaine, Frank Gerstle, George Marshall, Paul McVey, Gerald Mohr, Ruth Perrott, and John Stevenson)

86. The Big Lift (1/18/51; Tony Barrett, Paul Douglas, Paul DuBov, Byron Kane, Betty Lou Gearson, Eddie Marr, Ralph Moody, Henry Rowland, George Seaton, and Lurene Tuttle)

87. Spellbound (1/25/51; John Blyforce, Herbert Butterfield, Joseph Cotten, Alfred Hitchcock, Mercedes McCambridge, Howard McNear, James Nusser, and William Tracy)

88. Take a Letter, Darling (2/1/51; Jim Bacus, Arthur Q. Bryan, Mary Jane Croft, Fritz Feld, June Foray, Peter Leeds, Mitchell Leisen, Fred MacMurray, and Rosalind Russell)

89. Lucky Jordan (2/8/51; Paul DuBov, Verna Felton, Virginia Gregg, Alan Ladd, Sheldon Leonard, GeGe Pearson, Earle Ross, King Vidor, and Herb Vigran)

90. Dark Victory (2/15/51; Lynn Allen, Tallulah Bankhead, David Brian,

Edmund Goulding, Ralph Moody, Norma Varden, and Stan Waxman)

91. No Minor Vices (2/22/51; Dana Andrews, Jim Backus, Ann Diamond, Louis Jourdan, Maria Palmer, and Billy Wilder)
92. A Foreign Affair (3/1/51; Lucille Ball, Charles Brackett, Marlene Dietrich, Sam Edwards, Wally Maher, Dan Riss, Henry Rowland, Gil Stratton, Herb Vigran, and Billy Wilder)
93. Bachelor Mother (3/8/51; Lucille Ball, Arthur Q. Bryan, Bob Cummings, Garson Kanin, and Frank Nelson)
94. Thelma Jordan (3/15/51; Hy Averback, Jack Carroll, William Conrad, Wendell Corey, Ralph Moody, Ruth Perrott, Robert Siodmak, Barbara Stanwyck, Stan Waxman, and Peggy Webber)
95. The Great Lover (3/22/51; Jim Backus, Pinto Colvig, Fritz Feld, Rhonda Fleming, Paul Frees, Bob Hope, Sheldon Leonard, George Marshall, and Walter Tetley)
96. Next Time We Love (3/29/51; Bruce Cannon, Stanley Ferrar, E.H. Griffith, Leone Ledoux, Gerald Mohr, Joel Nessler, Eleanor Parker and Jimmy Stewart)
97. The Damned Don't Cry (4/5/51; Eleanor Audley, Tony Barrett, Ken Christy, Joan Crawford, Eddie Fields, Paul Frees, Frank Lovejoy, Sidney Miller, Vincent Sherman and Irene Winston)
98. Hired Wife (4/12/51; Jim Backus, Jeff Chandler, Ken Christy, Mary Jane Croft, Robert North, Earle Ross, Rosalind Russell, and William Seiter)
99. Humoresque (4/19/51; Lynn Allen, Tallulah Bankhead, Steve Cochran, Sheldon Leonard, Helen Marvintile, Jean Negulesco, Nestor Paiva, John Stevenson, and Ben Wright)
100. Jackpot (4/26/51; Jim Backus, Dawn Bender, Bill Bouchey, Ann Diamond, Betty Lou Gerson, Jerry Hausner, Walter Lang, Eddie Marr, Edwin Max, Sidney Miller, Jeffrey Silver, Jimmy Stewart, Margaret Truman, and Stan Waxman)
101. The Captain from Castile (5/3/51; Douglas Fairbanks, Jr., Henry King, and Paula Morgan)
102. No Time For Love (5/10/51; Claudette Colbert)
103. Rogue's Regiment (5/17/51; Dick Powell)
104. Back Street (5/24/51; Charles Boyer and Mercedes McCambridge)
105. Beyond Glory (5/31/51; Alan Ladd)
106. The Gunfighter (6/7/51; Gregory Peck)
107. D.O.A. (6/21/51; Edmund O'Brien)
108. The Lady Takes a Chance (6/28/51; Joan Caufield and John Lund)
109. Only Yesterday (7/5/51; Jeff Chandler and Mercedes McCambridge)
110. The Fugitive (7/12/51; Henry Fonda)
111. Remember the Night (7/19/51; William Holden)
112. Stairway to Heaven (7/26/51; Robert Cummings)
113. Caged (8/2/51; Eleanor Parker)
114. The Ghost and Mrs. Muir (8/16/51; Charles Boyer and Jane Wyatt)
115. Mother Was a Freshman (8/30/51; Loretta Young)

The Screen Guild Theater

At first this series was titled *The Camel Screen Guild Players*; then Camel dropped the product name by the fall of 1948, but continued sponsoring. It was broadcast from Hollywood over NBC, Thursday evenings. Beginning with episode 79, Camel dropped sponsorship, and the program moved to ABC as an hour-long dramatic program, still on Thursdays. Beginning April 6, 1952, *Screen Guild* was heard over CBS, Sunday evenings from 9 to 10 pm, EST.

1. Call Northside 777 (10/7/48; Richard Conte, Pat O'Brien, and Jimmy Stewart)
2. Welcome, Stranger (10/14/48; Bing Crosby, Barry Fitzgerald, and Mona Freeman)
3. The Babe Ruth Story (10/21/48; William Bendix, Charles Bickford, and Lurene Tuttle)
4. Kiss of Death (10/28/48; Leon Ames, Coleen Gray, Victor Mature, and Lurene Tuttle)
5. Take a Letter, Darling (11/4/48; Fred MacMurray and Rosalind Russell)
6. All My Sons (11/11/48; Burt Lancaster, Ona Munson, and Edward G. Robinson)
7. Rebecca (11/18/48; John Lund, Agnes Moorehead, and Loretta Young)
8. 13 Rue Madeline (11/25/48; Leon Ames, John Beal, Humphrey Bogart, and William Lundigan)
9. Night Song (12/2/48; Hoagy Charmicheal, Van Heflin, and Merle Oberon)
10. Michael and Mary (12/9/48; Claudette Colbert and Ronald Colman)
11. Where There's Life (12/16/48; Signe Hasso and Bob Hope)
12. Snow White (12/23/48; Edgar Bergen, Charlie McCarthy, Charles Ken, and Mary Jane Smith)
13. Pinocchio (12/30/48; Fanny Brice, Hans Conried, and Hanley Stafford)
14. Notorious (1/6/49; Ingrid Bergman, John Hodiak, and J. Carroll Naish)
15. So Evil, My Love (1/13/49; Deborah Kerr and Ray Milland)
16. The Fuller Brush Man (1/20/49; Janet Blair and Red Skelton)
17. The Walls of Jericho (1/27/49; Claire Trevor and Cornel Wilde)
18. The Big Punch (2/3/49; Wayne Morris)
19. Fury at Furnace Creek (2/10/49; Barbara Britton, Wendell Corey, Reginald Gardiner, Charles Kemper, and Victor Mature)
20. Deep Waters (2/17/49; Dana Andrews, Jean Peters, and Dean Stockwell)
21. One Way Passage (2/24/49; Lew Ayers, Charles Bickford, and Jane Wyman)
22. Command Decision (3/3/49; Edward Arnold, Brian Donlevy, Clark Gable, John Hodiak, and Walter Pidgeon)
23. Letters from an Unknown Woman (3/10/49; Joan Fontaine and Louis Jordan)
24. Dark Victory (3/17/49; Joan Crawford, Paula Winslowe, and Robert Young)
25. Enchantment (3/24/49; Jayne Meadows, David Niven, and Teresa Wright)
26. The Fighting O'Flynn (3/31/49; Helena Carter and Douglas Fairbanks, Jr.)
27. Good Sam (4/7/49; Gary Cooper and Ginger Rogers)
28. The Fighting O'Flynn (4/14/49; Helena Carter and Douglas Fairbanks, Jr.)
29. Blue Dalhia (4/21/49; Alan Ladd, Veronica Lake, and Will Wright)
30. Bachelor Mother (4/28/49; Lucille Ball, Charles Coburn, and Joseph Cotten)
31. Undercurrent (5/5/49; Barbara Stanwyck and Robert Taylor)
32. Temptation Harbor (5/12/49; Signe Hasso and Herbert Marshall)
33. The Bride Goes Wild (5/19/49; June Allyson and Van Johnson)
34. Flesh and Fantasy (5/25/49; Kirk Douglas and Ava Gardner)
35. Roadhouse (6/2/49; Ida Lupino, Lloyd Nolan, and Richard Widmark)
36. One Sunday Afternoon (6/9/49; June Haver and Dennis Morgan)
37. Together Again (6/16/49; Irene Dunne and Walter Pidgeon)
38. Stairway to Heaven (6/23/49; David Niven and Herbert Marshall)
39. The Old Lady Shows Her Medals (6/30/49; Ethel Barrymore, Lionel Barrymore, and James Cagney)
40. Homecoming (10/6/49; Clark Gable and Lana Turner)
41. Champion (10/13/49; Kirk Douglas and Marilyn Maxwell)
42. The Paleface (10/20/39; Bob Hope and Jane Russell)
43. A Kiss in the Dark (10/27/49; David Niven and Jane Wyman)

44. A Letter to Three Wives (11/3/49; Linda Darnell and Paul Douglas)
45. The Bribe (11/10/49; Joseph Cotten and Ava Gardner)
46. A Street with No Name (11/17/49; Lloyd Nolan and Richard Widmark)
47. Suspicion (11/24/49; Nigel Bruce, Joan Fontaine, and Cary Grant)
48. Command Decision (12/1/49; Edward Arnold, Brian Donlevy, Clark Gable, John Hodiak, Van Johnson, and Walter Pidgeon)
49. Alias Nick Beal (12/8/49; Ray Milland)
50. Family Honeymoon (12/15/49; Claudette Colbert and Fred MacMurray)
51. Little Women (12/22/49; June Allyson and Peter Lawford)
52. It's a Wonderful Life (12/29/49; Victor Moore and James Stewart)
53. You're My Everything (1/5/50; Anne Baxter and Dan Dailey)
54. The Ox-Bow Incident (1/12/50; Edward Arnold and Charlie Ruggles)
55. You Belong to Me (1/19/50; Don Ameche and Lucille Ball)
56. I Love You Again (1/26/50; Ruth Hussey and William Powell)
57. John Loves Mary (2/2/50; Patricia Neal and Ronald Reagan)
58. Calcutta (2/9/50; Alan Ladd and Gail Russell)
59. Double Indemnity (2/16/50; Barbara Stanwyck and Robert Taylor)
60. Laura (2/23/50; Dana Andrews, Gene Tierney, and Clifton Webb)
61. Everybody Does It (3/2/50; Linda Darnell and Paul Douglas)
62. A Foreign Affair (3/9/50; Joan Fontaine and John Lund)
63. What a Woman! (3/16/50; Brian Aherne, Joseph Cotten, and Rosalind Russell)
64. The Sun Comes Up (3/23/50; Jeanette MacDonald and Charles Ruggles)
65. Adventure in Baltimore (3/30/50; Preston Foster and Shirley Temple)
66. It Started with Eve (4/6/50; Charles Laughton and Diana Lynn)
67. The Shocking Miss Pilgrim (4/13/50; Betty Grable)
68. The Cowboy and the Lady (4/20/50; MacDonald Carey and Ginger Rogers)
69. The Shocking Miss Pilgrim (4/27/50; Betty Grable)
70. Hold Back the Dawn (5/4/50; Charles Boyer and Olivia de Havilland)
71. Mad About Music (5/11/50; George Brent and Alan Mobray)
72. The Maltese Falcon (5/18/50; Lauren Bacall and Humphrey Bogart)
73. The Seventh Veil (5/25/50; Ida Lupino and George Sanders)
74. The Dark Corner (6/1/50; John Hodiak and Brenda Marshall)
75. My Son, My Son (6/8/50; Angela Lansbury and Herbert Marshall)
76. The Mating of Millie (6/15/50; Robert Cummings and Barbara Hale)
77. -----(6/22/50)
78. You're My Everything (6/29/50; Anne Baxter and Dan Dailey)
79. Twelve O'Clock High (9/7/50; Ward Bond and Gregory Peck)
80. Ninotchka (9/14/50; Joan Fontaine and William Powell)
81. Secret Fury (9/21/50; Claudette Colbert and Robert Ryan)
82. The Captive (9/28/50; Lew Ayers and Teresa Wright)
83. Champagne for Caesar (10/5/50; Barbara Britton, Ronald Colman, Art Linkletter, Vincent Price, and Audrey Totter)
84. Any Number Can Play (10/12/50; Broderick Crawford and Alexis Smith)
85. The Informer (10/17/50; Paul Douglas)
86. Mother Didn't Tell Me (10/24/50; Dorothy McGuire)
87. Tell It to the Judge (11/2/50; Robert Cummings and Rosalind Russell)
88. The Dark Mirror (11/9/50; Dana Andrews, Bette Davis, and Gene Tierney)
89. Father Was a Fullback (11/16/50; Linda Darnell and Fred MacMurray)
90. Romance of Rosey Ridge (11/23/50; Janet Leigh and Ida Lupino)
91. Woman in Hiding (11/30/50; Howard Duff and Ida Lupino)

92. Tom, Dick and Harry (12/7/50; George Murphy, Dennis O'Keefe, and Ginger Rogers)
93. The Seventh Veil (12/14/50; Anne Baxter and Van Heflin)
94. Come to the Stable (12/21/50; Hugh Marlowe, Ruth Warrick, and Loretta Young)
95. Snow White / Pinocchio (12/28/50; Edgar Bergen, Fanny Brice, Charlie McCarthy, and Hanley Stafford)
96. The Paleface (1/4/51; Bob Hope and Jane Russell)
97. Brief Encounter (1/11/51; Stewart Granger and Deborah Kerr)
98. Birth of the Blues (1/18/51; Bing Crosby, Phil Harris, and Dinah Shore)
99. House of Strangers (1/25/51; June Havoc, Victor Mature, and Edward G. Robinson)
100. Free for All (2/1/51; Ann Blyth and Donald O'Connor)
101. The Postman Always Rings Twice (2/8/51; Ann Blyth and Donald O'Connor)
102. June Bride (2/15/51; Frank Lovejoy and Jane Wyman)
103. Miss Grant Takes Richmond (2/22/51; Eve Arden and William Holden)
104. The Guilt of Janet Ames (3/1/51; Joseph Cotten and Mercedes McCambridge)
105. All About Eve (3/8/51; Anne Baxter, Bette Davis, and George Sanders)
106. It's a Wonderful Life (3/15/51; Victor Moore, Donna Reed, and James Stewart)
107. Easter Parade (3/22/51; Fred Astaire and Judy Garland)
108. Kiss of Death (3/29/51; Victor Mature and Richard Widmark)
109. No Time for Comedy (4/5/51; Eve Arden and Ronald Reagan)
110. Twelve O'Clock High (4/12/51; Ward Bond, Hugh Marlowe, and Gregory Peck)
111. Mister 888 (4/19/51; Edmund Gwenn, Burt Lancaster, and Dorothy McGuire)
112. The Trouble with Women (4/26/51; Lucille Ball and John Lund)
113. Together Again (5/3/51; Charles Boyer and Irene Dunne)
114. Secret Heart (5/10/51; Joan Crawford)
115. Valley of Decision (5/17/51; Greer Garson and Barry Sullivan)
116. Michael and Mary (5/24/51; Helen Hayes and Walter Pidgeon)
117. Apartment for Peggy (5/31/51; Edmund Gwenn, William Lundigan, and Diana Lynn)
118. Ivy (3/13/52; Joan Fontaine and Stephen McNally)
119. Michael and Mary (3/20/52; Deborah Kerr and Herbert Marshall)
120. Night May Fall (3/27/52; Joseph Cotten and Angela Lansbury)
121. Circus Episode (4/3/52; Jeff Chandler and Audrey Totter)
122. Heaven Can Wait (4/6/52; Lynn Bari, John Brown, and Walter Pidgeon)
123. The Mating of Millie (4/13/52; John Lund and Donna Reed)
124. Bachelor Mother (4/20/52; Ann Sothern and Robert Stack)
125. Bluebeard's Eighth Wife (4/27/52; Diana Lynn and David Niven)
126. A Foreign Affair (5/4/52; Celeste Holm and Don Taylor)
127. The Great McGinty (5/11/52; Broderick Crawford and Ruth Warrick)
128. A Letter to Three Wives (5/18/52; Linda Darnell and Paul Douglas)
129. The Good Fairy (5/25/52; Ann Blyth and Robert Young)
130. Mad About Music (6/1/52; Piper Laurie and William Powell)
131. Christmas in July (6/8/52; Eddie Bracken and Nancy Gates)
132. Hold Back the Dawn (6/15/52; Jean Pierre Aumont and Barbara Stanwyck)
133. Family Honeymoon (6/22/52; Jeff Chandler and Barbara Stanwyck)
134. Over Twenty-One (6/29/52; MacDonald Carey and Irene Dunne)

The Sealed Book

Horror and supernatural tales by Robert A. Arthur and David Kogan, writers of *The Mysterious Traveler*, all of the scripts were repeats of *Traveler* episodes, with new casts. The series aired over the Don-Lee Mutual network, Sunday evenings from 10:30 to 11 pm, EST, hosted and narrated by Phillip Clarke.

1. The Hands of Death [aka "The Hands That Killed" when it was originally broadcast on *The Mysterious Traveler*] (3/18/45)
2. King of the World (3/25/45)
3. Death Spins a Web (4/1/45)
4. Devil Island (4/8/45)
5. Escape by Death (4/15/45)
6. Death at Storm House (4/22/45)
7. The Accusing Corpse (4/29/45)
8. Stranger in the House (5/6/45)
9. Out of the Past (5/13/45)
10. Welcome Home (5/20/45)
11. I'll Die Laughing (5/27/45)
12. Design for Death (6/3/45)
13. The Ghost Makers (6/10/45)
14. Broadway Here I Come (6/17/45)
15. Queen of the Cats (6/24/45)
16. Death Rings Down the Curtain (7/1/45)
17. Till Death Do Us Part (7/8/45)
18. The Man With the Stolen Face (7/15/45)
19. My Beloved Must Die (7/22/45)
20. Beware of Tomorrow (7/29/45)
21. Murder Must be Paid For (8/5/45)
22. To Have and To Hold (8/12/45)
23. Murderer Unknown (8/19/45)
24. Time on My Hands (8/26/45)
25. Death Laughs Last (9/2/45)
26. You Only Die Once (9/9/45)

Sergeant Preston of the Yukon*

A continuation of *Challenge of the Yukon*, still broadcast three times a week, *Preston* went twice a week on Tuesday and Thursday beginning January 8, 1952. Beginning June 29, 1952 the program went to once a week on Sunday afternoons, twice a week on Tuesday and Thursday beginning September 16, 1952, once a week on Tuesday beginning May 19, 1953, and finally back to twice a week on Tuesday and Thursday on September 15, 1953.

947. Sneak Gun (11/13/51)
948. Death in the Air (11/15/51)
949. Trap for a Killer (11/18/51)
950. Needed Cash (11/20/51)
951. Grim Journey (11/22/51)
952. Shag and the Fur Thieves (11/25/51)
953. The Vet in White Horse (11/27/51)
954. Jerry Goes Home (11/29/51)
955. Cave-In (12/2/51)
956. Frame-Up Victim (12/4/51)
957. Trail of Death (12/6/51)
958. The Trail of Gold (12/9/51)
959. Neil Holton's Vow (12/11/51)
960. Rainbow Gold (12/13/51)
961. King Proves His Worth (12/16/51)
962. Sins of the Father (12/18/51)
963. White Water (12/20/51)
964. McAllister's Bonanza (12/23/51)
965. The Christmas Mite (12/25/51)
966. Arms and the Girl (12/27/51)
967. The Little Mountie (12/30/51)
968. The Return of Red Gruver (1/1/52)
969. Mystery Boy (1/3/52)

*Compiled by Terry Salomonson. Copyright © 1988 Terry Salomonson.

1176. Maple Leaf Forever (5/20/54)
1177. Once a Thief (5/25/54)
1178. Double Courage (5/27/54)
1179. The Hanging Rock (6/1/54)
1180. Return of Moose Baker (6/3/54)
1181. The Stolen Malamutes (6/8/54)
1182. Maggie Kenley's Discovery
    (6/10/54)
1183. Return to Danger (9/14/54)
1184. The White Sable (9/16/54)
1185. Get Rich Quick (9/21/54)
1186. The Elusive Trio (9/23/54)
1187. Dog's Don't Lie (9/28/54)
1188. The Distance Finder (9/30/54)
1189. Trail of Crime (10/5/54)
1190. Hold the Lamp High (10/7/54)
1191. Murder By the Compass (10/12/54)
1192. Sellout (10/14/54)
1193. A Case for the Inspector (10/19/54)
1194. Wild Goose Chase (10/21/54)
1195. Midnight to Morning (10/26/54)
1196. Bad Company (10/28/54)
1197. Avalanche (11/2/54)
1198. The Eye Witness (11/4/54)
1199. The Long Trail (11/9/54)
1200. Lucky Seven Gold (11/11/54)
1201. The Third Strike (11/16/54)
1202. Capture (11/18/54)
1203. Dog Thieves (11/23/54)
1204. Trail of the Star (12/25/54)
1205. Hostages (11/30/54)
1206. Dangerous Prisoner (12/2/54)
1207. Till Proven Guilty (12/7/54)
1208. Betrayed (12/9/54)
1209. Fire Trap (12/14/54)
1210. Special Deputy (12/16/54)
1211. Lock, Stock, and Barrel (12/21/54)
1212. Christmas for Sally (12/23/54)
1213. Air Tight Frame-Up (12/28/54)
1214. Grubstake (12/30/54)
1215. Money or Your Life (1/4/55)
1216. Outlaw in Uniform (1/6/55)
1217. Ring Around the Heart (1/11/55)
1218. Gold Strike (1/13/55)

1219. Third Frame-Up (1/18/55)
1220. False Trail (1/20/55)
1221. Red Letter (1/25/55)
1222. Land Deal (1/27/55)
1223. Deed to the Future (2/1/55)
1224. Crooks at Large (2/3/55)
1225. Race Against Time (2/8/55)
1226. Gunfire (2/10/55)
1227. Express Robbery (2/15/55)
1228. A Scrap of Paper (2/17/55)
1229. Escape (2/22/55)
1230. Sled Ride to Death (2/30/55)
1231. Mail Robbers (3/1/55)
1232. The Trail of Curly (3/3/55)
1233. The Winner (3/8/55)
1234. Murder Plot (3/10/55)
1235. Cold Cash (3/15/55)
1236. Frame-Up (3/17/55)
1237. King's Capture (3/22/55)
1238. Yukon Showdown (3/24/55)
1239. Two Birds with One Stone
    (3/29/55)
1240. Scarface (3/31/55)
1241. Running Wild (4/5/55)
1242. The Fourth Man (4/7/55)
1243. Step-Brother (4/12/55)
1244. Klondike Land (4/14/55)
1245. Wild Trail West (4/19/55)
1246. First Case (4/21/55)
1247. Johnny Came Home (4/26/55)
1248. Lost Indian Mine (4/28/55)
1249. Chinook Gold (5/3/55)
1250. Sundown Jim (5/5/55)
1251. Cornered Killer (5/10/55)
1252. Freight Robbery (5/12/55)
1253. A Store for the Trader (5/17/55)
1254. Guardian for Jane (5/19/55)
1255. White River Gang (5/24/55)
1256. Glare of the Sun (5/26/55)
1257. Lucky Rabbit Foot (5/31/55)
1258. Bait for the Trap (6/2/55)
1259. The Yellow Streak (6/7/55)
1260. The Long Trail (6/9/55)

Shakespeare in Summer

Broadcast on local WNYC in New York 8:30 to 10:55 pm, EST, this series aired dramatizations of Shakespeare's plays presented by the Shakespeare Memorial Theater Production and the BBC.

1. Twelfth Night (7/13/59; Dorothy Tutin)   the Dublin Gate Players)
2. The Taming of the Shrew (7/20/59;   3. Measure for Measure (7/27/59)

Sherlock Holmes (1960 Series)

This series was broadcast over WBAI-FM in New York from 9:30 to 10 pm. *Sherlock Holmes* was previously a BBC production, rebroadcast months later in America. Scripts were adaptations of original Sir Arthur Conan Doyle stories.

1. The Man with the Twisted Lip (8/28/60)
2. The Beryl Coronet (9/4/60)
3. The Noble Bachelor (9/11/60)
4. The Blanched Soldier (9/18/60)
5. The Case of the Copper Beeches (9/25/60)
6. The Shoscombe Old Place (10/2/60)
7. The Beryl Coronet (10/9/60)

The Silver Theater

Sponsored by the International Silver Company, the 1847 Rogers Sterling Silver Division, this Sunday-afternoon drama program presented the best in writing and acting talent and was broadcast directly from Hollywood. Stars from almost every major Hollywood studio guested. Conrad Nagel was the host and director till 1942. From 1943 to 1944, John Loder took over. The 1945 season marked Nagel's return, taking over the announcing job from Loder.

Music was performed by Felix Mills and his orchestra for the entire run, except for a brief period in 1942 when Jack Miller and A. Newman supplied the music. J. Meaking was musician during the 1946 run, Oscar Bradley in 1947. Writers included Grover Jones, James Ruscoll, Ray Buffun, Charles Tazewell, Paul Franklin, True Boardman, and many others. John Conte was announcer until 1942, H. Charles during the 1943 to 1944 season, J. Bailey in 1945, and Clayton Collier in 1947. The final three seasons, 1945 to 1947, were short broadcast runs as summer fill-ins for *The Adventures of Ozzie and Harriet*.

The Silver Theater premiered on CBS, Sunday afternoons from 5 to 5:30 pm; 6 to 6:30 pm as of October 2, 1938. On October 5, 1941, *The Silver Theater* moved to Thursday evenings from 6 to 6:30 pm. Beginning July 4, 1943, *Theater* was heard Sunday afternoons from 6 to 6:30 pm. (The 1947 season was broadcast from New York.)

1. First Love [part one] (10/3/37; Cliff Arquette, Minerva Pious, Rosalind Russell, and James Stewart)
2. First Love [part two] (10/10/37;
Cliff Arquette, Minerva Pious, Rosalind Russell, and James Stewart)
3. First Love [part three] (10/17/37;

Cliff Arquette, Minerva Pious, Rosalind Russell, and James Stewart)

4. First Love [part four] (10/24/37; Cliff Arquette, Minerva Pious, Rosalind Russell, and James Stewart)

5. P.S. She Got the Job (10/31/37; Miriam Hopkins)

6. Honesty's Policy [part one] (11/7/37; Brian Aherne and Jane Wyatt)

7. Honesty's Policy [part two] (11/14/37; Brian Aherne and Jane Wyatt)

8. Medicine Girl (11/21/37; Constance Bennett, Cary Grant, and Barnett Parker)

9. Hospitals are for Sick People (11/28/37; Joan Fontaine and Lee Tracy)

10. Detour to Love (12/5/37; Clark Gable and Paula Winslowe)

11. Bright Shadow (12/12/37; Douglas Fairbanks, Jr. and Andrea Leeds)

12. The Queen Can Do No Wrong (12/19/37; Madeleine Carroll and Ray Milland)

13. Skyscraper (12/26/37; Chester Morris and Florence Rice)

14. Stronger Than Steel (10/2/38; Fredric March and Lurene Tuttle)

15. The Moon's Our Home (10/9/38; Bill Goodwin and Margaret Sullavan)

16. Wings in the Dark (10/16/38; Phyllis Brooks, Cary Grant, and Joseph Kearns)

17. Up from the Darkness [part one] (10/23/38; Rosalind Russell and James Stewart)

18. Up from the Darkness [part two] (10/30/38; Rosalind Russell and James Stewart)

19. Hollywood Legend (11/6/38; Rita Johnson and Franchot Tone)

20. Stars in Their Courses [part one] (11/13/38; Morgan Farley, Helen Hayes, Orson Welles, and Carlton Young)

21. Stars in Their Courses [part two] (11/20/38; Morgan Farley, Helen Hayes, Orson Welles, and Carlton Young)

22. The Captain Had a Daughter (11/27/38; Jack Arnold, William Farnum, and Ginger Rogers)

23. Danger Lights (12/4/38; Clark Gable and Paula Winslowe)

24. Broken Prelude [part one] (12/11/38; Pamela Caveness, Bette Davis, and Carlton Kadell)

25. Broken Prelude [part two] (12/18/38; Pamela Caveness, Bette Davis, and Carlton Kadell)

26. Challenge for Three [part one] (12/25/38; William Farnum, Joseph Kearns, Ida Lupino, and Conrad Nagel)

27. Challenge for Three [part two] (1/1/39; William Farnum, Joseph Kearns, Ida Lupino, and Conrad Nagel)

28. Study in Triangles (1/8/39; Leslie Howard and Rita Johnson)

29. Debutante (1/15/39; Elliott Lewis and Myrna Loy)

30. Misty Mountain [part one] (1/22/39; Jane Bryan, John Gibson, and James Stewart)

31. Misty Mountain [part two] (1/29/39; Jane Bryon, John Gibson, and James Stewart)

32. It May Be Forever (2/5/39; John Hiestand and Loretta Young)

32. Escape from Tomorrow [part one] (2/12/39; John Garfield and Andrea Leeds)

33. Escape from Tomorrow [part two] (2/19/39; John Garfield and Andrea Leeds)

34. Dear Victim (2/26/39; Herbert Marshall, Maureen O'Sullivan, and Eric Snowden)

35. Son of the Navy (3/5/39; Billy Cook, Elliott Lewis, and Ginger Rogers)

36. Love Is Where You Find It (3/12/39; Joseph Kearns, Shirley Ross, and Lee Tracy)

37. Timber Valley (3/19/39; Henry Fonda and Gail Patrick)

38. For Us, the Living [part one] (3/26/39; Joseph Kearns, Lindsay MacHarrie, Rosalind Russell, and Paula Winslowe)

39. For Us, the Living [part two] (4/2/39; Joseph Kearns, Lindsay MacHarrie, Rosalind Russell, and Paula Winslowe)

40. Man from Medicine Bow (4/9/39;

Glenda Farrell, Elliott Lewis, and Chester Morris)

41. Expert Opinion (4/16/39; Joseph Kearns, Elliott Lewis, and Robert Montgomery)

42. The Villain Still Pursues Her (4/23/39; Henry Brandon, Joseph Kearns, Robert Montgomery, and Helen Wood)

43. Love Is Our Destiny (4/30/39; Constance Bennett and Melvyn Douglas)

44. Train Ride (5/7/39; Joan Crawford, Carlton Kadell, and John Hiestand)

45. Understudy (5/14/39; Douglas Fairbanks, Jr. and Paula Winslowe)

46. Crossroads for Two [part one] (5/21/39; Roberto Bambers, Helen Hayes, and Carlton Young)

47. Crossroads for Two [part two] (5/28/39; Roberto Bambers, Helen Hayes, and Carlton Young)

48. Lost Yesterday [part one] (10/8/39; Loretta Young)

49. Lost Yesterday [part two] (10/15/39; Loretta Young)

50. Ex-Spy (10/22/39; David Niven)

51. Last Crossing (10/29/39; Merle Oberon)

52. The Road Goes Further [part one] (11/5/39; John Garfield)

53. The Road Goes Further [part two] (11/12/39; John Garfield)

54. Incredible Lady (11/19/39; Carole Lombard)

55. Speak of the Devil (11/26/39; William Powell)

56. With All My Love (12/3/39; Ginger Rogers)

57. For Richer, For Richer (12/10/39; Clark Gable)

58. Twice Upon a Time (12/17/39; Kay Francis)

59. Magic of Mistletoe (12/24/39; Margaret Lindsay)

60. Cresseida Calls (12/31/39; Wendy Barrie)

61. A Romeo for Juliet (1/7/40; Cary Grant and Margot Stevenson)

62. Return Engagement (1/14/40; Madeline Carroll and Fred MacKaye)

63. Meet Mr. Tomkins (1/21/40; Florence Baker and George Brent)

64. To the Memory of ... (1/28/40; Geraldine Fitzgerald)

65. Parent by Proxy (2/4/40; Rosemary DeCamp and William Powell)

66. Wild Blows the Wind (2/11/40; Joan Bennett and Elliot Lewis)

67. Heaven in Like That (2/18/40; Herbert Marshall and Frances Robinson)

68. Marriage Deferred (2/25/40; Cary Grant)

69. Lady by Preference (3/3/40; Kay Francis and Ned Le Fevre)

70. School Crossing (3/10/40; Humphrey Bogart)

71. Away from It All (3/17/40; Herbert Marshall and Paula Winslowe)

72. Hold That Tiger (3/24/40; Dennis Greene and Mary Martin)

73. Broken Destiny (3/31/40; Miriam Hopkins)

74. Prince and the Pauper (4/7/40; Douglas Fairbanks, Jr.)

75. Diana Discovers America (4/14/40; Madeline Carroll)

76. Census, 1940 (4/21/40; Edna Best, Joseph Kearns, and Thomas Mitchell)

77. Days of Grace (4/28/40; Carole Lombard)

78. Ice to the Eskimos (5/5/40; Carole Lombard)

79. I'll Never Forget (10/6/40; Laurence Olivier)

80. The Hour Shall Come [part one] (10/13/40; Bette Davis)

81. The Hour Shall Come [part two] (10/20/40; Bette Davis)

82. Nothing to Sneeze At (10/27/40; Douglas Fairbanks, Jr.)

83. For All Good Men (11/3/40; Virginia Bruce)

84. Who Done It? (11/10/40; Bob Hope)

85. World Without End (11/17/40; Martha Scott)

86. Not Without Publication (11/24/40; William Powell)

87. Critic on the Hearth (12/1/40; Greer Garson)

88. The Great Adventure (12/8/40; Ronald Colman)

89. Four on a Match (12/15/40; Kay Francis)

90. Christmas Armistice (12/22/40; Claire Dodd and Conrad Nagel)

91. All Things Come Home (12/29/40; Conrad Nagel and his daughter Ruth Nagel)
92. Child, Save My Fireman (1/5/41; Marsha Hunt, James Stewart, and Paula Winslowe)
93. Two Loves Have I (1/12/41; Linda Darnell, William Holden, and Kent Rogers)
94. Scene of the Crime (1/19/41; Dorothy Lovett, Ray Milland, and Paula Winslowe)
95. Love's New Sweet Song (1/26/41; Judy Garland, L. Lewis, and W. McCullom)
96. Bachelor Habit (2/2/41; Brian Aherne, Rosemary DeCamp, Harry Von Zell)
97. Light from These Shadows (2/9/41; John Heistand, Frank Martin, and Merle Oberon)
98. Heaven Is Like That (2/16/41; Charles Boyer and Constance Moore)
99. Drawn By Lot (2/23/41; Olivia De Havilland and Warren Hull)
100. Out of this World (3/2/41; John Archer and Thelma Hubbard)
101. Murder Unlimited (3/9/41; Reed Hadley, Jerry Hausner, Joseph Kearns, Carole Lombard, and Ed Max)
102. The Magic Darkness (3/16/41; Margaret Hayes, Jeffrey Lunn, and M. Reed)
103. Lady with Ideas (3/23/41; Hans Conried, Elliott Lewis, and Ann Sothern)
104. One Step Ahead (3/30/41; Joseph Kearns, Mary Schipp, Lurene Tuttle, and Orson Welles)
105. Niagara to Reno (4/6/41; Joseph Kearns, Kay Kyser, and Ginny Simms)
106. Tommy Malone Comes Home (4/13/41; Pat O'Brien and Frances Robinson)
107. A Man's Best Wife (4/20/41; Elliott Lewis and Myrna Loy)
108. The Better the Day (10/5/41; Leo Cleary and Mickey Rooney)
109. Eternally Yours [part one] (10/12/41; Edgar Barrier and Judy Garland)
110. Eternally Yours [part two] (10/19/41; Edgar Barrier and Judy Garland)
111. Case of the Evil Angel (10/26/41; Adolph Menjou)
112. Petticoat Fever (11/2/41; Red Skelton and Claire Trevor)
113. Alone in Paris (11/9/41; Madeline Carroll and Robert Young)
114. Father Darcy and the Beloved Blackguard (11/16/41; Pat O'Brien)
115. Ladies in Retirement (11/23/41; Berry Kroeger and Rosalind Russell)
116. For Richer, For Richer (12/7/41; Cliff Arquette and Errol Flynn)
117. Widow Wore a Black Eye (12/14/41; Alice Faye and Robert Preston)
118. Goodnight Galatea (12/21/41; Betty Field and Conrad Nagel)
119. Wings for the Lady (12/28/41; James Craig and Ellen Drew)
120. Lawyers Refer Eggs (1/4/42; William Powell)
121. The Awful Truth (1/11/42; Ann Southern)
122. Weekend in Havana (1/18/42; Bing Crosby)
123. Next Time We Love (1/25/42; Maureen Sullivan)
124. Public Enemy (2/1/42; Humphrey Bogart)
125. Seventh Man (2/8/42; Charles Boyer)
126. Talk of the Town (2/15/42; Joan Bennett)
127. Three on a Journey (2/22/42; Jean Hersholt)
128. Son of the Navy (3/1/42; Dorothy Lamour)
129. Christmas in July (3/8/42; Mickey Rooney)
130. The Whole Town's Talking (3/15/42; Kay Kyser)
131. Only Yesterday (3/22/42; Loretta Young)
132. Her Perfect Mate (3/29/42; Lorraine Day)
133. Summer Evening (4/5/42; Charles Boyer)
134. Pursuit (4/12/42; Paulette Goddard)
135. The Amazing Mr. Williams (4/19/42; Jack Benny)
136. Murder Unlimited (7/4/43; Kay Francis)
137. Timber Valley (7/11/43; Jon Hall)
138. Love Is Where You Find It (7/18/43; Janet Blair)

139. China Bridge (7/25/43; Ellen Drew)
140. Days of Grace (8/1/43; Edna Best)
141. Niagara to Reno (8/8/43; Dennis Day)
142. With All My Love (8/15/43; Marjorie Reynolds)
143. The Villain Still Pursues Her (8/22/43; Richard Whorf)
144. Son of the Navy (8/29/43; Ruth Hussey)
145. Out of This World (9/5/43; Henry Hull)
146. Lady with Ideas (9/12/43; Vera Vague)
147. Man from Medicine Bow (9/19/43; Roy Rogers)
148. Lost Yesterday [part one] (9/26/43; Loretta Young)
149. Lost Yesterday [part two] (10/3/43; Loretta Young)
150. Please Forgive Me (10/10/43; Charles Boyer)
151. What This Country Needs (10/17/43; Rosalind Russell)
152. Melody in Two Flats (10/24/43; Mickey Rooney)
153. Adventures in Algiers (10/31/43; Lorraine Day)
154. Once Upon a Weekend (11/7/43; John Garfield)
155. Appointment in the Sky (11/14/43; Alan Baxter)
156. A Little Journey (11/21/43; Betty Grable)
157. The Lady Grew Up (11/28/43; Kay Francis)
158. Help Wanted (12/5/43; Virginia Bruce and Herbert Marshall)
159. Ringside Table (12/12/43; Judy Garland and Alan Ladd)
160. The Juggler of Notre Dame (12/19/43; Ralph Bellamy and Robert Weede)
161. The Farmer's Son (12/26/43; Preston Foster and Ann Southern)
162. Here Swims the Bride (1/2/44; Richard Whorf)
163. Assignment in China (1/9/44; Claudette Colbert)
164. Mr. Margie (1/16/44; Bing Crosby)
165. Quite in Order (1/23/44; Basil Rathbone)
166. For This We Live (1/30/44; Dorothy Lamour)
167. Travel Is Broadcasting (2/6/44; William Powell)
168. Honeymoon Deferred (2/13/44; Alan Ladd)
169. She Looked Like an Angel (2/20/44; Hedy Lamarr)
170. One Day After Another (2/27/44; Bette Davis)
171. A Brown Study (3/5/44; Robert Young)
172. Someone Suitable (3/12/44; Chester Morris)
173. Steve Brodie (3/19/44; Brian Donlevy)
174. Wrong Number (3/26/44; Janet Blair)
175. The Steadfast Heart (4/2/44; Paul Lucas)
176. Miracle in the Rain (4/9/44; Helen Hayes)
177. William and Mary (4/16/44; Cornelia Otis Skinner and Roland Young)
178. The Woman I Killed (4/23/44; Herbert Marshall)
179. The Snow Goose (4/30/44; Ronald Coleman)
180. Bad Dream (5/7/44; Adolph Menjou)
181. Little Johnny Appleseed (5/14/44; Kate Smith)
182. The Guardsman (5/21/44; Ingrid Bergman and Herbert Marshall)
183. The Sun Field (5/28/44; Ruth Hussey and George Raft)
184. Nothing Ever Happens (6/4/44; Alan Baxter)
185. Heaven Is Like That (6/11/44; Edna Best)
186. Lady's Name Was Paris (6/18/44; George Brent and Ida Lupino)
187. Suez Road (6/25/44; Brian Donlevy and Ann Sothern)
188. Partners in Blue (7/2/44; Donna Reed)
189. Adventure for Two (7/9/44; Shirley Booth)
190. Home Again (7/16/44; K.T. Stevens)
191. Long Engagement (7/23/44; Shirley Booth)
192. Sound of Her Voice (7/30/44; Bill Goodwin)
193. For All Good Men (8/6/44; Louise Allbrittan)

194. My Wife's Other Love (8/13/44; June Vincent)
195. Two Loves Have I (8/20/44; Ann Rutherford)
196. Lucy Is a Lady (8/27/44; Diana Lynn)
197. Mr. Margie (9/3/44; John Conte)
198. Forever Walking Free (9/10/44; June Duprez)
199. What Kind of Girl Was Julie? (9/17/44; June Haver)
200. Imperfect Lady (9/24/44; Ruth Warrick)
201. Till Death Do Us Part [written by Leslie Charteris and Dennis Green] (10/1/44; John Loder and Maria Palmer)
202. One Day After Another (6/17/45; Mary Astor)
203. Study in Triangles (6/24/45; Conrad Nagel)
204. Bright Shadow (7/1/45; Ruth Hussey)
205. Broken Destiny (7/8/45; Sylvia Sidney)
206. Love Is Where You Find It (7/15/45; Robert Alda and Marilyn Maxwell)
207. With Pen in Hand (7/22/45; Diana Lynn)
208. Gilded Pheasant (7/29/45; Marguerite Chapman and Helmut Dantine)
209. A Charmed Life (8/5/45; Joan Davis and Harry Von Zell)
210. Return to Tomorrow (6/30/46; Dane Clark)
211. My Father and I (7/7/46; Peggy Ann Gardner and James Dunn)
212. Backfire (7/14/46; Brian Donlevy)
213. Bring Down the House (7/21/46; Marsha Hunt)
214. The Sea and Dennis Murphy (7/28/46; Pat O'Brien)
215. Sauce for the Gander (8/4/46; Eve Arden)
216. Private Eye (8/11/46; George Raft)
217. Until Forever (8/18/46; Claire Trevor)
218. Murder and Crumpets (6/15/47; Virginia Payne)
219. Penny Wise (6/22/47; Mason Adams)
220. At Home in Central Park (6/29/47; Lucille Wall)
221. Crystal (7/6/47; Anne Seymour and Ned Wever)
222. Pardon, My Heart's Showing (7/13/47; Karl Swenson)
223. You'll Never Be Far from Me (7/20/47; Conrad Nagel)
224. Leave it to Ethel (7/27/47; Ethel Merman)
225. Boiling Point (8/3/47; F. Lafferty)
226. Eager Beaver (8/10/47; Arnold Stang)
227. Horse in the Kitchen (8/17/47; Les Damon and Claudia Morgan)

The Six Shooter

The first appearance of the Six Shooter was in a western drama presented on the *Hollywood Star Playhouse*, broadcast April 13, 1952. The script was entitled "The Six Shooter," and on July 15, 1953, an audition recording using the same script was made. Starring in the role of Britt Ponset, a.k.a. "The Six Shooter," was James Stewart. Ponset was a frontier drifter who built a reputation by what everyone else said about him, even when it was against his own wish. Ponset, during his adventures, somehow found time to play "Hamlet" on a road company and advocated the right to have his name placed on a town ballet during an election, winning the offices of both Mayor *and* Sheriff at the same time! Ponset and a peddler conspired to advance a poor girl's fortune by reenacting a modern-day Cinderella, and when a young boy ran away from home, Britt told the boy the story of Dickens' *A Christmas Carol*, in a western style.

The series was produced in association with Revue Productions; Frank Burt was in charge of the series. He also wrote all of the scripts except for episode six, written by Les Crutchfield. Jack Johnstone was the director. Hal Gibney was the announcer until episode twenty-six, when John Wald took over. Basil Adlam supplied the music. Coleman Heating Products sponsored the first four broadcasts; afterwards the series remained sustaining. Broadcast over NBC, Sunday 8 to 8:30 pm, EST, beginning April 1, 1954, *The Six Shooter* was heard on Thursday evenings from 8 to 8:30 pm, EST.

Audition: The Six Shooter (7/15/53; Parley Baer and William Conrad)

1. Jenny (9/20/53; Harry Bartell, Jess Curt Patrick, George Neece, and D.J. Thompson)
2. The Coward (9/27/53; Michael Ann Barrett, Herb Ellis, Howard McNear, and Will Wright)
3. The Stampede (10/4/53; James McCallion and Lou Merrill)
4. Silver Annie (10/11/53; Parley Baer, Robert Griffin, Jeanette Nolan, Dan O'Herlihy, Herb Vigran)
5. Rink Larkin (10/18/53; Tony Barrett, Sammy Ogg, and Russell Thorsen)
6. Red Lawson's Revenge (10/25/53; Leone Ledoux, Shirley Mitchell, Barney Phillips, Paul Richards)
7. Ben Scofield [same script used for the audition episode] (11/1/53; Parley Baer, William Conrad, James McCallion, and Herb Vigran)
8. The Capture of Stacy Gault (11/8/53; Eleanore Audley, Parley Baer, Forrest Lewis, Barney Phillips)
9. Escape from Smoke Falls (11/15/53; Sam Edwards, Frank Gerstle, Robert Griffin, Forrest Lewis, and Jeanette Nolan)
10. Gabriel Starbuck (11/22/53; Lamont Johnson, William Johnstone, Del McKennon, John Stephenson, and Herb Vigran)
11. Sheriff Billy (11/29/53; Ken Christy, James McCallion, Howard McNear, and Alan Reed)
12. A Pressing Engagement (12/6/53; Sam Edwards, Barbara Eiler, Virginia Gregg, Bill Johnstone, and Herb Vigran)
13. More Than Kin (12/13/53; Michael Ann Barrett, Tony Barrett, Ted Bliss,

Marvin Miller, and Dan O'Herlihy)
14. Britt Ponset's Christmas Carol (12/20/53; Eleanor Audley, Dick Beals, Sam Edwards, and Howard McNear)
15. Cora Plummer Quincy (12/27/53; Parley Baer, Bert Holland, Virginia Gregg, Robert Griffin, and Jean Tatum)
16. A Friend in Need (1/3/54; Frank Gerstle, William Johnstone, Howard McNear, Shephard Menken)
17. Hiram's Goldstrike (1/10/54; Tony Barrett, Bill Johnstone, Howard McNear, Barney Phillips, and Herb Vigran)
18. The Silver Buckle (1/17/54; Eleanor Audley, Joe Cranston, William Conrad, Frank Gerstle, and Forrest Lewis)
19. Helen Bricker (1/24/54; Parley Baer, Lillian Buyeff, Ken Christy, Herb Vigran, and Will Wright)
20. Trail to Sunset (1/31/54; Harry Bartell, Robert Griffin, Lamont Johnson, Forrest Lewis, and Howard McNear)
21. Apron-Faced Sorrel (2/7/54; Sam Edwards, Bert Holland, and William Johnstone)
22. Quiet City (2/14/54; Virginia Gregg, Robert Griffin, Lamont Johnson, and Will Wright)
23. The Battle at Tower Rock (2/21/54; Eleanor Audley, Jess C. Patrick, Virginia Gregg, Bill Johnstone, and Les Tremayne)
24. The Cheyenne Express (3/7/54; Frank Gerstle, Barney Phillips, Paul Richards, and Herb Vigran)
25. Thicker Than Water (3/14/54; Dick Beals, Bob Grifin, Shirley Mitchell, and Barney Phillips)

26. Duel at Lockwood (3/21/54; Elvia Allman, Sam Edwards, Bert Holland, Howard McNear, and Will Wright)
27. Aunt Ema (4/1/54; Eleanor Audley and William Johnstone)
28. General Gillford's Widow (4/8/54; Parley Baer, Virginia Gregg, and Robert Griffin)
29. The Crisis at Easter Creek (4/15/54; William Conrad, Ted deCorsia, Virginia Gregg, and Marvin Miller)
30. Johnny Springer (4/22/54; Parley Baer, Harry Bartell, Joe Cranston, Virginia Gregg, and Barney Phillips)
31. The Revenge at Harness Creek (4/29/54; Eleanor Audley, Virginia Gregg, Bert Holland, Lamont Johnson, and Forrest Lewis)
32. Anna Norquest (5/6/54; Harry Bartell, Lillian Buyeff, William Johnstone, and Lou Merrill)
33. The Double Seven (5/13/54; Parley

Baer, Bob Griffin, Lamont Johnson, Howard McNear, and Gerald Mohr)
34. The Shooting of Wyatt King (5/20/54; Joe Cranston, William Johnstone, Junius Matthews, Barney Phillips, and Herb Vigran)
35. Blood Relations (5/27/54; Sam Edwards, Barbara Eiler, and Herb Ellis)
36. Silver Threads (6/3/54; Bert Holland, Barney Phillips, Ben Wright, and Will Wright)
37. The New Sheriff (6/10/54; Frank Gerstle, Junius Matthews, Del McKennon, Paul Richards, and Carlton Young)
38. When the Shoe Doesn't Fit (6/17/54; Eleanor Audley, Sam Edwards, Barbara Eiler, Sandra Gould, and William Johnstone)
39. Myra Barker (6/24/54; Parley Baer, Virginia Gregg, Howard McNear, and D.J. Thompson)

Somerset Maugham Theater

This Saturday morning anthology series featured dramatizations of Somerset Maugham stories. Various Hollywood stars guested on the broadcasts, but the series originated from New York, sponsored by Tintair. It was directed by Mitchell Grayson and produced by Ann Marlowe (later replaced by John Gibbs). First broadcast over CBS beginning at 11:30, it left the air for the summer, returning on NBC, still on Saturday mornings, but from 11 to 11:30 am.

1. The Colonel's Lady (1/20/51; Martha Scott)
2. Sanitorium (1/27/51; Berry Kroeger and Jessica Tandy)
3. The Kite (2/3/51; Dane Clark)
4. The Constant Wife (2/10/51; Joan Bennett)
5. Alien Corn (2/17/51; Anne Burr)
6. Mr. Know-It-All (2/24/51; Larry Adler and Anne Seymour)
7. Razor's Edge [part one] (3/3/51; John Conte and Jessica Tandy)
8. Razor's Edge [part two] (3/10/51; John Conte and Jessica Tandy)
9. Facts of Life (3/17/51; Lisa Kirk)

10. A String of Beads (3/24/51; Robert Cummings)
11. The Treasure (3/31/51; Dennis King)
12. Winter Cruise (4/7/51; Mady Christians)
13. Cakes and Ale (4/14/51; Nancy Kelly)
14. The Verger (4/21/51; Guy Kibbee)
15. Of Human Bondage [part one] (4/28/51; Nina Foch and S. Strudwick)
16. Of Human Bondage [part two] (5/5/51; Nina Foch and S. Strudwick)
17. The French Governor (5/12/51; Roland Young)

18. Painted Veil (5/19/51; Sarah Churchill)
19. Round Dozen (5/26/51; Eddie Dowling)
20. Rain (6/2/51; Sylvia Sidney)
21. The Letter (6/9/51; Judith Evelyn)
22. Up at the Villa (6/16/51; Hume Cronyn and Jessica Tandy)
23. Theater [part one] (6/23/51; Florence Reed)
24. Theater [part two] (6/30/51; Florence Reed)
25. Land of Promise (7/7/51; Alfred Drake)
26. Before the Party (7/14/51; Horace Bracken)
27. Moon and Six Pence (10/27/51; Dennis King)
28. Sanitorium (11/3/51; Hume Cronyn and Jessica Tandy)
29. The Verger (11/10/51; Thomas Mitchell)
30. String of Beads (11/17/51; Geraldine Fitzgerald)
31. Narrow Corner (11/24/51; Richard Greene)
32. The Colonel's Lady (12/1/51; Peggy Wood)
33. Louise (12/8/51; Veronica Lake)
34. The Constant Wife (12/15/51; Costance Bennett)
35. Raw Material (12/22/51; Peggy Ann Gardner)
36. Mr. Know-It-All (12/29/51; Everett Sloane)
37. End of Flight (1/5/52; Louise Rainer)
38. Razor's Edge (1/12/52; William Prince)
39. Before the Party (1/19/52; Stella Andrew)

Speed Gibson of the International Police

There were two stories in this series (but all one continuous story-line): The first was one hundred episodes in length, the second took up the balance of the series. The stories concerned Clint Barlow, Barney Dunlap, Marsha Windfield, and of course Speed Gibson, who traveled to the Orient to do battle with the evil Octopus. This juvenile serial starred John Gibson, Howard McNear, Hanley Stafford, Jack Mathers, and Elliott Lewis. Recorded and syndicated from California, each episode was fifteen minutes in length.

1. The Octopus Gang Active (1/2/37)
2. Speed Is Inducted Into the Secret Police (1/9/37)
3. Heading for Hong Kong (1/16/37)
4. A Shooting Attempt (1/23/37)
5. The Octopus Orders a Kidnapping (1/30/37)
6. Remaining at Wake Island (2/6/37)
7. Speed Is Missing (2/13/37)
8. Splinters Into Custody (2/20/37)
9. Splinters Gets Away (2/27/37)
10. Barney Flies the Mystery Plane (3/6/37)
11. The Trio Is Ambushed on Guam (3/13/37)
12. The Octopus Plans a Surprise (3/20/37)
13. The Arrival in Hong Kong (3/27/37)
14. Clint Suspicious of Mr. Wu (4/3/37)
15. Clint to Stay with Dr. Kingsley (4/10/37)
16. Hotel Rooms are Ransacked (4/17/37)
17. Marsha Is Kidnapped (4/24/37)
18. The Octopus Reveals His Plans (5/1/37)
19. Disguised as Collies (5/8/37)
20. Speed Is Knocked Out (5/15/37)
21. Leave on Bullet Plane (5/22/37)
22. Speed Tries to Warn Clint (5/29/37)
23. Shot at and Forced Down (6/5/37)

167. Safe Take-Off (3/9/40)
168. Speed Missing Again (3/16/40)
169. The Octopus Waits (3/23/40)
170. Car Crash (3/30/40)
171. Octopus Gang Member Is Questioned (4/6/40)
172. Clint Worried About Landing (4/13/40)
173. Clint's Plane Catches on Fire (4/20/40)
174. An Octopus Agent Confesses to Fire (4/27/40)
175. Desert Raider Attack (5/4/40)
176. Octopus Camp Is Reached (5/11/40)
177. Death Ray Blown Up (5/18/40)
178. The Octopus Finally Captured (5/25/40)

The Stan Freberg Show

This series lasted only fifteen broadcasts, making fun of numerous songs and skits, such as the "Banana Boat Song" and "Saint George and the Dragnet." Daws Butler, June Foray (later the voice of Rocky, the flying squirrel in *Rocky and Bullwinkle*), Peggy Taylor and Peter Leeds played supporting roles. Billy May supplied the music. The final broadcast featured various skits and songs from previous episodes. The series was broadcast over CBS, Sunday evenings from 7:30 to 8 pm, EST.

1. Incident at Varoses (7/14/57)
2. The Abominable Snowman (7/21/57)
3. Miss Jupiter and the Flying Zazzalof Family (7/28/57)
4. Paul Revere's Ride (8/4/57)
5. The Flying Saucer and a Symphony of Dogs (8/11/57)
6. Censoring an Elderly Man (8/18/57)
7. The Lone Analyst and Pronto (8/25/57)
8. The Flying Zazzalof Family — Revisited (9/1/57)
9. The Abominable Snowman Again (9/8/57)
10. Henry Cloverleaf (9/15/57)
11. The Canine Talent Agent (9/22/59)
12. The Rocket Powered Sled (9/29/59)
13. Gray Flannel Werewolves (10/6/57)
14. The Return of Miss Jupiter (10/13/57)
15. The Final Show (10/20/57)

The Star and the Story

The Columbia Broadcasting System's primary reason for airing another anthology series with various guest stars each week was Walter Pidgeon. For unknown reasons, he suddenly became available for radio appearances on a regular basis. CBS immediately signed Pidgeon to a twenty-six broadcast series — what type of a series was to be determined later.

Originally, *The Star and the Story* had no title — it was conceived only a week before its premiere — and was scheduled to be a Wednesday-evening presentation, beginning on Wednesday, February 2. Goodyear Tires, the sponsor of this series, signed only days before the first broadcast. CBS announced before the premiere that "each week Mr. Pidgeon will present screen players in their greatest roles." And did CBS find the talent! With Walter Pidgeon as the male lead each week, a female guest, reprising the roles she made famous, co-starred. Irene Dunne reprised her film role from "The Awful Truth," as did Merle Oberon in "Wuthering Heights" and Rosalind Russell in "His Girl Friday." By the middle of the run, numerous female leads were performing roles, regardless of whether it was their best-known role or not. Broadcast on Sunday evenings at 8 pm.

1. The Awful Truth (2/6/44; Irene Dunne)
2. The Pride of the Yankees (2/13/44; Teresa Wright)
3. A Man's Castle (2/20/44; Loretta Young)
4. His Girl Friday (2/27/44; Rosalind Russell)
5. Wuthering Heights (3/5/44; Merle Oberon)
6. The Love Affair (3/12/44; Miriam Hopkins)
7. Vivacious Lady (3/19/44; Ginger Rogers)
8. The Magnificent Obsession (3/26/44; Martha Scott)
9. Mayerling (4/2/44; Ingrid Bergman)
10. Strange Victory (4/9/44; Kay Francis)
11. The Straw (4/16/44; Barbara Stanwyck)
12. The Moon's Our Home (4/23/44; Virginia Bruce)
13. The Outsider (4/30/44; Donna Reed)
14. Lucky Partners (5/7/44; Lana Turner)
15. Heaven Can Wait (5/14/44; Gene Tierney)
16. A Star Is Born (5/21/44; Jennifer Jones)
17. A Kiss for Cinderella (5/28/44; Ida Lupino)
18. Accent on Youth (6/4/44; Anne Baxter)
19. My Favorite Wife (6/11/44; Joan Bennett)
20. Tovarich (6/18/44; Ann Sothern)
21. The Admirable Critchon (6/25/44; Olivia de Havilland)
22. Arrowsmith (7/2/44; Ruth Warrick)
23. Thief Is an Ugly Word (7/9/44; Agnes Moorehead)
24. No Time for Comedy (7/16/44; Claudette Colbert)
25. Romance (7/23/44; Hedy Lamarr)
26. Private Lives (7/30/44; Greer Garsonn)

Starring Boris Karloff

Also known as *Presenting Boris Karloff*, this Wednesday evening horror program featured horror star Boris Karloff in dramas of terror and murder. Mildred Natwick played the lead female roles, often the victimized wife or heroine being rescued from the killer or madman. Originating from New York, *Starring Boris Karloff* was broadcast over ABC from 9:30 to 10 pm, EST. Robert Corcoran wrote many of the scripts. Episodes eleven and thirteen were based on stories written by Cornell Woolrich. Episode three, "Mungahara," was written by Arch Oboler. George Gunn was the announcer. George Henninger was the organist.

1. Five Golden Guineas (9/21/49)
2. The Mask (9/28/49)
3. Mungahara (10/5/49)
4. Mad Illusion (10/12/49)
5. Perchance to Dream (10/19/49)
6. The Devil Takes a Wife (10/26/49)
7. The Moving Finger (11/2/49)
8. The Twisted Path (11/9/49)
9. False Face (11/16/49)
10. Cranky Bill (11/23/49)
11. Three O'Clock (11/30/49)
12. The Shop at Sly Corner (12/7/49)
13. The Night Reveals (12/14/49)

Stars in the Air

This anthology featured a wide variety of dramas (the majority being adaptations of movies) using Hollywood stars in the lead roles. Broadcast over CBS as a sustaining program, *Stars in the Air* premiered on Thursday evenings from 9:30 to 10 pm, EST. Beginning on May 3, 1952, the series moved to Saturday evenings from 10 to 10:30 pm, EST. Beginning May 31, the program moved back a half-hour, broadcast from 9:30 to 10 pm, EST. The final episode of the series was broadcast on Monday from 8 to 8:30 pm, EST. Johnny Jacobs hosted.

1. It's a Wonderful Life (12/13/51; James Stewart and Donna Reed)
2. John Loves Mary (12/20/51; Virginia Mayo and Ronald Reagan)
3. Mr. and Mrs. Smith (12/27/51; Jane Greer and Fred MacMurray)
4. You Belong to Me (1/3/52; Eve Arden and Ray Milland)
5. Take a Letter Darling (1/10/52; Cary Grant and Alexis Smith)
6. The Trouble with Women (1/17/52; Leif Ericson, Ruth Hussey, and John Lund)
7. Enchantment (1/24/52; Joseph Cotten and Marla Powers)
8. It Started with Eve (1/31/52; Vanessa Brown, Charles Cobourn, and Robert Stack)
9. The Yearling (2/7/52; Jean Hagen, John McGovern, and Gregory Peck)
10. Model Wife (2/14/52; Janet Leigh and Tony Curtis)
11. Suddenly It's Spring (2/21/52; MacDonald Carey and Betty Hutton)
12. The Bride Goes Wild (2/28/52; June Allyson and Dick Powell)
13. The Paleface (3/6/52; Bob Hope and Jane Russell)
14. Good Sam (3/13/52; Ann Sheridan and David Wayne)
15. Christmas in Connecticut (3/20/52; Gordon MacRea and Phyllis Thaxter)
16. Weekend for Three (3/27/52; Barbara Britton and Dennis O'Keefe)
17. Hail the Conquering Hero (4/3/52; Eddie Bracken, William Demarest, and Nancy Gates)
18. On Borrowed Time (4/10/52; Lionel Barrymore and Beula Bondi)
19. The Strange Love of Martha Ivers (4/17/52; Dan Duryea and Lizabeth Scott)
20. Deep Waters (4/24/52; Mona Freeman and William Lundigan)
21. The House on 92nd Street (5/3/52; Humphrey Bogart and Keefe Bresselle)
22. Jezebel (5/10/52; Jane Wyman and Carlton Young)
23. Night Song (5/17/52; Arthur Kennedy and Merle Oberon)
24. The Dark Corner (5/24/52; Howard Duff and Virginia Gregg)
25. Double Indemnity (5/31/52; Lydia Clark and Charlton Heston)
26. Kiss of Death (6/7/52; Victor Mature and Richard Widmark)
27. The Sun Comes Up (6/14/52; Percy Kilbride and Claire Trevor)

Stay Tuned for Terror

Robert Bloch is considered one of the masters of horror, having written numerous short stories and novels. His 1959 novel *Psycho* was filmed in Hollywood by director Alfred Hitchcock, setting a new standard for horror films throughout the sixties. On radio, however, it was a different story. *Stay Tuned for Terror* was produced and syndicated in Chicago and directed by Berle Adams. All of the scripts were based on stories written by Bloch, but after thirty-nine broadcasts, the series made no more fame for Bloch than when the program premiered.

The episodes themselves were, by the standards of the time, gruesome. Vampires, werewolves and witches were heard at least once on the show, but the majority of the evils were psychopaths and killers. The protagonists themselves often fell victim to horrible demises such as stabbings and beheadings. "Yours Truly, Jack the Ripper" invited the listeners on a modern-day man hunt for the real-life Jack the Ripper, supposedly still alive. "Lizzie Borden Took an Ax…" presented a different solution to the century-old crime, with horrifying results.

1. The Strange Flight of Richard Clayton (1/15/45)
2. The Bat Is My Brother (1/22/45)
3. Warm Up the Hot Seat (1/29/45)
4. The Soul Proprietor (2/5/45)
5. Satan's Phonograph (2/12/45)
6. The House of the Hatchet (2/19/45)
7. One Way to Mars (2/26/45)
8. The Hands of Loh Sing (3/5/45)
9. The Man Who Lost His Head (3/12/45)
10. Which Is the Witch? (3/19/45)
11. Black Bargain (3/26/45)
12. The Return of the Monster (4/2/45)
13. The Creeper of the Crypt (4/9/45)
14. The Secret of Sebek (4/16/45)
15. The Devil's Ticket (4/23/45)
16. The Secret of the Tomb (4/30/45)
17. The Man Who Cried Wolf (5/7/45)
18. Waxworks (5/14/45)
19. Beauty's Beast (5/21/45)
20. Sadini's Dummy (5/28/45)
21. Yours Truly, Jack the Ripper (6/4/45)
22. The Cloak of Darkness (6/11/45)
23. The Cat That Never Died (6/18/45)
24. Mad Scientist (6/25/45)
25. Totem Pole (7/2/45)
26. Contents, One Corpse (7/9/45)
27. Grandfather's Clock (7/16/45)
28. Lizzie Borden Took an Ax… (7/23/45)
29. The Heart of a Robot (7/30/45)
30. The Man Who Hated Machines (8/6/45)
31. The Grinning Ghoul (8/13/45)
32. Wine of the Wizard (8/20/45)
33. The Beasts of Barzac (8/27/45)
34. The Dark Demon (9/3/45)
35. I Hate Myself (9/10/45)
36. The Curse of the House (9/17/45)
37. The Man Who Raised the Dead (9/24/45)
38. The Boogie Man Will Get You (10/1/45)
39. Horror Show (10/8/45)

Straight Arrow

Another spin-off of *The Lone Ranger*, this one involved a Comanche Indian named Straight Arrow, who disguised himself as Steve Adams, the owner of the Broken Arrow cattle spread. With his faithful sidekick Packy McCloud, Straight Arrow fought for justice, usually battling murderers, thieves, and stage-coach robbers. Sheldon Stark wrote all of the scripts, having ten years of radio scripting experience under his belt before involving himself full-time with this project. Howard Culver played the lead role of Straight Arrow, Fred Howard was Packy, and Gwen Delano was Mesquite Molly, the Broken Arrow ranch housekeeper. Frank Bingham was the announcer. Milton Charles was the organist.

Straight Arrow was produced at KHJ, a Don-Lee Mutual network affiliate. The sound effects were handled by Ray Kemper, Bill James, and Tom Hanley, three men who would later work on *Gunsmoke*. Just like Roy Rogers, Straight Arrow rode a golden Palomino, a horse that was given its name months after the premiere via a contest. *Straight Arrow* remained a local show on the West Coast only, until February 7, 1949, when the series went national, alternating with Bobby Benson and the B-Bar-B Riders. J. Neil Reagan was the producer and director until the series went national, leaving Ted Robertson as his successor; it was sponsored by Nabisco Shredded Wheat.

On the West Coast (the first thirty-nine episodes) the series was broadcast on Thursday evenings from 8 to 8:30 pm, PST. Beginning February 7, 1949 (when *Straight Arrow* went national), the series was broadcast on Monday evenings from 8 to 8:30 pm, EST, and Tuesday and Thursday from 5 to 5:30 pm, EST. Beginning June 20, 1949, the show stayed on Monday evenings from 8 to 8:30 pm, EST. Beginning September 18, 1949, the show went back to its three-a-week format. Beginning February 7, 1950, the Monday night time slot was dropped, and the program remained on Tuesday and Thursday.

On February 6, 1949, a special live broadcast intended to gain enthusiasm for the show's national next-day premiere was presented. Entitled "Inaugural Pow-Wow," this special broadcast was not part of the regular programming.

Audition: Buffalo Hunt (1/5/48)
1. Stage from Calvaydos (5/6/48)
2. Trouble on the Trail (5/13/48)
3. False Friend (5/20/48)
4. The Dead Man Speaks (5/27/48)
5. Three on a Claim (6/3/48)
6. Wild Horse Mesa (6/10/48)
7. Ride for Justice (6/17/48)
8. Pioneer Editor (6/24/48)
9. The Haunted Desert (7/1/48)
10. War on the Range (7/8/48)
11. Oasis in the Desert (7/15/48)
12. The Iron Horse (7/22/48)
13. Danger Rides the Wind (7/29/48)
14. Fear Saddles a Samson (8/5/48)
15. The Gambler Holds the Cards (8/12/48)
16. Double for Danger (8/19/48)
17. Badmen Cross the Bravo (8/26/48)
18. The Ringer (9/2/48)
19. The Redman Traps a Killer (9/9/48)
20. Flame and Fury (9/16/48)
21. Spanish Gold (9/23/48)
22. Ambush at Eagle Pass (9/30/48)
23. The Hero (10/7/48)
24. Cry of the Wolf (10/14/48)
25. Pony Express (10/21/48)

26. Trail Blazer (10/28/48)
27. Rainbow's End (11/4/48)
28. The Sheriff Wins His Spurs [aka The Sheriff Earns His Spurs] (11/11/48)
29. The Boomer (11/18/48)
30. The Wild Turkey (11/25/48)
31. The Turncoat (12/2/48)
32. Bounty Hunter (12/9/48)
33. The Doctor and the Quack (12/16/48)
34. Sheep for the Manger [aka Sheep in the Manger] (12/23/48)
35. The Long Trail (12/30/48)
36. Rolling Stones (1/6/49)
37. The Widow's Mite (1/13/49)
38. The High Mountain (1/20/49)
39. Cattle Train (1/27/49)
40. The Roaring River (2/7/49)
41. The Hermit of Crosshollow Ridge (2/8/49)
42. Buffalo Hunt [restaged from audition recording] (2/10/49)
43. Grubstake (2/14/49)
44. Pioneer Crossing (2/15/49)
45. Ambush in the Desert (2/17/49)
46. Stampede for Justice (2/21/49)

253. Boundary War (2/6/51)
254. Double Danger (2/8/51)
255. Path to Peril (2/13/51)
256. Trial by Night (2/15/51)
257. Iron Wheels (2/20/51)
258. Mystery Ranch (2/22/51)
259. Corral a Killer (2/27/51)
260. Quicksand Crossing (3/1/51)
261. Fires of War (3/6/51)
262. Guns For Gold (3/8/51)
263. Medicine Man (3/13/51)
264. Finger of Manitou (3/15/51)
265. Track of Murder (3/20/51)
266. Drumbeat (3/22/51)
267. The Sheriff Learns the Law (3/27/51)
268. Broken Wheel (3/29/51)
269. Feathered Arrows (4/3/51)
270. Deadly Current [aka Deadly Smoke] (4/5/51)
271. Flash in the Pan (4/10/51)
272. False Rider (4/12/51)
273. Two Tribes West (4/17/51)
274. Calico (4/19/51)
275. Under Suspicion (4/24/51)
276. The Misfit (4/26/51)
277. The Dry Earth (5/1/51)
278. Spread Eagle (5/3/51)
279. Trail's End (5/8/51)
280. Reverse Proof (5/10/51)
281. Rustler's Run (5/15/51)
282. The Dark Cave (5/17/51)
283. Gamble for Gain (5/22/51)
284. The Conspirator (5/24/51)
285. Whiphand (5/29/51)
286. The Bitter Wind (5/31/51)
287. Rainbow's End (6/5/51)
288. Eagle Claw (6/7/51)
289. Owl Hoot (6/12/51)
290. Blanket Indian (6/14/51)
291. Flood Tide (6/19/51)
292. Long Summer (6/21/51)

The Strange Dr. Weird

A spin-off of *The Mysterious Traveler*, this horror series featured Maurice Tarplin (also host of *Traveler*) as the host, who lived in a "house on the other side of the cemetery." The listeners would be invited in, and the host would tell a different horror story each week, then invite them back for next week's story. David Kogan and Robert A. Arthur, the writers of *The Mysterious Traveler*, wrote the scripts, and the fifteen-minute broadcasts were actually abridged half-hour dramas from the *Traveler* series (the titles were changed from the originals). Sponsored by Ford Motors and later Adam Hats, *The Strange Dr. Weird* was broadcast over Mutual, Tuesday evenings from 7:15 to 7:30 pm, EST.

1. The House Where Death Lived (11/7/44)
2. The Summoning of Chandor (11/14/44)
3. Journey Into the Unknown (11/21/44)
4. Murder Comes Home (11/28/44)
5. Death in the Everglades (12/5/44)
6. The Man Who Talked with Death (12/12/44)
7. The White Pearls of Terror (12/19/44)
8. Stand in for Death (12/26/44)
9. Tiger Cat (1/2/45)
10. Murder Ship (1/9/45)
11. Beauty and the Beast (1/16/45)
12. Survival of the Fittest (1/23/45)
13. The Man Who Lived Twice (1/30/45)
14. Dark Wings of Death (2/6/45)
15. The Secret Room (2/13/45)
16. The Knife of Death (2/20/45)
17. Murder Will Out (2/27/45)
18. The Voice of Death (3/6/45)
19. The Two Faces of Death (3/13/45)
20. The Man Who Knew Everything (3/20/45)
21. He Woke Up Dead (3/27/45)
22. The Devil's Cavern (4/3/45)
23. When Killers Meet (4/10/45)
24. Dead Man's Paradise (4/17/45)

25. The Ghost Ship (4/24/45)
26. The Man Who Played Dead (5/1/45)

27. The Picture of a Killer (5/8/45)
28. Revenge from the Grave (5/15/45)

Strange Wills

Syndicated by ZIV Productions, this anthology series featured stories of missing heirs. Warren William, Lurene Tuttle, William Conrad, Howard McNear and Perry Ward played supporting roles. Marvin Miller starred in the audition program.

Audition: (1/15/46; Marvin Miller)
1. The Mad Concerto (6/8/46)
2. Alias Doctor Svengali (6/15/46)
3. Black interlude (6/22/46)
4. The Lady and the Pirate (6/29/46)
5. Prince of Broadway (7/6/46)
6. Treasure to Starboard (7/13/46)
7. One Shining Night (7/20/46)
8. Midnight on the Moor (7/27/46)
9. Seven Flights to Glory (8/3/46)
10. The Girl of Shadowland (8/10/46)
11. The Madman's Glory (8/17/46)
12. Emeralds Come High (8/24/46)
13. Emily (8/31/46)

14. Margain for Love (9/7/46)
15. They Met in Monte Carlo (9/14/46)
16. The Girl in Cell 13 (9/21/46)
17. So Deep the Stream (9/28/46)
18. The Miser's Gold (10/5/46)
19. East of Hudson's Bay (10/12/46)
20. Autograph Girl (10/19/46)
21. The Penthouse Orphan (10/26/46)
22. Singapore Liz (11/2/46)
23. Crosswinds (11/9/46)
24. The Dance Director (11/16/46)
25. Death Has Ten Words (11/23/46)
26. The Killer and the Saint (11/30/46)
27. Portsmith Square (12/7/46)

Streamlined Shakespeare

"The greatest actor we ever had was John Barrymore. I saw him four times in *Hamlet*.... He was extraordinarily simple, and he played the whole range of the character." So spoken by Eva Le Gallienne in 1982, describing John Barrymore, one of the great Shakespearean actors of all time. The National Broadcasting Company also thought so, because in June of 1937, NBC hired John Barrymore for a short-run series that ran only six episodes before being replaced by the four-week presentation of *NBC Presents Eugene O'Neill*.

This series was broadcast on Monday evenings at 9:30 to 10:15 pm; Barrymore was supported by his fourth (and last) wife, Elaine Jacobs Barrie, whom John had married less than a year before. Erin O'Brien performed numerous supporting roles as well. The scripts were adapted for radio by John Barrymore, along with the help of Forrest Barnes.

In August of 1950, Audio Rarities Records released excerpts from the 1937 program, deleted the original opening theme and monologue, and replaced it with a new one, entitling the 1950 series *John Barrymore and Shakespeare*. This second series, nothing more than a rebroadcast of the original 1937 run, was also broadcast on NBC, but only five productions were presented. The dates below belong to both series — the first are the dates of the 1937 series, the second are of the 1950 series, which was broadcast in a different order, and minus one presentation.

1. Hamlet (6/21/37; 8/10/50)
2. Richard III (6/28/37; 8/17/50)
3. Macbeth (7/5/37; 8/3/50)
4. The Tempest (7/11/37; 8/31/50)
5. Twelfth Night (7/19/37; 8/24/50)
6. The Taming of the Shrew (7/26/37)

Stroke of Fate

What would it be like had Truman not dropped the Bomb on Hiroshima? Would we be using yen instead of dollars? Would we be speaking Japanese instead of English? Would the Japanese theme song air over our television sets every morning? That was what this show concerned itself with. Presented in the *You Are There* tradition, this program featured that "what if" twist, leaning toward events in world history. History is just history. After each drama, a guest speaker with a degree in world history would talk about the historical significance of the dramatized events.

Professor Allan Nevins was on most of these broadcasts as speaker and lecturer. Walter Kiernan was the host of this series, broadcast on NBC, Sunday evenings from 8 to 8:30 pm. Episode twelve was broadcast an hour-and-a-half later, beginning at 9:30 pm. With no sponsor, the series dropped out of sight after thirteen broadcasts. The titles below are the actual script titles, which are probably some of the longest script titles for any radio program of that time.

1. What Might Have Happened if General Lee Had Accepted Lincoln's Offer to Command the Union Army? (10/4/53)
2. Queen Elizabeth I and the Earl of Essex (10/11/53)
3. What Might Have Happened Had Hamilton Killed Burr? (10/18/53)
4. What Might Have Happened Had Marie Antoinette Escaped the Guillotine? (10/25/53)
5. What Might Have Happened Had Lincoln Obtained the Consular Job He Wanted in 1841? (11/1/53; Stephan Lorant)
6. What Might Have Happened Had Benedict Arnold's Plot to Betray America Succeeded? (11/8/53)
7. What Might Have Happened Had Julius Caesar Wed Cleopatra? (11/15/53)
8. What Might Have Happened Had the French in 1936 Used Force to Oppose Hitler's Occupancy of the Rhineland? (11/22/53)
9. What Might Have Happened Had the French Won the Battle of Quebec in 1759? (11/29/53)
10. What Might Have Happened Had the Russians Purchased Alaska Instead of the U.S.? (12/6/53)
11. What Might Have Happened Had Alexander the Great Lived to Continue His Conquest of the West? (12/13/53)
12. What Might Have Happened Had America's First Secret Weapon — a One-Man Submarine — Succeeded in the Revolutionary War? (12/20/53)
13. What Might Have Happened Had Fate Prevented the Norman Conquest of England in 1066? (12/27/53; Dr. Richard Webb)

Studio One

This program was the brainchild of Fletcher Markle, who not only produced and directed, but occasionally starred and wrote a good many of the scripts. Initially broadcast over CBS radio on Tuesday evenings for a full hour, beginning 9:30 pm, EST, the program later moved to 10 pm. The series won critical approval from the start, due in part to Markle, who chose actors for voice contrast and ability to perform rather than for name status. Originating from New York, some were original scripts, and others were adaptations. Sheldon Stark was among the few who adapted original stories. Alexander Semmler supplied the music.

In Henrik Ibsen's "An Enemy of the People," one man spoke the truth against the wrath and greed of an entire town. The famous love story about a young soldier who turns from the military to a life of crime for the love of Carmen was presented on August 5, 1947. Although it was the basis of the famous opera by Bizet, no singing was performed. "Laburnam Grove" presented a comedy about a small Connecticut town and a retired chicken farmer who claimed he dabbled in counterfeiting. "Thunder Rock" presented the disturbing tale of a lighthouse keeper who imagined six people who died ninety years ago in a ship wreck were alive again. A wealthy girl fell in love with a young Jewish lawyer in "Earth and High Heaven." "Young Man of Manhattan," set in the Roaring Twenties, presented a humorous romance about a magazine writer and a sports columnist who marry and then go their separate ways. "Great Impersonation" presented Walter Slezak in an exciting adventure/spy story during the First World War. The story of an ambitious and heartless opera singer who thought nothing of stepping on her friends to get ahead, was entitled "Painted Veils." The broadcast of April 13, 1948, was later adapted for television when the series moved to TV. A preacher looked for new spiritual worlds to conquer, and found them in "One Foot in Heaven."

On November 7, 1948 (a few months after it left radio), *Studio One* made the transition to television, where the program was such a huge success, that the program continued on the air for almost ten years, providing work for such writers as Gore Vidal, Reginald Rose and Rod Serling.

1. Under the Volcano (4/29/47; Anne Burr, Joe Di Santis, and Everett Sloane)
2. Topaz (5/6/47; Anne Burr, Sebastian Cabot, Harold Dearenforth, Everett Sloane, and Hester Sondergaard)
3. An Enemy of the People (5/13/47; Frank Behrens, Ian MacAllaster, Paul McGrath, and Mabel Moore)
4. Alibi Ike (5/20/47; Anne Burr, Joe Di Santis, Ruth Gilbert, Everett Sloane, Howard Smith, and Bill Woodson)
5. Dodsworth (5/27/47; Santos Ortega)
6. Hay Fever [written by Noel Coward] (6/3/47; Anne Burr, Everett Sloane, Evelyn Varden, and William Woodson)
7. The Red Badge of Courage (6/10/47; Anne Burr, Joe Di Santis, Everett Sloane, Hester Sondergaard, and John Sylvester)
8. The Mysterious Mickey Finn

(6/17/47; Anne Burr and Everett Sloane)

9. Romantic Comedians (6/24/47; Anne Burr, Everett Sloane, and Hester Sondergaard)
10. Baby Cyclone (7/1/47; Anne Burr, Leon Janney, and Everett Sloane)
11. Payment Deferred (7/8/47; Agnes Moorehead)
12. Ah, Wilderness (7/15/47; Don Harran and Everett Sloane)
13. Holiday (7/22/47; Joan Alexander, Ed Begley, Anne Burr, Leon Janney, and Everett Sloane)
14. A Bill of Divorcement (7/29/47; Anne Burr and Everett Sloane)
15. Carmen (8/5/47; Anne Burr, Fletcher Markle, and Everett Sloane)
16. Pride and Prejudice (8/12/47; Anne Burr, Sarah Burton, Abby Lewis, Fletcher Markle, Gregory Morton, Hedley Rennie, and Miriam Wolfe)
17. Laburnam Grove (8/19/47; Anne Burr, Leon Janney, Lou Merrill, and Everett Sloane)
18. The Hunted [based on the Booth Tarkington story] (8/26/47; Anne Burr, Gregory Morton, Everett Sloane, Sidney Smith, Miriam Wolfe)
19. Thunder Rock (9/2/47; Robert Dryden, Clarence Durwin, Fletcher Markle, Stefan Schabel, and Hester Sondergaard)
20. The Barrets of Wimple Street (9/9/47; Anne Burr, Kathleen Cordell, and Fletcher Markle)
21. An Act of Faith* (9/16/47; Frank Behrens, Anne Burr, Robert Dryden, Lamont Johnson, Fletcher Markle, Mercedes McCambridge, Martin Wilson, and Miriam Wolfe)
22. Gentle Julia (9/23/47; Edwin Bruce, Anne Burr, Michael Dreyfus, Robert Dryden, Fletcher Markle, Joyce Van Patten, and Rosemary Rice)
23. Wuthering Heights (9/30/47; Anne Burr, Gregory Morton, Hester Sondergaard, and Miriam Wolfe)
24. A Tree Grows in Brooklyn (10/7/47; Betty Garde, Frank Readick, and Rosemary Rice)
25. Anthony Adverse (10/14/47; Bud Collyer and Mercedes McCambridge)
26. Singing Guns (10/21/47; Myron McCormick and Gary Merrill)
27. Kitty Foyle (11/4/47; Elspeth Eric, Fletcher Markle, Mercedes McCambridge, and John McGovern)
28. Let Me Do the Talking (11/11/47; John Garfield, Raymond E. Johnson, Mercedes McCambridge)
29. Young Man of Manhattan (11/18/47; Joe Di Santis, Mercedes McCambridge, and Robert Mitchum)
30. Payment Deferred (11/25/47; Charles Laughton and Hester Sondergaard)
31. Earth and High Heaven (12/2/47; Geraldine Fitzgerald, Mercedes McCambridge, Raymond Edward Johnson, Frank Richards, and Everett Sloane)
32. To Mary, with Love (12/9/47; Gene Kelly, Mercedes McCambridge, and Everett Sloane)
33. Experiment Perilous (12/16/47; Ralph Bellamy, Everett Sloane, Hester Sonergaard, and Gertrude Warner)
34. Painted Veils (12/23/47; Kathleen Cordell, Eileen Farrell, James Mason, Mercedes McCambridge, and Everett Sloane)
35. So Big (12/30/47; Joan Blondell, Edna Ferber, Everett Sloane, and Gertrude Warner)
36. Confidential Agent [based on the story by Graham Greene] (1/6/48; Raymond Massey and Mercedes McCambridge)
37. Wednesday's Child (1/13/48; Richard Arlen and Bonita Granville)
38. The Amazing Dr. Clitterhouse (1/20/48; Charles Irving, Paul Muni, Claire Niesen, and Everett Sloane)
39. The Great Impersonation (1/27/48; Bob Dryden, Fletcher Markle, Louise Rainer, Beverly Roberts, Walter Slezak, and Everett Sloane)
40. Dodsworth (2/3/48; Walter Huston)
41. Golden Boy (2/10/48; Dane Clark)
42. A Farewell to Arms (2/17/48; Madeleine Carroll, Joe Di Santis, Robert Dryden, Fletcher Markle, Everett Sloane, Hester Sondergaard, and Miriam Wolfe)

Because of a special broadcast on CBS, this episode ran thirty minutes instead of sixty.

43. King's Row (2/24/48; Robert Dryden, Leon Janney, Mercedes McCambridge, Cathy McGregor, Everett Sloane, Miriam Wolfe, and Robert Young)

44. Uncle Harry (3/2/48; Judith Evelyn, Brenda Forbes, Michael Redgrave, Everett Sloane, and Gertrude Warner)

45. Sometime Every Summertime (3/9/48; Burgess Meredith)

46. One More Spring (3/16/48; Glen Anders, Fletcher Markle, Susan Peters, and Everett Sloane)

47. The Thirty-Nine Steps (3/23/48; Kathleen Cordell, Glenn Ford, Mercedes McCambridge, Everett Sloane, John Stanley, and Miriam Wolfe)

48. Babbitt (3/30/48; Walter Huston, Mercedes McCambridge, Everett Sloane, and Hestor Sondergaard)

49. The Kimballs (4/6/48; Mercedes McCambridge, Everett Sloane, Franchot Tone, and Miriam Wolfe)

50. The Glass Key [based on the Dashiell Hammett story] (4/13/48; Alan Baxter, Joe Di Santis, Bob Dryden, Charles Irving, Elissa Landi, Cathy McGregor, and Everett Sloane)

51. Pride and Prejudice (4/20/48; Geraldine Fitzgerald)

52. South Riding (4/27/48; Charles Laughton, Everett Sloane, and Hester Sondergaard)

53. Private Worlds (5/4/48; Madeleine Carroll, Michael Fitzmaurice, Fletcher Markle, Mercedes McCambridge, and Claire Niesen)

54. Wine of the Country (5/11/48; Mercedes McCambridge, Robert Mitchum, and Everett Sloane)

55. The Last Tycoon [based on the F. Scott Fitzgerald story] (5/18/48; Betty Field, Fletcher Markle, Mercedes McCambridge, and Everett Sloane)

56. Angelic Avengers (5/25/48; Ann Blyth, Joe Di Santis, Margaret Phillips, and Everett Sloane)

57. One Foot in Heaven (6/1/48; Rosemary De Camp, Fletcher Markle, Everett Sloane, Franchot Tone, and Miriam Wolfe)

58. Let Me Do the Talking (6/8/48; Melvyn Douglas)

59. The Return of the Native (6/15/48; Michael Redgrave, Hedley Rennie, and Everett Sloane)

60. Arabesque (6/29/48; Marlene Dietrich, Joe Di Santis, Fletcher Markle, and Gary Merrill)

61. Topaz (7/6/48; Claude Rains)

62. Spanish Bayonet (7/20/48; Ian MacAllaster, Mercedes McCambridge, Burgess Meredith, Everett Sloane, and Gertrude Warner)

63. The Constant Nymph (7/27/48; Katherine Cordell, Hedley Rennie, and Rosemary Rice)

Suspense

"Radio's outstanding theater of thrills" was broadcast on CBS radio for more than twenty years. Numerous Hollywood and Broadway stars appeared in roles they were — or were not — associated with. In "To Find Help," Frank Sinatra starred as a psychopath, while in "Plan X," Jack Benny played a Martian. Lucille Ball was a murderer, Ronald Reagan was framed for murder, and Orson Welles kept a human brain alive in a jar. Twenty years of broadcasting involved numerous talented directors: William Spier, Ted Bliss, Anton M. Leader, William N. Robson, Bruno Zirato, Jr., Fred Hendrickson, Antony Ellis, Elliot Lewis, and others.

Suspense featured the best talent CBS offered, using their best script writers, sound effects men, radio actors, and directors taking turns bringing their own handiwork and style to the airwaves. The series was sustained, until Roma Wines became the first sponsor of the series, beginning in December of 1943. On November 20, 1947, the series went sustaining again, and on January 3, 1948, *Suspense* went to an hour-long format. On July 8, 1948, the series returned to the thirty-minute format, and under a new sponsorship, Auto-Lite. (Auto-Lite was responsible for later introducing *Suspense* to television for five seasons.) The show went sustaining in the summer of 1954, and by 1956 had various sponsors, including A.T.&T., Pepsi-Cola and Marlboro.

Episode 281 went under two titles, "Eve" and "The Black Angel," which were both announced during the broadcast. Episode 320 was untitled, but it was an adaptation of John Collier's short story "Back for Christmas." Glenn Ford was originally scheduled to star in episode 170, but instead, Lee Bowman took his place. Episode 375 was originally scheduled to be an adaptation of Edgar Allan Poe's "The Pit and the Pendulum," but for reasons unknown, a different script was used instead. Clifton Webb was originally scheduled to star in episode 160, but due to illness, Joseph Cotten took his place. The Kingston Trio's 1958 musical hit "Tom Dooley" was played for narration in episode 780. James Mason reprised his film role in "Odd Man Out," as did Dame May Whitty and Robert Montgomery in "Night Must Fall."

June Duprez and John Loder reprised their film roles in "The Brighton Strangler." Ben Hecht not only wrote episode 106, but acted in it as well. Lucille Ball fell ill shortly before the broadcast of October 19, 1944, so Nancy Kelly took her place. June Duprez took the place of an ill Ida Lupino on December 28, 1944. Episode 317 was originally scheduled to feature Sydney Greenstreet, but after he gave notice that he was unable to perform, Claude Rains and Vincent Price took his place.

Much of the music was composed and conducted by Wilbur Hatch, Leith Stevens, Lucien Morawek, Lud Gluskin, and Bernard Herrmann. By the mid-fifties, stock music was used in the background. Joseph Kearns, George Walsh, Elliott Lewis, William Johnstone, Larry Thor, Stuart Metz and Paul Frees were a few who announced for the series. Society Mistress Elsa Maxwell assisted in the Roma Wine commercials for a few months in 1945. The most popular episode, "Sorry, Wrong Number," was performed more than any other *Suspense* script, a total of eight broadcasts. The same script was later adapted into a big screen film in 1948 with Burt Lancaster and Barbara Stanwyck as the leads.

Episodes 83, 112 and 344 were written previously and performed on another CBS mystery program, *The Whistler*. A handful of scripts were written previously and performed for other radio programs such as *The Clock, Escape, Creeps by Night, The Mysterious Traveler, On Stage, Radio City Playhouse, Inner Sanctum Mysteries*, and *The Mercury Summer Theater on the Air*. Writers for *Suspense* were many, including William Spier, Robert L. Richards, Antony Ellis, Ross Murray, Tom Hanley, Lucille Fletcher, and Les Crutchfield. Episode 279 was actually two half-hour episodes from *The Adventures of Sam Spade* presented in an hour-long broadcast using much of the same cast as previous. William Shakespeare's "Othello" was broadcast in two parts in May of 1953, announced as the first time the play was dramatized over radio. The announcer for *Suspense* was mistaken; the same play was dramatized previously on radio programs such as *Radio Guild*.

Audition: *Forecast*: "The Lodger" (7/22/40; Noreen Gammill, Edmund Gwenn, and Herbert Marshall)

1. The Burning Court [based on the John Dickson Carr novel] (6/17/42; Julie Hayden, Charlie Ruggles)
2. Wet Saturday [based on the John Collier short story] (6/17/42; Clarence Derwent)
3. The Life of Nellie James (7/1/42; Jeanne Cagney)
4. Rope [based on the Patrick Hamilton stage play] (7/8/42; Richard Widmark)
5. The Third Eye [based on the R.W. Chambers short story] (7/15/42)
6. Witness on the Westbound Limited (7/22/42)
7. Philomel Cottage [based on the Agatha Christie story] (7/29/42; Eric Dressler and Alice Frost)
8. Finishing School [based on the story by Ethel Lina White] (8/5/42; Margo)
9. Suspicion [based on the short story by Dorothy Sayers] (8/12/42; Pedro de Cordoba, Helen Lewis)
10. The Cave of Ali Baba [based on the short story by Dorothy Sayers] (8/19/42; Romney Brent)
11. The Hitch-hiker (9/2/42; Orson Welles)
12. The Kettler Method (9/16/42; John Gibson, Roger De Koven, Guy Repp, and Gloria Stuart)
13. A Passage to Benares [based on the T.S. Stribling short story] (9/23/42; Horace Brent, Alan Hewitt, Guy Repp, and Paul Stewart)
14. One Hundred in the Dark [based on the Owen M. Johnson short story] (9/30/42; Alice Frost)
15. The Lord of the Witch Doctors (10/27/42; Nicholas Joy and Joseph Kearns)
16. The Devil in the Summer House (11/3/42; Martin Gabel and Leslie Woods)
17. Will You Make a Bet with Death? (11/10/42; Ted de Corsia, Michael Fitzmaurice, Nicholas Joy, and Leslie Woods)
18. Menace in Wax (11/17/42; Joseph Julian)
19. The Body Snatchers (11/24/42)
20. The Bride Vanishes (12/1/42; Hanley Stafford)
21. Till Death Do Us Part (12/15/42; Alice Frost, David Gothard, Peter Lorre, Mercedes McCambridge)
22. Two Sharp Knives [based on the Dasheill Hammett short story] (12/22/42; Stuart Erwin)
23. Nothing Up My Sleeve (1/5/43; George Coulouris and Elissa Landi)
24. The Pit and the Pendulum [based on the short story by Edgar A. Poe] (1/12/43; Henry Hull)
25. The Devil's Saint (1/19/43; Peter Lorre)
26. Death Went Along for the Ride (1/26/43; Ralph Bellamy)
27. The Doctor Prescribed Death (2/2/43; Geraldine Fitzgerald, Bela Lugosi, and Lou Merrill)
28. The Hangman Won't Wait (2/9/43; Sydney Greenstreet, Ian Martin, and Verna Felton)
29. In Fear and Trembling (2/16/43; Mary Astor and Verna Felton)
30. Will You Walk Into My Parlor? (2/23/43; Hans Conried, Geraldine Fitzgerald, and Sir Cedric Hardwicke)
31. The Night Reveals [based on the Cornell Woolrich short story] (3/2/43; Fredric March)

32. The Phantom Archer (3/9/43; Ralph Bellamy, Constance Bennett, and Walter Hampden)
33. Cabin B-13 (3/16/43; Ralph Bellamy)
34. The Customers Like Murder (3/23/43; Peggy Conklin and Roland Young)
35. The Dead Sleep Lightly (3/30/43; Lee Bowman, Walter Hampden, and Susan Hayward)
36. Fire Burn and Cauldron Bubble (4/6/43; Paul Lukas)
37. Fear Paints a Picture (4/13/43; Bea Benaderet and Nancy Colman)
38. The Moment of Darkness (4/20/43; Wendy Barrie, Peter Lorre, and George Zucco)
39. The Diary of Saphronia Winters (4/27/43; Ray Collins and Agnes Moorehead)
40. Death Flies Blind (5/4/43; Richard Dix, Montegue Love, and Gale Page)
41. Mr. Markham, Antique Dealer (5/11/43; Heather Angel, Bramwell Fletcher, and Paul Lukas)
42. The A.B.C. Murders [based on the Agatha Christie novel] (5/18/43; Bramwell Fletcher, Elsa Lanchester, and Charles Laughton)
43. Sorry, Wrong Number (5/25/43; Agnes Moorehead)
44. Banquo's Chair [based on the Rupert Croft Cooke story] (6/1/43; Hans Conried, Donald Crisp, John Loder, and Ian Wolfe)
45. Five Canaries in the Room (6/8/43; Lee Bowman, William Johnstone, and Ona Munson)
46. Last Night (6/15/43; Joseph Kearns, Kent Smith, and Margo)
47. The Man Without a Body (6/22/43; Wendy Barrie, John Sutton, and George Zucco)
48. Uncle Henry's Rosebush (6/29/43; Ellen Drew, Agnes Morrehead, and Ted Reid)
49. The White Rose Murders (7/6/43; Joseph Kearns and Maureen O'Hara)
50. Murder Goes Out for a Swim [based on a novel by Louis Joseph Vance] (7/20/43; Eric Blore and Warren William

51. The Last Letter of Dr. Bronson (7/27/43; George Coulouris, Laird Cregar, Harold Huber, Walter Kingsford, Theodore Von Eltz, and Ian Wolfe)
52. A Friend to Alexander [based on the short story by James Thurber] (8/3/43; Geraldine Fitzgerald and Robert Young)
53. The Fountain Plays [based on the short story by Dorothy Sayers] (8/10/43; Wendy Barrie, Edmund Gwenn, Dennis Hoey, and Ian Wolfe)
54. Sorry, Wrong Number (8/21/43; Hans Conried and Agnes Moorehead)
55. The King's Birthday (8/28/43; Dolores Costello, Martin Kosleck, Ian Wolfe, and George Zucco)
56. The Singing Walls [based on a story by Cornell Woolrich] (9/2/43; Dane Clark and Preston Foster)
57. Marry for Murder (9/9/43; Ray Collins, Bramwell Fletcher, Lillian Gish, and Otto Kruger)
58. The Cross-Eyed Bear [based on the novel by Dorothy B. Hughes] (9/16/43; Virginia Bruce, William Johnstone, and John Loder)
59. The Most Dangerous Game [based on the Richard Connell short story] (9/23/43; Orson Welles and Keenan Wynn)
60. The Lost Special [based on the short story by Sir Arthur Conan Doyle] (9/30/43; Orson Welles)
61. Philomel Cottage (10/7/43; Geraldine Fitzgerald and Orson Welles)
62. Lazarus Walks [based on a story by J.M. Speed] (10/19/43; Hans Conried and Orson Welles)
63. After Dinner Story [based on the short story by Cornell Woolrich] (10/26/43; Otto Kruger)
64. Statement of Employee Henry Wilson (11/2/43; Hans Conried and Gene Lockhart)
65. Cabin B-13 (11/9/43; Hans Conried, Phillip Dorn, Dennis Hoey, William Johnstone, and Margo)
66. Thieves Fall Out (11/16/43; Hans Conried, William Johnstone, Harry Lang, and Gene Kelly)

67. The Strange Death of Charles Umberstein (11/23/43; Hans Conried and Vincent Price)
68. The Black Curtain [based on the novel by Cornell Woolrich] (12/2/43; Bea Benaderet, Hans Conried, Cary Grant, William Johnstone, Harry Lang, Walter Tetley, and Lurene Tuttle)
69. The Night Reveals (12/9/43; Hans Conried, Margo, and Robert Young)
70. Wet Saturday (12/16/43; Hans Conried and Charles Laughton)
71. Back For Christmas [based on the John Collier short story] (12/23/43; Peter Lorre, John McIntire)
72. Finishing School (12/30/43; Janet Beecher, Elsa Lanchester, and Margo)
73. The One-Way Ride to Nowhere (1/6/44; Hans Conried, Alan Ladd, and John McIntire)
74. Dime a Dance [based on a Cornell Woolrich story] (1/13/44; Lucille Ball, Hans Conried, Patrick McGeehan, Jeanette Nolan, and Ian Wolfe)
75. A World of Darkness (1/20/44; Hans Conried, Paul Lukas, and Ian Wolfe)
76. The Locked Room (1/27/44; Virginia Bruce, Allyn Joslyn, Will Wright, and George Zucco)
77. The Sisters (2/3/44; Joseph Kearns, Ida Lupino, and Agnes Moorehead)
78. Suspicion (2/10/44; Hans Conried, John McIntire, and Charlie Ruggles)
79. Life Ends at Midnight (2/17/44; Fay Bainter, Dane Clark, William Johnstone, and Ralph Morgan)
80. Sorry, Wrong Number (2/24/44; Harry Lang, Cathy Lewis, John McIntire, and Agnes Moorehead)
81. Portrait Without A Face (3/2/44; Hans Conried, George Coulouris, Phillip Dorn, Michelle Morgan)
82. The Defense Rests (3/9/44; Hans Conried, Alan Ladd, John McIntire, and Will Wright)
83. Narrative About Clarence (3/16/44; Hans Conried, Laird Cregar, Wally Maher, and John McIntire)
84. Sneak Preview (3/23/44; Hans Conried, Joseph Cotten, Dennis Hoey, Cathy Lewis, John McIntire)
85. Cat and Mouse (3/30/44; Wendell Holmes, Lurene Tuttle, Sonny Tufts, and Will Wright)
86. The Woman in Red [based on the novel by Antony Gilbert] (4/6/44; Katina Paxinou and Ian Wolfe)
87. The Marvelous Barastro [based on the Ben Hecht story] (4/13/44; Hans Conried and Orson Welles)
88. The Palmer Method (4/20/44; Hans Conried, Ed Gardner, Jerry Hausner, and John McIntire)
89. Death Went Along for the Ride (4/27/44; Gene Kelly and Walter Tetley)
90. The Dark Tower [based on the stage play by George S. Kaufman and Alexander Woollcott] (5/4/44; Hans Conried, Verna Felton, Joseph Kearns, John McIntire, Jeanette Nolan, and Orson Welles)
91. The Visitor [based on the novel by Carl Randau and Leane Zugsmith] (5/11/44; Eddie Bracken)
92. Donovan's Brain [part one, based on the Curt Siodmak novel] (5/18/44; Hans Conried, Jerry Hausner, John McIntire, Jeanette Nolan, and Orson Welles)
93. Donovan's Brain [part two] (5/25/44; Hans Conried, Jerry Hausner, John McIntire, Jeanette Nolan, and Orson Welles)
94. Fugue in C Minor (6/1/44; Bea Benaderet, Ida Lupino, and Vincent Price)
95. Case History of Edgar Lowndes (6/8/44; Hans Conried, Donald Crisp, and Thomas Mitchell)
96. A Friend to Alexander (6/15/44; Hans Conried, Geraldine Fitzgerald, and Richard Whorf)
97. The Ten Grand (6/22/44; Lucille Ball, Harry Lang, Patrick McGeehan, and John McIntire)
98. The Walls Came Tumbling Down (6/29/44; Herb Butterfield, Hans Conried, Wendell Holmes, John

McIntire, Jane Morgan, and Keenan Wynn)

99. The Search for Henri Lefevre (7/6/44; Hans Conried, Joseph Kearns, Paul Muni, and Lurene Tuttle)

100. The Beast Must Die [based on the novel by Cecil Day Lewis] (7/13/44; Bea Benaderet, Hans Conried, Dennis Hoey, Joseph Kearns, Herbert Marshall, and John McIntire)

101. Of Maestro and Man (7/20/44; Richard Conte, Peter Lorre, John McIntire, and Lou Merrill)

102. The Black Shawl (7/27/44; Patrick McGeehan, Maureen O'Sullivan, and Dame May Whitty)

103. Banquo's Chair (8/3/44; Hans Conried, Donald Crisp, John Loder, Jane Morgan, and Ian Wolfe)

104. The Man Who Knew How [based on the short story by Dorothy Sayers] (8/10/44; Hans Conried, Joseph Kearns, Charles Laughton, and Ian Wolfe)

105. The Diary of Saphronia Winters (8/17/44; Ray Collins and Agnes Moorehead)

106. Actor's Blood [based on the short story by Ben Hecht] (8/24/44; Hans Conried and Fredric March)

107. The Black Path of Fear [based on the novel by Cornell Woolrich] (8/31/44; Brian Donlevy)

108. Voyage Through Darkness (9/7/44; Reginald Gardner and Olivia de Havilland)

109. You'll Never See Me Again [based on the novelette by Cornel Woolrich] (9/14/44; Joseph Cotten)

110. The Bluebeard of Belloc (9/21/44; Ludwig Dunath, Joseph Kearns, John McIntire, Merle Oberon)

111. The Man Who Couldn't Lose (9/28/44; Joseph Kearns, Gene Kelly, Wally Maher, and Lou Merrill)

112. Dateline : Lisbon (10/5/44; John Hodiak)

113. The Merry Widower [based on a short story by Roy Vickers] (10/12/44; Reginald Gardner)

114. Eve [based on a novel by Cornell Woolrich] (10/19/44; Joseph Kearns and Nancy Kelly)

115. Night Man (10/26/44; Virginia Bruce and Joseph Kearns)

116. The Singing Walls (11/2/44; Ken Christy, Van Johnson, and Wally Maher)

117. You Were Wonderful (11/9/44; Lena Horne, Joseph Kearns, and Wally Maher)

118. Dead of Night (11/16/44; Robert Cummings, Wally Maher, Walter Tetley, and Lurene Tuttle)

119. The Fountain Plays (11/23/44; Dennis Hoey, Charles Laughton, and Ian Wolfe)

120. The Black Curtain (11/30/44; Cary Grant, Wally Maher, Lurene Tuttle)

121. The Lodger [based on the novelette by Marie Belloc Lowndes] (12/14/44; Robert Montgomery)

122. The Brighton Strangler (12/21/44; June Duprez, Joseph Kearns, John Loder, Wally Maher, and Herbert Rawlinson)

123. A Thing of Beauty (12/28/44; June Duprez, Wally Maher, John McIntire, and Herbert Rawlinson)

124. I Had an Alibi (1/4/45; Cathy Lewis, Wally Maher, John McIntire, Lurene Tuttle, Keenan Wynn)

125. Drive-In (1/11/45; Joseph Kearns, Nancy Kelly, and Wally Maher)

126. To Find Help (1/18/45; John McIntire, Agnes Moorehead, and Frank Sinatra)

127. Drury's Bones (1/25/45; William Johnstone, Joseph Kearns, and Boris Karloff)

128. The Most Dangerous Game (2/1/45; Joseph Cotten and J. Carroll Naish)

129. Tale of Two Sisters (2/8/45; Patricia Hosley, Nancy Kelly, Walter Tetley, and Claire Trevor)

130. Sell Me Your Life (2/15/45; Lee Bowman, Wally Maher, John McIntire, and Lurene Tuttle)

131. John Barbie and Son (2/22/45; Verna Felton, Elliott Lewis, Jeanette Nolan, and Thomas Mitchell)

132. My Wife Geraldine (3/1/45; John

McIntire, Howard McNear, Jeanette Nolan, and E.G. Robinson)

133. Love's Lovely Counterfeit [based on the novel by James M. Cain] (3/8/45; Humphrey Bogart)

134. Cricket (3/15/45; Raymond E. Lawrence, Margaret O'Brien, and Dame May Whitty)

135. Heart's Desire (3/22/45; William Johnstone, Joseph Kearns, John McIntire, and Lloyd Nolan)

136. The Taming of the Beast (3/29/45; Helmut Dantine and Nancy Kelly)

137. A Guy Gets Lonely (4/5/45; Dane Clark, Howard Duff, Wally Maher, and Lurene Tuttle)

138. Pearls Are a Nuisance [based on the Raymond Chandler short story] (4/19/45; William Bendix)

139. Fear Paints a Picture (5/3/45; Joseph Kearns, Wally Maher, Lana Turner, and Will Wright)

140. Reprieve (5/10/45; John Garfield, Joseph Kearns, Cathy Lewis, Wally Maher, and John McIntire)

141. Two Birds with One Stone (5/17/45; Dana Andrews, Joseph Kearns, Cathy Lewis, Wally Maher)

142. My Own Murderer (5/24/45; Cathy Lewis, Norman Lloyd, Herbert Marshall, and Jane Morgan)

143. August Heat [based on the W.F. Harvey short story] (5/31/45; Ronald Colman and Dennis Hoey)

144. Two Sharp Knives (6/7/45; Wendell Holmes, Frank McHugh, and John Payne)

145. The Burning Court (6/14/45; Clifton Webb)

146. The Story of Ivy [based on the stage play by Marie Belloc Lowndes] (6/21/45; Verna Felton, Joseph Kearns, Patrick McGeehan, and Ann Richards)

147. The Dealings of Mr. Markham (6/28/45; Henry Daniell, Gavin Gordon, Joseph Kearns, and Joan Lorring)

148. The Last Detail (7/5/45; George Coulouris, Harry Lang, Howard McNear, and Ted Osborne)

149. Footfalls [based on the Wilbur Daniel Steele short story] (7/12/45; J. Carroll Naish, Ted Osborne)

150. Bank Holiday (7/19/45; Bonita Granville, Wendell Holmes, William Johnstone, and Elliott Lewis)

151. Fury and Sound (7/26/45; Norman Lloyd)

152. A Man in the House (8/2/45; William Johnstone and Joan Lorring)

153. Murder for Myra (8/9/45; Joseph Kearns, Cathy Lewis, and Lloyd Nolan)

154. Short Order (8/16/45; Conrad Binyon, Joseph Kearns, and Gerald Mohr)

155. This Will Kill You (8/23/45; Dane Clark, Elliott Lewis, and Wally Maher)

156. Nobody Loves Me (8/30/45; William Johnstone, Joseph Kearns, Peter Lorre, and Wally Maher)

157. Sorry, Wrong Number (9/6/45; Joseph Kearns and Agnes Moorehead)

158. The Furnished Floor (9/13/45; Don DeFore and Mildred Natwick)

159. The Library Book [based on a story by Cornell Woolrich] (9/20/45; Conrad Binyon, Cathy Lewis, Myrna Loy, and Wally Maher)

160. The Earth Is Made of Glass (9/27/45; Joseph Cotten, Gale Gordon, William Johnstone, Cathy Lewis)

161. Death on Highway 99 (10/4/45; William Johnstone, Cathy Lewis, and George Murphy)

162. Beyond Good and Evil [based on the story by Ben Hecht] (10/11/45; Joseph Cotten, Wally Maher, and Jane Morgan)

163. Summer Storm (10/18/45; Verna Felton, Henry Fonda, Elliott Lewis, Wally Maher, Lou Merrill)

164. A Shroud for Sarah (10/25/45; Lucille Ball, Wendell Holmes, Elliott Lewis, and Wally Maher)

165. The Dunwich Horror [based on the short story by H. P. Lovecraft] (11/1/45; Ronald Colman)

166. The Bet (11/8/45; Lee J. Cobb, Joseph Kearns, Cathy Lewis, Elliott Lewis, and Wally Maher)

Lewis, Wally Maher, Betty Moran, and Lurene Tuttle)

204. Commuter's Ticket (8/1/46; Jim Backus, Howard Duff, Jerry Hausner, and J. Carroll Naish)

205. Dead Ernest (8/8/46; Bob Bailey, Verna Felton, Jerry Hausner, and Wally Maher)

206. The Last Letter of Dr. Bronson (8/15/46; Herbert Butterfield, Henry Daniell, and Cathy Lewis)

207. The Great Horrell (8/22/46; Herb Butterfield, Howard Duff, and Joan Lorring)

208. Blue Eyes (8/29/46; Hume Cronyn, Howard Duff, and William Johnstone)

209. You'll Never See Me Again (9/5/46; Verna Felton, William Johnstone, Joseph Kearns, Cathy Lewis, Wally Maher, and Robert Young)

210. Hunting Trip (9/12/46; Lloyd Nolan and Vincent Price)

211. Till the Day I Die (9/19/46; Dane Clark, Betty Lou Gerson, and Cathy Lewis)

212. Statement of Employee Henry Wilson (9/26/46; Gene Lockhart)

213. Three Times Murder (10/3/46; Hans Conried, Rita Hayworth, William Johnstone, Wally Maher)

214. A Plane Case of Murder (10/10/46; Hans Conried and John Lund)

215. The Man Who Thought He Was Edward G. Robinson (10/17/46; Edward G. Robinson)

216. Dame Fortune (10/24/46; Hans Conried, Susan Hayward, William Johnstone, and Wally Maher)

217. Lazarus Walks (10/31/46; Hans Conried, Brian Donlevy, and Cathy Lewis)

218. Easy Money (11/7/46; Jack Carson and Paul Frees)

219. The One Who Got Away (11/14/46; Hans Conried, Hume Cronyn, and Joseph Kearns)

220. Drive-In (11/21/46; Judy Garland, Cathy Lewis, Raymond E. Lawrence)

221. The Strange Death of Gordon Fitzroy (11/28/46; Howard Duff, Chester Morris, and Lurene Tuttle)

222. The House in Cypress Canyon (12/5/46; Jim Backus, Hans Conried, Howard Duff, Paul Frees, Cathy Lewis, Wally Maher, and Robert Taylor)

223. They Call Me Patrice (12/12/46; William Johnstone, Susan Peters, and Wally Maher)

224. The Thing in the Window (12/19/46; Hans Conried, Joseph Cotten, Jerry Hausner, Joseph Kearns, Cathy Lewis, and Jeanette Nolan)

225. Philomel Cottage (12/26/46; Raymond E. Lawrence and Lilli Palmer)

226. Tree of Life (1/2/47; Hans Conried, Cathy Lewis, Elliott Lewis, and Mark Stevens)

227. The Will to Power (1/9/47; Howard Duff, Dan Duryea, Cathy Lewis, and Wally Maher)

228. Overture in Two Keys (1/16/47; Joan Bennett, Hans Conried, Howard Duff, William Johnstone)

229. One Way Street (1/23/47; Raymond E. Lawrence, Roddy McDowall, and Jeanette Nolan)

230. Three Blind Mice (1/30/47; Van Heflin)

231. End of the Road (2/6/47; Hans Conried, Glenn Ford, Bill Johnstone, Cathy Lewis, Wally Maher)

232. The Thirteenth Sound (2/13/47; Wally Maher, John McIntire, and Agnes Moorehead)

233. Always Room at the Top (2/20/47; Anne Baxter, Cathy Lewis, Wally Maher, and Jack Webb)

234. Three Faces at Midnight (2/27/47; William Bendix, Hans Conried, and Jack Webb)

235. Elwood (3/6/47; Eddie Bracken and Cathy Lewis)

236. You Take Ballistics (3/13/47; Howard daSilva and Jack Webb)

237. The Waxwork [based on the A.M. Burrage short story] (3/20/47; Claude Rains)

238. Trial by Jury (3/27/47; Howard Duff, Nancy Kelly, and Wally Maher)

239. The Swift Rise of Eddie Albright (4/3/47; Frank Lovejoy, Wally Maher, and Phil Silvers)

240. Community Property (4/10/47; Kirk Douglas, Paul Frees, Cathy Lewis, and Howard McNear)
241. Green-Eyed Monster (4/17/47; Cathy Lewis, Lloyd Nolan, and Alan Reed)
242. Win, Place and Murder (4/24/47; Hans Conried, Richard Conte, Cathy Lewis, and Wally Maher)
243. Lady in Distress (5/1/47; Howard Duff, Ava Gardner, and Wally Maher)
244. Dead Ernest (5/8/47; Howard Duff, Cathy Lewis, Elliott Lewis, and Wally Maher)
245. Death at Live Oak (5/15/47; Robert Mitchum)
246. Knight Comes Riding (5/22/47; Virginia Bruce, Howard Duff, and Wally Maher)
247. A Thing of Beauty (5/29/47; Hans Conried, Joseph Kearns, and Angela Lansbury)
248. Make Mad the Guilty (6/5/47; Hume Cronyn, Howard Duff, and Wally Maher)
249. Stand-In (6/12/47; Hans Conried, June Havoc, Cathy Lewis, Elliott Lewis, and Wally Maher)
250. Dead of Night (6/19/47; Cathy Lewis, Wally Maher, and Elliott Reid)
251. Phobia (6/26/47; Eva Le Gallienne, John McIntire, and Jeanette Nolan)
252. Money Talks (7/3/47; Alan Baxter, Berry Kroeger, Cathy Lewis, and Russell Thorson)
253. Murder by the Book (7/10/47; Berry Kroeger, Cathy Lewis, Gloria Swanson, and Lurene Tuttle)
254. Beyond Good and Evil (7/17/47; Vincent Price)
255. Murder by an Expert (7/24/47; Lynn Bari, Hans Conried, and Jack Webb)
256. Mortmain (7/31/47; Jerome Cowan and Wally Maher)
257. Quiet Desperation (8/7/47; Walter Abel, William Johnstone, Cathy Lewis, and Wally Maher)
258. Smiley (8/14/47; William Johnstone, Sidney Miller, Donald O'Connor, and Lurene Tuttle)
259. Murder Aboard the Alphabet (8/21/47; Jerry Hausner, William Johnstone, John Lund, Ben Wright)
260. Double Ugly (8/28/47; June Havoc, Wally Maher, and Lloyd Nolan)
261. The Argyle Album (9/4/47; Hans Conried, Edmund O'Brien, and Lurene Tuttle)
262. The Twist (9/11/47; Joseph Kearns, Sidney Miller, and Michael O'Shea)
263. The Visitor (9/18/47; Verna Felton, Joseph Kearns, Wally Maher, and Donald O'Connor)
264. The Blue Hour (9/25/47; Hans Conried, Wally Maher, Sidney Miller, and Claire Trevor)
265. The Story of Markham's Death (10/2/47; Kirk Douglas and Verna Felton)
266. The Man Who Liked Dickens [based on the short story by Evelyn Waugh] (10/9/47; Joseph Kearns and Richard Ney)
267. Self Defense (10/16/47; Marsha Hunt and Wally Maher)
268. The X-Ray Camera (10/23/47; Dennis O'Keefe and Lurene Tuttle)
269. Subway (10/30/47; June Havoc and Lurene Tuttle)
270. Dream Song (11/6/47; Joseph Kearns, Wally Maher, and Henry Morgan)
271. Riabouchinska [based on the short story by Ray Bradbury] (11/13/47; June Havoc, Joseph Kearns, Wally Maher, and Lurene Tuttle)
272. One Hundred in the Dark (11/20/47; Howard Duff, June Havoc, John McIntire)
273. The Pit and the Pendulum (11/28/47; Jose Ferrer)
274. The Clock and the Rope (12/5/47; Jackie Cooper, John McIntire, Paul McVey, and Lou Merrill)
275. The Man Who Couldn't Lose (12/12/47; Hans Conried, Dan Duryea, and Jack Webb)
276. Wet Saturday (12/19/47; Hans Conried and Boris Karloff)
277. Too Little to Live On (12/26/47; Harriet Hilliard and Ozzie Nelson)

278. The Black Curtain [based on the novel by Cornell Woolrich] (1/3/48; Jeff Chandler, William Conrad, Paul Frees, Sidney Miller, Jeanette Nolan, and Lurene Tuttle)
279. The Kandy Tooth (1/10/48; Hans Conried, Howard Duff, Jay Novello, and Lurene Tuttle)
280. Love's Lovely Counterfeit [based on the novel by James M. Cain] (1/17/48; James Cagney)
281. The Black Angel [based on the novel by Cornell Woolrich] (1/24/48; June Havoc, Alan Reed, Prince Michael Romanoff, Dick Ryan, and Lurene Tuttle)
282. Bet with Death (1/31/48; Lee Bowman and Otto Kruger)
283. Donovan's Brain (2/7/48; William Johnstone, Wally Maher, John McIntire, and Jeanette Nolan)
284. The Lodger [based on the story by Marie Belloc Lowndes] (2/14/48; Joseph Kearns, Robert Montgomery, Jeanette Nolan, and Peggy Webber)
285. Beyond Reason (2/21/48; William Johnstone, Howard McNear, Robert Ryan, and Ruth Warrick)
286. The House by the River [based on the novel by Alan Patrick Herbert] (2/28/48; Bill Johnstone, John McIntire, and Dan O'Herlihy)
287. In a Lonely Place [based on the novel by Dorothy Hughes] (3/6/48; William Johnstone, Robert Montgomery, and Lurene Tuttle)
288. Nightmare [based on a novel by Cornell Woolrich] (3/13/48; Eddie Bracken, William Conrad, William Johnstone, and Ben Wright)
289. Wet Saturday / August Heat (3/20/48; Hans Conried, Dennis Hoey, and Berry Kroeger)
290. Night Must Fall [based on the stage play by Emlyn Williams] (3/27/48; Heather Angel, Robert Montgomery, Richard Ney, and Dame May Whitty)
291. Suspicion [based on the short story by Dorothy Sayers] (4/3/48; Sam Jaffe)
292. Crossfire [based on the novel by Richard Brooks] (4/10/48; Julie Bennett, George Cooper, Marlo Dwyer, Sam Levene, Bill Lowly, Robert Mitchum, William Phipps, Luis Van Rooten, Robert Ryan, and Robert Young)
293. The Search (4/24/48; Howard Culver, Sandra Gare, and William Johnstone)
294. The Blind Spot (5/1/48; Frances Chaney, Jeff Corey, and Edmund O'Brien)
295. Life Ends at Midnight (5/8/48; Fay Bainter, Tony Barrett, Norman Field, and William Johnstone)
296. Deadline at Dawn [based on the novel by Cornell Woolrich] (5/15/48; John Beal, Rye Billsbury, Lillian Buyeff, Billy Gray, William Johnstone, Edith Lackner, and Helen Walker)
297. The Last Chance (7/8/48; Cary Grant)
298. Summer Night [based on the short story by Ray Bradbury] (7/15/48; Ida Lupino, Larry Dobkin)
299. Deep Into Darkness (7/22/48; Douglas Fairbanks, Jr. and Joseph Kearns)
300. The Yellow Wall-Paper (7/29/48; Agnes Moorehead)
301. An Honest Man (8/5/48; Charles Laughton and Cathy Lewis)
302. Beware the Quiet Man (8/12/48; William Conrad and Ann Sothern)
303. Crisis (8/19/48; Frank Lovejoy and Martha Scott)
304. Song of the Heart (8/26/48; Van Heflin)
305. The Morrison Affair (9/2/48; Madeline Carroll and Gerald Mohr)
306. The Big Shot (9/9/48; Burt Lancaster)
307. Hitch-hike Poker (9/16/48; Ed Begley, Kay Brinker, and Gregory Peck)
308. Celebration (9/23/48; Virginia Bruce and Robert Young)
309. The Man Who Wanted to Be Edward G. Robinson (9/30/48; Edward G. Robinson)

310. Night Cry [based on the novel by William L. Stewart] (10/7/48; William Conrad, Ray Milland)
311. A Little Piece of Rope (10/14/48; Lucille Ball)
312. Give Me Liberty (10/21/48; Ann Morrison and William Powell)
313. Death Sentence (11/4/48; Raymond Burr, John Garfield, and Wally Maher)
314. Muddy Track (11/11/48; Ann Blyth and Edmund O'Brien)
315. Sorry, Wrong Number (11/18/48; Eleanor Audley, Agnes Moorehead, and Ann Morrison)
316. The Screaming Woman [based on the short story by Ray Bradbury] (11/25/48; John McIntire, Agnes Moorehead, and Margaret O'Brien)
317. The Hands of Mr. Ottermole [from the short story by Thomas Burke] (12/2/48; Verna Felton, Vincent Price, and Claude Rains)
318. The Sisters (12/9/48; Rosalind Russell and Lurene Tuttle)
319. No Escape (12/16/48; James Cagney)
320. [Untitled] (12/23/48; Herbert Marshall)
321. Break-Up [based on the short story by Thomas Walsh] (12/30/48; William Bendix)
322. To Find Help (1/6/49; Ethel Barrymore, William Conrad, and Gene Kelly)
323. The Too-Perfect Alibi (1/13/49; Danny Kaye)
324. If the Dead Could Talk [based on a short story by Cornell Woolrich] (1/20/49; Dana Andrews, Ted de Corsia, Verna Felton, and Jeanette Nolan)
325. The Thing in the Window (1/27/49; Robert Montgomery)
326. Backseat Driver (2/3/49; Jim and Marion Jordan)
327. De Mortuis [based on the short story by John Collier] (2/10/49; Charles Laughton)
328. Catch Me If You Can [based on the novel by Patricia McGee] (2/17/49; Raymond Burr, Frank Lovejoy, and Jane Wyman)

329. Where There's a Will [based on the story by Agatha Christie] (2/24/49; James and Pamela Mason)
330. The Lovebirds (3/3/49; Joan Fontaine)
331. Three O'Clock [based on the short story by Cornell Woolrich] (3/10/49; Ted de Corsia, Van Heflin)
332. Murder Through the Looking Glass [based on a novel by Michael Venning] (3/17/49; Ed Begley, William Johnstone, and Gregory Peck)
333. Dead Ernest (3/24/49; Pat O'Brien)
334. You Can't Die Twice (3/31/49; Edward G. Robinson)
335. The Noose of Coincidence (4//49; Ronald Colman and Hans Conried)
336. Murder in Black and White (4/14/49; Verna Felton and Edmund Gwenn)
337. The Copper Tea Strainer (4/21/49; Raymond Burr, William Conrad, and Betty Grable)
338. The Lie [based on the short story by Cornell Woolrich] (4/28/49; Ed Begley and Mickey Rooney)
339. Death Has a Shadow (5/5/49; William Conrad and Bob Hope)
340. The Light Switch (5/12/49; Claire Trevor)
341. Consequence (5/19/49; Paul Ford and James Stewart)
342. The Night Reveals (5/26/49; Fredric March and Jeanette Nolan)
343. The Ten Years (6/2/49; Joan Crawford and Lurene Tuttle)
344. Lunch Kit (6/9/49; John Lund)
345. The Trap (6/16/49; Agnes Moorehead)
346. Ghost Hunt (6/23/49; Ralph Edwards and Joseph Kearns)
347. The Day I Died (6/30/49; Joseph Cotten, William Johnstone, and Cathy Lewis)
348. Nightmare (9/1/49; Gregory Peck)
349. Chicken Feed [based on the stage play by Guy Bolton] (9/8/49; William Conrad and Ray Milland)
350. Last Confession (9/15/49; Dorothy McGuire)
351. Experiment 6-R (9/22/49; William Conrad and John Lund)

352. Blind Date (9/29/49; June Havoc and Charles Laughton)
353. The Defense Rests (10/6/49; Van Johnson)
354. Account Payable (10/13/49; Edward Arnold)
355. Goodnight Mrs. Russell (10/20/49; Bette Davis and Elliott Reid)
356. Momentum [based on a short story by Cornell Woolrich] (10/27/49; Victor Mature, Lurene Tuttle)
357. The Search for Isabell (11/3/49; William Conrad and Red Skelton)
358. Murder of Aunt Delia (11/10/49; Van Heflin and Howard McNear)
359. The Red-Headed Woman (11/17/49; Desi Arnaz and Lucille Ball)
360. The Long Wait (11/24/49; Burt Lancaster)
361. Mission Completed (12/1/49; John Dehner and James Stewart)
362. For Love or Murder (12/8/49; Barney Phillips and Mickey Rooney)
363. The Flame Blue Glove (12/15/49; Lana Turner)
364. Double Entry (12/22/49; Eddie Cantor and Sidney Miller)
365. The Bullet (12/29/49; Hans Conried, William Conrad, John Dehner, and Ida Lupino)
366. I Never Met the Dead Man (1/5/50; Danny Kaye and John McIntire)
367. Four Hours to Kill (1/12/50; Robert Taylor)
368. The Escape of Lacy Abbott (1/19/50; John McIntire, Howard McNear, and William Powell)
369. Mr. Diogenes (1/26/50; Harriet Hilliard, John McIntire, Ozzie Nelson, and Jeanette Nolan)
370. Consideration (2/2/50; Rosalind Russell)
371. The Butcher's Wife (2/9/50; Kirk Douglas and Sidney Miller)
372. Murder Strikes Three Times (2/16/50; Hans Conried and Marlene Dietrich)
373. Slow Burn (2/23/50; Dick Powell)
374. Lady Killer (3/2/50; Loretta Young)
375. Banquo's Chair (3/9/50; Hans Conried, Joseph Kearns, and James Mason)
376. Motive for Murder (3/16/50; (3/16/50) John Dehner, Alan Ladd, and Howard McNear)
377. One and One's a Lonesome (3/23/50; Ronald Reagan)
378. Blood Sacrifice (3/30/50; Hans Conried, Joseph Cotten, John McIntire, and Jeanette Nolan)
379. Salvage (4/6/50; William Conrad and Van Johnson)
380. Six Feet Under (4/13/50; Dan Dailey, Barbara Eiler, John McIntire, and Jeanette Nolan)
381. Pearls Are a Nuisance (4/20/50; Howard McNear and Ray Milland)
382. The Chain (4/27/50; William Conrad, Agnes Moorehead, and Alan Reed)
383. Statement of Mary Blake (5/4/50; Joan Bennett, William Conrad, and John Dehner)
384. The Man in the Room (5/11/50; William Conrad and John Lund)
385. Angel Face [based on a short story by Cornell Woolrich] (5/18/50; Claire Trevor)
386. Very Much Like a Nightmare (5/25/50; Howard McNear, Dennis O'Keefe, and Alan Reed)
387. A Case of Nerves (6/1/50; Edward G. Robinson)
388. The Case of Henri Vibard (6/8/50; Charles Boyer and William Johnstone)
389. Deadline (6/15/50; Tony Barrett, Broderick Crawford, Georgia Ellis, John Hoyt, and Jay Novello)
390. The One Millionth Joe (6/22/50; Jack Carson and Howard McNear)
391. Love, Honor, or Murder (6/29/50; Cathy Lewis and Elliott Lewis)
392. True Report (8/31/50; Pat O'Brien and Larry Thor)
393. The Tip (9/7/50; Ida Lupino)
394. Over the Bounding Main (9/14/50; Dan Dailey)
395. The Crowd [based on the story by Ray Bradbury] (9/21/50; Dana Andrews and Howard McNear)
396. Fly by Night (9/28/50; Joseph Cotten)
397. The Rose Garden (10/5/50; Miriam Hopkins)
398. Rave Notice (10/12/50; Milton Berle, Howard McNear, and Sidney Miller)

399. The Wages of Sin (10/19/50; John Dehner and Barbara Stanwyck)
400. Too Hot to Live (10/26/50; Paul Frees, Howard McNear, and Richard Widmark)
401. The Victoria Cross (11/2/50; Herbert Marshall)
402. Blood on the Trumpet (11/9/50; William Holden and Barton Yarborough)
403. On a Country Road (11/16/50; Cary Grant, Cathy Lewis, Jeanette Nolan, and Larry Thor)
404. Going, Going, Gone (11/23/50; Harriet Hilliard, Howard McNear, and Ozzie Nelson)
405. The Lady in the Red Hat (11/30/50; Joan Banks, Van Heflin, and Lou Merrill)
406. After the Movies (12/7/50; William Conrad and Ray Milland)
407. A Killing in Abilene (12/14/50; Parley Baer, Alan Ladd, and Barton Yarborough)
408. Christmas for Carol (12/21/50; Dennis Day)
409. A Ring for Marya (12/28/50; Irene Tedrow, Larry Thor, and Cornel Wilde)
410. Alibi Me (1/4/51; Mickey Rooney)
411. Vamp Till Dead (1/11/51; Ed Max, Jeanette Nolan, Ginger Rogers, and John Hoyt)
412. The Well-Dressed Corpse (1/18/51; Eve Arden, Hy Averback, Verna Felton, and Larry Thor)
413. Aria from Murder (1/25/51; Howard McNear and Ezio Pinza)
414. Fragile — Contents Death (2/1/51; Paul Douglas, Lou Merrill, and Howard McNear)
415. The Windy City Six (2/8/51; Fred MacMurray, and Red Nichols and his Five Pennies)
416. The Death Parade (2/15/51; Agnes Moorehead)
417. Backseat Driver (2/22/51; Jim and Marion Jordan)
418. The Gift of Jumbo Brannigan (3/1/51; William Bendix)
419. A Vision of Death (3/8/51; Ronald Colman, Lawrence Dobkin, and Cathy Lewis)
420. Strange for a Killer (3/15/51; Van Johnson, Cathy Lewis, and Larry Thor)
421. Three Lethal Words (3/22/51; Hy Averback, Bea Benadaret, Lillian Buyeff, and Joan Crawford)
422. Death Notice (3/29/51; Jack Carson, Frances Chaney, Dick Crenna, and Ed Max)
423. Murder in G-Flat (4/5/51; Bea Benadaret, Jack Benny, Paul Frees, Jack Kruschen, Clayton Post)
424. Early to Death (4/12/51; Desi Arnaz, Lucille Ball, Tony Barrett, Tom Holland, and Jack Kruschen)
425. The Rescue (4/19/51; Joseph Kearns and James Stewart)
426. The Thirteenth Sound (4/26/51; Anne Baxter)
427. When the Bough Breaks (5/3/51; Rosalind Russell)
428. Death on My Hands (5/10/51; Alice Faye, Phil Harris, Gil Stratton, Jr., and Barbara Whiting)
429. Another Man's Poison (5/17/51; Charles Boyer, Paul Frees, Truda Marsden, and Irene Tedrow)
430. Fresh Air, Sunshine, and Murder (5/24/51; Jeff Chandler, Jack Kruschen, Cathy Lewis, Lou Merrill, Clayton Post, and Herb Vigran)
431. Overdrawn (5/31/51; Dick Crenna, Mary Jane Croft, Norman Field, Dick Powell, Benny Rubin)
432. Tell You Why I Shouldn't Die (6/7/51; Hy Averback, Cathy Lewis, Larry Thor, Richard Widmark)
433. The Truth About Jerry Baxter (6/14/51; Joan Banks, John Dehner, Gregory Peck, Clayton Post)
434. The Greatest Thief in the World (6/21/51; James Mason, Pamela Mason, and Ben Wright)
435. The Case for Dr. Singer (6/28/51; Edgar Barrier, Paul Frees, Truda Marsden, and Howard McNear)
436. Report on the Jolly Death Riders (8/27/51; Barbara Eiler, Eddie Firestone, and William Holden)
437. Steel River Prison Break (9/3/51; Jeff Chandler and Barton Yarborough)

438. The Evil of Adelaide Winters (9/10/51; Herbert Butterfield, Joseph Kearns, and Agnes Moorehead)
439. Neil Cream, Doctor of Poison (9/17/51; Charles Davis, Joseph Kearns, and Charles Laughton)
440. The McKay College Basketball Scandal (9/24/51; Tony Curtis and Martha Wentworth)
441. The Case Study of a Murderer (10/1/51; William Conrad, Jeanne Crain, and Howard McNear)
442. Betrayal in Vienna (10/8/51; Herb Butterfield, Herbert Marshall, John Stevenson, and Ben Wright)
443. The Flame (10/15/51; Harry Bartell, Cathy Lewis, Sidney Miller, and Cornel Wilde)
444. The Log of the Marne [based on a book by Lawrence Earl] (10/22/51; Ray Milland)
445. The Hunting of Bob Lee (10/29/51; William Conrad, Cathy Lewis, and Richard Widmark)
446. The Trials of Thomas Shaw (11/5/51; Joseph Cotten, Ramsey Hill, Paula Winslowe, Ben Wright)
447. The Mission of the Betta (11/12/51; Jerry Hausner, John Hodiak, and Ben Wright)
448. The Embezzler (11/19/51; Mary Jane Croft, John Lund, Lou Merrill, Sylvia Simms, Stan Waxman)
449. A Misfortune in Pearls (11/26/51; Joan Banks, Charles Calvert, Frank Lovejoy, and Sidney Miller)
450. A Murderous Revision (12/3/51; Jerry Hausner, Charlotte Lawrence, and Richard Widmark)
451. Blackjack to Kill (12/10/51; Eddie Firestone, Victor Mature, Clayton Post, and Steve Roberts)
452. The Case History of a Gambler (12/17/51; John Hodiak)
453. 'Twas the Night Before Christmas (12/24/51; Greer Garson, Irene Tedrow, and Anne Whitfield)
454. Rogue Male [based on the novel by Geoffrey Household] (12/31/51; Herbert Marshall)
455. The Case Against Loo Doc (1/7/52; Jeff Chandler, William Conrad, and Jack Kruschen)

456. The Fall River Tragedy (1/14/52; Agnes Moorehead, Rolfe Sedan, Stuffy Singer, Peggy Webber)
457. The Perfectionist (1/21/52; Richard Basehart, William Conrad, and Charlotte Lawrence)
458. Carnival (1/28/52; Charles Calvert, Joseph Cotten, Mary Jane Croft, and Dick Ryan)
459. The Treasure of Don Jose (2/4/52; Tony Barrett, J. Carrol Naish, Clayton Post, and Charles Seel)
460. Odd Man Out [based on the novel by F.L. Green] (2/11/52; James Mason and Dan O'Herlihy)
461. The Track of the Cat [based on Walter Van Tilburg Clark's novel] (2/18/52; Richard Widmark)
462. A Killing in Las Vegas (2/25/52; Linda Darnell, Jerry Hausner, and Lamont Johnson)
463. The Thirty-Nine Steps [based on the John Buchan novel] (3/3/52; Raymond Lawrence, Herbert Marshall, Tudor Owen, and Ben Wright)
464. A Watery Grave (3/10/52; Joseph Cotten, Mary Jane Croft, and Stan Waxman)
465. The Wreck of the Old '97 (3/17/52; Eddie Firestone, Roy Glenn, Frank Lovejoy, and Clayton Post)
466. A Murder of Necessity (3/24/52; Howard McNear, Lou Merrill, Paula Winslowe, Robert Young)
467. The Lady Pamela (3/31/52; Deborah Kerr, Peter Leeds, Ted Osborne, and Ben Wright)
468. Remember Me? (4/7/52; Dan Duryea, Joseph Kearns, and Charlotte Lawrence)
469. Mate Bram (4/14/52; Joan Banks, Roy Glenn, Steve Roberts, Richard Widmark, and Ben Wright)
470. The Diary of Captain Scott (4/21/52; Herbert Marshall)
471. The Shooting of Billy the Kid (4/28/52; Parley Baer, William Conrad, and Frank Lovejoy)
472. Frankie and Johnny (5/5/52; Harry Bartell, Lamont Johnson, Jack Kruschen, and Dinah Shore)
473. The Missing Person (5/12/52; MacDonald Carey, Jay Novello, and Irene Tedrow)

474. The Flight of the Bumblebee (5/19/52; Edgar Barrier, Jack Kruschen, and Fred MacMurray)
475. The Death of Me (5/26/52; William Conrad, Charlotte Lawrence, George Murphy)
476. A Good and Faithful Servant (6/2/52; Hy Averback, Jack Benny, Gerald Mohr, Doris Singleton)
477. Concerto for Killer and Eye Witnesses (6/9/52; William Conrad and Elliott Lewis)
478. Sorry, Wrong Number (9/15/52; Joseph Kearns and Agnes Moorehead)
479. Jack Ketch (9/22/52; Joan Banks, Charles Laughton, Raymond Lawrence, and Ben Wright)
480. Vidocq's Last Case [based on the autobiography of François Eugene Vidocq] (9/29/52; Parley Baer, Charles Boyer, William Johnstone, Victor Rodman, Paula Winslowe, and Ben Wright)
481. The Diary of Dr. Pritchard (10/6/52; Georgia Ellis, Sir Cedric Hardwicke, and William Johnstone)
482. How Long Is the Night? (10/13/52; Herb Butterfield, Jack Kruschen, and Richard Widmark)
483. The Death of Barbara Allen (10/20/52; Anne Baxter, Junius Matthews, and Jeanette Nolan)
484. Allen in Wonderland [based on a story by Curt Singer] (10/27/52; Edgar Barrier and Cornel Wilde)
485. Frankenstein [based on the Mary Shelley novel] (11/3/52; Paul Frees and Herbert Marshall)
486. The Frightened City (11/10/52; Hy Averback, Joan Banks, Frank Lovejoy, and Lou Merrill)
487. Death and Miss Turner (11/17/52; Charles Davis, Paul Frees, Agnes Moorehead, Jeanette Nolan)
488. Man Alive (11/24/52; William Conrad, Paul Douglas, and Jeanette Nolan)
489. The Big Heist (12/1/52; Ted Bliss, John Hodiak, Bert Holland, and Junius Matthews)
490. Joker Wild (12/8/52; Hy Averback, Lillian Buyeff, Bryon Kane, Joseph

Kearns, Charlotte Lawrence, Cathy Lewis, and Elliott Lewis)
491. The Man with Two Faces (12/15/52; Eddie Fields, Lloyd Nolan, Rolfe Sedan, and Tom Tully)
492. Arctic Rescue (12/22/52; Lillian Buyeff, Joseph Cotten, and Barney Phillips)
493. Melody in Dreams (12/29/52; John Lund, Junius Matthews, and Anne Whitfield)
494. The Mystery of Edwin Drood [part one; based on the unfinished novel by Charles Dickens] (1/5/53; William Johnstone, Terry Kilburn, Herbert Marshall, and Ben Wright)
495. The Mystery of Edwin Drood [part two] (1/12/53; William Johnstone, Joseph Kearns, Herbert Marshall, and Ben Wright)
496. Gold on the Adomar (1/19/53; Charles Calvert, John Hodiak, Joseph Kearns, and Clayton Post)
497. The Spencer Brothers (1/26/53; Parley Baer, William Conrad, John Dehner, and Richard Widmark)
498. Plan X (2/2/53; Jack Benny, William Conrad, John McIntire, and Howard McNear)
499. The Man Who Cried Wolf (2/9/53; John Dehner, Joseph Kearns, and William Powell)
500. The Love and Death of Joaquin Murieta (2/16/53; Hy Averback and Victor Mature)
501. St. James Infirmary Blues (2/23/53; Tony Barrett, Rosemary Clooney, Billy Hallop, Vivi Janniss)
502. The Storm (3/2/53; Joan Banks, Sharon Douglas, Jerry Hausner, Frank Lovejoy, and Rolfe Sedan)
503. The Dead Alive [based on the short story by Wilkie Collins] (3/9/53; Mary Jane Croft, Lamont Johnson, Joseph Kearns, Jeanette Nolan, and Herbert Marshall)
504. The Mountain (3/16/53; Paul Frees, John Hodiak, and Ben Wright)
505. The Signalman [based on Charles Dickens' story] (3/23/53; Joseph Kearns and Agnes Moorehead)
506. Tom Dooley (3/30/53; Joseph Cotten)

507. Around the World (4/6/53; Larry Haines, Alan Hewitt, and Van Johnson)
508. The Great Train Robbery (4/13/53; Hy Averback, Fred MacMurray, and Paula Winslowe)
509. Public Defender (4/20/53; Charles Calvert, Whitfield Connor, and Frank Lovejoy)
510. The Man Within [based on the novel by Graham Greene] (4/27/53; Joseph Kearns, Raymond Lawrence, Herbert Marshall, and Ben Wright)
511. Othello [part one; based on William Shakespeare's play] (5/4/53; William Conrad, Cathy Lewis, Elliott Lewis, Irene Tedrow, and Richard Widmark)
512. Othello [part two] (5/11/53; William Conrad, Cathy Lewis, Elliott Lewis, and Richard Widmark)
513. Vial of Death (5/18/53; Truda Marsden, Howard McNear, Lloyd Nolan, and Clayton Post)
514. Pigeon in the Cage (5/25/53; Dick Haymes, Joseph Kearns, and Charlotte Lawrence)
515. A Vision of Death (6/1/53; Hy Averback, Charles Calvert, Ronald Colman, and Mary Jane Croft)
516. The Mystery of the Marie Celeste (6/8/53; William Conrad, Paul Frees, and Van Heflin)
517. A Message to Garcia (9/14/53; Tony Barett, Edgar Barrier, and Richard Widmark)
518. The Empty Chair (9/21/53; Herb Butterfield, Agnes Moorehead, and Paula Winslowe)
519. Hellfire (9/28/53; Jerry Hausner, John Hodiak, Charlotte Lawrence, Clayton Post, and Dick Ryan)
520. Action [based on the short story by C.E. Montague] (10/5/53; Parley Baer, Herb Butterfield, Herbert Marshall, and Ben Wright)
521. The Shot [based on the short story by Alexander Pushkin] (10/12/53; Harry Bartell, Van Heflin, Joseph Kearns, Barney Phillips, and Jack Webb)
522. My True Love's Hair (10/19/53; Jeff

Chandler, Jack Kruschen, Clayton Post, Martha Wentworth)
523. Dutch Schultz (10/26/53; Hy Averback, Broderick Crawford, Paul Frees, and Sidney Miller)
524. Ordeal in Donner Pass (11/2/53; Parley Baer, Harry Bartell, John Dehner, Joseph Kearns, Charlotte Lawrence, Edmund O'Brien, and Paula Winslowe)
525. Needle in the Haystack (11/9/53; William Holden)
526. The Moonstone [part one; based on the novel by Wilkie Collins] (11/16/53; Dick Beals, Herbert Butterfield, Patricia Hitchcock, William Johnstone, Peter Lawford, and Ben Wright)
527. The Moonstone [part two] (11/23/53; Herbert Butterfield, William Johnstone, Peter Lawford, Eric Snowden, and Ben Wright)
528. The Wreck of the Maid of Athens [based on the diary of Emily Wooldridge] (11/10/53; Joseph Kearns, Jack Kruschen, Agnes Moorehead, and Ben Wright)
529. Trent's Last Case [based on the novel by E.C. Bentley] Dick Beals and Ronald Colman
530. The Mystery of the Marie Roget [based on the short story by Edgar Allan Poe] (12/14/53; Edgar Barrier, John Dehner, Lou Merrill, Jeanette Nolan, Cornel Wilde, and Paula Winslowe)
531. 'Twas the Night Before Christmas (12/21/53; Greer Garson and Anne Whitfield)
532. The Queen's Ring (12/28/53; James and Pamela Mason, Jeanette Nolan, and Ben Wright)
533. On a Country Road (1/4/54; Joan Banks, Frank Lovejoy, and Jeanette Nolan)
534. The One-Man Crime Wave (1/11/54; Dana Andrews)
535. The Face Is Familiar (1/18/54; Hy Averback, Jack Benny, Sheldon Leonard, and Clayton Post)
536. Want Ad (1/25/54; Charles Calvert, Mary Jane Croft, Robert Cummings, and Virginia Gregg)
537. Never Follow a Banjo Act (2/1/54;

Paul Frees, Jerry Hausner, and Ethel Merman)

538. Death at Skirkerud Pond (2/8/54; Jeff Chandler and Cathy Lewis)

539. The Outer Limit (2/15/54; Edgar Barrier and William Holden)

540. Murder by Jury (2/22/54; William Johnstone, Herbert Marshall, and Ben Wright)

541. The Barking Death (3/1/54; Hy Averback, Dick Beals, William Powell, and Paula Winslowe)

542. Circumstantial Terror (3/8/54; Charles Calvert, Victor Perrin, and Ronald Reagan)

543. The Girl in Car Thirty-Two [based on the story by Thomas Walsh] (3/15/54; Herb Butterfield, William Conrad, John Dehner, Roy Glenn, Cathy Lewis, and Victor Mature)

544. The Guilty Always Run (3/22/54; William Conrad, Jack Kruschen, Frank Nelson, Tyrone Power)

545. Somebody Help Me (3/29/54; Georgia Ellis, Cathy Lewis, Cornel Wilde, and Paula Winslowe)

546. Grand Theft (4/5/54; Mary Jane Croft, Truda Marsden, David Niven, and Victor Perrin)

547. Parole to Panic (4/12/54; Broderick Crawford, Barney Phillips, and Paula Winslowe)

548. The Card Game (4/19/54; Hy Averback, Eddie Field, Jay Novello, and Richard Widmark)

549. The Bertillion Method (4/26/54; Edgar Barrier, Charles Boyer, John Dehner, and Jane Webb)

550. The Giant of Thermopylae (5/3/54; Paul Frees, Jerry Hausner, and Frank Lovejoy)

551. The Last Days of John Dillinger (5/10/54; Parley Baer, Michael Ann Barrett, Sam Edwards, Roy Glenn, Van Heflin, Joseph Kearns, and Cathy Lewis)

552. The Revenge of Captain Bligh (5/17/54; Charles Davis, Antony Ellis, and Charles Laughton)

553. Weekend Special — Death (5/24/54; Hy Averback, Agnes Moorehead, and Barney Phillips)

554. Listen Young Lovers (5/31/54; Mona Freeman and Robert Wagner)

555. A Terribly Strange Bed [based on the short story by Wilkie Collins] (6/7/54; Peter Lawford)

556. The Earth Is Made of Glass (6/15/54; Herb Butterfield, Whitfield Connor, and Paula Winslowe)

557. Sequel to Murder (6/22/54; Whitfield Connor, and Betty Lou Gerson)

558. Too Hot to Live (6/29/54; Herb Butterfield, Charles Calvert, and Sam Edwards)

559. The Tip (7/6/54; Hy Averback, Dick Beals, Eddie Fields, and Lurene Tuttle)

560. Run Sheep Run (7/13/54; Cathy Lewis and Elliott Lewis)

561. Telling [based on the short story by Elizabeth Bowen] (7/20/54; Antony Ellis, Herb Butterfield, John Dehner, and Ben Wright)

562. Destruction (7/27/54; Parley Baer, John Dehner, Virginia Gregg, Jerry Hausner, and Clayton Post)

563. Goodnight Mrs. Russell (8/3/54; Virginia Gregg and Eleanor Tannin)

564. Never Steal a Butcher's Wife (8/10/54; Larry Dobkin and Paula Winslowe)

565. A Little Matter of Memory (9/30/54; Edgar Barrier, Lawrence Dobkin, and Joseph Kearns)

566. Chicken Feed (10/7/54; Edgar Barrier and Victor Perrin)

567. Lost (10/14/54; Tony Barrett, William Conrad, John Dehner, and Paula Winslowe)

568. Rave Notice (10/21/54; Edgar Barrier, Hans Conried, and John Stevenson)

569. The Shelter (10/28/54; Herb Ellis and Dick Ryan)

570. The Last Letter of Dr. Bronson (11/4/54; Parley Baer, John Dehner, and Virginia Gregg)

571. The Sure Thing (11/11/54; Hy Averback, Jerry Hausner, and Peter Leeds)

572. Blind Date (11/18/54; Shirley Mitchell and Victor Perrin)

William Conrad, and Sam
Edwards)

610. Love, Honor or Murder (8/9/55;
William Conrad, Jack Kruschen,
Charlotte Lawrence, and Barney
Phillips)

611. A Study in Wax (8/16/55; William
Conrad and Stacy Harris)

612. The Beetle and Mr. Bottle
(8/23/55; Eric Snowden)

613. The Lady in the Red Hat (8/30/55;
Jack Carroll and Virginia Gregg)

614. Strange for a Killer (9/6/55; Tony
Barrett, John Dehner, and Jack
Kruschen)

615. A Story of Poison (9/13/55; Herbert
Butterfield, Virginia Gregg, Paula
Winslowe, and Ben Wright)

616. The Stool Pigeon (9/20/55; Tony
Barrett, Edgar Barrier, and John
Dehner)

617. The Frightened City (9/27/55;
Harry Bartell and Charlotte
Lawrence)

618. Good-bye, Miss Lizzie Borden
[based on the play by Lillian de la
Torre] (10/4/55; Dick Beals, Virginia Gregg, Irene Tedrow, and
Paula Winslowe)

619. Heavens to Betsy (10/11/55; Hy Averback, Dick Beals, and Barbara Eiler)

620. Life Ends at Midnight (10/18/55;
Stacy Harris and Paula Winslowe)

621. To None and Deadly Drug
(10/25/55; Hy Averback, Harry
Bartell, Barbara Eiler, Jack
Kruschen)

622. The Mountain (11/1/55; Parley Baer
and Ben Wright)

623. Report on the X-915 (11/8/55; Stacy
Harris and Jack Kruschen)

624. Once a Murderer (11/15/55; Dick
Beals, Herb Butterfield, Joseph
Kearns, and Charlie Lung)

625. Classified Secret (11/22/55; Parley
Baer and Dick Beals)

626. This Will Kill You (11/29/55; Lillian
Buyeff, Sam Edwards, and Victor
Perrin)

627. When the Bough Breaks (12/6/55;
Dick Beals, Virginia Gregg, Stacy
Harris, and Joseph Kearns)

628. A Present for Benny (12/13/55;
Stacy Harris, Jack Kruschen, and

Junius Matthews)

629. The Cave (12/20/55; Dick Beals,
Billy Chapman, Hans Conried,
John Dehner, Lawrence Dobkin,
and Ben Wright)

630. The Mystery of the Marie Celeste
(12/27/55; John Dehner, Paul
Frees, and Joseph Kearns)

631. The Eavesdropper (1/3/56; Parley
Baer, Lawrence Dobkin, Herb
Ellis, and Charlotte Lawrence)

632. Two Platinum Capsules (1/10/56;
Edgar Barrier, Dick Beals, and
Stacy Harris)

633. The End of the String (1/17/56;
Mary Jane Croft, Stacy Harris, and
Jack Kruschen)

634. The Cellar Door (1/24/56; Paula
Winslowe)

635. Arctic Rescue (1/31/56; Lillian
Buyeff and George Walsh)

636. Variations on a Theme (2/7/56;
Parley Baer, Sam Edwards, and
Barbara Eiler)

637. Listen Young Lovers (2/14/56; Sam
Edwards, Joseph Kearns, and
Charlotte Lawrence)

638. Hollywood Hostages (2/21/56; Tom
Brown and Don Diamond)

639. The Diary of Captain Scott
(2/28/56; Hans Conried and Raymond Lawrence)

640. Quiet Night (3/6/56; Tony Barrett,
Stacy Harris, and George Walsh)

641. The Groom of the Ladder (3/13/56;
Hans Conried, Raymond E.
Lawrence, and Doris Lloyd)

642. Gallardo (3/20/56; Tony Barrett,
Virginia Gregg, and Victor Perrin)

643. The Murderess (3/27/56; Dick
Beals, John Dehner, Cathy Lewis,
and Paula Winslowe)

644. Game Hunt (4/3/56; Stacy Harris,
Jack Kruschen, and Raymond E.
Lawrence)

645. The Lonely Heart (4/10/56; Joseph
Kearns and Ben Wright)

646. The Seventh Letter (4/17/56; Parley
Baer, Dick Beals, Stacy Harris, Vic
Perrin, and George Walsh)

647. A Case of Nerves (4/24/56; Parley
Baer)

648. The Waxwork (5/1/56; William
Conrad)

649. The Phones Die First (5/8/56; Harry Bartell, Richard Crenna, and Barney Phillips)
650. The Death Parade (5/15/56; Jack Carroll, Stacy Harris, Howard McNear, Clayton Post, George Walsh, and Paula Winslowe)
651. Fragile: Contents Death (5/22/56; Ted Bliss and Victor Perrin)
652. The Flame (5/29/56; Tony Barrett)
653. The Twelfth Rose (6/5/56; Jack Carroll, Stacy Harris, and Paula Winslowe)
654. A Matter of Timing (6/12/56; Parley Baer, Sam Edwards, and Stacy Harris)
655. A Sleeping Draft [based on a Westin Martyr story] (6/19/56; Hans Conried and Abraham Sofaer)
656. The Treasure Chest of Don Jose (6/26/56; Edgar Barrier and Joseph Kearns)
657. The Music Lovers (7/3/56; Hans Conried and Ben Wright)
658. Want Ad (7/10/56; Mary Jane Croft and Stacy Harris)
659. The Man Who Threw Acid (7/17/56; Tony Barrett, William Conrad, and John Dehner)
660. The Tramp (7/25/56; Charlie Lung and Ben Wright)
661. Massacre at Little Bighorn (8/1/56; Stacy Harris)
662. Double Identity (8/8/56; Don Diamond, Charlotte Lawrence, and Paula Winslowe)
663. A Friend to Alexander (8/15/56; John Dehner and Charlotte Lawrence)
664. Hold-Up (8/29/56; Sam Edwards and Byron Kane)
665. The Security Agent (9/5/56; Parley Baer, Harry Bartell, Herb Butterfield, and Howard McNear)
666. A Case of Identity (9/25/56; Parley Baer, Michael Ann Barrett, and Joseph Kearns)
667. Waiting (10/2/56; Tom Hanley, Vivi Janniss, and Charlotte Lawrence)
668. The Digger (10/9/56; Parley Baer, Herb Butterfield, Lillian Buyeff, and Torin Thatcher)
669. The Prophesy of Bertha Abbott (10/16/56; Dick Beals, Richard Crenna, and George Walsh)
670. The Doll (10/23/56; Dick Beals and Patty McCormick)
671. Red Cloud Mesa [based on a story by William Derry Eastlake] (10/30/56; Reed Hadley)
672. The Signalman (11/4/56; Sarah Churchill and Ben Wright)
673. Three Skeleton Key (11/11/56; Vincent Price)
674. The Long Night [based on the short story by Lowell D. Blanton] (11/18/56; Frank Lovejoy)
675. The Man Who Stole the Bible (11/25/56; June Foray, Joseph Kearns, John Lund, Jay Novello, and Larry Thor)
676. The Rim of Terror (12/2/56; Tony Barrett and Barbara Whiting, and Ben Wright)
677. An Occurrence at Owl Creek Bridge [based on the short story by Ambrose Bierce] (12/9/56; Lou Merrill, Larry Thor, and Victor Jory)
678. Eyewitness (12/16/56; Tony Barrett, Howard Duff, Jack Kruschen, Lou Merrill, Barney Phillips)
679. Back for Christmas [based on the John Collier short story] (12/23/56; Herbert Marshall)
680. A Shipment of Mute Fate (1/6/57; Jack Kelly)
681. Russian New Year (1/13/57; Helmut Dantine)
682. Second Class Passenger (1/20/57; William Conrad, Hans Conried, and Sterling Holloway)
683. Freedom This Way (1/27/57; Hans Conried)
684. Frankie and Johnny (2/3/57; Daws Butler, Roy Glenn, Shirley Mitchell, and Margaret Whiting)
685. Door of Gold (2/10/57; Ramsey Hill, Myron McCormick, Shirley Mitchell, and Jay Novello)
686. Murder and Aunt Delia (2/17/57; Glenn Ford)
687. Two Hundred and Twenty-Seven Minutes of Hate (2/25/57; Charles McGraw)
688. Present Tense (3/3/57; Daws Butler and Vincent Price)
689. The Paralta Map (3/10/57; Raymond Burr, Stacy Harris, and Junius Matthews)

690. The Outer Limit (3/17/57; Hans Conried, Stacy Harris, Frank Lovejoy, and Barney Phillips)
691. Shooting Star (3/24/57; Hans Conried and June Lockhart)
692. A Good Neighbor (3/31/57; Jeff Chandler and Virginia Gregg)
693. The Vanishing Lady [based on the short story by Alexander Woollcott] (4/7/57; Edgar Barrier, Vanessa Brown, John Dehner, Virginia Gregg, and Ben Wright)
694. Thou Shalt Not Commit (4/14/57; Victor Jory and Joe di Santis)
695. Chicken Feed (4/21/57; Lloyd Bridges)
696. Escape to Death (4/28/57; Dick Beals, Ted de Corsia, Paul Dubov, Fritz Feld, and Francis Lederer)
697. Celebration (5/5/57; Jack Moyles and Joe di Santis)
698. Tarawa Was Tough (5/12/57; Dick Crenna, John Dehner, and John Lund)
699. Death and Miss Turner (5/19/57; Agnes Moorehead)
700. The Big Day (5/26/57; Daws Butler, William Keighley, John McIntire, and Jeanette Nolan)
701. Crossing Paris (6/2/57; Hans Conried and John Dehner)
702. The Green-and-Gold String [based on the short story by Philip MacDonald] (6/9/57; Byron Kane, Jeanette Nolan, Vincent Price, Irene Tedrow, and Ben Wright)
703. Trial by Jury (6/16/57; Kenny Delmar and Nancy Kelly)
704. A Load of Dynamite (6/23/57; Paul DuBov, Barney Phillips, and Bartlett Robinson)
705. The Yellow Wall-Paper (6/30/57; Ann Hunter and Agnes Moorehead)
706. Alibi (7/7/57; Ted de Corsia, Jack Kruschen, Peter Leeds, and Everett Sloane)
707. Flood on the Goodwins (7/14/57; Hans Conried, Charlotte Lawrence, and Herbert Marshall)
708. America's Boyfriend (7/21/57; Richard Crenna and Mercedes McCambridge)
709. Murder on Mike (7/28/57; Raymond Burr)
710. Fleshpeddler (8/4/57; Dick Beals, Daws Butler, DeForest Kelley, and Howard McNear)
711. Pigeon in the Cage (8/11/57; Lloyd Bridges)
712. Peanut Brittle (8/18/57; John Dehner, Skip Homeier, and Barney Phillips)
713. Leiningen Versus the Ants (8/25/57; William Conrad and Ben Wright)
714. Man from Tomorrow (9/1/57; Joan Banks, John Hoyt, Peter Leeds, and Frank Lovejoy)
715. Old Army Buddy (9/8/57; Paul Frees, Victor Jory, and Larry Thor)
716. Night on Red Mountain (9/15/57; Richard Crenna)
717. Shadow on the Wall (9/22/57; John Hoyt, Jackie Kelk, Charles Lung, and Jeanette Nolan)
718. Vamp Till Dead (9/29/57; Vanessa Brown and Jeanette Nolan)
719. Misfire (10/6/57; Jack Carson, William Conrad, John Dehner, and Barney Phillips)
720. The Well-Dressed Corpse (10/13/57; John Dehner and Margaret Whiting)
721. Sorry, Wrong Number (10/20/57; Virginia Gregg, Agnes Moorehead, and Jeanette Nolan)
722. The Country of the Blind (10/27/57; Raymond Burr and Ben Wright)
723. Firing Run (11/3/57; Dick Beals, Daws Butler, Ken Christy, Eddie Firestone, and Ruth Hussey)
724. The Pit and the Pendulum (11/10/57; John Hoyt, Vincent Price, and Ben Wright)
725. The City That Was (11/17/57; Francis X. Bushman)
726. The Star of Thessaly (11/24/57; Ray Noble)
727. Jet Stream (12/1/57; Virginia Gregg, Frank Lovejoy, and Sam Pierce)
728. Speed Trap (12/8/57; William Conrad, Lawrence Dobkin, Everett Sloane)
729. An Occurrence at Owl Creek Bridge (12/15/57; Harry Bartell, William Conrad, and Joseph Cotten)
730. Dog Star (12/22/57; Dick Beals,

Lou Krugman, Shirley Mitchell,
Sam Pierce, and Evelyn Rudie)
731. Never Steal a Butcher's Wife
(12/29/57; William Conrad and
Cathy Lewis)
732. A Week Ago Wednesday (1/5/58;
Dick Beals, Hillary Brooke, John
Dehner, Dee J. Thompson)
733. The Island (1/12/58; Lillian Buyeff,
Hans Conried, and John Lund)
734. The Crowded Void (1/19/58; John
Dehner, Shirley Mitchell, Barney
Phillips, Bartlett Robinson)
735. Nineteen Deacon Street (1/26/58;
Jack Kruschen, Jerome Thor, and
Paula Winslowe)
736. The Silver Frame (2/2/58; Charles
McGraw and Tracy Roberts)
737. The Long Shot (2/9/58; Herbert
Marshall, Florence Woollcott, and
Ben Wright)
738. One Chef Well Done (2/16/58;
Maurice Marsac)
739. Five Buck Tip (2/23/58; Ken
Christy, Jack Kruschen, Cathy
Lewis, Karl Swenson, Jerome
Thor)
740. Never Follow a Banjo Act (3/2/58;
Eddie Marr and Margaret Whit-
ing)
741. The Chain (3/9/58; John McIntire,
Agnes Moorehead, and Jay Nov-
ello)
742. Game Hunt (3/16/58; Lawrence
Dobkin, Roy Glenn, and Everett
Sloane)
743. Affair at Loveland Pass (3/23/58;
Jim Ameche, Vanessa Brown, and
Barney Phillips)
744. The Sisters (3/30/58; Frances
Farmer and Cathy Lewis)
745. Just One Happy Little Family
(4/6/58; Shirley Mitchell and Ray
Noble)
746. Win, Place or Die (4/13/58; Joan
Banks and Frank Lovejoy)
747. Alibi Me (4/20/58; Dick Beals and
Stan Freeberg)
748. Winner Lose All (4/27/58; Jack
Kruschen, John Lund, and Sam
Pierce)
749. Sundown (5/4/58; Jackie Kelk, Jack
Kruschen, and Victor Perrin)
750. Subway Stop (5/11/58; Virginia

Gregg, Skip Homeier, Jackie Kelk,
and Barney Phillips)
751. Zero Hour (5/18/58; Lillian Buyeff,
Victor Perrin, Evelyn Rudie, and
Karl Swenson)
752. Like Man, Somebody Dig Me
(5/25/58; Elliott Reid)
753. Rave Notice (6/1/58; Jack
Kruschen, Lou Merrill, and Barney Phillips)
754. The Invisible Ape (6/8/58;
Lawrence Dobkin, Byron Kane,
and Sam Pierce)
755. Strange for a Killer (6/15/58; Joan
Banks and Dan O'Herlihy)
756. The Last Kilometer (6/22/58; John
Dehner, Marsha Hunt, Ann
Hunter, and Ben Wright)
757. Rain Tonight (6/29/58; Tommy
Cook and Barney Phillips)
758. Rub Down and Out (7/6/58; Lloyd
Bridges)
759. The Long Night (7/13/58; Eddie
Firestone, Peter Leeds, Frank
Lovejoy, and Barney Phillips)
760. It's All in Your Mind (7/20/58;
Berry Kroeger, Lou Krugman,
Shirley Mitchell, and Sam Pierce)
761. The Steel River Prison Break
(7/27/58; Eddie Firestone, Barney
Phillips, and Bartlett Robinson)
762. The Voice of Company A (8/3/58;
Lillian Buyeff, John Dehner, Jack
Kruschen, Everett Sloane)
763. The Diary of Saphronia Winters
(8/10/58; Mercedes McCambridge
and Karl Swenson)
764. The Bridge (8/17/58; Virginia
Gregg, Jerry Hausner, and Cathy
Lewis)
765. Remember Me? (8/24/58; Jackie
Cooper, Sandra Gould, and Barney Phillips)
766. The Whole Town's Sleeping
(8/31/58; William Conrad, Charlie Lung, and Agnes Moorehead)
767. The Wait (9/7/58; John Dehner,
Howard McNear, Maria Palmer,
and Karl Swenson)
768. Command (9/14/58; Richard
Anderson and Sam Edwards)
769. No Hiding Place (9/21/58; Jim
Ameche, Lawrence Dobkin, Wendell Holmes, and Barney Phillips)

770. Affair at Eden (9/28/58; Frank Lovejoy)
771. The Man Who Won the War (10/5/58; Ted de Corsia, Herbert Marshall, and Abraham Sofaer)
772. The Treasure Chest of Don Jose (10/12/58; Raymond Burr and Tommy Cook)
773. Three Skeleton Key (10/19/58; Lawrence Dobkin and Vincent Price)
774. Headshrinker (10/26/58; Helmut Dantine and Nina Foch)
775. The Dealings of Mr. Markham (11/2/58; James and Pamela Mason)
776. Two for the Road (11/9/58; William Conrad and Charles McGraw)
777. My Dear Niece (11/16/58; Berry Kroeger and Jack Kruschen)
778. A Statement of Fact (11/23/58; John Dehner and Cathy Lewis)
779. Misfire (11/30/58; William Conrad and John Dehner)
780. Tom Dooley (12/7/58; Karl Swenson)
781. For Old Time's Sake (12/14/58; Virginia Gregg and John Lund)
782. Out for Christmas (12/21/58; Joan Banks, Raymond Burr, Dick Beals, and Karl Swenson)
783. The Thirty-Second of December (12/28/58; Joan Banks, Frank Lovejoy, and Barney Phillips)
784. Don't Call Me Mother (1/4/59; Agnes Moorehead and Barney Phillips)
785. Night on Red Mountain (1/11/59; Richard Crenna and Doris Singleton)
786. Ride Down Calhone (1/18/59; William Bishop and William Quinn)
787. Four of a Kind (1/25/59; Jack Kruschen, Barney Phillips, Alan Reed, and Elliott Reid)
788. Return to Dust (2/1/59; Dick Beals, Lawrence Dobkin, and Paula Winslowe)
789. Death Notice (2/8/59; Victor Jory and Barney Phillips)
790. The Signalman (2/15/59; Ellen Drew and Ben Wright)
791. Star Over Hong Kong (2/22/59; Ramsey Hill, Marie Wilson, and Ben Wright)
792. The Waxwork (3/1/59; Herbert Marshall)
793. Mad Man of Manhattan (3/8/59; Myron McCormick and Doris Singleton)
794. Death in Box 234 (3/15/59; Lou Krugman, Frank Lovejoy, and Edgar Stehli)
795. Script by Mark Brady (3/22/59; Victor Perrin, Marie Windsor, and Ben Wright)
796. John Barbie and Son (3/29/59; Jack Kruschen, John McIntire, and Karl Swenson)
797. Too Hot to Live (4/12/59; Van Heflin, Berry Kroeger, and Barney Phillips)
798. See How He Runs (4/19/59; Jim Backus, Dick Beals, Lou Krugman, and Sam Pierce)
799. Deep, Deep Is My Love (4/26/59; Lloyd Bridges)
800. The Amateur (5/3/59; Tommy Cook, Jackie Cooper, Berry Kroeger, and Peter Leeds)
801. On a Country Road (5/10/59; Howard Duff, Ida Lupino, and Jeanette Nolan)
802. A Friend of Daddy's (5/17/59; Dick Beals, Cathy Lewis, Frank Lovejoy, and William Quinn)
803. Spoils for Victor (5/24/59; Joan Banks, Georgia Ellis, and Berry Kroeger)
804. The Man Who Would Be King (5/31/59; Dick Beals, Lillian Buyeff, Jay Novello, Dan O'Herlihy, and Ben Wright)
805. The Pit and the Pendulum (6/7/59; Raymond Burr and Jay Novello)
806. Drive-In (6/14/59; Gail Lukas and Margaret Whiting)
807. Ivy's a Lovely Name for a Girl (6/21/59; Joan Banks and Frank Lovejoy)
808. Analytical Hour (6/28/59; Jack Carson, John Hoyt, and Sam Pierce)
809. Blood Is Thicker (7/5/59; Lawrence Dobkin, Sam Pierce, William Quinn, and Everett Sloane)
810. Eyewitness (7/12/59; John Lund)

811. An Occurrence at Owl Creek Bridge (7/19/59; Sam Edwards, Cathy Lewis, and Vincent Price)
812. Night Man (7/26/59; Lawrence Dobkin, and Marsha Hunt)
813. Red Cloud Mesa (8/2/59; Joseph Cotten, and Lawrence Dobkin)
814. Everything Will Be Different (8/9/59; Virginia Gregg, Peter Leeds, and Cathy Lewis)
815. Like Man, Somebody Dig Me (8/16/59; Lillian Buyeff, Dennis Day, Jack Moyles, and Bill Quinn)
816. Headshrinker (8/23/59; Lawrence Dobkin and Agnes Moorehead)
817. A Matter of Execution (8/30/59; Bill Adams, Harold Huber, Ginger Jones, and Santos Ortega)
818. After the Movies (9/6/59; Kevin McCarthy)
819. Death and the Escort (9/13/59; Bob Dryden, Elspeth Eric, Larry Haines, and Maurice Tarplin)
820. The Beetle and Mr. Bottle (9/20/59; Mason Adams, John Gibson, Ian Martin, and Guy Repp)
821. Room 203 (10/4/59; Ralph Bell, Eric Dressler, Bernard Grant, and Joseph Julian)
822. Infanticide (10/11/59; Ralph Bell, Frank Butler, and Santos Ortega)
823. The Crisis of Dirk Diamond (10/18/59; Eric Dressler, Bernard Grant, Ian Martin, and Maurice Tarplin)
824. The Easy Victim (10/25/59; Elspeth Eric, Leon Janney, Paul McGrath, and Robert Readick)
825. Re-Entry (11/1/59; Mason Adams, Jim Boles, Frank Butler, Robert Readick, Frank Thomas, Jr.)
826. The Last Trip (11/8/59; Ralph Bell, Bob Dryden, and Eugene Francis)
827. The Companion (11/15/59; Rita Lloyd and Virginia Payne)
828. The Thimble (11/22/59; Whitfield Connor, Joe Di Santis, Paul McGrath, Dan Ocko, Maurice Tarplin, and Ruth Tobin)
829. Leiningen Versus the Ants (11/29/59; Ralph Camargo and Luis Van Rooten)
830. Dynamite Run (12/6/59; Mason Adams, Bob Dryden, Larry Haines, and Bill Lipton)
831. The Country of the Blind (12/13/59; Jackson Beck, Ralph Camargo, Bernard Grant, and Santos Ortega)
832. A Korean Christmas Carol (12/20/59; Bill Lipton and Santos Ortega)
833. Moonlight Sail (12/27/59; James Boles, Guy Repp, and Luis Van Rooten)
834. Zero Hour (1/3/60; John Gibson and Ginger Jones)
835. The Long Night (1/10/60; Bill Adams and Sam Grey)
836. The Time, The Place, and The Death (1/17/60; Eric Dressler, Peter Fernandez, Claudia Morgan, Bryna Raeburn, and Maurice Tarplin)
837. Turnabout (1/24/60; Larry Haines, Raymond E. Johnson, Ginger Jones, and Melville Ruick)
838. End of the Road (1/31/60; Bernard Grant, Rita Lloyd, and Jane Seymour)
839. The Mystery of Marie Roget (2/7/60; Jackson Beck and Abby Lewis)
840. Sorry, Wrong Number (2/14/60; Virginia Gregg, Agnes Moorehead, and Jeanette Nolan)
841. Crank Letter (2/21/60; Lester Damon, Larry Haines, and Lyle Sudrow)
842. Lt. Langer's Last Collection (2/28/60; Murray Forbes, Jack Grimes, Ginger Jones, Ian Martin, William Mason, and Frank Thomas, Jr.)
843. Sleep Is for Children (3/6/60; Bill Adams, Ralph Bell, Elspeth Eric, and Ruth Tobin)
844. The Revolution (3/13/60; Ralph Camargo, Ronald Dawson, and Rosemary Rice)
845. Talk About Caruso (3/20/60; Mason Adams, Robert Dryden, and Stuart Foster)
846. Coffin for Mr. Cash (3/27/60; Leon Janney and Mandel Kramer)
847. A Shipment of Mute Fate (4/3/60; Bernard Grant)

848. Two Horse Parley (4/10/60; Larry Haines and Lyle Sudrow)
849. Tonight at 5:55 (4/17/60; Ralph Camargo, Whitfield Connor, John Gibson, Robert Readick, Larry Robinson, and Luis Van Rooten)
850. One More Shot (4/24/60; Jim Boles, Peter Fernandez, Jack Grimes, Joseph Julian, and Bill Lipton)
851. Bitter Grapes (5/1/60; Teri Keane, Rita Lloyd, and Edgar Stehli)
852. The Legend of Robbie (5/8/60; Eric Dressler, Joan Lorring, and George Matthews)
853. Dead Man's Story (5/15/60; Sam Grey, Kevin McCarthy, and Guy Repp)
854. Out the Window (5/22/60; Roger DeKoven and Ginger Jones)
855. Perfect Plan (5/29/60; George Petrie)
856. Two Came Back [based on a story by Jules Archer] (6/5/60; Bob Readick)
857. Elementals (6/12/60; Phil Meader and Santos Ortega)
858. Sixty Grand Missing (6/19/60; Ralph Bell and Bernard Grant)
859. Daisy Chain (6/26/60; Joan Lorring, Mercer McCloud, and Jane Rose)
860. Bon Voyage (7/3/60; Joseph Julian, Rita Lloyd, and Danny Ocko)
861. Report from a Dead Planet (7/10/60; Lester Damon, John Larkin, and Phil Meader)
862. Memorial Bridge (7/17/60; Ralph Bell, Roger De Koven, Robert Dryden, Sam Grey, Larry Haines)
863. Cold Canvas (7/24/60; Les Damon, Ginger Jones, William Redfield, and Guy Repp)
864. End Game (7/31/60; Michael Kane and Santos Ortega)
865. The Big Dive (8/7/60; Ralph Bell, Sam Grey, Leon Janney, Mandel Kramer, and Rosemary Rice)
866. Night Ferry to Paris (8/14/60; Robert Dryden and William Redfield)
867. Truck Stop (8/21/60; Larry Haines, Teri Keane, Mandel Kramer, and Dan Ocko)
868. The Girl in the Powder Blue Jag (8/27/60; Robert Dryden, Rita Lloyd, and Jane Rose)
869. A Rest for Emily (9/4/60; Ralph Bell, Abby Lewis, and Larry Robinson)
870. Rakovsky's Rubbles (9/11/60; Roger De Koven, Lynn Lorring, and Santos Ortega)
871. A Statement of Fact (9/18/60; Mason Adams, Jack Arthur, Rita Lloyd, and Lawson Zerbe)
872. Time on My Hands (9/25/60; Robert Dryden, Bill Lipton, Santos Ortega, and Ted Osborne)
873. Ivy's a Lovely Name for a Girl (10/2/60; Carl Frank, Phil Meader, and Johnny Spencer)
874. Witness for Death (10/9/60; Mary Jane Higby, Roger De Koven, Guy Repp, and Ruth Tobin)
875. Inferno (10/16/60; Robert Dryden, Dick Holland, and Mandel Kramer)
876. Night Man (10/23/60; Ginger Jones)
877. The City That Was (10/30/60; Bernard Grant, Martha Greenhouse, House Jameson, Michael Kane, Dan Ocko, and George Petrie)
878. The Green Lorelei (11/6/60; John Gibson, Elizabeth Lawrence, Robert Readick, and Bill Smith)
879. The Man Who Murders People (11/13/60; Allen Manson, George Petrie, and Maurice Tarplin)
880. Night on Red Mountain (11/20/60; Bill Adams, James Boles, Bob Dryden, Mandel Kramer, and Lawson Zerbe)
881. Home Is Where You Find It (11/27/60; Mandel Kramer and William Redfield)
882. Call Me at Half Past (6/25/61; Elspeth Eric and Bernard Grant)
883. Night of the Storm (7/2/61; Ralph Camargo, Teri Keane, and Rosemary Rice)
884. Epitaph (7/9/61; Barbara Becker, Joan Lorring, and Paul McGrath)
885. The Man Who Knew How to Hate (7/16/61; Robert Dryden and Leon Janney)

886. Stranger with My Face (7/23/61;
Bernard Grant and Lawson Zerbe)
887. You Can Die Laughing (7/30/61;
Larry Haines, Evelyn Juster, Ian
Martin, William Mason, and
Gertrude Warner)
888. Bells (8/6/61; Bill Lipton, Rosemary
Rice, Larry Robinson, and Lawson
Zerbe)
889. Murder Is a Matter of Opinion
(8/20/61; Bob Dryden, Bernard
Lenrow, Bill Lipton, and Lawson
Zerbe)
890. Sold to Satan [based on a story by
Jules Archer] (8/27/61; Bob Dry-
den, Elizabeth Lawrence, Ian Mar-
tin, and Kermit Murdock)
891. The Juvenile Rebellion (9/3/61;
Court Benson, Ronald Liss, and
Jimsey Summers)
892. The Green Idol (9/17/61; Parker
Fennelly, Abby Lewis, Ronald Liss,
and Mercer McCloud)
893. The Man in the Fog (9/24/61;
Robert Dryden, Mercer McCloud,
and Guy Repp)
894. No Hiding Place (10/1/61; Court
Benson, Leon Janney, and Grace
Matthews)
895. Dreams (10/8/61; Raymond E.
Johnson and Edgar Stehli)
896. Seeds of Disaster (10/15/61; Ralph
Camargo, Bob Dryden, Bernard
Grant, and Connie Lempke)
897. Witness to Murder (10/22/61;
Ronald Dawson, Bob Dryden,
Leon Janney, and Joan Lorring)
898. Death of an Old Flame (10/29/61;
Ralph Bell, Larry Haines, and Teri
Keane)
899. Till Death Do Us Part (11/5/61;
James Boles, Herb Duncan, Sam
Grey, and Bill Lipton)
900. The Impostors (11/12/61; Charita
Bauer, Arline Blackburn, Cliff
Carpenter, Bill Lipton, Reynold
Osborne, and Melville Ruick)
901. The Black Door (11/19/61; Ralph
Camargo)
902. Man Trap (11/29/61; Ralph Camargo,
Joseph Julian, and Teri Keane)
903. The Luck of the Tiger Eye (12/3/61;
Leon Janney, Raymond E. John-
son, and Mercer McCloud)

904. And So to Sleep My Love (12/10/61;
Bryna Rayburn, William Redfield,
and Elaine Rost)
905. Yuletide Miracle (12/17/61; Joe di
Santis, Larry Haines, Santos
Ortega, and Rosemary Rice)
906. The Old Man (12/31/61; Ralph
Camargo, Larry Haines, Leon Jan-
ney, Rita Lloyd, Reynold Osborne,
Guy Repp, and Lawson Zerbe)
907. Breakthrough (1/7/62; Robert Dry-
den, Dan Ocko, Guy Repp, and
Luis Van Rooten)
908. Feathers (1/14/62; Ian Martin,
Robert Readick, John Thomas,
and Lawson Zerbe)
909. Twenty-Four Sixty-Two (1/21/62;
Robert Dryden, William Mason,
Rosemary Rice, and Lawson
Zerbe)
910. Please Believe Me (1/28/62; Joan
Lorring and Robert Readick)
911. Friday (2/4/62; Robert Dryden,
Herbert Duncan, Ivor Francis, Bill
Lipton, and Mercer McCloud)
912. The Man Who Went Back to Save
Lincoln (2/11/62; Ralph Bell,
Court Benson, Cliff Carpenter,
and Ian Martin)
913. The Old Boyfriend (2/18/62;
Elspeth Eric, Joseph Julian, and
Lawson Zerbe)
914. Date Night (2/25/62; Freddie
Chandler, Sam Grey, Jack Grimes,
Bill Lipton, Rosemary Rice, Guy
Repp, and Lawson Zerbe)
915. Doom Machine (3/4/62; Cliff Car-
penter, Eugene Francis, Bernard
Grant, and Leon Janney)
916. Heads You Lose (3/11/62; Raymond
E. Johnson, Kermit Murdock, Bill
Redfield and Melville Ruick)
917. Perchance to Dream (3/18/62;
Robert Dryden, Bernard Grant,
Teri Keane, Paul McGrath, and
Guy Repp)
918. Memory of a Murder (3/25/62;
Ralph Bell, Connie Lempke, James
Monks, and Lawson Zerbe)
919. You Died Last Night (4/1/62; San-
tos Ortega and Robert Readick)
920. Let There Be Light (4/8/62; Ivor
Francis and Teri Keane)
921. Brother John (4/15/62; Sam Grey,

Tales of Fatima

This is another mystery program starring Basil Rathbone, one of the handful of programs he starred in after leaving *The New Adventures of Sherlock Holmes*. Rathbone played himself, and each week found himself caught up in a murder case. He was aided by Fatima, who gave the listeners a secret clue from her CBS echo chamber before the drama began. Sponsored by Fatima Cigarettes, this program ran a total of thirty-nine broadcasts before leaving the air, even when various Hollywood guests were added toward the end to pick up more listeners. Michael Fitzmaurice was the announcer. Jack Miller supplied music. Harry Ingram directed. The series was broadcast over CBS, Saturday evenings from 9:30 to 10 pm.

1. The Strange Mr. Smith (1/8/49)
2. The Mystery at Mirador (1/15/49)
3. The Fires at Scjuyler Square (1/22/49)
4. The Frozen Forest (1/29/49)
5. The Cairo Curse (2/5/49)
6. The Twisted Talisman (2/12/49)
7. The Jilted Juvenile (2/19/49)
8. The Invisible Caballero (2/26/49)
9. The Cry for a Cat (3/5/49)
10. The Tower of Ice (3/12/49)
11. Design for Death (3/19/49)
12. The Murder on Stage (3/26/49)
13. The Biggest Game (4/2/49)
14. The Murder at the Circus (4/9/49)
15. Duet and Death (4/16/49)
16. A Country Killing (4/23/49)
17. The Cautious Corpse (4/30/49)
18. Murder at the Ball Game (5/7/49)
19. Over My Dead Body (5/14/49)
20. A Much Expected Murder (5/21/49)
21. Time to Kill (5/28/49)
22. One Foot in the Grave (6/4/49)
23. Murder in Pig Latin (6/11/49)
24. Death Sits with the Baby (6/18/49)
25. Dead or Alive (6/25/49)
26. The Dark Secret (7/2/49)
27. The Sleeping Dog (7/9/49)
28. The Cargo of Death (7/16/49)
29. Memory of Murder (7/23/49)
30. The Next of Kin (7/30/49)
31. The Portrait of Death (8/6/49)
32. Dead and Buried (8/13/49)
33. Prescription for Death (8/20/49)
34. Intent to Kill (8/27/49; John Garfield)
35. A Dose of Death (9/3/49)
36. The Men in the Shadows (9/10/49; Bela Lugosi)
37. The Bend Sinister (9/17/49; Lilli Palmer)
38. The Most Dangerous Game (9/24/49; Rex Harrison)
39. Study in Suspicion (10/1/49)

Tales of the Texas Rangers

Similar to *Dragnet* and other detective series, this program featured dramatizations of various case files from the Texas Rangers. Joel McCrea starred as Ranger Jase Pearson, the lead detective who solved each week's case. Stacy Keach produced and directed the series. Hal Gibney was the announcer. Tony Barrett narrated. Joel Murcott, Charles E. Israel, Bob Wright, Will Gould, Robert A. White, Adrian Gendeaux and Arthur Brown, Jr., wrote the scripts. M.T. Lone Wolf Gonzaullas was the technical advisor assisting the script writers for the authenticity of the scripts. And, of course, names, dates and places were changed to protect the innocent. Trivia: For some strange reason, episode forty-three was almost the exact same script used on an episode of *Mr. District Attorney*.

The series was broadcast over NBC, and General Mills (Wheaties) sponsored the program for the first ten broadcasts. *Tales* premiered on Saturday evenings from 9:30 to 10 pm, EST. Frank Martin was the pitchman for Wheaties. Beginning with episode fourteen, the program was broadcast on Sunday evenings from 8:30 to 9 pm, EST. Beginning with episode forty-six, *Tales* was broadcast from 6 to 6:30 pm,

EST. *Tales of the Texas Rangers* returned to the airwaves via television in 1955 with Willard Parker in the role of Ranger Jace Pearson.

Audition: Just a Number (4/19/50)
1. Murder Money (7/8/50)
2. The White Elephant (7/15/50; Robert Bruce, Jeff Corey, and Jeanette Nolan)
3. Apache Peak (7/22/50; Paul DuBov, Sam Edwards, Virginia Gregg, and William Johnstone)
4. The Triggerman (7/29/50; Tom Holland, Byron Kane, Jack Kruschen, Tom McKee, and Jay Novello)
5. Quick Silver (8/5/50; Byron Kane, Lou Krugman, Russell Simpson, and Dee J. Thompson)
6. The Broken Spur (8/12/50)
7. Fool's Gold (8/19/50; Lillian Buyeff, Herb Butterfield, David Ellis, and Paul Frees)
8. The Open Range (8/26/50; Bob Cole, Paul DuBov, Bert Holland, Byron Kane, and Tom Tully)
9. Play for Keeps (9/2/50)
10. Dead Or Alive (9/9/50)
11. Candy Man (9/16/50; Reed Hadley, Wilms Herbert, Dick Ryan, and Lurene Tuttle)
12. Open and Shut (9/23/50; Joan Banks, Francis X. Bushman, and Vivi Janniss)
13. Clean Up (9/30/50; Herb Ellis, Paul Frees, Byron Kane, Lou Krugman, and Tom McKee)
14. Living Death (10/8/50; Lillian Buyeff, Ken Harvey, and Barney Phillips)
15. Dead Giveaway (10/15/50; Michael Ann Barrett, Paul Frees, Hal March, and Lurene Tuttle)
16. Murder Merry-Go-Round (10/22/50)
17. Soft Touch (10/29/50; Michael Ann Barrett, Paul Frees, Virginia Gregg, and Byron Kane)
18. The White Suit (11/5/50; Herb Butterfield, Lillian Buyeff, Herb Ellis, and Barney Phillips)
19. Blood Relative (11/12/50; Parley Baer, Virginia Gregg, William Johnstone, and Byron Kane)
20. Hanging by a Thread (11/26/50; Jeff Corey, Betty Lou Gerson, and Wally Maher)
21. Room 114 (12/3/50; Ann Diamond, Herb Ellis, Tom McKee, and Peggy Webber)
22. The Lucky Dollar (12/10/50; Wilms Herbert, Nestor Paiva, Barney Phillips, and Peggy Webber)
23. The Cactus Pear (12/17/50; Wilms Herbert, Tom McKee, and Gerald Mohr)
24. Christmas Present (12/24/50; Shephard Menken, James Nusser, and Victor Rodman)
25. The Devil's Share (12/31/50)
26. Dead Head Freight (1/7/51; Lillian Buyeff, Herb Ellis, Tom Holland, and Byron Kane)
27. Death in the Cards (1/14/51; Michael Ann Barrett, Ernie Newton, and Jeanette Nolan)
28. Blood Harvest (1/21/51)
29. Strange Confession (1/28/51)
30. Logger's Larceny (2/4/51)
31. The Hatchet (2/11/51; Parley Baer, Michael Ann Barrett, Tom Cook, and Gerald Mohr)
32. Sweet Revenge (2/18/51; Rye Billsbury, Stacy Harris, and Lamont Johnson)
33. The Trap (2/25/51; William Conrad, Paul DuBov, Herb Ellis, and Wilms Herbert)
34. Blind Justice (3/11/51; Ed Begley, Earl Keen, Tom Holland, and Herb Vigran)
35. Death by Adoption (3/18/51; Roy Glenn, Joseph Kearns, Barbara Luddy, and Tom McKee)
36. Breakdown (3/25/51; Tony Barrett, Herb Ellis, Betty Lou Gerson, William Johnstone, Byron Kane)
37. Pressure (4/1/51; William Conrad, Roy Glenn, Ernest Whitman, Will Wright, and Herb Vigran)
38. Bad Blood (4/8/51; Parley Baer, Whitfield Connor, Sam Edwards, Paul Frees, and Barbara Luddy)
39. Conspiracy (4/15/51)
40. Canned Death (4/22/51; Ken Christy, Joe Forte, Edmond McDonald, and Will Wright)

41. Hot Cargo (4/29/51)
42. No Living Witnesses (5/6/51; Parley Baer, Ed Begley, Herb Ellis, and Virginia Gregg)
43. Paid in Full (5/13/51)
44. Square Dance (5/20/51; Parley Baer, Joe Forte, Betty Moran, and Jeanette Nolan)
45. Joy Ride (5/27/51; Sam Edwards, John Frank, William Johnstone, Barney Phillips, Peggy Webber)
46. Death Shaft (9/30/51; Brad Brown, Ken Christy, Betty Lou Gerson, and Lamont Johnson)
47. The Wheel Chair Killing (10/7/51; Michael Ann Barrett, Frank Gerstle, and Tom Tully)
48. Play for Keeps (10/14/51)
49. Fugitive's Trail (10/21/51; Parley Baer, Sam Edwards, and Marion Richman)
50. The White Elephant (10/28/51)
51. The Helping Hand (11/4/51)
52. Open and Shut (11/11/51)
53. Wild Crop (11/18/51; Parley Baer, Sam Edwards, and Barney Phillips)
54. The Blowoff (11/25/51; Ed Begley, Betty Lou Gerson, Gerald Mohr, and Jeanette Nolan)
55. The Dead Give-Away (12/2/51)
56. Death Plant (12/9/51; Lamont Johnson, William Johnstone, and Charlotte Lawrence)
57. Pick-Up (12/16/51)
58. Christmas Pay-Off (12/23/51)
59. Killer's Crop (12/30/51; Ken Christy, Herb Ellis, Virginia Gregg, and Byron Kane)
60. Birds of a Feather (1/6/52)
61. Clip Job (1/13/52; Parley Baer, Ken Christy, Herb Ellis, Virginia Gregg, and Ernie Newton)
62. Blood Trail (1/20/52; Parley Baer, Tim Graham, and Barney Phillips)
63. Night Chase (1/27/52; Whitfield Connor, Herb Ellis, Betty Lou Gerson, and Jeanette Nolan)
64. The Rub Out (2/3/52; Herb Ellis, Nestor Paiva, Herb Vigran, and Peggy Webber)
65. The Hitch-Hiker (2/10/52)
66. Cold Blood (2/17/52; Parley Baer, Bob David, Herb Ellis, and William Johnstone)
67. Bright Boy (2/24/52; Whitfield Connor, Sam Edwards, Herb Ellis, and Paul McVey)
68. The Ice Man (3/2/52; Parley Baer, Lillian Buyeff, and Whitfield Connor)
69. Dream Farm (3/9/52; Dick Beals, Ken Christy, Barbara Luddy, and Barney Phillips)
70. Prelude to Felony (3/16/52; Ed Begley, Colleen Collins, and Forrest Lewis)
71. Con Man (3/23/52)
72. Night Hawk (3/23/52; Parley Baer, Michael Ann Barrett, Bert Holland, and Lou Krugman)
73. Troop Train (3/30/52; Sam Edwards, Herb Ellis, Peter Leeds, and Jeanette Nolan)
74. Uncertain Death (4/13/52)
75. Illusion (7/20/52; Parley Baer, Byron Kane, Jeanettte Nolan, and John Stevenson)
76. Address Unknown (4/27/52; Dick Beals, Leo Curley, Lillian Buyeff, Don Diamond, and Herb Ellis)
77. Little Sister (5/4/52; Herb Ellis, Betty Lou Gerson, Virginia Gregg, and Marion Richman)
78. Unleashed Fury (4/27/52; Whitfield Connor, Herb Ellis, Harry Lang, and Howard McNear)
79. Smart Kill (5/18/52; Parley Baer, Betty Lou Gerson, Virginia Gregg, and Barney Phillips)
80. Jailbird (5/25/52)
81. Sellout (6/1/52)
82. Illegal Entry (6/8/52)
83. Travesty (6/15/52)
84. Knockout (6/22/52; Parley Baer, Virginia Gregg, Jeanette Nolan, and Barney Phillips)
85. Ex-Con (6/29/52)
86. The Boomerang (7/6/52; Howard McNear, Ralph Moody, and Dee J. Thompson)
87. Fingerman (7/13/52; Hy Averback, Paul Frees, and Bob Israel)
88. Round Trip (7/20/52)
89. Stick-Up (7/27/52; Parley Baer, Junie Ellis, Lamont Johnson, and Leroy Leonard)
90. Double Edge (8/3/52; Parley Baer, Frank Gerstle, and Virginia Gregg)

91. Last Stop (8/10/52; Ken Christy, Leo Cleary, Whitfield Connor, Bert Holland, and Jeffrey Silver)
92. Cover Up (8/17/52; Leo Curley, Paul Frees, Betty Lou Gerson, and Lamont Johnson)
93. Three Victims (8/24/52; Ken Christy, Roy Glenn, Bert Holland, and Ernie Newton)
94. Misplaced Person (8/31/52; Dick Beals, Herb Ellis, Dan Riss, and Henry Roland)
95. Alibi (9/7/52; Paul Frees, Betty Lou Gerson, Dan Riss, and Herb Vigran)
96. Drive-In (9/14/52)

Tales of Tomorrow

Tales of Tomorrow was one of the earliest adult science-fiction series broadcast, first seen on television in August of 1951. In January of 1953, the program began broadcasting on radio as well, lasting only three and a half months. Titled *Beyond This World* during the audition stage, this radio program was not as successful as the television counterpart, which went off the air two months after the radio series.

1. Made to Measure (1/1/53)
2. The Biography Project (1/8/53)
3. Betelgeuse Bridge (1/15/53)
4. The Other Now (1/22/53)
5. The Stars are the Styk (1/29/53)
6. Syndrome Johnny (2/5/53)
7. The Unimars Plot (2/12/53)
8. Watchbird (2/19/53)
9. Inside Earth (2/26/53)
10. The Moon Is Green (3/5/53)
11. Martians Never Die (3/12/53)
12. The Girls from Earth (3/19/53)
13. The Old Die Rich (3/26/53)
14. Morrow on Mars (4/2/53)
15. The Drop (4/9/53)

Tarzan

Based on the fictional character created by Edgar Rice Burroughs, the famous bare-chested, long-haired, vine-swinging hero commanded the jungle animals, fought enemies of all shapes and sizes, and even took time to make primitive monkey-do to that blonde-haired damsel in distress, Jane. Lord and Lady Greystoke, the British birthparents of Tarzan, were stranded on a lonely African Coast, and soon murdered by wild apes. Tarzan, the only survivor and an infant at the time, was taken in by the apes, who raised him like one of their own offspring. Tarzan grew into a man, spending most of his time living in caves and trees and fighting off evil that invaded the sanctuary of the African jungle.

On September 12, 1932, a syndicated radio serial based on Burroughs' first Tarzan novel, *Tarzan of the Apes*, premiered. This three-a-week serial ran for a total of three hundred and sixty-four broadcasts. Joan Burroughs, the daughter of Edgar Rice Burroughs, played Jane Porter. Joan's real-life husband, James H.

Pierce, played the role of Tarzan. Others in the serial — some played more than one role: Hanley Stafford was Lord Tennington, Count Raoul de Coude, and Karanoff; Jeanette Nolan was La of Opar; Gale Gordon was Cecil Clayton; Ralph Scott was Lt. Paul D'Arnot; Frank Nelson was Nikolas Rokoff; Ted Osborne was Sheik Joseph; Allan Garcia was Vallons; Cy Kendall was Captain Tracy; and Lawrence E. Sterner was Professor Porter. Fred Harrington and Eily Malyan were Lord and Lady Greystoke in the first two broadcasts. Jane and Professor Porter are introduced in episode three. The director was James Knight Carden.

In 1934, the entire novel *Tarzan of the Apes* had run through, so another adventure was adapted for the series. Beginning with the second story, Fred Shields, became the director. Having previously played the role of Bill Fraser in the first adventure, Shields was also producer and director of numerous regional radio programs such as *The Pioneers, Rackety Hollow, The Radio Playmakers*, and *Hamlet in Hollywood*. Shields was also an announcer for transcontinental NBC productions originating in Hollywood, including *Hollywood Is on the Air, The Chase and Sanborn Hour* (with Jimmy Durante), and *The Fleischmann Sunshine Hour* with Rudy Vallee.

For the second and third adventure, Fred Shields narrated a few of the broadcasts, leaving John McIntire for the majority of the programs. Sound engineers were Jack Brundage and E. Dummel. Tarzan was played by Carlton Kadell, who would later become radio's *Red Ryder*. Jane was not featured in the second and third adventure, having returned to New York to think over the possible future she and Tarzan might have if she agreed to marriage. In the second adventure, Jeanette Nolan played the role of Magra, Ralph Scott was D'Arnot, Victor Rodman was Wolf, Cy Kendall was Atan Thome, Karena Shields was Helen, George Turner was Gregory, Don Wilson was Lal Taask, Fred Harrington was Mitchell, and Victor Potel was Larson. In the third adventure, Cy Kendall was Wong Tai, Ralph Scott remained D'Arnot, Fred MacKaye was Temur, Ted Meyers was Kailuk, Dan Davies was Ukah, Gale Gordon was O'Rourke (replaced by Jack Lewis beginning with episode four), Barbara Luddy was Ahtea, Dale Nash was Janette, Vernon Steele was Ashleigh, John Prince was Shahn, Thomas Freebairn was Smith and Poltar, and Victor Rodman played the role of Burton (replaced by Vernon Steele beginning with episode four).

1.–286. Tarzan of the Apes (9/12/32 to 7/9/34)
287.–325. Tarzan and the Diamond of

Asher (1934)
326.–364. Tarzan and the Fires of Tohr (1936)

Tarzan, Lord of the Jungle

Tarzan returned to the radio only one other time since the thirties serial. Broadcast on CBS, Saturday evenings from 8:30 to 9 pm, and syndicated by

Commodore Productions, this series replaced the *Hopalong Cassidy* that was also syndicated by Commodore. It was sponsored by Post Toasties and produced by Walter White, Jr. Edgar Rice Burroughs had died one year before this series premiered. All but two of the scripts were written by Bud Lesser. Three or four of the broadcasts appear as adaptations of Rice novels and three or four Tarzan films. The actors in each episode went uncredited, but the role of Tarzan was later revealed to be played by Lamont Johnson. This series, like its predecessor, was canned and made available to radio stations through syndication. In the West it was heard over the Don-Lee Mutual Broadcasting System. In 1952, CBS picked up the program and it debuted on March 22. It is not known exactly how many episodes were recorded (seventy-seven episodes are known at present), but what is known is that only sixty-seven were broadcast.

Under the radio contract agreement, Walter White, Jr., and Commodore Productions were to be offered refusal when Tarzan was offered to television, but Bud Lesser began preparing a television series in 1955, and a lengthy court battle followed. The result left a television pilot and no *Tarzan* television series.

1. The Siren of Omdur Mara (3/22/52)
2. Tarzan and the Monuema (3/29/52)
3. Black Gold of Africa (4/5/52)
4. Black Ivory (4/12/52)
5. Tarzan and the Coward (4/19/52)
6. The Female of the Species (4/26/52)
7. Tarzan and the Killer (5/3/52)
8. Jungle Legacy (5/10/52)
9. Jungle Orchids (5/17/52)
10. Gold Coast Robbery (5/24/52)
11. Life or Death (5/31/52)
12. D Is for Diamond and Death (6/7/52)
13. Pirates of Cape Bandero (6/14/52)
14. Lake of Blood (6/21/52)
15. Jungle Heat (6/28/52)
16. Jungle Hi-Jackers (7/5/52)
17. Tarzan and the Stranger (7/12/52)
18. Arab Vengeance (7/19/52)
19. Tarzan in Captivity (7/26/52)
20. Gold of the Sudan (8/2/52)
21. Stolen Jewels (8/9/52)
22. Drum Without a Heart (8/16/52)
23. Danger Off San Lorenco (8/23/52)
24. Terror at Night (8/30/52)
25. Head Hunters of Yambesi (9/6/52)
26. Trophy Room (9/13/52)
27. Death Has Small Wings (9/20/52)
28. Tarzan's Magic Amulet (9/27/52)
29. The Strange Book of Araby (10/4/52)
30. Cathedral in the Congo (10/11/52)
31. City of Sleep (10/18/52)
32. Jungle Odds (10/25/52)
33. Small Packages (11/1/52)
34. Adventure on the Road to Timbuktu (11/8/52)
35. Strange Island (11/15/52)
36. African Thanksgiving (11/22/52)
37. Hunter's Fury (11/29/52)
38. Congo Murder (12/6/52)
39. Black Gold of Africa (12/13/52)
40. Congo Christmas (12/20/52)
41. The Siren of Omdur Mara (12/27/52)
42. The Hand of Death (1/3/53)
43. The Man from Another World (1/10/53)
44. Quicksands of Wadihari (1/17/53)
45. Trail of Death (1/24/53)
46. Killer at Large (1/31/53)
47. Paradise Island (2/7/53)
48. The Demon of Rongue (2/14/53)
49. Hooded Death (2/21/53)
50. Simba Hodari (2/28/53)
51. Omen of the Emerald (3/7/53)
52. Volcano of the Sun (3/14/53)
53. Jungle Orchids (3/21/53)
54. End of the World (3/28/53)
55. The Arena of Death (4/4/53)
56. Jungle Smoke (4/11/53)
57. Evidence Destroyed (4/18/53)
58. The Missing Element (4/25/53)
59. New Death (5/2/53) [aka Rays of Death]

60. The Lipagor (5/9/53)
61. The Hot Rod Kid (5/16/53)
62. Mask of Monotiki (5/23/53)
63. None So Blind (5/30/53)
64. Night Riders of Tomkia (6/6/53)

65. The American Family Robinson (6/13/53)
66. The Long Journey (6/20/53)
67. Two in the Bush (6/27/53)

Syndicated programs, but not broadcast on CBS: Tarzan and the Decoy, Across a Continent, Curse of the Pharaohs, Tarzan's Mistake, Contraband, Congo Magic, First Prize, Death, The Ghost of the Karniki, Message to Fort Chavir, Trouble Comes in Paris.

Tell It Again

Children's program featuring classic novels instead of fairy tales or original dramas. Educational at its best. Marvin Miller was the narrator. Originated from Hollywood. First broadcast over CBS on Sunday afternoons from 1:30 to 2 pm, EST. On April 30, 1949, *Tell It Again* moved to Saturday from 10:30 to 11 am. Ernest Martin produced. Ralph Rose directed and wrote most of the scripts. Del Castillo supplied the organ music.

1. Treasure Island (1/18/48)
2. The Three Musketeers (1/25/48)
3. Oliver Twist (2/1/48)
4. The Adventures of Robin Hood (2/8/48)
5. Sinbad the Sailor (2/15/48)
6. The Spy (2/22/48)
7. Hiawatha (2/29/48)
8. A Trip to the Moon (3/7/48)
9. From the Earth to the Moon (3/14/48)
10. Huckleberry Finn (3/21/48)
11. Marco Polo (4/4/48)
12. The Odyssey (4/11/48)
13. Robinson Crusoe (4/25/48)
14. The Legend of Sleepy Hollow (5/2/48)
15. Ben Hur (5/9/48)
16. A Tale of Two Cities (5/16/48)
17. Quentin Durward (5/23/48)
18. Buffalo Bill (5/30/48)
19. Don Quixote (6/6/48)
20. Moby Dick (6/13/48)
21. Dr. Jekyll and Mr. Hyde (6/20/48)
22. Michael Strogoff (6/27/48)
23. The Man Without a Country (7/4/48)
24. The Adventures of Baron Munchausen (7/11/48)

25. Joan of Arc (7/18/48)
26. The Last of the Mohicans (7/25/48)
27. Black Arrow (8/1/48)
28. Casey at the Bat (8/8/48)
29. The Hunchback of Notre Dame (8/15/48)
30. Two Years Before the Mast (8/22/48)
31. The Luck of Roaring Camp (8/29/48)
32. A Midsummer Night's Dream (9/5/48)
33. Kidnapped (9/12/48)
34. The Mysterious Island (9/19/48)
35. Ramona (9/26/48)
36. Les Miserables (10/3/48)
37. Tom Sawyer (10/17/48)
38. The Man in the Iron Mask (10/24/48)
39. Frankenstein (11/7/48)
40. The Story of King Arthur (11/14/48)
41. The Swiss Family Robinson (11/21/48)
42. Peter Gynt (11/28/48)
43. The Little Minister (12/5/48)
44. Gullivers' Travels (12/12/48)
45. The Prince and the Pauper (12/19/48)
46. Silver Skates (12/26/48)
47. Typee Canoe and Tyler Too (1/2/49)
48. The Moonstone (1/9/49)

49. Black Beauty (1/16/49)
50. Huckleberry Finn (1/23/49)
51. The Spy (2/27/49)
52. Little Lord Fauntleroy (3/6/49)
53. Red Headed League (3/13/49)
54. Connecticut Yankee (3/20/49)
55. Heidi (3/27/49)
56. Buffalo Bill (4/3/49)
57. The Count of Monte Cristo (4/10/49)
58. Casey at the Bat (4/24/49)
59. Typee Canoe and Tyler Too (4/30/49)

60. Little Women (5/7/49)
61. Toby Tyler at the Circus (5/14/49)
62. Great Expectations (5/21/49)
63. Buffalo Bill (5/28/49)
64. Hoosier Schoolmaster (6/4/49)
65. Around the World in Eighty Days (6/11/49)
66. The Deerslayer (6/18/49)
67. The Tailsman (6/25/49)
68. The Man Without a Country (7/2/49)

Terror by Night

This late-night horror program was short lived, but featured adaptations of classic horror tales by masters of the macabre. At first broadcast, sustaining, over CBS, Sunday evening from 10 to 10:30 pm, EST, as of episode three, the program was broadcast from 10:30 to 11 pm, EST

1. The Phantom Rickshaw [based on the story by Rudyard Kipling] (3/1/36)
2. The Restless Dead (3/8/36)
3. The Bells (3/22/36)
4. The Tell-Tale Heart [based on the short story by Edgar Allan Poe] (3/29/36)

5. Death of a Friend (4/5/36)
6. The Half-Pint Flask (4/12/36)
7. Murder Ghost (4/19/36)
8. The Phantom Coach (5/3/36)
9. Death of a Friend (5/17/36)
10. The Open Door (5/24/36)

Texaco Star Theater

This musical variety program presented a half-hour of music and a half-hour of drama, sponsored by Texaco Gasoline. There are roughly two centers of entertainment: New York and California. It was very expensive and time consuming for a production unit on one coast to fly in an actor from another coast, so programs originating from New York were limited to New York performers, not Hollywood stars (unless that Hollywood star happened to be in New York for a few weeks for a stage performance). Likewise, programs originating from California were handicapped with West Coast performers. So Texaco executives came up with a very creative way to provide the listeners both, allowing almost anyone to appear on the program. The first thirty minutes were devoted to music and variety originating from Hollywood, and then, via remote pickup, the second thirty minutes were staged from New York.

The logs below consist of the dramas presented during the second half of the hour-long variety series, with full titles and guests listed. Lee Engle was the orchestra leader. Larry Elliott was the announcer. A. Stanford was the director. Adolph Menjou was the first master of ceremonies, replaced by John Barrymore on November 9, 1938. Eddie Cantor was emcee for the broadcast of January 18, 1939, with Ken Murray beginning January 25, 1939. John Barrymore returned as emcee beginning February 15, 1939, and here he remained until the end of the series. The dramas were broadcast over CBS, Wednesday evenings from 9:30 to 10 pm, EST. Beginning September 13, 1939, the dramas were broadcast Wednesday from 9 to 9:30 pm and beginning March 27, 1940, Saturday from 9:20 to 10 pm.

The premiere broadcast was an original written by Arch Oboler; it won an award for best original drama of 1938. Episode eight was written by Thornton Wilder. Alexander Woollcott was made special guest for three consecutive weeks in June of 1939, preempting dramas until afterwards. Maxwell Anderson's "Valley Forge" was broadcast in September of 1939. Walter Hampden starred in "The Goose Hangs High," a role he was respectfully recognized for. Ladislaus Fodor's "Church Mouse" featured Louis Calhern and Ruth Gordon.

1. Alter Ego (10/5/38; Bette Davis)
2. The Jest (10/12/38; John Barrymore and Noah Beery)
3. Romance (10/19/38; Miriam Hopkins)
4. Imitation of Glory (10/26/38; Vera Teasdale)
5. Happy Ending (11/2/38; John Barrymore)
6. Out of Thin Soil (11/9/38; Dead End Kids)
7. A Monument of Love (11/16/38; Fay Bainter)
8. Happy Journey to Trenton / Camden (11/23/38; Spring Byington)
9. Lend Me Your Eyes (11/30/38; Andrea Leeds and Adolph Menjou)
10. Your Honor (12/7/38; Edgar Barrier and John Barrymore)
11. Twilight Shore (12/14/38; Olivia de Havilland)
12. Chanson De Noel (12/21/38; Frances Dee and Adolph Menjou)
13. Each Wish of My Heart (12/28/38; Mary Astor)
14. Last Frontier (1/4/39; John Barrymore and Gail Patrick)
15. Stronger Man (1/11/39; John Barrymore and Basil Rathbone)
16. Rain on the Roof (1/18/39; J. Donald Wilson)
17. Ventriloquist (1/25/39; Reginald Gardner)
18. Manhattan Masquerade (2/1/39; Reginald Denny, Frances Langford, and Herbert Marshall)
19. Page Five, Column Two (2/8/39; Joan Blondell)
20. Twice Around the Clock (2/15/39; George Raft)
21. Breathes There a Man (2/22/39; Madeline Carroll)
22. Processional (3/1/39; Constance Bennett)
23. Doctor Jones (3/8/39; Edward Ellis)
24. Lovely Light (3/15/39; Olympe Branda)
25. Everything Happens to Me (3/22/39; Andy Devine and Ray Milland)
26. On Stage, Please (3/29/39; Allyn Joslyn and Andrea Leeds)
27. Happiness (4/5/39; Jim Ameche and Annabella)
28. Miracle at Lourdes (4/12/39; Constance Bennett)
29. Love Walked Beside Him (4/19/39; John Archer and Alice Eden)
30. Cathleen (4/26/39; Mary Gordon and Virginia Weidler)
31. We Were Such Kids (5/3/39; Tom Brown, Arthur Q. Bryan, and Alfred Shirley)
32. Sheriff Goes a Callin' (5/10/39; Gene Autry, Arthur Q. Bryan, and Frances Langford)

33. Wedding Present [written by Arch Oboler] (5/17/39; Elsa Maxwell and Priscilla Lane)
34. Merely Players (5/24/39; Kitty O'Neal and Basil Rathbone)
35. The Beach Boy (5/31/39; Jon Hall and Frances Langford)
36. Fugitive (6/7/39; Brian Aherne and Helen Mack)
37. [Alexander Woollcott tells about Dionne Quintuplets] (6/14/39)
38. Alexander Woollcott tells about his French poodle and dogs in general] (6/21/39)
39. [Alexander Woollcott tells about Charles Chaplin and more about dogs] (6/28/39)
40. Valley Forge (9/13/39; Philip Merivale)
41. Saturday's Children (9/20/39; Ilka Chase and D. Montgomery)
42. Secrets (9/27/39; Louis Calhearn, Dale Carnegie, and Jane Cowl)
43. Tomorrow and Tomorrow (10/4/39; Peter Lorre, Fredric March and wife)
44. Kind Lady (10/11/39; Grace George, Alice Marble, and Claude Rains)
45. Her Master's Voice (10/18/39; Edward Everett Horton)
46. Green Grows the Lilacs (10/25/39; John Boles)
47. A Bill of Divorcement (11/1/39; Walter Abel, Peter Lord, and Dr. M.S. Taylor)
48. Another Language (11/8/39; Theda Bara, John Beal, and Lillian Gish)
49. Criminal Code (11/15/39; Helen Claire and Burgess Meredith)
50. Candle Light (11/22/39; Glenda Farrell, Elsa Maxwell, and Franchot Tone)
51. Berkeley Square (11/29/39; Maurice Evans and Sylvia Field)
52. Bishop Misbehaves (12/6/39; Walter Connolly)
53. The Patsy (12/13/39; Joan Bennett)
54. The Goose Hangs High (12/20/39; Walter Hampden)
55. The Great Adventure (12/27/39; Elsa Lanchester and Charles Laughton)
56. Romance (1/3/40; Walter Abel, Sue Carol (Mrs. Alan Ladd), and Louise Rainer)
57. The Amazing Dr. Clitterhouse (1/10/40; Ruth Elder and Sir Cedric Hardwicke)
58. Five Star Final (1/17/40; Gene Baker, Walter Huston, and Gene Towne)
59. Farm of Three Echoes (1/24/40; Ethel Barrymore)
60. The Last of Mrs. Cheyney (1/31/40; Ruth Chatterton and Bill Thompson)
61. Kick-In (2/7/40; Margo and Chester Morris)
62. Jezebel (2/14/40; Miriam Hopkins and Edmund Lowe)
63. Church Mouse [written by Ladislaus Fodor] (2/21/40; Louis Calhern and Ruth Gordon)
64. Small Miracle (2/28/40; John Garfield)
65. Third Degree (3/3/40; Gladys George)
66. Juarez and Maximillian (3/10/40; Henry Hull and Edmund O'Brien)
67. Ceiling Zero (3/17/40; N. Carroll and Stanley Ridges)
68. Double Door (3/27/40; Helen Claire and Frances Reed)
69. Alias the Deacon (4/3/40; John Beal, Victor Moore, and Helen Twelvetrees)
70. Payment Deferred (4/10/40; A. Pringle and Claude Rains)
71. Icebound (4/17/40; Helen Hayes and Donald Woods)
72. Petticoat Fever (4/24/40; Mady Christians and Dennis King)
73. Milky Way (5/1/40; Joe E. Brown and Audrey Christie)
74. Let Us Be Gay (5/8/40; Walter Abel and Dorothy Gish)
75. Vinegar Tree (5/15/40; Mary Boland and Harold Vermilyon)
76. Daisy Mayme (5/22/40; Ethel Barrymore, Sabu, and Tom Powers)
77. Front Page (5/29/40; Jack Arthur and Lee Tracy)
78. Under Cover (6/5/40; Claudia Morgan and Conrad Nagel)
79. The First Year (6/12/40; John Craven and D. Dudley)
80. Ethan Frome (6/19/40; Ruth Gordon and Raymond Massey)
81. Broken Dishes (6/26/40; Charles Coburn and Helen Mack)

Textron Theater

One of many radio programs starring Helen Hayes, this one had her playing all of the female leads, leaving the male leads for the guests. This series was sponsored by Textron and broadcast over CBS, Saturday from 7 to 7:30 pm, EST. Textron dropped sponsorship on February 23, 1946, leaving the remaining four broadcasts sustaining. Without a sponsor, the series soon went off the air. Frank Gallop was the announcer. Lester O'Keefe directed. Vladimir Selinsky supplied the music. Episode twenty-three was scripted by Norman Corwin.

1. Madame Curie (9/8/45; Jose Ferrer)
2. To the Ladies (9/15/45; Chester Stratton)
3. Let the Hurricane Roar (9/22/45; Ralph Bellamy)
4. The Late Christopher Bean (9/29/45; Walter Huston)
5. Arrowsmith (10/6/45; Dean Jagger)
6. Chopsticks (10/13/45; Burgess Meredith)
7. Victoria Regina (10/20/45; Tonio Selwart)
8. Intermezzo (10/27/45; Brian Aherne)
9. My Little Boy (11/3/45; Carl Ewald)
10. Shadow Play (11/10/45; Alfred Drake)
11. The Ghost and Mrs. Muir (11/17/45; Maurice Evans)
12. Wuthering Heights (11/24/45; Martin Gabel)
13. Happy Journey to Trenton and Camden (12/1/45; Gene Lockhart)
14. Angel Street (12/8/45; Sir Cedric Hardwicke and Boris Karloff)
15. Miss Rhudabaker Takes Off (12/15/45; Michael O'Shea)
16. Family Portrait (12/22/45; Jose Ferrer)
17. Cinderella (12/29/45; Alfred Drake)
18. Kind Lady 1/5/46; Jose Ferrer)
19. Sobbin' Women (1/12/46; John Morley)
20. A Doll's House (1/19/46; Otto Kruger)
21. Run, Gabriel, Run (1/26/46; Wendell Corey)
22. Jane Eyre (2/2/46; Martin Gabel)
23. Ann Rutledge (2/9/46; John Morley)
24. My Little Boy (2/16/46; Donald Devlin)
25. Dick Swiveller and the Marchioness (2/23/46; Tom Helmer)
26. Romeo and Juliet (3/2/46; Maurice Evans)
27. Another Language (3/9/46)
28. Siren Song From Baltimore (3/16/46)
29. Mary of Scotland (3/23/46)

Theater of Romance

Previously titled *Romance*, the title was changed because the sponsors, Colgate, Palmolive and Halo Shampoo, wanted more than just a simple "romance." It was broadcast from New York until September 4, 1945, when the first episode premiered from Hollywood. Then the ratings skyrocketed. Arnold Moss was the host for the New York broadcasts, over CBS, Tuesdays from 8:30 to 9 pm, EST. Beginning October 2, 1946, *Romance* went back sustaining, and so CBS moved the program to Wednesdays from 5:30 to 6 pm, EST.

1. Good-bye, Mr. Chips (7/4/44; Karl Swenson and Gertrude Warner)
2. My Man Godfrey (7/11/44; Peggy Conklin and Peter Donald)
3. Stage Door (7/18/44; Joan Alexander, Joan Banks, Dick Kollmar, and Leslie Woods)
4. Having a Wonderful Time (7/25/44)
5. The Barker (8/1/44; Eric Dressler, Elspeth Eric, and Leon Janney)
6. Lady Hamilton (8/8/44; Peter Donald, Alfred Shirley, Gertrude Warner, and Joan Westmore)
7. A Star Is Born (8/15/44)
8. There's Always Juliet (8/22/44)
9. Pride and Prejudice (8/29/44; Myron McCormick)
10. Dark Victory (9/5/44)
11. Philadelphia Story (9/12/44)
12. Elizabeth Barrett and Robert Browning (9/19/44)
13. Accent on Youth (9/26/44)
14. Death Takes a Holiday (10/3/44; Raymond Edward Johnson)
15. Excess Baggage (10/10/44)
16. Waterloo Bridge (10/17/44)
17. Let Us Be Gay (10/24/44; Richard Kollmar)
18. The Last of Mrs. Cheyney (10/31/44; Mary Astor)
19. Soldier's Wife (11/14/44; Martha Scott)
20. Bachelor Mother (11/21/44; Shirley Booth)
21. Intermezzo (11/28/44; Ralph Bellamy and Martha Falconer)
22. Rendezvous at Mayerling (12/5/44; Geraldine Fitzgerald and Karl Swenson)
23. No Time for Comedy (12/12/44)
24. Casablanca (12/19/44; Victor Jory, Mercedes McCambridge, Santos Ortega, and Dooley Wilson)
25. The Messiah (12/26/44)
26. It Happened Tomorrow (1/2/45; Joan Allison, Ralph Bellamy, Frank Readick, and Edgar Stehli)
27. The Letter (1/9/45; Judith Evelyn)
28. The Dark Angel (1/16/45; Miriam Hopkins)
29. Ball of Fire (1/23/45; Shirley Booth and Shirley Smith)
30. Shining Hour (1/30/45; Mary Astor)
31. Lost Horizon (2/6/45; Paul Lukas, Edgar Stelhi, and Gertrude Warner)
32. Golden Boy (2/13/45; Claudia Morgan)
33. Destry Rides Again (2/20/45; Claire Trevor)
34. Springtime for Henry (2/27/45; Victor Moore)
35. The Man Who Came to Dinner (3/6/45; Richard Kollmar, Vicki Vola, and Clifton Webb)
36. Silver Chord (3/13/45; Gertrude Warner)
37. The Citadel (3/20/45; Claude Rains and Gertrude Warner)
38. Enchanted Cottage (3/27/45; Walter Abel)
39. Saturday's Children (4/3/45; Bonita Granville)
40. The Blue Danube (4/10/45; Martha Scott and Karl Swenson)
41. Penny Serenade (4/17/45; Ralph Bellamy)
42. Burlesque (4/24/45; Shirley Booth)
43. My Man Godfrey (5/1/45; Clifton Webb)
44. Interference (5/8/45; Helmut Dantine)
45. Call of the Siren (5/15/45; Sonny Tufts)
46. The White Cliffs (5/22/45; Constance Cummings and Karl Swenson)
47. Jezebel (5/29/45; Anne Baxter)
48. Winterset (6/5/45; Margo)
49. The Valiant (6/12/45; Ed Begley, Lloyd Nolan, and Ann Sheppard)
50. Love Is News (6/19/45; Dane Clark and Faye Emerson)
51. The Informer (6/26/45; Ed Begley, Frank Lovejoy, James Monks, and Will Smith)
52. Man Without a Country (7/3/45; John Hodiak)
53. Anne of Green Gables (7/10/45; Peggy Ann Gardner)
54. Suspicion (7/17/45; Judith Evelyn and Anthony Quinn)
55. Bringing Up Baby (7/24/45; Joan Alexander and Michael O'Shea)
56. Made for Each Other (7/31/45; Dane Clark)
57. My Sister Eileen (8/7/45; Shirley Booth and Judy Holiday)

58. Miracle in the Rain (8/14/45; Larry Haines)
59. Heaven Can Wait (8/21/45; Karl Swenson and Betty Winkler)
60. Mary, Queen of Scots (8/28/45; Judith Evelyn)
61. Seventh Heaven (9/4/45; Van Johnson and Susan Peters)
62. Conflict (9/11/45; Humphrey Bogart)
63. One Life to Lose (9/18/45; Joseph Cotten)
64. Hired Wife (9/25/45; Loretta Young)
65. Vivacious Lady (10/2/45; Lurene Tuttle and Robert Walker)
66. Angel Street (10/9/45; Anne Baxter, Sir Cedric Hardwicke, and Vincent Price)
67. Reverie (10/16/45; Ronald Colman and Lurene Tuttle)
68. 42nd Street (10/23/45; Robert Alda and Janis Paige)
69. Dust Be My Destiny (10/30/45; John Garfield and Cathy Lewis)
70. To Mary with Love (11/6/45; Michael Douglas)
71. Casanova Brown (11/13/45; Henry Fonda)
72. No Time for Comedy (11/20/45; Lou Merrill and James Stewart)
73. Penny Serenade (11/27/45; Cathy Lewis, Gerald Mohr, and Robert Walker)
74. Magnificent Obsession (12/4/45; Cathy Lewis, Earle Ross, Robert Taylor, and Lurene Tuttle)
75. Love Affair (12/11/45; Van Johnson, Lou Merrill, and Susan Peters)
76. One Way Passage (12/18/45; Joan Bennett and Humphrey Bogart)
77. The Messiah (12/25/45; Edward Arnold, Harris Brinn, and Jack McCarthy)
78. Intermezzo (1/1/46; Gregory Peck)
79. Corsican Brothers (1/8/46; Douglas Fairbanks, Jr.)
80. Ghost Goes West (1/15/46; Cary Grant and Cathy Lewis)
81. Kid Galahad (1/22/46; Jack McCarthy, Wayne Morris, and Claire Trevor)
82. Cradle Song (1/29/46; Earle Ross and Shirley Temple)
83. Gentleman Jim (2/5/46; Jim Bacus, Errol Flynn, and Joan Lorring)
84. Death Takes a Holiday (2/12/46; Alan Ladd, Cathy Lewis, and Lou Merrill)
85. The Uninvited (2/19/46; Ray Milland)
86. Enchanted Cottage (2/26/46; Herbert Marshall and Robert Young)
87. Random Harvest (3/5/46; Don Ameche and Lurene Tuttle)
88. Next Time We Love (3/12/46; Joan Blondell, Howard Duff, Gerald Mohr, and Lou Merrill)
89. The Hard Way (3/19/46; Robert Alda and Ida Lupino)
90. Woman in the Window (3/26/46; Cathy Lewis, Elliott Lewis, and Edward G. Robinson)
91. The Virginian (4/2/46; Wayne Morris)
92. Jamaica Inn (4/9/46; Louise Albritton)
93. Glass Key (4/16/46; Richard Conte)
94. Wait for Me, Darling (4/23/46; Claudia Morgan)
95. Shadow of a Doubt (4/30/46; Brian Donlevy)
96. Fifth Ave. Girl (5/7/46; Lucille Ball)
97. Blood on the Sun (5/14/46; James Cagney)
98. In Name Only (5/21/46; Shirley Booth)
99. Don't Ever Love Me (5/28/46; Jan Miner)
100. June Moon (6/4/46; Eddie Bracken)
101. There's Always Juliet (6/11/46; Gertrude Warner)
102. And Now Good-bye (6/18/46; Brian Aherne)
103. A Gentleman of the Press (6/25/46; Peter Lawford)
104. Tovarich (7/2/46; Mischa Auer)
105. Trial of Mary Dugan (7/9/46; Louise Albritton)
106. The Kind Lady (7/16/46; Mady Christians)
107. The Petrified Forest (7/23/46; Robert Alda)
108. Curtain Call (7/30/46; Vivien Blaine)
109. Morning Glory (8/6/46; Diana Lynn)

*Theater of Stars**

Broadcast over CBS, Sunday evenings from 6 to 6:30 pm, EST, originating from Hollywood, this program featured movie stars in original radio dramas, with a supporting cast including John Dehner, William Conrad, and Jeanette Nolan. Joan Banks guested in "The Remarkable Talent of Egbert Haw" with her real-life husband Frank Lovejoy.

1. The Guardsman (2/22/53; Edgar Barrier, John Dehner, Jeanette Nolan, and Joan Fontaine)
2. The Mango Tree (3/1/53; Joan Banks, Joseph Cotten, and Lawrence Dobkin)
3. Mail Order Bride (3/8/53; Parley Baer, Jeanne Bates, Robert Taylor, and Will Wright)
4. The Token (3/15/53; Dana Andrews, Georgia Ellis, and Theodore Von Eltz)
5. Impresario (3/22/53; Fay Baker, Don Diamond, Georgia Ellis, and Vincent Price)
6. Spring Thaw (3/29/53; Lillian Buyeff, MacDonald Carey, William Conrad, and Lawrence Dobkin)
7. Plough and Candle (4/5/53; Anne Baxter, Jack Kruschen, and Ralph Moody)
8. The New Man (4/12/53; Parley Baer, Donna Hanor, and Ronald Reagan)
9. Taos Incident (4/19/53; Dick Beals, John Dehner, Jeanette Nolan, and Claire Trevor)
10. The Long Run (4/26/53; Dan Dailey, John Dehner, Lawrence Dobkin, and Georgia Ellis)
11. Let There Be Honor (5/3/53; Parley Baer, John Dehner, Jeanette Nolan, and Ann Blyth)
12. The Remarkable Talent of Egbert Haw (5/10/53; Joan Banks, William Conrad, John Dehner, Byron Kane, Jack Kruschen, Frank Lovejoy, Lee Millar, and Jay Novello)
13. The Apple Tree (5/17/53; Georgia Ellis, Van Heflin, Ellen Morgan, and Ben Wright)

Theater Seminar

Broadcast from New York, 3 to 4 pm, EST, this series featured stage performers and directors, who talked about the importance of Shakespeare and what the plays mean to them.

*Compiled by Chris Lembesis.

1. Acting Shakespeare (9/6/53; Eva Le Gallienne)
2. Classic Revival of Shakespeare in America (9/13/53; Lawrence Langner)
3. Producing and Directing Shakespeare (9/20/53)
4. Understanding Shakespeare (9/27/53; Teresa Helburn)
5. Shakespeare, Master Craftsman (10/4/53; Maurice Evans)
6. The Genius of Shakespeare (10/11/53; Margaret Webster)
7. Direction: Analysis of the Script (10/18/53; Howard Lindsay)
8. The Director and the Actor (10/25/53; Sidney Kingsley)
9. Direction: Music (11/1/53; Mary Hunter)
10. Direction in the Round (11/8/53)

These Are the Men

A series of thirty-minute nationwide broadcasts telling the amazing stories of American military leaders who were currently winning the war, the broadcasts were presented to "give you a dramatic picture of the men who are making history." Sponsored by the Parker Watch Company and dedicated to the U.S. Treasury Department as part of the Sixth War Loan Drive, which was currently in production. The series was broadcast over NBC, Saturday afternoons from 2 to 3 pm, EST. Frank Sinatra made a special guest appearance at the end of the premiere broadcast in order to urge the listeners to "buy those bonds!"

1. President Roosevelt (12/2/44; Bill Adams)
2. General George C. Marshall (12/9/44)
3. General Dwight Eisenhower (12/16/44)
4. General Henry H. Arnold (12/23/44)
5. Admiral William F. Halsey (12/30/44)
6. Lt. General Jonathan M. Wainwright (1/6/45)
7. Admiral Ernest J. King (1/13/45)
8. General Douglas MacArthur (1/20/45)
9. Lt. General Alexander A. Vandegrift (1/27/45; Richard Arlen)
10. Admiral Chester W. Nimitz (2/3/45; Jack Benny)
11. General George F. Patton (2/10/45; Miriam Hopkins)
12. Brave Men (2/17/45)

This Is Hollywood

Hedda Hopper was the first gossip columnist to mention Norma Jean Dougherty (Marilyn Monroe) in upcoming films. Hopper and Joan Fontaine almost came to blows once at the Brown Derby. Gregory Peck had his film career launched due to Hopper's compliments in a revue. Hedda Hopper was one of the two most popular Hollywood columnists (Louella Parsons was the other) who not only had her own syndicated newspaper column, but her own radio series as well. Hopper began her radio career — believe it or not — as an actress on the NBC daytime serial *Brenthouse*. After appearing as a guest on a few radio series and announcing the latest Hollywood gossip, Hedda Hopper had her own radio program, first as a three-a-week, fifteen-minute series for Sunkist, and later for Armour and Company. By October of 1946, Hedda Hopper began hosting *This Is Hollywood*, a weekly thirty-minute radio series that presented dramatic sketches, adaptations of movies that were released within the past two years, with stars from the original films whenever possible. Ann Todd reprised her film role in the premiere broadcast, entitled "The Seventh Veil." Burt Lancaster and Edmund O'Brien reprised their film roles in "The Killers," as did Rex Harrison and Lilli Palmer in "Notorious Gentleman." Episode twenty-one was broadcast not from Hollywood, but from Salt Lake City, Utah. Ida Lupino subbed for Margaret Lockwood, who was originally scheduled to appear in "Bedelia."

After each drama, Hedda Hopper would give the latest scoop on what Hollywood star was sick, what director was planning to film what popular novel, who hit who at so-and-so's party, and other juicy gossip. The series was produced and directed by Frank Woodruff. The scripts (adaptations) were written by Bill Hampton. Adolph Deutsch supplied the music, and Bernard Dudley was the announcer. Proctor and Gamble sponsored the series, which was broadcast over CBS, Saturday evenings from 10:15 to 10:45 pm, EST, and 10 pm beginning April 26th. Hopper introduced each drama as well. Supporting cast included Gerald Mohr, Ed Begley, Jack Webb, and Roland Morris.

1. The Seventh Veil (10/5/46; Ray Milland and Ann Todd)
2. Angel on My Shoulder (10/12/46; Anne Baxter, Otto Kruger, and Paul Muni)
3. Canyon Passage (10/19/46; Susan Hayward and John Hodiak)
4. Lover Come Back (10/26/46; Louise Allbritton and George Brent)
5. Rendezvous with Annie (11/2/46; Eddie Albert and Marsha Hunt)
6. The Chase (11/9/46; Robert Cummings and Michele Morgan)
7. Bachelor's Daughters (11/16/46; Adolphe Menjou)
8. Scandal in Paris (11/23/46; David Niven and Akim Tamiroff)
9. Notorious Gentleman (11/30/46; Rex Harrison and Lilli Palmer)
10. The Stranger (12/7/46; Ruth Hussey and Edward G. Robinson)
11. So Goes My Love (12/14/46; Don Ameche and Myrna Loy)
12. White Tie and Tails (12/21/46; William Bendix and Dan Duryea)
13. Along Came Jones (12/28/46; Eddie Albert and Janet Blair)
14. The Egg and I (1/4/47; Claudette Colbert and Fred MacMurray)
15. Dark Mirror (1/11/47; Lew Ayres and Olivia deHavilland)
16. Magnificent Doll (1/18/47; Ginger Rogers)
17. Mr. Ace (1/25/47; George Raft and Sylvia Sydney)
18. Song of the South (2/1/47; James Baskett)
19. Wicked Lady (2/8/47; Brian Aherne and Joan Lorring)
20. The Spiral Staircase (2/15/47; George Brent and Ann Todd)
21. Ramrod (2/22/47; Veronica Lake and Joel McCrea)
22. Temptation (3/1/47; Merle Oberon and Edmund O'Brien)
23. Lady Love (3/8/47; Barbara Hale and Robert Young)
24. The Best Years of Our Lives (3/15/47; Dana Andrews and Harold Russell)
25. Kid from Brooklyn (3/22/47; Danny Kaye and Virginia Mayo)
26. Sinbad the Sailor (3/29/47; Douglas Fairbanks, Jr. and Maureen O'Hara)
27. Angel and the Bad Man (4/5/47; John Wayne)

28. The Strange Love of Martha Ivers (4/12/47; Van Heflin and Ida Lupino)
29. The Killers (4/19/47; Burt Lancaster and Edmund O'Brien)
30. The Private Affairs of Bel Ami (4/26/47; Ann Dvorak, Douglas Fairbanks, Jr., and Michele Morgan)
31. Centennial Summer (5/3/47; Virginia Bruce and Mark Stevens)
32. The Adventuress (5/10/47; Richard Greene and Maureen O'Sullivan)
33. Stairway to Heaven (5/17/47; Kim Hunter, David Niven, and Vincent Price)
34. The Magnificent Obsession (5/24/47; Lew Ayers and Susan Hayward)
35. Bedelia (5/31/47; Ida Lupino)
36. Fun on a Weekend (6/7/47; Eddie Bracken and Priscilla Lane)
37. That's My Man (6/14/47; Don Ameche and Catherine McLeod)
38. Mayerling (6/21/47; Charles Boyer and Merle Oberon)
39. Margie (6/28/47; Jeanne Crain and Alan Young)

This Is My Best*

Sponsored by Schenley Industries (Cresta Blanca Wines), this program presented Hollywood stars in flawless performances of top class dramas. Homer Fickett produced. Dave Titus directed. John McIntire was the announcer, and the writers included Norman Corwin, Robert Tallman, and Whit Burnett. Stories by James Thurber, John Steinbeck, Thorton Wilder, Robert Louis Stevenson, Joseph Conrad, Damon Runyon and Ring Lardner were adapted for the program. Broadcast over CBS, Tuesday evenings from 9:30 to 10 pm, EST. Beginning September 18, 1945, Orson Welles began producing and directing. Dane Clark produced the remaining run, beginning in May of 1946.

Edward Arnold was host for the first few months of the series. The Broadway cast of "Porgy and Bess" starred in episode three. Frank Morgan was scheduled to star in "Sleeping Beauty" on May 8, 1945, but the program was pre-empted; it was broadcast two weeks later. Rita Hayworth, real-life wife of Orson Welles, was featured in "Don't Catch Me." Hedda Hopper guested in "The Tin Crown" in February of 1946.

1. Hollywood Preview (9/5/44; Edward Arnold)
2. Tell Me a Love Story (9/12/44)
3. Porgy and Bess (9/19/44)
4. Leader of the People (9/26/44; Walter Brennan)
5. The Sea Gull (10/3/44)
6. Now I Lay Me Down to Sleep (10/10/44)
7. This Is the One (10/17/44)
8. Heaven's My Destination (10/24/44; Van Johnson)
9. Brighton Rock (10/31/44; Louis Hayward and Ida Lupino)
10. Career in C Major (11/14/44; Allan Jones)
11. Around the World in Eighty Days (11/21/44; Orson Welles)
12. Romance of Rosy Ridge (11/28/44; Robert Cummings)
13. Princess O'Hara (12/5/44; Lurene Tuttle)

*Compiled by Chris Lembesis.

14. Miracle in the Rain (12/12/44; Dorothy McGuire)
15. The Plot to Over-Throw Christmas (12/19/44; Ray Collins and Orson Welles)
16. The Secret Life of Walter Mitty (12/26/44; Robert Benchley)
17. The Sobbin Women (1/2/45; Paulette Goddard)
18. Harold Peavey's Fast Cow (1/9/45; Jack Carson and Stuart Erwin)
19. Let There Be Honor (1/16/45; Virginia Bruce and John Hodiak)
20. Storm (1/23/45; Burgess Meredith)
21. Jupiter Laughs (1/30/45; Gregory Peck)
22. The Hasty Heart (2/6/45; Fred Mac-Murray)
23. City of Illusion (2/13/45; Thomas Mitchell)
24. Biography (2/20/45; Rosaland Russell)
25. Down the Bayous (2/27/45; Ellen Rains)
26. Mdselle Irene, the Great (3/6/45; Ed Gardner)
27. The Heart of Darkness (3/13/45; Orson Welles)
28. Miss Dilly Says "No" (3/20/45; Ann Sothern)
29. Snow White and the Seven Dwarfs (3/27/45; Jeanette Nolan and Jane Powell)
30. Number One (4/3/45; Orson Welles)
31. Master of Ballantrae (4/10/45; Ray Collins, Agnes Moorehead, and Orson Welles)
32. Don't Catch Me (4/17/45; Rita Hayworth and Orson Welles)
33. Anything Can Happen (4/24/45; Orson Welles)
34. The Snow Goose (5/1/45; Herbert Marshall)
35. The Man Who Came to Dinner (5/15/45; Monty Woolley)
36. Sleeping Beauty (5/22/45; Frank Morgan)
37. Please, Charlie (5/29/45; Jack Benny and Keenan Wynn)
38. Turnips Blood (9/18/45; Herbert Marshall)
39. Coffee with Dorothy (9/25/45; George Murphy)
40. Hurry Kane (10/2/45; Joe E. Brown)
41. Guilded Pheasant (10/9/45; Sylvia Sydney)
42. Mr. Bisbee's Princess (10/16/45; Charlie Ruggles)
43. All the World Over (10/23/45; Nancy Kelly)
44. Venus Didn't Diet (10/30/45; Allan Joslyn and Brenda Joyce)
45. Passenger to Bali (11/6/45; Charles Laughton)
46. Col. Paxton and the Haunted Horse (11/13/45; Ray Collins and Agnes Moorehead)
47. This Is Violet (11/20/45; James Dunn and Ava Gardner)
48. Perfect Plan (11/27/45; Robert Walker and Keenan Wynn)
49. Mr. and Mrs. Cugart (12/4/45; Robert Young)
50. Can't Have Cake and Eat It (12/11/45; Nancy Colman)
51. The Night Before Christmas (12/18/45; Dick Powell)
52. Twenty-Two Years to Christmas (12/25/45; Virginia Bruce)
53. International Combustion (1/1/46; Keenan Wynn)
54. The Pink Hussar (1/8/46; Michael Chekhov)
55. Beautiful Pretense (1/15/46; Claire Trevor)
56. Park Avenue Blues (1/22/46; Virginia Mayo)
57. Cast the First Stone (1/29/46; Dick Foran)
58. The Tin Crown (2/5/46; Robert Alda and Hedda Hopper)
59. Jeff Raleigh's Piano Solo (2/12/46; Chester Morris and Gale Page)
60. Sitting Pretty (2/19/46; Garry Moore)
61. Blueprint for Happiness (2/26/46; Walter Brennan and June Lockhart)
62. Birdie, Birdie, Birdie, Birdie (3/5/46; William Bendix)
63. The Gentleman Dressed in Newspaper (3/12/46; Lee Bowman)
64. For Always (3/19/46; William Blythe)
65. That Man Is Here Again (3/26/46; Barry Sullivan)
66. Mr. Onion (4/2/46; Geraldine Fitzgerald)
67. The Way to the Heart (4/9/46; Conrad Nagel)
68. Outside Eden (4/16/46; Robert Young)
69. Wait Till the Sun Shines Kelly (4/23/46; Eddie Albert)

70. Love Life of Miss Stoneygate (4/30/46; Vera Vague)
71. The Pond (5/7/46; Ida Lupino)
72. Tugboat Annie Sails Again (5/14/46; Ray Collins)
73. She Left Her Flat (5/21/46; Joan Blondell)
74. The Furious Bride (5/28/46; John Lund)

This Is War

This thirteen-episode series, produced, directed, and written by Norman Corwin, was broadcast over all networks, documenting the forces of the United States during the war. Corwin directed all but one of the broadcasts (episode eight) and wrote many. Other writers included William N. Robson, Maxwell Anderson, Stephen Vincent Benét, George Faulkner, and Ronald MacDougall. Johnny Green, Frank Black, Tom Bennett, Donald Vorhees, Lyn Murray and Alexander Semmler supplied the music. Lt. Robert Montgomery narrated the first episode. Clifton Fadiman narrated episode nine. The broadcasts originated from New York, sustaining, Saturday evenings from 7 to 7:30 pm, EST.

1. This Is War (2/14/42; Joe di Santis, Theodore Goetz, House Jameson, Ted Jewett, Gerald Keane, Berry Kroeger, Archibald MacLeish, Ed Mayehoff, Robert Montgomery, Edward Racquello, Stefan Schnabel, the Almanac Singers, and Lilli Valenti)
2. White House and the War (2/21/42; Paul Muni)
3. Your Navy (2/28/42; Douglas Fairbanks, Jr. and Fredric March)
4. Your Army [written by Stephen Vincent Benet] (3/7/42; Tyrone Power)
5. The United Nations [written by George Faulkner] (3/14/42; Thomas Mitchell)
6. You're on Your Own (3/21/42; Claude Rains and Everett Sloane)
7. It's in the Works (3/28/42; Joan Banks, Peter Goo Chong, John Garfield, Henry Hull, Katherine Locke, Frank Lovejoy, Ed Mayehoff, Norman Ober, Jack Smart, Hester Sondergaard, Paul Stewart, and Martin Wolfson)
8. Your Air Force (4/4/42; Frank Albertson and James Stewart)
9. The Enemy (4/11/42; Clifton Fadiman)
10. Concerning Axis Propaganda (4/18/42; Donald Crisp)
11. Smith Against the Axis (4/25/42; James Cagney)
12. To the Young (5/2/42; Joseph Julian)
13. Yours Received and Contents Noted (5/9/42; Raymond Massey)

Time for Love

If you have never heard the great Marlene Dietrich sing "Où Vont les Fleurs" ("Where Have All the Flowers Gone?"), you don't know what you are missing. Those who had the opportunity to hear her over the radio during the forties and fifties are to be envied. Dietrich starred in *Time for Love*, as Dianne La Volte, a fictional crusader who fought for law and order. Some consider this series to be a spinoff of her previous radio program *Cafe Istanbul*, but sadly, no recordings of *Cafe* exist to date, leaving us only what was documented in newspapers and magazines to recollect what might have been great performances.

Robert Readick costarred with Dietrich, and the entire series was broadcast on CBS. The series, lacking a sponsor when it premiered, broadcast on Thursday evenings from 9 to 9:30 pm, EST. Beginning in September of 1953, Jurgen's Lotion signed up as a sponsor, and the series moved ahead, now 9:30 to 10 pm. Lee Vines was the announcer. Murray Burnett was the producer and director, replaced by Ernest Ricca beginning February 11, 1954.

1. The Meeting in Venice (1/15/53)
2. The Reunion in Paris (1/22/53)
3. The Lady and the Bullfighter (1/29/53)
4. Monte Carlo (2/5/53)
5. The Jewel Robbery (2/12/53)
6. The Adventure in the Alps (2/19/53)
7. The Neapolitan Interlude (2/26/53)
8. Cap Ferrat (3/5/53)
9. Vienna (3/12/53)
10. A Chapter in Singapore (3/19/53)
11. Rio de Janeiro (3/26/53)
12. Cairo (4/2/53)
13. Countess von Linden (4/9/53)
14. Flight to Nowhere (4/16/53)
15. -----(4/23/53)
16. The Carnation from Cadiz (4/30/53)
17. The Fur Coat (5/7/53)
18. Mill of the Gods (5/14/53)
19. Masquerade (5/21/53)
20. The Affair in Scotland (5/28/53)
21. Goodbye, Mike (9/3/53)
22. The Marrakech Mirage (9/10/53)
23. Maharajah (9/17/53)
24. The Episode of the Golden Snake (9/24/53)
25. Incident in Casablanca (10/1/53)
26. -----(10/8/53)
27. A Dangerous Cruise (10/22/53)
28. The Bandit (10/29/53)
29. Reunion in Nice (11/5/53)
30. The Conquest of Fear (11/12/53)
31. Night in Rome (11/19/53)
32. Sound of the Past (11/26/53)
33. The Recollections of Brittany (12/3/53)
34. The Orient Express (12/10/53)
35. The Stradivarius (12/17/53)
36. The Man on the Ferry (12/24/53)
37. Earthquake (12/31/53)
38. Tryst in Trieste (1/7/54)
39. The Lion Tamer (1/14/54)
40. The Mountain (1/21/54)
41. The Scarf (1/28/54)
42. Counterfeit Money (2/4/54)
43. The Trouble in Tanganyika (2/11/54)
44. The Man Who Wanted to Die (2/25/54)
45. Red Herrings (3/4/54)
46. The Hostage (3/11/54)
47. -----(3/18/54)
48. Beauty and the Beast (3/25/54)
49. The Episode in Algiers (4/1/54)
50. A Trap for a Traitor (4/8/54)
51. Ride the White Horses (4/15/54)
52. The Voice of the Dictator (4/22/54)
53. Fall Girl (4/29/54)
54. The Pharaoh's Curse (5/6/54)
55. Russian Roulette (5/13/54)
56. A Holiday in Portugal (5/20/54)
57. You're Dead (5/27/54)

Tish

This series featured adaptations of M. R. Rinehart stories, with Betty Garde in the lead role of Tish. Agnes Moorehead and Anne Elstner later took over the role. Directed by William N. Robson, the music was supplied by R. Starret, and orchestra led by Leith Stevens. The scripts (adaptations) were written by Leo Fontaine,

J. Raymond, A.L. Tyler, and J. Hammil. Beginning January 10, 1938, the series underwent two changes: Larry Menkin became the director, and the scripts became originals. It was broadcast over CBS on Thursdays, 9:30–10 pm, EST, on Wednesdays starting with episode three. The revamped version of this series was broadcast on Monday evenings from 8 to 8:30 pm, EST, beginning January 10, 1938. No relation to the 1932 series of the same name.

1. Like a Wolf in the Fold (10/14/37)
2. Simple Lifers [part one] (10/21/37)
3. Simple Lifers [part two] (11/3/37)
4. Mind Over Motor (11/10/37)
5. Tish Plays the Game (11/17/37)
6. Hijack and the Game (11/24/37)
7. Tish's Spy (12/1/37)
8. The Baby Blimp (12/8/37)
9. My Country Tish of Thee (12/15/37)
10. The Mouse (12/22/37)
11. Tish Goes to Jail (12/29/37)
12. Three Pirates of Penzance (1/5/38)
13. Cave on Thundercloud Mountain (1/10/38)
14. That Awful Night (1/17/38)
15. Tish and the Terrors (1/24/38)
16. Tish's Royal Welcome (1/31/38)
17. Hospital Mystery (2/7/38)
18. People's Choice (2/14/38)
19. A Romany Holiday (2/21/38)
20. Salvage (2/28/38)

To the President

One of a handful produced during the war that were written, produced and directed by Arch Oboler, this series was broadcast sustaining over the Blue Network, Sunday afternoons from 12:30 to 1 pm, EST.

1. The Martin Family (10/18/42)
2. The Story of Joe, Machinist (10/25/42)
3. They Are Hero for Me (11/1/42)
4. Marriage 1942 (11/8/42)
5. About My Mother (11/15/42)
6. Laughter (11/22/42; Gloria Blondell)
7. Miracle in 3B (11/29/42; Bette Davis)
8. The Hero (12/6/42; Harry Carey)
9. My Beloved Relatives (12/13/42; Conrad Veidt)
10. The Special Day (12/20/42; Deanna Durbin)

Tom Corbett, Space Cadet

"This is the age of the conquest of space, 2350 A.D. The world beyond tomorrow."

Based on the Robert A. Heinlein novel *Space Cadet,* this series soon became one of the most popular juvenile science-fiction series during the fifties. *Tom Corbett* began on CBS television, later moving to ABC, under the sponsorship of Kellogg's Pep Cereal. It is not known whose idea it was, but shortly after premiering on ABC television, *Tom Corbett* began a broadcast run over ABC radio, Tuesdays and Thursdays, live from New York, 5:30–6 pm. Drex Hines was the director. Jackson Beck was the announcer. Scripts were by Richard Jessup,

Jack Weinstock, Willie Gilbert, Gilbert Brann, Don Hughes, Elwood Holffman, Hal Rine, Peter Freedman, and Palmer Thompson. Many of the radio shows were adapted from television. Cast: Tom Corbet (Frank Thomas, Jr.), Dr. John Dale (Margaret Garland), Astro (Al Markim), Roger Manning (Jan Merlin), Captain Strong (Edward Bryce), Commander Arkwright (Carter Blake).

1. The Living Crystals of Titan [part one] (1/1/52; Peter Capel)
2. The Living Crystals of Titan [part two] (1/3/52; Peter Capel)
3. Rocket Into Danger [part one] (1/8/52)
4. Rocket Into Danger [part two] (1/10/52)
5. Space Station of Danger [part one] (1/15/52)
6. Space Station of Danger [part two] (1/17/52)
7. Shanghaied on a Deep Spacer [part one] (1/22/52)
8. Shanghaied on a Deep Spacer [part two] (1/24/52)
9. Operation Hide and Seek [part one] (1/29/52; Berry Kroeger)
10. Operation Hide and Seek [part two] (1/31/52; Berry Kroeger)
11. Doomed Cargo [part one] (2/5/52)
12. Doomed Cargo [part two] (2/7/52)
13. Interplanetary Space Tournament [part one] (2/12/52)
14. Interplanetary Space Tournament [part two] (2/14/52)
15. Ice Caves of Pluto [part one] (2/19/52)
16. Ice Caves of Pluto [part two] (2/21/52)
17. Trial in Space [part one] (2/26/52)
18. Trial in Space [part two] (2/28/52)
19. Asteroid of Danger [part one] (3/4/52)
20. Asteroid of Danger [part two] (3/6/52)
21. Giants of Mercury [part one] (3/11/52; Connie Lempke and James Monks)
22. Giants of Mercury [part two] (3/13/52; Connie Lempke and James Monks)
23. Atmosphere of Death [part one] (3/18/52; Peter Cappell, Elspeth Eric, and Maurice Tarplin)
24. Atmosphere of Death [part two] (3/20/52; Peter Cappell, Elspeth Eric, and Maurice Tarplin)
25. Mission of Mercy [part one] (3/25/52; Luis Van Rooten)
26. Mission of Mercy [part two] (3/27/52; Luis Van Rooten)
27. Double Cross in Space [part one] (4/1/52; Paul Ford, Gilbert Mack, and Ian Martin)
28. Double Cross in Space [part two] (4/3/52; Paul Ford, Gilbert Mack, and Ian Martin)
29. Mystery of the Sparkling Meteor [part one] (4/8/52; Sarah Bushel)
30. Mystery of the Sparkling Meteor [part two] (4/10/52; Sarah Bushel)
31. Holiday of Terror [part one] (4/15/52)
32. Holiday of Terror [part two] (4/17/52)
33. Riddle of Astro [part one] (4/22/52)
34. Riddle of Astro [part two] (4/24/52)
35. Escort of Death [part one] (4/29/52)
36. Escort of Death [part two] (5/1/52)
37. Danger in Deep Space [part one] (5/6/52; Luis Van Rooten)
38. Danger in Deep Space [part two] (5/8/52; Luis Van Rooten)
39. Marooned with Death [part one] (5/13/52; Susan Douglas and Ian Martin)
40. Marooned with Death [part two] (5/15/52; Susan Douglas and Ian Martin)
41. Greatest Show in the Universe (5/20/52; Leon Janney and Connie Lempke)
42. Greatest Show in the Universe (5/22/52; Leon Janney and Connie Lempke)
43. Revolt on Prison Rock [part one] (5/27/52; Joseph Ballow, William Keen, and James Monks)

44. Revolt on Prison Rock [part two]
    (5/29/52; Joseph Ballow, William
    Keen, and James Monks)
45. Vultures of Death [part one] (6/3/52;
    Maurice Tarplin)
46. Vultures of Death [part two] (6/5/52;
    Maurice Tarplin)
47. Satellite of Death [part one] (6/10/52;
    Dick Keith and Ian Martin)
48. Satellite of Death [part two] (6/12/52;
    Dick Keith and Ian Martin)
49. Pursuit of Danger [part one]
    (6/17/52; Ivor Francis and Ian Mar-
    tin)
50. Pursuit of Danger [part two]
    (6/19/52; Ivor Francis and Ian Mar-
    tin)
51. A Round Trip to Disaster [part one]
    (6/24/52)
52. A Round Trip to Disaster [part two]
    (6/26/52)

U.N. Workshop Series

This eight-episode series featured the agendas the U.N. was currently working on. Dr. John Stroessinger was the host for this entire series, produced and
sponsored by the United Nations. Mrs. Franklin D. Roosevelt was a featured
guest on the final episode. Syndicated across the country on various stations, in
New York, *Workshop* was heard from 4 to 5 pm, EST.

1. The United Nations and Economic
   Development (5/1/60)
2. Changing Africa: Nationalism vs.
   Colonialism (5/8/60)
3. The United Nations and Problems of
   Germany (5/15/60)
4. The U.S.S.R. and China (5/22/60)
5. The United Nations and the Middle
   East (5/29/60)
6. The Dilemma of Disarmament
   (6/5/60)
7. Problems of the United States in the
   United Nations (6/12/60)
8. Human Rights (6/19/60)

UNESCO at Work

David Thompson narrating, this series, documenting the work of UNESCO
in recent years, was broadcast over WNYC in New York from 9 to 9:30 pm, EST.

1. The Streams in the Desert (5/15/55)
2. UNESCO in the African Bush
   (5/22/55)
3. The Study of Earthquakes (5/29/55)

The United States Steel Hour

Previously entitled *The Theater Guild Dramas* and *Theater Guild on the Air*,
this program changed its name to *The United States Steel Hour* when the United
States Steel Corporation began sponsoring the program. For a full hour each

week, top stars of Hollywood and Broadway were featured in dramas ranging from originals to adaptations of novels, stage plays and movies. Most of the broadcasts originated from the Belasco Theater in New York, with a budget so high that the producers were able to fly Hollywood stars from the West Coast to the East to star in these broadcasts. Episode 152 was broadcast on Easter Sunday, an adaptation of Tennessee Williams' "Summer and Smoke," which told the tale of a young girl turning to prostitution. It created a small uproar. For episode 224, RCA joined U.S. Steel in co-sponsoring a special ninety-minute broadcast of William Shakespeare's "Hamlet" with Sir John Gielgud in the lead.

This series was broadcast over ABC on Sunday evenings, until September 11, 1949, when the program moved to NBC. George Kondolf produced and Homer Fickett directed. Harold Levey composed and conducted the music. Norman Brokenshire announced. Armina Marshall was executive producer. Roger Pryor and Elliott Reid were hosts near the end of the run.

1. Wings Over Europe (9/9/45; Burgess Meredith)
2. Jacobowsky and the Colonel (9/16/45; Annabella and Louis Calhern)
3. The Guardsman (9/23/45; Lynn Fontaine and Alfred Lunt)
4. Ah, Wilderness (10/7/45; Walter Huston)
5. Mr. Pim Passes By (10/14/45; Leo G. Carroll and Arlene Francis)
6. Sing Out, Sweet Land (10/21/45; Arthur Godfrey, Burl Ives, and Josh White)
7. At Mrs. Beam's (10/28/45; Paulette Goddard and Burgess Meredith)
8. Storm Over Patsy (11/4/45; Arline MacMahon, Martha Scott, and Richard Widmark)
9. Emperor Jones / Where the Cross Is Made (11/11/45; Boris Karloff and Canada Lee)
10. Pride and Prejudice (11/18/45; Joan Fontaine)
11. Mornings at Seven (11/25/45; Shirley Booth, Stu Erwin, and Arline MacMahon)
12. Elizabeth the Queen (12/2/45; Lynn Fontaine and Alfred Lunt)
13. Ned McCobb's Daughter (12/9/45; Shirley Booth and Alfred Lunt)
14. The Royal Family (12/16/45; Fredric March and Estelle Winwood)
15. Little Women (12/23/45; Katharine Hepburn and Oscar Homolka)
16. Knickerbocker Holiday (12/30/45; Walter Huston)
17. Three Men on a Horse (1/6/46; Shirley Booth, Stu Erwin, and Sam Levene)
18. The Silver Cord (1/13/46; Ralph Bellamy, Ruth Hussey, and Estelle Winwood)
19. Yellow Jack (1/20/46; Walter Abel, Luther Adler, and Alan Baxter)
20. The Front Page (1/27/46; Melvyn Douglas and Michael O'Shea)
21. The Second Man (2/3/46; Peggy Conklin, Jessie Royce Landis, and Alfred Lunt)
22. Prologue to Glory (2/10/46; Ed Begley, Susan Douglas, and Zachary Scott)
23. On Borrowed Time (2/17/46; Walter Huston)
24. Dead End (2/24/46; Alan Baxter, Richard Conte, and Joan Tetzel)
25. The Show-Off (3/3/46; Alfred Lunt)
26. The Barker (3/10/46; Pat O'Brien)
27. The Mask of Kings (3/17/46; Sir Cedric Hardwicke)
28. I Remember Mama (3/24/46; Mady Christians and Oscar Homolka)
29. Strange Interlude [part one] (3/31/46; Walter Abel and Lynn Fontaine)
30. Strange Interlude [part two] (4/7/46; Walter Abel and Lynn Fontaine)

31. Seven Keys to Baldpate (4/14/46; Walter Pidgeon and Martha Scott)
32. The Green Pastures (4/21/46; Hall Johnson Choir, Juano Hernandez, and Richard Huey)
33. Mary of Scotland (4/28/46; Helen Hayes and Helen Menken)
34. Mary, Mary Quite Contrary (5/5/46; Gertrude Lawrence)
35. Payment Deferred (5/12/46; Elsa Lanchester and Charles Laughton)
36. They Knew What They Wanted (5/19/46; Leo Carillo, John Garfield, and June Havoc)
37. Boy Meets Girl (5/26/46; Gene Kelly)
38. Call It a Day (6/2/46; Lynn Fontaine and Alfred Lunt)
39. Angel Street (6/9/46; Leo G. Carroll, Helen Hayes, and Victor Jory)
40. You Can't Take It With You (9/15/46; Kenny Delmar and Josephine Hull)
41. Craig's Wife (9/22/46; Florence Eldridge and Fredric March)
42. Our Town (9/29/46; Dorothy McGuire)
43. Dodsworth (10/6/46; Walter Huston and Jessie Royce Landis)
44. Berkeley Square (10/13/46; Rex Harrison)
45. The Green Goddess (10/20/46; Walter Abel, Ronald Colman, and Anita Louise)
46. Accent on Youth (10/27/46; Basil Rathbone and Jane Wyatt)
47. The Last of Mrs. Cheyney (11/3/46; Gertrude Lawrence)
48. Kind Lady (11/10/46; Lillian Gish and John Loder)
49. The Man Who Came to Dinner (11/17/46; Fred Allen and Sam Levene)
50. Burlesque (11/24/46; June Havoc and Bert Lahr)
51. A Bill of Divorcement (12/1/46; James Mason)
52. Golden Boy (12/8/46; Dana Andrews, June Havoc, and Sam Levene)
53. The Old Maid (12/15/46; Judith Anderson and Helen Menken)
54. Papa Is All (12/22/46; Peggy Conklin, Oscar Homolka, and Aline MacMahon)
55. Broadway (12/29/46; Shirley Booth and James Dunn)
56. The Great Adventure (1/5/47; Lynn Fontaine and Alfred Lunt)
57. The Male Animal (1/12/47; Peggy Conklin, Paul Douglas, and Elliott Nugent)
58. A Doll's House (1/19/47; Dorothy McGuire and Basil Rathbone)
59. Men in White (1/26/47; Marsha Hunt and Burgess Meredith)
60. The Farmer Takes a Wife (2/2/47; Kenny Delmar, William Holden, and Claire Trevor)
61. Abe Lincoln in Illinois (2/9/47; Alan Baxter, Raymond Massey, and Helen Menken)
62. The Time of Your Life (2/16/47; Mary Anderson, Dane Clark, and John Lund)
63. Blithe Spirit (2/23/47; Clifton Webb and Peggy Wood)
64. What Every Woman Knows (3/2/47; Helen Hayes)
65. No Time for Comedy (3/9/47; Florence Eldrige and Fredric March)
66. Gold (3/16/47; Angela Lansbury and Raymond Massey)
67. The First Year (3/23/47; Parker Fennelly, Betty Garde, and Gene Tierney)
68. Ladies in Retirement (3/30/47; Fay Bainter, Mildred Denham, and Estelle Winwood)
69. Still Life (4/6/47; Ingrid Bergman, Sam Wanamaker, and Peggy Wood)
70. The Importance of Being Ernest (4/13/47; Sir John Gielgud and Margaret Rutherford)
71. The Age of Innocence (4/20/47; Arthur Kennedy and Gene Tierney)
72. Escape (4/27/47; George Sanders)
73. The Animal Kingdom (5/4/47; Fred Astaire and Wendy Barrie)
74. Macbeth (5/11/47; Judith Anderson and Maurice Evans)
75. Uncle Harry (5/18/47; Geraldine Fitzgerald and Paul Henreid)
76. Ethan Frome (5/25/47; Mary Anderson, Pauline Ford, and Raymond Massey)
77. Three Men on a Horse (6/1/47;

Shirley Booth, Sam Levene, and David Wayne)

78. A Church Mouse (6/8/47; Pamela Brown and Basil Rathbone)
79. Clarence (6/15/47; Robert Walker)
80. Old Acquaintance (6/22/47; Ilka Chase, Dorothy Gish, and Roger Pryor)
81. Alice, Sit by the Fire (6/29/47; Helen Hayes)
82. One Sunday Afternoon (9/7/47; James Stewart)
83. Kiss and Tell (9/14/47; Dick Van Patten and Elizabeth Taylor)
84. Guest in the House (9/21/47; Walter Abel, Mary Anderson, and Wendy Barrie)
85. Saturday's Children (9/28/47; John Garfield)
86. The Admirable Crichton (10/5/47; June Duprez and Basil Rathbone)
87. Cyrano de Bergerac (10/12/47; Florence Eldridge and Fredric March)
88. Lady in the Dark (10/19/47; Gertrude Lawrence)
89. Apple of His Eye (10/26/47; Walter Huston)
90. The Petrified Forest (11/2/47; Peggy Conklin and Robert Montgomery)
91. Victoria Regina (11/9/47; Helen Hayes)
92. The Shining Hour (11/16/47; Joan Fontaine)
93. The Straw (11/23/47; Mary Anderson and Robert Mitchum)
94. Old English (11/30/47; Charles Laughton)
95. The Wisdom Tooth (12/7/47; Gene Kelly)
96. The Corn Is Green (12/14/47; Helen Hayes)
97. Little Women (12/21/47; Katharine Hepburn and Paul Lukas)
98. Her Master's Voice (12/28/47; Alfred Drake, Arlene Francis, and Betty Garde)
99. The Little Foxes (1/4/48; Thomas Mitchell, Agnes Moorehead, and Zachary Scott)
100. Holiday (1/11/48; Kent Smith and Margaret Sullavan)
101. Three-Cornered Room (1/18/48; Eddie Albert and Joan Caulfield)
102. Is Zat So? (1/25/48; Arlene Francis and Pat O'Brien)
103. Missouri Legend (2/1/48; Mary Anderson, Alfred Drake, and Raymond Massey)
104. Romeo and Juliet (2/8/48; Maurice Evans, Dorothy McGuire, and Florence Reed)
105. Dark Victory (2/15/48; Walter Abel and Madeleine Carroll)
106. The Far-Off Hills (2/22/48; Hume Cronyn, Mildred Natwick, and Jessica Tandy)
107. The Barretts of Wimpole Street (2/29/48; Brian Aherne and Madeleine Carroll)
108. Anna Christie (3/7/48; Oscar Homolka, Dorothy McGuire, and Burgess Meredith)
109. She Loves Me Not (3/14/48; Eddie Albert, Paul Douglas, and Judy Holliday)
110. Grand Hotel (3/21/48; Marlene Dietrich and Ray Milland)
111. Remember the Day (3/28/48; John Conte and Deborah Kerr)
112. The Philadelphia Story (4/4/48; John Conte, James Stewart, and Joan Tetzel)
113. Libel (4/11/48; June Duprez, Walter Hampden, and Michael Redgrave)
114. Anna Karenina (4/18/48; Ingrid Bergman)
115. Laburnam Grove (4/25/48; Charles Laughton)
116. Rebecca (5/2/48; June Duprez, Michael Redgrave, and Flora Robson)
117. The White-Headed Boy (5/9/48; Sara Allgood and Kenny Delmar)
118. Daisy Mayme (5/16/48; Dean Jagger and Ethel Merman)
119. Wednesday's Child (5/23/48; Walter Abel, Arlene Francis, and Ona Munson)
120. Reflected Glory (5/30/48; Audrey Christie and Irene Dunn)
121. A Bell for Adano (9/12/48; Robert Montgomery)
122. For Love or Money (9/19/48; Joan Caulfield and John Loder)
123. That's Gratitude (9/26/48; James Stewart)
124. The Letter (10/3/48; Marlene Dietrich and Walter Pidgeon)

125. Music in the Air (10/10/48; Peter Lawford and Mary Martin)
126. Laura (10/17/48; George Coulouris, June Duprez, and Burt Lancaster)
127. The Wind and the Rain (10/24/48; John Dall, Celeste Holm, and Otto Kruger)
128. Morning Star (10/31/48; Fay Bainter, Kenny Delmar, and Karl Malden)
129. The Criminal Code (11/7/48; Joan Chandler and Pat O'Brien)
130. Valley Forge (11/14/48; George Coulouris, June Duprez, and Claude Rains)
131. The Winslowe Boy (11/21/48; Frank Allenby, Alan Webb, and Valerie White)
132. The Two Mrs. Carrolls (11/28/48; Eddie Albert, MacDonald Carey, and Lilli Palmer)
133. Lovers and Friends (12/5/48; Madeleine Carroll and Walter Pidgeon)
134. Spring Again (12/12/48; Elizabeth Patterson and Monty Woolley)
135. Miss LuLu Bett (12/19/48; Jean Arthur)
136. Rip Van Winkle (12/26/48; Fred Allen)
137. The Game of Love and Death (1/2/49; Paul Henreid, Katharine Hepburn, and Claude Rains)
138. O Mistress Mine (1/9/49; Lynn Fontaine and Alfred Lunt)
139. The Late George Apley (1/16/49; William Eythe, Robert Morley, and Irene Rich)
140. Journey's End (1/23/49; Rex Harrison)
141. The Late Christopher Bean (1/30/49; Irene Dunne and Thomas Mitchell)
142. Beyond the Horizon (2/6/49; John Lund, Beatrice Pearson, and Richard Widmark)
143. Ah, Wilderness! (2/13/49; Walter Huston)
144. Mary of Scotland (2/20/49; Martita Hunt and Deborah Kerr)
145. Payment Deferred (2/27/49; Elsa Lanchester, Charles Laughton, and Jessica Tandy)
146. Interference (3/6/49; June Duprez, Raymond Massey, and Zachary Scott)
147. The Gioconda Smile (3/13/49; Charles Boyer)
148. Yesterday's Magic (3/20/49; Jean Arthur and Robert Morley)
149. June Moon (3/27/49; Eddie Albert, Kenny Delmar, and June Havoc)
150. Camille (4/3/49; Joan Fontaine and Louis Jourdan)
151. The Taming of the Shrew (4/10/49; Burgess Meredith and Joyce Redman)
152. Summer and Smoke (4/17/49; Todd Andrews and Dorothy McGuire)
153. Alien Corn (4/24/49; Bette Davis and Kirk Douglas)
154. The Skin Game (5/1/49; Sir Cedric Hardwicke, Martita Hunt, and Charles Laughton)
155. Of Mice and Men (5/8/49; June Havoc, George Matthews, and Burgess Meredith)
156. Ladies and Gentleman (5/15/49; Van Heflin and Ida Lupino)
157. Flare Path (5/22/49; Ian Hunter, Deborah Kerr, and Peter Lawford)
158. The Perfect Alibi (5/29/49; Boris Karloff and Joan Lorring)
159. John Loves Mary (6/5/49; Ann Blyth and Robert Cummings)
160. Dream Girl (9/11/49; Betty Field and John Lund)
161. Libel (9/18/49; June Duprez and Rex Harrison)
162. The Gentle People (9/25/49; Kenny Delmar, Dan Duryea, and Sam Levene)
163. Counselor-At-Law (10/2/49; James Cagney)
164. Burlesque (10/9/49; Bert Lahr and Ann Sothern)
165. Coquette (10/16/49; Dorothy McGuire and Cornel Wilde)
166. The Thunderbolt (10/23/49; Van Heflin and Celeste Holm)
167. Justice (10/30/49; Hume Cronyn, Robert Donat, and Jessica Tandy)
168. The Traitor (11/6/49; William Eythe, Nina Foch, and Tyrone Power)
169. Still Life (11/13/49; Helen Hayes and David Niven)

170. The Great Adventure (11/20/49; Lynn Fontaine and Alfred Lunt)
171. The Enchanted Cottage (11/27/49; Ray Milland)
172. The Amazing Dr. Clitterhouse (12/4/49; Madeleine Carroll and Basil Rathbone)
173. Street Scene (12/11/49; Shirley Booth, Richard Conte, and Diana Lynn)
174. The Browning Version (12/18/49; Edna Best and Maurice Evans)
175. The Passing of the Third Floor Back (12/25/49; Paulette Goddard and Sir Cedric Hardwicke)
176. While the Sun Shines (1/1/50; Peter Lawford)
177. The Scarlet Pimpernel (1/8/50; Rex Harrison, Lilli Palmer, and Francis L. Sullivan)
178. Another Language (1/15/50; Walter Abel, Richard Basehart, and Helen Hayes)
179. The Willow and I (1/22/50; Mel Ferrer, Beatrice Pearson, and Jane Wyman)
180. Dulcy (1/29/50; Lee Bowman, Celeste Holm, and Franchot Tone)
181. Autumn Crocus (2/5/50; Charles Boyer and Dorothy McGuire)
182. Goodbye Again (2/12/50; Madeleine Carroll, Linda Darnell, and Ezio Pinza)
183. The Druid Circle (2/19/50; Charles Laughton and Burgess Meredith)
184. Heaven Can Wait (2/26/50; Kirk Douglas and Walter Huston)
185. Lady in the Dark (3/5/50; MacDonald Carey, Hume Cronyn, and Gertrude Lawrence)
186. Our Town (3/12/50; Walter Huston and Elizabeth Taylor)
187. There's Always Juliet (3/19/50; Richard Widmark and Teresa Wright)
188. The Milky Way (3/26/50; Shirley Booth and Danny Kaye)
189. All That Money Can Buy (4/2/50; Walter Huston, Martha Scott, and Cornel Wilde)
190. Seventh Heaven (4/9/50; Robert Cummings and Joan Fontaine)
191. Great Expectations (4/16/50; Joan Fontaine, Francis L. Sullivan, and Richard Todd)
192. National Velvet (4/23/50; Peggy Ann Gardner and Mickey Rooney)
193. Double Door (4/30/50; Douglas Fairbanks, Jr. and Geraldine Fitzgerald)
194. Petticoat Fever (5/7/50; Gertrude Lawrence, Walter Pidgeon, and Arthur Treacher)
195. The Trial of Mary Dugan (5/14/50; Tom Drake, Paulette Goddard, and Pat O'Brien)
196. Page Miss Glory (5/21/50; Jack Carson, Betty Hutton, and Ronald Reagan)
197. Minick (5/28/50; Lee Bowman, Arlene Francis, and Sterling Holloway)
198. Call It a Day (6/4/50; Gertrude Lawrence and Franchot Tone)
199. Edward, My Son (9/10/50; Charles Laughton and Rosalind Russell)
200. The Barker (9/17/50; Paul Douglas and Ginger Rogers)
201. There Shall Be No Night (9/24/50; Lynn Fontaine and Alfred Lunt)
202. Brigadoon (10/1/50; Dennis Morgan and Patrice Munsel)
203. Blow Ye Winds (10/8/50; William Holden and Celeste Holm)
204. I Know Where I'm Going (10/15/50; Geraldine Fitzgerald and David Niven)
205. A Farewell to Arms (10/22/50; Joan Fontaine and Humphrey Bogart)
206. Michael and Mary (10/29/50; Joan Fontaine and Herbert Marshall)
207. Alice Adams (11/5/50; Judy Garland and Thomas Mitchell)
208. The Boysey Inheritance (11/12/50; Douglas Fairbanks, Jr. and Angela Lansbury)
209. Dr. Jekyll and Mr. Hyde (11/19/50; Barbara Bel Geddes and Fredric March)
210. Theater (11/26/50; Melvyn Douglas and Gloria Swanson)
211. Carousel (12/3/50; Patrice Munsel and Cornel Wilde)
212. Lottie Dundass (12/10/50; Dorothy McGuire and Jessica Tandy)
213. Boomerang (12/17/50; Kirk Douglas)
214. David Copperfield (12/24/50; Boris Karloff, Cyril Ritchard, and Flora Robson)

215. State Fair (12/31/50; Van Heflin and Gene Lockhart)
216. The Third Man (1/7/51; Joseph Cotten and Signe Hasso)
217. Trilby (1/14/51; Rex Harrison and Teresa Wright)
218. The Fortune Hunter (1/21/51; Jeanne Crain and John Lund)
219. The Morning Glory (1/28/51; Anne Baxter and John Hodiak)
220. Come Back, Little Sheba (2/4/51; Shirley Booth and Gary Cooper)
221. Within the Law (2/11/51; Ginger Rogers and Lee Tracy)
222. Promise (2/18/51; Hume Cronyn, Margaret Phillips, and Gloria Swanson)
223. Father of the Bride (2/25/51; Joan Bennett, Elizabeth Taylor, and Spencer Tracy)
224. Hamlet (3/4/51; Pamela Brown, Sir John Gielgud, and Dorothy McGuire)
225. The Hasty Heart (3/11/51; Richard Greene, John Lund, and Jane Wyatt)
226. Jeannie (3/18/51; Signe Hasso, Margaret Phillips, and Barry Sullivan)
227. A Tale of Two Cities (3/25/51; Douglas Fairbanks, Jr.)
228. The Fallen Idol (4/1/51; Signe Hasso, Jack Hawkins, and Walter Pidgeon)
229. This Side of Paradise (4/8/51; Nina Foch and Richard Widmark)
230. Light Up the Sky (4/15/51; Joan Bennett, Sam Levene, and Thelma Ritter)
231. The First Year (4/22/51; Kathryn Grayson and Richard Widmark)
232. Man in Possession (4/29/51; Rex Harrison and Lilli Palmer)
233. Candida (5/6/51; Katherine Cornell and Alfred Ryder)
234. Craig's Wife (5/13/51; Melvyn Douglas and Rosalind Russell)
235. Ethan Frome (5/20/51; Shirley Booth, Raymond Massey, and Margaret Phillips)
236. Elmer the Great (5/27/51; Paul Douglas)
237. Biography (6/3/51; Burgess Meredith and Rosalind Russell)
238. The Heiress (9/9/51; Betty Field, Basil Rathbone, and Cornel Wilde)
239. The Glass Menagerie (9/16/51; Montgomery Clift and Helen Hayes)
240. This Woman's Business (9/23/51; Nigel Bruce, David Niven, and Margaret Phillips)
241. Main Street (9/30/51; Joseph Cotten and Joan Fontaine)
242. Casanova Brown (10/7/51; Dan Dailey, Kenny Delmar, and Diana Lynn)
243. The Major and the Minor (10/14/51; Joan Fontaine and Ray Milland)
244. Pygmalion (10/21/51; Lynn Fontaine and Alfred Lunt)
245. Skylark (10/28/51; MacDonald Carey and Rosalind Russell)
246. A Foreign Affair (11/4/51; Marlene Dietrich and Richard Widmark)
247. Age of Innocence (11/11/51; Macdonald Carey and Claudette Colbert)
248. Twentieth Century (11/18/51; Claudette Colbert and Gregory Ratoff)
249. Allegro (11/25/51; Kenny Delmar, John Lund, and Jane Powell)
250. Good Housekeeping (12/2/51; Walter Abel and Rosalind Russell)
251. The Lost Weekend (12/9/51; William Holden and Brenda Marshall)
252. Arrowsmith (12/16/51; Tyrone Power and Loretta Young)
253. The Beloved Vagabond (12/23/51; Rex Harrison and Beatrice Pearson)
254. Goodbye, Mr. Chips (12/30/51; Margaret Phillips and Alan Webb)
255. I Know My Love (1/6/52; Lynn Fontaine and Alfred Lunt)
256. Look to the Mountain (1/13/52; Dorothy McGuire and John Ireland)
257. Daisy Mayme (1/20/52; Betty Hutton)
258. The Thief (1/27/52; Roddy McDowall, Dorothy McGuire, and David Niven)
259. The Old Lady Shows Her Medals (2/3/52; Lynn Fontaine)
260. The Traitor (2/10/52; Lauren Bacall and Humphrey Bogart)

261. The Meanest Man in the World (2/17/52; Coleen Gray, Josephine Hull, and James Stewart)
262. Oliver Twist (2/24/52; Boris Karloff, Leueen McGrath, and Basil Rathbone)
263. Portrait in Black (3/2/52; Barbara Stanwyck and Richard Widmark)
264. The Search (3/9/52; Fay Bainter and Montgomery Clift)
265. Love from a Stranger (3/16/52; Edna Best and Ray Milland)
266. Second Threshold (3/23/52; Fredric March and Dorothy McGuire)
267. An Ideal Husband (3/30/52; Rex Harrison and Lilli Palmer)
268. The Silver Whistle (4/6/52; Diana Lynn and James Stewart)
269. Florence Nightingale (4/13/52; Brian Aherne and Katherine Cornell)
270. The Truth About Blayds (4/20/52; Madeleine Carroll)
271. The Sea Wolf (4/27/52; Boris Karloff, Burgess Meredith, and Margaret Phillips)
272. Dear Brutus (5/4/52; Madeleine Carroll, Angela Lansbury, and David Niven)
273. Prologue to Glory (5/11/52; John Lund and Wanda Hendrix)
274. Over Twenty-One (5/18/52; Ruth Gordon and Van Heflin)
275. The Bishop Misbehaves (5/25/52; Vanessa Brown, Josephine Hull, and Charles Laughton)
276. Remember the Day (6/1/52; Macdonald Carey and Helen Hayes)
277. The Wisteria Trees (9/14/52; Joseph Cotten and Helen Hayes)
278. George Washington Slept Here (9/21/52; Kenny Delmar, Van Heflin, and Ann Rutherford)
279. Elmer the Great (9/28/52; Eddie Bracken and Wanda Hendrix)
280. Morning Star (10/5/52; Gertrude Berg and Sylvia Sidney)
281. Tommy (10/12/52; Wally Cox, Kenny Delmar, Wanda Hendrix)
282. The Sea Gull (10/19/52; Viveca Lindfors and John Lund)
283. Hobson's Choice (10/26/52; Madeleine Carroll, Melville Cooper, and Burgess Meredith)
284. Lo and Behold (11/2/52; Ann Blyth, Jeffrey Lynn, and Basil Rathbone)
285. Magnificent Obsession (11/9/52; Mel Ferrer and Rosalind Russell)
286. All About Eve (11/16/52; Tallulah Bankhead)
287. The Winslow Boy (11/23/52; Margaret Phillips, Basil Rathbone, and Alan Webb)
288. Liliom (11/30/52; Karl Malden, Geraldine Page, and Richard Widmark)
289. The Damask Cheek (12/7/52; Kevin McCarthy and Rosalind Russell)
290. The House of Mirth (12/14/52; Joan Fontaine and Franchot Tone)
291. The Pickwick Papers (12/21/52; Melville Cooper, Cyril Ritchard, and Alan Webb)
292. The Unguarded Hour (12/28/52; Nina Foch and Michael Redgrave)
293. State Fair (1/4/53; Van Johnson and Nancy Olson)
294. Jane (1/11/53; Edna Best and Michael Redgrave)
295. Trial by Forgery (1/18/53; Anne Baxter and Joseph Cotten)
296. The Scarlet Letter (1/25/53; Sir Cedric Hardwicke and Dorothy McGuire)
297. Reflected Glory (2/1/53; Macdonald Carey and Bette Davis)
298. Man and Superman (2/8/53; Maurice Evans and Deborah Kerr)
299. Cass Timberlane (2/15/53; Nina Foch and Fredric March)
300. The Show-Off (2/22/53; Paul Douglas and Jan Sterling)
301. O'Halloran's Luck (3/1/53; Gloria De Haven, John Lund, and James Stewart)
302. Vanity Fair (3/8/53; Joan Fontaine)
303. A Square Peg (3/15/53; Thomas Mitchell, Thelma Ritter, and Jane Wyatt)
304. The Old Maid (3/22/53; Betty Field and Nina Foch)
305. The Brass Ring (3/29/53; Melvyn Douglas and Gloria De Haven)
306. Great Expectations (4/5/53; Melville Cooper, Boris Karloff, and Margaret Phillips)
307. The Glass Menagerie (4/12/53; Shirley Booth)

308. The Petrified Forest (4/19/53; Tyrone Power)
309. 1984 (4/26/53; Richard Widmark)
310. Quiet Wedding (5/3/53; John Dall, Jessie Royce Landis, and Diana Lynn)
311. Black Chiffon (5/10/53; Judith Anderson and Burgess Meredith)
312. The Importance of Being Ernest (5/17/53; Rex Harrison and Lilli Palmer)
313. Kate Fennigate (5/24/53; Wendell Norey and Martha Scott)
314. The Grand Tour (5/31/53; Jean Arthur)
315. Julius Caesar (6/7/53; Maurice Evans and Basil Rathbone)

The Victory Theater

This was the CBS counterpart of NBC's *Victory Parade*, broadcast over CBS, Monday evenings from 9 to 9:30 pm, EST (with the exception of the premiere broadcast, which ran from 9 to 10 pm, EST). Amos 'n' Andy's first half-hour broadcast before a live studio audience was presented in episode six, which was also hosted by Cecil B. DeMille. Del Sharbutt announced for the series. Lud Gluskin supplied the music.

1. The Philadelphia Story (7/20/42; Cary Grant, Katharine Hepburn, and James Stewart)
2. [Musical broadcast] (7/27/42; Joan Edwards, Barry Wood, and the Warnow Orchestra)
3. Major Bowes' Original Amateurs (8/3/42)
4. A Nest of Eagles (8/10/42; Barbara Luddy and Les Tremayne)
5. The Big Town (8/17/42; Edward G. Robinson)
6. Amos 'n' Andy (8/24/42; Edward Arnold, Charles Correll, Cecil B. DeMille, Freeman Gosden, and Victor Moore)
7. Joe Smith, American (8/31/42; Ruth Hussey and Robert Young)

War Town

Sponsored by the Community Chest Fund Appeal, this short-run series featured true-life stories ranging from the courage of a United States sailor to a war prisoner's horrifying ordeal across the seas. One broadcast even documented U.S.O. Camp performances. Produced and directed by Robert Lewis Shayon, the entire series was recorded in New York City in 1944. Only fifteen episodes were recorded. Each broadcast ran fifteen minutes, and the entire series was syndicated on local stations in 1945. Jon Gart supplied the music. Jackson Beck was the announcer. Guest stars for each broadcast narrated, from Ralph Bellamy to Victor Jory. Phyllis Parker and Eloise Walton wrote the scripts.

1. Sergeant Joe (with Ralph Bellamy, Alice Frost, and Edmond O'Brien)
2. Larry Finds a Dad (with Ralph Bellamy and Skip Homier)
3. Escape (with Ralph Bellamy, Jack Hartley, Joseph Julian, Don

MacLaughlin, Myron McCormick, and James Monks)
4. Molly Malone (with Celeste Holm, Canada Lee, and Victory Jory)
5. Falling Stone (with Bill Adams, Raymond E. Johnson, Conrad Nagel, Michael O'Day, Frank Pacelli, and Maude Scheerer)
6. The Pint-Size War (with Jeannie Elkins, Michael Fitzmaurice, Nancy Kelly, Mary Michael, Conrad Nagel, and Vicki Vola)
7. Bad Girl (with Conrad Nagel)
8. Precious Gold [based on the book *They Shall Inherit the Earth*]
9. Too Young for Everything (with Joan Caulfield, Victor Jory, and Karen Morley)
10. Ex-Soldier (with Peggy Conklin and Edmond O'Brien)
11. Little Dictator (with Peter Fernandez, Michael Fitzmaurice, Victor Jory, and Ronald Liss)
12. Mama Merino (with Victor Jory and Hester Sondergaard)
13. On with the Show (with Edmond O'Brien)
14. General Janet, USO (with Dean Jagger, Bill Quinn, and Joan Tetzel)
15. Hands of Destiny (with Mady Christians, Ken Daigneau, Ray Ives, Jr., Victory Jory, Pat Ryan, and George Ward)

The Ways of Mankind

Produced by the National Association of Educational Broadcasters, this series portrayed the origin of customs and behavior patterns in various parts of the world, broadcast Sunday afternoons from 1 to 1:30 pm, EST. "Desert Soliloquy" was a docu-drama of a Hopi Indian's adventures in education. In "When Greek Meets Greek," a Spartan and Athenian boy contrast the values of two societies. "You Are Not Alone" was a study within workgroups in America, "Survival" was a drama of Native technology in the Arctic, and "All the World's a Stage" was a study in anthropology. The tracing of the growth of language was the subject of the first episode. The first thirteen broadcasts were repeated in consecutive order for a re-run in 1955, broadcast from 4 to 4:30 pm over WNYC in New York.

1. A Word in Your Ear: A Study in Language (12/14/52)
2. Stand-In for a Murderer (12/21/52)
3. Desert Soliloquy (12/28/52)
4. When Greek Meets Greek (1/4/52)
5. The Case of the Sea Lion Flippers (1/11/52)
6. Sticks and Stones (1/18/52)
7. Legend of the Long House (1/25/52)
8. You Are Not Alone (2/1/52)
9. All the World's a Stage (2/8/52)
10. Home, Sweet Home (2/15/52)
11. Survival (2/22/52)
12. But I Know What I Like (3/1/52)
13. The Museum of Man (3/8/52)
14. Laying Down the Law (9/6/53)
15. The Bamboo-Sized Pigs (9/13/53)
16. The Repentant Horse Thief (9/20/53)
17. Lion Bites Man (9/27/53)
18. The Forbidden Name of Wednesday (10/4/53)
19. The Case of the Borrowed Wife (10/11/53)
20. The Life of Yurok (10/18/53)
21. The Reluctant Shaman (10/25/53)
22. The Sea Monster and the Bride (11/1/53)
23. World Renewal (11/8/53)
24. Isle Full of Voices (11/15/53)

25. The Coming Out (11/22/53)
26. The Fighting Cock Refrain (11/29/53)
27. A Word in Your Ear: A Study in Language (7/3/55)
28. Stand-In for a Murderer (7/10/55)
29. Desert Soliloquy (7/17/55)
30. When Greek Meets Greek (7/24/55)
31. The Case of the Sea Lion Flippers (7/31/55)
32. Sticks and Stones (8/7/55)
33. Legend of the Long House (8/14/55)
34. You Are Not Alone (8/21/55)
35. All the World's a Stage (8/28/55)
36. Home, Sweet Home (9/4/55)
37. Survival (9/11/55)
38. But I Know What I Like (9/18/55)
39. The Museum of Man (9/25/55)

The Weird Circle

This series was syndicated in the late 1940s by Ziv Productions and broadcast on different networks. In New York, a four-episode broadcast run was presented from September to October of 1947. The series was recorded in New York. Performers through many of the dramas included Lawson Zerbe, Julie Stevens, Chester Stratton, Eleanor Audley, Audrey Totter, Gladys Thornton, Carl Eastman, Arnold Moss, Walter Vaughn, Regis Joyce, Alan Devitt, and Fred Barron. All of the stories were adaptations.

1. The Fall of the House of Usher [based on the story by Edgar Allan Poe] (4/15/46)
2. The House and the Brain (4/22/46)
3. The Vendetta (4/29/46)
4. Narrative of Arthur Gordon Pym (5/6/46)
5. Declared Insane (5/13/46)
6. A Terribly Strange Bed [based on the short story by Wilkie Collins] (5/20/46)
7. What Was It? [based on the short story by Fitz-James O'Brien] (5/27/46)
8. The Knight Bridge Mystery (6/3/46)
9. The Horla [based on the short story by Guy DeMaupassant] (6/10/46)
10. William Wilson [based on the short story by Edgar Allan Poe] (6/17/46)
11. Passion in the Desert (6/24/46)
12. Mated Falcone (7/1/46)
13. The Man Without a Country (7/8/46)
14. Dr. Manette's Manuscript (7/15/46)
15. The Great Plague (7/22/46)
16. Expectations of an Heir (7/29/46)
17. The Hand (8/5/46)
18. Jane Eyre [based on the novel by Emily Brontë] (8/12/46)
19. Murders in the Rue Morgue [based on the story by Edgar Allan Poe] (8/19/46)
20. The Lifted Veil (8/26/46)
21. The 4:15 Express (9/2/46)
22. A Terrible Night (9/9/46)
23. The Tell-Tale Heart [based on the short story by Edgar Allan Poe] (9/16/46)
24. The Niche of Doom (9/23/46)
25. The Heart of Ethan Brand (9/30/46)
26. Frankenstein [based on the novel by Mary Shelley] (10/7/46)
27. Feast of the Red Gauntlet (10/13/46)
28. Murder of the Little Pig (10/20/46)
29. Specter of Tappington (10/28/46)
30. Strange Judgment (11/4/46)
31. Wuthering Heights [based on the novel by Emily Brontë] (11/11/46)
32. Curse of the Mantle (11/18/46)
33. The Cask of Amontillado [based on the short story by Edgar Allan Poe] (11/25/46)
34. A Rope of Hair (12/2/46)
35. Falkland (12/9/46) [aka The Last Days of Pompeii]

36. The Trial for Murder (12/16/46)
37. The Werewolf (12/23/46)
38. The Old Nurse's Story (12/30/46)
39. The Middle Toe of the Right Foot (1/6/47)
40. The Dream Woman (1/13/47)
41. The Phantom Picture (1/20/47)
42. The Ghost's Touch (1/27/47)
43. The Bell Tower (2/3/47)
44. Evil Eye (2/10/47)
45. The Mark of the Plague (2/17/47)
46. The Queer Client (2/24/47)
47. The Burial of Roger Melvin (3/3/47)
48. The Fatal Love Potion (3/10/47)
49. Mad Monkton (3/17/47)
50. The Returned (3/24/47)
51. The Executioner (3/31/47)
52. Rapacini's Daughter [based on the short story by Nathaniel Hawthorne] (4/7/47)
53. The Wooden Ghost (4/14/47)
54. Last Days of a Condemned Man (4/21/47)
55. The Warning (4/28/47)
56. The Doll [based on the short story by Algernon Blackwood] (5/5/47)
57. The Diamond Lens (5/12/47)
58. The History of Dr. John Faust (5/19/47)
59. Duel Without Honor (5/26/47)
60. Specter Bride (6/2/47)
61. The Tapestry Horse (6/9/47)
62. The River Man (6/16/47)
63. The Rhyme of the Ancient Mariner [based on the poem by Samuel Taylor Coleridge] (6/23/47)
64. The Oblong Box [based on the story by Edgar Allan Poe] (6/30/47)
65. The Mysterious Bride (7/7/47)
66. The Thing in the Tunnel [based on the short story by Charles Dickens] (7/14/47)
67. The Moonstone [based on the novel by Wilkie Collins] (7/21/47)
68. The Pistol Shot (7/28/47)
69. The Possessive Dead (8/4/47)
70. The Goblet (8/11/47)
71. The Case of M. Valdemar [based on the story by Edgar Allan Poe] (8/18/47)
72. The Shadow (8/25/47)
73. Bride of Death (9/1/47)
74. Dr. Jekyll and Mr. Hyde [based on the story by Robert Louis Stevenson] (9/8/47)
75. The Red Hand (9/15/47)
76. The Haunted Hotel (9/22/47)
77. Markheim [based on the short story by Robert Louis Stevenson] (9/29/47)
78. The Black Parchment (10/6/47)

We Saw Tomorrow

This United Nations documentary series was a six-episode syndication reporting on Latin America. Melvyn Douglas was the narrator. First broadcast over NBC from 7:30 to 8 pm in June and July of 1953, this series was rebroadcast over WNYC in New York a couple of months later, from September to October of 1953, from 8:30 to 9 pm. The first set of dates is the NBC run, the second, the rebroadcast run.

1. Mexico (6/21/53; 9/12/53)
2. El Salvador (6/28/53; 9/19/53)
3. Columbia and Ecuador (7/5/53; 9/26/53)
4. Peru and Bolivia (7/12/53; 10/3/53)
5. Chile (7/19/53; 10/10/53)
6. Brazil (7/26/53; 10/24/53)

The Whisperer

Carlton Young was Peter Gault, a.k.a. "The Whisperer," a man who led a double life as a lawyer and as a crime syndicate front man — an interesting concept that never reached full potential. Betty Moran played the role of Ellen Morris. Jonathan Twice wrote the scripts. Johnny Duffy supplied the organ music. Broadcast sustaining over NBC, Sunday afternoons from 5 to 5:30 pm, EST, the series was produced and directed by Bill Karn.

1. Tea Time for Teenagers (7/8/51)
2. The Attempted Murder (7/15/51)
3. Hippity Hoppy (7/22/51)
4. A Policeman in Danger (7/29/51)
5. What Ye Sow (8/5/51)
6. The Fight Game (8/12/51)
7. Into Each Life (8/19/51)
8. Taken for a Bride (8/26/51)
9. Stanley Hayes (9/2/51)
10. Woman on Ice (9/9/51)
11. Never the Twain (9/16/51)
12. The Police Lieutenant (9/23/51)
13. Strange Bed Fellows (9/30/51)

Whitehall 1212

Whitehall 1212 featured dramatizations of case files from Scotland Yard. Written and directed by Wyllis Cooper, whose ear for detail was evident throughout the series with Cooper's insistence that an all–British cast perform the scripts. Broadcast over NBC, Sunday evenings from 10:30 to 11 pm, EST, the series was moved to 5 pm as of episode six, and 5:30 pm as of episode fourteen. Cast regulars included Harvey Hayes, Patricia Courtleigh, Horace Braham, Winston Ross, and Lester Fletcher.

1. The Blitz Murder Case (11/18/51)
2. The Show Mission (11/25/51)
3. The Fonier Case (12/2/51)
4. The Murder of Duncan Frazier (12/9/51)
5. The Man Who Murdered His Wife (12/16/51)
6. The Heathrow Affair (12/23/51)
7. The Murder of Charles Brooks (1/6/52)
8. Camere Is Murdered (1/13/52)
9. The Case of Donald Simms (1/20/52)
10. The Murder of Little Philip Avery (1/27/52)
11. The Peter Williams Case (2/3/52)
12. The Case of Arthur Freeman (2/10/52)
13. The Case of the Late Mrs. Harvey (2/17/52)
14. The Murder of Peter Amory (2/24/52)
15. The Murder of Margery Ashley (3/2/52)
16. The Case of Dr. Duncan Allen (3/9/52)
17. The Case of Thomas Applebee (3/16/52)
18. The Case of the Black Gladstone Bag (3/23/52)
19. The Murder of a Bloody Belguin (3/30/52)
20. The Case of the Fatal Bath (4/13/52)
21. The Case of Mrs. Minerva Bannamon (4/20/52)
22. The Case of Franchesca Nicholson (4/27/52)
23. The Case of William George Greenly (5/4/52)

24. The Case of Margery Tate (5/11/52)
25. The Case of Sidney Wolfe (5/18/52)
26. The Case of Maggie Ralenson (5/25/52)
27. The Case of Winifred Hog (6/1/52)
28. The Case of the Strange Bonfire (6/8/52)
29. The Case of the Homemade Handbag (6/15/52)
30. The Murder of Mrs. Ann Battersby (6/22/52)
31. The Case of the Weed Eradication (6/29/52)
32. The Murder of Mr. Sweet (7/6/52)
33. The Case of the Ankush (7/13/52)
34. The Case of the Unidentified Woman (7/20/52)
35. The Case of the Magneta Blotting Pad (7/27/52)
36. The Murder of Nora Brady (8/3/52)
37. The Case of the Missing Clarinet (8/10/52)
38. The Case of the Dugel Henry (8/17/52)
39. The Murder of Lady Madge Johnson (8/24/52)
40. The Case of the Madden Family (9/7/52)
41. The Case of the Eaton Brothers (9/14/52)
42. The Case of the Winchester Bottles (9/21/52)
43. The Case of the Inoperative Wireless (9/28/52)
44. The Case of the Electric Touch (9/28/52)

With Canada's Mounted Police

This short-run series, much like the later *Sergeant Preston of the Yukon*, but with more than one hero, was broadcast 10 to 10:30 pm, EST, over the Blue Network on Monday evenings. Stars were Eustace Wyatt and Allyn Joslyn.

1. The Case of Ernest Cashell (1/11/32)
2. -----(1/18/32)
3. The O'Brien Murders (1/25/32)
4. The Secret of Horatius (2/1/32)
5. The Idaho Kid (2/8/32)
6. -----(2/15/32)
7. -----(2/22/32)
8. The Island Affair (2/29/32)
9. The Mad Trapper of Rat River (3/7/32)
10. -----(3/14/32)
11. The Case of Wai Kuen (3/21/32)
12. Constable Whaley's First Patrol (3/28/32)
13. Rounding Out the Saga (4/4/32)

The Witness

Syndicated by the Episcopal Church and originating from Hollywood, this religious series was heard in the mid-forties. Only sixteen fifteen-minute episodes were made, and the order in which they were broadcast or recorded remains unknown. The log below is listed alphabetically.

1. Apart From (with Leon Ames and Rosemary De Camp)
2. Blend Ethnic Background (with J. Carrol Naish)
3. The Boy's Mother Dies (with Leon Ames and Alan Young)
4. A Child Abused (with Joseph Cotten and Rosemary De Camp)
5. The Farm Couple Adopts (with J. Carrol Naish)

6. A Friend in Need (with Joseph Cotten and Rosemary De Camp)
7. A Good Man's Anger (with J. Carrol Naish)
8. The Good Samaritan of the Highway (with Marvin Miller and Robert Young)
9. Kindness and Understanding (with Marvin Miller and Alan Young)
10. Labor Personnel Relations (with Robert Young)
11. Laugh and the World Laughs with You (with Leon Ames and Alan Young)
12. Love Children (with J. Carrol Naish)
13. Mixed Race (with Virginia Gregg)
14. Parents and Juvenile Delinquency (with J. Carroll Naish)
15. The Purpose to Live (with Jayne Meadows and Gene Raymond)
16. Who Is My Neighbor? (with J. Carrol Naish)

Words at War

Words at War presented stories concerning the war from books produced during the war. Premiered on NBC, Thursday from 8 to 8:30 pm, EST, beginning with episode three, the program moved to Saturdays from 8:30 to 9 pm, as a summer replacement for *Truth or Consequences*. Beginning with episode twelve, the series was heard on Thursdays from 11:30 pm to 12 am; beginning with episode seventeen, Tuesdays from 11:30 pm to 12 am. Beginning with episode fifty-two, Johnson's Wax took up sponsorship and aired the series as a summer replacement for *Fibber McGee and Molly*, Tuesdays from 9:30 to 10 pm, with Carl Van Dorn. Clifton Fadiman filled in for Van Dorn from episodes fifty-five to sixty-one. With episode sixty-seven, the series went back to Tuesdays from 11:30 pm to 12 am, sustaining.

1. Combined Operations (6/24/43)
2. One World (7/1/43; Wendel Wilke)
3. They Call It the Pacific (7/10/43)
4. The Last Days of Sevestopol (7/17/43)
5. The Ship (7/24/43)
6. Firm Hands, Silent People (7/31/43)
7. Prisoner of the Japs (8/7/43)
8. Love at First Flight (8/14/43)
9. The Last Days of Sevestopol (8/19/43)
10. Malta Spitfire (8/21/43)
11. Burma Surgeon (8/28/43)
12. Dynamite Cargo (9/2/43; Jackson Beck)
13. Free Lands (9/9/43)
14. Since You Went Away (9/16/43)
15. They Shall Not Have Me (9/23/43)
16. Battle Hymn of China (9/30/43)
17. Eighty Three Days (10/5/43)
18. Paris Underground (10/12/43)
19. Shortcut to Tokyo (10/19/43)
20. Who Dare to Live (10/26/43)
21. Here Is Your War [based on the book by Ernie Pyle] (11/2/43)
22. To All Hands (11/9/43)
23. Skyways to Berlin (11/16/43)
24. Escape from the Balkans (11/23/43; Robert St. John)
25. Fruits of Fascism / Sawdust Caesar / Balcony Empire [three dramas] (11/30/43)
26. The Book of War Letters (12/7/43)
27. Mother America (12/14/43; Jackson Beck and Bernard Lenrow)
28. Log Book-British Merchant Marine (12/21/43)
29. Ninth Commandment: The Invasion of Holland (12/28/43)
30. They Shall Inherit the Earth (1/4/44)
31. Eighty-Three Days (1/11/44)
32. War Tide (1/18/44)
33. Condition Red (1/25/44)
34. The White Brigade (2/1/44)
35. George Washington Carver (2/8/44; Canada Lee and Fredric March)

36. The New Sun (2/15/44)
37. Assignment U.S.A. (2/22/44)
38. I Served on Bataan (2/29/44; Tallulah Bankhead)
39. The Weeping Wood (3/7/44)
40. Science at War (3/14/44)
41. Der Feuhrer (3/21/44)
42. A Bell for Adano (3/28/44)
43. Assignment U.S.A. (4/4/44)
44. Wild River (4/11/44)
45. Silence of the Seas (4/18/44)
46. Tarawa (4/25/44)
47. The Curtain Rises (5/2/44)
48. Gunners Get Glory (5/9/44)
49. Lifeline (5/16/44)
50. Lend Lease: Weapon for Victory (5/23/44)
51. The Navy Hunts the CGR 3070 (5/30/44)
52. Fair Stood the Winds of France (6/27/44)
53. War Criminals and Punishment (7/4/44)
54. Captain Retread (7/11/44)
55. War Below Zero (7/18/44)
56. Lost Island (7/25/44)
57. Headquarters Budapest (8/1/44)
58. Nazis Go Underground (8/8/44)
59. Heaven Below / China Looks Forward [two dramas] (8/15/44)
60. Pastoral (8/22/44)
61. Simone (8/29/44)
62. The Veteran Comes Back (9/5/44)
63. One Man Air Force (9/12/44)
64. The Return of the Traveler (9/19/44)
65. Journey Through Chaos (9/26/44)
66. Pacific Victory, 1945 (10/3/44)
67. The Veteran Comes Back (10/10/44)
68. War, Criminals and Punishment (10/17/44)
69. Still Time to Die (10/24/44)
70. The Return of the Traveler (10/31/44)
71. One Thing After Another (11/14/44)
72. Barriers Down (11/21/44)
73. Camp Follower (11/28/44)
74. The Guys on the Ground (12/5/44)
75. Your School, Your Children (12/12/44)
76. The Cross and the Arrow (12/19/44)
77. Scape Goats in History / History of Bigotry in the United States (12/26/44; Bernard Lenrow)
78. It's Always Bright Tomorrow (1/2/45)
79. Borrowed Nights (1/9/45)
80. Verdict on India (1/16/45)
81. The Story of a Secret State (1/23/45)
82. Ten Escape from Tojo (2/6/45)
83. What to do with Germany (2/13/45)
84. Battle Report: Pearl Harbor to the Coral Sea (2/20/45)
85. Faith of our Fathers (2/27/45)
86. Rainbow (3/6/45)
87. Can Do (3/13/45)
88. Tomorrow We'll See (3/20/45)
89. Banshee Harvest (3/27/45)
90. Full Employment in a Free Society (4/3/45)
91. Apartment in Athens (4/10/45)
92. They Left the Back Door Open (4/17/45)
93. Brave Men (4/24/45)
94. The Hide Out (5/1/45; Arnold Moss)
95. The Road to Curftom (5/15/45; Luis Van Rooten)
96. Wartime Racketeers (5/22/45)
97. Soldier to Civilian (5/29/45)
98. My Country (6/5/45)

The World and the West

This documentary series about the countries in the Western world had Professor Arnold J. Toynbee as the speaker for each episode. Broadcast over ABC from 10:30 to 11 pm, EST, only six episodes were heard before it was replaced by *Discovery*, a science-panel program.

1. Russia (3/8/53)
2. Islam (3/15/53)
3. India (3/22/53)
4. The Far East (3/29/53)
5. Psychology of Encounters (4/5/53)
6. The Greeks and the Romans (4/12/53)

World Security Workshop

This dramatic series, designed to promote a better world of understanding, featured prize-winning scripts and stories. The premiere broadcast was Leon Meadow's script on New York City entitled "Citizen Delavan," about a scientist engaged in work on the atomic bomb. Episode eight was based on the prize-winning play by Ray Bradbury. Episode thirteen featured a reading of "The Decision to Use the Atomic Bomb," written by Henry L. Stimson. Episode twenty-three was written by John Farley, and Sheldon Stark wrote episode twenty-five. Joseph Julian not only narrated episode eighteen, but he wrote the script as well. Episode twenty-two featured Leo M. Cherne, executive secretary of the Research Institute of America. After half a year and a total of twenty-six broadcasts, the series was taken off the air, replaced by *Those Sensational Years*. The program remained sustaining the entire run, broadcast on ABC every Thursday evening from 10 to 10:30 pm, EST. The program was also known as *The ABC World Security Workshop*.

1. Citizen Delavan (11/14/46)
2. Psycho-Neurosis of a Sound Effect (11/21/46; Betty Jaffey)
3. Mrs. Campbell's One World (11/28/46)
4. Memo to the People (12/5/46)
5. Volts Times Amperes Equals Peace [based on the story by Ira Marion] (12/12/46)
6. War Is the Enemy (12/19/46)
7. A Night in Plainville (12/26/46)
8. The Meadow (1/2/47)
9. Sing a Song of Friendship (1/9/47)
10. The Ordeal of Mario Lanza (1/16/47)
11. Invitation to Life (1/23/47)
12. Arctic Attack (1/30/47)
13. The Decision to Use the Atomic Bomb (2/6/47)
14. The Vision of Steven Marlowe (2/13/47)
15. One Hungry Man (2/20/47)
16. The Sergeant Pays a Debt (2/27/47)
17. Shadow on the Bridge (3/6/47)
18. Welcome, Honorable Enemy (3/13/47; Joseph Julian)
19. The Price of Freedom (3/20/47)
20. John Lander Lived in a Rickety House (3/27/47)
21. The Man Who Conquered Devil's Island (4/3/47; Van Heflin)
22. The Unknown History of the United States (4/10/47)
23. April 17, 1977 (4/17/47; Marc Connelly)
24. Onward and Upward with the Short-wave (4/24/47)
25. Conspiracy Out of Space (5/1/47)
26. The Cave (5/8/47; Carl Van Dorn)

The World's Greatest Novels

This series featured faithful adaptations of popular novels, in consecutive parts. At first broadcast sustaining over NBC, Saturday evenings from 7 to 7:30 pm, EST, on February 23, 1945, *The World's Greatest Novels* moved to Fridays from 11:30 pm to 12 am, EST. On July 30, 1948, this program changed its title to *The NBC University Theater of the Air*.

1. Jane Eyre [part one] (2/23/45)
2. Jane Eyre [part two] (3/2/45)
3. Vanity Fair [part one] (3/9/45)
4. Vanity Fair [part two] (3/16/45)
5. Vanity Fair [part three] (3/23/45)
6. Vanity Fair [part four] (3/30/45)
7. Vanity Fair [part five] (4/6/45)
8. Madame Bovary [part one] (4/13/45)
9. Madame Bovary [part two] (4/20/45)
10. Les Miserables [part one] (4/27/45)
11. Les Miserables [part two] (5/4/45)
12. Les Miserables [part three] (5/11/45)
13. Les Miserables [part four] (5/18/45)
14. Les Miserables [part five] (5/25/45)
15. Les Miserables [part six] (6/1/45)
16. The House of Seven Gables [part one] (6/8/45)
17. The House of Seven Gables [part two] (6/15/45)
18. The House of Seven Gables [part three] (6/22/45)
19. Candide (6/29/45)
20. War and Peace [part one] (9/14/45)
21. War and Peace [part two] (9/21/45)
22. War and Peace [part three] (9/28/45)
23. War and Peace [part four] (10/5/45)
24. War and Peace [part five] (10/12/45)
25. War and Peace [part six] (10/19/45)
26. Huckleberry Finn [part one] (10/26/45)
27. Huckleberry Finn [part two] (11/2/45)
28. Huckleberry Finn [part three] (11/9/45)
29. Huckleberry Finn [part four] (11/16/45)
30. Cloister and the Hearth [part one] (11/23/45)
31. Cloister and the Hearth [part two] (11/30/45)
32. Cloister and the Hearth [part three] (12/7/45)
33. Cloister and the Hearth [part four] (12/14/45)
34. The Haunted Man (12/21/45)
35. Rip Van Winkle (12/28/45)
36. Ninety-Three [part one] (1/4/46)
37. Ninety-Three [part two] (1/11/46)
38. Ninety-Three [part three] (1/18/46)
39. Ninety-Three [part four] (1/25/46)
40. Crime and Punishment [part one] (2/1/46)
41. Crime and Punishment [part two] (2/8/46)
42. Tristram Shandy [part one] (2/15/46)
43. Tristram Shandy [part two] (2/22/46)
44. Crime of S. Bonnard (3/1/46)
45. Cranford [part one] (3/8/46)
46. Cranford [part two] (3/15/46)
47. The Last of the Mohicans [part one] (3/22/46)
48. The Last of the Mohicans [part two] (3/29/46)
49. Youth [part one] (4/5/46)
50. Youth [part two] (4/12/46)
51. The Way of All Flesh [part one] (4/19/46)
52. The Way of All Flesh [part two] (4/26/46)
53. Mayor of Casterbridge [part one] (5/3/46)
54. Mayor of Casterbridge [part two] (5/10/46)
55. Mayor of Casterbridge [part three] (5/17/46)
56. Mayor of Casterbridge [part four] (5/24/46)
57. Mayor of Casterbridge [part five] (5/31/46)
58. Anna Karenina [part one] (11/1/46)
59. Anna Karenina [part two] (11/8/46)
60. Anna Karenina [part three] (11/15/46)
61. Anna Karenina [part four] (11/22/46)
62. Vanity Fair [part one] (11/29/46)
63. Vanity Fair [part two] (12/6/46)
64. Vanity Fair [part three] (12/13/46)
65. Vanity Fair [part four] (12/20/46)
66. Adventures of Sinbad (12/27/46)
67. Moby Dick [part one] (1/3/47)
68. Moby Dick [part two] (1/17/47)
69. Moby Dick [part three] (1/24/47)
70. Moby Dick [part four] (1/31/47)
71. Old Wives Tales [part one] (2/7/47)
72. Old Wives Tales [part two] (2/14/47)
73. Old Wives Tales [part three] (2/21/47)
74. Old Wives Tales [part four] (2/28/47)
75. Gulliver's Travels (3/7/47)
76. The Brothers Karamozov [part one] (3/14/47)

77. The Brothers Karamozov [part two]
   (3/21/47)
78. The Brothers Karamozov [part
   three] (3/28/47)
79. The Brothers Karamozov [part four]
   (4/4/47)
80. Caesar Birroteau [part one] (4/11/47)
81. Caesar Birroteau [part two] (4/18/47)
82. Caesar Birroteau [part three] (4/25/47)
83. Caesar Birroteau [part four] (5/2/47)
84. The Heart of Midlothian (5/9/47)
85. Betrothed [part one] (5/16/47)
86. Betrothed [part two] (5/23/47)
87. The Return of the Native [part one]
   (5/30/47)
88. The Return of the Native [part two]
   (6/6/47)
89. The Return of the Native [part
   three] (6/13/47)
90. The Return of the Native [part
   four] (6/20/47)
91. Pere Goriot (6/27/47)
92. Moby Dick (7/4/47)
93. The Scarlet Letter (7/11/47)
94. Tom Sawyer [part one] (7/18/47)
95. Tom Sawyer [part two] (7/25/47)
96. The Pilot (8/1/47)
97. The Luck of Roaring Camp
   (8/8/47)
98. Ramona [part one] (8/15/47)
99. Ramona [part two] (8/22/47)
100. Hoosier Schoolmaster [part one]
   (8/29/47)
101. Hoosier Schoolmaster [part two]
   (9/5/47)
102. Life on the Mississippi (9/12/47)
103. The Legend of Sleepy Hollow
   (9/19/47)
104. Little Women [part one] (9/26/47)
105. Little Women [part two] (10/3/47)
106. Diana of the Crossroads [part one]
   (10/10/47)
107. Diana of the Crossroads [part two]
   (10/17/47)
108. Diana of the Crossroads [part three]
   (10/24/47)
109. Diana of the Crossroads [part four]
   (10/31/47)
110. Silas Marner [part one] (11/7/47)
111. Silas Marner [part two] (11/14/47)
112. A Tale of Two Cities [part one]
   (11/21/47)
113. A Tale of Two Cities [part two]
   (11/28/47)

114. A Tale of Two Cities [part three]
   (12/5/47)
115. A Tale of Two Cities [part four]
   (12/12/47)
116. A Child Is Born (12/19/47)
117. The Pickwick Papers (12/26/47)
118. Wuthering Heights [part one]
   (1/2/48)
119. Wuthering Heights [part two]
   (1/9/48)
120. Wuthering Heights [part three]
   (1/16/48)
121. Wuthering Heights [part four]
   (1/23/48)
122. Kennelworth [part one] (2/6/48)
123. Kennelworth [part two] (2/13/48)
124. Kennelworth [part three] (2/20/48)
125. The Man Without a Country
   (2/27/48)
126. The Rise of Silas Lapham [part one]
   (3/5/48)
127. The Rise of Silas Lapham [part two]
   (3/12/48)
128. The Rise of Silas Lapham [part
   three] (3/19/48)
129. The Rise of Silas Lapham [part
   four] (3/26/48)
130. The Moonstone [part one] (4/2/48)
131. The Moonstone [part two] (4/9/48)
132. The Moonstone [part three]
   (4/16/48)
133. The Moonstone [part four]
   (4/23/48)
134. Kidnapped [part one] (4/30/48)
135. Kidnapped [part two] (5/7/48)
136. Kidnapped [part three] (5/14/48)
137. Washington Square [part one]
   (5/21/48)
138. Washington Square [part two]
   (5/28/48)
139. A Connecticut Yankee in King
   Arthur's Court [part one] (6/4/48)
140. A Connecticut Yankee in King
   Arthur's Court [part two] (6/11/48)
141. A Connecticut Yankee in King
   Arthur's Court [part three]
   (6/18/48)
142. The Red Badge of Courage
   (6/25/48)
143. The Rise of Silas Lapham (7/2/48)
144. Free (7/9/48)
145. Pastorale (7/16/48)
146. The Works of Thomas Wolfe
   (7/23/48)

X Minus One

This science-fiction series premiered during the height of science-fiction. Each week for almost three years, this program presented some of the best in science-fiction writing, faithfully adapted from short stories. Many consider this an extension of *Dimension X*, since the first thirty-or-so scripts were previously performed on that series. For some reason, this revival gained more popularity, and George Lefferts and Ernest Kinoy, the program's primary writers, had to pen more scripts. Others who wrote scripts were William Welch and Jack C. Wilson. Daniel Sutter directed. Fred Collins announced (Bill McCord was announcer for episode thirty-seven).

Two broadcasts in particular, "The Tunnel Under the World" and "The Lifeboat Mutiny," are considered two of the best science-fiction productions on radio. Occasionally sponsored by Bromo Quinine and Pabst Blue Ribbon, the series was broadcast Sunday evenings from 8 to 8:30 pm, EST. Beginning July 7, 1955, it was Thursday from 8 to 8:30 pm, and on July 28, 1955, the series moved ahead, 9 to 9:30 pm. On November 16, 1955, the series moved to Wednesdays from 8 to 8:30 pm. Beginning January 4, 1956, the series was heard from 9:30 to 10 pm. Beginning April 3, 1956, *X Minus One* was heard on Tuesdays from 8:30 to 9 pm; beginning July 3, 1956, 8 to 8:30 pm; on September 26, 1956, Wednesdays from 9 to 9:30 pm. On June 20, 1957, the program moved to Thursdays from 8 to 8:30 pm.

On January 27, 1973, the Renaissance Radio Production, in cooperation with *Galaxy Magazine,* broadcast an episode using the same name and opening, in hopes of reviving the series. Heard over WRVR in New York City, the intent was to revive the series, supplementing the scripts used previously with new ones. However, NBC halted the rebroadcasts. Ira Sprintson was the director, and "The Iron Chancellor" became another part of radio history.

Audition: And the Moon Be Still and Bright (4/22/55; Staats Cotsworth, Roger De Koven, Bob Hastings)
1. No Contact (4/24/55; John Larkin and Nelson Olmstead)
2. The Parade (5/1/55; Donald Buka, Bill Griffis, Wendell Holmes, and Luis Van Rooten)
3. Mars Is Heaven (5/8/55; Joseph Curten, Berry Kroeger, and Alexander Scourby)
4. Universe (5/15/55; Margaret Curlen, Ethel Everett, Bill Griffis, Wendell Holmes, Ed Jerome, Peter Capel, Bill Lipton, Ken Williams, and Bill Zuckert)
5. Knock (5/22/55; Donald Buka, Bill Griffis, Abby Lewis, Peter Capell, Ian Martin, Jason Seymour, and Edgar Stehli)
6. The Man in the Moon (5/29/55; Laurie March, Luis Van Rooten, and Alexander Scourby)
7. Perigi's Wonderful Dolls (6/5/55; Joe Di Santis, Bob Hague, Ed Latimer, Ross Martin, Santos Ortega, Sidney Smith, and Luis Van Rooten)
8. The Green Hills of Earth (7/7/55; Denise Alexander, Joan Alexander, Les Damon, Leon Janney, and Joe Di Santis)

9. Dr. Grimshaw's Sanitarium (7/14/55; Matt Crowley, Bill Griffis, Wendell Holmes, Nelson Olmsted, and Ken Williams)

10. Nightmare (7/21/55; John Gibson, Joyce Gordon, Owen Jordan, Joseph Julian, Santos Ortega, John Seymour, and Luis Van Rooten)

11. The Embassy (7/28/55; John Gibson, Joyce Gordon, Joseph Julian, Santos Ortega, Luis Van Rooten)

12. The Veldt (8/4/55; Joseph Julian and Berry Kroeger)

13. Almost Human (8/11/55; John Larkin, Beverley Lunsford, Mary Patton, Charles Penman, David Pfeffer, and Bill Quinn)

14. Courtesy (8/18/55; Joan Allison, Lin Cook, Jack Grimes, Joseph Julian, Santos Ortega, Nat Pollen, and Guy Repp)

15. Cold Equations (8/25/55; Jack Arthur, Court Benson, Milo Bolton, Walter Kinsella, Bob Hastings, and Jane Meredith)

16. Shanghaied (9/1/55; Court Benson and Jill Meredith)

17. The Martian Death March (9/8/55; Bob Dryden, Jim Dukas, Ivor Francis, Jack Grimes, Ross Martin, Sid Raymond, Luis Van Rooten, Lyle Sudrow, and Jack Tarpley)

18. The Castaways (9/15/55; Ralph Bell, Roger De Koven, Dick Hamilton, Lawrence Kerr, and David Seffer)

19. And the Moon Be Still and Bright (9/22/55; Staats Cotsworth, Roger De Koven, Stan Early, Bob Hastings, Joseph Julian, Resse Taylor, Luis Van Rooten, and Karl Weber)

20. First Contact (10/6/55; John Larkin and Nelson Olmstead)

21. Child's Play (10/20/55; Clark Gordon, Bob Hastings, Wendell Holmes, and Bill Malley)

22. Requiem (10/27/55; Leon Janney and Karl Webber)

23. Hello, Tomorrow (11/3/55; James Boles, Joseph Di Santis, and John McGovern)

24. Dwellers in Silence (11/10/55; John Larkin and Jan Miner)

25. The Outer Limit (11/16/55; Ted Osborne, Anne Seymour, and Karl Webber)

26. Zero Hour (11/23/55; Joe Di Santis, Jim Dukas, Bob Hastings, Wendell Holmes, Joe Julian)

27. The Vital Factor (11/30/55; Rolly Bester, Les Damon, Bob Hastings, John Larkin, Peggy Luman, Nina Rieter, and David Seffer)

28. Nightfall (12/7/55; Raymond Edward Johnson, John McGovern, and Luis Van Rooten)

29. To the Future (12/14/55; John Larkin and Jan Miner)

30. Marionettes, Inc. (12/21/55; Fredricka Chandler, Arthur Cole, Les Damon, Ted Getz, Dick Hamilton, Bob Hastings, Ginger Jones, and Karl Swenson)

31. A Logic Named Joe (12/28/55; Bob Hastings, Wendell Holmes, Joseph Julian, Mandel Kramer, Guy Repp, and William Zuckert)

32. The Roads Must Roll (1/4/56; Ralph Bell and Wendell Holmes)

33. Time and Time Again (1/11/56; Ralph Bell, James Dukas, Peter Fernandez, Clark Gordon, Jack Grimes, Dick Hamilton, and Joseph Di Santis)

34. Perigi's Wonderful Dolls (1/18/56; Denise Alexander, Joan Alexander, Les Damon, Leon Janney, and Joe Di Santis)

35. The Parade (1/25/56; Joseph Curten, Berry Kroeger, and Alexander Scourby)

36. The Cave of Night (2/1/56; Bob Hastings and Alexander Scourby)

37. The C-Chute (2/8/56; Danny Auchal, Stan Early, John Gibson, Bob Hastings, Mercer McLeod, and Lyle Sudrow)

38. The Skulking Permit (2/15/56; Joseph Bolland, Ruby Dee, Dick Hamilton, Alan Hewitt, Wendell Holmes, Mandel Kramer, Bill Quinn, and Joe Di Santis)

39. Junkyard (2/22/56; Stan Early, Bob Hastings, John Larkin, Mercer McLeod, Jack Orrison)

40. Hello, Tomorrow (2/29/56; John Larkin and Jan Minor)

41. A Gun for Dinosaur (3/7/56; Donald

Buka, Alistair Duncan, Alan Hewitt, Wendell Holmes, and Warren Parker)

42. Tunnel Under the World (3/14/56; Larry Haines, Bob Hastings, Lymon Olmquist, Ken Raffitte, Norman Rose, Elaine Ross, and Amy Sedell)

43. $1000 a Plate (3/21/56; Ralph Bell, Bob Hastings, Alan Hewitt, Mandel Kramer, Mercer McLeod, and Karl Swenson)

44. A Pail of Air (3/28/56; Joe Di Santis, Pamela Fitzmaurice, Dick Hamilton, Ronnie Liss)

45. How To (4/3/56; Joe Bell, Jane Bunce, Alan Bruce, Les Damon, Ben Graver, Santos Ortega, and Ann Seymour)

46. Star Bright (4/10/56; Ralph Bell, Billy Harris, Bill Quinn, Sarah Thussel, Kate Wilkinson, and Lawson Zerbe)

47. Jaywalker (4/17/56; Bob Hastings, Raymond Edward Johnson, Teri Keane, Connie Lempke)

48. The Sense of Wonder (4/24/56; Vera Allen, James Bunce, Joe Di Santis, Rita Lloyd, and Bill Quinn)

49. Sea Legs (5/1/56; Ralph Bell, Fred Chandler, James Dukas, Stan Early, Jack Grimes, Dick Hamilton, Craig MacDonald, Kermit Murdock, Jack Orrison, Charles Penman, Bill Redfield, and Jim Stevens)

50. The Seventh Order (5/8/56; Wayne Chapel, W.W. Chaplin, Dick Hamilton, Bob Hastings, James Monks, Nelson Olmstead, James Rafferty, Jim Stevens, Reese Taylor, Kate Wilkinson)

51. Hallucination Orbit (5/15/56; Vera Allen, Dick Hamilton, Teri Keane, John Larkin, John Moore, William Redfield, and Hope Risman)

52. The Defenders (5/22/56; Lydia Bruce, Stan Early, Mike Ingram, Warren Parker, Grant Richards)

53. Lulungameena (5/29/56; Ralph Camargo, Jack Grimes, Bob Hastings, Kermit Murdock, and Ned Weaver)

54. Project: Mastodon (6/5/56; Dick Hamilton, Bob Hastings, Raymond Edward Johnson, Joseph Julian, John Larkin, Floyd Mack, Frank Maxwell, and Charles Penman)

55. If You Were a Moklin (6/12/56; Ralph Camargo, Joseph Julian, Karl Webber, and Pat Weil)

56. Project: Trojan (6/19/56; Alistair Duncan, Ivor Francis, Burford Hampden, Alfred Isliff, Bill Quinn, and Alfred Shirley)

57. Wherever You May Be (6/26/56; Jack Orrison, Patsy O'Shea, and William Redfield)

58. Mr. Costello, Hero (7/3/56; Joseph Di Santis, Bob Hastings, Wendell Holmes, Raymond Edward Johnson, Teri Keane, Mandel Kramer, and Jim Stevens)

59. Bad Medicine (7/10/56; Cliff Carpenter, Bill Griffis, Joe Julian, Alan Manson, and Norman Rose)

60. The Old Die Rich (7/17/56; Jim Boles, Ralph Camargo, Wendell Holmes, Jan Minor, Guy Repp, and Bill Zuckert)

61. The Stars Are the Styk (7/24/56; Dick Hamilton, Bob Hastings, Craig MacDonald, Charlotte Manson, and Patsy O'Shea)

62. Student Body (7/31/56; Charles Carou, Bob Hastings, M.E. Joels, John Radee, Jim Stevens, and Kate Wilkinson)

63. The Last Martian (8/7/56; Ralph Bell, Mandel Kramer, John McGovern, Elliott Reid, Santos Ortega)

64. The Snowball Effect (8/15/56; Peggy Allenby, Arthur Glum, Wendell Holmes, Ted Osborne, Warren Parker, and Mary Patton)

65. Surface Tension (8/28/56; Mason Adams, Danny Auchal, Larry Haines, Bob Hastings, Jim Stevens, Luis Van Rooten, and Lawson Zerbe)

66. Tunnel Under the World (9/4/56; Larry Haines, Bob Hastings, Lymon Olmquist, Ken Raffitte, Norman Rose, and Elaine Ross)

67. The Lifeboat Mutiny (9/11/56;

Mandel Kramer, John McGovern,
and William Redfield)
68. The Map Makers (9/26/56; Tom
Collins, Dick Hamilton, John
Larkin, and Ed Prentiss)
69. Protective Mimicry (10/3/56; Dick
Hamilton, Wendell Holmes, Teri
Keane, Mandel Kramer, and
Charles Penman)
70. The Colony (10/10/56; Alan
Bergman, Fredrica Chandler, John
Larkin, Larry Robinson, and Bill
Quinn)
71. Soldier Boy (10/17/56; Ralph Bell,
Larry Haines, Bob Hastings, Alan
Hewitt, Wendell Holmes, and
Kermit Murdock)
72. Pictures Don't Lie (10/24/56; John
Gibson, Sam Grey, Dick Hamil-
ton, and Joe Di Santis)
73. Sam, This Is You (10/31/56; Larry
Haines and Pat Holsey)
74. Appointment in Tomorrow
(11/7/56; Bob Hastings, Arthur
Hughes, Pat Holsey, and Ted
Osborne)
75. The Martian Death March
(11/14/56; Ralph Bell, Roger De
Koven, Dick Hamilton, Lawrence
Kerr, and David Seffer)
76. Chain of Command (11/21/56; John
Gibson, Wendell Holmes, and
John McGovern)
77. The Castaways (11/28/56; Staats
Cotsworth, Roger De Koven, Stan
Early, Bob Hastings, Leon Janney,
Joseph Julian, Reese Taylor, Luis
Van Rooten, and Karl Webber)
78. There Will Come Soft Rains / Zero
Hour (12/5/56; Rolly Bester, Les
Damon, Bob Hastings, John
Larkin, Peggy Luman, Nina Rieter,
and David Seffer)
79. Hostess (12/12/56; Les Damon, Teri
Keane, and Kermit Murdock)
80. Reluctant Heroes (12/19/56; Jim
Grauman, Dick Hamilton, Bob
Hastings, Mandel Kramer, and Jim
Stevens)
81. Honeymoon in Hell (12/26/56;
Wilma Cure, Roger deKoven, Jack
Grimes, Wendell Holmes, Leon
Janney, Charles Penman, and
William Redfield)

82. The Moon Is Green (1/2/57; Joyce
Gordon, Bill Lipton, Ian Martin,
and Frank Milano)
83. Saucer of Loneliness (1/9/57; Wendell Holmes, Bill Keane, Mandel
Kramer, Nat Polen, Elaine Ross)
84. The Girls from Earth (1/16/57; John
Gibson, Dick Hamilton, Bob
Hastings, and Mandel Kramer)
85. Open Warfare (1/23/57; Jack
Grimes, Larry Haines, and Wendell Holmes)
86. Caretaker (1/30/57; Mason Adams,
R.E. Johnson, Betty Kane, Bill
Lipton, and Ted Osborne)
87. Venus Is a Man's World (2/6/57;
Dennis Beabio, Fredricka Chandler, John Gibson, Bob Hague,
and Jarianne Raphael)
88. The Trap (2/13/57; Ralph Bell,
Donald Buka, and William
Redfield)
89. Field Study (2/20/57; Les Damon,
Teri Keane, Kermit Murdock,
Alfred Shirley, and Santos Ortega)
90. Real Gone (2/27/57; John Baragrey,
Harold Huber, and John McGov-
ern)
91. The Seventh Victim (3/6/57;
Arthur Hughes, Teri Keane, Ian
Martin, Frank Maxwell, and Law-
son Zerbe)
92. The Lights on Precipice Peak
(3/13/57; Court Benson, Jim
Boles, Joseph Helgeson, Ted
Osborne)
93. Protection (3/20/57; William
Keane, William Redfield, and
Elliott Reid)
94. At the Post (3/27/57; Fred Maxwell,
Arnold Moss, and Sam Raskin)
95. Martian Sam (4/3/57; Ivor Francis,
Santos Ortega, and William Zuckert)
96. Something for Nothing (4/10/57;
Danny Auchal, Ralph Bell, Karen
Forbes, John Gibson, Wendell
Holmes, Joseph Julian, and Jock
McGregor)
97. The Discovery of Morneal Mathe-
way (4/17/57; Les Damon, Wen-
dell Holmes, Leon Janney, and
Guy Repp)
98. Man's Best Friend (4/24/57; Bob

Hastings, Wendell Holmes, Raymond Edward Johnson, Leona Powers, Bill Redfield, and Santos Ortega)
99. Inside Story (6/20/57; Ralph Bell, Edwin Cooper, Dick Hamilton, Bob Hastings, Pat Hosley, and Leon Janney)
100. The Category Inventor (6/27/57; Joe Bell, Burt Cowlan, Betty Galen, Wendell Holmes, and Nelson Olmstead)
101. The Skulking Permit (7/4/57; Joseph Bolland, Ruby Dee, Joe Di Santis, Dick Hamilton, Alan Hewitt, Wendell Holmes, Mandel Kramer, and Bill Quinn)
102. The Early Model (7/11/57; Joe Bell, Anthony Campbell Cooper, Alistair Duncan, Bob Hastings)
103. The Merchants of Venus (7/18/57; Jackson Beck, Joe Julian, Ted Osborne, and Jarred Reed)
104. The Haunted Corpse (7/25/57; Walter Black and Lydia Bruce)
105. End as a World (8/1/57; Peter Fernandez, Jack Grimes, Larry Robinson and Alice Yorman)
106. The Scapegoat (8/8/57; Bobby Alford, Jane Aymar, Roger deKoven, Wendell Holmes, Guy Repp, and Karl Webber)
107. At the Post (8/15/57; House Jameson and Frank Maxwell)
108. Drop Dead (8/22/57; Joseph Bell and Lawson Zerbe)
109. Volpa (8/29/57; Nelson Olmstead)
110. Saucer of Loneliness (9/5/57; Wendell Holmes, Bill Keane, Mandel Kramer, Jock McGregor, Nat Polen, and Elaine Ross)
111. The Old Die Rich (9/12/57; Jim Boles, Ralph Camargo, Jan Miner,

Guy Repp, Bill Zuckert)
112. Tsylana (9/19/57; Walter Black, Guy Repp, Adele Ronson, and David Ross)
113. The Native Problem (9/26/57)
114. A Wind Is Rising (10/3/57; Burt Cowen, Les Damon, and Bill Griffis)
115. Death Wish (10/10/57; Joe Bell, Walter Black, Ralph Camargo, and Maurice Tarplin)
116. Point of Departure (10/17/57; Ron Dawson, Lymon Olmquist, and Jim Stevens)
117. The Light (10/24/57; Bob Hastings, David Kurmand, and Karl Webber)
118. Lulu (10/31/57; William Redfield)
119. The Coffin Cure (11/21/57; Joe Bell, Harvey Hayes, Raymond E. Johnson, and Betty Kane)
120. Shock Troop (11/28/57; Ralph Camargo, Edwin Cooper, Bernard Lenrow, and John Thomas)
121. The Haunted Corpse (12/12/57; Walter Black, Lydia Bruce, Lymon Olmquist, and Edgar Stanley)
122. Double Dare (12/19/57; Ralph Camargo, Ivor Francis, Harvey Hayes, and Michael Ingram)
123. Target One (12/26/57; Joe Bell, Allen Collins, Lymon Olmquist, Guy Repp, Frank Silvera, and Charles Webster)
124. Prime Difference (1/2/58; Evelyn Juster, John Thomas and Lawson Zebre)
125. Gray Flannel Armor (1/9/58; Betty Galen, Pat Hosley, Abby Lewis, and Guy Repp)
126. The Iron Chancellor (1/27/73; Jackson Beck, Donald Buka, Leon Janney, and Evelyn Juster)

You and Your Security

A Social Security Administration syndication, transcribed by our Allied Forces, these stories concerned the business and formation of the Social Security system and featured interviews with people who work for Social Security and families who live with Social Security: "A series of broadcasts designed to make clear the meaning of Federal Social Security to you and your family." John Byrne wrote, produced and directed each broadcast. Jack Ward supplied the music. Fred Uttal announced and narrated. Guest stars often narrated. Edwin C. Hill was commentator. Recorded in New York, it was broadcast in 1949.

1. A New Light (with Joe Di Santis, Ray Ives, Jr., Madeline Kaleen, and Clyde North)
2. Detective (with Dean Jagger)
3. Confidential (with John Gibson)
4. Widows and Children (with Vivian Barry, Art Carney, and Neil O'Malley)
5. Dan Cupid (with Neil O'Malley, Tony Rivers, and Gloria Strut)
6. Disaster (with Joan Barton, Dean Jagger, Barry Thomson, and Walter Vaughn)
7. Identification (with Art Carney, Madeline Collenn, Clyde North, and Santos Ortega)
8. Education (with Madeline Kaleen, Clyde North, and Patricia Shay)
9. Social Security Card (with Madeleine Kaleen and Santos Ortega)
10. Community (with Billy M. Green, Clyde North, and Patricia Shay)
11. Record Keeping (with John Shay and Patricia Shay)
12. Hoey-Pogge (with John Batchelder, Jane M. Hoey, and Oscar C. Pogge)
13. Altmeyer-Pogge (with Arthur J. Altmeyer, John Batchelder, and Oscar C. Pogge)

You Are the Jury

Broadcast over NBC and sponsored by the Gruen Watch Company. Each episode ran fifteen minutes.

1. The People vs. Professor Carver Grim
2. The People vs. Gilbert Wallace
3. The People vs. Fred Garland
4. The People vs. Henry Harper
5. The People vs. Morton Mayo
6. The People vs. Peter Slocum
7. The People vs. Philip Wayne
8. The People vs. Margaret Tildonn

You Are There

Originally titled *CBS Is There*, this is a continuation of the same series, with the title changed in an attempt to attract more listeners. This documentary drama presented historical events as they happened, with various anchormen and news correspondents interviewing on-lookers, witnesses, troops, and statesmen about events. This series remained sustaining during its entire run.

What sort of a day was it? A day like all days, filled with those events that alter and illuminate our times.... And you were there.

Canada Lee was the guest in episodes thirty-two and sixty; Martin Gabel, on episode eighty-two. Beginning April 4, 1948, *You Are There* was broadcast on Sunday afternoons beginning 2 pm, EST. On August 22, 1948, the series moved ahead half an hour, beginning at 2:30 pm. On June 12, 1949, *You Are There* left the airwaves, returning in October as a once-a-month Sunday-afternoon feature until July of 1950. The final episode was not broadcast in some areas. Werner Michael was the producer, Michael Sklar and Goodman Ace (often unbilled) wrote the scripts. In February of 1953, *You Are There* made the transition to television, with Walter Cronkite as the reporter.

24. The Battle of the Monitor and the Merrimac (4/4/48)
25. The Last Days of Pompeii (4/11/48)
26. The Battle of Plassey (4/18/48)
27. The Fall of Troy (4/25/48)
28. The Surrender of Sitting Bull (5/2/48)
29. The Burr-Hamilton Duel (5/9/48)
30. The Signing of the Magna Carta (5/16/48)
31. The Execution of the Emperor Maximilian (5/23/48)
32. Toussaint L'Ouverture Liberates Hatti (5/30/48)
33. The Battle of Hastings (6/6/48)
34. The Sailing of the Pilgrims (6/13/48)
35. The Impeachment of Andrew Johnson (6/20/48)
36. The Execution of Mary, Queen of Scots (6/27/48)
37. Philadelphia, July 4, 1776 (7/4/48)
38. -----(8/22/48)
39. The Death of Joan of Arc (8/29/48)
40. -----(9/5/48)
41. -----(9/12/48)
42. The Ratification of the U.S. Constitution (9/19/48)
43. The Trial of Ann Hutchinson (9/26/48)
44. The First Battle of Bull Run (10/3/48)
45. Columbus Discovers America (10/10/48)
46. The Trial of Marie Antoinette (10/17/48)
47. The Fall of Troy (10/24/48)
48. The Election of Thomas Jefferson (10/31/48)
49. Lee and Grant at Appomattox (11/7/48)
50. The Exile of Napoleon (11/14/48)
51. The Assassination of Abraham Lincoln (11/21/48)
52. Conquest of the Grand Canyon (11/28/48)

53. The Execution of the Emperor Maximillian (12/5/48)
54. The Conspiracy of Cataline (12/12/48)
55. The Death of Captain Kidd (12/19/48)
56. The Battle of the Montior and the Merrimac (12/26/48)
57. The Surrender of Sitting Bull (1/2/49)
58. The Sentencing of Charles I (1/9/49)
59. Mutiny in the Continental Army (1/16/49)
60. Toussaint L'Ouverture Liberates Hatti (1/23/49)
61. Colonel Johnson Eats the Love Apple (1/30/49)
62. The Trial of John Peter Zenger (2/6/49)
63. The Battle of Hastings (2/13/49)
64. The Plot to Kill Savonarola (2/20/49)
65. The Impeachment of Andrew Johnson (2/27/49)
66. The Rise of Alexander the Great: Peace Officer (3/6/49)
67. The Rise of Alexander the Great: Battle for Asia (3/13/49)
68. The Rise of Alexander the Great: Mutiny in India (3/20/49)
69. The Oklahoma Land Run (3/27/49)
70. The Execution of Mary, Queen of Scots (4/3/49)
71. Perry's Dash to the North Pole (4/10/49)
72. Napoleon Returns from Elba (4/17/49)
73. The Assassination of Julius Caesar (4/24/49)
74. Montezuma and the Spaniards (5/1/49)
75. The Impeachment of Supreme Court Justice Samuel Chase (5/8/49)

76. Lexington, Concord and Merriam's
   Corner (5/15/49)
77. April 1, 1861—Fort Sumter (5/22/49)
78. The Siege of Leyden (5/29/49)
79. The Capture of John Wilkes Booth
   (6/5/49)
80. Caesar Crosses the Rubicon
   (6/12/49)
81. The Trial of Aaron Burr (10/30/49)
82. The Trial Run of Tom Thumb
   (11/27/49)
83. The Crowning of Charlemagne

   (12/25/49)
84. The Surrender of New Amsterdam
   (1/22/50)
85. The Charge of the Light Brigade
   (2/19/50)
86. The Stamp Act Rebellion (3/19/50)
87. The Battle of Thermopylae
   (4/30/50)
88. The Trial of William Penn (5/21/50)
89. The Women's Rights Convention
   (6/18/50)
90. The Boston Tea Party (7/9/50)

Your Radio Theater

An anthology series of various stage dramas and movie adaptations, using recordings of previous programs such as *Best Plays*, and a newly recorded opening and closing theme, Herbert Marshall was host when the series premiered, replaced by Vincent Price in November. Marshall took over again as host by early January. Broadcast over NBC from 9:05 to 10 pm, EST.

The premiere broadcast featured Victor McLaglen as a man who betrayed fellow members of the Irish-Republican Army. The second broadcast, a rebroadcast of *Best Plays*, featured Fredric March and wife Florence Eldridge in a classic drama of the heroic resistance of a Finnish scientist and his American wife. "On Borrowed Time" concerned a grandfather who defied relatives and death.

1. The Informer (10/11/55; Victor
   McLaglen)
2. There Shall Be No Light (10/18/55;
   Florence Eldridge and Fredric
   March)
3. On Borrowed Time (10/25/55; Parker
   Fennelly and Mildred Natwick)
4. Of Mice and Men (11/8/55; Burgess
   Meredith and Anthony Quinn)
5. Moby Dick (11/15/55; Fredric March)
6. Lost Weekend (11/22/55; Joan Banks

   and Joseph Cotten)
7. Death of a Salesman (12/6/55; Paul
   Douglas and Willy Lowman)
8. Double Indemnity (12/13/55; Marilyn
   Maxwell)
9. Miracle of the Bells (12/20/55; Jeff
   Chandler)
10. The Snake Pit (1/3/56; Agnes Moorehead)
11. Angel Street (1/10/56; Melville Cooper,
   Judith Evelyn, and Vincent Price)

Your Story Parade

Also known as the *Texas School of the Air*, this children's program presented fifteen-minute sketches with John Arlen in the leads. Helen Kelly was the Story Parade Lady. Wesley Davis wrote the scripts.

INDEX

533